THE ELGAR COMPANION TO
FEMINIST ECONOMICS

The Elgar Companion to Feminist Economics

Edited by

Janice Peterson

Professor of Economics, State University of New York-Fredonia, USA

Margaret Lewis

Professor of Economics, College of Saint Benedict, USA

Edward Elgar
Cheltenham, UK • Northampton, MA, USA

Published by
Edward Elgar Publishing Limited
Glensanda House
Montpellier Parade
Cheltenham
Glos GL50 1UA
UK

Edward Elgar Publishing, Inc.
136 West Street
Suite 202
Northampton
Massachusetts 01060
USA

Paperback edition 2001
Paperback edition reprinted 2004

A catalogue record for this book
is available from the British Library

Library of Congress Cataloguing in Publication Data

The Elgar companion to feminist economics / edited by Janice Peterson,
    Margaret Lewis.
        1. Feminist economics.   2. Women—Economic conditions.
    I. Peterson, Janice.   II. Lewis, Margaret.
    HQ1381.E44   2000
    330'.082—dc21   99–33956
                                                                        CIP

ISBN 1 85898 453 X (cased)
        1 84064 783 3 (paperback)

Printed and bound in Great Britain by Antony Rowe Ltd, Chippenham, Wiltshire

Contents

Contributors to the Volume and their Entries

Aerni, April Laskey, Department of Business, Economics, and Management, Nazareth College of Rochester, USA.
Macroeconomics

Albelda, Randy, Department of Economics, University of Massachusetts Boston, USA.
Income Distribution; Marxist Political Economics; Welfare Reform

Anderson, Donna M., Department of Economics, University of Wisconsin–La Crosse, USA.
Tax Policy

Aslaksen, Iulie, Statistics Norway, Norway.
Gross Domestic Product

Avin, Rose-Marie, Department of Economics, University of Wisconsin–Eau Claire, USA.
International Economics

Badgett, Lee, Department of Economics, University of Massachusetts–Amherst, USA.
Sexual Orientation

Bakker, Isabella, Department of Political Science, York University, Canada.
Development Policies

Balakrishnan, Radhika, International Studies, Marymount Manhattan College, USA.
Population

Barker, Drucilla K., Department of Economics, Hollins University, USA.
Economic Welfare; Gender; Neoclassical Economics

Bartlett, Robin L., Department of Economics, Denison University, USA.
Committee on the Status of Women in the Economics Profession (CSWEP); Pedagogy

Beller, Andrea H., Department of Agricultural and Consumer Economics, University of Illinois at Urbana-Champaign, USA.
Divorce

Benería, Lourdes, City and Regional Planning Department and Women's Studies, Cornell University, USA.
Structural Adjustment Policies

Berger, Silvia, FLACSO, Argentina.
Economic History, South America

Bergeron, Suzanne, Women's Studies and Social Sciences, University of Michigan Dearborn, USA
Imperialism

Berik, Günseli, Economics and Women's Studies, University of Utah, USA.
Globalization

Bernasek, Alexandra, Department of Economics, Colorado State University, USA.
Informal Sector

Brown, Doug, College of Business, Northern Arizona University, USA.
Capitalism; Postmodernism

Bruegel, Irene, Local Economy Policy Unit, South Bank University, London, UK.
Urban and Regional Economics

Burnell, Barbara S., Department of Economics, College of Wooster, USA.
Occupational Segregation

Chamberlain, Mariam K., National Council for Research on Women, USA.
Glass Ceiling

Coleman, Margaret S., New York State Office of the Deputy Comptroller for New York City, USA.
Labour Force Participation; Unions and Union Organizing

Connelly, Patricia, Sociology Department, Saint Mary's University, Canada.
Economic History, Canada

Cornwall, Richard, Queer Insurgency, 155 Haight Street, #311, San Francisco, CA, USA.
Sexual Orientation

Deere, Carmen Diana, Economics Department, University of Massachusetts–Amherst, USA.
Agriculture (Third World)

Duggan, Lynn, Labor Studies Division, Indiana University–Bloomington, USA.
Family Policy

Elson, Diane, Development Studies Programme, Department of Sociology, University of Manchester, UK and UNIFEM, United Nations.
Development, Theories of

Ferber, Marianne A., Department of Economics, University of Illinois at Urbana-Champaign, USA.
Contingent Labour Force

Figart, Deborah M., Richard Stockton College, USA.
Comparable Worth/Pay Equity; Discrimination, Theories of; Wage Gap

Floro, Maria Sagrario, Department of Economics, American University, USA.
Double Day/Second Shift

Ghilarducci, Teresa, Department of Economics, University of Notre Dame, USA.
Pensions and Old Age Retirement

Graham, Patricia, Department of Economics, University of Northern Colorado, USA.
Banking and Credit

Grapard, Ulla, Department of Economics, Colgate University, USA.
Methodology

Grossbard-Shechtman, Shoshana, Department of Economics, San Diego State University, USA.
Marriage, Theories of

Hammond, Claire Holton, Department of Economics, Wake Forest University, USA.
Women in the Economics Profession

Hartmann, Heidi, Institute for Women's Policy Research, USA.
Comparable Worth/Pay Equity; Parental Leave

Headlee, Sue, Washington Semester Program in Economic Policy, American University, USA.
Economic History, Western Europe

Helburn, Suzanne W., Department of Economics, University of Colorado–Denver, USA.
Child Care

Hill, Marianne T., Center for Policy Research and Planning, USA.
Public Sector Economics/Public Finance

Himmelweit, Susan, Faculty of Social Science, The Open University, UK.
Domestic Labour

Hopkins, Barbara, Department of Economics, Wright State University, USA.
Socialism

Horrell, Sara, Faculty of Economics and Politics, University of Cambridge, UK.
Economic History, Great Britain

Hyman, Prue, Department of Women's Studies, Victoria University of Wellington, New Zealand.
Economic History, Australia and New Zealand

Jacobsen, Joyce P., Department of Economics, Wesleyan University, USA.
Human Capital Theory

Jennings, Ann, Department of Economics and Management, DePauw University, USA.
Dualisms; Labour Markets, Theories of

Katz, Elizabeth, Department of Economics, St Mary's College of California, Moraga, California, USA.
Migration

King, Mary C., Economics Department, Portland State University, USA.
Labour Market Segmentation

Kiss, D. Elizabeth, Department of Human Development and Family Studies, Iowa State University, USA.
Divorce

Lapidus, June, Department of Economics, Roosevelt University, USA.
Income Support and Transfer Policy

Laurence, Louise, Department of Economics, Towson University, USA.
Domestic Abuse

Lewis, Margaret, Department of Economics, College of Saint Benedict, USA.
History of Economic Thought; Macroeconomics

Lucas, Linda E., Department of Economics, Eckerd College, USA.
Environmental and Natural Resource Economics

MacDonald, Martha, Economics Department, Saint Mary's University, Canada.
Economic History, Canada

Manning, Linda M., Department of Economics, University of Missouri–Rolla, USA.
Banking and Credit

Matthaei, Julie, Department of Economics, Wellesley College, USA.
Patriarchy; Race

Mayhew, Anne, College of Arts and Sciences, University of Tennessee–Knoxville, USA.
Institutional Economics; Value

McCrate, Elaine, Department of Economics, University of Vermont, USA.
Class

McGoldrick, KimMarie, Department of Economics, University of Richmond, USA.
Economics Education; Education, Economics of

McKinney, Judith Record, Department of Economics, Hobart and William Smith Colleges, USA.
Economic History, Russia

Meurs, Mieke, Department of Economics, American University, USA.
Economic History, Eastern Europe

Mutari, Ellen, General Studies Program, Richard Stockton College, USA.
Family Wage; Protective Legislation

Nelson, Julie A., Department of Economics, University of Massachusetts-Boston, USA.
Econometrics; Economic Man

Nickless, Pamela J., Department of Economics, University of North Carolina-Asheville, USA.
Economic History, United States

Olmsted, Jennifer C., Economic Research Service, United States Department of Agriculture, USA.
Economic History, Middle East and North Africa

Peterson, Janice, Department of Economics, State University of New York–Fredonia, USA.
Feminization of Poverty

Power, Marilyn, Faculty in Economics, Sarah Lawrence College, USA.
Minimum Wage

Pyle, Jean Larson, Department of Regional Economic and Social Development, University of Massachusetts–Lowell, USA.
Economic History, Singapore; Economic Restructuring

Rives, Janet M., Department of Economics, University of Northern Iowa, USA.
Unemployment and Underemployment

Robertson, Linda, Writing and Rhetoric Program, Hobart and William Smith Colleges, USA.
Rhetoric

Seiz, Janet A., Department of Economics, Grinnell College, USA.
Feminism(s); Game Theory and Bargaining Models

Shackelford, Jean, Department of Economics, Bucknell University, USA.
International Association for Feminist Economics (IAFFE)

Sharp, Rhonda, Economics, School of International Business, University of South Australia, Australia.
Women's Budgets

Shaw, Lois B., Institute for Women's Policy Research, USA.
Poverty, Measurement and Analysis of

Sosin, Kim, Department of Economics, University of Nebraska at Omaha, USA.
Unemployment and Underemployment

Strassmann, Diana, Rice University, USA.
Feminist Economics

Summerfield, Gale, Office of Women in International Development, University of Illinois at Urbana-Champaign, USA.
Economic History, China; Economic Restructuring

Swaminathan, Madhura, Indira Gandhi Institute of Development Research, India.
Economic History, India

Tanski, Janet M., Department of Economics, New Mexico State University, USA.
Economic History, Mexico

Taylor, Susan K., Bank of America Corporation, USA.
Volunteer Labour

Tilly, Chris, Department of Regional Economic and Social Development, University of Massachusetts–Lowell, USA.
Income Distribution

Waldfogel, Jane, School of Social Work, Columbia University, USA.
Contingent Labour Force

Waller, William, Department of Economics, Hobart and William Smith Colleges, USA.
Austrian Economics; Post Keynesian Economics

Walters, Bernard, School of Economic Studies, University of Manchester, UK.
Growth Theory (Macro Models)

Woody, Bette, College of Arts and Sciences, University of Massachusetts–Boston, USA.
Affirmative Action

Woolley, Frances, Department of Economics, Carleton University, Canada.
Family, Economics of

Wyss, Brenda, Department of Economics, Wheaton College, USA.
Child Support

Young, Mary, Department of Economics, Southwestern University, USA.
Health, Economics of

Zein-Elabdin, Eiman, Department of Economics, Franklin and Marshall College, USA.
Economic History, Sub-Saharan Africa

Zepeda, Lydia, Department of Consumer Science, University of Wisconsin–Madison, USA.
Technological Change

Introduction

The principal objective of this Companion is to provide readers with an introduction to the extensive and evolving literature of feminist economics. The 99 entries included in this work address major concepts in feminist economics as well as feminist economic critiques and reconstructions of major economic theories and policy debates. In addition to providing definitional and historical background information and overviews of feminist and feminist economic contributions, the entries also contain suggestions for further research, cross references to other relevant entries in the volume and reference lists guiding readers to representative works. The use of technical language has been kept to a minimum to make the volume accessible to a broad audience of researchers, teachers and activists from a variety of disciplines.

Although there has been an increase in the recognition of feminist economic work during the last decade, feminist economics is not new and has deep roots in both the political economy and feminist literature. In the mid-nineteenth century, for example, classical economist John Stuart Mill and feminist Harriet Taylor Mill offered a passionate defense of the rights of women and criticized the exclusion of women from certain occupations. As criticisms of industrial capitalism intensified in the late nineteenth century, Friedrich Engels drew attention to the inferior status of women in the Victorian family as one of the flaws of the capitalist system. At the turn of the century, Thorstein Veblen focused a great deal of his scathing critique of US capitalism on the inferior ('barbarian' in his words) status of women, a condition that he felt in many ways defined the economy of that time. Many feminists of that era also addressed economic concerns and feminist writers, such as Charlotte Perkins Gilman and Beatrice Potter Webb, focused explicit attention on the importance of gender in economic relationships. Throughout the twentieth century, feminist economists have challenged the established doctrine on key concepts and issues within many economic traditions, enriching, and in many cases transforming, the literature on topics ranging from the economic significance of domestic labour to explanations of the gender wage gap and women's roles in economic history.

During the last decade, these unique feminist insights began to gain recognition as contributions to a new and distinct body of work, and 'feminist economics' began to be recognized as an emerging school of economic thought. The entries in this volume seek to examine the growing and diverse literature on feminist economics in terms of five broad topical categories: concepts, schools of economic thought, traditional economic fields (as categorized by the mainstream *Journal of Economic Literature*), current policy issues, and institutions of the economics profession. Thus, some entries focus on the fundamental theoretical foundations of both economic and feminist thought, examining such core concepts as 'value', 'economic man', 'economic welfare', 'class', 'race' and 'gender'. Other entries seek to provide readers with an overview of the characteristics of different schools of economic thought and the connections between these approaches and feminist economics. A number of entries address issues and models that are drawn from the traditional economic field designations such as labour economics, development economics and macroeconomics. These topics present a special challenge since many feminist economists, like other heterodox political economists, find these traditional definitions and distinctions problematic. They are used in this volume, however, to highlight the nature of feminist economic critiques and reconstructions of orthodox economic concepts and analyses as they are most commonly applied in research and teaching. Another group of entries address current policy issues, highlighting the importance of linking feminist economic theory to policymaking and activism. Additionally, some entries examine the experiences of women economists and the professional organizations that have been established to provide support for both the expanding presence of women in the profession and the further development of feminist economic thought.

Feminist economists are a very diverse group of scholars and activists, representing very different views on both economics and feminism. And feminist economics, like all forms of economic and social inquiry, is changing over time. Consequently, this volume does not attempt or presume to provide the definitive discussion of feminist economics, but rather seeks to provide the reader with an introduction to many of the major themes, issues and concerns reflected in the current feminist economic literature. The volume essentially provides a 'snapshot' of feminist economic thought at the time the volume was crafted (the mid to late 1990s) and, like all snapshots, it is a picture that reflects the location and position of the photographers. Thus, while every effort has been made to provide as comprehensive an overview as possible, the volume still largely reflects the interests and perspectives of a particular community, one comprised predominantly of academic economists in the industrialized world (particularly the USA). It is the hope of those involved in this project that future reference works in feminist economics will feature a new diversity of both topics and contributors.

The editors very much appreciate all of the excellent insights and suggestions received from the many contributors to the volume, and we thank them for all of their hard work. Many thanks also go to Joanne Foeller for her valuable assistance in preparing the manuscript. In addition, we greatly appreciate the understanding and cooperation of Edward Elgar and the members of his very fine staff who offered their advice and assistance throughout the project.

Affirmative Action

Affirmative action was first used in US policy by President Lyndon Johnson in the 1965 Executive Order 11246 directing federal government contractors to take affirmative action to end discrimination in the hiring and pay of minorities and women. This measure, along with Title VII of the Civil Rights Act of 1964 and the Equal Pay Act of 1963, established an executive enforcement apparatus for equal opportunity and firmly shaped affirmative action as the principal remedy for ending discrimination in employment. In the three decades following, affirmative action expanded to incorporate reporting and enforcement directives in the civil rights framework and litigation to clarify remedies and sanctions. Two government agencies were created to enforce affirmative action requirements, an independent Equal Employment Opportunities Commission (EEOC) and the Office for Contract Compliance (OFCCP) in the Department of Labor. The law directed employers to address inequalities caused by past discrimination based on sex, race and disability through affirmative action plans. A combination of government mandates and employer responses resulted in an evolution of affirmative action programme content to include a diverse array of remedies ranging from institutional changes such as personnel system restructuring to skills training and individual career development.

Government contractors were also required to prepare affirmative action plans and contracting agencies to further integrate contracting through 'set aside' programmes which reserved a percentage of contracted work for minority- and women-owned business enterprises. Over the years, despite evidence that affirmative action has been effective in reaching employment goals to reduce race and sex bias in the workplace and is widely supported by employers, attacks on affirmative action by increasingly vocal conservative interests seriously threatened programmes by the 1990s. The basis of opposition to affirmative action constitutes a wide range from the accusation that programmes cause inefficiencies by hiring unqualified women and minorities, to the arguments that such programmes impose costs on white males and unfairly stigmatize intended beneficiaries.

Globally industrialized and developing economies have been slow to institute affirmative action tools to correct visible lags in equal opportunity actions for women and other disadvantaged populations. The 1957 Rome Treaty establishing the European Union (EU) mandated equal opportunity which subsequent acts have expanded to require that affirmative action be undertaken by member states to end bias in employment of women. Many developing nations have also followed this pattern in progressive constitutions and legislation. As yet, however, both industrialized and emerging democracies have been slow to implement serious affirmative action measures routinely in the workplace. Research and theory, including feminist theories, have identified many aspects of labour market discrimination globally to challenge conventional economic thinking. There is a need for economists to undertake a fuller exploration of equity, fairness and the benefits of equal opportunity regulation to employers and the economy in order to support better policy.

Background
The history of affirmative action is rooted in social and economic trends of the immediate post-World War II period and political pressures to balance competing demands in the market place. Under pressure from the growing unrest of a frustrated black civil rights movement joined by women's consciousness activists, federal legislation and executive orders responded to failures to put an end to discrimination and economic barriers by voluntary means.

In 1961, President Kennedy issued Executive Order 10925, which banned racial discrimination by government contractors and established guidelines to promote equal hiring practices, borrowing the concept 'affirmative action' from a 1935 Labour Relations Act requiring unions to make up for past discrimination. He also appointed a Commission on Women to study legislation and hiring practices of women. Following Kennedy's death, President Lyndon Johnson pressed successfully for passage of the Civil Rights Act of 1964 with Title VII which outlawed discrimination in employment in firms employing 50 or more workers and created the Equal Employment Opportunity Commission (EEOC). This later body, an independent agency headed by a permanent, five-member commission was directed to set standards for compliance, collect compliance reports and receive complaints from individuals. Employment discrimination based on race, colour, religion, sex and national origin (later amended to include disability and age) was prohibited by employers, employment agencies and labour unions.

In 1965, President Lyndon Johnson issued Executive Order 11246 establishing non-discrimination rules for federal contractors and first-tier subcontractors of more than 50 employees (amended in 1972 to include 15 or more employees) or at least $50 000, and construction projects operating with federal assistance. Employers were required, in Johnson's words, to take 'affirmative action' to eliminate bias in employing or contracting firms. Executive Order 11246 also created the Office of Federal Contract Compliance Programmes (OFCCP) in the US Department of Labor to coordinate other federal agencies and specifically oversee and enforce government compliance programmes. The Office required that employers establish plans and timetables for achieving equity goals for minorities and women in hiring, promotion and compensation. For the first time sanctions were put in place using the leverage of 'debarment' or the threat of loss of federal contacts in the case of non compliance of the anti-discrimination law.

After a history of more than three decades, research has been limited in exploring the efficacy of compliance programmes in meeting goals or measuring other impacts of affirmative action on equal opportunity for women and minorities. In theory, affirmative action should increase the demand for women and minorities at all stages of the employment cycle, from hiring through advancement and promotion and retirement as well as potentially narrow the male–female pay gap (Gunderson 1994). Research is sketchy and results ambiguous, however, particularly for women. Beller (1979) analysed US Current Population Census Data (CPS) before and after enforcement was strengthened in 1974, and reported increases in female earnings over the period 1967–74 as a result of Title VII and affirmative action compliance programmes, concluding that stricter enforcement led to larger reductions in the gender gap. Impacts of affirmative action compliance reviews were examined by several researchers who found that occupational segregation, a significant problem in women's employment, was reduced following 1974 rule changes favouring women (Osterman 1982; Leonard 1984a, 1984b; Smith and Welch 1984). The impact of affirmative action programmes on black women, however, is less clear with some researchers finding gains superior to those of white women (Leonard 1984c, Smith and Welch 1984, p. 271), while others find more rapid progress by white women compared to blacks. This is particularly true when education and work experience are taken into account (Kilson 1977; Woody and Malson 1984).

The rise of the conservative movement in the USA and other western democracies spurred a strong challenge to affirmative action programmes. In the USA, conservative activists increased litigation in the courts and proposed changing the law to eliminate affirmative action in employment and education throughout the 1990s. Behind some successes in the challenge were effects of economic restructuring and deeply felt opposition to remedies perceived to contradict a strong American value that individual effort, motivation and innate ability, and not discrimination, are the cause of black–white economic disparities (Kluegel 1994). At the same time, public opinion polls and views by leading business enterprises indicate support for legislative reform rather than outright repeal of equal employment opportunity statutes (Glass Ceiling Commission 1995).

Globally, affirmative action has not been instituted widely, although major progress has been made in recent years in the European Union (EU) and in individual member states, particularly in France. Article 119 of the Treaty of Rome required equal compensation for women and men by member states. The European Council which oversees the EU, further endorsed affirmative action (*action positive*) programmes in 1984. From the 1980s up to the present, the European Union Council and Commission have debated measures and options for promoting member state enforcement strategies with only limited success (Nonon 1998). A 1993 study of 13 EU countries by the European Commission found uneven programme commitments among countries and a lack of monitoring and enforcement of affirmative action programmes specifically (European Commission 1993). In the UK, not yet a full EU member state, the situation is even worse. The only redress for discrimination by women is through individual complaints in the courts (Morris and Nott 1991), compared to EU members where the International Court of the Hague is increasingly available. The International Court of the Hague has successfully settled discrimination cases brought by women who failed to get relief in national courts (Nonon 1998, pp. 33–7).

At least one EU member state, France, has developed a comprehensive affirmative action policy in its labour relations regulation administration. This, along with recently passed equal wage legislation, parallels the affirmative action policy in the USA. Under the French law of 1983 employers are required to audit and file detailed reports of jobs and staff by sex along with other personnel data including vacancies, turnover and salary and benefits. A plan and timetable for affirmative action strategies, including attention to occupational stratification or concentration of women in 'women's jobs' is also required. Works councils (*comité d'entreprise*), a European institution designed to increase worker management collaboration in the workplace, is designated to oversee affirmative action plans while incentive grants are available to offset programme costs such as training (Grizeau 1994). To date, few evaluations have been made of the French programme. One analysis was critical and found that while affirmative action has been on the books for more than a decade, by the 1990s only 26 of some 300 plans filed have been approved by the government (Serdgenian 1994).

Feminist thinking to date only tangentially addresses many of the issues raised in the affirmative action debate and ensuing controversy. A few feminist scholars have examined theory more closely, however, and find a failure to account for inefficiencies caused by discrimination (Blau and Ferber 1986, p. 262) and note that neoclassical economics in particular does not respond to many failures in the market process to resolve special institutional problems associated with labour market discrimination such as nepotism (England and Farkas 1986; Williams 1993; Blau and Jusenius 1976). If discrimination results in a poor allocation of resources in economic production, or reduces the potential economic output of the firm, remedies should take into account the labour deployment in jobs and tasks as well as in the concentration or dispersal in particular occupational categories. These are issues which underscore much of the affirmative action debate and offer important clues to policy remedies. Research which probes and better isolates the costs of discrimination in disaggregated components of production and output, as well as benefits which firms reap as the result of eliminating bias, would help generate support for affirmative action regulations as well as identify strategies which may be most effective.

Affirmative action as the implementation side of employment opportunity policy is aimed at changing organizations and in particular, personnel and contracting systems and actions. Personnel actions are a central focus of the requirements of both the EEOC and the OFCCP. All personnel actions are considered appropriate for use in affirmative action remedies and include recruitment and hiring, job classification, compensation and benefits, work assignment, performance appraisal, promotion and advancement and termination rules (Tomaskovic-Devey 1993). The procedure for evaluation of affirmative action is similar to the EEOC and the OFCCP. Following Title VII and Executive Orders which prohibit discrimination based on race, colour, religion, sex or national origin, government regulators direct employers of more than 15 employees to review existing staffing and file statistical reports annually (Yakura 1996). Where deficiencies in status and pay of women and minorities compared to white males are identified, employers are required to develop an affirmative action plan, including goals and timetables to correct inequalities among employees. Affirmative action plans may be described as requiring a set of specific and results-oriented procedures to which contractors commit themselves to apply every good faith effort. Contractors who fail to file, or deficiencies identified as the result of complaints, audits or court orders, can cause sanctions to be taken in the form of court actions, fines and in the case of federal contracts and grants, suspension of eligibility to contract with the US government, although sanctions have rarely been enforced (Blau and Ferber 1986, p. 287; Yakura 1996, p. 26,)

To assess the economic impact of affirmative action programmes does require attention to operational aspects of the workplace and how these cause and promote bias. The economics literature on workplace discrimination is extensive, but for purposes of a discussion of affirmative action can be divided between effects of systemic discrimination and that of behaviour and attitudes. Systemic discrimination, which relates to the structure of personnel systems, including job groups, occupational systems, recruitment, hiring, termination, job assignment, promotion and reward systems, have represented the principal focus of affirmative action plans, because, even though such factors by themselves are considered unintended or 'disparate impact' effects (Gunderson 1994), they are still considered contributors to stratification, segregation and segmentation of women in education and work (Osterman 1979; Hartmann 1987). Discrimination based on attitudes and behaviour is also considered a serious cause of discrimination and can involve external discriminators and women themselves through so-called 'feedback effects' (Blau and Ferber 1986, p. 229). Behaviour further is interfaced with structural systems such as the informal determination of job ladders, performance and promotion decisions, particularly into top hierarchies. Considerable research has been made on attitudes and behaviour, including impacts of bosses and superiors (Harlan and Weiss 1982) and peers and subordinates (Kanter 1977; Woody 1988). The collective impacts of behaviours are to reinforce occupational segregation and maintain discriminatory job systems frequently beyond the reach of traditional affirmative action. Thus affirmative action programmes have placed less attention on behaviour change, despite evidence that advancement and promotion are particularly highly related to individual subjective choice.

Affirmative action encountered criticism from the beginning, but efforts escalated during the mid 1990s to dismantle legal mandates and regulatory systems supporting employment based on four principal criticisms: (1) preferential treatment is 'unfair', (2) quotas constitute 'reverse discrimination', (3) affirmative action stigmatizes intended beneficiaries, (4) affirmative action promotes inefficiency and poor performance. The argument of fairness for preferential treatment has been raised primarily by those opposed to the use of affirmative action to integrate jobs and higher education in favour of racial and ethnic minorities, but whose opposition does not include other traditional beneficiaries of absolute preferences such as veterans of military service, relatives or, in the case of admissions to educational institutions, the sons and daughters of alumni. While there are no requirements for preferential treatment in the law (Norton 1996), numerical goals in affirmative action have been used to accelerate integration of systems with particularly poor histories of integration, and where social need is high for female and minority staff such as police departments.

Quotas have been the single most controversial tool for affirmative action. One reason for opposition is the perception that employment constitutes a zero-sum game where one group's gain is another's loss (Yakura 1996, p. 4). Quotas are frequently called 'reverse discrimination', implying that a favoured majority suffers losses as the result of measures taken to equalize opportunity for those suffering discrimination. Quotas are not required by law and voluntary affirmative action plans rarely set quotas for minorities or women (Woody 1988; Cox 1993). When 'fast track' or executive training programmes are used, training slots are typically added on to a base number to accommodate women and minorities rather than redistributed (Woody 1988, p. 5). Numerical goals are preferred by many businesses, however, because they are easy to communicate, produce rapid compliance and are unambiguous (Fisher 1994), and current French regulations do direct employers to use numerical goals in affirmative action as the only feasible way to equalize men and women in occupational categories (Gadrey 1992).

Another criticism of affirmative action is that it stigmatizes minorities and women as 'deficient' and is based on the notion that minorities and women may be perceived as having gained something that they did not legitimately earn, or that they are chosen for arbitrary reasons of sex and race, not effort and performance (Carter 1991). Closely related is the argument that affirmative action promotes inefficiency by selecting inferior individuals, however, there is no evidence to date that employers hire unqualified minorities or women under affirmative action and this argument fails to account for any inefficiencies caused by exclusion of women and minorities from employment.

Alternative approaches to existing affirmative action strategies are not immediately clear. Because the range of current practices is so broad, and because there are no clear means for equalizing economic values across genders, the challenges facing feminist economists are twofold. First, feminist economists need to develop appropriate theoretical frameworks for analysing the economic status of women. Here such issues as the definition of terms (such as 'work' and 'equal opportunity') and how best to account for women's dual roles in social production and reproduction when evaluating equality, both warrant further investigation. Second, feminist economists need to develop better measures for evaluating actual affirmative action policies. Here an issue is determining what factors to include in constructing and assessing successful programmes. For this, previously ignored factors such as economic performance, professional development and advancement and promotion and succession systems might be incorporated. Another, more far-reaching issue is whether the affirmative action goal of equalizing labour value across the genders can even be achieved without changing the nature of the marketplace itself. In other words, achieving a level playing field might actually challenge traditional values such as status, mobility and compensation in order to distribute workplace rewards more equitably.

BETTE WOODY

See also
Discrimination, Theories of; Labour Market Segmentation; Labour Markets, Theories of; Occupational Segregation; Wage Gap.

Bibliography
Adler, Nancy J. and Dafna N. Izraeli (1994), 'Competitive Frontiers: Women Managers in a Global Economy', in Nancy J. Adler and Dafna N. Izraeli (eds), *Competitive Frontiers: Women Managers in a Global Economy*, Cambridge, Massachusetts: Blackwell, pp. 1–21.
Becker, S. Gary (1965), *The Economics of Discrimination*, Chicago: University of Chicago Press.
Beller, Andrea (1979), 'The Impact of Equal Employment Opportunity Laws on the Male/Female Earnings Differential', in Cynthia B. Lloyd, Emily Andrews and Curtis L. Gilroy (eds), *Women in the Labor Market*, New York: Columbia University Press, pp. 304–30.
Bergmann, Barbara R. (1986), *The Economic Emergence of Women*, New York: Basic Books.
Bergmann, Barbara R. (1996), *In Defense of Affirmative Action*, New York: Basic Books.
Blau, Francine D. and Marianne A. Ferber (1986), *The Economics of Women, Men and Work*, Englewood Cliffs, New Jersey: Prentice-Hall.

Blau, Francine D. and Carol Jusenius (1976), 'Economists' approaches to sex segregation in the labor market: An appraisal', *Signs: Journal of Women in Culture and Society*, **1** (3, Pt 2), (Spring), 181–99.

Carter, Stephen L. (1991), *Reflections of an Affirmative Action Baby*, New York: Basic Books.

Cox, Taylor H. Jr (1993), *Cultural Diversity in Organizations*, San Francisco: Berrett-Koehler.

Cox, Taylor H. Jr and Carol Smolinski (1994), *Managing Diversity and Glass Ceiling Initiatives as National Economic Imperatives*, Washington, DC: Glass Ceiling Commission, US Department of Labor.

England, Paula and George Farkas (1986), *Households, Employment and Gender*, New York: Aldine de Gruyter.

European Commission (1993), *La Segregation Professsionelle des Femmes et des Hommes dans la Communaute Europeenne, Europe Sociale*, Brussels: Office of Official Publications of the European Communities, p. 123.

Ferber, Marianne A. and Bonnie G. Birnbaum (1977), 'The new home economics: retrospect and prospects', *Journal of Consumer Research*, **4** (4), 19–28.

Ferber, Marianne A. and Julie A. Nelson (1993), 'The Social Construction of Economics and The Social Construction of Gender', in Marianne A. Ferber and Julie A. Nelson (eds), *Beyond Economic Man*, Chicago: University of Chicago Press.

Fisher, Anne B. (1994), 'Businessmen Like to Hire by the Numbers', in Paul Burstein (ed.), *Equal Employment Opportunity*, New York: Aldine de Gruyter.

Folbre, Nancy (1993), 'Socialism, Feminist and Scientific', in Marianne A. Ferber and Julie A. Nelson (eds), *Beyond Economic Man*, Chicago: University of Chicago Press, pp. 94–110.

Gadrey, Nicole (1992), *Hommes et Femmes au Travail*, Paris: Editions Marmattan.

Glass Ceiling Commission (1995), *A Solid Investment: Making Full Use of the Nation's Human Capital*, Washington, DC: US Department of Labor.

Grizeau, Fabienne (1994), *L'Egalite professionnelle*, Paris: Economica.

Gunderson, Morley (1994), 'Male–Female Wage Differentials and Policy Responses', in Paul Burstein (ed.), *Equal Employment Opportunity*, New York: Aldine de Gruyter.

Harlan, Anne and Carol Weiss (1982), 'Sex Differences in Factors Affecting Managerial Career Advancement', in Phyllis A. Wallace (ed.), *Women in the Workplace*, Boston: Auburn House, pp. 59–86.

Hartmann, Heidi I. (1981), 'The family as the locus of gender, class and political struggle: the example of housework', *Signs: Journal of Women in Culture and Society*, **6** (3), 366–92.

Hartmann, Heidi I. (1987), 'Internal Labor Markets and Gender: A Case Study of Promotion', in Clair Brown and Joseph A. Pechman (eds), *Gender in the Workplace*, Washington, DC: Brookings.

Hartmann, Heidi I. (1996), 'Who has Benefited from Affirmative Action in Employment?', in George E. Curry (ed.), *The Affirmative Action Debate*, Reading, Massachusetts: Addison-Wesley.

Jaynes, Gerald David and Robin M. Williams, Jr (1989), *A Common Destiny*, Washington DC: National Academy Press.

Kanter, Rosebeth Moss (1977), *Men and Women of the Corporation*, New York: Basic Books.

Kilson, Marion (1977), 'Black women in the professions, 1890–1970', *Monthly Labor Review*, **100** (May), 38–41.

Kluegel, James R. (1994), 'Trends in Whites' Explanations of the Black–White Gap in Socioeconomic Status, 1977–89', in Paul Burstein (ed.), *Equal Employment Opportunity: Labor Market Discrimination and Public Policy*, New York: Aldine de Gruyter.

Leonard, Jonathan (1984a), 'Anti-discrimination or reverse discrimination: The impact of changing demographics, Title VII and affirmative action on productivity', *Journal of Human Resources*, **19** (2), (Spring), 145–74.

Leonard, Jonathan (1984b), 'Employment and occupational advance under affirmative action, *Review of Economics and Statistics*, **66** (3), (August), 377–85.

Leonard, Jonathan (1984c), 'The impact of affirmative action on employment, *Journal of Labor Economics*, **3** (4), (October), 439–63.

Morris, Anne E. and Susan M. Nott (1991), *Working Women and the Law*, London: Routledge/Sweet and Maxwell.

Nonon, Jacqueline (1998), *L'Europe, un atout pour les femmes?'*, Paris: La Documentation Francaise.

Norton, Eleanor Holmes (1996), 'Affirmative Action in the Workplace', in George E. Curry (ed.), *The Affirmative Action Debate*, Reading, Massachusetts: Addison-Wesley.

Osterman, Paul (1979), Sex discrimination in professional employment: A case study', *Industrial and Labor Relations Review*, **32** (4), (July), 451–64.

Osterman, Paul (1982), 'Affirmative action and opportunity: A study of female quit rates', *Review of Economics and Statistics*, **64** (4), (November), 604–13.

Rose, David L. (1994), 'Twenty-Five Years Later: Where Do We Stand on Equal Employment Opportunity Law enforcement?', in Paul Burstein (ed.), *Equal Employment Opportunity*, New York: Aldine de Gruyter.

Serdgenian, Evelyne (1994), 'Women Managers in France', in Nancy J. Adler and Dafna N. Izraeli (eds), *Competitive Frontiers*, Cambridge, Massachusetts: Blackwell, pp. 190–205.

Skrentny, John David (1996), *The Ironies of Affirmative Action*, Chicago: University of Chicago Press.

Smith, James and Finis Welch (1984), 'Affirmative action and labor markets', *Journal of Labor Economics*, **2**, 155–82.

Strober, Myra (1997), 'The scope of micro-economics: implications for economic education', *Journal of Economic Education*, **18**, 135–49.

Tomaskovic-Devey, Donald (1993), *Gender and Racial Inequality at Work*, Ithaca, New York: ILR Press.

Williams, Rhonda M. (1993), 'Race, Deconstruction and the Emergent Agenda of Feminist Economic Theory', in Marianne A. Ferber and Julie A. Nelson (eds), *Beyond Economic Man*, Chicago: University of Chicago Press, pp. 144–52.

Woody, Bette (1988), 'Corporate Policy and Women Executives', Working Paper, Wellesley, Massachusetts: Wellesley College Center for Research on Women.

Woody, Bette and Michelene Malson (1984), 'In Crisis: Low Income Black Employed Women in the US Workplace', Working Paper, Wellesley, Massachusetts: Wellesley College Center for Research on Women.

Yakura, Elaine K. (1996), 'EEO Law and Managing Diversity', in Ellen Ernst Kossek and Sharon A. Logel (eds), *Managing Diversity: Human Resources Strategies for Transforming the Workplace*, London: Blackwell Business, pp. 16–29.

Agriculture (Third World)

The majority of women in the Third World reside in rural areas and engage in agricultural activities. It has been argued that 'although women do the majority of work in agriculture at the global level, elder men, for the most part, still own the land, control women's labour and make agricultural decisions in patriarchal social systems' (Sachs 1994, p. 6). One of the main accomplishments of the new inter-disciplinary field of Women in Development (WID, also known as Women and Development, WAD, or Gender and Development, GAD) as it evolved in the 1970s and 1980s was to make rural women's agricultural labour visible. Feminist scholarship also challenged a number of concepts in the field of peasant studies and rural household economics (Deere 1995).

Most definitions of the peasantry depart from the notion of the family farm as the basic unit of production and consumption (Chayanov 1966; Wolf 1966). The family farm is posited to rely primarily on family labour for its productive and reproductive activities, in contrast to a capitalist farm which relies on wage labour and engages only in productive activities. Implicit, if not explicit, is the assumption that peasant family farms are synonymous with male-headed households and that, with respect to farm activities, men are the primary agriculturalists, assisted by women and children.

Boserup (1970) was among the first to challenge this assumption demonstrating that, cross-culturally, peasant men are not always the principal farmers. She argued that an important distinction must be drawn between male and female farming systems, with the latter prevailing in many parts of Africa prior to colonization. While Boserup's work was path-breaking in illustrating that one could not assume that farmers were always men, various aspects of her work were challenged, including her conceptualization of modernization (Beneria and Sen 1981), her generalization of African agrarian history (Guyer 1991) and her reliance on census statistics to characterize farming systems.

The deficiency of census data in capturing women's economic participation has now been amply demonstrated (Dixon 1984, Kandiyoti 1985), particularly in the case of rural women in Latin America (Deere and León 1982). For example, census data led to the conclusion that Latin American peasant agriculture was male-based; moreover, this data suggested that with the development of agrarian capitalism over the course of the twentieth century women were being displaced from agricultural activities. While Latin America thus seemed to conform to Boserup's main propositions – that male farming systems were associated with plough agriculture, and that mechanization often resulted in displacing women from agricultural work – field research in the 1970s and 1980s revealed a much more complex picture (Deere and León 1982, 1987).

Prior to the rapid development of agrarian capitalism in Latin America in the 1950s and 1960s, peasant agriculture was generally family-based, rather than characterized by a male farming system. Nonetheless, women's participation in agriculture was most heterogenous, varying, for example, by region and with race and ethnicity (Deere and León 1987, pp. 3–5). Probably the most important contribution of the new generation of field research was to demonstrate that the family-based farm is often characterized by a division of labour by gender, not only in terms of farm activities (agriculture versus animal raising or agricultural processing) but also with respect to given tasks (ploughing versus seeding). The concept of the gender division of labour was increasingly employed to stress the social, rather than biological, construction of men's and women's roles. The gender division of labour in agriculture was found to vary not only cross-culturally and regionally in accordance with cultural constructions of femininity and masculinity (Harris 1978; Bourque and Warren 1981), but also within given regions in accordance with the prevailing social relations of production and income-generating opportunities, as well as with peasant social differentiation (differing access to means of production), suggesting the importance of material conditions in changing social constructs (Deere and León 1982; Stephen 1991).

Given this heterogeneity, it is difficult to establish any linear relationship between women's participation in agriculture and the degree of capitalist development. Nevertheless, there is sufficient evidence to suggest that, over time, rather than decreasing, as census statistics imply, women's participation in peasant agriculture in a number of Latin American countries has been increasing – a product of growing land shortage and male migration in search of wage work, women's lower opportunity cost in the labour market (that is, lower wages than men's), and the growth in the number of female-headed households, among other factors (Deere and León 1982; Crummett 1987).

The research effort on the gender division of labour and the variations in family farming systems also led to two other contributions. Gender analysis enriched the definitions of activities encompassed in the categorization of farming systems and raised the issue of the relationship between women's participation in production and women's status in the household. In addition to field labour, animal care and processing and transformation activities, it was shown that a gender-based understanding of farming systems also had to include farm decision making and control over the outcome of productive activities on the farm (Poats *et al.*, 1988).

Taking into account this broader set of variables to pursue the relationship between women's participation in production and women's status, a distinction was made between patriarchal and egalitarian family farming systems (Deere and León 1982). Patriarchal farming systems are characterized by women's participation in agricultural field work and animal raising, but male control over decision making and the product of family labour; egalitarian farming systems, in contrast, are those where there is a corresponding association between men's and women's participation in farm labour, decision making and disposition of the product. These distinctions have been found to be associated with class differences. In the Andean case, for example, the rich peasant strata most clearly corresponded to a patriarchal family farming system whereas more egalitarian family farming systems tended to predominate among the poorer strata of the peasantry.

A second major assumption of peasant studies which was challenged by feminist research was the posited undifferentiated return to family labour characterizing family-labour farms (Deere 1995). Chayanov's (1966) influential theory of the family-labour farm was based on the argument that such was a uniquely non-capitalist unit which could not be analysed with the toolkit of neoclassical economics. Since the category of wages did not exist, it was impossible to calculate the category of profits and to posit, as for capitalist firms, that the objective of family-labour farms was to maximize profits. Rather, according to Chayanov, the peasant family maximized the undifferentiated return to family labour subject to the drudgery constraint and the consumer/worker trade-off.

Underlying the concept of an undifferentiated return to family labour is the assumption that the family labour product goes into a household fund and that it benefits those who produced it; that is, it assumes income pooling and shared consumption. A growing feminist literature has demonstrated that not all the income generated by family labour is necessarily pooled; moreover, income pooling does not always result in shared consumption, particularly in equitable consumption among household members (Evers et al. 1984; Bruce and Dwyer 1988).

Whether the family labour product is used to benefit all who produce it largely depends on who controls the fruits of family labour. Income pooling is more likely the lower the degree of monetization of the economy, with the family labour product stored and consumed over the year. Once the family labour product consists of commodities, sold on the market, women's participation in decision making and in the direct marketing of farm products is often necessary to assure that the family labour product results in pooled income and shared consumption (Deere 1990). That is, income pooling is more likely in egalitarian farming systems where women participate in field work, decision making and in the final disposition of the product.

The specialization of household members in given occupations greatly influences the extent to which control over income is individualized rather than socialized. For example, when peasant men in Latin America generate wage income from selling their labour power, they are much more likely to dispose of this income as they so wish, with minimal contributions to the household fund. In a variety of settings, it has been found that women are more likely to pool the income which they have earned from their own independent income-generating activities with their spouses and children as compared to men (Roldán 1982; Flora and Santos 1985).

It has also been has demonstrated that there is not a one-to-one correspondence between income pooling and shared consumption. The practice of male preference in protein and caloric consumption is common to many societies, with men either eating first or being served the choice morsels. Folbre (1986), reviewing a broad range of cross-cultural material, thus concludes that women work more and consume less than men within rural households. This proposition suggests that the assumption of an undifferentiated return to family labour is a problematic building block for a theory of peasant economy.

Feminist work on intra-household relations has also questioned the appropriateness of the concept of household strategies (Schmink 1984). As Wolf (1990) argues, in the peasant studies literature individual and household behaviour is often merged and discussed interchangeably as if a household had a logic and an interest of its own. At the very least, the concept of a household strategy implies a unity or coincidence of interests among household members. Nevertheless, until recently, little attention was given within the peasant studies literature to how such a unity of interests might be achieved, imposed, or implemented.

Recent feminist analysis has shown that gender and generational hierarchies and the struggles within and among them are central to an understanding of peasant household economy, whether in South-East Asia, the Middle East, or Latin America (Hart 1986; Berik 1987; Wolf 1990, 1992, Stephen 1991). Household decision making – whether with respect to farm decisions, labour allocation among different income-generating activities, family size, consumption, and so on – is rarely democratic. Rather, those with more authority or bargaining power – men and adults – tend to make decisions over those with less – women and children. Women and children often do not participate in how 'household' goals are defined.

Moreover, 'household strategies' do not necessarily reflect the interests of all household members. For example, the common practice of sending daughters to school at a later age than sons may be a rational household strategy if young girls are more productive than boys at an earlier age, due to their significant contribution to domestic work and animal care. Moreover, sending girls to school for fewer years than their brothers may represent a rational household strategy if there is a greater return to education for men than for women due to unequal labour market opportunities. But such 'rational' household strategies do not serve the interests of young women very well.

As Folbre (1986, 1987) has argued in a more general context, the significant differences in economic welfare among household members in terms of consumption levels, noted earlier, also shed doubt on the assumption that altruism governs household behaviour. She contends, instead, that economic self-interest penetrates the most intimate aspects of household life. For Folbre, inequality within the household is linked to differences between men and women in bargaining power. She considers these differences not just culturally determined but directly related to the institutions of patriarchy, such as systematic differences in access to means of production, wealth and wages.

Other researchers highlight how gender relations are an arena of potential conflict and constant struggle. Benería and Roldán (1987), for example, propose that intra-household relations are characterized by a continuous process of negotiation, contracts, renegotiation and exchange. However, negotiations between men and women are rarely carried out as equals, but rather are constrained by the very system of authority structuring household relations.

In sum, there seems to be general agreement that rather than by cohesion and coherence, as implied by altruism, intra-household relations are governed by relations of domination and subordination, hierarchy and inequality, and struggle and conflict. This suggests that to posit the existence of household strategies, the cultural rules, attitudes and beliefs, and the material conditions which favour the pursuit of altruism rather than self-interest, as well as the conditions which favour negotiation, compromise and cooperation within the family, must be subject to scrutiny.

Recent research has focused on the role of rural women's rights in land in determining their bargaining position within and outside the household. In the bargaining power approach to the analysis of family relations, bargaining power depends on a number of factors, but particularly on a family member's 'fall-back position' if family cooperation fails to benefit all members (Sen 1983, 1990). Agarwal (1994a, 1994b) argues that among the factors determining rural women's fall-back position in intra-household bargaining, private land rights are even more important than access to employment. In her masterful survey of women's traditional land rights in South Asia, she demonstrates that in matrilineal and bilateral systems of inheritance (systems in which marital customs kept land within the kin group) women had considerable bargaining power in household relations.

Although in the post-1950s period most South Asian states adopted gender-progressive inheritance laws which established that women may have independent property rights in land, these legal changes have been hotly contested in regions with traditional patrilineal inheritance systems. Among the factors constraining women in exercising their land rights are patrilocal post-marital residency; low levels of female literacy; strong (at times, violent) opposition from male kin; the social construction of gender needs and roles; and male bias at all levels of public decision making. Agarwal argues that even the idea that women need independent rights in land (in terms of their welfare, to increase their efficiency, to ensure their equality with men and to secure their empowerment) is still an arena of struggle, one which requires contestation by women at all levels – the household, the community and the state.

In South Asia (Agarwal 1994a), Africa (Sachs 1994) and Latin America (Deere 1987) the main beneficiaries of state-directed agrarian reforms have been primarily male household heads. Nonetheless, Deere and León (1997) found that in the 1990s the growth of the feminist movement, both nationally and internationally, and of rural women's organizations, combined with the spread of governmental offices and ministries concerned with ending discrimination against women, have resulted in more gender-neutral agrarian legislation in Latin America. For example, a number of countries now provide that in state-directed land redistribution efforts, land must be titled in the name of both spouses.

A final concern in the literature has been with the persistence of the peasantry in the Third World, given the growth of agro-industry, large scale proletarianization, and high rates of rural–urban migration (Deere 1990). The persistence of the peasantry is often explained in terms of peasants' ability to produce cheap food or provide cheap seasonal labour for capitalist markets (de Janvry 1981). Peasants will accept a price less than that which capitalist farmers might accept since peasants do not need to earn a profit to stay in business but, rather, simply a positive return to their labour. Similarly, peasant wage workers can accept a wage less than that needed to reproduce the capacity to labour, since some portion of consumption requirements are met through subsistence production on the household plot.

It has been argued that what gives peasant units of production their competitive edge in capitalist markets is the non-transferability of family labour (Schejtman 1980). Specifically, because women, children and the elderly often have a zero or low opportunity cost (that is, few if any alternatives for generating income), the household is better off no matter how low the return to family labour in agricultural production.

Feminist researchers have probed further, asking why this might be the case. They have demonstrated that there is, indeed, a differential social valuation of male and female labour, both in the capitalist labour market and among and within peasant households, and that these factors are highly interactive (Roldán 1982; Spindel 1987; Collins 1993). In the labour market, the subordination of women allows capitalists to pay women lower wages than men, even for similar tasks and at comparable levels of productivity (Mones et al. 1987). Women also earn less than men because of gender segregation of the labour force and differential wage scales for male and female jobs and tasks (Arizpe and Aranda 1981; Lago 1987; CIERA et al. 1987). Moreover, often the structure of agricultural employment – whereby permanent wage employment is a male domain – limits women's potential income opportunities outside the household, relegating them to either seasonal, labour-intensive tasks, or household-based production – thus rendering their labour 'non-transferable'.

Another aspect of this non-transferability which must be taken into account in explaining why family labour is cheap, is the concept of 'joint production' and the gender division of labour which assigns to women the tasks of daily and generational reproduction. An often-noted characteristic of rural women's work is that they carry out several activities simultaneously in time, combining productive and reproductive tasks. If the notion of simultaneity is extended to cover the length of the working day, another general characteristic of rural women's work is the wide range of productive and reproductive activities in which they engage (Campana 1982; Floro 1994). In a typical day, a peasant woman might pasture her animals while spinning and collecting firewood, work three or four hours in the field after cooking for the field hands, in addition to spending six or seven hours on housework, food processing and child care. Each of these activities taken by itself may be lowly remunerated or unremunerated. But taken together they serve to enhance the household's level of reproduction, mitigating the effects of a low return to family labour implicit in low prices for peasant production or of low wages. In sum, gender analysis has revealed that the competitive edge of peasant units of production may in fact lie in the subordination of women and the undervaluation of female labour in productive and reproductive activities.

This entry has largely focused on conceptual issues and the contributions which feminist analysis has made to an understanding of the peasantry in the Third World. If in the 1970s and early 1980s the bulk of empirical work in this field centered on making rural women's work visible and in understanding changes in the gender division of labour in agriculture, the focus of the 1990s has been on understanding the impact of structural adjustment policies and the neo-liberal model in agriculture – in which the market is seen as the main and best allocator of resources in an economy, with government assuming a reduced role. Considerable research has been undertaken on gender and rural labour markets in this latter context, in particular, the conditions which give rise to a new feminization of agriculture (see, for example, Deere and León 1987, Collins 1993; Lara Flores 1995). Less attention has been given until recently to gender and rural land, water and credit markets. Since the adoption of the neo-liberal model in agriculture usually implies the privatization of communal land holdings, production cooperatives and water rights, in addition to the withdrawal of the state from the provision of subsidized credit and technical assistance to poor farmers, there is an ample research agenda for feminist researchers. Moreover, with the end of agrarian reform efforts throughout much of the Third World, women's access to land will increasingly depend on inheritance practices and the functioning of land markets, both under-researched topics. If women's bargaining position within the rural household is largely determined by women's access to property, as suggested above, there is much work ahead to be done.

CARMEN DIANA DEERE

See also
Development Policies; Development, Theories of; Double Day/Second Shift; Economic Restructuring; Family, Economics of; Game Theory and Bargaining Models; Migration; Structural Adjustment Policies; Technological Change.

Bibliography
Agarwal, Bina (1994a), *A Field of One's Own: Gender and Land Rights in South Asia*, Cambridge: Cambridge University Press.
Agarwal, Bina (1994b), 'Gender and command over property: a critical gap in economic analysis and policy in South Asia', *World Development*, 22 (10), 1455–78.
Arizpe, Lourdes and Josefina Aranda (1981) 'The "Comparative Advantages" of women's

disadvantages: women workers in the strawberry export agribusiness in Mexico', *Signs*, 7 (2), 453–73.

Benería, Lourdes and Martha Roldan (1987), *The Crossroads of Class and Gender*, Chicago: University of Chicago Press.

Benería, Lourdes and Gita Sen (1981), 'Accumulation, reproduction and women's role in economic development: Boserup revisited', *Signs*, 7 (2), 279–98.

Berik, Gunseli (1987), *Women Carpetweavers in Rural Turkey: Patterns of Employment, Earnings and Status*, Geneva: ILO.

Bourque, Susan and Kay Warren (1981), *Women of the Andes: Patriarchy and Social Change in Rural Peru*, Ann Arbor: University of Michigan Press.

Boserup, Ester (1970), *Women's Role in Economic Development*, New York: St Martin's Press.

Bruce, Judith and Daisy Dwyer (eds) (1988), *A Home Divided: Women and Income in the Third World*, Stanford: Stanford University Press.

Campaña, Pilar (1982), 'Mujer, trabajo y subordinación en la Sierra Central del Peru', in M. León (ed.), *Las Trabajadoras del Agro*, Bogotá: ACEP, pp. 143–60.

Chayanov, A.V. (1966), *The Theory of Peasant Economy*, ed. by D. Thorner, B. Verblay and R.E.F. Smith, Homewood, Illinois: Irwin.

CIERA, ATC, and CETRA (1987), *Mujer y agroexportación en Nicaragua*, Managua: Instituto Nicaraguense de la Mujer.

Collins, Jane (1993), 'Gender, contracts and wage work: agricultural restructuring in Brazil's São Francisco Valley', *Development and Change*, 24 (1), 53–82.

Crummett, María de los Angeles (1987), 'Class, household structure, and the peasantry: an empirical approach', *Journal of Peasant Studies*, 14 (3).

Deere, Carmen Diana (1987), 'The Latin American Agrarian Reform Experience', in C.D. Deere and M. León (eds), *Rural Women and State Policy: Feminist Perspectives on Latin American Agricultural Development*, Boulder: Westview Press, pp. 165–90.

Deere, Carmen Diana (1990), *Household and Class Relations: Peasants and Landlords in Northern Peru*, Berkeley: University of California Press.

Deere, Carmen Diana (1995), 'What difference does gender make? Rethinking peasant studies', *Feminist Economics*, 1 (1), 53–72.

Deere, Carmen Diana and Magdalena León (1982), *Women in Andean Agriculture: Peasant Production and Rural Wage Employment in Colombia and Peru*, Geneva: ILO.

Deere, Carmen Diana and Magdalena León (eds) (1987), *Rural Women and State Policy: Feminist Perspectives on Latin American Agricultural Development*, Boulder: Westview Press.

Deere, Carmen Diana and Magdalena León (1997), 'Women and Land Rights in the Latin American Neo-Liberal Counter-Reforms', Women in International Development Working Paper #264, Michigan State University.

de Janvry, Alain (1981), *The Agrarian Question and Reformism in Latin America*, Baltimore: Johns Hopkins University Press.

Dixon, Ruth (1984), *Women's Work in Third World Agriculture: Concepts and Indicators*, Geneva: ILO.

Evers, Hans-Dieter, W. Clauss and Diana Wong (1984), 'Subsistence Reproduction: a Framework for Analysis', in Joan Smith, I. Wallerstein and H.D. Evers (eds), *Households and the World Economy*, Beverly Hills, California: Sage, pp. 23–36.

Flora, Cornelia and Blas Santos (1985), 'Women in Farming Systems in Latin America', in J. Nash and H. Safa (eds), *Women and Change in Latin America*, So. Hadley: Bergin & Garvey, pp. 208–28.

Floro, Maria Sagrario (1994), 'Work Intensity and Time Use: What Do Women Do When There Aren't Enough Hours in a Day?', in G. Young and B. Dickerson (eds), *Color, Class and Country: Experiences of Gender*, London: Zed Books.

Folbre, Nancy (1986), 'Cleaning house: New perspectives on households and economic development', *Journal of Development Economics*, 22 (1), 5–40.

Folbre, Nancy (1987), 'The Black Four of Hearts: Toward a New Paradigm of Household Economics', in J. Bruce and D. Dwyer (eds), *A Home Divided: Women and Income in the Third World*, Stanford: Stanford University Press.

Guyer, Jane (1991), 'Female Farming in Anthropology and African History', in M. di Leonardo (ed.), *Gender at the Crossroads of Knowledge: Feminist Anthropology in the Postmodern Era*, Berkeley: University of California Press.

Harris, Olivia (1978), 'Complementarity and Conflict: An Andean View of Women and Men', in J. LaFontaine (ed.), *Sex and Age as Principles of Social Differentiation*, London: Academic Press.

Hart, Gillian (1986), *Power, Labour and Livelihood: Processes of Change in Rural Java*, Berkeley: University of California Press.

Kandiyoti, Deniz (1985), *Women in Rural Production Systems: Problems and Policies*, Paris: UNESCO.

Lago, M. Soledad (1987), 'Rural Women and the Neo-Liberal Model in Chile', in C.D. Deere and M. León (eds), *Rural Women and State Policy: Feminist Perspectives on Agricultural Development in Latin America*, Boulder: Westview, pp 21–34.

Lara Flores, Sara María (ed.) (1995), *El rostro femenino del mercado de trabajo rural en América Latina*, Caracas: Nueva Sociedad and UNRISD.

Mones, Belkis, Lidia Grant, Taracy Rosado and Pastora Hernandez (1987), 'Proletarizacion Femenina y el Limitado Mercado Laboral Agrícola', in F. Pou et al. (eds), *La Mujer Rural Dominicana*, Santo Domingo: CIPAF, pp. 167–84.

Poats, Susan, Marianne Schmink and Anita Spring (eds) (1988), *Gender Issues in Farming Systems Research and Extension*, Boulder: Westview.

Roldán, Martha (1982), 'Subordinación genérica y proletarización rural: un estudio de caso en el Noroeste Mexicano', in M. León (ed.), *Las Trabajadoras del Agro*, Bogotá: ACEP, pp. 75–102.

Sachs, Karen (1994), *Gendered Fields: Rural Women, Agriculture and Environment*, Boulder: Westview Press.

Schejtman, Alexander (1980), 'The peasant economy: internal logic, articulation, and persistence', *CEPAL Review*, no. 11, 115–34.

Schmink, Marianne (1984), 'Household economic strategies: Review and research agenda', *Latin American Research Review*, **19** (3), 87–101.

Sen, Amartya (1983), 'Economics and the family', *Asian Development Review*, **1**.

Sen, Amartya (1990), 'Gender and Cooperative Conflicts', in I. Tinker (ed.), *Persistent Inequalities*, New York: Oxford.

Spindel, Cheywa (1987), 'The Social Invisibility of Women's Work in Brazilian Agriculture', in C.D. Deere and M. León (eds), *Rural Women and State Policy: Feminist Perspectives on Latin American Agricultural Development*, Boulder: Westview Press, pp. 51–66.

Stephen, Lynn (1991) *Zapotec Women*, Austin: University of Texas Press.

Wolf, Diane (1990), 'Daughters, decisions, and domination: an empirical and conceptual critique of household strategies', *Development and Change*, **21**, 43–74.

Wolf, Diane (1992), *Factory Daughters: Gender, Household Dynamics, and Rural Industrialization in Java*, Berkeley: University of California Press.

Wolf, Eric (1966), *Peasants*, Englewood Cliffs, New Jersey: Prentice-Hall.

Austrian Economics

Austrian economics begins in 1871 with the publication of Carl Menger's *Grundsätze der Volkswirtschaftlehre* (Principles of Economics). It continued in the nineteenth century in the works of Friedrich von Wieser and Eugen von Böhm-Bawerk. Major theorists in the early twentieth century include Friedrich A. Hayek (1889–1992), winner of the Nobel Prize in 1974 and author of the classic book, *The Road to Serfdom*, and Ludwig von Mises (1881–1973). Major contemporary theorists include Israel Kirzner and the late Murray Rothbard (White 1984 pp. 4–7). In this entry the extant discussions of feminist economics by Austrian economists will be reviewed. Contributions to the literature regarding issues of gender by an Austrian economist will also be reviewed in order to explore the areas of convergence and divergence between Austrian and feminist approaches to both economics and gender.

Some elements of Austrian economics are essential to understanding both the convergence and divergence of Austrian, neoclassical and feminist economics. Austrian economists view human behaviour as the purposeful, goal-directed behaviour of people pursuing their individual plans which are constructed from the subjective values of each person. This creates an economic environment of pervasive uncertainty. The only proper subject matter of economics is the social consequences of this individual behaviour. People voluntarily come together to make exchanges in order to promote their plans. There is no supposition that the plans will necessarily conflict or coordinate. Through the process of competition, the different interests of the participants are meliorated, as they each adjust their plans in light of the new information being created and revealed as market processes continue. There is no belief that any equilibrium will necessarily emerge, only that the market process, if unfettered, will allow individuals to make adjustments in their plans to promote their interests. These purposeful individuals through market processes both create and use the knowledge that emerges in the form of prices.

Karen Vaughn, a contemporary Austrian economist, in her review of neoclassical contributions in *Beyond Economic Man* (Ferber and Nelson 1993) expresses sympathy with many of the criticisms levelled by feminist economists on the theory and practice of economics (Vaughn 1994, p. 309). She argues in contrast to the authors she is reviewing:

> these particular complaints do not imply that the economic approach to understanding human action is the culprit. Rather, it is the misunderstanding of the limits of the economic approach to human behavior and the misapplication of that approach to situations where it is unilluminating at best that leads to some of the problems the authors identify. (p. 309)

She argues that feminists mistake mathematical formalization for the economic approach to understanding human behaviour and notes that Austrians use verbal approaches (ibid., p. 310). But the core of her Austrian reactions to non-Austrian feminist writings is the differences between the Austrian view of the economic approach to human behaviour and orthodox neoclassical economics.

Vaughn asserts that 'economics is an approach to a particular subject matter – the study of exchange in markets' (pp. 310–11). She expands on this theme by describing Hayek's view of economics or 'catallactics' which focuses on how markets coordinate the complex interactions of many individuals

with no overall common goal, who pursue their own projects and plans in
cooperation with one another despite their differences and conflicts (p. 311).

> Catallactics takes the market as a primary focus of study because peaceful, con-
> tractual exchange is one way of producing order and wealth out of potential
> conflict. Hence the so-called 'privileging' of contract and markets in economics.
> (p. 311)

She notes that rationality in the Austrian framework has a very different
meaning from that employed in neoclassical economics: 'Rationality ... means
simply choosing the more highly valued alternative over the less valued
alternative according to one's own judgement' (p. 310).

Vaughn's presentation is only a book review but it highlights the important
differences that make the inclusion of gender less difficult, the discussion of
some issues of interest to feminists more difficult, and the approach to policy
fairly straightforward in the Austrian theoretical framework. The rational
individuals of Austrian economics pursue their objectives as fully enculturated
human beings; everyone comes to the market with cultural baggage, and the
results of patriarchy and sexism on market participants are only one kind of
baggage. The analysis of that cultural baggage is part of sociology, anthropology, psychology, or possibly biology, but not economics. Unlike neoclassical
economics, the Austrian individual's behaviour is not going to be modelled
mathematically, consequently the Austrian individual need not possess distinct, separable, well-ordered preferences. Thus the Austrian approach accepts
cultural phenomena, such as gender identities, as important in the construction of individuals' plans of action, but prior to the behaviour that is of
interest to the Austrian economist.

The Austrian economic approach to human behaviour explores the consequences of these purposeful, goal-directed individuals each pursuing their
diverse and possibly incompatible plans, who are 'radically ignorant' because
of pervasive uncertainty, each choosing in the market place those exchanges
that promote their plans. Of interest to Austrians is the emergence of sponta-
neous order out of these uncoordinated plans of individual agents. Thus only
the behaviour of market participants is clearly within the purview of Austrian
economists. Vaughn does note that there is no a priori reason not to use this
approach on the household (Vaughn 1994, p. 311) or other social institutions,
but that one could go beyond the boundaries of usefulness she articulates (see
above). However, Vaughn is made uncomfortable by Julie Nelson's characterization of economics as a science of provisioning for two reasons. She
notes that provisioning is undefined. This concerns Vaughn because it *might*
extend a household model based on essentialist assumptions about human
behaviour derived from the household experience to the entire economy. She
notes that households are traditionally the site of authoritarian behaviour

which is anathema to the Austrian libertarian perspective in its conceptualization of markets (pp. 311–12).

The understanding of market processes by Austrian economists needs to be elaborated to make clear Austrian economists' attempts to deal with issues of interest to feminists. Austrian economists understand competition as a dynamic process that includes traditional price competition behaviour, entrepreneurship and rivalry in a market system characterized by pervasive uncertainty. In the Austrian economic approach to market-place discrimination, like that of neoclassical economist Gary Becker, discrimination disadvantages all those who discriminate since they may incur higher costs by restricting the available pool of employees or pay higher prices as a result of discriminating among merchants from whom they purchase goods and services. Also individuals who object to discrimination will choose to exchange and interact with others who do not have a taste for discrimination. Consequently, Austrian economists conclude little in the way of governmental intervention is desirable. Moreover, this is consistent with most Austrian economists' commitment to a classical liberal approach to human behaviour where individual freedom is a primary value to be preserved. Consequently, collective action of any sort is morally, ethically, methodologically and theoretically suspect. All of this results in an admirable internal consistency in Austrian economic thought.

Since frequently the results of Austrian economics and neoclassical economics converge, and since their practitioners often share basic ideological commitments, it may seem that Austrian economics is simply another variant of mainstream thought. However, Horowitz (1995) argues that feminist and Austrian economists share certain epistemological and methodological criticisms of neoclassical economics. For example, Horowitz argues that the feminist economists' rejection of Cartesian masculine conceptions of science is similar to Austrian and Hayekian rejection of Cartesianism: 'many feminists argue that the official methodology of science, developed by Descartes and Bacon among others, privileges male notions of objectivity and rationality to the exclusion of subjectivity and emotion which were seen as predominantly female and, therefore, to be avoided' (Horowitz 1995, p. 261). From this Horowitz concludes that the feminist economics project includes 'the attempt to rehabilitate a real, acting subject'. He sees this as parallel to the 'extension of subjectivism from value to knowledge and, most recently, all the way to the interpretations and expectations of economic actors'. He is referring to moving away from the subjective utility framework of neoclassical economics to a position accepting the social construction of knowledge, interpretation, and expectation formation, which he claims Austrians and feminists share. He notes later, oddly in a different context, that Donald Lavoie has shown links between Austrian and 'post-positivist', 'non-objectivist' conceptions of knowledge (pp. 268–9). Presumably this indicates a post-structuralist turn shared by Austrians and feminists.

Horowitz bases his argument almost exclusively on Hayek's rejection of the possibility of objective social science which led Hayek to argue for subjective approaches to economics. However, unlike feminists, Hayek accepted the Cartesian dualistic disjunction between objective/subjective; he even accepted the dominance of objectivity in the natural sciences. He simply turned the dualism over, asserting a dominance of subjective over objective knowledge in the social sciences. Horowitz (except in his brief nod to Lavoie) thinks that feminist economists generally treat the Cartesian framework similarly, so he associates Austrian thought with radical feminist approaches to knowledge.

Horowitz addresses two substantive concerns regarding feminist economics. He responds to England's (1993, p. 42) argument that a more connective self would take into account empathy and allow interpersonal comparisons of utility. Horowitz notes that England is referring to the neoclassical notion of utility as hedonic (concerning feelings), whereas the Austrian conception of utility is the ranking of importance of various means and ends. Thus the absence of empathetic understanding, seen as the barrier to interpersonal utility comparisons by England, could only be resolved by completely knowing the mind of another in the Austrian framework (Horowitz 1995, pp. 269–70). Horowitz also notes that Strober's (1994) association of competition with masculinity as an example of androcentrism in economics, because it privileges male notions of social interaction, requires examination on two counts. First, her characterization of competition as aggressive, masculine behaviour is at odds with the extremely passive characterization of competition in the neoclassical purely competitive model. Second, such a criticism of competition as aggressive and destructive, while possibly consistent in Horowitz's view with the Schumpeterian characterization of entrepreneurship, are inconsistent with Austrian economists', particularly Israel Kirzner's, characterization of entrepreneurship.

Horowitz argues that Austrian economic notions of competition focus on how individual competition leads to unintentional social cooperation and that the false dichotomy in feminist economics between market competition (as masculine and aggressive) and intentional forms of cooperation (feminine) illustrates an opportunity for an expanded research agenda for both feminist and Austrian economists. Austrian economists could explore the effects of intentional cooperative efforts on both sides of the market and feminists could explore the effects of unintentional cooperation resulting from market exchange (Horowitz 1995, pp. 273–4).

Horowitz concludes that Austrian economists would benefit from exploring the gender-based critique of markets presented by feminists; and that feminists, who are more sceptical of markets than he views the profession at large, would benefit from exploring 'comparative epistemological advantages of alternative political and economic institutions' (Horowitz 1995, p. 273). And he believes feminists, who he sees as interventionists, should consider the non-interventionist arguments of the Austrian economic tradition.

Deborah Walker is an Austrian economist who writes on topics of particular interest to feminists. Walker's (1984, 1988) work focuses on legislative inadequacy in the case of comparable worth legislative initiatives and mandatory family leave legislation. Her critique focuses on hidden costs and unintended consequences of legislation. Hidden costs and unintended consequences are changes firms and individuals make in response to legislation that decrease opportunities that previously existed (for example, employees cannot choose to work for less than the minimum wage). The dynamic character of market competition is always viewed as meliorative through changes in people's opportunities leading to altered rational choices.

Walker (1994) summarizes Austrian economic views on matters of race and gender. Of particular interest are the views presented on discrimination. She notes that public policy in the area of employment discrimination was designed to 'promote equality of opportunity and to remedy both historical and current injustices in hiring practices' (Walker 1994, p. 362). She believes that the public policy debate has 'centered around perceived social injustices', but asks, 'are people in those markets making choices themselves which simply lead to some occupations being predominantly female and others being predominantly male?' clearly reflecting the methodological individualism of the Austrian approach (p. 362).

Walker admits discrimination exists, but argues, 'Generally, we cannot say that labour market discrimination is the problem' (Walker 1994, p. 363). This is because there are types of discrimination which are not undesirable from the Austrian economic perspective or from the Austrian ethical perspective. Her argument hinges on distinctions among the possible meanings of equality of opportunity. She identifies two meanings of the term: first, everyone can offer their services for a particular job; and second, employers have an obligation to consider everyone who makes an offer and are prohibited from using certain characteristics in evaluating those offers. She argues that free markets devoid of legal restrictions underly the former, and the latter is the motivation behind the US Civil Rights Act of 1964 (Title 7) (p. 363). She asserts that discrimination that is a social problem exists alongside rational desirable discrimination, such as discrimination that occurs when some physical characteristic not shared by all applicants is required for the job or safety of one group of potential employees over others (pp. 363–4).

Walker then addresses the question of whether markets decrease discrimination. She begins by noting that discrimination increases search costs and labour costs, thus it decreases the profitability of firms engaging in discriminatory hiring practices. Because of the cost disadvantage associated with discrimination, sufficiently competitive markets may punish the offending employers. Thus she concludes the competitive markets can eliminate discrimination. She also notes that as information about potential employees becomes available through market competition, the ability of individual job applicants to demonstrate their commitment to their employer by customizing their job contracts (for example by agreeing not to take extended medical or child care leave), is compromised by legislative action. Thus a free market can not only reduce undesirable discrimination, but could increase the ability of individual women to provide employers with information that might enhance their job opportunities. She notes that other legislation, notably minimum-wage legislation and Davis–Bacon legislation (which prohibits government from undercutting prevailing local wage rates on government projects), prevents workers from offering their services to employers on terms that may be mutually attractive, meaning at lower wages than the legislation allows.

Finally, Walker reviews the unintended consequences of affirmative action. Firms are less efficient because they have had to hire less productive employees which leads to lower economic growth and less job creation (Walker 1994, p. 369). Employers may only hire the 'cream of the crop' among women and minorities, who 'would have been able to find employment in the absence of anti-discrimination laws' (p. 369), so the employer never has to fire an employee and face a lawsuit alleging discriminatory employment practices. Thus other minorities, not the cream of the crop, will face diminished employment opportunities. She also addresses the psychological costs of affirmative action. Qualified individuals may feel that it is unfair that women and minorities are given preference in some hiring situations and take it out on women and minorities. Employers might hire unqualified women and minorities to avoid lawsuits, and as a result confirm negative stereotypes to the disadvantage of all women and minorities. And, 'affirmative action legislation sends the message to people that they do not have to achieve advancement on their own' (p. 369).

Walker's essay nicely presents the Austrian economic position on discrimination. Unfortunately her presentation does not present any of the empirical evidence that may support her argument. In addition, Walker jumps seamlessly from the theoretical argument that markets can reduce discrimination, to the assertion that markets *have historically* reduced discrimination. The Austrian faith in the superiority of unfettered market processes over legal intervention in those processes does not put them at odds with much theoretical neoclassical work on these subjects; but it certainly puts them at odds with most feminist and empirical work on these subjects.

Boettke (1995) addresses some issues of interest to feminists and economists from an Austrian perspective in his review of Richard Posner's book
Sex and Reason (1992). While Boettke commends Posner for his application
of rational choice theory to sexual behaviour, he also takes Posner to task for
accepting the positive/normative distinction and privileging 'scientific' discourse over civic discourse (Boettke 1995, p. 364). He also notes that where
the economic approach to human behaviour could be applied in a useful way
to human sexuality is in the exploration of how the choices made by different
people generate the rules and norms of sexual behaviour. Boettke shows how
Posner's neoclassical approach is unable to engage the issues raised by feminists such as those raised by Catherine MacKinnon (pp. 370–71).

Both Vaughn and Horowitz make a compelling case that there is nothing in
the epistemological or methodological foundations of Austrian economics
which precludes the development of a distinctly Austrian feminist economics
or theoretical consideration of issues of concern to feminists. Both indicate
that incorporation of gender constructions into the construction of people's
identity and plans is within their understanding of Austrian economics.
Vaughn's concern with the limits and boundaries for useful application of the
Austrian perspective on human behaviour suggests there might be some
subject matter of interest to feminists where application of the Austrian
perspective would not be useful. Walker's work shows how Austrian approaches can be used to explore issues of discrimination bearing out the
optimism of Vaughn and Horowitz. Boettke's review is interesting because he
explicates the limitations of neoclassical approaches to some issues of concern to feminists, shows how the Austrian approach might lead to better
questions and analyses, and makes a credible attempt to engage the work of
MacKinnon in a non-trivial way from the Austrian perspective. It seems that
an Austrian-feminist approach to economics is possible, but that potential is
significantly underdeveloped at present.

WILLIAM WALLER

See also
Affirmative Action; Discrimination, Theories of; Dualisms; Labour Markets, Theories of; Methodology.

Bibliography
Boettke, Peter J. (1995), 'Good economics – bad sex (and even worse philosophy): a review
essay', *Review of Political Economy*, 7 (3), 360–73.
England, Paula (1993), 'The Separative Self: Androcentric Bias in Neoclassical Assumptions',
in M. Ferber and J. Nelson (eds), *Beyond Economic Man: Feminist Theory and Economics*,
Chicago: University of Chicago Press, pp. 37–53.
Ferber, M. and J. Nelson (1993), *Beyond Economic Man: Feminist Theory and Economics*,
Chicago: University of Chicago Press.
Hayek, F.A. (1944), *The Road to Serfdom*, Chicago: University of Chicago Press.

Horowitz, S. (1995), 'Feminist economics: an Austrian perspective', *Journal of Economic Methodology*, **2** (2), 259–79.

Posner, Richard (1992), *Sex and Reason*, Cambridge: Harvard University Press.

Strober, M. (1994), 'Rethinking economics through a feminist lens', *American Economic Association Papers and Proceedings*, **84**, 143–7.

Vaughn, K. (1994), 'Beyond *Beyond Economic Man*: a critique of feminist economics', *Journal of Economic Methodology*, **1** (2), 307–13.

Walker, D. (1984), 'Value and Opportunity: The Issue of Comparable Pay for Comparable Worth', CATO Institute Policy Analysis, Number 38, 31 May.

Walker, D. (1988), 'Mandatory Family-Leave Legislation: The Hidden Cost', *CATO Institute Policy Analysis*, No. 108, 8 June.

Walker, D. (1994), 'Economics of Gender and Race', in P. Boettke (ed.), *The Elgar Companion to Austrian Economics*, Aldershot: Edward Elgar.

White, L. (1984), *The Methodology of the Austrian School of Economics*, Auburn, Alabama: The Ludwig von Mises Institute of Auburn University.

Banking and Credit

Women-owned businesses are growing in number worldwide. They include cottage industries in the developing world, established by women living in poverty and struggling to survive and feed their families (World Bank 1996); small businesses created by low-income women in developed countries like the USA and Canada, for whom entrepreneurship is a gateway to survival and getting off welfare rolls (US Department of Commerce 1997, Raheim 1997); and small to medium-sized businesses in the developed world established by middle- to high-income women to circumvent the glass ceiling (Mergenhagen 1996). Credit access is important to any business, but it is often difficult to obtain for small businesses with limited collateral and credit history. Consequently, access to credit for the purposes of financing such small businesses has important implications for the economic status of many women. Because of limited savings and personal assets, as well as the nature of their activities, women's businesses and their loan requirements tend to be small (Bakker 1994). Although lending to these types of businesses is often perceived as risky, a variety of 'microcredit' projects, offering small, unsecured loans to small businesses, have been found to be worthwhile in developing nations (Counts 1996). The success of these microcredit projects has led to interest in credit programs such as microfinance for low-income female heads of household in developed countries like the USA and Canada.

Although central banks view their policy actions as gender-neutral because they target aggregate variables like interest rates, women are disproportionately affected by monetary policy, especially during contractions. Because small businesses tend to be more dependent on local bank loans than larger firms (Hubbard 1995) and face more restrictive, more expensive access to bank credit, they bear a disproportionate burden of a credit crunch. But recent research on the role played by bank lending in the transmission of a monetary contraction policy (a reduction in the money supply leading to higher interest rates) has suggested that smaller firms are affected differently from larger businesses (Hubbard 1995). A reduction in the money supply reduces bank reserves and can increase uncertainty that results in a shrinking pool of credit that is extended only to those with the best credit ratings (Abell 1991). The burden tends to fall on less preferred customers, those with marginal credit ratings, along with smaller, riskier enterprises (Kashyap and Stein 1994). In addition, increases in market interest rates increase the charges to small firms because un-collateralized bank loans are more expensive (Hubbard 1995, Oliner and Rudebusch 1996). Thus women-owned businesses may experience greater negative effects from central bank policies since they are more likely to fall into this category of small firms with more restricted access to credit.

Recent developments in microfinance, which first emerged in developing countries in the form of microcredit, offer potential remedies for limited credit access. The numbers of women in the world gaining access to credit for small enterprises through various forms of microcredit peer-lending organizations is still relatively modest. But the experience of the last decades, as variations of microcredit networks have been developed in Asia, Africa and Latin America, is beginning to demonstrate that access to modest amounts of credit without collateral can transform the lives of low-income women and their families (Todd 1996). This success has captured the attention of development organizations such as the World Bank and the United States Agency for International Development (USAID) and has spawned projects such as GEMINI (Growth and Equity through Microenterprise Investments and Institutions) and even an international summit conference held in Washington, DC, in 1997. Nevertheless, academic scholars, especially academic economists, remain sceptical because of data and theoretical limitations associated with analysing microcredit groups.

In developing countries, two factors are recognized as common sources of credit restriction in the formal financial sector for women: their lack of control over economic resources and the nature of their economic activity. Many women in developing countries do not hold land rights, and so often cannot provide collateral to gain access to credit. Husbands often have to sign for and make spending decisions about the loans that women are responsible for repaying. Women's businesses tend to be especially small, often with only one worker. Characteristics of formal bank credit are often inappropriate for the needs of female micro entrepreneurs because of the time involved to process loan applications, inconvenient bank working hours, requirements for guarantors and the high margin charged on loans (Bayas et al. 1994). Projects have recently been implemented in many developing countries to address women's entrepreneurship and access to formal credit. Even in developed countries like the USA, women have typically used personal credit cards, personal assets, business earnings and supplier credit rather than bank loans, in addition to family and friends (Mergenhagen 1996).

Like those in developing countries, women's businesses in the developed world tend to be newer and concentrated in lower-return service sector businesses. The owners have competing family responsibilities, and there are many gender-related barriers to the establishment and growth of business concerns. Since women have lower incomes, they probably have less personal savings to offer as collateral. Even when their financial characteristics are the same as men's, discriminatory attitudes and practices on the part of lenders and creditors create barriers. For instance, in some cases women are still asked to have a spouse co-sign when applying for a loan (Bakker 1994).

As part of economic restructuring efforts in developing countries, programmes for increased credit access have been designed to target small entrepreneurs, who are predominantly women. More than eight million poor people worldwide, two thirds of whom are women, have used unsecured micro loans averaging US$75 to start businesses. This practice, which has taken place in developing countries for approximately 20 years, has become more common in the USA during the 1990s (Gaouette 1997). Microcredit lending in the USA has reached $130 million annually, and has grown from 50 programmes in 1991 to more than 200 operating in 44 states by 1996 (Gaouette 1997).

According to the World Bank, microcredit programmes have three key components that set them apart from other lending programmes: borrowers have very low incomes and no collateral; individuals must join a group of business peers in order to get a loan; and women are given preference for such loans, making up more than 80 per cent of total borrowers (World Bank 1996). The Grameen Bank in Bangladesh is often seen to be the international model of this type of microcredit project. In the Grameen system, a borrower must have four other friends who will qualify for loans. If one person in the group of five has difficulty, the others are obligated to assist or they risk having their lines of credit reduced, so support is coupled with peer pressure. The group receives some training on bank operations before it is approved and loans are made. Loan payments are made in weekly 'centre' meetings in villages. A centre includes 6–8 borrower groups of 5 members each. Centre meetings feature rituals designed to develop discipline and unity, such as singing songs and repeating a list of affirmations called 'Sixteen Decisions' (Counts 1996).

It is this peer group lending component coupled with the promise of continuing and increasing access to credit that provides the motivation to repay (Otero and Rhyne 1994). Borrowers start with a small loan, about US$50, but repeater loans of increasing amounts can be made as long as repayment of the loan is made. Continuing access is critical since it is believed that the poor need to have credit available for 8–10 years in order to escape poverty. This primary motivation has resulted in a repayment rate in excess of 95 per cent for most microcredit programmes (World Bank 1996). While training is provided for the financing process, no training is given for the activities to be financed. Borrowers can choose their own activities, which include projects such as poultry farming, petty trade and shopkeeping, cattle raising, or handicrafts (World Bank 1996).

In 1995, the Grameen Bank had 2 million borrowers spread through 34 000 villages in Bangladesh and the bank earned enough profits to hire 11 000 employees (Counts 1996). This success has inspired replications of the model in Asia, Africa and Latin America. The original idea of village-based microcredit has been moving toward 'microenterprise finance' in many areas. With this expansion to the formal financial sector, several themes are emerging. First, in order to reach large numbers of people, projects need to be self-sufficient because small, subsidized programmes are not viable. Second, to ensure the needed size and profits, informal sector techniques need to be adopted. These techniques include giving clients a strong motivation to repay via peer group lending, slashing administrative costs by decentralizing applications, approvals and collections. It is also important to have customer relations that are based on self-respect; borrowers should be seen as customers to be served, rather than as passive beneficiaries. Finally, it must be recognized that savings mobilization may be as important as credit. When there is no savings institution available, poor people save in forms like livestock or jewellery; the poor need savings to make the transition between seasons and to provide for family emergencies. If they can determine that their assets will be securely held and maintain value, are relatively liquid and in a convenient location, poor people prefer to save in a monetary form. But when institutions take savings and perform these functions, they become financial intermediaries (Otero and Rhyne 1994).

The microcredit model, as exemplified by the Grameen approach, is not without its controversies. Critics ask if working for income simply increases the burdens on already overworked women, and if women are targeted by microcredit projects because they are easier to discipline? In addition, critics point out that the staff of the Grameen Bank is predominantly male (Todd 1996). Despite these controversies, Todd (1996) found that ten years of membership in Grameen produced fundamental change in the family relationships of most of the women in her study. In two-thirds of Todd's sample, the Grameen borrowers contributed over half of net household income while a group of non-borrowers contributed only about one-fourth (Todd 1996, p. 48). Schuler and Hashemi (1994) found that when women have access to credit and control over their own resources, they gain status within the family and in the community as a result. On the other hand, Goetz and Gupta (1996) challenge these conclusions because the proportion of small loans to women in rural areas barely exceeds 5 per cent worldwide, and they question whether analysis of women's empowerment is about power or productivity. However, Todd (1996) maintains that it was the crucial nature of land and the critical function of the woman's capital in getting access to it that enabled most of the Grameen Bank borrowers she studied to obtain strong positions in their families. She points out that the alternative route to women's empowerment of getting education or training and escaping the household trap by working for wages is not yet a realistic option in most rural villages (Todd 1996).

There is a strong assumption in aid organizations supporting microcredit projects, that women will spend a greater share of their earnings on their families than men will. A frequently quoted survey finding from the Women's World Banking organization is that if a poor man in India earns 100 rupees, he will spend 40 of them feeding and educating his children. But if a poor Indian woman earns the same amount, she will spend 92 rupees on her children (Kuper 1996). If this finding is confirmed by additional formal research, it challenges many of the fundamental assumptions of neoclassical economics concerning individual behaviour and family decision making (see, for example, England 1993). This raises interesting questions for feminist research on the economics of the family and the ways in which the relative earnings of husbands and wives affect household decision making and family wellbeing.

In addition, feminist economists have an important role to play in the economic analysis of microcredit and microfinance projects necessary for effective policymaking in both developing and developed nations. Feminist economists have the challenge of identifying appropriate economic models and research methods to analyse the micro behaviour and macro impacts of these peer-lending programmes because the standard neoclassical approach with its assumptions of autonomous, self-interested behaviour in the market is inadequate.

In addition to the lack of appropriate economic models, the lack of data disaggregated by sex, particularly for larger-scale government as well as private lending in the formal sector, is a constraint for research. Questions that need to be examined include whether credit programmes increase women's power and status in the family and community or whether women are just working harder. The magnitude of gender differences in bank lending channel impacts, which is especially important since monetary policy is universally used as a policy tool, also needs to be examined. Finally, which characteristics leading to the success of microlending programmes in developing countries are universal and which are culture-specific need to be explored.

Feminist economists have a special challenge in finding appropriate ways to analyse microcredit groups and to examine how this approach can improve the welfare of women and their families, especially since traditional economic models are not particularly useful in analysing the microcredit behaviour of women entrepreneurs primarily motivated by cooperation with peers or the macroeconomic impact of a network of thousands of uncollaterized mini-loans. Small uncollaterized loans made available to women through peer-lending networks hold the promise of empowering not only women in developing countries, but low-income women in the developed world to lift themselves and their families out of poverty. But additional economic research is needed to move these projects from anecdotal stories in development to the economic mainstream.

LINDA M. MANNING AND PATRICIA GRAHAM

See also

Agriculture, Third World; Development Policies; Economic Restructuring; Informal Sector; Macroeconomics.

Bibliography

Abell, John D. (1991), 'Distributional effects of monetary and fiscal policy: Impacts on unemployment rates disaggregated by race and gender', *American Journal of Economics and Sociology*, **50** (3), (July), 269–84.

Bakker, Isabella (ed.) (1994), *Rethinking Restructuring: Gender and Change in Canada*, Toronto: University of Toronto Press.

Bayas, M.M., R.L. Meyer and N. Aguilera-Alfred (1994), 'Discrimination against women in formal credit markets: Reality or rhetoric?', *World Development*, **22** (7), (July), 1073–82.

Counts, Alex (1996), *Give Us Credit*, New York: Random House.

England, Paula (1993), 'Separative Self: Androcentric Bias in Neoclassical Assumptions', in Marianne A. Ferber and Julie A. Nelson (eds), *Beyond Economic Man: Feminist Theory and Economics*, Chicago and London: University of Chicago Press, pp. 37–53.

Gaouette, Nicole (1997), 'Mini loans help welfare mothers to create their own jobs', *The Christian Science Monitor*, 4 January.

Goetz, Anne Marie and Rina Sen Gupta (1996), 'Who takes the credit? Gender, power, and control over loan use in rural credit programs in Bangladesh', *World Development*, **24**, 45–63.

Hubbard, R. Glenn (1995), 'Is there a credit channel for monetary policy?', *St. Louis Federal Reserve Bank Review*, **77** (3), 63–77.

Kashyap, Anil K. and Jeremy C. Stein (1994), 'Monetary Policy and Bank Lending', in N.G. Mankiew (ed.), *Studies in Business Cycles Vol. 29*, Chicago and London: University of Chicago Press, pp. 221–56.

Kuper, Simon (1996), 'Small loans, big impact – children are often the beneficiaries when microbanks lend to female entrepreneurs', *Financial Times London Edition*, **2**, 11 February.

Mergenhagen, Paula (1996), 'Her own boss', *American Demographics*, December, 37–41.

Oliner, Stephen D. and Glenn D. Rudebusch (1996), 'Monetary policy and credit conditions: evidence from the composition of external finance: comment', *The American Economic Review*, **86** (1), (March), 300–309.

Otero, Maria and Elisabeth Rhyne (eds) (1994), *The New World of Microenterprise Finance*, West Hartford, Connecticut: Kumarian Press.

Raheim, Salome (1997), 'Problems and prospects of self-employment as an economic independence option for welfare recipients', *Social Work*, **42** (1), (January), 44–53.

Schuler, Sidney Ruth and Syed M. Hashemi (1994), 'Credit programs, women's empowerment, and contraceptive use in rural Bangladesh', *Studies in Family Planning*, **25** (2), 65–76.

Todd, Helen (1996), *Women at the Center: Grameen Bank Borrowers After One Decade*, Boulder: Westview Press.

US Department of Commerce (1997), 'Census Bureau Says Percent of Employer Businesses Owned by Women Continues to Increase', Apr 8, www.census.gov/Press-Release/cb97–57.html

Ward, Kathryn (ed.) (1990), *Women Workers and Global Restructuring*, Ithaca, New York: ILR Press.

World Bank (1996), 'Microlending gains momentum in Bangladesh', (97/1125), www.worldbank.org/html/extdr/extme/1125.htm.)

Capitalism

Capitalism is an economic system and a social formation that includes its own philosophical paradigm and ideology. Despite its relative youth and fairly recent expansion throughout the world, capitalism has come to dominate contemporary economic discourse and to be the economic system privileged by many economists and policymakers.

Most textbook definitions of capitalism emphasize that it is an economic system based upon private ownership of the means of production. In addition, that system is presumed to rely on the motive of profit in order to generate production, and the distribution of that production is assumed to occur most effectively through the market mechanism. While these features may reflect current understanding of the concept, the definition of capitalism has historically been the subject of intense debate. For example, perhaps the best known critic of capitalism, Karl Marx, emphasized that the essence of capitalism is the existence of a wage-earning class whose ability to live is unfairly dependent upon the purchase of its labour by the business class which only hire the workers if they stand to make a profit from the use of workers' labour. Neoclassical economists along with classical liberal philosophers, on the other hand, have focused on capitalism's philosophical tenets, emphasizing the individual freedom that capitalism provides by relying on private ownership, the ability of workers to sell their labour to the highest bidder in competitive markets, and the sovereignty of consumers to spend their money votes wherever they choose. Thus, understanding the concept of capitalism in contemporary economic discourse requires consideration of both the economic system and its philosophical and ideological influences.

It is important to state that capitalism is a 'market economy'. And although markets (that is, anywhere where an exchange takes place between buyers and sellers of products) have existed for thousands of years, capitalism is the first economic system to rely on markets for meeting the basic necessities of life. Prior to capitalism these basic necessities were largely met through nonmarket provisioning activities. Thus capitalism is a commercial society in this respect, and most people feel some of the competitive, market-induced anxiety and insecurity at one point or another in their lives as they contend with the uncertainties of market living (see Polanyi 1957).

The insecurities associated with market capitalism are not borne equally between men and women, illustrating the gendered nature of this type of economic system. The gendered nature of capitalism has had serious consequences for the economic and social status of women and, consequently, is an important topic of feminist economic inquiry. Early analysis of capitalism's gendered nature led feminist economists to examine how capitalism, not only as an economic system but also as a social formation, has interacted with the social system of patriarchy to construct and maintain economic and social hierarchies. More recently, feminist economists have expanded their analysis to consider how other social systems, such as race and sexual preference, have affected gendered economic experiences in both developed and developing nations with the goal of providing a better understanding of the gender inequality and subordination of women that is observed in most capitalist economic systems and social formations.

When examining the gendered nature of capitalism, there are some conspicuous observations relating to women and issues of gender injustice. For example, since it is involvement in commercial, market activities that defines economic visibility in a capitalist system, even a cursory glance at the past reveals that men have been conspicuously present in the capitalist, wealth-producing machine in their capacities as the 'captains of industry', the predominant factory personnel, the builders of machines and the great architectural monoliths of industry and finance. Women, whose work has been traditionally defined outside of the commercial sphere, have been less visible though no less vital to the system's overall functioning. This structure, and the associated economic invisibility, has meant that men have controlled much of the power and privilege associated with capitalism and thus women's economic subordination, a point noted by critics of capitalism since the nineteenth century.

Karl Marx's close associate, Friedrich Engels, emphasized the significance of women's exclusion from the commercial economy as the source of their subordination under capitalism, stating in his classic study, *The Origin of the Family, Private Property and the State*: 'we can already see from this that to emancipate woman and make her the equal of the man is and remains an impossibility so long as the woman is shut out from social productive labour and restricted to private domestic labour' (Engels 1972, p. 221). Thus, through their movement into the sphere of capitalist production, women would join the ranks of the working class. For Marxists of this period, however, class was the overriding social and economic distinction and all workers (regardless of their gender or race) would be reduced to the commonality of alienated labour. Workers would eventually unite under this umbrella and carry out social change that would create a classless society.

Other economists of the late nineteenth and early twentieth century also recognized the gendered effects of capitalism. For example, institutional economist Thorstein Veblen noted in *The Theory of the Leisure Class* (1899), that even women married to capitalism's 'captains of industry' were subordinated as well as privileged. Because 'it grates painfully on our nerves to contemplate the necessity of any well-bred woman's earning a livelihood by useful work' (Veblen 1912, p. 180), Veblen argued that these wives were often used by wealthy businessmen as a symbol of their financial success and status, thereby contributing to the social belief that a woman's sphere 'is within the household, which she should "beautify" and of which she should be the "chief ornament"' (ibid., p. 180). And because, 'by virtue of its descent from a patriarchal past, our social system makes it the woman's function in an especial degree to put in evidence her household's ability to pay', Veblen recognized that 'in the modern civilized scheme of life the woman is still, in theory, the economic dependent of the man' (ibid., pp. 180, 182).

Further discussion by economists of the gendered effects of capitalism effectively ceased until the 1960s and 1970s, when feminists began exploring how the concept of 'patriarchy' (defined as a system of male domination over women) interacted with other social and economic systems. In examining various economic systems throughout history, feminist scholars found that the patriarchal institutions of the feudal agricultural societies that preceded capitalism actually shaped the evolution of market capitalism to ensure continued male domination: 'in order to maintain men's domination within society, women had to be excluded from this newly emerging source of wealth, power, and prestige' (Brandt 1995, p. 35). This recognition, in turn, generated a great deal of feminist economic inquiry and debate, and has been a particularly important discussion for feminist economists examining capitalism from a Marxist perspective, with its emphasis on class relations as the essence of capitalism.

In her classic article, 'The Unhappy Marriage of Marxism and Feminism', feminist economist Heidi Hartmann argued that patriarchy is actually a relationship between men (a hierarchical one, to be sure), but a unique type of relationship that allows men through a variety of their own bonds to maintain economic leverage over women and by so doing dominate women in other, non-economic ways as well (Hartmann 1979, p. 11). Patriarchy, when viewed as a relationship between men, means that men must have at least an unarticulated consensus among them that they have something to gain as a group by holding women down, and this exists regardless of class and race differences among men.

As Hartmann suggests there is a 'material base' to patriarchy in capitalism and it 'does not rest solely on child-rearing in the family, but on all the social structures that enable men to control women's labour' (Hartmann 1979, p. 12). For example, in the nineteenth century, initially women and children were used extensively for tough and dirty, low-wage jobs in coal mines, textile factories and other industries. But these abuses were so glaringly exploitative that factory legislation was passed that prevented women and children from working in the paid labour force in many occupations. Men then 'sought to keep high wage jobs for themselves and to raise male wages generally' (ibid., p. 16).

So there were 'patriarchal prejudices' as capitalism evolved. Women were (1) kept at home under the 'cult of domesticity' (Kessler-Harris 1982, pp. 49–

50), (2) offered the worst jobs in the paid labour force, and (3) channelled into 'female professions' like nursing and teaching where this 'reinforced the belief that women are less skilled than men, or are only capable of performing work which is an extension of their "natural" nurturing tendencies' (Brandt 1995, p. 38).

This led to the 'family wages' policy that benefited men both as wage workers and capitalists. Men wanted wages that were high enough to support their families with the women and children thus kept at home. For example, Matthaei (1996) argues that, in the first half of the nineteenth century – the early industrial period of capitalism, capitalists found it difficult to entice men to leave their domestic production activity and come to work in the factories. Consequently, the notion of men as the family breadwinner was promoted, with men being told that they were not men if they did not earn a wage to support their family. All this occurred simultaneously with the emphasis on the 'cult of domesticity' (or 'cult of true womanhood') aimed at women. Thus changing social norms about the 'proper' work roles for men and women was a key development for nineteenth-century capitalist economies and reflected how the ideology underlying patriarchy reinforced the needs of capitalist employers and perpetuated the capitalist economic system (Matthaei 1996, pp. 31–4).

Women were allowed into some jobs where they were paid less *because they were women*, and this also encouraged them to stay at home as housewives and mothers. The material base for men's leverage over women, that is, patriarchy, was secured both by channelling women into the low-paying jobs that were frequently similar to householding and mothering activities and by keeping them at home (Hartmann 1979; Folbre 1994, p. 95). Thus the family wage 'cemented the partnership between patriarchy and capital' (Hartmann 1979, p. 18).

Many feminist economists argue that this complex interaction between patriarchy and capitalism is not captured by earlier critiques of capitalism, such as traditional Marxism, and are thus ill-equipped to analyse the status of women under capitalism. Hartmann argues, for example, that 'most Marxist analyses of women's position take as their question the relationship of women to the economic system, rather than that of women to men, apparently assuming the latter will be explained in their discussion of the former' (Hartmann 1979, p. 3). But today's feminist economists try to focus more specifically on the relationship between men and women and then examine the economic dimensions of this.

For example, Nancy Folbre has suggested that the relationship between patriarchy and capitalism is better analysed by talking about 'structures of constraint'. These structures are defining features of our lives and give us a sense of identity but can also create conflicts of interest, power and justice. Gender, age, sexual preference, race and class are typical structures of constraint (Folbre 1994, p. 59). Consequently, one might argue that within these structures, older, white, heterosexual males are also the majority of the capitalist class. And historically they have been. The structures overlap and can reinforce each other. For example, Folbre maintains that using this kind of approach provides a better way to tackle the problem of women and capitalism, because it can reveal the multiple and overlapping levels of sexist domination. It is thus more than simply the mechanisms of capitalism that result in women's domination, and to overcome this domination these structures of constraint have to be addressed.

What have been the experiences of women under capitalism? As the industrialization experience of the nineteenth century indicates, women's economic roles in both the home and the workplace have been vital in reproducing both patriarchy and capitalism. And they have been exceedingly diverse. The development of the 'family wage' norm is clearly more reflective of women's experiences in the industrialized capitalisms (see Amott and Matthaei 1991). Yet even in the USA, it was never a reality for many groups of women, such as women of colour, working-class women and immigrant women. There is ample evidence that women's productive efforts have been devalued and undercounted by the official statistics and national income accounts. In rural regions of Third World nations wage labour is less prominent. But women do much of the agricultural labour as well as the household and parenting labour (Shiva 1989; Ward 1990).

What has been the twentieth-century experience of women and capitalism? Clearly, women have moved into the labour force. In 1990 US women were 45 per cent of the paid labour force, and this included two-thirds of all married women with children and two-thirds of all single mothers (Brandt 1995, p. 39). But they have also been pressured into doing most of the domestic labour as well. This is the 'second shift' or 'double duty' phenomenon (Hochschild 1989). Also women have faced a variety of inequities in labour markets, such as wage discrimination, occupational segregation into low-paying service jobs and contingent work, and the 'glass ceiling' in professional employment. They still make only about 70 per cent of men's salaries (Amott 1993; Brandt 1995).

Over the last century, feminists have raised the concern that as women have increased their participation in the capitalist economy and become more economically independent of men, they have actually become poorer. One example of this concern is the 'feminization of poverty', the substantial increase in the number of poor persons living in families headed by a single mother in the USA during the 1970s. High rates of poverty for single mother families and other groups of women continue to be a serious concern in industrialized capitalist nations. The concern about women's poverty is also critical in analyses of women in developing capitalist nations, where 'women play a crucial economic role as the lowest rank in the global assembly line' (Brandt 1995, p. 42; see Ward 1990).

The issues facing women and their struggle for gender justice are many and complex. To what extent is the problem of subordination due to capitalism or patriarchy? The 'pauperization of motherhood', the 'glass ceiling', increased female labour-force participation and many other twentieth-century developments that concern women are not necessarily caused by capitalism or globalization. These issues and injustices have been equally observable in the former socialist nations as well. But as Folbre maintains there are many 'structures of constraint' and injustice at work simultaneously.

What remains for feminist economics and its examination of capitalism? In some respects the tasks are straightforward. Women suffer three economic injustices. As feminist economists have demonstrated, women living in a capitalist economic system and society are often underpaid, overworked and lack an equal democratic voice. And while women have recognized considerable gains, especially in the labour markets of developed countries, these gains have not typically translated into equal responsibilities for men in nonmarket economic activity. Because men have been able through the patriarchal power system to slough off responsibilities for these vital parts of the life process, women have had to pull more than their equal weight, leading feminist economist Nancy Folbre to argue that

> we need an economy based on equal opportunity that enforces equal responsibilities as well as rights. We need to reorient our economic goals away from increasing Gross National Product and toward improving social welfare. We need to provide greater recognition and support for labour devoted to the care and nurturance of children, the sick, and the elderly. (Folbre 1994 p. 252–3)

Thus, for the next century, the issues facing feminist economists are more about sharing the load of life than sharing the economic pie. Accomplishing this goal requires a unity among women and interested (feminist?) men that may be at odds with the logic of the market as exemplified in late twentieth-century capitalism. Therefore, the challenges facing feminist economists are to bridge the issues of race, ethnicity, class and other social structures that currently divide women and to create a 'unity through diversity' that will, in turn, effect the social and economic changes necessary for creating a gender-just world.

DOUG BROWN

See also

Class; Domestic Labour; Double Day/Second Shift; Family Wage; Feminization of Poverty; Glass Ceiling; Globalization; Institutional Economics; Labour Force Participation; Marxist Political Economics; Neoclassical Economics; Socialism.

Bibliography

Amott, Teresa (1993), *Caught in the Crisis: Women and the US Economy Today*, New York: Monthly Review Press.

Amott, Teresa and Julie Matthaei (1991), *Race, Gender, and Work: A Multicultural Economic History of Women in the United States*, Boston: South End Press.

Brandt, Barbara (1995), *Whole Life Economics: Revaluing Daily Life*, Philadelphia: New Society Publishers.

Engels, Frederick ([1942], 1972), *The Origin of the Family, Private Property and the State*, New York: International Publishers.

Folbre, Nancy (1991), 'The unproductive housewife: her evolution in nineteenth century economic thought', *Signs*, **16**,(Spring), 463–84.

Folbre, Nancy (1994), *Who Pays For The Kids?: Gender And The Structures of Constraint*, New York: Routledge.

Hardesty, Sarah and Nehama Jacobs (1986), *Success and Betrayal: The Crisis of Women in Corporate America*, New York: Simon and Schuster.

Hartmann, Heidi (1979), 'The unhappy marriage of Marxism and feminism: towards a more progressive union', *Capital and Class*, **8**, (Summer), 1–33.

Hochschild, Arlie (1989), *The Second Shift*, New York: Avon Books.

Kessler-Harris, Alice (1982), *Out to Work: A History of Wage-Earning Women in the United States*, New York: Oxford University Press.

Matthaei, Julie (1996), 'Why feminist, Marxist, and anti-racist economists should be feminist–Marxist–anti-racist economists', *Feminist Economics*, **2**, (Spring), 31–4.

Nelson, Julie (1993), 'The Study of Choice or the Study of Provisioning? Gender and the Definition of Economics', in Marianne Ferber and Julie Nelson (eds), *Beyond Economic Man*, Chicago: University of Chicago Press, pp. 23–36.

Polanyi, Karl ([1944], 1957), *The Great Transformation*, Boston: Beacon Press.

Shiva, Vandana (1989), *Staying Alive: Women, Ecology and Development*, Atlantic Highlands, New Jersey: Zed Books.

Veblen, Thorstein ([1899], 1912), *The Theory of the Leisure Class*, New York: Viking Press.

Ward, Kathryn (ed.) (1990), *Women Workers and Global Restructuring*, Ithaca, New York: ILR Press.

Child Care

Child care services include nonparental (usually paid) care of young children of working parents, preschool educational programmes and out-of-school-time programmes for school-aged children. Activists in the field prefer to use the phrase 'early care and education' rather than 'child care' to emphasize the dual functions of the services, to satisfy working parents' need for custodial services for their children as well as children's need for early education.

In the last 30 years the increasing labour force participation of young mothers has led to a steady increase in the social production of early care and education in industrialized nations. By 1995 in the USA, for instance, 60 per cent of children from birth to the age of five who were not already enrolled in school participated in some kind of nonparental, paid child care (Hofferth 1996). Government reaction to these profound shifts in child rearing and the commodification of child care have differed widely among nations. In response to increasing problems of availability, affordability and quality of child care services, public policy debates have focused on the degree to which government should guarantee universal availability of services, what form government subsidies should take (for example, direct subsidies to parents or public provision of services), the degree of public regulation of service quality, the need for public support of training and quality improvement and the efficacy of early childhood education as an intervention strategy to prepare poor children for school.

The governments of most industrialized countries accept some public responsibility for sharing the cost of rearing their nations' children and many have developed a comprehensive family policy. In particular, European nations provide publicly supported child care and other programmes that both encourage families to incur the costs of raising children and make it easier for women to juggle employment and child-rearing responsibilities. In most European countries for children aged two-and-a-half or three until their entry into primary school, publicly financed and operated child care is almost universally available, and it is virtually free for any children whose parents want them to attend regardless of the mother's labour market status. Child care for infants and toddlers is provided in a more diverse delivery system and is not as heavily subsidized (Kamerman and Kahn 1995). Scandinavian countries have made the greatest commitment to a family policy to support working parents through good quality, inexpensive child care for children over one year old, and parental leave policies that compensate parents for loss of income and guarantee the parent's job. Sweden also leads in school-aged programmes through a national policy to integrate elementary school and child care into full day programmes (Jaffe 1998).

The USA, England, Canada (except for Quebec), Australia and New Zealand have less well-defined family policies and spend less money on programmes to subsidize child care. They tend to leave the provision of child care to market forces so that for-profit centres provide a sizeable proportion of care (about one-third of centres in the USA according to Kisker et al. 1991). In the United States a rather chaotic system has evolved of profit and nonprofit centres, family child care providers and informal arrangements subsidized in part by philanthropic and government programmes. Working mothers still carry the major responsibility for and much of the increased cost of child rearing, facts that contribute to parental stress, the feminization of poverty, the high percentage of children (over 20 per cent) living in poverty, and, possibly, to disincentives to bear children (Folbre 1994c).

Except during World War II there was little federal support for early care and education in the United States until the 1960s when the federal government launched Head Start, a federally funded but locally managed intervention programme, originally a half day school year programme for at-risk three- and four-year-olds. It serves about 30 per cent of the eligible three- and four-year-olds, and since 1994 has begun to fund an Early Head Start for infants and toddlers (US General Accounting Office 1994). The federal government also channels funds through the states to reimburse child care providers for services to children of some poor working parents and for mothers leaving welfare for work. This funding is not an entitlement, and only a fraction of the families in need receive these subsidies. Middle- and upper-income families using child care do receive an entitlement in the form of a child care tax credit that provides limited financial relief.

Governments in developing countries also support child care and early education services. In particular, they recognize the value of early childhood education and are developing programmes targeted to poor children. In India, for instance, as early as 1944, a commission of the preindependent government recommended that the states establish free preschools. Today, a variety of federal, private and voluntary programmes exist. The national government operates the Integrated Child Development Services, a programme providing poor children from birth to six years old with health care and early childhood education through a network of Aganwadis (courtyards). It serves 16 million children a year and is supported by various international agencies (Pattnaik 1996).

Institutionalized child care is essential in China where more than 90 per cent of young mothers are employed, along with most grandmothers and aunts. Chinese parents, limited to raising one or two children, emphasize the importance of preschools in providing academic preparation and socialization as good citizens. Although preschools are more universally available than in many countries, attendance varies dramatically geographically, as does quality (Tobin et al. 1989).

Early childhood care and education policy is important to feminists for several reasons. First, affordable child care services are necessary for working mothers who still take the major responsibility for child rearing. Second, providing free, or virtually free, services can be a major component of any successful strategy to help single mothers and poor families escape poverty and prepare their children for success in school. Third, child care work is one of the most underpaid of female occupations. Commodified child care, like the caregiving provided by mothers in their own homes, is undervalued despite the complex of skills required and the responsibility involved. Fourth, child care provision as currently organized creates class divisions among women, pitting mothers seeking affordable child care against poorly paid female providers. Fifth, nonparental child care is a major setting for children's socialization, and as such the services can contribute to or discourage children from forming traditional gender identities.

Feminist scholarship on child care is a relatively new area of study. In the United States, the Center for the Child Care Workforce has tracked wages and working conditions of child care staff and carried out research to demonstrate the important link between the relatively low quality of care in the USA and the low wages earned by child care workers (Center for the Child Care Workforce 1998; Whitebook et al. 1990). Several studies of family child care providers who care for children in their own homes have focused on the relation between low pay and the psychological vulnerability of women who see their roles as substitute mothers (Nelson 1990), and the interplay of unpaid and paid caregiving work performed in the informal sector (Tuominen 1994).

Although a vast feminist literature exists on the caring responsibilities of women, not much of this discussion focuses specifically on child care (Abel and Nelson 1990; Baber and Allen 1992; Folbre 1994a). These feminist perspectives on caring, however, can help explain the low status and pay of child care workers. Abel and Nelson (1990), for example, characterize the disagreements among feminists about the effects of women's caregiving as being based on an instrumental focus on the oppressive nature of reproductive work and its effect in disadvantaging women in the labour market versus a psychological and ethical focus on the positive effects of caring in humanizing social relations. As Fisher and Tronto (1990) note, this controversy reflects the contradictory nature of caregiving which necessarily involves both labour and love.

In commodified child care, these aspects of caring are separated to some extent through a division of labour in which mothers provide the loving relations and retain responsibility for child rearing, but hire others to do the caring labour. This division of labour helps explain how fragmentation of the caring process can produce alienation in caregivers and parents, affecting both the quality of care and caregiver wages. Parents using paid child care accept the prevailing belief that child rearing is the private domain of the nuclear family. They see themselves as primarily responsible for child rearing despite the fact that much of it is being socially produced. This contradiction, as well as their absence from the actual caregiving while they are at work, may explain why parents tend to downplay the skills required in providing good quality child care (Hayes et al. 1990; Hofferth 1991; Kisker and Maynard 1991; Child Care Action Campaign 1992; Kontos et al. 1995; Modigliani 1997).

In fact, the research on early care and education indicates that provider training is one of the most important positive influences on good quality child care (Helburn and Howes 1996; Helburn 1995). To do her job effectively the paid caregiver must also be a teacher and be able to plan and revise her activities according to the needs of a diverse group of children congregated away from their homes. In her study of nannies, sociologist Julia Wrigley (1995), documents caregiver job dissatisfaction, high rates of nanny turnover and attempts by mothers to limit the nanny's child-rearing function to child tending, reserving the educating function for herself. Sociologist Margaret Nelson (1990) ascribes the rapid turnover of family child care providers to burnout caused by the contradictions inherent in the limited responsibility and authority these women can exercise over children to whom they become attached, combined with the low pay and low status of the work. Lyda Beardsley (1990), an early childhood educator, illustrates the danger to children from staff irritability and bad judgement from inadequate staffing and staff adherence to strict time schedules and rules. Routinization of procedures in child care centres allows management to hire less skilled workers, but it also inhibits true caring by staff.

Not only are there conflicting interests between mothers and their hired caregivers, there are also conflicting interests within the family. In two-parent families husband and wife must negotiate about satisfying alternative adult needs and about adults' versus children's interests. Even in families where mothers control finances, they must choose between their own personal needs and those of their children. The very decision of young mothers to work for pay requires weighing interests. Skold (1988) characterizes the feminist child care dilemma in countries like the USA as a conflict over women's interest in equality – the right to work and fully participate in all aspects of society – and children's interest in quality – the right to grow up in a healthy, loving and stimulating environment. Feminist groups have not always sided with the children. During the child care public policy debate in the late 1970s, for example, some feminist groups lobbied with for-profit interests against federal regulation of quality.

Economists, not necessarily feminist, have studied child care topics such as the effect of child care prices on maternal employment decisions (Council of Economic Advisors 1997), the effect of child care prices on the use of market care by working mothers (Council of Economic Advisors 1997), the effects of child care tax credits on maternal employment decisions (Averett et al. 1997; Altshuler and Schwartz 1996; Gentry and Hagy 1995), the child care labour market and the supply of labour (Walker 1991; Blau 1992, 1993; Mocan and Viola 1997), the effects of regulation on the child care industry (Chipty 1995; Chipty and Witte 1997; Hofferth and Chaplin 1997), the relative efficiency of for-profit and nonprofit centres (Helburn 1995; Mocan 1995; Mukerjee and Witte 1993; Preston 1993), and the presence of hidden action (the tendency to provide lower quality for services parents cannot monitor) among for-profit centres (Helburn and Morris 1998). While this represents a considerable range of topics, the scope and quality of empirical work by economists on child care is limited by a preference for econometric techniques and dependence on existing data sources. For instance, most studies of the relation between cost and quality have been flawed by the lack of good measures of quality and economists' unwillingness to collect their own data. The exception is found in Helburn (1995) where economists collaborated with child development specialists to collect classroom quality observations and detailed cost information from on-site interviews for 400 child care centres. This research was deliberately designed to inform public policy related to the need for higher quality child care, the economic conditions inhibiting market provision of such care and the cost of producing it. The research also examined the claim of child care advocates of excessively low pay in the field and found that child care teachers earned $5200 less than their counterparts in their regional labour markets.

Strober et al. (1994) also collected their own data, using qualitative research techniques to examine the labour market and work environment of caregivers. From interviews with staff and directors in four California centres, they found that job satisfaction was influenced by factors other than wages, such as the managerial competence of the director and training opportunities, and that tight supervision through strict rules interfered with job satisfaction.

Nancy Folbre has provided the most cogent feminist economic analysis of child care so far. She explores the reasons why modern economies do a poor job of caring for children. She suggests that they may be creating conditions that will reduce the supply of caring labour and argues that the process of economic development tends to penalize commitments to family labour (Folbre 1994a). Folbre explores women's motivations for supplying caring labour and why this labour is undervalued (1994b). She justifies public subsidies to share the costs of child rearing that now are disproportionately incurred by mothers, arguing that child care is a public good and child rearing is a public service (1994c). Folbre claims that society as a whole benefits from the services and sacrifices of those who raise the next generation. Therefore, those who do not raise children are free riding since they do not pay their share of child rearing costs. Further, if the public does not pay its share, the supply of caring labour (mainly services provided by women) could decline. She notes that the costs of child rearing for women are increasing with the increasing percentage of households headed by women, the declining percentage of fathers' income transferred to mothers and children and the tendency of women to pay the costs of child care. She argues that economists have failed to incorporate the role of nonmarket labour in human capital formation, and that economies where both women and men are pursuing individual careers provide little economic reward for parenting. She warns that this can lead in the long run to a decline in the supply of caring labour. Since parenting is increasingly a public service, to offset these externalities there should be a more equitable distribution of the costs of child rearing, and more equal opportunity for children through, for instance, public investment in early care and education, after-school programmes, and the like.

A few feminist economists have analysed child care-related public policies. Through a comparison of European (particularly French) and US family and child care public policy, Bergmann makes the case for large increases in public funding to reduce child poverty in the USA (1996, 1997). She argues that those European economies that provide liberal family allowances and free child care have much lower poverty rates for children, and that government provision of good quality child care for low-income families enables single mothers working full time at the minimum wage to live above the poverty line (1994). In encouraging labour force participation and increased labour force attachment, subsidizing child care would create long-run benefits for these families. In addition, more public funding of child care would help resolve the dilemma that forces feminists to take sides in choosing between mother's rights and children's. Essays in Helburn (1999) review research findings and discuss polices that could create an effective national child care system in the USA.

Yeager and Strober's case study (1992) of an unsuccessful local initiative to finance child care through local taxes, provides insight into the political strategies necessary to bring about the public policy changes advocated by Bergmann and illustrates the importance of moving away from traditional approaches to economic research. Using exit polls to analyse voter behaviour in a local election, Yeager and Strober report that the spending measure was defeated because supporters failed to make their case to the voters. They conclude that in order to expand public spending on child care significantly, voters will have to be convinced that providing child care is not just a private responsibility, but also a public responsibility.

Economic analysis of the child care industry is just beginning. Economists' tastes related to topics of study, their reliance on existing data sets, and their distaste for interdisciplinary collaboration limit their contributions. This is unfortunate since market imperfections probably account for the inadequacy of services and existing inequities. More research is needed to understand how competitive conditions in the child care industry affect the cost and quality of child care, why wages are low and what strategies might work in raising them, how working conditions affect turnover and low quality of care, what explains parental reluctance to pay for quality and how to increase their demand for quality, and how to finance improvements in quality. Some of these topics require interdisciplinary research, the use of qualitative research techniques and data gathering, procedures that economists are not used to employing. Feminist economists need to fill this void. In addition, theoretical insights provided by feminist economists will help move forward the research agenda on child care and help feminists develop public policy recommendations that further both women's and children's needs. In this regard, little has been written (Helburn 1998 provides an exception) envisioning the form and organization that early childhood care and education should take to promote a more egalitarian and humane society.

Suzanne W. Helburn

See also
Family, Economics of; Family Policy; Parental Leave.

Bibliography

Abel, Emily K. and Margaret K. Nelson (1990), 'Circles of Care: An Introductory Essay', in Emily K. Abel and Margaret K. Nelson (eds), *Circles of Care: Work and Identity in Women's Lives*, Albany: State University of New York Press.

Altshuler, Rosanne and Amy Schwartz (1996), 'On the progressivity of the child care tax credit: snapshot versus time-exposure incidence', *National Tax Journal*, **49** (1), 57–71.

Averett, Susan, H. Elizabeth Peters and Donald Waldman (1997), 'Tax credits, labour supply, and child care', *Review of Economics and Statistics*, **79** (1), (February), 125–35.

Baber, Kristine M. and Katherine R. Allen (1992), *Women and Families: Feminist Reconstructions*, New York and London: Guilford Press.

Beardsley, Lyda (1990), *Good Day Bad Day: The Child's Experience of Child Care*, New York and London: Teachers College Press.

Bergmann, Barbara R. (1994), 'Curing child poverty in the United States', *American Economic Review*, **84** (2), 76–80.

Bergmann, Barbara R. (1996), *Saving Our Children From Poverty: What the United States Can Learn from France*, New York: Russell Sage Foundation.

Bergmann, Barbara R. (1997), 'Government support for families with children in the United States and France', *Feminist Economics*, **3** (1), 83–92.

Blau, David (1992), 'The child care labour market', *Journal of Human Resources*, **11** (2), (Spring), 9–39.

Blau, David (1993), 'The supply of child care labour', *Journal of Labour Economics*, **11** (2), 324–47.

Center for the Child Care Workforce (1998), *Current Data on Child Care Salaries and Benefits in the United States*, Washington DC: Center for the Child Care Workforce.

Child Care Action Campaign (1992), 'Choosing Quality Child Care: A Qualitative Study Conducted in Houston, Hartford, West Palm Beach, Charlotte, Alameda, Los Angeles, Salem and Minneapolis', New York: EDK Associates.

Chipty, Tasneem (1995), 'Economic effects of quality regulations in the day-care industry', *American Economic Review, Papers and Proceedings*, **85** (2), (May).

Chipty, Tasneem and Ann Witte (1997), 'An Empirical Investigation of Firms' Responses to Minimum Standards Regulations', NBER Working Paper 6104, New York: National Bureau of Economic Research.

Council of Economic Advisors (1997), 'The Economics of Child Care', (December), Manuscript, Washington, DC: Council of Economic Advisors.

Fisher, Bernice and Joan Tronto (1990), 'Toward a Feminist Theory of Caring', in Emily K. Abel and Margaret K. Nelson (eds), *Circles of Care: Work and Identity in Women's Lives*, Albany: State University of New York Press.

Folbre, Nancy (1994a), *Who Pays for the Kids?*, London and New York: Routledge.

Folbre, Nancy (1994b), '"Holding hands at midnight": The paradox of caring labour', *Feminist Economics*, **1** (1), 73–92.

Folbre, Nancy (1994c), 'Children as public goods', *American Economic Review*, **84** (2), 86–90.

Gentry, William and Alison Hagy (1995), 'The Distributional Effects of Tax Treatment of Child Care Expenses', National Bureau of Economic Research, Working Paper 5088, New York: National Bureau of Economic Research.

Hayes, C.D., J.L. Palmer and M.J. Zaslow (eds) (1990), *Who Cares for America's Children: Child Care Policy for the 1990s*, Washington, DC: National Academy Press.

Helburn, Suzanne (ed.) (1995), *Cost, Quality, and Child Outcomes in Child Care Centres, Technical Report*, Denver, Colorado: Department of Economics, Center for Research in Economic and Social Policy, University of Colorado at Denver.

Helburn, Suzanne (1998), 'Child care and child rearing today and tomorrow', *Capitalism, Nature, Socialism*, **9** (1), 64–72.

Helburn, Suzanne (ed.) (1999), *The Silent Crisis in US Child Care, The Annals of the American Academy of Political and Social Science*, (March).

Helburn, Suzanne and Carollee Howes (1996), 'Child care cost and quality', *The Future of Children*, **6** (2), 62–82.

Helburn, Suzanne and John Morris (1998), 'Sector Quality Differences in a Mixed Industry: Child Care', Manuscript.

Hofferth, Sandra (1991), 'Comments on the Importance of Child Care Costs to Women's Decision Making', in David Blau (ed.), *The Economics of Child Care*, New York: Russell Sage Foundation.

Hofferth, Sandra (1996), 'Child care in the United States today', *The Future of Children*, **6** (2), 41–61.

Hofferth, Sandra and Duncan Chaplin (1997), 'State regulation and child care choice', *Population Research and Policy Review*, **16** (2), 1–30.

Jaffe, Ken (1998), 'Following world trends in child care', *Child Care Information Exchange*, **121** (May/June), 73–5.

Kamerman, Sheila B. and Alfred J. Kahn (1995), *Starting Right: How America Neglects Its Youngest Children and What We Can Do About It*, New York and Oxford: Oxford University Press.

Kisker, E. and R. Maynard (1991), 'Quality, Cost, and Parental Choice of Child Care', in David Blau (ed.), *The Economics of Child Care*, New York: Russell Sage Foundation.

Kisker, Ellen, Sandra Hofferth, Deborah Phillips and Elizabeth Farquhar (1991), *A Profile of Child Care Settings: Early Education and Care in 1990, Volume I*, Princeton, New Jersey: Mathematica Policy Research, Inc.

Kontos, S., C. Howes, M. Shinn and E. Galinsky (1995), *Quality in Family Child Care and Relative Care*, New York: Teachers College Press.

Modigliani, Kathy (1997), *Parents Speak About Child Care*, Boston: Wheelock College Family Child Care Project.

Mocan, H. Naci (1995), 'Quality-adjusted cost functions for child-care centers', *American Economic Review*, **85** (2), 409–13.

Mocan, H. Naci and Deborah Viola (1997), 'The Determinants of Child Care Workers' Wages and Compensation: Sector Differences, Human Capital, Race, Insiders and Outsiders', NBER Working Paper 6328, New York: National Bureau of Economic Research.

Mukerjee, Swati and Ann Witte (1993), 'Provision of child care: cost functions for profit-making and not-for-profit day care centres', *Journal of Productivity Analysis*, **4** (1–2), 145–63.

Nelson, Margaret K. (1990), 'Mothering Others' Children: The Experiences of Family Day Care Providers', in Emily K. Abel and Margaret K. Nelson (eds), *Circles of Care*, Albany: State University of New York Press.

Pattnaik, Jyotsna (1996), 'Early childhood education in India: history, trends, issues and achievements', *Early Childhood Education Journal*, **24** (1), 11–16.

Preston, Anne E. (1993), 'Efficiency, quality, and social externalities in the provision of day care: comparisons of nonprofit and for-profit firms', *Journal of Productivity Analysis*, **4** (1–2), 165–82.

Skold, Karen (1988), 'The Interests of Feminists and Children in Child Care', in Sanford M. Dornbusch and Myra H. Strober (eds), *Feminism, Children and the New Families*, New York and London: Guilford Press.

Strober, Myra H., Suzanne Gerlach-Downie and Kenneth E. Yeager (1994), 'Child care centres as workplaces', *Feminist Economics*, **1** (1), 93– 120.

Tobin, Joseph, David Wu and Dana Davidson (1989), *Preschool in Three Cultures: Japan, China, and the United States*, New Haven and London: Yale University Press, pp. 188–222.

Tuominen, Mary (1994), 'The hidden organization of labour: gender, race/ethnicity and informal economy', *Sociological Perspectives*, **37** (2).

US General Accounting Office (1994), *Early Childhood Programmes: Many Poor Children and Strained Resources Challenge Head Start*, GAO/HEHS-94-169BR.

Walker, J.R. (1991), 'Public Policy and the Supply of Child Care Services', in David Blau (ed.), *The Economics of Child Care*, New York: Russell Sage Foundation.

Whitebook, M., C. Howes and D. Phillips (1990), *Who Cares? Child Care Teachers and the Quality of Care in America*, Oakland, California: Child Care Employee Project.

Wrigley, Julia (1995), *Other People's Children: An Intimate Account of the Dilemmas Facing Middle-Class Parents and the Women They Hire to Raise Their Children*, New York: Basic Books.

Yeager, Kenneth E. and Myra H. Strober (1992), 'Financing child care through local taxes', *Journal of Family Issues*, **13** (3), 279–96.

Child Support

Child support refers to transfers of resources from noncustodial parents to custodial parents to help defray the costs of rearing children. Interest in child support has grown dramatically in response to growing numbers of impoverished single mother families worldwide (Beller and Graham 1993; Bruce et al. 1995). Governments increasingly emphasize enforcing private child support obligations over other policy responses to poverty among single mother families. In many countries efforts to stem the growth of single mother families have failed and ideological and political support for public spending on childrearing is waning. Also, where women's labour force participation conflicts with traditional ideals of good mothering, governments prefer enforcing paternal contributions to children over improving mothers' labour market outcomes (Millar 1994).

Prior to World War II, the vast majority of member countries of the Organisation for Economic Co-operation and Development (OECD) left child support decisions to the discretion of their judiciaries. Researchers fault systems of juridical discretion for their inconsistency (that is, treating similar noncustodial fathers differently), for failing to award child support to many single mother families, for setting award rates very low relative to the costs of raising children, for making it difficult to modify award levels, and for placing the burden of collection on custodial parents (Beller and Graham 1993; Millar 1994). Empirical studies from a wide range of countries show that many absent fathers paid very little child support, if any, under the old systems (Bruce et al. 1995).

Since the 1950s most OECD countries have more stringently codified paternal support obligations and have sought to establish more effective systems of collecting income support from absent fathers, often routinizing payment along the lines of taxation and social insurance (Garfinkel and Wong 1990; McFate 1995). Most countries have established clear guidelines for award amounts and have arranged for periodic updates of award levels to account for inflation or for changes in families' economic circumstances. To increase the portion of award money actually collected, OECD governments have established agencies authorized to use wage withholding, tax return intercepts, property liens and various other methods of enforcing payment. In the UK, the child support agency is part of the Department of Social Security, while Australia's child support agency is a unit of the Australian Tax Office (Oldham 1996).

One motive for OECD governments to reform their child support systems was to recover some of the growing amount of public money being spent on single mother families (Garfinkel et al. 1992; Millar 1994). In some contexts, objections to publicly supporting single mothers were associated with a changing racial and ethnic composition of the population receiving support (McFate 1995). Especially since the 1980s, government efforts to increase private child support transfers have been accompanied by reductions in public transfers. Increasingly countries are adopting hybrid strategies, using public funds and institutions to enforce private support obligations (or to make up for failures of private support), rather than to replace them.

Because English-language information about child support in the countries of Latin America and the Caribbean, Africa and Asia is very limited, this entry focuses on child support in Western Europe, North America and Australia. But Judith Bruce, a Senior Associate of the Population Council in New York, documents an active cross-cultural dialogue on family relationships that she believes is moving towards universal agreement on rights and responsibilities for family members (Bruce et al. 1995). Some developing countries have joined OECD countries in increasing government regulation of private child support obligations, but limited resources severely constrain enforcement in developing economies. And feminist scholars note unintended negative consequences for women and children when governments adopt child support systems without adequately considering local contexts (Burman 1992).

Feminist scholars not only evaluate how child support policy regimes affect women and children but also offer arguments for why collecting child support is so problematic in the first place. Feminists link fathers' default on childrearing responsibilities to changes in patriarchal relations. In this view, male support of women and children is contingent to some degree upon male power and authority in households, or is offered in exchange for women's housekeeping efforts, women's sexual fidelity and/or women's emotional support (Bergmann 1981; Ehrenreich 1983; Furstenberg 1992). From a feminist perspective, men have withdrawn economic support because they have lost patriarchal prerogatives and privileges. Further, feminists argue that women's gains in the paid labour force make it easier for men to withdraw support since men believe their ex-wives can easily support themselves (Bergmann 1981; Ehrenreich 1983).

Patriarchy also shapes institutional interventions into family economies. Feminists link low child support award levels to the invisibility and under-valuation of traditionally female household labour and to policymakers' and judges' lack of attention to the importance of human capital in modern economies (Weitzman 1988). Child support awards fail to fully account for the time (or opportunity) costs of rearing children. Overlooking or discounting caretaking time is consistent with an economic perspective that considers household production to be 'not really work' and childrearing to be a 'natural', non-economic activity. But inattention to caretaking labour ignores studies that attribute women's low market wages to the loss of human capital development opportunities on the job or to the depreciation of human capital when women take on childrearing responsibilities. In the UK, child support awards include a stipend intended to compensate the custodial parent either for child care services or for career damage due to child care responsibilities. But English social policy analyst, Jane Millar (1994), argues that the stipend accounts only for caring costs incurred after parents separate and not for the costs of caring incurred during a marriage.

Feminists also recognize that patriarchy and traditional conceptions of women's roles may limit the degree to which women benefit from child support reforms. Better enforcement of private child support obligations should raise living standards for single mother families and should result in men bearing a larger share of the costs of childrearing. But reforms may also reinforce a traditional gender division of family labour, with women depending on men for access to marketed goods and services, while women continue to bear most of the burden of household production (Millar 1994). In countries that dramatically reduce public support for childrearing, some women may be forced to rely on abusive ex-partners. Even when ex-spouses are not abusive, women may be drawn into patterns of obligation and control from which they had hoped single parenting would free them (Millar 1994).

Neoclassical economists explain inadequate child support levels very differently than feminists do. According to Weiss and Willis (1985, 1993), children are 'consumer durables' for parents, who spend money on children in hopes of reaping satisfaction from parenting and from their children's welfare. Using this framework, Weiss and Willis argue that many noncustodial parents stop paying support because their efforts to raise children's living standards are frustrated by custodial parents who spend part of every child support dollar on themselves and only a fraction on their children (see also Lerman 1989; Beron 1990). In Weiss and Willis's view, custodial parents inevitably misallocate family resources because custodians fail to account for the pleasure that noncustodial parents derive from spending money on the children. A second reason Weiss and Willis offer for nonpayment of child support is that noncustodial parents spend little time with their children and so lack a key source of satisfaction from investing in them.

From a feminist perspective, Weiss and Willis's analysis of child support default mirrors a common male excuse for non-payment: that mothers cannot be trusted to spend child support money appropriately. While Weiss and Willis's model is gender-neutral on the surface (in other words, equally applicable to both male and female noncustodial parents), it shifts responsibility for paternal default in the USA from fathers to mothers. On the other hand, feminist economists agree with Weiss and Willis that absent fathers have economic reason to avoid supporting children. Folbre (1983) argues that the process of capitalist economic development increases the net costs of raising children, giving both men and women an incentive to default on parental obligations. As market employment displaces home-based production in the course of capitalist development, children become increasingly reliant on their own earning power and rely less on inheriting family assets from their parents. In this context, children are less likely to work with their parents in family enterprises or to support parents in old age. And while the economic benefits of childrearing fall, the costs rise largely because children need more education in order to compete for skilled jobs in the wage economy and because women's wages rise with expanding labour markets, increasing the opportunity cost of time spent rearing children.

While capitalist development erodes the incentives for both men and women to invest in children, Folbre argues that men are in a stronger position than women to default on childrearing obligations. Folbre attributes the difference between maternal and paternal default rates to what she calls 'patriarchal structures of constraint'. In Folbre's words, structures of constraints are 'sets of asset distributions, rules, norms, and preferences that empower given social groups' (Folbre 1994, p. 51). For example, patriarchal constraints that shape parental behaviour include gendered norms of good parenting and rules governing the assignment of child custody.

Both Folbre (1994) and Burggraf (1997) link the gender distribution of the costs of raising children to the public/private distribution of the benefits of raising children. Both economists argue that children are public goods in advanced industrial economies (see also Dornbusch and Strober 1988). According to Folbre and Burggraf, industrialized countries have socialized many of the economic benefits of childrearing. For example, all citizens benefit from parents' investments in children by enjoying retirement benefits paid for by the next generation. Folbre and Burggraf both argue that the public nature of benefits from spending on children limits incentives for individual parents to support children. In other words, the public at large reaps benefits regardless of whether or not they help pay the costs, and this creates a free-rider problem. But Folbre and Burggraf offer diametrically opposed proposals for responding to parental default. Burggraf favours reprivatizing the benefits of raising children (through a dividend to responsible parents paid during retirement), while Folbre favours socializing more of the costs of raising children.

Neoclassical economists are pessimistic about the potential for efficiently collecting private child support, even with recent policy changes. Weiss and Willis (1993) argue that noncustodial parents' inability to control how child support payments are used makes enforcing private transfers highly problematic. Other economists maintain that even if private child support transfers could be collected efficiently, successful collection efforts would create perverse incentives. For instance Lerman (1993) argues that successful child support enforcement would create work disincentives for non custodial parents and might promote non-marital childbearing and family splitting by easing burdens for single parents. And Burtless (1987) argues that better enforcement would create disincentives to marriage or remarriage for single mothers. In light of the problems they associate with increasing private child support transfers, some neoclassical economists propose alternatives. For instance Lerman recommends promoting joint-custody arrangements and in-kind contributions, 'so the non custodial parent's contribution looks more like a consumption good and less like a tax' (Lerman 1989, p. 237).

Economists Beller and Graham (1993) are much more optimistic about private child support. Beller and Graham make extensive proposals for child support policy in the USA, many of which are beginning to be implemented. They advocate efforts to deter out-of-wedlock childbearing (particularly among teenagers), efforts to increase paternity establishment in out-of-wedlock births, formal presumptive guidelines that establish new child support awards as a proportion of the noncustodial parent's income, full indexing of award levels to inflation, explicit provisions for low-income noncustodial parents (requiring them to make at least a small regular payment), enhanced enforcement of child support payment, and policies to increase contact between children and noncustodial parents. Beller and Graham's empirical work suggests that changes in the legal environment in the USA during the 1980s and early 1990s did have a small positive impact on child support receipts (Beller and Graham 1993).

Some feminist economists propose taking child support reform a step further by implementing child support assurance programmes, such as those that exist in Austria, Belgium, Denmark, Israel, Norway and Sweden (Bergmann 1981; Garfinkel et al. 1992). With a child support assurance system (sometimes called an advanced maintenance scheme), the government assumes responsibility for collecting child support payments from noncustodial parents. Children with legally liable parents receive a socially assured minimum amount of child support each month, regardless of whether or not the state has been able to collect from the absent parent. Advanced maintenance schemes appeal to feminists because they guarantee a minimum standard of living for single mother families without making women depend on particular men for economic survival. Further, advanced maintenance programmes may reduce the stigma of receiving government support for childrearing (Lerman 1989).

Child support assurance systems also are appealing because they provide for children with low income fathers. Economist Elaine Sorensen (1997) demonstrates that a sizable fraction of noncustodial fathers in the USA are so disadvantaged economically that complying with child support awards would impoverish them and their current households. Sorensen argues that many fathers who find it difficult to pay support also fall out of contact with their children (either because of shame or because the children's mothers refuse them access). As philosopher Sara Ruddick puts it, 'when fathering is identified with economic support in a way that mothering is not, and when men cannot consider themselves mothers, unemployed, impoverished young men cannot take themselves to be "parents"' (Ruddick 1992, p. 186).

Feminist economists would combine a child support assurance programme with labour market policies that increase women's ability to support themselves and their children. Sweden has successfully kept single mother families out of poverty by reducing women's labour market inequality, rather than by relying on public or private income transfers (Gustafsson 1995). Of eight countries (Canada, France, Germany, Italy, the Netherlands, Sweden, the UK and the USA) surveyed by McFate, Sweden was the only country in which lone-parent families were not more likely to be poor than couple-headed families (McFate 1995).

Research possibilities for feminist economists in the field of child support are rich and varied. Empirical analyses of current child support practices and policies in the countries of Latin America and the Caribbean, Africa and Asia would enrich understanding of gender relations in these regions and could inform designing policy to improve women and children's living standards. And much work remains to fully evaluate the efficacy and gendered consequences of recent and ongoing child support reform efforts in the OECD countries. Perhaps the biggest challenge facing feminist scholars is to evaluate and promote strategies to increase men's direct involvement in childrearing activities (Folbre 1997; Bruce et al. 1995). Because even if men pay fully half of the costs of rearing children, feminist economists object to a division of labour that delegates all caring activity to women.

BRENDA WYSS

See also
Divorce; Family, Economics of; Family Policy; Feminization of Poverty; Patriarchy; Welfare Reform.

Bibliography

Beller, Andrea and John Graham (1993), *Small Change: The Economics of Child Support*, New Haven: Yale University Press.

Bergmann, Barbara (1981), 'The share of women and men in the economic support of children', *Human Rights Quarterly*, **3** (2), 103–12.

Bergmann, Barbara and Mark Roberts (1987), 'Income for the Single Parent: Child Support, Work, and Welfare', in Clair Brown and Joseph Pechman (eds), *Gender in the Workplace*, Washington, DC: The Brookings Institution, pp. 247–70.

Beron, Kurt J. (1990), 'Child support payment behaviour: An econometric decomposition', *Southern Economic Journal*, **56**, (January), 650–53.

Bruce, Judith, Cynthia Lloyd and Ann Leonard (eds) (1995), *Families in Focus: New Perspectives on Mothers, Fathers, and Children*, New York: The Population Council.

Burggraf, Shirley P. (1997), *The Feminine Economy and Economic Man: Reviving the Role of Family in the Post-Industrial Age*, Reading, Massachusetts: Addison-Wesley.

Burman, Sandra (1992), 'First-World Solutions for Third-World Problems', in Lenore Weitzman and Mavis Maclean (eds), *Economic Consequences of Divorce: The International Perspective*, Oxford: Clarendon Press, pp. 366–78.

Burtless, Gary (1987), 'Comments', in Clair Brown and Joseph Pechman (eds), *Gender in the Workplace*, Washington, DC: The Brookings Institution, pp. 263–7.

Dornbusch, Sanford and Myra Strober (1988), 'Our Perspectives' and 'Public Policy Alternatives', in Sanford Dornbusch and Myra Strober (eds), *Feminism, Children, and the New Families*, New York: The Guilford Press, pp. 3–24 and pp. 327–55.

Ehrenreich, Barbara (1983), *The Hearts of Men: American Dreams and the Flight from Commitment*, Garden City, New York: Anchor Books.

Folbre, Nancy (1983), 'Of patriarchy born: the political economy of fertility decisions', *Feminist Studies*, **9** (2), 261–84.

Folbre, Nancy (1994), *Who Pays for the Kids? Gender and the Structures of Constraint*, London and New York: Routledge.

Folbre, Nancy (1997), 'The future of the elephant-bird', *Population and Development Review*, **23** (3), 647–54.

Furstenberg, Frank F. (1992), 'Daddies and Fathers: Men Who Do for Their Children and Men Who Don't', in Frank Furstenberg, Kay Sherwood and Mercer Sullivan (eds), *Caring and Paying: What Fathers and Mothers Say About Child Support*, New York: Manpower Demonstration Research Corporation, pp. 34–56.

Garfinkel, Irwin, Sara S. McLanahan and Philip K. Robins (eds) (1992), *Child Support Assurance: Design Issues, Expected Impacts, and Political Barriers as Seen from Wisconsin*, Washington, DC: The Urban Institute Press.

Garfinkel, Irwin and Patrick Wong (1990), 'Child Support and Public Policy', in *Lone-Parent Families: The Economic Challenge*, Paris: Organisation for Economic Cooperation and Development, pp. 101–26.

Gustafsson, Siv (1995), 'Single Mothers in Sweden: Why is Poverty Less Severe?', in Katherine McFate, Roger Lawson and William Julius Wilson (eds), *Poverty, Inequality, and the Future of Social Policy: Western States in the New World Order*, New York: Russell Sage Foundation, pp. 291–325.

Lerman, Robert (1989), 'Child-Support Policies', in Phoebe Cottingham and David Ellwood (eds), *Welfare Policy for the 1990s*, Cambridge, Massachusetts: Harvard University Press, pp. 219–46.

Lerman, Robert (1993), 'Policy watch: child support policies', *Journal of Economic Perspectives*, **7** (1), 171–82.

McFate, Katherine (1995), 'Introduction: Western States in the New World Order', in Katherine McFate, Roger Lawson and William Julius Wilson (eds), *Poverty, Inequality, and the Future of Social Policy: Western States in the New World Order*, New York: Russell Sage Foundation, pp. 1–26.

Millar, Jane (1994), 'State, family and personal responsibility: The changing balance for lone mothers in the United Kingdom', *Feminist Review*, **48**, (Autumn), 24–39.

Oldham, J. Thomas (1996), 'Lessons from the new English and Australian child support systems', *Vanderbilt Journal of Transnational Law*, **29** (4), 691–733.

Ruddick, Sara (1992), 'Thinking About Fathers', in Barrie Thorne (ed.), *Rethinking the Family: Some Feminist Questions*, Boston: Northeastern University Press, pp. 176–90.

Sorensen, Elaine (1997), 'A national profile of nonresident fathers and their ability to pay child support', *Journal of Marriage and the Family*, **59**, 785–97.

Weiss, Yoram and Robert Willis (1985), 'Children as collective goods and divorce settlements', *Journal of Labor Economics*, **3** (3), 268–92.

Weiss, Yoram and Robert Willis (1993), 'Transfers among divorced couples: evidence and interpretation', *Journal of Labor Economics*, **11** (4), 629–79.

Weitzman, Lenore (1988), 'Women and Children Last: The Social and Economic Consequences of Divorce Law Reform', in Sanford Dornbusch and Myra Strober (eds), *Feminism, Children, and the New Families*, New York: The Guilford Press, pp. 212–48.

Class

Class is a central concept in several schools of nonneoclassical thought. It has received extended treatment at the hands of Weberians, institutionalists and, especially, Marxists. Karl Marx and his frequent collaborator Frederick Engels developed the foundations of Marxian political economy, in which 'class' is a relationship among groups of people characterized by conflicting interests in the production and distribution of the surplus product and surplus labour time (that is, that part of social output above and beyond what is necessary to reproduce society at its current level of production, and the time required to produce it). The definition of Marxian class relations centres on the idea of surplus extraction or exploitation: that a politically dominant group is able to appropriate and control a surplus which it has not produced, and thus the labour time embodied in that product.

The exact mechanisms of surplus extraction, and the corresponding form of class relations, differ across time and space. For example, feudal lords extracted surplus from serfs, who often delivered their products directly to lords, and who were bound to the lords through custom, faith and coercion. Slave owners extracted surplus from slaves, who were both the direct producers and a form of wealth. In contrast to feudalism and slavery, the integration of capitalist production with markets means that workers 'choose' their exploiters. However, they do not choose the fundamental fact of exploitation. Because capitalists own the means of production and control the labour process, workers depend upon the wages which capitalists provide, and submit in varying degrees to capitalist direction of their work. Whatever the historical setting, a principal tenet of Marxian class theory is that the material interests of exploiters and exploited conflict over the extraction of surplus. Dominant classes attempt to lengthen the working day, increase the pace of production and reduce compensation; subordinate classes resist these measures.

Marx expected that under certain historical conditions, workers would become conscious of their conflict with owners, and organize as a class to resist owner exploitation. The ensuing class struggle, according to Marx, would shape the trajectory of history, transforming old institutions and social relations into new forms. Moreover, the working class was the only class under capitalism with specifically revolutionary capacity, because only workers had the interests, and potentially the solidarity, to overthrow the capitalist system.

Marx is not the only writer to have developed a theory of class. Both institutional economists in the tradition of Thorstein Veblen and sociologists since Max Weber have used the concept of class extensively, but define it differently. Like Marxists, institutionalists regard property as the foundation of power and social class under capitalism; large corporations embody that power (Hunt 1994). Unlike Marxists, institutionalists tend to emphasize that attaining culturally defined social class is an economic goal of individuals and families. Institutionalists also disagree among themselves about the significance of class as a system.

According to the Weberian tradition in sociology, classes are distinguished by differential life opportunities rather than by exploitation. Thus Weber draws attention to family income and wealth, rather than to relationships in production (as with Marx). But because Marx saw the concentrated ownership of productive assets as constitutive of the wage–labour relationship, there is considerable overlap between the Marxian and Weberian class concepts. Furthermore, in much Marxist and feminist empirical work, investigators resort to Weberian definitions of class, simply because data is seldom collected in ways which more directly measure Marxian class locations.

The early formulators of class theory did not explore the relationship between class and gender in great depth. Marx clearly expected that individuals who were outside the capitalist production process, such as housewives, would be proletarianized as accumulation progressed. Differences among nonowners would be obliterated as labour was rendered increasingly homogeneous. Thus there would be little need for an independent analysis of gender and class. Engels speculated that the oppression of women originated in the need of property-owning men to ensure the 'legitimacy' of their heirs. The basis for female subordination among families who did not own property remained unspecified (Engels [1884] 1968).

More recently, the concept of class has been important for feminist economic thought in four ways. Two of them concern women's domestic labour. First, feminists have sought to establish the extent to which women's household labour may increase the rate of surplus extraction by dominant classes. Second, some feminists have reasoned that if class involves one group's control over another group's labour for the purpose of extracting a surplus, then wives may live in a *gender class* relationship with their husbands. The last two developments have focused on the reciprocal relationship between gender, race and class. First, feminists have increasingly recognized the ways in which the meaning and experience of gender is dependent upon one's location in national and global capitalist class systems, as well as in racial hierarchies. And finally, just as gender is mediated by class and race, so are class and race mediated by gender.

Developments in the theory of household labour and class
In some systems, such as slavery and sharecropping, in which producer households are closely integrated with production for the benefit of landowners, it is readily apparent that household production is necessary for the production of surplus. Owners of plantations or haciendas needed household labour in order to reproduce the direct producers, both daily and intergenerationally. In such systems, where children produced more than they consumed no later than the age of 12, there were consequently strong incentives for large families. Indeed, under slavery, slave owners exploited women both as direct producers and as reproducers (Davis 1981). On the Peruvian haciendas studied by Deere (1990), women had access to land only through husbands, who in turn had feudal or sharecropping relations with landlords, so that women had to perform surplus labour for the landlord class, as well as bear large numbers of children.

Under capitalism, in which women's household labour became physically much more separate from production for the market, the relationship of household labour to class exploitation was not as apparent. In 1972, Dalla Costa and James argued that women's household production is essential for capital because it reproduces the working class. Moreover, household labour creates surplus value, because the value of the portion of men's wages which maintains wives is less than the value of wives' production. Women's unwaged household labour thus subsidizes capitalist production, raising the rate of exploitation. Mies, following Rosa Luxemburg, also pointed out the importance of integrating this exploitation of women in the home with the parallel exploitation of other '"non-capitalist melieux and strata"' throughout the world (Mies 1986, p. 34, quoting Luxemburg 1923). Mies argued that the sexual division of labour and the international division of labour ought not to be regarded as separate phenomena, since they both involve the exploitation of non-wage labourers under conditions where the rules governing wage labour are not applied.

A debate raged for about ten years over whether household labour did indeed raise the rate of capitalist exploitation. The significance of the debate for the development of thought on class and gender is that it gave women's domestic labour unprecedented significance and centrality in Marxist thought.

The domestic labour debate did so, however, by framing the exploitation of family labourers as capitalist exploitation, a familiar and fully legitimated problem for the left. It asked whether women's struggles subverted the relationship between labour and capital. The debate did not raise the possibility of patriarchal exploitation, it did not explore the implications of the analysis for a concept of gender class in any systematic way, and it did not consider the revolutionary potential of women's struggles against husbands and fathers. However, it did set the stage for all these subsequent developments.

Precisely because the domestic labour debate treated women's household production as *labour*, it set the stage for a consideration of women's exploitation by male family members, be they capitalists or workers. Folbre (1982) argued that it was possible to define exploitation *within* the home. Other writers developed similar lines of thought into theories of gender class. Much as Marxists defined classes with respect to structural conflicts over the production and appropriation of surplus under capitalism, feudalism and other economic systems, gender class theorists viewed women and men in structural conflict over the production and appropriation of goods within household systems. Perhaps the earliest of these theorists was Delphy (1984) who argued that patriarchy has an economic base, which is the exploitation of women in the home, through the production of domestic services and childrearing. Since wives are 'maintained' rather than paid by their husbands, they are not domestic wage labourers. Therefore, the household labour system is distinct from capitalism. Nonetheless, it is driven by the same motive, material profit. Delphy concluded that patriarchal class locations, that is, men vs. women in the home, may disrupt the potential solidarity of what she called the 'industrial' classes (workers, capitalists).

Ferguson (1991) also wrote of women as a class, because women are dominated and exploited by men in 'sex/affective production'. (Going beyond Delphy, she saw this as including sexuality, the production of children, and social bonding.) Because of men's ownership of their own wages, men can impose upon women an unequal exchange in sex/affective goods. However, an individual man's degree of power depends crucially on his position in other hierarchies, especially race and 'family class' (similar to Delphy's 'industrial' class).

Ferguson, moreover, argued that women may achieve the social cohesion necessary to be a revolutionary class. Acknowledging that race and family class differences have almost always undermined that in the past, she nonetheless argued that the availability of jobs for women with living wages, women's increased control of their fertility, the existence of large social welfare programmes, and the greater instability of married couple families, may permit and indeed compel women to rely more on their gender class. Moreover, as the socializers of children and the reproducers of male wage earners, women are uniquely positioned to disrupt the patriarchal capitalist system by refusing to participate in unequal exchange.

Fraad et al. (1994) developed a third theory of gender class, which is elaborated within their framework of fundamental and subsumed class processes. A fundamental class process involves the production and appropriation of surplus labour. A subsumed class process maintains the conditions of existence of the fundamental class process(es); a subsumed class, such as merchants or moneylenders, is thereby able to claim some share of the surplus generated through the fundamental process. In the household, the fundamental class process is one in which men appropriate women's surplus labour time; the related subsumed class processes include the production of gendered meanings, which make women's exploitation appear natural or desirable.

According to Fraad et al., married couple households with a male wage earner and a female domestic labourer embody a fundamental class process which is feudal: men appropriate the surplus labour of their wives through cultural, political and economic mechanisms. (The cultural processes include gendered meanings, the political processes may include domestic violence, and the economic processes may include men's ownership of the means of household production.) Unlike capitalist exploitation, household feudal exploitation does not depend on markets; like medieval European feudalism, it does rely on custom and coercion.

Fraad et al. also describe a subsumed class process in which women secure the conditions of existence of their own exploitation. For example, gender processes in the production of cultural meanings often induce women to discipline themselves, to produce surplus for men without questioning the legitimacy of that process. Thus distinctly gendered cultural processes shape the fundamental process of appropriating surplus (and vice versa).

In conclusion, Fraad et al. find that these feudal households are full of contradiction and potential for revolutionary change. The class processes in the household interact with other cultural and political processes in ways which may undermine the viability of exploitation.

Developments in the theory of gender and capitalist class location

Feminists have often treated gender as a unitary category, having a common meaning for all groups of women, and providing an unproblematic basis for gender solidarity. But increasingly it has been recognized that this is an unfounded assumption, which may serve the interests of some women (affluent, white, or of dominant countries) over the interests of others (poor, racially subordinate, or colonized). (For early statements concerning gender and race, see Davis 1981, and hooks 1984. For a discussion of feminism and colonialism, see Alexander and Mohanty 1997.)

As Ngan-Ling Chow has recently put it (1996, p. xx), 'race and class are as significant as gender, each contributing bases for common bonds as well as generating divergent patterns of structural relationships and life experiences that shape the social construction of diverse kinds of women and men in different historical and sociocultural contexts'. In particular, men of subordinate classes, races and nations usually have less access to economic resources than more privileged men, and therefore wield less power over their female kin. Moreover, women of different positions within class, race and national hierarchies often experience gender oppression differently. For example, the pattern of husbands appropriating the surplus labour of women in the household does not apply to unmarried women, who are disproportionately poor women or some women of colour. A very different problem for unmarried low-income women is inadequate support for their household labour, via welfare payments. Similarly, the sex/affective production of children is more likely to involve coercive pronatal practices for white women of higher socioeconomic status, and coercive antinatal practices for poor women or women of colour (for example, sterilization abuse both in the USA and other countries).

Marxian theorists have often discussed the working class as if it were a male preserve. This is clearly unwarranted. Class theorists have begun to appreciate the extent to which gender influences class location, and the history, meaning and experience of class itself. The effect of gender on class location has been studied primarily in the context of twentieth-century patterns of class formation. Contrary to the expectations of early Marxists, these patterns have exhibited more, rather than less, fragmentation of the working class, a process in which gender has been one of several crucial determining variables. These developments have been described in somewhat different terms for less and more developed countries.

In many developing countries (and in many poor neighbourhoods of the USA), the process of globalization has tended to divide the working class into a proletariat and subproletariat. The latter is often very feminized. These two groups can be distinguished by their different 'means of remuneration' (Portes 1984; Benería and Roldán 1987). The proletariat engages in contractual labour subject to labour regulations, and is often unionized. The subproletariat performs more casual labour, receiving cash and in-kind payments, often under conditions violating labour codes (particularly in industrial homework), and often earning subminimum wages. The subproletariat includes homeworkers or workers in putting-out systems, personal servants, independent street peddlers and porters. Benería and Roldán found that women are heavily concentrated in the Mexico City subproletariat, particularly after marriage, when factory owners are unwilling to accommodate women's needs for flexibility to care for their families. Similar patterns appear in some countries of southeast Asia, where manufacturing operatives in export industries are overwhelmingly female, many of them performing industrial homework without the protection of labour codes and unions.

It is women's position within the family labour system which renders them particularly vulnerable to such extreme exploitation. 'Women's subordination to men as wives, mothers, and daughters makes them a particularly attractive source of low-cost labour at a time when investors seek to maintain an edge in fiercely competitive international markets' (Fernandez-Kelly and Sassen 1993, p. 25).

Class formation in advanced capitalist countries has also created some anomalies for traditional Marxian theory. By some very restrictive definitions, the working class actually became a minority of the labour force in some countries (Przeworski 1985). The working class also did not become homogenized; rather, it became highly segmented. (See Gordon et al. 1982 for a historical account of the segmentation of labour; see Albelda and Tilly 1994 for a feminist critique.) In general, the working class fragmented into those with more and less expertise, and more and less supervisory authority over others, creating a need for a theory of 'middle-class class locations' in highly developed capitalist countries (Wright 1996).

Wright (1996) conceptualized middle-class class locations as contradictory locations within class relations defined according to property, skills and authority in production. Wright's class location typology (p. 25) first divides owners from employees. Owners are further classified as petty bourgeoisie, small employers and capitalists, according to the number of employees. Nonowners are classified along two dimensions, relation to authority and relation to scarce skills. Employees who are unskilled and who have no supervisory or managerial authority are 'workers', narrowly defined. A broader definition of workers also includes skilled workers without authority and unskilled workers with minimal authority. Other employees with greater degrees of skill and authority are in middle-class class locations, where political and economic allegiances are much more complex and unstable.

Drawing upon special surveys with measures of expertise, workplace authority and ownership of productive assets in six advanced capitalist countries, Wright found that the distribution of employed persons across class locations is greatly influenced by gender. In particular, women comprise 55–62 per cent of workers (narrowly defined) in all the countries studied, even though they only constitute 40–45 per cent of the employed labour force. Also, over 80 per cent of expert managers are males (Wright 1996, pp. 61–4). Women are especially underrepresented in jobs involving authority (although there is tremendous international variation (p. 337)).

An important aspect of Wright's work is his recognition of the internal class heterogeneity of families. Husbands and wives often have very different capitalist class locations. Many feminists, including Ferguson and Delphy, have criticized empirical investigators of class for neglecting this issue. Wright (1996) gets around the problem by asserting that both men and women may have two kinds of class locations, direct and mediated. The direct location is based on one's own position in capitalist production. The mediated location is based on the direct location of family members. Families may thus have complicated internal class structures. For example, in the USA and Sweden, only 39 per cent and 44 per cent, respectively, of men and women in two-earner families had the same direct class location.

Feminists have not only examined how gender allocates people into capitalist class locations, but they have also begun to explore how gender affects the history, structure and experience of class. Concerning history, Mies (1986) argued that the earliest establishment of class relations was thoroughly interwoven with the development of patriarchal control over women. Concerning structure, Wright (1996) pointed out that some poorly paid occupations might not even exist if it were not for the exclusion of women from more desirable jobs, and their consequent availability for the poorly paid ones. Concerning the experience of class, England (1992) found that authority confers a much larger pay premium on men than on women in the United States.

Overall, the relationship between class and gender is one of mutual determination. Benería and Roldán (1987) conclude that the gender division of labour in wage work leaves women with fewer resources for the renegotiation of gender relations within the home, which in turn reduces women's chances of leaving the subproletariat. Similarly, Deere (1990) demonstrates that the distribution of resources and wealth among men and women influences their relative bargaining positions within the household, with direct implications for income pooling, shared consumption and the gender division of labour. Similarly, the domestic gender division of labour affects the class relations in which household members participate, in turn contributing to the relative position of men and women in society and in the home.

Directions for future research
Class and gender has been an important area of feminist research for several decades. Themes running through the literature for more and less developed countries concern the multiple class relations of households, the mutual relationship between women's domestic exploitation and their class position in nonhousehold production, the fragmentation of the working class, and the complexities introduced by racial and national hierarchies. Several important areas remain for future research by feminist economists.

To date, there has not been much work done on the effect of capitalist class location on gender class relations. The main exception is Wright (1996), who found that capitalist class location has basically no significant empirical effect on who does the housework. If this result is replicated, a theoretical problem arises: does relative capitalist class location not affect the relative bargaining position of men and women in the domestic arena?

There has also been little research on the relationship in the capitalist workplace and the political arena between women of different classes. Since women have become more economically fragmented in the United States, how does this affect the potential for alliances between women of different capitalist class locations? There is a large related body of research on race and gender, but relatively little specifically on class and gender.

Another important question for future research concerns women's longitudinal experience of class. Benería and Roldán (1987) explored this question in their study of women homeworkers in Mexico City, showing that marriage and the growth of family responsibilities tended to push women lower in the class structure. More studies of this nature need to be done for both the underdeveloped and developed world. Because of the complexity of their mediated and direct locations, and the greater family instability of the 1970s and 1980s, women may shift in and out of several class locations within their lifetimes. How does this affect their class and feminist consciousness?

Finally, how can women outside the labour force be conceptualized in class theories? Many of these women are unmarried and thus do not even have a mediated class location through their husbands. This issue requires further feminist reconstructions of class theory to fully incorporate the varied experiences of women.

ELAINE MCCRATE

See also

Capitalism; Domestic Labour; Family, Economics of; Marxist Political Economics; Race; Value.

Bibliography

Albelda, Randy and Chris Tilly (1994), 'Towards a Broader Vision: Race, Gender and Labor Market Segmentation in the Social Structure of Accumulation Framework', in David M. Kotz, Terrence McDonough and Michael Reich (eds), *Social Structures of Accumulation: The Political Economy of Growth and Crisis*, Cambridge: Cambridge University Press, pp. 212–30.

Alexander, M. Jacqui and Chandra Talpade Mohanty (1997), *Feminist Genealogies, Colonial Legacies, Democratic Futures*, New York: Routledge.

Benería, Lourdes and Martha Roldán (1987), *The Crossroads of Class and Gender: Industrial Homework, Subcontracting, and Household Dynamics in Mexico City*, Chicago: University of Chicago Press.

Dalla Costa, Mariarosa and Selma James (1972), *The Power of Women and the Subversion of the Community*, Bristol: Falling Wall Press.

Davis, Angela Y. (1981), *Women, Race and Class*, New York: Vintage Books.

Deere, Carmen Diana (1990), *Household and Class Relations: Peasants and Landlords in Northern Peru*, Berkeley: University of California Press.

Delphy, Christine (1984), *Close to Home: A Materialist Analysis of Women's Oppression*, London: Hutchinson (in association with The Explorations in Feminism Collective). Translated and edited by Diana Leonard.

Engels, Frederick ([1884] 1968), *The Origin of the Family, Private Property and the State*. Reprinted in *Karl Marx and Frederick Engels, Selected Works in One Volume*, London: Lawrence and Wishart, pp. 455–593.

England, Paula (1992), *Comparable Worth: Theories and Evidence*, New York: Aldine de Gruyter.

Ferguson, Ann (1991), *Sexual Democracy: Women, Oppression and Revolution*, Boulder: Westview Press.

Fernandez-Kelly, M. Patricia and Saskia Sassen (1993), 'Recasting Women in the Global Economy: Internationalization and Changing Definitions of Gender', Russell Sage Foundation Working Paper #36.

Folbre, Nancy (1982), 'Exploitation comes home: a critique of the Marxian theory of family labour', *Cambridge Journal of Economics*, **6**, 317–29.

Fraad, Harriet, Stephen Resnick and Richard Wolff (1994), *Bringing It All Back Home: Class, Gender and Power in the Modern Household*, London: Pluto Press.

Gordon, David M., Richard Edwards and Michael Reich (1982), *Segmented Work, Divided Workers: The Historical Transformation of Labor in the United States*, Cambridge: Cambridge University Press.

hooks, bell (1984), *Feminist Theory: From Margin to Center*, Boston: South End Press.

Hunt, E.K. (1994), 'Class, Social, in Institutional Economics', in Geoffrey M. Hodgson and Warren J. Samuels (eds), *The Elgar Companion to Institutional and Evolutionary Economics A–K*, Aldershot: Edward Elgar.

Luxemburg, Rosa (1923), *Die Akkumulation des Kapitals, Ein Beitrag zur okonomischen Erklarung des Kapitalismus*, Berlin.

Mies, Maria (1986), *Patriarchy and Accumulation on a World Scale: Women in the International Division of Labor*, London: Zed Books.

Ngan-Ling Chow, Esther (1996), 'Introduction: Transforming Knowledgment: Race, Class, and Gender', in Esther Ngan-Ling Chow, Doris Wilkinson and Maxine Baca Zinn (eds), *Race, Class, and Gender: Common Bonds, Different Voices*, Thousand Oaks: Sage Publications, pp. xix–xxvi.

Portes, Alejandro (1984), 'Latin American Class Structures: Their Composition and Change During the Last Decades', Occasional Paper No. 3, School of Advanced International Studies, Baltimore: Johns Hopkins University.

Przeworski, Adam (1985), *Capitalism and Social Democracy*, Cambridge: Cambridge University Press.

Veblen, Thorstein (1973), *The Theory of the Leisure Class*, Boston: Houghton Mifflin.

Wright, Erik Olin (1996), *Class Counts: Comparative Studies in Class Analysis*, Cambridge: Cambridge University Press.

Committee on the Status of Women in the Economics Profession (CSWEP)

The Committee on the Status of Women in the Economics Profession (CSWEP) was created and charged by the American Economics Association (AEA) in 1971 to monitor the progress of women in the profession and to engage in activities that would remedy the apparent gender imbalance in the profession. The committee, currently composed of 13 members who are appointed for three years by the President of the AEA, meets three times a year to plan the six sessions it sponsors for the AEA's national programme, to discuss content material for the next newsletter, to hear about the activities of the regional representatives and to develop new initiatives.

Out of a backdrop of social unrest and of the political disenchantment of the late 1960s and early 1970s, a group of economists got together and discussed the plight of women in the profession. The group became known as the Women's Caucus. The Caucus wanted to put before the AEA's executive committee at its business meeting seven resolutions to end the gender bias they experienced in the profession. Six of the seven proposed resolutions were adopted on 29 December 1971. The first resolution, declaring that economics was not exclusively a man's field, was intended to end discrimination against women at all levels of the profession. Undergraduate and graduate instructors were to encourage women to study economics. Graduate programmes in economics were to use the same admission standards and to provide the same financial aid to women as they did to men. Once admitted, women were to receive the same amount of encouragement and mentoring as their male counterparts did. And when it came to the time to find a job, women were to receive as much assistance as the male students did. In the job market, employers were to give women equal consideration for jobs. Once hired, promotion and tenure possibilities were to be the same as for men; and of course, salaries, fringe benefits and institutional resources were to be equal. Full time jobs were to be the same for both sexes. Finally, women were not to be discriminated against on the basis of existing relationships with other faculty members.

The AEA executive committee then passed a second resolution that created CSWEP, with four additional resolutions that pertained to initiatives the association could take on its own to further women's advancement. Thus, the association encouraged editors of its journals to put women on their editorial boards. Programme chairs were to include women on programmes at national meetings, and the AEA encouraged regional associations to do the same. A code of procedures for hiring and an open listing of all job opportunities were to be created. To accommodate the needs of two-career families or nontraditional families, the association was to encourage part-time employment options for both men and women and to support childcare initiatives at the national meetings. The seventh resolution, establishing a roster of women economists, was not passed.

Once the resolutions were passed, CSWEP went about its work. One of its first tasks was to determine how many women economists there were in the profession and where they were located. In December 1972, CSWEP sent a questionnaire to 2000 universities and colleges. Even with a letter from the President of the association, only 22 per cent of these institutions responded. Of the 43 PhD-granting departments known as the 'cartel', 42 responded. The survey found that there were 1194 economists at the cartel schools, of which 80, or 6 per cent, were women. Eleven per cent of those receiving PhDs and 13 per cent of those receiving MAs at the cartel schools were women. Eighteen of the universities had no women at all on their faculty. The percentages of professors who were women were small and progressively decreased up through the ranks: 9 per cent of the assistant, 4 per cent of the associate and 2 per cent of the full professors were women (Bell 1973, pp. 509–10). To discover women at other universities and outside of academia, CSWEP initiated a chain letter to all known women economists, asking them to identify other women economists and to send them a copy of CSWEP's letter. By the end of the first year over 1000 women economists had been identified.

These investigations further revealed that in 1972 no women were on the AEA's executive committee. The editor of the *American Economic Review* (*AER*) was male, and only two of its 17 editorial board members were women. *The Journal of Economic Literature* also had a male editor, and only one of its eight editorial board members was a woman. A crude count of who presented papers by gender at the national meetings revealed that two women presented papers, three women chaired sessions, and six women discussed papers in the 30 sessions which usually had 3 to 4 papers each. Despite the AEA's declaration, the percentages of women faculty and the numbers of women involved in the profession indicated that economics was a man's field.

Over the years, CSWEP has tried to affirm and recognize the economic contributions of women and, in particular, of women in the economics profession. This goal is compatible with that of feminist economics, which represents an economic, intellectual and political agenda that affirms the economic value of women and their contributions to economic life and the economics profession. It is also a goal that can be seen through the contributions of CSWEP's 10 chairs and their attendant boards.

CSWEP's first chair, Carolyn Shaw Bell (1972–73), focused on documenting the number of women in the profession so that the claim that there were no qualified women for jobs could be laid to rest. Its second chair, Barbara Reagan (1974–77), made CSWEP a standing committee of the AEA, while the third chair, Ann Friedlaender (1978–79), found herself and CSWEP in the midst of the politically charged debate over the ratification of the Equal Rights Amendment (ERA). Friedlaender and CSWEP unsuccessfully campaigned to have the AEA meetings moved from Atlanta, Georgia to a state that had ratified the ERA. CSWEP's next chair, Elizabeth Bailey (1980–82), began her tenure in Atlanta by placing an ad in the Atlanta Constitution with a list of over 900 economists who favoured the ERA. When Barbara Bergmann (1983–84) took over the reins, she focused on opening up the economics 'club'. Bergmann's energies were spent writing letters to economics departments pointing out that there were no women on their faculties. Institutions like the National Bureau of Economic Research that had few, if any, women, also received letters. Isabel Sawhill (1985–87) and Nancy Gordon (1988–90) encouraged several members of the committee to write grant proposals for research on why women were not being as successful as had been originally hoped. Elizabeth Hoffman (1991–93) made the tradition of publishing two CSWEP sessions in the *AER Papers and Proceedings* permanent and began the push for daycare at the national meetings. Rebecca Blank (1994–96) saw the daycare issue through, and she established a network of women at the PhD-granting schools who could act as liaisons for CSWEP; these women would collect data for the committee and distribute information. Robin Bartlett (1997–99), with the help of Andrea Ziegert, wrote a grant proposal on behalf of the committee to the National Science Foundation (NSF) for the purpose of setting up a series of team-mentoring workshops that would help younger female economists earn tenure. In January 1998, senior and junior women economists came together for two days to discuss each other's work and to discuss other issues related to surviving and thriving in the economics profession today.

Each CSWEP chair has tried to foster the advancement of women in the economics profession, and CSWEP's influence on the way that the economics profession conducts most of its business has been noticeable. While initial progress was slow, the percentage of women at all levels of the professorate has doubled from 1972 to 1998. Women are no longer overtly discriminated against in undergraduate or graduate school; admission requirements are identical for men and women. A greater percentage of women are making it through graduate school and into academic jobs, and it is hoped that as more female students see women as economists, these trends will continue. In addition, half of the 1998 AEA executive committee are women, and the percentage of women who are on the editorial boards of the association's journal has also doubled. These findings support CSWEP's belief that putting a critical mass of women economists in important positions will open up new doors for women economists.

CSWEP engages in a variety of ongoing activities that help promote women in the profession. The original chain letter evolved into the AEA's annual Universal Academic Questionnaire that is sent to all economics departments across the country. Information about graduate schools, the job market and departmental information by gender is requested. Also, despite the AEA's initial lack of support, CSWEP has constructed its Roster of Women Economists. The Roster includes over 7000 female economists in the US and abroad, listing women economists by field and speciality. As a result, it serves as a convenient resource for employers and other economists and policymakers.

The Roster also serves as the mailing list for the CSWEP newsletter, which provides its readers with job information, calls for papers, grant announcements and other information for career advancement. The newsletter also publishes reviews of the work of significant women economists in various subspecialities to document their contributions. The newsletter also regularly publishes biographies of deceased women economists and autobiographies of current board members to demonstrate the diversity of career paths that are taken. CSWEP has also used electronic media to disseminate information. The CSWEP web site (cswep.org) includes CSWEP's mission statement, a list of board members, membership information, a link to the Roster and an announcement page to keep the profession abreast of CSWEP's activities, while the CSWEP listserv, available to members, allows for time-sensitive information to be disseminated to associates.

As previously mentioned, in order to increase the visibility of women in the profession, CSWEP has lobbied for sessions at the annual meetings and for a select number of the papers presented there to be published in the *AER Papers and Proceedings*. At the 1977 meetings, the focus of the CSWEP sessions was on gender-related research. Almost 20 years later, three non-gender-related sessions had been added. The purpose of the gender-related sessions is to move scholarship on gender and economics forward, while the non-gender-related sessions profile the work of junior women economists and bring it to the attention of a wider audience.

CSWEP has also contributed to knowledge about gender and economic issues through conferences and reports. With a grant from the Carnegie Foundation, CSWEP and the AEA, along with the Center on Research on Women in Higher Education and the Professions, sponsored a conference on occupational segregation in May 1975 at Wellesley College. The proceedings from that conference were originally published as a supplement to the spring issue of *Signs: Journal of Women in Culture and Society* (1976) and later as Blaxall and Reagan (1976). Under CSWEP chair Bailey, a CSWEP/Brookings conference took place in November 1984 and resulted in another path-breaking work, *Gender in the Workplace* edited by Brown and Pechman (1987). Also that year, CSWEP members Edwards and Ferber (1986) reported that journals which used double-blind refereeing versus single-blind refereeing published proportionately more articles by women.

The critics of CSWEP would say that it has not done enough for women in the profession and of course that is true. A lot still needs to be done, but the task of identifying what the problems are is not trivial. Some, for example, would argue that CSWEP is too mainstream. It is probably true that most associates of CSWEP are more traditional in their views about what constitutes economics, yet there are associates who hold diverse perspectives and broader understandings of what constitutes economics. In 1992, the impatience of some of these critics, along with the absence of an international presence and the need for a more feminist agenda, led a number of CSWEP members and others to create the alternative organization, the International Association of Feminist Economics (IAFFE). Many women economists now hold membership and participate in both organizations.

Other critics would argue that CSWEP's focus is only on academics and specifically, academics at the top PhD-granting institutions. Historically, there is some truth to this criticism, especially about the period prior to microcomputers and the Internet. (Then, not only was it harder to locate women outside the academy, but CSWEP was still primarily concerned with improving women's dismal showing in PhD-granting schools.) While most of the members of CSWEP are academics, a significant number of government economists also belong although women in business are noticeably absent. Some critics have also argued that CSWEP has largely overlooked the experience of undergraduate women and what can be done to increase the numbers of women majoring in economics and going on to graduate school.

Despite these complaints, CSWEP has paved the way for many women economists to succeed in the profession. It showcases and values the contributions that women make to the discipline. It has sponsored sessions and conferences, and it has commissioned research to understand the historic and theoretical reasons for women's underrepresentation and undervaluation in the economics profession and in the economy as a whole. Its efforts have added to new understandings of how markets work and do not work, and it has worked to remedy many of the gender inequities within the profession. CSWEP has helped to open up the profession from the 'old boys' system that existed in the early 1970s to one where women economists are on most association committees and jobs are widely publicized in *Job Opportunities for Economists*. Nepotism laws, which had limited the access of married women to academic jobs, are artifacts of the past. In addition, CSWEP has acknowledged the lives of most of its members by making daycare available at the national meetings.

Yet, there is much to be done. First, CSWEP needs to address the one original resolution that has not been given much attention – part-time work. On today's faculties two-career couples are not unusual. However, given consulting opportunities, one or both members of the couple may want to be tenured as part-time or proportional-time faculty. How to promote this option in an equitable way needs to be studied. Second, CSWEP needs to address some of the criticisms that have been directed at it over the its first 25 years and decide what to do, if anything. As progress is made, expectations rise. However, the need to reach women in the non PhD-granting institutions and in government and business is critical to the success of CSWEP's mandate. There are more women teaching and doing research at these schools than at the larger research-oriented schools, as evidenced by recent CSWEP surveys (1993–97). These women need the support of CSWEP in achieving their goals too. CSWEP's new mission statement, developed for its 25th anniversary, declares that 'economics is as much of a woman's field as it is a man's field' (Bartlett and Small 1997). If women continue to progress at the rate of the last 25 years, it will take another 25 years for gender parity. CSWEP intends to devise new programmes to speed up that process.

ROBIN L. BARTLETT

See also

International Association for Feminist Economics (IAFFE); Women in the Economics Profession.

Bibliography

American Economics Association (1971 through 1997), 'Minutes of the Executive Committee Meetings', *The American Economic Review Papers and Proceedings*.
Bartlett, Robin and Kenneth Small (1997), *American Economic Association's Committee on the Status of Women in the Economics Profession Newsletter*, (Fall), Granville, Ohio: CSWEP.
Bell, Carolyn Shaw (1973), 'Report of the Committee on the Status of Women in the Economics Profession', *American Economic Review*, **63** (2), pp. 615–31.
Blaxall, Martha and Barbara Reagan (1976), *Women and the Workplace: The Implications of Occupational Segregation*, Chicago: The University of Chicago Press.
Brown, Claire and Joseph A. Pechman (eds) (1987), *Gender in the Workplace*, Washington, DC: The Brookings Institution.
Committee on the Status of Women in the Economics Profession (CSWEP). *Annual Departmental Surveys*, 1993 through 1997, unpublished.
Edwards, Linda N. and Marianne Ferber (1986), 'Journal reviewing practices and the progress of women in the economics profession: is there a relationship?', *American Economic Association 1986 Committee on the Status of Women in the Economics Profession Newsletter*, October, pp. 2–7.
Kahn, Shulamit (1993), 'Gender differences in academic career paths of economists', *The American Economic Review Papers and Proceedings*, **83** (2), 52–6.
Signs: Journal of Women in Culture and Society. Part 2, (1976), **1** (3), Spring.

Comparable Worth/Pay Equity

'Comparable worth' is a shorthand term for a policy designed to raise the wages of jobs held predominantly by women until they equal the wages of comparable jobs held predominantly by men. Specifically, comparable worth requires that jobs that are equivalent in their demands, measured by such factors as skill, effort, responsibility and working conditions, be paid equally. The policy is also known as 'pay equity' in the USA or 'equal value' in Europe, Australia and New Zealand. Although these terms are sometimes seen to have different meanings (see Figart and Kahn 1997), they will be used interchangeably throughout this entry.

Insofar as it works to raise women's wages in women's jobs, pay equity confronts forms of discrimination not addressed by better-established policies such as equal pay for equal work (which raises women's wages to equal those of men working in the same job) or affirmative or positive action (which helps women enter jobs typically held by men). The essential premise of comparable worth policy is that the wages of jobs held predominantly by women are depressed at least partially by discrimination: if men had these same jobs in large numbers, the jobs would pay more.

The need for comparable worth policy arises because of the substantial gender typing of jobs in the economy and the well-documented negative relationship between the proportion of women in an occupation and its pay rate, that is, the more women, the lower the pay, on average (see Treiman and Hartmann 1981; Sorensen 1994). Although the representation of women in the labour force has increased worldwide, occupational segregation is still extensive. The majority of male workers in the world work in an occupation that could be defined as male-dominated; women in the labour force also work generally with other women, though to a lesser extent (Anker 1998, chapter 10).

The key theoretical issue in the implementation of comparable worth is developing a credible approach to determining to what extent different jobs are equivalent in value. The key practical issue in implementation is getting employers to undertake determinations and adjust pay accordingly. Unless comparable worth policy has been established by law or collective bargaining, employers are unlikely to take action to raise the pay of female-dominated occupations. Thus pay equity is an important issue for feminist economic thought because it encourages discussion of the value of women's work, caring labour (for example, work that involves nurturing, personal contact and concern for others), and other activities that are gendered as female. Although pay equity has largely been a concern in industrialized nations thus far, it raises issues of importance to women workers worldwide.

Historically, the concept of comparable worth or equal pay for jobs of equal value developed in tandem with the concept of equal pay for equal work. Both World War I and World War II spurred efforts to adopt equal pay for equal work policies because, as women entered many jobs formerly closed to them, the differences between typical female pay scales and typical male pay scales became apparent. Both to help women and protect men from so-called lower-priced competition, interest in pay equity grew. In the 1940s and 1950s, the development of specific pay equity remedies was assisted by the widespread adoption of job evaluation systems in large firms. Designed to align the relative pay rates of diverse jobs, these systems compare jobs based on indicators of the skill, effort and responsibility required in each job and the working conditions in which it is performed. In 1951, an International Labour Organization policy ('Convention 100') required that countries promote the principle of equal pay for jobs of equal value (see ILO 1986, Gunderson 1994).

Although a great many countries have signed on to the convention, few countries have developed any systematic means of ensuring that the principle is implemented in practice. For example, when the USA passed the Equal Pay Act of 1963, the attempt to incorporate equal value language failed. Subsequent legal efforts to include comparable worth remedies under the more inclusive 1964 Civil Rights Act have generally failed in the Courts. Of 39 states with equal pay laws, 15 use language calling for equal pay for work of comparable value but none are currently enforced (Cook 1983). Twenty states have implemented pay adjustments for at least some of the female-dominated occupations in their state civil services, and some labour unions have won pay equity adjustments from private employers, but no national law specifically addresses comparable worth in the USA (Hartmann and Aaronson 1994).

In the industrialized countries of the European Union, Canada, Australia and New Zealand, greater steps have been taken to achieve pay equity. Because of different legal institutions and industrial relations systems, pay equity implementation has varied. Australia's centralized minimum wage tribunals have facilitated pay adjustments for female-dominated occupations. New, higher minimum wages in women's jobs have raised women's wages in the aggregate relative to men's, but these increases stop short of across-the-board pay equity. New Zealand's Equal Pay Act of 1972 includes language specifically requiring equal pay for 'work which is exclusively or predominantly performed by female employees' (Hyman 1994, p. 85). Implementation has been slow, however, due in part to a trend towards decentralized labour relations.

In the European Union, the European Court of Justice has held that the principle of equal pay for equal value is mandated under the Equal Pay Directive of 1975. The European legal tradition recognizes individual litigation but not class action lawsuits. As a result, equal value is complaint-driven by individual litigants using direct male–female job comparisons (Kahn and Meehan 1992). Comparable worth lawsuits are more extensive in the United Kingdom than in the other member countries (Gunderson 1994), reflecting both this tradition of individual litigation and the prevalence of job evaluation systems. Most of Canada's provinces and territories have adopted pay equity through legislation, and federal law applies to public entities. Ontario possesses the most far-reaching pay equity legislation in the world. The 1987 Pay Equity Act requires compensation that is free of gender bias in all public as well as private sector employers with ten or more employees. In general, realization of comparable worth in Canada has been effected through the collective bargaining process; unions have played a significant role in ensuring the practical application of the legislative provisions (Fudge and McDermott 1991).

The early research on pay equity documented the need for and potential efficacy of the policy through studies of labour market discrimination, occupational segregation and the male–female wage gap. This early feminist literature on pay equity generated a critique of the neoclassical economic model of wage determination, which posits that wages are determined by the interaction of labour supply and demand and reflect the rational choices and productivity of individuals in competitive markets. The central premise of this critique is that wages are determined by institutions that perpetuate gender inequality, including the division of labour in the household, practices within workplaces, public policies and cultural norms (see Figart 1997 for a review of this literature). Consequently, the role of institutions and power in wage-setting has been highlighted and analysed by feminist scholars from economics and other disciplines (Treiman and Hartmann 1981; Remick 1984; Sorensen 1984; Hartmann 1986; Amott and Matthaei 1988; Bergmann 1989; Kessler-Harris 1990; Peterson 1990; Steinberg 1990).

Feminists view the labour market as an aggregation of socially-constructed institutions with ideas of gender-appropriate work and pay embedded in them. For example, family wage ideology (the belief that men should earn wages high enough to support a family) traditionally legitimated gender-based wage differentials in many industrialized economies. Once jobs become identified as women's work, they pay less primarily because women do the work. Pay practices that incorporated discrimination in the past are carried forward into contemporary prevailing wages. Concepts such as 'skill', which have been used to explain wage inequality, are historically constructed, socially contingent, and strongly gendered (Phillips and Taylor 1980; Baron and Newman 1989).

Based on their view that wages are socially constructed and influenced by a variety of social and cultural forces, feminists have generally supported pay equity as a means to address the inequities they identify in the wage distribution. By contrast, traditional economists have largely opposed the policy, arguing that if you raise the price of a woman's job you are sending the wrong signal in labour markets – reinforcing occupational segregation, raising unemployment and causing other negative economic repercussions (Hill and Killingsworth 1989). As shown by feminist economists Mutari and Figart (1997), such neoclassical arguments against comparable worth have been used by opponents lobbying against the policy.

Recent feminist scholarship has focused on evaluating the process of pay equity implementation in the United States and other countries. Feminist scholars have highlighted the process of generating a social movement, the experiences of women workers and the impact of the movement on consciousness, finding that the benefits of comparable worth often go beyond what can be measured in wage changes (Evans and Nelson 1989, McCann

1994). Feminists have also criticized the technocratic nature of implementation via job evaluation and the tendency of bureaucracies to contain reform and reinforce the status quo by maintaining rather than challenging existing workplace hierarchies (Acker 1989; Evans and Nelson 1989; Fudge and McDermott 1991; Steinberg 1991; Figart and Kahn 1997). Researchers have also evaluated the actual and anticipated results of comparable worth policies, finding many instances of monetary gains for working women. These gains have been documented by scholars such as Aldrich and Buchele (1986), Michael et al. (1989), Sorensen (1994), Hartmann and Aaronson (1994) and through regular newsletters and research briefings by advocacy groups such as the National Committee on Pay Equity in the United States. Figart and Lapidus (1995) have estimated that comparable worth wage increases could significantly reduce the proportion of women among the working poor. Additionally, it would decrease overall earnings inequality, inequality between women and men, and inequality among women (Figart and Lapidus 1997).

Further feminist economic research on comparable worth and pay equity is needed in key areas. First is the issue of the valuation of work and the determination of wages. The wage-setting process in the firm is still little understood. How discrimination enters the process of valuing jobs and determining their relative wage rates needs further investigation. Job evaluation systems, classification schemes and wage and salary surveys all require greater scrutiny. Beyond the firm, understanding how particular occupations are affected, or not affected, by changes in demand and supply is critical to learning how labour market institutions may operate differently for women and men. How and how much are women's and men's choices constrained? How are gender-segregated labour markets perpetuated? As Bergmann (1989) has suggested, it would be extremely useful to have a model of the labour market that could predict what wage patterns would be like in a free market with no discrimination. Whether the relative valuations of jobs produced by current job evaluation systems approaches those discrimination-free wages could then be investigated using the model.

Second, the effectiveness of pay equity remedies needs further evaluation. Little research has been done on job evaluation methods and how to remove gender and other biases that are present in most available plans. In particular, research to improve measures of job content is needed. While several studies are now available of how pay equity has been implemented in practice in a variety of jurisdictions, and with what results, more studies are needed to allow for drawing conclusions about which strategies generally yield the best results. The role of labour unions and the collective bargaining process also need further examination. Moreover, few studies have tried to assess the spillover effects – positive and negative – of pay equity policies enacted in some occupations, sectors, or geographical areas, but not others. The overall effectiveness of pay equity remedies, relative to other forms of anti-discrimination enforcement, is also not known. The sustainability of pay equity reform is also relatively unexamined, as the reform is relatively recent. How political mobilization contributes to initiating, achieving and sustaining pay equity bears further study.

In addition, the impact of the changing global economy needs to be addressed more thoroughly. Economic restructuring and the political trend toward deregulation of labour markets has changed the context in which pay equity strategies can be pursued. Reforms targeted at the public sector are likely to be less effective in the future, as the legitimacy of the state as a 'model employer' and the size of government are challenged. Growing inequality and increased immigration in industrialized countries raise the issues of race, ethnicity and national origin. Further research is needed on the relationship between racial/ethnic and gender wage discrimination in order to explore the potential for pay equity remedies that target minority-concentrated as well as female-dominated occupations.

Given the persistence of the twin problems of extensive gender segregation and substantially lower pay for women than for men in most labour markets around the world, feminist economists face a rich set of opportunities and challenges in formulating both theory and empirical research that can help to improve the implementation of comparable worth wage policies and the adoption of other wage-enhancing strategies. Moreover, the continued involvement of feminist economics in the practical aspects of pay equity implementation is also needed, as activists, consultants, expert witnesses and policymakers.

HEIDI HARTMANN AND DEBORAH M. FIGART

See also

Affirmative Action; Family Wage; Discrimination, Theories of; Human Capital Theory; Labour Force Participation; Labour Market Segmentation; Labour Markets, Theories of; Minimum Wage; Occupational Segregation; Wage Gap.

Bibliography

Acker, Joan (1989), *Doing Comparable Worth: Gender, Class, and Pay Equity*, Philadelphia: Temple University Press.

Aldrich, Mark and Robert Buchele (1986), *The Economics of Comparable Worth*, Cambridge, Massachusetts: Ballinger Publishing Co.

Amott, Teresa and Julie Matthaei (1988), 'The promise of comparable worth: a socialist–feminist perspective', *Socialist Review*, **18** (2), 101–17.

Anker, Richard (1998), *Gender and Jobs: Sex Segregation of Occupations on the World*, Geneva: International Labour Office.

Baron, James N. and Andrew E. Newman (1989), 'Pay the Man: Effects of Demographic Composition on Prescribed Wage Rates in the California Civil Services', in Robert T. Michael, Heidi I. Hartmann and Brigid O'Farrell (eds), *Pay Equity: Empirical Inquiries*, Washington, DC: National Academy Press, pp. 107–30.

Bergmann, Barbara R. (1989), 'What the common economic arguments against comparable worth are worth', *Journal of Social Issues*, **45**, (Fall), 67–80.

Cook, Alice H. (1983), *Comparable Worth: The Problem and States' Approaches to Wage Equity*, Manoa, Hawaii: Industrial Relations Center.

England, Paula (1992), *Comparable Worth: Theories and Evidence*, New York: Aldine de Gruyter.

Evans, Sara and Barbara Nelson (1989), *Wage Justice: Comparable Worth and the Paradox of Technocratic Reform*, Chicago: University of Chicago Press.

Figart, Deborah M. (1997), 'Gender as more than a dummy variable: Feminist approaches to discrimination', *Review of Social Economy*, **55**, (Spring), 1–32.

Figart, Deborah M. and Peggy Kahn (1997), *Contesting the Market: Pay Equity and the Politics of Economic Restructuring*, Detroit: Wayne State University Press.

Figart, Deborah M. and June Lapidus (1995), 'A gender analysis of labor market policies for the working poor in the US', *Feminist Economics*, **1**, (Fall), 60–81.

Figart, Deborah M. and June Lapidus (1997), 'Reversing the Great U-Turn: Pay Equity, Poverty, and Inequality', in Ellen Mutari, Heather Boushey and William Fraher IV (eds), *Gender and Political Economy: Incorporating Diversity into Theory and Policy*, Armonk, New York: M.E. Sharpe, pp. 188–205.

Fudge, Judy and Patricia McDermott (eds) (1991), *Just Wages: A Feminist Assessment of Pay Equity*, Toronto: University of Toronto Press.

Gunderson, Morley (1994), *Comparable Worth and Gender Discrimination: An International Perspective*, Geneva: International Labour Office.

Hartmann, Heidi (1986), 'The Political Economy of Comparable Worth', in Garth Mangum and Peter Phillips (eds), *Three Worlds of Labor Economics*, Armonk, New York: M.E. Sharpe, pp. 217–34.

Hartmann, Heidi and Stephanie Aaronson (1994), 'Pay equity and women's wage increases: success in the states, a model for the nation', *Duke Journal of Gender Law and Policy*, **1**, 69–87.

Hill, M. Anne and Mark R. Killingsworth (eds) (1989), *Comparable Worth: Analyses and Evidence*, Ithaca, New York: ILR Press.

Hyman, Prue (1994), *Women and Economics: A New Zealand Feminist Perspective*, Wellington: Bridget Williams Books.

International Labour Office (1986), *Equal Remuneration, General Survey of the Reports on the Equal Remuneration Convention (No. 100) and Recommendation (No. 90), 1951*, Geneva: ILO.

Kahn, Peggy and Elizabeth Meehan (eds) (1992), *Equal Value/Comparable Worth in the UK and USA*, New York: St Martin's Press.

Kessler-Harris, Alice (1990), *A Woman's Wage: Historical Meanings and Social Consequences*, Lexington, Kentucky: University Press of Kentucky.

McCann, Michael W. (1994), *Rights at Work: Pay Equity Reform and the Politics of Legal Mobilization*, Chicago: University of Chicago Press.

Michael, Robert T. and Heidi I. Hartmann (1989), 'Pay Equity: Assessing the Issues', in Robert T. Michael, Heidi I. Hartmann and Brigid O'Farrell (eds), *Pay Equity: Empirical Inquiries*, Washington, DC: National Academy Press, pp. 1–19.

Michael, Robert T., Heidi I. Hartmann and Brigid O'Farrell (eds) (1989), *Pay Equity: Empirical Inquiries*, Washington, DC: National Academy Press.

Mutari, Ellen and Deborah M. Figart (1997), 'Markets, flexibility, and family: evaluating the gendered discourse against pay equity', *Journal of Economic Issues*, **31**, (September), 687–705.

Peterson, Janice (1990), 'The challenge of comparable worth: an institutionalist view', *Journal of Economic Issues*, **24**, (June), 605–12.

Phillips, Ann and Barbara Taylor (1980) 'Sex and skill: Notes toward a feminist economics', *Feminist Review*, **6**, 79–88.

Remick, Helen (ed.) (1984), *Comparable Worth and Wage Discrimination: Technical Possibilities and Political Realities*, Philadelphia: Temple University Press.

Sorensen, Elaine (1984), 'Equal pay for comparable worth: A policy for eliminating the under-valuation of women's work', *Journal of Economic Issues*, **18**, (June), 465–72.

Sorensen, Elaine (1994), *Comparable Worth: Is It a Worthy Policy?* Princeton: Princeton University Press.

Steinberg, Ronnie (1990), 'Social construction of skill: gender, power, and comparable worth', *Work and Occupations*, **17**, (November), 449–82.

Steinberg, Ronnie (1991), 'Job Evaluation and Managerial Control: The Politics of Technique and the Techniques of Politics', in Judy Fudge and Patricia McDermott (eds), *Just Wages: A Feminist Assessment of Pay Equity*, Toronto: University of Toronto Press, pp. 193–218.

Treiman, Donald J. and Heidi I. Hartmann (eds) (1981), *Women, Work, and Wages: Equal Pay for Jobs of Equal Value*, Washington, DC: National Academy Press.

Contingent Labour Force

During the 1990s increasing attention has been focused in the economically advanced countries on the growing proportion of workers who have non-standard or 'alternative' work arrangements, and hence are members of what is often called the contingent labour force. Comparable information about developing countries does not appear to be available, although it is entirely likely that non-standard employment is at least equally common there. In this entry the focus is, however, on the situation in the USA, because research here has been done on a wide variety of non-standard work, while information available for the other members of the European Union and Japan focuses almost exclusively on part-time workers, and on what are termed 'temporary workers'. Interestingly, to the extent that comparable data are available, developments in the USA appear to be well within the bounds of what has been happening in these other countries.

The term contingent labour force has been narrowly defined as consisting of workers who lack explicit or implicit contracts for long-term employment (Polivka 1996). It had earlier been defined to include those who work minimum hours that vary unsystematically (Polivka and Nardone 1989) but the first major survey of contingent workers and workers with alternative work arrangements conducted by the Bureau of Labor Statistics in 1995 did not include this category. The term is, however, frequently used more broadly to include a variety of alternative work arrangements that are not contingent, *per se*. These diverse categories are first briefly described, followed by a discussion of the reasons why feminist economists are particularly concerned about the rising incidence of this type of employment. Finally there are suggestions as to what might be done to minimize the disadvantages of holding such jobs.

Part-time workers are regularly employed with hours of work substantially shorter than is normal in the establishment. There is disagreement whether such workers, by far the largest category, should be included among workers with non-traditional employment, as they often are. It is rightly argued that many part-time jobs are not 'contingent' because they generally do have 'explicit or implicit contracts for long-term employment'. They are, however, plausibly included, because they share a number of the other characteristics of contingent and alternative work, such as a relatively high rate of turnover and low rates of benefits coverage.

Part-time work has long been a feature of the labour market. As early as 1950, part-time workers comprised 16 per cent of the labour force; by 1995 this figure had risen to 23.9 million, amounting to 19 per cent of the labour force. It has been calculated that about half of the new jobs between January 1993 and January 1995 have been part-time jobs. More than two-thirds of those who work part time by preference are women; most of the remainder are students and, to a lesser extent, elderly workers in transition to retirement. It is, however, involuntary part-time jobs, which have ranged from 17 per cent of the total in relatively prosperous times to 32 per cent in recessions, that have risen most rapidly in recent years (Tilly 1991). (In 1991, part-time workers in countries of the European Union constituted 15.0 per cent of the labour force, up from 13.6 per cent in 1983, and ranging from 3.4 per cent of the labour force in Greece and 4.5 per cent in Spain, to 22.6 per cent in Germany and 32.4 per cent in the Netherlands (DeGrip et al. 1997), while they comprised 16.1 per cent of the labour force in Japan in 1992, up from 11.0 per cent in 1982 (Houseman 1995). In all these countries a substantial majority of part-time workers were women.) Part-year workers have also long been common in a number of industries, among them seasonal farm workers, construction workers, clerks hired for the Christmas rush, and most school teachers.

Official data on the various categories of alternative workers did not become available till 1995 (Cohany 1996), but it appears that their numbers have risen rapidly. According to a report by the Bureau of Labor Statistics there were 1.2 million temporary help supply workers in that year. Such workers are typically employed by large agencies and sent out to other businesses as they are needed. Women, most of them working full time, constitute almost two-thirds of these temporary workers, predominantly in what are now called the administrative support occupations. Men in this category earn only slightly more than half as much as men in traditional work arrangements; a disproportionate number of them are non-white, work part time, and tend to be in industrial jobs. Some temporary workers receive such benefits as health insurance and contributions to pension funds from the agencies that employ them, and thus do better than many contingent and other alternative workers.

Among those who are least likely to have job security or benefits are on call workers. Their number reached 2.0 million in 1995. Recently these have increasingly included skilled white-collar workers as well as blue-collar workers, at times drawn from pools of retirees. Those that are highly trained confront a very different situation from the traditional crowded hiring halls or dock-sides, where unskilled labourers assemble in the morning in the hope of being chosen for a day's work; but these continue to exist as well (Southern Regional Council 1988). Women and blacks are not disproportionately represented in this category, but other minorities are.

Independent contractors added up to 8.3 million in 1995, and include a broad array of occupations, from textbook editors and real estate agents to building cleaners. Unlike other sole proprietors in many types of service industries, they work for corporate clients. Contrary to workers in the other categories, white men are represented far more heavily than in proportion to their representation in the labour force, and their earnings are high relative to their peers in traditional employment.

Finally, workers provided by contract firms to other companies, who tend to work at the customer's work site, comprise only 0.7 million. The contract firms provide such services as security, landscaping and computer programming, as well as many others. There are relatively few women among these workers, but disproportionately large numbers of blacks and other minorities.

Although there now is a reasonably precise count of workers who report that they belong to the above categories, there is still considerable uncertainty about the reliability of some of these numbers, and particularly about the total number of non-standard workers. First, it is not clear whether individuals always identify themselves correctly; for instance, a person employed by a temporary supply agency may or may not claim to be a temporary worker. Second, the same worker may be included in more than one of the categories; that is, a temporary help worker may also work part time. Third, individuals who work a total of 35 hours or more a week are counted as full-time workers, even if they reach this total by holding two or more part-time jobs. Nonetheless, estimates of the non-standard work force that include part-time workers consistently range between 25 and 30 per cent of the total labour force.

There is little agreement as to what extent growing numbers of people who prefer to work only part time, irregularly, or temporarily may have contributed to the recent increase in the non-standard labour force. Some women and men no doubt prefer such work arrangements, whether they are students, young people exploring career options, adults who value flexibility because of family responsibilities, or older people in transition to retirement. Also, some non-standard jobs can be very attractive, and on occasion may pay higher wages to compensate for the uncertainty and lower benefits. At the same time it is clear, however, that many of those currently in the non-standard work force would prefer regular full-time jobs if they were available (Rothstein 1996). Shank (1986) reported that among workers 25–54 years old, as many as 44 per cent of those working 1–14 hours a week, and 37 per cent of those working 15–29 hours a week would prefer to work longer hours in order to earn more money. Callaghan and Hartmann (1991) lend further support to this view by pointing out that many people have several part-time jobs, in order to piece together the equivalent of a full-time position. In addition, as already noted, women and minorities are very heavily represented among contingent workers, and they are least likely to have other options.

By way of contrast, there can be no doubt that as businesses have been downsizing, during upswings as well as recessions, demand for non-standard labour has increased at the expense of demand for full-time, regular workers. Among the explanations for this is that employers gain flexibility in staffing levels; that at times they use temporary hires as a way of screening potential permanent employees; and in some cases they are able to take advantage of economies of scale by using specialized services and hiring highly specialized workers. It is also clear, however, that they frequently pay lower wages and less overtime, and almost invariably provide fewer benefits. Such practices, together with the inherent lack of job security, can be a serious problem not only for people who are unable to find regular work, but also for many of those who 'voluntarily' choose contingent and alternative employment in order to combine paid work with family responsibilities.

Feminist economists care about issues of equity in general, and equitable treatment of workers in particular, rather than focusing single-mindedly on efficiency. Therefore they tend to believe that to the extent that reducing the regular work force enhances the profits of shareholders and executives, and perhaps the wages of the remaining 'permanent' workers, but simultaneously reduces the earnings and benefits of the workers who now have contingent or alternative rather than traditional jobs, is to be deplored, even if the gains to the former exceed the losses to the latter. The reason for this conclusion is that the overall gains would be achieved at the expense of redistribution to the relatively privileged from the more needy.

A second reason why feminist economists generally look askance at the growth of the contingent and alternative labour force is that, although a good deal of attention has been focused on contingent and other non-traditional workers in recent years (see, for example, Belous 1989; Blank 1990; duRivage 1992; Tilly 1991, 1996; Warme et al. 1992, as well as the papers in the special issue of the *Monthly Labor Review* October 1996), very little is known about the long-term impact of contingent and alternative work, so that even if people were as rational as neoclassical economists assume, they cannot be expected to make entirely rational decisions. Ferber and Waldfogel (1998) suggest that past temporary work and part-time work (except voluntary part-time work for women) is associated with lower wages, and that all past temporary work and part-time work, as well as self-employment, is associated with lower benefits, even after controlling for current employment type. The implications of these findings are all the more ominous when it is remembered that women and minorities, who in any case receive lower wages and benefits, on average, than white men, are disproportionately represented among contingent workers, and considerably overrepresented among both part-time and temporary supply workers. More research on this subject is urgently needed if individuals are to be able to make better informed decisions, and to have a better basis for policies that would minimize the costs and maximize the benefits of contingent and alternative work to all concerned.

Feminist economists are particularly interested both in discovering the causes and effects of economic developments, and in ways to shape the developments so that people's lives will be improved. If there is to be progress in answering the many questions that, as was made clear above, remain largely unresolved, considerably more research is needed. There is, first of all, a need for better data, and especially longitudinal data. In addition, better evidence of the extent to which the increase in non-traditional workers is driven by changes in demand and in supply would be useful, as would more information concerning the long-run impact of contingent and various forms of alternative employment on workers as well as concerning the long-run impact of the use of non-standard work arrangements on employers.

However, on the basis of what is known now, there is reason to believe that the following policy suggestions are warranted. First, because contingent and non-standard jobs can be useful to workers as well as employers, it would be a mistake to impose regulations that would make such arrangements difficult or impossible; but it is equally important to avoid instituting or perpetuating rules that make these arrangements especially advantageous to employers. Therefore such regulations as equal pay for equal work and affirmative action should apply equally to all workers. Similarly, as far as possible, employers should be required to pay the same benefits to all workers, pro-rated to the extent that they are employed less than full time and less than all year. Because, however, this is often difficult to arrange, and leaves many non-traditional workers inadequately covered, it would also be highly desirable for the government to provide some of these benefits, notably health care. Finally, government itself should avoid discriminating against non-traditional workers in its own programmes, such as for instance unemployment insurance. Although adopting these policies would certainly not solve all problems, it would substantially reduce the disadvantages associated with non-standard work today.

It is worth noting that some other countries have already adopted a number of the policies that are being suggested for the USA. For instance, France, Germany and Spain have adopted statutory principles of non-discrimination;

Belgium, Italy, Luxembourg, Portugal, Sweden and Switzerland apply all their labour social legislation to part-time workers, and Canada applies some minimum employment standards to these workers; many of the countries also provide proportional unemployment insurance (Thurman and Trah 1990). Nonetheless, many part-time workers face problems in these countries as well, for 'all countries set minimum thresholds in terms of hours or earnings that determine whether contributions to social security and unemployment insurance for a particular employee are required' (Houseman, 1995 p. 255).

MARIANNE A. FERBER AND JANE WALDFOGEL

See also
Unemployment and Underemployment; Wage Gap.

Bibliography

Belous, Richard S. (1989), *The Contingent Economy: The Growth of the Temporary, Part-Time, and Subcontracted Workforce*, McLean, Virginia: National Planning Assoc.

Blank, Rebecca M. (1990), 'Are Part-Time Jobs Bad Jobs?', in Gary Burtless (ed.), *A Future of Lousy Jobs?*, Washington, DC: Brookings Institution, pp. 123–55.

Callaghan, Polly and Heidi Hartmann (1991), *Contingent Work: A Chart Book on Part-Time and Temporary Employment*, Washington, DC: Economic Policy Institute.

Cohany, Sharon R. (1996), 'Workers in alternative employment arrangements', *Monthly Labor Review*, **119** (10), (October), 31–45.

DeGrip, A., J. Hoevenberg and E. Willems (1997) 'Atypical employment in the European Union', *International Labour Review*, **136** (1), (Spring), 49–71.

duRivage, Virginia L. (ed.) (1992), *New Policies for the Part-Time and Contingent Workforce*, Armonk: New York: M.E. Sharpe.

Ferber, Marianne A. and Jane Waldfogel (1998), 'The long-term consequences of non-standard work', *Monthly Labor Review*, **121** (5), (May), 3–12.

Houseman, Susan (1995), 'Part-time employment in Europe and Japan', *Journal of Labor Research*, **16** (3), (Summer), 249–62.

Polivka, Anne E. (1996), 'A profile of contingent workers', *Monthly Labor Review*, **119** (10), (October), 10–21.

Polivka, Anne E. and Thomas Nardone (1989), 'On the definition of "contingent work"', *Monthly Labor Review*, **112** (12), (December), 9–16.

Rothstein, Donna (1996), 'Entry into and consequences of nonstandard work arrangements', *Monthly Labor Review*, **119** (10), (October), 75–82.

Shank, Susan (1986), 'Preferred hours of work and corresponding earnings', *Monthly Labor Review*, **109** (11), (November), 40–44.

Southern Regional Council (1988), *Hard Labor: A Report on Day Labor Pools and Temporary Employment*, Atlanta, Ga: Southern Regional Council.

Thurman, Joseph E. and Gabriele Trah (1990), 'Part-time work in international perspective', *International Labour Review*, **129** (1), 23–40.

Tilly, Chris (1991), 'Reasons for the continuing growth of part-time employment', *Monthly Labor Review*, **114** (3), (March), 10–18.

Tilly, Chris (1996), *Half a Job: Bad and Good Part-Time Jobs in a Changing Labor Market*, Philadelphia: Temple University Press.

US Department of Labor (1995), 'Contingent and Alternative Employment Arrangements', Bureau of Labor Statistics, Report 900, August, Washington, DC: Bureau of Labor Statistics.

Warme, Barbara D., Katherine P. Lundy and Larry A. Lundy (eds) (1992), *Working Part-Time: Risks and Opportunities*, New York: Praeger.

Development Policies

Economic development policies in the so-called 'developing' countries reflect both mainstream and critical concerns about the pace and direction of growth through rapid capital accumulation and industrialization. More broadly, the processes of economic growth and human development have been the main targets of development policies.

Early modernization approaches (Rostow 1960, see Scott 1995 for a feminist critique) in tandem with human capital theories, advocated a massive expansion of education systems to create a stock of well-trained workers and managers who would steer essentially agrarian ('backward') societies toward industrial modern ones. The benefits of growth and modernization would lead to better living conditions, wages, education and wellbeing. However, by the early 1970s, reliance on an evolutionary model of social and political change had done little to improve the relative position of women (and many others). In particular, the representation of modernization as a universal and linear process reaffirmed a partial, masculinist view of development and posited a dualistic view of the traditional versus the modern world. Feminist economists began to take on both the epistemological foundations and the practical outcomes of a model that made women invisible and treated them paternalistically.

With the publication of Ester Boserup's pioneering critique *Women's Role in Economic Development* (1970) new ground was laid for feminist scrutiny of development planners and their neglect of women's role in the economy and agriculture. Her work inspired a new approach known as 'Women in Development' (WID) which influenced donor governments, international agencies and the women's movement during the 1970s and early 1980s. The WID approach sought to address the failure of development planners to consider women's needs and women's viewpoints which created a flawed integration of women in the process of development. Largely directed at micro-level projects, WID practitioners showed why development policies consistently failed to deliver resources to women. For example, early agricultural innovation practices and extension services fell short of meeting their objective of increasing rural productivity and income because they overlooked women's roles in the production process. WID policies were to recognize the significant economic and social costs of neglecting and undermining women's roles in the development process. Early development policy related to women primarily as mothers or would-be mothers; welfare programmes were devised which made women the primary targets of a 'basic needs' strategy addressed at health, education, housing, nutrition and home-based income-generating activities. Many studies uncovered the hidden role of women both as agents in development and as recipients of androcentric policies. However, the WID approach has also been criticized for its record in terms of integrating women into the development process and its limited understanding of the structural rigidities of patriarchal relations. As Kabeer and Humphrey (1990) point out, while WID agencies recognize gender asymmetries in crucial resources (land, credit, training, employment) their underlying explanations rested on cultural norms and the sexual division of labour. Linking women's empowerment to their participation in the market leaves out gender subordination in all its dimensions.

By the early 1980s, a shift in focus in feminist economics was fuelled by a change in the macro policy environment away from Keynesian thinking to neo-liberal economics which stressed stabilization and structural adjustment policies. For gender practitioners, the need to extend their critical insights beyond discrete micro-level projects to macroeconomic policies became quickly apparent as policy increasingly focused on cutting back aggregate public expenditure and the money supply in order to reduce deficits and curb inflation (Razavi 1996).

Along with these changes in the macro policy environment, serious criticism from feminists in the North and South began to eclipse the WID approach and paved the way for the emergence of more critical feminist approaches often referred to as Gender and Development (GAD). These heterodox approaches (including neo-institutional, Post Marxist and Post Keynesian) to development stressed the need to understand and question existing power relations among women and men in society by focusing on gender relationships, their social construction, and how gender differences have led to inequalities in power between women and men as well as among women. The GAD approach to development thinking and practice is more difficult to apply in practice than WID as it focuses on relationships between women and men as well as institutional change. The latter objective gave rise to the concept of gender mainstreaming in international agencies such as the United Nations Development Program (UNDP), the International Labour Organisation (ILO), the Food and Agricultural Organization (FAO) and the World Bank. Gender mainstreaming is a systematic process of situating gender equality issues at the centre of broad policy decisions, institutional structures and resource allocations and includes the views of women and their priorities in decision making about development (Schalkwyk et al. 1996). At the same time, grassroots efforts have pressured for more participatory and democratic structures that would allow men and women to respond to and benefit from economic opportunities without compromising the production of human resources (UNDP 1995b).

Feminist economic approaches and contributions to the policy debate

Debates and developments in feminist economic theory continue to inform policy insights. Three broad areas of theoretical analysis have shaped the collaboration efforts between feminist scholars and policy advocates of the development process in recent years. The first relates to one of the fundamental insights of feminist economics: that traditional economics has assumed the male norm to be the universal and focused on scarcity rather than provisioning. Feminist economics foregrounds the interaction of productive and reproductive activities creating the foundations for a more complete economics (Nelson 1996). Domestic work or 'reproductive work' is the work of managing a household, cooking, cleaning, keeping home, clothing and domestic equipment in good repair, and caring for family members and friends and neighbours. In principle, it is excluded from the gross national product; it is defined in the United Nations System of National Accounts as lying outside the production boundary. But the work of what Diane Elson calls the care economy (including voluntary community work) is vital for keeping the social framework in good repair, and for maintaining and reproducing the labour force. Reproductive work and voluntary community work could in principle be done by men or women – but provisioning has been socially constituted as more the responsibility of women than men in most countries. Global estimates suggest that women's unpaid work produces an output of $11 trillion, compared to a global GDP of about $23 trillion (UNDP 1995a, p. 97).

Second, feminist economists, particularly scholars and activists from the South, have criticized and revealed the hidden value system underpinning knowledge production in the West. These excavations into the methodological foundations of development policies uncovered a process of knowledge creation based on particular kinds of information (universal vs. local) and researchers (detached vs. involved). Feminist economists contributed to epistemological debates within development about how knowledge is constructed, making explicit the location of the knower in the social world being studied. The emergence of the 'feminist standpoint', based on the distinctive experiences of women's lives in a gendered social world, was applied to development paradigms with the idea that development theories and practice should start from the vantage point of those 'from below'; poor Third World women. The underlying premise was not to privilege this group but rather to indicate that no true development would take place unless it was accompanied by a structural transformation in the lives of the poorest and most oppressed.

Feminist practitioners and scholars were also challenged to make explicit their own standpoint. Mohanty (1988) criticizes white, Western feminists for their universalizing tendencies ('sisterhood is global') and their process of 'Othering' (Eurocentrism) Third World women. Mohanty and other Third World writers have been particularly critical of the victimology in western feminist accounts of global restructuring. For example, discussion of international restructuring of manufacturing industries and the rise of Export

Processing Zones frequently see Third World women as the passive victims of multinational capital. Newer approaches originating from writers outside of the western framework examine the interaction of constraining structures and women's varied responses to changing material incentives. Kabeer (1989) for instance, has demonstrated how women garment workers in Bangladesh have taken the new insecurities and opportunities of the government's active encouragement of garment industries, thereby reconstituting purdah norms and customary practices, toward a new, more participatory definition of women's roles. Such an approach has meant that scholars and practitioners have had to re-evaluate their notions of agency, especially poor women's agency and resistance, and it has also opened the door to new voices in the policy process.

More recent postmodern critiques such as some of the articles in Ferber and Nelson's *Beyond Economic Man* (1993), Crush's *Power of Development* (1995) and Nelson's 'Feminism, Objectivity and Economics' (1996) have facilitated the formulation of new questions about the nature of economics and its basic assumptions. Feminist postmodernism challenges both the inclusive universalism of feminist empiricism (the WID school) and the binary universalism of the standpoint approach. Emphasizing the fractured realities and identities created by modern life, feminist postmodernism deals with overlapping, interconnected concepts because it is experientially or contextually based (Nelson 1993, p. 30). Within economics, feminists have challenged discursive foundations, 'the Cartesian view (that) underlies the prestige given to mathematical models of individual rational choice' (Nelson 1993, p. 33) and needs, revealing their masculinist foundations (Pujol 1992). Often the goal of such interventions is to broaden the subject and methodology of economics in order to address the many different realities of men's and women's lives.

Feminist economic approaches to development policies span both mainstream and critical economics sharing the common conviction that development policies are not necessarily neutral with respect to gender. Following from this basic premise, challenges posed by feminist economists include putting value on women's unpaid work (such as caring for children and the elderly, growing food for domestic consumption) and demonstrating that economic growth and reform do not benefit all people, nor are women and men able to respond equally to new economic environments. In addition, feminist economics has provided a fundamental gender planning tool by distinguishing between development policies targeted at meeting women's practical gender interests or needs and more strategic gender needs (Molyneux 1985; Moser 1993). Practical needs refer to those needs identified by women themselves as responding to an immediate necessity within a specific context such as daily access to clean water, health care and sufficient nourishment. Strategic needs are formulated from the analysis of women's subordination to men and relate to more structural, long-term changes in such aspects as the gender division of labour, power and control, legal rights, women's control over their bodies, equal wages and measures against domestic violence.

Feminist economic approaches to development can be alternatively grouped according to schools of thought such as neoclassical and critical (structuralist, institutional, political economy), or according to WID and GAD. This section will group the underlying theoretical models which inform policy according to neoclassical and critical approaches.

The neoclassical approach
The economists within this framework have made substantial contributions to the analysis of the development process and, more recently, structural adjustment policies (see Razavi and Miller 1997). Using neoclassical tools of analysis in tandem with an understanding of intrahousehold inequalities in bargaining power, access and control over resources and income, this body of work seeks to illustrate how gender biases and rigidities affect adjustment polices and growth strategies and may indeed, ultimately contribute to their undermining. By targeting human capital through education and skills training, alleviating barriers to markets and focusing on households as economic agents, neoclassical economics focuses on the twin goals of individual utility maximization and increased output/growth.

Some economists working within the neoclassical framework have, however, been influenced by institutional economics which questions key assumptions of the neoclassical approach (that is, that information is perfectly available to all economic decision makers and that transactions are costless) and emphasizes the importance of norms, cultures and values in economic processes. Such studies have recognized the barriers that exist to achieving the neoclassical goals of utility maximization and efficient resource allocation. Haddad et al. (1995) for example, cite studies that show that women are, however, less able than men to reallocate their time between different activities. This is related to two factors stemming from the asymmetry in men's and women's obligations, rights and bargaining positions within the household: the gender-based assignment of household roles restricts the substitution of male and female labour time; and women's labour immobility is also explained by the failure of the household economy to transmit changing price incentives to women.

Palmer (1991) has referred to these gender-based distortions as a 'reproductive labour tax' which she sees as a kind of tithe levied against women's unpaid work in reproduction that distorts their ability to engage in income-generating activities, acting as a kind of externality to their maximal resource allocation. The thrust of her work and that of Haddad et al. (1995) is 'to show

how resources (especially female labour) may be allocated between sectors in a skewed and inefficient manner due to various constraints which arise from gender roles and inequitable gender relations' (Razavi and Miller 1997). Discrimination against women is recognized and variously attributed to prejudice, persistence of traditions or inadequate information about women such as their abilities and technical skills (Elson 1994).

The implications for public policy are targeted at enhancing the efficiency of markets and freeing up women's labour in unproductive (that is, nonmarket) sectors for greater mobility in the newer, dynamic sectors such as tradables and export processing. Overcoming market rigidities through public interventions (through redressing male bias in financial markets, social services, education and opening up many of the non-biological aspects of women's reproductive labour to market forces) would, it is posited, allow women to participate fully thereby reducing gender inequality and enhancing economic efficiency (World Bank 1995; Palmer 1991).

Such measures are not only to be carried out by individuals and market institutions but are also facilitated through public mechanisms of an enabling yet benevolent state, hence: regulation of land markets to remove gender-based distortions in inheritance and property rights laws; reform of financial markets through changes in collateral requirements, signatories in the case of loans and greater availability of credit; legal changes in the terms and conditions that govern the terms of marriage and family formation, divorce, violence against women; access to education and training; and social supports to facilitate women's movement into tradables and the formal sector (Bakker 1994).

Several shortcomings in this literature have been emphasized. The view of development espoused by this approach has been criticized for being too benign: everyone is seen as potentially benefiting from the process in the long run; markets are viewed as able to meet human needs and realizing wellbeing if properly functioning (there is little sense of how definitions of female labour, for example, are built into the way in which markets operate or how the sustainability of human resources is maintained); and state institutions and development agencies are not problematized as structures with embedded gender hierarchies themselves. To the extent that gender inequalities do persist, informational problems or cultural factors (socially-assigned roles, for example) are brought into the explanatory framework falling short of an examination of how patterns of subordination are created and reproduced. Strict boundaries between male and female sectors may not be the result of free choice but may in fact have been constructed and maintained through powerful agents in the economy. Most basically, the care economy which consists of reproducing and maintaining human resources is left largely invisible; the one way in which it does enter neoclassical analysis is as the burdens of reproduction – a constraint to women's supply-side behaviour (Razavi 1996).

The dual process of neo-liberal agendas of market-led efficiency and WID's emphasis on women's economic agency has, according to Kabeer, led to a 'gender trap'. If the market is to be the main mechanism for allocating resources, women will often be unable to buy the support services they need to reduce their unpaid work. At the same time, if they are unable to purchase substitute goods and services, they will be constrained in their pursuit of activities which could increase their purchasing power. Cutbacks in service expenditures tend to fall more on women because they put more time into non-leisure activities and home production activities (survival activities) than men. The policy implications of this are that the opportunity cost of women's time is not taken into account in programme design or policy formulations. Also, women's time and labour is assumed to be highly responsive to expansion and contraction in the formal economy (Moser 1993; Elson 1991). Yet time allocation studies concerning poor women suggest that particularly in rural areas, women's time and labour is extremely unresponsive to such changes (Tinker et al. 1990).

Despite these criticisms, this literature has been very instrumental in assessing the impact of gender differences on macroeconomic concerns (within the WID Division of the World Bank, for example) and empirically charting how the removal of gender biases will facilitate the achievement of adjustment policy goals (Razavi and Miller 1997). Under the rubric of 'investing in people' the World Bank has advocated a gender-sensitive neoclassical paradigm whose goal is to maximize all human capital potential in order to achieve higher rates of growth of output. However, as Elson notes: 'The depiction of people as autonomous owners of their own labour, concerned to satisfy their own preferences, tends to be blind to differences of social power which enable some people, but not others, to behave as "rational economic men"' (Elson 1994).

The critical approach

A major question which separates neoclassical and critical approaches within feminist economics is how gender bias in development policies is construed: is the problem with the actual policies which are gender biased or with pre-existing gender relations? Generally, feminist neoclassical economists would subscribe to the former view, feminist critical economists to the latter. One key starting point for feminist critical economics is the observation that gender imbalances cannot be rectified primarily through human capital accumulation, that more structural factors may persist which need to be addressed if women are to make economic gains. These structural factors are not simply the problems related to the 'incompleteness' of markets, but also due to the unequal distribution of resources and decision-making power, and the power relations that underpin a fluid and culturally determined gender division of labour reflected in markets and the reproductive sphere.

The tools of analysis of feminist critical economics rest on two premises: that there is an interdependence between the market and nonmarket sectors of the economy which is not recognized in most of economics, and that three distinct levels of analysis exist (macro, meso, micro) with corresponding gender biases built in at the analytical level which then shape subsequent policy responses (Elson 1994). Neoclassical economics treats the micro, meso and macro levels as fully integrated: the macro level focuses on monetary aggregates like total output and expenditure which are seen as the coherent result of the activities of millions of individuals (micro) which are integrated by the institutions of the meso level (markets, firms). Male bias is the result of omitting gender from the macro and meso levels and is rooted in the way in which gender is conceptualized at the micro level (Razavi and Miller 1997).

Feminist critical economics unpacks each level for male bias and critiques the microfoundations of neoclassical economics. At the *micro* level, differences and inequalities between women and men are not simply explained as a matter of differences in preference and resource endowments; power and preferences are problematized as socially constructed and socially entrenched asymmetries in rules and resources giving certain individuals power over others to shape their options. One of the major criticisms made by feminist economists of development policy starting with WID centred on the extremely flawed model of the household which initially consisted of a nuclear family with a male head responsible for breadwinning and women responsible for the family. Planners began to respond to WID critiques that women and children were often engaged in productive work but their efforts were still considered secondary with men retaining their role as principal decision makers as heads of household.

Two other levels of economic analysis and intervention have been scrutinized by feminist economists and activists. The *meso* level of markets are not intrinsically gendered (that is, biased toward men or women) but do become the 'bearers of gender', that is, gender relations shape the relations between women and men as they engage in markets. Labour markets, for example, create separate male and female spheres based on distinct gender hierarchies and social norms about femininity and masculinity. The *macro* level of monetary aggregates is criticized as male biased because it omits from its analysis a whole area of production – the unpaid production of human resources. Whilst micro level analysis is criticized for the way in which it conceptualizes gender, meso and macro level analyses are criticized for the activities and values which are left out. In particular, the view that the reproduction economy will continue to function no matter what the changes in the rest of the economy leads to policies which may not be sustainable (in economic and human terms) in the long run. The increased demand for women's time in paid and unpaid activities has meant an increased bias against girls' education, increased mental and physical stress, and in some communities a deterioration of the social fabric (Commonwealth Secretariat 1989; World Bank 1995).

A number of key suggestions (Benería 1995) from the feminist economics literature on Structural Adjustment Packages, economic restructuring and market liberalization illustrate this notion of a crisis in sustainability. One is that planners should not assume the infinite capacity of people to bear the costs of adjustment. Policies to reduce aggregate demand, for example, translate into a decreased economic capacity of individuals to meet their needs and those of their families. Falling real household incomes put pressure on women who carry the basic responsibility for meeting family needs. Policies should therefore take into consideration the hidden costs of adjustment such as deteriorating infrastructure, declines in schooling for girls in particular and the resultant long-term losses in productivity, intensification of domestic work and increased violence. Women only have a limited range of responses and their and their children's welfare is most dependent on public expenditure in education and health which are the areas most likely to be affected by budget cuts. Cuts in public sector employment are also more likely to have more significant impacts on employment prospects for women rather than men.

Some of the shortcomings of the feminist critical approach are that few empirical studies exist using these tools of analysis. Much of the work is still at the conceptual stages and has not had a big policy impact, although modelling has been initiated by a team of heterodox economists in a special issue of *World Development* (Çagatay et al. 1995) on gender, adjustment and macroeconomics. This approach also tends to be more complex given its insistence on incorporating how the gender division of labour came about and is sustained. Gender differentiation is derived from structural inequalities within varying institutional contexts (households, communities, markets, states) which calls for a dynamic not a static analysis. There are examples of recent training materials which rely on some of the tools of critical economics (The British Council, Canadian International Development Agency, UNDP) and many non-governmental organisations (NGOs) from the North and South are involved in developing an alternative approach based on a critique of unequal distribution and control of resources and power (for example, ALTWID and DAWN).

In addition feminist critical economics argues for a strong link between macroeconomic and human resource indicators. Human development targets should be a commitment alongside the fiscal and monetary targets set out in the financial plans of governments. This would require redefining efficiency of resource use to include resources applied to the unmarketed services that are critical for human resources production. The development by UNDP of a Gender Development Index (GDI) to complement their Human Development Index (HDI) is one influential example of the attempt to link macroeconomic and human indicators. The interdependence between marketed output and reproductive activities has also been recognized by the many signatory countries of the Beijing Platform for Action (1995).

A further link has been made between feminist economics and the broader human development debate. Human development strategies approach every issue in the traditional growth models from the vantage point of people who are viewed not only as the beneficiaries of economic growth but also as the real agents of change in society. A feminist perspective means inserting an additional level of understanding: that women stand at the crossroads between production and reproduction, between economic activity and the care of human beings. This makes women strong potential political actors in the human-centered development programme. Sen (1995) suggests that three sets of issues must be addressed in human development strategies. One is related to women's weak access to economic resources and their inability to make economic decisions that will enhance their and their families' wellbeing. Second, although broad commonalties exist with regard to policies which will lift women out of poverty and powerlessness, the specificity of different women needs to be addressed. Third, women's contribution to unpaid labour needs to be recognized as economically valuable and must be counted as well as supported through policies.

Underestimation of women's work has had numerous policy consequences as the United Nations Development Program noted in its 1995 *Human Development Report*. The Report notes that in almost every country, women contribute as much total labour as men, often more, yet they receive a much smaller share of the goods and services produced by total labour. In addition, they are assigned the role of maintaining and reproducing the unpaid sector including families and communities but not given adequate control of the necessary resources to carry out this vital function. Public policy intervention is called for in terms of incentives, investments and other measures that will provide supports for the work of reproduction and altering the division of labour between women and men. Traditionally, policy responses to unpaid work have been characterized by two basic approaches: policies that encourage a more equitable distribution of unpaid work between women and men through, for example, social spending in health, education and child care; and policies that attempt to provide economic and social recognition for unpaid work through such policy tools as government transfers, tax credits and actual valuation in National Income Accounts of unpaid work.

Future issues for feminist economics

Feminist economics has illustrated that mainstream development policies and strategies are not gender neutral because they assume the male actor as the standard and representative of the human actor. These policies have often focused on men's roles and on the household and the family with the underlying assumption that women would benefit as equally as men from project implementation. Projects specifically implemented for women are also often formulated in limited and stereotypical ways reinforcing the subordination of women in households and communities. The implementation of economic policies directed at enhancing human capital, investing in technologies, or emphasizing export-oriented production may not be intrinsically gendered yet gender-differentiated impacts result from preexisting inequalities grounded in both the division of labour and gender-differentiated social rights and obligations, as well as in the gendered nature of institutions through which macroeconomic policies are implemented.

Feminist economics has challenged development planners to include in their frameworks fundamental questions related to the reproductive economy. To what extent do policies increase the unpaid work that women do? Do they remove or reinforce prior barriers to women's participation in markets (product, labour, credit)? What are the impacts of policies on women's wellbeing: their health, nutritional status, access to basic needs, childcare, housing and education? The growth of feminist economics has also introduced new voices into economic policymaking. Many are academics but many are also grassroots women and NGOs who have documented the impacts of macroeconomic policies on their families and communities, and who have produced alternative development strategies centered on human development by extending Amartya Sen's (1990) notion of entitlements. A focus on women's entitlements (that is, material and non-material entities which enlarge economic, political, social and cultural choices) means policies which will increase women's access to land ownership and use, credit and other productive resources.

More recent research is focused on the complementarity of many efficiency and equity measures moving away from earlier formulations that specified a necessary trade-off between the two (see Çagatay et al. 1995). Research on trade, for instance, has documented how gender biases can have an impact on macroeconomic objectives such as continuous and higher growth (Joekes 1995). Women's Budget Statements in Australia and South Africa have integrated gender in appraisals of overall budget strategy in an effort to identify efficiency losses to society due to gender inequality. All of these issues and challenges provide a rich and critically important agenda for future research by feminist economists (Goetz 1997).

ISABELLA BAKKER

See also

Development, Theories of; Double Day/Second Shift; Economic Restructuring; Globalization; Growth Theory (Macro Models); Imperialism; Informal Sector; Population; Structural Adjustment Policies.

Bibliography

Agarwal, Bina (1994), *A Field of One's Own: Gender and Land Rights in South Asia*, Cambridge: Cambridge University Press.

Bakker, Isabella (ed.) (1994), *The Strategic Silence: Gender and Economic Policy*, London: Zed Press and The North/South Institute.

Bakker, Isabella (1997), 'Identity, Interests and Ideology: The Gendered Terrain of Global Restructuring', in Stephen Gill (ed.), *Globalization, Democratization and Multilateralism*, Tokyo, New York: Macmillan/United Nations University Press.

Benería, Lourdes (1992), 'Accounting for women's work: the progress of two decades', *World Development*, **20** (11), 1547–60.

Benería, Lourdes (1995), 'Toward a greater integration of gender in economics', 'Gender, Adjustment and Macroeconomics', Special Issue of *World Development*, **23** (11), (November), 1839–50.

Boserup, Ester (1970), *Women's Role in Economic Development*, London: George Allen and Unwin.

Çagatay, Nilufer, Diane Elson and Caren Grown (eds) (1995), 'Gender, Adjustment and Macroeconomics', Special Issue of *World Development*, **23** (11), (November).

Commonwealth Secretariat (1989), *Engendering Adjustment for the 1990s*, London: Marlborough House.

Crush, Jonathan (1995), *Power of Development*, London/New York: Routledge.

Elson, Diane (1991), *Male Bias in the Development Process*, Manchester: Manchester University Press.

Elson, Diane (1994), 'Micro, Meso and Macro: Gender and Economic Analysis in the Context of Policy Reform', in Isabella Bakker (ed.), *The Strategic Silence: Gender and Economic Policy*, London: Zed Press and the North–South Institute, pp. 33–45.

Ferber, Marianne A. and Julie A. Nelson (1993), *Beyond Economic Man: Feminist Theory and Economics*, Chicago: The University of Chicago Press.

Goetze, AnneMarie (ed.) (1997), *Getting Institutions Right for Women in Development*, London and New York: Zed Press.

Haddad, Lawrence, Lynn Brown, Andrea Richter and Lisa Smith (1995), 'The gender dimensions of economic adjustment policies: potential interactions and evidence to date', *World Development*, **23** (6), 881–96.

Joekes, Susan (1995), *Trade-related Employment for Women in Industry and Services in Developing countries*, Geneva: Occasional Paper No. 5, UNRISD and UNDP, Fourth World Conference on Women.

Kabeer, Naila (1989), 'Cultural dopes or rational fools? Women and labour supply in the Bangladesh garment industry', *The European Journal of Development Research*, (November).

Kabeer, Naila (1994), *Reversed Realities*, London: Verso.

Kabeer, Naila and John Humphrey (1990), 'Neo-liberalism, Gender, and the Limits of the Market', in Christopher Coclough and James Manor (eds), *States or Markets? Neo-liberalism and the Development Policy Debate*, Oxford: Clarendon Press.

Mohanty, Chandra (1988), 'Under western eyes: feminist scholarship and colonial discourses', *Feminist Review*, **30**, (Autumn).

Molyneux, Maxine (1985), 'Mobilization without emancipation? Women's interests, state and revolution in Nicaragua', *Feminist Studies*, **11** (2), 227–54.

Moser, Caroline (1993), *Gender Planning and Development: Theory, Practice and Training*, London and New York: Routledge.

Nelson, Julie (1993), 'The Study of Choice or the Study of Provisioning? Gender and the Definition of Economics', in Marianne Ferber and Julie Nelson (eds), *Beyond Economic Man: Feminist Theory and Economics*, Chicago: University of Chicago Press, pp. 23–30.

Nelson, Julie (1996), 'Feminism, Objectivity and Economics', in Julie Nelson (ed.), *Economics as Social Theory*, London and New York: Routledge.

Palmer, Ingrid (1991), *Gender and Population in the Adjustment of African Economies*, Geneva: ILO.

Pujol, Michele (1992), *Feminism and Antifeminism in Early Economic Thought*, New York: Gower Press.

Razavi, Shahra (1996), *Working Towards a More Gender Equitable Macro-Economic Agenda*, Geneva: UNRISD.

Razavi, Shahra and Carol Miller (1997), *Conceptual Frameworks for Gender Analysis within the Development Context*, Paper Prepared for Inter-Agency Review Meeting, Socio-Economic and Gender Analysis, Pearl River, New York, March 6–9.

Rostow, W.W. (1960), *The Stages of Economic Growth: A Non-Communist Manifesto*, Cambridge: Cambridge University Press.

Schalkwyk, Johanna, Helen Thomas and Beth Woroniuk (1996), *Mainstreaming: A Strategy for Achieving Equality between Women and Men*, Stockholm: SIDA.

Scott, Catherine (1995), *Gender and Development. Rethinking Modernization and Dependency Theory*, Boulder, CO: Lynne Rienner Publishers.

Sen, Amartya (1990), *Public Action to Remedy Hunger*, London: The Global Hunger Project.

Sen, Gita (1995), 'Alternative economics from a gender perspective', *Development*, 1, 21–6.

Sen, Gita (1996), 'Gender, markets and states: a selective review and research agenda', *World Development*, 24 (5), (May), 821–9.

Tinker, Irene, Grazia Borrini, Sheldon Margen and Ashok Desai (eds) (1990), *Human Energy*, New Delhi: Wiley Eastern Limited.

UNDP (1995a), *Human Development Report*, Oxford: Oxford University Press.

UNDP (1995b), *Restructuring Economic and Social Policy: Cross-Cultural Insights from the Grassroots*, New York: UNDP, July.

World Bank (1995), *Toward Gender Equality: The Role of Public Policy*, Washington, DC: World Bank.

Development, Theories of

Development, understood as a process of economic, social and political transformation that raises the general standard of living, has been a pre-occupation of social science from Adam Smith's *Wealth of Nations* and Karl Marx's *Das Kapital* onwards. No short entry can do full justice to such a huge field. This entry will be confined to the narrower field of contemporary theories of economic development (or lack of development) and to the interventions that feminist economics (or women-focused economics) has made within it.

Development economics, as taught in economics programmes today, dates back almost 50 years, to the setting up of the United Nations Organization with a mandate to promote the development of the poorer regions of the world, the efforts at economic reconstruction after World War II, and the beginning of decolonization, with the independence of India in 1946. It has always had a strong policy focus, concerned to influence policymakers in both national and international economic institutions.

There have been three dominant themes in the theories of economic development advanced in the last 50 years: first, a concern with national processes of accumulation, structural change and economic growth; secondly, a concern with poverty and wellbeing; and thirdly, a concern with the implications of international economic relations for national development. The field of development economics has always been contested, with continuing debates on the relative merits of the state and the private sector as engines of growth; on the relationship between growth, wellbeing and poverty; on the relative efficacy of planning and markets as means of co-ordination; and on the international economy as a facilitator or constraint upon the development of the countries of Asia, Africa, the Middle East and Latin America (once collectively referred to as the Third World, now more often referred to as the South)(for guides to these debates, see Toye 1987; Sen 1983; Lal 1985).

Until 1970, with the publication of Ester Boserup's *Women's Role in Economic Development,* the production of theories of economic development was an almost exclusively male activity, and women were largely invisible within those theories. Boserup's book was followed by a growing body of work by women scholars, some of it in continuation of Boserup's arguments, some of it in counterpoint to Boserup's arguments, but all of it insisting that theories of development have to take into account differences between men's and women's economic lives, and the inequalities of power between men and women.

This entry will first discuss some of the key, pre-Boserup, analyses of economic development, selecting those theories which are particularly relevant to the subsequent discussion of women-focused and feminist contributions to theories of development. A good starting point is Nobel prize-winning economist Arthur Lewis's 1954 article, 'Economic Development with Unlimited Supplies of Labour', in which Lewis draws upon the classical tradition in economics to emphasize the importance of mobilizing the surplus labour which he argued could be found in the 'subsistence' sector, for reinvestment in a 'capitalist' sector, which sought to maximize the surplus product left after the payment of wages. Lewis postulated that the subsistence sector could continue to sustain its customary level of output per head, while also supplying labour to the capitalist sector, for a wage somewhat higher than customary income per head in the subsistence sector. This transfer of labour would continue until the surplus labour in the subsistence sector had all been transferred, thus permitting the capitalist sector to grow rapidly. This process of structural change would, Lewis assumed, in turn raise the general standard of living.

The validity of the Lewis model as an encapsulation of how development takes place has been the subject of continuing debate. Does labour flow voluntarily to the modern sector, attracted by a higher wage than the customary level of income in the subsistence sector? Or is it extracted by coercive means, as argued for instance by Weeks (1970)? Are there any plausible grounds for supposing that the subsistence sector reacts to a transfer of labour out of the sector by redeploying the remaining labour so that its customary level of production per head is maintained? Sen (1975) implies that such redeployment is possible if there is a work-sharing rule in the family-based subsistence sector. But Lal (1983) points out that such behaviour would entail those who remain in the family-based sector giving up some leisure without getting any extra reward in compensation, which he describes as 'perverse'.

Gender relations were not specifically identified in this debate, as either a barrier to the redeployment of labour between sectors or within sectors, or as a source of motivation to work harder or longer, or of a source of power to extract more work without any extra compensation. Lewis himself implicitly assumed that producers in the subsistence sector were men, remarking that 'men will not leave the family farm to seek employment if the wage is worth less than they would be able to consume at home' (Lewis 1955, p. 409). However, he did identify 'the wives and daughters of the household', as a further source of labour for the capitalist sector, arguing that this would lead to gains 'because most of the things which women otherwise do in the household can in fact be done much better or more cheaply outside, thanks to large scale economies of specialisation, and also to the use of capital. (Grinding grain, fetching water from the river, making cloth, making clothes, cooking the midday meal, teaching children, nursing the sick etc.)' (p. 404). In other words, he envisaged what feminists subsequently called 'reproductive work' (that is, the unpaid work in households and communities that is necessary to reproduce the labour force and the social fabric) being transferred to the capitalist sector. In his book on the theory of economic growth, Lewis (1955) was in no doubt about the benefits to women: 'Women benefit from growth even more than men. ... Woman gains freedom from drudgery, is emancipated from the seclusion of the household, and gains at last the chance to be a full human being, exercising her mind and her talents in the same way as men' (Lewis 1955, p. 422). This reflects the widespread optimism of the 1950s that the benefits of economic growth would 'trickle down' to everyone, and an implicit assumption that the surplus in the capitalist sector would indeed be reinvested in ways that reduce women's drudgery, and allow women to be 'full human beings'.

There was also optimism that every country could enjoy economic growth, which was frequently understood as taking place through a series of stages. The countries which were labelled 'less developed' or, more optimistically, 'developing', were seen as being at an earlier stage of a process through which the richer, more industrialized countries (labelled developed) had already passed. This was explicit in Rostow's (1960) theory of the 'take-off into self-sustained growth' which described development in terms of a passage from a 'stable and traditional society' to a 'dynamic and modern society'.

The theories discussed thus far focused on development as a process of structural transformation and growth, rather than development as an object of policy. However, both Lewis and Rostow recognized that investment was risky, and that there was a need for the state to promote productive reinvestment of profits, including investment by the state itself. Development planning, based on the Harrod–Domar model at the macroeconomic level, and social cost–benefit analysis at the microeconomic level, was widely advocated in the 1950s and 1960s by economists in both the developing and developed countries; and because it was generally recognized that markets fail in co-ordinating large-scale investment decisions, producing a national plan became a requirement for receiving development aid (for further discussion, see Lal 1983 and Toye 1987).

Such plans very often focused on industrialization ('traditional' was equated with agriculture and 'modern' with industry) and were based upon the protection of domestic industry ('import-substituting industrialization'). The intellectual case for this was made by 'structuralist' economists, who argued that the agricultural structure of Third World economies hindered their development. One of the most important arguments for this was put forward by UN economists Prebisch (1950) and Singer (1950). They argued that the prices of primary products tended to fall relative to those of manufactured products over the long run. Since the exports of the Third World in the 1940s, 1950s and 1960s were made up mainly of agricultural goods, while their imports were manufactured goods, this meant that their terms of trade tended to fall and international trade did not promote their development. Over time, they would have to supply more and more primary products (for example, coffee) in order to import the same quantity of manufactured goods (for example, tractors). The solution was to change the structure of their production by limiting imports of tractors and producing tractors within the country. More broadly, structuralist economists shared the view that state intervention to promote specific sectors of industry and to overcome obstacles to growth was required to sustain development. Pronounced inequalities in land ownership were identified as one important obstacle, and lack of access to new technology was another.

The optimistic vision of development as a passage from traditional (and agricultural) to modern (and industrial), from less developed to developed, which could be brought about by national development planning and protection of national industries was challenged in the 1960s by the opposing vision of the 'dependency school'. A leading proponent of the dependency school was Andre Gunder Frank who proposed that underdevelopment is largely the result of past and continuing economic and other relations between satellite underdeveloped and the now developed metropolitan countries (Frank 1966). This school of thought, which is reviewed in detail by Palma (1978), rejected the dichotomy between traditional and modern sectors, on the grounds that so-called traditional society had already been reshaped by an international process of capitalist development. Moreover, it proposed that the key problem of development in the underdeveloped countries was the dependent and exploitative way in which they were integrated into the international capitalist economy, which was not fundamentally changed by import-substitution industrialization. The argument was buttressed by interpretations of Latin American history which proposed that integration into the international economy had served to transfer surplus out of the underdeveloped countries for investment in the developed countries and could not promote autonomous and self-sustaining national development. The answer lay in a complete disengagement from the international capitalist economy.

The dependency school brought the questions of international power and international inequality to the forefront of attention, but its focus on imperialism was not complemented by a focus on 'machismo'. Nor was it clear what practical action could be derived from its analysis or what guidance it provided to organizations struggling to improve the lives of poor people in what was then called the Third World, since underdevelopment was presented as a self-perpetuating structure.

By the 1970s both the growth and modernization paradigm and the dependency paradigm were being challenged. On the one hand, there were plenty of examples where industrial growth had been achieved, but the living standards of poor people had barely improved, and inequality had worsened (such as Brazil). On the other hand, newly industrializing countries (NICS) in Asia (Taiwan, South Korea, Hong Kong and Singapore) were challenging the domination of the developed countries in world markets for manufactured exports, and the mass of people living in the NICS had enjoyed sustained increases in income. In this ferment, women's voices, insisting women's concerns be addressed, began to be heard.

By common consent among development and feminist economists, the pioneer was Ester Boserup (1970) who challenged the optimistic view that capital accumulation, economic growth and modernization necessarily benefited women. In the case of agricultural modernization, she argued that women had been deprived of access to training, land rights, education and technology, by both colonial and post-colonial administrators, who could not conceive of women being farmers in their own right, even though in much of sub-Saharan Africa and South-East Asia women enjoyed a significant autonomous role in traditional agricultural production. This lack of access to resources meant that while men's productivity in farming increased, women's productivity did not. In the case of industrial modernization, she argued that women accounted for a much lower percentage of the industrial labour force in large-scale modern factories than they did in home-based handicraft manufacturing. She pointed to obstacles on the demand side, including labour market regulations, and employers' prejudiced perceptions of women's capacities and work commitment; and on the supply side, she suggested that women had difficulties combining work in the modern sector with their reproductive responsibilities, and were hindered by the view that work outside the home was not proper for women. Above all, women were hampered by their lack of appropriate skills, stemming from their lack of formal education, and confinement with the family. According to Boserup (1970, p. 214), 'Employment in the modern sector requires not only formal training, but also a certain attitude to work, which may best be described as the capacity to work regularly and attentively. Those who work within the confines of the home are not likely to acquire this attitude'. As a result of all these factors, women had been left marginalized and excluded from modernization. Boserup's remedy for this was investment in more and better education for women – planners must change their view that women were primarily housewives, and train women to compete equally with men in the market place, so that women could be included in economic modernization.

As Kabeer (1994) points out, Boserup's book laid the foundations for a large body of 'Women-in-Development' literature, and a large number of policy initiatives aimed at 'integrating women into development'. Tinker (1990), in describing the making of the field of Women-in-Development, calls Boserup's book, 'the fundamental text for the UN Decade for Women' (1975–85). Boserup's 'marginalization' thesis found support from other authors analysing development from women's perspective. For instance, as Pearson (1992) points out, the idea that development marginalized women was supported by some Latin America researchers, such as Saffiotti (1978) who examined the implications for women's employment of import-substitution industrialization in Brazil. Saffiotti found that during the 1950s and 1960s, while women's industrial employment increased overall, their share relative to men in the industrial labour force declined. In her view this was related to Brazil's dependent position in the world economy, which meant that import-substitution industrialization was reliant upon imported large-scale capital-intensive technology which created jobs for men rather than women.

But by no means all feminists agreed with Boserup. By the end of the 1970s there was a strong body of feminist opinion that identified the problem not in terms of exclusion of women from development but in terms of the ways in which women were incorporated into development. Benería and Sen (1981, 1982) argued that the key concept is subordination rather than exclusion and marginalization; and that women's subordination can take a wide variety of different forms because capitalist modernization takes a wide variety of different forms (plantations, small commercial farms, labour-intensive or capital-intensive technologies, and export-oriented or import-substitution industrialization). Women's disadvantage in new forms of paid work is not primarily the result of traditional cultural practices and prejudices, but of the way in which the new forms of production create insecure and hierarchical job structures. Benería and Sen also criticized Boserup for ignoring the crucial significance of reproductive work, (that is, the unpaid work in households and communities that is necessary to reproduce the labour force and the social fabric) and the need to focus on changing the way that production and reproduction are articulated. Without this, women would always be disadvantaged by having to do the bulk of unpaid reproductive work, as well as work in paid production.

Similar themes were also central to the analysis produced in the late 1970s by the Subordination of Women Group at the Institute of Development Studies, University of Sussex. The SOW Group made a significant contribution by promoting a multidisciplinary approach, in which economists such as Diane Elson, Maureen Mackintosh and Ruth Pearson worked with political scientists, such as Maxine Molyneux, and anthropologists, such as Kate Young, Penelope Roberts and Ann Whitehead, to analyse how both marriage and the market would need to be transformed if the subordination of women were to be ended (Young et al. 1981).

They argued that gender subordination takes many forms, and that new forms may be created as old ones fade away. For example, Elson and Pearson (1981) analysed female labour-intensive export-oriented industrialization, not as an inter-sectoral labour transfer, but as an interplay of conflicting tendencies: a tendency to *intensify* the existing forms of gender subordination; a tendency to *decompose* existing forms of gender subordination; and a tendency to *recompose* new forms of gender subordination. While policies to promote the expansion of employment in export factories did not in any simple way liberate women, the interplay of these tendencies opened up a space for women to act collectively to improve their conditions as wage workers and as members of household communities, and to build co-operation and solidarity between women.

The terrain on which feminists had to engage with development theory shifted in the 1980s. Planning for development was replaced by liberalization and privatization. The economics of development became dominated by neo-classical economics which identified the main obstacle to development as policy-induced price distortions, such as over-valued exchange rates, import controls and credit controls. It was argued that deregulation of the economy would remove such distortions and promote both growth and improved standards of living (for a guide to this shift, see Toye 1987). This theory was put into practice via IMF stabilization policies and World Bank structural adjustment policies, which made devaluation, decontrol and deflation conditions for the receipt of the funds that governments of developing countries urgently needed to enable them to service the debt they incurred in the late 1970s in the aftermath of the quadrupling of oil prices.

Nevertheless, a concern with the inter-sectoral transfer of labour continued – but now as a transfer from the non-tradable sector to the tradable sector. (The non-tradable sector includes all public sector and private sector production of goods and services which do not enter international trade – such as education or food for on-farm consumption; the tradable sector includes all production of goods and services which do enter international trade.) This transfer is expected to be brought about by devaluation and deregulation of markets (including import liberalization) (Lal 1988; Edwards 1988). Such a transfer is expected to lead to a reduction in the balance of payments deficit and a higher rate of economic growth (as a result of a lifting of the balance of payments constraint). Unlike the Lewis model, there is no appeal to surplus labour in the macroeconomics of structural adjustment; the development gains are supposed to come not from mobilizing surplus labour, but from reallocating a given stock of fully employed labour (Addison and Demery 1994).

A feminist critique of this theory was presented by Elson (1991) arguing that the theory of structural adjustment implicitly assumes unlimited supplies of female labour, available to make good any shortfalls in provision of public sector non-tradable services (such as health, education, water, sanitation) and to increase production of exports, while at the same time maintaining household food security and the social fabric of family and community networks. Adjustment theory does not confront this implication because it appears to treat labour as a non-produced means of production, and all consumption as discretionary. But since even devotees of structural adjustment do not believe that people can live on fresh air, there is a hidden assumption that whatever is necessary to sustain the given stock of labour will be done. This in practice is largely 'women's work'.

Gendered cultural norms about what is 'men's work' and 'women's work' mean that men's labour tends not to be reallocated to women's work where there is a decrease in what is considered to be men's work and an increase in what is considered to be women's work. Instead, a more likely outcome is unemployment and underemployment for men, and overwork for women. Failure to take this into account in analysing adjustment, argued Elson, results in extra burdens for women, and means that adjustment programmes are unlikely to be able to deliver the growth they promise:

> Ignoring the implications of macro-economic changes for unpaid domestic labour inputs is tantamount to assuming that women's capacity to undertake extra work is infinitely elastic – able to stretch so as to make up for any shortfall in income and resources required for the production and maintenance of human resources. However, women's capacity for work is not infinitely elastic and breaking point may be reached. There may simply not be enough female labour time available to maintain the quality and quantity of human resources at its existing level. This

may not have an immediate impact on the level and composition of gross national output, but in the longer run a deterioration in health, nutrition and education will have adverse impacts on output levels. (Elson 1991, p. 179)

There is thus an underlying continuity between theories of development which postulate a transfer from the subsistence or traditional or agricultural sector to the capitalist or modern or industrial sector, and theories of adjustment that postulate a transfer of labour from the non-tradable sector to the tradable sector. Similar questions arise: how will the transfer take place; is extra labour time required and, if so, how is it mobilized; what barriers might obstruct the productive use of labour and the reinvestment of profits so as to increase productivity and living standards? The critique of structural adjustment theory produced by feminist economics has some similarities with parallel critiques by structuralist economics: both emphasize discontinuities and non-substitutability as well as the role of power and cultural norms in structuring the use of resources. However, as Elson (1993) argues, structuralist economics prioritizes social relations of class and ignores the social relations of gender.

In the 1990s there has been a growing concern in feminist contributions with moving beyond critique to the construction of alternative models and analytical tools. For instance, Palmer (1991, 1992) has suggested that price distortions can be caused by gender discrimination as well as by inappropriate government controls. She identified four sources of gender-based price distortion: gender discrimination in access to resources or outlets for produce; the additional tasks women face (and men do not) in reproduction and family maintenance (which Palmer characterizes as a 'reproduction tax' on women which distorts their choice of activities); unequal terms of exchange between men and women within households; and a distribution of income within households that does not provide women with the same incentives as men to respond to new opportunities introduced by structural adjustment programmes. Palmer argued that adjustment programmes do not focus on reducing gender-based price distortions and may even worsen them. She suggested that the persistence of gender-based price distortions will weaken the supply response, especially in smallholder-based agricultural economies, so that adjustment programmes will fail to achieve their growth objectives. Her conclusion was that adjustment programmes should be redesigned to include reduction of gender-based distortions. In particular, fiscal policy should be designed to reduce the 'reproduction tax'.

Further contributions have come from a project on gender, adjustment and macroeconomics which promoted dialogue between feminist economics and non-orthodox macroeconomists (see Cagatay et al. 1995). For instance, Darity (1995) constructed a two-sector model of a gender-segregated low-income agrarian economy, and used it to show how a devaluation of the currency, which raises the relative price of export cash crops, means extra demand for women's labour and extra income for their husbands who control the sale of the crop. The key to women benefiting from an expansion of the cash crop sector is a reduction in the degree of power men exercise over women's labour, and a more equal sharing of the proceeds.

In contrast, Erturk and Cagatay (1995) focused on the investment behaviour of firms and savings behaviour of households in industrializing economies, drawing upon empirical research on patterns of economic development to identify some 'stylized facts' about the degree of feminization of the paid labour force and the extent of women's unpaid household work. They assumed that a rise in the feminization of the labour force stimulates investment by making available a new pool of low-cost and malleable labour, while a rise in the extent of women's unpaid household work is equivalent to an increase in savings because it reduces expenditure on marketed goods. The interaction of these two effects is examined in relation to recovery from economic crisis and recession, and it is concluded that recovery will be dampened if the positive impact of feminization of the paid labour force on investment is weaker than the positive impact of an intensification of women's household work on savings.

Both of these models are highly simplified (as all formal models must be) but they are important as heuristic devices which begin the task of showing how gender-sensitive variables, which capture reproduction as well as production, and power as well as choice, can be incorporated in analysis of how growth and structural change takes place (or fails to take place).

As well as new concepts and models for analysing production and growth, feminist writers have also insisted on the importance of new visions of what development should be. Particularly important have been the writings of an autonomous interregional organization of women from the South – DAWN, standing for Development Alternatives with Women for a New Era – which was set up just prior to the 1985 UN Conference of Women in Nairobi. DAWN emphasized not only gender equality, but also class and race equality, and international equality between countries, and put forward a critique of both states and markets (Sen and Grown 1987; Sen and Heyzer (eds) 1994). There were some parallels between DAWN's concern to articulate a new vision of development and the concept of human development articulated in the *Human Development Report*, published annually since 1990 by the United Nations Development Programme, and drawing its conceptual framework from the concepts of capabilities and entitlements developed by Amartya Sen (Sen 1984). Feminist economists generally welcomed this approach to development theory but were concerned to ensure that it became more gender-sensitive, and to ensure that some critical ambiguities in the concept of human development were resolved in a way that empowered women (DAWN 1995; Elson 1997).

The *Human Development Reports* themselves did become more gender-aware in their analysis and presentation of statistics, devoting an issue (1995) to the struggle for gender equality, and presenting measures of the economic value of women's unpaid reproductive work, and two new indexes of development, the gender-related development index and the gender-empowerment measure. However, the concept of human development has often been narrowly interpreted by international aid agencies as meaning simply an emphasis on investing in health and education as well as in infrastructure and equipment – investment in human capital as well as in physical capital. In this way, human development has been assimilated into the dominant model of adjustment and liberalization, and labour is still viewed as a factor of production and development a process of inter-sectoral reallocation of this factor, and the enhancement of its productivity (see, for instance, World Bank 1991).

Moreover, while the *Human Development Reports* themselves have stressed that people should not be regarded as simply factors of production (the means to an end) but as ends in themselves, Elson (1997) points out there is a lack of clarity in the Reports about the conditions under which this is possible. In particular, the fact that markets may be coercive as well as enabling is not fully confronted. DAWN (1995) argues for redefining and engendering human development, stressing values of self-realization together with sharing and reciprocity (DAWN 1995, p. 23). The challenge for feminist economics is to help translate this into a practical strategy. This will require more analysis of how both states and markets (national and international) can be transformed; of how new forms of property right that emphasize stewardship rather than ownership can be created; and of how forms of mutually supportive organization of production and reproduction can be created. A fruitful approach may be to reconceptualize development not as a transfer of labour between sectors, but as an interactive and contradictory process, in which there is potential (albeit often suppressed) for the transformation of labour from the object to the subject of the process, and for the creation of the conditions for women to truly be agents of their own development.

DIANE ELSON

See also

Agriculture (Third World); Class; Development Policies; Domestic Labour; Double Day/Second Shift; Gross Domestic Product; Globalization; Growth Theory (Macro Models); Imperialism; Informal Sector; International Economics; Population; Structural Adjustment Policies.

Bibliography

Addison, Tony and Lionel Demery (1994), 'The Poverty Effects of Adjustment with Labor Market Imperfections', in Susan Horton, Ravi Kanbur and Dipak Mazumdar (eds), *Labor Markets in an Era of Adjustment*, Washington, DC: World Bank, pp. 147–93.

Benería, Lourdes and Gita Sen (1981), 'Accumulation, reproduction and women's role in economic development', *Signs: Journal of Women in Cultural and Society*, **7** (2), 279–98.

Benería, Lourdes and Gita Sen (1982), 'Class and gender inequalities and women's role in economic development – theoretical and practical implications', *Feminist Studies*, **8** (1), 157–76.

Boserup, Ester (1970), *Women's Role in Economic Development*, New York: St. Martins Press.

Cagatay, Nilufer, Diane Elson and Caren Grown (eds) (1995), *Gender, Adjustment and Macroeconomics*, Special Issue of *World Development*, **23** (11).

Darity, William (1995), 'The formal structure of a gender-segregated low-income economy', *World Development*, **23** (11), 1963–8.

DAWN (1995), *Markers on the Way: The DAWN Debates on Alternative Development*, Barbados: Women and Development Unit, University of West Indies.

Edwards, Sebastian (1988), 'Terms of trade, tariffs and labor market adjustment in developing countries', *World Bank Economic Review*, **2**, 165–85.

Elson, Diane (1991), 'Male Bias in Macroeconomics: The Case of Structural Adjustment', in Diane Elson (ed.), *Male Bias in the Development Process*, Manchester: Manchester University Press, pp. 164–90.

Elson, Diane (1993), 'Gender aware analysis and development economics', *Journal of International Development*, **5** (2), 237–47.

Elson, Diane (1997), 'Economic Paradigms Old and New: The Case of Human Development', in A. Berry, R. Culpepper and F. Stewart (eds), *Global Governance and Development Fifty Years After Bretton Woods*, London: Macmillan, pp. 50–71.

Elson, Diane and Ruth Pearson (1981), 'The Subordination of Women and the Internationalisation of Factory Production', in Kate Young, Carol Wolkowitz and Roslyn McCullagh (eds), *Of Marriage and the Market – Women's Subordination in International Perspective*, London: CSE Books, pp. 144–66.

Erturk, Korkut and Nilufer Cagatay (1995), 'Macroeconomic consequences of cyclical and secular changes in feminization: an experiment in gendered macromodeling', *World Development*, **23** (11), 1969–77.

Frank, Andre Gunder (1966), 'The development of underdevelopment', *Monthly Review*, **18** (4), September, 17–31.

Kabeer, Naila (1994), *Reversed Realities: Gender Hierarchies in Development Thought*, London: Verso.

Lal, Deepak (1983), *The Poverty of 'Development Economics'*, London: Institute of Economic Affairs.

Lal, Deepak (1985), 'The misconceptions of "development economics"', *Finance and Development*, **22**, (June), 10–13.

Lal, Deepak (1988), 'A simple framework for analyzing various real aspects of stabilization and structural adjustment policies', *Journal of Development Studies*, **25**, (April), 291–312.

Lewis, W. Arthur (1954), 'Economic development with unlimited supplies of labour', *Manchester School*, **22** (2), 139–91.

Lewis, W. Arthur (1955), *The Theory of Economic Growth*, London: Allen and Unwin.

Palma, Gabriel (1978), 'Dependency: a formal theory of underdevelopment or a methodology for the analysis of concrete situations of underdevelopment', *World Development*, **6** (7/8), 881–924.

Palmer, Ingrid (1991), *Gender and Population in the Adjustment of African Economics: Planning for Change*, Geneva: ILO.

Palmer, Ingrid (1992), 'Gender Equity and Economic Efficiency in Adjustment Programmes', in Haleh Afshar and Carolyne Dennis (eds), *Women and Adjustment Policies in the Third World*, London: Macmillan, pp. 69–83.

Pearson, Ruth (1992), 'Gender Issues in Industrialisation', in Tom Hewitt, Hazel Johnson and

Dave Wield (eds) *Industrialisation and Development*, Oxford: Oxford University Press, pp. 222–47.

Prebisch, Raul (1950), *The Economic Development of Latin America and its Principal Problems*, New York: United Nations.

Rostow, W.W. (1960), *Stages of Economic Growth*, Cambridge: Cambridge University Press.

Saffiotti, Helieth (1978), *Women in Class Society*, New York: Monthly Review Press.

Sen, Amartya (1975), *Employment, Technology and Development*, Oxford: Clarendon Press.

Sen, Amartya (1983), 'Development: Which way now?', *Economic Journal*, **93**, 745– 62.

Sen, Amartya (1984), *Resources, Values and Development*, Oxford: Blackwell.

Sen, Gita and Caren Grown (eds) (1987), *Development, Crises and Alternative Visions: Third World Women's Perspectives*, New York: Monthly Review Press.

Sen, Gita and Noeleen Heyzer (eds) (1994), *Gender, Economic Growth and Poverty: Market Growth and State Planning in Asia and the Pacific*, New Delhi: Kali for Woman.

Singer, Hans (1950), 'The distribution of gains between borrowing and investing countries', *American Economic Review*, **40** (2) (Papers and Proceedings), 470–85.

Tinker, Irene (1990), 'A Context for the Field and the Book', in I. Tinker (ed.), *Persistent Inequalities. Women and World Development*, Oxford: Oxford University Press, pp. 27–53.

Toye, John (1987), *Dilemmas of Development*, Oxford: Blackwell.

United Nations Development Programme (1990–1998), *Human Development Report*, Oxford and New York: Oxford University Press.

Weeks, John (1970), 'The political economy of labor transfer', *Science and Society*, **1**, 463–80.

World Bank (1991), *World Development Report*, Oxford and New York: Oxford University Press.

Young, Kate, Carol Wolkowitz and Roslyn McCullagh (eds) (1981), *Of Marriage and the Market – Women's Subordination in International Perspective*, London: CSE Books.

Discrimination, Theories of

Empirical studies have demonstrated that women's economic status is significantly different from men's according to several key indicators such as wages and occupational distribution. Most feminists and some other schools of economists attribute this to labour market discrimination. Although labour market discrimination may take several forms, including discrimination in hiring, assignments and promotions, as well as sexual harassment, economists typically focus on wage differentials as a measurable manifestation of discrimination. From this perspective, labour market discrimination consists of remunerating employees differently when they have equivalent productivity.

Feminist economists have researched the extent and causes of labour market discrimination in order to explore the material aspects of gender inequality. In capitalist economies, wages are a crucial resource. Access to jobs paying relatively higher wages provides a degree of power and autonomy in the public sphere and within the household. Further, the ability to support a family and not be perceived as financially dependent is culturally valued in most industrialized countries. To eradicate barriers posed by discrimination, feminist economists have studied and advocated policies such as affirmative action, comparable worth/pay equity and raising the minimum wage.

When analysing discrimination, feminist economists have tended to respond to existing theoretical frameworks or to rely on existing analytical categories. While exposing the limits of neoclassical approaches, institutional models, segmentation theory and other constructs for understanding women's experiences has made an enormous contribution to the literature, there is little consensus on an alternative framework. However, the basis for an emerging feminist alternative is the assertion that the social construction of gender permeates men's and women's labour market experiences. Feminist economists are also pioneering the intersections of gender with race/ethnicity, age, class and sexual orientation.

The existence of labour market discrimination is controversial among neoclassical economists. Labour economists have struggled to reconcile the apparent persistence of discrimination by gender and race/ethnicity with the fluid workings of neoclassical wage theory. According to textbook models, unless men and women differ in their productivity, rational employers should hire cheaper categories of labour until wages equalize. Two mainstream perspectives disagree on whether differential outcomes are explained by discrimination. According to those focusing on labour supply issues, if women's economic status comes from rational decisions that they make themselves as individuals supplying labour, then there is no discrimination. That is, women's own educational and job choices would explain both occupational segregation and wage differentials. Alternatively, if women's economic status comes from gender-specific labour demand on the part of employers (due to their own preferences or the perceived preferences of coworkers and customers), there is labour market discrimination.

Neoclassical human capital theory has been used to argue that wage differentials do, in fact, result from productivity differences. Specifically, differences in wages reflect gender differences in employees' investment in human capital and stock of human capital as measured by years of schooling, experience, job tenure and other factors. Because women anticipate intermittent labour market participation in order to focus on child care and other aspects of social reproduction, they make lower human capital investments than male workers and different occupational choices. However, human capital theorists have only been able to statistically explain about 50 per cent of the wage gap with human capital variables (Gunderson 1989; England 1992). In a key study substantiated by other scholars, sociologist Paula England (1982) found that women with more continuous work experience are no more apt than other women to be employed in predominantly male occupations.

The tools of neoclassical analysis have also been used by economists who acknowledge the existence of demand-side discrimination (see Albelda et al. 1997 for a summary). Gary Becker has proposed that individuals (either employers or coworkers) may have a 'taste for discrimination', developed outside the labour market, that cause the employers who have or cater to such tastes to pay a wage premium for desirable workers. In the long run, competitive market forces will punish discriminating employers who have relatively high labour costs; discrimination should erode since it is not rational or economically efficient. However, imperfectly competitive markets permit discrimination to persist. In contrast, the theory of statistical discrimination (often attributed to Edmund Phelps or Kenneth Arrow) suggests that discrimination may be rational. Because employers have imperfect information about the potential productivity of future employees, they use screening devices to select between applicants, including generalizations about racial or gender groups.

Although aspects of each of these theories have been incorporated into feminist approaches, many feminist economists have been troubled by their emphasis on current labour market discrimination. Within most neoclassical frameworks, pre-labour force discrimination and socialization are treated as exogenous, not part of studying economics and markets. Yet feminists point out that there are feedback effects between the labour market and other social institutions including the family (England 1992, pp. 108–12; Bruegel and Perrons 1995, pp. 111–12). Women who perceive discrimination in the past may be discouraged from training for non-traditional jobs. Wage discrimination may encourage married couples to adopt a traditional division of labour between market and domestic labour. While traditional models present us with two options – either women choose certain jobs (supply-side) or employers discriminate (demand-side) – in reality, these dynamics of choice and constraint cannot be isolated from each other.

In a pathbreaking article, Bergmann (1974) has argued that past and current discrimination restrict women and people of colour to a small subset of occupations (that is, occupational segregation). An abundant supply of workers in these limited occupations drives down wages. This 'crowding hypothesis' synthesizes models proposed by F.Y. Edgeworth and other early twentieth-century economists with Becker's discrimination theory. However, Bergmann disputes Becker's contention that discrimination is irrational and unprofitable. Discrimination can be profitable if it is a generalized practice. Employers can afford to hire white men at a premium if they only compete with employers doing the same thing, passing higher prices on to consumers. Occupational segregation concentrates workers who experience discrimination involuntarily into industries where prices as well as wages are relatively low. The existence of separate labour markets for different groups maintains industry- and individually-based wage differentials.

The existence of discrete labour markets for different industries and sectors of the economy is a theme in institutional labour market theory. For example, dual labour market theory notes that the economy is divided between a primary sector and a secondary sector. The 'primary sector' is traditional manufacturing and skilled crafts, which are highly unionized and offer promotion opportunities. Jobs in the 'secondary sector' are low-wage and dead-end. Women and people of colour have difficulty gaining access to primary-sector jobs.

Within the primary sector, jobs beyond the entry level are filled by promotions, upgrades and other institutionally-determined procedures. These 'internal labour markets' deemphasize the role of competitive markets, undermining Becker's assertion that competition can eliminate discrimination. Discrimination is institutionalized because once workers are in different entry-level positions, their promotion opportunities are limited by the structure of the job ladder rather than individual prejudice. Nevertheless, dual labour market theory is limited in its scope since it is primarily descriptive in nature, it oversimplifies the complexity of labour market hierarchies, and it applies only to a particular historical period, that is, postwar industrialized countries.

Radical segmentation theory similarly evokes the concept of separable labour markets characterized by different firm size and structure as well as the gender and race/ethnicity of the labour supply. Labour market segmentation, it is argued, evolved historically within the capitalist economic system. Employers have an interest in maintaining discrimination because they use racial and gender differences to create divisions among workers. One implication of the theory is that white male workers do not benefit from discrimination; employers capture the benefits of discrimination by keeping workers from unifying and unionizing.

While feminist political economists have applauded segmentation theory's historical specificity, they have disputed the contention that employers are the sole beneficiaries from discrimination. Both Hartmann (1976) and Rubery (1978) have drawn upon this theoretical approach in their work. Yet they believe that traditional segmentation theory ignores the way working class men also benefit from women's restricted access to the highest paid occupations. A similar stance, albeit more critical of segmentation theory, is taken by Williams (1991) and other authors in the capitalist competition school. In this Marxian approach, competition for jobs exists between groups of workers, especially between 'skilled workers' and 'subordinate workers' (Williams 1991, p. 77). A competitive wage hierarchy is sustained by entrenched workers, typically white males, seeking to preserve their relative advantage.

Feminist economists influenced by institutional and radical theories have focused on the power dimensions of the wage-setting process, presenting historically and even geographically and organizationally specific accounts of the process of defining labour market segments. Through occupational segregation certain jobs have become identified as 'women's work', and these jobs pay less because they are feminized and deemed 'unskilled'.

Sociologists have also contributed to the literature on the process of discrimination, especially how it is replicated within organizations, evaluating the relative importance of both market and organizational forces in determining pay in male- and female-dominated job categories (Bridges and Nelson 1989; Acker 1990; Cockburn 1991; Pfeffer and Konrad 1991).

The task facing feminist economists is to merge the lessons gained from both neoclassical economists, who emphasize the measurable manifestations of wage discrimination, with those of political economists and feminist scholars in other disciplines who focus on historical and organizational processes of assigning jobs and wages. From institutional and radical analyses, feminist theories of discrimination recognize that the structure of labour markets and other economic and social institutions influence individual economic actors. Feminist approaches to the study of discrimination share some critiques of neoclassical discrimination models with institutionalist and radical analyses of labour markets, but also provide a unique contribution through the development of gender theory. Conventional economic methods tend to neglect the process by which gender interacts with and shapes social forces and institutions.

According to feminist economists, economic institutions do not develop independently of gender. This insight forms the basis of emerging feminist research and needs to be developed further. Many neoclassical and Marxist approaches argue that labour market structures develop according to strictly economic rationales, either profit maximization or class-based accumulation strategies. Then, discriminatory attitudes and/or institutions give women certain places within the structure. Gender theory argues that socially constructed notions of gender (and race/ethnicity, class, age, and so on) shape the available places. Gender is not only crucial in assigning people to places in the gendered division of labour, but in the very definition and value of occupations, and thus in shaping the division of labour as a whole (Murgatroyd 1982; Acker 1990). Acknowledging that cultural and psychological forces play such a role calls into question the extent to which labour market decisions are made by rational individuals. Feminist economists, along with sociologists and scholars in other disciplines, must continue to document the use of gender in drawing up new occupational classifications and their pay scales, as well as in the production and reproduction of gender-typed jobs during economic restructuring.

Recent work by feminist economists also asserts that the interactions between production and reproduction must be analysed in a way that overcomes the supply and demand dichotomy (Bruegel and Perrons 1995). Patriarchal relations within the household and society influence both suppliers and demanders of labour, and both dynamics are integral to understanding discriminatory processes and consequences. Thus, Figart (1997) has proposed a feminist definition of discrimination that emphasizes process as well as outcomes; measurable as well as unquantifiable repercussions. She defines labour market discrimination as 'a multidimensional interaction of economic, social, political, and cultural forces in both the workplace and the family, resulting in differential outcomes involving pay, employment, and status' (p. 4). Feminist economists can utilize this expanded definition of discrimination to embrace methodological pluralism in the ongoing project of documenting and theorizing discrimination. Such research could utilize or generate innovative data sets and employ qualitative research methodologies that elucidate the concrete experience of discrimination.

DEBORAH M. FIGART

See also

Affirmative Action; Comparable Worth/Pay Equity; Family Wage; Human Capital Theory; Labour Market Segmentation; Labour Markets, Theories of; Minimum Wage; Occupational Segregation; Wage Gap.

Bibliography

Acker, Joan (1990), 'Hierarchies, jobs, bodies: a theory of gendered organizations', *Gender and Society*, **4** (2), 139–58.
Albelda, Randy, Robert Drago and Steven Shulman (1997), *Unlevel Playing Fields: Understanding Wage Inequality and Discrimination*, New York: McGraw-Hill.
Bergmann, Barbara R. (1974), 'Occupational segregation, wages and profits when employers discriminate by race or sex', *Eastern Economic Journal*, **1** (2/3), 103–10.
Bruegel, Irene and Diane Perrons (1995), 'Where do the costs of unequal treatment for women fall?', *Gender, Work and Organization*, **2** (3), 110–21.
Bridges, William P. and Robert L. Nelson (1989), 'Markets and hierarchies: Organizational and market influences on gender inequality in a state pay system', *American Journal of Sociology*, **95**, 616–58.
Cockburn, Cynthia (1991), *In the Way of Women: Men's Resistance to Sex Equality In Organizations*, Ithaca: ILR Press.
England, Paula (1982), 'The failure of human capital theory to explain occupational sex segregation', *The Journal of Human Resources*, **17** (3), 358–70.
England, Paula (1992), *Comparable Worth: Theories and Evidence*, New York: Aldine de Gruyter.
Figart, Deborah M. (1997), 'Gender as more than a dummy variable: Feminist approaches to discrimination', *Review of Social Economy*, **LV** (1), 1–32.
Gunderson, Morley (1989), 'Male–female wage differentials and policy responses', *Journal of Economic Literature*, **27** (1), 46–72.
Hartmann, Heidi (1976), 'Capitalism, patriarchy, and job segregation by sex', *Signs*, **1** (3), 137–69.
Murgatroyd, Linda (1982), 'Gender and occupational stratification', *Sociological Review*, **30** (4), 574–602.
Pfeffer, Jeffrey and Alison K. Konrad (1991), 'The effects of individual power on earnings', *Work and Occupations*, **18** (4), 385–414.
Rubery, Jill (1978), 'Structured labour markets, worker organisation and low pay', *Cambridge Journal of Economics*, **2** (1), 17–36.
Williams, Rhonda (1991), 'Competition, Discrimination, and Differential Wage Rates: On the Continued Relevance of Marxian Theory to the Analysis of Earnings and Employment Inequality', in Richard A. Cornwall and Phanindra V. Wunnava (eds), *New Approaches to Economic and Social Analyses of Discrimination*, New York: Praeger, pp. 65–92.

Divorce

Mainstream and feminist economists alike have produced a growing stream of research on divorce. Family sociologists and lawyers have also made important contributions. June Carbone, a legal scholar, writes that 'feminist perspectives on divorce focus on the implications of divorce for the lives of women and their children' (1994, p. 183). This entry will focus specifically on the economic implications of divorce for women and children in the United States. After a brief discussion of economic theories of divorce, the empirical literature in the field concerning the trends, determinants, and consequences of divorce will be examined.

Divorce first came to the attention of economists in the 1970s. Gary Becker, Jacob Mincer and students in the Labor Workshop at Columbia University were the first to apply the rational choice models of neoclassical economics to the decisions of family life including marriage and divorce. This theoretical work in the 1970s laid the groundwork for the subsequent explosion of a largely empirical literature. More recently, this literature has expanded to include the economics of child support and the application of bargaining theory to the economics of divorce.

Following the neoclassical economic approach to divorce introduced by Becker et al. (1977), economists Beller and Graham (1993, p. 57) suggest that 'the economic argument for marital dissolution is that, given voluntary associations, one or both parties believe they will be better off alone (or with a different partner, since new partners are sometimes selected before a divorce occurs)'. One reason for this is likely to be that before marriage, partners have incomplete information about potential spouses; once married, they may be dissatisfied with their partner's performance, including their earnings as well as their ability or willingness to engage in household production, leading to divorce (Becker 1981; Beller and Graham 1993). There are a great many other possible reasons for divorce. For example, people may change, meet someone else they like better, or find they have different ideas about how to spend money or raise children. Grossbard-Schechtman (1993) extended the neoclassical economic analysis of divorce to incorporate a simultaneous relationship with labour supply, indicating how the two sometimes depend upon each other and how the effects of other variables, such as personal income, on divorce or on labour supply depend on that variable's effect on the other outcome.

Economists, including Lundberg and Pollak (1993, 1997) and feminist economists, including Folbre (1994), McCrate (1992) and Heath and Ciscel (1996) apply bargaining theory to the study of divorce. For example, divorce-threat models suggest that if the two spouses do not agree and one believes s/he can do better outside of the marriage, s/he will use the threat of divorce as a bargaining point to settle the disagreement. This model has implications for the distribution of resources within marriage. It 'predicts that policies improving the status of divorced women will shift resources within marriage to wives' (Lundberg and Pollak 1997, p. 32).

Growing levels of divorce have perhaps been the most conspicuous change in marital status in the USA since the late 1960s, and it is estimated that if current trends continue approximately one-half of all marriages will end in divorce (Blau et al. 1998). Although, as demographer Andrew Cherlin (1992) has shown, divorce is not a particularly new phenomenon in the USA, during the 1960s and 1970s divorce rates rose more rapidly than would have been expected based on historical trends. By 1997, 10 per cent of adults were divorced, with little difference by race or gender (US Census Bureau 1997a, 1997b). This increase in divorce has been associated with other changes in family structure, most particularly a decrease in the number of children living with two parents. In 1996, for example, 28 per cent of children under 18 years of age lived with only one parent, usually their mother, 36 per cent of whom were divorced (US Census Bureau 1998).

High levels of divorce in the USA have occurred in the context of two additional trends — an increased social acceptability of divorce and the spread of no-fault divorce laws. Although it is difficult to measure the increased acceptability of divorce, there is widespread agreement that 'divorce as a socio-legal process molds and reinforces social values. Its institutional availability helps to fashion individual action and choice' (Gibson 1994, p. 215). No-fault divorce laws allow marriages to be dissolved without proof that a spouse was guilty of any particular misconduct. California enacted the first no-fault divorce statute in 1969. Currently 17 states allow only no-fault divorce, while another 31 allow it in addition to traditional grounds for divorce (Elrod and Spector 1998). The impact of no-fault divorce statutes has been that 'marriage became, for all intents and purposes, terminable at will' (Carbone 1994, p. 187). Recent evidence indicates that these laws 'raised divorce rates significantly and strongly' (Friedberg 1998, p. 608).

It is possible that other policy changes may work to reduce the divorce rate. McCrate (1992), for example, argues that changes in the social safety net during the 1980s meant 'that a married mother with limited earning power contemplating divorce ... could expect substantially less assistance and more stigma from the government than in the 1970s' (p. 414). As welfare reform continues to dismantle the social safety net, that is even more likely to be the case. However, to date these changes do not appear to have had a significant effect on the divorce rate.

The literature on the determinants of divorce has differentiated between demographic factors, economic factors, and the overall legal and social environment and their relationship to divorce. Demographic determinants of marital dissolution include age at marriage and number and ages of children. Economic determinants of marital dissolution include earnings and the wife's labour force participation in terms of the number of years of work as well as number of hours of work (Cameron 1995).

Age at marriage is one of the strongest and most robust predictors of divorce. Marriages begun at later ages, after a more extended period of marital search, are more stable. There is some evidence, however, that the relationship may be nonlinear, with the probability of divorce rising beyond a certain age (Becker et al. 1977). Investments in spouse-specific human capital represent another key factor in marital stability. Children are the main form of such capital, and the birth of a child to a couple is a stabilizing influence. The effects are complex, however, varying with the number and ages of the children (Waite and Lillard 1991). In contrast, offspring from a previous union have an adverse effect on marital stability. Becker et al. (1977) interpret this result as indicating that children from another partnership are a source of friction in the current union. An alternative explanation is that such children make their parent a less attractive spouse, by diverting resources of time, energy and money away from the current marriage (Chiswick and Lehrer 1990; Lehrer 1996).

Becker's (1981) theory of marriage shows that in the optimal sorting of people into marriages, there is positive assortative mating (that is, likes marry likes) for traits that are mutually reinforcing, such as education, intelligence, age and religion. Substantial empirical evidence supports the notion that unions are indeed less stable when the partners differ along these dimensions (Becker et al. 1977; Michael 1979). In particular, marrying outside the religion has a significant adverse effect on marital stability, an influence that varies in magnitude depending on precisely which pair of religions is involved (Lehrer and Chiswick 1993). Studies have also found a negative relationship between practising an organized religion and divorce (for example, Ferber and Sander 1989). Finally, differences between spouses in gender role attitudes were also found to be significant. Typically attitudes as well as behaviour related to wives' paid employment and housework, including child care, are found to have some effect (for example, Huber and Spitze 1980).

The neoclassical economic model of marriage and marital dissolution predicts that increases in the husband's earnings should have a favourable impact on marital stability, a hypothesis that is consistently confirmed by empirical studies. There is less agreement regarding the relationship between measures of the value of female time and the probability of divorce, partly because of differences among studies in precisely when such value is measured (Lehrer 1988). The majority of the studies finds a positive relationship between wife's earnings and employment on the one hand and divorces on the other hand (for example, Huber and Spitze 1980; Ferber and Sander 1989; Heath and Ciscel 1996). But, the direction of causality is not unambiguous. Higher earnings and employment provide women with an alternative to marriage that allows them to support their family, but women may also increase their employment and earnings in anticipation of a divorce. Using data collected during the 1970s, Johnson and Skinner (1986) found that as divorce rates increased over time, 'women, anticipating a higher probability of separation, work more' (p. 468).

There is little agreement about the effect of relative income of husband and wife on marriage and marital dissolution. Folbre (1994) notes that after 1950 women's increased economic independence (a result of decreased fertility and increased employment) and the resulting increased bargaining power within the family made marriage more attractive to women. However, she goes on to say that at the same time marriage was becoming less attractive to men. She points out that, although men did not change their behaviour in large numbers until the 1970s, this 'male disaffection with domesticity' was 'a central theme of the beatnik and Playboy ethos of the 1950s and 1960s' (p. 205).

By contrast, McCrate (1992) suggests that during the 1980s as women's earnings increased relative to men's, it was easier for wives to seek a divorce. At the same time she notes that as real income fell sharply for many men, they became more dependent upon women and were 'thus more inclined to grant bargaining concessions to their wives' (p. 413). For wives then, being granted these concessions may mean remaining married is preferred to divorce.

Taking what they coined a radical bargaining approach, Heath and Ciscel (1996, p. 3) note that a woman 'remains in her marriage because she has limited fallback positions in the wage labor system'. They use data from both first and second marriages to examine the relationship between women's employment, divorce and bargaining within the family. They argue that 'women who are both participants in the labour market and who have experienced divorce may be expected to remarry only if their partner accepts a more balanced family bargaining environment, or places a high value on the economic independence or income these women generate' (p. 6). Their results indicate that women's labour force attachment is less disruptive of second marriages than of first.

In addition to the influences operating at the couple-level described above, the overall legal and social environment also influences divorce decisions. The cost of legal services related to marital dissolution and trends in property settlements, payments to spouses and child support payments as well as the availability of public assistance are examples of legal factors (McCrate 1992). Examples of social factors that may affect divorce are the influence of organized religion on society and what economists call the 'marriage market'. For instance, marriage market conditions can affect divorce probabilities: when there is a surplus of marriageable women, divorce is more likely (Grossbard-Shechtman 1993).

A major focus of the feminist literature on divorce is on its economic consequences. One important question is how the capital accumulated during the marriage is to be distributed. Financial assets, household durables and houses are generally shared according to a one-time property settlement. How much each spouse gets has been shown to depend upon the divorce laws in effect at the time. Viewed as advantageous to women when introduced, no-fault divorce laws have, according to many studies, in fact resulted in smaller settlements for women (Weitzman 1985, Peters 1986, Parkman 1992). However, recent work by Gray (1996), shows that the effect depends upon the state's laws governing the distribution of marital property at divorce. Further, if the woman has sacrificed her own career to invest in her husband's human capital, as was common in the past, she should be entitled to some portion of his lifetime income (Beller and Graham 1993), including pension and retirement income.

The most difficult questions about distribution when a marriage breaks up generally involve the children. Who shall gain custody of the children, and who shall bear the costs of rearing them? Typically, the mother retains physical custody of the children, although joint custody is becoming increasingly common (Maccoby et al. 1988). At the same time, mothers usually earn less than fathers do and often the fathers pay little, if any, child support (Beller and Graham 1993). As a result, the economic consequences of divorce are almost always negative and prolonged for mothers and their children, while they are sometimes positive for fathers (Weitzman 1985; Hoffman and Duncan 1988; Holden and Smock 1991). Many of the single-parent households headed by women fall into poverty and have little choice but to resort to welfare (Beller and Graham 1993); the increasing incidence of such households over time has led to the so-called 'feminization of poverty'.

To date the literature has mainly focused on describing the economic hardship women face following divorce, but a few studies have also attempted to explain why this situation occurs. Feminist explanations of the economic hardship of women following divorce reflect the differing perspectives among feminist scholars on the issue of 'equality' in marriage. Liberal feminists tend to attribute women's bleaker financial prospects at divorce largely to the traditional division of labour within the intact family, whereby women invest less in their human capital than men do and do much more of the housework and child care (Holden and Smock 1991; Carbone 1994). They believe that to remedy this disadvantage men must take on more domestic responsibilities (Carbone 1994, p. 183). 'Cultural feminists' or 'feminists of difference', on the other hand, believe that women care more about children than men do and are more willing to make sacrifices for them. They claim women do poorly at divorce because the child care role is so undervalued. Hence, they believe that increasing the importance society attaches to children and increasing rewards for child care will benefit women (Carbone 1994, p. 200 note 3). Despite these differences among them, feminists, in general, would tend to agree that justice requires the legal system to 'take responsibility for the vulnerable position in which marital breakdown places the partner who has completely or partially lost the capacity to be economically self-supporting' (Okin 1989, p. 183).

Other alternatives, such as investing more in education, participating more continuously in the labour market and engaging in training, would also help women to protect themselves against the exigencies of divorce (Mauldin 1990). Unfortunately, these strategies are rarely employed to the extent adequate to ensure women's financial wellbeing as well as remarriage does.

For divorced mothers, in general, remarriage is the surest way to improve their economic status and that of their children (Folk et al. 1992; Hill 1992; Holden and Smock 1991; Mauldin 1990). However, feminists note that seeking another husband is by no means unambiguously desirable, since there is once again likely to be economic inequality within that marriage (Catlett and McKenry 1996). Furthermore, being forced to find a new spouse too quickly due to economic exigencies can simply result in another unhappy marriage (Folk et al. 1992).

In the last decade, intense attention has been focused on the consequences of family structure for the wellbeing of children. A substantial body of literature has established that growing up in a single-parent family, the vast majority of which are headed by women, is disadvantageous for the children (see for example, Krein and Beller 1988; McLanahan and Sandefur 1994), although receiving child support tends to reduce the extent of this disadvantage (Beller and Chung 1988; Graham et al. 1994; Knox and Bane 1994). For instance, it has been found that children who spend time in a single-parent family are less likely to graduate high school and less likely to go on to college (Krein and Beller 1988). While negative effects of living in a single-parent family on children have been documented, children who live in dysfunctional families, such as many would be if people were prevented from getting divorced, may also suffer negative consequences.

The literature also shows that contact with the noncustodial father tends to be beneficial for children, unless such contact results in greater conflict between the ex-spouses (Seltzer et al. 1995). Beyond the direct benefits of a father spending time with his children, greater contact tends to be associated with more child support being paid. One legitimate concern is to avoid strict child support enforcement policies that are likely to promote domestic abuse, such as forcing a mother to cooperate in identifying and obtaining child support from the father of her child, whom she fears, as a condition of eligibility for welfare.

Much work still remains. Feminists could fill a gap in the existing literature by developing their economic theory of divorce, expanding upon existing approaches like bargaining, and applying their theory to the study of divorce. With respect to the determinants of divorce, more research is needed about the effect of relative income of husbands and wives, often used as a measure of bargaining power. A better understanding of these issues will help to explain not only why some couples divorce but also why some remain married.

Empirical evidence documenting the economic consequences of divorce for women and children is actually quite extensive and convincing. However, more work should be done to explain the sources of women's economic disadvantage following divorce, including the apparently detrimental effects of no-fault laws, as well as the effects of possible alternatives. Gary Becker, for instance, argues that divorce should only be allowed by mutual consent (see also Parkman 1992). Nancy Folbre (1994), however, suggests that this only gives 'the primary wage-earner (typically male) and the physically stronger partner (also typically male) tremendous power over the person specializing in family labour (typically female)' (p. 257). In any case, divorced mothers should not have to rely on remarriage to maintain the economic status of their children. This is especially important in light of the recently enacted time limits on welfare. Therefore, continued research on ways to improve enforcement of child support orders is crucial. Research on how to increase fathers' involvement with their children after divorce would also add useful information. Solving these problems would improve women's economic status and their children's outcomes after divorce. It is also important, however, to do more research on the relationship between child support enforcement and domestic violence. At the same time, while child support is important for maintaining the financial wellbeing of the wife and children after divorce, care must be taken that improvement in that respect does not come at the expense of their safety.

ANDREA H. BELLER AND D. ELIZABETH KISS

See also

Child Support; Family, Economics of; Feminization of Poverty; Game Theory and Bargaining Models; Marriage, Theories of; Welfare Reform.

Bibliography

Becker, Gary S. (1981), *A Treatise on the Family*, Cambridge and London: Harvard University Press.

Becker, Gary S., Elisabeth M. Landes and Robert T. Michael (1977), 'An economic analysis of marital instability', *Journal of Political Economy*, **85** (6), 1141–87.

Beller, Andrea H. and John W. Graham (1993), *Small Change: The Economics of Child Support*, New Haven and London: Yale University Press.

Beller, Andrea H. and Seung Sin Chung (1988), 'The Effect of Child Support Payments on the Educational Attainment of Children', Paper presented at the Population Association of America Annual Meetings, New Orleans, April 1988.

Blau, Francine D., Marianne A. Ferber and Anne E. Winkler (1998), *The Economics of Women, Men, and Work*, Upper Saddle River, New Jersey: Prentice-Hall, Inc.

Cameron, Sam (1995), 'A review of economic research into determinants of divorce', *British Review of Economic Issues*, **17** (41), 1–22.

Carbone, June R. (1994), 'A feminist perspective on divorce', *The Future of Children*, **4** (1), 183–209.

Catlett, Beth Skilken and Patrick C. McKenry (1996), 'Implications of feminist scholarship for the study of women's postdivorce economic disadvantage', *Family Relations*, **45** (1), 91–7.

Cherlin, Andrew J. (1992), *Marriage, Divorce, Remarriage*, Cambridge: Harvard University Press.

Chiswick, Carmel and Evelyn L. Lehrer (1990), 'On marriage-specific human capital: its role as a determinant of marriage', *Journal of Population Economics*, **3** (3), 193–213.

Elrod, Linda D. and Robert G. Spector (1998), 'A review of the year in family law: A search for definitions and policy', *Family Law Quarterly*, **31** (4), 613–66.

Ferber, Marianne A. and William Sander (1989), 'Of women, men, and divorce: not by economics alone', *Review of Social Economy*, **47** (1), 15–26.

Folbre, Nancy (1994), *Who Pays for the Kids: Gender and the Structures of Constraint*, London: Routledge Press.

Folk, Karen F., John W. Graham and Andrea H. Beller (1992), 'Child support and remarriage: implications for the economic well-being of children', *Journal of Family Issues*, **13** (2), 142–57.

Friedberg, Leora, (1998), 'Did unilateral divorce raise divorce rates? Evidence from panel data', *American Economic Review*, **88** (3), 608–27.

Gibson, Colin S. (1994), *Dissolving Wedlock*, London: Routledge.

Graham, John W., Andrea H. Beller and Pedro Hernandez (1994), 'The Effects of Child Support on Educational Attainment', in Irwin Garfinkel, Sara S. McLanahan and Philip K. Robins (eds), *Child Support and Child Well-being*, Washington: The Urban Institute Press.

Gray, Jeffrey S. (1996), 'The economic impact of divorce law reform', *Population Research and Policy Review*, **15** (3), 275–96.

Grossbard-Shechtman, Shoshana (1993), *On the Economics of Marriage: A Theory of Marriage, Labour and Divorce*, Boulder: Westview Press.

Heath, Julia A. and David H. Ciscel (1996), 'Escaping the fate of Sisyphus: Bargaining, divorce, and employment in the patriarchal family', *Review of Radical Political Economics*, **28** (1), 1–19.

Hill, Martha S. (1992), 'The role of economic resources and remarriage in financial assistance for children of divorce', *Journal of Family Issues*, **13** (2), 158–78.

Hoffman, Saul D. and Greg J. Duncan (1988), 'What *are* the economic consequences of divorce?', *Demography*, **25** (4), 641–45.

Holden, Karen C. and Pamela J. Smock (1991), 'The economic costs of marital dissolution: Why do women bear a disproportionate cost?', *Annual Review of Sociology*, **17**, 51–78.

Huber, Joan and Glenna Spitze (1980), 'Considering divorce: An expansion of Becker's theory of marital instability', *American Journal of Sociology*, **86** (1), 75–89.

Johnson, William R. and Jonathan Skinner (1986), 'Labour supply and marital separation', *American Economic Review*, **76** (3), 455–69.

Krein, Sheila F. and Andrea H. Beller (1988), 'Educational attainment of children from single-parent families: differences by exposure, gender, and race', *Demography*, **25** (2), 221–34.

Knox, Virginia W. and Mary Jo Bane (1994), 'Child Support and Schooling', in Irwin Garfinkel, Sara S. McLanahan and Philip K. Robins (eds), *Child Support and Child Well-being*, Washington, DC: The Urban Institute Press.

Lehrer, Evelyn (1988), 'Determinants of marital instability: a Cox-regression model', *Applied Economics*, **20** (2), 195–210.

Lehrer, Evelyn (1996), 'The determinants of marital stability: a comparative analysis of first and higher order marriages', *Research in Population Economics*, **8**, 91–121.

Lehrer, Evelyn L. and Carmel Chiswick (1993), 'Religion as determinant of marital stability', *Demography*, **30** (3), 385–404.

Lundberg, Shelly and Robert A. Pollak (1993), 'Separate spheres bargaining and the marriage market', *Journal of Political Economy*, **101** (6), 988–1010.

Lundberg, Shelly and Robert A. Pollak (1997), 'Bargaining and Distribution in Marriage', in Inga Peterson and Christina Jonung (eds), *Economics of the Family and Family Policies*, London: Routledge.

Maccoby, Eleanor E., Charlene E. Depner and Robert H. Mnookin (1988), 'Custody of Children Following Divorce', in E. Mavis Hetherington and Josephine D. Aresteh (eds), *Impact of Divorce, Single Parenting, and Stepparenting on Children*, Hillsdale, New Jersey: Lawrence Erlbaum.

Mauldin, Teresa A. (1990), 'Women who remain above the poverty level in divorce: Implications for family policy', *Family Relations*, **39** (2), 141–6.

McCrate, Elaine (1992), 'Accounting for the slowdown in the divorce rate in the 1980s: a bargaining perspective', *Review of Social Economy*, **50** (4), 404–19.

McLanahan, Sara and Gary Sandefur (1994), *Growing up with a Single Parent: What Hurts, What Helps*, Cambridge and London: Harvard University Press.

Michael, Robert (1979), 'Determinants of Divorce', in L. Levy-Garboua (ed.), *Sociological Economics*, Beverly Hills: Sage, pp. 223–68.

Okin, Susan Moller (1989), *Justice, Gender and the Family*, New York: Basic Books.

Parkman, Allen M. (1992), *No-Fault Divorce: What Went Wrong?*, Boulder: Westview Press.

Peters, H. Elizabeth (1986), 'Marriage and divorce: informational constraints and private contracting', *American Economic Review*, **76** (3), 437–54.

Saluter, Arlene F. and Terry A. Lugaila (1998), 'Marital Status and Living Arrangements: March 1996', in US Census Bureau, *Current Population Reports*, Series P20, Number 496, Washington, DC: US Census Bureau.

Seltzer, Judith, Thomas Hanson and Sara S. McLanahan (1995), 'Will Child Support Enforcement Increase Father–Child Contact and Parental Conflict after Separation?', Paper presented at the Conference on the Effects of Child Support Enforcement on Nonresident Fathers, Princeton University, September.

US Census Bureau (1997a), *Marital Status and Living Arrangements of People 18 Years Old and Older, By Sex: March 1997*, http://www.bls.census.gov/cps/pub/1997/m_status.htm

US Census Bureau (1997b), *Selected Characteristics of the Population by Race: March 1997*, http://www.bls.census.gov/cps/pub/1997/int_race.htm

US Census Bureau (1998), *Marital status and Living Arrangements: March 1996*, Current Population Reports, p20-426.

Waite, Linda J. and Lee A. Lillard (1991), 'Children and marital disruption', *American Journal of Sociology*, **96** (4), 930–53.

Weitzman, Lenore J. (1985), *The Divorce Revolution: The Unexpected Social and Economic Consequences for Women and Children*, New York: Free Press.

Domestic Abuse

In surveys of domestic abuse in a variety of countries, in excess of 20 per cent of the women have experienced physical violence in their relationships over their lifetimes (Heise et al. 1994, pp. 6–9). In any given year, 11.6 per cent of women in the USA are victims of physical abuse by a partner (Straus and Gelles 1990). Although definitions of domestic abuse are contested and subject to difficulties in measurement, it has been named as the major cause of women's injuries. One part of the controversy over the definition is what type of abuse is included. Domestic abuse can be narrowly defined as a pattern of physical abuse only. However, broader definitions include not only physical force, but a pattern of mental abuse including intense criticism, put downs and verbal harassment, sexual coercion and assaults, isolation due to restraint of normal activities and freedom, and denial of access to resources. Most researchers rely on the more narrow definition drawing from the Conflict Tactic Scales (CTS) used to measure physical violence, although some researchers do use a broader definition. Another part of the definitional problem is the relation to be used as the unit of analysis in defining domestic abuse, that is, whether the relation should be limited to married couples or should include all intimate relationships.

Domestic abuse in the USA did not become a public issue until the rise of the women's movement in the late 1960s and early 1970s. Starting at the grass roots level, feminists and battered women's advocates opened a network of shelters to provide safe havens for women and their children. The success of this movement in bringing domestic abuse to the public's attention resulted in the passage of laws, such as the Family Violence Prevention and Services Act of 1984 and the Violence Against Women's Act of 1994. It also increased development of programmes to train service providers, protocols to treat victims and mandated arrests of abusers in some states. Research to identify the extent and causes of the domestic violence problem, the impact and effectiveness of interventions, and the costs to society is still relatively young. Most of these early studies focused on sexual and/or physical violence. For economists, domestic abuse did not become an area of research until the 1990s, and it was feminist economists, for the most part, who took the lead.

The earliest studies by feminist economists (Tauchen et al. 1991; Anderson 1997; Farmer and Tiefenthaler 1997) develop models that draw heavily on Becker's altruistic model (1974, 1981) and cooperative game theoretic models (Manser and Brown 1980; McElroy and Horney 1981). Becker's model postulates that the family behaves as a rational single unit trying to maximize joint household utility (or satisfaction). Cooperative game theoretic models illustrate how family members coordinate decisions about the family. Feminist economists add a twist in that they use a noncooperative model of family decision making that introduces violent behaviour, but does not discard altruistic behaviour. The level of violence appears in the utility function of both spouses, but an increase in violence increases the utility of the husband and decreases the utility of the wife. Thus, the husband may transfer income to the wife to offset the negative impact of the violence on her level of utility. Should the level of utility within the marriage fall below the level of utility outside the marriage, the wife would leave the abusive relationship. The level of utility outside the marriage then acts as the 'threat point', the point at which the relationship between partners ends.

Tauchen et al. (1991) test the validity of this model using data on 125 women in Santa Barbara County, California, who had been physically abused by an intimate and had sought shelter. This study sought to identify the socioeconomic characteristics that determine the level of violence and the distribution of welfare in violent relationships. Later studies (Farmer and Tiefenthaler 1996; Anderson 1997; Farmer and Tiefenthaler 1997) that built on the work of this earlier study introduced the availability of services or external support as a means of raising the threat level of leaving the relationship. The empirical results are mixed for two reasons: the data differ as to the definition of violence and the socioeconomic characteristics measured, and the data differ from small samples that include only women who had sought shelter from the abuse (Tauchen et al. 1991) to national samples that include abused women who use services and those who do not (Riechers 1997). Regardless, the policy implications are the same: 'Increased opportunities outside the marriage made available through services provided by the government, charities, and family members and large divorce settlements for women are ... expected to decrease the level of violence ...' (Farmer and Tiefenthaler 1995, p. 18).

Rao (1997) introduced both qualitative and quantitative research that recognizes the broad social and cultural context in which women experience violence. His study of violence in three small villages in India is unique. He uses focus groups to determine that 'wife abuse is more likely when dowries are perceived as inadequate, when husbands are alcoholic, and when the cause of abuse is perceived as "legitimate" by the community' (Rao 1997, p. 1169). The qualitative findings act as an aid in the design of the survey and are supported by the empirical work. The policy conclusions differ, though, from those studies done in the USA and Canada. Specifically, 'strategies like the provision of women's shelters, or police intervention in cases of abuse, which may have been successful in other contexts would be of little value here unless the more fundamental problem of a woman's exclusive dependence on marriage is solved' (p. 1178). He concludes that 'the formation of women's groups within the community to combat violence may prove a more effective deterrent' by having the effect of reducing the community's tolerance for violence (p. 1178).

Little research has been done on the effectiveness of interventions in the case of domestic violence. Tauchen and Witte's (1995) work is the only economic study to evaluate the effectiveness of interventions. Specifically, they analyse the impact of three different treatments carried out by police officers in Minneapolis: advising the couple, separating the individuals temporarily and arresting the suspect. This model differs from previous research in that it looks at the effect over time. In a static model, arresting the suspect was seen as a deterrent to continued abuse. But, in Tauchen and Witte's dynamic model, they find that six months out the difference in the impact of the three methods is negligible.

The definition of domestic abuse is a crucial element in determining what to include in a measure of the economic costs associated with this social problem. A definition that relies solely on the use of physical force assumes that only assaults severe enough to result in injury will elicit costs. This narrow definition will result in lower cost estimates than a broader definition. Two of the first attempts at enumerating the various costs of domestic abuse occurred in New South Wales and Queensland, Australia (Women's Co-ordination Unit 1991; Sunshine Coast Interagency Research Group 1993). Feminist economists in Canada and the USA (Greaves et al. 1995; Day 1995; Laurence and Spalter-Roth 1995) have continued this research. The importance of these studies rests on the lack of awareness of the extent and costs of the problem to society at large. The costs of domestic abuse have a reach far beyond what one would ordinarily consider. It is known that battered women flood hospitals and mental health facilities; crowd courts, shelters and drug treatment centres; burden child welfare offices; and cost businesses millions in lost workdays and decreased productivity. Being able to measure 'the full economic impact of this issue is key to inspiring greater efforts to reduce the prevalence of violence against women. In addition, it is imperative that policies and programs be examined so that intervention and prevention in the area of violence against women are effective' (Greaves et al. 1995, p. 1).

A final area of research that has been largely ignored is the impact of public policy on victims of abuse. Recent legislation to reform welfare in the USA has brought the issue to the forefront. A report in Massachusetts (McCormick Institute and Center for Survey Research 1997) highlights the importance of such research. The change in the law afforded researchers the opportunity to interview and survey women who were reapplying for assistance. They found that 'One out of every five female TAFDC adult recipients in Massachusetts has been abused by a former or current boyfriend or husband within the last twelve months according to the definition of violence provided by Massachusetts law under the 1978 Abuse Prevention Act' (McCormick Institute and Center for Survey Research 1997, p. 3). This has important implications in shaping a welfare reform proposal. Although these women were found to 'have significant work experience and are eager to participate in school and training programs' (ibid., p. 39), abusive partners may prevent them from working or entering training programmes. From years of abuse, these women may have mental or physical consequences that prevent them from sustaining employment. If they cannot continue to receive public assistance, these women and their children may return to the abusive relationship. Such a study informs policymakers of the risk in designing a reform package that does not consider the special case of these women and their children. It encourages them to consider setting the requirements for the receipt of assistance in such a way as to reduce this risk.

Research on domestic abuse is a nascent area for feminist economists to explore. It is an area that allows feminist economists to work in interdisciplinary teams with others such as anthropologists and sociologists. Specifically, the focus on sexual/physical violence needs to be widened in two ways: the first to include psychological abuse, and the second to include women of colour, disabled women, lesbians, immigrant women and institutionalized women. For quantitative research, national and community level survey studies need to be undertaken. These surveys should yield the appropriate variables to carry out a more thorough analysis of the problem. These variables should include, but are not limited to, race, socioeconomic status, age and sexual orientation. In addition, there would be a benefit in understanding the problem if more qualitative studies such as Rao's (1997) were undertaken in countries other than India.

Important areas for further research in feminist economics may answer several questions. What are the consequences of violence on labour force participation, economic wellbeing, fertility decisions and divorce rates? What are the economic costs to society in terms of social services, lost productivity, the criminal justice system, medical care and victim assistance services? How could one evaluate both short- and long-term effects of preventive and treatment interventions? What causes some women to seek help, others to wait, and some never to seek respite from the abuse? These studies would help to inform policymakers about alternative approaches or settings for identifying and providing services to victims and the perpetrators of domestic abuse.

LOUISE LAURENCE

See also

Divorce; Family, Economics of; Game Theory and Bargaining Models; Marriage, Theory of; Welfare Reform.

Bibliography

Anderson, Deborah (1997), 'Domestic Violence: Returning to an Abuser', Cornell University, mimeo.

Becker, Gary S. (1974), 'A theory of marriage: Part II', *Journal of Political Economy*, **82** (2, Part II), (March/April), S11–S26.

Becker, Gary S. (1981), *A Treatise on the Family*, Cambridge: Harvard University Press.

Bloch, Francis and Vijayendra Rao (1997), 'Terror as a Bargaining Instrument: "Dowry" Violence in Rural India', Williams College, mimeo.

Day, Tanis (1995), *The Health-Related Costs of Violence Against Women in Canada*, Ontario: Centre for Research on Violence Against Women and Children.

Farmer, Amy and Jill Tiefenthaler (1995), 'Battered Women as Strategic Actors: A Model of

Asymmetric Information, Signaling, and Credible Threats', Colgate University, Department of Economics, Working Paper No. 9502.

Farmer, Amy and Jill Tiefenthaler (1996), 'Domestic violence: The value of services as signals', *American Economic Association Papers and Proceedings*, **86** (2), 274–9.

Farmer, Amy and Jill Tiefenthaler (1997), 'An economic analysis of domestic violence', *Review of Social Economy*, **15** (3), 337–58.

Greaves, Lorraine, Olena Hankivsky and JoAnn Kingston Riechers (1995), *Selected Estimates of the Costs of Violence Against Women*, Ontario: Centre for Research on Violence Against Women and Children.

Heise, Lori L., Jacqueline Pitanguy and Adrienne Germain (1994), *Violence Against Women: The Hidden Health Burden*, World Bank Discussion Paper No. 255, Washington, DC: The World Bank.

Laurence, Louise and Roberta Spalter-Roth (1995), 'Measuring the Costs of Domestic Violence Against Women and the Cost-Effectiveness of Interventions: An Initial Assessment and Proposals for Further Research', Washington, DC: Institute for Women's Policy Research.

Manser, M. and M. Brown (1980), 'Marriage and household decision making: a bargaining analysis', *International Economic Review*, **21** (1), (February), 31–44.

McCormick Institute and Center for Survey Research (1997), *In Harm's Way? Domestic Violence, AFDC Receipt, and Welfare Reform in Massachusetts*, Boston: University of Massachusetts Boston.

McElroy, M.S. and M.J. Horney (1981), 'Nash-bargained household decisions: Toward a generalization of the theory of demand', *International Economic Review*, **22** (2), (June), 333–49.

Rao, Vijayendra (1997), 'Wife-beating in rural South India: a qualitative and econometric analysis', *Social Science Medicine*, **44** (8), 1169–80.

Rao, Vijayendra (1998), 'Wife-abuse, its Causes and its Impact on Intra-Household Resource Allocation in Rural Karnataka: A "Participatory" Econometric Analysis', in M. Krishnaraj, R. Sudershan and A. Shariff (eds), *Gender Issues in Population, Health, and Development*, Oxford, England: Oxford University Press.

Riechers, JoAnn Kingston (1997), 'Does Economic Status Affect the Frequency of Domestic Abuse?', McMaster University, mimeo.

Straus, Murray A. and Richard J. Gelles (1990), 'How Violent are American Families? Estimates from the National Family Violence Resurvey and other studies', in M.A. Straus and R.J. Gelles (eds), *Physical Violence in American Families: Risk Factors and Adaptations to Violence in 8,145 Families*, New Brunswick, New Jersey: Transaction Publishers, pp. 95–112.

Sunshine Coast Interagency Research Group (1993), *Who Pays? The Economic Costs of Violence Against Women*, Queensland, Australia: Women's Policy Unit, Office of the Cabinet.

Tauchen, Helen V., Ann Dryden Witte and Sharon K. Long (1991), 'Domestic violence: a nonrandom affair', *International Economic Review*, **32** (2), 491–511.

Tauchen, Helen V. and Ann Dryden Witte (1995), 'The dynamics of domestic violence', *American Economic Association Papers and Proceedings*, **85** (2), 414–18.

Women's Co-ordination Unit (1991), *Costs of Domestic Violence*, New South Wales.

Domestic Labour

Although nineteenth-century economists took an interest in nonmarket forms of production, including subsistence agriculture and domestic labour, by the turn of the century the economy and economics had been more narrowly defined. The study of domestic labour was dispatched early in the twentieth century, in the United States at least, to the newly-created discipline of home economics (Gardiner 1997). Margaret Reid became one of the few successful economists to straddle the divide between home economics and mainstream economics, with her *Economics of Household Production* for which the University of Chicago awarded her a PhD in Economics in 1931. She defined household production as comprising those unpaid activities carried on by members of a household for each other which 'might be replaced by market goods or services, if circumstances such as income, market conditions and personal inclinations permit the services being delegated to someone outside the household group' (Reid 1934, p. 11). Similar definitions have been used by writers on domestic labour to this day.

The study of domestic labour resurfaced in the 1960s as married women's labour force participation increased in most advanced capitalist economies, particularly the USA and Northern Europe. Both orthodox and more radical economists began to recognize and attempt to explain the ways in which female labour did not conform to the patterns of male employment. As well as analysing discrimination in employment practices, both schools focused on the different conditions under which men and women entered the labour market and identified unequal domestic responsibilities as a major source of such differences. The New Home Economics used the individualist utility-maximizing methodology of neoclassical economics to analyse time spent within the home as 'nonmarket time', which they classified as neither consumption nor production. The radical approach, influenced by a growing interest in Marxist political economy, preferred to use the term 'domestic labour' to stress the difference in the social relations under which unpaid work within the home took place from those of commodity-producing wage labour. This entry will concentrate on the analysis carried out within the radical approach and, in particular, on the lively 'domestic labour debate' that ensued.

In the late 1960s and 1970s, the dominant intellectual programme within feminism, particularly Marxist feminism, focused on uncovering the material conditions of women's oppression. This programme of analysis represented an interpretation of Karl Marx's method of historical materialism, according to which the social relations under which work is organized provide the basis upon which all other aspects of society depend. The analysis of domestic labour, as characteristically women's work, would thus provide the material basis for an understanding of women's oppression in all its forms.

With the greater appreciation of the importance of culture that came in the 1980s, less feminist interest was shown in theoretical debates that concentrated on the material aspects of domestic labour. Nevertheless domestic labour had been rendered visible and the main insights from the analysis of domestic labour, that women's domestic contributions were important to society and that the unequal allocation of responsibilities for domestic labour between women and men prevented women from contributing to and benefiting materially from society on the same terms as men, became widely accepted. For example, an increasing number of countries have started to include some measure of domestic labour in the national accounts, or are debating whether and how to do so. At an international level, the 1993 revision of the System of National Accounts (SNA) recommended for the first time that *all* production of *goods* in households for their own consumption be included in the measurement of economic activity. The United Nations Human Development Report, which produced the first international Gender Development Index, took this a step further by examining the inequality of hours worked by women and men in household *service activities*, such as cooking, cleaning and the care of children and the elderly that remained excluded from the SNA (United Nations Development Programme 1995). The Beijing Conference on Women recommended that data collection on unremunerated work, including that which is currently outside national accounts, be improved and that methods be developed for valuing such work for presentation in satellite accounts, 'with a view to recognising the economic contribution of women and making visible the unequal contribution of remunerated and unremunerated work between women and men' (United Nations 1995, recommendation 206 (f) (iii)).

Further, the analysis of domestic labour is beginning to have an influence on policy, particularly with respect to developing countries where unpaid labour has to be taken into account as a constraint on the extent to which family labour can be shifted from one sector to another in economic restructuring (Catagay et al. 1995). In developed economies too, policy analysts are increasingly recognizing that the family wage model in which women are taken as financially dependent full-time domestic labourers is now outdated, and that without taking account of the relationship between gendered domestic and wage-earning potentialities, effective economic policies in many areas including pay equity, labour market regulation, fiscal policy and welfare reform cannot be developed.

Debates on how to characterize domestic labour were a formative influence on Marxist Feminism, a school of feminism characterized both by its use of Marxist methods of analysis and its critique of traditional Marxism. The common ground was the use of an historical materialist method of analysis whose starting point was the recognition of historically specific modes of production within which different economic processes applied. In contrast to neoclassical economics, there were no universal economic laws to be derived from trans-historical assumptions about human nature. Rather, different types of society could be characterized by their different relations of production, in particular the relation between a class of producers and a ruling class that, through its dominant position in the mode of production, had power over all other aspects of that society too. The power of any ruling class rested on its extraction and control of a surplus, over and above the level of production that was needed to reproduce the population.

However, as feminists pointed out, Marxist economic analysis had consistently ignored the existence of domestic labour, by talking as though all the working class needed to do to reproduce itself was to consume commodities bought with the wage. Up to then, Marxist political economy had failed to recognize the quantitative importance of the labour that turned purchased commodities into the cooked meals, washed clothes and clean houses that adult workers required, as well as provided the child care that was necessary if a future generation of workers was to be reproduced. More significantly, from a historical materialist perspective, existing Marxist analysis had ignored the distinctive social relations of domestic labour, seeing wage labour for capital as the only significant type of labour under capitalism. Marxist feminists pointed out that domestic labour was equally necessary to the continuation of the capitalist model of production as the wage labour on which Marxist analysis had focused. The common ground in what subsequently became known as 'the domestic labour debate' was the recognition of this lacuna in traditional Marxist analysis; the debate was about how exactly it should be filled.

One dispute centred on whether domestic labour constituted a mode of production in itself, with its own ruling class (husbands) and producing class (women). The non-Marxist materialist feminist, Christine Delphy, argued that marriage was a universal instrument for the subordination of women through husbands' appropriation of their wives' labour power (Delphy 1984). The trans-historical nature of the claim led her position to be rejected by many Marxist feminists, who saw domestic labour as having changing relations of production distinct from but shaped by those of the dominant modes of production with which they coexisted.

A related aspect of the debate centred on whether domestic labour should be seen as 'productive'. Productive labour within Marxist theory is the labour that directly produces surplus value, upon which the capitalist system of production for profit depends. The Wages for Housework campaign, led by Selma James and Mariarosa Dalla Costa, argued that domestic labour produced surplus value and was just like waged work in all respects except that it was unpaid (Dalla Costa and James 1972). Feminist strategy should therefore focus on gaining wages for housework to give all women the bargaining power of waged workers.

Against this, it was argued that wages for housework would entrench rather than remove the gender division of labour between family and economy. This was because domestic labour differed from waged work in more ways than just being unpaid; to understand the persistence of the gender division of labour, the specific social relations of domestic labour had to be analysed. Domestic labourers generally had more control of their own working practices than wage workers, but fewer opportunities through specialization and co-operation for productivity improvements. Further, domestic production was not subject to the pressure of competition to minimize labour time in order to improve productivity. In Marxist terms this meant that domestic labour was not subject to the law of value which imposed a common measure of labour time across different forms of capitalist production. There was therefore no process by which an hour of one person's domestic labour was made comparable to an hour of someone else's, or an hour of domestic labour applied to one task made comparable to an hour on another task. So to ask whether housework produced a surplus was a meaningless question, because the amount of time people devoted to housework could not be compared with the labour time embodied in the commodities they consumed (Himmelweit and Mohun 1977).

A third and again related debate turned on who gained from domestic labour. For those who saw domestic labour as producing a surplus, the question was how and by whom that surplus was appropriated. If a housewife's surplus product was appropriated by employers, through her domestic labour allowing lower wages to be paid to the wage earners in her household, then both housewives and wage earners had common oppressors. If, on the other hand, it was the direct consumers of a woman's domestic labour who appropriated her surplus labour, then it was the other members of her family who were her oppressors and against whom feminist struggle needed to be waged. In this case, exploitative relations within the home meant that housewives formed a class with interests in common with each other and distinct from those of wage earners.

Hartmann (1976) took a different approach to the question of who gained from domestic labour. She saw women's domestic labour and their exclusion from well-paying jobs as the result of a historic compromise between capitalism and patriarchy in which working class men's resistance to capital was bought off by paying them a 'family wage' that gave them access to and control of their wives' domestic labour. Against this Humphries (1977) argued that all members of the working class, including women, benefited from men's higher wages freeing married women from the need to take employment so that the whole family could gain from their domestic labour. In Humphries' view, the main dynamic involved was a negotiation between capital concerned about the deteriorating quality of its labour force and a working class keen to improve its standard of living. Barrett and McIntosh (1980) argued that the working class could have pursued a less gender-differentiated strategy and although some women gained some immediate benefits, there were deleterious effects on others in the short term and all in the longer term: women without male breadwinners in their households faced dire poverty and wives in general were made financially dependent on their husbands.

Looking back over this debate today, some of the theoretical issues seem arcane. The debate itself, however, proved useful to those who remained within the Marxist tradition, because it provided a focus for clarifying and refining the use of Marxist terms, as well as showing their limitations in analysing social relations outside those of capitalist production. The debate may seem old fashioned today partly because so many of its insights are taken for granted in modern feminist economic thought. The debate raised awareness that the household is a unit of production as well as consumption, even in modern capitalist economies, so that people's standard of living depends not only on the level of wages and the provision of public services, but on domestically produced goods and services too. Further, the debate demonstrated that capitalist production is not self-sufficient but depends on domestic labour that goes on outside capitalist relations, with many interesting issues turning on the changing relationship between the domestic and capitalist sectors of the economy across space and time (Gardiner 1997).

All these points have since led to interesting empirical work, for example, the reassessment of historical and contemporary growth rates by considering the extent to which they were boosted by an influx of labour from domestic production. Aslaksen and Koren (1996) calculated that over the past 20 years Norwegian growth rates have been overestimated by as much as 25 per cent through ignoring the increased labour force participation of women and the consequent shifting of much human capital formation from the domestic to the market sector. However, Wagman and Folbre (1996) showed that ignoring domestic labour does not always result in overestimation of growth rates. In a historical study of the US economy, they found that for the periods 1870–90 and 1910–30 growth rates were higher when domestic production was taken into account, although in the intervening period, 1890–1910, market GNP had a higher growth rate than it would if adjusted to take account of domestic production too. In a cross-sectional study estimating adjusted measures of GNP per capita for 132 contemporary economies, Cloud and Garrett (1997) found that measures such as GNP consistently but unevenly underestimated total production by leaving out the contribution of unpaid domestic labour to human capital formation.

Critiques of the domestic labour debate called into question two common features of its analysis: its tendency to universalize the position of the white Western housewife, and its failure to connect with the issue of gender divisions in society.

Molyneux (1979) criticized the domestic labour debate for being conducted at the wrong level of analysis, as if an ideal version of the domestic arrangements of Western capitalism were of the same level of generality as capitalist production itself. Instead, she argued that the historically specific contemporary domestic arrangements of a particular stage in European and

North American capitalism were but one way that reproduction could be arranged to coexist with capitalist production, not the only way. The empirical and historical analysis of domestic relations of production was a worthwhile project, but not the attempt logically to derive their existence from the form of capitalist production in an abstract way that ignored their historically specific and changing character.

Recognizing this changing character of domestic labour, Coulson et al. (1975) were among the first of many to criticize the debate for being conducted as though all domestic labour was done by housewives who did not also engage in wage labour. In practice, they pointed out, most women in most capitalist economies carry out both domestic and wage labour, so that the 'central feature of women's position under capitalism is not their role simply as domestic workers, but rather the fact that they are *both* domestic and wage labourers' (p. 60, their emphasis). This did not invalidate the whole idea of analysing domestic labour as a different type of labour from wage labour, but put the emphasis on understanding how women coped with the interface between two different types of relations of production.

This criticism of the debate for ignoring the reality of women's lives is closely related to another critique: while the intention of the debate was to uncover the material basis of women's oppression by focusing on the social relations under which a particular type of labour went on, it ignored the question of why there was specialization in that sort of labour and failed to explain how such specialization related to the gender division of labour. Some writers took a dual systems approach which invoked a notion of capitalist patriarchy, in which capitalism provided the positions for different types of workers, while patriarchy was the decisive force in dividing those positions between men and women. Hartmann's answer made patriarchy more structural than that, so that from an economic perspective 'the creation of gender can be thought of as the creation of a division of labour between the sexes, the creation of two categories of workers who need each other', that is, wage-earning men and domestic labour-performing women (Hartmann 1981, p. 371). So for her the existence of domestic labour and the gender of who did it were intimately related under patriarchal capitalism and she saw domestic labour as the primary economic way in which men exercised patriarchal power over women.

Maureen Mackintosh saw the failure to explain why it was women who performed the bulk of domestic labour as a consequence of ignoring the specific use-value content of domestic labour in concentrating on its private non-capitalist social relations. Only by explaining the link between the two meanings of 'domestic work as work done within the home, and domestic work as a particular kind of work, such as child care, cooking and cleaning, servicing the members of a household' would any understanding of the sexual division of labour between domestic and other types of labour be achieved (Mackintosh 1979, p. 175).

In concentrating on the specific content of domestic labour, Benería (1979) argued that the role domestic labour plays in human reproduction was key to understanding gender divisions. Himmelweit (1984) took this further by arguing that the separation between relations of production and reproduction is a historically specific one, taken to its extreme in the separation of home and workplace, work and leisure, production and consumption in advanced capitalist societies. Domestic labour has gradually been reduced to just those reproductive and other activities that cannot be part of production under capitalism and in doing so has become seen more as a characteristically feminine (leisure) activity than a form of work.

More recently writers have seen 'care' as the irreducible content of domestic labour, thus seeing it as women's work as a consequence of a gender division of labour in society in which caring labour, whether paid or unpaid, tends to be allocated to women (Gardiner 1997). This of course just displaces the question onto why caring should be nearly universally a woman's activity, for which explanations from outside economics, based in psychology, ethics and anthropology have been sought (Bubeck 1995).

The main methodological insight to come out of the debate and its critiques was the recognition that the reproduction of the next generation and the different social relations of domestic labour required a different sort of analysis, a different economic methodology, from that developed for the analysis of capitalist production relations. In particular it led to a recognition that what fundamentally distinguishes domestic labour was its caring and relational aspects and that these needed both empirical and theoretical analysis.

Jean Gardiner observes that empirical accounts, relying on time use studies, frequently do not recognise the significance of the care elements in domestic labour. Except when there are very young children, time use studies do not record child care as taking a sizeable portion of domestic time. Yet care responsibilities for children or elderly parents remain the most significant variable affecting women's labour force participation and hours of employment. Gardiner suggests that the solution to this apparent paradox is in the less tangible nature of caring labour, which time budget studies, focusing on physical tasks, fail to capture. An important part of child care consists of 'planning, supporting, supervising and communicating with children' (Gardiner 1997, p. 175). But these are often the least observable aspects of domestic labour and, even if child care is the reason the parent is at home, it is frequently the more physical tasks that go alongside child care that get recorded. Indeed many of those physical tasks may be taking place in the home only because child care is going on there; the carer, prevented from taking employment, has time to spend on other domestic tasks and less money to spend on substitutes, and home-based child care requires more domestic tidying, cooking and so on than nursery based care.

Gardiner argues that there is an increasing tendency for the 'care of people and the maintenance of social relationships' to be the central aspect of domestic labour, despite its failure to be recorded or even perceived as work by those who do it. She thinks, however, that this perception is changing; productivity increases in the physical tasks involved in domestic labour render the interpersonal, relational aspects of women's domestic labour more visible and make the emotional and educational aspects of caring for children assume more importance than their physical care. As with other types of work, technology cannot replace, and indeed may expand, some of the more skilled aspects of domestic labour, so that the interpersonal skills they require, so frequently devalued along with the work itself, should become more valued.

Indeed perhaps the fundamental personal and relational nature of women's domestic activities has been obscured by referring to domestic labour as unpaid 'work' (Himmelweit 1995). Certainly domestic activities have some characteristics in common with work as commonly defined. Such activities take time and energy and form part of a division of labour. However much domestic activity does not conform to a third characteristic of work, which applies to the production of most marketed goods and some services, that the performance of a task can be separated from the person who performs it. Many domestic activities cannot be transferred to another person without fundamentally changing the nature of the task performed. Indeed, to go back to Reid's definition with which this entry started, they can 'be replaced by market goods and services, if circumstances such as income, market conditions and personal inclinations permit'. However in so doing the 'product' is changed to one with a different relational content; buying someone a meal in a restaurant conveys a different meaning from cooking a meal at home; a paid worker can provide excellent child care but the relationship she builds with her charge is her own, not that of her employer (Himmelweit 1995).

A major task for feminist economics is to understand labour that is fundamentally relational, rather than defined by a distinct product. Such labour has its own motivations, forms of division and remuneration, is allocated and its results distributed differently from the types of labour typically considered in economics. Rather than arguing about the ways in which domestic labour does and does not conform to existing accounts of labour and production, a feminist economic analysis needs to analyse, both empirically and theoretically, the relational aspect of labour, an aspect which is not only fundamental to most domestic labour, but is also increasingly being recognized as relevant to much paid labour too.

SUSAN HIMMELWEIT

See also
Capitalism; Double Day/Second Shift; Family, Economics of; Family Wage; Labour Force Participation; Marxist Political Economics.

Bibliography

Aslaksen, Julie and Charlotte Koren (1996), 'Unpaid household work and the distribution of extended income: The Norwegian experience', *Feminist Economics*, 2 (3), 65–80.
Barrett, Michèle and Mary McIntosh (1980), 'The family wage: Some problems for socialists and feminists', *Capital and Class*, 11, 51–73.
Benería, Lourdes (1979), 'Reproduction, production and the sexual division of labour', *Cambridge Journal of Economics*, 3 (3), 203–25.
Bubeck, Diemut Elisabet (1995), *Care, Gender, and Justice*, Oxford: Clarendon Press.
Catagay, N., D. Elson and C. Grown (eds) (1995), Special Issue on Gender Adjustment and Macroeconomics, *World Development*, 23 (11).
Cloud, Kathleen and Nancy Garrett (1997), 'A modest proposal for inclusion of women's household human capital production in analysis of structural transformation', *Feminist Economics*, 3 (1), 151–77.
Coulson, Margaret, Branka Magas and Hilary Wainwright (1975), 'The housewife and her labour under capitalism – a critique', *New Left Review*, (89), 59–71.
Dalla Costa, Mariarosa and Selma James (1972), *The Power of Women and the Subversion of the Community*, Bristol: Falling Wall Press.
Delphy, Christine (1984), 'The Main Enemy', in Christine Delphy (ed.), *Close to Home: A Materialist Analysis of Women's Oppression*, London: Hutchinson, pp. 57–77 (originally published in French in *Partisans*, 54–5, 1970).
Folbre, Nancy and Michèle Pujol (eds) (1996), Special Issue in Honour of Margaret Reid, *Feminist Economics*, 2 (3).
Gardiner, Jean (1997), *Gender, Care and Economics*, London: Macmillan.
Hartmann, Heidi (1976), 'Capitalism, patriarchy and job segregation by sex', *Signs: Journal of Women in Culture and Society*, 1 (3) part 2, 137–69.
Hartmann, Heidi (1981), 'The family as the locus of gender, class and political struggle: the example of housework', *Signs: Journal of Women in Culture and Society*, 6 (3), 366–94.
Himmelweit, Susan (1984), 'The real dualism of sex and class', *Review of Radical Political Economics*, 16 (1), 167–83.
Himmelweit, Susan (1995) 'The discovery of "unpaid work": The social consequences of the expansion of "work"', *Feminist Economics*, 1 (2), 1–20.
Himmelweit, Susan and Simon Mohun (1977), 'Domestic labour and capital', *Cambridge Journal of Economics*, 1 (1), 15–31.
Humphries, Jane (1977), 'Class struggle and the persistence of the working class family', *Cambridge Journal of Economics*, 1 (2), 241–58.
Mackintosh, Maureen (1979), 'Domestic Labour and the Household', in Sandra Burman (ed.), *Fit Work for Women*, London: Croom Helm, pp. 173–91.
Molyneux, Maxine (1979), 'Beyond the domestic labour debate', *New Left Review*, (116), 3–27.
Reid, Margaret (1934), *Economics of Household Production*, New York: John Wiley.
United Nations (1995), *Report of the Fourth World Conference on Women*, Beijing, 4–15 September, 1995.
United Nations Development Programme (1995), *Human Development Report 1995*, New York: Oxford University Press.
Wagman, Barnet and Nancy Folbre (1996), 'Household services and economic growth in the United States, 1870–1930', *Feminist Economics* (1), 43–66.

Double Day/Second Shift

The term 'double day/second shift' (and other similar terms such as 'double burden', 'dual roles', 'double shift') has been commonly used to describe the nature and manner of work typically performed by women who are engaged in both paid and unpaid work. These expressions have been so popular in both feminist and general literature that their origins are somewhat lost. Over the last few decades, increasing numbers of women have taken on the role of income earners (paid work), yet at the same time they continue to perform their traditional roles as household managers and child care providers (unpaid work). Although men in some societies seem to be taking on more household chores as indicated in a number of time-use studies (Juster and Stafford 1991; Robinson and Godbey 1997), much of the unpaid work at home and in the community such as domestic chores, child care, care of the sick and backyard gardening still fall on women. This work burden is heightened even more during periods of economic recession and crises, cutbacks in government expenditures and declines in real wages. In addition to their dual roles, many poor women work as substitute service providers and as community managers, their 'third role' as feminists are quick to point out (Moser 1991; Benería 1992; Lind 1997).

The multiplicity of roles that women perform, as income earners, principal housework and child care providers as well as community managers, compels them to seek ways to relieve time pressure. For some, this means reducing the time for leisure and/or sleep. But for many working women, the biological limit as to the number of working hours they can do has already been reached. There is little room for lengthening the 'double (work) day' so that women end up developing a facility to juggle many tasks by performing two or more activities at a time. This particular coping strategy, referred to as overlapping activities in time-use studies, is defined as the simultaneous performance of two or more tasks by an individual.

More recently, however, feminists have pointed out that this dimension of time use conveys important information on the quality of life that existing measurements of living standards do not (Floro 1995a). After all, any inquiry into people's welfare must involve not only asking how much people earn but also how they conduct their work in order to acquire goods and services to meet their needs. Intensification of work, in the sense that a person is exerting more effort (physical and/or mental) per unit of time by simultaneously performing two or more activities, is a qualitative dimension of time use that is particularly relevant to women and their wellbeing. For example, a woman may be taking care of a child while working as a market vendor or washing clothes while cooking food.

Although the concept of work intensity has received little attention in both economic and feminist literature, there is growing evidence that suggests it is not an isolated nor trivial phenomenon. Several time-use studies in the United States and Australia show that the overlapping of activities particularly involving child care is quite common among women, more so than among men (Hill 1985; Bittman and Pixley 1997). Likewise, the findings of feminist studies on household strategies during economic crisis show that intensification of work has been an important coping mechanism for many women. Studies on homeworking and informal sector activities show a high incidence among women workers in Bangladesh, Mexico, the United States and Spain of combining market work and domestic activities such as cleaning, cooking and child care (Roldan 1985; Hossain 1988; Lozano 1989). Although most of these jobs are low paid, they can be started and interrupted at will and are easily combined with such tasks as the supervision of children and cooking. Some women take their household responsibilities with them to work. In a Delhi study of slum dwellers, for example, Karlekar (1982) points out that 30 per cent of women streetsweepers take their children with them. DeVanzo and Lee (1983) likewise find a high incidence of combining child care with paid work especially among Malaysian women without any child care substitutes. Deere (1990) and Creevey (1986) also have pointed out that overlapping activities is one characteristic governing peasant women's work throughout Latin America and the Sahel region in Africa.

The occurrence of 'double day' for working women and the incidence of 'work intensity' have generally been validated by the results of time-use surveys. These surveys have provided one of the most useful sets of data on women and men and their participation in activities. While varying in form and method of collection, time-use surveys typically record the various activities (such as work, child care, domestic chore, leisure, travel, personal care and sleep) an individual engages in a given period (usually a day) and the amount of time spent per activity. The first systematic collection of time allocation data originated in the former USSR by S.G. Strumilin in 1924 (Juster and Stafford 1991; Szalai 1966). Similar data were collected for specific topics such as leisure time and commuting time from selected population samples (mostly urban) over the next few decades in Europe and in the United States (Juster and Stafford 1991). In the mid 1960s, the Hungarian sociologist Alexander Szalai made the first attempt to collect methodologically comparable data for a large number of countries which include USA, USSR, Hungary, Germany, Yugoslavia, East Germany, Peru, Poland, Belgium, France and Bulgaria (Szalai 1966, 1972). Within the United States, time-use studies were conducted in 1965/66, 1975/76 and 1981 by the Survey Research Center at the University of Michigan and by the Survey Research Center at the University of Maryland in 1985 and 1992–94 (Juster and Stafford 1985, 1991; Stinson 1997).

National time-use surveys generally have been motivated by the need to construct more complete national income accounts and to develop a better picture of the quality of life that people have. Government agencies in several countries including Canada, Australia, Denmark and Germany have conducted time-use studies on a periodic basis for such purposes (Goldschmidt-Clermont and Pagnossin-Alligisakis 1995; Stinson 1997). Currently, the European Union countries are planning a harmonized set of national time-use surveys with a standard set of methodologies for the survey instrument and collection procedures (Ironmonger 1997). But the most critical gap remains in the developing countries. Although time-allocation surveys have been conducted in the 1960s and 1970s in several countries like Botswana, Cameroon and Bangladesh, the coverage and method vary widely, ranging from small samples of rural villages to more extensive survey coverage, and from anthropological field observation to usage of time-use diaries (Goldschmidt-Clermont 1987).

Over the last decade, feminist economists' challenges to the invisibility of unpaid work in economic analysis and policymaking have contributed to significant progress in accounting for unpaid work and in developing more comprehensive time-use data collection methods (Benería 1995). Presently, the United Nations Statistical Division and the United Nations Development Programme and Statistics Canada have pushed for the documentation and measurement of unpaid work in developing countries (United Nations 1995; Statistics Canada 1995). Several national governments including India, Laos and South Korea are currently conducting national time-use studies with special focus on unpaid work.

Nonetheless, there are some dimensions and aspects of wellbeing that have yet to be examined using such data, and the potential of time-use data for examining more rigorously the gendered effects of government policy has yet to be realized. For example, the measurement and documentation of work intensity has received little attention partly as a result of the methodological limitations of existing time use methods and analysis (Floro 1995b). Household surveys on time-use have not progressed much in terms of providing information on the incidence of work intensity. In early time-use surveys, overlapping activities were ignored in the time diary and recall methods, thus making their documentation problematic. This omission has in fact been acknowledged in a few studies of household time use and is considered by social scientists to be a serious methodological problem. It has also created a systematic bias in the reporting of unpaid work. For example, the amount of labour devoted to certain nonmarket work such as child care tends to be underestimated; as Robinson and Godbey (1997) found, adding secondary activity child care time increased the total amount of time devoted to child care. Australian time-use data suggest that as much as three-quarters of all time spent in child care may be accompanied by another activity (Bittman and Pixley 1997). Although most time-use surveys now collect data for primary as well as secondary activities, little systematic study of the nature of overlapping activities has been conducted, thus contributing to the under-recognition of the time-intensiveness of unpaid work.

There are serious welfare consequences of work intensity which makes its study an urgent research agenda for academics and policymakers. Studies on women homeworkers in Mexico, Germany and Spain respectively show that long hours of work coupled with prolonged periods of high levels of work intensity can have negative effects on women's health (Roldan 1985; Sichtermann 1988; Benton 1989). Women who find themselves to be both 'time-poor' and 'money-poor' are subject to considerable stress and eventual deterioration of health. This connection between work processes and women's health, in fact, has been reported in several medical and psychology studies (Baruch et al. 1987; Verbrugge 1987).

A working life characterized by double day and work intensity reflects a nontangible cost dimension of poverty and feeble social policies. There are adverse consequences on the social growth and learning process of children if women continue to perform a disproportionate share of housework and at the same time are compelled by economic necessity to work long hours for pay. The resulting intensification of work may lower the level of attention children receive for extended periods and, depending on the type of job available, may even expose the children to non-stimulating and potentially dangerous environments and hazardous materials (Roldan 1985; Benton 1989).

Any assessment of economic and social policies therefore requires a more comprehensive evaluation not only in terms of output or levels of (money) incomes but also of resulting changes in the unpaid work burden and the level of work intensity. For example, the removal of food price subsidies in developing countries is usually analysed in terms of shifts in money income and consumption levels which serve as indicators of how the policy reform affects living standards. But household income–consumption surveys do not adequately convey the other important changes that may have resulted from such a policy. Household members, particularly women, may be compelled to employ coping strategies such as working longer hours and increasing the intensification of work. The invisibility of increased unpaid work and incidence of overlapping tasks is likely to give a false impression of the effectiveness of policy reform (Floro 1995a).

Existing welfare indices also do not take into account the serious consequences of prolonged periods of work intensity particularly for women who maintain their families alone and who are likely to be both time-poor and money-poor (Folbre 1997). In addition, these indices neglect the intergenerational effects of women's greater work intensity, a situation made worse in recent years by the government downsizing that has occurred as a part of economic restructuring. As the production of basic social services and the costs of raising children are transferred from the government to the individual, these families in particular are likely to suffer negative repercussions from changes in women's work intensity.

Although there has been significant progress in the documentation of paid and unpaid work, there is still much to be done in terms of developing new methods of measuring and studying the processes of work that convey more complete information on the quality of life. This requires, however, several steps. First, conventional survey methods of collecting time-use data need to be revised to facilitate the measure of overlapping activities and to identify which households and their members are likely to engage in such activities. This would involve collecting data on multiple activity episodes obtained by diary or recall so that both the main or primary activity and any possible other activities (secondary and tertiary) during a given time period can be recorded. Secondly, there is a need to devise a means of ranking activities by the effort involved in order to determine the relation between overlapped activities and work intensification. Since some overlapping activities can actually be pleasing while others can be stressful, classifying activities according to the level of effort (mental or physical) expended is an important task as well.

Once this information is collected, it then needs to be presented in a composite index that includes a work intensity indicator. This would refine further the observable elements of work intensity. Fourthly, there is a need for researchers and academics to develop ways of incorporating this indicator and other observable dimensions of time use (for example, length of working hours or discretionary leisure time) into existing wellbeing or standard of living indices. Finally, the importance of a research study that explores more carefully the link between work intensity and observable aspects of women's health/level of stress and children's social development, academic performance and health levels cannot be underestimated. Ultimately, society bears the consequences when the wellbeing of its principal caregivers and household managers and that of the future generation are increasingly compromised.

MARIA SAGRARIO FLORO

See also
Domestic Labour; Economic Restructuring; Family, Economics of.

Bibliography
Barnett, Rosalind and G. Baruch (1987), 'Mother's Participation in Child Care: Patterns and Consequences', in Faye Crosby (ed.), *Spouse, Parent, Worker*, New Haven and London: Yale University Press.
Baruch, G., L. Beiner and Rosalind Barnett (1987), 'Women and gender research on work and family stress', *American Psychologist*, **42** (2), (February), 130–36.
Benería, Lourdes (1992), 'The Mexican Debt Crisis: Restructuring the Economy and the House-

hold', in Lourdes Benería and Shelley Feldman (eds), *Unequal Burden: Economic Crises, Persistent Poverty, and Women's Work*, Boulder, Colorado: Westview Press.

Benería, Lourdes (1995), 'Toward a greater integration of gender in economics', *World Development*, **23** (11), (November), 1839–50.

Benton, Laura (1989), 'Homework and industrial development: Gender roles and restructuring in the Spanish shoe industry', *World Development*, **17** (2), 255–66.

Berk, Richard and Sarah Fenstermarker Berk (1979), *Labour and Leisure at Home, Content and Organization of the Household Day*, Beverly Hills: Sage.

Bittman, Michael and Jocelyn Pixley (1997), *The Double Life of the Family: Myth, Hope and Experience*, Sydney: Allen Unwin.

Creevey, Lucy (1986), 'The Role of Women in Malian Agriculture', in Lucy Creevey (ed.), *Women Farmers in Africa*, Syracuse, New York: Syracuse University Press.

Deere, Carmen Diana (1990), *Household and Class Relations: Peasants and Landlords in Northern Peru*, Berkeley: University of California Press.

De Vanzo, Julia and Donald Lye Poh Lee (1983), 'The Comparability of Child Care with Market and Non-market Activities: Preliminary Evidence from Malaysia', in Mayra Buvinic et al. (eds), *Women and Poverty in the Third World*, Baltimore: Johns Hopkins University Press.

Floro, Maria Sagrario (1995a), 'Women's well-being, poverty and work intensity', *Feminist Economics*, **1** (3), 1–25.

Floro, Maria Sagrario (1995b), 'Economic restructuring, gender and the allocation of time', *World Development*, **23** (11), (November), 1913–29.

Folbre, Nancy (1994), *Who Pays for the Kids? Gender and the Structures of Constraint*, London: Routledge.

Folbre, Nancy (1997), 'A Time (Use Survey) for Every Purpose: Non Market Work and the Production of Human Capabilities', Paper Presented at the Conference on Time Use, Non-Market Work and Family Well-Being, Washington DC, November 20–21.

Goldschmidt-Clermont, Luisella (1987), *Economic Evaluations of Unpaid Housework: Africa, Asia, Latin America and Oceania*, Geneva: International Labour Office.

Goldschmidt-Clermont, Luisella and Elisabetta Pagnossin-Aligasakis (1995), *Measures of Un-recorded Economic Activities in Fourteen Countries*, United Nations Development Programme Working Paper, New York.

Hill, Martha (1985), 'Patterns of Time Use', in Thomas Juster and Frank Stafford (eds), *Time, Goods, and Well-Being*, Ann Arbor: University of Michigan, Institute for Social Research.

Hossain, H. (1988), 'Industrialization and Women Workers in Bangladesh: From Home-Based Work to the Factories', in N. Heyzer (ed.), *Daughters in Industry*, Kuala Lumpur: Asia Pacific Development Center.

Ironmonger, Duncan (1997), 'National Accounts of Household Productive Activities', Paper Presented at the Conference on Time Use, Non-Market Work and Family Well-Being, Washington DC, November 20–21.

Juster, Thomas and Frank Stafford (1985), *Time, Goods, and Well-Being*, Ann Arbor: University of Michigan, Institute for Social Research.

Juster, Thomas and Frank Stafford (1991), 'The Allocation of Time: Empirical Findings, Behavioral Models, and Problems of Measurement', *Journal of Economic Literature*, **29**, (June), 471–522.

Karlekar, M. (1982), *Poverty and Women's Work: A Study of Sweeper Women in Delhi*, New Delhi: Vika Publishing House.

Lind, Amy (1997), 'Gender, development and urban social change: women's community action in global cities', *World Development*, **25** (8), 1205–23.

Lozano, Beverly (1989), *The Invisible Force: Transforming American Business with Outside and Home-Based Workers*, New York: The Free Press.

Moser, Caroline (1991), 'Adjustment From Below: Low Income Women and Time and the Triple Role in Guayaquil, Ecuador', in H. Afshar and Carolyn Dennis (eds), *Women, Recession and Adjustment in the Third World*, London: Macmillan Press.

Ramu, G.N. (1989), *Women, Work and Marriage in Urban India*, New Delhi: Sage.

Robinson, John and Geoffrey Godbey (1997), *Time for Life: The Surprising Ways Americans Use Their Time*, University Park, Pennsylvania: Pennsylvania State University Press.

Roldan, Martha (1985), 'Industrial Outworking, Struggles for the Reproduction of Working Class Families and Gender Subordination', in N. Redclift and E. Mingione (eds), *Beyond Employment: Household, Gender and Subsistence*, Oxford: Basil Blackwell.

Sichtermann, Barbara (1988), 'The Conflict Between Housework and Employment', in J. Jenson, E. Hagen and C. Reddy (eds), *Feminization of the Labor Force*, Cambridge: Polity Press.

Statistics Canada (1995), *Households' Unpaid Work: Measurement and Valuation*, Studies in National Accounting, catalogue 13–693E, No. 3.

Stinson, Linda (1997), 'Using a Time Use Approach to Measure the Frequency and Duration of Non-Market Labor: Problems and Solutions', Paper Presented at the Conference on Time Use, Non-Market Work and Family Well-Being, Washington DC, November 20–21.

Szalai, Alexander (1966), 'Trends in comparative time budget research', *The American Behavioral Scientist*, IX (9), 3–8.

Szalai, Alexander (1972), *The Use of Time*, The Hague: Mouton.

Szebo, L. and E.A. Cebotarev (1990), 'Women's work patterns: a time allocation study of rural families in St. Lucia', *Canadian Journal of Development Studies*, 11 (2), 259–78.

United Nations (1995), *The World's Women 1995: Trends and Statistics*, Social Statistics and Indicators Series K., No. 12.

Verbrugge, L.M. (1987), 'Role burdens and physical health of women and men', in Faye Crosby (ed.), *Spouse, Parent, Worker: On Gender and Multiple Roles*, New Haven, Connecticut: Yale University Press.

Dualisms

Western feminist thought holds that gender relationships are integral to the larger patterns of social rank and authority, organization, practices and modes of thought in a society. Dualisms represent one mode of thought or manner in which important social distinctions, such as gender, can be articulated. They rest on a basic belief that phenomena are separable into two mutually exclusive categories or principles.

The expressions of dualism with which Western feminists may be most familiar are nineteenth-century distinctions between public and private spheres and the social doctrine of 'separate spheres' for men and women. These categories are fundamentally opposed, in the sense that their integrity depends on strict separation. Thus while men's sphere of 'the market' and women's sphere of 'the family' were defined as necessary, complementary adjuncts to one another, mixing them compromised the respective virtues of each (Rosaldo 1980). Market roles were thought to endanger women's familial morality, while charitable instincts associated with the family were deemed inconsistent with men's competitive market rationality. Moreover, separate spheres implied social hierarchy; despite their supposed moral superiority within the private family, women's exclusion from public market roles denied them public rights, privileges and authority. Such exclusionary asymmetry is characteristic of dualistic patterns of thought.

Western societies share a heritage of dualistic habits of thought and patterns of social distinctions extending back to the ancient Greeks. Dualisms have been most evident in Western philosophy, where they were first identified and criticized. Despite their philosophical inadequacies, dualisms have real social histories and effects that can bias social theories. Feminists have appropriated and extended philosophical critiques of dualism within analyses of gender relationships in society and in social theory, including feminist economics.

This entry begins with a discussion of dualism in Cartesian philosophy and in more recent positivistic philosophies of science, followed by descriptions of twentieth-century critiques of dualism that include important feminist developments. It then proceeds to a brief summary of feminist histories of dualistic principles in conventional social beliefs and their role in shaping exclusionary social principles and practices in (especially) Great Britain and the US. The final sections explore the prevalence of dualistic habits of thought within standard neoclassical economics and accompanying statements of methodology, as well as the social consequences of their expressions in social policy decisions.

Dualism and the philosophy of science
Dualistic philosophies view reality as systematically divided according to two irreducible, mutually exclusive, opposed and implicitly ranked principles. The earliest Western expressions of philosophical dualism include Plato's distinction between the eternal and the temporal, according to which transitory material phenomena are deceptive reflections, mere shadows of timeless, true and ideal essences. Other dualistic distinctions between mental, manual and reproductive functions were used by Aristotle to justify gender and class divisions in Greek society (Dewey 1929; Okin 1979, ch. 4).

Cartesian dualism, which has been highly influential in modern Western views of science, posits a radical detachment of the principle of 'mind' from the principle of 'body', or physical reality. The principles opposed in dualism are ranked and extended over a series of associated features and/or portions of reality. Thus Descartes prioritized mind over body, seeing it as the source of wisdom, rational powers and objective, universal knowledge. The physical body, meanwhile, was the seat of subjective emotions and misleading appearances and that which must be studied, disciplined, and manipulated to reveal her secrets (Keller and Grontkowski 1996). Descartes also regarded quantitative measures and mathematical logic as the ideal, 'objective' and universally reliable means for discovering unity among the diverse qualities of particular phenomena (Hadden 1994).

We can interpret Descartes' dualism as a chain of oppositions:

mind/body
reason/emotion
objective/subjective

> universal/particular
> reliable/misleading
> quantity/quality.

The oppositions are asymmetrical; terms on the left are thought to encompass or explain terms on the right, but not vice versa. Thus the left side is seen as transcendent, at the direct expense of terms on the right, which are limited and debased (see Bordo 1987).

The Cartesian view that science can be free of subjectivity is often referred to as 'modernism', particularly when science is thereby set forth as the impartial arbiter of truth, rational belief and (consequently) rational action in society. The best known justifications for the rightful social authority of science are those of 'positivism', which attributes science's special status to its unique methods. While the uniqueness of science has been variously described by different groups of positivists, in each case it has required the exclusion of some types of propositions from, or some bases for, legitimate 'scientific' knowledge. Karl Popper, who has been particularly influential among positivist economists, for example, sought to exclude propositions that were not 'falsifiable'. He thus banished Marxist historicism and Freudian psychology – two of the most important sources for contemporary feminist insights – from the realm of 'science'.

The basic positivist position is that impersonal, value-neutral, and disinterested scientific practice gradually establishes objective facts and/or successively eliminates subjective error. This requires the practitioner, *qua* scientist, to transcend all personal particularity and be distanced from his subject matter. We can now extend our chain of modernist dualisms:

> fact/value
> distance/immersion
> science/humanism.

Critiques of dualism

Dualistic, modernist views of science have fallen into disfavour in the philosophy of science. Though the critiques began with Peirce, Nietzsche and others in the late nineteenth century, Kuhn's (1962) argument is the best known. Kuhn attacked positivistic fact-value dualisms and detached-observer models of science by showing that the historical development of the natural sciences has been based on the emergence of what he called 'paradigms'. Paradigms represent a consensus of belief among interested scholars. They exemplify and codify those scholars' world view, establishing a set of central questions, priorities, values and prescribed methods then used to systematically structure and interpret observations of reality. Important phenomena may be identifiable only with the paradigm's guidance and facts only become facts when they are given interpretations consistent with other propositions within the paradigm. Arguments will be recognized as 'science' only when they conform to the accepted principles and methods of a community of scholars. Nonstandard methods, experiences, questions or values will be ignored. Kuhn described this as normal.

Kuhn's critique of positivism challenged only science's self-description, without faulting 'science as usually practiced' or questioning either the biases or the larger social origins and consequences of paradigmatic values and assumptions. It is significant, though, that most of Kuhn's examples came from physics, where the influence of social beliefs and values on scientific principles and priorities is less obvious than in the life sciences. Subsequent scholars have expanded Kuhn's analysis of the social nature of science and linked the standardized beliefs within paradigms to conventional beliefs in society. Gould (1981), a noted palaeontologist, has shown, for example, how late Victorian race and gender assumptions unconsciously biased the results of craniometric studies and early IQ testing in the USA. Similar cases abound (Keller and Longino 1996). What is taken for granted in society may become embedded in paradigms, be legitimated as science and is then protected from challenges by exclusionary methodological definitions of what types of experiences can warrant scientific belief.

Feminists have noted the androcentrism of positivistic claims to scientific objectivity, exploring their broader social foundations and effects. Because modernist values are (falsely) universalized, both their partiality and their social history are obscured; they are 'normalized', while 'other' values are tainted with abnormality. These dualisms have been studied as unconscious, habitual expressions of underlying social traditions and divisions by gender as well as race and class. Thus the philosopher of science Sandra Harding (1986) and others (see the essays in Harding 1993) argue that modernism promotes the exclusion of women and women's concerns from science; that quantitative, experimental methods are favoured over more intuitive, participant–observer methods; and that science has been used against those groups typically excluded from scientific practice. The social identities of those who sponsor or practise science are privileged in Cartesian positivist perspectives; the supposed radical detachment of scientists misrepresents the traditional exclusivity of scientific practices as transcendence.

Harding's arguments add a new pairing to the list of Cartesian oppositions

masculine/feminine

that recognizes how cultural views of women and femininity are dualistically associated with the terms of 'otherness' on the right side. While 'man' is a universalized category, 'woman' has been particularized, restricted, and disqualified from full participation in the social production of privileged – and thus potentially authoritarian – knowledge. If 'white' and 'middle class' are also normalized categories in social thought, then the disqualifying attributions of otherness will be compounded (Harding 1993).

Cultural dualism

Dualisms have a cultural history that can be examined. Feminists have contextualized questions of how science is practised, and by whom, through historical studies of exclusionary social beliefs and formations, thereby tracing the influence and evolution of cultural dualism in the modern West. Bordo (1987) has explained Descartes' dualism as an alienated response to the collapse of medieval views of social unity and to widespread social instability in the seventeenth century. Cartesian thought was a flight from the feminine connectivity of the medieval world, to masculine objectivity, as compensation for the traumatic loss of social unity. Hadden (1994) has also linked it to new commercial practices that constructed standardized social valuations through commensurate systems of money prices. He argues that new, algebraically-based business accounts provided the metaphor for Descartes' abstract, quantitative representations of disparate qualities in physical reality.

The masculine principles of Cartesian dualism also appeared in individualistic philosophies of self-determination and self-interest. Nicholson (1986) has tracked the history of individualism through public–private distinctions in Anglo-American society. Whereas medieval society recognized no private sphere, Locke's seventeenth-century theory of the social contract helped establish dualistic public–private distinctions as a new justification for state authority. Locke located the social basis of the (public) state in the free association of isolated heads of (private) landed households. Thus individualism implied autonomy and public rights based on private ownership – women and most men were excluded – and rested on dualistic divisions among social institutions (also see Pateman 1989). Since production was still organized within households, however, modern meanings of 'the family' did not yet exist.

Nineteenth-century industrialization inaugurated the social principle of 'separate spheres' for men and women. As wage labour expanded, households lost control over men's productive labour. They retained control over women's labour, but it was increasingly seen as 'unproductive' (Folbre 1991). Jennings (1993) has argued that the nineteenth-century developments added to the dualisms already noted:

public/private
market/family

man/woman
production/reproduction
money/love
autonomy/dependence
competition/cooperation
selfishness/nurturance
amoral/moral
exchange/charity.

Thus more exclusive definitions of men's and women's roles, domains and proper traits emerged, understood in terms of modified public–private distinctions and Cartesian patterns. Moreover, market economy and values were thereby elevated to positions of social preeminence. Monetary measures became the standard indices of the social worth of persons and pursuits, at the expense of persons, values and activities associated with the family.

Terms on the left formed the basis for the masculine American ethos of 'rugged individualism', while terms on the right associated women with noncompetitive, nonproductive, moral and emotional concerns for others. Men became 'breadwinners', the producers of the expanding flows of goods to meet human needs, and Economic Man appeared as the bearer of historical rationality and progress. Competition winnowed the economically fit from the unfit to yield an ever more efficient basis for further social advances (see Hofstadter 1944; Matthaei 1982). Though women reared the (masculine) actors for this historical drama and provided a necessary antidote to dehumanizing market struggles, their direct contribution to social progress was largely denied.

As 'animating myths' (Jones 1983), these dualistic constructions have constituted social norms and aspirations in the societies that produced them (particularly the USA and Great Britain), despite their misrepresentation of the actual lives of most men and women in the nineteenth (or any other) century. Paid labour by women was stigmatized, concealed and significantly undercounted (Peterson 1990) but about 20 per cent of US women were officially counted as wage earners in 1900 and their actual economic contributions were much higher. Women's domestic labour augmented standards of living, many urban women took in boarders, laundry or piecework and women contributed long hours to family shops and farms.

Over the nineteenth century, working class men struggled for higher family wages to satisfy the new, middle class norms (May 1985) while the corresponding moral, familial and dependent conceptions of women depressed their wages below subsistence levels. Living wages for women were perceived as a threat to the family, to women's moral and reproductive capacities, to proper childrearing practices and to men's breadwinner roles (Kessler-Harris 1990). Even the growing numbers of middle class, educated women who carved out new, feminine professions (teaching, nursing, social work), based on the metaphor of 'social homemaking' and public extensions of women's private moral roles, were poorly paid. Making wage labour an attractive alternative to women's dependent domesticity was deemed immoral (but see Glenn 1996 and Jennings and Champlin 1994 on somewhat different articulations of dualistic morality as applied to women of colour).

Although more privileged groups of (skilled, white, native-born) male workers had achieved the wages needed to maintain separate spheres by the turn of the century in the USA, new social forces gradually increased the numbers of women in paid labour. The growth of 'men's' market production led to new consumer goods and assigned new consumer roles to women. As consumerism spread, women in lower income households saw the need to meet rising standards through their own wages. Women's labour force participation rates increased in every decade of the twentieth century, though it was not until after World War II that the rationale gradually shifted from women's appointed concerns for the needs of their families to increasing recognition of their own rights and desires for public achievement (Kessler-Harris 1982). Despite increasing social acceptance of women's paid labour, however, the doctrine of separate spheres is still reflected in gendered job structures and occupational segregation that restrict women's opportunities, limit the market value of their skills and affirm their primary responsibility for childrearing and housework. 'Women workers' remain a special category, different from the masculine norm.

Dualism and conventional economics

The Cartesian aspects of standard economic thought are striking. Virtually every mainstream economic principles text opens with positive-normative distinctions and calls for objective analysis. McCloskey (1983) has identified the modernist aspects of traditional views of proper economic methodology and shown that modernist methodological prescriptions misrepresent the actual practices of economists. Though mathematical technique is greatly admired, no objective standards for good prediction exist and economists do not reject theoretical propositions that perform poorly. Instead, McCloskey draws on rhetoric to show that the persuasive power of economics rests on unacknowledged uses of metaphor, analogy and appeals to accepted authority. Mainstream economists' intolerance for explicitly qualitative and historical methods of study is disingenuous. Like Kuhn, however, McCloskey has called for few changes in 'economics as usually practiced'. 'Modernism is impossible', says McCloskey (1983, p. 327); economists should simply be more forthright, inclusive and civil.

McCloskey's (1993) call for greater recognition of 'feminine' (or 'conjective') styles of reasoning in economics is a step in the right direction but may be inadequate, for two main reasons. First, the descriptions of rational human beings found in standard economics conform to basic Cartesian principles; thus standard theories are themselves modernist expressions. Second, the stability of the mainstream scholarly paradigm rests on the exclusion of distracting, nonstandard methods and questions and, hence, of unorthodox practitioners from the community whose views the mainstream paradigm represents. Feminist economists have analysed each of these obstacles to greater inclusivity.

Despite the inaccuracy of economists' modernist methodological self-descriptions, modernist theoretical biases are evident in mainstream economics. The central agent of orthodox economic theory, 'Economic Man', is possessed of masculine Cartesian virtues and exclusions. England (1993) describes him as a 'separative self', a fictional Robinson Crusoe with no history or social origin. His autonomous tastes and preferences, insusceptible to interpersonal comparisons, form the irreducible basis for his calculating, selfish and rational behaviour in the competitive marketplace. Such atomistic individualism is required for the clear predictions expected from standard theory but precludes consideration of the underlying social processes of exclusion that might explain such phenomena as discrimination.

Modernist emphases on quantitative methods have also made mathematical precision an important limiting factor in the development of acceptable forms of neoclassical arguments. Historical explanations of economic processes are neglected, except when supported by statistical analysis, though even cliometric studies are relatively low-status in the profession. In game theory, which allows for somewhat less-than-deterministic outcomes, meanwhile, the mathematical need for simplifying assumptions has restricted the development of realistic explanations for social processes (like gender and power) that many feminists desire (Nelson 1996). Labour market theories have similar limitations. Mirowski (1989) has argued that the styles of mathematical reasoning still favoured in standard economics were the result of economists' attempts to mimic the successes of nineteenth-century physics. Thus the theoretical animus of standard economics is thoroughly imbued with masculine modernist principles that bias possible questions and results (see also Ferber and Nelson 1993).

Many of the concerns raised by feminist economists fall outside the central vision of neoclassical economics and/or challenge its modernist, individualistic foundations. Recognizing feminist concerns may thus require significant modifications to established principles, but paradigmatic commitments to existing standards, assumptions and styles of argument imply little reward for engagement with issues raised outside the paradigm's boundaries. Internal standards of excellence deflect potentially disruptive criticisms and devalue scholarship based on alternative perspectives or methods. In that case, simply admitting women's insights into economics may not increase women's status and influence or reduce their isolation within the profession.

Disciplinary communities also recreate their basic commitments partly through the training and socialization of new generations. The Committee on the Status of Women in the Economics Profession (CSWEP) regularly documents the small numbers of women on faculties at prestigious graduate schools and the insufficient mentoring of women students in economics. Moreover, research by women is most often cited by other women, while men tend to cite other men; professional networks are also highly segregated by gender. Given the preponderance of men, especially in the higher ranks of the profession, this effectively reduces both the impact and the visibility of women – and women's insights – within the profession (Kahn 1995; Ferber 1988). Gender segregation in society, based on cultural dualism, tends to be professionally reproduced.

Social consequences of dualistic beliefs

The dualistic biases of standard economic theories have real social consequences through both prescriptions for public policy and accepted economic indices. In the USA, the dominance of market values and faith in the rationality of market outcomes promote strong preferences for health care rationed by market prices, profits and the ability to pay, for example, rather than by methods that could improve access, especially for women, minorities and children. Standard classifications of market vs. non-market activities in National Income Accounts (GDP) also reinforce traditional views of the economic significance of men's and women's activities. Social security benefits that favour traditional households with male breadwinners and female homemakers reflect such gender divisions (Folbre 1994). In addition, income support and transfer payments programmes are divided into 'social insurance', which is legitimated by past productive contributions and market earnings, and 'social assistance' to families, which is stigmatized and made vulnerable to political challenge by the belief that it is unearned (and perhaps undeserved) public 'charity'. Men tend to be more eligible for the former, women for the latter, thus reinforcing continuing dualistic distinctions and amplifying discriminatory disadvantages in assessments of the value of men's and women's labour. Efforts to reduce discriminatory wage differentials, through policies such as comparable worth, are also hampered by the sway of dualistic beliefs. Opponents of comparable worth argue that subjective criteria for (re)counting women's occupational skills and contributions are no substitute for the rational, objective criteria reflected in market outcomes (Raisian et al. 1988). Even attempts to improve standard social and accounting classifications by representing nonmarket activities and relationships theoretically as 'market equivalents', as in Becker's (1981) view of the family, may sustain cultural dualism, however. Such attempts may only reinforce universalized masculine market norms and further obscure devalued categories.

David Chioni Moore, a scholar of feminist accounting and postmodernism, also argues that modifying methods of social valuation may be very difficult. Policies are based on standard accounting categories and practices that reflect conventional economic categories and preconfigure the raw data for economic theories and policies, thereby reproducing a circular, 'self-confirming apparatus of value recognition' (Moore 1994, p. 595). The costly social processes of attributing value and measuring social outcomes are themselves biased, as when both national income accounts and economic theory conventionally attribute the production of economic value to firms rather than households. Although alternative interpretations might be more equitable, the massive commitment of social resources to the existing apparatus for assigning value yields powerful material commitments to the measures and value attributions thereby constructed. Meanwhile, effective dissent and the construction of alternative interpretations are made prohibitively expensive for disprivileged groups. These 'technologies of gender' (or race or class) constitute a social infrastructure that channels resources and material encouragements to various social groups, thus contributing to the reproduction of their current status assignments in society, while dualistic beliefs defend the objectivity of social accounting constructions.

Perhaps nowhere are masculine modern Western market values and statistical measures more consequential than in policies to promote global economic development (Waring 1988). Dualistic constructions of value in standard economic accounts lead to systematic undercounting of the vital economic contributions of subsistence-oriented, informal or nonmarket production in poorer countries. These activities fall disproportionately to women who, in turn, have been disproportionately burdened by the dislocations of standard development policies. Moreover, though the same biases undervalue women's social contributions in much of the West, theories or policies that deny their own social construction and valuational context will not only misunderstand alternatives but may undervalue entire cultural systems. Thus the imposition of Western development policies remakes non-Western societies in the image of the modern West, reconfirms the exclusionary interpretive apparatus and may involve a wholesale disregard for all indigenous social values, arrangements, supports and environmental conditions.

Simple calls for greater inclusivity and tolerance for the insights of marginalized groups in scholarly disciplines or policy circles, like McCloskey's, can obscure the material reality of large scale investments in the existing social infrastructure of belief, practice and assessment. Greater concern and recognition for the perspectives devalued by dualistic habits of thought may require more radical reconsideration of the foundations of conventional economic thought and contemporary economic struggles to achieve more equitable policies and relations in society.

ANN JENNINGS

See also

Class; Domestic Labour; Feminist Economics; Gender; Methodology; Neoclassical Economics; Postmodernism; Race; Value.

Bibliography

Becker, Gary (1981), *A Treatise on the Family*, Cambridge, Massachusetts: Harvard University Press.

Bordo, Susan (1987), *The Flight to Objectivity*, Albany: State University of New York Press.

Dewey, John (1929), *The Quest for Certainty*, New York: Capricorn Books.

England, Paula (1993), 'The Separative Self', in Marianne Ferber and Julie Nelson (eds), *Beyond Economic Man*, Chicago: University of Chicago Press, pp. 23–36.

Ferber, Marianne (1988), 'Citations and networking', *Gender and Society*, (2), 82–9.

Ferber, Marianne and Julie Nelson (eds) (1993), *Beyond Economic Man*, Chicago: University of Chicago Press.

Folbre, Nancy (1991), 'The unproductive housewife', *Signs*, **16** (3), 463–84.

Folbre, Nancy (1994), *Who Pays for the Kids?*, London: Routledge.

Glenn, Evelyn Nakano (1996), 'From Servitude to Service Work', in Cameron Lynne Macdonald and Carmen Sirianni (eds), *Working in the Service Society*, Philadelphia: Temple University Press, pp. 115–56.

Gould, Stephen Jay (1981), *The Mismeasure of Man*, New York: W.W. Norton.

Hadden, Richard (1994), *On the Shoulders of Merchants*, Albany: State University of New York Press.

Harding, Sandra (1986), *The Science Question in Feminism*, Ithaca: Cornell University Press.

Harding, Sandra (ed.) (1993), *The Racial Economy of Science*, Bloomington: Indiana University Press.

Hofstadter, Richard (1944), *Social Darwinism in American Thought*, Philadelphia: University of Pennsylvania Press.

Jennings, Ann (1993), 'Public or Private? Institutional Economics and Feminism', in Marianne Ferber and Julie Nelson (eds), *Beyond Economic Man*, Chicago: University of Chicago Press, pp. 111–29.

Jennings, Ann and Dell Champlin (1994), 'The Cultural Contours of Race, Gender and Class Distinctions', in Janice Peterson and Doug Brown (eds), *The Economic Status of Women Under Capitalism*, Cheltenham: Edward Elgar, pp. 95–110.

Jones, Gareth Stedman (1983), *Languages of Class*, Cambridge: Cambridge University Press.

Kahn, Shulamit (1995), 'Women in the economics profession', *Journal of Economic Perspectives*, **9** (4), 193–205.

Keller, Evelyn Fox and Christine R. Grontkowski (1996), 'The Mind's Eye', in Evelyn Fox Keller and Helen Longino (eds), *Feminism and Science*, Oxford: Oxford University Press, pp. 187–202.

Keller, Evelyn and Helen Longino (1996), *Feminism and Science*, Oxford: Oxford University Press.

Kessler-Harris, Alice (1982), *Out to Work*, Oxford: Oxford University Press.

Kessler-Harris, Alice (1990), *A Woman's Wage*, Lexington: University Press of Kentucky.

Kuhn, Thomas S. (1962), *The Structure of Scientific Revolutions*, Chicago: University of Chicago Press.

Matthaei, Julie (1982), *An Economic History of Women in America*, New York: Schocken.

May, Martha (1985), 'Bread Before Roses', in Ruth Milkman (ed.), *Women, Work and Protest*, London: Routledge and Kegan Paul, pp. 1–21.

McCloskey, Donald (1983), 'The rhetoric of economics', *Journal of Economic Literature*, **21** (2), 481–517.

McCloskey, Donald (1993), 'Some Consequences of a Conjective Economics', in Marianne Ferber and Julie Nelson (eds), *Beyond Economic Man*, Chicago: University of Chicago Press, pp. 69–93.

Mirowski, Philip (1989), *More Heat than Light*, Cambridge: Cambridge University Press.

Moore, David Chioni (1994), 'Feminist Accounting Theory as a Critique of What's "Natural" in Economics', in Philip Mirowski (ed.), *Natural Images in Economic Thought*, Cambridge: Cambridge University Press, pp. 583–609.

Nelson, Julie (1996), *Feminism, Objectivity and Economics*, London: Routledge.

Nicholson, Linda (1986), *Gender and History*, New York: Columbia University Press.

Okin, Susan Moller (1979), *Women in Western Political Thought*, Princeton: Princeton University Press.

Pateman, Carole (1989), *The Disorder of Women*, Stanford, CA: Stanford University Press.

Peterson, Janice (1990), 'What's in a Number', mimeo, State University of New York at Fredonia.

Raisian, John, Michael Ward and Finis Welch (1988), 'Implementing Comparable Worth', in Garth Mangum and Peter Philips (eds), *Three Worlds of Labor Economics*, Armonk, New York: M.E. Sharpe, pp. 183–200.

Rosaldo, Michelle (1980), 'The Use and Abuse of Anthropology', *Signs*, 5, 391–417.

Waring, Marilyn (1988), *If Women Counted*, San Francisco: Harper and Row.

Econometrics

A currently popular PhD-level econometrics textbook defines econometrics as 'the field of economics that concerns itself with the application of mathematical statistics and the tools of statistical inference to the empirical measurement of relationships postulated by economic theory' (Greene 1997, p. 1). In the eighteenth and nineteenth centuries, empirical work in economics stressed data collection and inductive reasoning. The rise of econometrics signalled a move towards a tighter relationship between neoclassical economic theories arrived at through deduction, and statistical theory regarding probability and inference (Darnell 1994). As the constitution of the Econometric Society states, the object is to create 'studies which aim at a unification of the theoretical–quantitative and the empirical–quantitative approach to economic problems and that are penetrated by constructive and rigorous thinking similar to that which has come to dominate in the natural sciences' (Frisch 1933, p. 1). In addition to providing empirical measures of theoretically posited parameters (for example, price elasticities), econometrics has also increasingly come to be used for 'testing' the theories themselves (Darnell 1994). Undergraduate and graduate economics education in econometrics tends to centre around the theory underlying regression models (that is, models in which variation in one measure is thought to be related to one or more other variables and a random disturbance or error term), and the problems of statistical inference when the disturbance term is not well-behaved.

Probably the most important use of econometrics in an area of feminist concern has been the frequent use of regression models to estimate how a worker's wage is related to job and personal characteristics, including the worker's sex. The wage difference attributable to sex that is 'left over' after taking into account other variables that might influence wages (for example, years of education) – or, as it is called, the 'unexplained residual' – is often taken as evidence of labour market discrimination (for example, Blau and Ferber 1992, pp. 191–5).

Feminist economists have varied in their evaluation of the general usefulness of the econometric research methodology, for this and other topics. Some, following accepted practice, explicitly or implicitly endorse the search for 'testable' models with manageable stochastic properties (for example, Redmount 1995). Others are somewhat less sanguine about the possibility of gaining useful knowledge through econometric analysis.

For example, while some early supporters of the econometric approach had high hopes regarding the ability of 'quantitative argument and exact proof' (Schumpeter 1933, p. 12) to settle differences among economists, the abovementioned econometric studies of labour market discrimination give one clear example of the ambiguity which in fact may plague such studies, no matter how technically sophisticated they may be. Consider regression results suggesting that a wage gap still exists between men and women, even when they have the same observable skills, experience, and so on. Those who do not believe discrimination exists commonly argue that such results could be explained by the omission of important – perhaps unobservable – variables (for example, greater ambition on the part of men). On the other hand, those who believe that the impact of discrimination is actually understated by such studies will argue that some of the included variables (for example, seniority) themselves reflect labour market discrimination (Blau and Ferber 1992, p. 195; Bergmann 1989, pp. 44–5). Because of the different underlying beliefs, econometric testing will never be able to settle the argument.

While the founders of the Econometric Society glorified the melding of mathematical deduction and statistical theory, Bergmann characterizes the dominant methodology as a combination of 'musing and regression running on second-hand data' (1987, p. 192). That is, economists' primary way of theorizing is by introspection combined with 'mulling over a few factual crumbs' (p. 192), while regression analysis is used only to provide weak and inconclusive backing for one theory over another. Since 'systematic, first-hand observation of economic functioning' (p. 192), which Bergmann argues is crucial to economic science, is not part of most economists' methodology, the result has been 'silliness and confusion and fruitless controversy' (p. 198).

MacDonald (1995a, b) argues that economics exhibits masculine biases at the levels of epistemology (theory of knowledge), methodology (plan of research) and methods (techniques for gathering evidence). The resulting limitation of economic knowledge to those results regarding mathematical models which can be garnered by econometric analysis of large, secondary data sets leaves economists 'lack[ing] a "feel" for many real world issues they address' (1995a, p. 177). Without such an understanding, issues of data collection, questionnaire design and other factors which have substantial implications for how the data can be legitimately interpreted 'remain largely invisible' to the economist (1995a, p. 177). (Problems in the measurement of unpaid work – especially domestic labour and volunteer work – are a particular case in point for feminist scholars.) MacDonald suggests that progress might be made by 'borrowing methods from the other social sciences, including survey research, case studies and participant observation' (1995a, p. 175).

The source of economists' preference for theoretical precision and secondary data may lie in masculinist notions of the relationship between detachment and objectivity, according to Nelson (1993, 1996). Getting Bergmann's 'first-hand observation' or MacDonald's 'feel' for the issues requires a degree of closeness between the researcher and the subject. For researchers who confuse objectivity with detachment, closeness may seem to threaten contamination by fostering undue subjectivity. Feminist scholarship on the origins of scientific ideals have associated this fear of connection with distinctly masculine psychological and historical phenomena (for example, Harding 1995), and with the gendered cultural dualism of separation and connection. While not arguing that the standard econometric approach has no usefulness, Nelson does argue for more attention to data collection and data quality and for broader and deeper standards of reasonableness in empirical work.

Not all feminist economists agree with the critiques of Bergmann, MacDonald and Nelson, nor are all proponents of such changes in empirical methodology explicitly feminist. Gustafsson (1995), for example, responding to MacDonald, suggests that first-hand data analysis be left to the sociologists while economists, due to 'comparative advantage' gained in training, stick to the use of large, multipurpose data sets. Nelson (1996) points out that mainstream economist Lawrence Summers's (1991) advocacy of more informal and pragmatic empirical methods, as contrasted to formal econometric testing, has much in common with the above mentioned methodological concerns.

Feminist work on econometrics takes one immediately into engagement with some of the deepest epistemological foundations of the discipline, as well as with some of the most mathematically and technically sophisticated arenas of economic discourse. Feminist economists can continue to make progress in direct critique and potential modification of econometrics itself, but also may more quickly further the goal of knowledge-building in empirical economics by exploring alternative methodologies of empirical investigation.

JULIE A. NELSON

See also

Discrimination, Theories of; Dualisms; Methodology; Wage Gap.

Bibliography

Blau, Francine D. and Marianne A. Ferber (1992), *The Economics of Women, Men, and Work*, 2nd edition, Englewood Cliffs, New Jersey: Prentice Hall.
Bergmann, Barbara R. (1987), '"Measurement" or finding things out in economics', *Journal of Economic Education*, **18** (2), (Spring), 191–203.
Bergmann, Barbara R. (1989), 'Does the market for women's labour need fixing?', *Journal of Economic Perspectives*, **3** (1), (Winter), 43–60.
Darnell, Adrian C. (1994), 'Introduction', in Adrian Darnell (ed.), *The History of Econometrics: Volume I*, Brookfield, Vermont: Edward Elgar, pp. ix–xx.
Frisch, Ragnar (1933), 'Editorial', *Econometrica*, **1** (1), 1–4.
Greene, William H. (1997), *Econometric Analysis*, Upper Saddle River, New Jersey: Prentice Hall.
Gustafsson, Siv. S. (1995), 'Economic Measurement: Comments on Chapters by MacDonald, Perrons and Redmount', in Edith Kuiper and Jolande Sap (eds), *Out of the Margin: Feminist Perspectives on Economics*, London: Routledge, pp. 223–7.
Harding, Sandra (1995), 'Can feminist thought make economics more objective?', *Feminist Economics*, **1** (1), (Spring), 7–32.

MacDonald, Martha (1995a), 'The Empirical Challenges of Feminist Economics', in Edith Kuiper and Jolande Sap (eds), *Out of the Margin: Feminist Perspectives on Economics*, London: Routledge, pp. 175–97.
MacDonald, Martha (1995b), 'Feminist economics: from theory to research', *Canadian Journal of Economics*, **29** (1), 159–76.
Nelson, Julie A. (1993), 'Value-free or valueless? Notes on the pursuit of detachment in economics', *History of Political Economy*, **25** (1), 121–45.
Nelson, Julie A. (1996), *Feminism, Objectivity, and Economics*, London: Routledge.
Redmount, Esther (1995), 'Toward a Feminist Econometrics', in Edith Kuiper and Jolande Sap (eds), *Out of the Margin: Feminist Perspectives on Economics*, London: Routledge, pp. 216–22.
Schumpeter, Joseph (1933), 'The common sense of econometrics', *Econometrica*, **1** (1), 5–12.
Summers, Lawrence H. (1991), 'The scientific illusion in empirical macroeconomics', *Scandinavian Journal of Economics*, **93** (2), 129–48.

Economic History, Australia and New Zealand

On many criteria, Australia and New Zealand (referred to collectively as Australasia) score well on the position of women. Women have achieved high office in the public sector and political life, with Aotearoa (the indigenous Maori name for New Zealand) currently having women leaders of both major political parties. Both countries were pioneers in women's suffrage and political participation, each has taken equal opportunity initiatives and has a narrow gender earnings gap by international standards, each has active and vocal feminist movements, and both bureaucracies have specific structures to take account of gender issues. Developed through lobbying by some feminists in the community, treated with suspicion by others as token and ineffective, these public sector structures were sufficiently significant for the term 'femocrats' to be coined to describe them in Australia (Eisenstein 1996).

Historically, too, some feminists argue that nineteenth-century Australian society, more egalitarian and less tradition-bound than Europe, saw greater political reform and a less restrictive family life for women compared with the 'home countries' of Great Britain (Grimshaw 1980). However, the Australasian experience provides some paradoxes in interpreting the position of women. Other Australasian feminists have judged their countries to be now, and through history, at least as gender-biased as most western countries (Mercer 1975; James and Saville-Smith 1994). Further, feminist scholars have shown that women were omitted from traditional male-centred histories, which emphasize the colonial experience, public life and economic development (Summers 1975), while the masculinist portrayal of leisure culture dominated by rugby, racing and beer is still a disturbingly accurate stereotype. Generalizations which overemphasize either the positive or negative side of historical and current Australian experience for women, however, are misleading, particularly when class and race differences are considered.

Many economic issues, problems and opportunities are common to Australia and New Zealand, reflecting that these geographically isolated and sparsely populated countries (18 million people in Australia, 3.7 million in New Zealand) share more similarities than differences, particularly in patterns of settlement, economic history, labour market structures, industrial relations systems and the economic and social position of women. Consequently, the entry will largely focus on the shared economic experiences of women in the two countries, although significant differences will also be addressed.

The entry will begin by examining how British colonization, class-based immigration and the marginalization of indigenous peoples in Australasia affected women's economic status in both countries. This discussion will be followed by examining how more recent economic and political developments have affected this status.

Women's participation in paid work

Both before and after British settlement in the late eighteenth and early nineteenth centuries, the range of activities undertaken by Aboriginal and Maori women, who had been in New Zealand since around 800 AD, was wider than that of their immigrant counterparts. These activities encompassed both spiritual (the 'dreamtime' in Aboriginal culture) and economic functions, with Aboriginal women in isolated areas mustering cattle, building roads and fences and mining ochre (McGrath 1990). In New Zealand, many older Maori women were respected as 'kamatua' or elders, and they were leaders in tourism and weaving (Te Awekotuku 1991). While colonization was instrumental in economic development from which the indigenous peoples received some benefits, the costs were enormous. British colonialism in both countries involved conquest, wars, missionary activity and land confiscations and purchases for derisory recompense. In some Australian regions, Aboriginals were confined to reservations and their numbers decimated. Later, many children were taken from their mothers and brought up by Europeans (McGrath 1990).

Recently, both governments have paid some attention to past mistreatment and acknowledged the need for reparations to their indigenous people. The resurgence of Maori language, culture and political influence was more rapid than that for Aboriginal culture due to the greater relative proportion of the population (about 14 per cent Maori versus 3 per cent Aboriginal), less rural isolation and somewhat less socioeconomic disadvantage through oppressive treatment. Women have been active in this resurgence through political activism and grassroots organizing, as illustrated by the development of 'Te Kohanga Reo' (total Maori language immersion kindergartens). However, Maori and Aboriginal people continue to be disadvantaged in the crime and prison statistics and have poorer education, health, income and judicial outcomes than white Australasians, attributed by many to alienation arising from the history of colonization and ongoing domination of white European values and institutions (Spoonley 1988).

British settlement of Australasia was motivated by a complex combination of push and pull factors, with advances in transport, the spirit of adventure and opportunity in undersettled lands and missionary zeal among the pull factors. Push factors included ridding the home country and individual families of extra mouths to feed, wastrels and convicts, many of whom were more victims than real criminals, driven to petty crime by poverty. Most women in the early British migration to Australia in the late eighteenth century were transported convicts, who constituted over half the 'First Fleet' of 1480 people. Women comprised about 10 per cent of the convict group, but made up 40 per cent of the 328 000 total colonial population by 1850 (Butlin 1994, p. 28).

White women settlers in Australia have been graphically portrayed by Ann Summers as 'Damned Whores' or 'God's Police' (Summers 1975), depending on their class. Sexually abused on the transport ships, convict women had few options on arrival beyond prostitution, with employment as servants the main alternative for a few. From the 1830s, 'respectable' families and single women were enticed to migrate, and these became the wives or God's Police, having large numbers of children. For those remaining single, domestic service was the main option, with teaching an alternative for a few (Aveling and Damousi 1991).

As settlement accelerated, agricultural and service expansion was accompanied by small-scale, craft-based industrialization. Both countries were reasonably prosperous, but low population size and density led to long-term dependence on a small range of largely primary sector exports including minerals, with gold rushes contributing to boom-and-bust cycles. Although major two-way trade and inward capital ties were to the 'mother country' until the 1970s, trans-Tasman (that is Australia/New Zealand) trade has also been significant, and diversification of products and markets is now accelerating for both countries.

While women's labour force participation rose with population growth, gender-based divisions of labour remained strong, both between paid and unpaid work and within paid work. From the 1860s, clerical, factory and shop work became options in both countries for some single young women, while others trained as teachers and telegraphers, but domestic service remained the largest occupation for New Zealand women throughout the nineteenth century (Porter and Macdonald 1996). Women's factory work was largely in the clothing and footwear sectors. Australia's greater size and diversity provided alternative opportunities more rapidly, with women moving into most industries, including the public sector, so constituting a quarter of urban wage earners in Australia by 1891 (Aveling and Damousi 1991).

In both countries participation in World War I created more varied industrial and service opportunities for women, but with the return of men from the Army, women were expected to make way for them (Aveling and Damousi 1991). This was repeated in the depression of the 1930s following increasing participation in the paid labour force during the 1920s, and again after World War II. However, the rapid increase in women's employment in general, and married women's in particular, since 1950 has not been reversed, thanks partly to the dismantling of formal and informal marriage bars. Much of the recent increase, however, is in part-time work, with slow output growth, labour-saving technological change and structural adjustment policies resulting in periods of decline in total paid work hours for both men and women (Hyman 1994). This reflects a continuation of the trend to ebbs and flows in the situation of women with economic conditions. (An earlier example of this is the elimination in the 1930s depression of women from all but low level public service.) Total female labour force participation is now about average for First World countries, with levels for sole mothers somewhat low internationally, due to relatively ungenerous parental leave, family support packages and child care subsidies.

Overall, however, the range of jobs available to women in both countries has expanded rapidly in the last 50 years, in both blue- and white-collar work. In spite of this, occupational segregation by gender remains high (O'Donnell and Hall 1988). Women in principle have access to the full range of apprenticeships and skilled trades, where until the 1970s few ventured beyond hairdressing. Nevertheless, socialization and the attitudes of employers and fellow employees to female trainees mean that areas such as building, electrical and mechanical trades and welding remain heavily male. Women have entered all the professions, with the total university undergraduate population and the flows of newly-trained recruits into areas like medicine, accountancy and law now over half women. However, the highest levels in such occupations, such as medical consultants and judgeships, are still heavily male, with glass ceilings even more evident in the private sector (Hyman 1994). Self-employment in a wide range of occupations is a fast growing alternative adopted by many women.

Earnings and conditions of work
Low levels of pay and poor conditions of work in factories were common to men and women during industrialization in the nineteenth century, with women's home work particularly poorly rewarded. Skilled women tailors earned less than half what was paid to male tailors (Coney 1986). This ratio was virtually unchanged in many areas of work in New Zealand until the late 1960s, buttressed by the family wage principle recognizing men's supposed need for higher wages, and supported by industrial relations institutions, with

the first minimum wage for women set in 1936, at 47 per cent of the male rate. In the 1970s, legislation led to rapid improvements, with differentials in minimum wages disappearing, and the female–male ratio for average ordinary time hourly earnings increasing from 72 per cent to 78 per cent by 1978, creeping up slowly to 81 per cent in the subsequent 20 years (Hyman 1994).

Australia's experience is similar, with a 1907 tribunal decision implementing a minimum male or family wage, and a 1919 decision setting women's basic wages at 54 per cent of men's (O'Donnell and Hall 1988). The female–male ratio for average weekly earnings for full-time adult non-managerial employees in the private sector increased from 59 per cent in 1970 to 81 per cent in 1976, and reached 83 per cent by the late 1980s (Australia Federal Department of Employment, Education and Training Women's Bureau 1987), but has shown little change since then. Total weekly and annual earnings show wider gaps than hourly levels, with women's preponderance in part-time work and less access to overtime (Hyman 1994). Further, gains for some women from greater opportunities to enter higher paid occupations and higher levels are counterbalanced in aggregate by widening overall differentials arising mainly from deregulation of the labour market. With women still overrepresented in low-paid occupations, most female dominated jobs are losing ground, often being defined or socially constructed as lower skilled.

In the 1880s, descriptions of working conditions in New Zealand such as 'long rows of women in impossible seating, who wrapped rags around their legs as protection from the cold that seeped from the concrete floors' were common (Coney 1986, p. 19). Such crowding, unsanitary conditions and long hours in factories led to investigations by a Sweating Commission and subsequently to legislation regulating conditions in factories and other work sites. Similar sweated labour conditions were seen in Australia, with women 'the industrial cannon fodder for manufacturing growth' (Markey 1980, p. 89), both in factories and outwork, again later remedied through legislation.

Conditions of work have improved dramatically in the last hundred years. However, more recently, economic downturns and structural adjustment policies have led to increased casualization of the workforce in both countries, with low and variable weekly hours and work on call common, together with the contracting out of many jobs and the removal of employment protections. Women are overrepresented in small workplaces and service industries such as commercial cleaning, retailing and restaurant and hotel work where one or more of these trends are particularly common (O'Donnell and Hall 1988).

Overall, then, women in Australasia currently have emerged from their colonial history to enjoy reasonable economic opportunity and status by international standards. However, more market-oriented structural adjustment policies pose a threat to those outside the highly educated professional and administrative groups, producing accentuated differences between women, as class and ethnic inequalities grow, with indigenous women particularly disadvantaged.

Activism and legislation

The paradoxes associated with Australasian women's economic status are also apparent in the history of women's activism and the evolution of relevant legislation. Early Australasian women were among the first to gain some political influence through suffrage, and hence feminists were instrumental in establishing legislation and policy for improving the welfare of women and children. In addition, feminist activists participated in early unionization attempts and promoted economic equality for all women. Despite these progressive actions and positions, Australasian women have not fully achieved pay equity, equal opportunity or gender neutral treatment in welfare and social policies. Consequently, the paradoxes discussed in Australasian women's economic status are similarly observed in legislative and policy areas.

Early Australasian feminist activism saw strong links between the temperance and suffrage/equality movements, nationally and regionally. Women's suffrage was the major early target, and in 1893 New Zealand became the first country in the world where women won the vote in national parliamentary elections. Australia implemented women's suffrage in 1902 for federal elections, with some states preceding and others following the national change. Suffragists in both countries also fought for reforms to the educational system, married women's property laws, women's health care and adoption laws (Summers 1975). The effect of women's enfranchisement was speedily seen in the New Zealand Parliament, especially with respect to the welfare of women and children. Legislation provided for improved economic rights of women after divorce or separation, adoption and infant protection reform, old age pensions for both sexes, admission of women to the legal profession and amendments to Factory Acts to improve health and safety and increase the wages of female apprentices (Sheppard 1903).

Historically, the most influential group lobbying for women's rights in New Zealand has been the National Council of Women (NCW), with the Maori Women's Welfare League also influential for the last half century. Founded in 1896, the NCW focused attention on problems associated with the public–private spheres distinction, working on issues ranging from child welfare to labour protection, to emphasizing the recognition of women's unpaid work and suggesting the right to a share of a husband's earnings. Because of its large membership, moderation arising from the need to reach consensus among disparate member groups, and generally good leadership, the NCW has been influential, being listened to by governments of all shades. It remains active today, lobbying and writing submissions to Government bodies on issues in similar areas, but also extending to the environment, macroeconomic policy, local government, health and education (Page 1996).

In the late 1960s and 1970s, the emergence of second wave feminism in New Zealand included attempts to bring together a single 'women's liberation movement', illustrated by the holding of four large United Women's Conventions. More recently, however, the trend has been to single issue organizations dealing, for example, with violence against women, peace, labour rights and welfare issues. Over the years, feminist organizations have made strategic use of possibly conflicting notions of women's equality with and difference from men. However, differences in position and needs between groups of women were, until recently, as poorly acknowledged as in many countries, with suffrage and later fights led by white middle-class women.

In Australia, much of the feminist organizing has been at the state level, with suffrage societies in all states by the early 1890s. Once the vote was won, feminist groups developed broader agendas. For example, the platform of the Victoria Women's Political Association, founded in 1909, covered women's disadvantage in many aspects of family law and life, protection of children, equal pay and opportunity in the labour market, education, food and milk supply and international issues. Progress was achieved in several of these areas, although it has been argued that there were contradictions between feminist concepts of the ideal family and of an independent identity for women (Summers 1975).

In the 1920s, housewives, country women's and professional women's organizations were formed in most states, fostering concerns relevant to their areas, while the position of women in paid work has been an ongoing focus of Australian feminist activity. Organizations were formed inside and outside the union movement, with a strong socialist feminist influence in politics and economic analysis (Sharp and Broomhill 1988), demonstrated by the holding of biannual Women and Labour Conferences in the late 1970s and early 1980s (and revived in the mid-1990s). The push for equal pay and then pay equity has been a major concern, with coalitions forming at federal and state levels to make joint submissions. For example, in the 1983 National Wage case, the National Council of Women, Union of Australian Women and Women's Electoral Lobby all supported centralized wage bargaining and a proper work value evaluation of women's jobs (O'Donnell and Hall 1988). The current New South Wales pay equity inquiry similarly received detailed joint submissions from key groups, such as the Women's Electoral Lobby, the National Pay Equity Coalition and the Australian Federation of Business and Professional Women.

Lobbying over the exploitation of women's labour led in both countries to gender-specific protective legislation to improve working conditions and limit hours. In New Zealand, limitations on the working day contained in the 1873 Employment of Females Act were widely ignored, with 18-hour days common, and agitation led to the appointment of a Sweating Commission in 1890. Many of its recommendations on hours and conditions, minimum age of workers and institution of a factory inspectorate were enacted in legislation during the 1890s (Coney 1986). Similarly, Victoria's 1873 Act 'to supervise and regulate workroom and factories and the employment of women therein', limited hours to eight per day, when 60-hour weeks had been common (Aveling and Damousi 1991). Australasia feminists were divided on the issue of gender-specific protective legislation, both on principle, and because it could and did lead to a reduction in opportunities for women, with exclusion from some jobs. Over time, it was repealed in both countries.

In both countries, unionization grew fast from the 1880s, with legislation recognizing union rights and responsibilities, and provision for collective bargaining and arbitration gradually enacted. In Australia, for example, a specific Female Employees' Union was formed in 1891, with laundry workers, barmaids and waitresses most prominent as members (Aveling and Damousi 1991). By the post-World War II period, women's growing labour force participation in Australasia saw almost equal union membership by gender. Until the 1980s, Australasian unions achieved one of the highest levels of labour force coverage in the world, and women assumed positions of union leadership. In New Zealand, however, the 1991 Employment Contracts Act 1991 began a deregulation of the labour market and a movement from centralized towards enterprise-based bargaining. This has substantially reduced levels of unionization and collective bargaining, thus contributing to the widening wage differentials noted earlier, and disadvantaging women (Hyman 1994). Australian unionists are fighting to resist similar moves from a Liberal government. The previous Labour administration had implemented a government–trade union Accord which included principles for wage settlement and other labour market policies.

Although equal pay for equal work was an important item on the agenda of early suffragists in Australia and New Zealand, it was a long process to convince male policymakers. Despite a stated commitment to equal pay, Labour governments in the depression of the 1930s supported the family wage concept and higher wages for men, regardless of whether individual men or women actually had dependants. Public sector equal pay legislation was finally enacted in New Zealand in 1960, providing for equal remuneration for identical work. This was extended to the private sector in 1972 with the Equal Pay Act, following sustained feminist pressure, which led to a Royal Commission which supported the move (Hyman 1994).

Despite playing a positive role in narrowing of the male–female earnings gap, the 1972 Equal Pay Act was interpreted as covering only identical work, leaving other pay and opportunity inequities unaddressed. More general gender employment discrimination became unlawful under the New Zealand Human Rights Commission Act of 1977. Positive initiatives and programmes for equal opportunity for women (as well as ethnic minorities and people with disabilities) are now required to remove barriers to recruitment and advancement, but only in the public sector, under the State Sector Act of 1988. Larger private sector firms were briefly covered under the 1990 Employment Equity Act, which also included broader pay equity measures, but this legislation was repealed before it could have any effect. Although the Equal Pay Act remains operative, there are concerns about its efficacy with enterprise level individual and collective contracts replacing wage agreements for larger groups (Hyman 1994).

Australia has had a similar history, although its equal opportunity legislation is stronger, with sex discrimination and affirmative action legislation covering the private as well as the public sector. Equal pay implementation has occurred through industrial relations institutions rather than legislation, with key decisions requiring not only equal pay for identical work, but also work value comparisons across different types of work by 1974. However, pay equity advocates argue that this was never properly implemented and that productivity increases under the government–trade union Accord of the 1980s were largely confined to highly organized male dominated manufacturing industries (O'Donnell and Hall 1988). Some new initiatives towards pay equity are currently under way, with the New South Wales inquiry mentioned earlier, and publication by the Human Rights and Equal Opportunity Commission of an Equal Pay Handbook that contains guidelines for pay equity.

Entitlements to parental leave exist in both countries, although these are generally for only a year and unpaid, with some provisions in the public sector for short periods of paid leave. While there are some subsidies for child care, general family and child support for both two-parent and one-parent families is comparatively ungenerous compared to European countries (Stephens and Bradshaw 1995). Although tax systems in both countries are individual based, giving positive incentive effects for partnered women to enter the labour market, the income maintenance system's incentives can be perverse. For example, the unemployment and sickness support systems are dependent on the joint income of a married or *de facto* married couple. Thus if the wife of an employed man loses her job, she will not be entitled to unemployment relief if he has significant earnings (Shaver 1995). This arises partly because the major emphasis in such programmes is on categorical systems rather than social insurance.

Further, high effective marginal tax rates (EMTRs) act as disincentives for entry into paid work or for increases in hours for sole parents and second income earners in low income households. These high EMTRs arise from rapid abatement of targeted family support and other benefits if additional income is earned beyond a low free area. The combined effect of these factors is a comparatively low labour force participation rate for women with young children, especially sole parents. However, levels of benefits for sole parents and large families are not particularly generous, so that poverty incidence among these groups is relatively high while the sole mother proportion of all families is growing rapidly (Stephens 1995). Welfare state cutbacks ('welfare reform') to reduce government expenditure further and to increase incentives to avoid dependence are currently on the agenda in both countries, with New Zealand introducing a community wage or 'work for the dole' scheme and reducing the youngest child's age-level at which sole parents must be available for training and work.

The presence of feminists both in the bureaucracy ('femocracy') and in pressure groups outside the bureaucracy helped obtain legislative and administrative structures aimed at reducing gender bias. One important Australian development, initiated in 1984 at the federal level and also implemented in a number of states, but now downgraded, was an officially produced supplementary Women's Budget, in which government departments were required to assess the gender impacts of policies under their control (Eisenstein 1996). In New Zealand, the autonomous Ministry of Women's Affairs has published a guide to gender analysis in order to pressure and assist other government departments and private sector organizations in considering gender (and ethnic) impacts when analysing and changing policies and practices (Ministry of Women's Affairs 1996). The gains and losses for women in labour markets, welfare and other areas over the period of femocracy has produced ambivalent attitudes among feminists with respect to the roles of the state, the roles of femocrats within it and the usefulness of women's budgets.

Feminists in Australasia have made considerable progress in analysing the gender impacts of past and present economic systems, theories and policies and in suggesting directions of change. However, there remains much to be done. Gender divisions of labour remain strong in both paid and unpaid work, and the realities and undervaluation of household, caring, emotional and community work in which women are overrepresented, need regular reiteration. These issues have ongoing prominence in both countries (Waring 1988), with Australia making official estimates of household contributions to national income. Further, Australia has pioneered calculations from time-use surveys of household input–output tables throwing light on inputs of time and goods and services into household production including the raising of children (Ironmonger 1989). With estimates that the household sector comprises as much as half of the total economy, more work is needed on the policy implications of these results.

It is already clear that current economic orthodoxy, manifested in deregulation and structural adjustment policies, is increasing inequalities by ethnicity and class, with some women benefiting but many losing through being unemployed, underemployed or employed in casualized low-paid work. Recent trade agreements, in which trade and investment are being deregulated, are of growing concern to feminist economists in this region, in the light of the long history of heavy dependence on international trade. Thus, another area for further research is to analyse the gender, race and class aspects of such agreements.

Of particular concern are how these aspects are affected by international movements of goods and services and changes in investment flows. In addition, the impact of these agreements on environment and intellectual property rights is crucial, particularly to indigenous people. One final area for further cross-national research is an analysis of how specific institutions, particularly transnational corporations, may affect income distribution within and across countries: evidence suggests that movements of plants to the cheapest labour and total cost sources are damaging low-waged workers, often women, in a number of countries (Hyman 1994). The approaches and tools of feminist economics are critical to adequate research in these areas.

PRUE HYMAN

See also

Comparable Worth/Pay Equity; Parental Leave; Protective Legislation; Structural Adjustment Policies; Women's Budgets.

Bibliography

Australia Federal Department of Employment, Education and Training Women's Bureau (1987), *Pay Equity: A Survey of 7 OECD Countries, Canberra: DEETWB Information Paper no 5.*

Aveling, Marian and Joy Damousi (eds) (1991), *Stepping Out of History: Documentation of Women at Work in Australia,* North Sydney: Allen and Unwin.

Butlin, N.G. (1994), *Forming a Colonial Economy: Australia 1810–1850,* Cambridge: Cambridge University Press.

Coney, Sandra (1986), *Every Girl: a Social History of Women and the Y.W.C.A. in Auckland 1885–1985,* Auckland: YWCA.

Eisenstein, Hester (1996), *Inside Agitators: Australian Femocrats and the State,* Philadelphia: Temple University Press.

Grimshaw, Patricia (1980), 'Women in the Family in Australian History', in Elizabeth Windschuttle (ed.), *Women, Class and History: Feminist Perspectives on Australia 1788–1978,* Melbourne: Fontana/Collins, pp. 37–52.

Hyman, Prue (1994), *Women and Economics: A New Zealand Feminist Perspective,* Wellington: Bridget Williams Books.

Ironmonger, Duncan (ed.) (1989), *Households Work: Productive Activities, Women and Income in the Household Economy,* North Sydney: Allen and Unwin.

James, Bev and Kay Saville-Smith (1994), *Gender, Culture and Power: Challenging New Zealand's Gendered Culture,* 2nd edition, Auckland: Oxford University Press.

Markey, Ray (1980), 'Women and Labour, 1880–1900', in Elizabeth Windschuttle (ed.), *Women, Class and History: Feminist Perspectives on Australia 1788–1978,* Melbourne: Fontana/Collins, pp. 83–107.

McGrath, Ann (1990), 'Spinifex Fairies: Aboriginal Workers in the Northern Territory, 1911–1939', in Elizabeth Windschuttle (ed.), *Women, Class and History: Feminist Perspectives on Australia 1788–1978,* Melbourne: Fontana/Collins, pp. 237–62.

Mercer, Jan (1975), 'The Sexist Society: An Introduction', in Jan Mercer (ed.), *The Other Half: Women in Australian Society*, Ringwood Victoria: Penguin.

Ministry of Women's Affairs (1996), *The Full Picture: Te Tirohanga Whanui-Guidelines for Gender Analysis*, Wellington: Ministry of Women's Affairs.

O'Donnell, Carol and Philippa Hall (1988), *Getting Equal: Labour Market Regulation and Women's Work*, North Sydney, Allen and Unwin.

Page, Dorothy (1996), *The National Council of Women: A Centennial History*, Auckland: Auckland University Press/Bridget Williams Books with National Council for Women.

Porter, Frances and Charlotte Macdonald (eds) (1996), *My Hand Will Write What My Heart Dictates: The Unsettled Lives of Women in Nineteenth-Century New Zealand as Revealed to Sisters, Family and Friends*, Auckland: Auckland University Press/Bridget Williams Books.

Sharp, Rhonda and Ray Broomhill (1988), *Short Changed: Women and Economic Policies*, Sydney: Allen and Unwin.

Shaver, Sheila (1995), 'Women, Employment and Social Security', in Anne Edwards and Susan Magarey (eds), *Women in a Restructuring Australia*, St Leonards, New South Wales: Allen and Unwin, pp. 141–57.

Sheppard, Kate (1903), 'Editorial', *The White Ribbon*, (February), pp. 6–7.

Spoonley, Paul (1988), *Racism and Ethnicity*, Auckland: Oxford University Press.

Stephens, Robert (1995), 'Measuring poverty in New Zealand', *Social Policy Journal of New Zealand*, **5**, 88–112.

Stephens, Robert and Jonathan Bradshaw (1995), 'The generosity of New Zealand's assistance to families with dependent children: an eighteen country comparison', *Social Policy Journal of New Zealand*, **4**, 53–75.

Summers, Anne (1975), *Damned Whores and God's Police: The Colonisation of Women in Australia*, Ringwood, Victoria: Penguin.

Te Awekotuku, Ngauhuia (1991), *Mana Wahine Maori: Selected Writings on Maori Women's Art, Culture and Politics*, Auckland: New Women's Press.

Waring, Marilyn (1988), *Counting for Nothing: What Men Value and What Women are Worth*, Wellington: Allen and Unwin/Port Nicholson Press.

Economic History, Canada

As in other countries the economic contributions of Canadian women have traditionally been neglected in much of mainstream economic history. However in the past 30 years feminist scholars have rewritten the economic history of Canada with women as important participants. This entry shows that women's work, both paid and unpaid, has been made visible in primary production such as farming and fishing, in factories and offices and in homes and communities. It also shows how women activists in unions, churches, communities and in the women's movement shaped economic policy throughout Canada's history.

Canada developed as a staples economy exploiting for export natural resources such as fur, timber, wheat, minerals and fish. Most accounts of the opening up of the country focus on the work of men in these sectors and in building the infrastructure such as railways and canals to help exploit these resources. Feminist scholars, however, have demonstrated the role of women in this process. For example white explorers and fur traders depended on native women for many of the skills necessary to survive in the harsh land

(Van Kirk 1980). With settlement men and women worked together in household production units to produce the necessities for family survival which included both products for the market and for home consumption. Both market and non-market production were important. As has been documented by Cohen (1988) for farming in Ontario and by Connelly and MacDonald (1983) for fishing in Atlantic Canada, Canadian women's labour was essential to the economy of the household and the broader process of capital accumulation. Women grew gardens, preserved food, cared for small livestock, dried fish, wove cloth and made clothes, as well as doing the important work of social reproduction in their families and communities. While there was mutual interdependence and a gender division of labour, women were subordinated by male ownership of capital and patriarchal relations in the family and society, reinforced by the law. Production in the home continued and overlapped with the growth of factory-based production in the nineteenth century, as Grant and Inwood (1990) illustrate in a study of home weaving.

With industrial development in the nineteenth century, wage labour became important for both men and women. As in the household production units there was a strong gender division of labour. Throughout the nineteenth century women typically represented little more than 10 per cent of the waged workforce, however in certain industries and occupations their presence was strong. Women constituted almost 50 per cent of employment in textile mills and were an important part of the workforce in other light manufacturing industries such as shoes, printing, confectionery, biscuit, tobacco and furniture (Kealey 1973; Acton et al. 1974; Altman 1990; Phillips and Phillips 1993; Muise 1995). In Montreal and Toronto in 1871 women and children made up 34 per cent of the industrial labour force (Phillips and Phillips 1993, p. 14). While women were thus an important part of the industrial workforce, the largest number of women worked in services as domestic servants (41 per cent of the female labour force in 1891), launderers, teachers and saleswomen. In 1901 the female labour force participation rate was 14 per cent, and women comprised 13 per cent of the total labour force (Connelly 1978, p. 85).

From the beginning of industrialization women workers earned less than their male counterparts, with the gender–wage ratio being about 50–60 per cent, a figure which remained relatively constant from the earliest days of industrialization in Canada until the 1980s (Phillips and Phillips 1993, p. 15). For the most part it was young unmarried women who were in the labour force. Married women's continued work outside the home was largely precluded by their heavy domestic workloads and the ideology that married men should earn enough to support a wife and children (Connelly 1978). This male family wage was as much myth as reality, however, and many women supplemented their family income by activities such as taking in boarders, doing laundry or sometimes piecework (Phillips and Phillips 1993, p. 19).

From the early days of industrialization there was controversy over the economic position of women. Middle-class reformers sought to mitigate the worst abuses of industrial work by promoting protective legislation for women and children which limited their participation in some of the more dangerous, but higher paid, work in factories and mines and helped reinforce sex segregation in the labour market. From the 1880s until about 1920 so-called maternal feminists argued for these changes for the good of mothers and children, while male workers and unions often supported them as a way to protect themselves from cheap female labour (Kealey 1979). Many of the protections all workers now enjoy such as minimum wages and health and safety regulations were first legislated just for women (McCallum 1986).

Women's labour force participation grew slowly through the first half of the twentieth century, with temporary surges during the two World Wars. A dramatic development in the early part of the century was the growth of white-collar work and the feminization of clerical work (Lowe 1987). By 1931 45 per cent of clerical jobs were held by women (Lowe 1987, p. 2) and the office tasks done by these women, along with their pay, bore little resemblance to the tasks and pay of the male clerks who preceded them. However women flocked to this growing occupation since it represented an improvement in opportunities over domestic service and factory work. From 1901 to 1921 the percentage of the female labour force in clerical work increased from 5.3 per cent to 18.5 per cent and it continued to increase, representing one-third of female employment by the 1970s (Lowe 1987, p. 49). Over the same time period, women's share of manufacturing jobs gradually declined. After the 1920s women's employment was concentrated in a narrow range of occupations, including clerical, sales, teaching and nursing. From 1890 to 1930 women constituted about half of all employment in the service sector (Altman 1990). The female/male wage ratio stood at 43 per cent in 1900 and increased to 53 per cent by 1930, reflecting the growth of relatively more attractive clerical jobs (Altman 1990).

The female labour force continued to consist mainly of unmarried women (including those who were divorced, widowed and separated). The participation rate of married women in 1931 was still only 3.5 per cent (Connelly 1978, p. 84). This changed briefly during World War II when employers actively recruited married women and the government supported their employment with child care help and tax concessions. These incentives were withdrawn after the war and married women were encouraged, and sometimes regulated, to leave the labour market.

In the first half of the twentieth century women gradually gained more legal rights which affected their economic prospects. The suffrage movement in Canada succeeded in getting the federal vote in 1918, and by 1922 women had won the right to vote in all provinces except Quebec. The famous 'Persons Case' in 1929 recognized women as persons in their own right under the law and established their right to hold seats in the Senate. Women were also activists within the trade union movement. In the first two decades of the century many women workers including garment workers, telephone operators and retail clerks joined unions. However the rate of unionization was much lower for women than men, reflecting the higher job turnover and domestic responsibilities of women as well as the structural challenges of organizing in the low-wage sectors where women predominated. Furthermore male unionists were ambivalent towards women's wage labour due to fear of low-wage competition and patriarchal assumptions about women's proper place (Briskin and Yanz 1983; Sangster 1985; White 1980). Women continued to be underrepresented by unions throughout the first half of the century, though they played an active role in some of the major organizing drives by the industrial unions in the 1930s and 1940s. Attempts were also made to organize service and retail workers, including a drive to organize the department stores and manufactories of the Timothy Eaton Company in Toronto between 1948 and 1951, which narrowly failed (Parr 1985).

By 1951 women comprised 22 per cent of the labour force and the female labour force participation rate was 24 per cent (Connelly 1978, p. 84). From then until the early 1990s the participation rate increased slowly at first and then dramatically through the 1960s, 1970s and 1980s. The growth in participation was mainly fuelled by married women, whose participation rate increased from 11 per cent in 1951 to almost 62 per cent by 1996 (Phillips and Phillips 1993, Statistics Canada 1997). By 1994, over 60 per cent of women with preschool children were in the labour force. This increase in participation was not accompanied by changes in the structural inequalities women encountered in the labour market. The earnings ratio remained stubbornly at around 60 per cent (for full-year, full-time workers) until the late 1970s (Phillips and Phillips 1993, p. 51). Furthermore the growth in women's employment was mainly fuelled by the growth of the service sector (both public and private) and the need for increased numbers of workers in traditional female-dominated occupations. Women were pulled into the labour market by the expansion of the economy and they were also pushed into the labour market by the increased cash needs of households (Connelly 1978). By 1992 over 60 per cent of two-parent families had both spouses employed and more than 16 per cent of these families would have been below the poverty line without the wives' earnings. However, despite the growing importance of women's paid work the gender division of labour in the home changed little, creating a double day for most women in two-earner households (Marshall 1993).

In response to these changing and yet unchanging conditions of women's lives, an active women's movement developed in the 1960s, which led to the

1970 Royal Commission on the Status of Women (Pierson et al. 1993; MacDonald 1995). Government structures for addressing women's issues, such as Status of Women Canada and the Canadian Advisory Council on the Status of Women, were set up, and coalition groups organized an umbrella group, the National Action Committee on the Status of Women (Canadian Advisory Council on the Status of Women 1993; MacDonald 1995). Women organized to achieve legal rights such as marital property rights, abortion rights, equal employment opportunity and equal pay. They fought for reforms of social security programmes to serve the needs of women, recognition of the unpaid work of women in the design of pensions, maternity benefits and support for child care (Pierson et al. 1993; Pierson and Cohen 1995). In the late 1980s and early 1990s employment equity and pay equity law were adopted in most provinces as a result of pressure from the women's movement.

Women also joined unions in increasing numbers and, with the organizing of public sector employees, 29.6 per cent of female employees were union members by 1997 (double the ratio for 1967). In 1997 women constituted 45 per cent of total union membership (Akyeampong 1997, p. 46). Women have campaigned strongly, and sometimes successfully, within their unions for gender equity policies (Briskin and Yanz 1983; Canadian Labour Congress 1997).

Since at least the mid 1980s Canada, like other industrialized nations, has experienced profound economic restructuring which has had distinct gender dimensions. There has been an increase in non-standard, or contingent jobs, that is, part-time, casual, part year and contract jobs, which are disproportionately filled by women. About a quarter of employment is now part-time and over one-third of that part-time work is involuntary (Canadian Labour Congress 1997). Cutbacks in the public sector have resulted in the loss of some of women's best job opportunities as civil servants, hospital workers and teachers. Cuts in health, education and social services have also increased the unpaid work of women in their families and communities. In 1993 60 per cent of all families headed by lone parent women and 56 per cent of elderly women had incomes below Statistics Canada's low-income cut-off, which is the standard poverty measure used in Canada (the low-income cut-offs represent levels of gross income where people spend disproportionate amounts of money for the basic necessities of food, shelter and clothing, and they vary by size of family and community size). Restructuring has resulted in a decrease in economic security and an increased workload for women.

In this context women's struggle for equality becomes even more difficult, although they continue to work toward that goal. Women have been active in resisting the undermining of the social safety net in Canada, including vocal participation in the government's 1994 Social Security Review and critical analysis of subsequent changes to unemployment insurance and the funding of social services. They have also turned their attention increasingly to macro-economic policy, bringing a feminist perspective to policies ranging from free trade, to monetary policy, to constitutional reform (MacDonald 1995; Pierson and Cohen 1995).

Despite these difficulties some gains have been made. Although most women remain in female-dominated occupations (70 per cent of women are still employed in clerical, sales, service, teaching and health-related occupations), women have dramatically increased their representation in some male-dominated fields, particularly in professional and management occupations. Women have also achieved greater equality in higher education. The wage gap has been gradually narrowing over the past 15 years. The female–male earnings ratio for full-time full-year workers increased from 64 per cent in 1980 to just over 70 per cent throughout the 1990s (Statistics Canada 1996). Thus the labour market experience for women in the 1990s, as for the labour force in general, is one of increased polarization in terms of earnings, hours of work and opportunities. While some women have achieved success in previously male-dominated professions, others have been caught in the growth of non-standard work and have seen their hours and incomes deteriorate.

This review of the economic history of Canada as it pertains to the economic status of women has shown continuity amid change. The gender division of labour has changed remarkably little over the course of Canada's history, nor has the fundamental inequality in the valuing of women and men's labour been much altered. Thus Canadian women still face many challenges if they are to achieve equal economic status with men.

There has been a burst of scholarship in the past 20 years, primarily by labour historians, recovering the economic history of women in Canada. Some work has also attempted to use that information to reinterpret and reconsider the broad sweep of Canadian economic history. But much research remains to identify more fully the reasons for the continuing gender differences.

Feminist economists are playing an important role in developing this gendered analysis of the Canadian economy and its transformation over time. This work is proceeding at different levels, from an understanding of a particular industry (Connelly and MacDonald 1983; Grant and Inwood 1990), to the political economy of a region, to national transformations such as industrialization in the nineteenth century (Cohen 1988) and economic restructuring in the late twentieth century (Bakker 1996). In Canada, because of its economic history, there is a strong scholarly interest in a gender analysis of primary production and the movement of economic activity across the paid/unpaid divide. Feminist economists are also contributing to the analysis of the development and ongoing transformation of the welfare state in Canada (Bakker 1996; Woolley et al. 1996; Phipps 1998,). Another important area for further research is a comparative analysis of the similarities and differences in the gendered economic histories of countries related by economics, heritage and/or geography, such as Canada, the United Kingdom and the United States.

MARTHA MACDONALD AND PATRICIA CONNELLY

See also

Comparable Worth/Pay Equity; Contingent Labour Force; Double Day/Second Shift; Economic Restructuring; Family Wage; Labour Force Participation; Protective Legislation; Wage Gap.

Bibliography

Acton, Janice, Penny Goldsmith and Bonnie Shepard (1974), *Women at Work: Ontario, 1850–1930*, Toronto: Canadian Women's Educational Press.

Akyeampong, Ernest (1997), 'A statistical portrait of the Canadian trade union movement', *Perspectives on Labour and Income*, (Winter), Statistics Canada.

Altman, Morris (1990), 'Aspects of Female Employment and Pay Inequality in Canada 1900–1930', Discussion Paper No. 89–10, Department of Economics, University of Saskatchewan.

Bakker, Isabella (ed.) (1996), *Rethinking Restructuring: Gender and Change in Canada*, Toronto: University of Toronto Press.

Bitterman, Rusty (1995), 'Farm Households and Wage Labour in the Northeastern Maritimes in the Early 19th Century', in David Frank and Gregory S. Kealey (eds), *Labour and Working-Class History in Atlantic Canada*, St John's: Institute of Social and Economic Research, pp. 9–41.

Bradbury, Bettina (1987), 'Women's history and working class history', *Labour/Le Travail*, **19**, (Spring), 23–45.

Briskin, Linda and Lynda Yanz (eds) (1983), *Union Sisters: Women in the Labour Movement*, Toronto: Women's Educational Press.

Canadian Advisory Council on the Status of Women (1993), *Expanding Our Horizons*, Ottawa: The Canadian Advisory Council on the Status of Women.

Canadian Labour Congress (1997), *Women's Work: A Report*, Ottawa: Canadian Labour Congress.

Cohen, Marjorie Griffen (1988), *Women's Work, Markets and Economic Development in Nineteenth Century Ontario*, Toronto: University of Toronto Press.

Connelly, Patricia (1978), *Last Hired, First Fired*, Toronto: The Women's Press.

Connelly, Patricia and Martha MacDonald (1983), 'Women's work: domestic and wage labour in a Nova Scotia community', *Studies in Political Economy*, **10**, 45–72.

Grant, Janine Roelens and Kris Inwood (1990), '"Labouring at the loom": a case study of rural manufacturing in Leeds County, Ontario, 1870', *Canadian Papers in Rural History*, **VII**, 215–36.

Kealey, Greg (ed.) (1973), *Canada Investigates Industrialism*, Toronto: University of Toronto Press.

Kealey, Linda (ed.) (1979), *A Not Unreasonable Claim: Women and Reform in Canada, 1880s-1920s*, Toronto: Women's Educational Press.

Kinnear, Mary (ed.) (1987), *First days, Fighting days: Women in Manitoba History*, Regina: Canadian Plains Research Centre.

Lowe, Graham (1987), *Women in the Administrative Revolution: The Feminization of Clerical Work*, Toronto: University of Toronto Press.

MacDonald, Martha (1995), 'Economic restructuring and gender in Canada: Feminist policy initiatives', *World Development*, **23** (11), 2005–17.

Marshall, Katherine (1993), 'Employed parents and the division of housework', *Perspectives on Labour and Income*, (Autumn), Statistics Canada.

McCallum, Margaret (1986), 'Keeping women in their place: the minimum wage in Canada, 1910–25', *Labour/Le Travail*, **17**, (Spring), 29–59.

McGrath, Carmelita, Barbara Neis and Marilyn Porter (eds) (1995), *Their Lives and Times: Women in Newfoundland and Labrador*, St John's Newfoundland: Killick Press.

Muise, D.A. (1995), 'The Industrial Context of Inequality: Female Participation in Nova Scotia's Paid Labour Force', in David Frank and Gregory S. Kealey (eds), *Labour and Working-Class History in Atlantic Canada*, St John's: Institute of Social and Economic Research, pp. 163–88.

Parr, Joy (1985), 'Women at Work', in W.J.C. Cherwiniski and Gregory S. Kealey (eds), *Lectures in Canadian Labour and Working Class History*, St John's: Committee on Canadian Labour History.

Parr, Joy (1990), *The Gender of Breadwinners*, Toronto: University of Toronto Press.

Phillips, Paul and Erin Phillips (1993), *Women and Work: Inequality in the Canadian Labour Market*, Toronto: Lorimer Press.

Phipps, Shelley (1998), 'Potential Access to Maternity and Parental Benefits in Canada: Implications of the Switch from UI to EI', Working Paper No 98–01, Department of Economics, Dalhousie University.

Pierson, Ruth Roach and Marjorie Griffen Cohen (1995), *Canadian Women's Issues Volume II: Bold Visions: Twenty-five Years of Women's Activism in English Canada*, Toronto: Lorimer Press.

Pierson, Ruth Roach, Marjorie Griffen Cohen, Paula Bourne and Philinda Masters (1993), *Canadian Women's Issues Volume I: Strong Voices: Twenty-five Years of Women's Activism in English Canada*, Toronto: Lorimer Press.

Prentice, Alison and Marjorie R. Theobald (eds) (1991), *Women Who Taught: Perspectives on the History of Women and Teaching*, Toronto: University of Toronto Press.

Sangster, Joan (1985), 'Canadian Working Women in the Twentieth Century', in W.J.C. Cherwiniski and Gregory S. Kealey (eds), *Lectures in Canadian Labour and Working Class History*, St John's: Committee on Canadian Labour History, pp. 59–79.

Statistics Canada (1996), *Earnings of Men and Women*, Catalogue No. 13–217–XPB.

Statistics Canada (1997), *Historical Labour Force Statistics*, Catalogue No. 71–201–XPB.

Van Kirk, Sylvia (1980), *Many Tender Ties: Women and Fur-trade Society in Western Canada, 1670–1870*, Winnipeg: Watson and Dwyer.

White, Julie (1980), *Women and Unions*, Ottawa: The Canadian Advisory Council on the Status of Women.

Woolley, Frances, Arndt Vermaeten and Judith Madill (1996), 'Ending universality: The case of child benefits', *Canadian Public Policy*, **XXII** (I), 24–39.

Economic History, China

An old Chinese saying observes, 'Investing in a daughter is like throwing water on the ground'. Although women have played an active role in the thousands of years of Chinese history, they have rarely controlled resources or had opportunities similar to men. A few archeological sites such as that of Banpo Village in Xi'an – where women are buried in larger, more abundantly laden caskets than men – indicate that the patriarchal image conveyed by the old saying above was not ubiquitous. Most Chinese women, however, have faced severe limits on their capabilities.

China's economic history covers too many centuries and regional variations to be summarized well in one volume, much less in a few pages. Therefore, after a brief background, this entry will focus on women's roles in contemporary Chinese economic history since the founding of the People's Republic of China (PRC) in 1949 when the socialist government announced that women would be 'liberated' from traditional discrimination. This period has been marked by waves of political change that have affected women's ability to participate fully in the economy; the key ones addressed below are the radical, socialist movements of the Great Leap Forward (1958–61) and the Cultural Revolution (1966–76) and the post-Mao, market-oriented Economic Transition (1976–present).

The next section provides an overview of women's participation in the economy followed by a discussion of key laws affecting women and a section that discusses women's activism and agency. The presentation addresses the complexity of the situation faced by women where patriarchal bias contrasts with the key roles women actually played in Chinese development, where official socialist views on employment and women's equality contrast with continuing discrimination after 1949, and where the relationship between independent sources of income and women's wellbeing has proven to be more complex than anticipated. Finally the relevance of the Chinese case for feminist economics and issues for future research are addressed.

Background

After marriage, young rural women traditionally lived with their husband's family in a different village and had little contact with their own parents (a tradition that continues to the present); so resources invested in daughters would be lost to the birth family (and village) while those used for the education and training of sons would remain, possibly with significant pay-offs, and would be security for the parents' old age. Proper women were supposed to be obedient to the males in the household and 'invisible' to outsiders both economically and physically. Women were *nei ren* (inside people) who did unpaid labour at home, while men were *wai ren* (outside people) who dealt with the world beyond the household. Rural women provided the support functions of caring for the children and their elderly in-laws, processing the products grown on the farm, engaging in sideline production, such as raising chickens and pigs, and doing handicrafts, such as weaving, basket-making and embroidery.

Women also worked outside the house and its courtyard, especially doing unpaid labour in agriculture since most of the population has always lived in rural areas. The women whose labour was most needed in the fields (especially those in southern China where several crops could be grown annually) were likely to escape the brutal practice of foot binding that began in the tenth century and was finally abolished after the PRC was founded in 1949. That poor women who had to work outside the home were less likely to have bound feet provides a counter-example to the 'conventional wisdom' that women's status, wellbeing and agency will automatically improve as income increases. Although access to formal education was generally denied to women until the early 1900s, some found ways to become literate, most dramatically illustrated by the secret script they developed in Hunan province. Still, more than 90 per cent of Chinese women were unable to read in 1950 (UNDP 1995).

The minority of women who worked in the cities usually found employment in industries that have typically hired women throughout the world, such as textiles. These urban women workers, especially in Shanghai, were active in labour organizations (Ono 1989). Middle- and upper-class women in the cities engaged in educational and charitable activities. They marched in the May 4th Movement in 1919 and joined the Communist Party or other political parties.

Since 1949, Chinese officials have stressed paid employment as the means for women to gain equality with men, and the country has one of the highest labour force participation rates of women in the world (70 per cent in 1993, UNDP 1995, p. 58). The rural–urban distinction continued, however, with official restrictions on migration to the city that were supposed to prevent the squalor of urban areas found in other developing countries; 70–80 per cent of Chinese women remained in agricultural and sideline activities until the Economic Transition of the late 1970s.

Women's involvement in the Chinese economy after 1949

With the founding of the PRC, land was redistributed to poor farmers, including women; although women had their names on the titles, their control was diluted because the papers were given to the male heads of household. Private ownership, however, was temporary as the goal of the socialist government was collectivization of agriculture. Officials pursued successive policies to achieve this, encouraging agricultural producer's cooperatives in the early 1950s and then communes during the Great Leap Forward (1958–61). The large communes were difficult to administer and resulted in famine; organization of production was scaled back to smaller level management during the Agriculture First plan in the early 1960s, but the Cultural Revolution (1966–76) revitalized the effort to collectivize farming on a large scale.

The greatest change in lifestyle for women in the 1950s was that they were brought into the paid labour force. In agriculture they usually worked in teams with other women and mainly performed tasks that women traditionally did, such as weeding. Women faced limits based on traditional discrimination; they were not supposed to plough the fields or put up beams in houses for fear that their participation would bring bad luck. During slack times, they worked along with men in public works projects such as terracing hillsides or building irrigation systems. The traditional system of rural markets operated except in the more radical periods of the Great Leap Forward and Cultural Revolution, and women were active traders in these markets. During the radical periods, women were encouraged to take non-traditional jobs like tractor and truck drivers and to form 'Iron Girls' teams to do strenuous work. Attempts to collectivize women's housework in these radical periods – through group eating halls, child care centres and support services – were relatively unsuccessful in the countryside.

Entering the agricultural labour force meant that a woman received a form of payment in her own name. Everyone was paid according to a share of the harvest based on accumulated, individual work points, determined at group meetings several times a year. Typically the best male workers would be allocated ten points for a full day's work, but women would earn at most eight since the farmers believed that men's strength was an important factor (Gao 1994, Croll 1995). Although central authorities discouraged this differential, they did not stop it. Envelopes with payment were sent home at intervals with the work points of each member delineated on the outside; the payment, however, was usually made to the male head of household.

The Household Responsibility System introduced in the post-Mao Economic Transition (late 1970s) reversed collectivization to stress material incentives tied to production; it returned use rights to individual families, though the state retains ownership of the land. Most Chinese women still work in agriculture, but now the work is once more done on a family basis and compensation of each individual is not explicit. More women are again doing traditional sideline activities. They are selling these products at the revived rural markets and some have started exporting their goods. By the mid 1980s, non-state rural industry at township, village and private levels was booming. A decade later, 40 to 50 million rural women are working in these businesses, usually in assembly jobs. Outside the home, young unmarried women are more likely to be the workers. Within the home, non-traditional businesses are often run by men while women are in charge of traditional agriculture and sideline activities (Entwisle et al. 1995).

More than 75 million rural men have left the farm to seek better opportunities in the cities. Another 25 million young women have also moved to the cities to do child care, clean houses, cook, wait tables in restaurants or work on assembly lines. Middle-aged women are left to run the farms by themselves, with some help from any children remaining at home and the husband's elderly parents (though they must take care of these in-laws). While the family strategy of having the husband, and possibly unmarried adult children, migrate may increase family income, it also adds to the burden of the wife in doing the farm work. Many of them pull their children, especially their daughters, out of school to help with the work or to earn wages in the non-state industry. If the whole family migrated to the city, they would lose the use rights to the land and their main form of security (Summerfield 1997).

Because migration was strictly controlled between 1949 and 1976, the rural–urban dichotomy is more pronounced than in many developing countries where family members move back and forth between countryside and city. The state promoted employment as the key to equality for women and provided jobs in state-owned enterprises for many urban women; state firms provided many benefits including health care, maternity leave, child care and pensions. Almost one-third of urban women, however, especially those middle-aged were encouraged to work in collectives at lower pay and with fewer benefits (Research Institute 1991, p. 239). Women and men made the same wage for the same job, but women tended to be concentrated in fields such as textiles and services where they had traditionally worked and that paid relatively low wages. During the Cultural Revolution there was an attempt to get women into more non-traditional jobs, but overall occupational segregation remained.

Since the reforms of the late 1970s, urban women have many opportunities to start their own businesses or work in joint ventures or for hotels with higher pay than they previously could get in state-owned enterprises. They have also, however, faced renewed discrimination in hiring and lay-offs or forced early retirement that is only partly related to the costs of health care and maternity leave. The pattern of concentration in lower-paying jobs continues with most women working in light industry; the only areas where women constitute more than half of the work force are health care and social work (State Statistical Bureau 1995, p. 50).

Because the economy has been flourishing, women have fared well overall despite the rising discrimination referred to above, but problems facing state-owned enterprises where millions of women still work are leading to more lay-offs in the late 1990s. The pattern that emerged in the late 1980s is for firms to lay off two women for every man. These negative effects are felt more by middle-aged, less-educated women, but even young women with university degrees are less likely than men to get the jobs that are available in state enterprises. While young, pretty women and those with more education are prospering, the women who are laid off from elite state jobs face reduced family incomes and lower status jobs such as housekeepers unless they have the entrepreneurial ability to start a business.

Development indicators: poverty, education, health care

Although inequality is increasing, the majority of Chinese have experienced economic gain during the Economic Transition of the 1980s and 1990s. Widespread benefits from the market reforms have been assured by the gradualist approach that has, for the most part, permitted people to stay in state jobs unless they voluntarily relocate and has given rural residents rights to land. Absolute poverty fell substantially in the thriving Chinese economy during the early 1980s, stagnated in the late 1980s, and resumed its downward trend in the 1990s. Based on international standards, absolute poverty has dropped from over half the population to approximately 30 per cent (over 300 million people) (World Bank 1995). Those still living in absolute poverty are concentrated in sparsely populated provinces in remote regions and minority areas, but the majority of poor people live in the crowded provinces near the coast interspersed among those with much higher incomes. Statistics do not show absolute poverty hitting women much harder than men (World Bank 1992).

Relative poverty, however, has a definite gender aspect because women have fewer opportunities in the economy than men, especially in higher-level positions regardless of whether they are under the state, private or government management. Relative poverty can be expected to increase as the reforms emphasize incentives and efficiency rather than equal distribution of income. In addition, as men leave the farms to find higher pay, the women who remain face a variant of the 'feminization of poverty'. Although they may remain married, they become *de facto* heads of households and many of them do not receive income from their husbands (the reports of migrant men setting up new families in the cities are numerous). By the segregation of most middle-aged women in China into the lower paid occupations associated with agricultural production, relative opportunities are reduced and relative poverty gains in importance.

Urban women have received more state subsidies either directly or indirectly (as part of a family) than those in rural areas. Health care, education for children and housing have all been highly subsidized in the cities, but rural communities have had to cover most of these benefits from their own funds. Still, most of the population had access to at least minimal health care and education at the beginning of the reform period in 1976. Women have greatly benefited from the basic needs policies implemented after 1949 and continue to benefit in the mid 1990s as indicated by long life expectancy (70.4 years), low infant mortality (44 per 1000 live births) and maternal mortality rates (95 per 100 000 live births), and closing gaps in educational attainment between young women and men (the female/male enrolment ratios are 95 for primary education, 78 for secondary education and 75 for tertiary or post-secondary education) (UNDP 1995). China presents an excellent case study of how government policies can improve basic living conditions at low levels of income.

With the market reforms, contradictory effects have appeared in education and health care. The quality has improved in the cities and some rural areas, but the problem of rural girls being kept out of school has increased (as discussed above): rural girls comprise 75–80 per cent of school drop-outs (Gao 1994, p. 94). In addition, about half of rural residents lost their access to health care in the 1980s (World Bank 1992). Furthermore, during the post-reform period of rising incomes, the sex ratio still indicates a disadvantage in basic survival for women (the male/female sex ratio was 106 in the census of 1990, while an unbiased sex ratio for a population would be expected to be between 95 and 100).

Legislation affecting women's economic status

Although the legal framework of the PRC is incomplete, several laws have given women explicit legal rights and the various versions of the Constitution include statements about equality for women. The two marriage laws (1950 and 1980) granted women the right to choose whom they marry, to divorce, and for widows to remarry; this gives them much greater capabilities in choosing what type of work they will be involved in as well. Several regulations on protective legislation are based on biological differences mainly related to child-bearing. The Labour Protection Regulations of 1988, for example, specify a paid maternity leave of 90 days, rest breaks during pregnancy, two 30-minute breaks daily for nursing mothers and provision of child care facilities by the employer. The protective legislation also prohibits women from some highly-paid work that is deemed dangerous to their health (Woo 1994, p. 281). The Women's Law of 1992 addressed the problems of increasing discrimination, particularly in employment. Despite restricting 'certain work categories or positions that are unfit for women' (Woo 1994, p. 280), the law appears mainly positive for women theoretically, but it has not been tested much in the courts.

The One-Child Policy requires some mention as legislation that has been implemented in ways disadvantageous to women. While the goal of reducing population growth in the world's most populous country is understandable, officials have slighted their own, and world, evidence on the effectiveness of incentives based on opportunities – especially in terms of women's employment and education – in reducing the fertility rate. More resources poured into countering the rise in discrimination against women's employment and in expanding their educational opportunities would be likely to achieve the same results with fewer punitive measures (see Sen 1995). The Household Responsibility System, while positively contributing to rising incomes in rural areas, is problematic in creating counter-incentives to lowering the fertility rate by reorganizing production on the basis of the agrarian family where sons contribute to the wealth of the family throughout their lives. The conflicting incentives of the Household Responsibility System and the One-Child Policy combine with traditional bias to increase selective abortion, infanticide, neglect and abandonment of girls since 1979.

Women's activism in the economy

Between 1949 and 1976, women could pursue their rights to the extent that they coincided with state policy, but efforts to point out shortcomings of the

Communist Party were dealt with severely. The All China Women's Federation had been set up in 1947 by the Communist Party to promote women's equality, but in practice its main task has been to promote Party policies among women. Although it has been criticized by activists, the Women's Federation has published articles condemning discriminatory employment practices, initiated training programmes in rural areas, and implemented projects to help urban women who have lost their jobs in the reform process.

The main new institutional form for activism by women is through non-governmental organizations (NGOs). While they may not be free of government involvement, many groups are more independent than organizations like the Women's Federation (see listing of NGOs in Ford 1994). The women's hotline in Beijing, for example, has received international attention as a new approach to women helping each other in China and for its candid discussions at conferences.

Although the NGOs provide some outlet for women's energy and activism, they provide only a modest political voice. Political reform has yet to emerge in the Chinese Economic Transition where the emphasis has been on increasing efficiency and economic growth. By the early 1990s, elections of village committees in rural areas garnered the enthusiasm of foreign researchers for their potential for democratic participation. The percentage of women in office, however, has fallen throughout rural China (Rosen 1995). Before the reforms a larger percentage of women were placed in rural office through pro forma elections to promote the Party's policies with a single voice; now the percentage of women elected in rural areas has fallen but those who make it are able to speak with a greater variety of voices.

Most of women's activism in the economy since the end of the 1970s has tended toward individual and family strategies rather than organized group activities. Women's agency has increased in several notable ways through the ability to change jobs, set up a business, export and work in some of the new enterprises that have opened. The increase in agency has been offset by the discriminatory practices in hiring, lay-offs and forced early retirement. Overall, however, the economy is doing well, and benefits have been widely distributed because China does not have the large landless or unemployed populations observed in many developing countries; more people have gained than lost in the thriving atmosphere, but those who are losing could benefit from appropriate policies. Women comprise more than half of those who are losing, and thus the problem becomes a gendered one.

Although differing in detail and context, the reform policies in China are typical of the transition policies of Eastern and Central European post-socialist countries and the structural adjustment policies of many developing countries around the world. Issues of intrahousehold effects of social policies can be studied in the Chinese experience as well. The case is especially useful for feminist economics because it illustrates how supposedly gender-neutral policies can have 'unanticipated' negative effects on women even in a successful case where growth rates have been phenomenal. These negative effects limit women's agency, but they can be anticipated when studies show that they are manifested in economic policies in country after country. Whether officials address the expected gender issues as they design and reform policies then becomes an issue of political will as these studies provide needed material for all of those concerned with this process.

In addition, China provides an example that a poor country can make significant gains in wellbeing through policies without waiting for income per capita to reach higher levels. Indicators of these changes for Chinese women include life expectancy, infant mortality, maternal mortality, literacy and employment rates. The origins of these policies precede the current economic reforms. The experience with continuing discrimination against women despite their high labour force participation since the 1950s demonstrates that while employment opportunities are significant factors in women's agency and wellbeing, they are not sufficient.

The relationship between independent income and women's agency and wellbeing is a critically important area for further feminist economic research. The question asked by Kabeer (1995) in her work on Bangladesh can also be asked for China: Is independent income necessary, sufficient, or irrelevant? In addition, while gender remains a unifying factor in examining the effects of policies on women's lives, more work also needs to explore the differences by region, age and education, especially in a large country like China. Coercion versus reliance on economic incentives in population policies continues to require more research. Related to this is the issue of whether having children is an individual choice or a social one, in what ways children are public goods, and whether the model of Asian values alters the analysis. Housing and property rights are being studied from gendered perspectives mainly by a few researchers outside the country and are not yet included in policies in the late 1990s. Environmental damage has reduced growth in China and negatively affects development; studies need to address what women are doing to create pollution and also to work in ways that are sustainable and that may reduce the damage. With all of the emphasis on the role of microcredit and increased funding since the Fourth World Conference on Women in 1995, studies should focus on what happens to those who fail as well as those who succeed. Finally, the incipient processes of democratic reform such as the village committees will benefit from a feminist economic perspective. Neither democracy nor development can flourish if women are omitted from the opportunities.

GALE SUMMERFIELD

184   *Economic History, Eastern Europe*

See also

Eeconomic Restructuring; Population; Socialism; Structural Adjustment Policies.

Bibliography

Aslanbeigui, Nahid, Steven Pressman and Gale Summerfield (1994), *Women in the Age of Economic Transformation: Gender Impact of Reforms in Post-Socialist and Developing Countries*, London: Routledge.

Croll, Elisabeth (1995), *Changing Identities of Chinese Women: Rhetoric, Experience and Self-Perception in Twentieth-Century China*, Hong Kong: Zed Books.

Entwisle, Barbara, Gail E. Henderson, Susan E. Short, Jill Bouma and Zhai Fengying (1995), 'Gender and family businesses in rural China', *American Sociological Review*, **60**, (February), 36–57.

Ford Foundation (1994), *Interim Directory of Women's Organizations*, Beijing.

Gao, Xiaoxian (1994), 'China's Modernization and Changes in the Social Status of Rural Women', in C. Gilmartin et al. (eds), *Engendering China: Women, Culture, and the State*, Cambridge: Harvard University Press, pp. 80–97.

Kabeer, Naila (1995), 'Necessary, Sufficient or Irrelevant? Women, Wages and Intra-Household Power Relations in Urban Bangladesh', Working Paper #25, Sussex: Institute of Development Studies.

Ono, Kazuko (1989), *Chinese Women in a Century of Revolution, 1850–1950*, Stanford: Stanford University Press.

Research Institute of All China Women's Federation (1991), *Zhongguo Funu Tongji Ziliao: 1949–1989*, Beijing: China Statistical Publishing House.

Rosen, Stanley (1995), 'Women and political participation in China', *Pacific Affairs*, **68** (3), (Fall), 315–41.

Sen, Amartya (1995), 'Agency and Well-Being: The Development Agenda', in Noeleen Heyzer (ed.), *A Commitment to the World's Women*, New York: Unifem, pp. 103–12.

State Statistical Bureau (1995), *Women and Men in China: Facts and Figures 1995*, Beijing.

Summerfield, Gale (1997), 'Economic transition in China and Vietnam: Crossing the poverty line is just the first step for women and their families', *Review of Social Economy*, **55**, (Summer), 201–14.

UNDP (1995), *Human Development Report 1995*, Oxford: Oxford University Press.

Woo, Margaret (1994), 'Chinese Women Workers: The Delicate Balance between Protection and Equality', in C. Gilmartin et al. (eds), *Engendering China: Women, Culture, and the State*, Cambridge, Massachusetts: Harvard University Press, pp. 279–95.

World Bank (1992), *China: Strategies for Reducing Poverty in the 1990s*, Washington, DC: World Bank.

World Bank (1995), 'Poverty in China: What do the numbers say?', Background Note, Washington, DC: World Bank.

Economic History, Eastern Europe

Understanding fully the economic history of women in Eastern Europe is complicated by two problems. First, the role of women has received little attention from most scholars of East European economic history. The word 'women' cannot be found in the index of any of the major works, and women barely receive mention even in sections on human resources. The economic history of East European women has been studied as a separate topic, mainly by women, in a small number of publications and a good deal of scholarly work remains to be done on the issue. Secondly, the countries of Eastern

Europe (for the purposes of this entry, the former countries of Czechoslovakia, the German Democratic Republic and Yugoslavia, as well as Poland, Hungary, Romania, Bulgaria and Albania) are far from homogeneous and, especially in the period prior to World War II, differences in level of economic development, religion and other factors resulted in very different roles and outcomes for women. While some important distinctions will be noted in this short entry, many will be overlooked and significant analytical subtlety will be lost.

Prior to World War II, most Eastern European economies were predominately agrarian. Only in Czechoslovakia and what would become the German Democratic Republic (GDR) was less than 50 per cent of the population dependent on agriculture in the 1930s (Wolchik 1985, p. 32). The majority of East Europeans farmed small plots. The majority of East European women therefore worked on peasant farms. It appears that women's roles on these farms differed significantly by country. In Bulgaria, for example, scholars argue that women were recognized as producers and partners in the labour process; women could own and inherit land and control the income from the farm products they sold. In Albania, on the other hand, women were regarded as male property and largely confined to their own yards.

But large numbers of women were also employed in wage labour prior to World War II. In Czechoslovakia, women made up 30 per cent of the paid labour force in 1921 (Graver 1985, p. 70), in Bulgaria they made up 22 per cent of the (small) industrial labour force by 1909 and 36 per cent by 1944 (Todorova 1993). While the 'cult of domesticity' may have played a role in keeping women of bourgeois families out of the labour market in some countries (Hungary, for example), it did not affect the majority of East European women in the prewar period.

In part, the high level of female labour force participation was due to the devastation wrought by World War I, which decimated the male labour force in many countries. But women's participation in paid labour can also be traced to the relatively high rates of higher education attained by middle-class women in much of Eastern Europe. A large share of East European women remained illiterate into the 1950s (30–35 per cent in Romania, Bulgaria and Yugoslavia, a smaller share in Hungary and Czechoslovakia and a larger share in Albania), but among the middle classes the education of girls was common. In higher education, women made up from 17 per cent (Czechoslovakia) to 28 per cent (Poland) of all students in the 1930s (Wolchik 1985, p. 33).

The process of integrating women into the paid labour force was accelerated by the Communist Party governments after World War II. The collectivization of agriculture brought many peasant women into paid labour, and governments mobilized other women into industrial work in order to meet industrialization goals. By 1960, about 40 per cent of women in East European countries worked in paid employment, compared to about 30 per cent of women worldwide (Scott 1974, p. 82). By the 1970s, between 80 to 90 per cent of women in East European countries participated in paid work (ILO 1980).

East European states supported women's integration into paid labour through rapid extension of universal primary education, and by apprenticing young women in fields previously closed to women, like heavy industry and metallurgy. Traditional patterns of occupational segregation proved persistent, however. Many of the girls who entered non-traditional jobs found the working conditions in these jobs unsatisfactory and left. Those who stayed found that they faced more stringent requirements for advancement than their male colleagues. In the 1970s and 1980s, across Eastern Europe women workers were clustered in low-paying service and commercial sectors. Some of the predominantly female occupations in these sectors were highly skilled and traditionally male positions – engineers and doctors – but salaries in these jobs had fallen with their feminization. In skilled industrial jobs, which offered the highest wages in centrally-planned economies, women were significantly underrepresented. Within a given sector, too, women tended to be clustered in jobs with less responsibility and lower pay. In Hungary, for example, in 1977 skilled female manual workers earned 73 per cent of what their male counterparts earned, while unskilled female manual workers earned 75 per cent of male wages (Kulcsar 1985, p. 203). Only 8 per cent of workers in heavy industry were women, and this sector paid wages almost double the national average (Volgyes 1985, p. 226).

The new constitutions implemented by Eastern European Communist Parties after World War II specified equal rights and equal pay for women, rights which were not constitutionally guaranteed in many West European countries until the 1970s. Family Codes were passed in the 1950s, mandating the sharing of family responsibilities between the two marital partners. In addition, women's labour force attachment was facilitated by a set of social supports which many women still struggle for in other countries. Maternity leave was extended to women across Eastern Europe in the late 1940s and early 1950s. In Czechoslovakia, for example, women were granted 18 weeks of maternity leave at 100 per cent pay in 1948. Women could take additional unpaid leave, usually up to three years, and be guaranteed employment at their old place of work in a similar position upon return. Heavily subsidized child care was also provided. Although there were never enough places for all who wanted them, especially in rural areas, 80–90 per cent of children aged three to six years attended kindergartens in the 1970s as their mothers worked, while between 10 to 80 per cent of children aged zero to three years attended nurseries (ILO 1980). Women were also granted generous leave to care for sick children, early retirement, and in the GDR one day off a month to catch up on housework. Beginning in the 1960s, protective legislation was introduced to prevent women's employment in jobs considered hazardous to female health, including jobs requiring night work, exposure to toxic chemicals or radiation, or excessive lifting.

This legislation did not offer only benefits to East European women, however. The generous leave policies and the provision of housework days in the GDR reflected and helped to perpetuate an unequal division of labour at home. Family Codes notwithstanding, women were expected to continue to perform their 'natural' role of wife and mother in the home, caring for children and aging parents, cooking, cleaning and preserving a happy home life under conditions of shortage. This double burden contributed to women's exclusion from the most responsible and best paid jobs, as employers (correctly in most cases) expected women to lose work time when a child was born or a family member became ill. Protective legislation also kept women from some of the best paid jobs, which were often in shift work in heavy industry.

The double burden, housing shortages and other stresses of socialist modernization led to birth rates below replacement levels by the 1960s. By the late 1970s, states also faced slowing growth rates, declining enterprise performance and strained government budgets. Planners hoped to solve these varied problems by encouraging mothers to stay at home. By expanding maternity leaves and child payments, East European governments looked to free state enterprises from short-run labour surpluses, produce a labour force which could support the aging population and provide what they saw as a cheaper form of child care. Many younger women took advantage of the longer leaves, seeing them as an escape from the double burden and the tedium of dead-end jobs.

The radical economic transformation which began in Eastern Europe in 1989 has significantly changed the legal and practical conditions for women's employment. Although equal rights for men and women and equal pay for equal work are still enshrined in the constitutions, support services for employed women have begun to erode. State subsidies for child care have been cut radically and state child payments, while not eliminated, have not kept pace with inflation. Maternity leave, child sick leave and early retirement are still legal obligations for state firms, but state firms employ many fewer people. Regulation of the newly emerging private sector is minimal.

In this context, women's employment is complicated by a number of factors. First, as economic crises have created high prices and shortages of medicines, food and child care, women have carried much of the burden of searching for alternatives or providing substitutes. These tasks detract from their ability to advance in paid employment. Second, in some places, women's employment under socialism has been criticized as desertion of the family and collaboration with an emasculating state. Now that the socialist state has collapsed, women face pressure to return to their 'natural' role, allowing men to regain their masculinity. Despite these dual pressures, only a minority of women in Eastern Europe reported in the early 1990s that they would like to leave the labour force (16 per cent in Bulgaria, 35 per cent in Hungary) (Petrova 1993, Toth 1993). In any case, few women can afford to quit – the loss of income would plunge their households into real poverty. But a third force is also squeezing women from employment: high rates of dismissal by state employers. Parental leave, leave to care for sick children and protection from hazardous working conditions make women relatively more expensive and less desirable to state employers, despite the gender wage gap, and many employers prefer to lay off women rather than male 'household heads'. Further, many of the sectors where women have traditionally worked (state-run commerce, government services and light industry) have been among the first to collapse in the face of economic restructuring.

These changes have had an impact on women's employment, but not a simple one. Initially, in all countries but Hungary, women faced higher unemployment rates than men. By the mid 1990s, however, the ratio of women's to men's unemployment rates had begun to differ significantly from country to country. While in Poland women continued to experience higher rates of unemployment than men in 1994, in Bulgaria male and female unemployment rates and labour force participation rates are almost equal. In part, the difference may result from differences in previous structures of occupational segregation and in newly emerging industries. For example, service jobs in banking, finance, commerce and information technology, where women have been concentrated, have grown quickly as markets develop. Such growth may offer jobs for women displaced from state firms. It remains to be seen, however, whether women will continue to dominate these occupations and what impact privatization will have on relative male and female wages. High unemployment rates and lack of unionization or labour regulation may depress private sector wages, although wages in the state sector where more men continue to work have also fallen, and many state firms pay wages only intermittently, when cash flow permits.

Women's activism has both shaped and been shaped by these changes in women's roles over the last century. With the exception of Czechoslovakia, Poland, and what became the GDR, women in Eastern Europe could not vote until after World War II. This did not prevent women, especially middle-class women, from actively organizing in the prewar period, however. In Czechoslovakia, where women won the vote in 1919, women formed the National Council of Women in 1921 to coordinate 53 independent women's organizations. Women ran for office and after the 1930 elections, 4 per cent of members of parliament were women (Wolchik 1985, p. 79). In Bulgaria, where women did not gain the vote until 1944, the Bulgarian Women's Union was formed in 1901, and by 1931 this national organization had 8400 members (Todorova 1993, p. 34).

The victory of Communist Party governments after World War II greatly expanded women's participation in institutionalized politics. While women's participation varied greatly over time and between countries, all Communist Parties explicitly promoted the participation of women in politics and social organizations. In 1989, women accounted for approximately 30 per cent of national and local legislators across Eastern Europe. Still, women were systematically excluded from the highest level of political participation, making up about 5 per cent of full members of the Central Committee of the Romanian Communist Party from the 1950s until 1979 (when a resolution was passed to expand women's participation) (Fischer 1985, pp. 128–32). In Poland, women made up 11 per cent of Central Committee members in 1986 (Titkow 1993, p. 254). Women were more likely to participate in local party, government or trade union organizations. In the late 1970s, women made up 25 per cent of members of local People's Councils in Poland and about 30 per cent in Romania, but even at the local level women seldom held the positions of the highest responsibility (Nelson 1985, pp. 159–62). Women were also encouraged to participate in the separate women's organization, which advised women on how to manage their joint duties of socialist worker and socialist mother.

Strict restrictions on civil society limited independent organizing during the socialist period. By the 1970s, however, dissident movements had begun to challenge the state and women were active in these movements. In Poland in 1981, women made up an estimated 50 per cent of membership in Solidarity, although only 8 per cent of delegates to the union congress were women. In Czechoslovakia, women made up 21 per cent of signers of the Charter 77, and 4 of the 17 'spokespersons' (Jancar 1985, p. 171). While politically active, Polish and Czechoslovak women did not organize as women or put forth a feminist agenda. In contrast, in the GDR, where opposition emerged only in the 1980s, explicitly feminist organizations played an important role in the opposition movements.

The end of the political monopoly of the Communist Parties in 1989 opened new space for women's organizing. Response has been minimal in many places, however. Women's participation in mainstream politics declined radically with the removal of Communist Party guidelines. After the first free parliamentary elections, women's representation varied from 4 per cent of national legislators in Romania (Harsanyi 1993) to 12 per cent in Bulgaria (Todorova 1993, p. 36). In the early 1990s, reformed Communist Party women's organizations remained the only mass membership women's organizations in Eastern Europe, having retained many of their pre-1989 members. Some of these organizations, like the Polish Women's League, adapted significantly to new conditions, organizing unemployment counselling and retraining programmes for women. In other places, however, adaptation has been more limited.

Explicitly feminist organizations have emerged in all countries, but are mainly marginal organizations of urban, intellectual women. Only in the former GDR do feminist organizations play an important role. In the 1990 Roundtable government, for example, the feminist Independent Women's Association won recognition of women as an interest group and replaced majoritarian voting with compromise-based decision making. With unification, the organization (along with most other East German political forces) lost much of its influence, but it continues to support two representatives in Parliament. More importantly, the feminist movement is broadening feminist culture, through bookshops, cafes and clinics.

Ironically, attacks on abortion rights have contributed importantly to the emergence of significant new women's organizations in some countries. Some of these organizations, including the Polish Feminist Association and the Hungarian Feminist Network, frame their pro-choice position explicitly in feminist terms. Others have instead defended abortion on the grounds that it is impossible to provide for poor mothers and children. Where abortion rights are not under attack, as in Bulgaria and Romania, women's organizing has been less extensive and has continued to focus mainly on women's maternal and homemaking roles (Einhorn 1993; Harsanyi 1993; Petrova 1993).

Explanations of women's limited organizing are diverse. Some authors point to the double burden, which over the years has exhausted women. As women are pressed back into the household, their opportunities for political participation may diminish even further. Others argue that women's tokenistic representation under state socialism made women cynical about formal politics and reduced the legitimacy of women politicians. But most male politicians, too, were little more than puppets under the old regimes, and many men currently work two jobs in order to make ends meet, yet they have taken a much more active role in current politics than women.

One legacy of state socialism which may have contributed to women's political inaction is the tendency in state socialist ideology to reduce all interests to collective, class interests. This contributed to women's lack of consciousness of themselves as individuals and as a group so that, for example, '(w)henever the serious problems of women are debated in the Czech lands, someone, usually a woman, raises the question: "What about the problems of men?"' (Havelkova 1993, p. 62). This perspective was reinforced by the East European dissident movements, which emphasized the importance of the unified family in the struggle against the state. Well-worn arguments about the need to win the general battle before addressing 'special' women's interests were used to suppress discussions of gender difference. As a result of this legacy, many East European women lack a language with which to conceptualize their individual problems or a collective solution.

Further, over the past decades women's political activity has focused on women's interests as wives and mothers, a focus acceptable to and supported by the state socialist governments. Focused on these interests, women mainly participated in politics at the local level, where they addressed the immediate concerns of their family and community such as schools, transport, food distribution and local environmental problems. After 1989, however, politics was quickly institutionalized around a hierarchical liberal model, which channels political activism into national, competitive elections. Local institutions were stripped of resources as strained national governments changed tax policy to shift resources to the national level. This form of centralized, national politics may feel particularly foreign to East European women.

As previously noted, East European economic history is an area in which feminist economics has barely begun to make its contribution. A great deal of empirical work remains to be done to fill in the details of the outline provided here. The period prior to World War II is almost unexamined by feminists, and differences in prewar ideology, politics and economic structures may be important in explaining differences in women's experience with socialism and with the current transition on women. Study of the impact of the current transformation is also just beginning, and this will permit important comparisons with the experiences of women in other regions undergoing economic restructuring. One important question will be the impact of the high levels of education and political and social rights in Eastern Europe on women's experiences with and responses to economic restructuring.

But the economic history of women in Eastern Europe also raises more general theoretical questions for feminist economists. One issue is how to understand the prerequisites for women's emancipation. In Eastern Europe, women tremendously increased their access to paid employment and to the social services necessary for combining paid work and family. Some of these developments were the envy of women in other countries, who were still fighting for the right and ability to work outside the home. Yet few women experienced the developments in Eastern Europe as emancipation, and few today would argue that state socialism emancipated women. A wide range of social norms and expectations remained unchallenged and prevented women from taking full advantage of the structural changes. Detailed comparisons of the experiences of women in Eastern Europe and other regions may improve understanding of the conditions which enable women and men to participate in the economy and benefit equally from their work.

Recent history in Eastern Europe also focuses attention on the prerequisites for women's equal 'political' participation. After five decades of enforced political passivity and having attained near parity in education, men and women in Eastern Europe would appear to have historically unprecedented equality in their preparation for political participation. And yet the introduction of institutions of liberal democracy coincided with the rapid masculinization of East European politics. This raises important questions about the impact of institutional form on women's political participation. Would women feel more affinity for more political activity in decentralized institutions, institutions which address issues in both the private and public spheres or institutions which work through methods other than majoritarian voting? These are questions which remain for feminist economists and political economists to address.

MIEKE MEURS

See also
Double Day/Second Shift; Economic Restructuring; Socialism; Unemployment and Underemployment.

Bibliography
Einhorn, Barbara (1993), *Cinderella Goes to Market: Citizenship, Gender, and Women's Movements in East Central Europe*, London: Verso.
Fischer, Mary Ellen (1985), 'Women in Romanian Politics: Elena Ceausescu, Pronatalism, and the Promotion of Women', in Sharon Wolchik (ed.), *Women, State, and Party in Eastern Europe*, Durham: Duke University Press, pp. 121–37.
Fong, Monica and Gillian Paull (1993), 'Women's Economic Status in the Restructuring of Eastern Europe', in Valentine Moghdam (ed.), *Democratic Reform and the Position of Women in Transitional Economies*, Oxford: Oxford University Press, pp. 217–47.
Graver, Bruce (1985), 'Women in the First Czechoslovak Republic', in Sharon Wolchik (ed.), *Women, State, and Party in Eastern Europe*, Durham: Duke University Press, pp. 64–81.
Harsanyi, Doina Pasca (1993), 'Women in Romania', in Nanette Funk and Magda Mueller (eds), *Gender Politics and Post-Communism*, New York: Routledge, pp. 39–52.
Havelkova, Hana (1993), 'A Few Pre-Feminist Thoughts', in Nanette Funk and Magda Mueller (eds), *Gender Politics and Post-Communism*, New York: Routledge, pp. 62–73.
ILO (International Labour Office) (1980), *Work and Family Life: The Role of the Social Infrastructure in East European Countries*, Geneva: ILO.
Jancar, Barbara (1985), 'Women in the Opposition in Poland and Czechoslovakia in the 1970s', in Sharon Wolchik (ed.), *Women, State, and Party in Eastern Europe*, Durham: Duke University Press, pp. 168–88.
Kulcsar, Rozsa (1985), 'The Socioeconomic Conditions of Women in Hungary', in Sharon Wolchik (ed.), *Women, State, and Party in Eastern Europe*, Durham: Duke University Press, pp. 195–213.
Nelson, Daniel (1985), 'Women in Local Politics in Romania and Poland', in Sharon Wolchik (ed.), *Women, State, and Party in Eastern Europe*, Durham: Duke University Press, pp. 152–67.
Petrova, Dimitrina (1993), 'The Winding Road to Emancipation in Bulgaria', in Nanette Funk and Magda Mueller (eds), *Gender Politics and Post-Communism*, New York: Routledge, pp. 22–9.
Scott, Hilda (1974), *Does Socialism Liberate Women?*, Boston: Beacon Press.
Titkow, Anna (1993), 'Political Change in Poland: Cause, Modifier, or Barrier to Gender Equality', in Nanette Funk and Magda Mueller (eds), *Gender Politics and Post-Communism*, New York: Routledge, pp. 253–6.

Todorova, Maria (1993), 'The Bulgarian Case: Women's Issues or Feminist Issues', in Nanette Funk and Magda Mueller (eds), *Gender Politics and Post-Communism*, New York: Routledge, pp. 30–38.

Toth, Olga (1993), 'No Envy, No Pity', in Nanette Funk and Magda Mueller (eds), *Gender Politics and Post-Communism*, New York: Routledge, pp. 213–23.

Volgyes, Ivan (1985), 'Blue-Collar Working Women and Poverty in Hungary', in Sharon Wolchik (ed.), *Women, State, and Party in Eastern Europe*, Durham: Duke University Press, pp. 221–33.

Wolchik, Sharon (1985), 'Introductions', 'The Precommunist Legacy, Economic Development, Social Transformation' and 'Women's Roles in Eastern Europe', in Sharon Wolchik (ed.), *Women, State, and Party in Eastern Europe*, Durham: Duke University Press, pp. 1–13, 31–46, 189–95.

Economic History, Great Britain

Economic history, like its parent economics, has inherited a blindness to gender issues. Too often the typical experience has been male and the economic agent a man. But, like Plato's willing captives in the cave whose understanding of the world was through shadows on the wall, this representation has resulted in a limited comprehension. Escape into sunlight and realization that objects have three dimensions has its analogy not just in illuminating women's experience and history but also in offering revisionist interpretations to key debates. For instance, the emergent optimistic consensus on Britons' standard of living over the industrialization period has a less rosy glow when households are the unit of analysis and the losses and exploitation of women and children are set against the wage gains of men. Quantification of industrialization as growth in output and productivity too is affected by the incorporation of all gainfully employed individuals (Berg and Hudson 1992; Horrell and Humphries 1995). Light has penetrated some of the shadowy recesses of the cave and a recent verdict that 'in the field of economic history, gender is still rarely considered' is overly pessimistic, although there are many areas where torchbearing is still required (Sharpe 1995, p. 353).

Women's experience of and contribution to the dramatic upheaval that accompanied industrialization (circa 1750 to 1850) has been an area of considerable research and provides many clues to understanding the recent economic status of women in Great Britain, so this is the primary focus of the entry. Pre-industrial life has been portrayed as a world centred around the family unit where there was near equality in the participation of both spouses in the main arenas of activity: production, consumption and reproduction. Industrial revolution changed more than methods of production, it reorganized the household, tasks became demarcated as domestic or labour market and men and women played distinctly different roles. By 1920 less than one-third of women of working age were economically active and married women were almost solely engaged in domestic labour. How did this transition occur?

Pinchbeck's (1930) classic account of women's work documents the loss of jobs in agriculture as capitalistic methods of production demanded muscular, full-time work and in domestic industries where competition from new technologies rendered these jobs obsolete. But against this she cites the creation of jobs for women in factory work, in associated outworking activities (work performed outside the factory or shop) and as day labourers in some agricultural areas. On balance, she thought, women probably gained jobs. Further consideration of women's work has been hampered by lack of evidence. Although population censuses started in 1801 they either omitted or unreliably recorded female activities until 1851. However studies of individual occupations have provided insight into local patterns, and collection of household budgets documenting earnings and employment of family members have facilitated the search for overall trends (Horrell and Humphries 1995). These confirm the varied patterns of change and a weighted average of the occupational experiences indicates a decline in married women's labour force participation after the Napoleonic Wars (1793–1815), some recovery in the 1830s but then further decline to mid-century. Linking this information to the census data has suggested a second retreat of women from the labour force from 1861–71 to 1881–91, leaving women's work at low levels until after World War II.

The initial limited growth in job availability did not translate to financial independence for women in Great Britain. Information on married women's pay is sketchy, but where wives were working they earned very little relative to their husband's: one sixth to, exceptionally, half of his annual earnings. This reflected both low rates of pay for the work women did and the intermittent or seasonal nature of much of the work undertaken. Although women worked in most sectors in early industrialization (agriculture, underground in mines, textile factories and outworking activities) occupational segregation by sex existed. As the nineteenth century progressed women's work became confined to 'traditional' areas. In 1841 over half of working women were employed in domestic and personal services and nearly one-third in textiles and clothing occupations, proportions that decreased to a third and a fifth respectively by 1931 with the growth in secretarial work and service sector employment (Mitchell 1988). However for many women work was not full-time employment or just one job. Because of domestic commitments women often engaged in part-time home or outworking activities and even when employed in agriculture or cotton mills started work later and finished earlier than men; additionally, some women would have engaged in a variety of activities. Take, for instance, the married woman cited by the Poor Law Commissioners who would have spent six weeks haymaking, two weeks at each of reaping, cutting beans and raking oats and barley and would also have earned by her needle and washtub. Low pay, short hours and restricted occupations are enduring characteristics of women's paid labour amidst overarching change.

Although working class families relied on husbands/fathers to provide some three-quarters of their income throughout industrialization, the small size of women's and children's contributions belies their importance. Women's earnings were crucial in supporting families through critical life-cycle phases. Men's earnings did not vary with the demands of a growing family, instead it was so-called dependants' earnings which augmented incomes in the face of additional needs as family size and the ages of children rose.

Women earned income necessary for family survival through a patchwork of employment activities. Alongside this paid work women also contributed resources through an economy of makeshift. In rural areas women could add the equivalent of their own annual earnings to the household budget through gleaning, fuel gathering and keeping cows and pigs on the communal resources of commons and wastelands. These traditional rights were eroded with the advent of capitalist agriculture and enclosure, rendering women increasingly dependent on men and men's wages (Humphries 1990). But the removal of this traditional source of self-provisioning did not deter women from finding other avenues to exploit in the interests of family maintenance. Women took in lodgers, laundered, sold pies and lemonade and pawned clothing, as documented by oral histories collected in the twentieth century (Roberts 1977). However the nineteenth-century trend was curtailment of women's involvement in remunerated activities.

The causes of this trend remain in dispute. Some argue that the transition to the male breadwinner household was the consequence of greater opportunity cost of labour market participation with increasing productivity in homemaking. Under this scenario women's withdrawal was voluntary and aided by the significant growth in male earnings apparent by the end of the nineteenth century. Ideology, too, played its part. Women's primary role in domestic labour was emphasized and having a sole-earner husband became a symbol of working-class respectability. However these factors cannot explain declining participation over industrialization as real incomes showed consistent growth only from the 1840s and household technology remained unchanged. Carrying water was particularly time consuming, even in 1850 it took two days per week to fetch the water for a labouring family's needs.

Other scholars have seen a darker route to dependency which originated in an alliance between capitalism and patriarchy occasioned by industrialization. In these accounts the movement of production from the family unit in the home to individual employment in the factory threw workers into competition with one another and undermined patriarchal authority. The resultant conflict caused women to be excluded from some occupations as industrialization progressed, thus confined to insecure, badly paid jobs and consequently rendered dependent on men (Seccombe 1986). The picture needs shading, however. For many families dependence on a male earner preceded industrialization and no one route to dependency is evident. In mining, high male wages allowed other family members to retire from the labour force; in agricultural jobs in the south and east the move to capitalistic modes of production curtailed job opportunities for women and boys and reduced families to a state of grinding poverty; in contrast factory workers continued family employment strategies despite high earnings (Horrell and Humphries 1995). Grand theorizations lack explanatory power: women's experience was in part determined by local custom and employment availability. Indeed the continued decline in women's participation in the later nineteenth century brings into question the role of industrialization in women's oppression. This decline coexists with labour conflict over attempts to introduce cheap female workers to do men's jobs and slack labour markets, culminating in male trade unionists' demands for a family wage and exclusionary labour legislation to protect their employment (Rose 1988). Regulation started with the 1842 Mines Regulation Act (restricting the employment of women and children underground) and the passing of the Ten Hour Act in 1847 (limiting the hours of women and children in factories), but was not widespread nor effective till later. The early legislation may have curtailed the employment of women and children in these specific industries but it did not prevent them working, instead pushing them into unregulated areas of employment. The first legislation regulating the hours and conditions of non-factory labour was the Workshop Act of 1867, but the legislation was not deemed to be effective until a further Act in 1878. Women were increasingly ousted from paid work with detrimental consequences for their status, health and wealth.

In the mid-nineteenth century women had less education and training than men; girls were apprenticed less frequently than boys and fewer young women could sign their name in the marriage register in the 1840s. Compulsory schooling was not introduced until 1870 and it is likely that girls more often than boys would be absent, kept at home to help mothers and look after younger siblings. Secondary education was the privilege of the middle class and access to higher education was effectively prevented: London University was the first to award women degrees on the same terms as men in 1878.

The change in women's status in the economy impacted on their health. Industrialization brought increased work opportunities in the insanitary factory town and the unhealthy environment of the textile mill, and in availing themselves of these opportunities women endangered themselves and the lives of their offspring. Any increased independence brought about by regular employment and higher wages was bought at the cost of shorter life expectancy and increased morbidity. But women's lack of work as well as too much work had deleterious consequences for health. Women fared better when the local environment provided opportunities to contribute to the family purse. The commercialization of agriculture reduced these options and women in rural areas suffered excess female mortality and had poor health, as reflected in falling heights, when compared with their urban sisters. But the poor conditions of the factories also took their toll; work, not overwork, was the precondition for female wellbeing. Later in the century women benefited from the general improvements in medicine, living standards and public health but more research is needed to determine whether they shared in these gains equally with men or whether differential household resource allocation related to employment opportunities continued to determine relative outcomes. In the 1930s many working-class women, worn down by numerous pregnancies and miscarriages and with problems exacerbated by poverty, continued to suffer chronic ill health.

Indeed poverty was a state which afflicted many women's lives. Early quantification revealed large proportions of the working-class population living in poverty at the end of the nineteenth century, with costly life-cycle phases likely to induce periods of want over the typical lifetime. But this was hardship faced by the representative family, women without the support of a husband fared worse. The high incidence of female-headed households in the early industrial economy is only just being recognized, yet some 10–20 per cent of households in Britain at the time were headed by women (Humphries 1998). Households left reliant on the earnings of women and children through the death, incapacity or desertion of a male were in grievous circumstances. Disappearing job opportunities, poor pay and institutional constraints on employment curtailed earning opportunities and the option of exploiting common land to provide subsistence was removed, leaving the widow and her cow in the realm of the fairy tale. Reliance on the Poor Law to survive probably increased over time but the attitude towards needy women by those who managed the welfare system was ambiguous and became harsher. The Old Poor Law provided outrelief to supplement any income the widow and her children could earn and sometimes provided the equipment to establish income-earning activities, such as a wash-tub for laundering. The Act of 1834 changed the system of relief and aimed to withdraw poor relief from the able-bodied, instead confining them to the workhouse. Things did not improve. Long hours, poor conditions and pay too meagre to lift the family above subsistence was the lot of widows and deserted wives in the early twentieth century. The parlous circumstances of female-headed households and this example of the early feminization of poverty demonstrates another aspect of continuity in women's history.

Not all women were in poverty but the law made all married women propertyless and legally subordinate to and dependent upon their husbands

(Holcombe 1983). Single women were allowed property and common law traditionally provided the widow with dower rights (a life interest in one third of her husband's real property) although this could be substituted with jointure, a guaranteed annual revenue from land payable to a wife should she survive her husband. But these rights were eroded and the Dower Act of 1833 made them largely defeasible at the will of the husband. Case law shows a reduced access to, and control over, property for women over the eighteenth century, although law and practice may not have always coincided. Indeed, feminism, as an organized movement appearing in England in the 1850s, made its priority reform of the laws relating to the property of married women. Progress in getting reform through Parliament was slow and, when eventually enacted, the Married Women's Property Act of 1870 sadly disappointed its proponents. It had been hijacked in the House of Lords and far from asserting women's rights to her own property was a feeble compromise allowing a woman to keep her own earnings (but not, as it later transpired, savings from earnings while single), specified types of financial assets, and a limited amount of any property bequeathed to her. It was not until the Married Women's Property Act of 1882 that married women were allowed the same rights over property as their single sisters. They were then allowed to acquire, hold and dispose of property and to carry on trades and businesses separately from their husbands.

The law affected other areas of women's lives. Protective legislation, initially introduced to regulate the conditions of employment of women and children in mines and factories, was extended. Women's work in dangerous trades, in work gangs in agriculture and in workshops was regulated, although poorly enforced. The Factory and Workshop Consolidation Act of 1878 tried to make legislation more effective, but had the consequence of increasing home working and also exempting workshops that employed only female labour. Women were vulnerable to exploitation and were earning less than half of average male full-time weekly earnings.

Women's work conditions and pay came under increasing scrutiny in the late Victorian and Edwardian periods in part because of women's increased involvement in unions. The Women's Trade Union League was formed in 1874 to encourage women to form and join trade unions. An estimated 36 980 women members in 1886 had grown to 433 000 by 1913. This represented impressive growth but even so only 10 per cent of occupied women were in unions in 1911, compared with 30 per cent of men. However, women's unions were very visible, they were willing to strike and they were good at publicizing their cause. The successful strike at Bryant and May in 1889 against the system of fines for absenteeism and the poor working conditions suffered by the matchgirls was a high profile case which demonstrated the power of unionization.

Women's unions and other pressure groups, such as the Women's Industrial Council and Women's Labour League, also sought to improve women's pay through legislation. Arguments for a minimum wage were brought before Parliament. Feminists conducted extensive investigations into women's work which revealed the appalling conditions, hazards to health, inhumane hours and paltry pay endured by female homeworkers who were often solely responsible for themselves and their children (Pennington and Westover 1989). Irregularity of work was also a problem for these women and the Select Committee on the Sweating System acknowledged the frequent resort to prostitution this occasioned for women in these trades. Campaigning took many forms, including a Sweated Industries Exhibition, a Consumer League which tried to get consumers to boycott the products of employers who paid low wages, and the formation of an Anti-Sweating League. The women involved with these groups were instrumental in achieving social reform. A Select Committee was set up in 1907 and the Trades Board Act was passed by the Commons in 1909. This Act fixed a minimum hourly wage for workers in the chain making, paper-box making, readymade and bespoke tailoring and machine lace-making industries. The Act had a large impact on some workers' pay, raising rates for chainmakers by 150 per cent and improving pay for the 68 per cent of women in tailoring who had received below the minimum. In 1913 and 1918 more trades were added under the Trade Boards Act so that by 1921 there were 35 trade boards in existence. Even so women were still only paid half of male average pay within the trades and these Boards have been criticized for perpetuating the idea that women's work was low paid and secondary to that of a male family wage earner.

Women's unions exerted further influence in the years of industrial unrest between 1907 and 1914. In the Black Country (West Midlands) women chainmakers went on strike because employers were evading the Trade Board provisions. The workers conducted a highly publicized campaign that depicted Britain's womanhood in chains and the success of the strike sparked militancy throughout the Midlands. In Bermondsey workers had a successful strike over low pay at a number of food processing and confectionery establishments. Women's ability to improve their pay and conditions became increasingly apparent in the prewar years and reforms were achieved that improved working women's lives.

A further aspect of legislation which affected all women was the denial of the vote. There had been demand for the enfranchisement of women from the time of the 1832 Reform Bill but reform acts throughout the nineteenth century ignored their suffrage. By the twentieth century a number of suffrage campaigns were active, some organized by the National Union of Women's Suffrage Societies and the militant Women's Social and Political Union, set up in 1903 (Liddington and Norris 1978). Highly publicized action and campaigning was curtailed by the declaration of war in 1914 but women were given the vote afterwards when a new extension of the franchise was brought in. However the Act of January 1918 only gave women over the age of 30 the right to vote and it was not until 1928 that all women over the age of 21 were put on the electoral roll.

The dimensions of women's lives over a period of economic transition are no longer obscured by darkness. The impact on work and wellbeing of altered modes of production, changed property rights and recast welfare systems over industrialization have been mapped. But the economic history of later periods still remains a shadowy image of the original. Poorly lit corners persist in the interwar years, where women's experience of unemployment, the relationship between the growth of the new industries and the creation of female jobs, and women as victims of poverty require investigation. Researching grand themes provides an aggregate viewpoint but feminist economic historians have also pointed to the necessity of recovering the history of categories of women; female experience was as differentiated by class and occupation as it was unified by gender.

SARA HORRELL

See also
Economic History, Western Europe; Family Wage; Protective Legislation.

Bibliography
Berg, Maxine and Pat Hudson (1992), 'Rehabilitating the industrial revolution', *Economic History Review*, **XLV**, 24–50.

Holcombe, Lee (1983), *Wives and Property*, Oxford: Martin Robertson.

Horrell, Sara and Jane Humphries (1995), 'Women's labour force participation and the transition to the male-breadwinner family, 1790–1865', *Economic History Review*, **XLVIII**, 89–117.

Humphries, Jane (1990), 'Enclosures, common rights and women: the proletarianisation of families in the late eighteenth and early nineteenth centuries', *Journal of Economic History*, **L**, 17–42.

Humphries, Jane (1998), 'Female-headed households in early industrial Britain: the vanguard of the proletariat', *Labour History Review*, **63**, 31–65.

John, Angela V. (ed.) (1986), *Unequal Opportunities: Women's Employment in England 1800–1918*, Oxford: Basil Blackwell (especially chapters by Joanna Bornat, Ellen F. Mappin and Deborah Thom).

Liddington, Jill and Jill Norris (1978), *One Hand Tied Behind Us: The Rise of the Women's Suffrage Movement*, London: Virago.

Mitchell, B.R. (1988), *British Historical Statistics*, Cambridge: Cambridge University Press.

Pennington, S. and B. Westover (1989), *A Hidden Workforce: Homeworkers in England, 1850–1985*, Basingstoke and London: Macmillan Education.

Pinchbeck, Ivy (1930), *Women Workers in the Industrial Revolution*, London: Frank Cass.

Purvis, June (ed.) (1995), *Women's History: Britain 1850–1945*, London: UCL Press (especially chapters by Pat Hudson, Jane Humphries, Jane McDermaid, Barbara Harrison and Sandra Stanley Holton).

Roberts, Elizabeth (1977), 'Working-class standards of living in Barrow and Lancaster 1890–1914', *Economic History Review*, **XXX**, 306–21.

Rose, Sonya (1988), 'Gender antagonism and class conflict: exclusionary strategies of male trade unionists in nineteenth-century Britain', *Social History*, **XIII**, 191–208.
Seccombe, Wally (1986), 'Patriarchy stabilized: the construction of the male breadwinner wage norm in nineteenth-century Britain', *Social History*, **XI**, 53–76.
Sharpe, Pamela (1995), 'Continuity and change: women's history and economic history in Britain', *Economic History Review*, **XLVIII**, 353–69.

Economic History, India

The development of society requires that the well-being of all persons is enhanced and that women, like men, participate fully in the process of development. The 50 years since India's Independence from the British in 1947 have been a period of remarkable progress in certain aspects of women's development but sadly also a period of mass deprivation. This entry first outlines the changes in the economic status of women over this period. It then discusses legal changes for gender justice and the role of the women's movement in furthering gender equality.

Women's involvement in the Indian economy

Women are active participants in the Indian economy even though their participation is not always adequately captured by standard economic measures. For example, official statistics reveal that women's labour force participation (that is, participation in work involving production of goods and services for the market) in India is both low and lower than that found in other countries of East- and South-East Asia. As in most nations, a narrow definition and undercounting of work conceals much of the work performed by Indian women (though the task is made more difficult by specific features of the economy such as subsistence production), thus contributing to the low numbers for women's labour force participation.

The two major national sources of data on labour force participation are the Census of India, conducted decennially, and sample surveys of the National Sample Survey Organization (NSSO) conducted at regular intervals. When work participation is defined conventionally, both sources of data indicate that women's work participation is low and has declined over time. According to the Census, the rate of work participation among rural women was 37 per cent in 1961 and 27 per cent in 1991. Among urban women, the work participation rate fell from 13 per cent in 1961 to 10 per cent in 1991 (Census of India 1981, Census of India 1991).

Under pressure from scholars and activists, the concept of work used by the Census and NSSO has changed over time. In 1991, for the first time, the Census included unpaid work on the farm or family enterprise in its definition of work. Since 1977–78, the NSSO has included all nonmarket agricultural activities in its definition of work and collects information on an extended list of activities that includes domestic duties (code 92). There is another work category (code 93) defined as 'attended domestic duties and also engaged in free collection of goods (vegetables, roots, firewood, cattle feed, etc.), sewing, tailoring, weaving, etc. for household use' (NSSO 1986).

In 1983, using the conventional NSS work activity categories, 28 per cent of rural females above the age of five were in the work force; the corresponding rate for men was 61 per cent. In addition, 24 per cent of females were engaged in 'domestic duties only' and another 18 per cent were categorized under code 93. In other words, 42 per cent of women were working at unpaid tasks that involved production for the market or home. Given the drudgery of domestic labour in India, it can be argued that the burden of domestic work limits women's participation in the labour market. A decade later, in 1993–94, the proportion of women engaged only in domestic duties had declined to 18.8 per cent, and work participation in the paid work categories also had declined to 23.4 per cent (NSSO 1997). This could, perhaps, be related to the recession of the early 1990s and a shift of economic activity towards the informal sector.

The majority of workers in India, particularly women workers, are concentrated in the agricultural sector of the economy and they are, in large part, unskilled manual workers. In 1961, 85 per cent of the female labour force was in the agricultural sector and this proportion was a high as 77 per cent in 1992 (Visaria 1997). Over time, the proportion of women agricultural labourers in total workers has increased, from 32 per cent in 1951 to 44 per cent in 1991, when there were around 29 million female agricultural labourers in the country. Agricultural labour is undoubtedly the major occupation of women workers in the country.

Another important feature of women's employment in India is that the majority of women workers are in the informal or unorganized sector; only 4 per cent of all working women (and about 10 per cent of working men) are employed in the formal sector. The unorganized sector is characterized by the absence of regulation of the terms and conditions of work and by diverse forms of employer–employee relations. In the 1990s, with the introduction of structural adjustment policies, there has been a tendency towards 'informalization' and 'casualization' of the labour force. Data from the National Sample Surveys show that the proportion of casual labourers, that is, workers paid on daily or periodic contracts, in the total female work force rose from 41 per cent in 1990–91 to 45.3 per cent in 1993–94. The proportion of regular workers, or workers paid wages and salaries on a regular basis, fell from 4.5 per cent to 3.4 per cent over the same period. There has also been a fall in the rate of growth of female employment in the public sector due to expenditure reduction accompanying structural adjustment programmes.

The Indian economy is a low wage economy with wages below the minimum wage in a large number of occupations and activities. In addition, there is a huge disparity between male and female wages. In some regions of the country, women's wages are a mere one-third of men's wages. Over time, the wage gap has declined in certain occupations and risen in certain other occupations. In rural areas, wage disparities have worsened. Among agricultural labourers employed on a casual basis, the single most important occupational category for women, the male–female wage ratio was 144 in 1977–78 and 155 in 1987–88 (Visaria 1997). In the case of manual labour at public works, the male–female wage gap has narrowed significantly. In urban areas, the male–female wage gap seems to have narrowed for casual workers in the non-agricultural sector: the ratio fell from 211 in 1977–78 to 185 in 1987–88. The wage gap is relatively narrow in the public sector but this is a sector where growth of employment of women has slowed.

Given these factors, it is not surprising that poverty remains an important issue for Indian women. The overall extent of poverty, as measured by the headcount ratio, is very high in India and has increased in the early 1990s after declining for over a decade. Using standard household expenditure data and the 1993–94 official income-poverty line (which identifies persons unable to meet even the minimum nutritional requirements for survival) indicated that about 36 per cent of the population, or 323 million people, in India were poor. While it is difficult to identify the extent of income-poverty among women in India, it has been observed that among households below the poverty line, there tends to be a high proportion of women and girls. An analysis of the expenditure data for 1987–88 showed, for example, that whereas 44.9 per cent of all households were below a specified poverty line, 47 per cent of female-headed households fell below the same poverty line (Tendulkar et al. 1993).

Access to productive assets including land is another indicator of poverty. Although the data on land ownership by women are fragmentary and ethnographic, they indicate that few women own land and even fewer are really able to exercise control over the land they own (Agarwal 1994). In a rural economy, land is the asset par excellence and women's lack of ownership and control over land governs their economic and social status.

Indicators of health and education further reveal the low status of women. Life expectancy or longevity is an indicator of female survival; it is also correlated with good health and nutrition. Female life expectancy has risen from 37 years in the 1950s to 61.4 years in the 1990s but despite better biological survival chances, it is barely half-a-year longer than male life expectancy (as compared to about 7 years in industrialized nations). The discrimination against females in India is also captured by the sex ratio, or the ratio of females per 1000 males, which was 971 in 1991, and has declined since the beginning of the century. The adverse female–male ratio is particularly evident in countries of West Asia, South Asia and North Africa; the average for the industrial world was 1060 in 1991.

The low life expectancy and low and falling sex ratio reflects the existence of sex differentials in mortality and excess female mortality. These in turn are due to sex discrimination that starts at an early age; mortality rates for girls are much higher than that for boys and this difference persists until the age of 35. Maternal mortality is 50 times higher than in the industrialized countries. The high mortality among girls and women is due to several factors including the low social and economic status of women, the double day endured by women, and the neglect of or (worse) bias against girl children. Access to health services is also unequal. Evidence indicates that women receive less health care than men, that treatment of illness among women is usually of lower quality, received later and more frequently ineffective than among men (Chatterjee 1990; Kynch and Sen 1983).

Indicators of educational attainment also reveal the backwardness of women in India. Although literacy among women has risen, from 7.9 per cent in 1951 to 39.1 per cent in 1991, the majority of women are still illiterate. The absolute number of illiterate women has increased and the gender gap in literacy has not narrowed. Furthermore, there are huge differences across states, rural–urban areas, castes and communities. Among women from the scheduled castes (erstwhile 'untouchables'), only 19 per cent were literate in 1991 and among persons from scheduled tribes (that is, communities classified as belonging to tribes in the schedules of the Constitution), 18 per cent were literate. There are numerous barriers to the education of girls. Fewer girls enrol in school than boys and more girls drop out of school than boys. Even in urban areas, female school enrolment is not universal.

A striking contrast to the picture drawn above of discrimination against girls and women comes from the small southern state of Kerala (Ramachandran 1996). Life expectancy for women in Kerala is 15 years more than the Indian average, mass literacy has been attained among women, and there is little evidence of discrimination against girls in terms of health and nutrition. The factors that have contributed to these achievements include a transformation of backward agrarian relations, positive attitudes towards the survival of girls and government interventions after the formation of the state in 1957. Women's agency has been important in the process of social and economic development in Kerala. In particular, female education has affected progress in many health and demographic indicators. Historically, women have participated in trade unions, peasant and labour movements, and the movement for food. Women's participation in the work force, however, remains limited, there is large-scale female unemployment and the social position of women remains low in certain respects.

In sum, despite some progress over the last 50 years, women in India remain economically underprivileged. The majority of women workers are in agriculture where wages are low. Women's access to land is restricted and their health and educational attainments are unsatisfactory. The experience of Kerala shows that a different development strategy and committed public action can enhance the well-being of women and men.

Legislation and political activisim affecting women's economic status

The women's movement has attempted to use the law to advance its struggle and improve the well-being of women while being aware that laws alone cannot bring about fundamental changes in women's economic status. There is a long history of legislative reform starting from the social reform movement of the late nineteenth century that attempted to reform Hindu law and to end discrimination against women. The issues taken up by social reformers pertained mainly to marriage and included polygamy, bigamy, age of marriage, registration of marriage, dowry and *sati* (widow burning). In the post-Independence period, there have been three areas of contestation: personal laws, labour laws and laws relating to violence against women (AIDWA et al. 1995).

Questions of women's rights to property are complicated by the fact that marriage and inheritance laws, placed under the rubric of personal laws, vary with religion and region. In the 1950s, there was intense debate over the codification of Hindu law ending with the passage of the Hindu Succession Act (1956). A progressive feature of this Act was that it recognized the right of women to inherit property and it stipulated equal rights of succession between male and female primary heirs (ICSSR 1975). The Act has, however, not eliminated gender inequalities. There remain, for example, differences in how children of predeceased boys and girls are treated as primary heirs and the Act also excludes certain types of agricultural land and rights to tenancy (Agarwal 1994). Control over agricultural land is further constrained by the fact that legal powers with respect to agricultural land and land reform have been vested with state legislatures. Amendments are necessary in all personal laws to bring about gender justice.

Turning to labour laws, a basic weakness of existing legislation is that there are very few laws for workers in the unorganized sector of the economy (GOI 1988), particularly for home-based workers, a sector that is likely to expand with the deregulation of the labour market. The Equal Remuneration Act (1976), aims to eliminate sex discrimination in employment (both at the time of recruitment and further promotion) and in earnings (by assuring equal remuneration to men and women for the same work or work of a similar nature). Unfortunately, there are no guidelines to determine work of comparable or equal worth.

Another important labour law affecting women workers is the Minimum Wages Act (1948), which provides a mechanism for fixing and revising minimum wage rates for different occupations. A major drawback of this legislation is that it does not specify the bases for determining minimum wages. Minimum wages differ across occupations, and jobs in which women are a majority get classified as 'light work' and paid less than jobs in which male workers are a majority and that get classified as 'heavy work'. In addition, when wages are for piece-rate work, there appears to be no systematic basis for determining output and therefore contribution of the worker. This lacuna affects a large proportion of women workers in the informal sector. Minimum wages are not specified for many jobs in the informal sector, although governments have the power to update and expand the list of occupations in the schedule. The women's movement has demanded the stipulation of a national minimum wage.

Struggles by women's organizations have resulted in new laws and amendments to existing laws that govern Indian women's property and labour rights. All existing laws for women workers, however, suffer from problems of enforcement, implementation and interpretation. And, in many areas of the law, further reform is needed to end discrimination against women.

Indian women's political activism outside the legal institutions has also affected their economic status. Women participated in large numbers in the freedom struggle and were involved in all types of protests including armed struggles. The anti-colonial movement was critical in raising women's consciousness at a mass level. Women also became active in struggles to improve their economic status. There were two major peasant struggles in the 1940s, the Tebhaga movement in Bengal, and the Telengana struggle against feudal landlords in the south. In both these Communist Party-led movements, women participated in large numbers and took part in political as well as military activities (Chaktravartty 1980).

At Independence, the new Constitution pledged equality for women but in reality the avenues for women's development were restricted. The major struggle of the 1950s was around the Hindu Code Bill. This was an agitation in which women faced tremendous hostility and were ridiculed and attacked by the Hindu orthodoxy (Chaktravartty 1980). Women did make some gains in legal terms although implementation lagged behind. By the 1970s, the contemporary women's movement was coming to life with the growth of a large number of women's organizations and struggles against violence and economic issues such as price increases, low wages, distribution of land and government policy (Agnihotri and Mazumdar 1995).

The contemporary women's movement in India has taken up a diverse set of issues and widened its scope over time from a focus on domestic violence to issues relating to water, sanitation, food, fuel and other civic issues, that is, issues concerning women as citizens and participants in development. The broadening of the agenda stems from an understanding of poverty and differentiation within women. Since the late 1970s, the women's movement has taken a more comprehensive view of different dimensions of oppression, both within the family and that outside the family, namely that of caste or tribe, religion and class.

One example of women's activism in the contemporary period is the Chipko movement in the Garhwal Himalayas, a grassroots movement against the commercial exploitation and destruction of forests that began in 1972. Women had large economic stakes in the protection of forests as they depended on forests for food, fuel and fodder. Another example is the anti-*arrack* (liquor) campaign initiated by rural women in the southern state of Andhra Pradesh in 1992 that demanded and obtained a ban on the sale of *arrack*. The movement grew out of an economic crisis in which women encountered lower family expenditures, on the one hand, and rising alcoholism and violence on the other hand.

A landmark event in the women's movement was the Report of the National Committee on the Status of Women (CSW), *Towards Equality*, which systematically presented the issues of concern to Indian women (ICSSR 1975). The Report led to an expansion of research on women's issues, and brought activists and academics together. Drawing on the CSW, a national network of women's organizations presented a Memorandum demanding specific provisions for women's development including programmes of health, education and employment (Agnihotri and Mazumdar 1995). This resulted in the introduction of a chapter on Women and Development in the Sixth Five Year Plan. The Plan stipulated that women be included in all programmes for poverty alleviation and also promised that government redistribution programmes would try to give joint titles to husband and wife. Women are now included in many anti-poverty programmes.

The CSW also recommended the constitution of statutory, autonomous commissions at the level of central and state governments that would monitor and promote measures to ensure equality between men and women. The draft legislation, prepared in 1989, did not, however, grant autonomy to the Commissions and did not give it adequate investigative powers. Women's groups intervened again with concrete proposals for revision, and a redrafted Bill was passed in Parliament in August 1990.

While women's political participation at the national level remains limited (only 7 per cent of Members of Parliament in 1996 were women), a visible change has occurred in many states with respect to women's participation in the three-tier structure of elected local bodies, *panchayats*. This follows the 73rd and 74th Amendments to the Constitution (in 1993) that reserved one-third of positions in *panchayat* institutions for women. In West Bengal, one of the first states to seriously devolve power to *panchayats*, about 45 000 rural women were candidates in the fourth round of elections held in 1993. Around 24 000 women were elected members of the *panchayats* and a good number of them, particularly those representing the left parties, are from landless or small cultivator households and from traditionally oppressed castes and communities.

In conclusion, during the contemporary period, women's organizations and movements have been active in struggles for women's economic betterment both through legislative channels and extra-parliamentary political activism. Organizations with differing perspectives have come together on specific demands and have waged collective struggles for equality, as in the case of joint land titles for men and women, but much work remains, especially since only a few organizations currently work among the mass of rural women in India.

India is a country where the large majority of women suffer different forms of poverty and deprivation and where most women workers are employed in low-paid activities in the unorganized sector of the economy. Economists who seek to understand issues concerning the economic status of women in India and to inform and intervene in policy in this sphere have a large research agenda before them. With the continuing expansion of the unregulated labour market, exacerbated by policies of structural adjustment and liberalization, an important conceptual problem is to define the basis of wage determination for women workers, particularly home-based workers and rural workers. In terms of measurement issues, the task of measurement and valuation of women's work is incomplete. There is much scope for empirical work, for example, to document the impact of recent changes in the economy on work opportunities and wages and on women's paid and unpaid work. Lastly, the research agenda needs to include work that can inform the debates over important policy issues, such as control over resources and payment of fair and equal wages since Indian women's economic status is likely to be enhanced through continuing legislative change and action.

MADHURA SWAMINATHAN

See also
Development Policies; Development, Theories of; Informal Sector; Structural Adjustment Policies.

Bibliography
Agarwal, Bina (1994), *A Field of One's Own: Gender and Land Rights in South Asia*, Cambridge: Cambridge University Press.

Agnihotri, Indu and Vina Mazumdar (1995), 'Changing terms of political discourse: women's movement in India, 1970s–1990s', *Economic and Political Weekly* **30** (29), (July) 22.

All India Democratic Women's Association (AIDWA) et al. (1995), *Towards Beijing: A Perspective from the Indian Women's Movement*, New Delhi.

Chaktravartty, Renu (1980), *Communists in the Indian Women's Movement*, New Delhi: People's Publishing House.

Chatterjee, Meera (1990), 'Indian Women, Health and Productivity', World Bank, Population and Human Resources Department, Working Paper WPS 442, Washington, DC.

Government of India (GOI) (1988), *Shram Shakti*, Report of the National Commission on Self Employed Women and Women in the Informal Sector, New Delhi.

Indian Council of Social Science Research (ICSSR) (1975), *Status of Women in India: A Synopsis of the Report of the National Committee on the Status of Women* (1971–74), New Delhi.

Kynch, Jocelyn and Amartya Sen (1983), 'Indian women: well-being and survival', *Cambridge Journal of Economics*, **7**, 363–80.

National Sample Survey Organisation (NSSO) (1986), *Sarvekshana*, **IX** (4), April.

National Sample Survey Organisation (1997), *Employment and Unemployment in India, 1993–94*, Government of India, Department of Statistics, New Delhi.

Ramachandran, V.K. (1996), 'Kerala's Development Achievements: A Review', in Jean Dreze and Amartya Sen (eds), *Indian Development: Selected Regional Perspectives*, Oxford: Oxford University Press.

Registrar General and Census Commissioner, *Census of India 1981, Series-1, India Comparative Primary Census Abstract, 1971 and 1981*, Paper 3 of 1986, New Delhi.

Registrar General and Census Commissioner, *Census of India 1991, Series-1, India, Provisional Population Totals: Workers and Their Distribution*, Paper 3 of 1991, New Delhi.

Tendulkar, S.D., K. Sundaram and L.R. Jain (1993), 'Poverty in India 1970–71 to 1988–89', International Labour Office, ARTEP Working Papers, New Delhi.

Visaria, Pravin (1997), 'Women in the Indian working force: trends and differentials', *Artha Vijnana, Journal of the Gokhale Institute of Politics and Economics*, **39** (1).

Economic History, Mexico

This entry focuses on a typical example of women's participation in Latin American economies since pre-Hispanic times: the case of Mexico. Since before the Conquest of Mexico by the Spaniards in 1521, women in Mexico have played an important part in the economy (formal and informal sectors, households and farms), yet they have faced varying degrees of discrimination, exploitation and violence from their employers, the military and the men in their own families.

In the pre-Hispanic Aztec and Mayan societies, the fundamental role of women was that of reproduction, caring for children and subservience to men, husbands in particular. Aztec women were of two classes: the nobility (the *Pipiltin*) and the broad sector of the dominated and exploited classes that paid tribute to the dominant group, the *macehualtin*. In spite of the nobility of their blood, the *Pipiltin* women were completely excluded from public office or political activities and were barred from priesthood; they produced weavings and clothing and/or cared for their children (Rodriguez 1987, pp. 15–17). The *macehualtin* (or lower-class women) had to not only care for the children and carry out domestic chores, sewing and weaving for their family, but they also had to carry firewood, work in the agricultural and artisan labours of their husbands, and they had an obligation to contribute to the tribute to be paid to the dominant class. Mayan women married at an early age in order to start having as many children as possible, and their subservience to their husbands appears to have been extreme. The man was served his meal first and the woman ate her meal later; when a wife offered her husband something to drink, she had to then turn her back while the husband drank; it was considered dishonest for a woman to address a man unless he was the one to initiate the conversation. However, a major difference between the Aztec and Mayan societies is that Mayan women were sometimes allowed to be priestesses and *caciques* or rulers (Landa nd, p. 128; de la Torre 1987, both cited in Izquierdo 1989, pp. 8–13).

With the Spanish Conquest and the dawning of the colonial period (1521–1821) a new social hierarchy was imposed, in which the Spaniards or *peninsulares* were at the top, followed by *criollos* (children of Spaniards born in 'New Spain'), *mestizos* or *castizos* (children from the union of Spanish and Indian blood), Indians (native-born or indigenous Mexicans of pre-Hispanic origins, called Indians because the conquistadores thought they had come upon India in their first voyages to the New World), mulattos (cross between White or Spaniard and African) and blacks or Africans at the bottom. While women of both upper and lower classes had primary responsibility for the home and children during the colonial period, the workload of the indigenous women, mulattos, blacks and the poorer mestizo classes was much heavier. These women had to carry firewood, take food to their husbands in the fields, spin yarn and thread, weave, sew clothing, and function as servants for the hacienda lords and in the cities, sell fruits, vegetables, flowers, poultry and fish on the city streets. Domestic service and child care were the primary formal occupations of women in colonial Mexico (Arrom 1985, p. 157; Giraud 1987, pp. 65–8,).

Women in Mexico City were far from marginal participants in the economy in the late colonial period, for they constituted almost one-third of the paid labour force in 1753 as well as in 1811. But the extent of a woman's participation in the labour force was determined by her class and race. In 1811 in Mexico City, only 12.5 per cent of Spanish women were employed, whereas 35.6 per cent of mestizo and 45.7 per cent of Indian women were employed (Arrom 1985, p. 159). Thus mestizo women were three times, and Indian women nearly four times more likely to work than Spanish women.

Between 1753 and 1811 there was a diversification of women's employment. In 1753 a full 88 per cent of all identified female workers fell into just two occupational categories: domestic servants (77 per cent) and seamstresses

(11 per cent) whereas in 1811 only 54 per cent of the female labour force were employed as domestic workers and 3 per cent as seamstresses. In some cases, women were entering trades formerly restricted to male guild members, such as apprentices, weavers and cobblers. In spite of the greater diversity of women's occupations, they were still barred from the clergy, the military, and the government bureaucracy – the three careers with the most opportunity for upward mobility (Arrom 1985, pp. 161–3).

Women participated in the war of independence (1810–21), and at this time a group of women petitioned the government to have the same rights as men, to be full citizens. However, the constitutions of the new states primarily ensured that the control of resources and governmental power would pass to an American-born (that is, born in 'New Spain') male elite. A woman's legal status was determined through her relationship to the male head of household and to the male property owner (Miller 1991 p. 39).

Towards the end of the nineteenth century, during the regime of Porfirio Diaz (1877–1911) an extended national railway system and huge amounts of foreign investment stimulated the growth of the economy. In 1895, almost as many women were employed in industry (183 292) as were employed in domestic service (190 413). Important areas of women's employment were the tobacco industry, the textile and garment industries, shoe, food, beverage, pottery and glass factories (El Colegio de Mexico 1960, p. 304 cited in Escandon 1987, pp. 156–7; Soto 1977, p. 18). Between 1895 and 1910 women represented one-third of all employees in manufacturing. The benefits of this modernization, however, were reserved for the elite. Facing deplorable working and living conditions, including sexual abuse by male foremen and wages that were one-half to two-thirds of what men received for approximately the same jobs, female factory workers were the first Mexican women to organize in the nineteenth century (Soto 1977, pp. 18–21).

The birth of feminism in Mexico, as in other Latin American countries, seemed to have a correlation with the education of young women. In mid-nineteenth-century Mexico, Benito Juarez's government, which sought to weaken the church, passed legislation providing for public secondary schools for girls. The secular, state-supported education for women was seen as a means of weakening women's traditional loyalty to the church (Miller 1991, p. 51). According to Miller (1986) it was the female school teachers who formed the nucleus of the first women's groups to articulate what may be defined as a feminist critique of society. The female schoolteachers represented a new educated middle sector of society, they were conscious of their precarious social, economic and legal status and they were in touch with one another through a number of *congresos femininos* ('feminine congresses') which took place in this era from Merida in the Yucatan, Mexico to Buenos Aires in Argentina (Miller 1991, p. 35).

Women fought in the Mexican Revolution (1910–17) not only as *soldaderas* (mostly Indian or poor mestizo women who fought in armies and also cooked, nursed and performed a multitude of other services), but also as feminists, working to legislate complete rights of citizenship to women, including suffrage and the right of women to run for office. The Mexican Constitution of 1917 (resulting from the revolution) was hailed as the most advanced social and political document of its day, but women continued to be excluded. 'Political rights, including the right to vote, were granted to all Mexican citizens; women were excluded from the category of citizen' (Miller 1991, p. 77). It was not until 1953 that Mexican women finally secured the right to vote.

As men who had fought in the revolution returned to the work force in the 1920s, women were pushed out of their jobs. Workers' unions, far from protecting women, proved to be bastions of male supremacy (Miller 1991, p. 91). With the modernization of the traditional industries like textiles, clothing, tobacco and food, machines also often replaced women's labour (Rendon 1990, p. 34). For these reasons, women's labour force participation fell from 17.0 per cent of the economically active population in 1900 to 6.9 per cent in 1930 (Rendon y Salas 1987 cited in Rendon 1990, p. 44).

Since 1930, however, there has been a fairly steady increase in women's participation in production for the market despite the fact that sectoral changes have occurred. While women's participation in the economically active population (EAP) was estimated at 6.9 per cent in 1930, by 1970 it was 20.6 per cent of the total, 24.0 per cent of the total EAP in 1979 and 32.1 per cent of the EAP by 1990 (Rendon y Salas 1987; Rendon 1990; INEGI 1993, 1997a). While women's participation in the labour force has increased since 1930, the distribution of female employment by sector has also changed. During the period between 1940 and 1980, the Mexican government followed a strategy of import substitution industrialization, a strategy that emphasized national production of consumer goods with the help of high tariffs against imports, an overvalued exchange rate for the importation of capital goods and government-run enterprises, among other policies. During the period of import substitution, manufacturing employment for women fell from 30.9 per cent of the female labour force in 1930 to 20.4 per cent in 1970 but government services absorbed more and more female employees. Although the service sector is the main sector in which women were employed during this period, there were changes in service sector opportunities between 1940 and 1970. For example, in 1940, 72 per cent of the women occupied in the service sector were domestic workers, whereas by 1970 this percentage had fallen to 43 per cent. Women were increasingly employed in areas of teaching, health, housing, food preparation, custodial services (Rendon 1990, p. 36) and government services.

By 1980 Mexico was already faced with the constraints of its import-substitution industrialization strategy, but internal and international pressures to totally restructure the economy also mounted with the debt crises of 1982–88. By 1986 the country was facing the full impact of *neo-liberal* structural adjustment, which included currency devaluations, export promotion and export diversification, price and trade liberalization, foreign investment liberalization, privatization of government-run enterprises, deregulation and massive cutbacks in government spending. All of these measures have implied a reversal of import-substitution policies and have totally restructured the economy away from the strong participation of the public sector.

The participation of women in the economy has increased since the debt crisis began. As noted above, while women represented 24.0 per cent of the economically active population in 1979, this had increased to 32.1 per cent by 1990 (Rendon 1990; INEGI 1997b). Women's increasing market participation has not, however, resulted in greater gender equality. Of those who received an income for their work in 1990, 65.1 per cent of employed women received 2 monthly minimum wages or less, while the percentage of employed men in this income category was 53.1 (INEGI 1990, cited in INEGI 1993, p. 97). (It has been estimated that the average household needs to have at least four minimum wages just to survive.) Female unemployment rates have also been generally higher than those for males between 1987 and 1997. No matter what their extra-domestic participation, domestic work is still the responsibility of women: child care, cleaning, cooking. For the entire employed population in 1995, it was found that women's *extradomestic* labour hours were an estimated average of 32.7 hours per week and men's was 39.9 average hours; however, employed women worked an average of 28.4 hours per week in domestic labours, while for men the average was 11.9. Therefore, total average hours worked per week was 61.1 hours for women and 51.8 hours for men (INEGI 1997b).

Besides increasing women's labour force participation, the further impact of structural adjustment on Mexican women has been high rates of un- and underemployment and increasing participation in 'flexible' and informal labour markets, which include subcontracting and the revival of homework and of domestic and family labour systems. In increasing numbers, women are resorting to selling (mostly imported) articles on city streets, working in their homes for large textile and garment firms, assembling plastic flowers, toys, and paper boxes, and so on. In 1995 an estimated 4.6 per cent of the employed economically active female population were street vendors (*vendedores ambulantes*) while the percentage of all employed males who were street vendors for the same year was 3.2 (INEGI-STPS 1995 cited in INEGI 1997b, p. 53). In other words, of the total number of working men and women, there is a higher percentage of women in the precarious job of street vendor than men, even though in absolute terms there were more men than women street vendors in 1995 (approximately 729 thousand men versus 500 thousand women, INEGI-STPS 1995 cited in INEGI 1997b, p. 53). At the same time, small workshops have expanded in rural Mexico and in squatter towns outside major cities in which home-based assembly workers subcontract with local factories (Wilson 1991; Benería and Roldán 1987). Although the informal sector provides greater flexibility for employers and a certain level of independence for the 'micro-entrepreneur', and also sometimes allows the latter to achieve higher income levels than by working in the formal sector, there are often major disadvantages of informal sector employment and domestic outwork for the workers. The employment tends to be unstable, it is characterized by low wages (often below the legal minimum) and the absence of any form of insurance, it is labour-intensive, it involves specialized and monotonous tasks, no fringe benefits are provided, it bypasses protective legislation and the workers are usually unconnected and therefore unlikely to unionize. In some cases, the workers are forbidden from unionizing (see Roldán 1988, p. 231). Also, work is not continuously available, since it is subject to market conditions.

With structural adjustment, the Mexican government's economic development strategy has been to emphasize the assembly and export of manufactured goods in industries such as electronics, garments and pharmaceuticals, that is, an increased emphasis on *maquiladora* production, in which women play an important role. The growth in the *maquiladora* industry has increasingly integrated Mexico's women into the 'global assembly line'. Whereas 539 *maquiladoras* employed 74 770 women workers in 1980, by February 1997, 2601 *maquiladoras*, 77.3 per cent of which are located along Mexico's northern border, employed a total of 392 453 women workers (INEGI 1997a). This represents an increase of 382 per cent in the number of *maquiladoras*, and a 425 per cent increase in the number of women employed (INEGI 1998). Although the gender composition of the *maquiladora* work force has changed (roughly 58 per cent of all *maquiladora* workers are women today as opposed to 77 per cent in 1980 (INEGI 1997a), partially due to the increased skill and strength needed for more technologically advanced operations), their high level of employment still poses many questions about the conditions of women's employment and its effects on their health as well as their political and social status. These questions do not yet have definitive answers, and cause controversy in the border cities as well as in the literature. Low birth weights of babies born to some *maquila* workers in Tijuana have been the object of study (Eskenazi et al. 1993), and the several cases of anencephalitis from Tijuana to Matamoros and Brownsville have as yet not been thoroughly explained (Albrecht 1994, Bacon 1995). Women's continued segregation into the lowest paid unskilled jobs in the *maquiladoras* also suggests that their economic position is not improving within the companies (see, for example, Kopinak 1995; Ruiz and Tiano 1991). Also, women's increasing participation in the labour force has occurred in the context of a male-dominated labour movement which has been strongly influenced by the corporatist strategies of the ruling party.

Women in Mexico still play a significant role in Mexico's agricultural sector, both as small producers and as wage workers on large capitalist farms (especially in the Northwestern states of Sinaloa and Sonora). In 1990, more than eleven and a half million women were living in Mexico's countryside, constituting 49.7 per cent of the total rural population (Robles et al. 1993, p. 26). In 1995 1.2 million women (or 11.0 per cent of employed females) worked in agricultural activities (INEGI 1997b).

As a result of the agrarian reforms carried out under the presidency of Lazaro Cardenas (1934–40) the system of *ejidos* (government-owned land given to peasants in usufruct) was created. The vast majority of rural women who live on *ejidos*, however, do not hold use rights since Mexico's original agrarian reform law (which emerged out of the 1910–17 Revolution) established that the benefactor of land reform was to be male. While this changed with Article 200 of the Federal Law of Agrarian Reform in 1971, by then most of the land that was going to be distributed had already been distributed and most families (some 80 per cent of Mexico's *ejidos* and Indian communities) had already established other forms of survival outside of subsistence farming, since they could not survive on the meagre income they could eke out from the *ejido* (Stephen 1996, p. 292).

The 1992 reform to Article 27 of the Mexican Constitution provides land titles to *ejidatarios*, but since most of these are men, the many rural women who live and work on *ejido* land will still have no rights to the newly privatized land. Also, given that the only means by which women can own land is through purchasing it from their husbands and other family members and that the average rural wage is less than $4.00 per day, most women are unlikely to be able to purchase land (Stephen 1996, p. 292). This continues to be an important economic and political issue for women. For example, one of the demands of the indigenous women in Chiapas has been to have more equal rights over land (Rojas 1994).

The women with the most difficult economic and social circumstances of all continue to be the indigenous women, especially in the southern states of Chiapas, Oaxaca and Guerrero. Compared to women in other states, women in these states have the least access to education, are the first to abandon school, are the most likely to get the lowest wages, and they must bear the entire burden of domestic labour without access to clean water, electricity, gas stoves, and so on. On top of this, markets, transportation, health care facilities, and so on are far away from their homes (INEGI 1997b). All of this implies that indigenous women have a lower economic status than other women and the opportunities for these women to improve their economic status are extremely limited.

In the Highlands of Chiapas for example, in the mostly indigenous *municipios* (equivalent of US counties) of Altamirano, Margaritas, Ocosingo and San Cristobal, 64.1 per cent, 59.5 per cent, 60 per cent and 32.3 per cent respectively of the women 15 years of age or older cannot read or write, a reflection of the educational marginalization to which they are subjected. Those who work for pay generally receive less than one minimum wage per month (less than $100 US currency equivalent), while for the state as a whole 80 per cent of the families receive incomes of up to two minimum wages. In Altamirano, women in 93 per cent of the houses cook with firewood, 64.3 per cent do not have running water and 74.2 per cent have no electricity. The figures are similar for the other mostly-indigenous counties (Rojas 1994, p. 75). Using firewood inside the shelters for cooking, and lack of clean accessible water have grave health consequences for women and their families.

Given the economic conditions in which most indigenous women live in Chiapas, many have joined indigenous men in the Zapatista Army of National Liberation (EZLN) uprising, whose beginning coincided with and was a response to the North American Free Trade Agreement (NAFTA), which took effect 1 January 1994. It is estimated that 30 per cent of all combatants in the EZLN army are women. Some of them were founders of the organization, and have led units that have taken over entire towns and cities (Rojas 1994, pp. 27–9).

Violence against women has formed part and parcel of Mexico's economic history. Current statistics are cause for concern and further research into the relationship between economic factors and family/social violence against women. In the state of Mexico alone (near Mexico City) 85 000 rapes occur each year (SourceMex 3/20/91). Also, in a study of hospitals and clinics in Mexico City from 1989 to 1994, it was found that of approximately 6700 women who had suffered intentional injuries each year, 78 per cent of them had been injured by their spouse or by a male member of the family; only 28 per cent filed charges, and only 1.5 per cent resulted in convictions (Diaz and Sotelo 1996, p. 1940). The problem is not a recent one, nor is it confined to Mexico City. In a study on violence within the home against women and girls 12 years of age or older in the state of Jalisco, it was found that 44 per cent of rural women and girls, and 57 per cent of urban women and girls reported being physically abused in their homes. They reported that the abuse was inflicted by husbands in 60 per cent of cases and by parents in 40 per cent (Ramirez and Vazquez 1993, pp. 148–60, cited in Diaz and Sotelo 1996, p. 1937). Placing this issue on the feminist economist research agenda would help expose the facts and would address the economic causes of such attacks on women as well as policies that might help prevent such violence.

Another important research issue is that of the economic conditions of female-headed households. In 1990, for the country as a whole, 15.3 per cent of households with children were headed by women; by 1995 the figure increased to 17.8 per cent. The rate for Mexico City is greater, with 21.0 per cent of the households being headed by women in 1995 (INEGI 1990; INEGI-STPS 1995). The economic determinants of this circumstance and the survival strategies of the women involved have received relatively little attention in the literature.

Other important issues that have received relatively little attention in academic studies are the plight of domestic workers, and the differential impact of structural adjustment policies on Mexico's women. Feminist economic research on these and other issues has the potential not only to raise awareness and increase our knowledge of women's participation, but it also can contribute to the objectives of placing women on the national development agenda and empowering women at the family, community, and national levels.

JANET M. TANSKI

See also

Agriculture (Third World); Economic Restructuring; Globalization; Informal Sector; International Economics; Structural Adjustment Policies.

Bibliography

Albrecht, Laura J. (1994), 'Mystery in Cameron County', *Texas State Journal of Medicine*, **90** (4), (April), 16.

Arrom, Silvia Marina (1985), *The Women of Mexico City 1790–1857*, Stanford, California: Stanford University Press.

Bacon, David (1995), 'After NAFTA', *Environmental Action*, **27** (3), (Fall), 33–9.

Benería, Lourdes and Martha Roldán (1987), *The Crossroads of Class and Gender: Industrial Homework, Subcontracting, and Household Dynamics in Mexico City*. Chicago: University of Chicago Press.

De la Torre, Tomas (1987), 'Desde Salamanca, España, hasta Ciudad Real, Chiapas: diario de viaje 1544–1545', *Viajeros en Tabasco: Texto*, Ciprián Cabrera Bernart (ed.), Gobierno del Estado de Tabasco, Tabasco (Biblioteca Básica Tabasqueña).

Diaz Olavarrieta, Claudia and Julio Sotelo (1996), 'Domestic violence in Mexico: Letter from Mexico City' *The Journal of the American Medical Association*, **275** (24), June 26, 1937–1941.

El Colegio de Mexico (1960), *Estadísticas económicas del porfiriato*, Mexico, DF.

Escandon, Carmen Ramos (1987), 'Señoritas Porfirianas: Mujer e Ideología en el México Progresista 1880–1910', in Carmen Ramos Escandon et al. (eds), *Presencia y Transparencia: La Mujer en la Historia de Mexico*, Mexico, DF, El Colegio de Mexico, pp. 143–61.

Eskenazi, Brenda, Sylvia Guendelmen and Eric P. Elkin (1993), 'A preliminary study of reproductive outcomes of female Maquiladora workers in Tijuana, Mexico', *American Journal of Industrial Medicine*, **24** (6), (December), 667–76.

Giraud, François (1987), 'Mujeres y Familia en Nueva España' in Carmen Ramos Escandon, et al. (eds), *Presencia y Transparencia: La Mujer en la Historia de Mexico*, Mexico, DF, El Colegio de Mexico, pp. 63–77.

INEGI (Instituto Nacional de Estadística, Geografía e Informática) (1990), Population Census, Aguascalientes: Instituto Nacional de Estadística, Geografía e Informática.

INEGI (1993), *La Mujer en Mexico*, Aguascalientes: Instituto Nacional de Estadística, Geografía e Informática.

INEGI (1997a), *Estadisticas de la Industria Maquiladora de Exportacion*, Aguascalientes: Instituto Nacional de Estadística, Geografía e Informática.

INEGI (1997b), *Mujeres y Hombres en Mexico*, Aguascalientes: Instituto Nacional de Estadística, Geografía e Informática.

INEGI (1998), "Industria Maquiladora de Exportacion', in *Banco de Informacion Economica*, Aguascalientes: Instituto Nacional de Estadistica, Geografía e Informática. Http://dgcnesyp. inegi.gob.mx/BDINE/J15/j150001.HTM.

INEGI–STPS (Instituto Nacional de Estadística, Geografía e Informática–Secretaria de Trabajo y Promocion Social) (1995), *Encuesta Nacional de Empleo*, cited in INEGI (1997a).

Izquierdo, Ana Luisa (1989), 'La Condición de la Mujer en la Sociedad Maya Prehispánica' in Patricia Galeana de Valadés (ed.), *Seminario sobre la Participacion de la Mujer en la Vida Nacional*, Mexico, DF: Universidad Nacional Autónoma de México.

Kopinak, Kathryn (1995), 'Gender as a vehicle for the subordination of women maquiladora workers in Mexico', *Latin American Perspectives*, **22** (1), Issue 84, (Winter), 30–48.

Landa, Diego de (nd), *Relacion de las Cosas de Yucatan*, translated and edited by Alfred M. Tozzer, Peabody Museum of American Arcaeology and Ethnology, Harvard University, Cambridge, Massachusetts, cited by Izquierdo (1989), p. 9.

Miller, Francesca (1986), 'The international relations of women of the Americas, 1890–1928', *The Americas: A Quarterly Review of Inter-American Cultural History*, 43, October.

Miller, Francesca (1991), *Latin American Women and the Search for Social Justice*, Hanover and London: University Press of New England.

Ramirez, J. and G. Vazquez (1993), 'Mujer y violencia. Un hecho cotidiano', *Salud Publica Mexicana*, **35**, 148–60.

Rendon, Teresa y Carlos Salas (1987), 'Evolución del empleo en México: 1895–1980', *Estudios Demográficos y Urbanos*, Num 5, mayo–agosto, México, DF: El Colegio de México.

Rendon Gan, Teresa (1990), 'El Trabajo Femenino Remunerado en México durante el Siglo XX, Cambios, Tendencias y Perspectivas', in Elia Ramirez Bautista and Hilda R. Davila Ibanez (eds), *Trabajo Femenino y Crisis en Mexico. Transformaciones y Tendencias Actuales*, Mexico, Universidad Autonoma Metropolitana, Xochimilco, Division de Ciencias Sociales y Humanidades, Departamento de Producción Económica, pp. 29–51.

Robles, Rosario, Josefina Aranda and Carlota Botey (1993), 'La mujer campesina en la epoca de la modernidad', *El Cotidiano*, **52**, 25–32.

Rodriguez, Ma. De Jesus (1987), 'La Mujer y la Familia en la Sociedad Mexica' in Carmen Ramos Escandon et al. (eds), *Presencia y Transparencia: La Mujer en la Historia de Mexico*, Mexico, DF: El Colegio de Mexico, pp. 13–31.

Rojas, Rosa (ed.) (1994), *Chiapas, Y Las Mujeres Que?*, Mexico: Ediciones La Correa Feminista, Centro de Investigación y Capacitación de la Mujer A.C.

Roldán, Martha (1988), 'Renegotiating the Marital Contract: Intrahousehold Patterns of Money allocation and Women's Subordination Among Domestic Outworkers in Mexico City', in Daisy Dwyer and Judith Bruce (eds), *A Home Divided: Women and Income in the Third World*, Stanford, California: Stanford University Press, pp. 229–47.

Ruiz, Vicki L. and Susan Tiano (eds) (1991), *Women on the U.S.–Mexico Border: Responses to Change*, Boulder, San Franciso and Oxford: Westview Press.

Soto, Shirlene Ann (1977), 'The Mexican woman: a study of her participation in the Revolution 1910–1940', dissertation, Albuquerque, University of New Mexico.

SourceMex – Economic News and Analysis on Mexico, 3/20/91, Latin America Data Base, Albuquerque: Latin American Institute. Http://ladb.unm.edu

Stephen, Lynn (1996), 'Too Little, Too Late? The Impact of Article 27 on Women in Oaxaca', in Laura Randall (ed.), *Reforming Mexico's Agrarian Reform*, Armonk, New York and London: M.E. Sharpe, pp. 289–303.

Wilson, Fiona (1991), *Sweaters: Gender, Class and Workshop-Based Industry in Mexico*, New York: St Martin's Press.

Economic History, Middle East and North Africa*

Before discussing women in the economies of the Middle East and North Africa, the terms and geographical parameters must be defined. The term Middle East is geographically vague, as well as Eurocentric and colonialist, locating the region *vis à vis* Europe. Therefore the term Southwest Asia and North Africa (SWANA) will be used in this text to refer to Sudan, Egypt, Algeria, Morocco, Tunisia, Yemen, Saudi Arabia, Kuwait, Oman, Qatar, Iran, Iraq, Syria, Jordan, Lebanon, the West Bank, Gaza, Israel, the United Arab Emirates (UAE), Bahrain, Cyprus and Turkey. Although most of the countries of the region are considered Arab and Muslim, all contain non-Arab, non-Muslim communities, and in some, such as Cyprus, Iran, Turkey and Israel, these groups are the majority.

SWANA contains some of the globe's earliest civilizations, dating back at least 10 000 years. Knowledge of these cultures or how women fared in them is limited. El Saadawi (1993, p. 139) has argued that women in Ancient Egypt, Iraq and Palestine 'enjoyed respect and high status in all domains of life'. Early mythology suggests women were valued particularly for their contributions to economic survival in farming, weaving, water collecting and child bearing and rearing. Feminists have argued that patriarchy usurped matriarchal societies in these ancient cultures with the coming of urban societies and monotheism. All three of the monotheistic religions in the region, Judaism, Christianity and Islam, are patriarchal.

Although Islam, introduced in Arabia in the seventh century AD, is often viewed as particularly patriarchal, Nashat (1999) argues that the religion became so as it spread beyond Arabia, to areas where women's movements were already restricted. At the time of Muhammad women held important economic positions, as exemplified by Muhammad's first wife, Khadija, a rich, older woman and a businesswoman in her own right. Islam assured women's property and inheritance rights and historical records show that there were a number of women in early Islam who controlled fortunes and were active participants in the economy. Women's occupations included weaving, silk production, farming, music, peddling, midwifery, prostitution and trading. Women's access to the public sphere, though, diminished with increased urbanization.

Religion remains an important factor determining women's legal status in the region. Most countries use *Shari'a* (Islamic law) to define their legal system and thus women's rights. Israel, as a Jewish state, also uses religion as the basis for much of its legal system. Marriages, for instance, must take

---

* The views expressed herein are the author's and do not necessarily reflect the views of the US Department of Agriculture.

place within a particular religious tradition, whether in Israel, Iran or the Arab countries. The only exceptions are Turkey and Cyprus, which have civil marriages. The strong link between religion and the state has serious implications for defining the space within which women are able to manoeuvre, particularly as women's economic wellbeing is generally linked to their marital status and laws governing marriage. Access to employment, birth control and education, the public discourse on women's roles, and control of women's fertility can all be linked to family law and religious interpretation. Although in theory it is possible to protect women by linking religion and family law, and some liberal interpreters of the *Qur'an* have argued for equality between men between women, in practice these laws have often been used to control and isolate women.

Colonialism and neocolonialism, particularly by the English and French and more recently by the USA, have left their economic and political mark on the region. Given the tumultuous colonialist history, women have often struggled more for basic human rights, economic survival and political freedom than for equal rights with men. Women's circumstances cannot be separated from the local geopolitical conditions. SWANA's recent history has included foreign occupations, numerous wars and heavily militarized societies. The region is among the most highly armed in the world and has experienced high levels of conflict, particularly since the turn of the century. Women often bear the brunt of economic hardship during wars and military conflicts, as they struggle to survive, often without male providers. A common statement made by Palestinian feminists is that they bear a triple burden: oppression as a colonized people, as workers and as women.

Historical records show that women have acted as a collective group, protesting political or economic conditions which they felt were unjust. Tucker (1999) recounts how Palestinian women organized early in the twentieth century to protest against the British occupation of Palestine and the large-scale immigration of European Jews, which they perceived as threatening their economic survival. Egyptian women also protested against English occupation, marching in the streets of Cairo in 1919.

There has also been a feminist movement in the region for quite some time. Huda Sha'rawi, an early Egyptian feminist, among her many other accomplishments, is famous for taking off her veil in 1923 in a symbolic gesture. El Saadawi (1993) recounts how early Palestinian feminist May Ziyada was sent to a mental hospital after expressing her feminist sentiments. Yet, as Ahmed (1992) points out, feminism was closely associated with the oppressive forces of colonialism in the region, and therefore has not always been embraced. Nassef, a contemporary of Sha'rawi and Ziyada, articulated a 'feminism that did not automatically affiliate itself with westernization' (Ahmed 1992, p. 179), but she died young and her voice and ideas were lost in subsequent years. Calls for indigenous forms of feminism are now reemerging.

Concerning women's contemporary social and economic position, considerable differences exist between communities in SWANA. The degree to which religious law is followed and the way *Shari'a* is interpreted vary considerably. Huge income disparities also exist in the region within countries, but even more acutely between countries. Compared to other developing regions, SWANA has relatively low absolute poverty rates, but poverty remains a serious problem for many countries. Egypt, Yemen and Sudan are among the poorest countries, while the UAE, Saudi Arabia, Kuwait, Qatar and Israel are quite wealthy. This has profound effects on the economic wellbeing of women in various parts of the regions as well as the issues of concern to women in various communities.

Breakdowns of poverty by sex are unavailable, and given the low rate of households headed by single women in the region this statistic would be of limited use. A more important issue which remains largely unanswered is how much access women have to resources within their households. If standard measures such as female literacy and labour force participation are used, the conclusion would be, not much. But the question remains, do such measures accurately capture women's economic empowerment?

Two rather controversial stylized facts about women of SWANA are that they have among the lowest labour force participation and the highest fertility rates in the world. (Israel is excluded from this discussion, as it is categorized as industrial and has low fertility rates and high female labour force participation rates.) Women's share in the adult labour force ranges from 7 (Saudi Arabia) to 34 per cent (Turkey) (UNDP 1996). A number of reasons have been put forth to explain these statistics. These include measurement problems, Islam, culture, patriarchy and the structure of the economy. While a commonly held belief is that low labour force participation rates are somehow linked to Islam, some scholars have disputed this claim. A number of Islamic countries, particularly those outside SWANA, do not have low labour force participation rates. Papps (1993) found that religiosity was not a factor in predicting people's attitudes about women's economic roles in four countries: Egypt, Jordan, Morocco and Turkey. She concludes that culture and the strength of patriarchy in the region are far more important considerations than religion.

Moghadam (1995) argues that the type of 'modernization' which occurred in the region, favouring import substitution strategies and extraction, has also been a contributing factor to women's marginalization. Import substitution and resource extraction based economies tend to be more capital intensive. The heavy technological capital these economies invest in is often in male-dominated sectors. She provides the examples of Morocco and Tunisia, where women's labour force participation rates have been higher and the economies are more export oriented, as counter-examples.

One explanation for low labour force participation rates then is the lack of opportunities for women in the industrial sector. Increased women's labour force participation though is no panacea, as women who do find work often end up as textiles workers and carpet weavers, where they face very low wages and unsafe work conditions. Women have also become active participants in the informal economy. While for some informal sector work is well paid and rewarding, for others the income may be low and highly uncertain, work conditions may be dangerous and benefits and job security nonexistent. Women's household duties, which require a more flexible work structure, as well as the economic stress of structural adjustment, have led some women to seek out this type of work.

Labour force participation rates in the region are also underestimated. This problem, while not unique to the region, may be particularly acute for a number of reasons. First, the transition from the unpaid to the paid economy is often linked to industrialization, and the region has been rather late in industrializing. Women work in agriculture in many of these countries, yet their work is not counted. Family businesses absorb women's time, although this may not be acknowledged by men when answering household surveys. Women's participation in the informal economy may also not be captured. In addition, women put in long hours in the house, raising large families and coping economically on very little. Anker and Anker (1995) point out that in Egypt experiments with survey techniques led to labour force participation rate estimates which varied from 6.2 to 41.3 per cent. Varying the definition of work further increased the rate to about 91 per cent.

Whatever the reason for low rates historically, women's labour force participation in the region has been increasing. Economic need and higher education have been two factors leading women to seek employment, although most women are still in traditionally female occupations. A recent study by Anker (1998) found considerable occupational segregation in Bahrain, Iran, Jordan and Kuwait, but less in Tunisia and Egypt. It should be noted that within the region only Saudi Arabia practises complete sex segregation in labour markets which, while it has restricted women's roles and mobility, has also created a demand for female workers to serve women.

Literacy in the region has risen tremendously in the twentieth century, with Israeli, Lebanese, Turkish and Palestinian women in particular having both high literacy rates and education levels. Women in the Gulf states have lagged behind, but are now catching up. Kuwait, Bahrain, Qatar and the UAE now all have female literacy rates over 70 per cent. Illiteracy in some countries, such as Sudan, Egypt and Yemen, which have low literacy rates for both men and women, can be linked to poverty as well as sex discrimination.

While overall literacy, particularly in rural areas, remains low in these countries, many more women are now graduating from high school and college and going on to professional occupations, particularly in urban areas. Occupations which educated women enter are still closely sex linked and include nursing, administration, teaching and social work.

When women do enter the labour force, they are more likely to suffer from unemployment. Al-Qudsi et al. (1993) found that female unemployment rates in Bahrain, Egypt, Jordan and Iraq were double male rates. There is also evidence that women's wages are lower than men's. According to UN estimates, women's wages as a percentage of men's in agriculture are 84.5 per cent in Turkey, 79.5 per cent in Egypt, 60 per cent in Cyprus and Syria, compared to 75 per cent in the USA, although more research is needed to determine women's labour contributions and the degree of discrimination and occupational segregation they face.

Another interesting 'puzzle' in the region is the fertility issue. Economic theory suggests that fertility is inversely related to economic growth. Kuwait fits this model, with a current total fertility rate or TFR (an estimate of the average number of children a woman will have in her lifetime) around 3.1 and high income and literacy rates, as compared to average TFRs in the Arab world of around 4.6. In contrast, high national income countries such as Saudi Arabia and Libya have TFRs over 6. Literacy and fertility are also generally inversely related, yet the Palestinians and Jordanians, who have very high literacy rates, still have high fertility rates as well. This trend, though, is not universal. Despite low income and literacy rates, the average TFR in Egypt dropped from 5.9 to 3.8 between the years 1970–80 and 1982–92.

A number of factors explain SWANA's high fertility rates. Fertility rates may initially increase before they decrease as income rises. In addition, children in the region are still perceived as contributors to family income and an insurance policy for parents, particularly since many countries do not have well-developed safety nets. While the opportunity cost of women staying home has increased, this has primarily affected the small elite of educated women, who have increased their labour force participation and lowered their fertility rates. Another reason why fertility rates have remained high is that the family unit is highly valued and status is placed on having large families. Women often articulate the desire to have many children. In addition, some states have followed pro-natalist policies.

The centrality of the family in SWANA has been both a positive and a negative force in women's lives. Women are honoured for their roles as mothers and are considered the backbone of the society and the family. Hijab (1988) states that it is important not to conflate equality with respect when discussing Arab societies. Although women do not receive equal treatment to men, they are treated with respect. This, Hijab argues, is why women who have attempted to enter male-dominated professions have not had too much difficulty. Also, because the family is valued, many states have laws guaranteeing women paid maternity leave and access to child care as women have begun entering the paid labour force in increased numbers. Women enjoy excellent maternity leave policies in countries such as Libya, Iraq and Saudi Arabia.

Feminist economists have barely begun covering issues pertaining to women's economic position in SWANA. The extent of and changes in wage discrimination and occupational segregation have not been adequately addressed. Detailed microeconomic as well as comparative studies of women's wellbeing in individual communities are missing. The question of whether policymakers can improve women's economic conditions without cultural changes remains an open one, and the role of conflict in the region and its effect on women's economic wellbeing has been understudied. The role of the family in either empowering or controlling women is also not well understood and has important economic implications.

Many of the regional structural adjustment analyses have ignored gender issues. The situation facing women in countries such as Egypt and Yemen, where poverty is widespread and structural adjustment painful, have not been adequately addressed. Documentation of women's role in the informal sector remains inadequate. The growing problem of unemployment for people of the region, which impacts women both as labour market participants and household managers, must be addressed. Little is understood about the link between women's wellbeing and safety nets, whether family or government based. The list is practically endless.

Data availability remains a serious problem. Many countries have collected very limited data on women, and other countries do not allow access to their data. This is particularly true of the Gulf states. Military conflicts and political tensions in the region have also impeded research efforts and data collection. Accurate, comprehensive data on the Palestinians' economic conditions have been difficult to obtain, and as a result the Palestinian economy has been excluded from almost all tables listing macroeconomic conditions in the region. Because of wars, data from Lebanon, Iraq, Sudan and Yemen are limited. All of these factors contribute to the lack of published information on women in the region.

Still, the most important issue facing feminist economists studying the region is the appropriateness of existing theory and methodology. North American and European feminist scholars have critiqued economics for its androcentrism, but feminist economic theory must also be critiqued for its cultural biases. Culturally appropriate research which addresses local concerns is necessary. Women in SWANA, as well as in other parts of the world, need forums for determining what their primary economic concerns are. For example, is lowering fertility an objective of local women, or a goal imposed by outsiders? Do women of the region see entry into the paid labour force as the answer to economic insecurity?

Will obtaining more data necessarily address these issues? Olmsted (1997) and Berik (1996), who have both conducted field work in the region, point out that feminist researchers need to move beyond survey analysis. More interactive research methods such as focus groups and in-depth interviews may be required to address gender concerns in SWANA.

While the women of SWANA are often viewed by the rest of the world as being among the most oppressed, the reality is far more complex. Broader, more culturally sensitive definitions of economic empowerment are needed to understand gender dynamics in the region. Women, while often denied official representation in governments and access to the labour market, have still been powerful economic and political activists within both the home and the public sphere. In addition there are huge differences in the achievements of women of the region, based on their geographical and class locations. Western scholars, including feminists, have tended to stereotype Islam, Arab culture and more generally women in SWANA, and much more research is needed to undo these myths, while also providing policymakers with better and more accurate information about where these women do lack political and economic access because of their sex.

JENNIFER C. OLMSTED

See also

Development, Theories of; Family, Economics of; Imperialism; Informal Sector; Labour Force Participation; Methodology; Patriarchy; Population; Occupational Segregation; Structural Adjustment Policies.

Bibliography

Ahmed, Leila (1992), *Women and Gender in Islam: Historical Roots of a Modern Debate*, New Haven, Connecticut: Yale University Press.

Al-Qudsi, Sulayman, Ragui Assaad and Radwan Shaban (1993), 'Labor Markets in the Arab Countries: A Survey', paper presented at the First Annual Conference on Development Economics, Cairo, Egypt.

Anker, Richard (1998), *Gender and Jobs: Sex Segregation of Occupations in the World*, Geneva: International Labour Office.

Anker, Richard and Martha Anker (1995), 'Measuring Female Labour Force with Emphasis on Egypt', in Nabil Khoury and Valentine Moghadam (eds), *Gender and Development in the Arab World: Women's Economic Participation: Patterns and Policies*, London: Zed Press, pp. 148– 76.

Berik, Gunseli (1996), 'Understanding the Gender System in Rural Turkey: Fieldwork Dilemmas of Conformity and Intervention', in Diane Wolf (ed.), *Feminist Dilemmas in Fieldwork*, Boulder, Colorado: Westview Press, pp. 56–71.

El Saadawi, Nawal (1993), 'Women's Resistance in the Arab World and in Egypt', in Haleh Afshar and Mary Maynard (eds), *Women in the Middle East: Perceptions, Realities and Struggles for Liberation*, (Women's Studies at York), London: Macmillan, pp. 139–45.

Hijab, Nadia (1988), *Womanpower: The Arab Debate on Women at Work*, Cambridge: Cambridge Middle East Library.

Hijab, Nadia (1994), 'Women and work in the Arab world', *Middle East Report Special Publication*, July.

Moghadam, Valentine (1995), 'The Political Economy of Female Employment in the Arab Region', in Nabil Khoury and Valentine Moghadam (eds), *Gender and Development in the Arab World: Women's Economic Participation: Patterns and Policies*, London: Zed Press, pp. 6–34.

Nashat, Guity (1999), 'Women in the Middle East: 8000 B.C.E.–C.E. 1800', in Guity Nashat and Judith E. Tucker, *Women in the Middle East and North Africa: Restoring Women to History*, Bloomington, Indiana: Indiana University Press, pp. 5–72.

Obermeyer, Carla Makhlouf (ed.) (1995), *Family, Gender, and Population in the Middle East: Policies in Context*, Cairo: The American University Press.

Olmsted, Jennifer C. (1997), 'Telling Palestinian women's economic stories', *Feminist Economics*, 3 (2), 141–51.

Papps, Ivy (1993), 'Attitudes towards Female Employment in Four Middle Eastern Countries', in Haleh Afshar and Mary Maynard (eds), *Women in the Middle East: Perceptions, Realities and Struggles for Liberation*, (Women's Studies at York), London: Macmillan, pp. 96–116.

Swirski, Barbara and Marilyn Safir (1991), 'Living in a Jewish State: National, Ethnic and Religious Implications', in Barbara Swirski and Marilyn Safir (eds), *Calling the Equality Bluff: Women in Israel*, New York: Pergammon Press, pp. 7–17.

Tucker, Judith (1988), 'Women in the Middle East and North Africa: The Nineteenth and Twentieth Centuries', in Guity Nashat and Judith E. Tucker, *Women in the Middle East and North Africa: Restoring Women to History*, Bloomington, Indiana: Indiana University Press, pp. 73–131.

UNDP (United Nations Development Programme)(1996), *Human Development Report*, New York: Oxford University Press.

World Bank (1995), *Claiming the Future: Choosing Prosperity in the Middle East and North Africa*, Washington, DC: The World Bank.

Economic History, Russia

The history of Russia includes experience with a variety of economic systems, including serfdom, Soviet-style socialism and the recent attempt to move to a market-based private-enterprise economy. The nature of women's participation in Russian economic life over time has been shaped both by the very different institutional arrangements of the different periods and by the remarkably unchanging views of women's domestic and nurturing roles. The former, combined with changing state goals and political forces, have determined the extent of women's involvement in the paid labour force; the latter have ensured women's continuing responsibility for work in the home.

Pre-Soviet Russia

Prior to the twentieth century, Russia was characterized by enormous class differences. For women of the privileged classes economic and legal rights varied significantly over the centuries, while for peasant women life was shaped more by custom than by law and thus changed very slowly. What changes did occur in the lives of peasant women in the pre-Soviet period were due more to changes in the relationships between peasants and land-lords than to explicit changes in women's rights or obligations.

In the medieval period, women of the noble or landowning classes in Russia enjoyed the right to hold (and sell) property, to engage independently in a variety of financial transactions and to participate on their own in the legal system. Their dowries remained their own property, as did anything they inherited or acquired during marriage (Pushkareva 1997, pp. 47–50). During the sixteenth and seventeenth centuries, the Russian rulers consolidated their power over society, the rights of these women diminished and women of the aristocracy found themselves confined to special women's quarters (*terem*), closed off from the larger society, with their duties (mainly 'to devote all their strength to their family and their home') spelled out in the manual of household management called the *Domostroi* (Pushkareva 1997, pp. 63, 83, 88). With the attempt by Peter the Great to westernize the country in the early eighteenth century, noble-women emerged from seclusion and began again to be granted certain economic and legal rights, a process which continued under Elizabeth and Catherine the Great, the powerful women who ruled after Peter's death. In the mid-nineteenth century, as revolutionary activity and demands for social justice increased, the focus for people concerned with the position of women was on the rights to work and to receive an education (Pushkareva 1997, p. 236).

For peasant women, however, the right to work was never an issue. These women, who constituted around 90 per cent of Russian women up until the Bolshevik Revolution in November 1917, spent their lives engaged in arduous and endless labour, attempting to meet the economic demands imposed by heavy taxation and, between the sixteenth century and 1861, by the institution of serfdom. Under serfdom, peasants faced heavy obligations to their landlords in cash, in kind and in service. Despite laws intended to limit it, the power of the landlords over the lives of their serfs was in practice nearly absolute. Landlords could transfer serfs to other landowners, exile them to Siberia or send them to serve in the army, even when this meant the break-up of families; they could refuse permission for a female serf to marry a serf from another estate, require that one of their serfs marry another, or charge fees before allowing marriages desired by the serfs themselves (Blum 1969, pp. 423–35).

Economic pressures were not eased by the emancipation of the serfs in 1861, since the peasant communities were required to pay the government for the plots of land they received at the time of emancipation. To meet these annual redemption payments, many young men were sent by the village communes to work in the cities, so that agricultural work was increasingly the responsibility of the women who remained behind. Nor was life easier for those women who migrated to the cities. Women working in factories earned only 42 per cent as much as men, lived with their families in crowded dormitories far from their place of work, and often had to bring their babies to the workplace and leave their young children at home unsupervised (Pushkareva 1997, pp. 223–5). While there were attempts to introduce some protective (labour) legislation in the early 1900s, many women workers were illiterate and knew nothing of the legislation, and even those who did were often too poor to take advantage of it (Pushkareva 1997, p. 238).

The Soviet period

The seizure of power by the Bolsheviks in 1917 introduced a period of dramatic social and economic change which brought both enormous opportunities and enormous hardships to Russian women. Nonetheless when the Soviet Union was formally dissolved on 25 December 1991, 74 years after the Revolution, Russian women still faced, as they had prior to the Soviet experiment, gender divisions in the workplace and in the home and a patriarchal society which permitted the Minister of Labour to say without apology 'Why do we have to give work to women when there are men unemployed?' (*Moscow Times*, 16 February 1993).

The 1920s

In the early Soviet period, legislation was shaped both by the demands of the Civil War and by the Marxist beliefs of the new leaders. While the new regime placed far greater emphasis on class than on gender, it recognized that men and women had not been equal in tsarist Russia. The Bolsheviks believed that the precondition for equality between men and women was the economic independence of women. Those concerned with women's status thus focused their attention on employment issues and on the social provision of household services such as child care, laundry and food preparation. They believed that if women were freed from responsibilities in the home, they would be able to obtain jobs and end their dependence on their husbands.

This belief underpinned the Family Codes of 1918 and 1926, which made marriage a civil rather than religious institution, dissolvable by either party without the need to establish grounds for divorce, and with the right to receive alimony determined by disability and poverty rather than by gender (Goldman 1993, pp. 51–2). While philosophically far ahead of legislation in the rest of the world, these Family Codes proved a mixed blessing for Soviet women. As Wendy Goldman explains in *Women, the State and Revolution*, 'the right to divorce [was considered] particularly important to women, whose true feelings and abilities were so often stifled by the unbreakable bonds of marriage' (Goldman 1993, p. 101) and yet 'high unemployment, low wages, and lack of daycare created a sharp contradiction between the harsh reality of life and a legal vision of freedom' (p. 103).

In the wake of the devastation caused by years of war (World War I, revolution and civil war), the Bolsheviks in 1921 retreated temporarily from their commitment to establish an economic system free of the 'anarchy of the market' and the evils they believed sprang from private ownership of the means of production. With the introduction of the New Economic Policy, most small enterprises reverted to private ownership and even those enterprises which remained in the hands of the state were to be managed with attention to profit. This concern with profit led to sharp increases in the unemployment rate, and women were hurt disproportionately by the cutbacks in jobs.

Less skilled, less educated and less experienced, women were also put at a disadvantage in the labour market by the law giving priority to war veterans, by the protective labour legislation intended to ensure that their reproductive abilities were unimpaired, by the inability of the financially-strapped government to provide sufficient child care facilities and by the patriarchal attitudes of employers. Although the law promised equal pay for equal work (decades before such a law was even considered in Western Europe or the United States), far too many women were unable to find jobs and thus remained dependent on husbands who in startling numbers took advantage of the newly liberal marriage and divorce laws to leave their wives for other women, especially if their wives became pregnant (Goldman 1991, p. 128).

The 1920s were thus a period of enormous economic hardship for Russian women. Many found it necessary to earn money through prostitution. Many were forced to abandon their children because they could not provide for them unless they were employed and they could not get or keep jobs if they had child care responsibilities. On the other hand, the 1920s was also the decade of active work by the *Zhenotdel*, the women's department of the Communist Party. While the primary goal of the *Zhenotdel* was the political mobilization of women, the means used were diverse and included a drive to increase literacy, the organization of communal child care and dining facilities, internship programmes in various institutions and general consciousness raising (Lapidus 1978, pp. 63–5).

The 1930s and World War II

With the end of the New Economic Policy and the introduction of rapid industrialization and central planning by Joseph Stalin in the late 1920s and early 1930s, the problem of unemployment disappeared and the demands of the economy made female participation in the industrial labour force essential. Excess demand for labour resulted from the commitment to extremely rapid increases in output and from an incentive system which rewarded enterprise managers and workers for fulfilling gross output targets rather than for keeping costs low or profits high. The need to draw women into the labour force was greatly intensified by the demographic imbalances resulting from the loss of so many young men in the wars, in the forced collectivization of agriculture in the early 1930s and in the Stalinist purges of the late 1930s. Between 1930 and 1932, the number of women employed doubled from 3 to 6 million and between 1933 and 1937, 3.35 million more women joined the industrial labour force. Women made up 82 per cent of all newly-employed workers in this period, and by 1937 they made up 34 per cent of the total work force (Lapidus 1978, p. 99). Protective legislation, which made women more expensive employees and limited the kinds of work women could legally perform, did not significantly reduce their opportunities, especially since there was a tendency to ignore such legislation when it proved an obstacle to plan fulfilment.

New employment opportunities offered women considerable upward social mobility, as did new educational opportunities. Russian women were being educated in unprecedented numbers. Between 1926 and 1939, the official female literacy rate rose from 42.7 to 81.6 per cent; by 1937, 43 per cent of the students in higher educational institutions were female, up from 28 per cent in 1927 (Lapidus 1978, pp. 136, 149).

Despite these gains, the 1930s were not easy for Russian women. The high share of the country's resources devoted to investment meant that wages were extremely low. The emphasis on heavy industry meant that consumer goods and services were severely neglected, and it was primarily the women who had to cope with the difficulties this created. The purges meant the arrest and incarceration in labour camps of many women, and the disruption of family life of many more, especially since the arrest of a husband or father often meant the loss of one's apartment and the impossibility of finding any but the most menial job.

The difficulties of life in the Soviet Union intensified with the onset of World War II. Production was necessarily directed almost exclusively to the war effort and was increasingly the responsibility of women, as men were sent to the front. Women in the factories worked 10–12 hours a day, while those in the countryside worked as much as 22 hours a day (Pushkareva 1997, p. 262); in addition, by 1943 women made up 8 per cent of those serving in the military (Clements 1991, p. 271). The material cost of the war was enormous, one estimate equating it to the total wealth created in the industrialization drive of the 1930s. The human cost was also staggering and exacerbated the already pronounced demographic imbalance. According to Soviet censuses, in 1939 there were 7.5 million more women than men in the Soviet Union, and by 1959 this difference had risen to over 20 million (*Narodnoe khoziaistvo SSSR v 1982 godu* 1983, p. 6).

Post-World War II Soviet socialism

Although the end of the war brought some relief, it was not until after Stalin's death in 1953 that Soviet leaders relaxed both the political terror and the economic pressure. Under Nikita Khrushchev housing construction increased sharply, reducing the number of families forced to live in communal apartments with shared kitchen and bathroom facilities. There were also increases in the provision of child care services and in the production of consumer goods and services, as the Party attempted to shift its source of legitimacy from a reliance on terror to a social contract with the population. For the first time these improvements extended to rural areas, although change there was much slower than in the cities. As Clements notes (1991, p. 273), 'many peasant women [still] lugged water in buckets from wells, lit their huts with oil lamps, and heated and cooked with the traditional brick stoves until the late 1960s'.

There were also gains in education and in political representation for women during this period. The percentage of peasant women who had completed high school rose from 21 in 1959 to 48 in 1970, although this continued to lag behind the level in cities, where 75 per cent of the women had high-school educations in 1970 (Clements 1991, p. 274). Under Khrushchev the first (and only) woman was appointed to the Politburo, and women's councils (*zhensovety*) were set up to work at the local level to improve the quality of women's lives, primarily by addressing issues of child care, social services, culture and health.

During this mature period of Soviet socialism, the lives of most Russian women were easier than at any other time during the century, yet many difficulties and inequities remained. Despite the promises of the early years of Bolshevik rule, the state had found it impossible to take over the tasks associated with running a home and raising a family, and these responsibilities fell almost entirely upon women. Not only was there no attempt by Soviet leaders to change the gender division of roles within the family or increase male participation in housework and child care, but the demographic imbalance meant that many Russian women were raising children as single parents. In 1959, almost 30 per cent of Soviet households were headed by women (Lapidus 1978, p. 169).

In addition to their work in the home, the overwhelming majority of Soviet women of working age also held paying jobs, a consequence of both ideology and economic necessity. In the late 1970s 'if all agricultural employment [were] included, female participation rates approach[ed] the demographic maximum, with over 85 percent of able-bodied women between the ages of twenty and fifty-five ... employed full time' (Lapidus 1978, p. 161).

For this work, women received on average about 70 per cent of the pay men received, a function of both the industries in which they worked and the positions they held (Lapidus 1978, pp. 193–4). Women were concentrated in light industry and in the trade, public catering, heath and culture sectors, all of which were assigned low priority by the leaders (Lapidus 1978, pp. 171–3). According to one Russian author, in the late 1980s 'nearly 80 percent of working women [were] employed in so-called "female" sectors and jobs' (Mezentseva 1994, p. 111). Despite high levels of education and regardless of the sector in which they were employed, women were over-represented in the lower ranks and under-represented at the higher levels (Lapidus 1978, p. 185), a pattern that was also true in the political hierarchy (Nechemias 1996). Women tended to choose jobs for proximity to home or child care rather than for wage rates or opportunities for advancement and they had less time than men to devote to political meetings and educational seminars at their places of employment.

Post-Soviet Russia

Soviet living standards improved significantly in the 1960s and early 1970s, but by the late 1970s falling rates of economic growth, increased exposure to the West and growing awareness of such social ills as juvenile delinquency, alcoholism and petty crime were contributing to widespread dissatisfaction and cynicism about Soviet achievements. Mikhail Gorbachev's attempts to restructure the economy and reinvigorate the population in the late 1980s simultaneously opened up new possibilities for Soviet women and created new obstacles. With the dissolution of the USSR in 1991 and the Russian government's commitment to convert to a market economy based on private ownership, the difficulties for women soon outweighed the opportunities, as many of the gains achieved under Soviet socialism were threatened by the transition process and the promises offered by democracy and the market remained largely unrealized.

The disruption of the economy initially resulted in severe shortages of food and other consumer goods, making the task of feeding and clothing one's family even more time-consuming than before. The renewed focus on profit meant, as it had in the 1920s, that women were especially vulnerable to unemployment. The laws providing for generous maternity leaves remained on the books, making women workers expensive; the restructuring of the economy eliminated many of the kinds of positions which had been predominantly filled by women; the dramatic reduction in government revenues meant low – and often long-deferred – wages for state jobs in the primarily female education and health sectors. While official unemployment figures in Russia are admittedly unreliable, it is nonetheless clear that women today constitute at least 70 per cent of the unemployed (Bridger et al. 1996, pp. 51–2).

Official figures on poverty are also unreliable, but there are strong reasons to believe that women are disproportionately represented as well among the almost 21 per cent of the Russian population who are officially identified as having incomes below the subsistence level (*Jamestown Monitor* 16 October 1997). According to the *World Development Report 1996* (World Bank 1996, p. 71), in Russia and the other former Soviet republics the characteristics most likely to be associated with poverty are belonging to a large or single-parent family, being out of work, being old, lacking assets and lacking education. Of these, all but the last are significantly more likely to characterize women than men in Russia.

Along with these economic difficulties have come political and social changes. The end of censorship has led to a flourishing industry in pornography and to the open expression of patriarchal values. While the view that women are responsible for creating a warm and nurturing home life is not new in Russia, and there were many campaigns during the Soviet period which stressed the importance of this role, these earlier campaigns assumed that women would also participate fully in the labour force. Now women are being told that they should confine themselves to the home.

Not only are women supposed to withdraw from the labour force they are also apparently expected to withdraw from the political sphere. Under the quotas which characterized the Soviet period, women held roughly one-third of the seats in the legislative body. With the elimination of these quotas in 1989, the number of women elected fell by half, and the trend has continued (Marsh 1996, p. 288). The elections of 1993 reduced the share of women in the Duma to 13.5 per cent (60 of 450 members), and those of 1995 brought it down to 9.8 per cent (Rule and Shvedova 1996, pp. 45, 55). In addition, the 1995 elections marked the failure of the Women of Russia party to acquire the 5 per cent of the vote needed to qualify for party-list representation (Rueschemeyer 1997, p. 7).

On the other hand, the freedom to engage in political discourse and to form public organizations has given women a new channel for effecting change in their lives and society. In the Soviet period, feminism was associated with the bourgeois West and feminist analysis was prohibited by the authorities. (In the late 1970s, four women were deported for their refusal to halt publication of an unofficial feminist magazine, see Clements 1991, p. 277 and Marsh 1996.) Although there is still a tendency for Russian women to associate feminism with Western values with which they are uncomfortable (in particular a denial of 'femininity'), a number of women are beginning to establish organizations and pursue research addressing feminist concerns (see Posadskaya 1994; Marsh 1996; Rotkirch and Haavio-Mannila 1996).

The experience of women in Russia suggests that differences in economic systems do not necessarily lead to fundamental differences in the economic lives of women, and a comparison of the experience of Soviet and USA women reinforces this conclusion. Under both serfdom and Soviet socialism, the work of Russian women was essential for the leaders' goals as well as for the survival of the family, but this did not eradicate patriarchal attitudes. Under both the New Economic Policy of the 1920s and the transition to the market in the 1990s women have borne the brunt of unemployment, while in the period of Soviet socialism they tended to be employed in low-status and low-paying occupations. Under both twentieth-century American capitalism and twentieth-century Soviet socialism, women have experienced occupational segregation, glass ceilings and the double day.

Neither in a market system oriented toward the maximization of profit nor in a planned system oriented toward the maximization of heavy industrial output has the contribution of women in the domestic sphere been assigned significant value. Nor has the employment outside the home of the majority of women significantly affected either the distribution of obligations within the home or the balance of power between men and women in the public sphere. The explanation of the phenomena which characterize women's economic lives must therefore lie beyond the nature of particular economic systems, or else economic systems bear far more similarities to one another than is generally recognized. Both feminist economics and the study of economic systems can be enriched through further exploration of these issues.

JUDITH RECORD MCKINNEY

See also
Socialism; Marxist Political Economics; Economic Restructuring.

Bibliography
Blum, Jerome (1969), *Lord and Peasant in Russia*, New York: Atheneum.
Bridger, Sue, Rebecca Kay and Kathryn Pinnick (1996), *No More Heroines? Russia, Women and the Market*, New York and London: Routledge.
Buckley, Mary (ed.) (1992), *Perestroika and Soviet Women*, New York and Cambridge: Cambridge University Press.
Clements, Barbara Evans (1991), 'Later Developments: Trends in Soviet Women's History, 1930 to the Present', in Barbara Evans Clements, Barbara Alpern Engel and Christine D. Worobec (eds), *Russia's Women: Accommodation, Resistance, Transformation*, Berkeley, CA: University of California Press, pp. 267–78.
Goldman, Wendy Z. (1991), 'Working-Class Women and the "Withering Away" of the Family', in Sheila Fitzpatrick, Alexander Rabinowitch and Richard Stites (eds), *Russia in the Era of NEP*, Bloomington, Indiana: Indiana University Press, pp. 125–43.
Goldman, Wendy Z. (1993), *Women, the State and Revolution: Soviet Family Policy and Social Life, 1917–1936*, New York and Cambridge: Cambridge University Press.
Jamestown Monitor (1997), 16 October.
Lapidus, Gail Warshofsky (1978), *Women in Soviet Society: Equality, Development, and Social Change*, Berkeley, California and London: University of California Press.
Marsh, Rosalind (1996), 'The Russian women's movement', in *Women in Russia and Ukraine*, New York and Cambridge: Cambridge University Press, pp. 286–304.
Mezentseva, Yelena (1994), 'Equal opportunities or protectionist measures? The choice facing women', in Anastasia Posadskaya (ed.), *Women in Russia*, New York and London: Verso, pp. 109–22.
Moscow Times (1993), 16 February.

Narodnoe khoziaistvo SSSR v 1982 godu (1983), Moscow: Finansy i statistika.

Nechemias, Carol (1996), 'Women's Participation: from Lenin to Gorbachev', in Wilma Rule and Norma C. Noonan (eds), *Russian Women in Politics and Society*, Westport, Connecticut and London: Greenwood Press, pp. 15–30.

Posadskaya, Anastasia (ed.) (1994), trans. by Kate Clark, *Women in Russia: A New Era in Russian Feminism*, New York and London: Verso.

Pushkareva, Natalia (1997), trans. and ed. by Eve Levin, *Women in Russian History: From the Tenth to the Twentieth Century*, Armonk, New York and London: M.E. Sharpe.

Rotkirch, Anna and Elina Haavio-Mannila (eds) (1996), *Women's Voices in Russia Today*, Brookfield, Vermont and Aldershot: Dartmouth Publishing Company.

Rueschemeyer, Marilyn (1997) 'Ongoing transformations: women in the politics of post-communist societies', *AAASS NewsNet*, **37** (2), (March), 7–8.

Rule, Wilma and Nadezhda Shvedova (1996), 'Women in Russia's first multiparty election', in Wilma Rule and Norma C. Noonan (eds), *Russian Women in Politics and Society*, Westport, Connecticut and London: Greenwood Press, pp. 40–59.

World Bank (1996), *World Development Report 1996: From Plan to Market*, Oxford: Oxford University Press.

Economic History, Singapore

Singapore, a small island economy of just over three million people in Southeast Asia, has had high rates of economic growth and remarkable increases in its standard of living since independence in the 1960s. The economic roles of women – in the labour force, in the household and as reproducers of the next generation of workers – have been critical components of these outcomes although women have not shared equally in the gains.

Singapore has been widely cited as an economic success story. Although the Asian economic crisis that arose in other countries in 1997 may affect Singapore, growth through 1997 remained close to 8 per cent. Singapore considers itself a model for Asian development – one based on Asian values that stress the importance of family, community, hard work and respect for authority. In recent years statesmen such as Senior Minister Lee Kuan Yew have suggested that transitional economies in the region emulate its form of capitalism rather than the United States model. Because of its renown and the relevance of women's economic activities to the goals of short- and long-term growth, Singapore is the Southeast Asian nation chosen for this volume.

Pre-independence

Singapore was under British colonial rule from 1819 until 1959 when it obtained self-rule status. During this time period, Singapore was an entrepot economy, or a centre for transshipment of goods into and out of the region, because its location as an intermediary was ideal. Shipbuilding and repair and petroleum refining were the major industries. According to Kuo and Wong (1979), Singapore did not have a settled population until the 1930s. Before then many inhabitants were Chinese male immigrants who came to work on a temporary basis in these industries and remit earnings to their families abroad. Immigration controls were imposed by the colonial government in the 1930s to curtail transient migration and promote permanence. Women's economic activities became more a part of economic life; by the mid-1950s about half of women workers were engaged in community, social and personal services, one-eighth were in agriculture and one-sixth in commerce. In all these categories, many women were in informal sector activities that had long working hours and small earnings (Wong 1981).

Singaporean women first became active in the early 1950s when, as part of a larger anti-colonial movement for democracy and equal rights, women fought for equal rights in marriage, education and work. They particularly focused on a woman's right to a monogamous marriage and an end to the economic insecurities and abuses of polygamy. The newly-formed Singapore Council of Women proposed legislation in 1953 to abolish polygamy. The People's Action Party Women's League, formed in 1956, encouraged women to lobby for an end to polygamy and in favour of other equal rights. Such actions occurred simultaneously with shifts in the composition of the voting public. Until 1955, voters were largely men, who registered voluntarily. However, a reform in the mid-1950s provided for automatic registration of voters, bringing women to one-half of the voting population. Additionally, voting in the 1959 elections was deemed mandatory for men and women. Given such events, attention to issues concerning women became important to winning an election. The People's Action Party (PAP), a party that rose to prominence in 1955 and has held almost total dominance of the political scene since then, sought women's votes by pledging support for them in politics, in the economy and in terminating polygamy (Lin 1993).

The PAP won, and the Singapore Legislative Assembly subsequently fulfilled campaign promises and enacted the Women's Charter in 1961. It applied to all non-Muslim Singaporeans; the Muslim minority were exempt due to religious convictions allowing polygamy. It was considered a major breakthrough, remarkable for its time, and was thought to establish women as legal equals of men. It outlawed polygamy and mandated that married as well as single women had rights to act in their own legal capacity. They could use their own surname, own or sell property, enter contracts, and engage in any trade, profession or social activity (Liew and Leong 1993; Lin 1993; *The Singapore Woman* 1988).

Singapore's export-oriented development strategy

Singapore became formally independent in 1965. It chose to aggressively pursue an export-oriented development strategy after a brief foray during the early 1960s with import-substitution, a strategy designed to promote domestic production of consumer goods by erecting protective tariffs and quotas.

Given its lack of domestic entrepreneurs, Singapore developed a comprehensive package of financial incentives to attract multinational corporations (MNCs). At the time, MNCs seeking export-production platforms abroad were in the garment/textile and electronics industries, sectors that typically employed largely female work forces. Women were hired because they could be paid lower wages and were perceived to be more amenable to painstaking tasks and less likely to resist adverse working conditions. The availability of female labour in Singapore was therefore critical for attracting MNCs in these industries (*The Singapore Woman* 1988; Pang 1988; Wong 1981).

Singapore has modified its export-oriented development strategy to adjust to changes in the global and regional economies over time. By the mid-1980s, it was reducing its emphasis on garments/textiles and had expanded the electronics, finance and business services, and transportation and communications sectors (Pang 1988). In the 1990s, Singapore has been promoting itself as a regional hub for production, marketing and finance. It is the higher-skilled member of a growth triangle that includes Malaysia and Indonesia as partners who provide manufacturing sites, lower-skilled labourers and markets.

An ongoing supply of female labour has been central to the success of the evolving export-oriented development strategy. Although women benefited from increases in the standard of living and improvements in social services (with gains in wages and incomes and access to upgraded housing and better education), they remain in subordinate positions to men in the economic and political spheres (disproportionately in lower occupational levels, earning less than men within the same occupation, and with few female political representatives). Further, the view that the household is headed by males persists in many places. This entry will first examine the overall results of the Singaporean development strategy, then women's changing economic position and how they fared, followed by their status in terms of broader measures that include education, health and political participation.

Results of Singapore's development strategy

Since independence, the Singaporean government has chiefly focused on achieving rapid rates of growth, increasing per capita incomes and providing jobs and housing in a stable society. Although improvements in education and health have been goals, they have not been top priorities. The results in terms of targeted goals have been impressive. Gross domestic product (GDP) grew at a spectacular rate of 10 per cent per year from 1965 to 1980, pushed by a 13 per cent annual increase in manufacturing (Pyle 1994). Growth continued at over 6 per cent annually during the 1980s and at almost 9 per cent a year from 1990 to 1995. Per capita income rose to 26 730 a year in 1995 US dollars, among the highest in the world (United Nations Development Programme 1997; World Bank 1997). The unemployment rate fell to levels considered very low internationally, averaging 1.8 per cent for the period 1989–91 and 2.0 per cent for the period 1992–95 (Research and Statistics Department 1996). The form of housing changed dramatically as the populace moved from traditional *kampung* or squatter housing into high-rise complexes with electricity and sanitation. Although the population is ethnically diverse (77.5 per cent Chinese, 14 per cent Malay and 7 per cent Indian), its composition has been stable and ethnic peace has been maintained (Department of Statistics 1994).

The Singapore success story has, however, included very controversial political and social dimensions. The authoritarian PAP has ruled Singapore since 1959, led by Lee Kuan Yew as Prime Minister until 1990 (he remains as Senior Minister). The PAP has actively suppressed opposition throughout its history. In the late 1960s, the government effectively established control over labour unions, depoliticizing them and shifting power from employees to the employers (Pang 1988). The government has restricted people's freedom to speak in opposition to it. In the 1997 elections, voters were told their housing estates would not be considered for upgrading unless their area elected a PAP candidate. In addition, the government has been so interventionist in social planning that its actions are widely considered social engineering (Deyo 1991; Pyle 1997). This will be illustrated below in the examination of fertility and housing policies.

Economic outcomes for women

Women's participation in the labour force changed dramatically from 1957 (the only Census data available near the transition from British colonial rule) to 1996. Female labour force participation (that is, the proportion of women aged 15 and over in the labour force) rose from 21.6 per cent to 51.5 per cent during this period; women became 41.5 per cent of the labour force by 1996, in sharp contrast to their 17 per cent share in 1957 (Research and Statistics Department 1996; Wong 1981). Although younger, single women were the first to rapidly increase their participation, married women and women aged 25 and older followed. The biggest increases in women's employment came first in the manufacturing sector, followed later by the financial and business services sector; however women typically were employed in lower level jobs of the occupational hierarchy (Pyle 1994; Research and Statistics Department 1996).

Although women made some gains in the paid labour force (their labour force activity increased, their limited share of higher occupations rose and some dimensions of the male–female wage gap fell), they remain in disadvantaged positions *vis-à-vis* men. Women still hold only a small percentage of jobs in higher level occupations. In 1996 two-thirds of working women were employed in the lowest occupational categories – clerical workers, service workers, shop and market sales workers, plant and machine operators and assemblers, and cleaners, labourers and related workers (Research and Statistics Department 1996). Women have also been more vulnerable to unemployment than men, disproportionately suffering layoffs in the economic downturns of 1974 and 1985. Women earn substantially less than males. Although there was some improvement in female income as a percentage of male income from 1978 to 1989 as it rose from 63 per cent to 73 per cent (Pyle 1994), the ratio deteriorated in the 1990s. According to Yim and Ang (1997), women earned 73 per cent of male income in 1990 but only 59 per cent in 1995. The gender gap widened in the 1990s for all age groups over 24.

The role of government policies in shaping economic outcomes for women
The increases in women's labour force participation rates did not simply occur spontaneously. State policies – fertility and family policies, housing policies and the structure of the legal framework itself – were very influential in shaping them. For example, throughout the past three decades, the government actively developed, then reversed, sets of policies designed to influence fertility and, in turn, to alter women's activities in the labour force and household in ways that benefited its growth strategy. Although the unemployment rate was a relatively high 9 per cent in the mid-1960s, the government developed antinatalist policies to reduce fertility rates and ensure an adequate supply of female workers. Fertility rates were then about five, meaning that a women would have five children if, over her lifetime, she were to bear children at each age in accordance with prevailing age-specific fertility rates. To reduce this rate, the state established family planning clinics throughout the island and a range of disincentives whereby families having more than the designated number of children would lose priority in access to educational opportunities, tax deductions and maternity leave. Fertility rates fell to two by the mid-1970s (Saw 1980). Women's labour force participation rates increased rapidly in the 1970s, propelled by these policies as well as by the increased demand for female labour, rising levels of education and changes in social attitudes (Pang 1988).

However, this set of development policies (combining export-oriented and fertility policies) contained a serious problem for long-term growth. These policies involved conflicts among women's roles as workers and reproducers of the future supply of workers and the short-term and long-term needs of the development strategies. Singapore's prospects for continued growth were threatened because it soon encountered a labour shortage; the shortage was compounded by fertility rates that had fallen below replacement levels and Singapore's xenophobic reluctance to utilizing immigrant workers. Therefore, in the 1980s, women once again became a central focus of a newly revised development strategy. This occurred in two ways. First, in 1985, a Special Economic Committee recommended increasing the labour supply primarily by encouraging more women to enter the labour force (Ministry of Trade and Industry 1986). Second, the government selectively reversed the existing antinatalist policies to encourage the 'more educated' women (chiefly the Chinese, the majority group) to have additional children. These more educated women would be given handsome tax incentives if they had their second child by a certain age, as well as childcare subsidies, priority in housing and more flexible work schedules. The 'less educated' (largely the Malay, the minority ethnic group) were still offered the preexisting incentives to reduce fertility (Ministry of Health 1991; Pyle 1997; Saw 1990). This strategy was designed to increase the supply of future workers selectively, by augmenting it from a gene pool of the more educated.

These two types of policies placed the targeted women in the contradictory position of being urged to participate in the workforce and simultaneously have more children. In addition, many women were outraged by the underlying elitist notions of the revised fertility policies, particularly as they pertained to access to education (Lin 1993). Many noted that these policies discriminated by class and by race. In response, the government suggested a range of social policies to help alleviate this most recent contradiction. For example, alternative work arrangements such as part-time work, job sharing and homework could help. In addition, since a study in the late 1980s identified childcare as the biggest single factor limiting women's labour force participation (Singapore Council of Women's Organizations 1989), the government could provide financial incentives to encourage provision of more affordable childcare. Last, Lee Kuan Yew, then the Prime Minister, even suggested that men share more in household duties, thereby alleviating the time constraints women face. However, upon closer examination, he was actually suggesting that women educate their sons to become more equal domestic partners in the future (Henson 1990). This not only made women (rather than men) responsible for bringing about changes but left at least a generation of women without relief.

In reality, immigrant maids have alleviated the time constraints faced by some mothers in the formal labour force. However, this strategy is based on upper-income women shifting much of the burden to often vulnerable lower-income immigrant women. In addition, the government has carefully limited immigration. It has increased the tax on immigrant workers, thereby curtailing one possible solution to the problem of encouraging Singaporean women to simultaneously increase labour force activity and have more children.

In addition to fertility policies, government policies regarding housing and urban development have also reshaped women's economic activities. The Housing and Development Board (HDB) was established in the 1960s to alleviate overcrowding and poor living conditions in the central city by replacing traditional dwellings with high-rise housing estates spread throughout the island. New towns were established in rural areas. The planned communities included light industry mixed in the housing estates along with shops, schools and recreational facilities. Such development had a major impact on the nature of women's work lives. It tended over time to preclude continued existence of many informal economic activities that women had pursued as hawkers or workers in shop-houses (where living and work space flowed together, allowing women to combine home duties with economic activity). However, many of the women displaced from these activities became a supply of workers for the light manufacturers locating in the housing estates. These were often MNCs seeking female workers. Thus, the high-rise housing estates facilitated moving women from informal sector economic activities into wage employment for MNCs (Pyle 1999).

As more women entered the labour force, it became obvious that there were omissions in the law that made it difficult for women to achieve equality. For example, the Constitution of Singapore does not explicitly guarantee equality between the sexes. Although it states that 'All persons are equal before the law and entitled to the equal protection of the law', gender is not mentioned in a list of ascriptive characteristics which cannot be grounds for discrimination in employment or business (Liew and Leong 1993). This is not corrected by the Employment Act, passed in 1985, which provides several weeks of paid maternity leave but does not ensure equal pay for equal work or protect against either sexual discrimination in employment or sexual harassment at work (Liew and Leong 1993). Women are not granted medical benefits for their families whereas men are (Liew and Leong 1993; Lin 1993).

Women and other indicators of development
Although Singapore ranks high internationally in per capita income level, the traditional measure of economic development, it ranks considerably lower in broader measures of development, particularly those including gender differences. For example, while eighth highest in GDP per capita in 1995, Singapore ranked twenty-sixth in terms of the human development index (HDI), an indicator that includes life expectancy and education as well as per capita income. Singapore was twenty-seventh in the gender development index (GDI) which extends the HDI to include gender differences. Worse, Singapore is forty-seventh internationally in the gender empowerment measure (GEM) which assesses women's representation in parliament, in administrative and managerial jobs, in professional and technical work and in percentage of earned income. Singapore's rankings in the HDI and GDI are, however, higher than all other countries in East, South and Southeast Asia (United Nations Development Programme 1997).

Singaporean women's life expectancy of 79 years exceeds male expectancy of 75 years. Health care, safe water and sanitation are available throughout the country. The maternal mortality rate, the infant mortality rate and the mortality of children under five are all below the average for industrialized countries (United Nations Development Programme 1997). Women have substantial control over reproduction. However, female adult illiteracy (14 per cent) is substantially higher that than of males (4 per cent) (World Bank 1997). Although there is relatively even enrolment of men and women in primary and secondary education systems, considerable disparity still remains at the tertiary or university level. Women have long been streamed into different areas of study than men (Lin 1993). Within the region, Japan, Hong Kong, the Philippines and South Korea all rank higher on the United Nations Development Programme's education index than Singapore (United Nations Development Programme 1997).

Women's representation in formal political settings in Singapore has always been low. Women's activism has been stronger at certain times, particularly the 1950s, than at others. In the 1960s, activism declined because women felt most of their demands had been met with the Women's Charter. In addition, many women were attending school or taking jobs as a result of the industrialization programme. By 1970 there were no female members of parliament (MPs); there would be none until 1984 (Lin 1993). Women's highest level of representation came in 1988 when 4 out of 87 were female.

Gradually, however, with rising international interest in women's issues in the 1970s, Singaporean women began reorganizing. Two groups that focused on changing discriminatory laws and practices were the Singapore Association of Women Lawyers (SAWL) established relatively early (1974) and the Association of Women for Action and Research (AWARE), established later (1985) in reaction to the government's changes in fertility policies in the 1980s. Women's activism has been shaped by their socialization in Asian cultures which have long posited that women should obey or acquiesce to their fathers, then their husbands. Many reject the label 'feminism' and proceed with a more subdued form of activism in their quest for change (Lin 1993). The government-sanctioned Singapore Council of Women's Organizations (SCWO) was established in 1980 as an umbrella organization representing women in Singapore. Singapore was the last country of the ASEAN nations to form such a federation, a fact many women's groups found embarrassing and which held up formation of an ASEAN Confederation of Women's Organizations. SCWO has actively worked on issues of violence against women, the need for employment training, and it has conducted a survey to find out why some married women were not in paid occupations (Singapore Council of Women's Organizations 1989).

Controversies have continued in the mid 1990s, most notably over the government's reaffirmation that it should provide benefits to the family through the male, in line with the traditional balance of responsibility between a man and a woman in the household. The issue came to a head in 1994 when Prime

Minister Goh Chok Tong announced in his National Day Rally speech that, although women's groups have lobbied for the government to provide medical benefits to the families of female civil servants commensurate with benefits provided to families of male civil servants, it would not do so (*The Straits Times Weekly Edition*, 27 August, 1994). Men have been deemed financially responsible for the family. Following Dr Goh's speech, the government said it would review all policies to see what changes needed to be made to ensure that all rights and benefits meant for the family would be channelled through the male. Although many in Singapore support the notion of the male as head of household, women's organizations took issue with this line of government action. They also objected to the government's opposition to unmarried single-parent families and the ban against single mothers' purchase of HDB flats (Chua 1994).

Agenda for the future

Understanding the history of women's economic roles in Singapore is important for feminist economics because it illuminates the relationship between women's economic activities and the economic development process and highlights a number of complex issues women and society face. Specifically, it shows clearly that women's economic roles were critical for the success of Singapore's development strategy. Future growth in Singapore depends significantly on the success of policies to increase women's labour force participation and on policies that integrate women of all ethnic groups more equally into all levels of the labour force.

Further, the Singapore case demonstrates that women's economic roles encompass not only work in the paid labour force, but also in the household and in reproducing future generations of workers. It highlights the very complex relationships that exist between work in the paid labour force and in the household, particularly as they impact on short- and longer-term economic development. It reveals the need for innovative and carefully thought-out social policies that recognize the importance of all aspects of women's economic contributions to development and that help to alleviate inequities and contradictory demands on women's time. These issues are important for many countries – whether industrialized, transitional or developing.

Inequities between men and women in Singapore remain on many fronts that relate to economic issues – the workplace, the household and the political sphere. Much work in understanding and alleviating them remains to be done. The approach of feminist economics can be insightful. As shown, although many gains have been made, women have not been guaranteed equal rights at work. State policies have been designed to bring women into the labour force, not to incorporate them equally. Further, women's roles in the household and how they relate to the development process could be more fully recognized and valued. All of this is compounded by the fact that women have been very underrepresented in government, meaning they have a reduced voice in shaping the political economy of Singapore.

Therefore, much additional research could be done to shed more light on women's economic roles in Singapore. Survey research at the household and firm level would help researchers and policymakers understand more fully what precludes women's entry into the labour force, what types of jobs women moving into the housing estates chose, how women are integrated into jobs, what the obstacles are to their advancement and why they leave the labour force. In addition, surveys could be designed to understand the impact of various social policies that have been enacted. At a broader level, as in other countries, Singaporean national income accounts do not include the value of all work done in the household and therefore misrepresent women's true economic contribution. Quah et al (1993) were the first to value household work in Singapore, estimating it at 5 per cent of GNP in 1986. Wong and Leong (1993) challenge the methodology, saying proper adjustments to their procedures would increase the value to 17 per cent of GNP. More research clarifying the value of work performed in the household is needed. Last, comparative studies could be undertaken among women in different ethnic groups in Singapore and among Singaporean women and women in other countries in the region.

Finally, an agenda for the future could include development of additional policies to address the problems identified. To provide a few examples, policymakers could work on issues of equitable pay, glass ceilings and sexual harassment. Singapore, like many other countries, faces challenges in resolving the work–family conflict. The range of child care options should be increased, whether provided by the government, employers, unions or family members. There is need for more sharing of work in the household, well-paid flexible work arrangements (flextime, part-time work, home-based work) and expanded leaves of absence. Policies regarding the operation of the retirement fund could be revised in light of a full understanding of the value of women's work in the official labour force and in the household. At the same time, the remaining inequities in citizenship rights could be eliminated, making women fully equal.

JEAN LARSON PYLE

See also
Development Policies; Gross Domestic Product; International Economics.

Bibliography
Chua Mui Hoong (1994), 'Gender roles: debate hotting up', *The Straits Times Weekly Edition*, 17 September, p. 14.
Department of Statistics (1994), *Yearbook of Labour Statistics Singapore 1994*, Singapore: SNP Publishers.

Deyo, Frederic C. (1991), 'Singapore: Developmental Paternalism', in Steven M. Goldstein (ed.), *Minidragons: Fragile Economic Miracles in the Pacific*, Boulder, Colorado: Westview Press, pp. 48–87.

Henson, Bertha (1990), 'Men's attitudes as husbands, fathers must change: PM', *The Straits Times*, 2 July.

Kuo, Eddie C.Y. and Aline Wong (1979), 'Some Observations on the Study of Family Change in Singapore', in Eddie C.Y. Kuo and Aline Wong (eds), *The Contemporary Family in Singapore*, Singapore: Singapore University Press, pp. 3–14.

Liew Geok Heok and Leong Chooi Peng (1993), 'Legal Status', in Aline K. Wong and Leong Wai Kum (eds), *Singapore Women: Three Decades of Change*, Singapore: Times Academic Press, pp. 252–83.

Lin, Jenny Lam (ed.) (1993), *Voices and Choices: The Women's Movement in Singapore*, Singapore: Singapore Council of Women's Organizations.

Ministry of Health (1991), 'Social Policies Related to Family Formation', (brochure), Singapore.

Ministry of Trade and Industry (1986), *The Singapore Economy: New Directions Report of the Economic Committee*, Singapore.

Pang Eng Fong (1988), 'Development Strategies and Labour Market Changes in Singapore', in Pang Eng Fong (ed.), *Labour Market Developments and Structural Change: The Experience of ASEAN and Australia*, Singapore: Singapore University Press, pp. 195–242.

Pyle, Jean L. (1994), 'Economic Restructuring in Singapore and the Changing Roles of Women, 1957–Present', in Nahid Aslanbeigui, Steven Pressman and Gale Summerfield (eds), *Women in the Age of Structural Transformation*, London: Routledge, pp. 129–44.

Pyle, Jean L. (1997), 'Women, the family and economic restructuring: the Singapore model?', *The Review of Social Economy*, LV (2), 215–23.

Pyle, Jean L. (1999), 'Economic Development, Housing and the Family: Is the Singapore Approach an Appropriate Model?', in Irene Tinker and Gale Summerfield (eds), *Women's Rights to House and Land: China, Laos, Vietnam*, Lynne Rienner, pp. 27–52.

Quah, Euston, David Lee, Linda Low and Toh Mun Heng (1993), 'The Homemaker and the Economy', in Aline K. Wong and Leong Wai Kum (eds), *Singapore Women: Three Decades of Change*, Singapore: Times Academic Press, pp. 125–68.

Research and Statistics Department, Ministry of Labour (1996), *Report on the Labour Force Survey of Singapore*, Singapore.

Saw Swee-Hock (1980), *Population Control for Zero Growth in Singapore*, Singapore: Oxford University Press.

Saw Swee-Hock (1990), *Changes in the Fertility Policy of Singapore*, Singapore: The Institute of Policy Studies.

Singapore Council of Women's Organizations (1989), *Report on Survey of Married Women in Public Housing*, Singapore: SCWO.

The Singapore Woman (1988), Singapore: AWARE (Association of Women for Action and Research).

The Straits Times Weekly Edition, various issues.

United Nations Development Programme (1997), *Human Development Report 1997*, New York: Oxford University Press.

Wong, Aline K. (1981), 'Planned development, social stratification, and the sexual division of labor in Singapore', *Signs*, 7 (2), 434–52.

Wong, Aline K. and Leong Wai Kum (1993), 'Singapore Women: An Overview', in Aline K. Wong and Leong Wai Kum (eds), *Singapore Women: Three Decades of Change*, Singapore: Times Academic Press, pp. 1–19.

World Bank (1997), *World Development Report 1997*, New York: Oxford University Press.

Yim Seow Hua and Ang Seow Long (1997), 'Income trends: the gender income gap', *Statistics Singapore Newsletter*, **19** (3).

Economic History, South America

During the twentieth century, women in South America have experienced considerable changes in their economic status as a result of deep transformations in the region's societies. More specifically, since the colonization process in the sixteenth century, the exploitation of natural resources led an important part of the population to remain in non-capitalist structures or in a subsistence economy. The deficiencies in nutrition and health care, the lack of access to education and to the most elemental rights mark the life conditions of most of these women. From 1930 up to now the region's emphasis on industrial growth, the internal migration to and development of urban areas, a weakening of traditional social, political and economic structures in the rural areas, and new social movements, have all greatly transformed the conditions of women's lives.

South America is comprised of twelve countries: Brazil, Uruguay, Argentina, Paraguay, Chile, Bolivia, Peru, Ecuador, Colombia, Venezuela, Surinam and Guyana. Its geographical area represents 40 per cent of the Americas and its population constitutes 6 per cent of the world's population. In 1995, South America's Gross Domestic Product (GDP) amounted to 1.2 billion USA dollars, or about 5 per cent of world GDP, with Brazil and Argentina having the largest economies in the region; these two countries constitute two-thirds of the region's population and generate three-fourths of its GDP (FLACSO 1995). Despite South America's global standing as a region with an intermediate income level, important structural differences and economic circumstances exist across the individual nations (for example, the 1995 per capita product in Bolivia was six times lower than that in Chile) thus contributing to significant differences in the economic status of women across the region.

Because the activities of South American women were considered insignificant and even unworthy of attention prior to 1930, their stories were largely excluded from the histories of this region. Consequently, this entry will focus on the changing status of women in South America after 1930. In addition, two distinct periods will be differentiated, based on changes in development strategies: the first, from 1930 to 1975, will be referred to as the 'industrialization through import substitution' period; the second, from 1975 to the present, as 'an open economy process with internationalization of markets and capital'.

Industrialization through import substitution 1930–75

Immediately after the worldwide economic depression, economic development policy in the wealthier South American countries focused on industrial development, with the purpose of producing consumer goods that the contraction of exports prevented from buying abroad. Twenty years later, especially in Argentina, Brazil, Venezuela and Colombia, the emphasis shifted to import substitution of intermediate and capital goods. The expansion and diversification of the productive structure allowed the absorption of a growing population, the incorporation of more advanced technologies (both in the urban and the rural area) and the construction of an important infrastructure, mainly in transport, communications and energy. The impulse given by the public sector was shown in policies that encouraged industrialization, enlarged infrastructure and, in some cases, reformed tax, tariff and agrarian structures. It also extended public education and health and created social security services that, although not enough to cover the whole population (about 30 per cent of the work force was excluded from them), implied significant social progress. The shift to a policy of import substitution had significant effects on women throughout South America although rarely were these effects intended. In other words, changes in women's economic status were not typically considered in either development policy.

The preference for industrialization over agricultural development during this period propelled South Americans into urban areas. Combined with an unequal distribution of land and the prevalence of outdated social relationships in rural sectors, the process of industrialization caused rapid migration into the capital of each country, with women forming the largest contingent among the migrants. As women migrated into urban areas, their labour force participation increased slightly. Between 1950 and 1970, for example, female participation rates moved from 18.3 per cent to 20.6 per cent for the entire region (Schkolnik 1985). These relatively low levels may be attributed to several factors. First, because South American women's labour force participation was strongly limited and conditioned by 'caring labour' in the family reproduction process, South American women tended to leave the labour force upon reaching their child-bearing years. More specifically, their participation rates peaked in the age groups before maternity (ages 20–24), and in many countries, especially in the Southern Cone (Argentina, Chile, Uruguay), Brazil, Colombia and Venezuela, there is little indication that these women eventually returned to the paid labour force. This pattern, however, was not universal. For example, in families with low household incomes, women's employment in domestic work was often what made family subsistence possible (León and Deere 1982); consequently, many of these women remained in the labour force after age 24. In addition, educational attainment differentiated women's participation. For example, in Bolivia, Ecuador, Paraguay and Peru, those women with a higher level of schooling tended to remain in the labour market (Psacharopoulos and Tzannatos 1994) after maternity.

Women's labour force participation was also affected by a slow increase in paid job opportunities available during this time. Initially, the concentration of women in urban areas, combined with the limited work opportunities available to them, often meant that women ended up unemployed, employed in the informal sector, or underemployed. By the mid 1970s, however, the 54 per cent of female workers (and 40 per cent of male workers) worked in urban areas and experienced considerably lower unemployment rates than in the period prior to industrialization. In spite of this, significant underemployment remained (Gatica 1986). The emphasis on import substitution, for example, opened up jobs for women in a few branches of industry, such as textiles and garments. In a related development, the rise in the number of small-sized companies dedicated to meeting the basic needs of the low income domestic population, led to the emergence of a large informal sector which employed more than 30 per cent of all active women during this time (United Nations 1995). In addition, growth in the infrastructure necessary for industrialization further increased job opportunities for those women with higher levels of educational attainment. These women were able to find jobs in the formal sector as shop clerks, secretaries, teachers, officers and nurses as a result of expanding state services in public education, health and social security.

Demographic and political changes were also significant during this period. Decreases in the mortality rate, increases in life expectancy and the fall in fertility rates signified a healthier population and fewer family responsibilities for women. A more permanent and pervasive educational system served to reduce illiteracy for women and men and urban immigration reduced traditional rural poverty. The increased urban population also brought about conditions of social and political interaction, mobilization and participation. Specifically during this time, women gained the right to vote and demonstrated an ever-growing political and social activism.

All these changes parallelled an increase of 44 per cent in the per capita income for the whole area between 1950 and 1975 (an annual cumulative rate of 1.48 per cent), with increases of an average 76 per cent in the smaller countries (CEPAL 1978; 1996). While this growth reduced differences in the per capita incomes among South American countries, it did not reverse the highly unequal distribution of income and wealth that existed in the region, and inequality was found to increase as certain sectors benefited more from import substitution strategies. In addition, unemployment continued to affect over half of the rural population and almost a third of the urban population and, more significantly, more than 35 per cent of the rural and urban households remained below the poverty line (FLACSO 1995). Deep inequalities also persisted among South American women at the end of this period, a result that garnered the attention of feminist scholars beginning in the late 1960s. As these scholars stressed the existence of a multiplicity of contradictions that arose from the analysis of gender and also encouraged the study of the relationship of inequalities between class and gender (see, for example, Benería and Sen 1982), the economic status of South American women gained increased attention in social science research, thus leading to a more complete picture for the post-1975 period.

The open economy process with internationalization of markets and capital 1975 until the present

By the mid 1970s, South American economies were in crisis as a result of the import substitution strategies and because of world economic conditions. This crisis was intended to be palliated with external debt. Reagan's policy increased the interest rate in the United States and determined the impossibility of payment of this debt, the interruption of external capital inflow and a massive flight of local capital. The strategy of the import substitution was rapidly replaced by structural adjustment policies (SAPs) in the 1980s.

The shift to structural adjustment policies coincided with a gradual return to democracy across South America during this period, and it was also influenced by the 1982 debt crisis. This crisis led the State in almost every country to assume private external debt, a move that increased State deficits and exerted inflationary pressure across the region. In addition, the globalization of the world economy affected both the structural adjustment policies adopted and the region's economies. More specifically, the liberalization of international financial markets, the relocation of external investment towards production for the world market, increasing deregulation by the more advanced countries and the push from international financial agencies to adopt similar measures across the region influenced not only the SAPs for each country, but also contributed to the region's move toward an open economy process emphasizing the internationalization of the region's markets and capital.

While evaluating the results of this process is complex and ongoing, some of the economic, social and political effects of SAPs on South American women can now be assessed. One apparent result is that SAPs are not gender-neutral development strategies, so that the changing economic status of South American women since 1975 has differed from that of South American men. And like those changes observed during the 'industrialization through import substitution' period, South American women have experienced both economic gains and losses as a result of these new development strategies.

These mixed results correspond to three changes in South American labour markets since 1975: a decrease in overall employment rates, a decrease in real wages and a modification of the type of employment generated, combined with an increase of informal sector employment and underemployment. It is important to note that these factors mask the multiplicity of occupational experiences across the region, making it difficult to draw connections between full-time stable formal jobs that have been created and the economic inactivity that persists.

Since 1975, South American women's labour force participation has increased, and by 1995 it had reached 33.5 per cent, with women also working more hours than before. (It is also important to note that while the 1995 rate represents gains over the earlier period, it is still below that for women in developed countries and remains much lower than the 80 per cent rate for South American men (FLACSO 1995).) The reasons for women's gains in labour force participation can be attributed to several factors. First, the employment in the tertiary (services) sector, which offers more opportunities for women, has grown since 1980 (CEPAL 1978, 1996). The processes of economic restructuring have contributed to the decline of manufacturing-dominated industrial complex.

During this time women also experienced, on average, increases in educational attainment, although great differences among countries, between rural and urban areas and between native, indigenous and black populations remain. This improvement in the quality of the labour force has, in turn, expanded women's labour market opportunities. Finally, the social perceptions that the growing presence of women in the labour force was necessary for contributing to households' budgets and that wives bore a greater responsibility to support these budgets (Berger 1995) produced, together with the restored force of feminism, a social legitimization of female employment.

Other sources for women's increasing presence in the labour force, have, however, not generally been viewed as positive for women. One explanation for women's increased labour force participation is that women can be and are paid lower wages than men, a common feature in economies emphasizing export production and international competitiveness. Evidence of this may also be reflected in the growing gender wage gap across the region. In 1980, for example, the gender wage gap was 55 per cent, but by 1994, it had increased to 62.7 per cent. In addition, a comparison of the gender salary gap reveals a disparity of 62 per cent in 1992 that reached 70 per cent by 1994 (United Nations 1997).

Another key source for this growth is the systematic increase in the number of South American women between 25 and 49 years of age now in the labour force. Specifically, South American women seem to be moving into the labour force not because they are secondary workers whose income provided access to nonessential goods, but because of the severe unemployment and low wages that have accompanied SAPs in the region (Arriagada 1994).

Despite women's greater labour force participation, high unemployment rates remain an issue across South America, with women continuing to face higher rates than men do. Women also continue to experience greater variation in their unemployment rates, thus reflecting greater susceptibility to economic fluctuations, and greater underemployment rates than men. In 1994, the open unemployment rate was 6.7 per cent for men and 9.5 per cent for women, while underemployment was 3.1 per cent for men and 6.1 per cent for women (United Nations 1997).

The contraction and reorganization of the region's industrial sectors, a shift of jobs to the informal sector and continuing occupational segregation all seem to be contributing factors here. The SAPs had a pronounced impact on the structure of consumption, which in turn had an impact on the organization of work to meet the new consumption demand. Part of the demand for goods and services feeding the expansion of the informal economy comes from the mainstream economy and the fragmentation of what were once mostly homogeneous middle class markets (Sassen 1996). The informal sector includes independent workers, domestic service and people who work for companies with not more than five employees. In this, 56.4 per cent of women and only 47.5 per cent of men worked in 1994 (United Nations 1997).

In fact, for every urban area in South America, the employment of women continues to fall into the traditional patterns of female occupation and shows few signs of expanding into traditionally male occupations. At the same time it is interesting to point out that domestic service makes up 20 per cent of Latin America's economically active female population. According to studies by Chaney and García Castro (1989), Latin American society places this kind of job at the lowest level of the social scale, just above prostitution and begging. In Argentina, for example, 70 per cent of the women in the 1997 labour force worked: as maids, 18 per cent; as shop clerks, 12 per cent; as health workers, 7 per cent; as education workers, 10 per cent; and as spinners, tailors and dressmakers, 8 per cent (Berger 1998).

The disturbing trends in output across the region also converge to explain labour market factors. Between 1975 and 1995, per capita product growth was only 0.45 per cent per year, significantly lower than the 1.48 per cent rate between 1950 and 1975 (CEPAL 1978, 1996), which suggests that SAPs may not have been as successful as import substitution policies for improving economic wellbeing. In addition, income differences persist across gender. Interestingly, the greatest income difference between men and women occurs in Brazil, where the economic activity rate of women grew the fastest among all the South American countries between 1950 and 1996, while the smallest difference was found in Chile, where the activity rate is also the lowest (United Nations 1997). It may thus be assumed that in those countries where women have been forced to accept lower relative wages, a higher increase in their activity rate became necessary, a fact which in turn contributed to the deterioration of their relative wages.

It has been observed that income differences are less between younger South American men and women, although these differences do increase with age. While these findings suggest that, in the future, the income gap might continue to decrease as women continue to acquire more education, evidence indicates that the current income gap cannot be attributed to women's lower levels of education. For example, even when men and women had the same level of educational attainment, men's average income in 1994 remained higher than that of women, especially among those with 10–12 years of schooling (United Nations 1997).

The reasons for the weak education–income connection are complex and may relate back to the occupational segregation and employment in the informal sector noted above. In addition, women's various skills and training are still typically not as appreciated in the region's labour markets as are men's. This may be a reflection of societal attitudes about women's appropriate role in society, a position often reinforced by educational systems themselves. For example, female education is still often related to certain abilities, identified from a cultural standpoint, as more appropriate for women, even though it is increasingly obvious that women now acquire education more and more often so they can work in a professional job (Bianchi 1994) rather than only engaging in the family work of social reproduction.

While increases in educational attainment and labour force participation offer hope for improving the future economic status of South American women, challenges remain. One dilemma facing some South American countries, especially those with high illiteracy rates such as Paraguay and Bolivia, is that women remain a minority in school enrolment and a majority in the drop-out rate (United Nations 1992); a trend which must be reversed if women are to make economic gains. In other countries such as Uruguay and Argentina women in the labour force have a higher educational level than men do. Additionally, the concentration of health services in urban areas, which are also mostly private, makes access to adequate health care difficult for most of the population. When combined with the hard socioeconomic conditions facing many South Americans, the frequent pregnancies, poor nutrition and lack of rest not only produce high maternal and infant mortality rates but also affect women's ability to obtain and maintain work in the paid labour force. These problems are also reinforced by cultural discrimination against girls and women, who are considered to be less deserving of health care and nutrition than males, and by the increasing tendency of adolescent pregnancies and voluntary abortions, most of which are illegal (Subbarao 1994).

Another challenge facing South American women arises from the increasing percentages of women-headed households. This is a trend that seems to be due to the fact that the crisis leads to a decrease in the importance of the function of man as a 'money supplier' and more separations take place.

However, there are different interpretations. In most South American countries, there is a direct relationship between female-headed households and absolute poverty, with over 30 per cent of women-headed households being poor and indigent (United Nations 1995). However, in Argentina and in Uruguay, the percentage was less than 30 per cent, which appears to be the result of female-headed households being more frequent among higher socioeconomic levels (Berger 1995).

South American women also continue to bear most of the domestic burden. Thus while the increase of South American women in the labour force has contributed to a growing social acceptance of women's own development independent from their families, it has not meant a reduction in the housework they do. This has implied a serious deterioration in living conditions, especially for those women who have no access to private child care institutions or to market substitutes for home-produced goods and services, such as ready-made clothes, take-away food and laundry and ironing services. There has also been a deterioration of State services as a result of the region's countries' general acceptance of the deregulation and privatization of state-owned companies' provisions of SAPs – as advocated in the Washington Consensus. In 1990 a group of Latin American and Caribbean policymakers, representative of international agencies, and members of academic and think-tank communities participated in a conference sponsored by the Institute for International Economics in Washington. At the conclusion of the group's deliberations, Williamson (1990) wrote that they have reached a substantial degree of consensus regarding ten policy instruments: fiscal discipline; public expenditure priorities in education and health; tax reform; positive but moderate market-determined interest rates; competitive exchange rates; liberal trade policies; openness to foreign direct investment; privatization; deregulation and protection of property rights (Burki and Perry 1998). All these moves have also reduced women's employment opportunities since the State has historically been more receptive to hiring women than has the private sector. These factors have led to an increase in the number of working hours for adult women, particularly for women in the poorer income groups who have had to join the labour force in addition to continuing their multiple reproductive tasks.

As the positive and negative effects of SAPs on women are being identified, South American women are increasingly engaged in political and social activities to mitigate the negative effects and encourage the positive ones. In 1979, for example, the Convention on the Elimination of All Forms of Discrimination against Women adopted by the General Assembly of the United Nations on 28 December 1979 was signed by all countries of the region. It refers to women's rights in work, education, politics, access to property, social and reproductive health, family planning and so on. For the first time, positive discrimination is established in the world in an international document. Argentina is the only country in the world that included this in its Constitution. By ratifying this document, the countries are compelled to adopt their legislation and to report about the achievements in this issue. Fortunately, every country of South America, except for Paraguay, has subsequently ratified it. This has led most of the region's governments to create boards for promoting the improvement in the status of women and to adopt plans and policies aimed at ensuring equality of opportunities. However, as in many other nations outside South America, although these instruments for insuring equality exist, not enough resources have been made available thus far to execute the programmes.

At the same time, South American women have also demonstrated how the organization and defence of living conditions constitute a real and potential sphere of political participation. Through their struggles in women's groups, such as family consumer protection organizations, community soup kitchens (*'ollas populares'*) and food collectives and production workshops, as well as in movements against human right abuses such as Mothers of Plaza de Mayo and Mujeres de Chile, thousands of women have invaded the public sphere to combat the deterioration of their world. An important example of South American women's activism occurred in the feminist movement in Chile in the early 1980s. Originating the slogan 'Democracy in the Nation and at Home', this group called attention to the association between the fight for political participation and the fight for the sharing of household tasks, arguing that the sharing of power begins in the basic social unit, the family (León 1986). Subsequent time-use studies performed in some countries have reinforced this position when it was revealed that, in almost all countries surveyed, women worked more combined hours in the market and the home than did men (PNUD 1996).

South American women still face considerable obstacles to improving their economic status. Thus, while South American societies have experienced significant transformations during the periods surveyed, women's economic roles continue to be conditioned by the place they have traditionally occupied within the social and economic systems and by the ways in which South American societies have viewed biological and social reproduction (Guzmán and Todaro 1995). These ongoing patterns of discrimination may, in turn, help explain why occupational segregation and the gender income gap persist as well as why women continue to experience greater unemployment, employment in the informal sector and underemployment. And as long as wives, who now have the opportunity of finding a job at times when their husbands find it impossible to get one, continue to earn low wages, the remarkable increase of the population in absolute poverty is not likely to be reversed.

Feminists and feminist economists have contributed, and can continue to contribute, to improved understanding of the economic status of South American women and to recommendations for change. Their criticisms of the supposed gender neutrality of labour market theories have demonstrated that the organization of work processes is not independent of the workers' sex (Ferber and Nelson 1993; Maruani 1991). Gender studies during the 1980s also stressed the radical character of the contradiction between production and reproduction, stating that domestic work could only be reduced through a mass relocation of resources to the process of reproduction and through a modification of the ongoing relation between production of goods and reproduction of people (Picchio 1992). Likewise, feminists have struggled to demonstrate that certain needs, traditionally viewed as private, are actually social needs. They have also shown that the State has not been neutral in generating gender inequalities in society and have therefore argued that it cannot be neutral in overcoming them, especially when the burden of economic restructuring has fallen mainly on women. Women have reached a critical mass, that is they have succeeded in taking over spaces in such numbers and proportions that they allow them to stop being self-considered and considered by others a minority without power. In this way, they are now able to develop strategies that allow them to use the institutional resources for the purpose of improving their own economic position and that of their communities (Presidencia de la República 1997).

Thus, future research should include the design and incorporation of equal opportunity strategies as part of State agendas and the analysis of the political, social and economic circumstances that affect their degree of feasibility and acceptability. It is also vital for citizens of South America to be involved in these State-originated policies, particularly since they offer the opportunity for generating new gender relationships in which women and men participate equally in all aspects of the economy.

SILVIA BERGER

See also

Agriculture (Third World); Class; Development Policies; Development, Theories of; Double Day/Second Shift; Dualisms; Economic History, Mexico; Economic Restructuring; Globalization; Growth Theory (Macro Models); Informal Sector; International Economics; Population; Structural Adjustment Policies.

Bibliography

Aguiar, Neuma (1990), 'Las mujeres y la crisis latinoamericana', *Mujer y Crisis. Respuestas ante la Recesión*, Río de Janeiro: DAWN/MUDAR, pp. 11–30.

Arriagada, Irma (1994), 'Transformaciones del trabajo femenino urbano', *Revista de la Cepal*, (53), pp. 91–110.

Benería, Lourdes and Gita Sen (1982), 'Desigualdades de clase y de género y el rol de la mujer en el desarrollo económico. Implicaciones teóricas y prácticas', in Magdalena León (ed.), *La Realidad Colombiana. Debate Sobre la Mujer en América Latina y el Caribe. Sociedad, Subordinación y feminismo, Vol. III*, Bogotá, Colombia: Asociación Colombiana para el Estudio de la Población, pp. 65–80.

Berger, Silvia (1995), 'Mujeres en sus puestos. Clases Sociales y Oferta de Trabajo en la Reestructuración del Capitalismo Argentino', *Estudios Sobre Reestructuración Socioeconómica y Subordinación de Género en Argentina*, (3), Buenos Aires: FLACSO.

Berger, Silvia (1998), 'Structural adjustment policies in Argentina. Changes in regional and gender employment', *Out of the Margin 2/IAFFE Conference*, mimeo, University of Amsterdam.

Bianchi, Marina (1994), 'Mas alla del doble trabajo', in Cristina Borderías, Cristina Carrasco and Carmen Alemany *Las Mujeres y el Trabajo, Rupturas Conceptuales*, Barcelona: ICARIA, pp. 493–502.

Burki, Shahid Javed and Guillermo E. Perry (1998), *Beyond the Washington Consensus: Institutions Matter*, Washington: The World Bank.

Buvinic, Mayra (1996), 'Promoting employment among the urban poor in Latin America and the Caribbean: a gender analysis', *Issues in Development Discussion*, (12), Geneva: International Labour Office.

CEPAL (1978), *Anuario Estadístico de América Latina*, Santiago de Chile: Naciones Unidas.

CEPAL (1984), *La Mujer en el Sector Popular Urbano: América Latina y el Caribe*, Santiago, Chile: United Nations.

CEPAL (1994), *Mujer y Trabajo Urbano en América Latina: el Significado de los Cambios en los Años Noventa*, Santiago de Chile: Naciones Unidas.

CEPAL (1996) *Quince Años de Desempeño Económico. América Latina y el Caribe. 1980–1995*, Santiago de Chile: Naciones Unidas.

Chaney, Elsa M. and Mary García Castro (eds) (1989), *Muchachas no more. Household workers in Latin America and the Caribbean*, Philadelphia: Temple University Press.

Ferber, Marianne and Julie A. Nelson (1993), *Beyond Economic Man. Feminist Theory and Economics*, Chicago: The University of Chicago Press.

FLACSO (1995), *Latin American Women. Compared Figures*, Chile: Ministerio de Asuntos Sociales de España.

Gatica, Jaime (1986), 'La evolución del empleo formal e informal en el Sector Servicios Latinoamericano', *PREALC* (279), Santiago de Chile: OIT.

Guzmán, V. and R. Todaro (1995), 'La Discriminación Laboral Ingresa a la Agenda Pública', in Rosalba Todaro and Regina Rodríguez (eds), *El Trabajo de las Mujeres en Tiempo Global*, Ediciones de las mujeres (22), Santiago de Chile: Isis Internacional–CEM, pp. 93–116.

León, M. and C. Deere (1986), 'Introducción: hacia una síntesis de la década', *La Mujer y la Política Agraria en América Latina*, Bogotá: Siglo Veintiuno.

Maruani, Margaret (1991), *La Construcción Social de las Diferencias de Sexo en el Mercado de Trabajo*, Madrid: Economía y sociología del trabajo.

Picchio, Antonella (1994), 'El trabajo de reproducción, tema central en el análisis del mercado laboral', in Cristina Borderías, Cristina Carrasco and Carme Alemany (eds), *Las Mujeres y el Trabajo. Rupturas Conceptuales*, Barcelona: ICARIA, pp. 451–87.

PNUD (1996), *Human Development Report 1995*, New York: Oxford University Press, pp. 97–110.

Presidencia de la República, Secretaria de la Mujer (1997), *Plan Nacional de Igualdad de Oportunidades para las Mujeres. 1997–2001*, Asunción, Paraguay: La Rural Ediciones.

Psacharopoulos, George and Zafiris Tzannatos (1994), 'Women's employment and pay in Latin América', *Regional and Sectorial Studies*, Washington, DC: The World Bank.

Sassen, Saskia (1996), *New Employment Regimes in Cities: the Impact on Immigrant Workers*, New York: Journals Oxford Ltd.

Schkolnik, Susana (1985), 'Población y fuerza de trabajo en América Latina, 1950–1980', *PREALC* (259), Santiago de Chile: OIT.

Subbarao, K. (1994), *Enhancing women's participation in economic development*, Washington, DC: The World Bank.

United Nations (1992), *Situación de la Mujeres en el Mundo 1970–1990. Tendencias y Estadísticas*, Nueva York: UNICEF.

United Nations (1995), *Panorama Social de América Latina 1995*, Santiago de Chile: CEPAL.

United Nations (1997), *Panorama Social de América Latina 1996,* Santiago de Chile: CEPAL.

Wainerman, Catalina (1992), 'Improving the accounting of women workers in population censuses. Lesson from Latin America', *World Employment*, Working Papers (178), Geneva: ILO.

Williamson, John (1990), *What Washington means by Policy Reform, Latin American Adjustment: How much has Happened*, Washington, DC: The Institute for International Economics.

Economic History, Sub-Saharan Africa

Much of 'African History' presents European constructions of Africa (Mudimbe 1988). The literature on economic history in particular is quite limited but generally follows the major paradigms of Western economic thought. Literature grounded in neoclassical economic analysis perceives African history as a series of rational, risk-minimizing individual decisions in response to different equilibria-disturbing forces (for example, Hopkins 1973). Marxian interpretations emphasize the role of structural, supra-individual factors in shaping the region's economic path, with the classical Marxian tradition (for example, Freund 1984) giving primacy to class relations within different modes of production, and more contemporary perspectives (for example, Wallerstein 1976) highlighting the influence of centre–periphery relations within the global division of labour. Although the two schools differ on the question of what constituted the economy in the African past, they share an underlying 'stages of growth' view in which African economies reflect an earlier episode of an industrialized market society. Institutionalist analysis on the other hand defines the economy as a substantive process of material provisioning embedded in culture and social institutions and hence situates African economic history within specific local traditions (for example, Polanyi 1966).

In all these interpretations very little is said about women or gender relations, therefore overlooking some significant historical themes and leaving much of the gap to be filled by anthropologists and other social scientists. Ester Boserup's *Woman's Role in Economic Development* (1970) was the first text in economics to contain substantial analysis of the role of women in the evolution of Africa's economic systems and the impact of change on African women. Adopting a neoclassical approach, Boserup documented a much more important role for women in African economies than historians had previously believed, and brought to attention the negative impacts of both colonial rule and post-colonial development policies on women. Boserup dealt with women's issues worldwide; as yet, there is no text in economics devoted to the subject of women in African history. Large gaps in data and several unanswered questions remain. Some of the major unanswered questions concern gender-differentiated patterns of technological adaptation in different production systems, women's role in long-distance trade, the effect of colonialism and development in widening differences among women and the dynamic effects of particular gender relations on the growth of African economies.

The pre-colonial period

This vast period conventionally refers to all history prior to the partition of Africa at the Berlin Conference of 1884. Current descriptions of pre-colonial African societies present a static picture, indicating little of the process or pace of change. The descriptions suggest that the most prevalent material provisioning activity in this period was swidden (extensive) agriculture supported by cattle herding, fishing or hunting. Some societies were predominantly pastoral; others relied primarily on hunting and gathering. In west Africa, the middle Nile valley and the Ethiopian highlands the level of technological development up to the eighteenth century is believed to have parallelled that in the Middle East, China, India and Medieval or early modern Europe (Freund 1984).

Considerable diversity between societies existed, yet invariably a distinct gender specification determined the roles of women and men in production and their relative shares of output. In Kenya among the Gikuyu, who trace their history to the fifteenth century AD, men were responsible for home-building, cultivation, tending animals and hunting. Women's tasks included harvesting, food production and processing, and home maintenance (House-Midamba and Ekechi 1995). In the seventeenth century Kingdom of Dahomey elephant hunting was one of the responsibilities of the army which was entirely female (Polanyi 1966). Among the pastoral Somali in the horn of Africa men tended cattle, women milked and processed milk products or tended the small grain fields sometimes used to support herding. Women had a central role in production in most agricultural societies. Boserup used the term 'female farming systems' to describe those areas where women performed most tasks, while men only prepared land for cultivation. The main tool used in these systems, prevalent mostly in central Africa, was the hoe. According to Boserup men dominated in plough agriculture, for instance in Ethiopia and generally among Muslim communities. She also suggested that combined male–female work was common only in intensive agriculture because of the relatively high demand for labour. The division of labour in agriculture often specified different crops for men and women, but women's specialization in food crops production seems to be a later development that emerged during the colonial period.

Women were also active in industry and trade, in addition to their responsibilities in home maintenance and reproduction. The industries in which women participated were primarily cloth weaving, pottery and palm oil processing. In sixteenth-century Zimbabwe the Portuguese reported that women were occupied in gold mining. Women's role in trade was more noticeable. Although in the literature trade is mostly associated with the 'market women' of west Africa, this activity could be found in communities from Senegal to northern Sudan, perhaps dating back to the late fifteenth century. Economic historians had originally believed that long-distance trade was exclusively dominated by men. Recent scholarship disputes this claim (House-Midamba and Ekechi 1995). For example, in the seventeenth-century kingdom of Benin (part of present day Nigeria) women participated in the coastal cloth trade with Europeans. All of these activities were carried out together with home maintenance, food preparation (which included water fetching and firewood gathering) and child and elderly care. This prominent role of women in material life was probably consolidated as a result of the Atlantic slave trade from the sixteenth to the nineteenth century, and earlier on the East African slave trade, since mostly males were exported (Robertson and Klein 1983).

Nevertheless, in many societies women had a subservient social status incongruent with their contributions to economic activity. Gender articulated with other hierarchies, primarily age and ethnicity, to function as a sub-category within each hierarchy. In the kingdom of Burundi, for example, where the Tutsi maintained a superior feudal relation to the Hutu, there was a clear patriarchal order of female subservience to men within each group (Hay and Stichter 1984). In all societies men appeared to be in control of resource management and ceremonial activity, while women carried out material production. The king, clan or the family male elders determined the appropriate use of land, the key source of livelihood. Women's labour and reproductive abilities were carefully controlled through the practices of polygyny and bride's wealth. Austen (1987) believes that this exploitation was such a significant source of inefficiency that it may have inhibited the growth of many African economies. Men were also responsible for conducting religious rituals and political affairs, including warfare. As a corollary, property ownership was an exclusively male domain in the majority of societies. In the few matrilineal groups such as the Senufo in today's Ghana, women were able to own and inherit property (Hay and Stichter 1984). Muslim communities followed the Shari'a law which grants women an inheritance from husband and kin, but it is not clear how this law was rendered in practice. Still, in several societies, women held a prominent social status and wielded great power. In Dahomey women held the public office of the census, thereby determining the basis for annual taxation. The Igbo of Nigeria had a 'dual-sex' political system, designating male and female counterparts for each public office, including the king (Hafkin and Bay 1976).

The colonial and post-colonial era
European rule introduced new institutions to Africa while altering the character of preexisting ones. The crucial development in this period was the

establishment of private property and commodity production as the organizing principles of African economies. Wage labour was instituted as a requisite
for the development of commercial agriculture and mining. In east and west
Africa agriculture was the primary activity, organized in African or European
settler farms. Mining dominated the economies of central and southern Africa, with European concessions transforming the landscapes of the Congo,
Rhodesia, South Africa and Zambia (Austen 1987). The restructuring of
African economies that took place during this period produced greater gender-
based disparities in income and wealth. Moreover colonial rule magnified
economic inequalities among women by establishing race and class as additional parameters of intra-gender stratification.

The main factors behind increased gender inequalities were the enlarge-
ment of the monetary economy, the mechanization of agriculture, the expansion
of formal education and the privatization of land ownership. Men were recruited to cultivate cash crops and work in mines, leaving women to attend to
subsistence production, thereby excluding them from access to cash income
and property ownership. The introduction of machinery in agriculture widened the productivity gap between women and men as new technologies were
made available only to male farmers. Boserup argued that, given their cultural biases, European settlers and colonial administrators perceived agriculture
to be a male occupation and consequently promoted men's farming. Similarly
formal education was available to far more boys than girls. The privatization
of land ownership had a detrimental effect on women's access to land which
accumulated in the hands of men since they had the requisite financial resources to purchase it. In other cases, such as in Rhodesia and Transkei
(southern Africa), many women lost their rights to common lineage lands
because colonial administrators assigned land titles to husbands. The erosion
in women's land rights was behind some of the well-known resistance movements to colonialism. The 1959 revolt of Kon women in British Cameroon
was a direct reaction to this phenomenon (Boserup 1970). Of course, the
deterioration in the status of women did not always originate in European
rule. For example, recent literature suggests that fifteenth-century Benin witnessed intense gender struggles around the time of the boom in the
female-dominated cotton trade, that eventually led to the loss of women's
control over land (House-Midamba and Ekechi 1995).

The mining economies of southern Africa were shaped by the migrant
labour system. As men migrated, most women were left behind in 'native
reserves' to grow food and care for children and elders. This system was
fostered by consolidation of the patriarchal authority of African men through
a number of legal enactments in the first decades of the twentieth century.
Colonial rulers granted chiefs and heads of homesteads extensive powers to
recruit labour and ensure the compliance of women. Most women remained

behind, although many moved to towns. Single migrants became part of an urban 'proletariat', deriving their livelihood from beer brewing and prostitution. This proletariat was joined by many Asian women brought over as indentured workers. In consequence, as men became part of a new industrial, relatively skilled working class, most women either remained in unpaid food production in native reserves or took low-paying jobs as domestic servants in European settler homes.

Accounts of African economic history typically miss these gendered impacts of colonial rule. Wallerstein (1976) has noted that the incorporation of Africa into the 'world economy' since 1900 entailed the division of local economies into three zones: the first specialized in generating primary products (crops, minerals) for European markets; the second engaged in food production to support producers in the first zone; and the third zone supplied the labour force for the first two. Historical evidence supports this conceptualization. However, Wallerstein seems oblivious to the clearly gendered nature of this economic space in which men carried out production in the first zone, and were monetarily remunerated; meanwhile women were occupied in unpaid or relatively low-wage food production in the second zone, and in biological and social reproduction in the third.

The literature on economic history has paid even less attention to the intra-gender repercussions of colonial rule. These patterns were most sharply pronounced in southern Africa where, in addition to the general divide between subsistence and market economies, the female category was racially fractured into European, African and Asian. European settler women were initially confined to unpaid reproductive roles. As a result of more rapid industrialization and higher demand for labour, they became increasingly incorporated into the labour market. Black African women found employment mostly as domestic servants in European women's homes, and missionary education played an important role in preparing them for this social class (Walker 1990). Boserup identified a distinct race–sex hierarchy that placed black African women at the bottom of the wage scale, followed by Asians and coloureds, then European women. In effect, colonial rule in southern Africa transformed the pre-colonial socioeconomic structure from one where gender and age were the primary axes of female domination to one in which they articulated with race and class to generate deeper and more complex forms of oppression for women.

Most assessments of the impact of colonial rule on Africa perceive women as a homogeneous category. By and large it is held that colonialism engendered a universal deterioration in the status of women (for example, Boserup 1970). This argument overlooks the differential impacts noted above. Women's varied responses to colonial rule testify to the complexity of the economic and social transformations that took place during this period. Responses that show unambiguous discontent are signified in events such as the 1929 Igbo women's war in protest of taxation and exclusion from the Native Administration set up by the British (Boserup 1970). The case of the Kenyan Kowe Luo women who managed to maintain their living standards via a series of innovations in agriculture presents a successful attempt to cope with the new processes initiated by colonial administrators and settlers (Hafkin and Bay 1976). Women who belonged to social groups that benefited economically and politically from these processes later became part of the post-colonial African elite, sharing little in common with the majority of the population. One may argue that European colonial rule was beneficial to African women to the extent that it weakened the grip of some traditional patriarchal institutions and expanded education. The historical records indicate that while this may have been true for some, in many instances European practices undermined the social institutions that ensured women's livelihood and political voice (Walker 1990). Coquery-Vidrovitch (1997) argues that by introducing Victorian values of domesticity Western education imposed an additional layer of inequality on African women. In general, therefore, whether one is critical or sympathetic it is highly inaccurate to speak of a monolithic effect of colonialism.

Most of the structures created under colonialism continued unchanged in the post-colonial era, generally dated from the early 1960s. African economies became more entrenched in their role as a world supplier of primary products. As a region, sub-Saharan Africa has struggled with ecological stress, foreign debt and general economic decline since the 1970s. Most women experienced only a slight change in their conditions relative to men. The gender bias in national economic policy continued, as modernization efforts targeted large-scale, male-owned agricultural enterprises, and almost entirely neglected the heavily female, smallholder sector. The erosion in women's land rights persisted as the region moved toward greater privatization in compliance with structural adjustment policies. Many women entered new trades and made gains in employment, health and education, nonetheless they still lag far behind men. The average adult illiteracy rate for women is 54 per cent compared to 35 per cent for men (World Bank 1997). Although women comprise 40 per cent of the labour force in Africa, the majority of them are employed in the 'informal sector', at low wages and with limited access to commercial credit, efficient technology and legal protection. Women's share of administrative and managerial jobs is less than 10 per cent. The wage gap between women and men is substantial; on average women earn 45 per cent of men's income. In some countries such as Mali and Chad the gap is staggering, women earn 13 per cent and 20 per cent of men's incomes in the two countries respectively (United Nations Development Programme 1995).

Feminist economics and future research

Feminist economics has shed tremendous light on the history and contemporary conditions of women in the industrialized countries, and there are important parallels between the historical narratives of women in those societies and women in Africa. For example, wage gaps and occupational segregation are common to both experiences. However, the process of economic development has also produced significant differences in each case. In most industrialized market economies the removal of material production from the family to the market was accompanied for a long time by the confinement of large numbers of women to unpaid domestic roles. In Africa, because of a truncated process of industrialization, women's roles in material provisioning have not diminished. Indeed, as a result of historical factors (the slave trade) and contemporary ones (rapid population growth, male-dominated emigration) these roles have expanded even further. The position of women in Africa, therefore, cannot be considered a mere reflection of an earlier stage in the history of women in the industrialized societies.

Nor can women in Africa be subsumed under a global female category. As much as there are significant disparities among women within the industrialized economies there are substantial historical and cultural contrasts between the market traders of Ghana, Muslim pastoralists in Somalia, Afrikaner settlers in South Africa, and many others. This multiplicity requires judicious application of concepts and analytical categories. For instance, labour force participation statistics grossly underestimate the economic contributions of African women because they are mostly engaged in subsistence production beyond the monetary boundaries of labour markets. On the other hand, many women in Muslim societies contribute to the monetary economy from their domestic confines, without formally entering the 'labour force'.

An important task for future research in economic history lies in filling the gaps in current knowledge about women in Africa. Some of the phenomena identified in previous research, including Boserup's distinction between women's use of the hoe *vis-à-vis* men's reliance on the plough, remain unexplained. Moreover, as feminist economists have pointed out, Boserup's analysis narrowly focused on employment and productivity, leaving unaddressed more fundamental economic and social factors. Filling these gaps is complicated by some larger epistemological issues in written African history such as the systematic dismissal of local, oral material (see Mudimbe 1988). As Coquery-Vidrovitch has argued recently (1997) the epistemic authority of African women in particular is altogether disregarded by historians. Given its methodological emphasis on narrative and experience, feminist scholarship can make a great contribution to research in African women's economic history, and indeed African history in general.

EIMAN ZEIN-ELABDIN

See also

Agriculture (Third World); Informal Sector; Structural Adjustment Policies.

Bibliography

Austen, Ralph (1987), *African Economic History: Internal Development and External Dependency*, London: James Currey.

Boserup, Ester (1970), *Woman's Role in Economic Development*, New York: St Martin's Press.

Coquery-Vidrovitch, Catherine (1997), *African Women: A Modern History*, Boulder, Colorado: Westview Press.

Freund, Bill (1984), *The Making of Contemporary Africa: the Development of African Society since 1800*, Bloomington, Indiana: Indiana University Press.

Hafkin, Nancy and Edna Bay (eds) (1976), *Women in Africa: Studies in Social and Economic Change*, Stanford, California: Stanford University Press.

Hay, Margaret and Sharon Stichter (eds) (1984), *African Women South of the Sahara*, New York: Longman.

Hopkins, A.G. (1973), *An Economic History of West Africa*, New York: Columbia University Press.

House-Midamba, Bessie and Felix Ekechi (eds) (1995), *African Market Women and Economic Power: the Role of Women in African Economic Development*, Westport, Connecticut: Greenwood Press.

Mudimbe, V.Y. (1988), *The Invention of Africa: Gnosis, Philosophy, and the Order of Knowledge*, Bloomington: Indiana University Press.

Polanyi, Karl (1966), *Dahomey and the Slave Trade: An Analysis of an Archaic Economy*, Seattle, Washington: University of Washington Press.

Robertson, Claire and Martin Klein (eds) (1983), *Women and Slavery in Africa*, Madison, Wisconsin: University of Wisconsin Press.

United Nations Development Programme (1995), *Human Development Report*, Washington, DC: UNDP.

Walker, Cherryl (ed.) (1990), *Women and Gender in Southern Africa to 1945*, Cape Town: David Philip.

Wallerstein, Immanuel (1976), 'The Three Stages of African Involvement in the World-Economy', in Peter Gutkind and Immanuel Wallerstein (eds), *Political Economy of Contemporary Africa*, Beverly Hills: Sage Publications.

World Bank (1997), *World Development Report*, Washington, DC: The World Bank.

Economic History, United States

Economists and economic historians have focused their attention on the history of capitalist development, thus most economic histories of the United States are the story of industrial development as it spread from early beginnings in New England to the west and south. Studies of the economic role of women have followed a similar pattern leading to a concentration on the experience of northern native-born white women and the impact of the changing economy on their economic and social roles. The intense re-examination of slavery beginning in the late 1950s has likewise led to some scholarship on the role of African-American women under slavery and in decades immediately following emancipation. Luckily economists and economic historians are not alone in studying the economic role of women and there is a rich literature by social historians which can supplement economists' work. (See Ruiz and DuBois 1994 for studies on the experience of various ethnic groups.)

As both economic and other social historians began to examine the experiences of diverse regional, ethnic and racial groups, the ability to make meaningful generalizations about women's economic status became more limited. The story of US economic development is complicated by the state-by-state variation in not only women's legal status but also in approaches to social policy. The question of women's agency also looms large – are women passive victims of societal and economic forces or active participants in shaping their own history? In the 1980s, this controversy spilled over to the courtroom as Sears successfully argued that they had not failed to recruit women for higher-paid positions but that women had historically preferred low-paying dead-end jobs (Kessler-Harris 1994).

One question that has fascinated students of women's economic history is the connection between economic organization, the division of labour and women's social status. It has long been claimed that economic development improves women's status, indeed the European colonists were convinced that their more developed economic organization lightened woman's drudgery and elevated her status. Social historians' studies of the impact of European contact on the changing status of Native-American women cast some doubt on that hypothesis (Jensen 1994, Perdue 1994).

While Native-American traditions and economic organizations varied widely, it seems clear that among the nations which experienced European contact in the eastern USA, women often played an important and recognized economic role. Among the nations of the eastern woodlands and the nations of the Southeast, matrilineal descent and female controlled agriculture were not unusual. While there appears to have been a fairly rigid division of labour by sex, sexual inequality did not necessarily follow. Women often wielded power and influence in the community to the amazement and consternation of Europeans. Because Native-American ideas of appropriate gender roles contradicted the dominant European notions, increasing and prolonged pressure was applied to 'civilize' the natives. These sometimes well-intentioned efforts to change gender roles disrupted traditional economies. Well into the twentieth century Native-American children were often removed from their homes to be educated in white-run schools which usually trained girls in domesticity. The disruption of traditional forms of land-holding and the removal of the eastern nations to the west often further undermined women's traditional roles. There was, of course, resistance, as in the successful attempt by the Cherokee to give women their share of tribal lands when the Federal government forced a cessation of communal land-holding in Oklahoma, but resistance was not always successful (Amott and Matthaei 1996, Chapter 3).

European-American women in the colonial and early federal period also experienced changes in status and gender ideology, but unlike Native-American women this was not imposed from without but developed in a community in which women were active, if lesser, participants. While women's experience in the colonial period varied from colony to colony, the economic contribution of women was probably viewed as more important for community and family survival than would be the case later. In the seventeenth century, the world view of the colonists was such that the idea of a man supporting a wife was not a common one. Families were viewed as economic units with husband and wife supporting children. Childhood was shorter for both girls and boys and consisted mainly of training for adult duties. Gendered division of labour was the rule and in the patriarchal world of the seventeenth century, male work was to rule both house and society. Positions of power and prestige were reserved for men, yet studies by social and economic historians of women's work before the revolution reveals women in a surprising number of unusual jobs. Women whose husbands, brothers or fathers were away were found exercising male authority in a variety of circumstances. Single women, who were few in number in a period where virtually every woman married, owned property, ran businesses and, in some localities, voted (Goldin 1990, pp. 46–54; Ulrich 1991). While there is some evidence of protest against societal restrictions on access to education or the restrictions on property-holding for married women, these protests were isolated and sporadic. By the end of the eighteenth century, the world view of the colonists was changing. Influenced by Enlightenment thought and the changes brought about by the Industrial Revolution in Britain, men and women would find their old notions of women's proper role challenged.

In the 1820s, the USA began to experience the stirring of industrialization in the Northeast and the ideology of women's proper role began to change. As men increasingly worked away from the home in the developing urban centres and more workers were employed in industrial pursuits, the division between public and private spheres became more important. Beginning first in the developing middle class in the north and eventually spreading to other classes and regions, an ideology known as the 'cult of domesticity' developed. Women's role in the family was elevated as mothers were given responsibility for the spiritual education of children. The notion of women working outside the home became morally repugnant and evidence of a debased moral nature or a disordered family. It is ironic that this ideology developed and took hold in the very region where the first industrial workers were predominantly women. Young women, recruited from the declining agricultural areas of New England, worked in the mills for five to seven years before marriage, usually contributing much of their pay to the family coffers. As a literate, temporary labour force, the New England mill girls captured

worldwide attention and Americans bragged that they had managed to indus-
trialize without degrading labour or creating a permanent working class. It
did not go unnoticed that the mill girls worked for about a third to half the
wages of unskilled male labour. Some of these early women organized against
slavery, for the ten-hour day and participated in and organized turn-outs
(strikes) to protest against cuts in wages, speed-ups and lengthening of working hours. Like other workers of this period their organizations were short-lived,
seldom surviving downturns in the business cycles (Ryan 1981; Kessler-
Harris 1982; Milkman 1985).

The developing ideology of separate spheres for men and women accommodated the mill girls because they were 'temporary' workers forced to work
outside the home by family circumstances, but women of the middling classes
would find their opportunities further restricted in the decades before the
Civil War (1861–65). It became less acceptable for women to actively participate in the work of their husbands and less possible as husbands' work was
removed from the home. The necessity to contribute to family income did not
always disappear, however. Careful work by feminist economists with the
manuscript census, business directories and city directories has revealed that
much of married women's work for cash went unnoticed. Women took in
boarders, did laundry, sold vegetables and in many instances ran farms,
plantations and stores just as they had done in the colonial period, and yet
they were listed in the census as 'At Home', 'No Occupation'. Society simply
did not see women's work (Folbre 1991; Goldin 1990, pp. 43–6).

Middle-class women also began to feel constrained by the restrictions on
married women's ability to hold property. Children were considered much
like property and women had no legal power or authority over their children
either within marriage or at marital dissolution. Divorce was difficult and, in
most states, rarely given even in cases of abuse or neglect (Salmon 1986).
Even a cursory reading of the Declaration of Sentiments from the 1848
Woman's Rights Convention at Seneca Falls cannot fail to notice the demands for married women's equal status before the law in property holdings.

Was women's economic status elevated in this period? Work outside the
home for young single women and the immigrant women who would quickly
follow to the mills in the late 1840s and 1850s became more plentiful and
better paid than other alternatives. But prevailing middle-class ideology now
argued that women at work outside the home was not only shameful but
possibly immoral. Middle-class women by the 1860s would witness the
beginnings of the professionalization of medicine and law which will deny
women entry to the practice of medicine and law. Their alternatives were
certainly more restricted, yet the profession of teaching opened to women as
Massachusetts and other Northern states began systems of public education
that required cheap teachers and the prejudice against women teachers slowly

crumbled. Perhaps most importantly, women used the notion of the moral superiority of women to justify their violation of separate spheres as women's groups agitated for not only suffrage but changes in the status of married women, temperance (a social movement concerned with the impact of alcohol addiction and its impact on family welfare and domestic violence), and other social legislation (Gordon 1995, p. 412).

In general this agitation will not be found in the south until the twentieth century. Southern society remains tied to an economy based on slavery until the forced emancipation of African-Americans during the Civil War. Women's economic status remained within a patriarchal model perhaps more akin to the pre-Revolutionary period. The economy for slaveholders and non-slaveholders alike revolved around slave production and was increasingly dominated by the production of cotton. Women, particularly within the yeoman households but also in the plantation households, contributed to this economy by manufacturing household goods, occasional agricultural work and, in the case of the plantation mistress, supervising the household side of the plantation. Slave women's work also reflected a gendered division of labour, particularly on large plantations where slave women were often in charge of household tasks for the slave family. But field work for slave women was the rule with even pregnant women and nursing mothers participating in field work at times of peak labour needs (Jones 1985).

The Civil War (1861–65) changed women's work in the south for both African-American and European-American women. One dramatic change in the postwar organization of agriculture was the widespread withdrawal of African-American adult women from field work. African-American married women supplemented family income in other ways, not unlike the yeoman farmers' wives. They took in washing, cultivated small vegetable gardens, raised chickens, kept a cow and made butter, performed domestic labour in the homes of white people and wealthier blacks. We also should not overlook the black middle class that developed rapidly during the decades before the white backlash known generally as 'Jim Crow' which disenfranchised black men and imposed social segregation in the southern states. Black women's clubs flourished and many women combined work and family, usually in ways related to race uplift like teaching, running small newspapers or in the case of Maggie Walker of Richmond, Virginia, establishing and running a penny savings bank (Brown 1994). African-American middle class women were active in the late nineteenth century organizing for suffrage and pushing for labour legislation, a cessation to lynching and other causes. As the south became increasingly hostile, many of these middle-class reformers relocated to northern states and continued to work for reform (Jones 1985).

Southern white women also found their work changed after the Civil War. In response to economic dislocation or the death or incapacity of male household heads, women probably entered into a wider variety of jobs. In general, married women's property rights were strengthened as the states rewrote and modified state constitutions and laws during reconstruction. It became easier in many southern states for married women to run businesses and hold property in their names. However, agitation for economic or social reform among southern white women remained isolated and sporadic with the exception of clubs formed to celebrate and preserve southern tradition (Lebsock 1977).

As industry continued to develop and spread in the late nineteenth-century north, women continued to work as unskilled mill operatives. Many of these workers would be recent immigrants or the daughters of immigrants as wave after wave of European immigrants arrived. Although each ethnic group had different experiences and often settled in different areas, it was usually single women who worked outside the home in domestic labour as well as unskilled factory work. Wages remained about one-half of men's wages and jobs for women were more likely to be piece-rate jobs with little or no advancement possible (Amott and Matthaei 1996).

While medicine, law and other professions continued to become increasingly difficult for middle-class women to enter, a new vocation was 'feminized'. Clerical work, long a male occupation with a job ladder to managerial positions, was transformed into a white, usually native-born, female occupation with lower pay and little possibility of upward mobility. Partially because this work required more education, women in the labour force in this period had higher average levels of formal schooling than their male counterparts (Goldin 1990; Rotella 1981).

Permanent labour organizations such as the American Federation of Labor developed in the late nineteenth century and while the most long-lasting and successful unions were skilled men, women were surprisingly active in the trade union movement. Women workers organized with the more radical unions like the International Workers of the World and in industries where women dominated the labour force. In the early twentieth century, working-class women were attracted to the revitalized suffrage movement and some rather interesting and strange alliances among wealthy women and immigrant women resulted (Milkman 1985; Tax 1994).

Indeed, in the first part of the twentieth century women from the suffrage movement, the temperance movement, the settlement house movement, the Progressive movement and the labour movement formed ever-shifting alliances that agitated for the reform of labour laws, protective labour legislation for women and children, better health care, better sanitation, pure food and drug laws and a whole variety of other reforms. They achieved many surprising successes including the extension of voting rights to women, prohibition of alcohol, protective labour legislation in some states and the creation of a

Women's Bureau in the Department of Labor. Frances Perkins' appointment in 1932 as the first woman in the Presidential cabinet and the first woman Secretary of Labor came after decades of women's activism on local and state levels (Kerber and DeHart 1995, Section II).

Women's wages remained half that of men, and by the 1930s women were still employed in largely unskilled jobs working within a predominantly female labour force. Women were still barred from admission to most professional schools or only admitted in very small numbers regardless of their qualifications. While universities in the United States were quicker to allow women in graduate programmes and award women degrees, universities, in general, did not hire women. In the 1920s, many firms and schools instituted marriage bars denying work and education to married women. In the 1930s during the Great Depression, married women's work was increasingly attacked as taking jobs from male household heads, even though most women did not work in jobs that were considered appropriate for men (Amott and Matthaei 1996; Goldin 1990).

In the decades of the 1920s, 1930s and 1940s, the US economy was transformed from an industrial economy to a service economy. These decades saw astonishing changes as immigration was severely limited, African-Americans began a mass migration to northern jobs and relative freedom, and the world was torn by depression and war. For women workers, the biggest change was the entry of married women into the labour force. This trend, beginning in the 1930s and continuing to the present has transformed society (Jones 1985, Goldin 1990).

In the world of women's work in 1930, most full-time women workers were single. Less than 12 per cent of married women worked in 1930 while the overall labour force participation rate for all women was about 25 per cent (Goldin 1990, pp. 13–17). By 1994, the overall participation rate for women would be close to 60 per cent with rates for married women also 60 per cent and even married mothers of children under three having rates close to 60 per cent. Today women workers are over half of the labour force (Blau et al. 1998, pp. 84, 95).

The reasons for this astonishing change are many-fold. As the service sector grew, the demand for women workers grew as well. Real wages for women increased throughout the period pulling women into the labour market. Societal attitudes toward working mothers shifted as more mothers worked for pay. The feminist movement of the 1970s revitalized the women's movement and created much needed support for many working women struggling with the late twentieth-century version of the 'cult of domesticity' known as the 'feminine mystique'. The Civil Rights Act of 1963 opened schools and professions to middle- and upper-class women. And expectations of what it took to live the good life escalated in the post-World War II period requiring a two-income family (Blau et al. 1998, Chapter 8).

It might be expected that it could be confidently asserted that women's status has been significantly improved since World War II, yet women are still predominantly in 'women's jobs'. Most women are found in the service sector working at relatively low-paying dead-end jobs, and women have had difficulty breaking through the 'glass ceiling' to top level management. Likewise, medicine and law have opened to women but the top positions and most prestigious jobs still seem reserved for men. Relative wages were stuck at 59 per cent of male wages for most of the post-World War II period with the gap narrowing to around 65 per cent in the 1980s and 75 per cent by 1996 (Goldin 1990, Chapter 3; US Department of Labor 1998).

The reasons for the narrowing wage gap are debated but it seems likely that the decline in real wages for men in the manufacturing sector played a significant role. Women are increasingly found below the poverty level as the incidence of poverty among female-headed households has grown in the last two decades. While it seems certain that women's economic status today is superior to that of one hundred years ago, the experiences of women of different classes, races and ethnic groups is so varied as to make a joyful conclusion about the more recent period suspect.

Feminist economists have contributed in important ways to the economic history of American women. The work of Amott and Matthaei (1996) has highlighted the economic experiences of women of diverse racial and ethnic backgrounds. Folbre (1991) has done diligent work in studying the social construction of the numbers used to measure economic growth and participation. Bergmann (1986) has explored the astonishing increase in women's labour force participation in this century and done pioneering work in studying discrimination. Likewise economic historians Goldin (1990) and Rotella (1981) have done pioneering work about women workers in the field of US economic history. But feminist economists need to do more of such work. Much of what economists (feminists and others) know and theorize about the current economic situation is based on stylized facts about the past. Explanations of the wage gap, the occupational crowding of women, and other labour market phenomena often rely on notions of how women behaved in the past that are suspect. Did women really choose low-wage, dead-end jobs so that they could devote more energy to their families? Women's struggles to enter lucrative jobs reserved for men belies this. Are women's wages lower because women have intermittent labour force participation? Past behaviour of birth cohorts makes this suspect.

Broader philosophical issues require more work. The economic role of women in the household and in reproductive labour is too dimly understood. The interaction between the expansion of the market and women's economic, social and legal status also cries out for more study from a feminist perspective. Economic theory itself might be strengthened by a better understanding of the multitude of experiences women have had, not only in the labour market and as social reproducers, but also as consumers. Feminist economists might consider borrowing some techniques and methods from other disciplines and begin to use case studies, oral histories and perhaps even ethnographic studies in the analysis of women and their economic role. After all, the economic world looks considerably different from the perspective of a young immigrant woman from Honduras than from the office of a college professor.

PAMELA J. NICKLESS

See also
Family Wage; Feminization of Poverty; Glass Ceiling; Labour Force Participation; Occupational Segregation; Wage Gap.

Bibliography

Amott, Teresa and Julie Matthaei (1996), *Race, Gender and Work: A Multicultural Economic History of Women in the United States*, Boston: South End Press.

Bergmann, Barbara (1986), *The Economic Emergence of Women*, New York: Basic Books, Inc.

Blau, Francine D., Marianne A. Ferber and Anne E. Winkler (1998), *The Economics of Women, Men and Work*, New Jersey: Prentice Hall.

Brown, Elsa Barkley (1994), 'Womanist Consciousness: Maggie Lena Walker and the Independent Order of Saint Luke', in Vicki L. Ruiz and Ellen Carol DuBois (eds), *Unequal Sisters: A Multicultural Reader in US Women's History*, New York: Routledge, pp. 268–83.

Folbre, Nancy (1991), 'The unproductive housewife: Her evolution in nineteenth-century economic thought', *Signs: A Journal of Women in Culture and Society*, **16** (3), 463–85.

Goldin, Claudia (1990), *Understanding the Gender Gap: An Economic History of Women in America*, New York: Oxford University Press.

Gordon, Linda (1995), 'The Powers of the Weak: Wife-Beating and Battered Women's Resistance', in Linda K. Kerber and Jane Sherron DeHart (eds), *Women's America: Refocusing the Past*, New York: Oxford University Press, pp 411–25.

Jensen, Joan M. (1994), 'Native American Women and Agriculture: A Seneca Case Study', in Vicki L. Ruiz and Ellen Carol DuBois (eds), *Unequal Sisters: A Multicultural Reader in US Women's History*, New York: Routledge, pp. 70–84.

Jones, Jacqueline (1985), *Labor of Love, Labor of Sorrow: Black Women, Work and the Family from Slavery to the Present*, New York: Basic Books, Inc.

Kerber, Linda K. and Jane Sherron DeHart (eds) (1995), *Women's America: Refocusing the Past*, New York: Oxford University Press.

Kessler-Harris, Alice (1982), *Out To Work: A History of Wage-Earning Women in the United States*, New York: Oxford University Press.

Kessler-Harris, Alice (1994), 'Equal Employment Opportunity Commission vs Sears, Roebuck and Company, A Personal Account', in Vicki L. Ruiz and Ellen Carol DuBois (eds), *Unequal Sisters: A Multicultural Reader in US Women's History*, New York: Routledge, pp. 545–59.

Lebsock, Suzanne (1977), 'Radical reconstruction and the property rights of southern women', *Journal of Southern History*, **43**, May, 195–216.

Milkman, Ruth (ed.) (1985), *Women, Work and Protest: A Century of US Women's Labor History*, Boston: Routledge and Kegan Paul.

Perdue, Theda (1994), 'Cherokee Women and the Trail of Tears', in Vicki L. Ruiz and Ellen Carol DuBois (eds), *Unequal Sisters: A Multicultural Reader in US Women's History*, New York: Routledge, pp. 32–43.

Rotella, Elyce (1981), *From Home to Office: US Women at Work, 1870–1930*, Ann Arbor, Michigan: UMI Research Press.

Ruiz, Vicki L. and Ellen Carol DuBois (eds) (1994), *Unequal Sisters: A Multicultural Reader in US Women's History*, 2nd edn, Routledge: New York.

Ryan, Mary P. (1981), *Cradle of the Middle Class: The Family in Oneida County, New York, 1790–1865*, Cambridge: Cambridge University Press.

Salmon, Marylynn (1986), *Women and the Law of Property in Early America*, Chapel Hill: University of North Carolina Press.

Tax, Meredith (1994), 'The Uprising of the Thirty Thousand', in Vicki L. Ruiz and Ellen Carol DuBois (eds), *Unequal Sisters: A Multicultural Reader in US Women's History*, New York: Routledge, pp. 203–27.

Ulrich, Laurel Thatcher (1991), *Good Wives: Images and Reality in the Lives of Women in Northern New England 1650–1750*, New York: Vintage Books.

US Department of Labor Website (1998), http://www.dol.gov/dol/wb/public/wb-pubs/7996.htm

Economic History, Western Europe

This entry will examine the economic status of women in Western Europe over the nineteenth and twentieth centuries, the time period in which capitalism and the industrial revolution emerged in Western Europe, giving this region much economic and political power in the world. In this context, Western Europe is understood as the region containing seventeen countries: Austria, Belgium, Denmark, Finland, France, Germany, Greece, Ireland, Italy, Luxembourg, the Netherlands, Norway, Portugal, Spain, Sweden, Switzerland and the United Kingdom. In the nineteenth century, industrial capitalism spread from Britain, the country of its origin, to the continent: to Belgium and France initially, and then to Germany and northern Italy. In the same period, modern economic growth occurred in Denmark, the Netherlands, Switzerland, and Sweden, with balanced growth of agriculture and industry. Societies and economies remained traditional in southern Italy, Norway, Finland, Spain, Portugal, and Greece. In the twentieth century, additional countries in the region were introduced to industrial capitalism and many already industrialized countries established welfare states and saw the development of the tertiary (service) sector of their economies.

This entry places particular emphasis on how the economic roles and status of women change with the development of industrial capitalism. The basic pattern that has been observed in Britain, France, and the United States is that capitalism's initial effect was to lower the status of women because it undercut their role in production, as manufacturing moved from the home to the factory. Eventually, however, as feminist economist Barbara Bergmann has maintained, the productivity of labour became so great that rising wages drew women into the paid labour force and provided them with an opportunity for a role in production and, thus, a chance for economic independence (Bergmann 1986). Many feminist historians and economists emphasize, however, that a role in production is necessary, but not sufficient, for women to attain higher economic and social status. Other key determinants of women's status are the nature of existing institutions, governmental policies, culture, religion, as well as women's own capacity for effective political action. Patriarchy, defined by feminist historian Gerda Lerner as the 'institutionalization of male dominance over women and children in the family and the extension of male dominance over women in society in general' (Lerner 1986, p. 239), is critically important in shaping the economic status of women. Indeed, feminist economist Heidi Hartmann argues that the status of women must be understood in terms of the interaction of capitalism and patriarchy (Hartmann 1976).

This entry will consider three key indicators to measure the economic status of women: the extent of labour force participation of women, the extent of occupational segregation by gender, and the size of the wage gap by gender (Blau et al. 1998). In addition, the legislation passed in countries in response to the rise of capitalism and the activism of women in the form of feminism and other reform movements will be examined.

The nineteenth century up to 1914

The economic status of women was transformed dramatically during the transition to capitalism. In the second half of the eighteenth century, Great Britain became the first nation to see the industrial revolution and the emergence of capitalism. Britain's economic history presaged many of the social and economic trends that would occur on the continent as industrial capitalism spread to other nations of Western Europe. Emerging capitalism interacted with the existing patriarchy that stemmed from European feudalism. The result was that the potential liberation that wage employment offered women was only partially realized due to the reproduction of a hierarchical gender division of labor within the capitalist firm (Hartmann 1976). For example, the exclusion of British women from high-skilled jobs in production and other forms of occupational segregation were the main mechanisms that kept pay low for women. Put forth in 1819 as protective legislation, the Factory Acts really did not protect women, but rather kept them out of desirable jobs left to 'unprotected' male labour (Folbre 1994, p. 142). English Poor Laws, enacted over the period from 1572 to 1834, regulated the poor women and children who lost their economic independence as a result of the enclosure of medieval common fields (Piven and Cloward 1971, p. 15). Organized feminism arose in Britain in 1856 with the Society for Promotion of Employment of Women. It fought for women's rights to employment and for married women's property rights (Pinchbeck 1930, p. 304).

Industrial capitalism spread to the continent in the first half of the nineteenth century. Starting in Belgium which, like Britain, enclosed the common fields of feudalism, the emergence of industrial capitalism ended many of the economic and social relationships of the feudal agricultural economy, and brutally created an industrial working class dependent on wages to live. In countries such as France, capitalism developed more slowly than it did in Britain and Belgium. Peasants had gained control of land in the French Revolution, and thus it took longer to develop a working class. Because peasants retained their feudal ability to be self-sufficient in food and fibre and were thus not forced to live by wage labour, the development of capitalism was slowed and France remained agrarian for a longer period than Britain and Belgium. Germany and northern Italy were also later in developing capitalism because they were not politically united until late in the nineteenth century, and they lacked numerous institutional prerequisites for capitalism, such as legal reforms to permit labour mobility. Southern Italy and Spain had traditional, feudal-like agriculture which held back industrial development. Portugal and Greece were perhaps too far from the core of Western Europe to feel much of the economic and military competition from Britain that pushed Germany and Italy to introduce industrial capitalism from above by state-led initiatives. Balanced growth without much industrialization took place in Denmark, the Netherlands, Switzerland and Sweden. Thus these countries largely avoided the brutal aspects of the emergence of industrial capitalism (Morris and Adelman 1988).

Before the emergence of capitalism, Western European men and women worked together in what has been called 'the family economy' (Tilly and Scott 1978). Production and living both occurred in the household, and the division of labour was by gender and age with the relative status of women being directly related to women's role in production (Blau et al. 1998, p. 17). Consequently, in agricultural societies of feudal Europe, the status of women was relatively high because women were involved in production, helping in the fields, caring for small animals, growing gardens and processing food and fibre. However, an equally important determinant of economic status was property rights which were assigned to men. Industrialization under capitalism separated production from the home and initially left women behind at home without much of a role in production. This lowered their status. However, with time, women were drawn out of the home into the productive labour force, and thus their status began to change.

Some feminist economists refer to this changing pattern of women's status as a U-shaped curve. Status is high in agricultural societies when women work in production (left side of the U), then status falls as industrial capitalism emerges in the society and women are excluded from production (low centre of the U), and, with time, status rises again as capitalism draws women into the productive labour force (right side of the U). At the low centre of the U, social norms tend to condemn women working for pay outside the home, especially doing manual labour in factories (see Tilly and Scott 1978, on England and France; and Blau et al. 1998, p. 24, on Germany). Although elements of this pattern are seen in the case of Western European women, their economic history throughout the nineteenth century yields a much more complex picture.

Textile manufacturing was one of the key industries in the early industrial revolution and was a particularly important source of manufacturing employment for women. Working for a wage in the new textile factories was liberating for women in Western Europe in comparison to domestic service and the needle trades (which continued to be the main occupations for women in Western Europe) in that it allowed women to live beyond the command of their husbands, fathers, or brothers in the domestic workshop or on the farm. It was also emancipatory for women to be together in the factory and see their collective contribution to production. The percentage of a nation's women working for pay who were employed in textile mills can be used as an indicator of the status of women in the early stages of the transition to industrial capitalism. By 1851, 20 per cent of working women in Britain were in the textile mills. Nothing comparable was to be seen in France or Germany until much later. Only in 1866 were 10 per cent of French working women found employed in the mills and, as late as 1882, only 12 per cent of Prussian employed women worked in textile factories (Scott 1993, p. 404).

Although the opportunities to move into wage labour created by industrial capitalism provided women with some liberation from patriarchal power in the family, patriarchal power was imposed in the capitalist workplace in the form of occupational segregation. For example, in mid-nineteenth-century France, men produced sewing machines and earned a high wage, whereas women *used* the sewing machines to produce garments and earned a low wage (Coffin 1996, p. 111). The liberating effects of wage work were often limited by this hierarchical gender division of labour. Occupational segregation acted to keep women's wages down, contributed to the 'double burden' of paid and unpaid employment and limited women's opportunities. In addition, industrialization and wage labour introduced women to new forms of workplace hazards and economic insecurity. Also, men in trade unions blocked women's entry into high-skilled jobs (Hartmann 1976).

While the new factories allowed women to earn a wage (as opposed to the unpaid labor in the family economy of feudal Europe), there was a gender wage gap. Although statistical data for the nineteenth century is limited, estimates for the 1850–1914 time period indicate that in France, women earned 50 per cent of what men earned (Stewart 1989, p. 26); in Germany, women earned from 60 to 80 per cent of a man's wage (Frevert 1988, p. 184); in Italy, women earned less than 50 per cent of men's pay (Bettio 1988, p. 245); and in Belgium, women earned between 33 to 50 per cent of what men earned (Hilden 1993, p. 76).

As the early factory system turned to working-class women and children to create the first generation of wage earners, concerns about exploitation and working conditions increased and led to the enactment of various types of 'protective' legislation. This legislation was supported by political elites who feared social upheaval, trade unions that feared competition from women, and progressive reform movements pushing for genuine protection (Martens 1997, p. 19). Starting in 1819 in Britain, the Factory Acts prohibited women from working in coal mines, from working in the textile mills at night, and it limited their working day to twelve hours. Half a century later, France and Germany passed similar laws. The idea was to protect women and children, but not adult males, from the vagaries of the market and the horrible health and safety conditions of factories. Belief in laissez-faire economics prevented laws from protecting all wage workers. Consequently, this 'protective' legislation had the effect of keeping women out of high-paying and high-skilled jobs, reserved for unregulated male labour (Stewart 1989). Belgium, alone among the Western European countries that experienced the spread of the factory system and of the use of coal as fuel, passed no protective legislation. Women had a long tradition of working for pay in Belgium, and it was the only country that did not exclude women from underground coal mining. One result of this was the emergence in Belgium of radical women-worker movements (Hilden 1993, p. 4).

In addition, during the nineteenth century, Western Europe saw women's activism grow in early feminist and other social reform movements. The French Revolution and other nineteenth-century reform movements provided favourable conditions for feminism in that they affirmed egalitarian ideals. Activism of European women began with the 'Declaration of the Rights of Women' by Olympe de Gouge in 1789, just as French men were declaring the rights of man. By 1881, French feminists obtained some property rights for married women, but not as many as were obtained in Britain in 1882 (Folbre 1994, p. 148). German women were active in trade unionism and social democratic politics for the purpose of achieving women's equality and improving working conditions for women (Frevert 1988, p. 326). Women's activism in response to the effects of capitalism gave them experience in the political sphere, but achieved only minor gains.

The twentieth century after 1914
Three developments in the twentieth century affected the economic status of women in Western Europe. First was the rise of the welfare state after World War I from its earlier roots in the 1880s Germany of Bismarck. Second was the rise of the tertiary or service sector of the economy due to the growth of productivity in the primary sector of agriculture and secondary sector of industry. The rise of the tertiary sector began in Britain after 1850, and in continental Europe toward the end of the nineteenth century in countries where industrial capitalism had taken root. Third was the beginning

of industrial capitalism in Ireland, Spain, Portugal and Greece, as global capitalism discovered the cheap labour of women there in the 1980s and 1990s.

The welfare state emerged in Western Europe in response to the economic insecurity and strains on the family that accompanied the development of industrial capitalism. For example, intergenerational transfers of income that had previously taken place within the extended family were no longer adequate as the social and economic importance of the family diminished. Early welfare state programmes replaced these intra-family income flows with public pensions provided through taxation, a process shaped by patriarchy and traditional gender norms (Folbre 1994, p. 150). Across Western Europe, welfare states took on different characteristics reflecting the nature of the interaction of capitalism and patriarchy in different societies. The 'liberal' welfare state in Great Britain, for example, gave old-age insurance only to the poor, while the 'corporatist' welfare states of France and Germany developed old-age insurance for full-time workers which, in effect, meant that only men qualified, making women dependent on them in old age. The least patriarchal welfare state was the social democratic welfare state, as in Sweden, where old-age insurance was universal (Folbre 1994, p. 150). Despite the patriarchal nature of the welfare state, it is argued that its development has helped raise the standard of living of women by helping them reduce the risk of poverty in old age (Barr 1993, p. 13; Duncan 1996, p. 74).

Beginning in the early twentieth century, as industrial capitalism evolved and transformed the economies of Britain, France, Germany and northern Italy, the tertiary sector of the economy grew, providing new employment opportunities for women. The expanding welfare states needed teachers and nurses, and both the expanding government sectors and the growing corporate sectors needed office workers to fill the jobs of typist, secretary and file clerk. As the communications industries developed, post offices needed clerks to sell stamps and telephone operators were needed. And in the expanding retail sector, sales clerks were needed. New services for the growing middle classes created jobs, and the increased demand for labour was met largely by hiring women (Bettio 1988, p. 44; Frevert 1988, p. 334; Scott 1993, p. 407; Martens 1997, p. 20).

In the late twentieth century, global capitalism led by the United States began to employ the cheap labour of women in southern Europe and Ireland (Garcia-Ramon and Monk 1996, p. 247; Pyle 1990). Revolutions in communications and transportation made it possible for capitalists in the US, the UK and Japan to set up industrial production in countries where capitalism had not yet penetrated and thus labour was in surplus and cheap. Moreover, with the expansion of the European Union to include 15 of the 17 states of Western Europe, capitalists from the UK, France, Germany and the Netherlands moved to Ireland and southern Europe, again in search of cheap female labour. Since Ireland, Spain, Portugal and Greece had not evolved industrial capitalism on their own, they did not have welfare states. To make it possible for women to work for pay, the patriarchal family was called on to care for children, the sick, and other dependents, so that mothers could be employed outside the home. In addition, the patriarchal family continued to provide old-age security which the welfare states to the north provided in the form of public social insurance (Garcia-Ramon and Monk 1996, p. 1).

The establishment of welfare states and the growth of services and other types of 'white-collar' work in the more industrialized nations of Western Europe, and the more recent impact of globalization and the expansion of industrial capitalism to the less industrialized Western European nations, contributed to the increases in women's labour force participation in this region throughout the twentieth century. In 1994, labour force participation rates of women in Western Europe ranged from 79 per cent of women in the population in Sweden and Denmark to 40 per cent in Ireland. In between, women in Finland and Norway participate at a rate of 71 per cent; the UK at 65 per cent and Portugal at 62; France and Germany at 59 per cent; Austria and Switzerland at 58 per cent; the Netherlands at 56 and Belgium at 54 per cent; Italy at 47, Spain at 42, and Greece at 41 per cent (Blau et al. 1998, p. 336). Compared to the nineteenth century, the economic status of women in Western Europe has improved steadily throughout the twentieth century with an acceleration after World War II. In some countries, the labour force participation rates of women are nearly the same as that of men. There are, to be sure, important differences. For example, while many women work full time, as in France, women in Sweden work part time for long periods each week and receive benefits, and many women in the UK work part time for only short periods each week and receive no benefits. The increase in labour force participation after World War II came in different decades in different countries. It has levelled off in most countries (Duncan 1996, p. 1; Martens 1997). Whether or not women have widespread access to full-time, paid work over their adult lives is a crucial indicator of women's economic and social status (Duncan 1996).

In contemporary analyses, occupational segregation is measured with an index consisting of the percentage of working women that would have to change jobs in a nation in order to duplicate the distribution of men across occupations. In 1994, occupational segregation indices in Western Europe ranged from 25 per cent in Italy to 44 per cent in Ireland, with gender segregation in Greece at 26 per cent, 34 per cent in Switzerland, 35 per cent in Sweden, 36 per cent in Germany and the Netherlands, 37 per cent in Belgium, 41 per cent in Finland and 42 per cent in Denmark and Norway (Blau et al. 1998 p. 351). To interpret these indices requires further context.

The index for Italy is low because women work in agriculture and blue-collar jobs alongside of men, not because many women are in the professions or management. The index for Sweden is relatively high because so many women work in white-collar jobs in the government (Blau et al. 1998, p. 351).

These statistics demonstrate that occupational segregation is still present and significant in Western Europe at the end of the twentieth century. Bergmann argues that sex segregation on the job is the major determinant of women's earning less than men (Bergmann 1986, p. 87). Hartmann argues that occupational segregation by gender is the basic mechanism of patriarchal domination of women by men and the cause of women's lower social status (Hartmann 1976, p. 137). On the other hand, the variations in the extent of occupational segregation by gender in the nations described above provide an experimental laboratory for studying why societies differ in their rigidity regarding what work men can do and what work women can do.

The most widely-reported statistic on earning differentials in contemporary analyses, the gender wage gap, is generally measured as the ratio between women's and men's hourly wages. In 1990, Swedish women earned the highest percentage of men's earnings, 90 per cent, while British and Irish women earned the smallest percentage of men's earnings, 68 per cent. In between, one finds 87 per cent in Denmark, 86 per cent in Norway, 83 per cent in Italy, 81 per cent in France, 78 per cent in Finland, 76 per cent in Belgium and Greece, 75 per cent in the Netherlands, 73 per cent in West Germany and 72 per cent in Portugal and Spain (Duncan 1996, p. 80).

It has been suggested that the low relative earnings of women in the Netherlands, West Germany, Ireland and the UK are due to the domestic focus of women's work there. Moreover, the low relative earnings of women in the UK has been attributed to the prevalence there of short, part-time and poorly paid work (Duncan 1996, p. 80). It has also been argued that the small wage gap in Sweden is due to the extensive paid family leave system there, and that the small wage gap in France is due to the extensive, publicly-financed child-care system there (Headlee and Elfin 1996, pp. 107, 127). Furthermore, researchers have found that the overall wage structure in a country has an important impact on the gender wage gap. Sweden's generally more equal wage structure helps women who tend to work in low-skilled, low-paying jobs. In addition, the activism of Swedish trade unions is seen to have played a role in significantly lowering the gender gap in Sweden between 1960 and 1990. Egalitarian trade unions in Italy are credited with contributing to a substantial reduction in the gender wage gap between the early 1960s and mid 1980s (Bettio 1988, p. 100). Within Europe, Sweden has stronger unions than Britain and this explains some of the gender wage gap differences between the two countries. Unions in the USA are weaker than in Sweden and this partially explains why the US gender wage gap is larger than Sweden's (Blau et al. 1998, p. 353).

Legislative responses to capitalist development in the twentieth century took two major forms. First, social policies of the welfare state protected families from the vagaries of the market. Second, replacing the protective legislation of women workers of the previous century, legislation in the post-World War II period defended women's employment rights and their right to equal treatment and opportunity in labour markets. In addition to the old-age insurance mentioned earlier, after World War II, many Western European welfare states provided family allowances to help families pay for the costs of child rearing. However, the welfare states in 10 of the 17 Western European countries are more generous to the elderly, as only 10 per cent of social spending in these countries goes to families with children (Folbre 1994, p. 160). Nevertheless, family allowances, when combined with publicly-subsidized child care, have reduced the risk of poverty for women with children (Bergmann 1996). In France, 100 per cent of child care needs are provided for publicly (for children aged 3 to 7), whereas in the UK, only 37 per cent are met publicly for children of this age. A correlation exists between these statistics and lost lifetime earnings for women due to childbearing: in France women lose only 12 per cent, while UK women lose 57 per cent when they have children. In Germany, child care support for working women is so low that they lose 49 per cent of their potential lifetime pay when they bear children, while in Sweden, women lose only six per cent of lifetime earnings when they have children (Folbre 1994, p. 161). Paid parental leave is an achievement of many continental Western European countries, with Sweden in the lead. As of 1991, Swedish couples can share up to eighteen months of paid family leave when they have children (Headlee and Elfin 1996, p. 111).

In addition to this social legislation, laws on women's employment rights have been passed in several Western European countries. Employment rights are civil rights in the public sphere of labour markets and the workplace. Laws were passed to outlaw discrimination against women in employment, pay, promotion, hiring and firing. It has been a hard, long battle in the twentieth century to achieve these employment rights. In 1907, French women won the right to spend their own earnings rather than have to turn them over to their husbands (Folbre 1994, p. 148), and they could go to work for pay without the permission of their husbands only as of 1965 (Folbre 1994, p. 145). French women obtained the right to equal pay for equal work in 1972 and anti-discrimination rights in 1983 (Headlee and Elfin 1996, p. 130). Italian women were forbidden to work in the public sector until 1923 (Bettio 1988, p. 44). Until 1976, German men could forbid their wives to work for pay (Folbre 1994, p. 148). As to equal employment opportunity, Sweden led the way in 1947 with 'equal pay for equal work' laws, followed in 1980 by laws against employment discrimination against women. When the six nations of France, Germany, Italy, Belgium, the Netherlands and Luxembourg created the European Community in 1957 by signing the Treaty of Rome, this founding document mandated equal pay for equal work (Garcia-Ramon and Monk 1996, p. 12).

A second wave of feminism in Western Europe began after World War II. The first wave had achieved the right of women to vote in Scandinavia and Britain, earlier in the twentieth century. It is common to date the second wave from the publication of Simone de Beauvoir's *The Second Sex* in French in 1949. Her chapter on the history of women from the French Revolution onward is entitled 'The Vote and a Job', clearly identifying the two achievements of modern feminism. Later, building on the Treaty of Rome, European feminists have worked through the European Union as it expanded to include Denmark, Greece, Spain, Ireland, Portugal, the UK, Sweden, Austria and Finland; only Switzerland and Norway are not members. One feminist goal has been to bring member country gender relations up to the standard of Sweden. Feminists have also organized around women's exploitation in sweatshops and industrial homework. One hundred different kinds of homework were identified by Dutch women's unions in a 1979 survey leading to the creation of support centres (Tate 1994, p. 206). In France, home workers went on strike over changes in piece rates, lack of payment for expenses and inaccurate crediting of work (Tate 1994, p. 208). Laws against exploiting home workers have been passed in France and Italy, but are not widely enforced. Feminists have learned that passing laws is not enough; it takes additional activism to get the laws enforced (Folbre 1994, p. 51).

These historical facts about the economic status of women in Western Europe are of great importance for feminist economists. As advocates of economic rights for women equal to those for men, feminist economists stress the important distinction between sex (the biological givens) and gender (the culturally-created) roles and expectations. Since the biological givens remain the same, historical changes in economic status are matters of gender. By studying the economic status of women over time and across 17 societies, feminist economists can demonstrate the commonalities and the differences that technology, culture and society can make in gender roles and expectations. The history of Western Europe shows that the social and technical changes associated with the rise of industrial capitalism created a common pattern of women's participation in production and, consequently, of their status. That is, the U-shaped curve of women's labour force participation can be observed as capitalism spread from England to the continent and Scandinavia, and now in Ireland and southern Europe. This common pattern strongly suggests that the status of women is not biologically determined but rather changes over time with developments in technology and the social organization of production and distribution. This pattern also suggests that what is known as the traditional family, a male breadwinner and a female homemaker, is of recent origin (the past 200 years) and is related to women's low status.

Equally important to these commonalities are the differences found in the status of women within the 17 countries of Western Europe, and between them and other industrial capitalist countries such as the United States and Japan. These differences demonstrate the role that culture, society, institutions and policies can play in retarding or enhancing the status of women. Some countries value the traditional family and discourage the labour force participation of married women. Other countries enact legislation to help women work outside the home so that gender equality can be pursued. One profoundly important factor determining the status of women is the wage structure in a country: how much are skill and higher education rewarded and how compressed or how unequal are the wage distributions? Since women tend to work in low-skill, low-paying jobs, the gender wage gap is less where egalitarian unions compress the wage distribution. This is true of many nations in Western Europe in comparison to the USA, and true within Europe where Swedish wage structure is more egalitarian than that in, say, the UK.

The 17 countries of western Europe provide an excellent database for future comparative research on the source of gender inequalities, on the mechanisms that maintain them, and the conditions of changing them. Economists need to describe the differences in gender relations in different societies under different historical conditions, and to develop theories to explain the differences. When women take up paid work outside the home, traditional gender roles in capitalist patriarchy are challenged as women are seen as workers as well as homemakers. Further research is needed not only on the social and economic conditions of this transformation, but also to identify those strategies that can enhance women's collective activity to free themselves and their families from the gender constraints of capitalist patriarchy.

SUE HEADLEE

See also

Capitalism; Child Care; Economic History, Great Britain; Labour Force Participation; Occupational Segregation; Parental Leave; Patriarchy; Protective Legislation; Wage Gap.

Bibliography

Barr, Nicholas (1993), *The Economics of the Welfare State*, Stanford, California: Stanford University Press.

Bergmann, Barbara (1996), *Saving Our Children From Poverty: What the United States Can Learn from France*, New York: Russell Sage Foundation.

Bergmann, Barbara (1986), *The Economic Emergence of Women*, New York: Basic Books.

Bettio, Francesca (1988), *The Sexual Division of Labour; The Italian Case*, Oxford: Clarendon Press.

Blau, Francine, Marianne Ferber and Anne Winkler (1998, third edition), *The Economics of Women, Men, and Work*, Englewood Cliffs, New Jersey: Prentice-Hall.

Coffin, Judith G. (1996), 'Consumption, Production, and Gender: The Sewing Machine in

Nineteenth Century France', in Laura L. Frader and Sonya O. Rose (eds), *Gender and Class in Modern Europe*, Ithaca, New York: Cornell University Press, pp. 111–41.

Duncan, Simon (1996), 'The Diverse Worlds of European Patriarchy', in Maria Doloros Garcia-Ramon and Janice Monk (eds), *Women of the European Union: The Politics of Work and Daily Life*, London: Routledge, pp. 74–110.

Folbre, Nancy (1994), *Who Pays for the Kids? Gender and the Structures of Constraint*, London: Routledge.

Frevert, Ute (1988), *Women in German History: From Bourgeois Emancipation to Sexual Liberation*, translated by Stuart McKinnon-Evans, Oxford: Berg.

Garcia-Ramon, Maria Doloros and Janice Monk (eds) (1996), *Women of the European Union: The Politics of Work and Daily Life*, London: Routledge.

Hartmann, Heidi (1976), 'Capitalism, patriarchy, and job segregation by sex', *Signs: Journal of Women in Culture and Society*, **1** (3, Pt.2), (Spring), 137–69.

Headlee, Sue and Margery Elfin (1996), *The Cost of Being Female*, Westport, Connecticut: Praeger.

Hilden, Patricia Penn (1993), *Women, Work, and Politics: Belgium, 1830–1914*, Oxford: Clarendon Press.

Lerner, Gerda (1986), *The Creation of Patriarchy*, New York: Oxford University Press.

Martens, Lydia (1997), *Exclusion and Inclusion: The Gender Composition of British and Dutch Work Forces*, Aldershot: Avebury Publishing, Ltd.

Morris, Cynthia Taft and Irma Adelman (1988), *Comparative Patterns of Economic Development 1850–1914*, Baltimore: Johns Hopkins University Press.

Pinchbeck, Ivy (1930), *Women Workers and the Industrial Revolution, 1750–1850*, London: Frank Cass and Co. Ltd. Reprinted (1960), New York: Augustus M. Kelly Publishers.

Piven, Francis Fox and Richard A. Cloward (1971), *Regulating the Poor: The Functions of Public Welfare*, New York: Pantheon.

Pyle, Jean Larson (1990), *The State and Women in the Economy: Lessons from Sex Discrimination in the Republic of Ireland*, Albany: State University of New York Press.

Scott, Joan W. (1993), 'The Woman Worker', in Genevieve Fraisse and Michelle Perrot (eds), *A History of Women in the West, Vol. IV, Emerging Feminism from Revolution to World War*, Cambridge: Harvard University Press, pp. 399–426.

Stewart, Mary Lynn (1989), *Women, Work, and the French State: Labor Protection and Social Patriarchy, 1879–1919*, Kingston: McGill-Queen's University Press.

Tate, Jane (1994), 'Homework in West Yorkshire', in Sheila Rowbotham and Swasti Mitter (eds), *Dignity and Daily Bread: New Forms of Economic Organizing Among Poor Women in the Third World and the First*, London: Routledge, pp. 193–217.

Tilly, Louise A. and Joan W. Scott (1978), *Women, Work, and Family*, London: Routledge.

Economic Man

The concept of 'economic man' refers to the assumption that people can be characterized as self-interested, rational and autonomous. The concept originated with John Stuart Mill. Writing in the nineteenth century, Mill argued that it would be useful for political economy to assume 'an arbitrary definition of man, as a being who inevitably does that by which he may obtain the greatest amount of necessaries, conveniences, and luxuries, with the smallest quantity of labour and physical self-denial with which they can be obtained in the existing state of knowledge' (Oakley 1994, p. 155), or 'who desires to possess wealth, and who is capable of judging the comparative efficacy of means for obtaining that end' (Persky 1995, p. 223). Although Mill did not himself use the exact term economic man anywhere in his writings, Mill is generally credited with the origination of the idea. The actual first use of the term economic man may have been as a derogatory reference to such a set of assumptions in John Kell Ingram's *A History of Political Economy* in 1888 (Persky 1995, p. 122). The common use of a Latin synonym, *homo economicus*, to refer to the same concept may have been initiated by Vilfredo Pareto in 1906 (Persky 1995, p. 122).

This concept played a major role in the methodological development of (classical and) neoclassical economics. While it is apparent in Mill's writings that he recognized a much richer psychology of actual human nature, Mill argued for this abstraction on the basis of methodological principles. The method of science, Mill believed, was axiomatic–deductive. Therefore the science of political economy must start with simplified 'laws of human nature' and from there deduce the laws of social functioning related to production of wealth (Oakley 1994, pp. 150–51). Some scholars have also explored the relationship between the image of economic man and the rise of modern capitalism. Nancy Folbre (1994), for example, is one writer who has contrasted the images of human nature that historically underlie neoclassical vs. Marxist thought.

A more contemporary understanding of economic man retains the assumptions of self-interest and rationality, but replaces Mill's notion of maximization of wealth with the notion of maximization of utility. The notion that persons are autonomous was not explicitly stated by Mill nor by later theorists, but can be seen to be implicit in the assumptions of individual choice and action.

Economic man has been a frequent target of criticism, since well before the development of feminist economic critiques, from both inside and outside the economics profession, for the lack of realism implied by his rather one-dimensional psychology (for example, Leibenstein 1976; Meeks 1991). Sometimes the critiques focus on the aspect of selfishness, in light of observations of apparently non-self-interested human behaviour. Other times, they review the assumptions that economic man knows what is best for himself and pursues this logically, in the face of contrary evidence about actual human cognition from the disciplines of psychology and philosophy. Yet another critique is based on the recognition of economic man's social isolation: 'What remained missing in ... economic man, was any recognition that "human thought, feeling, and action" are all profoundly functions of intersubjective relations with others' (Oakley 1994, p. 178). Methodological debates concerning the uses of economic man are also legion. In spite of these numerous critiques, however, Persky (1995) is probably correct in saying that 'the majority of economists remain confident of the survival of their favorite species' (p. 221).

Feminist economists have used the concept of economic man, and participated in debates about him, in many different ways. Some implicitly accept the concept, by starting their analysis with the usual assumptions of self-interest, rational choice and autonomy. Some feminist economists have used the sexism of term economic *man* (since it is now widely recognized that such usage of 'man' is not perceived as gender-neutral) simply as an example of how the language of the discipline reflects the centrality of the activities of men in economic analysis (for example, Cohen 1982). Recently, feminist economists have gone more deeply to criticize both the substantive assumptions behind economic man – like the non-feminist critiques referred to above – and to add a new dimension to the critique. The new dimension is to show how the substantive and methodological assumptions which give him his staying power are rooted in more general cultural gender (and sometimes race) biases. The feminist contribution to the critique of economic man is not limited to pointing out (again) that assumptions of narrow rationality, self-interest and autonomy are inadequate to the job of explaining human behaviour. The new contribution is to show that science need not be conceived of only in terms of axiomatic–deductive methods, and that such methodological biases are strongly associated with cognitive and cultural understandings of gender and value. As the preface to *Beyond Economic Man: Feminist Theory and Economics* states,

> We intend for the title to be read with the emphasis on the word 'man'. As economists and social scientists, we want to retain and improve economic analysis by ridding the discipline of the biases created by the centrality of distinctively masculine concerns. (Ferber and Nelson 1993, p. iii)

Implicit in the assumptions underlying economic man are the dualisms of self-interest vs. other interest, rationality vs. emotion, and separation from others vs. connection to others. These dualisms are loaded with gendered and evaluative meaning, in the sense that the first term in each pair tends to be both associated with masculinity in Western culture, and accorded higher status within economic theorizing. These themes have been explored by various scholars, with somewhat varying emphases.

For example, Folbre and Hartmann (1988) examine the assumption of self-interest in economic models, contrasting the assumed self-interest of men in the market place to the assumed altruistic motivations of women and men within the female realm of the home. Examining both Marxist and neoclassical thought, they suggest that the notions of harmonious homes serve both to hide conflict and to rationalize women's economic disadvantages. Interestingly, John Stuart Mill – author of *The Subjection of Women*, it should be remembered, as well as of *Principles of Political Economy* – again enters the discussion, this time in regard to his arguments that women could have interests distinct from those of their fathers and husbands (Folbre and Hartmann 1988, pp. 193–4).

Folbre (1994) and Nelson (1996) are among the feminist economists who discuss gender biases in the notion of rationality. Folbre suggests that people are 'imperfectly rational', in that they use their powers of reasoning, but are not perfectly rational in the traditional economists' sense. Nelson contrasts narrow definitions of rationality based on strict logic and precision, to broader notions which include the use of metaphor and language and the influence of one's personal position and experiences.

England (1993) explains how the assumptions of selfishness, exogenous tastes, and the impossibility of interpersonal utility comparisons are examples of a model of a 'separative' self. Nelson (1996) elaborates further on the gendered aspects of this presumed autonomy:

> Thomas Hobbes ... wrote, 'Let us consider men ... as if but even now sprung out of the earth, and suddenly, like mushrooms, come to full maturity, without all kind of engagement to each other'. ... *Homo economicus* is the personification of individuality run wild. 'Economic man', the 'agent' of the prototypical economic model, springs up fully formed, with preferences fully developed, and is fully active and self-contained. He has no childhood or old age; no dependence on anyone; no responsibility for anyone but himself. The environment has no effect on him, but rather is merely the passive material, presented as 'constraints', over which his rationality has play. He interacts in society without being influenced by society: his mode of interaction is through an ideal market in which prices form the only, and only necessary, form of communication. *Homo economicus* is the central character in a romance of individuality without connection to nature or to society.
>
> Yet humans simply do not spring out of the earth. Humans are born of women, nurtured and cared for as dependent children, socialized into family and community groups, and are perpetually dependent on nourishment and shelter to sustain our lives. These aspects of human life, whose neglect is often justified by the argument that they are unimportant or intellectually uninteresting or merely 'natural', are, not just coincidentally, the areas of life thought of as 'women's work'. (Nelson 1996, pp. 30–31)

Thus autonomy is not a fact of human existence, but rather a construct that is coherent with distinctly masculine-biased world views.

There is room for discussion among feminists, however, on both the source of the notion of economic man and on the issue of what, if anything, should replace this image of human nature. Raising questions about the role of gender, philosopher Harding (1986, Chapter 7) points out the 'curious coincidence' between feminist critiques of economic man and criticism from an 'African-oriented' view, expressed by economist Vernon Dixon. In Dixon's (1977) view, the African-oriented approach also rejects the notion of economic man in favour of an image that is less individuated and self-interested. Issues of both race and gender have also been explored by Williams (1993) and by scholars deconstructing a much-used allegory for economic man: the story of Robinson Crusoe (Samson 1995; Grapard 1995).

McCloskey (1993) suggested that along with *vir economicus* (his term for a distinctly masculine economic man) we consider an image of a *feminina economica* who has a greater sense of social solidarity. This particular solution to the problem of replacing economic man would probably only receive a minority vote from feminist economists, however. More commonly, feminist economic analysis tends towards unpacking, rather than reinforcing, the sexist dualisms implicit in the dividing up of the world into selfish/rational/autonomous and altruistic/emotional/connected realms. Nelson (1996), for example, suggests that the selfish/altruistic dualism has prevented the discussion of interpersonal interactions motivated by responsibility or commitment (p. 70). Harding (1986), Williams (1993) and others have taken a more explicitly deconstructionist approach to understanding these dualisms, along the lines of postmodern theory.

A neoclassical economist, however, may reply to feminist critiques with the argument that economic man is not meant to be realistic, and so criticisms of his adequacy as a model of human selfhood is beside the point. Such an argument is advanced, for example, by Persky who claims that any suggested alternative 'must be parsimonious' in its assumptions, including only a 'manageable' set of human motivations, lest the ability of the model to yield 'tightly reasoned generalizations' be lost (1995, p. 230). Such an argument, of course, assumes that economics, to be a science, must necessarily proceed by the methods of abstraction and deduction – an assumption heavily called into question by other scholarly research on epistemology and methodology – explicitly feminist (for example, Nelson 1993) and otherwise (for example, Oakley 1994).

Yet work remains to be done. This work need not be so much in continuing to critique the model of economic man, nor of seeking, necessarily, a global replacement for this image in economic thinking. Rather, what is necessary is to continue to investigate the ways in which use of this model may have biased economic investigations – and perhaps even influenced actual economic behaviour – and of seeking, on a case-by-case basis, to develop ways of thinking about human individuality, situatedness and motivation which are more adequate to the tasks at hand.

JULIE A. NELSON

See also

Dualisms; Methodology; Neoclassical Economics; Postmodernism; Race.

Bibliography

Cohen, Marjorie (1982), 'The Problem of Studying "Economic Man"', in Angela Miles and Geraldine Finn (eds), *Feminism in Canada: From Pressure to Politics*, Montreal: Black Rose Books, pp. 89–101.

Dixon, Vernon J. (1977), 'African-oriented and Euro-American-oriented world views: research methodologies and economics', *The Review of Black Political Economy*, **7** (2), 119–56.

England, Paula (1993), 'The Separative Self: Androcentric Bias in Neoclassical Assumptions', in Marianne A. Ferber and Julie A. Nelson (eds), *Beyond Economic Man: Feminist Theory and Economics*, Chicago: University of Chicago Press, pp. 37–53.

Ferber, Marianne A. and Julie A. Nelson (eds) (1993), *Beyond Economic Man: Feminist Theory and Economics*, Chicago: University of Chicago Press.

Folbre, Nancy (1994), *Who Pays for the Kids? Gender and the Structures of Constraint*, London: Routledge.

Folbre, Nancy and Heidi Hartmann (1988), 'The Rhetoric of Self-Interest: Ideology and Gender in Economic Theory', in Arjo Klamer, Donald N. McCloskey and Robert M. Solow (eds), *The Consequences of Economic Rhetoric*, Cambridge: Cambridge University Press, pp. 184–203.

Grapard, Ulla (1995), 'Robinson Crusoe: The Quintessential Economic Man?', *Feminist Economics*, **1** (1), (Spring), 33–52.

Harding, Sandra (1986), *The Science Question in Feminism*, Ithaca: Cornell University Press.

Leibenstein, Harvey (1976), *Beyond Economic Man: A New Foundation for Microeconomics*, Cambridge, Massachusetts: Harvard University Press.

McCloskey, Donald N. (1993), 'Some Consequences of a Conjective Economics', in Marianne A. Ferber and Julie A. Nelson (eds), *Beyond Economic Man: Feminist Theory and Economics*, Chicago: University of Chicago Press, pp. 69–93.

Meeks, Gay (1991), *Thoughtful Economic Man: Essays on Rationality, Moral Rules and Benevolence*, Cambridge: Cambridge University Press.

Nelson, Julie A. (1993), 'The Study of Choice or the Study of Provisioning? Gender and the Definition of Economics', in Marianne A. Ferber and Julie A. Nelson (eds), *Beyond Economic Man: Feminist Theory and Economics*, Chicago: University of Chicago Press, pp. 23–36.

Nelson, Julie A. (1996), *Feminism, Objectivity and Economics*, London: Routledge.

Oakley, Allen (1994), *Classical Economic Man: Human Agency and Methodology in the Political Economy of Adam Smith and J.S. Mill*, Brookfield, Vermont: Edward Elgar.

Persky, Joseph (1995), 'The ethology of homo economicus', *Journal of Economic Perspectives*, **9** (2), (Spring), 221–31.

Samson, Melanie (1995), 'Towards a "Friday" model of international trade: a feminist deconstruction of race and gender bias in the Robinson Crusoe trade allegory', *Canadian Journal of Economics*, **28** (1), (February), 143–58.

Williams, Rhonda M. (1993), 'Race, Deconstruction, and the Emergent Agenda of Feminist Economic Theory', in Marianne A. Ferber and Julie A. Nelson (eds), *Beyond Economic Man: Feminist Theory and Economics*, Chicago: University of Chicago Press, pp. 144–53.

Economic Restructuring

Economic restructuring is a broad term, encompassing an array of economic policies that overall involve a shift to more market-oriented economic systems with less government intervention. It is used in four main contexts: in establishing either general development policies or structural adjustment programmes (SAPs) in developing countries, in forming transition policies of post-socialist countries, in devising changes in government spending and labour market reforms in the more developed or OECD countries, and in characterizing changes in the global economy as a whole. Although the effects of economic restructuring on women are often examined in the context of developing countries or post-socialist economies, economic restructuring is a global phenomenon that has similar policy components worldwide. To design effective policies to counter the often negative effects of economic restructuring, it must be understood and addressed as a global phenomenon.

Key policy elements of economic restructuring are trade liberalization (reduced trade barriers such as tariffs and quotas, floating exchange rates, freer flows of portfolio or foreign direct investment), privatization (of sectors, industries, or services formerly run or provided by the state), a decrease in government spending and regulation of the economy (regarding health and safety, environmental standards, anti-trust, or measures to ensure fair treatment of workers), and reduction of the power of organized workers. These policies lead to increased globalization of production, financial flows and the movement of people. Economic restructuring also typically involves the promotion of the export-led development strategy by international agencies such as the World Bank or International Monetary Fund (IMF), an expanded role of multinational corporations (MNCs) in industrialized and developing countries with their burgeoning networks of subcontractors and home workers (long referred to as the 'global assembly line'), and major repositioning of the relative power of international institutions.

The particular subset of these restructuring policies and their outcomes have varied somewhat across countries. Concerns about low-level jobs for women in export processing, microenterprises and the informal sector, and problems of discrimination in layoffs and hiring are common in studies of developing and post-socialist countries (Aslanbeigui et al. 1994; Ward and Pyle 1995). Research on reforms in the industrialized countries has centered on the missing middle, the trends toward 'flexible' production and 'flexible' forms of work, and the feminization of the labour force (MacDonald 1995). In the 1980s and into the early to mid 1990s, many East and Southeast Asian economies were stellar performers, Latin America experienced a lost decade of development, the human costs of government cutbacks were clearly evident in sub-Saharan Africa, and the industrialized countries saw gains for those at the top but losses for the middle class and poor. Despite the variations, the policies in these countries have been remarkably similar and part of global economic transformation.

Economic restructuring policies have set the economic environment for hundreds of millions of women and men throughout the world during the 1980s and 1990s. There are, however, serious questions about whether these policies support sustainable human development. Although the policies were to have taken on a more human face in the 1990s, the deaths of over one thousand in Indonesia in the summer of 1998 illustrate that the reform package with currency devaluations and layoffs of workers (promoted by the IMF and the World Bank) has not adequately addressed the human dimension of the process.

Economists usually portray changes associated with economic restructuring in terms of macroeconomic variables, such as the growth of gross domestic product (GDP), omitting different effects by gender as well as the human costs. The focus is on efficiency and profit in line with the tenets of the neoclassical approach to economics. Economic restructuring, however, involves changes in the international division of labour and the international distribution of power and access to resources. The consequences are complex; it is not a gender-neutral process (Bakker 1994; Benería 1995). Economic restructuring has offered enhanced opportunities for some women, but for many the opposite is the case. The widespread move to more market orientation typically leads to rising inequality between women and men (and among women in different countries and from different age groups, ethnicities, social strata) because the market rewards those with assets and access to resources. Women often receive few of the benefits accruing and bear a disproportionate share of the burden of these changes (Benería and Feldman 1992; Aslanbeigui et al. 1994; Thomas-Emeagwali 1995; Seager 1997; Pyle 1999).

Globalization of market activities has occurred unevenly. Women in marginalized countries have limited opportunities, and women in countries that have become much more part of the global market economy generally find work only in the lowest occupational levels (United Nations 1995b). In addition, with economic restructuring there is reduced support for education, housing and social services (such as health care or food and fuel subsidies) and less regulation in the economy (of product standards, environmental conditions, or working conditions such as pay or health and safety). These changes make it harder to maintain standards of living in the household, an endeavour that is largely women's responsibility. This further widens inequalities between women and men.

Economic restructuring policies, the result of widespread applications of policy prescriptions from traditional economic theory, are linked with increases in women's small-scale self-employment endeavours (microenterprise), employment in the informal sector, female poverty and women's relatively disadvantaged status in the home as well as in society. The United Nations Development Programme (1995) estimates that 70 per cent of the world's poor are women and attributes this to unequal treatment of women in the labour market, their position in the family, and the way government deals with them.

Feminist economics can shed considerable light on how the unequal impact of economic restructuring on women can, in turn, have an adverse effect on sustainable human development. Specifically, because gender is not addressed in traditional analyses, policies are often poorly constructed and the actual outcomes are not predicted. They can in turn undermine the development process. Some of the main themes in the large literature by feminists and feminist economists on the effect of economic restructuring are: women and their work (paid and unpaid, in the formal sector, informal sector or microenterprise and in the household), women in the family/household (allocation of labour, income and bargaining power between women and men), women and the environment (environmental degradation, chemicals in agricultural or industrial production and indoor pollution) and institutional change and bases for empowerment (transformation of the social and cultural institutions that place men systematically in dominant positions throughout society). These themes and their relation to sustainable human development are explored below, stressing women's strategies as active economic agents as well as issues of their wellbeing with respect to the international forces of economic restructuring.

Women and work

Economic restructuring has reshaped women's working lives around the world. Although neoclassical economics examines how labour market choices and outcomes differ by gender, feminist economics brings a wider vision to the analysis of work because it examines a broader range of activities: unpaid as well as paid, informal and formal sector work and household work (analysing it from the viewpoint of the individual as well as the family/household). In further contrast to neoclassical economics, feminist economists recognize the unequal power relations between women and men and the gender bias of development policies that result in women facing dramatically different choices regarding their work options (and education and training) than men (Elson 1995; *World Development* 1995).

The overall liberalization of the world economy and the shift to more market orientation have resulted in the globalization of many agricultural, industrial and service activities (including tourism and the sex industry) in ways that change women's work opportunities. Some of the more visible aspects of economic restructuring over the past two decades that affect women's work lives are the shift to export-led development strategies, the spread of MNCs and their subcontracting networks internationally, the use of structural adjustment policies (SAPs) that decrease public sector employment and public expenditures on social services and the resultant larger role of informal sector and microenterprise endeavours.

The increased market and trade orientation involves gains for some, losses for others. In industrialized countries (and many transitional economies) it often involves retrenchment of women workers as jobs move abroad, the resurgence of sweatshops that tend to employ immigrant women and children and expansion of home-based work. In developing countries, women usually do not have the resources necessary to become business owners in the expanding tradable goods sectors. They therefore acquire jobs in export sectors (whether in agriculture, manufacturing or service) or increase their informal sector activities. Throughout the world, women face discrimination in pay or access to jobs and often disproportionately bear the burden of layoffs (Aslanbeigui et al. 1994; Seager 1997; United Nations 1995b).

Export-led development (a set of financial incentives designed to encourage production for export) was perceived as successful in several countries in East and South-East Asia for decades. In negotiations with borrowing countries throughout Latin America and Africa in the 1980s and 1990s, the IMF and World Bank have actively promoted adoption of this development approach to increase growth and generate the required foreign exchange to repay loans. In the crisis of the late 1990s, the Asian countries themselves are being pressured to make their markets and financial institutions more open to global competition. Export industries are typically engaged in light manufacturing (clothing, shoes, electronics, toys and sporting goods) or service endeavours (reservations for travel industries or data entry and processing for insurance and banking firms). They normally employ largely female work forces because they perceive women as willing to perform monotonous tasks for relatively low wages (Pyle 1999; United Nations 1995a). In most cases, women's wages are substantially lower than men's (Seager 1997; Seguino forthcoming).

The increasing globalization of powerful MNCs has further contributed to economic restructuring. MNCs now originate from a wide variety of countries (not only from the United States, Western Europe and Japan but also from Taiwan, Singapore, Hong Kong and South Korea), locate production in successive tiers of new countries (for example, Eastern European countries, Bangladesh, Sri Lanka, Vietnam, China and many Central American nations), and utilize extensive networks of subcontractors to provide low-cost production flexibility. MNCs in the consumer goods and service sectors hire large percentages of women workers. Although MNCs may offer wages and working conditions that are slightly better than in indigenous firms, the negative aspects of working in them are readily obvious in the short run (long hours often with forced overtime, harassment from managers, speedups and poor housing conditions) and in the longer run (lack of benefits, deterioration of eyesight and health, absence of advancement opportunities and even retrenchment). In addition, MNCs have developed an array of cost-cutting strategies to employ in the event workers seek to improve wages or working conditions – automation, relocation, subcontracting networks that involve informal sector workers and suppression of worker discontent. Each of these has adverse impacts on the women involved (Pyle 1999).

Still, another form of economic restructuring, the stabilization and structural adjustment policies required by the IMF and World Bank as conditions for receiving loans, create a climate favourable for corporations with little attention to employment or income inequality. In many countries, SAPs have resulted in increasing unemployment, rising poverty, environmental degradation and deteriorating working conditions (Sparr 1994; Safa 1995; G. Sen 1995; Wee and Heyzer 1995). Policy changes to reduce government deficits hurt women – both via their loss of public sector employment, and through cuts in social services like health and education. These changes affect women's abilities to provide the desired standard of living in the household and they must increase their workload to compensate. This typically leads to increases in women's informal sector economic activities.

Women's involvement in informal sector activities have grown rapidly due to several of these aspects of economic restructuring. For example, as MNCs increase their global spread and their use of layers of subcontractors, larger numbers of women are drawn into employment in these networks spawned by, but outside of, the MNCs. The work site ranges from medium size enterprises to individual piecework done in the home. Employment in smaller enterprises or in the home has lower pay, no benefits, no opportunity for advancement and can be terminated at will. Similarly, women who have lost their public sector jobs as a result of SAPs or who must supplement meagre household incomes because of cutbacks in government provided social services increasingly turn to informal sector work (United Nations 1995a, b; UNDP 1995).

The informal sector involves a wide range of activities. It encompasses home-based industrial or service work or setting up a microenterprise (preparing and selling street foods, producing small items, selling magazines and sundries, cutting hair at curbside). Increasingly, informal sector activities entail migration of large numbers of women to urban areas or to other countries where they work as domestics, in manufacturing, or in the sex industry. Abuses are prevalent. In addition to the lack of recognition of the value of their work in official national accounts, the low wages and often poor working conditions, some women (particularly those who have migrated) have been physically and sexually abused.

Women have developed a wide range of strategies to counteract the undesirable effects of economic restructuring on their work lives. Some actively resist MNC policies, seeking better wages and working conditions, although it is dangerous to do so since MNCs frequently have police provided by the state to break up worker actions. Other women have developed passive resistance strategies at work that undermine production but which are difficult to prove. In addition, women homeworkers have organized and have the International Labour Organization's (ILO) support to counteract the lack of recognition and the low pay of home-based work (Boris and Prugl 1996). Others are working to document instances of and press for laws to prohibit enforced servitude and sexual slavery.

In many places, microenterprises have been a significant survival strategy for poor women although few women make more than in formal sector jobs (Tinker 1990; Rowbotham and Mitter 1994). Establishment of these small business activities has been constrained by the lack of available credit for women. Many development programmes in the 1980s and 1990s have focused on microcredit, although there is concern that in some cases males may control the resources targeted toward women.

Women and the family/household
A key area for feminist analysis is how economic restructuring policies play out within the family or household. In contrast to the neoclassical approach that treats the family as fully cooperative, feminist economists view the family as involving both cooperation and conflict, where the members work together for some goals but may have serious disagreements over issues such as the allocation of labour and income (see A. Sen 1990, 1995; Tinker 1990; Folbre 1995; Haddad et al. 1995; MacDonald 1995). Thus, it is necessary to examine policy effects at the individual and family levels.

Restructuring policies lead to changes in how income is earned, who is earning it, how much of their time is involved and how needed household work is supplied – whether by women, men, the extended family, or via government provided services. Most researchers agree that a woman is likely to spend a larger proportion of her income on the children, that her income provides security to the family through the diversification of earnings and that the ability to earn some income improves a woman's standing in the household (Blumberg 1995; A. Sen 1995). These outcomes are influenced, however, by perceived contributions based on how income is earned (A. Sen 1990).

In countries where structural adjustment policies have led to lower family incomes, such as most of Latin America and sub-Saharan Africa, women's increased labour market participation has provided support without necessarily improving their standing in the family. At times, unemployed men's stress over changing roles has contributed to increased domestic violence. In addition, women often work longer at home doing work that is essential to family wellbeing but which typically is not recognized or appropriately valued. Women frequently do unpaid work to grow vegetables or process cheaper goods that previously would have been purchased at a more refined stage. Cuts in health care and other social services fall heavily on women who are the caretakers in the family and must improvise to try to provide for the needed services being eliminated (Aslanbeigui et al. 1994).

Even in places where economic restructuring has led to a growing economy and higher average per capita incomes, such as China and Vietnam, women's gains have been offset to some degree by labour market discrimination and loss of traditional family support systems that are not replaced adequately by the market or the state. Although the government potentially could supply support such as subsidized child care, government spending in these areas is being cut rather than expanded (Aslanbeigui et al. 1994).

In both growing and contracting economies, the need to combine productive and reproductive activities and the continuing discrimination in the labour market have contributed to two overlapping trends. One is the expansion of the informal sector discussed in the preceding section. The other is the trend toward home-based work, or using housing as a location for income-earning activities, such as piecework outsourced by firms, provision of services to subcontractors, microenterprise, or renting rooms (Summerfield and Tinker 1997; Boris and Prugl 1996; Safa 1995; Sparr 1994).

Family strategies frequently conflict with individual strategies and often adversely affect women. Emphasis on exports has given new sources of income to some women but also resulted in crops that were traditionally considered women's area to be taken over by men as they became more profitable (beans in Zambia, for example). This has occurred with respect to women's microenterprises as well. In addition, higher school fees (that occur with most restructuring policies as governments are required to cut back spending) and opportunities for home-based work mean that daughters may lose the access to education in a conflict with their parents and brothers. Opportunities for men and unmarried women in the cities result in family migration strategies that may increase overall family income but usually increase the workload of the wife/mother who remains in the countryside to work on the farm; the need for help may also lead to keeping a daughter home from school. The lack of understanding of intrahousehold dynamics by officials and development workers has exacerbated these policy-related disadvantages for women (Aslanbeigui et al. 1994).

Women have been active in addressing the way economic restructuring affects them as members of families. Women in Latin America have sheltered their families from falling income by growing vegetables and setting up community kitchens. In the 1990s, SEWA (Self Employed Women's Association) and the ILO, for example, have been vigorously promoting recognition of home work (piece production or service work done under contract) and seeking better wages and benefits (Prugl and Boris 1996).

Women and the environment
Restructuring policies – with their emphasis on economic growth, export promotion, cuts in government spending and deregulation of market activities – have affected the environment in a variety of ways, often detrimental and usually with differential gender impacts (see Wee and Heyzer 1995). Neoclassical economics measures the gains from market transactions, such as exports

of timber, but does little to account for the vanishing forests or other environmental problems that are 'external to the market'. Resource and environmental economists make some effort to calculate nonmarket values (for use and existence of resources), but typically omit gender issues (considering policies gender neutral). Feminist economists (such as Waring 1989) at times address gender and the environment, especially with respect to sustainable human development, but the nexus of economic restructuring (particularly trade liberalization), environmental issues (both brown and green) and gender studies is not yet well integrated into the feminist approach to economic policy analysis. Women's knowledge of crops, animals, land and forests is now being undermined, but the contribution that this knowledge can make to sustainable development (Sachs 1996) has not been adequately recognized or explored.

In addition, women and children are usually hit harder by pollution and environmental degradation because they comprise the majority of the poor and are frequently cut off from traditional sources of sustenance as forests disappear, common lands are privatized and waterways become too polluted to drink from or to support fish. In many developing countries, their unpaid family labour takes longer as they have to spend more hours searching for fuel or clean water (see Summerfield and Tinker 1997). Their children are more frequently stillborn or born with afflictions that require more care. In the North, women are often blamed for over-consumption of goods even though they control fewer resources than men, and they suffer from increased health threats related to environmental pollutants, such as the high incidence of breast cancer in the Silicon Valley area of California.

Women comprise a larger share of the farmers in many developing countries (China, Vietnam, sub-Saharan Africa) as men and older children migrate to the cities to search for work (Sachs 1996; Summerfield and Tinker 1997). The women left to run the farms face threats to their land from new sources of industrial pollution nearby, new roads and problems associated with the growing use of fertilizers and pesticides (frequently imported from countries where their use is banned). These female farmers and their customers in the city and in foreign markets face health threats from the chemicals. As export and population pressures lead to deterioration of overused crop lands and deforestation results in more frequent floods and changing weather patterns, women are increasingly susceptible to endemic hunger and famine.

Restructuring policies encourage foreign direct investment that often centres on export-processing firms that are allowed to bypass pollution regulations and expose their predominately female work force to high levels of indoor pollution and hazardous chemicals. Local firms that compete for the export markets usually operate with a smaller profit margin and frequently violate regulations to cut current costs. These processes affect women directly as workers and indirectly through location effects (Pyle 1999).

Women's strategies in the face of environmental degradation include forming non-governmental organizations to protect areas and promote environmental policies and participating in community efforts to develop sanitation methods. Women are active in finding ways to combine the new opportunities occurring after restructuring with environmentally friendly processes, such as growing agricultural products and medicinal herbs to sell in urban and international markets, producing and marketing traditional crafts and supplementing family nutrition with community gardening. In the more developed countries, women address health issues by forming organizations that advocate spending a larger proportion of cancer research funds on breast cancer and in raising issues of environmental justice when waste sites are located near the poor and minorities. At the macroeconomic level, feminist economists are working for inclusion of environmental values and women's nonmarket contributions in the national income accounts (Waring 1989).

Institutional change and bases for empowerment
Feminist economists recognize the importance of both the institutional framework within which women live and work and the changes that occur in social institutions over time, topics which are typically overlooked by mainstream analyses of economic restructuring. Social institutions may be broadly defined as 'the means of social coordination, ranging from organizations such as the firm, the family, and the state to the political rules and social norms that help such organizations function' (Folbre 1995, p. 2). They range from the local to the global and include culture and traditions. Feminist social scientists recognize that institutions are not gender neutral but embody gender preferences, norms and practices (Goetz 1997, p. 5). The structure of social institutions and the way they change over time not only mediate the impact of economic restructuring policies on women in different societies but also shape the opportunities women have for economic empowerment. Elson (1995) argues that the development process is biased because of the gendered nature of economic structures and processes that do not consider existing gender inequalities (wherein females are disadvantaged) and that do not build in policies to remedy these inequities.

Economic restructuring takes place within societies that have diverse cultures. Culture and tradition, however, institutionalize discrimination against women to some degree in every society studied, including those with matrilineal traditions (though patriarchy is the most common structure). Culturally women and men typically have distinct roles; women's economic contributions, although constituting a substantial portion of work done, are generally undervalued. Laws either do not grant equality to women or frequently are not enforced. Traditional bias against women has even re-emerged in socialist countries making the transition to market-oriented economies as the socialist ideology that promoted equality for women loses its prominence in society.

In addition, economic restructuring over the past two decades has involved significant changes in the structure and composition of the major global institutions, the power structures within which the world's women must function and struggle for change. Understanding the effects of economic restructuring on women therefore requires a survey of the major global institutions, whether gender equity is a primary goal, and, if so, what the extent of their ability to promote it might be, in terms of financial capacity and authority to enforce.

Global institutions can be divided into several general categories: MNCs and their production networks, international financial institutions (such as the World Bank and the IMF), the United Nations (UN) and subsidiaries such as UNIFEM and the ILO focused on human development issues, prominent national governments (such as the G-7), and non-governmental organizations (NGOs) or grassroots organizations. These organizations differ widely in terms of their motivations and their ability to meet their goals. The venues where women's voices may be heard have been limited but are growing. Women have been active in organizing to improve their lives.

MNCs, one of the key international institutions as global economic restructuring has proceeded, are motivated to cut costs, acquire new markets and increase profits; their priorities do not include treating people (including women) equally, reducing unemployment or income inequalities, or preserving the environment. As discussed above, changes in MNCs have had complicated, often negative, effects on women's long-term economic self-sufficiency. Although there are countless examples worldwide of women attempting workplace organization to counteract the effects of this form of economic restructuring, they face the considerable power of the corporations to suppress their efforts, which often includes the police power of the state.

The World Bank and the IMF, two key international institutions prominent throughout economic restructuring endeavours, seek to shape borrowing countries' macroeconomic policies in line with their vision (based on the neoclassical economic paradigm of economic development). They are fundamentally concerned with the borrowers' ability to repay debt, lowering trade and government deficits, and opening markets, rather than with increasing employment and reducing societal inequality. As shown, the structural adjustment policies they require typically have an adverse impact on women's lives. A number of feminist economists have questioned this macroeconomic approach and have begun to develop macro models that incorporate feminist concerns (Benería 1995; *World Development* 1995). Since 1994, the World Bank has committed to mainstreaming gender concerns, establishing more participatory approaches to development planning and promoting social development (Murphy 1997). However, projects with gender-related actions were only 30 per cent of the bank's investment portfolio from 1994 to 1996, down from 45 to 50 per cent in the early 1990s (Murphy 1997). In addition, there are often breakdowns between the plan and how it is implemented, and gender concerns may be downplayed.

Although many UN organizations seek to enhance the economic and social status of women and address the adverse impact of many economic restructuring policies, their efforts are diluted by the multi-agency structure of the UN and they lack the necessary funding and power to implement or enforce their recommendations. Since 1975, the UN has sponsored four international conferences focusing on assessing women's progress (or lack of it) and formulating strategies to improve them, the most recent being the Fourth World Conference on Women in Beijing in 1995. UN agencies have produced several key reports designed to increase the informational base regarding women's socioeconomic and political status (UNDP 1995, United Nations 1995b). They have developed new measures of development that incorporate gender differences as variables (the Gender Development Index (GDI) and the Gender Empowerment Measure (GEM)). Agencies such as UNIFEM have developed a range of programmes to increase women's capabilities, include women in development planning and support experimental programmes that benefit women and, in turn, the development of their countries (UNIFEM 1995). Similarly, the ILO has enacted many conventions that would improve the place of women in the workplace, but it, too, lacks enforcement capabilities. It has developed an action guide to improve the quantity and quality of employment opportunities for women (Lim 1996).

Although various national governments have power internationally, most do not incorporate gender in their planning for future development. National governments typically are more concerned with GDP growth rates, price stability, maintaining a favourable position during global economic restructuring and surviving financial, political, or military crises, rather than with unemployment, inequality, or gender differences. Women's representation, and therefore women's voices, in governing national bodies is very small, although growing in some areas. There have been a few female heads of state recently, but most are women succeeding a male family member.

It is in NGOs that women's positions and concerns are increasingly voiced. Many NGOs addressing gender and development issues have arisen from a great variety of countries in the past 25 years and have played an increasingly visible role in international conferences (Chen 1995). Although many are small grassroots organizations with limited power, some have formed regional coalitions that provide a power base with considerable leverage (Tinker 1990). Chen (1995) traces how NGOs were a major force in pushing for the international conferences on women and how they have used their increased skills and competencies to forge linkages with other international move-ments, such as those concerned with the environmental and human rights.

Women's strategies to address the changed institutional environment that has accompanied economic restructuring include organizing in MNCs, offer-ing alternative macroeconomic policies to the World Bank and IMF, developing a greater presence in the UN and ILO, strengthening NGO networks, devel-oping new institutions that can provide a base for political power (such as NGOs), transforming other institutions (such as the family) and altering laws (such as those specifying property rights) so that women have full ownership and control rights comparable to men's.

Issues for future research
As economic restructuring policies and the dynamic they generate continue to play a major role in the lives of people around the world, more work needs to address the strategies that women can use to reduce the costs of adjustment and take advantage of any emerging opportunities. At this point, the most common strategies that have emerged are microenterprise, microcredit and education. Although these are important, the micro ventures are mainly sur-vival strategies for the poorest women and their families. While increasing women's educational levels gives them greater flexibility, it is, by itself, an insufficient strategy to improve women's lives given the context of the key policy elements of economic restructuring (shift to more market-oriented economic systems with trade liberalization, privatization, decreasing govern-ment regulation, suppression of workers, use of export-oriented development strategies, and involvement of multinational corporations).

As globalization and marketization continue, more work is needed on how women can organize for better wages and working conditions on a regional or global basis in different sectors of the economy. Researchers and policymakers could further examine the importance and extent of home-based work and strive in new forums for appropriate recognition of the value of the work and adequate remuneration. Others could more systematically evaluate the actual effects of microenterprise programmes – to determine to whom the benefits really accrue and what additional changes in male–female power relations may be necessary for microcredit and microenterprise pro-grammes to succeed. In addition to microcredit programmes, research is needed on structural changes in international financial institutions that could give women and poor people more access to resources. Studies should exam-ine issues faced by women in the context of the family and community (local, national and international) as well as individual aspects of their wellbeing and agency. More work needs to focus on the nexus of areas that are often addressed separately such as gender, trade and the environment. Increasing urbanization calls for more research on urban survival strategies, food security and opportunities for increasing agency and wellbeing, including housing rights and changing institutions to provide a social safety net. Researchers and policymakers can continue assessing the gender inclusiveness or gender sensitivity of the major global institutions discussed and how they can be altered to systematically address gender inequities as a part of their standard operation procedure. Perhaps, more importantly, researchers, practitioners (such as NGO workers) and policymakers can work together to construct new institutional arrangements and more humane policies that could be substituted for current economic restructuring policies.

JEAN LARSON PYLE AND GALE SUMMERFIELD

See also

Banking and Credit; Development Policies; Globalization; Informal Sector; International Economics; Structural Adjustment Policies; Unemployment and Underemployment.

Bibliography

Aslanbeigui, Nahid, Steven Pressman and Gale Summerfield (eds) (1994), *Women in the Age of Economic Transformation*, London: Routledge.

Bakker, Isabella (ed.) (1994), *The Strategic Silence: Gender and Economic Policy*, London: Zed.

Benería, Lourdes (1995), 'Toward a greater integration of gender in economics', *World Development*, **23** (11), November, 1839–50.

Benería, Lourdes and Shelley Feldman (eds) (1992), *Unequal Burden: Economic Crises, Persistent Poverty, and Women's Work*, Boulder, Colorado: Westview Press.

Blumberg, Rae Lesser, Cathy A. Rakowski, Irene Tinker and Michael Monteon (eds) (1995), *EnGENDERing Wealth and Well-Being*, Boulder, Colorado: Westview Press.

Boris, Eileen and Elisabeth Prugl (1996), *Homeworkers in Global Perspective: Invisible No More*, New York: Routledge.

Chen, Martha A. (1995), 'Engendering world conferences: the international women's movement and the United Nations', *Third World Quarterly*, **16** (3).

Elson, Diane (1995), *Male Bias in the Development Process*, Second edn, Manchester: Manchester University Press.

Folbre, Nancy (1995), *Engendering Economics: New Perspectives on Women, Work, and Demographic Change*, World Bank.

Goetz, Anne Marie (ed.) (1997), *Getting Institutions Rights for Women in Development*, London: Zed Books.

Haddad, Lawrence, Lynn Brown, Andrea Richter and Lisa Smith (1995), 'The gender dimensions of economic adjustment policies: potential interactions and evidence to date', *World Development*, **23** (6), 881–96.

Lim, Lin Lean (1996), *More and Better Jobs for Women: An Action Guide*, Geneva: ILO.

MacDonald, Martha (1995), 'The Empirical Challenges of Feminist Economics: The Example of Economic Restructuring', in Edith Kuiper and Jolande Sap (eds), *Out of the Margin: Feminist Perspectives on Economics*, London: Routledge, pp. 175–97.

Murphy, Josette (1997), *Mainstreaming Gender in World Bank Lending: An Update*, Washington, DC: The World Bank.

Prugl, Elisabeth and Eileen Boris (1996), 'Introduction', in Eileen Boris and Elisabeth Prugl (eds), *Homeworkers in Global Perspective: Invisible No More*, New York: Routledge, pp. 3–17.

Pyle, Jean L. (1999), 'Third World Women and Global Restructuring', in Janet S. Chafetz (ed.), *Handbook on Gender Sociology*, New York: Plenum Publishing, pp. 81–104.

Rowbotham, Sheila and Swasti Mitter (eds) (1994), *Dignity and Daily Bread: New Forms of Economic Organising Among Poor Women in the Third World and the First*, London: Routledge.

Sachs, Carolyn (1996), *Gendered Fields: Rural Women, Agriculture, and Environment*, Boulder, Colorado: Westview Press.

Safa, Helen I. (1995), 'Gender Implications of Export-Led Industrialization in the Caribbean Basin', Rae Lesser Blumberg, Cathy A. Rakowski, Irene Tinker and Michael Monteon (eds), *EnGENDERing Wealth and Well-Being*, in Boulder, Colorado: Westview Press, pp. 89–112.

Seager, Joni (1997), *The State of Women in the World Atlas*, New Edition, London: Penguin.

Seguino, Stephanie (forthcoming), 'Economic liberalization, export-led growth, and gender wage differentials in South Korea and Taiwan', *Cambridge Journal of Economics*.

Sen, Amartya (1990), 'Gender and Cooperative Conflicts', in I. Tinker (ed.), *Persistent Inequalities*, New York: Oxford University Press, pp. 123–49.

Sen, Amartya (1995), 'Agency and Well-Being: The Development Agenda', in Noeleen Heyzer (ed.), *A Commitment to the World's Women*, New York: UNIFEM, pp. 103–12.

Sen, Gita (1995), 'Alternative economics from a gender perspective', *Development: Journal of the Society for International Development*, (1), (Special issue prepared for the 4th UN World Conference on Women), pp. 10–13.

Sparr, Pamela (ed.) (1994), *Mortgaging Women's Lives: Feminist Critiques of Structural Adjustment*, London: Zed.

Summerfield, Gale and Irene Tinker (1997), 'The Family and Economic Transformation in Developing Countries: Impacts and Strategies, A Symposium Based on Issues Raised at the NGO Forum of the United Nations' Fourth World Conference on Women, Huairou, China August 30–Sept. 9, 1995', *Review of Social Economy*, **55**, (Summer).

Thomas-Emeagwali, Gloria (ed.) (1995), *Women Pay the Price: Structural Adjustment in Africa and the Caribbean*, Trenton, New Jersey: Africa World Press, Inc.

Tinker, Irene (ed.) (1990), *Persistent Inequalities: Women and World Development*, New York: Oxford University Press.

United Nations (1995a), *Women in a Changing Global Economy: 1994 World Survey on the Role of Women in Development*, New York: United Nations.

United Nations (1995b), *The World's Women 1995: Trends and Statistics*, New York: United Nations.

United Nations Development Fund for Women (UNIFEM) (1995), *Commitment to the World's Women*, New York: UNIFEM.

United Nations Development Programme (UNDP) (1995), *Human Development Report 1995*, New York: Oxford University Press.

Ward, Kathryn and Jean Larson Pyle (1995), 'Gender, Industrialization, Transnational Corporations, and Development: An Overview of Trends', in Christine E. Bose and Edna Acosta-Belen (eds), *Women in the Latin American Development Process*, Philadelphia, Pennsylvania: Temple, pp. 37–64.

Waring, Marilyn (1989), *If Women Counted: A New Feminist Economics*, Macmillan: London.

Wee, Vivienne and Noeleen Heyzer (1995), *Gender, Poverty, and Sustainable Development*, Singapore: Engender.

World Development (1995), Special Issue 'Gender, Adjustment and Macroeconomics', **23** (11), (November).

Economic Welfare

Economic welfare, or wellbeing, has traditionally been associated with the amount of material goods and services available to society. It has been an enduring concern throughout the history of economics, and since the time of Adam Smith, classical and neoclassical economists have been committed to the notion that economic welfare is best served by allowing markets to work with as little state regulation and intervention as possible. Questions regarding the appropriate role of the state in the functioning of markets remain at the centre of contemporary neoclassical conceptions of economic welfare. Among the classical economists, discussions of economic welfare concerned questions regarding both aggregate growth in goods and services and income distribution. Today, however, neoclassical economists conceive of economic welfare almost solely in terms of economic efficiency, and questions regarding income distribution and other equity considerations are outside the domain of what has come to be called welfare economics. This relatively narrow focus leaves out many important questions about the qualitative aspects of economic wellbeing, many of which are of particular interest to women. To address this problem feminist economists are reexamining the notion of economic welfare and conceptualizing it in ways that expand its definition, accommodate equity considerations and account for gender differences in economic wellbeing.

The contemporary concept of economic welfare has its origins in the interwar period in Britain, particularly in the work of Pigou (1932). Pigou viewed national income, an aggregate measure of economic activities, as an objective indicator of economic welfare, and was concerned with examining the ways in which it was defined and measured. He recognized that there are instances when economics activities create either costs or benefits to people not directly involved in those activities. For example, in Pigou's time railroad trains emitted sparks and smoke that caused damage to crops and woodlands. The social and private costs of railroad transportation diverged, and so national income would be overestimated if this damage was not accounted for. Pigou advocated using taxes to force railroad companies to account for the costs of the damages they caused. Similarly when economic activities generate benefits to others, he advocated the use of subsidies to encourage these activities. He also argued that economic welfare would be increased if national income were more equally distributed.

Pigou's insight concerning the distinction between social and private costs and benefits remains an enduring contribution to welfare economics. However, his notion that a more equal distribution of income increases economic wellbeing was soon challenged. This prescription was based on the common sense idea that a small increase in income means more to a poor person than it does to a rich one. In economics the argument goes like this: economic wellbeing depends on the level of utility or satisfaction that people derive from consuming goods and services. The law of diminishing marginal utility states that as a person's consumption of a good increases the marginal, or additional, utility of that good decreases. Therefore it follows that redistributions of income from the rich to the poor increase social welfare because the marginal increase in utility to a poor person from an additional increment of income is greater than the marginal loss of utility to a wealthy person.

During the 1930s, however, the conception of utility was changing. Utility was no longer conceived of as a measurable amount of satisfaction or pleasure, but rather as an ordering of consumer preferences. Since utility was no longer conceived of as a measurable quantity, it was not possible to compare the utility of one person to another (what economists refer to as interpersonal comparisons of utility). This meant that it was no longer possible to claim that income transfers from the rich to the poor would increase economic welfare because there was no way of comparing the gain in utility to the poor with the loss in utility to the wealthy.

England's (1993) analysis reveals some of the gendered assumptions implicit in this line of reasoning. She argues that assuming the impossibility of interpersonal comparisons of utility flows from particular assumptions about the nature of the self and its connection to others. Neoclassical economists assume a concept of the self that is radically separate from other people; however one could also assume a connected, empathic self, and a person conceived of in this way would be able to imagine how someone else feels in a given situation. Thus scholars could make the inferences about the subjective feelings of others that are necessary for interpersonal comparisons of utility. England argues that although there would still be practical measurement problems with such inferences these would be analogous to other measurement problems in economics and empirical estimates would not be impossible in principle.

England's analysis is, of course, a contemporary one. During the 1930s neoclassical economists were concerned with establishing economics as a science and considered such value judgments as unscientific (Barker 1995). The methodological tensions between the unscientific nature of value judgments and the desire to professionally assess economic welfare were resolved by the development of what is today referred to as welfare economics. Contemporary welfare economics is concerned with examining the conditions under which the decisions of rational economic agents in a decentralized market economy will lead to an optimal allocation of resources.

The conditions for an optimal allocation of resources, also referred to as an economically efficient allocation, is generally stated in terms of Pareto optimality (after the Italian economist Vilfredo Pareto). For any given distribution of income, an allocation of resources is optimal if changing that allocation to benefit one individual without making another individual worse off is not possible. It can be shown that this condition will be met when any economic activity is carried on up to the point where the marginal benefits are just equal to the marginal costs; this equality, in turn, provides an operational standard for evaluating efficiency. This criterion is ubiquitous in mainstream economics, where it is standard practice to construct a mathematical model, from that model deduce the conditions necessary for a Pareto optimum, and then compare these conditions to market outcomes. This methodology implies that economists can identify, for example, an optimal level of pollution, an optimal level of product safety, an optimal level of resources devoted to child care and even an optimal rate of crime.

Economists recognize that any economically efficient, or Pareto optimal, outcome is always contingent upon a given distribution of income which may or may not be equitable. Sen (1987) has eloquently pointed out that economic systems characterized by extreme income inequality, poverty and other ills may still be Pareto optimal. Neoclassical economists argue that promoting equitable economic outcomes may require a tradeoff between equity and efficiency. This answer privileges efficiency over equity in discussions of economic welfare because any steps to change an inequitable distribution of income or other resources to a more equitable one is always presented as a cost to society.

The efficiency/equity tradeoff is embedded in the notion that good scientific inquiry should separate facts from value judgments about them. In this account value neutrality furthers the development of economics as an objective science. The goal of value neutrality, however, has been contested. Harding (1995) argues that it weakens standards for maximizing objectivity because it does not allow for an examination of the influence of implicit shared values on scientific inquiry, and it allows the objections of those outside the scientific community to be marginalized or dismissed as special interests. In economics the nearly unquestioning acceptance of economic efficiency as the appropriate criterion for evaluating economic welfare closes off a critical examination of the implicit values and interests embedded in that criterion.

Barker (1995) argues that despite its purported differences from earlier conceptions of economic welfare, welfare economics still implicitly identifies improvements in economic welfare with increases in physical productivity and real income. Real income, in practice, is measured by the market value of goods and services. Thus it excludes activities that are important to economic wellbeing but that do not take place in markets. Housework, child rearing, volunteer work and subsistence labour are just a few examples. Although there is an increasing awareness of the economic significance of nonmarket activities, national income and labour force statistics continue to underestimate the value of this sort of work (Benería 1995).

Barker argues that another serious problem with using Pareto optimality as a criterion for economic welfare is that it implicitly assumes that all goods have a relative price and therefore measures of economic wellbeing can be collapsed into a single metric, market value, and that all human needs can be met through some type of market exchange. Feminist economists have pointed out that market exchange is only one of the ways that society organizes the provisioning of its material needs (Folbre 1995; Nelson 1996; Strassmann

1993). Children, in particular, have their needs met through relationships based on care, obligation and responsibility rather than on contractual exchange. Disregarding ways of provisioning that do not fall under the rubric of market exchange effectively obscures their significance, especially when empirically assessing economic efficiency.

Theoretically, economic outcomes are efficient when the marginal benefits are just equal to the marginal costs. In practice, however, efficiency gains are noted whenever the costs of production are decreased or output is increased. Thus the emphasis on market exchange, and its attendant lack of attention to tasks traditionally considered as women's work, may entail serious distortions in empirically evaluating economic phenomena on efficiency grounds. For example, firms that reduce their overheads by eliminating day-care centres may appear more efficient to their stockholders; hospitals may increase productivity by sending their patients home earlier and governments may find it efficient to eliminate subsidies for home-care for the elderly. These efficiencies, however, are mainly illusory: work previously done for wages is shifted to the unpaid labour of the household. Similar phenomena have been shown in Elson's (1992) work on the effects of structural adjustment policies. She shows that policies which appear to increase productivity and efficiency often do so by shifting costs from the paid economy to the unpaid economy. This both increases women's burdens and leads to socially inefficient outcomes.

Another important part of the feminist critique of economic efficiency is an examination of the role it plays in determining which theories will be accepted by the mainstream of the economics profession. Humphries (1995) examines this issue in the context of neoclassical analyses of labour markets. She argues that economists' interpretation of the wage gap between men and women hinges on their belief in the efficiency of markets. Wage differentials can be explained as a result of sex discrimination or they can be manifestations of the rational choices that men and women make to jointly maximize the wellbeing of the household. Economists tend to discount explanations based on sex discrimination in favour of the joint maximization hypothesis because discrimination is economically inefficient. Since inefficiencies will be eliminated by rational individuals pursuing their own self interest in markets and other institutions, any economic phenomena that are inefficient must be temporary. The implications for economic policy are a shift in emphasis from policies that encourage affirmative action, equal-pay legislation, and outlaw sex discrimination to policies that relax these efforts in favour of non-intervention in market outcomes and processes. These policy recommendations are consistent with the mainstream commitment to the notion that economic welfare is best served by allowing markets to work with as little government regulation as possible. Similarly the lack of attention to gender-specific inequities resulting from market outcomes reflects the fact that questions regarding equity considerations remain outside the domain of neoclassical conceptions of welfare economics.

Feminist economics is beginning to recast questions about economic welfare in ways that do not privilege efficiency over equity and that construct multidimensional conception of economic wellbeing. Social welfare is defined not only in term of the availability of material goods and services but also in terms of the quality of peoples' lives, including qualitative indicators that reflect how people perform their work and spend their time. Feminist economists also examine the detrimental effects of gender and class inequalities on both individual and social wellbeing. These lines of inquiry are consistent with Nelson's (1996) notion that feminist economics should be conceptualized as the study of provisioning and should examine the various ways in which human needs are met. A few examples will be considered in the discussion that follows. These examples are not meant to be an exhaustive accounting of the new feminist work in this area, but rather to suggest new avenues of feminist research on economic welfare.

Qualitative accounts of women's working lives are one important area of research. Floro (1995) discusses the importance of accounting for both the length and intensity of work time in evaluating economic wellbeing, especially women's wellbeing. The multiplicity of women's productive, reproductive and community roles often compel them to find new ways to deal with time pressures, and one way they do this is by reducing their sleep or leisure hours. Poor women, however, may have already reached the biological limits as to the number of hours they can work, and so they cope by combining tasks which intensifies their work. For example, street sweepers both care for their children and attend to their cleaning tasks. Conventional household production models are inadequate for assessing the welfare of poor women and children, because they either would account for one task or the other, or they would ignore any interactive effects between the two tasks. To understand fully the welfare effects in this situation, Floro argues that the analytical framework must account for the effects of time use on women's health, children's wellbeing and overall social welfare.

The consequences of gender bias in education on social welfare is another important area of feminist inquiry. Hill and King (1995) show that educating women and girls has both private and social benefits that are often not reflected by market outcomes. For example, the education of females results in increases in family health, child survival and increases in parental investments in children's human capital. Given these significant contributions to social welfare, Hill and King suggest policy interventions that will foster increases in female education.

On the macroeconomic level, the work being done by Çagatay et al. (1995) has developed alternative models for assessing economic policies that will contribute to the provisioning of human needs and the enhancement of human capacities. Explicit recognition of the contributions of reproductive labour, generally considered women's work, to the functioning of the market economy is a central part of their project. As Benería (1995) argues, conceptually sophisticated, gender-sensitive statistics are necessary to generate quantitative estimates of women's work. Such statistics will also facilitate examinations of disaggregated indicators of social wellbeing such as gender inequalities in domestic work and leisure, productivity changes in household production and changes in family welfare that result from changes in the income and employment status of household members.

The role of caring labour in assessing economic welfare is another aspect of the feminist research agenda. As Himmelweit (1995) argues, the concept of women's work in both feminist and neoclassical economics is based on a notion of work that is derived from the model of commodity-producing wage labour, and this renders invisible those aspects of domestic activities and needs that do not fall neatly into a work/non-work dichotomy. Child care and elder care are just two examples. One of the effects of this invisibility is that more and more of the needs and desires of workers and their families are being constructed in a form that has to be met through the market by consumer goods. Success is gauged by the money income available for purchasing consumption goods. This tendency perpetuates income inequality because the profitability of substituting purchased commodities for domestic activities requires that the purchased goods be relatively low priced. This in turn requires a low-wage labour pool, which contributes to income inequality. Himmelweit concludes that if feminist economists want to recognize the contributions of caring labour to the wellbeing of society then a non-dichotomous conception of these activities is required.

Feminist economics has the potential to make significant contributions to a gender- and class-sensitive conception of economic wellbeing. Part of that project will include the development of conceptually sophisticated and gender-sensitive statistical indicators of women's work that will provide both quantitative and qualitative valuations. Explicitly accounting for gender and class inequality in evaluating economic wellbeing is another important area for research. Also necessary is a critical examination of the construction of market-oriented economic concepts such as work, leisure and consumption with an eye to determining their function in mainstream theory and their usefulness to feminist economics. As this sort of work progresses, feminist economists will continue to make an important contribution to a complex and nuanced understanding of the determinants of economic welfare.

DRUCILLA K. BARKER

See also

Domestic Labour; Feminist Economics; Neoclassical Economics; Public Sector Economics/ Public Finance.

Bibliography

Barker, Drucilla K. (1995), 'Economists, social reformers, and prophets: a feminist critique of economic efficiency', *Feminist Economics*, **1** (3), 26–39.

Benería, Lourdes (1995), 'Toward a greater integration of gender in economics', *World Development*, **23** (11), 1839–50.

Çagatay Nilüfer, Diane Elson and Caren Grown (1995), 'Introduction', *World Development*, **23** (11), 1827–36.

Elson, Diane (1992), 'From Survival Strategies to Transformation Strategies: Women's Needs and Structural Adjustment', in Lourdes Benería and Shelley Feldman (eds), *Unequal Burden: Economic Crises, Persistent Poverty, and Women's Work*, Boulder: Westview Press, pp. 26–48.

England, Paula (1993), 'The Separative Self: Androcentric Bias in Neoclassical Assumptions', in Marianne A. Ferber and Julie A. Nelson (eds), *Beyond Economic Man: Feminist Theory and Economics*, Chicago: University of Chicago Press, pp. 37–53.

Floro, Maria Sagrario (1995), 'Women's well-being, poverty, and work intensity', *Feminist Economics*, **1** (3), 1–25.

Folbre, Nancy (1995), '"Holding hands at midnight", the paradox of caring labor', *Feminist Economics*, **1** (1), 73–92.

Harding, Sandra (1995), 'Can feminist thought make economics more objective?', *Feminist Economics*, **1** (1), 7–32.

Hill, M. Anne and Elizabeth King (1995), 'Women's education and economic well-being', *Feminist Economics*, **1** (2), 21–46.

Himmelweit, Susan (1995), 'The discovery of "unpaid work": the social consequences of the expansion of "work"', *Feminist Economics*, **1** (3), 1–20.

Humphries, Jane (1995), 'Economics, Gender and Equal Opportunities', in Jane Humphries and Jill Rubery (eds), *The Economics of Equal Opportunities*, Manchester: Equal Opportunities Commission, pp. 55–86.

Nelson, Julie A. (1996), *Feminism, Objectivity, and Economics*, London: Routledge.

Pigou, Arthur, C. (1932), *The Economics of Welfare*, London: Macmillan.

Sen, Amartya (1987), *On Ethics and Economics*, Oxford: Basil Blackwell.

Strassmann, Diana (1993), 'Not a Free Market: The Rhetoric of Disciplinary Authority in Economics', in Marianne A. Ferber and Julie A. Nelson (eds), *Beyond Economic Man: Feminist Theory and Economics*, Chicago: University of Chicago Press, pp. 54–68.

Economics Education

What constitutes economics education has been widely interpreted. Research covering this broad topic has included issues of assessment, content, process and economics as a profession. Examples of what constitutes assessment research include the measurement of student learning, evaluation of teaching methods and, more recently, the use of learning theories to enhance the educational experience. Alternative presentations of course-specific materials, such as the Phillips curve and prisoner's dilemma, as well as literature focused on the inclusion of diversity (based on race, class and gender) in the economic classroom are consistent with content research. New learning processes such as experiments, simulations/computer labs, writing, service-learning and active-learning experiences might be included in the process category. Finally, a segment of the literature addresses the labour market for economists as well as the ongoing analysis of trends in the economic major.

The field of economics education has had a long and continuously evolving history. Significant interest in economics education among American Economic Association members, for example, can be demonstrated since the association's inception in 1885. In fact, 'sessions on economics education frequently constituted ten percent or more of the annual meetings before the turn of the century' (Elton and Siegfried 1991, p. 373). While such professional meetings provide the opportunity for presentation and discussion of pedagogical practices, the impact of research in this area is limited by what appears in print. In this regard, what has been defined as economics education has been largely influenced by the criteria laid forth in the *Journal of Economic Education*. Established in 1969, the *Journal of Economic Education* is the only journal completely dedicated to publishing research on economics education and its focus is clearly traditional.

Traditional views on what constitutes economics education are best exemplified by the introduction of 'Voluntary National Content Standards in Economics' by the National Council of Economic Education (NCEE) in January 1997. The focus of these content standards is on neoclassical economic concepts and skills that develop *the* economic way of thinking coupled with suggestions of pedagogical exercises intended to reinforce these concepts and skills. Not only are these standards too simplistic, as argued by some mainstream economists (Pennar 1997), but feminist economists would add that the standards reinforce the marginalization and exclusion of many economic identities from the neoclassical portrayal of the economy. Compounding this exclusion is the presentation of exercises designed to lead students to a single 'correct' solution, thereby de-emphasizing differences among students and their learning styles. 'Consequently, the standards developed by the NCEE construct a classroom where few students gain the economic understanding necessary to fully participate in their economies' (McGoldrick and Lewis 1998).

Feminist pedagogical scholarship, on the other hand, challenges pedagogies and course content to allow for inclusivity and participation by all potential students. While the most basic of this research includes developing examples in which women and minorities are added as specific cases for analysis, the more advanced applications consider student background and experience as important components that inform students' perceptions of the world in which they participate. Whether focused on transforming course content or on pedagogical practices aimed at identifying and incorporating student diversity, each of these forms of research is a movement toward building a community of learning in which all contribute to what is learned.

Although most of this feminist scholarship has its origins in women's studies, some feminist pedagogical scholarship has made inroads into the hard sciences. (See for example, McIntosh 1983, 1990; Rosser 1990, 1995.) Despite the depth of literature on pedagogical practices consistent with feminist visions in other disciplines, advances in economics education along similar lines have been slow in developing and a majority of the most notable publications on feminist pedagogy in economics had appeared in print since 1990 and in journals other than the *Journal of Economic Education.*

Although it might at first appear that applications of feminist pedagogical ideals are a recent phenomenon in economics, some economists recognized long ago that these feminist pedagogies were appropriate for the economics classroom. For example, Sarah Lawrence professor Jean Carol Trepp (1939) suggested expanding the walls of the classroom to include fieldwork in economic education. Her work led her to search 'for other ways in which the traditional forms of instruction might be modified to serve the needs and interests of the students' (p. 6). Newcomer (1946) revisited this alternative teaching technique in her report on 'Undergraduate Teaching of Economics – Report of the Undergraduate Economics Curriculum and Related Areas of Study'. In this report, Newcomer questioned whether the (then) current methods for studying economics (lecture and discussion) were adequate and suggested the possibility of fieldwork or job experiences as a complement in student education (p. 847).

The development of an economics education research agenda that is analogous to the incorporation of feminist pedagogy to the degree to which it is integrated in women's studies suggests a discussion of inclusivity within course content, in pedagogical practices and combinations of the two. Traditional economics education research focusing on developing course content often neglects a discussion of diversity based on race, class, gender or alternative economic paradigms and it is even more rare to find a published article that discusses inclusive pedagogy or a combination of diversity in content and inclusive pedagogy. Given the limited published research in each of these three potential areas of feminist scholarship, it is clear that feminist pedagogy as applied in economics is in its infancy. A consideration of the research that has been published in the areas of course content, pedagogical practice and combinations of the two will help to motivate an agenda for further incorporation of feminist scholarship and pedagogy into economics.

Most of the literature that advocates a reconsideration of course content toward incorporating diversity issues is motivated by improving student performance in a specific economics class. For example, Tuma (1995) demonstrates that race, ethnic and gender biases can be purged from a macroeconomics class in a way that not only allows the instructor to avoid compromise on course content coverage, but also uses basic economic tools in the process. For example, he suggests disaggregating the population by race, ethnicity and gender, estimating multiple production possibilities curves and developing economic policies that focus on groups that have the greatest potential for increasing their productivity to increase the gains to society (p. 354). By using race, ethnicity and gender differences as a vehicle for the application of basic economic tools throughout the course, Tuma claims to provide adequate content coverage while demonstrating the pervasiveness of biases in economic modelling. (For a similar discussion see also Tuma and Haworth 1991.)

Feiner and Roberts (1995) argue that the use of competing paradigms (as opposed to materials identifying race, gender and class issues) in the principles course can provide the opportunity to develop students' critical thinking skills. When considering income distribution, for example, they suggest that the standard treatment of simply identifying income gaps by race or gender is not sufficient in understanding the problem; what is missing is the historical context in which these differences are grounded. By revealing the historically grounded social and political influences on the economic position of women and different racial groups, students have the background and tools to better argue for or against suggested interventionist policies.

The case for redesigning the introductory microeconomics course to contain examples that are 'gender-inclusive' is built by Lage and Treglia (1996). They accomplish this by incorporating additional readings that cover 'the topics of price discrimination based on gender, affirmative action in the labor market and in higher education and comparable worth' and test the resulting learning differences (p. 27). Although gender alone was not a significant factor in determining student performance, results indicate that exposure to scholarship on women increased the performance of all students, but most dramatically so for women.

Bartlett (1996) offers examples for exploring the diversity among students as a basis for challenging traditional textbook content and providing a better learning environment. By asking students to specify and share examples of groups they would consider part of their identity, the diversity within the classroom is exposed. The revealed differences can then be used by the instructor as a basis for discussion when materials incorporating diversity are added to a principles course. By also adding a consideration of differences in learning styles and a variety of testing techniques, the economics classroom can be transformed into one in which students have greater opportunities to learn and professors have better indicators of what they have learned.

Incorporating race and gender into the principles of economics course is the element through which the move to a feminist economics classroom is most advanced. In addition to the four articles identified above, the recently published *Introducing Race and Gender into Economics* (Bartlett 1997) provides examples of how race and gender can be made explicit within the principles of economics courses. Some of the articles in this volume not only indicate where race and gender could be included, but also provide a step-by-step process for integrating such issues into class discussion. Although not all entries outline exercises in such great detail, this volume is the first that includes a set of such explicit exercises.

Despite the differences in approach, each of the above authors focus on expanding course content as their primary change from the traditional economics class. While adding diversity of course content is clearly consistent with the direction feminist economists would like to see economics education take, this single component is far from sufficient in defining the path towards a feminist economics classroom. Rather, it is the combination of diversifying content, introducing alternative methodologies and using more inclusive pedagogical techniques that move the classroom to one that is consistent with feminist visions. As such, a feminist economics classroom can be envisioned as one in which students learn about the social construction of economics, critically assess the assumptions underlying differing methodological approaches to identifying and solving economic problems, learn from a variety of sources and through a variety of mediums and use their knowledge to better participate in society.

Only a few published articles attempt to define what this new feminist economics classroom might look like or the process by which it might be developed. As Bartlett and Feiner (1992) argue, content, methodology and pedagogy must change simultaneously if the economics classroom is to be reconstructed. More specifically, they suggest that content must become multicultural by recognizing race, gender, sexual orientation and class differences; alternative methodologies, especially those other than formal, abstract mathematical models, must be included; and a more balanced pedagogical approach, with the goal of developing a community of learning, must be developed.

Shackelford (1992) identifies recurring themes of feminist pedagogy and shows how they might be applied to promote critical thinking and creativity in the classroom. She uses examples of course content and materials, classroom environment and attitudes, assignments and evaluation of students to discuss how economics courses can be restructured to be consistent with feminist pedagogical goals of ending patriarchy, validating alternative methodologies and emphasizing learning processes over content memorization. McGoldrick (1998, forthcoming) provides examples of how service-learning can be used to achieve these goals. Applied in economics, service-learning suggests that students volunteer at local nonprofit community agencies and discover information that will allow them to better examine the realities associated with economic theory associated on such issues as poverty and unemployment. When students use first-hand experiences in applying theories to the realities of economic problems, they become the authority. Thus, by the very nature of service-learning, some of the patriarchal or authority-laden classroom environment is eliminated.

A feminist–institutionalist perspective is offered by Lewis (1995). This approach stresses the link between the economic theory developed in the classroom and the economic realities in the world. It is argued that the traditional classroom environment does little to encourage student interest. By 'breaking down' this traditional model, through changes in pedagogy, content, methodology and definition, Lewis demonstrates how to 'transform the economics classroom into a site for social action' (p. 556). Through this approach to teaching economics, students learn how complex economies work and understand how to use economic tools to make better decisions and become active participants in society.

The process of changing the economics classroom to become consistent with feminist economics is described in Aerni et al. (1999). They suggest that once an instructor begins to change either course content (making it more diverse) or pedagogical techniques (building towards a community of learning), the process will naturally lead to evolutions in both content and pedagogy. For example, an instructor may begin making changes to the classroom environment through an active learning approach that encourages more discussion. This process will lead some students to share their experiences, note how they differ from textbook examples and question the more traditional treatment of many groups within economics. It is expected that this will induce the instructor to supplement traditional content in the process of responding to these questions, thus adding diversity to the economics class. This process will eventually transform the classroom (through subsequent changes in content and pedagogy) to one that is consistent with a feminist economics classroom.

While each of these articles contributes a piece of the puzzle picturing what such a feminist economics classroom might look like, there are still many pieces missing. First, a feminist research agenda needs to include a variety of studies expanding the depth and breadth of examples for inclusive course content. Much of the work along these lines is merely suggestive of how course content should change, recommending, for example, that a discussion of gender and race differences be included in analyses of the decision to go to college. But to encourage the integration of diversity into this discussion feminist economists need to develop exercises that promote this integration. Second, more work needs to be done to define alternative learning environments, such as the community of learning, with references to the economics classroom. Third, more 'how to' course-specific case studies are needed to indicate the impact of these alternative content and pedagogical methods on learning in economics. (See, for example, McGoldrick 1998, forthcoming.) Fourth, despite the vast literature available suggesting that active learning and similar pedagogies are beneficial in the learning process, the lecture mode still dominates in economics (Becker and Watts 1996). It would be useful to go beyond a documentation of what styles are employed in the classroom and investigate why these dominate the economics discipline. Fifth, the development of learning communities and the acknowledgment of shared knowledge authority of instructor and student suggest alternative methods of evaluating knowledge acquisition, yet only Shackelford (1992) has made any attempt at discussing how the feminist approach to teaching economics will affect evaluation or assessment issues. And finally, very few articles have been published documenting international differences in economics education. Most of the literature is dominated by North American authors, examples and classroom constructs. It would be instructive to compare methods used around the world so that feminist economists might learn alternative methods and share in the process of developing a feminist economics classroom.

KimMarie McGoldrick

See also
Feminist Economics; Pedagogy.

Bibliography

Aerni, April Laskey, Robin L. Bartlett, Margaret Lewis, KimMarie McGoldrick and Jean Shackelford (1999), 'Toward a feminist pedagogy in economics', *Feminist Economics*, **5** (1), 29–44.

Bartlett, Robin L. (1996), 'Discovering diversity in introductory economics', *Journal of Economic Perspectives*, **10** (2), (Spring), 141–53.

Bartlett, Robin L. (ed.) (1997), *Introducing Race and Gender into Economics*, London: Routledge Press.

Bartlett, Robin L. and Susan F. Feiner (1992), 'Balancing the economics curriculum: content, method, and pedagogy', *American Economic Review*, **82** (2), (May), 559–64.

Becker, William E. and Michael Watts (1996), 'Chalk and talk: a national survey on teaching undergraduate economics', *American Economic Review*, **86** (2), (May), 448–53.

Blank, Rebecca (1991), 'The effects of double-blind versus single-blind reviewing: experimental evidence from the *American Economic Review*', *American Economic Review*, **81** (4), (December), 1041–67.

Borg, Mary O. and Stephen L. Shapiro (1996), 'Personality type and student performance in principles of economics', *Journal of Economic Education*, **27** (1), (Winter), 3–25.

Elton, Hinshaw C. and John J. Siegfried (1991), 'The role of the American Economic Association in economic education: a brief history', *Journal of Economic Education*, **22** (4), (Fall), 373–81.

Feiner, Susan and Bruce Roberts (1995), 'Using alternative paradigms to teach about race and gender: a critical thinking approach to introductory economics', *American Economic Review*, **85** (2), (May), 367–71.

Lage, Maureen J. and Michael Treglia (1996), 'The impact of integrating scholarship on women into introductory economics: evidence from one institution', *Journal of Economic Education*, **27** (1), (Winter), 26–36.

Lewis, Margaret (1995), 'Breaking down the walls, opening up the field: Situating the economics classroom in the site of social action', *Journal of Economic Issues*, **29** (2), (June),
555–65.

McGoldrick, KimMarie (1998), 'Service-learning in economics: a detailed application', *Journal of Economic Education*, **29** (4), (Fall), 365– 76.

McGoldrick, KimMarie (Forthcoming), 'The Road Not Taken: An Example of Feminist Pedagogy in Economics', in April Aerni and KimMarie McGoldrick (eds), *Valuing Us All:
Towards Feminist Pedagogy in Economics*, Ann Arbor: The University of Michigan Press.

McGoldrick, KimMarie and Margaret Lewis (1998), 'Moving Beyond the Neoclassical Class-
room: Using Critical and Active Pedagogical Practices to Reconceptualize the Concept of
Work', Presentation at the 1998 International Association for Feminist Economics Summer
Conference.

McIntosh, Peggy (1983), 'Interactive Phases of the Curricular Re-Vision: A Feminist Perspective', Center for Research on Women, Working Paper No. 124, Wellesley, Massachusetts,
Wellesley College.

McIntosh, Peggy (1990), 'Interactive Phases of Curricular and Personal Re-Vision with Regard
to Race', Center for Research on Women, Working Paper No. 219, Wellesley, Massachusetts:
Wellesley College.

National Council on Economic Education (1997), *Voluntary National Content Standards in
Economics*, New York: National Council on Economic Education.

Newcomer, Mable (1946), 'Undergraduate teaching of economics – Report of the Subcommittee on the Undergraduate Economics Curriculum and Related Areas of Study', *American
Economic Review*, **36** (4), December, 845–7.

Pennar, Karen (1997), 'Economics made too simple', *Business Week*, 20 January, 32.

Rosser, Sue V. (1990), *Female-Friendly Science: Applying Women's Studies Method and Theories to Attract Students*, New York: Pergamon Press.

Rosser, Sue V. (ed.) (1995), *Teaching the Majority: Breaking the Gender Barrier in Science,
Mathematics, and Engineering*, New York: Teacher College, Columbia University.

Shackelford, Jean (1992), 'Feminist pedagogy: a means for bringing critical thinking and
creativity to the economics classroom', *American Economic Review*, **82** (2), May, 570–76.

Siegfried, John J., Robin L. Bartlett, W. Lee Hansen, Allen C. Kelley, Donald N. McCloskey
and Thomas H. Tietenberg (1991), 'The status and prospects of the economics major',
Journal of Economic Education, **22** (3), (Summer), 197–224.

Trepp, Jean C. (1939), *The Uses of Field Work in Teaching Economics*, Bronxville, New York:
Sarah Lawrence College.

Tuma, Elias H. (1995), 'Macroeconomics and discrimination in teaching', *American Economic
Review*, **85** (2), May, 352–6.

Tuma, Elias H. and Barry Haworth (1991), *Cultural Diversity and Economic Education*, Palo
Alto: Pacific Books.

Williams, Mary L., Charles Waldauer and Vijaya G. Duggal (1992), 'Gender differences in
economic knowledge: an extension of the analysis', *Journal of Economic Education*, **23** (3),
Summer, 219–31.

Education, Economics of

The specialization defined as the economics of education can be traced back
to the 1960s. It is in this time period when articles analysing the rate of return
to education and human capital links to the economic development of nations
first appeared. Since that time the field has grown beyond these two research
areas, but this transformation has not been without its growing pains. (For
example, the 1970s were a time of controversy between the human capital

and screening and signalling model explanations of wage determination. Specifically, the human capital model suggests that additional years of education generate higher earnings because the more highly-educated worker is more productive on the job, whereas signalling and screening models posit that pre-existing abilities, as evidenced by educational attainment or performance, are used by employers and employees to predict *a priori* the productivity contributions, and thus determine the wage, of a potential employee.) Until very recently the field boundaries have not been well defined, often overlapping into related fields such as labour economics, as indicated in the preceding discussion. The works of Blaug (1992) and Cohn and Johnes (1994) have made a significant impact on the definition of the field by outlining and presenting lead articles on various areas of study within the field.

Yet even in these works there is a seeming lack of attention to issues that are important to feminist thought. For example, the potential for policy changes resultant from the documentation of differential resources leading to inequities across labour market groups (by race, class and gender) provide a fertile ground for contributions by economists informed by feminist theory. What is necessary is a recognition by scholars of the implications of completed research and the formulation of a feminist agenda expanding and enlightening the work that has already begun within the field.

The economics of education covers a wide variety of topics that may be gathered under three more general themes: the provision of quality education, returns to education, and the link between education and economic development. The first of these themes include topics such as equity and efficiency, externalities and the role of government subsidies, the economics of school choice, the cost of providing educational services and the market for educators. Rate of return to education research generally includes links between education and the labour market including the educational choice and wage determination models. The final theme includes research analysing issues of access to education, household allocation of resources and women's contribution to economic development.

Although these three themes are seemingly broad, they contain issues that provide a path for feminist scholarship. Given previous data limitations, much of the research that would be of interest to feminist scholars has barely begun. Issues of race, class and gender appear most often in discussions of equity and efficiency, links between education and the labour market and economic development. While research in these areas is not always consistent with feminist theory, there are a number of studies within the field that either directly address issues of importance to feminist scholars or provide a motivation for further research. In the following discussion, examples from each of these three themes are explored to show how current analysis might be expanded to include issues relevant to feminist theory. The first theme to be considered is that of the provision of quality education within which research detailing equity and efficiency arguments and school choice will be addressed.

Equity and efficiency arguments, based in large part on public choice theory, focus primarily on the implications of resources invested in education and on school choice debates. In this context, equity refers to the equal access and use of resources across schools, most notably across inner city and suburban school districts. Efficiency arguments question the allocation of these resources and debate whether it is appropriate to focus the use of resources toward those that have the greatest potential to develop into productive citizens. Educational resources are a primary concern of researchers investigating equity and efficiency in the educational system because of their related future impacts on educational achievement and earnings. For example, school resource gaps between black and white students have been shown to lead to similar gaps in educational attainment and earnings (Card and Krueger 1996). In addition, there is some evidence that differences in teacher time allocation by student social class reinforces achievement disparities by class (Brown 1991). This is an important potential area of research for feminist scholars since it allows for a consideration of environmental influences on the success of a student instead of relying completely on data about the individual.

Proponents for family determination in the choice of schooling alternatives argue that increases in efficiency and equity can be obtained by relying more on a market-based approach to the provision of education. In a review of family choice studies, Catterall (1992) indicates that this approach is countered by the argument that decision-making processes are influenced by characteristics such as race and class and thus further segregation is the expected outcome. The argument that family choice improves class equity has been more recently challenged by suggesting that imperfect information (due to preference and information cost differences) can actually increase class segregation (Ambler 1994). The more general debate surrounding the family choice issue is best exemplified through a discussion of educational vouchers. Proponents of educational vouchers base their arguments on parental choice and operational efficiency. Yet the counter-argument suggests that the voucher system not only minimizes equity goals but can also lack efficiency gains once hidden costs are considered (Waring 1996). Feminist scholars already engaged in equity versus efficiency arguments in other fields within economics could enlighten this debate and highlight the implications for race, class and gender.

Although investigation of the second theme of research in the economics of education field, educational attainment links to the labour market, is dominated by labour economists performing wage market studies, the economics of education field delves deeper into the questions of labour market success. Thus, it is also concerned with issues such as investigating the determinants of educational attainment and how school characteristics impact on labour market success.

The educational choice decision process has been examined from a variety of angles. Much of the research has focused on finding an explanation for the differential rate of college attendance by attempting to pinpoint the characteristics that enter into the decision-making process for men and women. Characteristics of the individual, family and expected future occupation have all been shown to play a role in this decision. For example, Averett and Burton (1996) find that the expected college wage premium has a positive impact on the decision of men to go to college, but no impact on women's decision. The question that remains unanswered in this line of research is *why* these characteristics have a differential impact by gender.

The link between school characteristics and labour market success is widely documented. Since the early 1990s a significant portion of this research has been dedicated to the consideration of characteristics that may have unique consequences for minorities, women and lower-class students. For example, Solnick (1990) considers a sample of graduates from historically black colleges to test the hypothesis that socialization differences can have a negative impact on career advancement. Her findings indicate that although these graduates begin at a higher salary than comparable graduates of non-black colleges, they suffer from a lower promotion rate. What is missing from this type of research is the more detailed study of the socialization process that is hypothesized to negatively impact labour market success. Although feminist theory would consider socialization as an important determination of labour market success, feminist scholars in economics should be charged with an investigation of this process as opposed to simply pinpointing it as a potential drawback.

One characteristic that is often associated with school quality is location. It is widely reported that inner-city schools provide a lower quality education to students. If this is indeed the case, or if employers use school location as a signal of school quality, then graduates of inner-city schools would be expected to earn less in the labour market. Sexton and Nickel (1992) find that both white and black students earn significantly less in the labour market if they graduated from an inner-city school. Again this brings the feminist scholar back to question issues of equity and efficiency in educational provision, especially since a majority of inner-city school students are from minority populations. This question begs similarities with the statistical discrimination issues raised around gender differences in labour market attachment. Many of the lessons learned in this area of research could be used to enlighten the discussion and policy implications of this locational differential.

The final theme within the economics of education field, the relation of education to economic development, has received notable attention since 1990. In October 1996 the *Economics of Education Review* devoted a special issue to the economics of education in developing countries and included articles focused on issues of equity and efficiency, school choice and financial reform. It is interesting to note that these did not discuss gender, race, or class-specific issues, despite the significant impact that feminist theory appears to have had on studies of education and economic development. Research that has been consistent with feminist theory includes a variety of topics such as women's access to education, the invisibility of women in developing economies and policy implications.

Subbarao et al. (1994) investigate women's participation in higher education in developing countries. This extensive document explores the time trends underlying women's enrolment in higher education programmes, the underlying constraints inhibiting gender equity in higher education and the impact that World Bank policies have had on the participation of women in the sciences. This is one of the few areas of research in which economists have not only investigated the inequities, but have also critiqued programmes and policies designed to rectify these disparities.

A critique of the analysis of rural education in less-developed countries reveals that biases in measurement and perspective distort the perceived labour contributions of women (Bowman 1991). Since many of these contributions are invisible, women have been long thought to be unprepared for (and thus typically excluded from) vocational training provided in rural schools. Bowman suggests that these countries look to the early American land-grant colleges for a model that has the potential to increase the economic welfare of workers and their families.

Although each of the topics discussed above has the potential of presenting a forum for feminist debate, little of this has occurred to date. There is much room for applying already well-defined arguments made by feminist economists to the economics of education topics. Unfortunately, there is no particularly well-defined feminist agenda in the field of the economics of education and thus much of the work that could contribute to the building of a feminist agenda has been completed in isolation.

One of the main contributions that feminist theory can make to the economics of education is the push to a more inclusive research agenda. Although researchers have, to various degrees, considered the implications of race, class and gender for their work, often this work falls short of its potential. For example, the documented race, class and gender differential impacts of family choice programmes provide no policy alternatives that would improve equity and efficiency in educational provision. Alternatively, the work documenting educational policies for developing countries often neglects a discussion of race and class. Yet an even more pressing problem is inherent methodological and measurement biases that run rampant in empirical studies. In a 1997 *Feminist Economics* exploration devoted to addressing the need for economic research to utilize field work and other alternative methodologies, Berik (1997, p. 121) suggests that, 'survey-generated data bear the imprint of values and ideological beliefs in survey design and implementation, and often produce male-biased accounts'. This problem may find its solution as feminists continue to argue for alternative data collection techniques and research methods. The groundwork for a feminist agenda in the economics of education has been laid, the challenge is now to better define the path by which to achieve a more inclusive field of study.

KimMarie McGoldrick

See also
Development Policies; Human Capital Theory; Labour Market, Theories of.

Bibliography

Ambler, John S. (1994), 'Who benefits from educational choice? Some evidence from Europe', *Journal of Policy Analysis and Management*, **13** (3), (Summer), 454–76.

Averett, Susan L. and Mark L. Burton (1996), 'College attendance and the college wage premium: differences by gender', *Economics of Education Review*, **15** (1), (February), 37–49.

Berik, Günseli (1997), 'The need for crossing the method boundaries in economics research', *Feminist Economics*, **3** (2), (Summer), 121–5.

Blaug, Mark (ed.) (1992), *The Economic Value of Education: Studies in the Economics of Education*, Aldershot: Edward Elgar.

Boozer, Michael and Cecilia Elena Rouse (1995), 'Intraschool Variation in Class Size: Patterns and Implications', National Bureau of Economic Research, Working Paper No. 5144, June.

Bowman, Mary Jean (1991), 'The formation of human resources for farming and household work as vocations: lessons for less developed countries', *Economics of Education Review*, **10** (1), (February), 1– 5.

Brown, Byron W. (1991), 'How gender and socioeconomic status affect reading and mathematics achievement', *Economics of Education Review*, **10** (4), (December), 343–57.

Card, David and Alan B. Krueger (1996), 'School resources and student outcomes: an overview of the literature and new evidence from North and South Carolina', *Journal of Economics Perspectives*, **10** (4), (Fall), 31–50.

Carnoy, Martin (1996), 'Education and racial inequality: the human capital explanation revisited', *Economics of Education Review*, **15** (3), (June), 259–72.

Catterall, James S. (1992), 'Theory and practice of family choice in education: taking stock – review essay', *Economics of Education Review*, **11** (4), (December), 407–16.

Cohn, Elchanan and Geraint Johnes (eds) (1994), *Recent Developments in the Economics of Education*, Aldershot: Edward Elgar.

Grogger, Jeff (1996), 'Does school quality explain the recent black–white wage trend?', *Journal of Labor Economics*, **14** (2), (April), 231–53.

Grogger, Jeff and Eric Eide (1995), 'Changes in college skills and the rise in the college wage premium', *Journal of Human Resources*, **30** (2), (Spring), 280–310.

Hill, Elizabeth T. (1995), 'Labor market effects of women's post-school-age training', *Industrial and Labor Relations Review*, **49** (1), (October), 1995, 138–49.

Hoenack, Stephen A. (1996), 'The economics of education in developing countries: an assessment of the state of the art', *Economics of Education Review*, **15** (4), (October), 327–38.

Levine, Phillip B. and David J. Zimmerman (1995), 'The benefit of additional high-school math and science classes for young men and women', *Journal of Business and Economics Statistics*, **13** (2), (April), 137–49.

Sexton, Edwin A. and Janet F. Nickel (1992), 'The effects of school location on the earnings of black and white youths', *Economics of Education Review*, **11** (1), (March), 11–18.

Solnick, Loren M. (1990), 'Black college attendance and job success of black college graduates', *Economics of Education Review*, **9** (2), 135–48.

Subbarao, K., Laura Raney, Halil Dundar and Jennifer Haworth (1994), 'Women in Higher Education: Progress, Constraints, and Promising Initiatives', World Bank, Working Paper No. 244.

Waring, Jim (1996), 'Educational vouchers: the case for public choice reconsidered', *Public Budgeting and Finance*, **16** (3), (Fall), 63– 73.

Environmental and Natural Resource Economics

The field of environmental and natural resource economics considers the use of natural physical resources in provisioning activities. The field is methodologically characterized by neoclassical assumptions such as self-interest, homogeneity and competition, and by the application of cost–benefit analysis, cost-effectiveness analysis and environmental impact analysis (Tietenberg 1994). The field developed from three influential papers. The first two, 'The economic theory of a common property resource: the fishery' by H. Scott Gordon published in the *Journal of Political Economy* (1954) and Anthony Scott's 'The fishery: the objectives of sole ownership' in the same journal (1955) describe the economic problem inherent in use of a common resource for which no rent is charged. The third, 'The tragedy of the commons' by Garrett Hardin (1968), sets the metaphorical basis for the field.

The tragedy of the commons predicts that a common (unmanaged) resource will be an overexploited resource. The tragedy results when a rational economic agent, driven by self-interest, exploits the natural resources beyond the sustainable level. This over-exploitation occurs because the full opportunity cost of the action (for example, fishing, fuelwood gathering) is not paid when the resource is free for the taking or because the cost is pushed onto a third party as an externality. In order to achieve an efficient outcome, the tragedy model calls for internalizing the cost through some institutional means such as taxation or sole owner management (for example, by a government agency). Natural resource models generally specify that if the common resource is either privatized or nationalized, an incentive is created to internalize the cost or at least to preserve the resource for future exploitation. The tragedy metaphor has become in economics the central metaphor which explains natural resource degradation and supports implementation of private property rights. However, simple privatization or nationalization may not lead to an optimal solution because that solution needs to take into account not only the resource management regimes and the models which generate those regimes but also the discount rates of resource users as well as the institutional framework within which the resource is being utilized.

Although feminist scholarship is still in the early stages in this field, current work can be classified into three threads. First, feminist economists are challenging the behavioural assumptions of the neoclassical economic model and the tragedy of the commons model which represent the theoretical and metaphorical bases of natural resource and environmental economics; secondly, they are using empirical approaches and case studies to make women visible as natural resource users, managers and owners; and thirdly, they are engaged with ecofeminists in exploring the connections between women, nature and natural resources in the economic development process. While most of this scholarship is still being integrated into the traditional natural resource literature, it has had an impact on policy and awareness in both industrialized and unindustrialized countries.

The first thread of feminist inquiry is theoretical and follows feminists in microeconomics who have critiqued the behavioural assumptions of the rational economic agent as limiting and counter-intuitive. Feminist economists ask why the economic agent in the environmental model places such a low value on future uses of the resource that they intentionally exhaust the resource from which they draw their current income or livelihood. That is, rather than assuming a particular type of behaviour, feminist economists suggest that it might be more useful to explore the causes of the behaviour and identify alternatives. Lucas (1993) offers a feminist critique which points out that the tragedy metaphor is flawed in assuming only one type of human behaviour: behaviour which is self-interested and engaged only in competition. Cooperative or sustainable management regimes are assumed away in the typical natural resource model. It may be that the resource is managed differently in the short run if used for subsistence rather than for exchange; or, a village unit might manage resources differently from the corporate or government monopoly. Agarwal (1998) moves the critique of the commons in new directions when she asks if 'the very values of caring for others, especially children, might lead women not toward conserving nature but its opposite' (unpaginated) in an attempt to provide for their family.

The traditional approach in natural resource economics not only assumes away cooperative behaviour, it also has no consideration of any learning, information or knowledge feedback which might either mitigate or worsen the outcome of the tragedy. Research on the commons opens broad opportunities for feminists to explore forms of cooperative management of resources which heretofore have been invisible and to challenge the behavioural assumptions which underlie the model.

A second thread of feminist economics research is empirical and focuses on documenting the gendered aspects of natural resource production ranging from fishing to fuelwood collection. Women are primary users and owners of natural resources and yet these activities, paid and unpaid, are often invisible in analysis and in subsequent policy decisions. Case studies and empirical analysis serve to overcome this invisibility. Connelly and MacDonald (1992) document women's role, which is often unpaid and therefore economically unseen, in the Canadian Atlantic Ocean fishery. They found that state policy related to the fishery is based on implicit assumptions about gender relations in the household and that a focus on gender was necessary to fully understand the implications of that policy. This approach is unique in that only the rare fisheries analysis considers gender at all, presuming either that women are not active in the fishery or that women have the same economic experience as the men. Humphries (1990) takes a similar empirical approach to gender in the economic history of the commons when she traces the impact of the enclosure movement in England on women. The research shows that women were major users of the commons and that they were displaced from the commons and their source of income by early enclosure. Agarwal (1994) focuses on the gendered aspects of economic development in India by making women resource users visible. While documenting women's economic activities Agarwal stresses that because of patriarchal structures these women have less access to cash and to market work and so they become more dependent on gathering activity such as wood gathering from common property. Zein-Elabdin (1996) extends this theme and says that the relationship between women and nature is contextual and 'molded by institutional contexts such as the sexual division of labor' (p. 931). She proposes that the 'human–environmental relationship is dialectical' and looks explicitly at the differential hardships on women from the exclusion of women from the African forestry management programmes of the World Bank (Zein-Elabdin 1997). Compared to the men in her analysis, women have more frequent contact with the forest and yet they are not participants in rulemaking or dispute resolution. These empirical studies identify women interacting with nature for economic purposes and help us observe and theorize more clearly.

The third thread of feminist economics research comes out of a dialogue in the literature of economic development. This literature offers a rich feminist debate between ecofeminists and feminist economists on the relationship between humans and their natural environment and the causes of degradation of that environment. In many situations, women are observed working more directly than men with natural resources in the production of food, textiles, fuel and other household activities. Why women are identified more closely with nature and the implications of that association are at the source of deep debates within the feminist community (Merchant 1995).

Ecofeminism in its various forms posits that women have a special relationship to nature either because of social and economic structures or because of biological or spiritual reasons. Regardless of the source of the relationship with nature, many ecofeminists argue that this unique relationship conveys special knowledge of the environment to women and that this special knowledge prepares women to be superior stewards of the environment, in particular in the process of economic development (Griffin 1995; Reuther 1996; Sontheimer 1991; Warren 1994). Following this line of argument, some ecofeminists call for more women to be involved in the development decision process, for nature to be considered an equal partner with humans in the development process and for the values of equality, diversity and interconnectedness to be central to economic development policy. Ecofeminist Vandana Shiva has been a strong critic of the western development model as it is applied in India, suggesting, for example, that the General Agreement on Tariffs and Trade (GATT) is a mechanism for separating women from food and causing a restructuring of power around food. She argues that rural women have sophisticated knowledge that should be supported in an agriculturally-driven development model rather than in a pro-industrial model (Mies and Shiva 1993; Shiva 1994).

Feminist economists have been critical of some elements of ecofeminism such as that, in a reductionist way, it simply replaces male domination of nature with female superiority and that it romanticizes the peasantry. For example, Agarwal (1994, 1997) argues that ecofeminism does not adequately reflect the reality of political economy. She says that women are not uniquely connected to nature because of biology but because they are more economically dependent, made so by the power structures created by patriarchy. Within these debates, economists also find themselves in agreement with many of the critiques particularly those that recommend that women should be fully involved in development decisions. There is plenty of space for the arguments to expand in the future to include some common ground from the various feminist positions. This dialogue offers one of the few experiences where feminist economists are engaging in debates beyond the discipline.

Feminist economics' contributions to natural resource and environmental economics and to the debates in economic development have the potential to frame major research questions such as the role of scarcity and natural resources in economic provisioning. The future might also hold research which reframes the nature of woman's struggle: Is woman's struggle fundamentally a natural resource struggle and, if so, what are the elements of that struggle? There can be more research exploring from an economic perspective the parallels between instrumental views of women and views of the environment. Carolyn Merchant's early work argued that the practices of patriarchy link the environment with women in an instrumental way, a theme elaborated on by ecofeminists but given little attention by economists. Empirical analysis could shed some light on questions of patriarchal practice and natural resource exploitation. Lastly, economists might examine more thoroughly the unwritten assumptions of the typical natural resource or commons model to ask why the resource is not paid appropriate levels of rent or why markets do not exist for certain resources. A similar perspective asks what are the characteristics of natural physical resources which make them different in analysis from other inputs or resources. Given the trend in the field toward discounting these differences and treating natural resources as natural capital or a depreciable asset, feminist economists in the future could be teasing out important distinctions between natural and other resources and building models which reflect these insights.

LINDA E. LUCAS

See also
Development Policies; Development, Theories of.

Bibliography

Agarwal, Bina (1994), *A Field of One's Own: Gender and Land Rights in South Asia*, Cambridge: Cambridge University Press.

Agarwal, Bina (1997), 'Gender, environment and poverty interlinks: regional variations and temporal shifts in rural India, 1971–91', *World Development*, 5 (1), 23–52.

Agarwal, Bina (1998), 'The Future of Feminist Economics', *Conference Report*, Amsterdam: Out of the Margin/International Association for Feminist Economics Annual Conference, University of Amsterdam.

Connelly, M. Patricia and Martha MacDonald (1992), 'State policy, the household and women's work in the Atlantic Fishery', *Journal of Canadian Studies*, **26**, 18–32.

Elson, Diane (ed.) (1991), *Male Bias in the Development Process*, Manchester: Manchester University Press.

Griffin, Susan (1995), *The Eros of Everyday Life*, New York: Doubleday.

Gordon, H. Scott (1954), 'The economic theory of a common property resource: the fishery', *Journal of Political Economy*, **62**, 124–42.

Hardin, Garrett (1968), 'The tragedy of the commons', *Science*, **162**, 13 (December), 1243–8.

Humphries, Jane (1990), 'Enclosures, common rights, and women: the proletarianization of families in the late eighteenth and early nineteenth centuries', *Journal of Economic History*, **50**, 17–42.

Lucas, Linda E. (1993), 'Feminist Critique of the Tragedy of the Commons' (unpublished). Paper presented at the annual meetings of the American Economic Association, Boston.

Merchant, Carolyn (1995), *Earthcare. Women and the Environment*, New York: Routledge.

Mies, Maria and Vandana Shiva (1993), *Ecofeminism*, Washington: Fernwood Publications.

Reuther, Rosemary Radford (ed.) (1996), *Women Healing Earth*, New York: Orbis Books.

Scott, Anthony (1955), 'The fishery: the objectives of sole ownership', *Journal of Political Economy*, **62**, 112–24.

Shiva, Vandana (ed.) (1994), *Close to Home: Women Reconnect Ecology, Health and Development Worldwide*, Philadelphia: New Society Publishers.

Sontheimer, Sally (1991), *Women and the Environment*, New York: Monthly Review Press.

Tietenberg, Tom (1994), *Environmental Economics and Policy*, New York: HarperCollins.

Warren, Karen (1994), *Ecological Feminism*, London: Routledge.

Zein-Elabdin, Eiman (1996), 'Development, gender, and the environment: theoretical or contextual link? Toward an institutional analysis of gender', *Journal of Economic Issues*, **30** (4), 929–47.

Zein-Elabdin, Eiman (1997) 'Gender equity and sustainable development in Sub-Saharan Africa: The World Bank strategy for the forest sector', *Scandinavian Journal of Development Alternatives*, **16** (1), 75–95.

Family, Economics of

The economics of the family is concerned with how decisions are made and resources are allocated within families. The applications of the economics of the family include the topics of divorce, domestic labour, population, labour force participation and theories of marriage. This entry will focus on issues which cut across all of these applications: how do the individuals inside a family reconcile their interests and come to collective decisions, whether it be on how many children to have, how to allocate time, or how to allocate consumption between family members. It is not limited to feminist models of the family, but rather discusses the major developments in the economics of the family, both within and outside the mainstream neoclassical literature, from a feminist perspective.

Until the late 1960s or early 1970s, neither neoclassical nor critical (Marxist) economists tried to explain how decisions are made in families. Neoclassical economists adopted a 'unitary' or 'black box' view of the family. They assumed that the family acts as a unit, and has a single, unified set of interests. The family makes the consumption, labour supply and intra-household allocation decisions which produce the greatest 'household' utility, satisfaction or wellbeing, given the resources available. Formally, the family maximizes a 'household utility function' subject to an aggregate budget constraint. Critical economists also defined people in terms of the class position of their families, and treated the household as an undifferentiated unit. A good analysis of traditional and critical approaches to the family can be found in Folbre (1986).

There are fundamental problems with the unitary view of the family. First, the assumption that all family members have a single set of interests prevents analysis of conflict or inequality inside households. Yet there is considerable evidence that resources such as food and leisure time are unequally divided among family members, and women and girls suffer disproportionately from this inequality (Woolley and Marshall 1994). Second, the unitary view of the family is methodologically unsound. Neoclassical economists, in particular, advocate 'methodological individualism'. This means economic outcomes should be explained in terms of individual choices and external constraints. In this view, there is no methodological reason to substitute family choice for individual choice.

The unitary view of the family has its only theoretical justification in the work of Gary Becker. Becker (1991) argued that transfers from an altruistic 'head' to other family members induce them to act in his [sic] interests. The family has a single unified set of interests: those of the male household head. Becker's model has well-known problems. It makes the odd assumption that the male head cares about other family members, but that other family members are completely selfish. Also, Becker's argument only holds if the head controls enough of the household income that others depend on transfers from him, and if certain other conditions are satisfied (Bergstrom 1989). These unrealistic assumptions may be one reason why the unitary model is not supported by empirical evidence. It predicts that household decisions should depend only on total household income, while studies of family consumption patterns show that it matters, for example, who receives government transfer payments (Lundberg et al. 1997).

Becker's work matters to feminist economists for three reasons. First, it reveals the patriarchal foundations, the assumption of women's dependency, underlying the unitary model of the family. Second, it encapsulates the beliefs many feminist economists challenge: that there is altruism in the family and selfishness in the market place. Third, Becker's work matters because many economists and feminists have used his research as a basis for their own work (see Grossbard-Shechtman's entry on 'Marriage, Theories of' or Grossbard-Shechtman 1984), as a basis for critiques (Folbre 1986, Bergmann 1995), or as a stimulus towards the development of a different, better understanding of family behaviour.

Neoclassical, critical and feminist economists have now developed new approaches to understanding the family. The work draws attention to the process of cooperation and conflict in families. Family members cooperate in production and reproduction. Yet there is conflict, negotiation and bargaining over the gains from cooperation.

The economics of the family is concerned with how resources are allocated within families. Time is one resource men and women allocate very differently. Women spend time in household production, men in market production. Some of the earliest analysis of the value of household production was carried out by Margaret Reid, a pioneer in the field of 'home economics' (for a feminist analysis of Reid's work, see Yi 1996). Reid's colleagues at the University of Chicago, Theodore Schultz and Gary Becker, incorporated Reid's idea of household production into their 'new home economics'. The new home economics argued that women specialize in household production because they have a 'comparative advantage' in household work. Women's productivity in household work relative to their market wage is supposedly higher than men's. Thus a family sacrifices less money income when a given amount of housework is done by women, rather than men, and so women do the housework.

The new home economics, as it is presented in economics textbooks (Blau et al. 1998), is essentially a trade model without any trade. There is specialization (women specialize in household work, men in market), but no exchange. The commodities produced through household work are shared equally by all family members. Apps (1981) gives household production models a feminist edge by making explicit the process of exchange and the terms of trade within the family. Women exchange household work for market goods. Apps argues that if the terms of trade are unfavourable to women, for example because women are 'crowded' into the household sector, women will receive less in exchange for their household production.

The idea of a 'market' in household production can be found in Becker (1991) and Grossbard-Shechtman (1984), as well as Apps (1981). However neither neoclassical nor feminist economics makes much use of the household production market idea. One reason for the neglect is a romanticization of love and marriage. Another is that the idiosyncratic, non-monetary and personal exchanges inside a household are very different from competitive market transactions. Yet the idea of a market in household production can be used to link exchanges inside the household to influences outside the household. For example, marriage practices and institutions (monogamy, polygamy), women's and men's labour market opportunities and changes in the ratio of women to men in the population (due to say, neglect of girl children or war) change the supply of and demand for household production. This, in turn, influences the 'wage' women receive for their household work, and therefore the division of resources inside marriage and women's wellbeing.

Household production models have been anathema to many feminist economists because they are often based on the presumption that women have a natural comparative advantage in household work. They justify on efficiency grounds the traditional division of labour feminists seek to change. Yet it appears that there is a growing interest among feminist economists in measuring exchanges within the household (Katz 1995). Household production's potential as a source of bargaining power or a sphere of female control within the household needs to be better understood by feminist economists, as do the barriers to achieving a more equal division of household work.

For the most part, however, new research on the economics of the family has concentrated less on the household as a place of exchange and more on the household as a place of negotiation. One of the most popular ways of modelling that negotiation is using 'game-theoretic' models.

Game theoretic models can be divided into 'cooperative' and 'non-cooperative' models. In cooperative bargaining models, players divide the gains from cooperating on the basis of what each person would get if cooperation broke down, that is, based on his or her 'threat' or 'fall-back' position. Manser and Brown (1980) and McElroy and Horney (1981) apply cooperative bargaining theory to marriage with divorce taken as the 'threat point'. This highlights the influence of divorce laws, employment opportunities and other parameters on each partner's wellbeing during marriage. Lundberg and Pollak (1993) take the threat point to be staying married but reverting to traditional gender roles, thereby bringing social norms into the economics of the family. A person's threat point is also changed by, and in turn can influence, fertility and labour market decisions (Ott 1995).

Cooperative bargaining seems to be a 'natural' way to model the family, where people cooperate in caring for children, in sharing jointly-consumed goods such as housing, and in doing household work. Yet group cooperation has individual costs. Every hour spent on something that benefits the whole family, such as cleaning the house, means less time for personal activities, such as reading. Why should people cooperate, that is, not shirk their household chores? One way of exploring the evolution of cooperation is with a non-cooperative approach.

The essence of the non-cooperative approach is that each family member chooses how much income to spend on household goods, and how much time to spend on paid and unpaid work, by maximizing his or her utility, which depends upon the wellbeing (if there is altruism) and the choices of other family members. The advantages of the non-cooperative approach are that it makes explicit the processes of negotiation and the nature of cooperation within the family. Also the evolution of cooperation over time can be explained as the outcome of a non-cooperative game played repeatedly (see Bergstrom 1996). Even though there may be an immediate pay-off from free-riding on other people's contribution to the family, over the longer term the pay-offs to cooperation are higher.

Non-cooperative and cooperative bargaining models attempt to correct gender bias 'by stricter adherence to existing norms of scientific inquiry' (Harding 1986). They represent what feminist philosopher Sandra Harding calls 'feminist empiricism'. First, the models adhere to the neoclassical standard of methodological individualism more strictly than the unitary approach. Second, gendered assumptions, for example, that the household is headed by a benevolent male dictator, or that women have a comparative advantage in household work, are replaced by a symmetrical treatment of men and women. Third, substantial contributions to the literature have been made by women and, therefore, the bargaining models incorporate women's, as well as men's, views of reality. Here bargaining models differ from the household exchange models discussed above and the collective approach discussed below, both of which have been developed primarily by male neoclassical economists. Finally, by existing norms of economic inquiry, bargaining models are better models. They provide more plausible explanations of household expenditure patterns and labour supply behaviour; they explain how inequality in men's and women's labour market and other opportunities can result in inequality within marriage; they identify factors influencing the division of resources, such as divorce laws and social programmes (Phipps and Burton 1995); and they generally fit the data better. The value of the approach is evidenced by its success in raising issues such as intra-household distribution in widely-read and influential journals (Lundberg and Pollak 1993).

Yet with its emphasis on formal modelling, derivation of demand and supply equations and rational choice, game-theoretic modelling retains neoclassical economic methods. Indeed, a growing number of economists who pay little attention to gender issues are now using game-theoretic models to explain family behaviour (Bergstrom 1996), suggesting that there is nothing inherently feminist about the game-theoretic approach.

In fact, a substantial number of feminist economists, such as McCrate (1987), Seiz (1995) and Nelson (1996), are now rejecting formal game-theoretic approaches for several reasons. First, the requirements imposed by formal modelling restrict what can be studied. For example, formal models require that people have well-defined utility functions, assuming away issues of agency, that is, people's awareness of their own interests and their ability to act on those interests. Children are usually omitted from formal bargaining models because cooperative bargaining models with three or more players are often intractable, or do not yield unique solutions. Second, internalized gender norms, such as women's responsibility for keeping up the household, are hard to incorporate except as 'differences in tastes', an explanation too broad and too easily invoked to be intellectually satisfying. Third, there is little analysis of the process of negotiation. There is no bargaining in bargaining models, instead family members instantaneously arrive at the cooperative outcome. Finally, the benefits of using a mathematical model to formulate testable hypotheses are greatest when working with quantitative data; mathematical modelling often contributes little to the analysis of qualitative data. Yet an increasing number of feminist economists are using qualitative data in their research. A number of these researchers are rejecting game-theoretic models in favour of the 'cooperative conflicts' approach, developed by Sen (1990) and Agarwal (1994).

The cooperative conflicts work retains the fundamental insights from the cooperative bargaining approach: people gain from cooperating, are in conflict over the division of gains to cooperation, and each person's share of the gains to cooperation depends crucially upon her threat or fall-back position. Yet it differs from the cooperative bargaining approach most obviously by rejecting mathematical modelling. Instead, Agarwal and Sen identify influences on women's and men's threat or fall-back positions and their bargaining power, and predict the direction of these influences on household outcomes. Perhaps because the approach is non-mathematical, Sen and Agarwal incorporate hard-to-quantify influences on household outcomes often omitted from more formal models, such as the influence of children, extended family and community on household bargaining, historical practices and ideologies about gender, perceptions of a person's needs and contribution, and processes of negotiation and bargaining.

The influence of community and culture on family outcomes highlights the dynamic, ongoing interaction between the household and other social structures. For example, Agarwal argues, in the South Asian context, that the most effective way of strengthening women's position inside the household is by supporting women's right to hold land. However, the process of gaining land rights involves challenging prevailing norms governing gender roles and behaviour. Gaining rights for women is a process of 'women's empowerment at multiple levels along the way' (Agarwal 1994, p. 477). This ties the economics of the family into the growing feminist literature on 'empowerment'. In this sense the cooperative conflicts approach is a promising direction for feminist economic research.

The 'collective' approach provides a second alternative to game-theoretic models of household decision making. Collective models assume that whatever outcome a family reaches, it is Pareto efficient; that is, it is not possible to make one family member better off without making another one worse off. The model does not predict where the unimprovable outcome will occur, nor does it identify theoretically factors influencing the outcome. Instead, collective models use information on household expenditures or labour supplies to discover the family 'sharing rule', that is, the share of family income received by each family member. For example, Browning et al. (1994) study spending on women's clothing and conclude from this that women's share of (overall) family expenditure is higher when women's earnings account for a larger share of the household's income, or when the household's income is higher.

The collective approach deliberately neglects issues of power, bargaining and negotiation within families. For example, the Browning et al. (1994) study cited above offers no explanation of how or why women's earnings change the outcome of household decisions. Some recent work by feminist economists (notably Katz 1995), adopts the collective focus on observing household transactions, rather than specifying *a priori* the determinants of household interactions. Yet the collective approach can be seen to represent a real threat to the development of a feminist economics of the family. First, because the collective approach purports to be a general theory, it reduces the status of all other models to 'special cases' of the general collective approach. Second, it turns attention away from the question of central importance to feminist economists: creating a theoretical understanding of the causes of unequal gender relations within families.

Achieving more equal gender relations within families is crucial to feminists because women's lives are often structured by their responsibilities as daughters, mothers and wives. Yet, because the family has been defined as part of the private sphere, public policy can rarely influence gender relations in families directly. The crucial question for people concerned with achieving greater equality for women is what changes in the market, government or other arenas will produce more equal gender relations in the household.

The economics of the family has shown how women's employment opportunities, land rights, social programmes, divorce laws and other factors influence outcomes within the family. Yet many unresolved issues remain. One puzzle for economists studying the family is the consistency of gender roles in the face of massive economic change. For example, most Western countries have seen dramatic increases in female labour force participation over the past 25 years, yet these have been associated with decidedly undramatic changes in the division of household work, suggesting that something not captured in existing models strongly influences what happens in families. One possible explanation for the consistency of gender roles is that people have deeply-rooted norms and ideologies about gender. For example, Agarwal argues that ideologies are important in establishing what is *'doxa'* – taken for granted and not negotiable – and what can be negotiated. Yet so far there is not much research linking the large feminist literature on the social construction of gender (such as Weedon 1996) with the economics of the family.

Individualism is an ideology, inherent in neoclassical economics, which has been questioned by feminist economists. Individualism states, first, that choices are made by individuals acting in their own (possibly selfish, possibly altruistic) interests. Second, people's wellbeing is identified with their choices: given the range of options available, the option a person chooses is the option which gives her the greatest wellbeing. So if a mother chooses to give her child the last scoop of rice, she must get greater well-being from watching her child eat than she would from eating herself. Feminist studies of the family have begun to question the ideology of individualism. Sen (1990) argues that women and other oppressed people may not have a sense of their own interests, while Nelson (1996, p. 70) argues that a mother's or father's care for others may be better understood as a 'commitment' than an action motivated by own interests. Although there is not yet a well-developed non-individualistic non-unitary model of the family, this research agenda is, as the title of Nelson's paper suggests, a way of moving 'Towards a Feminist Theory of the Family'.

Ideologies about gender roles and other ideologies influence people's behaviour in part because they are embodied in marriage and other institutions. Many of the approaches surveyed here, including game-theoretic models, the collective approach and some of the household exchange literature, take institutional constraints as given. Yet an understanding of the family which takes institutions as exogenous cannot explain the existence of institutions or how to change them. Focusing on the evolution of institutions is a potential route for gaining greater insight into the economics of the family.

One agenda for feminist economics is to identify the sources of inequality in the family and identify policies which promote more equal gender relations in families. The feminist research described in this entry has opened up the black box of the household. In doing so it has answered many questions, but raised other ones: questions about the usefulness of formal modelling, the evolution of gender norms and ideology, the value of individualism and the formation of institutions. Answering these questions will lead not just to a better understanding of the family, but also to better economic thought.

FRANCES WOOLLEY

See also
Divorce; Domestic Labour; Double Day/Second Shift; Family Policy; Game Theory and Bargaining Models; Labour Force Participation; Marriage, Theories of; Methodology.

Bibliography
Apps, Patricia (1981), *A Theory of Inequality and Taxation*, Cambridge: Cambridge University Press.
Agarwal, Bina (1994), *A Field of One's Own: Gender and Land Rights in South Asia*, Cambridge: Cambridge University Press.
Becker, Gary S. (1991), *A Treatise on the Family, Enlarged Edition*, Cambridge: Harvard University Press.
Bergmann, Barbara (1995), 'Becker's "Theory of the Family": preposterous conclusions', *Feminist Economics*, **1** (1), 141–50.
Bergstrom, Theodore C. (1989), 'A fresh look at the rotten kid theorem – and other household mysteries', *Journal of Political Economy*, **97** (5), 1138–59.
Bergstrom, Theodore C. (1996), 'Economics in a family way', *Journal of Economic Literature*, **34** (4), 1903–34.
Blau, Francine, Marianne Ferber and Anne Winkler (1998), *The Economics of Women, Men, and Work, Third Edition*, Upper Saddle River, New Jersey: Prentice Hall.
Browning, Martin, François Bourguignon, Pierre-Andre Chiappori and Valerie Lechene (1994), 'Incomes and outcomes: a structural model of intra-household allocation', *Journal of Political Economy*, **102** (6), 1067–96.
Folbre, Nancy (1986), 'Hearts and spades: paradigms of household economics', *World Development*, **14** (2), 245–55.
Grossbard-Shechtman, Shoshana (1984), 'A theory of allocation of time in market for labor and marriage', *Economic Journal*, **94**, 863–82.
Harding, Sandra (1986), *The Science Question in Feminism*, Ithaca: Cornell University Press.
Katz, Elizabeth (1995), 'Gender and trade within the household: Observations from rural Guatemala', *World Development*, **23** (2), 327–42.
Lundberg, Shelly and Robert Pollak (1993), 'Separate spheres bargaining and the marriage market', *Journal of Political Economy*, **101** (6), 988–1010.
Lundberg, Shelly, Robert Pollak and Terence Wales (1997), 'Do husband and wives pool their resources? Evidence from the U.K. Child Benefit', *Journal of Human Resources*, **32** (3), 463–80.
Manser, M. and M. Brown (1980), 'Marriage and household decision-making', *International Economic Review*, **21**, 31–44.
McCrate, Elaine (1987), 'Trade, merger, and employment: Economic theory of marriage', *Review of Radical Political Economics*, **19** (1), 73–89.
McElroy, Marjorie and Mary Jean Horney (1981), 'Nash-bargained household decisions: toward a generalization of the theory of demand', *International Economic Review*, **22**, 333–49.
Nelson, Julie (1996), *Feminism, Objectivity and Economics*, London and New York: Routledge.
Ott, Notburga (1995), 'Fertility and the Division of Work in the Family: A Game Theoretic Model of Household Decisions', in Edith Kuiper and Jolande Sap (eds), *Out of the Margin: Feminist Perspectives on Economics*, London and New York: Routledge.

Phipps, Shelley and Peter Burton (1995), 'Social/institutional variables and behavior within households: an empirical test using the Luxembourg Income Study', *Feminist Economics*, **1** (1), 151–74.
Seiz, Janet (1995), 'Bargaining models, feminism and institutionalism', *Journal of Economic Issues*, **29** (2), 609–18.
Sen, Amartya K. (1990), 'Gender and Cooperative Conflicts', in Irene Tinker (ed.), *Persistent Inequalities: Women and World Development*, New York: Oxford University Press, pp. 123–49.
Weedon, Chris (1996), *Feminist Practice and Poststructuralist Theory*, 2nd edition, Cambridge, Massachusetts: Blackwell.
Woolley, Frances and Judith Marshall (1994), 'Measuring inequality within the household', *Review of Income and Wealth*, **40** (4), 415–31.
Yi, Yun-Ae (1996), 'Margaret G. Reid: life and achievements', *Feminist Economics*, **2** (3), 17–36.

Family Policy

Shiela Kamerman and Alfred Kahn, professors of Social Work at Columbia University known for their work on comparative family policy, define family policy as 'a field in which certain objectives regarding the family are established ... and various policies and measures are developed to achieve these goals' (1978, p. 5). Examples include public childcare programmes; tax policy; income support and transfer policy; child support levels, enforcement, and assurance programmes; and legislation affecting maternity and parental leave. Kamerman and Kahn distinguish between 'explicit' family policy, designed to achieve specific goals or outcomes (such as transmission of societal values, inducement of women to leave or enter the labour force, provision of day care, child welfare, family counselling, family planning, income maintenance, tax benefits and housing policies); and 'implicit' family policy, which is not aimed primarily at families, but affects them indirectly (for example, via consequences of industrial locations, construction of roads, international trade policy, or immigration policy). In this sense, family policy can be seen as a 'perspective' on all other policy. Kamerman and Kahn contend that 'raising the issue of implicit family policies in multiple-policy domains may serve to underscore the pervasiveness of government activity with regard to the family in those societies which deny having any family policy at all' (1978, p. 4).

For economists' purposes family policy may be described as the set of a society's institutions that influence the distribution of costs and responsibilities for children, the elderly, and other persons who are unable to care for themselves. Feminist economists are concerned with the ways in which family policy regimes or individual policy measures enhance or constrain the economic and political progress of different groups of women, relative to men and relative to women of other generations, classes, races, ethnicities and family situations. Analysis of family policy can be used to explore the relationship between theory and practice for certain branches of feminist economic theory. This entry begins with a discussion of family policy and ideology, moves to family policy as a strategy for reconciling family and employment, and concludes with a schematic overview of research by feminist economists on family policy and suggested directions for further research. In view of the short space of this entry, the focus will be on explicit family policy in the USA and Europe.

Ideological foundations of family policy are similar to those of social policy in general, including redistributive justice, social solidarity (the level of commitment by social groups to one another), universality, and subsidiarity (the belief that policy should be neutral toward existing forms of responsibility, as within the family). In addition, principles underpinning family policy may include conservatism, maternalism, pronatalism (encouragement of population growth) or population control. The form and acceptability of family policy vary depending on the strength of ideological norms and on the degree of consensus as to a definition of 'the family' (broadly defined in this entry as involving two or more people who have a primary emotional commitment and relationship to one another). As noted by Linda Hantrais (Director, European Research Centre, Loughborough University) and Marie-Therese Letablier (Centre d'Etudes de l'Emploi, Paris) authors of a European Commission initiative comparing family policy in Europe, controversies in this policy realm include questions concerning the nature of the family, the degree to which it varies across cultures and the role of the state in creating or destroying family solidarity (Hantrais and Letablier 1996). Over time, policy measures exert influence on norms, values and demographic patterns, with cumulative effects over generations. For example, legal and income constraints affecting single-parent or gay and lesbian families can result in marginalization or greater inclusion of these groups in society.

In her analysis of the ideological foundations of family policy, political scientist Annette Borchorst uses the concept 'familism' to identify tensions between feminist goals and family goals (both of which are subject to change), defining familism as the belief that the family is 'the basic unit of society, rather than men, women and children as individuals, each with their own rights' (Borchorst 1993, p. 168). Familist taxation systems – prevalent in the United States, the United Kingdom, Germany, France, Luxembourg, and to some extent Belgium – treat married couples as a unit, providing social security and other entitlements to stay-at-home spouses regardless of whether they perform caring work in their home. Social benefits to non-earners who care for other people are chiefly provided via their attachment to labour force participants.

To varying degrees all countries' family policies privilege labour force work over household work. A non-familist policy regime would provide equal social benefits to those involved in labour force and non-labour force work, using as a criterion for social insurance a person's engagement in market and nonmarket work, rather than marital status (see Nelson 1991). Borchorst characterizes family policy in Scandinavia and the Netherlands as 'indirect familism'; spouses are taxed as individuals, but social rights, such as old-age pensions and health care, are based on labour force attachment.

Hantrais and Letablier's classification of Western European nations' family-employment policies into three groups further illustrates how nations' ideological foundations and principles influence family policy. A first group of countries promotes parents' employment and provides policy support based on principles of gender equality or a commitment to family wellbeing. Sweden, Denmark and Finland promote equality through providing a combination of paid parental leave (with incentives for fathers to use leave options), public child care, reduced working hours, and other supports that allow for women's continuous employment, although often part time and interrupted by periods of parental leave. France and Belgium are also included in this first grouping; the ideological basis for support of mothers' employment in these two countries is a commitment to child wellbeing, however, rather than gender equality. Emphasis is placed on public child care and flexible work-time arrangements, with much less attention to fathers' responsibility for children.

In a second group of countries, Austria, Germany, Luxembourg and the Netherlands, government policy encourages sequential ordering of work and family, with state support based more on concern to maintain the family as an institution than on protecting the individual rights of its members. While transfers to families are extensive in these countries, public provision of child care is low, and mothers are assumed to bear responsibility for the care of young children. German half-day and irregular public school hours, for example, are predicated on the assumption that mothers spend little time in the labour force and are primarily homemakers.

A third set of countries is classed as 'non-interventionist', generally promoting sequential ordering of employment and family life at lower levels of support, either due to deliberate non-interference, as in Britain and Ireland, or to financial constraints, as in Greece, Spain and Portugal. In this third group of countries, 'market forces or family networks may be substituted for state support, depending on the willingness or otherwise of governments to intervene in the private lives of families and on the financial resources at their disposal' (Hantrais and Letablier 1996, p. 125).

In addition, all European Union member nations must conform to the Council of Ministers' 1992 directive on the protection of pregnant women. This directive provides for uninterrupted maternity leave of at least 14 weeks at pay equivalent to at least 80 per cent of the woman's previous salary. No

Europe-wide directive has been issued which makes child-rearing leave available to fathers.

The United States is most similar to Hantrais and Letablier's third group of European states favouring non-intervention, except that US law contains no right to paid maternity leave (though pregnancy is considered a disability and compensated by employers in states with laws requiring disability insurance). US non-interventionism is deliberate, rather than due to financial constraints. Whereas most European polities acknowledge the need for some degree of protection of a 'personal sphere from market forces', US policy is based on the assumption that individuals and families must be buffered as little as possible from the market; any protections are seen to result in work disincentives. Neither explicit nor implicit family policy is a concept familiar to the US public, despite widespread acceptance of other forms of social entitlements, though even these are minimal by European standards (Ginsburg 1992). Since 1992, the Family and Medical Leave Act (FMLA) mandates 12 weeks of unpaid leave in certain businesses and all government occupations to care for a newborn or adopted child or a sick family member. While the FMLA may indicate a move away from non-interventionism, the USA remains the only industrial country with no national legislation on paid maternity leave.

Eastern European family policy regimes have tended to be more pronatalist and more redistributive than those of Western European nations. From the 1950s through the 1980s, central planning and extensive incorporation of women in the paid labour force gave rise to rapidly falling birth rates, inspiring a pronatalist policy agenda. Government control of pricing and incomes allowed massive redistribution of child-rearing costs, along with incomes in general. Most East European countries also restricted abortion rights for women who did not already have several children. Abortion remained free and legal in East Germany, where the pronatalist impulse led to larger child-rearing subsidies and universal free day care, with the goal of reconciling *motherhood* with employment. Policy allocated household work to women; for example, married women and single mothers in East Germany received one day off work monthly to perform household chores (see Duggan 1995). Although Eastern European feminists criticized aspects of state socialist governments' family policies, as these nations are integrated into the world market, feminists are concerned about falling benefit levels and an accelerating gender and income divide between public and private spheres (Posadskaya 1993).

The ideological bases of family policy noted above give rise to economists' varied approaches to this relatively new and limited field within economics. The scant economics literature on family policy reflects the fact that mainstream economics' tools of analysis exclude most questions regarding nonmarket work and power relations (except for a small but grow-ing literature on bargaining power), omissions that discourage dynamic analysis of families. Power differences within households and society are conflated with exogenously determined individual preferences, so the work of caring for family members is seen, by definition, as a freely made individual choice.

In addition to limited theory, there is also little (especially English lan-guage) empirical economic research on families. American exceptions include the extensive literature on the economic incentives of welfare (see Moffitt 1992, and Haveman and Wolfe's 1994 book analysing investments in chil-dren). Another important mainstream contribution to the literature on family policy is Barbara Bergmann's comparison of the extensive French and mini-mal US public child care programmes (Bergmann 1993). Her work profiles French successes, such as greater equality of children's achievement and relatively high labour force participation rates of mothers. Other notable exceptions include Davies and Joshi's (1990) detailed comparisons of women's foregone earnings due to child-rearing in several European countries; Davies and Joshi document the extent to which family policy measures, such as public child care in Sweden and France, reduce the gender gap in lifetime earnings relative to the gap in Germany and the United Kingdom. Also significant is Waldfogel's (1998) examination of the wage or 'family' gap between mothers and non-mothers in the USA and Great Britain. Her time series analysis shows that job-protected maternity leave coverage offsets some of the negative wage effects of children.

While mainstream economic categories and concepts may be usefully ap-plied to family policy analysis, as shown by the research noted above, the mainstream toolbox is too small to provide insights into most of the richly complex topics in this field. Interdisciplinary by nature, nonmarket exchanges require new, more comprehensive, analytic frameworks. Perhaps the clearest illustration of economism in models of the family is the literature on the economics of fertility decisions, in which children are viewed as consumer durables and parents as rational utility maximizers. Models of individual choice subject to budget constraints may be used for limited inquiries into fertility behaviour; however, a thorough approach to the 'production' of chil-dren requires an understanding of the socioeconomic and socio-psychological contexts of child-rearing (Turchi 1975).

The addition of political economy to economic theory enlarges both the analytic framework and the project of understanding family policy. Feminist political economists challenge the philosophical and epistemological basis of mainstream economics, leading to insights into the relationship between compensated labour force work and uncompensated caring work (see Beasley 1994). As this body of theory allows analysis of power relations between nonmarket and market actors, it is possible to conceptualize, for example, competitive firms 'externalizing' the care of labour force participants onto the 'caring sphere', similarly to firms externalizing environmental costs onto communities, as mainstream theory holds. Folbre (1994) has examined changes in parents' ability to defray the cost of children historically, focusing on ways in which the growth of labour force work expanded women's and children's autonomy and correspondingly diminished individual patriarchs' control. Children's new options (and reduced obligation to parents) gave rise to social security, a new policy constellation to insure mainly fathers. Other noteworthy feminist political economy research on family policy includes Cannan's (1995) analysis of the United Kingdom's retreat from entitlements into 'enterprise culture', and Trzcinski's (1995) use of an ecological perspective, highlighting the value of diversity of family forms, to critique analytic frameworks for family policy.

In addition, McElroy (1990) and others have explored family policy as a source of intrahousehold bargaining power. Along with culture, labour market trends and the general legal setting, family policy can exert considerable influence on the bargaining arena or 'rules of the game' within which bargaining takes place, for example, through increasing women's ability to earn income, providing child support assurance, or enforcing legislation on domestic violence (see also Duggan 1995; Phipps and Burton 1995). Such policy measures affect both the bargaining framework and the fall-back positions (resources with which the 'player' will 'walk away' from the relationship should bargaining break down) of partners within a marriage or other family relationship. In turn, women's power in families affects their power in society, potentially leading to further legitimation of, or disregard for, the concerns of women, older children and other groups who do caring work.

Some theoretical and empirical research directions that feminist economists may usefully pursue include analysis of children as public goods worthy of societal investments, development of standards to measure 'successful' investments in children and inquiry into path dependence (for social evolution) of certain types of investment in children, building, for example, on the work of Bergmann (1993) and Haveman and Wolfe (1994). Related questions may include the following: How should 'efficiency' in the provision of caring work be defined? To what extent do markets allocate time (for market and nonmarket work) 'efficiently'? As an alternative to efficiency, what criteria might be used to measure success in political economic exchanges? What is the optimal role for markets in the provision of caring? Can states mediate gender conflict and, if so, how? What institutional boundaries should be placed around 'subsistence' caring? Can a nonmarket-centred epistemology be used to understand the effects of markets on nonmarket practices? Might 'equality of fall-back position' be used as a measure of equity and a policy goal? What roles have labour organizations played historically in promoting different types of family policy around the world?

Because feminist economics brings to the field of family policy elevated concern for and theoretical tools to revalue nonmarket work, this perspective provides insights into class-based as well as gender-based trends. The context of current family and social policy is global liberalization (government deregulation, privatization, structural adjustment and austerity measures) and consequently rapid economic restructuring. This liberalization and the accompanying trend of increasing inequality can be seen as implicit family policy that steers societies in certain directions with regard to gender roles, time use, caring work and asset differentiation among families. Explicit family policy may be used to moderate the effects of such changes, providing the basis for greater solidarity and political power among different generations, classes, races and ethnicities of women and other groups who have a stake in a thriving nonmarket sphere.

LYNN DUGGAN

See also
Child Care; Child Support; Divorce; Domestic Labour; Domestic Abuse; Double Day/Second Shift; Family, Economics of; Income Support and Transfer Policy; Labour Force Participation; Pensions and Old Age Retirement; Parental Leave; Tax Policy; Welfare Reform.

Bibliography
Beasley, Chris (1994), *Sexual Economyths: Conceiving a Feminist Economics*, New York: St Martin's Press.
Bergmann, Barbara (1993), 'The French Child Welfare System: An Excellent System We Could Adapt and Afford', in William Julius Wilson (ed.), *Sociology and the Public Agenda*, Boulder, Colorado: Sage, pp. 341–50.
Bock, Gisela and Pat Thane (eds) (1991), *Maternity and Gender Policies: Women and the Rise of the European Welfare States, 1880s–1950s*, New York and London: Routledge.
Borchorst, Annette (1993), 'Working Lives and Family Lives in Western Europe', in Carlsen and Larsen (eds), *The Equality Dilemma*, Copenhagen: The Danish Equal Status Council.
Cannan, Crescy (1995), 'From Dependence to Enterprise? Women and the Western Welfare States', in Barbara Einhorn and Eileen Janes Yeo (eds), *Women and Market Societies: Crisis and Opportunity*, Brookfield, Vermont: Edward Elgar.
Duggan, Lynn (1995), 'Restacking the deck', *Feminist Economics*, **1** (1), (Spring), 175–94.
Davies, Hugh and Heather Joshi (1990), 'The foregone earnings of Europe's mothers', *Discussion Papers in Economics*, **24**, Birkbeck College, University of London.
Folbre, Nancy (1994), *Who Pays for the Kids: Gender and the Structures of Constraint*, London: Routledge.
Ginsburg, Norman (1992), *Divisions of Welfare: A Critical Introduction to Comparative Social Policy*, London: Sage.
Hantrais, Linda and Marie-Therese Letablier (1996), *Families and Family Policies in Europe*, London and New York: Longman.
Haveman, Robert and Barbara Wolfe (1994), *Succeeding Generations: On the Effect of Investments in Children*, New York: Russell Sage Roundation.
Kamerman, Shiela, and Alfred J. Kahn (eds) (1978), *Family Policy: Government and Families in Fourteen Countries*, New York: Columbia University Press.

Kamerman, Shiela, and Alfred J. Kahn (eds) (1991), *Childcare, Parental Leave, and the Under 3s: Policy Innovation in Europe*, New York: Auburn House.

Lewis, Jane (ed.) (1993), *Women and Social Policies in Europe*, Aldershot, England: Edward Elgar.

McElroy, Marjorie (1990), 'The empirical content of Nash-bargained household behaviour', *Journal of Human Resources*, **25** (4), (Fall), 559–98.

Moffitt, Robert (1992), 'Incentive effects of the US welfare system: a review', *Journal of Economic Literature*, **30**, 1–61.

Nelson, Julie (1991), 'Tax reform and feminist theory in the United States: incorporating human connection', *Journal of Economic Studies*, **18** (5–6), 11–29.

Orloff, Ann (1993), 'Gender and the social rights of citizenship: the comparative analysis of gender relations and welfare states', *American Sociological Review*, **58** (3), (June), 318–22.

Phipps, Shelley and Peter Burton (1995), 'Social/institutional variables and behaviour within households: an empirical test using the Luxembourg income study', *Feminist Economics*, **1** (1), (Spring), 151–74.

Posadskaya, Anastasia (1993), 'Changes in Gender Discourses and Policies in the Former Soviet Union', in Valentine Mogahadam (ed.), *Democratic Reform and the Position of Women in Transitional Economies*, Oxford: Clarendon Press, pp. 162–79.

Trzcinski, Eileen (1995), 'An ecological perspective on family policy', *Journal of Family and Economic Issues*, **16** (1), (Spring), 7–33.

Turchi, Boone A. (1975), 'Microeconomic theories of fertility: a critique', *Social Forces*, **54** (1), (September), 107–25.

Waldfogel, Jane (1998), 'The family gap for young women in the United States and Britain: can maternity leave make a difference?', *Journal of Labor Economics*, **16** (3), 505–45.

Family Wage

The 'family wage' is a term that developed in the nineteenth and twentieth centuries to signify an individual's wage that is sufficient to support a family. Sometimes used interchangeably with the concepts of a 'living wage' or a 'just wage' the term family wage has taken on a specifically gendered meaning. A family wage has become identified with the division of labour between a male breadwinner and a woman performing unpaid domestic labour. It also expresses sentiments codified in legal and social prohibitions against child labour. Thus, by earning a family wage a male worker can support a nonemployed spouse and other dependants. The family wage is distinct from legislated minimum wages, which have historically been and still remain below a family-sustaining level.

The family wage has both material and ideological dimensions. In industrialized countries, it has served as the basis for legislative and collective bargaining initiatives pursued by trade unions, middle-class reformers, social investigators and policymakers since the nineteenth century (Humphries 1977; Hartmann 1981; Lewis 1984; Rose 1992; Horrell and Humphries 1995; Frader 1996). It was inextricably linked to the historic development of protective legislation policies that reduced married women's labour force participation rates at the turn of the century. Some of these measures led to real wage increases for male workers in specific occupations and industries. Further, the concept of the family wage articulates the gender ideology of separate spheres. It supports a vision of masculinity as linked to being a provider (Kessler-Harris 1990; Baron 1991; Rose 1992; Frader 1996). The link between masculinity and wage earning has supported the assertion of feminist economists and historians that gender is fundamental to the construction of class relations. However, ideological constructs of masculinity have been differentiated by race. Men of colour are generally excluded from breadwinner jobs and married women of colour's labour force participation has been a social norm in the USA since the abolition of slavery (Matthaei 1982, pp. 134–5; Amott and Matthaei 1996, p. 165). Thus, despite the pervasiveness of this gender ideology, not all men, or even all male workers, have had access to jobs with a family wage, creating a tension that has motivated various political and economic reform movements over time.

To the extent that it has been the basis of concrete pay practices, the family wage is part of institutionalized social relations fostering the wage gap between male and female workers. Family wage ideology historically justified unequal pay for equal work as well as wage differentials between men's and women's jobs. Therefore, the legacy of family wage policies in the twentieth century includes segregated employment in lower paid jobs for those women who are in the paid labour force and the promulgation of women's economic dependence on male breadwinners and, in their absence, the state.

The family wage has been a subject of interdisciplinary study and analysis. Within economics, Marxist, socialist and institutionalist feminists have taken the lead in incorporating the concept of a family wage as a crucial aspect of the critique of neoclassical wage theory. Feminist economists argue that actual wages are not necessarily equivalent to workers' productivity (that is, marginal revenue product). Social institutions and gender/racial ideologies influence the development of pay practices historically and within specific workplaces. Therefore, the history of family wage policies shed light on the limits of abstract wage theory, and point to the need for concrete analyses of wage setting.

Early debates among feminist economists over the family wage centred on whether it was a unified working-class strategy or a means by which male workers gained privileges at the expense of working women. The family wage represented a demand for subsistence and survival on the part of working-class families. At the same time, it reinforced patriarchy. Because of this dual nature of the family wage, it has been a lightning rod for debates over the relationship between class and gender struggles.

In her early work, Humphries (1977) explicitly articulated the position that the family wage was a working-class strategy to minimize family members' labour force participation while maintaining family income. Although acknowledging that the family wage may have reinforced patriarchal social relations in the long run, Humphries viewed the restriction of female labour supply, accompanied by the demand for a family wage, as the only strategy to raise wages that could also mobilize support from middle-class reformers. Her research was a response to Marxist feminists who argued that the domestic division of labour was perpetuated primarily because it was functional for capitalism; Humphries sought to establish that class agency influenced the development of economic institutions.

Humphries' account has been critiqued for overemphasizing class struggle over gender conflict. Her critics stress the gendered impact of family wage policies in bestowing power upon male breadwinners within the household. In her classic exposition of the relationship between capitalism and patriarchy, Hartmann (1981) maintained the family wage was divisive for the working class because it furthered men's over women's interests. By focusing on the benefits for married couples, Humphries' analysis ignored the situation of women who needed to stay in the labour force, especially unmarried and widowed women workers (Sen 1980). Historians have documented instances of nineteenth-century English working-class women's active resistance to the family wage doctrine, especially single women employed in the textile industry (Benenson 1991, Rose 1992). Asserting that the real purpose of the family wage was women's exclusion from well-paid jobs, Benenson contended that the primary beneficiaries were skilled male artisans who already earned breadwinner wages. The lack of support for family wage policies by unmarried working-class women implies the absence of working class unity in support of a family wage strategy.

May (1982) has suggested that campaigns for a family wage contained elements from both sides of this debate. Each aspect has been salient in different historical periods. In the early nineteenth century, 'the family wage challenged the ideology of working class poverty, invoking social justice and high wages in the name of the family' (p. 401). The historical context for this assertion was *laissez-faire* capitalism and Malthusian views of working-class immorality. Only at the end of the nineteenth century, as the ideology of separate spheres emerged, did the family wage become 'an adult male prerogative' (see also Horrell and Humphries 1995). Nevertheless, May's study of the development of the Five Dollar Day at Ford Motor Company indicates that the realization of jobs paying a family wage lagged behind its ideological development. During the twentieth century the family wage was finally extended beyond a small aristocracy of labour. In fact, sociologist Kim Blankenship (1993) argues that the ideological basis of Title VII of the US Civil Rights Act of 1964 was the extension of the male breadwinner family model to African Americans during a period of tight labour markets.

Recent analyses by feminists in economics and related disciplines continue to emphasize the historical development of family wage ideology and policies. In particular, the family wage is depicted as one dimension of a set of historically contingent gender relations that are subject to change as part of the process of social and economic restructuring. This research, primarily on the contemporary UK and USA, examines the decline in jobs earning a family wage (reflected in men's declining real wages) and married women's increased labour force participation (McDowell 1991; Bruegel and Perrons 1995; Bakker 1996; Mutari and Figart 1997). These changes suggest that the ideological hegemony of a gender order based upon separate spheres is eroding. The potential exists for a new set of gender relations.

Thus, the family wage has represented one of various possible institutionalized responses to the question posed by Folbre (1994): how does society pay for the costs of social reproduction? The demise of the family wage as a method of supporting social reproduction, while potentially liberatory, also poses challenges. This is an important area for future research by feminist economists. As McDowell (1991, p. 415) has noted, two-earner families 'are now doing three jobs for the price of one previously: two in the paid labour force and one unpaid at home ... if it is accepted that previously the male "family wage" reflected some contribution towards the unpaid domestic labour of female partners'. Alternatives to the family wage, including comparable worth/pay equity, family policy and policies to shorten the paid work week hold promise. Most importantly, feminist economists have argued that the family wage should be degendered and that all workers should earn a family-sustaining wage.

ELLEN MUTARI

See also
Class; Comparable Worth/Pay Equity; Discrimination, Theories of; Domestic Labour; Family Policy; Labour Force Participation; Minimum Wage; Patriarchy; Protective Legislation; Wage Gap.

Bibliography
Amott, Teresa and Julie Matthaei (1996), *Race, Gender, and Work: A Multi-Cultural Economic History of Women in the United States*, Boston: South End Press.
Bakker, Isabella (ed.) (1996), *Rethinking Restructuring: Gender and Change in Canada*, Toronto: University of Toronto Press.
Baron, Ava (ed.) (1991), *Work Engendered: Toward a New History of American Labor*, Ithaca: Cornell University Press.
Benenson, Harold (1991), 'The "Family Wage" and working women's consciousness in Britain, 1880–1914', *Politics and Society*, **19** (1), 71–108.
Blankenship, Kim M. (1993), 'Bringing gender and race in: US employment discrimination policy', *Gender and Society*, **7** (2), 204–26.
Bruegel, Irene and Diane Perrons (1995), 'Where do the costs of unequal treatment for women fall? An analysis of the incidence of the costs of unequal pay and sex discrimination in the UK', *Gender, Work and Organization*, **2** (3), 110–21.
Folbre, Nancy (1994), *Who Pays for the Kids? Gender and the Structures of Constraint*, London: Routledge.

Frader, Laura L. (1996), 'Engendering Work and Wages: The French Labor Movement and the Family Wage', in Laura L. Frader and Sonya O. Rose (eds), *Gender and Class in Modern Europe*, Ithaca: Cornell University Press.

Hartmann, Heidi I. (1981), 'The Unhappy Marriage of Marxism and Feminism: Towards a More Progressive Union', in Lydia Sargent (ed.), *Women and Revolution: A Discussion of the Unhappy Marriage of Marxism and Feminism*, Boston: South End Press.

Horrell, Sara and Jane Humphries (1995), 'Women's labour force participation and the transition to the male-breadwinner family, 1790–1865', *Economic History Review*, **XLVIII** (1), 89–117.

Humphries, Jane (1977), 'Class struggle and the persistence of the working class family', *Cambridge Journal of Economics*, **1**, 241–58.

Kessler-Harris, Alice (1990), *A Woman's Wage: Historical Meanings and Social Consequences*, Lexington: The University Press of Kentucky.

Lewis, Jane (1984), *Women in England, 1870–1950: Sexual Divisions and Social Change*, Bloomington: Indiana University Press.

Matthaei, Julie A. (1982), *An Economic History of Women in America*, New York: Schocken Books.

May, Martha (1982), 'The historical problem of the family wage: the Ford Motor Company and the five dollar day', *Feminist Studies*, **8** (2), 399–424.

McDowell, Linda (1991), 'Life without father and Ford: the new gender order of post-Fordism', *Transactions of the British Institute of Geographers*, **16**, 400–419.

Mutari, Ellen and Deborah M. Figart (1997), 'Markets, flexibility, and family: evaluating the gendered discourse against pay equity', *Journal of Economic Issues*, **31** (3), 687–705.

Rose, Sonya O. (1992), *Limited Livelihoods: Gender and Class in Nineteenth-Century England*, Berkeley: University of California Press.

Sen, Gita (1980), 'The sexual division of labor and the working-class family: towards a conceptual synthesis of class relations and the subordination of women', *Review of Radical Political Economics*, **12** (2), 76–86.

Feminism(s)

'Feminism', in the singular, might be defined as the belief that inequality between women and men should be eliminated, but to attempt to be more concrete is to engender debate. For as long as feminist movements have existed, feminists have held a variety of conflicting views on quite fundamental questions, from the nature and sources of women's oppression to the goals of feminist political activity.

To bring order to this diversity, many writers have sought to construct taxonomies of feminist schools of thought: Jaggar (1983) is an influential and still-valuable early example, and Tong (1998) is a recent one. Such efforts are fraught with hazards: oversimplification is unavoidable, and the attempt to construct a few boxes into which all feminist thinkers can be fitted is never fully successful. Classifications are becoming even more difficult over time: as feminist activism and writing grow around the world, feminisms proliferate; feminist scholarship becomes ever more specialized; and to varying degrees in different locales, the separation of feminist theorizing from feminist activism means that any taxonomy of schools of (academic) feminist thought will be only loosely related to the varieties of feminist political efforts.

This entry will by no means try to provide a comprehensive overview of contemporary feminist thought. Its aims are far more modest: to supply background information so that readers unfamiliar with Anglo-American feminist literature outside economics might better understand references encountered elsewhere in this volume, and to suggest useful readings for those interested in further exploration. The entry will describe three varieties of feminism – labelled 'liberal', 'socialist' and 'postmodernist' – that have influenced contemporary English-language feminist economics. The discussion will highlight the relevance for feminist economics of several important ongoing debates in feminist theory. The history and literature treated here will emanate mostly from the USA and Britain. In other locales, the debates among feminists may of course be very different; readers interested in 'Third World' feminist thought, for example, may wish to consult Marchand and Parpart (1995); Mohanty et al. (1991); Narayan (1997), and Sen and Grown (1987).

Liberal and socialist feminisms arose in the USA and Britain in the 1960s (liberal feminism was the more visible strain in the USA, and socialist feminism in Britain). Their differences were reflected in their analytical frameworks, their views on the dimensions and causes of women's oppression and their goals as activists.

Liberal feminism is characterized by its acceptance of the basic institutional structures of capitalism and representative democracy as seen in the industrialized West; its goal is to obtain 'equal rights' and 'equal opportunity' for women within those structures. Just as the 'first wave' feminists of the nineteenth century fought for women's rights to own property and to vote, 'second wave' liberal feminists campaign to end private-sector and governmental discrimination against women, so that women might have equal access to (and receive equal rewards for) education, employment and political participation.

Like their predecessors Mary Wollstonecraft (1792), Harriet Taylor Mill (1851) and John Stuart Mill (1869), contemporary liberal feminists argue that the rights upheld by classical liberalism must be extended to women as well as men. Women should be as able as men to pursue happiness and to fulfil their individual potential; this requires that women have as much freedom of choice as men. The book credited with galvanizing liberal feminism in the USA was Friedan (1963), which decried the confinement of women to marriage, motherhood and housework. Like Wollstonecraft and the Mills, Friedan argued that this confinement, by making women economically dependent on men and preventing them from fully developing their abilities, both harmed individual women and imposed costs on society in general.

To define liberal feminism by its aim of achieving gender equality within capitalism leaves room for disagreement about many issues. Two questions are particularly central to liberal feminist policy debates. The first concerns the extent to which state intervention on women's behalf is necessary and desirable. Liberal feminists might all agree, for example, that women are more vulnerable than men to poverty, but hold a range of views about how the state ought to respond. The second question – often referred to as the 'equality vs. difference' debate – concerns whether the achievement of gender equality requires that gender be ignored or that differences between women and men be taken into account (see Scott 1988; Williams 1982). The 'equality' argument is that gender should be irrelevant to the way individuals are treated by the law, employers, educators, and so on, and thus women should be treated just the same as men. The 'difference' side argues that if women are offered admission to the public sphere on the same terms as men, given that male-dominated occupations have been constructed for individuals who are not subject to pregnancy and who have little responsibility for child care and housework, access will remain *de facto* unequal. On this view, to give women an equal chance in the labour market might require providing gender-specific benefits such as pregnancy and maternity leave.

Thus it is not always obvious what must be done to remove gender-specific obstacles to women's participation (much depends, as will be discussed below, on one's views regarding the extent, mutability and desirability of gender differences). And the debates become even more complex when those are not the only obstacles women face. To focus only on gender-based disadvantages is in effect to argue that women should have the same opportunities as their brothers. This is less than adequate for addressing the situations of women who confront additional constraints linked to other aspects of social identity, such as race, class or nationality. Liberal thought can readily incorporate opposition to racial discrimination: the social order endorsed by liberalism is conceived as meritocratic, meaning that individuals' economic status should be determined primarily by ability and effort, not by irrelevant personal characteristics such as race and sex. But liberalism's acceptance of capitalist property rights and of the principle of market determination of incomes limits liberal feminists' ability to address inequalities associated with class. Similarly, liberal feminist efforts on behalf of women in the global South have tended to focus on 'integrating women into the mainstream of (capitalist) development', eschewing more wide-ranging challenges to intranational and international power relations (see Chowdhry 1995 and Sen and Grown 1987 for critiques).

Since it is unusual for feminists working within economics to explicitly identify the variety of feminism they espouse, and since individuals may support liberal feminist policy proposals while holding more radical views regarding ultimate goals, it is difficult to reliably classify feminist economists as 'liberal' or 'other'. It can be said, however, that much of the published writing of feminist economists, particularly writing within the neoclassical framework, is consistent with liberal feminist views (see, for example, Bergmann 1986). There is a certain philosophical congruence between liberal feminism and neoclassical economics: both focus on the autonomous individual, freedom of choice and of contract, rationality and voluntary interactions in markets. And economic analyses that emphasize the need for women to gain freer access to education and to labour and capital markets are well matched to liberal aims. This is not to suggest, of course, that neoclassical economics has been congenial to feminism: as many feminists have attested, quite the opposite has been true (Ferber and Teiman 1981; Pujol 1992; Bergmann 1987).

Socialist feminism arose in the late 1960s and early 1970s among women active in leftist, black civil rights, and antiwar movements in the USA and Britain. Socialist feminists saw themselves as part of a 'women's liberation' movement, in contrast to the 'women's rights' approach of liberal feminism. The liberation of women required not just the abolition of gender inequality, but much larger social transformations. In particular, in order to end inequality based on class, race and nationality, capitalism had to be replaced by socialism, institutions perpetuating racial dominance had to be dismantled, and the international power structure had to be radically reformed.

Socialist feminist analytical frameworks were to varying degrees modelled on the historical materialism of Marx and Engels, in which analysis begins from a society's material life (the activities of production and reproduction) rather than from its ideas. In such analyses, the source of gender inequality is not prejudice against women or the persistence of outmoded tradition (as often suggested by liberals), but the conflicting material interests created by a specific social structure.

Marx and Engels had provided some discussion of gender inequality in their writings (see Vogel 1983). In particular, Engels (1845) linked the subordination of women to the establishment of private property under men's control. Women's consequent economic dependence on men enabled men to benefit from women's labour and to restrict women's sexuality. Eliminating gender inequality would require the abolition of private property, women's full entry into the labour force and the socialization of domestic work. Although this analysis left many questions unanswered, few Marxists before the late 1960s had been interested enough in gender relations to build upon it.

Marxist–feminist writers extended the analysis by focusing on the gender division of labour and paying attention to reproductive as well as productive activities. They examined women's distinct roles as workers, seeking to explain more fully how women's subordination was functional for maintaining capitalism. For example, women's domestic labour was essential to the day-to-day maintenance of the working class and the production of the next generation of workers; and the fact that this domestic labour was unwaged helped to keep employers' labour costs lower than they would otherwise be. Women formed a 'reserve army of labour' that could be drawn into and ejected from employment according to changing capitalist needs. And the fact that women workers' wages were much lower than men's meant that women's market labour produced extra profit for capital.

It soon became apparent, however, that viewing gender inequality simply as an outgrowth of capitalism was inadequate. It could not explain the widespread gender inequality seen in noncapitalist societies; it neglected aspects of women's oppression that could not easily be related to the gender division of labour; and it ignored the ways in which the subordination of women benefited noncapitalist men. To address these problems, socialist feminists supplemented Marxist theory in a variety of ways. Rubin (1975) proposed that societies' 'sex-gender systems' (governing family relations, sexuality and gender ideology) required analysis separate from that of their economies. Mitchell (1974) argued that gender inequality was as much ideological as material in origin, and that feminists should build upon psychoanalytic theory to explain the formation of female and male personalities. Ferguson and Folbre (1981) defined and analysed a special category of work, 'sex-affective production', done mostly by women. A number of socialist–feminists (for example, Eisenstein 1979; Hartmann 1976; Rowbotham 1974) elaborated 'dual systems theories', which posited that capitalism and 'patriarchy' were separate and semi-autonomous systems of social dominance. The systems operated harmoniously in many ways, but could come into conflict in some times and places: for example, as more women were drawn into the labour market, benefiting capitalists, women's economic dependency on husbands declined, reducing husbands' patriarchal power.

Some writers have distinguished 'Marxist' from socialist feminism, using the former term for inquiry focused on the relationship of gender inequality to capitalism, and the latter for work that went far beyond orthodox Marxism to posit separate systemic forces creating male power and privilege. Since many of the key participants in the development of socialist feminism were economists, the history of socialist feminism is also part of the history of feminist economics. For example, Hartmann (1976, 1981a, 1981b) wrote some of the most influential early works on dual systems theory. Nancy Folbre explored the gender allocation of tasks and consumption within the household (Folbre 1982) and developed a theory of fertility decisions (Folbre 1983). Elson and Pearson (1981) analysed the growing employment of Third World women in manufacturing. Other participants in these early discussions who have continued to contribute to feminist economic scholarship include Lourdes Benería, Jean Gardiner, Susan Himmelweit, Jane Humphries, Maxine Molyneux and Gita Sen. It is unclear whether this strain of feminist theory should still be called 'socialist' feminism, given that advocacy of socialism has virtually disappeared from discussions of gender inequality. Several recent works within or about this body of thought (for example, Hennessy and Ingraham 1997) have proposed 'materialist feminism' as an alternative label.

Much early socialist feminist work, consistent with the Marxist methodological tradition, relied on structural–functional arguments, which show how dominant groups benefit from others' subordination without explaining just how individuals are induced to behave in the ways the structure requires. As socialist feminism developed further, theorists' attention turned to the construction of subjectivity, or how individual wants and beliefs are tailored to (and by) the social structure. Chodorow (1978) drew upon psychoanalytic theory to explain the formation of masculine and feminine personalities under the material conditions of women's primary responsibility for child care. The male child, she suggested, has to separate and distinguish himself from the mother much more sharply than does the female child; as a result, adult men tend to repress their relational needs and seek autonomy, while women tend to define and experience themselves in relationship with others. In another important contribution, Hartsock (1983) extended the Marxist idea of the determination of consciousness by material life to the notion of a 'feminist standpoint'. Because of the gender division of labour, women's daily lives differed dramatically from those of men. Women's experiences, Hartsock argued, offered distinct perceptions of the social world, from which a feminist understanding of gender relations could be developed (although for women to come to a feminist interpretation of their experience was by no means inevitable). This way of linking socially-differentiated experiences to individuals' 'knowledge' about the world came to be referred to as 'standpoint epistemology' (Harding 1986, 1991).

Chodorow's and Hartsock's writings, which were influential far beyond the community of socialist feminism, contributed to a growing body of feminist work that emphasized differences between women and men; this tendency was later dubbed 'difference' or 'gynocentric' feminism (Nicholson 1997). Feminist writers explored assertions that women and men differed in their 'ways of knowing' (Belenky et al. 1986), their patterns of moral reasoning (Gilligan 1982; Ruddick 1980), their relationships to the natural environment (Merchant 1980), and many other characteristics. In many cases, the argument was that attributes and attitudes associated with women had been unjustly devalued and that feminists should embrace and affirm rather than renounce them. These alleged gender differences were usually viewed as socially constructed rather than as strictly biologically determined and immutable; but while some writers clearly sought to have the devalued qualities adopted by men as well as women, others appeared content to have differences persist, so long as the 'female' characteristics received the respect they deserved.

Disagreements regarding the tractability and desirability of gender differences have continued to spark debate among feminists. In economics, many such debates centre on the gender division of labour. For example, does one view some women's full-time engagement in child care and work in the home as freely chosen or as coerced? Does one seek to have that occupation afforded greater respect and economic security, or to have it abolished, either by dividing the labour equally between women and men or by moving the work out of the home? Similarly, does one focus more on pay equity and comparable worth efforts that aim to raise wages in traditionally female occupations, or on affirmative action and other reforms that seek to make women's occupational distribution like that of men? 'Difference' arguments also appear in some feminist discussions of economic methodology (for example, England 1993; McCloskey 1993; Nelson 1992).

Debates over gender difference remain ubiquitous. In the 1980s, however, those who emphasized differences between women and men came increasingly under attack for their neglect of differences among women. The challenges came first from women of colour, lesbians, and others whose experiences and concerns had been poorly represented in feminist writing and activism. Additional blows were then inflicted by proponents of postmodernist or poststructuralist feminism.

While both liberal and socialist feminists frequently lamented the existence of racial inequality, race was rarely given very extensive attention in the feminist writing of the 1960s and 1970s, and feminists rarely inquired whether their statements about the lives of 'women' applied across racial/ethnic groups. Thus when feminists of colour (and a few white allies) began to write critiques of the racial/ethnic biases in US and British feminism (for example, Anthias and Yuval-Davis 1983; hooks 1981, 1984; Joseph 1981; Lorde 1984; Lugones and Spelman 1983; Moraga and Anzaldua 1983; Spelman 1988), all schools of thought were found wanting.

Just as men had often written of the 'human' in ways that really only referred to males, the white, mostly middle-class women who did most feminist writing through the 1970s tended (to varying degrees) to describe 'women' and gender relations by generalizing from their own experiences, failing to acknowledge that women of different classes and racial/ethnic communities often had sharply different experiences of gender. To define women's central problem as their confinement to the home, for example, failed to address the situations of most African-American women, who had high rates of labour force participation. Further, these other dimensions of identity were linked to a multitude of conflicts of interest among women, such as those between a low-wage worker and the affluent consumer of her product, or between the victim and the beneficiary of racial discrimination in hiring.

One response to these problems was 'identity politics', the idea that individuals should work with others 'like themselves' to articulate their particular perspectives and pursue their particular needs. Organizations were formed, and books and articles written, for example, on Black feminism (in addition to the works cited in the previous paragraph, see Collins 1990; hooks 1990; King 1988; Mirza 1997). Although such efforts yielded many fruits, the difficulties surrounding identity were far from resolved. A women's group based on ethnicity could still be fractured by differences of class, age and sexual orientation, for instance; and people with a shared social identity could nevertheless have very different interpretations of social reality. These issues would become central in discussions of postmodernist feminism.

Postmodernist feminism is the newest of the feminisms discussed here, and the one most closely identified with the world of the academy, where it arose in the 1980s and rapidly gained influence. The term 'postmodern' (which has been applied to trends in art and architecture and to alleged changes in the global economy as well as to arguments regarding social theory) is an unusually problematic one. It is often rejected by the very scholars whom others view as postmodernism's exemplars; and 'postmodernism' is often used (as it will be here) interchangeably with 'poststructuralism', which refers to a set of ideas drawn from the work of French philosophers and social theorists including Jacques Derrida, Michel Foucault, Jacques Lacan, Louis Althusser and Julia Kristeva.

Postmodernism/poststructuralism can perhaps better be characterized as an intellectual disposition than as a set of specific claims about the world (useful introductions include Dickens and Fontana 1994, Nicholson 1990 and Weedon 1996). Parpart and Marchand (1995, p. 2) describe postmodernism as 'an amalgam of often purposely ambiguous and fluid ideas'. Friedman (1998, p. 209) suggests that the 'poststructuralist imperative' is the demand, 'Always problematize'. Among the central ideas associated with postmodernist/ poststructuralist thought (including its feminist strands) are scepticism toward all truth claims; a view of identities as multiple and unstable; and a rejection of 'grand theories' of human history.

Regarding epistemology, postmodernists are 'antifoundationalist': they argue that rationality, philosophy and the practices of scholarly disciplines are unable to provide foundations that will assure the production of timeless and universal 'truth'. Rather, all knowers are socially situated, and all knowledge is necessarily partial and fallible. Since interpretations and beliefs have social effects, contention over knowledge has political dimensions.

Poststructuralists view language as not simply conveying meaning, but rather as creating it, particularly through the construction of binary oppositions such as culture/nature, objective/subjective, male/female, sex/gender.

Analysing and subverting – 'deconstructing' – these dualisms is a central tool of poststructuralist criticism.

Postmodernists/poststructuralists are severely critical of universalizing generalizations (such as statements about 'women') and tend to emphasize 'difference' (the diversity within all social groups) in the face of claims of commonality. This stance was influenced by earlier critiques of overgeneralization in feminist thought; but instead of embracing identity politics, postmodernist feminists question all such identities. Assertions about the experiences and interests of 'women' – including those advanced by feminists – are rejected as 'essentialist', that is, as falsely implying that there is some unvarying essence shared by all members of the group (see Fuss 1989; Riley 1988). Individual identity is seen as necessarily multiple, and as always in the process of construction: individuals constantly revise their ideas about identity in interaction with discourses surrounding them (Butler 1990). Which aspects of one's identity seem salient varies: one sees oneself at one moment as woman, at another as a rural dweller, or lesbian, or immigrant, and so on. The meanings ascribed to these identities change over time as well.

Finally, postmodernist/poststructuralist thought rejects grand theories about the nature of societies and meta-narratives about the course of human history (including the European Enlightenment's optimistic vision of the triumph of reason and the liberal and Marxist visions of social progress descended from it). False generalizations and mechanistic accounts of the workings of abstract social structures are to be avoided. Analyses should be disaggregated and localized in time and place. Rather than theorize about the primary cause of women's subordination, one might seek to explain, say, competing images of femininity in Indian cinema or discourse on sex and mental illness in mid nineteenth-century England.

Within feminist economics, postmodernist influence has been manifest in a number of ways: epistemological modesty sometimes explicitly grounded in poststructuralism (as in the works of Diana Strassmann); close critical attention to the ways in which meanings are created in economic 'texts' (Grapard 1995; Strassmann and Polanyi 1995); examination of the relationship between knowledge and power in the economics discipline (Strassmann 1993a, 1993b); and insistence that feminist economists pay more attention to 'difference' (Williams 1993). Hewitson (1999) offers a wide-ranging exploration of the relevance of poststructuralism to feminist economics, and shows how poststructural theory can illuminate policy debates.

Outside economics, the growing influence of postmodernism/poststructuralism has been associated with significant changes in (academic) feminist thought; there is a 'gulf between feminist theory of the 1970s and 1990s' (Barrett and Phillips 1992, p. 2). Feminist theorists now tend to focus less on 'material' relations and more on the construction of meanings in 'texts' or 'discourses'. Many writers are disinclined to use many of the central terms of earlier feminist writing – terms such as oppression, power, social structure, patriarchy, the state and sometimes even 'women'. There is less analysis of the accuracy or validity of claims, and more of their 'discursive effects'. These changes are the subject of intense controversy (see Friedman 1998; Marchand and Parpart 1995; Nicholson 1990). Some feminists see them as necessary correctives to earlier oversimplifications. Others (for example, Alcoff 1988) express concern that the changes may have disempowering effects on both feminist inquiry and feminist activism. How, for example, can feminists make political demands in the name of women if the category 'women' is held to be illegitimate because there is no important shared experience or attribute by which 'women' can be defined? And if all knowledge is perspectival and partial, what hope can feminist scholars have that their research may persuade nonfeminists?

Postmodernist/poststructuralist feminism clearly poses enormous challenges to liberal and socialist feminisms. Perhaps the most profound of these, from the point of view of feminist economics, is the problematization of individuals' identities and interests, which economic analyses typically take as a starting point. Liberal feminism, like liberalism more broadly, posits individuals with given, presumably coherent, sets of beliefs and desires (the origins of which are rarely addressed); and socialist feminism, like Marxism, posits 'objective' interests determined by individuals' positions in the social structure (allowing that the 'subjective' recognition of these interests may require effort). If, as poststructuralists argue, the identity of every 'subject' is multiple and always changing, this raises important questions for feminist economists. First, on this view, neoclassical notions of 'preferences' and 'rationality' seem distinctly naive. An individual's wants may be both inconsistent and unstable, violating the fundamental neoclassical assumptions regarding preference-orderings that underpin optimization modelling. Further, even if individuals' preferences are consistent and stable, if subjectivity is socially constructed, then one must ask, what is the relationship between what people want (or choose) and their genuine wellbeing? On what basis can economists make judgments about economic welfare, if people's own choices are imperfect guides? Finally, if each individual has many identities, and the perceived salience of each is continually changing, what does this mean for people's perceptions of their interests and for the possibility of collective action? While these questions themselves are far from new to economics, their reiteration by economists influenced by poststructuralism may cause them at last to receive wider discussion.

To peruse this volume is to be made aware of the huge array of problems that feminist economists are urgently seeking to address. How are (diverse) women (diversely) affected by the shifts of financial and industrial capital associated with 'globalization'? What does the transition to capitalism in the former Soviet bloc mean for (different) women? Can the attacks on the welfare state in the industrialized countries be reversed? To answer such questions effectively, feminist economists (whether liberal, socialist, poststructuralist or other in orientation) will have to address both 'material interests' and the realms of 'culture' and 'ideology' in which those interests are defined and contested. Feminist economics must avoid both the extremes of 'the problematic essentialism of a universalized feminism' and 'a politically empty social constructionism which dissolves any notion of commonality in the acid bath of difference' (Pearson and Jackson 1998, p. 6). The philosophical and methodological issues associated with poststructuralist challenges to liberal and socialist feminism are being grappled with by feminists in all branches of the humanities and social sciences. One may hope that feminist economists will both benefit from and contribute to these important debates.

JANET A. SEIZ

See also
Capitalism; Class; Dualisms; Feminist Economics; Gender; Marxist Political Economics; Methodology; Patriarchy; Postmodernism; Race; Sexual Orientation; Socialism.

Bibliography

Alcoff, Linda (1988), 'Cultural feminism versus poststructuralism: The identity crisis in feminist theory', *Signs*, **13** (3), 405–36. Reprinted in Nicholson (1997).

Anthias, Floya and Niva Yuval-Davis (1983), 'Contextualizing feminism – gender, ethnic and class divisions', *Feminist Review*, **15**. Reprinted in Terry Lovell (ed.) (1990), *British Feminist Thought: A Reader*, Oxford, UK and Cambridge, Massachusetts: Basil Blackwell.

Barrett, Michèle (1988), *Women's Oppression Today: The Marxist/Feminist Encounter*, revised edition, New York and London: Verso Books.

Barrett, Michèle and Anne Phillips (1992), *Destabilizing Theory: Contemporary Feminist Debates*, Stanford, California: Stanford University Press.

Belenky, Mary Field, Blythe McVicker Clinchy, Nancy Rule Goldberger and Jill Mattuck Tarule (1986), *Women's Ways of Knowing*, New York: Basic Books.

Bergmann, Barbara R. (1986), *The Economic Emergence of Women*, New York: Basic Books.

Bergmann, Barbara R. (1987), 'The Task of a Feminist Economics: A More Equitable Future', in Christie Farnham (ed.), *The Impact of Feminist Research in the Academy*, Bloomington: Indiana University Press.

Butler, Judith (1990), *Gender Trouble: Feminism and the Subversion of Identity*, London and New York: Routledge.

Chodorow, Nancy (1978), *The Reproduction of Mothering: Psychoanalysis and the Sociology of Gender*, Berkeley: University of California Press.

Chowdhry, Geeta (1995), 'Engendering Development? Women in Development (WID) in International Development Regimes', in Marianne H. Marchand and Jane L. Parpart (eds), *Feminism/Postmodernism/Development*, New York and London: Routledge.

Collins, Patricia Hill (1990), *Black Feminist Thought: Knowledge, Consciousness and the Politics of Empowerment*, Boston: Unwin Hyman.

Dickens, David R. and Andrea Fontana (eds) (1994), *Postmodernism and Social Inquiry*, New York and London: Guilford.

Eisenstein, Zillah (ed.) (1979), *Capitalist Patriarchy and the Case for Socialist Feminism*, New York: Monthly Review Press.

Eisenstein, Zillah (1986), *The Radical Future of Liberal Feminism*, New York: Monthly Review Press.

Elson, Diane and Ruth Pearson (1981), 'Nimble fingers make cheap workers', *Feminist Review*, **7**, 87–107.

Engels, Friedrich (1845), *The Origin of the Family, Private Property and the State*, Reprinted (1972), New York: International Publishers.

England, Paula (1993), 'The Separative Self: Androcentric Bias in Neoclassical Assumptions', in Marianne Ferber and Julie A. Nelson (eds), *Beyond Economic Man: Feminist Theory and Economics*, Chicago and London: University of Chicago Press.

Ferber, Marianne A. and Michelle L. Teiman (1981), 'The Oldest, the Most Established, the Most Quantitative of the Social Sciences – and the Most Dominated by Men: The Impact of Feminism on Economics', in Dale Spender (ed.), *Men's Studies Modified: The Impact of Feminism on the Academic Disciplines*, New York: Pergamon Press.

Ferguson, Ann and Nancy Folbre (1981), 'The Unhappy Marriage of Patriarchy and Capitalism', in Lydia Sargent (ed.), *Women and Revolution: A Discussion of the Unhappy Marriage of Marxism and Feminism*, Boston: South End Press.

Folbre, Nancy (1982), 'Exploitation comes home: a critique of the Marxian theory of family labor', *Cambridge Journal of Economics*, **6** (4), 317–29.

Folbre, Nancy (1983), 'Of patriarchy born: The political economy of fertility decisions', *Feminist Studies*, **9** (3), 269–84.

Folbre, Nancy (1994), *Who Pays for the Kids? Gender and the Structures of Constraint*. London and New York: Routledge.

Friedan, Betty (1963), *The Feminine Mystique*, New York: W.W. Norton.

Friedman, Susan Stanford (1998), *Mappings: Feminism and the Cultural Geographies of Encounter*, Princeton, New Jersey: Princeton University Press.

Fuss, Diana (1989), *Essentially Speaking: Feminism, Nature, and Difference*, London and New York: Routledge.

Gilligan, Carol (1982), *In a Different Voice: Psychological Theory and Women's Development*, Cambridge: Harvard University Press.

Grapard, Ulla (1995), 'Robinson Crusoe: the quintessential economic man?', *Feminist Economics*, **1** (1), 33–52.

Harding, Sandra (1986), *The Science Question in Feminism*, Ithaca New York: Cornell University Press.

Harding, Sandra (1991), *Whose Science? Whose Knowledge? Thinking from Women's Lives*, Ithaca, New York: Cornell University Press.

Hartmann, Heidi (1976), 'Capitalism, patriarchy, and job segregation by sex', *Signs* **1** (3, pt 2), 137–69. Reprinted in Karen V. Hansen and Ilene J. Philipson (eds) (1990), *Women, Class and the Feminist Imagination: A Socialist Feminist Reader*, Philadelphia: Temple University Press.

Hartmann, Heidi (1981a), 'The Unhappy Marriage of Marxism and Feminism: Toward a More Progressive Union', in Lydia Sargent (ed.), *Women and Revolution: A Discussion of the Unhappy Marriage of Marxism and Feminism*, Boston: South End Press. Reprinted in Nicholson (1997).

Hartmann, Heidi (1981b), 'The family as the locus of gender, class and political struggle: the example of housework', *Signs*, **6** (3), 366–94.

Hartsock, Nancy (1983), 'The Feminist Standpoint: Developing a Grounding for a Specifically Feminist Historical Materialism', in Sandra Harding and M. Hintikka (eds), *Discovering Reality: Feminist Perspectives on Epistemology, Metaphysics, Methodology and Philosophy of Science*, Boston and Dordrecht: D. Reidel. Reprinted in Meyers (1997) and Nicholson (1997).

Hennessy, Rosemary and Chrys Ingraham (eds) (1997), *Materialist Feminism: A Reader in Class, Difference and Women's Lives*, London and New York: Routledge.

Hewitson, Gillian (1999), *Feminist Economics: Interrogating the Masculinity of Rational Economic Man*, Northampton, MA, and Cheltenham, UK: Edward Elgar.

hooks, bell (1981), *Ain't I a Woman*, Boston: South End Press.

hooks, bell (1984), *Feminist Theory: From Margin to Center*, Boston: South End Press.

hooks, bell (1990), *Yearning: Race, Gender and Cultural Politics*, Boston: South End Press.

Jaggar, Alison M. (1983), *Feminist Politics and Human Nature*, Totowa, New Jersey: Rowman and Allenheld.

Joseph, Gloria (1981), 'The Incompatible Menage a Trois: Marxism, Feminism, and Racism', in Lydia Sargent (ed.), *Women and Revolution: A Discussion of the Unhappy Marriage of Marxism and Feminism*, Boston: South End Press.

King, Deborah K. (1988), 'Multiple jeopardy, multiple consciousness: the context of black feminist ideology', *Signs*, **14** (1), 42–72. Reprinted in Meyers (1997).

Lorde, Audre (1984), *Sister Outsider*, Trumansburg, New York: Crossing Press.

Lugones, Maria C. and Elizabeth V. Spelman (1983), 'Have we got a theory for you! Feminist theory, cultural imperialism and the demand for "The Woman's Voice"', *Women's Studies International Forum*, **6** (6), 573–81.

Marchand, Marianne H. and Jane L. Parpart (eds) (1995), *Feminism/Postmodernism/Development*, New York and London: Routledge.

Matthaei, Julie (1996), 'Why feminist, Marxist, and anti-racist economists should be feminist–Marxist–anti-racist economists', *Feminist Economics*, **2** (1), 22–42.

McCloskey, Donald [now Deirdre] N. (1993), 'Some Consequences of a Conjective Economics', in Marianne Ferber and Julie A. Nelson (eds), *Beyond Economic Man: Feminist Theory and Economics*. Chicago and London: University of Chicago Press.

Merchant, Carolyn (1980), *The Death of Nature: Women, Ecology and the Scientific Revolution*, San Francisco: Harper and Row.

Meyers, Diana Tietjens (ed.) (1997), *Feminist Social Thought: A Reader*, New York and London: Routledge.

Mill, Harriet Taylor (1851), 'The Enfranchisement of Women', reprinted in Ann P. Robson and John M. Robson (eds) (1994), *Sexual Equality: Writings by John Stuart Mill, Harriet Taylor Mill, and Helen Taylor*, Toronto: University of Toronto Press.

Mill, John Stuart (1869), 'The Subjection of Women', reprinted in Ann P. Robson and John M. Robson (eds) (1994), *Sexual Equality: Writings by John Stuart Mill, Harriet Taylor Mill, and Helen Taylor*, Toronto: University of Toronto Press.

Mirza, Heidi Safia (ed.) (1997), *Black British Feminism: A Reader*, London and New York: Routledge.

Mitchell, Juliet (1974), *Psychoanalysis and Feminism*, New York: Pantheon Books.

Mohanty, Chandra Talpede, Ann Russo and Lourdes Torres (eds) (1991), *Third World Women and the Politics of Feminism*, Bloomington: University of Indiana Press.

Moraga, Cherrie and Gloria Anzaldua (eds) (1983), *This Bridge Called My Back: Writings by Radical Women of Color*, Second edition, New York: Kitchen Table Press.

Narayan, Uma (1997), 'Contesting Cultures: "Westernization", Respect for Cultures, and Third World Feminists', in Linda Nicholson (ed.), *The Second Wave: A Reader in Feminist Theory*, New York and London: Routledge.

Nelson, Julie A. (1992), 'Gender, metaphor and the definition of economics', *Economics and Philosophy*, **8** (1), 103–25.

Nicholson, Linda J. (ed.) (1990), *Feminism/Postmodernism*, London and New York: Routledge.

Nicholson, Linda J. (ed.) (1997), *The Second Wave: A Reader in Feminist Theory*, London and New York: Routledge.

Parpart, Jane L. and Marianne H. Marchand (1995), 'Exploding the Canon: An Introduction/Conclusion', in Marianne H. Marchand and Jane L. Parpart (eds), *Feminism/Postmodernism/Development*, New York and London: Routledge.

Pearson, Ruth and Cecile Jackson (1998), 'Introduction: Interrogating Development: Feminism, Gender and Policy', in Cecile Jackson and Ruth Pearson (eds), *Feminist Visions of Development: Gender Analsysis and Policy*, London and New York: Routledge.

Pujol, Michele A. (1992), *Feminism and Anti-Feminism in Early Economic Thought*, Brookfield, Vermont and Aldershot: Edward Elgar.

Riley, Denise (1988), *Am I That Name? Feminism and the Category of 'Women' in History*, Minneapolis: University of Minnesota Press.

Rowbotham, Sheila (1974), *Woman's Consciousness, Man's World*, Baltimore, Maryland: Penguin Books.

Rubin, Gayle (1975), 'The Traffic in Women: Notes on the "Political Economy" of Sex', in Rayna Rapp Reiter (ed.), *Toward An Anthropology of Women*, New York: Monthly Review Press. Reprinted in Karen V. Hansen and Ilene J. Philipson (eds) (1990), *Women, Class and the Feminist Imagination: A Socialist Feminist Reader*, Philadelphia: Temple University Press, and in Nicholson (1997).

Ruddick, Sara (1980), 'Maternal thinking', *Feminist Studies*, **6** (2), 342–67. Reprinted in Meyers (1997).

Scott, Joan W. (1988), 'Deconstructing equality-versus-difference: or the uses of poststructuralist theory for feminism', *Feminist Studies*, **14** (1), 35–50. Reprinted in Meyers (1997).

Sen, Gita and Caren Grown (1987), *Development, Crises, and Alternative Visions: Third World Women's Perspectives*, New York: Monthly Review Press.

Spelman, Elizabeth V. (1988), *Inessential Woman: Problems of Exclusion in Feminist Thought*, Boston: Beacon Press.

Strassmann, Diana (1993a), 'The stories of economics and the power of the storyteller', *History of Political Economy*, **25** (1): 147–65.

Strassmann, Diana (1993b), 'Not a Free Market: The Rhetoric of Disciplinary Authority in Economics', in Marianne Ferber and Julie A. Nelson (eds), *Beyond Economic Man: Feminist Theory and Economics*, Chicago and London: University of Chicago Press.

Strassmann, Diana and Livia Polanyi (1995), 'The Economist as Storyteller: What the Texts Reveal', in Edith Kuiper and Jolande Sap (eds), *Out of the Margin: Feminist Perspectives on Economics*, London and New York: Routledge.

Tong, Rosemarie Putnam (1998), *Feminist Thought: A More Comprehensive Introduction*, Second edition, Boulder, Colorado and Oxford: Westview Press.

Vogel, Lise (1983), *Marxism and the Oppression of Women: Towards a Unitary Theory*, New Brunswick, New Jersey: Rutgers University Press.

Weedon, Chris (1996), *Feminist Practice and Poststructuralist Theory*, Second edition, New York and Oxford: Basil Blackwell.

Williams, Rhonda M. (1993), 'Race, Deconstruction, and the Emergent Agenda of Feminist Economic Theory', in Marianne Ferber and Julie A. Nelson (eds), *Beyond Economic Man: Feminist Theory and Economics*, Chicago and London: University of Chicago Press.

Williams, Wendy W. (1982), 'The equality crisis: some reflections on culture, courts and feminism', *Women's Rights Law Reporter*, **175**, 15–34. Reprinted in Meyers (1997) and Nicholson (1997).

Wollstonecraft, Mary (1792), *A Vindication of the Rights of Women*. Reprinted (1975), New York: W.W. Norton.

Feminist Economics

Feminist economic research has a long history, but has only recently gained recognition as a distinct set of new perspectives. Perhaps the most revolutionary aspect of contemporary feminist economics is its contesting of the purpose of economic inquiry: to whom is economic thought accountable and how can it help human lives? By and large feminist economists hold economic thought to a standard that requires it to be more responsive to the needs and well-being of women and their families. In seeking to further such inquiry, feminist economists have also sought to understand and to challenge disciplinary resistances to feminist thought. Such efforts have led feminist economists to consider the underlying intellectual and institutional dynamics of economics.

They have also endeavoured to change the institutional forms that have marginalized feminist economic thought since its earliest beginnings. This entry describes some major themes of recent feminist economic research.

As more women entered the economics profession during the 1960s and later, they began to uncover flaws in economic accounts produced almost solely by men, flaws that could be identified without abandoning either mainstream theory or methods. Drawing from women's lives and supporting their models with detailed empirical studies, these scholars have shown how many well-accepted models or 'stylized facts' have been based on stereotypical assumptions about gender. Much of this work has enhanced the rigour of mainstream economic thought by raising neglected concerns and by showing the inadequacy of accepted economic accounts, particularly those built on uninvestigated assumptions. Until the 1960s, for example, the issue of 'female labour supply' was scarcely addressed, as most economists had assumed that women did not 'work'.

Important research by mainstream feminist economists has led to better economic understanding of many subjects, principally in labour economics. Occupational segregation, employment discrimination and the gender wage gap are among the many areas where women economists have contributed to reducing gender bias in mainstream economic knowledge. Madden (1973), for example, showed how the potential for monopsonistic discrimination could adversely affect the pay of women in certain markets. Similarly, Myra Strober showed how men's behaviour and power relations between women and men could be key factors in causing occupational segregation; her work disputes earlier theories that attributed occupational segregation to women's choices alone (Strober 1984; Strober and Catanzarite 1994). More recently, Blau and Kahn (1994) demonstrated how claimed differences between male and female quit rates fail to hold up when the level of pay is controlled; they concluded that the presumed evidence of women's greater propensity to quit any job is simply an artifact of women's lower average pay. (See Blau et al. 1998, and Jacobsen 1998 for extensive further references to such contributions.)

While many feminist scholars agree that mainstream economics can be improved, a growing number seek more than mere revisions. These researchers feel that flaws in the core conceptual categories of the mainstream paradigm prohibit adequate explanations of a wide range of economic phenomena. (For examples, see the many papers in Ferber and Nelson (eds) 1993; Kuiper and Sap et al. (eds) 1995.) For these scholars, the issue is not whether some phenomena could be worked into a reformulated mainstream model; improvements to mainstream models have addressed some feminist concerns. Rather, they perceive that, in general, mainstream accounts are inherently more limited than alternative explanatory approaches in their capacity to explain some key phenomena.

While other empirically-oriented disciplines, such as the physical and biological sciences, have tended to define themselves around an empirical domain to be understood, mainstream economists have increasingly identified 'economics' as an explanatory approach. An 'economic' theory, according to the received mainstream view, is one that is built on the core concepts identified as the discipline's 'microfoundations'. Prominent among these microfoundations are the core concepts of self-interested individualism, contractual exchange and constrained optimization. The explanatory approach built on these and other core concepts constitutes the central paradigm of late twentieth-century economic theorizing. (See Strassmann 1993a for a more elaborated discussion of these points.)

The conceptual framework of the paradigm is centred on the autonomous agent: able-bodied, in control, independent, rational and heterosexual – a self-contained adult able to choose from an array of options, limited only by untheorized constraints. This agent's identity and behaviour, particularly his assumed independence, adulthood and ability to make choices, underlie many key features of mainstream models and imply other less obvious assumptions. The assumption of individual autonomy, for example, directs attention away from the connectedness of human life and the complexities of interdependent relationships. Further, the notion of people as independent agents and unique selves, responsible for only their own needs, reflects a disproportionately male, adult and privileged world view. A theoretical structure built on the experience of independent adults ignores the limited autonomy of children, the elderly and the infirm, as well as others who critically depend on the decisions of others. (For more discussion, see Nelson 1992; England 1993; Strassmann 1993a.)

Many feminist economists believe that this framework poorly characterizes the lives of those whose economic circumstances are more distinctly structured by factors beyond their personal control, and hides the fact that many people have little opportunity to self-determine their lives through making 'choices' (Strassmann 1993a; Folbre 1994). Further, the assumption of rational decision making is hardly apt for choices that are not characterized by rational exchange, such as those prompted by violence and coercion or decisions made under the influence of drugs or alcohol. (See Christensen 1998 for an in-depth discussion of this point.)

But more subtly, and perhaps more importantly, the emphasis on choice rather than on the conditions that critically underlie choices misleads by giving the impression that outcomes may be adequately understood without theorizing key structural circumstances. While mainstream economists commonly include certain types of structural features in their models, particularly those they view as 'economic', they have paid little theoretical attention to factors that do not cohere well with the microfoundational framework or that are difficult to incorporate into formal models. Mainstream economists typically dismiss these factors as outside the purview of the field.

The requirement that 'economic' analyses be built on the microfoundational concepts of the disciplinary paradigm has led mainstream practitioners to conclude that research oriented towards retheorizing the paradigm cannot be 'economics', or that theory built with words cannot be 'theory'. According to the mainstream view, 'legitimate' economic theory must take a form, expressed in both microfoundational assumptions and mathematical language, that mainstream economists consider a defining feature of theory (Strassmann 1994; Humphries 1995). Further, defining economics as an explanatory approach precludes the possibility of theorizing subjects that are not clearly explicable through the central disciplinary paradigm. For example, how cultural perceptions and social norms influence economic life is rarely treated as a central feature of mainstream economic investigation; these subjects are more likely to be relegated to the realm of 'constraints' or 'exogenous factors'. And yet, as feminist economists have shown, some decisions, such as whether to take on more work as a single parent or whether to breastfeed an infant, are intensely influenced by social and cultural factors, norms that are often embedded in workplace and other institutional structures.

Duncan and Edwards (1997), for example, show how the likelihood that single British mothers will take on market work is influenced far more by cultural factors, such as the moral context in which these mothers consider market work, than by such 'economic' factors as levels of human capital and policy constraints. Similarly, Galtry (1997), demonstrates that, contrary to cultural perceptions of breastfeeding as an individual choice, breastfeeding norms embedded in workplace structures prohibit breastfeeding as a realistic choice for many mothers, to the detriment of children's health. Disagreeing with the economic view that cultural factors should be treated as exogenous, Agarwal (1997) explains how social norms and social perceptions are interlinked with the market, the community and the state. She argues persuasively that those who hold greater social, familial and economic power decisively influence the social norms and social perceptions that prevail in any given setting. Consistent with Agarwal's insights, other feminists show how standard economics teaching materials are infused with the privileged perspectives of dominant economic practitioners (Feiner and Roberts 1990; Strassmann and Polanyi, 1995a).

Further, some feminist scholars have shown how the exclusion of non Western voices from participation in the construction of much economic theory has led to theories that claim a false universality for Western economic phenomena. For example, while most mainstream economic models treat income as the primary determinant of economic well-being, property and land rights are far more important than income as determinants of well-being in

South Asia (Agarwal 1994). Moreover, women's lack of land rights in this part of the world has been a key source of gender inequality and a barrier to women's well-being. Since many development policies do not consider the economic role of land rights and, more generally, fail to consider gender in development planning, many policies have been biased and less effective (Elson 1991; Agarwal 1995).

These and other feminist economic insights show how the pervasive requirement that legitimate 'economics' research cohere with the microfoundational paradigm narrowly limits the range of acceptable economic theories, and provides unsatisfactory explanations of women's economic status. As feminist economists have begun to reconstruct economics into a discipline more accountable to the well-being of all people, they have begun to contest a disciplinary definition that so adversely restricts economic theorizing.

More generally, models that begin with a presumption of human equality in resources and choices distort through failing to recognize the wide variety of important influences on women's lives. These include gendered social norms, cultural prohibitions on women's full participation in economic life, inequitable treatment of reproductive issues, power imbalances in relationships, coercion and threatened violence, gendered legal and social institutions and discrimination of various sorts. (See, for example, Benería 1979, 1995; Bergmann 1986; Agarwal 1994; Hopkins 1995; Trzcinski 1995). By denying alternative approaches status as legitimate economic inquiry, the discipline shields itself from potentially transformative critiques and reconstructions.

Further, the conceptual hierarchy of the microfoundational paradigm de-emphasizes issues of particular importance to women. The result is that many subjects especially salient for women have been seriously neglected in economic analyses. The neglected subjects disproportionately reflect aspects of economic life in which the traditional core conceptual categories obscure critical features of economic life, as elaborated in the following sections. Many feminist economists therefore feel that serious analysis of economic phenomena requires conceptual approaches that go beyond foundational assumptions.

In calling for a body of knowledge more accountable to the diversity of human lives, some feminist economists have sought to reorient the field to answer questions of more immediate importance to broader populations. How to provide for human needs, for example, is a more compelling question to the hungry than how to understand human wants and choices (Sen 1984; Nelson 1993; Renwick and Bergmann 1993). Similarly, efforts to assess human well-being may be more useful to many than simple measures of productive output. More generally, however, permitting discussions of disciplinary goals requires reconceptualizing the field beyond approaches made possible through the microfoundational framework.

Some of the most important theoretical innovations of feminist economic research challenge the traditional economic conceptual categories of selfhood, agency, family and work. In so doing, this work deconstructs the presumed correspondence between market and social values and retheorizes economic life in consideration of neglected diverse influences on women's economic outcomes.

In taking on the implications of human interdependencies for economic behaviour, feminist economic scholars have begun to explore the consequences for economic theory of alternative concepts of being – what it means to be living in relation to others – as well as new ways of thinking about the discipline's existing models of familial and sexual interrelationships. Related to this work is the recognition that familial and other interpersonal relationships are themselves often built upon and supported through specific valuable activities, such as taking care of family material and emotional needs. Because of their nonmarketed status, however, these activities have been undervalued by economists and more generally by patriarchal societies in which men have more power in incorporating social values into institutional structures. (See, for example, Agarwal 1995; Folbre 1995; Himmelweit 1995.)

Feminist inquiry into assumptions about selfhood and the nature of 'being' begins with recognizing that humans do not begin life as fully autonomous and independent adults. Humans instead start life as infants, completely dependent on nurturance from others. Deconstructions of the separative economic 'self' have led to models of humans as relational beings, giving primacy to core human relationships, such as the parent–child bond and the family, and explorations of human domesticity, sexuality and reproductive life (Hartsock 1983; Held 1990; Kondo 1990). New understandings of being more generally recognize a diversity of human actors in economic theories, including women and children and people with different sexualities, as well as the influence of cultural norms and intrasocietal positioning on perceptions of selfhood and being.

Reproductive life, ignored by a framework in which humans emerge as fully formed adults, is also a growing area of feminist economic inquiry. Recent research includes economic studies of breastfeeding, family planning, abortion, surrogate parenthood, infertility, neonatal death and prostitution (see Smythe 1996; Galtry 1997; and Hewitson 1999 for examples). Related work examines the influence of reproductive life on economic outcomes through the mediating influences of social norms and legal and political institutions. These studies explore how policies towards maternity, family leave and child care interact with specific business practices to affect women's relative success in the paid labour force. (See, for example, Duggan 1995; Bergmann 1997; Rubery et al. 1998.) Among many questions, they ask: how do institutions, cultural norms and business practices influence women's workplace decisions? How do expectations about the appropriate gender division of housework and cooking, or the perceived legitimacy of mothers' taking on marketed work, influence women's position in the marketplace?

In considering the implications of human interdependencies, feminist economists have also explored the consequences of how people spend their time. More specifically, they have asked: what are the consequences of human activities that support human relationships, and how should these be theorized in relation to other economic activities? (For more discussion, see Floro 1995 and Himmelweit 1995.)

Supportive activities can take many forms: attending to emotional needs, breastfeeding, child care, elder care, cooking, gathering firewood, coordinating the satisfaction of family needs, and so forth. These activities are regarded in many (perhaps all) cultures as less valuable than activities that produce money income. Within families, money income is often viewed as more valuable than unpaid family supportive activities, even when money income is not spent on family needs (Elson 1991; Agarwal 1997).

Despite initiatives to understand unpaid work in disciplinary subfields such as development and public economics, core economic theories as yet fail to incorporate the insights of this scholarship. While sometimes mentioned in passing, productive unpaid work is rarely substantively incorporated into major economic models and policy measures, despite research showing that such omissions are by no means benign. Economic analyses that fail to consider divergences between social and market values distort through undervaluing work where pay has been suppressed through discrimination or through lack of alternative employment options; by placing no value on unpaid work; and by failing to recognize that people who participate in markets may not altruistically represent the wishes of their dependants. (See Sen 1984; Waring 1988; Wagman and Folbre 1996 for more extensive discussion of the above points.)

A growing body of feminist research addresses such related issues as the consequences of undervaluing women's marketed work and of excluding nonmarketed work from assessments of national output and in specific policy analyses. Feminist economic research is also exploring what methods might be used to include unpaid household work into measures of output, in estimating income distribution, in considering the time intensity of work, and for assessing the production of household human capital. (The essays in the 1996 special issue of *Feminist Economics* on unpaid work, guest-edited by Folbre and Pujol, extensively discuss these points.) Efforts to retheorize work also address many neglected concerns relating to women's experience of market employment. For example, do employment and government policy practices recognize differences between women's and men's bodies and lives, or does the

configuration of the workplace directly influence women's relative opportunities? (For more discussion, see Bergmann 1997; Colander and Woos 1997.)

Economists have been slow to consider that human interactions need not
be production oriented to enhance wellbeing, a fact long recognized by
noneconomists and economic anthropologists (Sahlins 1972; Gagnier and
Dupré 1995). While insisting on the productivity of many unpaid activities,
feminists have also been quick to emphasize that economics should focus on
overall wellbeing, since increases in aggregate wellbeing do not always go
hand in hand with greater output. (See, for example, the special explorations
in *Feminist Economics*, guest-edited by Aslaksen and Koren (1999) on
quality-of-life indicators.) Moreover, the distribution of wellbeing within a
society (women compared with men, children compared with adults, some
ethnicities compared with others, and so forth) may be very unequal. The
failure to count nonmarketed activities as work, or to consider the role of
such factors as time intensity, has obscured the greater work burden that large
numbers of women endure relative to men (Floro 1995). Developing better
assessments of total wellbeing and the relative wellbeings of specific groups
is a feminist economic research priority. Further, feminists have critiqued the
tendency in dominant economic writings to assume that all families can
obtain a minimally satisfactory level of well-being through rational optimization (Strassmann and Polanyi 1995a).

Closely connected with rethinking selfhood and being is a recognition of
the heterogeneity of human relations. Mainstream economic views of the
family parallel the heterosexual, consensual marital arrangements that characterize the domestic lives of most American economists. Mainstream
approaches have taken two general forms: first, the family as economic agent,
characterized internally by cooperation and altruism, and second, the family
as bargaining game in which spouses are presumed to stay together only
through mutual consent. (See Ott 1995 for a review of these approaches.)

Feminist economists have argued that formal models of the family are deeply
inadequate for a variety of reasons. First, they capture only a very narrow slice
of human domestic and sexual arrangements. Absent are non-marital heterosexual relationships, non-sexual shared living arrangements, lesbian and gay
relationships. Formal models also fail to problematize consent in cases with
dramatic differences in bargaining power. (See Seiz 1991; Badgett 1995; Agarwal
1997; Katz 1997; and Christensen 1998 for more discussion.) Until the advent
of feminist inquiry, the issue of bargaining power and the consequences of the
two players having widely unequal initial starting positions were barely addressed in explanatory models and led to little acknowledgement of the potential
for exploitative sexual and domestic relationships.

Sexuality in mainstream economic models is implicitly treated as confined
to consensual heterosexual relations, with a resounding silence on how un-

equal initial situations, including overwhelming social constraint, coercion and poverty may lead some to tolerate abusive and exploitative relationships as an alternative to financial or employment jeopardy. The trading of domestic and sexual services for financial support – by no means limited to prostitution – is left out of most analyses of the family. More generally, the 'economics of the family' ignores relations induced or maintained through financial need, sexual harassment, fear of physical abuse, or the explicit trading of embodied sexual or domestic labour for financial support, as in concubinage or prostitution, both of which were particularly prevalent during colonialism, and whose legacy remains (Stoler 1991). While not perhaps characteristic of the sexual and domestic experience of American male economists, substantial differences in relational bargaining power are an important feature of the economic landscape for many women.

Explorations of family decision making that fail to acknowledge the significance of differences in bargaining situation therefore fail to capture some of the most important influences on final outcomes. Recent feminist economic research explores the consequences of inequality in domestic and sexual relations, including the potential for coercion and violence, possibilities ignored in a choice-centred framework. As Agarwal (1997) has argued, women's inequality in family bargaining is not an independent phenomenon, but is integrally linked to women's unequal social status in societies at large.

In calling for an economics more responsive to the voices of women and other disempowered groups, feminist economists have sought to understand how feminist voices have been kept out, whether through institutional barriers or through intellectual restrictions that have limited the scope and nature of economic theorizing. The fields of history of thought, economic education and methodology have therefore risen to greater prominence in feminist economic inquiry than is the case for the discipline more generally.

As part of such research, feminist scholars have shown how important work by women, present in economics since its beginnings, has been lost, ignored or relegated to other disciplines (Pujol 1992). In so doing, they have also attempted to demonstrate how the neglect or exclusion of the work of women scholars may have been facilitated by institutional developments in the field, such as the exclusion of 'home economics' from economics (Folbre 1991) or the prejudicial treatment of women economists, as manifested in biased disciplinary conventions in publication, employment and promotion practices (Ferber and Teiman 1981). Other feminist economists have traced Western and masculinist biases in economics through their implementation into the methodological and rhetorical norms of the field (Strassmann 1993a; Weintraub (ed.) 1993; Williams 1993; Grapard 1995).

In attempting to understand the neglect of important women's ideas and the more general proscription of feminist insight, feminist economic scholars have sought to probe more deeply into how ideas are sorted and preferred in the discipline. The conventional modernist view is that proper scientific methods are the key to objective research and that the identity of the researcher should be irrelevant to properly conducted scholarship. This understanding of the research process is disputed by feminists and scholars in other fields (cultural studies, social studies of science, philosophy of science), who do not accept that it is possible for research to be so completely detached from the context of its production (Harding 1986; Traweek 1988). Helen Longino, for example, has argued that the social context in which knowledge is produced renders it vulnerable to the influence of social values (Longino 1990). Similarly, rhetorical scholars, critical interpretive anthropologists and scholars in social studies of science claim the existence of a direct, though complex, interrelationship between the construction of knowledge and the characteristics of intellectual communities. (For more discussion, see Strassmann 1993b.)

In accordance with these positions, feminist economists show how conventional economic methodological views fail to explain why it has taken the entry of women and other excluded groups into economics to produce more rigorous inquiry on subjects involving gender. In related research, feminist scholars in economic education and feminist pedagogy show how conventional economics instructional materials and pedagogy reinforce racial and gender bias in disciplinary instruction, thereby reinforcing a masculinist disciplinary status quo. (See, for example, Feiner and Roberts 1990; Aerni et al. 1999.)

These insights lead to a critical dilemma: how can feminists negotiate the desire, on the one hand to claim that economic accounts are necessarily situated in the specific lives and communities of their producers, while at the same time seeking to promote feminist accounts as more credible than established ones? (Longino 1992). In addressing these and other complex concerns, feminist economists draw from feminist epistemology, cultural studies, and poststructural and postcolonial theory in producing a variety of insights into the construction of economic knowledge and the quest for a more useful economics. (See, for example, Seiz 1992; Barker 1998; Hewitson 1999; and Charusheela forthcoming.)

Related research challenges traditional notions of rigour in economic scholarship, particularly in methods of argument, empirical investigation and the form of theoretical representation (Nelson 1992; Strassmann and Polanyi 1995b). By revealing an array of insights that could not be expressed through formal models, Agarwal (1997) demonstrates how a rigorous analysis may take an alternative mode and lead to a richer and more useful understanding of economic phenomena. More generally, feminist economists call for a broadening of economic methods, with tools chosen for their usefulness in providing insight, rather than for their coherence with a specific methodological definition of economics. (For extensive further discussions, see the special issue in *Feminist Economics* (Strassmann (ed.) 1997), *Expanding the Methodological Boundaries of Economics*.)

Feminist economic views in the late twentieth century are themselves situated in the lives of current researchers in feminist economics, and may not represent the directions the field will take in the future or fully convey potential shifts in economic terrain. New feminist economic ideas, some perhaps not even imaginable to current participants, may emerge as barriers to economic research are eroded and as scholars currently excluded from the field become able to participate in feminist economic discussions. Nonetheless, feminist economists have initiated a sweeping debate on economic theory and policy issues vital to the economic wellbeing of the majority of humans.

While necessarily incomplete, the selection of the ideas represented in this entry indicates how feminist economic ideas may lead to major new initiatives in economic inquiry and a possible transformation of the field. In challenging the merits of narrowly situated economic theories, feminist economists have begun to construct an economics that serves the interests of a broader and more representative group of people.

DIANA STRASSMANN

See also

Economic Man; Economic Welfare; Family, Economics of; Feminism(s); Game Theory and Bargaining Models; History of Economic Thought; Methodology; Neoclassical Economics; Pedagogy; Rhetoric; Women in the Economics Profession.

Bibliography

Aerni, April Laskey, Robin L. Bartlett, Margaret Lewis, KimMarie McGoldrick and Jean Shackelford (1999), 'Exploring the intersections of more inclusive course contents and learning environments: toward a feminist pedagogy in economics', *Feminist Economics*, **5** (1), (March), 29–44.

Agarwal, Bina (1994), *A Field of One's own: Gender and Land Rights in South Asia*, Cambridge: Cambridge University Press.

Agarwal, Bina (1995), 'Gender, Property, and Land Rights: Bridging a Critical Gap in Economic Analysis and Policy', in Edith Kuiper and Jolande Sap with Susan Feiner, Notburga Ott and Zafiris Tzannatos (eds), *Out of the Margins: Feminist Perspectives on Economics*, London: Routledge, pp. 264–94.

Agarwal, Bina (1997), 'Bargaining and gender relations: within and beyond the household', *Feminist Economics*, **3** (1), (Spring), 1–51.

Aslaksen, Iulie and Charlotte Koren (eds) (1999), 'Explorations on quality of life indicators', *Feminist Economics*, **5** (2), (July).

Badgett, M.V. Lee (1995), 'Gender, sexuality, and sexual orientation: all in the feminist family?', *Feminist Economics*, **1** (1), (Spring), 121–39.

Barker, Drucilla K. (1998), 'Dualisms, discourse, and development', **13** (3), (Summer), 83–94.

Benería, Lourdes (1979), 'Reproduction, production, and the sexual division of labour', *Cambridge Journal of Economics*, **3** (3), (September), 203–25.

Benería, Lourdes (1995), 'Towards a greater integration of gender in economics', *World Development*, **23** (11), (November), 1839–50.

Bergmann, Barbara R. (1986), *The Economic Emergence of Women*, New York: Basic Books, Inc.

Bergmann, Barbara R. (1997), 'Government support for families with children in the United States and France', *Feminist Economics*, 3 (1), Spring, 83–92.

Blau, Francine D. and Lawrence Kahn (1994), 'Rising wage inequality and the US gender gap', *American Economic Review*, 84 (2), (May), 23–8.

Blau, Francine D., Marianne A. Ferber and Anne E. Winkler (1998), *The Economics of Women, Men, and Work*, 3rd edn, Upper Saddle River, New Jersey: Prentice-Hall.

Charusheela, S. (forthcoming), 'Women's Choices and the Ethnocentric/Relativism Dilemma', in Stephen Cullenberg, Jack Amariglio and David Ruccio (eds), *Postmodernism, Economics and Knowledge*, London: Routledge.

Christensen, Kimberly (1998), 'Economics without money; sex without gender: a critique of Philipson and Posner's *Private and Public Health: The Aids Epidemic in an Economic Perspective*', *Feminist Economics*, 4 (2), (Summer), 1–24.

Colander, David and Joanna Wayland Woos (1997), 'Institutional demand-side discrimination against women and the human capital model', *Feminist Economics*, 3 (1), (Spring), 51–62.

Duggan, Lynn (1995), 'Restacking the deck: family policy and women's fall-back position in Germany before and after unification', *Feminist Economics*, 1 (1), (Spring), 175–94.

Duncan, Simon and Rosalind Edwards (1997), 'Lone mothers and paid work: rational economic man or gendered moral rationalities?', *Feminist Economics*, 3 (2), (Summer), 29–62.

Elson, Diane (1991), 'Male Bias: An Overview', in Diane Elson (ed.), *Male Bias in the Development Process*, Manchester, United Kingdom: Manchester University Press, pp. 1–28.

England, Paula (1993), 'The Separative Self: Androcentric Bias in Neoclassical Assumptions', in M.A. Ferber and J.A. Nelson (eds), *Beyond Economic Man: Feminist Theory and Economics*, Chicago: University of Chicago Press, pp. 37–53.

Feiner, Susan and Bruce Roberts (1990), 'Hidden by the invisible hand: neoclassical economic theory and the textbook treatment of women and minorities', *Gender and Society*, 4 (2), (June), 159–81.

Ferber, Marianne and Julie Nelson (eds) (1993), *Beyond Economic Man: Feminist Theory and Economics*, Chicago: University of Chicago Press.

Ferber, Marianne and Michelle L. Teiman (1981), 'The Oldest, the Most Established, and the Most Quantitative of the Social Sciences – and the Most Dominated by Men: The Impact of Feminism on Economics', in Dale Spender (ed.), *Men's Studies Modified: The Impact of Feminism on the Academic Disciplines*, New York: Pergamon Press, pp. 125–39.

Floro, Maria (1995), 'Women's well-being, poverty, and work intensity', *Feminist Economics*, 1 (3), (Fall), 1–25.

Folbre, Nancy (1991), 'The unproductive housewife: her evolution in nineteenth-century economic thought', *Signs*, 16 (3), (Spring), 463–84.

Folbre, Nancy (1994), *Who Pays for the Kids?: Gender and the Structures of Constraint*, London: Routledge.

Folbre, Nancy (1995), '"Holding hands at midnight": the paradox of caring labor', *Feminist Economics*, 1 (1), (Spring), 73–92.

Folbre, Nancy and Michèle Pujol (eds) (1996), *A Special Issue in Honor of Margaret Reid*, *Feminist Economics*, 2 (3), (Fall).

Gagnier, Regenia and John Dupré (1995), 'On work and idleness', *Feminist Economics*, 3 (1), (Spring), 96–109.

Galtry, Judith (1997), 'Suckling and silence in the USA: costs and benefits of breastfeeding', *Feminist Economics*, 3 (3), (Fall), 1–24.

Grapard, Ulla (1995), 'Robinson Crusoe: the quintessential economic man?', *Feminist Economics*, 1 (1), (Spring), 33–52.

Harding, Sandra (1986), *The Science Question in Feminism*, Ithaca, New York: Cornell University Press.

Hartsock, Nancy (1983), *Money, Sex, and Power: Toward a Feminist Historical Materialism*, New York: Longman.

Held, Virginia (1990), 'Mothering versus Contract', in Jane Mansbridge (ed.), *Beyond Self-Interest*, Chicago: University of Chicago Press, pp. 287–304.

Hewitson, Gillian (1999), *Feminist Economics: Interrogating the Masculinity of Rational Economic Man*, Aldershot: Edward Elgar.

Himmelweit, Susan (1995), 'The discovery of "unpaid work": the social consequences of the expansion of "work"', *Feminist Economics*, **1** (2), (Summer), 1–20.

Hopkins, Barbara (1995), 'Women and Children Last: A Feminist Redefinition of Privatization and Economic Reform', in Edith Kuiper and Jolande Sap with Susan Feiner, Notburga Ott and Zafiris Tzannatos (eds), *Out of the Margins: Feminist Perspectives on Economics*, London: Routledge, pp. 249–63.

Humphries, Jane (1995), 'Introduction', in Jane Humphries (ed.), *Gender and Economics*, Aldershot: Edward Elgar, pp. xiii–xxxix.

Jacobsen, Joyce P. (1998), *The Economics Of Gender, 2nd edn*, Cambridge, Massachusetts: Blackwell Publishers.

Katz, Elizabeth (1997), 'The intra-household economics of voice and exit', *Feminist Economics*, **3** (3), (Fall), 25–46.

Kondo, Dorinne (1990), *Crafting Selves: Power, Gender, and Discourses of Identity in the Japanese Workplace*, Chicago: University of Chicago Press.

Kuiper, Edith and Jolande Sap with Susan Feiner, Notburga Ott and Zafiris Tzannatos (eds) (1995), *Out of the Margins: Feminist Perspectives on Economics*, London: Routledge.

Longino, Helen (1990), *Science as Social Knowledge*, Princeton, New Jersey: Princeton University Press.

Longino, Helen (1992), 'Essential Tensions – Phase Two: Feminist, Philosophical, and Social Studies of Science', in Ernan McMullin (ed.), *In Social Dimensions of Science*, South Bend, Indiana: Notre Dame University Press, pp. 198–218.

Madden, Janice (1973), *The Economics of Sex Discrimination*, Lexington, Massachusetts: Lexington Books.

Nelson, Julie A. (1992), 'Gender, metaphor, and the definition of economics', *Economics and Philosophy*, **8** (1), (April), 103–25.

Nelson, Julie A. (1993), 'The Study of Choice or the Study of Provisioning? Gender and the Definition of Economics', in M.A. Ferber and J.A. Nelson (eds), *Beyond Economic Man: Feminist Theory and Economics*, Chicago: University of Chicago Press, pp. 23–36.

Ott, Notburga (1995), 'Fertility and Division of Work in the Family: A Game Theoretic Model of Household Decisions', in Edith Kuiper and Jolande Sap with Susan Feiner, Notburga Ott and Zafiris Tzannatos (eds), out of the Margins: Feminist Perspectives on Economics, London: Routledge, pp. 80–99.

Pujol, Michèle (1992), *Feminism and Anti-Feminism in Early Economic Thought*, Aldershot: Edward Elgar.

Renwick, Trudi J. and Barbara R. Bergmann (1993), 'A budget-based definition of poverty, with an application to single-parent families', *Journal of Human Resources*, **28** (1), 1–24.

Rubery, Jill, Mark Smith and Colette Fagan (1998), 'National working-time regimes and equal opportunities', *Feminist Economics*, **4** (1), (Spring), 71–102.

Sahlins, Marshall (1972), *Stone Age Economics*, New York: Aldine De Gruyter.

Seiz, Janet (1991), 'The bargaining approach and feminist methodology', *Review of Radical Political Economics*, **23** (1–2), 22–9.

Seiz, Janet (1992), 'Gender and Economic Research', in Neil de Marchi (ed.), *Post-Popperian Methodology of Economics: Recovering Practice*, Boston: Kluwer-Nijhoff, pp. 273–319.

Sen, Amartya (1984), *Resources, Values and Development*, Cambridge, Massachusetts: Harvard University Press.

Smythe, Ines (1996), 'Gender analysis of family planning: beyond the feminist vs. population control debate', *Feminist Economics*, **2** (2), (Summer), 63–86.

Stoler, Anne (1991), 'Carnal Knowledge and Imperial Power', in Michaela di Leonardo (ed.), *Gender at the Crossroads of Knowledge: Feminist Anthropology in the Postmodern Era*, Berkeley: University of California Press, pp. 51–101.

Strassmann, Diana (1993a), 'Not a Free Market: The Rhetoric of Disciplinary Authority in Economics', in M.A. Ferber and J.A. Nelson (eds), *Beyond Economic Man: Feminist Theory and Economics*, Chicago: University of Chicago Press, pp. 54–68.

Strassmann, Diana (1993b), 'The stories of economics and the power of the storyteller', *History of Political Economy*, **25** (1), (Spring), pp. 147–66.

Strassmann, Diana (1994), 'Feminist thought and economics; or what do the visigoths know?', *The American Economic Review*, **84** (2), (Summer), 153–8.

Strassmann, Diana (ed.) (1997), *A Special Issue: Expanding the Methodological Boundaries of Economics, Feminist Economics*, **3** (2).

Strassmann, Diana and Livia Polanyi (1995a), 'The Economist as Storyteller: What the Texts Reveal', in Edith Kuiper and Jolande Sap with Susan Feiner, Notburga Ott and Zafiris Tzannatos (eds), *Out of the Margins: Feminist Perspectives on Economics*, London: Routledge, pp. 129–50.

Strassmann, Diana and Livia Polanyi (1995b), 'Shifting the paradigm: value in feminist critiques of economics', *Forum for Social Economics*, **25** (1), (Fall), 3–19.

Strober, Myra H. (1984), 'Toward a General Theory of Occupational Sex Segregation: The Case of Public School Teaching', in Barbara Reskin (ed.), *Sex Segregation in the Workplace: Trends Explanations, Remedies*, Washington, DC: National Academy Press, pp. 144–56.

Strober, Myra H. and Lisa Catanzarite (1994), 'The Relative Attractiveness Theory of occupational Segregation by Gender', in Petra Beckman and Gerhard Englebrech (eds), *Arbeitsmarkt für Frauen 2000: Ein Schritt vor oder ein Schritt zuruck?*, Nurnberg, Germany: Institut für Arbeitsmarkt-und Berufsforschung der Bundesanstalt für Albeit, pp. 116–39.

Traweek, Sharon (1988), *Beamtimes and Lifetimes: The World of High Energy Physics*, Cambridge, Massachusetts: Harvard University Press.

Trzcinski, Eileen (1995), 'The Use and Abuse of the Neoclassical Theory in the Political Arena: The Example of Family and Medical Leave in the United States', in Edith Kuiper and Jolande Sap with Susan Feiner, Notburga Ott and Zafiris Tzannatos (eds), *Out of the Margins: Feminist Perspectives on Economics*, London: Routledge, pp. 231–48.

Wagman, Barnet and Nancy Folbre (1996), 'Household services and economic growth in the United States, 1870–1930', *Feminist Economics*, **2** (1), (Spring), 43–66.

Waring, Marilyn (1988), *If Women Counted: A New Feminist Economics*, San Francisco: Harper & Row.

Weintraub, E. Roy (ed.) (1993), 'Minisymposium: feminist theory and the history of economic thought', *History of Political Economy*, **25** (1), (Spring), 117–201.

Williams, Rhonda (1993), 'Race, Deconstruction and the Emergent Agenda of Feminist Economic Theory', in M.A. Ferber and J.A. Nelson (eds), *Beyond Economic Man: Feminist Theory and Economics*, Chicago: University of Chicago Press, pp. 144–52.

Feminization of Poverty

In 1978 sociologist Diana Pearce introduced the concept of the 'feminization of poverty' with the assertion that 'Poverty is rapidly becoming a female problem' (Pearce 1978, p. 28). In support of her claim she cited a variety of trends in US poverty, emphasizing in particular the increase in the share of the poverty population living in 'female-headed families' (the term used by the United States Bureau of the Census to indicate families maintained by women alone) from roughly one-third to one-half over the decade of the 1970s (Pearce 1978, p. 28, 1983, p. 70). Thus, the concept of the 'feminization of poverty' quickly became associated with analyses of the proportion of the poor living in female-headed families and increases in this proportion over time (Pearce 1989). As female-headed families continued to represent roughly one-half of the poverty population through the 1980s and into the 1990s (Albelda and Tilly 1996, p. 8), the phrase was often given a more general meaning and used to reflect the observation that 'the most common face of poverty in the United States among adults is a woman's'(Albelda and Tilly 1996, p. 23).

The assertion that US poverty had been 'feminized' over the decade of the 1970s raised important questions for feminist research in the United States and internationally. In the United States, feminist scholars stressed the paradox of women bearing an increasing burden of poverty during a decade often associated with important social and economic gains for women (Pearce 1978; Ehrenreich and Piven 1984). International scholars questioned whether this trend was inherent in the development of mature industrial societies or a phenomenon unique to the United States. Comparative studies found that while women and their children were over-represented among the poor throughout the industrialized world, the feminization of poverty was 'most pronounced in the United States where it was first identified' (Goldberg and Kremen 1990, p. 201). Consequently, this entry will focus on the discussion of the feminization of poverty as it evolved in the United States.

Poverty became an important policy issue in the United States during the 1960s with the exposure of the depth and extent of economic deprivation in the United States in works such as Michael Harrington's *The Other America* (1962). At that time, however, poverty was not seen to be a problem faced especially by women, and policies to promote economic growth and enhance labour market productivity were generally viewed as the best anti-poverty strategies by policymakers (see, for example, Council of Economic Advisers 1964). Pearce explicitly challenged this view, arguing that 'The "other America" is a changing neighborhood: men are moving out; women and children are moving in' (Pearce 1983, p. 70). She argued that the feminization of poverty had 'profoundly altered the needs of today's poor, as well as the nature of public policy required to meet those needs' (Pearce 1990, p. 226).

Pearce contended that while poor women and men shared many characteristics, there were causes of women's poverty that were unique to women, most particularly their responsibilities for children and their disadvantaged position in the labour market. She argued that women who headed families often bore most or all of the economic burden of raising children, a burden that was increased by the lack of adequate child support payments from absent fathers or public assistance from the state (Pearce 1983, 1990). In the labour market, women faced occupational segregation and discrimination, contributing to wages that were below those earned by men and often below what was necessary to support a family (Pearce 1978, 1983). In addition, Pearce argued that the structure of the welfare system institutionalized gender inequality and perpetuated women's poverty. She described welfare as a 'workhouse without walls', keeping women trapped in a system where they alternated between poorly paid work and inadequate welfare benefits, neither of which were sufficient to move them out of poverty (Pearce 1978, 1990).

Feminist writers popularized and extended Pearce's analysis of poverty in numerous works throughout the 1980s. Ehrenreich and Piven (1984), for example, emphasized the importance of the 'family wage' ideology (that is, the belief that men should earn a wage sufficient to support a wife and children) in defining women as secondary workers and thus contributing to occupational segregation and low wages. The feminization of poverty was seen to reflect the fact that although increasing numbers of women could no longer rely on the economic security provided by the male family wage, they had to seek income to support themselves and their families in a labour market shaped by this ideology. Ehrenreich and Piven also argued that this created a situation where the social welfare system, though inadequate and flawed, was increasingly important for the economic security and independence of many women. Thus, the cuts in social welfare spending initiated by the Reagan administration during the early 1980s were seen as a serious threat to this economic security and independence, and the feminization of poverty became an issue closely associated with critiques of 'Reaganomics' as well as with calls for broader economic reforms focused on women (Ehrenreich and Piven 1984).

In addition to highlighting the uniqueness of female poverty, the feminization of poverty literature also stressed the potential for mobilizing women around a common economic agenda. And while many poverty analysts and activists did credit this work with increasing public awareness of the plight of poor women, many also cautioned that the feminization of poverty literature's focus on gender was very narrow and obscured the importance of class and race in understanding poverty and downplayed the significant race and class differences that exist among women. Critics argued that attempts to organize women across these differences were 'naive' and that analyses that ignored these differences provided a distorted picture of the history and political–economic context of women's poverty in the United States (Sarvasy and Van Allen 1984).

Sparr (1984) and Malveaux (1985), for example, argued that the discussion of women's poverty as a relatively recent phenomenon in the United States ignored the histories of working-class women and women of colour, who had experienced substantial and persistent poverty long before the 1970s. In addition, Sparr argued that the contention of female poverty being different from male poverty ignored the fundamental nature of capitalism which 're-quires and maintains a class of impoverished people' (Sparr 1984, p. 14). Burnham (1985) further argued that in the USA race had played a critical role in determining the composition of this impoverished class, and thus an analysis of poverty that ignored the class context of capitalist development was seen to be particularly problematic when it was applied to the black community. Malveaux (1985) also argued that the exclusion of male poverty from the analysis distorted perceptions of the nature of poverty in the black community, and that the emphasis on male–female inequality obscured the serious inequalities that exist between white and black women in the labour market.

These criticisms of the feminization of poverty concept drew attention to the complex interaction of race, class and gender in the US economy and to the dangers of focusing too narrowly on gender in the analysis of poverty and in the development of policy alternatives. This raised important questions for feminist poverty analysis and challenged feminist writers to broaden their analyses. Sarvasy and Van Allen (1984), for example, argued that the gender approach to poverty was valid but could be strengthened through the adoption of a socialist–feminist approach that incorporated the class and race differences between women. They proposed an analysis of women's poverty based on the concept of women's 'unjust dual role' (that is, the need to combine unpaid domestic work with underpaid market work), but in a context where the class and race differences in the construction of the 'unjust dual role', and in the vulnerability to poverty that it implied, were explicitly addressed. And, while they expressed sympathy with the calls for government action to improve the status of women found in much of the feminization of poverty literature, they stressed the importance of recognizing the contradictory nature of the capitalist welfare state and its complex role in both improving and diminishing the economic status of women (Sarvasy and Van Allen 1984).

Folbre (1984) added that it was mothers who were particularly vulnerable to poverty in the United States, a condition she named the 'pauperization of motherhood'. Folbre argued that the impoverishment of mothers reflected the 'patriarchal bias' in state policy in the United States that had 'consistently benefited men and disadvantaged women and children' (Folbre 1984, p. 73). She emphasized the inequitable distribution of the benefits and costs associated with children, and argued that while children provided benefits to society as a whole, many non-parents and fathers were able to enjoy these benefits without paying for them. Thus, Folbre identified the ability of individual fathers and society as a whole to shift the economic costs of raising children onto mothers as a critical component of women's poverty.

Within a decade of its introduction, the feminization of poverty had become a widely known concept. In response to the issues raised by this concept, poverty analysts from a variety of disciplines and perspectives established an extensive literature on poor women and female-headed families. Numerous studies documented the trends in poverty for poor single mothers and their children, empirically examined the various factors contributing to the disproportionate poverty of female-headed families, and offered proposals (often based on the family policies of Western Europe and Scandinavia) for social welfare policy reform (see, for example, Rodgers 1986; Sidel 1986; Zopf 1989; Starrels et al. 1994). Feminist economists contributed to this evolving literature, stressing the relationship between women's paid and unpaid work and applying their analyses to policy discussions of critical importance to poor women, such as welfare reform.

Welfare reform presented a particularly important challenge for feminist economists in the 1990s, when the assumption that single mothers could simply 'work their way of poverty' became one of the defining characteristics of welfare reform proposals (Tilly and Albelda 1994). Feminist economists responded to these proposals with research examining the economic realities faced by single mothers and questioning the validity of the assumptions behind such strategies. Researchers at the Institute for Women's Policy Research, for example, found that single mothers receiving public assistance did in fact engage in significant amounts of paid work, but even if they worked full time they did not earn enough income to support a family above the poverty level. Like other mothers, poor single mothers 'packaged' their labour market income with income from other sources, such as income from other family members and public assistance (Spalter-Roth 1994). Chris Tilly and Randy Albelda described the particular disadvantages faced by poor single mothers as a 'triple whammy' – 'job discrimination against women, the time and money it takes to care for children, and the presence of only one adult' – which 'combine to make it nearly impossible for women to move off welfare through work alone' (Tilly and Albelda 1994, p. 8; Albelda and Tilly, 1996).

Thus, a critical insight from feminist economic work on welfare reform is that single mother families are poor because one female adult has the sole responsibility for both raising and supporting a family, and real welfare reform must recognize this reality and institute a 'set of thorough changes in the relations among work, family and income' (Tilly and Albelda 1994, p. 9). The need to evaluate the impacts of recent changes in the welfare system, and to continue to propose and advocate for progressive alternatives, provides many opportunities and challenges for feminist economic research and activism. Other areas for further research in feminist economics include extending the analysis of the poverty status of working poor women and assessing the potential for labour market reforms to reduce women's poverty (see, for example, Figart and Lapidus 1995), and extending the analysis of the poverty status of older women and evaluating the impacts of Social Security reform on the economic status of women in retirement (see, for example, Shaw et al. 1998). These contemporary policy issues present important avenues for feminist economists to contribute to the public discussion of the economic realities faced by poor women in the United States. They also raise important challenges to feminist economists to continue the work of incorporating race, class and gender into the analysis of women's poverty.

JANICE PETERSON

See also
Divorce; Family Wage; Income Support and Transfer Policies; Wage Gap; Welfare Reform.

Bibliography
Albelda, Randy and Chris Tilly (1996), *Glass Ceilings and Bottomless Pits: Women's Work, Women's Poverty*, Boston: South End Press.
Burnham, Linda (1985), 'Has poverty been feminized in black America?', *Black Scholar*, **16** (2), 14–24.
Council of Economic Advisers (1964), *Economic Report of the President*, Washington, DC: United States Government Printing Office.
Ehrenreich, Barbara and Frances Fox Piven (1984), 'The feminization of poverty: when the "family-wage system" breaks down', *Dissent*, **31** (2), 162–70.
Figart, Deborah M. and June Lapidus (1995), 'A gender analysis of US labor market policies for the working poor', *Feminist Economics*, **1** (3), 60–81.
Folbre, Nancy (1984), 'The pauperization of motherhood: patriarchy and public policy in the United States', *Review of Radical Political Economics*, **16** (4), 72–88.
Goldberg, Gertrude Schaffner and Eleanor Kremen (1990), *The Feminization of Poverty: Only in America?*, New York: Praeger.
Harrington, Michael (1962), *The Other America*, New York: Macmillan.
Malveaux, Julianne (1985), 'The economic interests of black and white women: are they similar?', *The Review of Black Political Economy*, **14** (1), 5–27.
Pearce, Diana (1978), 'The feminization of poverty: women, work and welfare', *Urban and Social Change Review*, **11** (1,2), 28–36.
Pearce, Diana (1983), 'The feminization of ghetto poverty', *Society*, **21** (1), 70–74.
Pearce, Diana (1989), 'The Feminization of Poverty: An Update', *First Annual Women's Policy Research Conference Proceedings*, Washington, DC: Institute for Women's Policy Research, pp. 147–52.
Pearce, Diana (1990) 'Welfare is Not For Women: Why the War on Poverty Cannot Conquer the Feminization of Poverty', in Linda Gordon (ed.), *Women, the State, and Welfare*, Madison, Wisconsin: The University of Wisconsin Press, pp. 265–79.
Rodgers, Harrell R. Jr. (1986), *Poor Women, Poor Families: The Economic Plight of America's Female-Headed Households*, Armonk, New York: M.E. Sharpe.
Sarvasy, Wendy and Judith Van Allen (1984), 'Fighting the feminization of poverty: socialist–feminist analysis and strategy', *Review of Radical Political Economy*, **16** (2), 89–110.
Shaw, Lois, Diana Zuckerman and Heidi Hartmann (1998), *The Impact of Social Security Reform on Women*, Washington, DC: Institute for Women's Policy Research.
Sidel, Ruth (1986), *Women and Children Last: The Plight of Poor Women in Affluent America*, New York: Viking.
Spalter-Roth, Roberta (1994), 'The real employment opportunities of women participating in AFDC: what the market can provide', *Social Justice*, **21** (1), 60–75.
Sparr, Pamela (1984), 'Re-evaluating feminist economics: "feminization of poverty" ignores key issues', *Dollars and Sense*, (September), 12–14.
Starrels, Marjorie E., Sally Bould and Leon J. Nichols (1994), 'The feminization of poverty in the United States: race, gender, ethnicity, and family factors', *Journal of Family Issues*, **15** (4), 590–605.
Tilly, Chris and Randy Albelda (1994), 'It's not working: why single mothers can't work their way out of poverty', *Dollars and Sense*, (November/December), 8–10.
Zopf, Paul E. Jr (1989), *American Women in Poverty*, New York: Greenwood.

Game Theory and Bargaining Models

Although game theory entered economics with great fanfare in the 1940s, as late as the 1970s the approach was being applied in only a few areas of the discipline. Dramatic advances occurred in the 1980s, however, and game theory has now become one of the standard tools of mainstream microeconomics. Many economists interested in gender inequality have found game theory appealing. Indeed, exploration of the potential of game-theoretic frameworks for analysis of gender relations is today one of the most intriguing frontiers in feminist economic theory.

Game theory applies to situations in which 'individuals have some understanding of how the outcome for one is affected not only by his or her own actions but also by the actions of others' (Hargreaves Heap and Varoufakis 1995, p. 2). It has been used to analyse a wide variety of economic and political phenomena, including military strategy, the price and output decisions of oligopolistic firms, wage bargaining between unions and employers, the conduct of monetary policy, the establishment of social institutions such as property rights and political systems, and the decision to pursue collective action.

Feminist economists have so far used game theory primarily for modelling household decisions. This entry will begin by selectively surveying this literature, discussing the strengths and limitations of formal household models. It will then address the potential usefulness of game-theoretic frameworks for analysing gender relations beyond the household.

Feminist economists became interested in game-theoretic modelling because the existing neoclassical and Marxist portrayals of the household were seriously flawed (see Folbre 1986; Kabeer 1998; Katz 1997). Neoclassical work on phenomena such as labour supply, consumption and fertility had long taken the household as the decision-making unit, positing that it sought to maximize a household utility function. If asked how this 'household well-being' function was related to household members' individual utility functions, analysts might cite either Samuelson's (1956) suggestion that households be viewed as having reached consensus on economic decisions or Becker's (1974, 1981) 'rotten kid theorem' formulation, in which the household's utility function is that of an altruistic 'head' whose economic power compels other household members to comply with his wishes. Neither of these derivations of a household utility function – often referred to as the 'unitary' or 'common preferences' household model – is fully satisfactory from a technical point of view; and feminists criticized both models for obscuring the power relations present in the heterosexual household. Analogously, Marxist economists, although they forcefully challenged the exploitation of workers by capitalists, typically neglected to investigate the allocation of tasks and consumption within the household, obscuring the possibility that the home might also be a site of exploitation (Folbre 1982, 1986). Thus both neoclassical and Marxist feminists sought alternative models that would show the household to be an arena of inequality and conflict as well as of caring and cooperation. More recently, other economists have been attracted to game-theoretic modelling because of the accumulation of empirical evidence that (*contra* the unitary model) the intrahousehold distribution of consumption depends significantly on which household members receive or control income (Lundberg and Pollak 1996; Haddad et al. 1997).

Game-theoretic household models generally portray a husband and wife trying to decide how their time will be allocated and how the items they produce or purchase will be distributed. Being together may increase both partners' wellbeing in many ways, including the joys of loving companionship, the economies of joint consumption and the efficiencies of coordinated work efforts. But there are many ways in which tasks and consumption might be divided between the partners, and their interests conflict regarding these.

The situation can be modelled in two ways, corresponding to the two basic types of game theory. In *noncooperative* games (such as the Prisoners' Dilemma), the players are unable to make binding agreements, so each must act without being able to coordinate choices with the other. In a noncooperative household model, husband and wife might make unilateral 'moves' regarding work and consumption until a stable (equilibrium) division is achieved. In *cooperative* games, players can make binding agreements. To identify a cooperative game's outcome, one does not refer to a series of individual strategic choices. Typically, the analyst simply specifies which of the possible agreements should be viewed as optimal, according to some set of criteria, and identifies that as the outcome the players will choose.

The first applications of game theory to the household were the cooperative 'bargaining' models of Manser and Brown (1980) and McElroy and Horney (McElroy and Horney 1981; McElroy 1990). In these models, each partner's utility is a function of his/her consumption of public (shared) goods (such as housing), private goods and leisure. Being together confers potential gains of three sorts: due to the shared goods, each partner gets more for a given level of expenditure than if single; if the partners are altruistic, each gets utility from the other's consumption; and the pleasures of companionship may further add to wellbeing.

The models assume the partners will stay together ('cooperate') only if doing so leaves them at least as well off as they would be apart. Their expected utility levels if their relationship ended are referred to as the threat point (or 'fallback position'). What each will gain from cooperating is the difference between his/her utility at the chosen cooperative outcome and his/her utility at the threat point. What, then, determines how the total gains from the relationship will be distributed? How much will each partner work and consume? What determines 'bargaining power', one's ability to get one's own wants met at the expense of the partner's?

To answer these questions, the models' outcomes are selected by applying the 'Nash cooperative bargaining solution', in which the partners agree on an allocation that maximizes the *product* of their individual gains from cooperation (Manser and Brown apply two other solutions as well). In the Nash solution, bargaining power depends crucially on the 'threat point'. If one partner's outside options improve, so that s/he would lose less than before from ending the relationship, then s/he will get a more favourable deal in the relationship than s/he did earlier. This solution essentially makes the household utility function a weighted average of the partners' individual utility functions, with the relative weights determined by their outside options.

The Manser–Brown and McElroy–Horney models have many limitations. For example, since they present the time-allocation problem as a choice between market work and leisure, they ignore within-household tasks and cannot address controversies over the gender division of labour. And since outcomes are a function of the partners' outside options, they must be renegotiated whenever those options change even slightly. If this is interpreted to imply that the threat of divorce is repeatedly being invoked, it is implausible. If one's outside options improve but remain worse than what one is receiving in the relationship, a divorce threat would not be credible, and it would seem no new deal need be struck.

Later modellers have addressed those limitations and extended the game-theoretic approach to new questions and situations. A brief description of some of these models' basic features may convey some of the flavour of this line of inquiry; more extensive surveys may be found in Haddad et al. (1997), Katz (1997), and Lundberg and Pollak (1996). In Lundberg and Pollak (1993), husband and wife bargain over consumption and over the labour time each will devote to producing public (shared) goods. The Nash solution is used to identify the cooperative outcome, but the threat point here has the partners not leaving the relationship, but withdrawing into a noncooperative 'separate spheres' division of labour, said to be determined by gender role ideology. In Carter and Katz (1997), which also combines cooperative and noncooperative elements, husband and wife control separate gender-specific spheres of activity, each allocating his/her own labour time and controlling the resulting income. Their activities are linked by a 'conjugal contract' according to which each may contribute to the production of public goods and/or transfer income to the other. The higher-income partner can use transfers to induce the other to allocate more labour time to the public good. Ott (1992, 1995) extends the bargaining approach to fertility decisions, and constructs a dynamic cooperative model in which the partners' labour supply decisions in each period have human capital implications that affect their bargaining power later. Women's withdrawal from the labour force to care for children reduces their subsequent earning power, worsening their bargaining position in the household. Finally, Tauchen et al. (1991) use a noncooperative model to address domestic violence. The dominant partner may exercise violence, which both yields him direct satisfaction and induces his partner to behave in ways that increase his wellbeing.

How should feminists assess these models? Like all economic models, they are of course unrealistic, leaving out many features of reality and distorting some others. They include some things that the conventional 'unitary' models do not, and this might be seen as advantageous for analysis of gender relations; but they also leave out a great deal that feminists might regard as crucial.

The basic message of the cooperative models is that 'bargaining' outcomes are a function of the factors that determine the partners' threat points. From a feminist point of view, even these simplest models might be seen as superior in some ways to the 'unitary' household (Seiz 1991, 1995). First, in contrast to the image of harmony generally seen in unitary models, the bargaining models portray both mutually beneficial and conflictual aspects of household relationships: they show the household as both a cooperative unit important to its members' wellbeing and an institution in which gender inequalities may be manifest and perpetuated. Second, the centrality of the threat point focuses attention on the external or structural factors that produce unequal outcomes for women and men – although, as several feminist commentators have noted, these gender asymmetries are rarely emphasized in presentations of the models (Agarwal 1997; Folbre 1997; Katz 1997). The explanatory variables in the McElroy–Horney model include 'in principle', McElroy (1990, p. 578) states, 'every variable that affects how well each family member could do in the next best alternative outside of the family'. These would include employment opportunities and wages; nonwage income; remarriage prospects; access to support from natal families, social networks and the state; and rules regarding child custody, child support, property settlements and alimony (in practice, unfortunately, most studies focus only on measured wage and nonwage incomes). Given the sizable gender asymmetries in these external factors in most societies, the bargaining framework can offer a clear account of why household 'bargains' often leave women working longer hours and consuming less than men. Finally, the bargaining models have important policy implications with which feminists can concur (although again, these often are left unexplored in the modelling literature). First, policymakers should not assume that increasing the incomes or assets of male 'household heads' will necessarily lead to equitable increases in the wellbeing of other family members; and second, policies that improve women's outside options may also improve their treatment within the family (see Haddad et al. 1997 and Lundberg and Pollak 1996 on policy implications and empirical evidence).

But if these inclusions constitute virtues, it is equally true that the models have exclusions that may be seen as serious weaknesses. There are problems in the models' treatment of the processes by which outcomes are determined, and the models are very incomplete in identifying and explaining the factors that shape intrahousehold allocations.

The cooperative bargaining models, as mentioned earlier, say nothing about the process through which the players come to agreement. Nash (1950, 1953) chose his solution – maximizing the product of the players' gains from cooperation – because it alone exhibited all of four mathematical properties he considered desirable (see Luce and Raiffa 1957 for details). Later game theorists have shown how something close to the Nash solution might emerge, under some conditions, from offer-and-counteroffer negotiations (Binmore et al. 1986; Harsanyi and Selten 1988), and other cooperative solutions besides Nash's have been proposed. But much work remains to be done to see whether the processes and outcomes posited are appropriate as representations of what occurs in households.

Noncooperative games do specify the processes of rational individual action that determine their outcomes, but they too are problematic. Severe restrictions must be imposed if the models are to have unique equilibrium solutions: players' options must be quite limited, and strong assumptions must be made about players' knowledge. The structure of a game must be taken as given, leaving open the question of how the rules are established. And little progress has been made in matching noncooperative game structures with observed institutional realities, including those in households.

Some feminist economists have cautioned against expecting much descriptive realism from formal household models. Katz (1997, p. 37) notes that household allocation is probably far more complex than existing models allow: 'different types of resources may be allocated according to different logics – unitary, cooperative and noncooperative decision-making rules may all co-exist in the same household'. Nelson (1994, p. 130) argues, 'If … marital bargaining takes place on many different levels and with strong outside influence, mathematical tractability of theoretical … formulations is likely to be the exception rather than the rule'. Lundberg and Pollak (1993) suggest that it is the very complexity of household bargaining that makes cooperative modelling attractive. And Ott (1995) proposes that if the cooperative bargaining models' outcomes have predictive value, the lack of attention to process is not really important. Much more discussion of these issues by feminist economists is needed.

Another set of problems arises because existing household models ignore altogether some factors that might significantly affect outcomes, and take as given much of what feminist analysts would like to explain. The distribution of tasks and consumption among household members is surely not shaped exclusively by the relative attractiveness of their outside options; and many phenomena concerning the scope of bargaining and the determinants of bargaining power, matters which must be assumed in formal models, require explanation. Questions along these lines have been raised by a number of feminist scholars (Folbre 1997; Hart 1995; Katz 1997; Lundberg and Pollak 1996; Sen 1990); the most wide-ranging feminist examination of these issues is offered by Agarwal (1994, 1997).

Among the questions Agarwal addresses are the following: In household bargaining, do both women and men simply pursue their individual self-interest, or might their motivations differ markedly? How do ethical principles regarding fairness and appropriateness affect the household distribution of work and consumption? How do social norms impinge upon what is and is not bargained over, and how do they affect women's bargaining power relative to men's? And how is bargaining within the household related to contestation in other arenas such as the community and the state?

Several feminist writers suggest that women and men may approach household allocation with very different motives and that this may significantly affect outcomes. In an influential early critique of household bargaining models, Sen (1990) proposes that in many contexts, while men may be guided by a clear sense of their own individual welfare, women may see their wellbeing as subsumed in that of their households. England and Kilbourne (1990) argue that women are socialized to be more altruistic than men, and thus are less likely to drive hard bargains on their own behalf. Agarwal (1994, 1997) explores these questions at length, cautioning against assuming the existence of such gender differences without sufficient evidence. While women may sometimes appear to accept inequitable treatment, this may simply reflect the limitedness of their options, not lack of concern for their own welfare. And women's seemingly greater concern with family wellbeing, Agarwal observes, is often consistent with their self-interest, since women tend to be more dependent than men on family support.

Agarwal also broadens the discussion, initiated by Sen, of the role of ethical principles. Sen (1990, p. 134) argues that intrahousehold distribution will depend not only on individuals' outside options, but also on 'conceptions of desert and legitimacy'. A household's assessment of its members' deservingness, he suggests, will be strongly influenced by how much each is perceived as contributing to the household's wellbeing. Agarwal (1994, 1997) proposes that families are likely to invoke other principles of distributive justice as well, including distribution according to needs. Any such principles might be gender-biased; for instance, due to social biases in perceptions, just as women's contributions tend to be underestimated, so may their needs be.

Although modellers sometimes note that social norms might influence household economic decisions, they rarely go much further in exploring either the effects or the origins of norms. Agarwal (1994, 1997) provides an extensive discussion of these issues. Social norms, Agarwal (1997, pp. 15–16) suggests, may define which matters can and cannot legitimately be bargained over, and may also 'set limits to bargaining by admitting something as contestable but restricting the range of contestation'. It might be considered unquestionable, for instance, that women are responsible for child care, or that productive assets are managed by men. Social norms also operate in myriad ways to shape women's and men's bargaining power, for example when they limit women's employment opportunities and control over property. Further, Agarwal proposes, social norms need not be viewed as immutable, as most economic analyses assume them to be; rather, many norms can be seen as contestable. This leads to the question of the usefulness of game-theoretic approaches for understanding gender relations beyond the household.

To understand what goes on within the household, Agarwal's work shows, we need a much richer understanding of cultural and institutional phenomena outside the household. Similar suggestions have come from other feminist economists. 'Today', Folbre (1997, p. 263) notes, 'the microeconomics of household bargaining seems better developed than the macroeconomics of gender- and age-based inequalities. Many economists are modeling the consequences of differences in bargaining power, but few are exploring the causes'. Lundberg and Pollak (1996, p. 152) observe that current household models 'focus on the subgame of bargaining within a particular marriage ... [while] the real action is elsewhere – in the prior game that determines social norms and gender roles'.

Gender relations are obviously the products of action and contestation in a variety of sites other than the household. As Agarwal (1994, 1997) elaborates, women's options are shaped in particular ways by employers and other transactors in (typically imperfectly-competitive) markets for labour, credit, productive assets and products; by 'communities' (defined by locality, religion, race/ethnicity and other factors); and by governments. These arenas are linked in complex ways: for example, a community's restrictive notions of proper female behaviour may limit women's educational and work opportunities in ways that reduce their bargaining power in the labour market and therefore also in the household; and laws regarding child custody, division of marital assets and access to state support often make household 'exit' options very different for women than for men. Formal household models, as emphasized earlier, must take such factors as given, whereas feminists would like to have them explained. Might the bargaining framework be useful for analysing gender-related contestation in these external arenas as well, including the construction of social norms and state policies?

This sort of inquiry has so far received little attention from economists. While much game-theoretic work has been done on employer–worker interactions in the labour market and workplace, few of these models focus specifically on women or on gender (a very interesting exception is Sap (1993)). Gender contestation at the levels of community and state has been almost completely unexplored in these terms (although work by Folbre (1994, 1997) and Molyneux (1998) on gender-related collective action is closely related). Agarwal however helps point the way for such analysis. (See Agarwal (1994, 1997) for discussion of women's 'bargaining' with communities.)

Extending Agarwal's analysis very slightly provides an illuminating discussion of women's interaction with the state. Men and women (as individuals and as members of organized groups) seek to induce the state to act in ways that serve their gender interests; Folbre (1997) refers to 'gender coalitions'. Such interactions can often be viewed, Agarwal suggests, as bargaining situations. Suppose a feminist group is campaigning for state action that would benefit women. Both the state actors and the feminists can enjoy gains if they can reach agreement, but there are conflicts between them over the precise nature of their agreement. How would the outcome be determined?

State actors may have a variety of objectives that a feminist group can either promote or impede. They might wish to maintain or enlarge their control over state power; to increase the degree to which their rule is regarded, both domestically and abroad, as legitimate and constructive; to increase the economic resources at the state's disposal; and to alter the lives of their citizens, in ways that either benefit or harm women. A feminist group might be able to influence elections, through their own votes and through affecting the votes of others. They might undertake demonstrations that could cause the government to lose face domestically and internationally. And they might, perhaps working in concert with organizations abroad, be able to affect the country's access to aid, trade, and investment. The anticipated costs and benefits of state cooperation with the feminists will also depend on the expected reaction of the state's male subjects. Although it would appear quite difficult to incorporate all these complexities into a formal game-theoretic model, a broader approach framed by game-theoretic concepts such as 'bargaining power' might be quite useful in analysing states' actions on gender issues.

Further, 'games' take many other forms besides bargaining. Analysts have gained considerable insight into business decisions, military strategy, collective action, political decision making and many other phenomena by characterizing the 'payoff structures' facing actors in terms of very simple games such as the Prisoners' Dilemma (Davis 1997 and Dixit and Nalebuff 1991 give many examples). In the Prisoners' Dilemma, two prisoners accused of committing a crime together are questioned separately by police and offered the following deal: if you confess and your partner does not, you will receive a short jail sentence and he will get a long one. The prisoners know that if neither confesses, both will go free. They will do best, obviously, if both keep silent; but since they are unable to make a binding agreement to that effect, each prisoner will confess. Thus both will be convicted, even though a better outcome for them was possible. This payoff structure might be seen, as Ott (1992, 1995) demonstrates, as characterizing some house-holds' fertility decisions. Suppose a husband and wife want to have a child, but the wife would have to leave the labour force for some years to care for the child. Assume this withdrawal would reduce her earning power and her intrahousehold bargaining power so much that her economic losses would make her worse off overall than she would be without the child. The husband might promise to compensate her for her lost earnings; but if no binding agreement can be made for all future periods, he will have an incentive to renege as the wife's bargaining power deteriorates over time. Knowing this, the 'rational' wife will be unwilling to have the child, even though both partners could have been better off with the child, given a suitable redistribu-tion of their income.

Thinking in terms of 'payoff structures' might illuminate many other deci-sions women face – such as whether to pursue nontraditional employment (given the possibility of harassment by male coworkers), whether to seek legal redress for sexual assault or domestic violence (given the ability of agents for the accused to besmirch one's character), and whether to sue a discriminating employer – as well as showing how policy interventions that alter payoffs could produce more equitable outcomes.

Game theory also offers powerful tools for the analysis of collective ac-tion, as is shown by Chong's (1991) study of the US civil rights movement. Sometimes using formal models, and sometimes constructing verbal narra-tives that draw on game-theoretic concepts, Chong analyses a variety of historical events, including changes in individuals' willingness to undertake collective action, strategic choices made by civil rights groups and govern-mental bodies' responses to the movement. Similar work might be done by feminists to help understand (and perhaps guide) collective actions over gender issues.

It remains to be seen how useful game theory will be to feminist econo-mists. Some have wondered whether game-theoretic models will actually provide new insights into economic phenomena, as opposed to simply taking ideas long accepted by dissident (including feminist) economists and ex-pressing them in a language respected by the profession's mainstream (Seiz 1991, 1995). The question is posed more harshly on the back cover of Hargreaves Heap and Varoufakis (1995): 'Does game theory simply repeat what everyone already knows in a language that no one understands?' As a prominent practitioner and popularizer of game theory admitted in 1990, 'Few if any of the conclusions of successful game-theoretic analyses are startling or mysterious or arcane; after the fact, it is usually easy to say, "Well, I think I already knew that"' (Kreps 1990, pp. 87–8).

But to give in to pessimism about a line of inquiry that feminists have just begun to explore would be foolish. Already, game-theoretic models (in conjunction with a wealth of empirical work) have begun to shift economists' views of the household: as Folbre (1997, p. 363) puts it, '(it) is no longer acceptable to ignore inequalities of power and welfare among household members, or to assume that the household itself can be treated as an undifferentiated optimizing unit'. A great deal of work remains to be done. As several feminist economists have argued, formal household models must focus much more than they do now on gender asymmetries, and they must be elaborated and supplemented to deal more adequately with extrahousehold and nonquantitative phenomena such as social norms (Agarwal 1997; Folbre 1997; Katz 1997; Lundberg and Pollak 1996). Modelling will need to be informed by qualitative empirical work, including historical studies, surveys, ethnographies and other sorts of analysis to which economists are unaccustomed. Thus, in this area as in others, feminist economists must pursue an interdisciplinary research agenda.

What feminists take from game theory need not be limited to formal modelling. Game-theoretic modes of reasoning, employed heuristically rather than being restricted to formal model construction, may provide a very fruitful approach to gender relations both in and outside the household. Thinking in terms of 'bargaining power', or of the 'payoff structures' of situations in which women interact with partners, employers, communities and governments, may sometimes help feminists both to better understand the world, and to change it.

JANET A. SEIZ

See also

Divorce; Domestic Abuse; Domestic Labour; Family, Economics of; Family Policy; Marriage, Theories of; Methodology; Migration.

Bibliography

Agarwal, Bina (1994), *A Field of One's Own: Gender and Land Rights in South Asia*, New York and Cambridge, UK: Cambridge University Press.

Agarwal, Bina (1997), '"Bargaining" and gender relations: within and beyond the household', *Feminist Economics*, **3** (1), 1–51.

Becker, Gary S. (1974), 'A theory of marriage part II', *Journal of Political Economy*, **82**, S11–S26.

Becker, Gary S. (1981), *A Treatise on the Family*, Cambridge, Massachusetts: Harvard University Press.

Binmore, Kenneth, Ariel Rubinstein and A. Wolinsky (1986), 'The Nash bargaining solution in economic modelling', *Rand Journal of Economics*, **17** (2), 176–88.

Carter, Michael R. and Elizabeth G. Katz (1997), 'Separate Spheres and the Conjugal Contract: Understanding the Impact of Gender-Biased Development', in Lawrence Haddad, John Hoddinott and Harold Alderman (eds), *Intrahousehold Resource Allocation in Developing Countries: Methods, Models and Policy*, Baltimore and London: Johns Hopkins University Press.

Chong, Dennis (1991), *Collective Action and the Civil Rights Movement*, Chicago: University of Chicago Press.

Davis, Morton D. (1997), *Game Theory: A Nontechnical Introduction*, Mineola, New York: Dover Books.

Dixit, Avinash and Barry Nalebuff (1991), *Thinking Strategically: The Competitive Edge in Business, Politics and Everyday Life*, New York and London: W.W. Norton.

England, Paula and Barbara Kilbourne (1990), 'Markets, Marriages, and Other Mates: The Problem of Power', in Roger Friedland and A.F. Robertson (eds.), *Beyond the Marketplace: Rethinking Economy and Society*, New York: Aldine de Gruyter.

Folbre, Nancy (1982), 'Exploitation comes home: a critique of the Marxian theory of family labour', *Cambridge Journal of Economics*, **6** (4), 317–29.

Folbre, Nancy (1986), 'Hearts and spades: paradigms of household economics', *World Development*, **14** (2), 245–55.

Folbre, Nancy (1994), *Who Pays for the Kids? Gender and the Structures of Constraint*, London and New York: Routledge.

Folbre, Nancy (1997), 'Gender Coalitions: Extrafamily Influences on Intrafamily Inequality', in Lawrence Haddad, John Hoddinott and Harold Alderman (eds), *Intrahousehold Resource Allocation in Developing Countries: Methods, Models and Policy*, Baltimore and London: Johns Hopkins University Press.

Haddad, Lawrence, John Hoddinott and Harold Alderman (eds) (1997), *Intrahousehold Resource Allocation in Developing Countries: Methods, Models and Policy*, Baltimore and London: Johns Hopkins University Press.

Hargreaves Heap, Shaun P. and Yanis Varoufakis (1995), *Game Theory: A Critical Introduction*, London and New York: Routledge.

Harsanyi, John and R. Selten (1988), *A General Theory of Equilibrium Selection in Games*, Cambridge, Massachusetts: MIT Press.

Hart, Gillian (1995), 'Gender and Household Dynamics: Recent Theories and Their Implications', in M.G. Quibria (ed.), *Critical Issues in Asian Development: Theories, Experiences and Policies*, Oxford and New York: Oxford University Press.

Kabeer, Naila (1998), 'Jumping to Conclusions? Struggles over Meaning and Method in the Study of Household Economics', in Cecile Jackson and Ruth Pearson (eds), *Feminist Visions of Development: Gender Analysis and Policy*, London and New York: Routledge.

Katz, Elizabeth G. (1997), 'The intra-household economics of voice and exit', *Feminist Economics*, **3** (3), 25–46.

Kreps, David M. (1990), *Game Theory and Economic Modeling*, New York: Oxford University Press.

Luce, R. Duncan and Howard Raiffa (1957), *Games and Decisions: Introduction and Critical Survey*, New York: John Wiley and Sons. Reprinted 1989, New York: Dover Books.

Lundberg, Shelly and Robert A. Pollak (1993), 'Separate spheres bargaining and the marriage market', *Journal of Political Economy*, **100** (6), 988–1010.

Lundberg, Shelly and Robert A. Pollak (1996), 'Bargaining and distribution in marriage', *Journal of Economic Perspectives*, **10** (4), 139–58.

Manser, Marilyn and Murray Brown (1980), 'Marriage and household decision making: a bargaining analysis', *International Economic Review*, **21** (1), 31–44.

McElroy, Marjorie B. (1990), 'The empirical content of Nash-bargained household behavior', *Journal of Human Resources*, **25** (4), 559–83.

McElroy, Marjorie B. and Mary Jean Horney (1981), 'Nash-bargained household decisions: toward a generalization of the theory of demand', *International Economic Review*, **22** (2), 333–49.

Molyneux, Maxine (1998), 'Analysing Women's Movements', in Cecile Jackson and Ruth Pearson (eds.), *Feminist Visions of Development: Gender Analysis and Policy*, London and New York: Routledge.

Nash, John (1950), 'The bargaining problem', *Econometrica*, **18**, 155–62.

Nash, John (1953), 'Two person cooperative games', *Econometrica*, **21**, 128–40.

Nelson, Julie A. (1994), 'I, thou, and them: capabilities, altruism, and norms in the economics of marriage', *American Economic Review*, **84** (2), 126–31.

Ott, Notburga (1992), *Intrafamily Bargaining and Household Decisions*, New York: Springer-Verlag.

Ott, Notburga (1995), 'Fertility and Division of Work in the Family', in Edith Kuiper and Jolande Sap (eds), *Out of the Margin: Feminist Perspectives on Economics*, New York and London: Routledge.

Samuelson, Paul (1956), 'Social indifference curves', *Quarterly Journal of Economics*, **70**, 1–22.

Sap, Jolande (1993), 'Bargaining power and wages: a game-theoretic model of gender differences in union wage bargaining', *Labour Economics*, **1**, 25–48.

Seiz, Janet A. (1991), 'The bargaining approach and feminist methodology', *Review of Radical Political Economics*, **23** (1–2), 22–9.

Seiz, Janet A. (1995), 'Bargaining models, feminism, and institutionalism', *Journal of Economic Issues*, **29** (2), 609–18.

Sen, Amartya K. (1990), 'Gender and Cooperative Conflicts', in Irene Tinker (ed.), *Persistent Inequalities: Women and World Development*, Oxford and New York: Oxford University Press.

Tauchen, Helen V., Ann Dryden Witte and Sharon K. Long (1991), 'Domestic violence: a nonrandom affair', *International Economic Review*, **32** (2), 491–511.

Gender

The distinction between sex and gender is central to contemporary feminism. Whereas sex refers to the biological differences between men and women, gender refers to the social construction of sexual identity, a construction that assigns differing roles, rights and opportunities to persons based on their sex. Gender difference entails hierarchical difference: the social construction of maleness is of higher status and privilege than the social construction of femaleness. Since gender is a relational term, referring to the interaction between male and female gender roles, the study of one entails a study of the other. It is by using gender as a category of analysis that feminist scholarship has the potential to transform disciplinary paradigms, and the impact of gender analysis is clearly seen in many disciplines within the academy such as philosophy, sociology, anthropology and literary criticism. Economics, however, has been remarkably resistant to canonical change, although it has a relatively rich history of the inclusion of women's issues.

During the 1950s neoclassical economics pioneered the analysis of women's labour force participation, and later the economics of nonmarket activities were examined under the rubric of the new home economics. However, neither of these efforts incorporated the sort of gender analysis that would transform the economics discipline (Benería 1995). Transformative gender analysis requires more than simply adding topics that bear on women's lives and experiences. It requires an examination of the role of gender in shaping the premises and values that have guided scholarly inquiry. Unexamined, these implicit assumptions result in biases and distortions in traditional disciplinary accounts. Moreover purportedly gender-neutral concepts, theories and methodologies serve to hide, protect and naturalize gender privilege. By way of illustration, in neoclassical economics the wage gap between men and women is explained as a result of women's rational choices, an explanation that justifies the higher earnings of men. A gender analysis, on the other hand, entails an examination of the ways in which gender-specific social expectations about women's roles as wives and mothers affect their labour market experiences.

Gender will, however, be only one part of the explanation because gender is always part of a complex social construction of identity, hierarchy and difference. Race, ethnicity, class and sexuality are other socially constructed categories that intersect with gender to determine the cultural, social and economic locations of individuals. Folbre (1994) refers to these as 'structures of constraint', and points out that people occupy multiple and often contradictory positions because people belong to multiple groups. An individual's economic options depend on the interaction between the different dimensions of collective identity.

Since gender analysis is always contextual and interrelated with other structures of constraint, the feminist economics project is multifaceted. Gender is common to all these facets, and many feminist analyses in economics begin with an examination of the role that the sexual division of labour plays in the social construction of gender.

In its most general sense, the sexual division of labour is a division between productive labour and reproductive labour. Productive labour is what is normally thought of as paid work or market work. Reproductive labour consists of housework, raising children and the physical and emotional care of others, all things that are generally considered women's work. Absent a gender analysis, it may seem appropriate to assume that the sexual division of labour arises because women are naturally adept in the practice of child rearing and the performance of other household tasks. Feminist economists, however, question this assumption and examine the ways in which social expectations about the meaning and substance of women's work create and perpetuate gender inequality.

Folbre's (1991) analysis of the treatment of women's domestic labour in nineteenth-century economic thought illuminates part of this process. She argues that during the eighteenth century domestic work was recognized as economically productive, but during the nineteenth-century, work came to be defined as something that was performed outside the home for wages. Market values, expressed in monetary terms, became the new arbiter of value, while activities not amenable to the money metric were relegated to the background. This definition of productive labour valorized participation in the market and devalued the nonmarket contributions of women. Housework was clearly labelled unproductive and treated as such by the census and in national income accounts. This gender bias, in ostensibly objective and scientific statistics, continues to discount the value of women's domestic labour and obscures its contributions to economic welfare.

The importance of appropriately accounting for and valuing reproductive labour is a major theme in efforts to take gender into account in macroeconomic theory and modelling. Accounting for reproductive labour is necessary in order to understand the conditions required for the functioning of the market economy. Moreover, adequate measures of the value of household production are required to understand the extent of gender inequality, and to avoid bias in measurements of economic growth when female labour force participation increases or when production shifts from the household to the market (Benería 1995). Accounting for the importance of reproductive labour has played a key role in the arena of women and development as well. Feminist scholars have shown that structural adjustment programmes implicitly rely on the unpaid labour of women to alleviate the adverse effects of policies that reduce public expenditures on health and welfare, increase food prices and reduce the role of the government. In part, policymakers are able to ignore the costs that these policies impose on women because household labour does not show up in the traditional statistics or in mainstream economic policy models (Elson 1992).

Economists of all persuasions are cognizant of the fact that women's roles in the household negatively affect their remuneration in paid labour markets. Neoclassical economics, however, takes women's responsibility for domestic labour as a given, and explains the wage gap as the result of women's rational choices to jointly maximize household income. This analysis assumes that women have a comparative advantage in household labour because the wages they give up in the market to devote more time to the household are less than men's wages. Thus women choose jobs and careers which, although lower paying, are compatible with their household responsibilities. Besides being an exercise in circular reasoning, this analysis assumes that all women will marry, that heterosexual marriage is the norm and that household income will be divided equitably. As the many entries in this volume attest, feminist economists question these assumptions and construct gender analyses that examine the ways that sex discrimination, race prejudice and occupational segregation contribute to the unfavourable labour market outcomes of women and people of colour relative to white males.

While neoclassical economics is not the only school of economics to suffer from androcentric bias, it is perhaps the most resistant to integrating gender into its theories, models and policies. Feminist economists show how neoclassical methodology seriously limits the type of explanations that count as economics and this in turn limits the ways in which economic issues can be studied. These limitations bias and distort economic knowledge. Rather than representing scientifically rigorous models of economic phenomena, neoclassical theory reflects a distinctly androcentric, or male-centred, view of the world. Neoclassical models and explanations are based on self-interested individualism and contractual exchange, both purportedly gender-neutral concepts. Economic agents, the individual members of an economic system, are assumed to be rational, self-interested individuals with no contingent obligations who choose to enter into exchange relations when it serves their own interests. Their individual economic decisions are coordinated through markets, and economic outcomes are simply the collective results of their choices.

This conception of economic agency and human relations is an idealized representation of only one part of people's economic lives, pertaining only to impersonal market interactions. Since it does not describe any relations other than those based on calculated self-interest it is not a universal description of all behaviour and relationships. It does not describe the parent–child relationship nor any other relationships based on affection or obligation. Folbre and Hartmann (1988) argue that both neoclassical and Marxist economists assume that individual self-interest motivates men's decisions in markets but does not motivate either men or women in the home. This assumption idealizes the family and legitimates gender inequality. Pujol (1992) reveals the Victorian patriarchal ideology at the root of this conception of women and the family. Examining the history of economics she shows that women, to the extent that they appear at all in classical political economy, are implicitly assumed to be married, mothers, economically dependent, unproductive and irrational.

The new home economics is similarly inadequate in its conceptions of women's agency and interfamily relations. It treats the household as an entity of unified interests, with the head of the household, assumed to be an altruist, acting in the best interest of the whole. The only economic actor in the family is the head, all others disappear from the analysis. This treatment of the family reflects a theoretical dichotomy between relations in the private realm of the family and relations in the realm of the market and public life. Rationality, objectivity and freedom are associated with the public sphere; emotion, subjectivity and necessary obligations are associated with the private sphere.

The public/private distinction has a long history in the Western liberal tradition and is closely related to a whole series of gendered dualisms characteristic of that tradition such as mind/body, reason/emotion, subjective/objective, positive/normative, masculine/feminine and freedom/necessity. These dualisms order the human and physical world into binary and purportedly natural oppositions that reflect and perpetuate gender hierarchy. Feminist economists have recognized the importance of such dualisms in economic theory and have developed various strategies for analysing and deconstructing them. Jennings (1995), for example, argues that the concept of economic man has its origins in the nineteenth-century cultural ethos that conflated men with dynamic market activity and women with unchanging familial roles. The association of women with family is still deeply embedded in our culture and remains the main foundation of contemporary gender distinctions. Recognizing that dualisms both separate and privilege the market over other spheres of life, Jennings posits a feminist institutionalism that rejects dualisms and understands markets and economies as embedded in a matrix of culture, beliefs and practices.

Nelson (1996) suggests a different strategy, constructing a new metaphor she refers to as 'the gender/value compass'. This strategy retains gender as a category of analysis, but increases the number of categories under consideration to four: masculine positive and negative and feminine positive and negative. She argues that the central task of the feminist project on gender is to explore and value the feminine positive while exposing the masculine negative. Nelson goes on to argue that this will promote an understanding of economics as centrally concerned with the provisioning of everyday life, and facilitate an understanding of human behaviour that incorporates both choice and material connection.

Other feminist economists work toward deconstructing gendered dualisms by analysing the context in which they occur and displacing their hierarchical construction. For example, Feiner and Roberts (1990) examine the treatment of race and gender in introductory economics textbooks. In these texts the economic status of white men is treated as the norm and the economic experiences of women and people of colour are represented as deviant or anomalous. Feiner and Roberts examine the way that the efficiency/equity tradeoff is used to justify economic inequality and show that this tradeoff is a false dichotomy resting on an inappropriate use of the positive/normative distinction.

Explicitly examining the implications of the intersection of gender with other stratifiers such as race, ethnicity, sexuality and class is another important area of research in feminist economics. In Western culture race is one of the most powerful, creating difference and inequality among individuals according to physical appearances in the same way that gender creates difference and inequality according to sex. Williams (1995) argues that racism was an integral part of nineteenth-century British social thought and was embedded in another set of binary oppositions such as culture/nature, civil/savage and progressive/backward. These dualisms continue to reflect and perpetuate race hierarchy. Her analysis demonstrates that economic man is not simply a masculine construction, but is also race and class specific.

Daniel Defoe's *Robinson Crusoe* is an important example of the intersections of race, gender and class in the nineteenth-century imagination. Interestingly, the character of Robinson Crusoe has become an important figure in microeconomic theory as a paradigm example of the rational economic agent. Grapard's (1995) analysis of the use of the Robinson Crusoe metaphor reveals its grounding in a racist and gendered perspective. Economists remove Crusoe from the world of violence, coercion and exploitation and place him in a social vacuum: a world without women or history. Thus economic exploitation is effectively masked by the rhetoric of contractual exchange, and the socially constructed Western male individual is presented as the human norm. Economic man is alleged to be universal and gender neutral, a ploy that effectively obscures the role of economic theorizing in maintaining race, class and gender hierarchies.

Sexuality is another important category of analysis for feminist economics. Badgett (1995) examines the relationship between gender and sexual orientation, and points out that gender alone is inadequate for understanding the lives of gays, lesbians and bisexuals. Since the families of same-sex couples face quite different legal, political and cultural constraints, gender and sexuality constitute two separate analytical axes. Ignoring the latter seriously misinterprets or implicitly omits the lives of gay people. Moreover, considering the effects of variations in sexual orientation on people's economic lives will facilitate a rethinking of the influence of gender norms and family legal institutions on economic behavior.

Gender is now a central category of analysis for both applied and theoretical feminist economics. It allows feminist economists to examine the ways in which traditional disciplinary accounts have misrepresented the lives and experiences of women, people of colour and other less economically privileged people. These examinations reveal the biases and distortions entailed by androcentric theorizing, as well as the ways that such theorizing naturalizes and protects gender, race and class privilege. Applying the lens of gender to all aspects of economics has the potential to transform the ways that feminist economists think about the economy and their own discipline. One of the challenges to feminist economics is to further incorporate analyses of the intersections race, class, sexuality and other structures of constraint into its project.

Feminist economists can broaden our understanding of economic processes and institutions by exploring the ways in which people's economic opportunities, choices and constraints are influenced by their multiple and often contradictory social locations. Examining the ways in which ostensibly universal categories are constituted by oppositional dualisms can reveal the ways that false universalism naturalizes and reproduces social hierarchy and inequality. Finally, taking gender seriously, as well as other significant dimensions of collective identity, will result in less partial and less distorted accounts of people's actual lives in all their many varieties. This can lead to economic theorizing that illuminates economic realities and facilitates socially progressive policy analyses.

DRUCILLA K. BARKER

See also

Class; Dualisms; Economic Man; Gross Domestic Product; Methodology; Patriarchy; Race; Sexual Orientation.

Bibliography

Badgett, M.V. Lee (1995), 'Gender, sexuality and sexual orientation: all in the feminist family?', *Feminist Economics*, **1** (1), 121–40.

Benería, Lourdes (1995), 'Toward a greater integration of gender in economics', *World Development*, **23** (11), 1839–50.

Elson, D. (1992), 'From Survival Strategies to Transformation Strategies: Women's Needs and Structural Adjustment', in Benería Lourdes and Shelly Feldman (eds), *Unequal Burden: Economic Crises, Persistent Poverty and Women's Work*, Boulder: Westview Press, pp. 26–48.

Feiner, Susan F. and Bruce B. Roberts (1990), 'Hidden by the invisible hand: neoclassical economic theory and the textbook treatment of race and gender', *Gender and Society*, **4** (2), June, 159–81.

Folbre, Nancy (1991), 'The unproductive housewife: her evolution in nineteenth century economic thought', *Signs: Journal of Women in Culture and Society*, **16** (31), 463–84.

Folbre, Nancy (1994), 'Collective Action and Structures of Constraint', in *Who Pays for the Kids?: Gender and the Structures of Constraint*, London: Routledge, pp. 51–90.

Folbre, Nancy and Heidi Hartmann (1988), 'The Rhetoric of Self-Interest: Ideology and Gender in Economic Theory', in Arjo Klamer, Donald McCloskey and Robert Solow (eds), *The Consequences of Economic Rhetoric*, Cambridge: Cambridge University Press, pp. 184–206.

Grapard, Ulla (1995), 'Robinson Crusoe: the quintessential economic man?', *Feminist Economics*, **1** (1), Spring, 33–52.

Jennings, Ann L. (1995), 'Public or Private: Institutional Economics and Feminism', in Marianne A. Ferber and Julie A. Nelson (eds), *Beyond Economic Man: Feminist Theory and Economics*, Chicago: University of Chicago Press, pp. 111–30.

Nelson, Julie, A. (1996), *Feminism, Objectivity, and Economics*, London: Routledge.

Pujol, Michèle (1992), *Feminism and Anti-Feminism in Early Economic Thought*, Aldershot: Edward Elgar.

Williams, Rhonda M. (1995), 'Race, Deconstruction, and the Emergent Agenda of Feminist Economic Theory', in Marianne A. Ferber and Julie A. Nelson (eds), *Beyond Economic Man: Feminist Theory and Economics*, Chicago: University of Chicago Press, pp. 144–52.

Glass Ceiling

The term 'glass ceiling' first came into use in 1986 when two *Wall Street Journal* reporters coined the phrase to describe the invisible barrier that blocks women from top jobs in corporate America (Catalyst 1992, p. 1). In their article, which was part of a *Wall Street Journal* 'Special Report on the Corporate Woman', the authors, Carol Hymowitz and Timothy Schellhardt, described a corporate world in which access to the top was blocked by a variety of factors largely related to corporate tradition and prejudice. The expression came into widespread use, primarily in the United States, although by 1989 usage had spread to the United Kingdom (Ayto 1990, p. 155). Elsewhere in the world, and in the parlance of international organizations concerned with the status of women, there are relatively few references to the term.

Although the glass ceiling is not a concept that originated in economic analysis, it has clear implications for the study of inequality of economic opportunities between men and women, specifically inequality in returns from investment in education and training. Also implied is the issue of the effectiveness of affirmative action policies and practices to overcome obstacles to women in the upper reaches of corporate management.

With the passage of time the glass ceiling metaphor was extended to include obstacles hindering the advancement of minority men as well as women (Federal Glass Ceiling Commission 1995a, p. iii). Occasionally the term has also been applied to the situation of women in the government and non-profit sectors of the economy. To what extent the glass ceiling applies to these populations will be discussed further below.

In 1991 the US Congress passed the Glass Ceiling Act pursuant to Title II of the Civil Rights Act of 1991. Under the Act, a Federal Glass Ceiling Commission was established as a 21-member bipartisan body chaired by the Secretary of Labor. Its mandate was to identify the glass ceiling barriers that have blocked the advancement of women and minorities in management and decision-making positions in the business sector of the economy and to make recommendations for eliminating such barriers. The Commission undertook an extensive research and information-gathering effort, including background studies, public hearings, surveys of chief executive officers and interviews with focus groups. This work culminated in the spring of 1995 with the Commission's fact-finding report, entitled, *Good for Business: Making Full Use of the Nation's Human Capital*, followed at the end of the year with the publication of its recommendations in *A Solid Investment: Making Full Use of the Nation's Human Capital*.

As evidence of the prevalence of the glass ceiling, the Commission presented statistics on the underrepresentation of women and minorities in the upper levels of the corporate world. A survey of senior managers in the top corporations, the *Fortune* 1000 industrial and 500 service companies, showed that 97 per cent are male. Of the *Fortune* 2000 industrial and service companies, only 5 per cent of senior managers are women, almost all of them white. African American men and women hold less than 2.5 per cent of these positions. Moreover, women and minorities earn significantly less than their white male counterparts in senior management (Federal Glass Ceiling Commission 1995a, pp. iii–iv).

The glass ceiling is less pervasive in the public and not-for-profit sectors. In fact, most women and minority professionals and managers work in these sectors. One of the background studies conducted for the Glass Ceiling Commission reported that 83 per cent of white and Hispanic women professionals and fully 90 per cent of black women professionals held positions in these sectors, as compared to 53 per cent of white male professionals (Burbridge 1994). For that reason, the glass ceiling is usually used to refer to the corporate sector rather than the government or non-profit sectors. It should be noted, however, that while women and minorities are better represented in the non-corporate management sectors the salary levels there are considerably lower than those in business.

What is the nature of the barriers that constitute the glass ceiling? Some are societal factors and others are internal to the firm. Societal factors include limitations in access to educational and training opportunities of the type required for advancement in business. These barriers have been substantially reduced over the past 25 years, in part through affirmative action efforts, and women are moving towards parity in attainment of graduate degrees in business and law. This has resulted in a significant and growing proportion of entry- and mid-level managers in corporations (Catalyst 1995). It is indicative that in a 1993 survey by Korn/Ferry International, an executive search firm, over 40 per cent of senior female executives had MBAs and 25 per cent had law degrees (Korn/Ferry International and UCLA Anderson Graduate School of Management 1993).

Clearly, the main barriers to the advancement of women into the executive ranks are those within the firm. Groundbreaking research on the subject was carried out by Ann Morrison and her colleagues at the Center for Creative Leadership in which they examined the experience of the 76 top female executives in *Fortune* 100 companies (Morrison et al. 1987; Morrison 1992). In 1992, a survey of the literature in the field was conducted for the Glass Ceiling Commission by Catalyst, an organization that works with corporations to advance women in executive positions (*Cracking the Glass Ceiling* 1992). As part of its ongoing work, Catalyst conducted a large-scale study of women in corporate management in 1995 (*Women in Corporate Leadership: Progress and Prospects*). The Catalyst study was based on a survey questionnaire regarding career paths and strategies that was sent to 1251 women who hold titles of vice-president and above in *Fortune* 1000 companies, supplemented by a survey and interviews with *Fortune* 1000 CEOs.

The overwhelming conclusion, based on these and other studies, is that the foremost barrier to the advancement of women and minorities into the executive ranks is male prejudice. While other barriers have been identified, they are often related to or the result of biased perceptions on the part of CEOs. In its 1995 survey, Catalyst examined the following barriers: male stereotyping and preconceptions of women; exclusion from informal networks of communication; lack of opportunities for general management/line experience; inhospitable corporate culture; lack of mentoring; too little time in the pipeline; lack of awareness of organizational politics; commitment to family responsibilities; lack of personal initiative or ability; ineffectual leadership style. The study results clearly demonstrate the critical role of male stereotypes and preconceptions of women. Although a majority of executive women (52 per cent) designated this factor as the chief obstacle to their advancement, most of the CEOs (82 per cent) attributed the scarcity of women in top management to lack of general management/line experience. Interestingly, there does not seem to be a similar disconnect with regard to commitment to family responsibilities as an obstacle. Only 15 per cent of executive women and 16 per cent of CEOs cite this as a factor. Undoubtedly this is because executives have the means to ensure adequate child care and other household services.

The Federal Glass Ceiling Commission used a broadened definition of the glass ceiling, one that applies to minority males as well as women. However, it was clear that the CEOs interviewed perceived the glass ceiling primarily in terms of women. They attributed the scarcity of minorities at the top to the external shortage of qualified candidates rather than to internal factors. This view is shared by the minority men interviewed, who perceived the barrier as a brick wall obstructing entry rather than a glass ceiling. While it is true, according to census data, that the pool of African-American minorities with the educational credentials required for senior management positions remains small, it has expanded since the 1960s at a rate not reflected in corporate recruitment.

Carrying the metaphor one step further, women's groups have extended the view of invisible barriers in the corporation downward from the glass ceiling at the top to the 'sticky floor' at the bottom. This view brings into the picture the large number of women in low-paying and low-mobility jobs who also face artificial barriers, including but not limited to those that make up the glass ceiling (Harlan and Bertheide 1994). The needs of women in these positions extend far beyond those of executive women, needs such as child care or opportunities for educational preparation. The 'classic' glass ceiling applies to women, including minority women, in the upper ranks. Remedies such as affirmative action legislation, while relatively effective in gaining access to employment in business organizations for women and minorities, have been less successful in advancing them to leadership positions. In principle, a corporation could be in compliance with affirmative action guidelines while promoting very few women to senior management positions.

Although women have made steady advances into management positions in recent years, progress has been slow. The 1995 Catalyst study examined the role of both individual career strategies of successful female executives and corporate management development initiatives for the advancement of women. The survey finds that while both individual and company efforts are required, corporate initiatives have been less critical than women's own efforts. A similar conclusion was reached in a study of women's advancement in the upper reaches of the legal profession (Epstein et al. 1995). In the Catalyst survey, thirteen career advancement strategies were identified. In order of their importance, as seen by women executives, they are: consistently exceed performance expectations; develop a style that men are comfortable with; seek difficult or high-visibility assignments; have an influential mentor; network with influential colleagues; gain line management (as against staff) experience; move from one functional area to another; initiate discussion regarding career aspirations; be willing to relocate; upgrade educational credentials; change companies; develop leadership outside office; gain international experience.

On the corporate side, there are a number of possible strategies to advance women into senior management but little evidence is available about the extent to which such strategies have been put into practice. In order of potential effectiveness they are: giving women high visibility assignments, succession planning, mentoring programmes, management accountability for women's advancement, in-house leadership training, external executive development programmes, women's employee networks within the firm and numerical targets. How far companies are prepared to go in adopting such practices remains to be seen.

Much will depend on changes in the business environment. The impact of such changes on the glass ceiling was investigated by Lois Shaw and her associates at the Washington-based Institute for Women's Policy Research (Shaw et al. 1993). In particular, they studied the process of corporate restructuring and globalization during the 1970s and 1980s and its influence on women's share of managerial positions. They found that restructuring during this period presented both problems and opportunities for women and minorities in management. On the plus side, there has been a long-term shift of employment from manufacturing to services, where women tend to be better represented at the managerial level. Also, to the extent that restructuring occurs through encouraging early retirement, some higher level positions become available. On the negative side, restructuring raises several kinds of problems for women and minorities: the reduction in the number of supervisory and low-level managerial positions that were formerly routes into management; the use of independent contractors instead of permanent staff; high pressures on those who remain after downsizing, which make combining career with family life more difficult; increased emphasis on geographical mobility and foreign experience for operating in the global marketplace. In spite of these disadvantages, women's share of managerial positions made progress during the 1980s, including progress at the top. Minority males made gains also but less so than women.

Although the term glass ceiling is not in widespread use worldwide, the basic concept is well known in feminist circles and organizations concerned with women's issues. Generally it is viewed as part of the broader problem of the underrepresentation of women in positions of influence in social, economic and political arenas. The Platform for Action emanating from the Fourth United Nations World Conference on Women, held in Beijing in 1995, identifies twelve critical areas of concern for the advancement of women. One of these areas is the underrepresentation of women in power and decision-making positions. Particular attention is given to the situation of women in government. The United Nations publication *The World's Women 1995: Trends and Statistics* provides comparative data on women in top positions in government, business and the media in various countries. As in the United States, women are shown to be least well represented by far in business. Further research will show whether progress in this area, however slow, continues to be made and what strategies or conditions are conducive to higher levels of participation by women.

It is notable that much of the literature on the glass ceiling emanates from sources outside of feminist economics. The most systematic data on the subject is collected by Catalyst as part of its ongoing efforts to promote women in managerial positions and on corporate boards. For understandable reasons, feminist economists have focused attention more on women at the bottom than the top of the labour market. For example, the recent book by Randy Albelda and Chris Tilly, entitled, *Glass Ceilings and Bottomless Pits*, deals almost exclusively with the bottomless pits, that is, women's poverty and welfare reform.

The scope and persistence of the glass ceiling is an issue that clearly warrants further research. An important future source of information for such research is the growing body of case law on the subject – legal actions that have taken place to enforce affirmative action at the managerial level, the testimony presented, and the court decisions reached.

MARIAM K. CHAMBERLAIN

See also
Affirmative Action; Discrimination, Theories of; Labour Market Segmentation; Labour Markets, Theories of.

Bibliography
Albelda, Randy and Chris Tilly (1997), *Glass Ceilings and Bottomless Pits: Women's Work and Women's Poverty*, Boston, Massachusetts: South End Press.
Ayto, John (1990), *Longman Register of New Words, Volume Two*, Essex: Longman Group UK Limited.

Burbridge, Lynne (1994), 'The Glass Ceiling in Different Sectors of the Economy: Differences Between Government, Non-Profit and For-Profit Organizations', Paper prepared for the Glass Ceiling Commission.

Catalyst (1992), *Cracking the Glass Ceiling: Strategies for Success*, New York: Catalyst.

Catalyst (1996), *Women in Corporate Leadership: Progress and Prospects*, New York: Catalyst.

Epstein, Cynthia Fuchs, Robert Saute, Bonnie Oglensky and Martha Gever (1995), 'Glass ceilings and open doors: women's advancement in the legal profession', *Fordham Law Review*, **LXIV** (2), November, 295–449.

Federal Glass Ceiling Commission (1995a), *Good for Business: Making Full Use of the Nation's Human Capital*, Washington, DC: US Government Printing Office.

Federal Glass Ceiling Commission (1995b), *A Solid Investment: Making Full Use of the Nation's Capital*, Washington, DC: US Government Printing Office.

Harlan, Sharon L. and Catherine Waite Bertheide (1994), *Barriers to Workplace Advancement Experienced by Women in Low Paying Occupations*, Albany: Center for Women in Government, State University of New York.

Korn/Ferry International and UCLA Anderson Graduate School of Management (1993), Decade of the Executive Woman, New York: Korn/Ferry International.

Morrison, Ann M. (1992), *The New Leaders: Guidelines on Leadership Diversity*, San Franciso: Jossey-Bass Inc., Publishers.

Morrison, Ann M., Randall P. White, Ellen Van Velsor and the Center for Creative Leadership (1987), *Breaking the Glass Ceiling*, Reading, Massachusetts: Addison-Wesley Publishing Company.

Shaw, Lois B., Dell P. Champlin, Heidi I. Hartmann and Roberta Spalter-Roth (1993), *The Impact of the Glass Ceiling and Structural Change on Minorities and Women*, Washington, DC: Institute for Women's Policy Research.

United Nations (1995), *The World's Women 1995: Trends and Statistics*, New York: United Nations.

Globalization

Globalization refers to the growing integration of national economies through increasingly unfettered flows of trade, investment and financial capital across national borders. It is an economic process that began with the emergence of capitalism in the sixteenth century and gained new impetus in the 1990s owing to trade and financial liberalization and rapid diffusion of information technologies. This process has implications for economies of both Third World and industrial nations, and feminist researchers have examined the gender implications in both contexts.

The latest phase in the process of globalization began in the 1970s as industrial economies gradually reduced trade barriers under the General Agreement on Tariffs and Trade (GATT). This was followed by a reduction in capital controls in the early 1980s. The turning point, indeed the main force driving the recent globalization, is the implementation of supply-side (neoloberal) macroeconomic policies in the industrial and Third World economies alike after 1980. In most Third World economies these policies were adopted under the rubric of structural adjustment policies (SAPs) and as a solution to the balance of payments crisis induced by these countries' heavy international debt. The supply-side policies call for the liberalization of trade and capital inflows, restrictive fiscal policy, domestic deregulation, privatization of state-owned enterprises and specialization in economic activities based on comparative advantage as key components of a successful strategy for economic growth.

The emphasis on specialization according to comparative advantage has brought about a dramatic shift in Third World economies to export-oriented growth based on either labour-intensive manufactures or agro-exports. The integration of Eastern European economies into this global trade and investment network in the post-1989 period has followed a similar process of adjustment. The key agents that have extended this network to the Third World and to Eastern Europe are the Bretton Woods Institutions, primarily the World Bank and the International Monetary Fund (IMF), which have forced the adoption of a uniform set of policies in debtor countries and have regarded their rate of integration into the global economy as the main indicator of their success in development. The international trade agreements of the early 1990s (North American Free Trade Agreement (NAFTA), the Uruguay Round of GATT, and the creation of the World Trade Organization) have given a further impetus to both the growth of international trade and trade liberalization. Other agreements under negotiation, such as the Multilateral Agreement on Investment (MAI), seek to reduce government restrictions on international investment. As a result of this increasing international homogenization of economic policies there has been an unprecedented extension of markets and deepening of capitalist relations on a global scale.

The second major force driving the recent globalization is the application of information technologies, which reduced the costs of communication and thereby the time and space that separate national markets, and changed the skill requirements of many jobs. The new technologies have thereby boosted the mobility of capital in new ways. First, they have allowed the transnational corporations (TNCs) to minimize costs by outsourcing, either relocating standardized, labour-intensive segments of manufacturing processes to lower cost sites or creating global electronic outworking in services that were previously non-tradeable, and dispersing corporate departments in different parts of the globe. Second, the new technologies have facilitated the massive growth of cross-border, short-term financial capital flows in foreign exchange, derivative and equity markets, and the resurgence of portfolio investment (in part as a response to the privatization of state-owned enterprises in Third World countries and Eastern European economies) (Lall 1997).

There are differing positions on the *consequences* of globalization, which correspond to the longstanding divide in economic theory and policy between neoclassical and non-neoclassical economics. The proponents of globalization are neoclassical economists, who emphasize the benefits associated with the 'free' flow of goods and resources internationally and minimal government involvement in the domestic economy. Indeed, neoclassical theory underpins the economic policies guiding the recent globalization. Critics of globalization are predominantly non-neoclassical economists, who emphasize the social costs of globalization and support government policies to address these costs.

The optimistic views on globalization are exemplified by Krugman (1995) and the World Bank/IMF position embodied in the SAPs. The proponents of globalization assume that this process is inevitable and beneficial to all countries willing to pursue the prescribed economic policies. Production and trade based on comparative advantage is expected to bring about greater growth and a rise in standards of living everywhere through a better division of labour, bigger economies of scale, the flow of investment toward activities with the highest returns, and lower prices. The proponents of this view either downplay or dismiss the costs of globalization. Most acknowledge that during the adjustment process to the new pattern of international specialization unskilled workers in industrial countries will be hurt by the decline in demand for their labour. However, they view these adverse effects as temporary and small, and attribute the growing wage inequality or persistent unemployment to technological change, rather than import competition. Their argument is based on the relatively small size of industrial country trade with Third World countries and the weak empirical support for trade as the cause of growing wage inequality (Freeman 1995; Cline 1997). They also oppose any measures that would impede the working of the principle of comparative advantage and limit the free mobility of goods and capital (such as protection of industries facing import competition or enactment of minimum international environmental, health, safety and labour standards that would raise the costs of investing in the Third World). The proponents predict that the working and living conditions in the Third World will improve as the outcome of the unfettered growth process, such that they will look more like those in industrial countries (that is, an 'upward harmonization' will take place) as workers increasingly demand better living and working conditions.

Critics of globalization represent a wide range of perspectives, including neoclassical economics. The main focus of critics is the employment and distributional effects of globalization on industrial economies. By contrast to the proponents, the critics view trade with low income economies as an important, if not the main, explanation for growing wage inequality (Wood 1994; Rodrik 1997; Feenstra 1998). Critics within the neoclassical school, Rodrik (1997) and Feenstra (1998), respectively fault neoclassical analyses for overlooking the substantial restructuring of national economies (and job losses) that are needed to bring about the much-hailed benefits of freer trade and the adverse employment effects of international outsourcing by TNCs. Rodrik argues that, even if the direct impact of trade is small, globalization is likely to exacerbate the downward movement of wages and labour standards in three ways. First, globalization weakens the bargaining power of workers, who now become substitutable for one another on a global scale. Second, trade erodes industrial country norms as imports produced under weaker labour standards outcompete those produced under higher standards. Third, freer mobility of capital erodes the tax base and makes it increasingly difficult to finance social programmes, as the tax burden shifts away from the TNCs and the wealthy, to workers who are neither internationally mobile nor able to pay higher taxes. Neoclassical critics argue for new government spending in order to ease social tensions and hardships arising from increasing inequality, poverty, and unemployment (Kapstein 1996; Rodrik 1997). Specifically, there are calls for 'positive adjustment policies' (Greenaway and Milner 1995), the need for continuous upgrading of skills (Freeman et al. 1995), changes in multilateral rules that allow for industrial countries to protect their labour standards through trade restrictions (Rodrik 1997), and extension of wage subsidies to low-skilled workers hurt by shifting trade patterns (Feenstra 1998).

Non-neoclassical critics are similarly concerned with rising wage and class inequality and consequent disruptions in the social fabric. In addition, they are concerned with the detrimental effects of globalization on the environment (Korten 1995; Mander and Goldsmith 1996). In this view, globalization is weakening the capacity of the state to regulate the actions of increasingly powerful financial speculators and the TNCs in a number of ways. First, non-neoclassical critics are concerned about a 'downward harmonization' of standards in industrial countries under the threat of capital flight and job losses. Their second major concern is about the restrictions imposed by capital mobility and the recent trade agreements on the state's ability to set its own economic and social policies and address the needs of its citizens whose lives have become more economically insecure (Cohen 1996). A third concern is about the opening up of Third World economies to capital flows without adequate environmental, health and safety protections in place (Sen 1997). Fourth, there is growing concern about the costs of financial liberalization to the low-income groups in the Third World and industrial countries alike, who may have to bear the brunt of the crises that are precipitated by the whims of financial speculators and that may spread from one country to another. These costs may be borne either in the form of SAPs or allocation of tax revenues for bail-outs. Non-neoclassical critics view the enactment of international standards and greater regulation of capital as the main means for countering these adverse effects of globalization.

Much of the above literature has ignored the gender-, race- and even class-differentiated consequences of globalization. Neoclassical economists identify the adverse effects only on the specific group referred to as 'unskilled' workers. To the extent that they discuss gendered effects, these are couched in

arguments against the adoption of protective, anti-discrimination or minimum wage legislation and in favour of dismantling existing labour regulations.
These studies argue that women workers are likely to be the losers from
having such regulations (World Bank 1996). While the non-neoclassical perspective focuses on the adverse implications of globalization on the working
class in general terms, it has been more open to examining the interactions of
class and gender (MacEwan and Tabb 1989; Sklair 1992). Indeed, the growing feminist and feminist economics literature on globalization has been
informed by the non-neoclassical perspective.

With few exceptions (Benería 1989; Connelly et al. 1995; Sen 1997), feminist
economists have not written on globalization generally, but rather on the effects
of various *processes* of globalization on the gender division of labour and gender
division of control over economic resources in both the Third World and industrial countries. Specifically, feminist economists have focused on the effects of
the implementation of the supply-side model and the recent international trade
agreements on both the employment prospects and working conditions of men
and women workers and the unpaid work of women. Recently, feminist economists have also shown how gender inequality may either constrain or underlie the
success of macroeconomic policies, thereby highlighting the feedback effects
between gender inequality and macroeconomic outcomes.

Among the first group of studies, feminist empirical research on Third
World and Eastern European countries has focused on the detrimental effects
of SAPs and market reforms on the employment prospects and livelihoods of
the low-income groups, among whom women, minority race and ethnic groups
are overrepresented (Palmer 1991; Benería and Feldman 1992; Bakker 1994;
Aslanbeigui et al. 1994; Sparr 1994). This research has also shown that the
implementation of SAPs has increased the female share of the industrial
labour force and overall employment (that is, brought about the 'feminization
of employment'). This has been the outcome of both the entry of increasing
numbers of women into wage labour as a result of worsening living standards
and the increased demand for women workers in export-oriented industries.
Most of the early case studies of newly-industrializing economies and recent
cross-country evidence supports the association of export-orientation of Third
World economies with the feminization of employment (Wood 1991; Çagatay
and Ozler 1995).

Feminist researchers have long problematized the poor working conditions
in export-oriented jobs (Nash and Fernandez-Kelly 1983). However, the recent consensus is that these jobs are nonetheless superior to the alternatives
for women in the domestic economy (Lim 1990; Joekes 1995; Sen 1997).
Feminist research has explained the employer preference for women workers
in export-oriented industries in terms of the unit labour cost advantage provided by women (Elson and Pearson 1981), brought about by the concerted

efforts of governments and firms to mobilize gender ideals and stereotypes to create women as secondary workers (Elson 1995; Seguino 1997). While early research suggested that country comparative advantage in export of labour-intensive manufactures is based on women's disadvantages (Arizpe and Aranda 1981), recent research provides preliminary evidence that gender wage in-equality may indeed be an important source of export growth (Seguino 1997).

Recent case studies suggest, however, that the concentration of women in manufacturing jobs may be a historically limited phase in export-oriented industrialization (Joekes 1995; Pearson 1995). To the extent that countries are able to upgrade the quality of their exports and move away from standard labour-intensive products, as is the case in a small number of newly-industri-alizing countries, the demand for female labour declines. In addition, there is evidence that the diffusion of just-in-time organizational innovations is lead-ing to a defeminization or masculinization of manufacturing as men emerge as the more flexible, cost-effective workers compared to women (Roldan 1993). Since the high female share in manufacturing employment is a sign of women's secondary status in the labour market, this decline is not necessarily an adverse development (Joekes 1995). The interpretation of these labour market adjustments clearly depends on whether the emerging employment opportunities for women represent better pay and working conditions.

Until recently, research by feminist economists on gendered labour market outcomes in industrial countries has not been framed by questions related to globalization. In the last decade, Standing (1989) has proposed the 'global feminization' thesis and suggested that in industrial economies this tendency reflects the substitution of low-waged women workers for men workers in the context of deskilling of jobs and weakening of labour regulations. While the precise mechanisms have yet to be understood, Wood (1991) has found empirical support for feminization of manufacturing employment in indus-trial countries up to the mid-1980s. Feminist economists have also shown that since the mid-1980s the employment losses and dislocation brought about by the recent trade agreements are disproportionately borne by women, especially minority women (Cohen 1987; Gabriel and MacDonald 1996). They have also raised concerns about the constraints on social policy im-posed by these trade agreements that endanger future redistributive policies in favour of women and minorities (Cohen 1996).

The second major concern of feminist economists has been the conse-quences of the implementation of the supply-side model for the unpaid labour of women. Elson (1995) has criticized macroeconomics for treating labour as a non-produced input to economic growth and disregarding the role of the unpaid labour of women in reproducing the labour force. According to Elson, the neglect of gender division of labour in macroeconomic theory has conse-quences for not only equity but also efficiency of policy outcomes. As

SAPs increase the pressures on women to engage in paid work, the rigidity of gender division of labour in the household results in the intensification of women's unpaid labour. If, in response, daughters are withdrawn from school, then this will likely impede future economic growth via the quality of the future labour force. In addition, the rigidity of gender division of labour and the consequent inflexibility of labour allocation may prevent SAPs from achieving the intended adjustment in the composition of output away from non-tradeables to tradeables. By demonstrating the weaknesses of the macroeconomic model that underpins the supply-side policies, such critiques point the way for developing macroeconomic models consistent with the goal of human development rather than simply economic growth (Elson 1997) and such efforts by feminist economists have already begun (Palmer 1991; Çagatay et al. 1995).

Feminist economists have proposed a number of strategies to address the detrimental effects of globalization. Reinterpreting the politics of social movements, Sen (1997) argues that women's organizations have to work both globally and locally and forge coalitions with groups engaged in class- and race-based politics. The goals of this political action are to make the state and the TNCs accountable, to reform the IMF and the World Bank, and to push for new international agreements in order to reshape the global economy. Gibson-Graham (1996), on the other hand, emphasizes the politics of representation. She argues that in order to devise strategies that make use of the contradictions in the global economy, scholars and policymakers have to avoid representing the 'globalizers' and the 'globalized' in homogeneous ways, specifically the TNCs as all-powerful, invincible entities.

Many issues raised by the recent globalization process have yet to be examined by feminist economists. First, feminist economists have to examine the gendered employment impact of information technologies, especially the implications of the internationalization of services (building on the recent research by Mitter and Rowbotham 1995). Second, feminist economists need to work on engendering international trade models and continue the empirical research on the gendered employment and wage effects of macroeconomic and trade policies. The task of assessing the 'price' of the Third World macroeconomic success stories or 'miracles' in terms of gender and class inequalities is far from complete. Third, feminist economic research on industrial countries has to adopt a global lens in the examination of labour market outcomes, macroeconomic policies, social safety net, education, and training policies, as exemplified by Bakker (1996). Heightened global awareness in industrial country research is imperative for feminist economists to break the 'industrial country–Third World country' dichotomies in analysis and policy. The challenge for feminist economics is to examine the *connections* between industrial country and Third World country developments, and to identify the processes that link the fortunes of disadvantaged workers globally, in order to enable the broadest political coalitions based on common interests. Fourth, there is the urgent need for feminist economists to continue the work (begun with Çagatay et al. 1995) on developing alternative macro-economic models and policies to the supply-side model, which currently underpins globalization.

GÜNSELI BERIK

See also
Development Policies; Economic Restructuring; Growth Theory (Macro Models); International Economics; Macroeconomics; Structural Adjustment Policies.

Bibliography

Arizpe, Lourdes and Josefina Aranda (1981), 'The comparative advantage of women's disadvantages: women workers in the strawberry industry in Mexico', *Signs*, **7** (2), 453–73.

Aslanbeigui, Nahid, Steve Pressman and Gail Summerfield (eds) (1994), *Women in the Age of Economic Transformation: Gender Impact of Reforms in Post-Socialist and Developing Countries*, London and New York: Routledge.

Bakker, Isabella (ed.) (1994), *The Strategic Silence: Gender and Economic Policy*, London: Zed Books.

Bakker, Isabella (ed.) (1996), *Rethinking Restructuring: Gender and Change in Canada*, Toronto, Buffalo, London: University of Toronto Press.

Benería, Lourdes (1989), 'Gender and the Global Economy', in Arthur MacEwan and William K. Tabb (eds), *Instability and Change in the World Economy*, New York: Monthly Review Press, pp. 242–58.

Benería, Lourdes and Shelley Feldman (eds) (1992), *Unequal Burden: Economic Crisis, Persistent Poverty and Women's Work*, Boulder: Westview Press.

Çagatay, Nilufer, Diane Elson and Caren Grown (eds) (1995), 'Gender, adjustment and macroeconomic models', Special Issue, *World Development*, **23** (11).

Çagatay, Nilufer and Sule Ozler (1995), 'Feminization of the labour force: the effects of long-term development and structural adjustment', *World Development*, **23** (11), 1883–94.

Cline, William R. (1997), *Trade and Income Distribution*, Washington, DC: Institute for International Economics.

Cohen, Marjorie (1987), *Free Trade and the Future of Women's Work*, Toronto: Garamond Press.

Cohen, Marjorie (1996), 'Democracy and the Future of Nations: Challenges for Disadvantaged Women and Minorities', in Robert Boyer and Daniel Drache (eds), *States against Markets: The Limits of Globalization*, London and New York: Routledge, pp. 399–414.

Connelly, Patricia, Tania Murray Li, Martha MacDonald and Jane L. Parpart (1995), 'Restructured worlds/restructured debates: globalization, development and gender', *Canadian Journal of Development Studies*, Special Issue, 17–38.

Elson, Diane (1995), 'Male bias in Macroeconomics: The Case of Structural Adjustment', in *Male Bias in the Development Process*, Manchester: Manchester University Press, pp. 164–90.

Elson, Diane (1997), 'Economic Paradigms Old and New: The Case of Human Development', in Roy Culpeper, Albert Berry and Frances Stewart (eds), *Global Development Fifty Years After Bretton Woods*, New York: St Martin's Press, pp. 50–71.

Elson, Diane and Ruth Pearson (1981), 'The subordination of women and the internationalization of factory production', in Kate Young, Carol Wolkowitz and Roslyn McCullagh (eds), *Of Marriage and the Market*, London, Boston, Melbourne and Henley: Routledge and Kegan Paul, pp. 18–40.

Feenstra, Robert C. (1998), 'Integration of trade and disintegration of production in the global economy', *Journal of Economic Perspectives*, **12** (4), 31–50.

Freeman, Chris, Luc Soete and Umit Efendioglu (1995), 'Diffusion and the employment effects of information and communication technology', *International Labour Review*, **134** (4–5), 587–604.

Freeman, Richard B. (1995), 'Are your wages set in Beijing?', *Journal of Economic Perspectives*, **9** (3), 15–32.

Gabriel, Christine and Laura MacDonald (1996), 'NAFTA and Economic Restructuring: Some Gender and Race Implications', in Isabella Bakker (ed.), *Rethinking Restructuring: Gender and Change in Canada*, Toronto, Buffalo, London: University of Toronto Press, pp. 165–86.

Gibson-Graham, J.K. (1996), *The End of Capitalism (As We Knew It): A Feminist Critique of Political Economy*, Cambridge, Massachusetts: Blackwell Publishers.

Greenaway, David and Chris Milner (1995), 'The world trade system and the Uruguay round: global employment implications', *International Labour Review*, **134** (4–5), (July–October), 497–517.

Joekes, Susan (1995), *Trade-Related Employment For Women in Industry and Services in Developing Countries*, Geneva: United Nations Research Institute For Social Development, Occasional Paper 5.

Joekes, Susan and Ann Weston (1994), *Women and the New Trade Agenda*, New York: UNIFEM.

Kapstein, Ethan B. (1996), 'Workers and the world economy', *Foreign Affairs*, **75** (3), 16–37.

Korten, David (1995), *When Corporations Rule the World*, West Hartford and San Francisco, California: Kumarian Press and Berrett-Koehler Publishers.

Krugman, Paul (1995), 'Growing world trade: causes and consequences', *Brookings Papers on Economic Activity*, (1), 327–77.

Lall, Sanjaya (1997), 'TNCs: the New Custodians of Development?', Roy Culpeper, Albert Berry and Frances Stewart (eds), *Global Development Fifty Years After Bretton Woods*, New York: St Martin's Press, pp. 169–91.

Lim, Linda (1990), 'Women's Work in Export Factories: The Politics of a Cause', in Irene Tinker (ed.), *Persistent Inequalities*, New York: Oxford University Press, pp. 101–19.

MacEwan, Arthur and William Tabb (eds) (1989), *Instability and Change in the World Economy*, New York: Monthly Review Press.

Mander, Jerry and Edward Goldsmith (eds) (1996), *The Case Against the Global Economy: and for a Turn Toward the Local*, San Francisco: The Sierra Club Books.

Mitter, Swasti and Sheila Rowbotham (eds) (1995), *Women Encounter Technology: Changing Patterns of Employment in the Third World*, London and New York: Routledge.

Nash, June and Maria Patricia Fernandez-Kelly (eds) (1983), *Women, Men and the International Division of Labour*, Albany: State University of New York Press.

Palmer, Ingrid (1991), *Gender and Population in the Adjustment of African Economies: Planning for Change*, Geneva: International Labour Office.

Pearson, Ruth (1995), 'Male Bias and Women's Work in Mexico's Border Industries', in Diane Elson (ed.) *Male Bias in the Development Process*, Manchester: Manchester University Press, pp. 133–63.

Rodrik, Dani (1997), *Has Globalization Gone Too Far?*, Washington, DC: Institute for International Economics.

Roldan, Martha (1993), 'Industrial restructuring, deregulation and new JIT labour processes in Argentina: towards a gender-aware perspective?', *IDS Bulletin*, **24** (2), 42–52.

Seguino, Stephanie (1997), 'Gender wage inequality and export-led growth in South Korea', *Journal of Development Studies*, **34** (2), 102–32.

Sen, Gita (1997), 'Globalization, justice and equity: a gender perspective', *Development*, **40** (2), 21–26.

Sklair, Leslie (1992), *Capitalism and Development*, London and New York: Routledge.

Sparr, Pamela (ed.) (1994), *Mortgaging Women's Lives: Feminist Critiques of Structural Adjustment*, London and New Jersey: Zed Books.

Standing, Guy (1989), 'Global feminization through flexible labour', *World Development*, **17** (7), 1077–95.

Wood, Adrian (1991), 'North–South trade and female labour in manufacturing: an asymmetry', *Journal of Development Studies*, **27** (2), 168–89.

Wood, Adrian (1994), *North–South Trade, Employment and Inequality: Changing Fortunes in a Skill Driven World*, Oxford: Oxford University Press.
World Bank (1996), *Involving Workers in East Asia's Growth*, Washington, DC: The World Bank.

Gross Domestic Product

The gross domestic product (GDP) represents the value added of all production activities of resident producer units encompassed by the production boundary of the national accounts. The international guidelines for compilation of national accounts were earlier issued by the United Nations. Most recently the revised System of National Accounts (SNA) has been published jointly by the five organizations: United Nations, OECD, IMF, World Bank and Commission of the European Communities (Eurostat) (United Nations et al. 1993).

As indicated by the term 'value added', GDP measures the total value of output of the economy without 'double counting' the value of input in the production process. Hence, GDP as a measure of production is defined as output minus intermediate consumption. Equivalently, GDP is defined as the final uses of goods and services that pass from the producer units into final demand, that is, goods and services that are not used again in the production of other goods. Final demand is generally defined as comprising final consumption expenditure, gross capital formation and net exports (exports less imports).

GDP is the value of all goods and services produced in a country without regard to its allocation among domestic and foreign claims, whereas gross national product (GNP) or gross national income (GNI) as it is called in SNA 1993, is the sum of total domestic and foreign primary incomes of all residents of a country, and so it includes net income received from abroad. Thus, for countries with a large migrant labour force, or where a large part of the capital stock is owned by overseas residents, there may be large differences between domestic product (what is produced inside the economic territory of the country) and national product, or national income (what accrues to the residents of the country). For purposes of comparisons of the economic welfare of a nation the national income is probably more relevant than the domestic product. Gross national income (GNI) minus consumption of fixed capital, that is net national income (NNI), is thus referred to as national income. Conceptually, both GNI and NNI are measures of income and not product.

All activities producing goods and services that are supplied, or in principle could be supplied, to other units are encompassed within the production boundary of the national accounts. Own-account production of all goods that are retained by their producers is included in the production concept, whereas own-account production of services is confined to housing services by owner-occupied dwellings and domestic and personal services produced by employing paid domestic staff. The 1993 revision of SNA comprises a thorough discussion of the production boundary. In order to include women's unpaid work, it is now recommended that unpaid household work is imputed in satellite accounts, that is, supplementary accounts that are separate from but consistent with the national account framework.

Interest in measuring the national product or national income of a country goes back a long way in history (Studenski 1958). The first estimates of national income were made in England by Sir William Petty in 1665 and Gregory King in 1698. Petty adopted a comprehensive income concept, defining the 'Income of the people' as the sum of the 'Annual value of the Labour of the people' and the 'Annual Proceed of the Stock of wealth of the nation'. On the other side of this double-entry account, he included the 'Annual Expense of the people', comprising consumption outlays and, in principle, the surplus remaining after current consumption.

In the late eighteenth century the French physiocrats, led by François Quesnay, identified national income with agricultural product, believing that only agriculture produced a rent over and above costs. The physiocratic framework provided a useful tool for showing the connections between agriculture and the so-called nonproductive sectors of the economy into a *tableau économique*, which showed that the national income would be obtained by adding up all the outputs produced in the economy – amounting to the national product.

Statistical implementation of estimates of national product required more extensive and sophisticated data, and it came much later. By the early 1900s, however, estimates of both national income and national product had been made in a number of countries. At that time the measurement of national income focused on a comprehensive production concept, encompassing all productive resources in economies where agricultural subsistence production was still widespread. Within this historical context it seemed natural to consider nonmarket work as a contribution to national income. In several countries the early national income estimates included imputed values for the unpaid work of women in the household, for example for Norway (Kiær 1913) and the United States (King et al. 1921). These figures were based on census numbers of housewives and daughters living at home, multiplied by the average wage rate for domestic servants.

During the 1930s the influence of Keynesian thought on national accounting was reflected in the shift in the focus away from its earlier primary concern with measuring national income to measuring GDP and its final demand components as instruments for fiscal policy and income determination. At the same time the availability of statistical material was greatly improved. The statistical developments in some cases preceded the theoretical: Kuznets' (1934) first data came well before Keynes's theory, but both reflected the same need and reinforced and stimulated each other. Part of this development was Leontief's pioneering work of input–output analysis. This theoretical and empirical effort reached an important point at the end of World War II, when comprehensive national accounts were published in a number of countries, among them Great Britain, the United States, Norway, Denmark, the Netherlands, France, Canada and Australia.

In Norway and the other Scandinavian countries the national account estimates included the value of unpaid household work: for Norway in 1943 estimated to be 15 per cent of the national product. The purpose of including the value of unpaid household work in the national accounts was to provide a comprehensive picture of all economic activity in society. Despite the apparent undervaluation as compared to recent estimates, they represented a pioneering effort to record women's economic contribution to society. The Scandinavian national accounting tradition of the 1930s was characterized by its emphasis on both real and financial flows being part of the national account system. In contrast, the Anglo–American tradition, here represented by Pigou, emphasized the financial flows and suggested that national income should include 'everything that people buy with money income, together with the services that a man obtains from a house owned and inhabited by himself' (Pigou, quoted in Waring 1989). According to this view, unpaid household activities clearly belong within the production boundary, regardless of whether money changes hands or not.

The first international standard for national accounts, *A System of National Accounts and Supporting Tables* published in 1953 (United Nations 1953), came to be based on a market approach, where only goods and services that were exchanged for money or could be exchanged for money should be included. Goods and services produced by unpaid household work were excluded by this choice of production boundary (United Nations 1953). Concern for internationally comparable figures led Norway in 1950 to omit unpaid work in the national accounts.

As the national account framework found widespread use as a tool for macroeconomic policies and business-cycle management, methodological improvements focused on those uses rather than on expanding the production boundary to own-account production of goods and services. During the 1970s, a new interest emerged in extending national accounting to social accounting, following the discussion of GDP as a welfare indicator (Nordhaus and Tobin 1972). Both time-use in nonmarket activities and environmental concerns were seen as crucial issues to include in welfare measurements (United Nations 1977). As appropriate data became available in the form of time budget surveys, the question of women's unpaid work in the household was brought back on the agenda. In this process the pioneering work of Reid (1934) was rediscovered. Eisner (1989) provided a framework for extended national accounts, including imputed values for unpaid household work (see, for example, Chadeau 1992 and Goldschmidt-Clermont 1993). Waring (1989) won a wide audience for her book *If Women Counted: A New Feminist Economics*. Ironmonger (1996) pioneered a practical application of the extended national account in his proposal to compute the Gross Household Product, in addition to Gross Market Product, the total of which is Gross Economic Product. Not only is the level of productive activity biased when unpaid household production is not included, but so is the level of growth rates of the economy as well (see, for example, Devereux and Locay 1992; Wagman and Folbre 1996; Eisner 1997). Thus, a feminist perspective on national accounting has argued that a more comprehensive valuation of production is needed, in order to give visibility both to women's unpaid work and to nature and the natural environment (see, for example, Clark 1995; Duchin 1998; Nelson 1997).

As unpaid household work has not been included in national accounts, the contribution of women's work to society is undervalued in economic terms. This is due in part to a somewhat restrictive definition of economic activity. But part of the problem is the notion of value itself. For the purposes of economic valuation, value is synonymous with market value. But many goods and services with economic value are not marketed. In theory, this problem is resolvable if these items could be sold, for a market value could then be imputed to them on this basis – as is done for subsistence crops consumed by the producers themselves. The question of value is simplified in practice by assuming that an hour of market work and an hour of nonmarket work have the same value. This implies that productivity differences between market and nonmarket work are disregarded.

An additional consideration is that the value of much household and community work transcends market value, because this activity may have an intrinsic value that is not fully captured by its market value. Indicators for quality of life represent an attempt to measure values that are not fully reflected in market values (Nussbaum and Sen 1993). The pursuit of good health, the acquisition of knowledge, the time devoted to fostering social relationships, the hours spent in the company of relatives and friends – all are worthwhile activities, yet they carry no price tag.

For *Human Development Report 1995*, extensive research was undertaken on the amount of time women and men spend on market and nonmarket activities. Spanning industrial and developing countries, the data generated by this research are used to provide estimates of the value of household and other unpaid work (Goldschmidt-Clermont and Pagnossin-Aligisakis 1995).

A review of the 31 countries in the sample shows that women work longer hours than men in nearly every country. Of the total burden of paid and unpaid work, measured by labour market statistics and time budget surveys, women carry on average 53 per cent in developing countries and 51 per cent in industrial countries. Of men's total work time in industrial countries, roughly two-thirds is spent in paid market activities and one-third in unpaid non-market activities. For women, these shares are reversed. In developing countries, more than three-quarters of men's work is in market activities, while women spend two-thirds of their total work time in unpaid nonmarket work (United Nations 1995, pp. 88, 89).

To aggregate the output of household goods and services and compare it with the aggregates of conventional national accounts, such as gross domestic product, the value of household production is usually computed at the cost of inputs – labour and capital. For unpaid labour, a market wage is imputed to the labour time needed to produce household goods and services. The market wage selected is usually that of a substitute household worker – a worker who can perform, within the household, most of the economic activities carried out by unpaid household members. Because such workers tend in industrial countries to be women with relatively low pay, using their wage as a yardstick gives a conservative estimate of the value of household labour. After selecting this wage, the choice is among using net wages (after taxes), gross wages (before taxes) or extra gross wages, which include employers' social security contributions. Most satellite accounts are based on extra gross wages for estimating value added household production, as this is the case in market sectors (Goldschmidt-Clermont 1993).

With extra gross wages as the yardstick, a conservative estimate of the value of nonmarket production in households is about half the value of gross domestic product in industrialized countries. Most of the value of nonmarket output is attributable to labour; for example, labour valued at extra gross wages accounts for 72 per cent of GDP in Australia, 53 per cent in Germany and 45 per cent in Finland. Clearly, the value of nonmarket production in households in industrial countries is considerable, whatever the standard (United Nations 1995, p. 97).

Further improvements of the national accounting framework in the directions outlined above involves two aspects that need to be addressed separately. First, in order to find more comprehensive measures of economic activities taking place within the economy as a whole, supplementary statistics like satellite accounts for household production are needed. In connection with this, many methodological issues need elaboration, for example, the use of market wage rates in evaluating unpaid work, the assessment of productivity in household production, and the question of valuing output directly rather than measuring value added from the costs of input. Future research as well as statistical implementation, based on time budget surveys, should aim at developing satellite accounts in all countries as a tool for evaluating economic policies. As part of this methodological improvement it will be useful to develop an input–output approach to the interrelations between the market and nonmarket spheres (Ironmonger 1996).

Secondly, a more general question is the validity of using measures of aggregate production or consumption as an indicator of welfare. GDP was never meant as a welfare indicator, yet for lack of more suitable measures, welfare evaluations are often based on GDP comparisons. The United Nations has now developed Human Development Indicators (HDI) that capture several dimensions of welfare, that is, life expectancy, educational attainment and adjusted real income. Since 1995 the HDI has been supplemented by the gender-related development index (GDI) and the gender empowerment index (GEM) (United Nations 1995). The GDI concentrates on the same variables as the HDI but focuses on inequality between women and men as well as on the average achievement of all people taken together. In other words, the GDI is the HDI adjusted for gender inequality. The GEM concentrates on participation – economic, political and professional. It focuses on three variables: income-earning power, share in professional and managerial jobs and share of parliamentary seats. Due to data limitations it cannot capture aspects of empowerment such as status within the household, in community life or in rural areas.

While both GDI and GEM are important supplements to HDI in describing women's situation, these indicators quantify only those aspects that are readily measurable. They do not cover quality of life dimensions such as participation in community life, decision making within the family, dignity and personal security. These dimensions are powerful determinants of the relative status of women over and above income levels. In order to find a more comprehensive measure of women's wellbeing it is crucial to develop quality of life indicators. In addition to capturing the above-mentioned aspects, quality of life indicators need to address women's situation in the workplace, covering a wide range of issues, from protection of workers' rights, availability of jobs and access to quality child care, to women's participation in corporate decision making. Both the existing indicators, GDI and GEM, and future quality of life indicators to be developed are highly useful tools as they serve as constant reminders to policymakers to evaluate consequences of economic policy for the situation of women. It is a great challenge to develop indicators for quality of life that can better represent the connections between economic conditions and the ecological and human conditions, and to link such indicators to a national account framework.

IULIE ASLAKSEN

See also
Domestic Labour; Economic Welfare.

Bibliography
Chadeau, Ann (1992), 'What is household's non-market production worth?', *OECD Economic Studies*, **18**, 85–103.

Clark, Mary E. (1995), 'Rethinking ecological and economic education: a Gestalt shift', *Ecological Economics*, **18**, 400–415.

Devereux, J. and L. Locay (1992), 'Specialization, household production and the measurement of economic growth', *American Economic Review*, **82**, 399–403.

Duchin, Faye (1998), *Structural Economics: Measuring Changes in Technology, Lifestyles, and the Environment*, Washington, DC and Covelo, CA: Island Press.

Eisner, R. (1989), *The Total Incomes System of Accounts*, Chicago: University of Chicago Press.

Eisner, R. (1997), 'Black holes in the statistics', *Challenge*, **40**, January–February, 6–16.

Goldschmidt-Clermont, L. (1993), 'Monetary valuation of non-market productive time. Methodological considerations', *Review of Income and Wealth*, **39**, 419–33.

Goldschmidt-Clermont, L. and E. Pagnossin-Aligisakis (1995), *Measures of Unrecorded Economic Activities in Fourteen Countries*, New York: United Nations Human Development Report Office, Occasional Paper No. 20.

Ironmonger, Duncan (1996), 'Counting outputs, capital input and caring labor: estimating gross household product', *Feminist Economics*, **2**, 37–64.

Kiær, Anders N. (1913), 'Norges nationalindtægt og nationalformue samt kapitalverdien av vort folks arbeidsevne' (National income and national wealth of Norway including capitalized value of the work force), *Statsøkonomisk tidsskrift*, **27**, 124–42.

King, W.I., W.G. Mitchell, F. Macaulay, and O.W. Knauth (1921), *Income in the United States, Its Amount and Distribution*, National Bureau of Economic Research, New York: Harcourt, Brace & Co.

Kuznets, S. (1934), *National Income 1929–1932*, US Congress, S. Doc. 124, 73rd Congress, 2nd session.

Nelson, Julie A. (1997), 'Feminism, ecology and the philosophy of economics', *Ecological Economics*, **20**, 155–62.

Nordhaus, W. and J. Tobin (1972), 'Is Growth Obsolete?', in *Economic Growth*, Fiftieth Anniversary Colloquium, Vol. 5, New York: NBER, pp. 509–32.

Nussbaum, Martha C. and Amartya Sen (eds) (1993), *The Quality of Life*, Oxford: Clarendon Press.

Reid, Margaret G. (1934), *Economics of Household Production*, New York: John Wiley.

Studenski, P. (1958), *The Income of Nations*, New York: New York University Press.

United Nations (1953), *A System of National Accounts and Supporting Tables* ST/ESA/STAT/SER.F/2

United Nations (1977), *The feasibility of welfare-oriented measures to supplement the national accounts and balances: A technical report*. Statistical Office of the UN Studies in Methods. Series F, no. 22.

United Nations (1995), *Human Development Report 1995*, New York: Oxford University Press.

United Nations, OECD, IMF, World Bank and Commission of the European Communities (Eurostat) (1993), *System of National Accounts 1993*. ST/ESA/STAT/SER.F/2/Rev. 4

Wagman, B. and N. Folbre (1996), 'Household services and economic growth in the United States, 1870–1930', *Feminist Economics*, **2**, 43–66.

Waring, Marilyn (1989), *If Women Counted, A New Feminist Economics*, London: Macmillan.

Growth Theory (Macro Models)

Growth theory seeks to identify the reasons for the radically different historical and contemporary experiences of growth of per capita and national income. It is premised on the view that relatively simple, aggregative relationships are capable of capturing, at least in part, the causal influences on the complex real processes of change which economic growth entails. Its particular focus is the factors responsible for altering society's capacity to produce goods and services rather than how a given capacity is utilized over a shorter period. This means that a time scale of decades rather than years is the appropriate correlate in calendar time; even small differences in growth over such time periods cumulate to large differences in the standards of living between countries and through time. As well as attempting to provide explanations for different rates of growth much of the recent work asks whether policy may systematically improve growth performance. In fact, understanding the reasons for growth and, hopefully, being able to design policies that encourage higher rates of growth has become one of the central concerns of economists and policymakers in recent years. Crucially, it represents the best and, perhaps, the only realistic prospect of eliminating poverty and expanding life chances for all people – but especially for women who bear a disproportionate share of the suffering imposed by endemic poverty.

Growth theory has a number of important strands reflecting the methods and interests of different schools of thought and different historical periods. The early theorists of capitalism struggled to make sense of the radical changes taking place in Western European societies, particularly Britain, in the late eighteenth and nineteenth centuries. A major result of their classical analysis was an aggregative, class-based theory of economic growth and distribution. By contrast, the central focus of the neoclassical economists of the later years of the nineteenth and the twentieth century was not growth but allocation and exchange. Nevertheless, the impetus of Keynes's *General Theory* (1936) stimulated a new generation of primarily, but not exclusively, neoclassical economists to produce new types of aggregative macro models to explain economic growth in mature capitalist economies. This quickly extended to a project to provide developmental growth theories to understand how poor and less-developed economies might shift onto higher growth trajectories.

A feminist critique and the lineaments of a gender-aware reconstruction of macroeconomics, of which growth theory is one small element, is a very recent project. Of course, macroeconomics has, to some degree, been subject to the critique of being excessively technicist and formalistic (for example, Nelson 1993). However, the development of a specific feminist critique of macroeconomics seems to have been associated with the fuller analysis of the position of women in development and particularly the gender distribution of poverty in developing countries. This developed from the late 1970s and throughout the 1980s and is largely associated with the analysis of the impact of structural adjustment programmes. These studies (for example, the Commonwealth Secretariat 1989, Afshar and Dennis 1992) demonstrated that structural adjustment programmes were very far from gender-neutral; women bore a large share of the hardship and poverty associated with such programmes while providing a disproportionate share of the labour and effort. This fuelled a demand, particularly of the international aid organizations, to become gender aware in their distribution of aid projects and their evaluation of their impact and, in turn, required an analytical structure in which to capture the economic circumstances of women in such societies. The evidence of vastly different time allocations and rewards also re-focused the objection to the gender distribution of poverty from one of equity to one of efficiency (Elson 1991; Palmer 1992). Economic efficiency requires that all agents be able to shift their resources, principally labour, between uses on equal terms. Gender inequality means that women have unequal access to market participation and prior commitments within the reproductive sector, which make it impossible for them to compete on equal terms. The removal of such distortions will raise both the static and dynamic efficiency of a market economy (Palmer 1992), thereby contributing to economic growth.

These arguments are essentially microeconomic in nature, that is, based on the analysis of individual choice within given economic circumstances, even though with clear macroeconomic implications. However, the realization that gender inequality was itself a constraint on economic development suggested the extension of this insight to other levels of economic analysis and contributed to the development of the idea of the economy as a gendered structure (Elson and McGee 1995; Goetz 1995; Elson et al. 1996). The extension of the analysis from the micro level proceeded by identifying further levels of analysis in terms of the meso and macro. (The meso level of analysis is based on the institutional structures which mediate individual behaviour to the aggregate level and, in turn, determine how aggregate and, in particular, macro policy variables impact at the micro level (Elson 1994).) The analysis of key governmental and economic institutions in terms of their gender composition and, in particular, their decision-making characteristics, has made some progress (Elson et al. 1996; Goetz 1995). These studies demonstrate that the gendered nature of institutions in terms of how their agendas are set, and the gender composition of those making decisions, have a powerful influence over whether development policies can be successfully implemented and, therefore, have important macro implications. However, the specifically macro or aggregate level of analysis has remained somewhat elusive until recently. The attempt to address a macro level of analysis in gender terms is a project which has only been addressed in the 1990s. The publication of the World Development Special Issue, *Gender, Adjustment and Macroeconomics* (1995) is a convenient starting point, although some earlier work, for example Bakker (1994), foreshadows some of the key issues.

The first stage in the reconstruction of macroeconomics, and of growth theory in particular, requires the identification of the gender biases inherent in the traditional mode of theorizing. However, this has been much more problematic than for the micro or meso levels of analysis. The theoretical structure of micro and meso analysis is directly derived from the behaviour of the stylized agents who people these models. The method is to endow such actors or representative agents with preferences and resources and allow them to act against an environment of constraints according to a set of rules defining rational behaviour. This approach is often dubbed the 'rational actor model'. The behaviour of these actors become the hypotheses of the model. In this framework the possibility of re-specifying preferences, resources and constraints to reflect the different stylized positions of women and men provides a relatively straightforward method of acquiring a gender-sensitive perspective. However, applying representative agents of this kind to macroeconomics is much less satisfactory.

The domain of macroeconomics is the behaviour of aggregates such as overall consumption, investment or government spending, and the way these aggregate categories interact. Of course, representative agents can be used to rationalize such a structure. Reconsidering such agents in terms of gender may then radically change the behaviour of such models (see, for example, Darity 1995). However, the extent to which stylized individuals can successfully capture the behaviour of aggregates is very limited. Aggregates submerge differences in individual behaviour – whether these differences arise from gender, class, income or race. A more appropriate metaphor for thinking about macroeconomics may be in terms of flows of money and resources which are not directly linked back to individual circumstances. Such disembodied flows can then be conceived as being channelled by constraints arising from the various capacities of the economy to produce.

A conceptualization of the aggregate economy in terms of this 'hydraulic' model of aggregate stocks and flows appears to leave little room for introducing gender as an analytical category. Nevertheless, the gendered nature of the division of labour, both within and between the productive and reproductive sectors, means that the recognition of and the importance attached to different aggregate stocks and flows reflects a gendered perception of the macroeconomy. Activities of particular importance to women are simply not recognized, or if recognized, not valued. Macroeconomics becomes a bearer of gender even if not formally gendered in the same manner as the micro and meso levels of analysis (Elson 1994). Of course, this links to the longstanding feminist critique of the national accounts as only a partial and misleading picture of economic life (Benería 1979). The failure to include those goods and, in particular, services not mediated through the market renders invisible to the policymaker and theorist much of women's contribution to welfare. However, it also reflects the presumption of macroeconomics that market relationships and the aggregate money flows corresponding to them are the legitimate domain of macroeconomics.

Traditional macroeconomics is a reflection of a conceptualization of the world of economics as being divided into a productive sector of market or marketable activities and a reproductive sector of activities supporting and reproducing human beings with a very particular relation to each other. To justify the exclusive attention on market interactions, the reproductive sector of nonmarket relationships must operate as a buffer which absorbs shocks to the productive and produces inputs for the productive but simultaneously has no significant feedback effects on the productive (Humphries and Rubery 1984; Elson 1994). Recognizing the implausibility of this dichotomy allows the behaviour of the reproductive sector to enter the domain of 'hydraulic' macroeconomics. It also allows the re-specification of traditional models to take account of constraints and feedbacks from the reproductive to the productive and therefore provides a method alternative to the re-specification of representative agents from introducing gender into macroeconomics.

Growth theory can be placed within this framework. Walters (1995) suggests that reproductive sector variables may be incorporated into traditional growth theory to give greater insights into the process of economic growth. He argues that this is possible by re-examining how traditional growth theory isolated itself from the reproductive sector. The modern impetus to growth theory began with Harrod's transfer of Keynes's short-run analysis to a long-run setting. Harrod discussed the likelihood of full employment occurring through a time period sufficiently long for the capital stock to change its employment capacity. In order to concentrate on this he assumed that the evolution of the labour force was independent of the process of growth. This assumption of labour supply exogeneity isolated his model from the reproductive sector. A similar isolation is evident in the literature that emerged in response to Harrod's model. The neoclassical developments (Solow 1956; Swan 1956) and the Keynesian (Kaldor 1956; Passinetti 1961) emphasized the importance of the evolution of the physical capital stock. Although they differed in their specification of the processes by which this stock evolved, like Harrod, they pushed into the background, or exogenous category, the evolution of labour supply and its response to the changes in the growth of capital. The behaviour of these models may be enriched by their re-specification of labour supply to take account of the labour force's origin within the reproductive sector. In addition, a recognition that labour is itself a produced means of production, representing the stock of human attributes largely developed and supported within the reproductive sector, alters the perception of these models (Walters 1995). It suggests that a fully macro perspective should recognize the prior claims of the reproductive sector on resources and time if this stock of human potential is to be reproduced and grow (Walters 1995). However, the formal reconstruction of these models to take account of these criticisms has, as yet, not taken place,

Traditional growth theory's isolation from the reproductive sector of the economy in part reflects the schism between classical and neoclassical modes of analysis. The classical economists had, as one of their central theoretical devices, the subsistence wage, which determined the minimum cost of production by reflecting the necessary cost of reproducing the labour force. The difference between this minimum and the price obtained in the market established the available surplus generated by the process of production which capitalists, by bearing down on wages, could capture for investment. The subsistence wage, therefore, was a crucial component in classical growth theory as it established a 'non-economic' upper limit on the extent of surplus extraction, the level of investment and, therefore, the rate of growth. The early classical economists always allowed that this wage included a complex of factors reflecting both traditional ideas of fairness as well as physical reproduction costs of human beings. However, the classical concept of the subsistence wage has remained rudimentary. Picchio (1992) has recently demonstrated that such a concept may be rigorously reinvented from a feminist perspective. In particular, she investigates the central role of housework in its determination and how it evolves under the influence of the state's social and economic policies. This approach provides the basis for a gender-aware classical growth theory.

The importance of the classical tradition in growth theory lingered longest in development theory where Lewis's (1954) growth model of a labour surplus economy self-consciously adopted a classical structure. This model analyses the growth process in a model with fixed real wages in which there is an overabundance of labour. Growth proceeds due to the extraction and investment of the surplus value generated by the difference between the exchange value of output and the fixed, and implicitly subsistence, cost of labour. This process simultaneously draws the surplus labour into the progressive capitalist sector. Ranis and Fei (1961) attempted to make this process more precise by transferring this model to an essentially neoclassical setting in which Lewis's subsistence wage is identified with the value of the additional output of the marginal worker, the marginal product, which is subject to diminishing returns. This innovation means that, initially, it is easy to draw workers out of the traditional sector without subsistence output suffering because the marginal product of such workers is very low or zero. However, barriers to growth emerge as the marginal product of those remaining in subsistence rises. This requires that the wage in terms of industrial goods must rise to attract further labour, and ultimately, that the industrial sector must compete for labour with the traditional sector. The wage increases erode the surplus available for investment and thereby reduce growth.

This uneasy mixture of classical and neoclassical can be given a more convincing structure by reconsidering movements between the sectors from a gender-aware perspective. A broad conception of the subsistence wage would recognize that only one dimension is reflected in immediate remuneration in either subsistence or money terms with other important dimensions, in particular women's labour time, established in the reproductive sector. Such a re-evaluation points to the importance of the reproductive sector in establishing the conditions necessary for labour transfer between the traditional and progressive sectors which constitutes the growth process. It emphasizes the payback in growth terms to investment in resources to support reproductive activities and points to the existence of a fresh set of constraints to growth if the claims made on the reproductive sector exhaust its capacity. This is especially pertinent when combined with the recognition that, from the perspective of many of the world's women, even developing countries constitute labour shortage economies for basic reproductive activities.

The analysis of growth theory from a classical perspective has obvious attractions for a feminist reconstruction because it never attempted a complete divorce of productive and reproductive activities. In addition, it never subscribed to the fetish that all value arises from exchange. This meant that it recognized the dependence of the productive on the reproductive and realized the need, however inadequately expressed, for some characterization of reproductive activity. Neoclassical macro theory, by contrast, has no historical foundation upon which feminist scholarship can easily lay claim except through the importation of microeconomic ideas into macroeconomics via the device of the representative agent. Despite the limitations of this approach there are a number of new avenues opening for a macroeconomics which is more sensitive to the importance of gendered structures and institutions for the overall behaviour of the economy. The new endogenous growth models provide one such avenue.

Endogenous growth theory developed because of the perceived weaknesses of the traditional neoclassical growth model which analysed growth in terms of the accumulation of physical capital while making the other key identified determinants of growth – labour and technical progress – exogenous or outside the domain of explanation. However, as there are diminishing returns to capital, this means that the model, in effect, is failing to address the fundamental causes of economic growth. In addition, the model's prediction of long-run convergence of per capita income is not supported by the evidence (Romer 1994). Endogenous growth theory attempts to address these failures of the traditional neoclassical growth model by making the evolution of all the key determinants of growth endogenous or determined within the model in a way that more closely matches the stylized facts of experience. This framework provides a number of important avenues for a more gender-aware characterization of the processes of growth.

An example is provided by Lucas's (1988) influential growth model which emphasizes the importance of education spending as a determinant of growth. This is chosen by the interaction of income with the preferences for education of a representative agent. However, whose preferences this represents is not addressed. Women arguably have different revealed preferences for activities which benefit children (Alderman et al. 1995). For this reason, the characterization of this representative agent and the intrafamily distribution of income, or, as comes to the same thing, control over its disposition, become crucial issues influencing the rate of growth; by implication they should become important policy objectives to increase the long-run rate of growth.

Many of the major endogenous growth models exhibit a similar capacity to be re-interpreted from a gender-aware perspective. For example, the Barro growth model (1990) makes growth a function of the externalities generated by government infrastructural spending. These have so far been rather narrowly interpreted. However, expenditures such as the social provision of childcare and health, the extension of networks supporting domestic or reproductive activities such as, for example, clean water as well as the importance of other, more traditionally recognized, networks such as roads and railways, are captured by this form of argument. In addition, the recognition of a potential role for government highlights the importance of the possible gendered nature of governmental institutions and provides a bridge to meso levels of analysis.

A further dimension of endogenous growth theory emphasizes knowledge and its dissemination as the basis of economic growth. However, the specificity of such knowledge is not addressed by the literature, and the key role of women in inculcating, and transferring, the necessary knowledge and skills is apparently not recognized. Of course, the endogenous growth literature has also extended its method to the area of fertility (see, for example, Becker et al. 1990). Although not, perhaps, as persuasive in its application, this literature nevertheless addresses the key issues of the determinants of fertility and the reasons for its variability across different cultures and time periods. Furthermore, it restores to a central position changes in population growth, composition and quality as among the chief causes, and consequences, of the process of economic change.

A reconstruction of growth theory to take account of the emerging feminist critique is evidently at a preliminary stage. However, a number of clear directions have become evident. First, the importance of explicitly taking account of the feedbacks and constraints arising from the reproductive sector provides a wide range of opportunities for reinterpreting traditional growth theory. Second, the pivotal importance of the social or subsistence wage determined in the reproductive sector allows a feminist reinterpretation of classical models of accumulation such as Lewis (1954). Finally, a more thorough examination of the specification of the representative agent suggests a distinct feminist interpretation of the burgeoning field of endogenous growth theory. Thus, the production of a gender-aware growth theory does not constitute a project alternative to that of previous theorists. The objective remains that of understanding, and therefore being able to encourage, the processes of economic growth which will extend life chances to all people. The introduction of gender is part of the attempt to make these models more adequate to the task.

BERNARD WALTERS

See also
Development Policies; Development, Theories of; Gross Domestic Product; Macroeconomics; Structural Adjustment Policies; Technological Change.

Bibliography
Afshar, H. and C. Dennis (eds) (1992), *Women and Adjustment Policies in the Third World*, London: Macmillan.

Alderman, H., P. -A. Chiappori, L. Haddad, J. Hoddinott and R. Kanbur (1995), 'Unitary versus collective models of the household: is it time to shift the burden of proof', *The World Bank Research Observer*, **10**, 1–19.

Bakker, I. (ed.) (1994), *The Strategic Silence: Gender and Economic Policy*, London: Zed Books with the North–South Institute.

Barro, R.J. (1990), 'Government spending in a simple model of endogenous growth', *Journal of Political Economy*, **98**, S103–S125.

Becker, G.S., K.M. Murphy and R. Tamura (1990), 'Human capital, fertility, and economic growth', *Journal of Political Economy*, **98**, S12–S37.

Benería, L. (1992), 'Accounting for women's work: the progress of two decades', *World Development*, **20** (11), 1547–60.

Commonwealth Secretariat (1989), *Engendering Adjustment for the 1990s*, London: Commonwealth Secretariat.

Darity, W. Jr (1995), 'The formal structure of a gender-segregated low-income economy', *World Development*, **23** (11), November, 1963–8.

Elson, D. (1991), 'Male Bias in Macro-economics: The Case of Structural Adjustment', in D. Elson (ed.), *Male Bias in the Development Process*, Manchester: Manchester University Press.

Elson, D. (1994), 'Micro, Meso, Macro: Gender and Economic Analysis in the Context of Policy Reform', in I. Bakker (ed.), *The Strategic Silence: Gender and Economic Policy*, London: Zed Books with the North–South Institute.

Elson, D., B. Evers and J. Gideon (1996), 'Gender Aware Country Reports: Concepts and Sources', Working Paper No. 1, Genecon Unit, University of Manchester Graduate School of Social Sciences.

Elson, D. and R. McGee (1995), 'Gender equality, bilateral programme assistance and structural adjustment: policy and procedures', *World Development*, **23** (11), November, 1987–94.

Goetz, A.-M. (1995), 'Macro-Meso-Micro Linkages: Understanding Gendered Institutional Structures and Practices', paper presented to the SAGA workshop on Gender and Economic Reform in Africa, Ottawa, 1–3 October.

Harrod, R.F. (1939), 'An essay on dynamic theory', *Economic Journal*, **49**, 14–33.

Humphries, J. and J. Rubery (1984), 'The reconstitution of the supply side of the labour market: the relative autonomy of social reproduction', *Cambridge Journal of Economics*, **23**, 331–7.

Kaldor, N. (1956), 'Alternative theories of distribution', *Review of Economic Studies*, **23**, 94–100.

Keynes, J.M. (1936), *The General Theory of Employment, Interest and Money*, London: Macmillan.

Lewis, W.A. (1954), 'Economic development with unlimited supplies of labour', *The Manchester School*, **22**, 139–91.

Lucas, R.E. (1988), 'On the mechanics of economic development', *Journal of Monetary Economics*, **21**, 3–42.

Nelson, J.A. (1993), 'The Study of Choice or the Study of Provisioning? Gender and the Definition of Economics', in M. Ferber and J. Nelson (eds), *Beyond Economic Man: Feminist Theory and Economics*, Chicago: University of Chicago Press.

Palmer, I. (1992), 'Gender equity and economic efficiency in adjustment models', in H. Afshar and C. Dennis (eds), *Women and Adjustment Policies in the Third World*, London: Macmillan, pp. 69–83.

Passinetti, L. (1961), 'Rate of profit and income distribution in relation to the rate of economic growth', *Review of Economic Studies*, **29**, 267–79.

Picchio, A. (1992), *Social Reproduction: The Political Economy of the Labour Market*, Cambridge: Cambridge University Press.

Ranis, G. and J.C.H. Fei (1961), 'A theory of economic development', *American Economic Review*, **51**, 500–565.

Romer, P.M. (1994), 'The origins of endogenous growth', *Journal of Economic Perspectives*, **8** (1), 3–22.

Solow, R.M. (1956), 'A contribution to the theory of economic growth', *Quarterly Journal of Economics*, **70**, 65–94.

Swan, T.W. (1956), 'Economic growth and capital accumulation', *Economic Record*, **32**, 334–61.

Walters, B. (1995), 'Engendering macroeconomics: A reconsideration of growth theory', *World Development*, **23** (11), November, 1869–80.

World Development Special Issue (1995), *Gender Adjustment and Macroeconomics*, **23** (11), November.

Health, Economics of

The economics of health and health care, particularly within industrialized nations, has not been a field of research that has yet been strongly influenced by feminist economists, although there is much scholarship on health care issues by feminists from other disciplines, especially public health and sociology (Fee 1983; Kane 1991; Fee and Krieger 1994; Moss 1996; Ruzek et al. 1997). Research published in the major journals on health economics generally reflects a standard neoclassical approach when examining issues such as the demand and supply for health services, financing issues, the economics of medical technology, regulation and competition, and externalities in health and medical care. Another major research focus is on the cost-effectiveness of various medical services and treatments. There are virtually no explicit references to feminist approaches to health care economics within the major journals and relatively few with respect to even gender issues. The textbooks used to teach health-care economics reflect this lack of attention to gender issues in the field. A prominent textbook, for example, only notes 'gender factors' on four occasions (Phelps 1997).

Health economics research that more accurately reflects gender, age, and racial/ethnic variations in both developed and developing countries is more likely to be found in publications with a strong policy orientation. In the RAND Institute's (1997) bibliography, for example, articles on health issues of importance to women can be found, including studies on mammography use among older minority women, gender life-cycle differentials in the patterns of adult health in developing countries, differences in quality of care for hospitalized men and women, and sample design for HIV infection among prostitutes (RAND 1997). Another policy-oriented group, the Institute for Women's Policy Research (IWPR), has conducted research on women's access to health insurance, the costs and benefits of preventative health care, and the costs of domestic violence (IWPR 1998). Yet other recent research on US health care policy reform still gives little, if any, attention to the unique needs of women or to how women may be disproportionately affected by policy changes (Ginzberg 1994; Aaron 1996; Rice 1998; Glied 1997).

Despite the lack of formal feminist economic scholarship on health care, gender differences in health have been noted and studied for at least 300 years (Kane 1991). It is often noted, for example, that women live longer than men do (currently this is true in both developing and developed countries, with some exceptions in South Asia). Research reveals, however, that this health advantage is not universal. Young girls and women in their reproductive years have historically been vulnerable to death and illness, and in some countries this continues to be the case (Kane 1991). As health scholar Penny Kane notes, the reduction of illness and death rates in the reproductive years is largely responsible for the overall improvement in female life expectancy relative to males (Kane 1991). It is not clear, however, that any advantage women have in terms of average life expectancy will be maintained over time: life expectancy has actually declined in some Eastern European countries, smoking has increased among women almost worldwide, and hazards related to work outside the home have also increased (Frankenhaeuser et al. 1991).

Drawing on the various literatures documenting gender differences in health status and raising concerns about pervasive gender bias in health care systems, feminists have identified a large number of health care issues that are worthy of additional study. To date, feminist economists have made contributions in two broad areas: research on domestic health policy in industrialized nations, and health-related research in the areas of development theory or policy. This entry will address developments in the first area of study, emphasizing feminist contributions to the study of health care in the USA.

Fee and Krieger (1994) offer one of the most comprehensive recent volumes on the political economy of health care. Their contribution is unique in that it presents a framework for studying the relationship of sexual politics to health and the health care system and includes several theoretical perspectives ranging from liberal feminism to Marxism, a variety of issues, and methodologies. They investigate women's health according to race, ethnicity and class and also examine the occupation of health care, the health of women workers and public health policy. Their work, along with Fee (1983) and Ruzek et al. (1997), provide an excellent starting point for feminist researchers because it provides a broad and theoretically diverse and challenging introduction to important research questions.

In addition, recent analyses of health care policy by Laurence and Weinhouse (1994), Rosser (1994) and Moss (1996) illustrate how gender stereotyping and institutional bias have distorted clinical and epidemiologic knowledge and practice, as well as having shaped health care policy in ways that undermine women's health. Rosser (1994) emphasizes how research on women's health has been systematically excluded or underfunded, with the possible exception of studies of reproduction and female contraception. In basic research and in clinical trials, too often male animal and human models have been the norm and thus not enough is known about heart disease in women, AIDS treatment in women, and even about breast cancer. Laurence and Weinhouse (1994) provide a compelling, journalistic account of gender bias in medical research. They cite a General Accounting Office (GAO) report that found that while the National Institutes of Health (NIH) had a policy to encourage researchers to include women as subjects, most researchers were unaware of the policy since no mention of it was made by the NIH in its grant application materials (Laurence and Weinhouse 1994, p. 60). Further, the

GAO audit of 50 NIH-funded studies found that 'one-fifth made no mention of gender and over one-third said the subjects would include both sexes but did not give percentages' (Laurence and Weinhouse 1994, p. 61). Moss (1996) and Haseltine (1997) provide a more academic discussion of many of the same issues and also offers excellent chapters on AIDS, mental health, immigrant women, women with disabilities and incarcerated women.

Largely in response to criticism about gender bias in medical research and treatment in the USA, the Office of Research on Women's Health was established in 1990 at the National Institutes of Health. Observational and interventional medical studies have since expanded to include more women and greater diversity, especially with respect to post-menopausal and Asian, African-American and Hispanic women (*Harvard Women's Health Watch* 1996). In the 1993 Commonwealth Fund Survey of over 3000 women and men, for example, researchers found that women were more likely to be diagnosed with particular mental illnesses, have chronic disabilities and to use health services (Falik and Collins 1996). Recent and ongoing studies such as *The Women's Health Initiative, The Nurses Health Study,* and the *Study of Women's Health Across the Nation* are collecting large sample longitudinal data that will be most helpful for future research (*Harvard Women's Health Watch* 1996).

A common criticism regarding health research and policy is that it has focused far too much on female reproductive capacities. Contraceptive research, for example, has been limited almost exclusively to women and much of the research on infertility has favoured high income, heterosexual women while clinical tests to control fertility have focused on poor and minority women. There is, however, a growing feminist literature on female reproductive health, which broadens the analysis by addressing a wider range of topics and specifically examining the impacts on women's status. Feminists have, for example, examined the impact of newly emerging reproductive technologies on both women's health and their reproductive rights (see, for example, Nygaard 1992; Raymond 1993; Adams 1994; Sen and Snow 1994). Other recent work about reproduction includes Blank's (1995) study of teen pregnancy. Blank refutes the idea that public assistance spending has resulted in higher birth rates among unwed women and instead finds that lower fertility among married women and lower rates of marriage in the USA are the cause of rising nonmarital birth rates. In addition, Morello-Frosch (1997) offers an excellent example of feminist analysis of reproductive hazards in the workplace, using lead as an example. She argues that current policies reinforce occupational segregation by gender without significantly improving the level of occupational safety.

Feminists also have presented research on the economic impact of domestic violence, both on a microeconomic level and on a macroeconomic level as it burdens the health care system. It is estimated that as many as one-third of the women seen in emergency rooms exhibit symptoms of ongoing abuse, and that the health care costs of women who are abused are about two-and-a-half times greater than for women who are not battered (Heise et al. 1994). In addition to the direct medical costs, the psychological effects – fear, anxiety, fatigue and depression – can be severely debilitating and interfere with productivity at home and in the workplace. Battered women are four to five times more likely to require psychiatric care and more likely to suffer from major depressions (Stark and Flitcraft 1991; Heise et al. 1994). Finally, the economic and health effects of domestic violence also extend to fetuses and to children – women who are pregnant are more likely to be battered, violence victims are more likely to abuse multiple substances, and are at much higher risk of miscarriage or having a low-birth weight infant (Heise et al. 1994; Laurence and Spalter-Roth 1996).

The availability and cost of health care for women and their families is another area where feminist economists have already contributed much to the policy debate in other areas, such as welfare reform (IWPR 1998). Bergmann and Hartmann (1995), for example, argue that assistance with health insurance must be an essential part of any welfare reform programme that requires parents to work. Instead of welfare reform, they propose the 'Help for Working Parents' plan as an alternative to move families out of poverty by provision of child care, health care and housing assistance.

Other interesting work that illustrates feminist economic contributions includes Galtry's (1997) article on the possible costs and benefits of breastfeeding in the USA. She draws from feminist theory, health-related research and economic literature to conclude that feminist analyses of labour market issues could be improved if the costs and benefits of breastfeeding were incorporated. Braithwaite and Taylor (1992) and Dula and Goering (1994) also provide excellent overviews of health care issues from the perspective of African-Americans and other underrepresented groups. It is noted in Braithwaite and Taylor, for example, that only 61 per cent of African-American women receive prenatal care in the first trimester, over half of young African-American women reported themselves in psychological distress, and African-American women disproportionately suffer from serious illnesses such as diabetes, cardiovascular diseases, cancer and AIDS (1992, pp. 35–51).

The possibilities for feminist research with respect to even traditional and well-defined subjects within health economics seem almost endless. Topics such as human cloning and human genome research will offer new areas for research by feminist economists; additional research that would benefit women in both developed and developing countries is also needed on the demand and supply for reproductive services, third-party payment for reproductive services, and so on. Other examples of topics might include: the effects on women's health of particular types of private insurance programmes; gender analysis of coverage under Medicaid, Medicare or other governmentally-supported programmes; medical malpractice as it relates to women; the cost and availability of new medical technologies to women, and regulatory issues.

There has also been relatively little research by economists about women as suppliers (either formally or informally) of health care services. In their study of Canadian home health care workers, Neysmith and Aronson (1997) found that immigrant women of colour were disproportionately represented in this low-paid labour pool that intertwines domestic and caring labour. They conclude that current health care policies tended to reinforce this labour's gendered and racist history, and ultimately this results in a lower quality of long-term care. Karon (1991) considered how the gender of a family caregiver affects the cost and quality of long-term care services for older women receiving services in a managed-care system, and found that older women who had daughters to provide 'caring labour' essentially provided a subsidy to the health care insurers.

Feminist economists interested in learning more about feminist approaches to health care should also investigate materials from sociology, medical anthropology, health care service delivery and administration, and nursing. The possibility for making positive contributions to women's lives is tremendous if more economists chose to focus on this field, particularly if they incorporated a multidisciplinary approach.

MARY YOUNG

See also
Development Policies; Domestic Abuse; Population; Welfare Reform.

Bibliography
Aaron, Henry (ed.) (1996), *Reforming US Health Care Financing*, Washington, DC: Brookings Institution.

Adams, Alice E. (1994), *Reproducing the Womb: Images of Childbirth in Science, Feminist Theory, Literature*, Ithaca, New York: Cornell University Press.

Bergmann, Barbara and Heidi Hartmann (1995), 'A welfare reform based on help for working parents', *Feminist Economics*, **1** (2), (Summer), 85–90.

Blank, Rebecca (1995), 'Teenage pregnancy: government programs are not the cause', *Feminist Economics*, **1** (2), (Summer), 47–58.

Braithwaite, Ronald and Sandra Taylor (eds) (1992), *Health Issues in the Black Community*, San Francisco, California: Jossey-Bass Publishers.

Dula, Annette and Sara Goering (1994), *It Just Ain't Fair: The Ethics of Health Care for African Americans*, Westport, Connecticut and London: Praeger.

Falik, Marilyn M. and Karen Scott Collins (eds) (1996), *Women's Health: The Commonwealth Fund Survey*, Baltimore, Maryland: Johns Hopkins Press.

Fee, Elizabeth (ed.) (1983), *Women and Health: The Politics of Sex in Medicine*, Amityville, New York: Baywood.

Fee, Elizabeth and Nancy Krieger (eds) (1994), *Women's Health, Politics, and Power: Essays on Sex/Gender, Medicine, and Public Health*, Amityville, New York: Baywood.

Feiner, Susan F. (ed.) (1994), *Race and Gender in the American Economy*, Englewood Cliffs, New Jersey: Prentice-Hall.

Frankenhaeuser, Marianne, Olf Lundberg and Margaret Chesney (eds) (1991), *Women, Work, and Health: Stress and Opportunities*, New York and London: Plenum Press.

Galtry, Judith (1997), 'Suckling and silence in the USA: the costs and benefits of breastfeeding', *Feminist Economics*, **3** (3), Fall, 1–24.

Ginzberg, Eli (ed.) (1994), *Critical Issues in US Health Reform*, Boulder, Colorado: Westview Press.

Glied, Sherry (1997), *Chronic Condition: Why Health Reform Fails*, Cambridge Massachusetts: Harvard University Press.

Harvard Women's Health Watch (1996), **4** (1), (September), 6.

Haseltine, Florence (1997), *Women's Health Research: A Medical and Policy Primer*, Washington, DC: American Psychiatric Press, Inc.

Heise, Lori L., Jacqueline Pitanguy and Adrienne Germain (1994), *Violence Against Women: The Hidden Health Burden*, Washington, DC: World Bank Discussion Papers.

Institute for Women's Policy Research (IWPR) (1998), http://www.org.IWPRRESEARCH.HTM

Kane, Penny (1991), *Women's Health: From Womb to Tomb*, New York: St Martin's Press.

Karon, Sarita L. (1991), 'The Difference It Makes: Caregiver Gender and Access to Managed Long Term Care Services in the Social HMO', Unpublished doctoral dissertation, Brandeis University.

Laurence, Leslie and Beth Weinhouse (1994), *Outrageous Practices*, New York: Ballantine Books/Random House.

Laurence, Louise and Roberta Spalter-Roth (1996), 'Measuring the Costs of Domestic Violence Against Women and the Cost-Effectiveness of Interventions', Washington DC: Institute for Women's Policy Research, Publication #B223.

Morello-Frosch, Rachel (1997), 'The Politics of Reproductive Hazards in the Workplace: Class, Gender and the History of Occupational Lead Exposure', *International Journal of Health Services*, **27** (3), 501– 21.

Moss, Kary L. (ed.) (1996), *Man-Made Medicine: Women's Health, Public Policy, and Reform*, Durham, North Carolina: Duke University Press.

Neysmith, Sheila and Aronson, Jane (1997), 'Working conditions in home care: negotiating race and class boundaries in gendered work', *International Journal of Health Services*, **27** (3), 479–99.

Nygaard, Vicki Leanne (1992), 'Using Feminist Sociology as a Theoretical Approach in Examining Issues Concerning Reproductive Technologies', Unpublished master's thesis, University of Victoria, Canada.

Phelps, Charles E. (1997), *Health Economics*, New York: Addison-Wesley.

Raymond, Janice G. (1993), *Women as Wombs*, New York: Harper SanFrancisco/Harper Collins.

RAND (1997), 'Health–Related Research: 1990–1997', A bibliography of selected RAND publications, RAND, Santa Monica, California.

Rice, Thomas (1998), *The Economics of Health Reconsidered*, Chicago: Health Administration Press.

Rosser, Sue V.(1994), *Women's Health – Missing from US Medicine*, Bloomington: Indiana University Press.

Ruzek, Sheryl, Virginia Olesen, and Adele Clarke (eds.) (1997), *Women's Health*, Columbus, Ohio: Ohio State University Press.

Sen, Gita and Rachel Snow (eds.) (1994), *Power and Decision: The Social Control of Reproduction*, Cambridge, Massachusetts: Harvard University Press.

Stark, Evan and Anne Flitcraft (1991), 'Spouse Abuse', in Mark Rosenburg and Mary Ann Fenley (eds), *Violence in America: A Public Health Approach*, New York: Oxford University Press.

History of Economic Thought

Historians of economic thought examine how thinking about economies, economic activities and the discipline of economics has evolved through time. Their explorations may delineate the contributions by individuals or by schools of thought to the development of key economic concepts and theories, or they may seek to explain how historical, political and cultural factors shaped those contributions. Many historians of thought focus on features that dominate mainstream economic thinking or on economists who have been most visible and influential in orthodox economic discourse, but some do analyse contributions that have been forgotten, ignored or marginalized in the evolution of the history of thought canon. Because women's voices and theorizing about 'women's issues' often fall into this latter category, the field of the history of economic thought offers important opportunities for feminist economic analysis. But prior to the 1990s, women's contributions were rarely discussed by historians of economic thought, which led to a common but mistaken belief that 'before World War I, as today, a (distressingly) few women were contributing to the literature' in economics (Baumol 1985, p. 11). Additionally, little historical analysis of economic thinking about women's activities and issues had been undertaken, again implying that women fell outside the purview of economic thought. And while there may be plausible non-sexist reasons for these omissions, recent work by feminist historians of economic thought reveals not only that women have been very much a part of economic thought, both as subject and object, over the past 200 years, but also that women's absence from these discussions says a great deal about the masculinist biases inherent in the economics discipline as well as in economic thought itself.

Feminist historians of economic thought have pursued several avenues of inquiry. One focus has been the rediscovery of women economists' voices that have been lost or marginalized over time. As discussed below, this work has examined both women who were feminists and those who were not as well as those who were known in the economics profession and those who were not, and it has also identified a few male voices that spoke about women as economic actors. Much of this scholarship has also been concerned with the reasons why these female voices are often unacknowledged in economic thinking, thus leading to the second focus of feminist inquiry, which is the exploration of masculinist biases in economic discourse and the economics profession. This latter avenue not only seeks to explain the silence of women economists as contributors, but also why economics has historically been unconcerned with women's economic activities and issues. These two inter-related areas of research by feminist historians of economic thought offer a more complete picture of economic thought and, more importantly, they may provide contemporary feminist economists with ideas for reconstructing economic discourse so that it explains more effectively the economic activities of and economic issues facing all economic actors.

Women's participation in economic discourse began shortly after the advent of modern economics in 1776 (with the publication of Adam Smith's *Wealth of Nations*), and it might be marked by the 1816 publication of Jane Marcet's *Conversations on Political Economy, in which the Elements of that Science are Familiarly Explained*. According to most contemporary historians of thought (Schumpeter 1954, p. 477, is an exception), Marcet contributed little to the evolution of mainstream economic thinking, but that was not her goal. Instead, Marcet wished to educate young people about the free-market economics of Smith, Thomas Robert Malthus and David Ricardo and in that, she was quite successful as hers 'became the best selling text of the nineteenth century' (Polkinghorn 1995, p. 72). But Marcet's success as a popularizer may also be why she is often relegated to a footnote in histories of economic thought. As Thomson notes in *Adam Smith's Daughters*, Marcet's role as an economics educator, which was historically only one of the few opportunities available to women, combined with her belief in 'the moral responsibility and the need for social relevance' in economics (Thomson 1973, p. 6), may explain why Marcet's voice is missing in contemporary discussions of economic thinking's evolution. However, as Polkinghorn (1995) argues, it is precisely this role as an educator that should make Marcet's work, and that of her contemporary, Harriet Martineau, of particular interest to historians of economic thought since 'the achievements of the popularizers' help explain 'how the general public acquires its understanding of economic principles', which in turn 'affects their actions' (Polkinghorn 1995, p. 71). Indeed, given the success of Marcet's and Martineau's work in popularizing the tenets of classical political economy, further work by feminist historians of thought is warranted to better understand the roles they and other women played in perpetuating economic ideas through popular formats, particularly if these roles differed from male popularizers.

While Marcet and Martineau are notable for the popularity of their work, most female participants in nineteenth-century economic discourse did not enjoy similar distinction, as suggested by their absence in contemporary histories of economic thought. However, while their omission might indicate that women did not engage in economic conversations during the nineteenth and early twentieth centuries, feminist historians of thought Pujol (1992), Groenewegen (1994a), Robert Dimand (1995), Mary Ann Dimand (1995), Forget (1995) and Sockwell (1995) have clearly demonstrated that women were in fact active participants in the scholarly discourse of academic journals and conferences and that they were earning college and graduate degrees in economics and teaching in newly-established institutions of higher education. Additionally, women were engaged not only in political debates about equal rights and economic independence for women, but also in other policy discussions throughout the Victorian era and into the early decades of the twentieth century (Libby 1990; M.A. Dimand 1995; Forget 1995). Thus the commonly held perception that women contributed little to the economics literature during the nineteenth and early twentieth century has been effectively disproven by this recent scholarship.

Identifying this large number of women economists represents an important first step, but perhaps the more important one facing feminist historians of thought is why women's voices have been largely absent and forgotten in contemporary histories. Not surprisingly, the answers are necessarily varied and complex, reflecting the diverse circumstances of the women involved as well as the historical and cultural contexts in which these women worked. Some recurring reasons have emerged, however, which reflect the emergence of professional standards and the topics women often chose to analyse.

The 'relatively standardized qualifications' for being a professional economist at the turn of the century 'included having the Ph.D., membership in the AEA [American Economics Association], and an academic job; publishing in the scholarly journals, not the popular press; and exercising care over one's reform activities' (Hammond 1993, p. 357). Given the opportunities available to women, many women economists between the late nineteenth century and the interwar period did not meet at least one of these qualifications. For example, many were avowed feminists, and their contributions frequently corresponded to their activism in often-radical political and social movements; three of the best-known voices from this period, Beatrice Webb, Rosa Luxemburg and Charlotte Perkins Gilman were well-known socialists, while others, such as Barbara Bodichon, Millicent Garrett Fawcett and Harriet Taylor, were vocal advocates for women's suffrage and equal pay for women. In addition to and because of their political activism, these women often published their work outside academic journals (M.A. Dimand 1995), further placing them outside professional boundaries. Women economists also did not have the same access to graduate education as men, and they were typically not considered for academic teaching jobs in economics, except at some women's colleges; instead women economists often were channelled into less prestigious positions at settlement houses, home economics programmes and government institutions (Hammond 1993; M.A. Dimand 1995). Finally, while women were never officially barred from the AEA, they were not welcomed (Hammond 1993; Forget 1995), although it is interesting to note that British women were key in establishing at least one field, economic history, during this time (Berg 1992).

One woman economist who did not have the appropriate credentials but was well-known for her economic writings is Charlotte Perkins Gilman (1860–

1935). Her contributions on the economic independence for women have been the focus of historians, feminist scholars and feminist historians of economic thought since her 'rediscovery' in 1966 by historian Carl Degler. As most scholars note, Gilman's work is 'understandably' omitted from histories of economic thought: Gilman was not a trained economist; she published in the popular press (including works of fiction); and she was a political and social activist, supporting herself as a public speaker and advocating reform, including the socialization of such domestic activities as the rearing of children. Thus one question facing contemporary feminist historians of thought is: was Gilman simply a historical curiosity, or does her work contribute to a better understanding of women's economic roles and activities?

Feminist historians of thought place Gilman's economic thought in the latter category, highlighting her economic analysis of women's economic dependence on men. Much of this work has focused on casting Gilman's contributions in terms familiar to contemporary economists. O'Donnell (1994), for example, argues that Gilman's *Women and Economics* offers a supply and demand analysis of nineteenth-century marriage markets with a particular focus on how wives were valued in these markets. O'Donnell and M.A. Dimand (1995) further note that Gilman considered the roles of wives as domestic producers to be both exploitative (in that women were economically dependent on their husbands for their livelihoods) and inefficient. To reduce the inefficiencies, which derived from domestic services being overproduced by individual households, Gilman advocated establishing formal markets to provide these services to the entire neighbourhood; this would not only take advantage of existing scale economies, but would also provide women with economic independence by compensating them for their work. Additionally, Dimand argues that Gilman provided one of the first economic analyses of externalities and considered factors that previous economists had not recognized, leading her to conclude that 'Gilman deserves recognition as an economist and attention from the profession which she has not previously received' (M.A. Dimand 1995, p. 146).

Other feminist economists have focused on Gilman's contributions in the context of transforming current economic thinking. Grapard (1996) and Lewis and Sebberson (1997) both argue that Gilman's text actually conforms to the disciplinary standards and conventions of knowledge of her time, and thus posit alternative explanations for Gilman's exclusion from the economics canon. While Grapard notes Gilman's 'lack of academic credentials and ... the obsolescence of her [evolutionary] theoretical framework' (Grapard 1996, p. 4), she highlights Gilman's explicit consideration of women's work as wives and mothers as the most compelling reason for Gilman's omission from mainstream economic knowledge, which even today typically fails to consider caring work as economic activity. On a complementary note, Lewis and Sebberson focus explicitly on Gilman's economic rhetoric, arguing that Gilman was an economist 'engaged in developing not only alternative theories of economics, but also alternative modes of theorizing about economics' thereby employing a rhetoric of social action rather than the so-called impassive science of mainstream economics (Lewis and Sebberson 1997, p. 418). These scholars thus view Gilman's work as offering contemporary economists insights on restructuring economic discourse that is more appropriate for a feminist economic agenda, thereby placing Gilman at the centre of historical economic thinking relevant to feminist economists.

While many women's omitted voices, like Gilman's, may be relatively easy to explain within their historical and cultural contexts, other voices are not so easily dismissed from histories of economic thought. Indeed, a particularly important contribution by feminist historians of thought has been finding largely unknown women economists whose work actually predates that of the traditionally-credited theorists. The recent feminist scholarship on Margaret Reid, for example, demonstrates that several Nobel-winning theories may actually derive from her pioneering studies.

Margaret Reid (1896–1991) came to economics via a home economics education, a common route for women of her generation. This background influenced the focus and method of Reid's work and may be part of the reason for Reid's less-known status (Forget 1996). Along with her mentor Hazel Kyrk and colleague Elizabeth Hoyt, Reid was not only instrumental in reshaping home economics to focus explicitly on the economic wellbeing of families and households, she was also an important mentor to young women economists and a major writer of textbooks in consumer economics (Thorne 1995; Forget 1996; Yi 1996), all factors which have typically not been of interest to historians of economic thought. However, the silence on Reid's contributions to economic theory is less easily explained, particularly when they are viewed as providing the antecedents to several ideas that have been awarded the Nobel Memorial Prize in economics.

Reid's work on household production represents perhaps her most extensive contribution to economics as the fall 1996 volume of *Feminist Economics* in honour of this work evidences. Reid, along with Kyrk, was one of the first to conceptualize the economic contributions of housework, and in her 1934 *Economics of Household Production,* she argued that the household was a locus of production as well as of consumption, a conclusion at the centre of Gary Becker's 1965 Nobel-prize winning theory of time allocation. As several feminist economists have noted (see, for example, Hirschfeld 1994 and Yi 1996), Reid's contribution has been largely ignored in the histories of the 'New Home Economics', which Becker is credited with 'fathering'. And while Becker himself has, to date, never acknowledged Reid's contributions to his work, it seems likely that her work did have an effect on Becker's since they were colleagues at the University of Chicago and Reid was known as an active participant in critiques of her colleagues' work (Yi 1996). Additionally, as Hirschfeld (1994) suggests, feminist economists might do well to examine Reid's contributions since her work may avoid the sexist biases many feminists find in Becker's work.

While Reid's contributions to conceptualizing housework as production may not be well known or acknowledged by the economists subsequently working on that topic, Reid's work has not been completely ignored by the economics profession nor have all her contributions been unacknowledged. In 1980, for example, Reid was the first woman economist to be chosen as an AEA Distinguished Fellow (although she was not awarded other professional honours typically accorded such contributors to the profession). Additionally, Nobel winners Franco Modigliani and Milton Friedman have acknowledged Reid's fundamental contributions to their work on the life-cycle model and permanent income hypothesis, respectively (Yi 1996, pp. 20–21, 25–6), which derived from Reid's extensive empirical analyses of household consumption patterns by income class. Reid also made significant contributions in the areas of housing and health; her analysis in *Housing and Income* of the income elasticity of housing 'changed the way economists now understand housing expenditures and related consumer behavior' (Yi 1996, p. 26), and her work on the correlation between income and death rates 'clears up the confusion about the income–health relationship, and provides detailed explanation about the other factors interrelated with either variable' (Yi 1996, p. 27). Thus, explaining Reid's absence from histories of economic thought is a much more difficult task than understanding Gilman's absence and can, in fact, be considered an egregious oversight by historians of thought.

One factor usually cited as contributing to the absences of voices such as Gilman's and Reid's is the topics they chose to analyse. Women economists often wrote about so-called 'women's issues', such as women's labour force activities and wages, which seemed to be of little interest to male economists (Baumol 1985). However, as Forget (1996) has contemplated, it is not clear if the lack of focus on women's issues were the result or the cause of the economics profession's inhospitality to women. In either case, as Madden (1972) noted in an early article on this subject, economists' historical contributions to discussions of 'the "woman problem"' have been relatively few and are often filled with untenable theoretical assumptions and stereotypical views toward women, exemplifying what Pujol (1992) has called the 'malestream' of economics.

This 'concern to expose and explain "androcentrism" or "male bias"' in economics (Seiz 1993, p. 185) represents the second major contribution by feminist historians of thought. As numerous scholars have demonstrated, all schools of economic thought, but particularly neoclassical economics, have exhibited androcentrism in their theoretical constructions, methodology and discourse. This recognition led Michèle Pujol, in her pathbreaking work, *Feminism and Anti-Feminism in Early Economic Thought* (1992) to note that the biases in neoclassical economic thought 'which characterize the school's treatment of women and their place in a capitalist economy' often construe women 'explicitly or implicitly, as exceptions to the rules developed, as belonging "elsewhere" than in the economic sphere, and as participating only marginally if at all in the nation's economic activity' (Pujol 1992, p. 1). (Likewise, Folbre (1993) and Folbre and Hartmann (1988) have explored the gendered biases inherent in Marxist economic paradigms, while Jennings (1993) has indicated aspects of institutional economics that require feminist reconstruction.)

Pujol's 1992 work is notable for several reasons. It was one of the first extended analyses of how neoclassical economics' methodology and ideology exclude women economists and women as economic actors from its discourse. Pujol not only explores how Adam Smith's economics set in motion the gender biases that persist today, but she also argues that the compelling feminist economic voices of Barbara Bodichon, Millicent Garrett Fawcett, Eleanor Rathbone and Ada Heather-Bigg are worth hearing. Moreover, Pujol exposes several nineteenth-century male standard bearers in economics both as sexists and as poor practitioners of the paradigm they helped to establish. For example, Pujol's analysis reveals how two articles written by F.Y. Edgeworth, who has long been considered a noted advocate of women's economic equality and an exemplary practitioner of neoclassical economic science, illustrate not only 'how the dogmatism of neoclassical economists and their profound and blind acceptance of the patriarchal structure of society lead to a completely incoherent theoretical position' regarding the equal pay issue but also to an 'acrobatic sophistry' in an attempt for theoretical consistency and finally to 'outright normative edicts' (Pujol 1992, p. 117) when explaining women's wage rates. But what troubles Pujol more, and what is particularly important for contemporary feminist economists, is how these theoretical acrobatics have endured as part of the neoclassical paradigm, even in those instances when the theory's creator recognized its internal inconsistencies and ideological biases. This concern, in turn, leads Pujol to analyse the economic contributions of Alfred Marshall and A.C. Pigou. Again Pujol finds that their work reflects not so much the neoclassical claims of economic science as the Victorian male biases regarding women's proper roles as wives and mothers and not as participants in the public economic sphere. Her findings guide Pujol to call for 'continued feminist critiques of malestream economic theory and ... the building of a feminist economics' that is free of the patriarchal biases of neoclassical economics (Pujol 1992, p. 203).

While Pujol's work is considered crucial in identifying the male biases in economic thought, she is not the only historian of thought concerned with exposing androcentrism. Peter Groenewegen, for example, notes Alfred Marshall's 'certain selectiveness in his use of evidence, and a tendency to reject factual material not congenial to him' in the neoclassical economist's discussion of women's proper role in the labour force (Greoenwegen 1994b, p. 93), leading to what Deborah Redman has called 'Marshall's split person-ality on the women's question' (Redman 1997, p. 202). White (1994) demonstrates how marginalist Stanley Jevons's dogmatism sometimes con-quered a dispassionate appeal to the facts in his argument that women's employment caused excess child mortality, while Forget (1997) examines how Jean-Baptiste Say's argument that women's wages are naturally below those of men (since men must support a family) provided the foundation for the separate-spheres argument inherent in the work of economists like Marshall and Jevons. And while these findings certainly deserve mention in histories of economic thought, they are perhaps more important for understanding the origins of sexist beliefs that still pervade contemporary economic thinking.

These analyses of androcentric biases in economic thought have been of particular interest to feminist economists as increasing numbers conclude that women's issues and concerns cannot simply be integrated into the domi-nant paradigm. In addition, the scholarship on locating women's forgotten voices provide feminist economists with possible sources of ideas for recon-structing neoclassical economics as well as the other androcentric paradigms. Thus, while it is possible to conclude that considerable gains have been made in finding women's contributions to economic discourse and in identifying how economists have evaluated women's economic activities, much more research is needed.

One area for further work is related to the rediscovery of women econo-mists since after finding these voices, feminist historians of thought still face the task of determining how to evaluate their contributions. In other words, further inquiry is needed to better understand why these women's voices were omitted from economics' histories of thought. Is it due to their gender (richly constructed), or is it because their contributions were not noteworthy? To answer this question, feminist economists must either adopt or adapt existing history of thought methods or develop new ones. One attempt has been made by Madden (1998), who not only considers why women's contri-butions have been ignored, but also the questions of how historians of thought might 'effectively and efficiently rank the "worthiness" of the publications' and of 'what constitutes a "contribution" in the field' (Madden 1998, p. 2). Cognizant of potential biases in existing methodologies, she advocates an 'explicit recognition of the factors influencing judgement of the relevance of the work for the disciplinary archives' (Madden 1998, p. 2) and offers a classification system which she applies to the case of the economics of consumption. Madden's work represents an important contribution to the systematic analysis of women economists' place in the history of economic thought and will hopefully be followed by additional efforts.

Another avenue for future research is further exploration of the connections between economics and the woman-friendly disciplines of home economics, social work and sociology as well as the social reform in which many women were engaged. As Forget (1996) discusses, the 'ethos of home economics ... was woman-centered, applied' (p. 9) and was 'at its core, a reform movement' (p. 8). Since this reflects the goals of many feminist economists, the work done in home economics, as in the other two fields, may offer contemporary scholars new conceptual, theoretical and methodological ideas for analysing issues of concern to a broader range of economic actors. Additional insights may result, as well, from further examination of the non-academic writings contributed by women activists and popularizers (as suggested by Polkinghorn). Relatedly, it would be interesting to explore if women economic educators offered views of economics that differed from the dominant paradigms or incorporated innovative pedagogies in the education of young women.

Finally, feminist historians of thought need to continue to identify biases other than gender that pervade existing economic theories. While Pujol (1992) and Folbre (1993), among others, have started this analysis, further work is needed to make explicit the origins of race, class and sexual preference biases in economic thinking. By looking at the discipline's history, feminist economists may learn how to avoid the biases and errors of our intellectual fathers as well as embrace the forgotten contributions of our intellectual mothers.

MARGARET LEWIS

See also
Dualisms; Feminist Economics; Women in the Economics Profession.

Bibliography
Baumol, William J. (1985), 'On method in US economics a century earlier', *American Economic Review*, **75** (6), 1–12.

Berg, Maxine (1992), 'The first women economic historians', *Economic History Review*, **XLV** (2), 308–29.

Dimand, Mary Ann (1995), 'Networks of Women Economists before 1940', in Mary Ann Dimand, Robert W. Dimand and Evelyn L. Forget (eds), *Women of Value: Feminist Essays on the History of Women in Economics*, Aldershot: Edward Elgar, pp. 39–59.

Dimand, Robert W. (1995), 'The Neglect of Women's Contributions to Economics', in Mary Ann Dimand, Robert W. Dimand and Evelyn L. Forget (eds), *Women of Value: Feminist Essays on the History of Women in Economics*, Aldershot: Edward Elgar, pp. 1–24.

Folbre, Nancy (1993), 'Socialism, Feminist and Scientific', in Marianne A. Ferber and Julie A. Nelson (eds), *Beyond Economic Man: Feminist Theory and Economics*, Chicago and London: University of Chicago Press, pp. 94–110.

Folbre, Nancy and Heidi Hartmann (1988), 'The Rhetoric of Self-Interest and the Ideology of Gender', in Arjo Klamer, Donald N. McCloskey and Robert M. Solow (eds), *The Consequences of Economic Rhetoric.* New York: Cambridge University Press, pp. 184–203.

Forget, Evelyn (1995), 'American Women Economists, 1900–1940: Doctoral Dissertations and Research Specialization', in Mary Ann Dimand, Robert W. Dimand and Evelyn L. Forget (eds), *Women of Value: Feminist Essays on the History of Women in Economics,* Aldershot: Edward Elgar, pp. 25–38.

Forget, Evelyn (1996), 'Margaret Gilpin Reid: a Manitoba home economist goes to Chicago', *Feminist Economics,* **2** (3), 1–16.

Forget, Evelyn (1997), 'The market of virtue: Jean-Baptiste Say on women in the economy and society', *Feminist Economics,* **3** (1), 93–111.

Grapard, Ulla (1996), 'The Trouble with "Women and Economics": A Postmodern Perspective on Charlotte Perkins Gilman', unpublished paper for the 1996 Allied Social Science Association meetings.

Groenewegen, Peter (1994a), 'Introduction: Women in Political Economy and Women as Political Economists in Victorian England', in Peter Groenewegen (ed.), *Feminism and Political Economy in Victorian England,* Aldershot: Edward Elgar, pp. 1–24.

Groenewegen, Peter (1994b), 'Alfred Marshall – Women and Economic Development: Labour, Family and Race', in Peter Groenewegen (ed.), *Feminism and Political Economy in Victorian England,* Aldershot: Edward Elgar, pp. 79–109.

Hammond, Claire (1993), 'American women and the professionalization of economics', *Review of Social Economy,* **51** (3), 347–70.

Hirschfeld, Mary (1994), 'Antecedents of the New Home Economics', unpublished paper for the 1994 Allied Social Science Association meetings.

Jennings, Ann L. (1993), 'Public or Private? Institutional Economics and Feminism', in Marianne A. Ferber and Julie A. Nelson (eds), *Beyond Economic Man: Feminist Theory and Economics,* Chicago and London: University of Chicago Press, pp. 111–29.

Lewis, Margaret and David Sebberson (1997), 'The rhetoricality of economic theory: Charlotte Perkins Gilman and Thorstein Veblen', *Journal of Economic Issues,* **XXXI** (2), 417–24.

Libby, Barbara (1990), 'Women in the economics profession, 1900–1940: factors in their declining visibility', *Essays in Economic and Business History,* **8**, 121–30.

Madden, Janice F. (1972), 'The development of economic thought on the "woman problem"', *Review of Radical Political Economy,* **4** (3), 21–39.

Madden, Kirsten (1998), 'Female Economists in the History of Economic Thought: Methodological Issues and a Case Study in Consumption Theory', unpublished paper for the 1998 History of Economics Society meetings.

O'Donnell, Margaret G. (1994), 'Early analysis of the economics of family structure: Charlotte Perkins Gilman's *Women and Economics*', *Review of Social Economy,* **LII** (2), 86–95.

Polkinghorn, Bette (1995), 'Jane Marcet and Harriet Martineau: Motive, Market Experience and Reception of Their Works Popularizing Classical Political Economy', in Mary Ann Dimand, Robert W. Dimand and Evelyn L. Forget (eds), *Women of Value: Feminist Essays on the History of Women in Economics,* Aldershot: Edward Elgar, pp. 71–81.

Pujol, Michèle A. (1992), *Feminism and Anti-Feminism in Early Economic Thought,* Aldershot: Edward Elgar.

Redman, Deborah (1997), 'Review of T. Raffaelli, E. Biagini and R. McWilliams Tullberg (eds), *Alfred Marshall's Lectures to Women* and Peter Groenewegen, *A Soaring Eagle: Alfred Marshall 1842–1924*', *Feminist Economics,* **3** (1), 201–9.

Schumpeter, Joseph A. (1954), *History of Economic Analysis,* New York: Oxford University Press.

Seiz, Janet (1993), 'Feminism and the history of economic thought', *History of Political Economy,* **25** (1), 185–201.

Sockwell, William D. (1995), 'Barbara Bodichon and the Women of Langham Place', in Mary Ann Dimand, Robert W. Dimand and Evelyn L. Forget (eds), *Women of Value: Feminist Essays on the History of Women in Economics,* Aldershot: Edward Elgar, pp. 103–23.

Thomson, Dorothy Lampen (1973), *Adam Smith's Daughters,* New York: Exposition Press.

Thorne, Alison Comish (1995), 'Women Mentoring Women in Economics in the 1930s', in

Mary Ann Dimand, Robert W. Dimand and Evelyn L. Forget (eds), *Women of Value: Feminist Essays on the History of Women in Economics*, Aldershot: Edward Elgar, pp. 60–70.

White, Michael V. (1994), 'Following Strange Gods: Women in Jevons's Political Economy', in Peter Groenewegen (ed.), *Feminism and Political Economy in Victorian England*, Aldershot: Edward Elgar, pp. 46–78.

Yi, Yun-Ae (1996), 'Margaret G. Reid: Life and achievements', *Feminist Economics*, 2 (3), 17–36.

Human Capital Theory

Human capital, the investment by persons in skills linked to productive capability, has engendered an important element of the feminist critique of neoclassical economic theory. While on the surface a noncontroversial explanation of why persons would choose to spend time in formal education and on-the-job training and why earnings would tend to rise with experience and job tenure, in reality human capital theory has numerous embedded assumptions which make it objectionable to those seeking to explain gender differences in earnings.

The concept of human capital is quite old, and serious references to it are found in economics writings back to 1676 (Rosen 1987, p. 682). As used in the writings of some economists, including A.C. Pigou and John Stuart Mill, the term 'human capital' appeared to be applied to the notion that the population of a country was a significant asset, and this usage links it to the idea of women as either being or providing 'reproductive capital' (Pujol 1992). However, most economists use the term following the meaning in Adam Smith, in which a worker chooses to acquire talents 'during his education, study, or apprenticeship', which 'as they make a part of his fortune, so do they likewise of that of the society to which he belongs' (Smith [1776] 1991, II.I.17). Smith appears to draw quite forcefully a distinction between unproductive and productive work in which reproductive work is considered unproductive (although it includes the means of creating the human capital!) (Pujol 1992, p. 18).

The modern rendition of human capital theory is commonly dated to the writings of Mincer (1958), Schultz (1961) and Becker (1993) and is strongly identified with the Chicago school of economics. It blossomed in the 1970s into a research programme, or, more accurately, as Blaug (1992a, p. 207) states, into 'a subprogram within the more comprehensive neoclassical research program' (see Rosen 1987 for a thorough statement of the conventional neoclassical formulation). It then led to the general application of neoclassical theory into what is now known as economics of the family, or the 'new home economics', most notoriously in the subsequent work of Becker (1976). This entry concentrates on human capital theory's best-known application in the area of feminist and gender economics: its application to the question of what causes the gender wage gap.

Human capital theory leads to several explanations for why women earn less than men do. First, women may have less human capital than men have. Secondly, women could have the same amount of human capital as men, but it could vary in type in the following four ways: women may be more likely to invest in human capital that has high nonmarket return; women may be more likely to invest in human capital that increases satisfaction with time spent in market work, nonmarket work, or leisure, while men may invest in human capital with a high return in wages but little increase in satisfaction; women may be less likely to invest in specific human capital; and women may invest in human capital that depreciates less rapidly than the human capital that men invest in. In all four cases, women's monetary return will therefore be lower than men's will.

There is strong empirical evidence that systematic differences in men's and women's human capital stocks do account for part of the wage gap (Jacobsen 1998, Chapter 7). In developing countries, women receive less formal education. In developed countries, while women and men have roughly comparable mean years of formal education, men are more likely to receive degrees in higher-paying fields and are more likely to go on to receive professional degrees. Women are underrepresented in formal apprenticeship programmes and appear to receive less informal on-the-job training. They have lower mean years of tenure (considered a proxy for receipt of specific capital) and lower mean years of total work experience. And they have much higher rates of intermittent labour force attachment. Studies using wage equations designed to measure the net effect of these differences generally report that some 30–50 per cent of the gender wage difference is attributable to these gender differences in human capital.

But why would men and women differ in their investment strategies regarding human capital? First, preferences for types of return may differ systematically by gender. Second, if women anticipate spending less total time in paid labour, their total monetary return is reduced relative to that of men's. Third, even if they anticipate as many total years of paid work, if they anticipate intermittent labour force attachment, it could lead to them choosing less rapidly-depreciating forms and less firm-specific capital, both of which would tend to have lower returns than more risky capital. Fourth, discrimination against women in the labour market in either hiring or pay takes the form of providing them with a lower rate of return on human capital. Anticipating discrimination, women might, therefore, invest less in market work-specific human capital. Fifth, discrimination in access to human capital attainment may occur, creating a barrier to women's achieving their desired level of investment. In the case of on-the job training, this could be partly due to the perception on the part of employers to make less specific human capital investments in women if they anticipate lower tenure on their parts (that is, statistical discrimination). In the case of formal education, the gatekeepers of educational institutions serve as the discriminating agents.

While it is quite clear that discrimination in access to education, training and labour markets was the critical determinant of women's lower human capital investments in historical periods, it has proved more difficult to design satisfactory tests for these hypotheses using recent data (Jacobsen 1998, Chapter 7). The issue of whether or not women choose occupations that require less rapidly-depreciating human capital has not been resolved, with researchers finding opposing results. There is evidence that women's expectations regarding child rearing and labour force intermittency can affect their formal education options, such as college major, and their acquisition of on-the-job training. There is also evidence that women value the nonmonetary aspects of work relatively more than do men. However, these expectations may themselves be formed by realizing that access to lucrative forms of employment is curtailed for women, making it difficult to argue that discrimination has not played an indirect part in shaping women's choices at this critical phase.

One of the main feminist critiques of human capital theory has been its narrow focus on labour market activity, which has tended to ignore interactions with marriage markets and choices made prior to entry into the prime labour market years. For example, while the first two explanations above imply free choice on the part of the woman in making investment decisions, critics have argued that women's choice to spend less time in labour force participation is not freely made. If there are social norms and customs governing choice, as institutional economists would argue is the case, then free choice is an oxymoron. Ability and/or desire to acquire various forms of human capital, which may vary systematically by sex, may nonetheless be shaped by such norms and customs. In particular, to the extent that the double day/second shift is automatically assigned to women, women may choose forms of human capital that are compatible with this requirement. Additionally, parents, husbands and other persons may make the choices regarding human capital investment for the woman. Clearly the feedback issues regarding society's expectations of women's roles becoming self-fulfilling have not been carefully modelled, nor is this issue readily tractable given current empirical and theoretical tools.

This critique has been particularly trenchant and well-founded with regard to the empirical literature on wage differentials, nearly all of which is based on the human capital model of wage determination. Generally, researchers try to control for all human capital-related measures in order to explain differences in wages between two groups. They then ascribe the unexplained component to a combination of omitted variables and discrimination, providing an apparent upper bound on the percentage of the wage gap that can be ascribed to discrimination against one of the groups. However, to the extent that the less-favoured group has less human capital because of experiencing discrimination or constrained choice in one of the ways mentioned above, this effect cannot be separated from freely choosing to invest in less human capital.

Another critique is that human capital theory, in its atomistic focus on the individual's decision, ignores the effect of others' actions on that decision. This is true not only in the senses described in the two preceding paragraphs, but also when incorporating ideas from crowding theory. To the extent that women are only allowed into a narrow range of occupations, the rate of return on human capital in the female-dominated occupations is reduced below what it would be in a freely-operating labour market. Also, if occupations differ in terms of the wage differential paid to women and men of equal productivity, women will be more likely to invest in specific human capital for the less discriminatory occupations. This creates a different occupational choice process for women than for men. In particular, occupations that are lower-earning but less discriminatory are relatively more attractive to women than they would be in a world with no discrimination.

A third critique, voiced by a wide range of labour market theorists, including Marxist and institutionalist scholars, is that all of the phenomena reported above are also compatible with alternative models of wage determination (see Blaug 1992b, Part II). Education may serve as a screening device to determine who is more or less able rather than as a way to increase ability, or as a method of acculturating workers to the capitalist production mode and segmenting them so as to inhibit formation of worker coalitions (Bowles and Gintis 1975). Rising wage profiles could be a pure function of linking wages to seniority, rather than evidence of increased productivity through accrual of more human capital.

Expanding these lines of thought into a feminist critique would attribute the differences between returns to men's and women's human capital to the desire to maintain patriarchy. Therefore one might imagine that if women are successful in, say, achieving entry into the academy, that the patriarchal order will be maintained by reducing access to another area and reordering wages so as to privilege this area instead. Occupational segregation and labour market segmentation theorists, particularly those focusing on the apparent relationship between lower earnings and higher percentage female, have pointed out that occupations that have become feminized appear simultaneously to undergo reduced relative status and reduced relative earnings (Reskin and Roos 1990). Also projected returns to increasing women's human capital endowments may be spurious if glass ceiling effects persist (that is, subtle discrimination which prevents women from achieving equal returns to those of men).

A final critique is whether people really make the types of forward-looking calculations assumed by the theory (which, as generally implemented, does not consider incomplete information or uncertainty). For instance, one study found that young women systematically underestimate the number of work years and therefore underinvest in human capital (Sandell and Shapiro 1982). The degree of uncertainty introduced by changes in marriage market workings (for example, rising divorce rates during the 1970s, lower rates of ever-marrying in the 1980s) might lead to a rejection of the principles of human capital calculation, or alternatively to a risk-reduction strategy of overinvestment in human capital, leading to lower returns than those predicted in a riskless world. Additionally, uncertainty regarding future payoffs might lead to differential behaviour by gender regarding human capital investment if men and women differ systematically in risk-aversion and/or appraisal.

Human capital theory continues to stimulate much research, with researchers continuing both to expand the programme and to critique it. A search of the EconLit database turned up 6793 abstracts referencing human capital; 590 were published in 1996 alone. The field of the economics of education has both expanded on the notion of human capital and developed various lines of critiques of it. A recent area of interest in development economics has been the link between women's education in developing countries and improved indicators of their wellbeing as well as decreased fertility (see Schultz 1995). To this extent, it appears that higher levels of education and female labour force participation have potentially positive feedback effects.

The debate over the relevance and potential uses of human capital theory also has implications for many other issues of current interest to feminist economists. These issues include expansion of national income accounts to account for nonmarket output stocks and flows, the relevance of workfare and training programmes to real welfare reform, and appropriate forms of development aid programmes. While it appears that the human capital portion of the neoclassical paradigm is firmly entrenched, no doubt additional extensions of relevance to feminist economics – and additional feminist critiques – will be forthcoming.

JOYCE P. JACOBSEN

See also
Discrimination, Theories of; Double Day/Second Shift; Education, Economics of; Glass Ceiling; Labour Force Participation; Labour Market Segmentation; Labour Markets, Theories of; Occupational Segregation; Wage Gap.

Bibliography
Becker, Gary S. (1976), *The Economic Approach to Human Behavior*, Chicago: University of Chicago Press.

Becker, Gary S. (1993), *Human Capital: A Theoretical and Empirical Analysis, with Special Reference to Education*, Third Edition, Chicago: University of Chicago Press.

Blaug, Mark (1992a), *The Methodology of Economics*, Second Edition, Cambridge: Cambridge University Press.

Blaug, Mark (ed.) (1992b), *The Economic Value of Education: Studies in the Economics of Education*, Aldershot and Brookfield: Edward Elgar.

Bowles, Samuel and Herbert Gintis (1975), 'The problem with human capital theory – A Marxian critique', *American Economic Review*, **65** (2), May, 74–82.

Jacobsen, Joyce P. (1998), *The Economics of Gender*, Second Edition, Cambridge, Massachusetts: Blackwell.

Mincer, Jacob (1958), 'Investment in human capital and personal income distribution', *Journal of Political Economy*, **66**, (August), 281–302.

Pujol, Michèle A. (1992), *Feminism and Anti-Feminism in Early Economic Thought*, Aldershot and Brookfield: Edward Elgar.

Reskin, Barbara F. and Patricia A. Roos (1990), *Job Queues, Gender Queues: Explaining Women's Inroads into Male Occupations*, Philadelphia: Temple University Press.

Rosen, Sherwin (1987), 'Human Capital', in John Eatwell, Murray Milgate and Peter Newman (eds), *The New Palgrave: A Dictionary of Economics*, London: Macmillan, pp. 681–90.

Sandell, Steven H. and David Shapiro (1982), 'Work expectations, human capital accumulation, and the wages of young women', *Journal of Human Resources*, **15** (3), (Summer), 335–53.

Schultz, T. Paul (ed) (1995), *Investment in Women's Human Capital*, Chicago: University of Chicago Press.

Schultz, Theodore (1961), 'Investment in human capital', *American Economic Review*, **51** (1), March, 1–17.

Smith, Adam (1991), *Wealth of Nations*, Buffalo: Prometheus Books.

Imperialism

In common usage, the term imperialism refers to the economic, political and cultural subjection of the Third World by Europe and the United States. While various theories of imperialism attribute its existence to such factors as geopolitical rivalry, psychological drives to dominate people from other cultures, or rampant nationalism, economic explanations tend to emphasize the role of capitalist expansion and competition for profits on a world scale as a determining factor. Economic theories of imperialism contend that unequal power relations between the two regions are developed and maintained to secure access to cheap raw materials, cheap labour, profitable investment outlets and/or product markets for capitalist firms.

There is widespread agreement that imperialism is one of the major forces in recent history, but in terms of identifying and assessing its impact the consensus breaks down. Imperialism is not contained within easily recognizable chronological or analytical boundaries, resulting in a certain amount of ambiguity associated with the use of the term. In some writings, the word designates the international expansion of capitalism from the early colonial encounters of the sixteenth century to the spread of transnational corporations in the present day. Some use the term to refer to a distinctly twentieth-century stage of monopoly capitalism, using other terms to describe European expansionism of earlier periods. Some associate imperialist domination with the use of military force or at least the threat of armed intervention, while others argue that the sources of differential power are more varied and subtle. There are also authors who write about the concept of imperialism yet do not use the term at all.

Most economic theories of imperialism come out of the Marxian and political economy traditions. It should be noted that Marx did not develop a theory of imperialism as such. Defining and explaining these processes was a task left to later generations of authors. The first sustained investigation of the problem emerged in the early twentieth century in an attempt to make sense of increased imperialist expansion and rivalry during that time. Here, most authors emphasized that imperialism was a political expression of an economic effect of capitalism. Hobson was one of the first to link imperialism with the capitalist development (Hobson 1902). Lenin argued that imperialism represented a stage of monopoly capitalism, with large firms exporting capital in order to increase their profits. Political and military rivalries occurred as competition between national monopolies spurred a contest between the countries of Europe for control over the 'backwards' areas (Lenin 1917, pp. 72–4). Other early writers who emphasized the relationship between capitalist development and imperialism include Hilferding, Bukharin and Luxemburg (Brewer 1990).

Most early theories of imperialism stress that increased competition between monopoly firms accelerates the spread of capitalism throughout the world. Whether this process spurs development and modernization in the colonies and semi-colonies, or whether it results in the 'development of underdevelopment' in these regions, was the subject of debate among a second generation of theorists writing during the 1950s, 1960s and 1970s. On one side of the debate were those who contended that the diffusion of capitalism would lead to development and progress throughout the globe, with the peripheral economies of the colonies and semi-colonies on lower rungs of the same ladder that the European centres had already climbed (for example, Warren 1980). The opposing view predicted a more pernicious outcome from the internationalization of capital: far from creating the conditions for the non-capitalist regions to catch up to the West, capitalist expansion would fix into place a two-sector world divided into exploiter and exploited nations. This thesis is the origin of the core–periphery (or centre–periphery), North–South model that underlies theories of underdevelopment, dependency and neo-colonialism associated with writers such as Baran (1957), Frank (1967) and Amin (1976).

One thing that nearly all of these authors have in common is their failure to recognize the gender dimensions of imperialism. The lives of women are shaped in particular ways by the spread of capitalism around the globe, and in turn the gender dimensions of imperialism affect the character of the encounter between different regions, cultures and economies. These aspects of imperialism have nonetheless been absent from many theoretical analyses. Since the 1970s, however, an emerging feminist scholarship has amply demonstrated the importance of gender to the understanding of imperialism and its effects. Various projects have charted the exploitation of Third World women workers by multinational corporations, the complex and sometimes contradictory interactions of gender, class and globalization and the gendered and colonial hierarchies that have influenced the way that Western social scientists have made sense of Third World women and imperialism itself. The concept of imperialism has not only formed the basis of feminist analyses, it has in turn been transformed by feminist thought.

One of the first feminists to write about imperialism was Rosa Luxemburg. It is interesting to note that while she wrote extensively on the 'woman question' in her lifetime, her analysis of imperialism in *The Accumulation of Capital* (1913) did not explicitly address the gender dimension. Nonetheless her theories have been viewed as a basis for a feminist theory of imperialism by later writers as described in the paragraph below. Luxemburg argued that the development of capitalism depended on a contradictory relationship with non-capitalist, or what she alternatively dubbed 'natural', economies such as peasant subsistence production in the colonies. On the one hand, there are pressures to maintain these subsistence economies. They are important sources of cheap non-wage goods and services and they serve as a market for capitalist output. Their existence could also provide a surplus population to keep wages low. On the other hand, there are pressures to integrate them more fully into the capitalist system, for instance by making subsistence workers wage workers. In either case, Luxemburg contended, these subsistence communities would be both exploited and destroyed.

In the 1980s, German social theorists C.K. Von Werlhof and Maria Mies built upon Luxemburg's thesis to produce a feminist theory of imperialism. Luxemburg considered only the non-gendered category of peasants in her discussion of non-wage subsistence workers. In separate essays in the book *Women: The Last Colony* (Mies et al., 1988), Von Werlhof and Mies argue that Luxemburg's non-wage workers include housewives throughout the world and the marginalized subsistence workers of both sexes. Von Werlhof's writing focuses on the role of women as non-capitalist subsistence workers who play multiple economic roles as providers of goods and services (such as food and caring labour) to the household, as a reserve army of labour and as wage workers in the capitalist economy. Mies's research on capitalist penetration in India and its impact on women shows that capitalism increases the marginalization of women in many rural areas. The subsistence production of these women is tapped by capitalist firms in various ways to increase local and global profits. For example, the food that women produce in the non-wage sector may decrease the wage needed to reproduce the labour of capitalist wage workers. She also demonstrates the relationship between sexism and the expansion of capital in these areas, showing how they interact to decrease the wellbeing of rural women. Mies argues that neither class nor patriarchy is the dominant oppression in these cases and suggests that anti-imperialist struggles need to confront both problems simultaneously.

Mies and Von Werlhof emphasize the relationship between capitalist expansion and the subsistence labour of women in their theories of imperialism. Other feminist studies have focused more on the effects of capitalist expansion and the movement of Third World women into the wage labour force. Since the 1970s, multinational firms have increasingly relocated production from Europe and the United States to areas of Asia and Latin America. Many of the jobs in these factories consist of labour-intensive assembly work and most of the workers in these plants are women with little bargaining power. These women workers are typically paid less than male workers. For example, women's wages in South-East Asia are 20–50 per cent lower than men's for comparable jobs, even though male productivity is lower (Elson and Pearson 1981, p. 148). Research by anthropologists such as Safa (1995) on the Caribbean and the contributors to the volume edited by Nash and Fernandez-Kelly (1983) on Latin America suggests that it is the low wages of female workers that attracts multinational firms. These writers emphasize that patriarchal and imperialist cultures, which give rise to incorrect assumptions such as the notion that Third World women are less skilled and thus deserve a lower wage, combine with the legacy of underdevelopment and lack of alternative opportunities to keep the wages of women low. These studies also demonstrate that firms frequently justify the low wages they pay women by assuming that women are not the primary breadwinners but are temporary earners of 'extra' income as a natural consequence of their child-bearing capabilities.

In addition to providing a source of cheap labour, Third World women, particularly South-East Asian women, are attractive to multinational firms because of assumptions that their natural skilfulness and docility will make them good employees. A brochure put out by the Malaysian government states that 'the manual dexterity of the oriental woman is famous the world over. Her hands are small and she works fast with extreme care' (Elson and Pearson 1981, p. 149). Feminist economists Elson and Pearson cite this as an example of the sexism and racism that motivates hiring and relocation decisions of multinational firms. 'Oriental' women are thought to be naturally suited to tedious, repetitive work, as well as to delicate work. It is believed that they will be less likely to complain or to organize because of their docility. The supposed passivity of these women has been challenged by a number of studies, most notably Ong's (1987) study of Malaysian factory workers. Ong's work shows how these women workers claim 'spirit possession' in order to gain control over the pace of work at their factories. The elimination of spirits from their bodies and machines is done through time-consuming rituals, resulting in something analogous to a sit-down strike. Ong's work does more than provide a counterpoint to ethnic stereotypes of passive Asian women, it provides a reminder that forms of resistance can be multiple and varied.

There has been a great deal of debate about whether the expansion of capital has improved Third World women's lives. Does working in a factory in a multinational corporation make women better off or does it increase their exploitation? Has the spread of capitalism and western culture led to an increase in women's freedoms or has it led to a decline in women's access to resources and power in the public sphere? These questions lie at the heart of a feminist theory of imperialism. The debate echoes the more general debates on imperialism as to whether the expansion of capitalism from Europe and the USA is a progressive force or whether its effects are more pernicious as discussed above. Many feminist development economists believe that the movement of women out of non-wage work and into the capitalist labour market is their best hope for fighting gender oppression (Kabeer 1994). Once women are integrated into the labour market, it is argued, the old system of patriarchal domination will break down. Whether the actual experiences of women bear this thesis out is another matter. Safa (1995) reports that women factory workers in export manufacturing firms in the Caribbean use their earnings to bargain for increased authority within the household. Mies's research on India (discussed above), in contrast, shows that women's exploitation has increased and their power has decreased due to capitalist penetration. Enloe's (1989) description of the exploitation of young women and girls within the sex-tourism industries of Thailand and the Philippines provides another example of how the influx of foreign capital has a negative effect on women's lives.

Anthropologist Fernández-Kelly's (1983) landmark study of women factory workers in the maquiladora region on the Mexico–US border demonstrates that the role of capitalist penetration can sometimes affect women's lives in complex and contradictory ways. She presents evidence that these women work long hours, face terrible working conditions and are offered little in terms of job security. These women are poorly educated, young and recent migrants to the area, they have few other opportunities because of their gender and many are the sole supporters of their children. This makes them vulnerable to the exploitative labour practices of the assembly plants. At the same time, however, they are able to break free of the sometimes stifling patriarchal relations of their society by working in the factories and having access to their own income. They are also able to develop a sense of solidarity which provides a base to challenge male authority in the plant and in the broader community. Considering the complex interactions between capitalism, patriarchy and imperialism that are possible, some researchers contend that it would be best to examine the effects of transnational capital on a case-by-case basis, locating where it intensifies gender oppression in some cases, challenges it in others, and transforms it in still others (for example, Elson and Pearson 1981; Mohanty 1991). Other researchers have added the insight that the expansion of capitalism affects different groups of women in a particular community, for instance benefiting upper-class women while decreasing the wellbeing of very poor women (for example, Benería and Roldan 1987).

In addition to providing insight into the contemporary relationship between gender and the spread of western capitalist economy and culture, feminist theorists have begun to explore the historical transformation of gender relations that resulted from colonization. Much of this research shows that contact between European cultures and the peoples of Africa, the Pacific and the Americas has played an important role in forming the basis of women's inequality in these societies which influences social structures in the present day. Studies by feminist anthropologists have challenged the presumption that pre-colonial societies were 'backward' in the sense that they were characterized by a great deal of gender inequality (and that contact with the 'modern' west somehow liberated indigenous women), showing that in many cases these societies were organized on an egalitarian basis. The example of Rothenberg's (1980) study of the Seneca Nation in what is now western New York, USA is a representative case. In this society, women had control of the means of subsistence production and a great deal of public power. The influence of European settlers, however, led to a decrease in the power of Senecan women because European men would not buy land or exchange goods with women, thus giving men exclusive access to the emerging money economy. The inculcation of ideals of femininity and European norms of family organization through religious and/or cultural indoctrination also had a negative effect on women's status in the Seneca community. Other feminist anthropological studies demonstrate that the impact of colonization tended to exacerbate existing gender oppression or promote it in previously egalitarian societies (Leacock and Etienne 1980).

The complexity of colonial social relations and the gendered nature of imperial rule have been described in a number of recent studies by feminist historians (for example, Stoler 1989; Chaudhuri and Strobel 1992). Some of this work emphasizes the ways that the colonial encounter changed women's lives in the imperial centres. Other studies emphasize the often uneasy relationships between European and indigenous women in the colonies, particularly those between mistresses and their female servants and/or slaves. Feminist historians have also investigated the different ways in which notions of masculinity and femininity have interacted with ideas of western superiority and native inferiority. 'Native' men, for instance, were often represented by colonial powers as inferior, feminine creatures, while women were often judged against rigid codes of European femininity and found wanting. Some historical and sociological accounts have also charted the relationship between gender relations and Third World nationalist and anti-imperialist movements (Chatterjee 1993; McClintock et al. 1997; Yuval-Davis and Anthias 1997).

A number of analyses of the gendered social and cultural dimensions of economic imperialism have been published in the last couple of decades. These works call attention to the imperialist biases of western knowledge of the Third World, including many western feminist accounts. For example, much of the writing on women in developing countries has focused on the 'traditional' male breadwinner/female housewife household as the locus of the oppression of women. Anti-imperialist feminists have revealed that these accounts better reflect the realities of white, western, middle-class women than the diversity of experiences of Third World women (for example, Jayawardena 1986). While western feminists might project their own experiences onto women from other regions, there is also sometimes a tendency to define these women as the backward, passive and oppressed 'other' of the liberated western woman. Mohanty (1991) challenges this portrayal of an 'average third world woman' who bears the burden of being poor, backwards, traditional and victimized, showing that it is produced by an imperialistic mind-set that views the other as inferior and in need of our salvation. She argues instead for the appreciation of the heterogeneity of women's experiences and the ways that different class and ethnic identities intersect with gender. She also stresses the importance of recognizing Third World women's capabilities and strengths in solving their own problems. Perhaps the most important point raised by the work of Mohanty and others working in this area is the need to develop an awareness of the kinds of biases that western scholars can bring to the study of Third World women in order to avoid them.

Finally it should be noted that feminists have recently begun to examine the gendered nature of the discourse of imperialism itself. Economic geographer Gibson-Graham (1996), for example, contends that the story of capitalist imperialism, which tells of a dominant, unified and intentional force penetrating the passive and receptive regions of the world, replicates the script of 'masculine' force and 'feminine' passivity found in patriarchal discourse. The effect of this kind of story is that it gives capitalism more power than it really has. Because analysts of imperialism think of capitalism as a powerful, irresistible force, they are not able to conceptualize outcomes where multinational firms can fail to meet their goals and/or lose out to community initiatives. Echoing Mohanty's theme, Gibson-Graham also suggests that such a story portrays Third World agents (including women) as passive victims of imperialism, and fails to recognize their potential for resistance to exploitation.

Feminist accounts of imperialism have raised a number of important questions about the gendered nature of imperialism and provide theoretical challenges for economists engaged in feminist scholarship. One challenge facing feminist economists is to develop economic theories of women in the Third World that can capture the complex interactions of class, ethnicity, nationality and gender in the economy. Another challenge to feminist economists is to provide a historical understanding of the impact of colonialism and modern imperialism on the economic status of women in both the core and periphery regions. Yet another avenue for feminist research is to trace the relationship between gendered and imperialistic discourses in both the history of economic thought and in contemporary theories. Some gestures in this direction have been provided in papers by Williams (1993) and Grapard (1995) and form a basis for further study. Grapard's deconstruction of the Robinson Crusoe metaphor shows how gendered and imperialist notions have become embedded into mainstream economic discourse, while Williams provides a challenge to the Eurocentric tendencies of contemporary feminist economic scholarship. Feminist economists have also recently begun to take into account the economic, social and cultural effects of imperialism in policy discussions concerning women in the Third World (Bakker 1994). The need for a better understanding of the intersection between the social, cultural and economic aspects of imperialism nonetheless continues to provide an important challenge for feminist economists around the globe.

SUZANNE BERGERON

See also

Development Policy; Development, Theories of; Economic Restructuring; Globalization; International Economics; Marxist Political Economics; Structural Adjustment Policies.

Bibliography

Amin, Samir (1976), *Unequal Development*, New York: Monthly Review Press.
Bakker, Isabella (1994), *The Strategic Silence: Women and Economic Policy*, London: Zed Press.
Baran, Paul (1957), *The Political Economy of Growth*, New York: Modern Reader Paperbacks.
Benería, Lourdes and Martha Roldan (1987), *The Crossroads of Class and Gender: Industrial Homework, Subcontracting and the Household Dynamics in Mexico City*, Chicago: University of Chicago Press.
Brewer, Anthony (1990), *Marxist Theories of Imperialism: A Critical Survey*, London: Routledge.
Chatterjee, Partha (1993), *Nationalist Thought and the Colonial World: A Derivative Discourse*, London: Zed Press.
Chaudhuri, Nupur and Margaret Strobel (eds) (1992), *Western Women and Imperialism: Complicity and Resistance*, Bloomington: Indiana University Press.
Donaldson, Laura (1992), *Decolonizing feminisms: race, gender and empire-building*, Chapel Hill: University of North Carolina Press.
Elson, Diane and Ruth Pearson (1981), 'The Subordination of Women and the Internationalization of Factory Production', in Kate Young, Carol Wolkowitz and Roslyn McCullagh (eds), *Of Marriage and Market: Subordination in International Perspective*, London: CSE Books, pp. 144–66.
Enloe, Cynthia (1989), *Bananas, Beaches, Bases: Making Feminist Sense of International Politics*, Berkeley: University of California Press.
Fernández-Kelly, María Patricia (1983), *For We are Sold, I and My People: Women in Industry in Mexico's Frontier*, Albany: State University of New York Press.
Frank, Andre Gunder (1967), 'The development of underdevelopment', *Monthly Review*, **18**, 17–31.
Gibson-Graham, J.K. (1996), *The End of Capitalism (As We Knew It): A feminist critique of Political Economy*, Oxford: Blackwell.
Grapard, Ulla (1995), 'Robinson Crusoe: quintessential economic man?', *Feminist Economics*, **1** (1), 33–52.
Hobson, J.A. (1902), *Imperialism: A Study*, London: Allen and Unwin.
Jayawardena, Kumari (1986), *Feminism and Nationalism in the Third World*, London: Zed Press.
Kabeer, Naila (1994), *Reversed Realities*, London: Verso.
Leacock, Eleanor and Mona Etienne (eds) (1980), *Women and Colonization: Anthropological Perspectives*, New York: Praeger Press.
Lenin, V.I. (1917), *Imperialism: Highest Stage of Capitalism*, Moscow: Foreign Languages Publishing House.
Luxemburg, Rosa (1913), *The Accumulation of Capital*, London: Routledge, Kegan Paul.
McClintock, Ann, Amir Mufti and Ella Shohat (1997), *Dangerous Liaisons: Gender, Nation and Postcolonial Perspectives*, Minneapolis: University of Minnesota Press.
Mies, Maria, Claudia Von Werlhof and Veronika Bennholdt-Thomsen (1988), *Women: The Last Colony*, London: Zed Press.

Mohanty, Chandra (1991), 'Under Western Eyes: Feminist Scholarship and Western Discourses', in Chandra Talpade Mohanty, Ann Russo and Lourdes Torres (eds), *Third World Women and the Politics of Feminism*, Bloomington: Indiana University Press, pp. 51–80.

Nash, June and María Patricia Fernández-Kelly (eds) (1993), *Women, Men, and the International Division of Labor*, Albany: State University of New York Press.

Ong, Aihwa (1987), *Spirits of Resistance and Capitalist Discipline: Factory Women in Malaysia*, Albany: State University of New York Press.

Rothenberg, Diane (1980), 'The Mothers of the Nation: Seneca Resistance to Quaker Intervention', in Eleanor Leacock and Mona Etienne (eds) (1980), *Women and Colonization: Anthropological Perspectives*, New York: Praeger Press, pp. 63–87.

Safa, Helen (1995), 'Gender Implications of Export-Led Industrialisation in the Caribbean', in Rae Blumberg, Irene Tinker, Cathy Rakowski and Michael Monteon (eds), *Engendering Wealth and Well-Being*, Boulder: Westview Press, pp. 89–173.

Said, Edward (1979), *Orientalism*, New York: Vintage Books.

Stoler, Ann Laura (1989), 'Rethinking colonial categories: European communities and the boundaries of rule', *Comparative Studies in Society and History*, 31 (1), 134–61.

Warren, Bill (1980), *Imperialism, Pioneer of Capitalism*, London: New Left Books.

Williams, Rhonda (1993), 'Race, Deconstruction, and the Emergent Agenda of Feminist Theory', in Marianne Ferber and Julie Nelson (eds), *Beyond Economic Man*, Chicago: University of Chicago Press, pp. 144–52.

Yuval-Davis, Nira and Floya Anthias (eds) (1997), *Unsettling Settler Societies*, London: Macmillan Press.

Income Distribution

Income distribution refers to the dispersion of income among households in any society. Income distribution addresses a wide range of income allocation mechanisms in economics, which has almost always been linked with discussions of growth theory and labour markets. Non-neoclassical economists have also linked discussions of income distribution with inequality, fairness, societal stability and poverty.

Income distribution is an important topic in feminist economics because it not only addresses issues of economic equality and fairness, but also because it calls attention to how households generate income (and with it the distribution of income within households) and how family structure and women's labour force participation contribute to income distribution. Women traditionally have had less direct access to income than men – usually depending on male family members because of reduced income-earning capacity – but the sexual division of labour has typically been absent from income distribution discussions (Albelda and Tilly 1996).

Income distribution in the United States has come in for renewed attention recently because since the 1970s individual earnings and family incomes have become dramatically more unequal (Gottschalk 1997). Ironically, as the US gender wage gap narrowed from the mid 1970s onward (after widening for 20 years), wage disparities along virtually every other dimension – level of education, race, industry – grew wider. Internationally, in the 1980s virtually every other industrialized capitalist country saw either the end of a trend toward earnings equalization (France, Germany, Italy) or an outright turn towards sharper inequality (Australia, Canada, Japan, Sweden, United Kingdom) (Freeman and Katz 1994). The United States, and to a lesser extent the United Kingdom, experienced the most rapid polarization in incomes. Moreover, the income gap between rich and poor countries continued to widen, as it has for most of the last century (Pritchett 1997). This entry will focus primarily on debates and evidence from the United States, although many of the insights and arguments are applicable elsewhere as well.

Much of the US literature on earnings inequality has focused on the fate of *male* wages, which have declined and become more dispersed in the last two decades. However, a few scholars have paid attention to the distribution of income among women workers – which has also become more unequal, but in the context of *rising* average female wages (see for example, Blau 1993; Cancian et al. 1993). In addition, while those discussing the causes of increased income inequality have noted the importance of changes in family structure, most analysts have still focused on changes in the labour market, downplaying feminist economics' concerns about family income generation and women's access to income. Feminist economics has much to contribute in this field by integrating dynamics of family formation and women's labour force participation into macroeconomic models of growth and labour markets and by questioning the subordination of income distribution to growth.

Over the last 50 years, conventional *microeconomic* views of income distribution have focused on individual earning capacity – the main source of income in wage-based economies. Mainstream *macroeconomic* views of income distribution, meanwhile, have subordinated distribution to economic growth.

Neoclassical economics has a considerable literature on earnings differences between individuals, all of which centres on labour markets. In deriving individual choices about work, initial endowments (that is, inheritance and talent) – perhaps the most important determinant of one's future income – are assumed to be given. The resulting short-run model then, derives labour supply from individual preferences and prices bereft of historical and institutional patterns of income generation, and demand from marginal revenue product, with prices (wages, in this case) clearing the market. The long-run model incorporates human capital investment such as education that affects individual productivity, but neoclassical analysts have paid little attention to the long-run household and community contexts for this investment.

Whereas the key blind spot of neoclassical microeconomics is the social context of income generation, conventional macroeconomics has a different weakness: viewing income distribution as secondary to growth. The ideas of Simon Kuznets and Arthur Okun illustrate the evolution of this notion. In

1955, Kuznets proposed that as economies shift from agricultural to industrial, income inequality first decreases, then increases. For mature industrial economies, Kuznets' proposition counsels focusing on growth, since equity follows directly from it. In developing countries, it calls for enduring current inequality for the sake of future equity and prosperity. In both cases, income distribution is a corollary to growth.

Twenty years later, Okun (1975) took the discussion in a different direction, suggesting that, as far as government redistribution policies were concerned, equity is not a corollary to growth, but an alternative to it. Okun posited a 'big tradeoff': redistributive equity comes at the expense of efficiency, largely because income redistribution reduces incentives for work and investment. Okun argued for the 'humane' side of the trade-off. But as soon as Okun's idea was coined, conservatives used it to justify a US transfer system that was (and remains) meagre compared with the country's industrial counterparts and to rationalize a growing wealth concentration in the United States.

But the theoretical subordination of income distribution to growth is theoretically indeterminate and empirically unwarranted. Three durable theoretical traditions within economics – neoclassical, Marxian and Keynesian – can (and do) accommodate a wide range of views on the relationship between equity and growth. Moreover, there is new empirical evidence that greater equality leads to greater growth, not the other way around (Glyn and Millaband 1994).

Feminist economics has enriched the discussion of income inequality by expanding current critiques and developing new ways of thinking about labour markets, earnings and family structure. This has been most effectively accomplished by emphasizing the role that nonmarket economic and social activity has in determining and supplementing income. In addition, feminist economists have argued forcefully for fairer distribution – including distribution of resources within the family – as an important objective in its own right.

Where neoclassical microeconomics presents participants in the labour market as atomistic individuals, feminist approaches stress the social context of labour market participation. Like institutional and Marxian models, feminist economics recognizes that the labour market itself is institutionally dense and historically contingent, so that the tools from other disciplines (namely sociology and history) as well as the conventional tools of economic market analysis are required to understand it. Research on the history of wage structures, marriage bars, the role of evolving ideologies of work, patterns of unionization and labour legislation have enriched the understanding of labour markets and how discrimination in labour markets have worked to impede women's wage-earning capacity (see for example Goldin 1990; Amott and

Matthaei 1996; Figart 1997). Feminist research has revealed that occupational segregation is universal, though patterns of segregation vary widely across societies.

But even more fundamental to understanding income distribution than particular factor markets, such as the labour market, is the simple fact that that humans must find ways to satisfy their physical, emotional and social needs. There are three chief ways to meet such needs: make, share, or buy. Under capitalism, a growing share of needs are commoditized: fulfilling them requires buying. Thus, income becomes essential – a prerequisite for consumption and, by extension, a measure of status. Indeed, in countless analyses economists have used income as a readily measurable proxy for consumption of goods and services, and even for wellbeing. But even in a capitalist mode of production, needs are also met via sharing and making – most notably in the household and via government transfers. Adequately analysing these locations of income distribution requires looking beyond market relations to the family and the state.

In industrialized capitalist economies, the family is the main site where people make or share goods rather than buying and selling them. As is well known, neither macroeconomic national income accounts nor most microeconomic data series measure unpaid household labour at all (see Benería 1992). Further, family structure greatly affects the income to which family members have access. This is true in an epochal sense: the shift from extended family to nuclear family, the reduction of child labour and increases in life expectancy have all profoundly affected income distribution, and it is also true in a cross-section among families in any given time period. Recent work has empirically explored the income consequences of the number of working-age adults in the family, the gender of those adults, and the presence of children requiring care (Albelda and Tilly 1997; Tilly and Albelda 1994). These factors conspire most dramatically against single-mother families, which (by definition) consist of one female adult with one or more dependent children. It is not surprising, therefore, to discover that poverty rates for single mothers are nearly four times as high as for the average family.

Income opportunities also affect family structure. Once again, this is true in both an epochal and a short-term sense. The centuries-long process of separation of home and workplace undermined the extended family, pulling workers centrifugally toward their own jobs and nuclear family units. The growing incorporation of women into the paid work force in the United States and other industrialized countries shifts power relations within the family, alters the type of care children receive, and makes single motherhood more thinkable for women and men alike (Bergmann 1986; Hartmann 1987; Folbre 1994). Debt-linked structural adjustment in Africa and Latin America has in many cases thrust women into the labour market while pushing men out, turning family structures topsy-turvy (Benería and Feldman 1992). This causal link between income and family structure means that the family is not simply a stable sphere of reproduction: it is a moving target.

Existing economic theory offers an unsatisfactory analysis of the distribution of work and rewards within the family. For neoclassical economics, the family – like production – can be seen as a black box. How work gets done and who does it is largely a technical question (comparative advantage) or a question of preferences – not subject to analysis by economists. Standard Marxian models offer little more, given their focus on class actors and interests. However, research driven by a feminist critique of economics has begun to crack open these issues (Hartmann 1981). Most importantly, feminist theory points to the importance of *power*, not just individual talents and preferences, in the allocation of work and consumption. Folbre (1982) extends the standard Marxian model of exploitation to allow exploitation of one family member (say, a wife) by another (say, a husband). Recent empirical research confirms that intrafamily resource allocation is shaped by age and gender. Notably, studies of Asia and Africa have pointed to the higher mortality rates of women due to the systematic denial of resources to women (Sen 1989). In one of the few studies of intrahousehold distributions in the United States, Lazear and Michael (1988) found that division of consumption between parents and children changes dramatically with the number of adults in a household: as the number of adults increases, children's share decreases more than proportionally. Moreover, access to paid work itself shifts power balances in the family. Women who earn wages, on average, gain decision-making power within the family, and those who earn more wages gain more power (England and Kilbourne 1990).

The state is the chief agent of redistribution in most industrialized economies. Feminist analysts have pointed out that state income transfer policies have often either assumed or worked to explicitly support traditional nuclear families. While states have long offered economic aid to women without men, that aid is often provided in a way that is designed to control women (especially poor women) or paternalistically 'protect' them (Abramovitz 1996). Feminists have generally argued instead for income policies that recognize the interdependence of all members of society that value nonmarket work. In terms of policies to ameliorate income inequality, feminist economists have noted that institutions aiding those at the bottom of the labour market – such as unions or minimum wages – disproportionately help women workers. Pay equity or comparable worth, which would require equal pay for work of equal value, could also substantially boost women's wages (England 1992; Figart and Lapidus 1995). But most fundamentally, eliminating gender income inequalities requires transforming the relationships among income, market work and family. Feminist economists have argued that income support and transfer policies must be linked to family policies that compensate for women's low wages and child care responsibilities since being female brings structural earnings disadvantages (Albelda and Tilly 1997; Bergmann and Hartmann 1995; Folbre 1994). Such family policies could include family allowances to all parents of young children; government-guaranteed health benefits, child care and other supports for low wage workers; and requirements that employers provide added flexibility to meet family care needs.

However, feminists have in many countries been losing the political debate with mainstream economists over the state's appropriate role in income distribution. Since most neoclassical economists subsume income distribution to growth, they would advocate that the state structure incentives to encourage paid work rather than reliance on transfers, and saving (and hence a future stream of property income) rather than consumption, although most would also support state provision of at least some minimal safety net. Supply-side and New Classical economists have put forward an extreme version of these views, claiming not only that income redistribution creates disincentives for hard work and savings, but that these disincentives overwhelm any positive redistributive effects. Further, building on the conventional macroeconomic view that rapid growth offers the solution to distributional problems, they argue that the best way to achieve growth is to enrich the wealthy, whose investments will spur economic expansion. Bolstered by these ideas, governments in industrialized counties cut back welfare state redistribution programmes while reducing taxes on the rich over the past 20 years – with the United States and United Kingdom undertaking the most radical cuts. Debt-burdened developing countries, under pressure from multilateral lenders such as the International Monetary Fund and World Bank to adopt structural adjustment plans, pursued similar policies.

Feminist economists have marshalled empirical research to contest these policies. For example, they have demonstrated that cross-section and time-series evidence contradict the mainstream notion that higher government transfers (such as welfare payments to single mothers) depress labour force participation and encourage births. Sweden, which has a relatively generous social support system, boasts a 93 per cent labour force participation rate among single mothers – in large part because much of the cash grant is kept intact as a mother works more – though most work only part time (Hauser and Fischer 1990). Further, the negative income tax experiments in the United States showed that higher transfers do not encourage single mothers to have more children – but they *do* result in more women living on their own.

But again, the contribution of feminist economics is not just empirical documentation but more fundamental theoretical reconceptualization of the state's role. One starting point is to question the neoclassical conceit that state policies are impositions on a logically prior market economy. In fact the state has historically always been the guarantor, builder and shaper of that economy. Redistribution is no more of an imposition than the right to private property itself. Thus, the feminist approach to income distribution seeks simultaneously to illuminate gender distinctions in access to income, to call attention to the broader social and political context that influences and supplements market earnings, and to open up the 'black boxes' of decision making within the family and the state.

RANDY ALBELDA AND CHRIS TILLY

See also

Comparable Worth/Pay Equity; Discrimination, Theories of; Growth Theory (Macro Models); Human Capital Theory; Income Support and Transfer Policy; Labour Markets, Theories of; Minimum Wage; Occupational Segregation; Structural Adjustment Policies.

Bibliography

Abramovitz, Mimi (1996), *Regulating the Lives of Women: Social Welfare Policy from Colonial Times to the Present*, 2nd edn, Boston, Massachusetts: South End Press.

Albelda, Randy and Chris Tilly (1996), 'Not Market Alone: Enriching the Discussion of Income Distribution', in Charles Whalen (ed.), *Political Economy for the Next Century*, Armonk, New York: M.E. Sharpe.

Albelda, Randy and Chris Tilly (1997), *Glass Ceilings and Bottomless Pits: Women's Work, Women's Poverty*, Boston, Massachusetts: South End Press.

Amott, Teresa and Julie Matthaei (1996), *Race Gender and Work*, 2nd edn, Boston, Massachusetts: South End Press.

Benería, Lourdes (1992), 'Accounting for women's work: Assessing the progress of two decades', *World Development*, **20** (11), 1547–60.

Benería, Lourdes and Shelley Feldman (eds) (1992), *Unequal Burden: Economic Crises, Persistent Poverty, and Women's Work*, Boulder, Colorado: Westview.

Bergmann, Barbara R. (1986), *The Economic Emergence of Women*, New York: Basic Books.

Bergmann, Barbara and Heidi Hartmann (1995), 'A welfare reform based on help for working parents', *Feminist Economics*, **1** (2), (Summer), 85–9.

Blau, Francine (1993), 'Gender and economic outcomes: the role of wage structure', *Labour*, **7** (1), 73–92.

Cancian, Maria, Sheldon Danziger and Peter Gottschalk (1993), 'Working Wives and Family Income Inequality Among Married Couples', in Sheldon Danziger and Peter Gottschalk (eds), *Uneven Tides: Rising Inequality in America*, New York: Russell Sage Foundation, pp. 195–221.

England, Paula (1992), *Comparable Worth: Theories and Evidence*, New York: Aldine de Gruyter.

England, Paula and Barbara Stanek Kilbourne (1990), 'Marriages, Markets, and Other Mates: The Problem of Power', in Roger Friedland and A.F. Robertson (eds), *Beyond the Marketplace: Rethinking Economy and Society*, New York: Aldine de Gruyter, pp. 163–88.

Figart, Deborah (1997), 'More than a dummy variable: feminist approaches to discrimination', *Review of Social Economy*, **55** (1), (Spring), 1–66.

Figart, Deborah and June Lapidus (1995), 'A gender analysis of U.S. labor market policies for the working poor', *Feminist Economics*, **1** (3).

Folbre, Nancy (1982), 'Exploitation comes home: a critique of the Marxian theory of family labor', *Cambridge Journal of Economics*, **6**, 317–29.

Folbre, Nancy (1994), *Who Pays for the Kids: Gender and the Structure of Constraints*, London: Routledge.

Freeman, Richard B. and Lawrence F. Katz (1994), 'Rising Wage Inequality: The United States vs. Other Advanced Countries', in Richard B. Freeman (ed.), *Working Under Different Rules*, New York: Russell Sage Foundation, pp. 29–62.

Glyn, Andrew and David Millaband (eds) (1994), *Paying for Inequality: The Economic Costs of Social Injustice*, London: IPPR/Rivers Oram Press.

Goldin, Claudia (1990), *Understanding the Gender Gap: An Economic History of American Women*, Oxford: Oxford University Press.

Gottschalk, Peter (1997), 'Inequality, income growth, and mobility: the basic facts', *Journal of Economic Perspectives*, **11** (2), Spring, 21–40.

Hartmann, Heidi (1987), 'Changes in Women's Economic and Family Roles in Post-World War II United States', in Lourdes Benería and Catherine Stimpson (eds), *Women, Households, and the Economy*, New Brunswick, New Jersey: Rutgers University Press, pp. 33–64.

Hartmann, Heidi (1981), 'The Family as the Locus of Gender, Class, and Political Struggle', in Sandra Harding (ed.), *Feminism and Methodology*, Bloomington, Indiana: Indiana University Press, pp. 109–34.

Hauser, Richard and Ingo Fischer(1990), 'Economic Well-Being Among One-Parent Families', in Timothy Smeeding, Michael O'Higgins and Lee Rainwater (eds), *Poverty, Inequality and Income Distribution in Comparative Perspective*, Washington, DC: Urban Institute Press, pp. 126–57.

Kuznets, Simon (1955), 'Economic growth and income inequality', *American Economic Review*, **45**, 1–28.

Lazear, Edward P. and Robert T. Michael (1988), *Allocation of Income Within the Household*, Chicago: University of Chicago Press.

Okun, Arthur (1975), *Equality and Efficiency: The Big Trade-off*, Washington, DC: The Brookings Institution.

Pritchett, Lant (1997), 'Divergence, big time', *Journal of Economic Perspectives*, **11** (3), Summer, 3–17.

Sen, Amartya (1989), 'Women's survival as a development problem', *Bulletin of the American Academy of Arts and Sciences*, **43**, November.

Tilly, Chris and Randy Albelda (1994), 'Family structure and family earnings: the determinants of earnings differences among family types', *Industrial Relations*, **33** (2), (April), 151–67.

Income Support and Transfer Policy

Income support and transfer policy refers to government programmes to redistribute income for the purpose of addressing economic insecurity. In the case of the United States, a national system of such programmes began with the Social Security Act of 1935. The Act was passed as part of a larger set of programmes that together comprised the New Deal of the 1930s. These programmes were enacted in response to the severe economic depression in the United States, and to pressure from social movements in the early part of the twentieth century. In many ways, the complicated history of income support and transfer programmes since the 1930s reflects its dual origins: maintaining consumer demand in times of economic downturn and meeting radical demands for state relief from the effects of capitalism. While providing economic stimulus, they may have also provided a safety valve that, in turn, may have weakened the very social movements that advocated for them. For feminist economists, the history of income support and transfer programmes has raised equally contradictory questions about the role of the state in simultaneously reinforcing and undermining women's economic dependence on men. While these questions and debates are not unique to the United

States, the USA provides an interesting illustration of these contradictions and will be the focus of this entry.

Prior to the passage of the Social Security Act, aid to those in need came from private charities and limited state and local programmes. The establishment of a federal role for income support and income transfer programmes marks the emergence of a 'welfare state'. Resistance to federal involvement in public assistance was embedded in larger discussions about states' rights and federal responsibilities within a federalist system of government. The controversy over which level of government, if any, should provide relief has resulted in a mix of federal, state and local programmes with varying and overlapping degrees of responsibility for funding and administration. This debate has now come full circle: federal programmes are being dismantled and transferred to the states as block grants in the name of welfare reform.

From its inception, the Social Security Act created a matrix of programmes stratified by gender and race. The basic distinction created by the Social Security Act was between social insurance programmes and public assistance programmes, the former including Social Security or 'old age pensions' and Unemployment Insurance and the latter Aid to Families with Dependent Children (AFDC) and aid to the indigent elderly not eligible for Social Security. (Until 1962 AFDC was named Aid to Dependent Children (ADC). With the welfare reform legislation of 1996, this programme was restructured and renamed Temporary Aid to Needy Families (TANF). The term AFDC is used throughout the entry to avoid confusion.) The social insurance programmes are contributory in that there are specific taxes linked to each of them paid by employers and employees. Unlike the social insurance and income support programmes in other industrial countries, the United States does not include guaranteed medical coverage in its social insurance programmes. The public assistance programmes are 'means tested', that is, recipients must prove economic hardship in order to qualify. Public assistance is therefore viewed as charity and has been inferior to social insurance in the level of benefits paid. Its recipients have been stigmatized since its inception. It is public assistance programmes that people think of today under the umbrella term 'welfare'.

While the Social Security Act of 1935 signals the beginning of income support and transfer programmes as they are known currently in the US, the various programmes in effect today did not emerge as a piece. Rather, excluded groups such as racial minorities and unmarried mothers won inclusion through legal and political battles covering some 40 years (Gordon 1994). For example, agricultural and domestic jobs were initially excluded from coverage in the unemployment insurance programme. Gordon attributes this to the power of wealthy southern Democrats who did not want to see blacks in the economic position to refuse low-waged agricultural and domestic employment. Similarly, aid to single mothers began as state aid to mothers who had been widowed or deserted: the deserving poor. 'Suitable family homes' were a necessary criteria for receiving AFDC, and residency requirements were established to disqualify migrant workers. State and local eligibility requirements and benefits levels reflected the racism of the 1930s. Black women were often excluded from AFDC as white officials saw no reason why black mothers should not continue in domestic and farm labour. It took the combined efforts of the Civil Rights, anti-poverty, feminist and welfare rights movement to win court cases and legislative victories to establish the principle of entitlement to AFDC.

The difference in fundamental assumptions underlying the structures of social insurance and public aid programmes reflect what feminist thinkers in sociology, history and economics call a two-channel or dual welfare state. The differences both reflect and reinforce differential access to income based on gender and race. While Social Security and Unemployment Insurance are income replacement programmes intended to replace the labour market, AFDC is an income replacement programme designed to replace the marriage market.

Feminist scholarship on the welfare state

Feminist scholars in disciplines other than economics have written extensively on the relationship between gender and the state. An excellent overview of this work is available in Gordon (1990), *Women, the State, and Welfare*. In her essay in that volume, political scientist Barbara Nelson argues that US welfare policy is actually two policies: one aimed at white industrial workers and the other at impoverished, white, working-class widows with young children. Sociologist Diana Pearce, the coiner of the term 'the feminization of poverty', argues in the same volume that these programmes are segmented along much the same lines as segmented labour markets. For example, workers receiving Unemployment Insurance are not expected to accept a job at lower wages than what they were receiving in their previous job. In contrast, AFDC mothers are now being expected to accept any job, or to perform community service in the absence of employment.

From its inception, AFDC was restricted so as not to enable women to live comfortably without male support. Even its early advocates

> believed that social-insurance programmes for unemployed and retired breadwinners would ultimately take care of dependent women and children. Assuming that women did not normally face the economy as individuals, as workers, there was no problem in grounding women's social rights in their dependent position. (Gordon 1997, p. 258)

There is disagreement among feminists about whether welfare programmes should be defended by feminists: that is, do they provide women access to resources (albeit inadequate) independent of a male income, or do these programmes merely replace one form of patriarchal control with another? During the US welfare rights movement in the 1970s, advocates of welfare did attempt to change the existing system, so that it would provide women with a higher level of economic independence, *and* so it would recognize the work of rearing children as labour. These feminists and welfare rights advocates, who saw public aid received by mothers of young children as payment for work done, viewed welfare as a *right*, affording poor women the same opportunity to stay home and raise their children that middle-class women had. (This movement is described by Teresa Funiciello, one of its participants, in *Tyranny of Kindness* 1993.)

The opposing view of the welfare state, as reinforcer of women's subordinate status, was labelled 'public patriarchy' by Brown (1981) to describe the ways in which men collectively, often acting through the state, control women. According to Abramovitz (1996), a particular view of family life – what she calls a family ethic – in which women's role is to marry and remain home, trading 'femininity, protection, economic support, and respectability' for economic independence (p. 38), is embedded in US social welfare policy. Middle-class women, that is, women who embrace this ethic, are considered deserving of public aid while women who do not, particularly unmarried mothers, are targeted for public disapproval. In her discussion of the origins of the Social Security Act, Abramovitz describes the federal government as 'systematically subsidiz[ing] the familial unit of reproduction' (p. 228).

The contradictory nature of the welfare state is also evident when viewing comparisons across industrialized countries. In her introduction to the wonderful collection *Gendering Welfare States* (1994), Sainsbury argues that while the welfare state has provided some independence from the market, it also reinforces women's economic dependence on men by failing to account for the sexual division of labour. Paradoxically, public responsibility for care enhances women's civil, political and social status.

The limited nature of the state subsidy in the US reflects the fact that reproductive labour is viewed as a private responsibility. Unlike Britain which pays a family allowance, or France which provides universal early childhood education, or Sweden with its generous parental leave policies, US policy is built on the premise that the family and labour market should be the primary systems of income distribution. The US is the only OECD country with almost no national programme of family allowances, day care, or parental leave.

Economists' views of income support and transfer programmes

Mainstream economic views of income support and transfer programmes generally follow ideological lines. Consistent with its focus on the rational behaviour of individual actors, neoclassical economists argue that social insurance and public assistance distort incentives. As a result, they claim that these programmes represent a drag on the economy, by syphoning off tax dollars that would be better used for private investment and by undermining individual initiative to work and save. The individualist methodology of neoclassical economics leads those interested in social policy and anti-poverty programmes to ask the question: Why is this person poor? In this framework, cutting public assistance and replacing social insurance with incentives for private insurance is good public policy because it restores the economic incentive to work and marry. On a political level, the emphasis on individual incentives has been used by representatives of the 'New Right' to argue that the welfare state was responsible for the poor performance of the US economy in the 1970s. This case was perhaps most forcefully made by George Gilder in *Wealth and Poverty* (1981). Gilder's thesis was that the taxes necessary to fund welfare programmes reduced disposable income, thereby forcing women into the labour market. This in turn lowered men's incentive and therefore their productivity. *Wealth and Poverty* was frequently cited by candidate, and then President, Reagan in his campaign to cut spending for social programmes.

In contrast, Keynesian economic theory, with its emphasis on maintaining the demand for goods and services in order to keep the economy from recession, provided much of the theoretical basis for the Social Security Act. Neoclassical economic theory was undermined by the extent and persistence of unemployment: it was hard to argue in the 1930s that the business cycle was self-correcting and the labour market if left alone would eliminate unemployment as wages fell. In addition, labour unions, communists, socialists and others were emphasizing the endemic nature of unemployment and poverty in capitalist economies. The Keynesian emphasis on aggregate demand and the importance of maintaining consumer purchasing power during the depression, thereby stimulating the economy and creating a demand for goods and services and the requisite workers to produce them, provided an economic justification for social income support and transfer programmes. Public works programmes, old age pensions and unemployment compensation were essential to lift the US economy out of the depression and to provide a counterpoint to radical organizing. Much of the support given by liberals to these economic policies is rooted in Keynesian theory: the role of the state is to mediate the extremes of the business cycle and to offer some protection to its victims.

Marxian economic theory, following its class emphasis, views the welfare state as created to mediate the class conflict in the USA in the 1930s in order to maintain capitalism as an economic system. There is an extensive and somewhat contentious literature on Marxian theories of the state. In the broadest terms, this debate is between those who view the capitalist state as the 'executive committee of the bourgeoisie', that is, merely reflecting the needs of the capitalist class, and those who view it as a site of class struggle. Whether the state does the bidding of the ruling class due to the interests of the people in government (agency theory) or because of the economic pressure the ruling class can bring to bear on the government (structuralist theory), the state represents the interests of the ruling class. In contrast to this, other Marxists view the state as a site of conflict in which the rules of democracy and the rules of the economy contest each other. These conflicting views offer different interpretations of the role of income support and transfer programmes. Where the state is seen as representing the needs of the economic ruling class, social insurance and public assistance programmes merely temper the extremes of capitalism in an effort to dissipate radical working class activity. On the other hand, those who view the state as a contested arena argue that these programmes represent hard fought gains for the working class that should be defended. Proponents of this view point to the explicit goals of Swedish social democratic policy which include social rights and the decommodification of labour power (that is, decreased reliance on wage labour), both of which serve to increase the relative power of the working class. In either case, Marxist analyses of social insurance and public assistance are viewed through the lens of class relations.

Because neither Marxian, neoclassical, nor Keynesian economics can explain the particularly gendered character of the US welfare state, many feminist economists have turned to a socialist feminist approach in their analysis of income support programmes in the United States. Abramovitz's version of such an approach interweaves the Marxist analysis of class with that of a radical feminist analysis of patriarchal social relations to explain that 'The state protects capitalism and patriarchy by enforcing their respective requirements, but also by mediating any conflicts that arise from the state's simultaneous commitment to both' (Abramovitz 1996, p. 19).

Feminist economists' views of the welfare state

Much of the contemporary feminist economic scholarship on the welfare state has arisen in response to attacks on public assistance since 1980. In defending social programmes against cuts feminist economists argued that there was a 'gender agenda' to these attacks. Socialist feminist economists in particular argued that this was not incidental; that part of the political programme of supply-side economics was an attack on the economic gains women had made in the USA since the 1960s. That is, as women's economic independence increased with increased female labour force participation rates, affirmative action and equal opportunity legislation and the growth of social programmes, the attack on social programmes came to be understood by some feminist economists as an attempt to decrease women's economic options outside of marriage (Albelda et al. 1986; Amott 1993)

In addition, feminist economists have entered the debates about the successes and failures of public assistance by empirically evaluating its effect on women and children. In her recent book *It Takes A Nation* (1997), Blank states:

> Many public assistance programmes have accomplished exactly what they set out to accomplish: food assistance has improved nutrition among the poor, health insurance has increased access to medical care, job training programs for single mothers increase their labour market involvement, and cash transfers seem to generally provide more cash income to families than they would obtain otherwise' (Blank 1997, p. 189).

She then argues that in the current political climate policy advocates must be armed with hard facts about which programmes have an impact, and she encourages research in policy and programme evaluation. In a more populist vein, Albelda and Folbre (1996) provide empirical documentation for advocates to use in response to the conservative attack on welfare. Their introduction to *The War on the Poor: A Defense Manual* reflects the contradictory nature of feminist scholarship on the welfare state noted above.

> Our purpose is not to defend the major public assistance programmes that remained in effect through 1995: Aid to Families with Dependent Children, Food Stamps, and Medicaid. We agree that these programmes have serious shortcomings. However, many criticisms of them have been inaccurate and misleading, and most of the proposed alternatives would do even greater harm' (Albelda and Folbre 1996, p. 7).

Feminist economists have also brought attention to the fact that income support and transfer policy doubles as family policy. An example of this is the structure of Social Security benefits for married women. Married women maximize benefits by filing as wives of workers rather than as wage workers themselves, in spite of the fact that a majority of women are employed in their own right. If women choose to collect benefits based on their own wages they will have been penalized for any time taken out of the labour market for bearing and raising children or for any other family labour since benefits are based only on contributions to market labour. In this context, women's work as wives and mothers is recognized but their economic dependence on men is simultaneously reinforced. The Social Security taxes women pay on their own labour is often lost because women's benefits are higher as wives than they are as workers. Thus, by valuing market and non-market labour differently, the social welfare system reinforces marriage as an income maximizing strategy for women.

Feminist economic scholarship on the welfare state has illustrated the role of gender ideology in shaping income support and transfer programmes and the contradictions for poor women that arise from this. These contradictions have placed many feminist scholars and activists in the position of supporting social programmes they have never believed in. Through a combination of advocacy and research that has long been the hallmark of feminist scholarship, feminist economists need to develop an integrated model of social insurance and public aid that explicitly recognizes the sexual division of labour and provides women with economic independence and economic well-being. This work is particularly important at a time when increasing globalization of the economy may limit the ability of nations to provide the types of public support for the labour of caring for children and others that feminists would like to see. Competitive pressures and free-trade pacts are putting pressure on governments to cut social programmes; feminist research and advocacy can provide a counterpoint to those pressures.

JUNE LAPIDUS

See also

Feminization of Poverty; Pensions and Old Age Retirement; Poverty, Measurement and Analysis of; Segmented Labour Markets; Welfare Reform.

Bibliography

Abramovitz, M. (1996), *Regulating the Lives of Women: Social Welfare Policy from Colonial Times to the Present*, Boston: South End Press.

Albelda, R. and N. Folbre (1996), *The War On the Poor: A Defense Manual*, New York: The New Press.

Albelda, R., J. Lapidus and E. McCrate (1986), *Mink Coats Don't Trickle Down: The Impact of Reaganomics on Women and People of Color*, Boston: South End Press.

Amott, T. (1993), *Caught in the Crisis*, New York: Monthly Review Press.

Blank, R.M. (1997), *It Takes a Nation: A New Agenda for Fighting Poverty*, New York and Princeton, New Jersey: Russell Sage Foundation and Princeton University Press.

Brown, Carol (1981), 'Mothers, Fathers and Children: From Private to Public Patriarchy', in Lydia Sargent (ed.), *Women and Revolution: A Discussion of the Unhappy Marriage of Marxism and Feminism*, Boston: South End Press, pp. 239–67.

Funiciello, T. (1993), *Tyranny of Kindness: Dismantling the Welfare System to End Poverty in America*, New York: The Atlantic Monthly Press.

Gilder, G. (1981), *Wealth and Poverty*, New York: Basic Books.

Gordon, L. (ed.) (1990), *Women, the State and Welfare*, Madison: The University of Wisconsin Press.

Gordon, L. (1994), *Pitied But Not Entitled: Single Mothers and History of Welfare*, New York: The Free Press.

Nelson, B.J. (1990), 'The Origins of the Two-Channel Welfare State: Workmen's Compensation and Mother's Aid', in L. Gordon (ed.) *Women, the State and Welfare*, Madison: The University of Wisconsin Press, pp. 123–51.

Pearce, D. (1990), 'Welfare is Not *for* Women: Why the War on Poverty Cannot Conquer the Feminization of Poverty', in L. Gordon (ed.), *Women, the State and Welfare*, Madison: The University of Wisconsin Press, pp. 265–79.

Sainsbury, D. (ed.) (1994), *Gendering Welfare States*, Sage Modern Politics Series Volume 35, London: Sage.

Informal Sector

The term 'informal sector' (also 'informal economy', 'hidden economy' or 'underground economy') is used to describe a heterogeneous group of economic arrangements with the common feature that they are not subject to regulation by the government or other societal institutions in an environment where similar activities are (Castells and Portes 1989). It is this absence of regulation that represents the essential distinction between the informal and formal sectors of the economy. The specific nature of the informal sector depends on the institutional context within a country, and thus varies across countries. Although informal sector activities have been identified in developed as well as developing countries (Portes et al. 1989), the literature has focused more heavily on the informal sector in developing countries, which will also be the focus of this entry.

Informal sector enterprises tend to be small-scale family-owned enterprises that make use of family labour, low levels of technology and labour-intensive methods of production. These enterprises tend to operate under conditions of easy entry and intense competition. The nature of employment includes both self-employment, such as home production and petty trading, and wage employment, such as casual labour, contract labour and piece work. Studies of the informal sector in developing countries have revealed it to be a significant source of employment and output. For example, Mazumdar (1975) estimated that in Bombay the informal sector accounted for 55 per cent of total employment, in Jakarta 50 per cent, and in Lima 53 per cent, and DeSoto (1989) estimated that 48 per cent of the economically active population in Peru was employed in the informal sector, and 38.9 per cent of national output was produced from informal sector activities.

Two broad theoretical perspectives that have informed work on the informal sector, including the work of feminist economists, can be identified in the literature. One takes a positive view of the sector and emphasizes its potential for creating employment opportunities in developing countries. This view is most commonly associated with the International Labour Organization (ILO). Often referred to as the 'dualist' perspective, the origins of this view can be found in an ILO mission report which identified a subsector of the urban labour market in Kenya that existed despite the fact that its activities were unaided, unregulated and unrecognized by the state (ILO 1972). The notion of economic dualism was used to distinguish the informal and formal sectors of the labour market in terms of excess labour supply. It was suggested that those who could not find employment in the formal sector created their own employment and in turn created an informal sector of economic activity. Since the workers in the informal sector were not seen as competing with those in the formal sector, the relationship between the two sectors was thought to be relatively benign. The International Monetary Fund (IMF) and the World Bank are adherents to a neo-liberal strand of the dualist view, associated most closely with the work of DeSoto (1989). The informal sector is seen as a reaction to excessive government controls in the formal sector such as minimum wage laws and labour regulations, and to the policies of organized labour, such as collective bargaining agreements. In contrast to the ILO's advocacy of active government support for the informal sector, the IMF/World Bank position has been to advocate liberalization of the formal sector from government regulations and the effects of organized labour.

The second theoretical perspective takes a negative view of the informal sector and emphasizes the vulnerability of the labour that is employed there. This view is most commonly associated with the work of Alejandro Portes and Manuel Castells. Often referred to as the 'structuralist' perspective, this view rejects the dualist theory of the informal sector in favour of a structural explanation, drawing upon Marx's notion of 'petty commodity production' to characterize informal sector activities (Moser 1978). The term 'petty commodity production' refers to production for the market by independent producers who own the means of production (for example, craftspeople). Structuralists argue that instead of a dichotomy between the formal and informal sectors, there exists a *continuum* of production processes that can be distinguished by their relationships to the capitalist sector. The capitalist mode of production involves production for the market by a class of owners of the means of production which confronts a class of workers. The structuralists view the informal sector as resulting from the incomplete transition to advanced capitalism. The informal sector, employing those who are the most socially and economically vulnerable, is seen as existing to serve the interests of capitalist production in the formal sector and is thus dependent and subordinate to that sector (Moser 1984). Structuralists argue that global competition has led formal sector enterprises to search for cheaper, more flexible modes of production, thereby shifting more of their production to the informal sector in the form of piece-work, out-work and contract work. On the basis of this view, it is argued that government policy should be used to assist in the transition to advanced capitalism and in the resulting disappearance of the informal sector.

Feminist sociologist MacEwan Scott (1995) notes that early research on the informal sector focused almost exclusively on men's activities. Mazumdar (1975) was the first to mention women in relation to the informal sector but only did so in the context of defining informal sector labour by its low opportunity cost. Because women who chose to work in the informal sector were not giving up time that could have been spent in productive activities, their labour was considered to have very little value. Subsequent research demonstrated women's heavy involvement and low remuneration in the informal sector. Feminist economist Benería (1989) noted that the majority of people employed in the informal sector in developing countries tend to be poor, and certain marginalized groups – women, the young, the elderly, racial and ethnic minorities, immigrants – tend to be disproportionately represented in this sector.

The discovery of women's involvement in the informal sector prompted feminist scholars to search for reasons to explain this. Some studies focused on specific groups of women workers, such as outworkers, street vendors, and domestic servants, while others focused on the theoretical significance of women's work for the family, economy and society. Many of these studies have suggested that patriarchal norms in the family and society can help explain the status of women in the informal sector. Some of the most well-known studies of particular groups of women employed in the informal sector include Moser's (1977) article on market sellers in Bogota, Colombia, Mies's (1982) book on the lacemakers of Naraspur in India, and several studies in a book edited by Benería and Roldan (1987) on homework and subcontracting in Mexico City. These studies helped tell the stories of women and their work in the informal sector, in diverse circumstances, in different parts of the Third World and have paved the way for feminist reconceptualizations of the informal sector.

To feminist economists, the growing evidence of women's participation in the informal sector was both further evidence of, and ammunition against, the gender bias inherent in mainstream development economics. The mainstream approach consistently underestimated the economic contributions of women, a flaw that became more apparent as feminist economists undertook case studies of women in developing countries. As women's heavy involvement in income-earning activities in the informal sector became more apparent, the significance of their economic contributions to the household also became so, challenging the traditional view of the household and household decision making, with its assumptions of a male head. It was found that women not only often contributed significantly to household income, but also that women's income had more beneficial effects on the family in general and children in particular than did men's income. Income earning opportunities for women thus became seen as the most direct way of promoting not only their own welfare, but also their children's welfare and economic development on a larger scale. Additionally, the bargaining power of women in the family and in society was thought to be enhanced by income earning. Even if only at the level of rhetoric, women quickly went from being largely invisible or unproductive to being the dynamic force to promote economic development.

In the context of this 'revolution' in thinking about women and development, a debate emerged among feminist economists on the subject of women in the informal sector. The debate closely mirrored that associated with the competing theoretical perspectives on the informal sector, but the contributions of feminist scholars on both sides have had a profound effect on both theoretical and practical understandings of the informal sector.

Some feminist economists accepted, at least pragmatically, the dualist view of the informal sector as a starting point. The feminist version of the dualist view accepts that women work in the informal sector because they lack other income-earning opportunities, and suggests that, especially if they are working from home, the informal sector can be advantageous for women. For example, Berger (1989) argues that the most effective policies to help women in the informal sector are those that provide them with access to credit, training, marketing and technical support; and at the legal level, reforms of property ownership, banking laws and other practices that constrain their opportunities to earn an income.

The feminist dualist view of the informal sector has stimulated a vast literature on women and micro-enterprise development. The small-scale enterprises run by women in the informal sector are characterized as 'micro-enterprises' and the women owners as 'micro-entrepreneurs' (see chapters in Berger and Buvinic 1989; Dignard and Havet 1995). This literature has primarily emphasized women's involvement in productive activities and the barriers that they face, as women, to earning a decent income from their work in these activities. These barriers include socially defined limits to their mobility, discrimination by formal lenders, reliance upon moneylenders, and exploitative relationships with merchants and middlemen. Access to credit has in particular become one of the central issues in promoting women's micro-enterprises and at a policy level has been accepted as a development priority by international development agencies like the World Bank, the United Nations and USAID (Berger 1995). Bernasek and Stanfield (1997), for example, argue that the Grameen Bank (a micro-enterprise lending scheme for women in rural Bangladesh), by facilitating women's involvement in informal sector activities, has been successful at encouraging progressive social change in terms of improving the socioeconomic status of its women borrowers.

Not all feminist economists accept the dualist view of the informal sector and many have criticized it. Approaching the informal sector from the structuralist perspective, this group emphasizes issues surrounding women's heavy participation in the most vulnerable sector of the economy (see, for example, Moser 1978, 1984; Benería 1989; Kalpagam 1994; MacEwan Scott 1995). Structuralist feminists thus view the informal sector as dependent and subordinate to the formal sector and argue that a development strategy based on informal enterprise will do little to help women because it ignores certain facts – one being that women's enterprises have low levels of capital and backward technology and that their dependence upon the large capitalist firms keeps them in a supplementary and subordinate position (Benería 1989). The micro-enterprise approach associated with the dualist view is also criticized for its failure to recognize that women's work in the informal sector indirectly subsidizes the formal sector by allowing men working in the formal sector to be paid wages that are lower than what is required for the family to subsist (Kalpagam 1994). Along the same lines, it has been suggested that women represent a reserve of cheap labour that can be utilized through outwork when demand is high (MacEwan Scott 1995).

Structuralist feminists have emphasized the specific problems women face in different types of informal sector work. They reject the idea that the informal sector provides women with the advantage of working at home and balancing work and domestic responsibilities. Kalpagam (1994) has argued that patriarchal structures within the family and within society combine with survival pressures to limit women's income-earning opportunities, thus leaving them concentrated in the worst and lowest-paying jobs and keeping them in a permanent state of vulnerability. MacKewan Scott (1995) points out that the gender division of labour within the family determines the gender division of labour in small-scale home production – men specialize in the larger-scale commercial activities and women in the smaller-scale activities that are extensions of housework. Occupational segregation and discrimination were thus found to occur for women within the informal sector itself.

Not surprisingly, the policy prescriptions of the two groups differ. Feminists from the dualist perspective favour providing greater access to resources for women and greater support for their informal sector activities. They tend to support initiatives like the Grameen Bank in Bangladesh which provide credit to poor women for self-employment. Feminists from the structuralist perspective favour providing women with greater access to formal sector employment opportunities and letting the informal sector shrink and ultimately disappear. Kalpagam (1994) for example, argues against supporting women's informal sector activities: 'Rather than confront the oppressive forces directly, it withdraws the oppressed from the scene completely, and does not increase their bargaining power' (Kalpagam 1994, p. 242).

Feminist economic scholarship on the informal sector has contributed to the growing acceptance of a different view of women and their role in economic development. On the one hand, theorists and policymakers are now more aware of the extent of women's economic contributions to the family from their participation in informal sector activities, as well as the extent to which they are involved in productive activities in addition to their reproductive responsibilities. Credit for this lies to a large extent with the work of feminists from the dualist school. (See for example, Berger 1989, 1995; Bhatt 1995; Tinker 1995.) On the other hand, theorists and policymakers are also more aware of the vulnerability of women employed in the informal sector –

the impediments that women face in their income-earning activities, such as access to credit and purchasing and distribution channels, as well as exploitative relationships with moneylenders, middlemen and merchants, and the occupational segregation and discrimination they experience. Credit for this lies to a large extent with the work of feminists from the structural school. (See for example, Young and Moser 1981; Benería and Roldan 1987; MacEwan Scott 1995). Despite their differences, feminists from both sides of the debate have been instrumental in focusing the attention of scholars, international development agencies and non-governmental organizations (NGOs) on women's involvement in the informal sector, and in economic development.

There will be numerous research possibilities in this area with a growing number of development projects targeting women. In particular, it will be important to evaluate the extent to which these projects improve the socio-economic status of women. To some extent this experience and the research evaluating it should contribute to a resolution of the debate that exists among feminist economists on the subject of the informal sector. One issue that seems likely to be important in future research is the issue of organizing women working in the informal sector. Although traditional trade union methods have not proven to be effective means for organizing these women, there are non-traditional methods that have developed that hold promise. Examples include the Self-Employed Women's Association (SEWA) and the Working Women's Forum (WWF), both in India (other examples may be found in Leonard, 1989). While assessments of these organizations differ among feminist economists – some more favourable and hopeful (Chen 1989; Bhatt 1995) than others (Kalpagam 1994) – they are being studied by feminist economists from both the dualist and structuralist perspectives. Promoting income-earning opportunities for women in the informal sector through organized activity would seem to have some potential to address the concerns of feminists from both perspectives – more resources for women and a greater recognition and support of common interests.

ALEXANDRA BERNASEK

See also
Banking and Credit; Development Policy; Development, Theories of; Globalization; Structural Adjustment Policies.

Bibliography
Benería, L. (1989), 'Subcontracting and Employment Dynamics in Mexico City', in A. Portes, M. Castells and L. Benton (eds), *The Informal Economy: Studies in Advanced and Less Developed Countries*, Baltimore: The Johns Hopkins University Press, pp. 173–88.
Benería, L. and M.I. Roldan (1987), *The Crossroads of Class and Gender: Homework, Subcontracting and Household Dynamics in Mexico City*, Chicago: University of Chicago Press.
Berger, M. (1989), 'An Introduction', in M. Berger and M. Buvinic (eds), *Women's Ventures: Assistance to the Informal Sector in Latin America*, Hartford: Kumarian Press, pp. 1–18.

Berger, M. (1995), 'Key Issues on Women's Access to and use of Credit in the Micro- and Small Scale Enterprise Sector', in L. Dignard and J. Havet (eds), *Women in Micro- and Small Scale Enterprise Development*, Boulder: Westview Press, pp. 189–216.

Berger, M. and M. Buvinic (eds) (1989), *Women's Ventures: Assistance to the Informal Sector in Latin America*, Hartford: Kumarian Press.

Bernasek, A. and J.R. Stanfield (1997), 'The Grameen Bank as progressive institutional adjustment', *Journal of Economic Issues*, **31** (2), 359–66.

Bhatt, E. (1995), 'Women and Development Alternatives: Micro- and Small Scale Enterprises in India', in L. Dignard and J. Havet (eds), *Women in Micro- and Small Scale Enterprise Development*, Boulder: Westview Press, pp. 85–100.

Castells M. and A. Portes (1989), 'World Underneath: The Origins, Dynamics and Effects of the Informal Economy', in A. Portes, M. Castells and L. Benton (eds), *The Informal Economy: Studies in Advanced and Less Developed Countries*, Baltimore: The Johns Hopkins University Press, pp. 11–40.

Chen, M. (1989), 'The Working Women's Forum: Organizing for Credit and Change in Madras, India', in A. Leonard (ed.), *SEEDS: Supporting Women's Work in the Third World*, New York: The Feminist Press, City University of New York, pp. 51–72.

DeSoto, H. (1989), *The Other Path: The Invisible Revolution in the Third World*, New York: Harper and Row.

Dignard, L. and J. Havet (eds) (1995), *Women in Micro- and Small Scale Enterprise Development*, Boulder: Westview Press.

Hart, K. (1973), 'Informal income opportunities and urban employment in Ghana', *Journal of Modern African Studies*, **11**, 61–89.

International Labour Organization (1972), *Employment, Incomes and Equality: A Strategy for Increasing Productive Employment in Kenya*, Geneva: ILO.

Kalpagam, U. (1994), *Labour and Gender: Survival in Urban India*, New Delhi: Sage Publications.

Leonard, A. (ed.) (1989), *SEEDS: Supporting Women's Work in the Third World*, New York: The Feminist Press, City University of New York

MacEwan Scott, A. (1995), 'Informal Sector or Female Sector? Gender Bias in Urban Labour Market Models', in D. Elson (ed.), *Male Bias in the Development Process*, Second Edition, Manchester: Manchester University Press.

Mazumdar, D. (1975), *The Theory of Urban Unemployment in Less Developed Countries*, World Bank Staff Working Paper No. 198, Washington DC: World Bank.

Mazumdar, V. (1989), 'Seeds for a New Model of Development: A Political Commentary', in A. Leonard (ed.), *SEEDS: Supporting Women's Work in the Third World*, New York: The Feminist Press, City University of New York, pp. 213–15.

Mies, M, (1982), *The Lacemakers of Narsapur: Indian Housewives Produce for the World Market*, London: Zed Books.

Moser, C. (1977), 'The dual economy and marginality debate and the contribution of micro analysis: market sellers in Bogota', *Development and Change*, **8** (2), 465–89.

Moser, C. (1978), 'Informal sector or petty commodity production: dualism or dependence in urban development?', *World Development*, **6**, 1041–64.

Moser, C. (1984), 'The informal sector revisited: viability and vulnerability in urban development', *Regional Development Dialogue*, **5**, 135–78.

Portes, A., M. Castells and L. Benton (eds) (1989), *The Informal Economy: Studies in Advanced and Less Developed Countries*, Baltimore: The Johns Hopkins University Press.

Tinker, I. (1995), 'The Human Economy of Micro Entrepreneurs', in L. Dignard and J. Havet (eds), *Women in Micro- and Small Scale Enterprise Development*, Boulder: Westview Press, pp. 25–40.

Weeks, J. (1975), 'Policies for expanding employment in the informal sector of developing economies', *International Labour Review*, **111**, 1–13.

Young, K. and C. Moser (eds) (1981), 'Women and the informal sector', *IDS Bulletin*, **12** (3).

Institutional Economics

Institutional economics is an approach to the study of economies, in which economies are understood as social organizations for the provisioning of society. Founded by US economists Thorstein Veblen and John R. Commons in the late nineteenth and early twentieth centuries, this school of thought differs from the more recent new institutional economics (NIE) of Richard Coase, Douglass North and Oliver Williamson. While both approaches share the proposition that institutions, recurring patterns of behaviour and perception, are important, institutional economists reject the NIE proposition that such patterns derive from the process of individual choice that is central to neoclassical economics. Instead, institutional economists consider institutions as shared cultural norms that evolve in non-teleological adaptations to new circumstances and experiences (Neale 1987). This process of cultural evolution is one of conflict and resolution, which in modern, complex societies most often takes place through political processes.

The original institutional economics developed in the United States in response to rapid social and economic change and in response to new ideas in the social sciences. Both Veblen and Commons sought to explain the rapid, in many ways traumatic, changes that accompanied the commercialization of American agriculture, the rise of big business and the growth of labour unions, which were all part of American industrialization (Mayhew 1987). In so doing they did not look at English neoclassical economic thought, with its emphasis on stability and equilibrium, but used instead a variety of 'homegrown' ideas, some of which had been coloured by American economists who studied in Germany during the last half of the nineteenth century. There they encountered the arguments of the German Historical School whose members placed emphasis on economic change, the positive role of the State and on the importance of different national histories. However, the major inspiration for the new approach came from the developments in other social sciences, and particularly from anthropology and sociology. What the early institutionalists shared with early anthropologists and sociologists that set them apart from other economists, including those of the German Historical School, was centrality of focus on the analytical concept of 'culture', the totality of time- and place-specific institutions that changed through time. Individuals were agents in that change, but were not the primary focus of analysis.

The concept of culture as a set of variable patterns that could be described through use of ethnographic and historical data was of greatest importance in the other social sciences. The use of statistical evidence for the same purpose was central to institutional economics as elaborated by Wesley C. Mitchell (1925), a student of Veblen's, and by his students. Commons and his students and colleagues used a combination of ethnographic, historical and statistical tools and, like Mitchell's intellectual progeny, laid stress on the idea that socioeconomic change could be actively and effectively managed once institutional patterns were described and understood.

The emphasis on historically-influenced cultural patterns and their importance in economic provisioning made women and socially-gendered roles central to Veblen's earliest work. Veblen used the anthropological thought of the 1890s to support his proposition that modern notions of property are not biologically innate in humans, but rather the product of a long process of cultural evolution. In particular he argued that the idea of property probably began with the capture of women (Veblen 1898) and that gendered social roles and the patriarchal household were a byproduct of predation among groups (Veblen 1899). As he turned his attention to the modern world, Veblen stressed the similarities between an earlier age when 'the dress of the women was an exponent of the wealth of the man whose chattels they were' and late nineteenth century society where 'the woman's dress sets forth the wealth of the household to which she belongs' (Veblen 1894, p. 64). Even more fundamentally, however, Veblen stressed the fact that 'pecuniary' activities, those of buying and selling, were not synonymous with provisioning. Veblen's approach to the historically gendered process of provisioning was similar to that of the early feminist economist Charlotte Perkins Gilman (Lewis and Sebberson 1997).

For institutionalists, and for feminists, economies are societies' organizations for provisioning, rather than the locus of an assumed universal rationality as is often asserted in neoclassical textbooks. Provisioning is the process of trying to assure culturally appropriate levels of food, housing, clothing and care. Many feminist economists have also focused on provisioning, rather than on rationality or buying and selling, as the subject area of economic analysis (Folbre 1994; Lewis 1995; Nelson 1996; Peterson 1995).

The continued overlap of feminist and institutionalist views can be understood by elaboration of each of the four core concepts of institutionalism. The first of these core ideas is that the patterns of behaviour that are the institutions of a society are culturally specific and culturally shared. For institutionalists this means that the entire range of organizations and behaviours that economists normally describe, meaning markets, 'rational' choice, preferences in work and consumption, and related activities, are not the product of individual 'tastes and preferences' but of cultural patterns whose histories can be unravelled. The idea that patterns of behaviour and belief are cultural and changeable is important for feminist economics because this view is in sharp contrast to the idea that attitudes and prejudices about women and their role in the economy emerge from individual black boxes of tastes and preferences. In the words of the famous song from *South Pacific* 'you have to be carefully taught', in this case to absorb most of the ideas about gender capacities and responsibilities. But the institutionalist emphasis on culture goes beyond the idea that bigotries are learned rather than innate; most importantly the idea of culture shifts the focus of analysis.

The fundamental neoclassical assumption, from which most modern economic analysis proceeds, is that individuals employ a kind of commercial rationality in which costs and benefits of action are measured and compared by use of money as a common denominator. The monetary 'benefits' of, for example, a mother of young children working outside the home is assumed to be implicitly or explicitly calculated by each individual, and then compared to the similarly valued 'costs' of alternative child care. The choice made is assumed to be arrived at without unwarranted coercion. Given this assumption, variable patterns of female participation in economies can only be described as a consequence of rational reactions to different factor endowments (women and/or their offspring are scarce or abundant relative to men, or have differentiated comparative advantages), or as consequence of unexplained tastes and preferences of the discrete individuals who constitute a neoclassically conceived economy.

The methods of institutional economics (ethnographic, historical, and statistical) allow discovery of patterns of female participation and entitlement in different times and places (Deere 1995; Zein-Elabdin 1996). For example, Zein-Elabdin uses ethnographic information to show that current discourse on economic development, gender and the environment fails to take into account the drastically different roles that women play in the provisioning processes in different parts of the world. The goal of her work is not to show that these differences are rational responses, but rather to argue that assumptions about the relationship of women to economic development and to the environment cannot be accurate without knowledge of local patterns. The descriptions of spatial and historic variation are not simple starting points for what the neoclassical approach deems the important work of explaining the rationality of each arrangement, but are rather the major purpose of analysis. This allows a richness of description not permissible in the formal work of neoclassicism.

Within both institutional and feminist economics great importance is also given to historical change. Of particular importance to institutionalists is the understanding that the modern integrated market system has involved production for sale of an ever-increasing range of human output and activity. As feminists have stressed, this has drastically altered the family and the role of women (Folbre 1994; Waller and Jennings 1991). In the United States and Western Europe, until sometime in the nineteenth century, commercial activity (that is, buying and selling) was peripheral to many household economies. As commercial activity became increasingly important with industrialization and low-cost transport, economic activity outside the household became of greater and greater importance and, to the extent that this was understood to be male activity, women were separated and made inferior to that world (Jennings 1993).

One example of the contrast between the institutionalist approach and that of rational choice economists are the explanations offered by institutionalists for changing trends in labour force participation. In recent years white women's participation in the labour force in the USA has increased. Institutionalists explain this change as a result of changing cultural norms and evolving work roles. Changing consumption norms and what it means to be adequately provisioned, interacting with economic growth, have encouraged women to enter the workforce in order for the family to maintain its relative social standing (Brown 1987).

As institutionalists understand the ongoing evolution of human society, there are few constants across time and space. Instead, current patterns replace past patterns and those will be replaced in the future. Neither markets nor any other aspect of modern society can be assumed to be part of other places and other times in the absence of evidence. However, institutionalists also think that some patterns are discernible in this ongoing change. Although great emphasis is placed upon cultural variation across time and space, a biological unity among humans is recognized, and it is from that biological unity that there emerges the idea of a universal process of innovation and valuation, often called by institutionalists 'instrumental valuing'. This process of valuing, the third core concept of institutional economics, is one that proceeds from human ability to use language so that learning can be carried through time, and it stems from the tool-using nature of humans (Ayres 1962).

By use of tools (defined here as all man-made devices) and of language, humans have accumulated knowledge about the world in which they live, and about ways in which to manipulate that world. That all such knowledge is always seen through the lens of a particular culture does not alter the fact that there are cross-cultural commonalities to such learning. These commonalities, shared appreciations of the nature of metals, of plants, of soil and other physical phenomena, and shared human biological goals of survival and reproduction lead people of different cultures to share in their valuation of many aspects of human learning. What is of particular importance to institutional economists in their understanding of this process is that learning and the accumulation of 'human capital' is a social, and not an individual, process. For feminist economists the idea that women of many different cultures value public and reproductive health information and processes is important, and is closely related to the institutionalist argument that there is a universal process of instrumental valuation.

From the institutionalist understanding of the role of technology in the ongoing process of instrumental valuation there follows the proposition that technological change is a major source of socioeconomic change, whether by virtue of exchanges between cultures or by the additive and cumulative process of innovation within a culture. Institutionalists share with Marxist economists this emphasis on technology, but differ because institutionalists see the process as one of cumulative causation, as a process of evolutionary change, rather than as a process of increasing contradiction that results in dramatic overhauls of entire systems. A similar perception of the ongoing, cumulative and often subtle effects of technological change has been pervasive in feminist economics, in discussion of the impact of factory employment, of changing forms of agricultural practice, and of modern communication and office equipment on gender roles and family organization (Kessler-Harris 1989; Folbre 1994).

The fourth core concept of institutionalism is an understanding that derives from all three of the characteristics of thought already outlined: socioeconomic structure and perception are always socially constructed and can, therefore, be *reconstructed*. That is, human societies are the creation of the people who constitute them, and people can (and do) remake them. The process can be a largely unconscious reaction to events, or it can be deliberately achieved.

Those who have identified themselves as institutionalists, in spite of their keen interest in reform, offer no formulas for welfare maximization, nor do they attempt to state the substantive conditions that would prevail in a utopian world. Institutionalist thought shares with the American pragmatic tradition the view that means and ends are part of a continuum, a continuum in which both means to a better society, and the ends that define that good society, change as society changes. Given this understanding there can be no substantive statement of the conditions of the best. What institutionalists do offer, however, is an understanding of reform as inevitable, and a process where wide participation by affected groups is reasonable. The role that institutionalists assign themselves in this process is that of knowledgeable participants.

To understand how institutional economists see the role of knowledgeable participants it is useful to talk of the early institutionalist, John R. Commons. Commons was part of a reformist group that flourished among American economists in the early part of this century and he made two contributions to institutionalist thought that have been of lasting importance (Ramstad 1986). By his own work and that of his students (who were largely responsible for the design of the US Social Security system), he provided examples of how detailed work of social reformation could be effective in achieving reform. He modelled socioeconomic change as a process whereby the conflict of interests that inevitably arise in the ongoing process of socioeconomic change are adjudicated to arrive at new 'reasonable values' (through the judicial process in the Anglo-American system on which Commons focused, but through other processes in other settings).

In his model of socioeconomic change Commons stressed the inevitability of conflict. In subsequent institutionalist work, economic organization has been understood as the consequence of conflicting interests among groups who make use of power and of the accepted processes of adjudication in the society in question. This is as true of the organization, functioning, and outcome of 'markets', which is to say of processes of buying and selling, as it is of political processes. In markets buyers and sellers have power to provide and power to withhold, and exercise these powers subject to the social and political constraints of the rest of society as it is affected by the behaviour of the buyers and sellers. There is an always ongoing process of redefining those constraints.

That the social and political power involved in market exchange has been ignored in most neoclassical analysis does not make it less real, and it has been a major task of institutionalists throughout this century to describe the relationships of power in the economic processes of production and distribution. In these descriptions the state is not accorded an inferior position, nor are buyers and sellers accorded a privileged position. Individuals, business firms of many kinds and sizes, governments, and a variety of social groups are all recognized as participants in social processes that determine, at any time, the distribution of goods, services and power.

Feminist economists, entering the discussion about provisioning in modern economies at a different time, and from a different point of evolution in the social sciences, have used a somewhat different language, but have arrived at a similar emphasis on the importance of power. Not only are gender roles socially constructed, but so are the economic advantages and disadvantages, entitlements and penalties associated with those gendered roles in the economy.

A major thrust of feminist economics has been to claim legitimacy for the use of negotiating power in redefining gendered roles and for negotiated reform. From the institutionalist perspective, there is no question that such negotiation is legitimate, for all socioeconomic outcomes are seen as negotiated and all current arrangements are subject to further negotiation. This is what economic reform entails.

The direction of future work by institutionalists writing as feminist economists is indicated by articles that have appeared in the *Journal of Economic Issues* in recent years. The use of ethnographic data by Zein-Elabdin (1996) in order to clarify the actual roles of women in agriculture and in response to environmental crises in various parts of the world has already been noted. Lewis (1995) and Peterson (1995) have stressed the importance of provisioning in teaching college students to think about the economy. Grapard (1997) has described changing gender roles in economies in Eastern and Central Europe. Kim (1997) and Mutari and Figart (1997), among others, have used statistical and other descriptions of the US economy to talk of conflicts and emerging resolutions involving gender and distribution. Though the commonalities of assumption and analytical approach require further exploration, the most promising directions for work that combines the institutionalist and feminist perspectives will involve the use of the institutionalist tools – historical and ethnographic accounts and descriptive statistics – to focus on changing gender roles and economic relationships. And, true to the institutionalist tradition, effective studies of this kind will necessarily contribute to the ongoing discussions of reform in the ways in which women's contributions to the provisioning process are defined and valued.

ANNE MAYHEW

See also
Feminist Economics; Marxist Political Economics; Neoclassical Economics; Value.

Bibliography

Ayres, Clarence E. (1962), *The Theory of Economic Progress,* New York: Schocken Books.

Brown, Clair (1987), 'Consumption Norms, Work Roles, and Economic Growth, 1918–1980', in Clair Brown and Joseph A. Pechman (eds), *Gender in the Workplace,* Washington, DC: The Brookings Institution, pp. 13–49.

Deere, Carmen Diana (1995), 'What Difference Does Gender Make? Rethinking Peasant Studies', *Feminist Economics,* 1, Spring, 53–72.

Folbre, Nancy (1994), *Who Pays for the Kids?,* London: Routledge.

Grapard, Ulla (1997), 'Gender in the transition of socialist regimes', *Journal of Economic Issues,* 31, (September), 665–86.

Jennings, Ann (1993), 'Public or Private? Institutional Economics and Feminism', in Marianne Ferber and Julie Nelson (eds), *Beyond Economic Man: Feminist Theory in Economics,* Chicago: University of Chicago Press.

Kessler-Harris, Alice (1989), *Women Have Always Worked,* New York: McGraw Hill.

Kim, Marlene (1997), 'The working poor: lousy jobs or lazy workers?', *Journal of Economic Issues,* 32, (March), 65–78.

Lewis, Margaret (1995), 'Breaking down the walls, opening up the field: situating the economics classroom in the site of social action', *Journal of Economic Issues,* 29, (June), 555–66.

Lewis, Margaret and David Sebberson (1997), 'The rhetoricality of economic theory: Charlotte Perkins Gilman and Thorstein Veblen', *Journal of Economic Issues,* 31, (June), 417–24.

May, Ann Mari (1996), 'The Challenge of Feminist Economics', in Charles J. Whalen (ed.), *Political Economy for the 21st Century,* Armonk, New Jersey: M.E. Sharpe.

Mayhew, Anne (1987), 'The beginnings of institutionalism', *Journal of Economic Issues,* 21, (September), 971–98.

Mitchell, Wesley C. (1925), 'Quantitative analysis in economic theory', *The American Economic Review,* 15, (March), 1–12.

Mutari, Ellen and Deborah M. Figart (1997), 'Markets, flexibility, and family: evaluating the gendered discourse against pay equity', *Journal of Economic Issues,* 31, (September), 687–706.

Neale, Walter C. (1987), 'Institutions', *Journal of Economic Issues,* 21, September, 1177–206.

Nelson, Julie (1996), *Feminism, Objectivity and Economics,* London and New York: Routledge.

Peterson, Janice (1995), 'For whom? Institutional economics and distributional issues in the economics classroom', *Journal of Economic Issues,* 29, (June), 567–74.

Ramstad, Yngve (1986), 'A pragmatist's quest for holistic knowledge: the scientific methodology of John R. Commons', *Journal of Economic Issues*, **20**, (December), 1067–105.

Veblen, Thorstein (1894), 'The economic theory of woman's dress', *Popular Science Monthly*, **46**, (November). Reprinted in Leon Ardzrooni (ed.) (1964) *Essays in Our Changing Order*, New York: Augustus M. Kelley.

Veblen, Thorstein (1898), 'The beginnings of ownership', *The American Journal of Sociology*, **4**.

Veblen, Thorstein (1899), 'The barbarian status of women', *The American Journal of Sociology*, **4**.

Waller, William and Ann Jennings (1991), 'A feminist institutionalist reconsideration of Karl Polanyi', *Journal of Economic Issues*, **25**, (June), 485–98.

Zein-Elabdin, Eiman (1996), 'Development, gender, and the environment', *Journal of Economic Issues*, **30**, (December), 929–47.

International Association for Feminist Economics (IAFFE)

The International Association for Feminist Economics (IAFFE) is a non-profit, non-governmental organization established in 1992 to provide a feminist perspective in the economics profession. The organization actively promotes research and action on economic issues of concern to women, children and men around the world, and it provides a framework for an international network of feminist economists. As of 1999, IAFFE had 600 members, women and men, from 38 different countries and including feminists from both economics and other social science disciplines.

IAFFE emerged as the result of concerns by feminist economists who believed that existing economics organizations did not adequately address issues of particular interest to them. While other organizations had been formed in the profession in response to women's growing presence, they had never had an explicitly feminist focus. In 1971, for example, members of the Union of Radical Political Economy (URPE) formed the women's caucus, making it the first modern day women's organization in economics. In 1973, the Committee on the Status of Women in the Economics Profession (CSWEP) was formed as an arm of the American Economics Association (AEA) to address the concerns of women economists about their positions in the economics profession. However, neither organization was explicitly devoted to promoting feminist research, developing feminist economic policies and policy responses, or engaging in action on feminist issues. Consequently, economic issues important to the well-being and empowerment of women worldwide – including gender perspectives on caring labour and household production, structural adjustment and economic history – received little institutional attention within the economics discipline prior to the 1990s. Indeed, economics is unique among the social science disciplines in failing to organize a separate feminist caucus or association during the 1970s, thereby losing twenty years of feminist research, networking and perspectives on policy. Thus IAFFE faces the challenge of making up considerable ground if economics is to achieve the integral feminist traditions found in other social science disciplines.

Groundwork for IAFFE's formation was laid in the fall of 1990, when April Laskey Aerni and Jean Shackelford began to construct a network of feminist economists who were interested in knowing of other feminist economists and of feminist work being conducted in economics. This network was expanded during the December 1990 AEA session, 'Is There a Home for Feminism in Economics?', organized by Diana Strassmann for the Allied Social Science Associations (ASSA) meetings in Washington DC, when session attendees were invited to join. A follow-up survey in February 1991 led to the August publication of the first 'Feminist Economists Network Update' newsletter, and in September, Iona Thraen, Barbara Bergmann, Aerni and Shackelford met to establish a format for a more formal association. In November, those interested were invited to become 'founding members' of the emerging organization, and the e-mail network, *femecon-1*, went on-line to give feminist economists worldwide instant communication. This last action dramatically increased the dialogue among feminist economists and provided a venue for building the organization and for encouraging discussion of feminist research and resources.

IAFFE was formally created at the January 1992 ASSA meetings in New Orleans. During the next six months, a number of standing committees were established and staffed, the first *IAFFE Newsletter* was published by Nancy Folbre, and the first IAFFE summer conference was planned by Barbara Bergmann. Held in July 1992 at American University in Washington DC, over 100 participants gathered to share research and ideas and to elect the organization's first set of officers, including Shackelford as IAFFE's first president. (Subsequent Presidents include Marianne Ferber, Myra Strober, Barbara Bergmann, Rhonda Sharp and Jane Humphries.)

Since its formation, IAFFE has served as a catalyst for advances in feminist economics. In its attempt to add feminist perspectives to economic research and analysis, the organization has worked to increase the visibility and the range of theoretical, methodological and empirical research by utilizing such traditional professional avenues as participation in academic conferences and the publication of the scholarly journal, *Feminist Economics*. IAFFE has also expanded its activities into outlets historically less valued by the economics profession; these have included attention to the teaching of economics and to participation in policy discussions worldwide.

In addition to sponsoring sessions at international, national and regional academic conferences, IAFFE holds an annual summer conference in which a diverse group of feminist economists and other social scientists from all over the world, from both inside and outside the academy, convene. These meetings are devoted to formal paper presentations, round table discussions, workshops and collaborative discussions. The great international diversity of participants has made possible new linkages for research and policy collaboration, and in order to encourage this continuing collaboration, the association has received grants to fund the attendance of feminists from the South (or Third World) and Eastern Europe.

The organization's journal, *Feminist Economics*, promotes cutting-edge feminist scholarship in economics and provides a forum for theoretical, empirical, policy-related and methodological work on economic issues from a feminist perspective. Along with the organization's other publications (*IAFFE Newsletter* and *femecon-1*), the journal intends to stimulate dialogue among economists, policymakers and the general public on feminist perspectives on economic issues. First published in spring 1995, *Feminist Economics* has consistently and successfully encouraged high-quality research, a fact noted by the Council of Editors of Learned Journals when they awarded the journal the prestigious 'Best New Journal' award in 1997.

IAFFE has also acknowledged the importance of feminist economic perspectives in the teaching of economics through the establishment of its Teaching and Pedagogy Committee. Under the leadership of Margaret Lewis and KimMarie McGoldrick, the committee has sponsored annual pedagogy workshops; organized sessions on feminist pedagogy at regional, national and IAFFE conferences; and compiled and disseminated via the world wide web course syllabi, a video guide and other classroom resources. By providing a lens through which disciplinary attention is focused on feminist pedagogy, IAFFE has contributed to making the economics classroom a more inclusive and hospitable environment for all.

To further international discussion of feminist inquiry into economic issues and further expand international linkages for collaboration, IAFFE also organizes panels on topics of interest to feminist economists at conferences throughout the world. In 1995, the chairs of IAFFE's International Committee, Bina Agarwal and Janet Seiz, structured a complete programme of eight panels on the theme 'Feminist Economics: Subverting the Mainstream' for the Fourth World Conference on Women held in Beijing, China. This kind of involvement has led to IAFFE's designation as a non-governmental organization in special consultative status with the Economic and Social Council of the United Nations .

Another way in which IAFFE maintains its international presence is through the establishment of regional branches. The first regional branch, ANZAFFE (the Australia New Zealand Association for Feminist Economics), organized formally in 1994. Under the guidance of Prue Hyman and Rhonda Sharp, ANZAFFE has organized panels and regional conferences and circulated a newsletter in an effort to foster international cooperation, collaboration and resource sharing. Additionally, regional branches for Europe and Africa are now currently being considered.

IAFFE's presence and agenda continues to enable a wide array of feminist economic projects – from books (such as this one) to a travelling graduate course to international conference collaborations. The importance of the Association's role as catalyst for furthering feminist thought (in its very short life), and its continuing potential for the future, should not be underestimated.

JEAN SHACKELFORD

See also
Committee on the Status of Women in the Economics Profession; Feminist Economics; Women in the Economics Profession.

International Economics

What do international trade theory and policy imply for women in the world economy? International trade affects the lives of men and women everywhere. Feminist economists, however, argue that trade has a different impact on women than on men, given the patriarchal structures of societies, labour market segmentation, discrimination and the marginalization of women in the Third World. The question is: Does trade merely reinforce women's inferior economic status, or does it contribute to their empowerment?

This question has raised a serious debate among feminist economists and other scholars as they attempt to understand the effects of trade theory and policy on the status of women in both industrialized and less-developed countries, especially within the context of the new trends toward globalization and trade liberalization. Feminist economists have contributed significantly to the debate, focusing mainly on the employment and wage effects of various trade policies. While feminist economists agree that women are affected by trade policies differently and usually more negatively than men, the specific impacts of these policies, and the analytical frameworks needed for understanding them, continue to be topics of debate. Therefore, feminist economists have called for a feminist perspective on trade theory in order to inform policymakers about the impact of trade policies on women, thus recognizing the interconnectedness between trade theory and policy and the need to include gender as a 'category of analysis' (Bakker 1996, p. 9).

This entry examines the impact of trade policies on the status of women in the world economy. After explaining the mainstream economic rationale for free trade, this entry gives a short discussion of the interconnectedness between trade theory and policy and the role of the major international institutions in promoting the free trade ideology, followed by a section on the effects of trade policies on women. This entry concludes with some suggestions for further research that would broaden and deepen feminist economics.

Theories of International Trade: Comparative Advantage

Mainstream international trade theory addresses the question: Why do countries trade and what are the benefits from free trade? Adam Smith, writing in the mid-eighteenth century, was the first major contributor to mainstream trade theory. Smith advocated free trade because of his fundamental belief that a market-run system without any government intervention will increase society's economic welfare. According to Smith, a nation should specialize in and export the goods it can make absolutely cheaper than its trading partner. The basis for trade is therefore the differences in costs of production across nations, as determined by differences in labour productivity. By specializing and trading, a nation will use its resources more efficiently and experience an increase in output, income and consumption. David Ricardo, writing early in the nineteenth century, refined Smith's ideas and developed a model to show that mutually beneficial trade can still take place even if one nation is absolutely more efficient than its trading partner in the production of all goods. The more efficient nation specializes in and exports the good in which it is relatively more efficient, while the less efficient nation specializes in and exports the good in which it is relatively less inefficient. Ricardo's trade theory is known as the principle of comparative advantage and is the basis for mainstream trade theory and policy advocating free trade (Carbaugh 1998, pp. 20–22).

Ricardo's principle of comparative advantage is supported by the vast majority of mainstream economists, who advocate free trade as a way to promote economic efficiency and growth in both industrialized and less-developed countries. What happens to factors of production (land, labour and capital) when countries engage in free trade? In this model, the free market will in the long run eliminate a short-run problem of unemployed workers in declining sectors as these workers retrain themselves for other jobs. This view has been strongly challenged by feminist economists who question the validity of this result for female workers in declining industries in both industrialized and less-developed countries.

Ricardo's comparative advantage model was refined in the early twentieth century by Eli Hecksher and Bertil Ohlin in order to take into account differences in the relative abundance of factors of production across nations and to analyse the impact of free trade on income distribution within a nation. According to the Hecksher–Ohlin model, differences in costs of production exist not because of differences in labour productivity but because countries are endowed with different factor supplies. Countries specialize in and export the products that use their abundant (and cheaper) resources intensively and import the products that use their scarce (and more expensive) resources more intensively. The model implies that, in the long run, the income of the more abundant factor of production will rise in relation to the income of the less abundant factor as the abundant factor is more intensively used. In Third World countries, this implies a rise in the share of national income going to labour (Carbaugh 1998, pp. 66–71). Feminist economists who have analysed the impact of trade on the wages and incomes of mostly female workers in export manufacturing industries have extensively debated this result.

This international division of labour implied by the mainstream trade model has shaped world trade since the nineteenth century when many Third World countries joined the world economy as independent nations, and it was reinforced during the 1960s when owners of capital from industrialized nations shifted production to less-developed nations where a cheap labour force was available. This has led to an emphasis on export manufacturing, the creation of Free Trade Zones (FTZs) in Third World countries and the proliferation of maquiladoras (industrial parks) along the Mexico–United States border.

The free trade model developed by Ricardo and refined by Hecksher–Ohlin has been widely promoted and gone unchallenged by mainstream economists in industrialized nations for almost 200 years. During the 1980s, however, a small number of mainstream economists started advocating government intervention to help specific industries develop a comparative advantage in the world market. This emerging view is associated with the pioneering work of Krugman (1986) and others. According to Krugman, trade needs not be based exclusively on relative factor endowments. He argues that economies of scale or decreasing costs of production may be the crucial factor in determining a nation's trading patterns. In this case, national firms can develop their comparative advantages with help from the government, as evidenced by the remarkable growth of the East Asian economies that have received considerable government support. Krugman thus advocates the development of an industrial policy to enable firms to expand their production and be the first ones to capitalize on economies of scale (Carbaugh 1998, pp. 85–7). This new theory of international trade is currently being debated in the United States and is highly controversial, given that it challenges the free trade model supported by most economists. This new theory is, however, significant for development and feminist economists because it recognizes the role of monopolies, oligopolies and national governments in shaping trade patterns, a fact long ago acknowledged by development and feminist economists who argue that multinational corporations have too much economic and political power in industrialized and less-developed countries.

In spite of this new development in trade theory, Ricardo's theory of comparative advantage remains the major influence in trade theory and policy.

While feminist economists have not yet developed a systematic critique and reconstruction of this model, they have contributed significantly to the understanding of the impact of specific trade policies on women. The following section discusses the role of international organizations in promoting the free trade ideology in the world economy and some major policies that have been put into effect to stimulate trade.

Several agreements have been signed and various institutions have been created to facilitate trade and to promote economic growth worldwide. The first important agreement, signed in 1947, was the General Agreement on Tariffs and Trade (GATT). GATT was created to encourage member nations to reduce their trade barriers, and between 1947 and 1993 industrialized nations participating in GATT have significantly lowered their trade restrictions. In 1995, GATT was replaced by the World Trade Organization (WTO) to improve the mechanisms for resolving trade disputes among member nations (Carbaugh 1998, p. 175). The International Monetary Fund (IMF) and the World Bank (also known as the International Bank for Reconstruction and Development) are two other institutions that have had a significant effect on international trade policies. During the 1980s and 1990s, these institutions have promoted free trade as a way to deal with the debt crisis in Third World nations and to foster economic growth in both the industrialized and less-developed nations. To that end, Structural Adjustment Policies (SAPs) have been put into effect in both industrialized and less-developed nations to increase their international competitiveness. Also there has been a significant trend toward regional trade agreements to promote trade liberalization within specific regions. The European Union (EU), the Canadian–United States Free Trade Agreement (CUFTA) and the North American Free Trade Agreement (NAFTA) are examples of the new emphasis on regional integration.

Given the hegemony of the comparative advantage model and the creation of so many institutions to promote free trade in the world, various policies have been put into effect since World War II to promote free trade in both industrialized and less-developed countries. Feminist economists and other scholars have provided important insights by analysing the impacts of these free trade policies on the status of women. Development economists have also contributed significantly to the understanding of these issues because many of these policies were to stimulate economic development in Third World countries.

Two examples of the internationalization of production as dictated by the principle of comparative advantage are the policies of Free Trade Zones (FTZs) and maquiladoras. As previously noted, during the 1960s, many producers of labour-intensive manufactured goods in industrialized nations, in response to increased competition, shifted production to Third World nations to take advantage of their cheap labour force (Elson and Pearson 1981, pp. 89–90). In order to encourage foreign investment, many developing countries created FTZs, areas that give producers tariff and tax breaks. At the same time, the respective governments of these producers changed their countries' tariff policies to allow the goods assembled abroad to reenter their economies duty-free. This export-oriented industrialization strategy, first adopted by South Korea, Taiwan, Hong Kong and Singapore and later by many poorer Third World countries (Shoesmith 1986, p. 1), was intended to generate growth, income, employment and earn foreign exchange. Some governments thus promoted export manufacturing under pressure from the IMF and the World Bank in order to earn foreign exchange to repay their debts.

Another early free trade programme, similar to the FTZs, is the Maquiladora Program, established in the early 1970s along the Mexico–United States border by the Mexican and United States governments 'to encourage foreign investment in export manufacturing through a combination of stimuli stemming from tariff flows and fiscal incentives' (Fernandez-Kelly 1983, p. 25). Maquiladoras are industrial parks created to benefit the Mexican economy and US producers by making the latter's products more competitive in the world market. These producers import parts and supplies tax-free from the United States, assemble them and re-export them to the United States duty-free (Carbaugh 1998, pp. 294–5).

What has been the impact of these various policies on the status of women? According to the free trade model, workers in the FTZs and in the maquiladoras will experience an improvement in their economic welfare through higher wages, incomes and consumption. This view was and is still shared by many development economists who view the process of trade expansion and industrialization as having a positive impact on women's status as they have more employment opportunities created by export manufacturing. The general consensus in the 1970s was that integrating women in the 'worldwide factories' would improve their status by moving them away from the informal sector of street vending, domestic services and subsistence agriculture, where the vast majority of the female labour force was employed. Lim (1978, 1990), who is one of the first development economists to study the impact of export manufacturing, writes that this form of development unlike others benefits women because it 'creates employment disproportionately for women' (Lim 1990, p. 119).

The early feminist literature on zones (Elson and Pearson 1981; Shoesmith 1986) rejects this view by arguing that women in the FTZs and in the maquiladoras are poor young women who are being exploited by multinational corporations. Management in these factories exploits the young women by paying them low wages relative to men, suppresses their labour rights, provides poor and unhealthy working conditions and exercises great control over their lives. Therefore, the integration of young women in 'world market factories' is not the solution to their subordination, as has been argued in the development literature, but may be part of the problem. Elson and Pearson argue that the ability of these women to earn a wage does not necessarily increase their status or their decision-making power within the household, and two recent studies, Kopinak (1995) on Mexico and Seguino (1995) on South Korea, support Elson and Pearson's arguments.

This 'exploitation' view has been criticized on two grounds. First, Lim (1990) believes that there are serious methodological weaknesses in the literature, which are caused by Marxist and feminist ideologies, ethnocentrism, vested political interests and poor research methods. She calls the 'exploitation' analysis a stereotype that does not fit the reality of all women working in export factories in Third World countries. Lim believes that export manufacturing provides jobs disproportionately for women and should be encouraged in the future. Second, as Safa (1995) and Joekes and Weston have argued, the issue of employment of young women by multinational corporations is highly complex and cannot be generalized from country to country. They argue that trade expansion in the past has benefited women in the Third World because it has increased women's access to paid employment. Safa also argues that, in Puerto Rico and the Dominican Republic, the increased participation of women into the industrial labour force, albeit in dead-end and low-paying jobs, combined with the decreasing employment of men, has augmented women's authority within the household.

The debate among feminist and non-feminist scholars with respect to the impact of FTZs and maquiladoras on the status of women suggests that the impact is varied, complex and multidimensional. Feminist and mainstream economists agree that free trade is an important stimulus to economic growth and creates employment for women in so far as women are employed in the expanding industries. They disagree, however, on whether or not employment in the export sector improves women's status in the household and in society. Feminists point to occupational segregation, labour market discrimination, the existence of strong patriarchal institutions and the growing influence of large multinational corporations to argue that free trade just reinforces the marginalization of women in Third World countries. Feminist economists have therefore called for government regulation of the powerful multinational corporations to improve the working conditions and the wages of the women working in these industries.

Feminist economists have also contributed significantly to the debate surrounding SAPs and two important free trade policies: CUFTA (the free trade agreement between Canada and the USA) and NAFTA (the free trade agreement between Canada, Mexico and the USA). Unlike the debate on FTZs and maquiladoras where feminist economists analysed the status of women in expanding manufacturing export industries, the focus in this debate is on the status of women in declining industries caused by trade liberalization.

SAPs were put into effect at the beginning of the 1980s in Africa, Asia and Latin America at the request of the World Bank and the IMF. The proposed goal of this restructuring was to help Third World countries deal with their crushing debt and increase the level of efficiency of their economies in order to prepare them for a more competitive world economy. Wherever SAPs are used, this usually entails a greater emphasis on free trade with the removal of most trade barriers and/or the creation of FTZs, a decrease in government spending, less government regulation and privatization of state enterprises (Bakker 1996, p. 3). Feminist economists argue that trade liberalization within the context of SAPs have increased the marginalization of women in Third World countries (Elson 1991; Aslanbeigui et al. 1994; Sparr 1994); and increased the economic vulnerability of women in labour-intensive industries in Canada (Bakker 1996; Cohen, 1987, 1995).

While SAPs have galvanized feminist economists all over the world, CUFTA has galvanized feminist economists in Canada. CUFTA, which became effective in 1989, eliminated all import tariffs and many nontariff trade barriers over a ten-year period (Carbaugh 1998, pp. 255–8). Cohen (1987) has provided one of the first (and few) empirical studies on trade liberalization within the context of a regional trade agreement. In her pioneering work, she argues that labour-intensive industries such as clothing, textiles, footwear and electronics that employ a high percentage of women will be negatively affected because of their comparative disadvantage *vis-à-vis* the United States. During the first three years after CUFTA took effect, employment in Canada decreased sharply, with most of the job losses being permanent and mostly in industries that employ large numbers of women (Cohen 1995, p. 11). In addition, these industries experienced downward pressure on wages. In clothing, for example, female employment decreased by 23 per cent between 1989 and 1992 while 'wages fell from 65 per cent of the average manufacturing wage in the early 1980s to 58 per cent in the early 1990s' (Cohen 1995, p. 11). Furthermore, service industries such as data processing, financial services, communications, transportation and cultural services are likely to be negatively impacted in the future because of the superior cost advantage of the United States. Women again will be the major losers because the majority of women work in the service sector. As a result of all these changes, Cohen argues, the female participation rate in the labour force declined from 58.6 per cent to 57.5 per cent during the four years after CUFTA (Cohen 1995, p. 12).

Gabriel and MacDonald (1996) extend the analysis of trade liberalization and restructuring policies to examine their effects on minority women in Canada and Mexico after NAFTA. They argue that the new economic environment of restructuring must be understood within the context of class, race and gender together rather than by gender alone (Gabriel and MacDonald 1996, p. 166). Many minority women in Canada are overrepresented in declining industries such as clothing, textiles and leather products, and these are the sectors that are likely to be negatively affected by NAFTA. At the same time, Mexican women will also be affected because NAFTA involves the 'maquiladorization' of the Mexican economy and increased exploitation for women. NAFTA then presents a common rallying point for struggle for minority women in Canada and Mexico – a point of encounter to explore differences and similarities.

Not all feminist economists, however, agree that trade liberalization as in CUFTA and NAFTA will necessarily have a negative impact on women's economic welfare. First, Joekes and Weston (1994) and Benería and Lind (1995) argue that it is difficult to generalize about the gender dimensions of trade expansion because of a lack of empirical research. Much of the literature has focused on the sectoral impact of specific trade policies such as the FTZs and maquiladoras. More research is needed to analyse the macroeconomic effects of trade liberalization on production, income and consumption given that women are both producers and consumers. Second, these scholars argue, female workers in industries with a comparative advantage are likely to benefit from free trade because their incomes will go up (although the increase is not automatic), while women in industries with a comparative disadvantage will experience higher unemployment and lower wages. Third, Benería and Lind argue that trade expansion can have significant non-economic implications that may impact women's lives. For example, trade liberalization may negatively impact the environment, making life more difficult for rural women in Third World countries who rely on the environment (wood, water, and so on) for survival. Or trade liberalization may accelerate the appropriation of women's indigenous knowledge, such as herbal knowledge, by multinational corporations, thereby negatively impacting women's power in their societies.

Feminist thinking has illuminated the debate concerning the impact of trade policies on the status of women. Feminist scholars have challenged the notion that women employed in the FTZs and maquiladoras have experienced an improvement in their economic welfare. Furthermore, feminist insights on the power of social and cultural institutions, patriarchy, labour market segmentation and discrimination, challenge many of the key theoretical arguments of the comparative advantage model, such as the prediction that women who lose their jobs in declining industries will be absorbed into expanding ones.

More feminist economic research is, however, necessary to capture the complexity of women's lives and the multidimensional effects of free trade: its microeconomic, macroeconomic and non-economic implications. In particular, researchers need to gain a more in-depth understanding of women's daily lives in order to discuss the multiplicity of their experiences under trade liberalization. It is important to give a voice to these women so that they can tell their stories, which calls for research methods such as surveys and interviews to capture their voices more completely than traditional economic statistics.

In addition, there are some important theoretical questions that need to be explored. Feminists need to deconstruct Ricardo's comparative trade theory and its core assumptions of competitive markets and factor mobility as feminist economists in Canada have recognized this issue. Bakker (1996, p. 9), for example, argues that 'the analytical framework of the rational economic man is not appropriate and hides the interconnectedness between economic factors and political, social, and cultural factors'. In an attempt to reconstruct international trade theory Ellie Perkins argues for 'sustainable trade', which she defines as 'exchanges which can continue indefinitely' (Perkins 1996, p. 2). She rejects the free trade model based on comparative advantage because free trade 'endangers the ecological, physical, social, cultural, economic or political foundations of the trading communities or regions' (Perkins 1996, pp. 2–3), thus with large-scale trade come environmental degradation, loss of local control over communities and resources, social deterioration and loss of cultural identity (Perkins 1996, p. 4).

More empirical research is also needed to analyse the various impacts of trade policies on the status of women. First, it is important to recognize the interconnectedness between economic factors and political, social and cultural factors. The gains from trade postulated by the free trade model are not automatic, but rather depend on how these interrelated factors play out in women's respective societies. For example, women in Nicaragua, where there is a strong feminist movement, have won the rights to organize labour unions in the FTZs after a long struggle with management. Second, there is also a need to explore the sectoral implications of trade policies. How are they different for women in the manufacturing, agricultural and service sectors? It is important, for example, to analyse the impact of NAFTA on women in the service industries in Canada as opposed to women in the labour-intensive manufacturing industries. Third, it is important to acknowledge differences in women in terms of race, class and ethnicity. For example, the impact of free trade may be different for indigenous women and for middle-class women in Mexico, or for minority women in the United States and Canada. Fourth, the link between free trade and the environment has to be explored in more empirical studies. Will free trade accelerate the deforestation of Latin America, which will then have a negative impact on rural women? Fifth, more research is needed to study the impact of free trade on indigenous knowledge. Given the strong interest in natural medicine by multinational corporations, for example, how can women use their knowledge of plants to increase their economic power? All of these factors will be critical in determining the future impact of 'free trade' on the economic status of women.

ROSE-MARIE AVIN

See also

Development Policies; Development, Theories of; Economic Restructuring; Globalization; Informal Sector; Structural Adjustment Policies.

Bibliography

Aslanbeigui, Nahid, Steven Pressman and Gale Summerfield (eds) (1994), *Women in the Age of Economic Transformation: Impact of Reforms in Post-Socialist and Developing Countries*, New York: Routledge.

Bakan, Abigail B. and Daiva K. Stasiulis (1996), 'Structural Adjustment, Citizenship, and Foreign Domestic Labour: The Canadian Case', in Isabella Bakker (ed.), *Rethinking Restructuring: Gender and Change in Canada*, Toronto: University of Toronto Press, pp. 217–42.

Bakker, Isabella (ed.), 1994, *The Strategic Silence: Gender and Economic Policy*, Canada, UK, USA: Zed Books Ltd with the North–South Institute.

Bakker, Isabella (ed.) (1996), *Rethinking Restructuring: Gender and Change in Canada*, Toronto: University of Toronto Press.

Benería, Lourdes and Amy Lind (1995), 'Engendering International Trade: Concepts, Policy, and Action', in Noelleen Heyzer (ed.), *A Commitment to the World's Women: Perspectives on Development for Beijing and Beyond*, New York: UNIFEM, pp. 69–86.

Carbaugh, Robert J. (1998), *International Economics*, 6th edn, Cincinnati: South-Western College Publishing.

Cohen, Marjorie Griffen (1987), *Free Trade and the Future of Women's Work: Manufacturing and Service Industries*, Toronto, Ontario: Garamond Press and Canadian Centre for Policy Alternatives.

Cohen, Marjorie Griffen (1995), 'Macho economics: Canadian women confront free trade', *Real World International: A Reader in Economics, Business, and Politics from Dollars and Sense*, 3rd edn, Somerville (Massachusetts): Economic Affairs Bureau, pp. 10–13.

Cohen, Marjorie Griffen (1996), 'New International Trade Agreements: Their Reactionary Role in Creating Markets and Retarding Social Welfare', in Isabella Bakker (ed.), *Rethinking Restructuring: Gender and Change in Canada*, Toronto: University of Toronto Press, pp. 187–202.

Coote, Belinda (1992), *The Trade Trap: Poverty and the Global Commodity Markets*, Oxford: Oxford University Press.

Elson, Diane (ed.) (1991), *Male Bias in the Development Process*, Manchester: Manchester University Press.

Elson, Diane and Ruth Pearson (1981), '"Nimble fingers make cheap workers": an analysis of women's employment in third world export manufacturing', *Feminist Review*, 7, 87–106.

Fernandez-Kelly, Maria Patricia (1983), *For We Are Sold, I and My People: Women and Industry in Mexico's Frontier*, Albany, New York: State University of New York Press.

Gabriel, Christina and Laura MacDonald (1996), 'NAFTA and Economic Restructuring: Some Gender and Race Implications', in Isabella Bakker (ed.), *Rethinking Restructuring: Gender and Change in Canada*, Toronto: University of Toronto Press, pp. 165–86.

Joekes, Susan (1987), *Women in the World Economy: An INSTRAW Study*, New York, Oxford: Oxford University Press.

Joekes, Susan and Ann Weston (1994), *Women and The New Trade Agenda*, New York: UNIFEM.

Kerr, Joanna (1996), 'Transnational Resistance: Strategies to Alleviate the Impacts of Restructuring on Women', in Isabella Bakker (ed.), *Rethinking Restructuring: Gender and Change in Canada*, Toronto: University of Toronto Press, pp. 243–60.

Kopinak, Kathryn (1995), 'Gender as a vehicle for the subordination of women maquiladora workers in Mexico', *Latin American Perspectives*, **22** (1), 30–48.

Krugman, Paul R. (1986), *Strategic Trade Policy and the New International Economics*, Cambridge: MIT Press.

Lim, Linda Y.C. (1978), *Women Workers in Multinational Corporations: The Case of the Electronics Industry in Malaysia and Singapore*, Michigan Occasional Papers (9), Women's Studies Program, University of Michigan.

Lim, Linda Y.C. (1990), 'Women's Work in Export Factories: The Politics of a Cause', in Irene Tinker (ed.), *Persistent Inequalities: Women and World Development*, New York, Oxford: Oxford University Press.

Perkins, Ellie (1996), 'Following the example of women initiatives: building communities to limit trade', *Alternatives*, (January–February), 10–15.

Safa, Helen I. (1995), 'The New Women Workers: Does Money Equal Power?', in Fred Rosen and Deidre McFadyen (eds), *Free Trade and Economic Restructuring in Latin America: A NACLA Reader*, New York: Monthly Review Press.

Seguino, Stephanie (1995), 'Gender wage inequality and export-led growth in South Korea', *Women Studies Forum*, **11**, 187–210.

Shoesmith, Dennis (ed.) (1986), *Export Processing Zones in Five Countries: The Economic and Human Consequences*, Hong Kong: Asia Partnership for Human Development.

Sparr, Pamela (ed.) (1994), *Mortgaging Women's Lives: Feminist Critiques of Structural Adjustment*, Atlantic Highlands, New Jersey: Zed Books Ltd.

Labour Force Participation

Labour Force Participation (LFP), or labour force participation rate, is an index measuring the ratio of the number of individuals in the waged labour market to the adult population of working age. It reflects the number of people in a defined population (nation, city) who are working for wages, usually during one year, and can be broken down in many ways, such as by gender, age, race or ethnicity. This index is important to feminist economists for several reasons. First, LFP can be used to compare the involvement of women and men in the waged labour force within a nation or region. Trends that indicate an increase of women's LFP compared to men's, for example, might be used to discuss numerous subjects such as changing gender roles, the increased importance of women's labour to an economy or the need for state sponsored day/elder care in order to replace women's traditional roles in the home. A second reason is the use of national LFP statistics to compare international labour trends. As the economies of all countries become more interconnected and industrialized, there has been a worldwide trend toward increasing numbers of women in waged labour. Comparisons of trends are useful in development economics and for activists seeking to promote world-wide improvement of the conditions that labouring women face.

LFP is one of the most difficult concepts to define in economics, yet it is a crucial theoretical building block. Many of the difficulties revolve around the implications attached to the words in the phrase. Labour is assumed by most economists to mean waged labour rather than the specific activities performed. Yet all societies pay men and women differently for the same labour, with women frequently receiving no wage for work which becomes waged labour when performed by men (Benería 1979). By inference, then, if economists only count waged labour, they must routinely undercount the labour of women. In addition, some forms of labour are both unpaid and paid, making it unclear as to when this labour (such as child/elder care, teaching, housecleaning and cooking) should be counted in LFP statistics. Since the definition of paid labour is frequently unclear, the definition of who is an actor in the labour force also becomes problematic. Indeed, the very size of the labour force changes with the definition of what labour is, with the variable portion comprised almost entirely of women.

Statistically relevant LFP is strongly identified with demographic characteristics such as gender, race, ethnicity and class. As an example, take Mrs Diaz, the building superintendent's wife, who runs an unlicensed daycare centre. Most of the mothers who send their children to Mrs Diaz work in illegal garment shops where their wages are not reported to the government, and where the piece rate is less than the minimum wage. On tax forms and census documents all these women are listed as housewives and/or welfare recipients, but do they count as labour force participants? While a feminist economist would argue they do, most non-feminist economists either would have no knowledge of these women's existence, or they would say this unrecorded workforce represents a small group in relation to the recorded workforce and are thus statistically insignificant. Increasingly, feminists have discovered that women's waged work is so frequently under-recorded as to call into question the reliability of all LFP statistics as recorded by official government agencies. In short, participation rates change with both the definition of labour and the composition of the labour force.

An accurate definition of LFP is critical to the ability of women to exercise power over their own lives and within their particular society. If women are considered full participants in the labour force, then the importance of women's contributions to the economy cannot be ignored by policymakers when they determine who has the right to access the economic surplus within society. However, if women are seen instead as tangential to the LFP of men in an economy, they are considered a drain on resources. Under these latter circumstances, women's power is greatly reduced.

Most twentieth century economists have assumed male waged labour to be the standard by which all other labour is judged; thus female LFP is viewed as an exception to the normal male model (Grapard 1995). While some work on female LFP was conducted in the early twentieth century, it was only in the 1960s and 1970s, during the Domestic Labour debates, that gender was incorporated into labour market theories (Himmelweit and Mohun 1977). Subsequent feminist scholars added to the Domestic Labour debates by gendering and expanding the definitions of labour force and participation. This scholarship took different forms: incorporating domestic labour into theories of surplus value (Folbre 1982), exposing the exploitation of women's labour in the household (Hartmann 1981; Folbre 1986; McCrate 1987), discussing the ongoing discrimination of occupational segregation in the labour market (Reskin and Hartmann 1985; Bergmann 1986; Bertaux 1991) and starting an examination of the international experiences of women waged workers (Leacock and Safa 1986).

Traditional economists also began to acknowledge the need to incorporate issues of gender into neoclassical models of labour supply. Gary Becker's theory of household decision making, while frequently taken to 'preposterous conclusions' (Bergmann 1995), was the first work by a neoclassical economist to recognize time allotted to production in the home as a factor in the decision to supply labour to the market. Before this, the labour supply decision was seen in terms of a trade-off between waged work and leisure, reflecting the male standard of waged work in the labour market and leisure in the home. In this analysis, not only were women viewed as an exception in the labour market, but their work in the home was also treated as incidental to the principle male activity in the home – leisure. Becker's recognition of the time spent in household labour allowed traditional economists to begin examining real world phenomena which had previously been unexplained. For example, Becker's model enabled the entry of married women of child-bearing age into the waged labour force in large numbers following World War II to be discussed in the same marginalist structure which had previously only been applied to male LFP decisions.

Gendering the concept of LFP has also resulted in an important reassessment of economic history. Coleman (1997) has found, for example, that in 1830s Massachusetts, women's LFP in waged, non-farm labour can conservatively be estimated to have been higher than 45 per cent. Adding together the ante-bellum years in New England, when women were a majority of the manufacturing labour force, and the war years for the Civil War, World War I, and World War II as well as the years since 1955, indicates that women's LFP in the United States has been under 40 per cent in only about one third of the years since industrialization began (just prior to the War of 1812). This makes the most recent rise in women's LFP since World War II not simply a twentieth century phenomena. Thus from a historical perspective, the relegation of women's LFP as an exception to the male norm of LFP is clearly incorrect. If wage earning women are as 'normal' as wage earning men, then the contribution of women to the economy, to productivity, and to the GDP statistics is more central to a functioning economy than has been generally recognized.

Including gender in LFP also permits examination of the interactive roles of race, ethnicity and class with gender (Feiner 1994). While poor women have always had a much higher LFP rate than more well-to-do women, different ethnic and racial groupings have differing LFP rates as well. There are numerous examples of these differences. For instance, prior to the Civil War, freed African women almost always worked for wages, and this high LFP has remained constant throughout the twentieth century. Thus the movement of women in the population at large out of waged work following the Civil War and World War I never happened for most African-American women (Hine et al. 1995). More recently, the incorporation of diversity into feminist analysis of LFP reveals that in the United States today the bulk of unrecorded labouring women engaged in the informal sector are not of European descent. This activity occurs in a wide range of occupations, such as illegal garment shops, maids, live-in child care and field help, which are neither tracked nor protected by labour laws and as a result, tend to be extremely exploitative and low paid (see, for example, Romero 1992). In addition, allowing demographic categories to interact also highlights the different international experiences of working women. For example, the woman factory worker in Malaysia who juggles Islamic religious restrictions with the need to earn a living has a vastly different work experience from a chicken worker in the United States who contracts carpal tunnel syndrome (see, for example, Ong 1989; Goldoftas 1995).

Including gender in discussions of LFP also has allowed feminist economists to broaden the theoretical work that examines the decision to offer labour to the market. The social and academic assumption about LFP for men is that they are all engaged in market labour from the time shortly after schooling is completed until a socially acceptable retirement age, with few if any absences from the labour force. Consequently, one reason that labour supply determination for men is so simple is that society's expectations of men are more simply defined: men are expected to work and receive monetary remuneration. The expectations of women, however, are more complex, hence the decision of women to supply labour also tends to be more complex.

Gender differences have historically driven men and women to make different economic decisions in all societies. Prior to industrialization in most countries, work tends to be located in the household or farm, although there are always gender differences in the labour performed there. After industrialization, the definition of work is expanded to include work out of the home or off the farm, a result which has historically affected women and men differently. For example, during US industrialization (beginning about 1810), women's work was the first to be commodified as women followed their work off the farms into the textile mills, and their work on the farm frequently became waged labour or 'outwork'. The heavy industries, which engaged the bulk of male labour in wage work, did not grow significantly until after 1850, 40 years after women's work had been industrialized. This pattern of gendered differences in the effect of industrialization can be seen in all countries (for example, Ong 1989).

Building on this, feminists have examined female labour supply within gendered parameters. While many women work because they must, rather than out of a dispassionate choice made through a labour/leisure trade-off, they still have decisions to make based on their gender-defined responsibilities. Since women are primarily in charge of that production which has remained in the household, they juggle child care and household maintenance responsibilities with the necessity of working for wages. Ultimately, for all but a few wealthy women who can afford to pay others to perform their gender assigned work, the labour supply decision of women is based on a complex of needs including financial necessity, social goals for wellbeing, gender determined non-market responsibilities and personal interests.

The examination of women's LFP has received different emphases in the feminist academic community. That women's responsibility in the home is not reduced with the advent of industrialization, thus resulting in their tending to work a double day both at home and work, has been noted by many feminists. Gendered roles continue in the face of dramatic economic changes, leading to the conclusion by many feminists that men reap a strong reward from having women in charge of household production, making men unwilling to give up the gendered division of labour (Hartmann 1982; Folbre 1982, 1986). Other feminist economists find that blaming male household members for the increased exploitation of women with the introduction of wage labour is too simplistic. Rather, existing gender divisions adapt to new economic situations and the exploitation of women's labour comes not primarily from the male members of the household but from the structure of the economy (Tilly and Scott 1980). Finally, there are different emphases placed on the primacy of gender as opposed to other demographic characteristics such as race, class and ethnicity (Amott 1993).

With all the differences within the feminist community, the overall debate about LFP has brought new vision to economics. By battling to include gender, feminists have challenged all of economics to attempt to be more inclusive of the diverse characteristics within the workforce. However, labour supply, or LFP, remains one of the most under-examined areas in economics. Many current economic publications still sidestep the gendered nature of LFP, and ignore the statistical inaccuracies caused by systematic undercounting of women's labour, as well as the issue of not including unpaid household labour in macroeconomic statistics. As other social sciences have begun to rewrite knowledge through gendered lenses – because gender affects every aspect of society profoundly – so too does economics need to reassess all economic wisdom through gendered eyes if it is to produce quality work that more accurately reflects the world which academics seek to illuminate.

MARGARET S. COLEMAN

See also
Domestic Labour; Double Day/Second Shift; Gender; Informal Sector; Race.

Bibliography
Amott, Teresa (1993), *Caught in the Crisis: Women and the U.S. Economy Today*, New York: Monthly Review Press.
Benería, Lourdes (1979), 'Reproduction, production and the sexual division of labor', *Cambridge Journal of Economics*, 3, 203–25.
Bergmann, Barbara (1986), *The Economic Emergence of Women*, New York: Basic Books.
Bergmann, Barbara (1995), 'Becker's theory of the family: preposterous conclusions', *Feminist Economics*, 1 (1), Spring, 141–50.
Bertaux, Nancy E. (1991), 'The roots of today's "Women's Jobs" and "Men's Jobs": using the index of dissimilarity to measure occupational segregation by gender', *Explorations in Economic History*, 28, 433–59.
Coleman, Margaret S. (1997), 'Female Labor Supply During Early Industrialization: Women's Labor Force Participation in Historical Perspective', in Mutari, Boushey and Fraher (eds), *Gender and Political Economy: Incorporating Diversity into Theory and Policy*, Armonk, New York and London: M.E. Sharpe.

Feiner, Susan (ed.), (1994), *Race and Gender in the American Economy: Views from Across the Spectrum*, Englewood Cliffs, New Jersey: Prentice-Hall, Inc.

Folbre, Nancy (1982), 'Exploitation comes home: a critique of the Marxian theory of family labour', *Cambridge Journal of Economics*, **6** (4), 317–29.

Folbre, Nancy (1986), 'Hearts and spades: paradigms of household economics', *World Development*, **14** (2), 245–55.

Goldoftas, Barbara (1995), 'To Make a Tender Chicken: Technological Change and Cost Cutting Take Their Toll', *Real World Micro, a Microeconomic Reader from Dollars and Sense*, 5th edn, Somerville, Massachusetts, pp. 48–50.

Grapard, Ulla (1995), 'Robinson Crusoe: the quintessential economic man?', *Feminist Economics*, **1** (1), Spring, 33–52.

Hartmann, Heidi (1981), 'The family as the locus of gender, class, and political struggle: the example of housework', *Signs*, **6** (9), 366–92.

Himmelweit, Susan and Simon Mohun (1977), 'Domestic labour and capital', *Cambridge Journal of Economics*, **1**, March, 15–29.

Hine, Darlene Clark, Wilma King and Linda Reed (1995), *'We Specialize in the Wholly Impossible': A Reader in Black Women's History*, Brooklyn, New York: Carlson Publishing.

Leacock, Eleanor and Helen I. Safa (1986), *Women's Work: Development and the Division of Labor by Gender*, New York, Westport, Connecticut and London: Bergin and Garvey Publishers.

McCrate, Elaine (1987), 'Trade, merger and employment: economic metaphors for marriage', *Review of Radical Political Economics*, (Spring), 73–89.

Ong, Aihwa (1989), 'State versus Islam: Malay families, women's bodies, and the body politic in Malaysia', *American Ethnologist*, **17** (2), 258–76.

Reskin, B. and H. Hartmann (eds) (1985), *Women's Work, Men's Work: Sex Segregation on the Job*, Washington, DC: National Academy Press.

Romero, Mary (1992), *Maid in the U.S.A.*, New York, London: Routledge.

Tilly, Louise A. and Joan Scott (1980), 'Women's Work and the Family in Nineteenth Century Europe', in Alice Amsden (ed.), *The Economics of Women and Work*, New York: St Martin's Press, pp. 91–124.

Labour Market Segmentation

The essence of the theory of labour market segmentation is that the labour market is best characterized as segmented into separate markets which reward their participants differently, rather than as one large labour market in which the same rules apply to everyone. In its most basic formulation, labour market segmentation theory describes the labour market as divided into 'good jobs' and 'bad jobs'. Good jobs provide job security and promotion possibilities, and pay workers more as they gain education, skills and seniority. Bad jobs are insecure, dead-end and poorly paid regardless of an individual's qualifications or tenure.

The roots of labour market segmentation theory are Averitt's (1968) dual industrial structure linked with Dunlop's (1957, 1966) early concepts about structure in the labour market. Averitt (1968) described a split between 'centre' industries and 'key' firms (later generally referred to as the 'core') that enjoyed steady demand and high profits and 'peripheral' industries that were vulnerable to cyclical swings in product demand and acted as a buffer for the core. Dunlop's (1957, 1966) work outlined labour market structures, that he termed wage contours and clusters, that underlay wage differentials for apparently similar workers, and internal labour markets, or job ladders within firms that provide training and mobility for some workers in some organizations.

The notion of a dual labour market linked to a dual industrial structure was quickly picked up by a number of researchers in the United States working in each of the neoclassical, institutional and radical literatures. Notable scholars included Bennet Harrison, Peter Doeringer and Michael Piore, who were particularly interested in explaining the relatively poor fortunes of black men in the US labour market. Black men were theorized to be disproportionately stuck in poorly paid secondary labour market positions without opportunities for mobility, regardless of their individual skills.

The version of labour market segmentation that emerged as the standard was that propounded by Reich et al. (1973), situated in the Neo-Marxist theoretical context of social structures of accumulation. This construction posited a primary labour market that included the economy's good jobs and a secondary labour market composed of the bad jobs. The primary labour market was described as further divided into the primary independent segment, which includes managerial and professional positions; and the primary subordinate segment, composed of union manufacturing jobs and clerical work in large organizations. In addition, women and members of racial and ethnic minority groups were observed to be often employed in sub-segments within each larger segment. For example, women are concentrated into a few professional occupations, primarily teaching, nursing and social work, that are not as well remunerated as are the male-dominated professions in the primary independent segment.

The concept of labour market segmentation, or dual labour markets as the concept was termed in much of the neoclassical and institutional literature, caught on and spread rapidly. Labour market segmentation theory is probably the single most important theoretical development in institutional and radical labour market theory of the last 25 years. However, it was difficult to distinguish empirically among segments as it became clear that most industries, occupations and even firms included elements of each segment.

Gittleman and Howell (1995) appear to have recently accomplished the empirical distinction of labour market segments in the US economy at the level of the job, by agglomerating similar occupation/industry cells using cluster analysis. Segments are distinguished from each other by earnings and benefits, unionization, sector, level of unemployment and short hours, skill requirements and working conditions. On the basis of this technique, Gittleman and Howell (1995) have identified a two-part primary independent segment, dividing work in the public sector from the private sector, a two-part primary subordinate sector, including high-wage blue-collar positions and clerical work, and a two-part secondary sector, composed of low-wage blue-collar jobs and service positions.

After an initial flurry of interest, labour market segmentation theory was dismissed by the neoclassical mainstream as atheoretical and empirically invalid (Cain 1976). Then in the mid-1980s the concept of labour market segmentation was revived in neoclassical economics, as discussed in Dickens and Lang (1988), due in part to the work of Dickens and Lang themselves. Dickens and Lang (1985, 1993), placing dual labour markets theoretically in the efficiency wage literature, have used sophisticated econometrics to establish the empirical superiority for men of a dual labour market model over a single labour market model.

Feminist economists have been both receptive to and critical of the theory of labour market segmentation. Many feminists have found segmentation to be a very useful construct, as it potentially provides a better explanation than does human capital theory of the high degree of occupational segregation by gender, the relatively low returns women tend to earn for tenure and experience and the enduring gender wage gap. The notion that women are disproportionately stuck in the secondary labour market resonates with the feminist understanding that women experience a 'glass ceiling' throughout the labour market, are shut out of the most lucrative positions and are relatively poorly paid, regardless of their level of education, skills, experience, tenure or commitment to the labour force. Further, the idea that women of colour are even more limited in their labour market opportunities than are white women, on average, fits with the conception that women may be differentially distributed among segments by race, ethnicity and class.

Consequently, feminist economists, particularly those working in the heterodox traditions, have made use of the structure of labour market segmentation as a descriptive device. A good example is Amott and Matthaei's (1996) economic history of women in the United States. Amott and Matthaei use the framework of segmentation to characterize the kinds of jobs obtained by women of different ethnicities and to assess occupational mobility over time.

However, feminist economists have also found the notion of labour market segmentation to be problematic. The historical development of segments, as articulated by Reich et al. (1973, 1982) is based upon the experience of white men. Their historiography conceptualizes segments as a post-World War II phenomenon that effectively divides the working class politically as well as on the job, succeeding a period of homogenization during which workers were rendered more similar, interchangeable and, consequently, organizable by the introduction of skill-replacing technologies. But, as Albelda (1985) and Albelda and Tilly (1994) have pointed out, women and people of colour have always been extremely differentiated from white men at work in the

USA, and in fact since World War II have held positions more similar to white men than ever before. Only after World War II were most women and people of colour in the USA working for wages and employed by organizations, rather than working (paid and unpaid) in private homes or in agriculture, often under sharecropping arrangements. Rather than being a period of segmentation, Albelda and Tilly (1994, p. 218) assert that the post-World War II period is better characterized as a period of proletarianization for white women, who dramatically increased their labour force participation, and one of integration for people of colour into 'the mainstream of the capitalist economy'.

Not only does the historical development of segmentation in the labour market not reflect the experience of women, the tripartite structure does not capture the differences among women's jobs or between women's and men's jobs (Hartmann 1987). Although women categorized in the primary segments do enjoy personnel systems and job security, they do not receive the payback to education, skill and experience that is earned by men in these segments, nor do they tend to enjoy the autonomy or authority. Internal labour markets, job ladders within firms that are considered to be a characteristic of the primary segment, provide much less opportunity for mobility to women. Critically, the pay for 'women's jobs', those jobs filled disproportionately by women, is far below that of men's jobs in the same segment, and frequently below that of men in lower segments.

This point has been demonstrated empirically by Friedberg et al. (1988, p. 118), who show that women do not appear to work in different segments of the labour market, but that 'the overwhelming majority of women are in what we call the "women's sector", one with virtually no returns to work experience, but significant returns to education'. In other words, women's jobs do not seem to fall squarely into the primary sector, which is theorized to reward both education and experience, nor into the secondary, which is conceptualized as rewarding neither.

Some critics have argued that weaknesses in traditional job classification schemes have contributed to the definition of labour market segments that do not accurately capture the nature of women's jobs. Women's jobs, as a group, are less well described and distinguished than are men's. One reason for this is that unionization lends itself to detailed job descriptions, and men and men's jobs have been more likely to be represented by unions than have women. Probably more important is the phenomenon described by social psychologists such as Baron (1991) as 'in-group bias', resulting in far better and more finely detailed job descriptions for occupations held by 'in-group' members.

A prime example is the relative paucity of categories in the occupational classification system of the 1990 US Census to describe 'women's jobs', particularly clerical work, as compared with men's occupations. Of the 501 occupational categories, 'secretary' is by far the single largest, including over three million workers and 2.5 per cent of the labour force in 1996. The second largest is registered nurse, which in 1996 included over two million people and 1.5 per cent of the labour force. Secretaries are 98 per cent women; nurses are 95 per cent women. On the other hand, 101 occupational categories are required to classify the 7 per cent of the labour force employed as 'Operators, Fabricators and Labourers', who are predominantly male (US Bureau of the Census 1996).

In the USA, researchers tend to rely upon the *Dictionary of Occupational Titles* (DOT) to characterize different jobs. This structure is notorious for underestimating the content of women's jobs, as demonstrated anecdotally by citing the famous example that the third edition of the DOT found the job Dog Pound Attendant to be more complex than either Nursery School Teacher or Practical Nurse. In response to criticism, the DOT was amended with an ad hoc procedure that upgraded many women's jobs, but it still fails to accurately describe or evaluate the demands of women's jobs. In particular the DOT classifications entirely overlook the aspect of many women's jobs having to do with nurturing and managing people. The concept that Hochschild (1983) has called 'emotion work' appears to be completely missing from the DOT analysis. Difficult working conditions noted by the DOT include only physical demands such as extreme temperatures and heavy lifting. Nowhere does the DOT account for the stress induced by having to be nice to people who may be angry, upset or hostile. The very job attributes overlooked by the DOT are those that may be said to characterize 'women's jobs'.

The jobs held disproportionately by members of racial and ethnic minority groups may be similarly ill-described. Malveaux (1985/86) has shown that comparable worth-inspired re-evaluation of job descriptions and pay may elevate the pay of occupations held disproportionately by both men and women in minority communities. Historians have noted the tendency of employers to hire people of colour for jobs that are particularly dirty, arduous, stigmatized or involve very personal service. If the assessment of difficult working conditions is understated, or if skills are overlooked by the DOT for jobs where minority workers are concentrated, then these jobs may also be inappropriately classified in labour market segmentation analysis.

A consistent weakness of the segmentation analysis then, ironically, is its inability to explain the particular labour market situation of women and people of colour. Though created in part to provide a rationale for the differential outcomes in the labour market associated with race and gender by hypothesizing that ascriptive characteristics are important in the allocation of labour to different segments, segmentation theories do not account well for the dynamics of race and gender. The concept of segments is designed to capture the idea that different bargains hold in different parts of the labour market, yet race and gender seem to significantly affect the bargain obtainable within each segment.

A major challenge for feminist economists and other segmentation theorists is to develop Reich et al.'s (1973) skeletal suggestion of race and gender sub-segments, a project that requires the creation of a completely different taxonomy and historical understanding of labour market segments. At a minimum, feminist economists need to study women's jobs with the same degree of interest as has been focused previously only on men's work, to conceptualize the evolution and contemporary dynamics of the labour markets in women's jobs, and to supplement our understanding of labour market segments with a well-developed picture of 'women's segments'. Ultimately, feminist economists will need to replace the theory of segmentation with one that examines all jobs with an eye to the kinds of dynamics apparent most obviously in women's work. Finally, as feminist economic research develops, feminist economists need to be alert to other possible axes of segmentation, so that they do not create a new theoretical foundation that adequately characterizes the work of the majority of women and men, while ignoring or misrepresenting jobs held by people distinguished by other characteristics such as race or ethnicity.

MARY C. KING

See also

Comparable Worth/Pay Equity; Glass Ceiling; Human Capital Theory; Occupational Segregation; Race; Unions and Union Organizing; Wage Gap.

Bibliography

Albelda, Randy (1985), '"Nice work if you can get it": segmentation of white and black women in the post-war period', *Review of Radical Political Economics*, **17**, (Fall), 72–85.

Albelda, Randy and Chris Tilly (1994), 'Towards a Broader Vision: Race, Gender and Labour Market Segmentation in the Social Structure of Accumulation Framework', in David Kotz, Terrence McDonough and Michael Reich (eds), *Social Structures of Accumulation*, Cambridge: Cambridge University Press, pp. 212–30.

Amott, Teresa and Julie Matthaei (1996), *Race, Gender and Work: A Multicultural Economic History of Women in the United States*, Boston: South End Press.

Averitt, Robert (1968), *The Dual Economy: The Dynamics of American Industry Structure*, New York: W.W. Norton.

Baron, James N. (1991), 'Organizational Evidence of Ascription in Labour Markets', in Richard R. Cornwall and Phanindra V. Wunnava (eds), *New Approaches to Economic and Social Analyses of Discrimination*, New York: Praeger, pp. 113–43.

Cain, Glenn, (1976), 'The challenge of segmented labour market theories to orthodox theory', *Journal of Economic Literature*, **14**, (December), 1215–57.

Dickens, William T. and Kevin Lang (1985), 'A test of dual labour market theory', *American Economic Review*, **75**, (September), 792–805.

Dickens, William T. and Kevin Lang (1988), 'The reemergence of segmented labour market theory', *American Economic Review*, **78**, (May), 129–34.

Dickens, William T. and Kevin Lang (1993), 'Labour Market Segmentation Theory: Reconsidering the Evidence', in William Darity, Jr (ed.), *Labour Economics: Problems in Analyzing Labour Markets*, Boston: Kluwer Academic Publishers, pp. 141–80.

Dunlop, John T. (ed.) 1957, *The Theory of Wage Determination: Proceedings of a Conference Held by the International Economic Association*, New York: Macmillan and Co.

Dunlop, John T. (1966), 'Job Vacancy Measures and Economic Analysis', in *The Measurement and Interpretation of Inflation*, New York: National Bureau of Economic Research.

Friedberg, Rachel, Kevin Lang and William T. Dickens (1988), 'The Changing Structure of the Female Labour Market, 1976–1984', in *Industrial Relations Research Association Series: Proceedings of the Forty-first Annual Meeting*, pp. 117–24.

Gittleman, Maury B. and David R. Howell, (1995), 'Changes in the structure and quality of jobs in the United States: effects by race and gender, 1973–1990', *Industrial and Labour Relations Review*, **48**, (April), 420–40.

Hartmann, Heidi I. (1987), 'Internal Labour Markets and Gender: A Case Study of Promotion', in Clair Brown and Joseph A. Pechman (eds), *Gender in the Workplace*, Washington, DC: The Brookings Institution, pp. 59–105.

Hochschild, Arlie (1983), *The Managed Heart*, Berkeley, California: University of California Press.

Malveaux, Julianne (1985/86), 'Comparable worth and its impact on black women', *Review of Black Political Economy*, **14**, (Fall/Winter), 47–62.

Reich, Michael, David M. Gordon and Richard C. Edwards (1973) 'A theory of labour market segmentation', *American Economic Review*, **63**, (May), 359–65.

Reich, Michael, David M. Gordon and Richard C. Edwards (1982), *Segmented Work, Divided Workers: The Historical Transformation of Labour in the United States*, Cambridge: Cambridge University Press.

US Bureau of the Census (1996), *Data Ferret: Federal Electronic Research and Review Extraction Tool*. Data available on-line from the March 1996 Current Population Survey. http://ferret.bls.census.gov/cgi-bin/ferret.

Labour Markets, Theories of

Labour market theories attempt to explain the processes of employment and wage determination in market societies. While most labour market theories focus on paid labour, some also consider unpaid, domestic labour; some are individualistic while others emphasize social and historical causation; some focus on the characteristics of labour supply while others focus on discrimination; some are microeconomic in their focus while others are macroeconomic in orientations. The main varieties of labour market theory considered here are the standard neoclassical perspective (and its recent 'transactions cost' variant); dual labour market theory; the segmented labour market approach; and relatively new efficiency–wage theories.

Feminist economists have responded to these various labour market theories with concerns about their underlying assumptions, their implicit gender biases, and their applicability to women's experiences. Because feminist economics encompasses a range of philosophical and theoretical orientations, within both feminism and economics, both the degree and type of feminist work done with various labour market theories differs. This entry first considers the general features of labour market theories and then the kinds of feminist arguments that can be made with them. Brief notes on applications of labour market theories to non-Western societies and areas for further research conclude the entry.

Types of theory

Before the 1960s, labour market theory emphasized both the special nature of labour markets and the historical determination of working conditions and relative wages across various industries and occupations. Circumstances at the time when particular occupations or industries emerged, such as the relative availability of various types of labour, were important in the patterns of job classifications and wages that resulted (Dunlop 1979). Workers, meanwhile, were socialized human beings whose job experiences and struggles congealed into habituated expectations, informal work rules and norms of fair treatment governing various classes of workers or jobs. Employers who violated the norms for working conditions, promotions or prevailing wages could encounter costly resistance, making labour markets function quite differently from the markets for most other goods. These older theories are often described as 'institutionalist' (Kaufman 1988).

Neoclassical labour market theory, which displaced institutionalist theories in the 1960s, holds that labour markets are governed by standard microeconomic principles of constrained optimization by individual workers and employers with autonomous (a priori, non-socially determined) tastes and preferences. In effect, labour markets function no differently than the markets for other types of goods (Brown 1988). Wages and employment are determined jointly by the firm's physical capital and position in the goods market (labour demand) and workers' self-investment in human capital, their willingness to sacrifice leisure for wages and market goods, and their preferences for various occupations or working conditions (labour supply). Wages and wage differentials are then taken to fairly reflect workers' actual productivity, where fairness means that wages are equal to marginal revenue product (MRP, or the contribution of the last worker hired to the revenues of the firm). Wage flexibility, or workers' willingness to let wages change with supply or demand, also ensures both market-clearing and the most efficient use of labour if competitive conditions prevail.

The approach does admit some 'unfair' wage differentials, particularly if some individuals possess 'tastes for discrimination', defined as the disutility, or pain, of associating with persons from a disliked group, such as women or blacks. Since discriminating persons will demand compensation to endure such contact, discrimination yields higher costs; competitive goods markets should therefore eliminate it (Becker 1971). Noncompetitive influences like labour unions may also promote unfair wage differentials, as well as unemployment, by restricting either labour supply, or wage flexibility, or both.

In this context, male–female wage differentials are generally viewed as reflections of different market productivities or, in some cases, 'statistical discrimination'. According to the neoclassical 'New Home Economics' of Becker (1981) and Mincer and Polachek (1974), men and women choose to acquire specialized human capital for producing market or domestic goods, respectively. When these goods are exchanged in the family, overall wellbeing increases through comparative advantage principles. Though men's and women's market wages differ as a result, they are still fair, rational and efficient. 'Statistical discrimination' occurs when employers find it costly to predict or monitor the productivity of an individual. They then substitute cheaper experiential knowledge of average group productivities in hiring and wage decisions. Though an individual's wage might be unfair as a result, group wages will be fair on average and cost structures will remain efficient.

Information costs have been generalized in the version of neoclassical theory known as the 'transactions cost' approach (TCA). Incomplete information on individual worker productivity prevents full rationality and maximum efficiency in the use of labour. Limited information leads to 'bounded rationality' and use of 'rules of thumb' and workplace institutions (such as seniority systems and firm-specific job-ladders) that serve as (the most) cost-effective substitutes for elaborate monitoring systems and complete information (Williamson et al. 1975). Such TCA arguments reincorporate some pre-neoclassical, institutionalist positions in labour market theory, but the commitment of TCA theorists to neoclassical economics' basic principles of constrained optimization is weakened only by their admission of incomplete information in firms' decision-making processes. In particular, there is no challenge to standard assumptions of autonomous individual tastes.

TCA has so far considered women mainly in its extensions within the New Home Economics to joint, husband–wife decisions about market and household labour allocations (Pollak 1985). There, incomplete information has been modelled as a problem in game theory, but neoclassical assumptions and results still generally hold (Nelson 1996). The individualistic perspective severely limits any consideration of social norms or power relationships.

Dual labour market theory (DLMT) is the main heir of the 'old' institutionalist labour economics that emphasized the special nature of labour markets and workers' socialization to historical workplace conditions and norms. Closely associated with Michael Piore (Doeringer and Piore 1971), current DLMT also emphasizes the firm-specific nature of many productive skills. The consequent need for on-the-job training by experienced co-workers is commonly satisfied though firm-specific job ladders that ration skill acquisition. Trainers who would otherwise be threatened by competition from newer workers might establish and maintain firm-specific skill monopolies to protect their own status and job security, thus refusing to train new workers, unless clear promotion structures and rules are instituted within the firm.

DLMT posits several aspects of 'duality' in labour markets (Doeringer and Piore 1971). First is a distinction between 'internal' and 'external' labour markets. Only entry-level positions are filled from the external market, while positions on the higher rungs of job ladders are filled by internal promotion. The second duality is a good jobs–bad jobs distinction between the 'primary labour market', where workers have promotion prospects, and the 'secondary labour market', where few skills are needed and, hence, few promotion prospects exist. This duality reflects DLMT's original concern with racial inequality and the lack of access to good, skilled jobs with promotion prospects for many minority groups (Vietoricz and Harrison 1973). The third duality, within the primary labour market, is between production jobs needing mostly on-the-job training and managerial or professional jobs that also involve skills obtainable outside the firm and that are relatively transferable from firm to firm (for example, 'general' skills acquired by formal education). Thus, although both 'tiers' of the primary labour market exhibit internal job ladders, job- and skill-rationing ladders are stronger in 'lower-tier' (blue-collar) primary labour market jobs. The segregated jobs and promotion paths implied by DLMT are hospitable to segregations of workers by race or gender because of immobility between the three labour markets, across job ladders within firms, and among firms. Enduring inequalities in access to occupations, promotions and wages can be established early in the work histories of different groups of workers (according to their entry-level positions at hiring) and more privileged workers will face little competition from disadvantaged groups thereafter.

Segmented labour market theory (SLMT) is similar to DLMT, particularly in the 'dualities' that delineate general job categories and the emphasis on historical evolution in employment relationships. SLMT rests on neo-Marxist views that social divisions reinforce the power and profits of the capitalist class, thereby weakening worker solidarity and depressing wages. How this is manifested is historically specific; under different material (technological) conditions of production, differing 'social structures of accumulation' become entrenched for a time, only to be undermined when new conditions emerge. The tripartite, two-primary-plus-secondary labour market divisions of DLMT are, according to SLMT, characteristic of postwar US labour relations and help explain the strong blue-collar unions of the period. The dominant industrial position of the USA after the war encouraged labour peace, through the acceptance of limited unionism in blue-collar production jobs in the most concentrated and capital-intensive industries, to exploit unusual profit opportunities. These circumstances are now giving way in the face of increasingly globalized goods and labour markets (Gordon et al. 1982).

SLMT views pre-existing social divisions by race and gender as wedges used by the capitalist class to maintain economic hegemony and reduce the extent and/or benefits of unions. Thus occupational segregation may exclude women from many benefits of unionism, for example, while racial divisions might prevent strong unions. SLM theorists generally argue that such divisions reduce all wages, including those of relatively privileged (white, male) workers. The latter are less able to make strong wage demands and have greater fear of job loss, since they must support some of those excluded from high-wage jobs (Gordon et al. 1982).

Efficiency wage theories (EWT) have recently emerged from the neoclassical 'new Keynesian' research agenda in macroeconomics. Troubled by the inability of flexible, market-clearing wages in neoclassical labour economics to explain unemployment, new Keynesians theorize that wage rigidities and above-equilibrium 'efficiency' wages are normal in most labour markets (see Blinder 1989). Although such wages result in unemployment, many workers prefer waiting for a stable, higher status, high-wage job to accepting a low status, low-wage job. Since better wages and working conditions increase worker satisfaction and motivation, employers can benefit from more efficient workers; greater fear of job loss may also raise productivity on the job (Akerlof and Yellen 1990).

Like institutionalist, DLM and SLM theories, efficiency wage theories view labour as different from other goods or resources. Though EWT retains many elements of neoclassical theory, its arguments that flexible, market-clearing wages may not be most efficient and that workers' choices can reflect social 'fairness' norms and status relationships with others both involve nonstandard microeconomic positions. The future development of EWT is uncertain, however. It could strengthen either its ties to TCA (with which it shares concepts of bounded rationality; see Solow 1990) or its institutionalist tendencies and move in the direction of DLMT.

Assessments of feminist potential and/or limitations
All of the labour market theories described above have some potential for feminist applications. Feminist perspectives also differ widely, however; they range from a general interest in women's status, to the 'liberal' view that women should, but do not now, receive the same treatment as men, to more radical views holding that gender inequalities are entrenched in larger social values and arrangements and infect social theories themselves with gender biases. More conservative varieties of feminist economics tend to apply existing neoclassical labour market theories to measure discriminatory labour market outcomes for women, while more radical feminist economists think biased theories help legitimate injustice and call for new kinds of theory.

Neoclassical labour market theories rest on methodological individualism and the standard rational choice framework. This is perhaps clearest in Becker's (1981) view of marriage and the family, which holds that women's low market wages are due to women's free choice of domestic skills and a high return on their domestic labour. Why women would consistently choose domestic labour specializations that result in low market wages is unclear, however. Becker finds it convenient to use biological explanations for different choices by men and women but, strictly speaking, he needs no explanation, since tastes are autonomous, 'primary data' in the theory. Only fairly conservative versions of feminist economics are fully consistent with neoclassical labour market theory, since it treats discrimination as a matter of personal taste rather than a systemic problem. Many feminist economists find these positions unacceptable but continue to use human capital arguments despite their reservations, especially in statistical estimates of discrimination in male–female wage differentials. (Figart (1997) offers an excellent summary of these issues.)

Most feminists question the autonomous tastes and free choices of strict methodological individualism; they emphasize the role of social gender-conditioning in the acquisition of skills and goals. Women tend to acquire the skills that society encourages them to have and may be discouraged from acquiring 'masculine' skills that are more highly valued in markets. Labour markets may reward women's traits at lower rates than men's, may fail to reward less traditional skills when women do acquire them and/or may exclude women from many opportunities open to men (Ferber and Green 1991). Wages may be below women's actual productivity or their productivity may be reduced by 'crowding' into a small range of occupations (Bergmann 1974). Then, however, the neoclassical view that markets are fair when wages are equal to marginal revenue product (MRP) may come into doubt.

Inquiries into the social origins of tastes and choices encourage more historical approaches to labour markets processes, such as those of DLMT. DLMT explicitly recognizes both fairness concepts and wages as social and historical products. Since good jobs and skills are rationed to reduce threats to current workers and trainers, 'fairness' may reflect the interests and prerogatives of incumbents over new groups of workers in labour markets. These views can be applied to gender (and race) concerns. If blue-collar 'trainers' (or professional/managerial 'mentors') feel threatened by more equal treatment of women (or minorities), attempts to train or promote them could meet resistance in many occupations. Occupational segregation and crowding by gender (or race) then remain convenient bases for discriminatory male–female (or black–white) wage differentials (Blau and Jusenius 1976). Job structures that ration opportunities also cause underemployment for many (perhaps most) workers (Brown 1988).

Quite radical arguments can also be made with DLMT, once it is recognized that DLMT does not require any theoretical link between wages and 'measurable' individual productivity or potential. Administered wages that ensure workplace cooperation by sustaining divisions among workers may simply devalue the work of less privileged groups through low wages. Such thinking supports demands for comparable worth policies to reassess the skills and contributions of men's and women's work and realign their wages across different occupations (Acker 1989). Since 'fairness' is understood as a fully historical, socially produced concept with no universal meaning, DLMT can also support the view that both fairness and productivity concepts in theory may themselves reinforce traditional inequalities. The neoclassical view that fair wages are equal to MRP may be only a theoretical assertion that what is, is fair. If, for example, the value a worker adds to a firm's revenues reflects what the worker's wage adds to the price of the product, higher wages can imply both higher output prices and a higher MRP. Since wages are the only observable indicator of MRP, 'wages = MRP' becomes a circular argument justifying prevailing wages linked to gender (or other) hierarchies, while it reproduces job structures that restrict workers' potential.

SLMT also rejects neoclassical productivity theory and has been openly receptive to discussions of gender (and racial) inequality in paid labour markets; such divisions are thought to weaken working class resistance to capitalist authority and profits. The SLMT framework has generated many empirical and historical studies of unionism, occupational segregation, unemployment patterns, and wage differentials by gender and race (Rubery 1978; Albelda 1985). Some feminists have objected to the approach's apparent subordination of gender and race relations to the logic of class relations, however.

SLMT's somewhat monolithic view of working class interests seems to represent the perspective of those workers least affected by racial and gender disadvantages as that of all workers (Power 1984), while its Marxist concern with the 'sphere of production' may reproduce broader historical tendencies to define domestic labour as 'unproductive' (Folbre 1991, 1993). Others have disputed whether social divisions hurt relatively privileged workers. Hartmann (1981) argues that working class men derive a surplus from women's responsibility for unpaid domestic labour, thus benefiting from working class gender divisions (though her work has been similarly criticized for inattention to racial divisions among women; see Joseph 1981). Williams (1991), using a somewhat different Marxist perspective, also argues that reduced competition from excluded groups of workers strengthens the hold of privileged groups on the best jobs. Efforts are underway to make SLMT more inclusive (for example, Albelda and Tilly 1994). The explicit discussions of race and gender divisions by SLM theorists also remain important and unusual in labour market theory.

The feminist potential of new Keynesian EWT has not yet received much attention (Nelson 1996). Though the acceptance of social influences on 'fairness' norms and individual preference formation seems promising, its discussions of social influences so far include mainly bounded rationality principles and productivity gains from respecting workers' status concerns. Thus EWT, like TCA interpretations of neoclassical labour market theory, presently does not advance feminist concerns with discrimination. If new

Keynesian reinterpretations of microeconomics eventually prove more dramatic, however, something closer to the feminist potential of DLMT could result. The outcome may be influenced by future uses of EWT by feminists.

The macroeconomic inspiration for EWT also suggests another reason for feminist interest in it. Neoclassical microeconomics admits no significant role for money (apart from reducing 'friction' in market mechanisms); it is essentially a 'barter' approach. Only by virtue of this can Becker extend human capital arguments to the unpaid domestic labour of women. If money were recognized as an essential part of market transactions, however, distinctions between paid and unpaid labour would be less easily dismissed and social relations within the family might not be so readily deemed 'fair' and 'rational'. That men receive payment for work in the form of general purchasing power (money), while women's unpaid labour yields specific, in-kind rewards, may imply significant social asymmetries in the opportunities of women and men that standard, microeconomics-based theories simply cannot consider (Jennings 1994). Since it is mainly within macroeconomics that the importance of money is discussed, the macroeconomic origins of EWT may be important. The gender significance of money might become a pivot point for further developments in both feminist macroeconomics and in interpreting the social devaluation of women's unpaid labour.

Issues for non-Western societies
The varieties of labour market theories described here were all developed within the English-speaking world. Neoclassical theories are usually understood as universally applicable and in need of little modification for non-Western or less-developed country cases. Their barter assumptions are particularly important for universal applicability, since only then can the lack of formal markets or the importance of subsistence economic relationships in many countries be ignored. Feminists have been among the strongest challengers to such universalism and have argued that, since so many of (especially) women's economic activities in poorer countries are not organized through formal markets, neoclassical labour market theories and development policies are particularly inappropriate to them and particularly damaging to women's economic fortunes (Benería and Feldman 1992; Waring 1988).

DLMT and SLMT have always affirmed that their respective accounts are historically and socially specific; thus they require further studies to describe the particular labour arrangements and conditions of non-Western and less-developed countries. Most of these studies have been undertaken by development economists (see Benería 1995). They are not described here because, although even Western cases are historically specific, 'special cases' in both perspectives, non-Western cases have still been somewhat underprivileged in their theoretical elaborations of labour market processes.

Areas for further research

There is no shortage of opportunities for further research in feminist labour economics. Only a few important areas where additional work is needed can be noted here. First, feminists with neoclassical allegiances still need to resolve inconsistencies between individualistic neoclassical assumptions and basic feminist views of social conditioning and power in gender relations and discrimination. The greatest potential for doing so may well lie in future feminist developments of EWT. The implied macroeconomic reorientation might also assist work in a second area, concerned with how monetized (paid) and nonmonetized (unpaid) economic relationships are socially linked. Recognition of the social importance of differences in forms of payment may, in turn, help illuminate a third area for further work, on cultural differences in labour relationships and labour concerns in developing countries as well as in the transitional economies of Eastern Europe.

A fourth area of concern is greater attention to institutional factors and sociopolitical context in econometric studies of male–female (or white–nonwhite) wage differentials. Without such attention, discrimination may appear only as a coefficient on a dummy variable or an inference from unexplained residuals in a regression equation, leaving open the possibility that discrimination estimates are merely incorrect inferences from poorly specified models or data. This also implies a fifth area of need, for more inductive, historical case studies to explore how political power and strategic decision making have influenced the evolution of job structures in the workplace and reflect prevailing gender and racial hierarchies in society. Though histories of job structures will vary across firms, they should still exhibit larger social patterns susceptible to theoretical development by methods such as pattern modelling (see Diesing 1971; Wilbur and Harrison 1978). Sixth, additional work is needed on relationships among race, gender and class divisions in society. Studies focused on only one dimension of inequality, such as gender or class, can marginalize other dimensions and may reproduce social biases if the divisions are integral to one another (see Glenn 1996).

Finally, the use of market metaphors to describe labour relationships in society also needs critical study (Galbraith 1997, Nelson 1996). 'Old' institutionalist labour economists regularly questioned the use of market metaphors (Dunlop 1984), while current DLMT and SLMT both suggest that closely associated 'productivity', 'efficiency', 'competition' and 'fairness' concepts may only justify, rather than illuminate, existing labour processes, outcomes and inequalities. Socially pervasive market metaphors (and market rhetoric) may limit how relationships in labour processes are understood and thereby help to recreate the discriminatory processes that feminists wish to challenge.

ANN JENNINGS

See also

Discrimination, Theories of; Dualisms; Human Capital Theory; Institutional Economics; Labour Market Segmentation; Marxist Political Economics; Neoclassical Economics; Occupational Segregation.

Bibliography

Acker, Joan (1989), *Doing Comparable Worth*, Philadelphia: Temple University Press.

Akerlof, George and Janet Yellen (1990), 'The fair wage-effort hypothesis and unemployment', *Quarterly Journal of Economics*, **105** (2), 255–83.

Albelda, Randy (1985), 'Nice work if you can get it', *Review of Radical Political Economics*, **17** (3), 72–85.

Albelda, Randy and Chris Tilly (1994), 'Towards a Broader Vision: Race, Gender, and Labor Market Segmentation in the Social Structures of Accumulation Framework', in David Kotz, Terrence McDonough and Michael Reich (eds), *The Political Economy of Growth and Crisis*, Cambridge: Cambridge University Press, pp. 212–30.

Becker, Gary (1971), *The Economics of Discrimination*, 2nd ed., Chicago: University of Chicago Press.

Becker, Gary (1981), *A Treatise on the Family*, Cambridge, Massachusetts: Harvard University Press.

Benería, Lourdes (1995), 'Toward a greater integration of gender in economics', *World Development*, **23** (11), 1839–50.

Benería, Lourdes and Shelley Feldman (1992), *Unequal Burden: Economic Crisis, Persistent Poverty, and Women's Work*, Boulder: Westview Press.

Bergmann, Barbara (1974), 'Occupational segregation, wages and profits when employers discriminate by race or sex', *Eastern Economic Journal*, **1** (April–July), 103–10.

Blau, Francine and Carol Jusenius (1976), 'Economists' approaches to sex segregation in the labor market', *Signs*, **1** (Spring), 181-9.

Blinder, Alan (1989), *Macroeconomics Under Debate*, New York: Harvester Wheatsheaf.

Brown, Clair (1988), 'Income Distribution in an Institutional World', in Garth Mangum and Peter Philips (eds), *Three Worlds of Labor Economics*, Armonk, New York: M.E. Sharpe, pp. 51–63.

Diesing, Paul (1971), *Patterns of Discovery in the Social Sciences*, New York: Aldine.

Doeringer, Peter and Michael Piore (1971), *Internal Labor Markets and Manpower Analysis*, Lexington, Massachusetts: D.C. Heath.

Dunlop, John (1979), 'Wage Contours', in Michael Piore (ed.), *Unemployment and Inflation*, White Plains, New York: M.E. Sharpe, pp. 63–74.

Dunlop, John (1984), 'Industrial relations and economics', *IRRA 37th Annual Proceedings*, 9–23.

Ferber, Marianne and Carol Green (1991), 'Occupational Segregation and the Earnings Gap', in Emily Hoffman (ed.), *Essays on the Economics of Discrimination*, Kalamazoo: W.E. Upjohn Institute, pp. 145–65.

Figart, Deborah (1997), 'Gender as more than a dummy variable', *Review of Social Economy*, **55** (1), 1–32.

Folbre, Nancy (1991), 'The unproductive housewife', *Signs*, **16** (3), 463–84.

Folbre, Nancy (1993), 'Socialism, Feminist and Scientific', in Marianne Ferber and Julie Nelson (eds), *Beyond Economic Man*, Chicago: University of Chicago Press, pp. 94–110.

Galbraith, James (1997), 'Dangerous Metaphor: The Fiction of the Labor Market', Public Policy Brief no. 36, Annandale-on-Hudson, New York: Jerome Levy Economics Institute.

Glenn, Evelyn Nakano (1996), 'From Servitude to Service Work', in Cameron Lynne Macdonald and Carmen Sirianni (eds), *Working in the Service Society*, Philadelphia: Temple University Press.

Gordon, David, Richard Edwards and Michael Reich (1982), *Segmented Work, Divided Workers*, Cambridge: Cambridge University Press.

Hartmann, Heidi (1981), 'The Unhappy Marriage of Marxism and Feminism', in Lydia Sargent (ed.), *Women and Revolution*, Boston: South End Press, pp. 1–41.

Jennings, Ann (1994), 'Towards a feminist expansion of macroeconomics', *Journal of Economic Issues*, **28** (3), 555–65.

Joseph, Gloria (1981), 'Incompatible Ménage à Trois: Marxism, Feminism, and Racism', in Lydia Sargent (ed.), *Women and Revolution*, Boston: South End Press, pp. 91–107.

Kaufman, Bruce (1988), *How Labor Markets Work*, Lexington, Massachusetts: D.C. Heath.

Mincer, Jacob and Solomon Polachek (1974), 'Family investments in human capital', *Journal of Political Economy*, **82** (March–April, Suppl.), S76–S108.

Nelson, Julie (1996), *Feminism, Objectivity, and Economics*, New York: Routledge.

Pollak, Robert (1985), 'A transactions cost approach to families and households', *Journal of Economic Literature*, **23**, 581–608.

Power, Marilyn (1984), 'Unity and division among women', *Economic Forum*, **15** (Summer), 39–62.

Rubery, Jill (1978), 'Structured labour markets, worker organization, and low pay', *Cambridge Journal of Economics*, **2** (March), 14–36.

Solow, Robert (1990), *The Labor Market as a Social Institution*, Cambridge, Massachusetts: Basil Blackwell.

Vietoricz, Thomas and Bennett Harrison (1973), 'Labor market segmentation', *American Economic Review*, **63** (May), 366–76.

Waring, Marilyn (1988), *If Women Counted*, New York: Harper & Row.

Wilbur, Charles and Robert Harrison (1978), 'The methodological basis of institutional economics', *Journal of Economic Issues*, **12** (1), 61–90.

Williams, Rhonda (1991), 'Competition, Discrimination, and Differential Wage Rates', in Richard Cornwall and Phanindra Wunnava (eds), *New Approaches to Economic and Social Analysis of Discrimination*, New York: Praeger, pp. 65–92.

Williamson, Oliver, Michael Wachter and Jeffrey Harris (1975), 'Understanding the employment relation', *Bell Journal of Economics*, (Spring), 250–78.

Macroeconomics

Macroeconomics is defined as the study of whole economic systems, with particular emphasis on general levels of total production, employment and the general price level and on the interrelations among sectors of the economy. Typically, macroeconomic theories have either explored the long-term growth of an economy's total production or the short-run fluctuations in that production as well as in employment and the general price level. This entry will explore those orthodox macroeconomic theories concerned with short-run economic fluctuations in production or output, employment and prices in developed economies. The reader is directed to 'Growth Theory (Macro Models)' for a discussion of theories concerned with the long-term growth in an economy, to the various schools of thought for discussion of heterodox macroeconomic models, and to entries related to developing nations for macroeconomic analyses of economic development.

Macroeconomic theory's focus on the levels of aggregate output, employment and prices reflects many nations' macroeconomic goals of steady growth in total production, full employment of the labour force, and stable prices across the economy. Consequently, macroeconomic theory is intimately connected with macroeconomic stabilization policies for limiting economic fluctuations, maintaining full employment and controlling changes in the overall price level. Thus discussions of macroeconomic theories and policies are often intertwined.

Most economists agree that modern macroeconomic thought began with John Maynard Keynes. In *The General Theory of Employment, Interest and Money* (1936), Keynes sought to explain the Great Depression then affecting capitalist market economies, a situation that existing classical theory could not adequately explain. He argued that short-term economic fluctuations were the result of market failures in labour and goods markets; these failures in turn led to insufficient aggregate demand, which then prevented a capitalist market economy from achieving full employment. To correct this situation, Keynes recommended government intervention in the economy.

Publication of Keynes's *General Theory* initiated the Keynesian revolution, perhaps the most significant development in twentieth-century macroeconomics. Since 1936, most macroeconomic theorists have either elaborated on Keynes's basic model, as in the IS–LM and new Keynesian traditions, or they have challenged its underlying assumptions, as in the monetarist, new classical, and real business cycle traditions. More specifically, the critics of Keynesian macroeconomics share the belief that the economy will self-correct in the long run as a result of relative prices adjusting to equate supply and demand in efficient and unfettered markets where economic agents engage in rational economic behaviour. Keynesians believe that 'understanding economic fluctuations requires ... appreciating the possibility of market failure on a grand scale' (Mankiw 1990, p. 1654). Consequently, Keynesians see the potential need for activist government macroeconomic policies to a much greater extent than do critics of Keynesianism. In addition, a key element for understanding what type of stabilization policies are recommended by the various macroeconomic traditions is the role money is said to play within each tradition.

Since macroeconomics purports to describe and analyse political economies and because macroeconomic stabilization policies have considerable impact on a nation's citizens, it is crucial that feminist economists understand, critique and reconstruct orthodox macroeconomic theory and policy. While feminist economic critiques of macroeconomic theories and policies in the context of developing nations began prior to the 1990s, feminist economists have only recently begun to examine those macroeconomic theories and policies pertaining to capitalist market economies. As discussed below, much of this work relates to critiquing specific aspects of these macroeconomic models and their attendant methodology and to identifying the gender biases in stabilization policies. Some feminist economists have gone beyond these critiques and attempted to reconstruct what constitutes the macroeconomy. While these efforts have largely been ignored by most of the economics profession, they do offer ideas for a feminist reconstruction of macroeconomics.

Prior to the 1990s, feminist macroeconomists concentrated on critiques of gross national and domestic products (GNP/GDP), which are the most frequently used measures of a country's total production output, and on macroeconomic policies for developing nations. In her scathing indictment of the gendered assumptions and policies related to national income accounting, Waring (1988) provided probably the best known feminist critique and reconstruction of national income and product accounts, such as GNP/GDP, which constitute the majority of macroeconomic statistics. As other feminist economists have also discussed (Goldschmidt-Clermont 1982; Elson 1991; Benería 1992), Waring explored the ramifications of these gendered assumptions for the effectiveness of development aid and structural adjustment policies.

Many feminist economists have criticized the microeconomic foundations of contemporary macroeconomic models. The underlying assumption that economic agents' behaviour can be reduced to the autonomous, rational 'economic man', combined with the exclusion of nonmarket activities from macroeconomic models, has been particularly criticized for generating inaccurate and incomplete descriptions of whole economic systems. As Nancy Folbre has argued, economic actors 'are not perfectly rational utility maximizers, but they are purposeful agents who make decisions to buy, to sell, and to engage in various social activities' influenced by both efficiency considerations and 'the social construction of individual preferences and cultural norms' (Folbre 1994, p. 39), which often lead to conflicting identities and interests. Other feminist economists, such as Nelson (1993) and Jennings (1993), also argue that individual decision making is socially and culturally determined and is motivated by concerns other than self-interest.

When this recognition of the complexity of human behaviour is combined with a definition of the economy broader than currently found in most macro-economic models, then economists can better understand how an economy develops. According to Folbre:

> The economy is much bigger than the sum of private and public enterprise, the goods and services currently valued in monetary terms. The current vocabulary of macroeconomics systematically distorts perceptions of current trends ... [because it excludes] (t)ime spent in family labor, investments in human capital through child care and education, depletion of natural resources, and degradation of the environment. (Folbre 1994, p. 253)

Thus as Nelson (1993, 1996) and Jennings (1993) argue, the economy must be studied in terms of provisioning to meet human needs rather than scarcity combined with unlimited wants. This disciplinary focus could, in turn, 'delin-eate a subject matter without using sexist assumptions about what is and is not important' (Nelson 1995, p. 142) by incorporating market and nonmarket activities and complex human behaviour into the analysis. In addition, this focus might further challenge the economic profession's preference for effi-ciency arguments thereby shifting macroeconomic theoretical analysis and policy toward equity and fairness considerations.

Feminist economists have also critiqued macroeconomic theoretical mod-els for their formal mathematical nature. Nelson, for example, challenges the method underlying the New Classical macroeconomic model, arguing that it makes sense 'only if one accepts that economies are essentially abstract Walrasian auctions; that all theory must conform to the formal dictates of such a model; and that all empirical knowledge about the economy must come via formal tests of hypotheses rigorously derived from such a model' (Nelson 1996, p. 121). However, such a limited method may well lead to 'rigidity ..., empty, out-of-touch exercises in pointless deduction' that 'serve inhuman ends' (Nelson 1995, p. 139). Instead, Nelson agrees with Myra Strober that the 'increased use of the technique of "hobnobbing with one's data"' is necessary if economic models and methods are to analyse actual economic problems (Nelson 1995, p. 140).

These feminist economic critiques have led to ideas as to how macroeco-nomic models and methods might be revised. The summer 1997 'Explorations' section in *Feminist Economics*, for example, examines how greater use of

qualitative methods as a complement to quantitative data helps feminist economists uncover and correct biases in survey data and expand the range of
topics and theories. Gunseli Berik discusses how national surveys and data
collection methods undercount women's economic activity, especially in developing nations. These methods not only limit the scope of macroeconomic
models but also have important implications for the analysis of effective
macroeconomic policies (Berik 1997). Irene van Staveren also notes the
problems for both theory and policy and advocates using focus groups as a
method

> necessary to bring economics back to economic agents of flesh and blood, women
> and men. Such approaches both broaden economics by embedding it in a social
> and life-historical context, and deepen it by replacing standard assumptions of
> economic behavior with concepts and interpretations arising from a selection
> from the researched group itself. (van Staveren 1997, p. 132)

While promising, the possibilities for creating feminist macroeconomic methods as well as the ramifications for reassessing macroeconomic models and
for analysing macro policies are still only beginning to be recognized.

The opportunities for restructuring macroeconomic models are also being
explored. Feminist economists are employing insights and critiques of existing models to reconstruct them. For example, in 'Toward a Feminist Expansion
of Macroeconomics' (1994), Jennings criticizes the pecuniary logic of orthodox macroeconomic models. Specifically, she challenges both the assumption
that money's primary economic function is as a medium of exchange (which
serves to reduce the economy to a barter system) and the monetarist assumption that money is simply a veil over real productive activity. Instead, she
argues, in capitalism, money, not real production, is what matters. Because
'money's social primacy, then, requires the social legitimacy of accumulation
and of property relationships linked to money profits' (Jennings 1994, p. 557),
'pursuits that yield monetary gain appear as social contributions' while those,
such as women's traditional domestic activities, are not viewed as productive,
thereby reinforcing existing gender hierarchies (p. 558), a point also argued
by Waring and other critics of GNP/GDP statistics.

Jennings then proposes 'a feminist agenda for macroeconomics' that uti-
lizes a monetary theory of production and addresses three issues. First, theorists
must be cognizant of 'the gender dimensions of contemporary social belief
and practice' when developing the behavioural assumptions for their macroeconomic models' (Jennings 1994, p. 561). Second, 'nonmarket exchanges
within the family must be examined as aspects of pecuniary logic', and
because money is a social prerogative, 'the absence of equal access to money
should be afforded larger theoretical consideration' (pp. 560–61). Finally,
because contemporary macroeconomic stabilization policies 'serve the reign-

ing economic interests', leading to 'both existing government and families/consumers hav(ing) been assigned roles in service to the existing configuration of gendered, raced, and classed profit interests', the gender, race and class dimensions of such policies must be considered (pp. 562–3).

Another approach taken by several feminist economists is abandoning existing macroeconomic models in favour of alternative models more consistent with feminist concerns. For example, futurist economist Hazel Henderson has constructed a macroeconomic model that includes non-monetized, productive work and an economy's natural resource base, as well as the traditional output of GNP, to account for more economic activity and the interaction between human action and the natural world. Her model of the economy is presented as a picture of a layer cake with the official market economy, all cash transactions, as the top half of the cake. This layer not only includes private sector production resting on public sector production of such things as government, infrastructure and formal education as measured in GNP, but also underground activities in which cash is exchanged. This layer is atop a non-monetized but productive bottom half of the cake which consists of a social cooperative counter-economy including sweat equity, unpaid family and community work, volunteering, home-based production for use, and subsistence agriculture. The two layers then rest upon nature's layer, our natural resource base, that also absorbs and recycles if tolerances are not exceeded (Henderson 1978, 1988, 1991).

Finnish feminist economist, Hilka Pietila, offers another variant of a broader model of the economy, postulating that the household is the core of human economies and that it interfaces with nature/ecology. Only recently in human history has an industrialized, monetized, and commercialized economy developed as a third aspect of human economies. Her theory of a national economy is pictured as concentric circles. The centre circle, most critical for human welfare, is 'the free economy' which is non-monetary, 'unpaid work for one's own and family needs, community activities, mutual help and cooperation' (Pietila 1996, p. 10). Surrounding this the next concentric circle, 'the protected sector', contains production that is protected and guided by official means for domestic markets in food, construction, services, administration, health, schools and culture. Finally, the fettered economy forms the outermost circle. In this sector manufactured goods are produced for export and to compete with imports. The fettered economy is characterized by large-scale competition, and with terms dictated by world markets, and its activities form the bulk of official GNP measurements. In addition, Pietila has begun to collect data based on this model for the economy of Finland. Her preliminary figures for the 1990 Finnish economy indicate that 48 per cent of people's time and 38 per cent of their money was spent on the free economy; 40 per cent of their time and 50 per cent of their money was spent on the protected sector; and only 12 per cent of their time and 13 per cent of their money was spent on the fettered economy (Pietila 1996, p. 10). Thus, by her definitions and estimates, much of GNP, which focuses on the fettered economy, measures only a very small part of a human economy.

The work of Jennings, Henderson and Pietila suggest possible directions for reconstructing macroeconomic theory from a feminist economic perspective; yet much work remains to be done. First, feminist economic challenges to the basic assumptions underlying macroeconomic models must be assessed. Feminist economists not only need to consider how more complex ideas about human behaviour might affect the models but also whether these assumptions about, for example, rational economic man, are actually linchpins for existing models. Therefore rather than simply adding-and-stirring women into existing models, feminist economists might re-vision the macroeconomy, developing models that more accurately represent the complexity of human behaviour within the complete sphere of economic activity.

Second, future feminist economic research must improve and expand existing macroeconomic data if nonmarket economic activity is to be captured. Changing existing data collection and methods is crucial not only for better evaluation of current macroeconomic models but, more importantly, for more complete accounting of a nation's total economic activity. Thus incorporating alternative methods, such as fieldwork, focus groups and oral histories, may offer further insights as to the economic activities performed by people as well as to what constitutes economic activity itself.

Revising macroeconomic models and providing better economic research would not only have implications for macroeconomic theory, but also for the analyses of macroeconomic policy, the final area in which future macroeconomic work by feminist economists must occur. As Jennings suggests, feminist economists must address how existing gender, race and class hierarchies affect and are affected by macroeconomic stabilization policy, particularly in developed nations where little of this work has been done. Another direction for feminist economists would be to examine how effectively macroeconomic policies achieve economic goals other than efficiency, particularly those related to human interaction with the environment, to economic justice and equity, and to social reproduction such as the raising of children. Only by broadening what constitutes macroeconomic activity and legitimate economic goals will feminist economists be able to fully assess the adequacy of macroeconomic theory and policy.

APRIL LASKEY AERNI AND MARGARET LEWIS

See also

Development Policies; Development, Theories of; Gross Domestic Product; Globalization; Growth Theory (Macro Models); Post Keynesian Economics; Structural Adjustment Policies; Unemployment and Underemployment.

Bibliography

Benería, Lourdes (1992), 'Accounting for women's work: the progress of two decades', *World Development*, **20** (11), 1547–60.

Berik, Genseli (1997), 'The need for crossing the method boundaries in economics research', *Feminist Economics*, **3** (2), (Summer), 121–5.

Elson, Diane (1991), 'Male Bias in Macroeconomics: The case of structural adjustment', in *Male Bias in the Development Process*, Manchester: Manchester University Press.

Folbre, Nancy (1994), *Who Pays for the Kids?*, New York: Routledge.

Folbre, Nancy and the Center for Popular Economics (1995), *The New Field Guide to the U.S. Economy*, New York: The New Press.

Goldschmidt-Clermont, Luisella (1982), *Unpaid Work in the Household*, Geneva: International Labour Office.

Henderson, Hazel (1978), *Creating Alternative Futures: The End of Economics*, New York: Putnam & Sons.

Henderson, Hazel (1988), *The Politics of the Solar Age: Alternatives to Economics*, Indianapolis, Indiana: Knowledge Systems Inc.

Henderson, Hazel (1991), *Paradigms in Progress: Life beyond Economics*, Indianapolis, Indiana: Knowledge Systems Inc.

Jennings, Ann (1993), 'Public or Private? Institutional Economics and Feminism', in Marianne Ferber and Julie Nelson (eds), *Beyond Economic Man: Feminist Theory and Economics*, Chicago: University of Chicago Press, pp. 111–29.

Jennings, Ann (1994), 'Towards a feminist expansion of macroeconomics: money matters', *Journal of Economic Issues*, **2**, (June), 555–65.

Keynes, John Maynard (1936), *The General Theory of Employment, Interest and Money*, New York: Harcourt Brace Jovanovich.

Levin, Lee (1995), 'Toward a Feminist, Post-Keynesian Theory of Investment', in Edith Kuiper and Jolande Sap, *Out of the Margin: Feminist Perspectives on Economics*, New York: Routledge, pp. 100–119.

Mankiw, N. Gregory (1990), 'A quick refresher course in macroeconomics', *Journal of Economic Literature*, **XXVIII** (4), (December), 1645–60.

Nelson, Julie (1993), 'The Study of Choice or the Study of Provisioning? Gender and the Definition of Economics', in Marianne Ferber and Julie Nelson (eds), *Beyond Economic Man: Feminist Theory and Economics*, Chicago: University of Chicago Press, pp. 23–36.

Nelson, Julie (1995), 'Feminism and economics', *Journal of Economic Perspectives*, **9**, (Spring), 131–48.

Nelson, Julie (1996), *Feminism, Objectivity and Economics*, See especially Chapter 8 'Feminist Economics, Empirical Economics, and Macroeconomics', New York: Routledge.

Pietila, Hilka (1996), 'The Triangle of the Human Economy: Household, Cultivation, Industrial Production: An Attempt at Making Visible the Human Economy in Toto', presented at the IAFFE Summer Conference, June 21–23, Washington, DC. Another version of this paper is in *Ecological Economics Special Issue*, **20**, (February), 1997, 113–28.

van Staveren, Irene (1997), 'Focus groups: Contributing to a gender-aware methodology', *Feminist Economics*, **3** (2), (Summer), 131–5.

Waring, Marilyn (1988), *If Women Counted: A New Feminist Economics*, San Francisco: Harper & Row.

World Development, Special Issue, Gender, Adjustment and Macroeconomics (1995), **23**, (November).

Marriage, Theories of

Economists who perform empirical studies on labour supply, consumption and a few other topics typically take account of marital status. However, most economists, including many feminist economists, do not give much weight to economic theories that analyse how decisions are made in marriage and how marriages are formed. The lack of attention economists pay to marriage theories is puzzling given the importance of the institution of marriage. Most families in the world include a married couple (ignoring legal distinctions between formal marriage and common-law marriage). Thus it is strange that economists tend to be much more interested in firms and governments, the other two major institutions that regulate and govern processes of production, allocation of resources and distribution. This entry discusses possible reasons why economists have paid relatively little attention to marriage and then reviews existing economic theories of marriage. The review is organized by school of economic thought, and while it starts with the oldest schools (Marxist and institutional economics), the entry's emphasis is on more recent work, especially theories following various neoclassical traditions. The theories reviewed deal either with marriage formation and dissolution or with intra-marriage allocation of resources.

Economic theories dealing with firms and their economic environment have attracted much more talent and attention than theories of marriage. The under-emphasis on theories of marriage is one aspect of the asymmetric treatment of families and firms by social scientists, whereby research on marriage is allocated mostly to sociology, and research on firms is allocated mostly to economics and business. This division of labour among the disciplines is in part the result of a dualism that encourages economists to study decisions with a monetary dimension. Also, those who traditionally study marriage and family (mostly sociologists and psychologists) lack interest in economic theory. In turn, this intellectual division of labour may be related to the traditionally high ratio of men to women in economics, an earlier trend to establish predominantly female home economics departments, and a tendency in Western societies to give higher status to activities predominantly performed by men than to activities predominantly performed by women. Most early economic theories have ignored issues of intra-marriage allocation of resources and distribution of consumption and wellbeing inside the household.

Marxist economists provided the first theory of production in marriage. Ever since Friedrich Engels published his *Origins of the Family, Private Property, and the State* more than a hundred years ago, Marxist economists have recognized that much production occurs within families and that women play an important economic role in this production. Early Marxists such as

Engels also dealt with the economics of marriage formation when they emphasized the impact of property structures on marriage and family. Marxist feminist economists including Hartmann (1976, 1981), Himmelweit and Mohun (1977) and Folbre (1982) have criticized these earlier Marxist models for the legitimization they offered to the traditional division of labour in the home, their focus on women's reproductive role, and some of the coercive mechanisms behind traditional gender roles.

A number of early institutionalist economists wrote on women's economic dependence on the institution of marriage. This includes Thorstein Veblen (see Waller and Jennings 1990; Jennings 1994) and Charlotte Perkins Gilman (see Folbre and Hartmann 1988). Pujol (1992) noted the similarity between Gilman's position on women's economic dependence on marriage and that of John Stuart Mill and Harriet Taylor. But mainstream economists mostly ignored this analysis of household production and family formation until recently.

In the 1960s mainstream economists began to pay serious attention to household decisions, when Mincer's (1962, 1963) and Becker's (1965) pioneering work in new home economics (NHE) imported quantitative methodologies developed in business economics to analyse household decision making. While early research in NHE recognized the separate contributions of family members to production in marriage, it failed to address the issue of distribution and consumption inside the household and marriage. The assumption of a single household utility function found explicitly in Becker (1965) and implicitly in Mincer has been criticized by many, including feminist economists Ferber and Birnbaum (1977) and bargaining theorists Manser and Brown (1980).

An early and influential alternative to the household utility models is found in Becker's (1973) theory of marriage formation (also in Becker 1992). This theory derives from a neoclassical framework and assumes rational choice. It also contains a market theory of marriage, which assumes voluntary exchange and the existence of marriage-related markets. Becker also assumes that some gains from marriage are based on a division of labour between men and women and, in some of his models, that men work outside the home while women specialize in household production. This assumption of a traditional division of labour is not, however, central to Becker's theory of marriage.

In his theory of marriage Becker also argued that laws such as a prohibition on polygamy have an impact on marriage rates and consumption of men and women in marriage. Assuming competitive marriage markets operating without restrictions, Becker concluded that a higher demand for marriage by men implies a higher market value to women participating in marriage markets in a polygamous regime than in a monogamous regime. Bergmann (1995) has criticized Becker's theory of marriage and polygamy by pointing out that in reality women living in polygamous societies do not appear to be better off than women living under monogamy. Becker's theory can be reconciled with observations about the difficult life of women living in polygamous regimes by recognizing that marriage markets do not operate freely. Instead, women may be coerced to marry even when they are not capturing their value in marriage markets (see Guttentag and Secord 1983; Grossbard-Shechtman 1993).

Becker's adoption of individual utility maximization by marriage-bound men and women did not lead him to totally reject the assumption of household utility maximization with respect to all household-related decisions. Becker (1976) proposed altruism within the household as a justification for models that assume a combined household utility function. His use of examples of male altruists and female egoists contributed to further critiques of Becker by feminist economists, including Bergmann (1995). Feminist antagonism to Becker's assumptions of household utility and male altruism help explain the lack of interest that feminist economists have expressed in all of Becker's theories, including his economic theories of marriage (see Woolley 1996).

Grossbard-Shechtman's (1984, 1993) theory of marriage follows Becker (1973) in assuming rationality and marriage market effects when modelling individual choice of marriage, consumption and work. Central to this theory is the concept of work performed for the benefit of a spouse. Grossbard (1976) recognizes that married women are often in a situation similar to that of domestic workers working for an employer, especially in poor countries. Grossbard-Shechtman (1993) includes discussions of power in marriage and of many institutional factors which influence allocation in marriage and marriage formation (see also Grossbard-Shechtman and Neuman 1998).

One of the advantages of Grossbard-Shechtman's market theory of marriage lies in its ties to conventional labour supply theory. If work is viewed as an unpleasant activity that ultimately adds to consumption opportunities, fluctuations in women's opportunities to make a living as workers for a husband will affect their willingness to participate in the labour force (Grossbard-Shechtman 1984; Grossbard-Shechtman and Granger 1998). This view of work and marriage as substitute forms of income has been criticized by Strober (1995). In particular, Strober questions the absence of educational attainment and non-traditional relationships as other choices women may prefer over traditional marriage or work.

Heer and Grossbard-Shechtman (1981) have applied a market theory of marriage to hypothesize that unfavourable marriage market conditions may motivate women to organize themselves collectively to improve their legal rights. This argument is compatible with the view of men and women as engaged in a gender war presented by Folbre (1994), who has argued that patriarchal norms and capitalist control over the labour process contributed to early feminist movements to improve women's economic wellbeing.

Cherry's (1998) marriage market theory also deals with both marriage formation and wellbeing in marriage. It follows Becker in the sense that Cherry defines markets for marriage and not for spousal labour, in contrast to Grossbard-Shechtman, but his emphasis on fairness in marriage is reminiscent of Marxist feminist analyses of marriage. Like Grossbard-Shechtman and Marxist feminist economists, Cherry discusses legal and political factors and integrates power relations into his analysis of marriage. Cherry then applies his model to analyse the effects of recent social policies on women's relative wellbeing. He shows that policies forcing women to move from welfare to work may be less advantageous to women's wellbeing in marriage than policies leading to improved employment conditions for men.

Bargaining theories model allocation of resources and distribution of goods in marriage by mechanisms other than the market mechanism. Bargaining theories typically take marriage as given and do not analyse marriage formation. The oldest bargaining theories by Manser and Brown (1980) and McElroy and Horney (1981) are based on cooperative game theories. A variation on cooperative game theories are the collective theories pioneered by Chiappori (1988) which recognize that cooperation takes place without specifying specific mechanisms (games) leading to allocation within the household. Recently, non-cooperative game theories have also been applied to marriage (for example, Chaudhuri and Epstein 1995; Bergstrom 1996; Lommerud 1997). Feminist critiques of the bargaining approach can be found in Seiz (1991) and Nelson (1996).

Empirical applications of bargaining theories emphasize distribution of consumption in marriage (see for example, Thomas 1990; Lundberg and Pollak 1996), a topic also addressed by feminist economists such as Agarwal (1994). Peters (1986) also contributed an empirical study of the effects of divorce laws on women's labour force participation that is rooted in bargaining theories of marriage.

Feminist economists in the Marxist tradition, such as Folbre, Hartmann and Himmelweit, have pursued the Marxist emphasis on coercive mechanisms organizing production. Their emphasis has not been on class oppression, however, but on men's oppression of women, with the focus on understanding decision making in marriage rather than marriage formation. A major theme of research in this tradition has been the effect of women's access to resources on the relative wellbeing of women, men and children. For example, Agarwal (1994) has shown how Indian women's access to land affects their consumption.

Recently marriage-related research by feminist economists has been encouraged thanks to the creation of the International Association for Feminist

Economists and its journal, *Feminist Economics*. The focus of this research has been on intra-marriage allocation rather than marriage formation. At the same time, institutions such as the American Economic Association and mainstream economics journals have contributed to the growing popularity of bargaining theories and game theory in dealing with intra-household allocation.

Moreover, demography institutions, such as annual meetings of the Population Association of America, and demography journals have encouraged the production of increasing numbers of empirical studies on marriage formation and intra-marriage allocation. Demographic studies related to marriage are authored mostly by sociologists (and some economists) and emphasize empirical analysis using minimal theoretical constructs. It is expected that as more and more empirical studies accumulate, there will be more of a demand for theories that integrate a variety of interesting findings.

Some of this integration is already occurring. Increasing integration of the marriage-related work contributed by researchers trained in various schools of thought is evident from the increasing popularity of rational choice models in the work of economists not clearly identified as neoclassical economists (for instance, see Folbre 1994); the growing interest in effects of legal and political constraints on individual marriage-related choices by economic demographers (for instance, see Whittington and Alm 1997); the increasing recognition by neoclassical economists that political interests influence public choice; the abandonment by neoclassical economists of the 'classic' working assumption that tastes do not change (see, for instance, Becker 1996); and the emergence of forums which bring economists from different backgrounds together such as a conference on the economics of gender recently organized by Persson and Jonung (1997).

Despite all these encouraging trends, cooperation and communication between experts on marriage trained in various traditions is limited. Sessions on marriage formation tend to be found mostly at demographic meetings, which have traditionally included few sessions related to intra-marriage allocation. In contrast, economics meetings have focused on intra-household allocation but not on marriage formation. Within economics, there tends to be a separation between different types of analysis of intra-marriage allocation: sessions on those topics organized by mainstream economists tend to emphasize theoretical or technical discussions (especially discussions based on game theory) and rarely discuss issues such as family violence and spousal abuse. In contrast, sessions organized by feminist economists often deal with policy-relevant issues such as equality in marriage and spousal abuse, and place less emphasis on theory. There is no organization where market theories of marriage are currently popular.

A better understanding of the determinants of marriage formation and allocation of resources in marriage is needed. Such understanding can benefit the study of consumption, labour supply, fertility and other demographic questions, transportation, taxation, ideologies and politics. A better understanding of marriage involves the creation of more opportunities for followers of the various schools of economics of marriage to interact with each other and with the empirical researchers. Such opportunities can be created by changing existing institutions for economists and creating new institutions. Feminist economists who have a tradition of questioning the status quo may rise to the forefront of such efforts. This process will hopefully encourage the development of better and more research, both theoretical and empirical. The construction of better theories of marriage is expected to promote scientific knowledge and improve our understanding of production, allocation and distribution in marriage.

SHOSHANA GROSSBARD-SHECHTMAN

See also

Divorce; Domestic Labour; Family, Economics of; Game Theory and Bargaining Models; Neoclassical Economics.

Bibliography

Agarwal, Bina (1994), *A Field of One's Own: Gender and Land Rights in South Asia*, Cambridge: Cambridge University Press.

Becker, Gary S. (1965), 'A theory of the allocation of time', *Economic Journal*, 75, 493–515.

Becker, Gary S. (1973), 'A theory of marriage: Part I', *Journal of Political Economy*, 81, 813–46.

Becker, Gary S. (1976), 'Altruism, egoism, and genetic fitness: economics and sociobiology', *Journal of Economic Literature*, 14, 817–26.

Becker, Gary S. (1992), *A Treatise on the Family*, Cambridge: Harvard University Press, 2nd edition.

Becker, Gary S. (1996), *Accounting for Tastes*, Cambridge: Harvard University Press.

Bergmann, Barbara (1995), 'Becker's theory of the family: preposterous conclusions', *Feminist Economics*, 1, 141–50.

Bergstrom, Theodore C. (1996), 'Economics in a family way', *Journal of Economic Literature*, 34, 1903–34.

Chaudhuri, Anita and Gil Epstein (1995), 'Perceptions, Threats, and Accumulation of Partnership Capital', Paper presented at the Western Economic Association, San Diego.

Cherry, Robert (1998), 'Rational choice and the price of marriage', *Feminist Economics*, 4 (1), 27–49.

Chiappori, Pierre-Andre (1988), 'Rational household labour supply', *Econometrica*, 56, 63–90.

Ferber, Marianne A. and Bonnie G. Birnbaum (1977), 'The new home economics: retrospect and prospects', *Journal of Consumer Research*, 4, 19–28.

Folbre, Nancy (1982), 'Exploitation comes home: a critique of the Marxian theory of family labour', *Cambridge Journal of Economics*, 6, 317–29.

Folbre, Nancy (1994), *Who Pays for the Kids? Gender and the Structures of Constraint*, London: Routledge.

Folbre, Nancy and Heidi Hartmann (1988), 'The Rhetoric of Self-Interest and the Ideology of Gender', in A. Klamer, Donald McCloskey and Robert Solow (eds), *The Consequences of Economic Rhetoric*, Cambridge: Cambridge University Press.

Grossbard [-Shechtman], [Shoshana] Amyra (1976), 'An economic analysis of polygamy: the case of Maiduguri', *Current Anthropology*, 17, 701–7.

Grossbard-Shechtman, [Shoshana] Amyra (1981), 'A Market Theory of Marriage and Spouse Selection', paper presented at the Population Association of America, Boston.

Grossbard-Shechtman, [Shoshana] Amyra (1984), 'A theory of allocation of time in markets for labour and marriage', *Economic Journal*, **94**, 863–82.

Grossbard-Shechtman, Shoshana A. (1993), *On the Economics of Marriage*, Boulder, Colorado: Westview Press.

Grossbard-Shechtman, Shoshana A. (1995), 'Marriage Market Models', in Mario Tommasi and Kathryn Ierulli (eds), *The New Economics of Human Behavior*, Cambridge: Cambridge University Press.

Grossbard-Shechtman, Shoshana A. and Clive W.J. Granger (1998), 'Women's jobs and marriage: baby-boom versus baby-bust', *Population*, **53**, 731–52. (In French)

Grossbard-Shechtman, Shoshana A. and Shoshana Neuman (1998), 'The extra burden of Moslem wives – clues from Israeli women's labor supply', *Economic Development and Cultural Change*, **46** (3), 491–518.

Guttentag, Marcia and Paul Secord (1983), *Too Many Women: The Sex Ratio Question*, Beverly Hills: Sage Publications.

Hartmann, Heidi (1976), 'Capitalism, patriarchy, and job segregation by sex', *Signs*, **1** (3), pt. 2, (Spring), 137–69.

Hartmann, Heidi (1981). 'The family as the locus of gender, class and political struggle: the example of housework', *Signs*, **6**, 366–94.

Heer, David M. and Amyra Grossbard-Shechtman (1981), 'The impact of the female marriage squeeze and the contraceptive revolution on sex roles and the women's liberation movement in the United States, 1960 to 1975', *Journal of Marriage and the Family*, **43**, 49–65.

Himmelweit, Susan and Simon Mohun (1977), 'Domestic labour and capital', *Cambridge Journal of Economics*, **1**, 15–31.

Jacobsen, Joyce P. (1994), *The Economics of Gender*, Cambridge, Massachusetts: Blackwell.

Jennings, Ann L. (1994), 'Feminism', in Geoffrey M. Hodgson, Warren J. Samuels and Marc R. Tool (eds), *The Elgar Companion to Institutional and Evolutionary Economics A–K*, Aldershot: Edward Elgar, pp. 225–9.

Lemennicier, Bertrand (1988), *Le Marche du Marriage et de la Famille*, Paris: Presses Universitaires de France (in French).

Lommerud, Kjell Erik (1997), 'Battles of the sexes: non-cooperative games in the theory of the family', in Inga Persson and Christina Jonung (eds), *The Economics of the Family and Family Policies*, London: Routledge.

Lundberg, Shelly and Robert A. Pollak (1996), 'Bargaining and distribution in marriage', *Journal of Economic Perspectives*, **10**, 139–58.

Manser, Marilyn and Murray Brown (1980), 'Marriage and household decision making: a bargaining analysis', *International Economic Review*, **21**, 31–44.

McElroy, Marjorie B. and Mary Jane Horney (1981), 'Nash bargained household decisions: toward a generalization of the theory of demand', *International Economic Review*, **22**, 333–49.

Mincer, Jacob (1962), 'Labour Force Participation of Married Women: a Study of Labour Supply', in H. Gregg Lewis (ed.), *Aspects of Labour Economics*, Princeton, New Jersey: Princeton University Press.

Mincer, Jacob (1963), 'Market Prices, Opportunity Costs, and Income Effects', in C. Christ (ed.), *Measurement in Economics*, Stanford, California: Stanford University Press.

Nelson, Julie (1996), *Feminism, Objectivity and Economics*, London and New York: Routledge.

Persson, Inga and Christina Jonung (eds) (1997), *The Economics of the Family and Family Policies*. London: Routledge.

Peters, Elizabeth H. (1986), 'Marriage and divorce: informational constraints and private contracting', *American Economic Review*, **76**, 137–54.

Pujol, Michele A. (1992), *Feminism and Anti-Feminism in Early Economic Thought*, London: Edward Elgar.

Seiz, Janet (1991), 'The bargaining approach and feminist methodology', *Review of Radical Political Economics*, **23** (1–2), 22–9.

Strober, Myra H. (1995), 'Do young women trade jobs for marriage? A skeptical view', *Feminist Economics*, **1**, 197–206.

Thomas, Duncan (1990), 'Intra-household resource allocation: an inferential approach', *Journal of Human Resources*, **25**, 635–64.
Waller, William and Ann Jennings (1990), 'On the possibility of a feminist economics', *Journal of Economic Issues*, **24**, (June), 613–22.
Whittington, Leslie A. and James Alm (1997), ''Til death or taxes do us part. The effect of income taxation on divorce', *Journal of Human Resources*, **32**, 388–412.
Woolley, Frances (1996), 'Getting the better of Becker', *Feminist Economics*, **2**, 114–20.

Marxist Political Economics

Writing in the mid and late nineteenth century, Karl Marx, and his collaborator Frederick Engels, developed a theory of capitalist production and a critique of prevailing economic thought. Those writings on the political, social and economic aspects of capitalist production form the basis for Marxist political economics. Marx's most famous economic work is *Capital*, a three-volume work on the dynamics of capitalist production. For Marx, and Marxist political economists, the relations of capitalist production are a driving determinant of all aspects of social life.

Marxist political economics analyses capitalism, making class the basis unit of analysis. Borrowing from classical political economists Adam Smith and David Ricardo, Marx used a labour theory of value to develop his theory of class exploitation. Exchangeable commodities receive their value from the average amount of labour time it takes to produce them using the level of technology available. Profits exist because workers, while paid a wage equal to their value, actually produce more than their value. The value of workers, like the value of other commodities, is the time it takes to reproduce the worker at the socially and historically necessary standard of living. The value of the output workers produce minus their wages (workers' value) is what Marx called surplus value or profits.

The process of extracting surplus value from workers when generalized to the entire system is called the process of accumulation, and it is the process of accumulation – the drive for profits – that is the cornerstone of understanding capitalist production and Marxist political economy. Analytically, the process of accumulation is to Marxist political economy what supply and demand curves are to neoclassical economics: it lays the foundation for explaining why and how goods and services are produced and allocated, the level and role of technology in a society, the conflict between workers and capitalists, the necessity of struggle and change, and even the roles governments and culture play.

Marx outlined several dynamics and tendencies that result from the process of accumulation, many still ring true today. For example, Marx predicted the expansion of capitalist class relations historically and geographically. In order for any capitalist to realize and continually accumulate, he or she must expand production and at the same time seek to minimize competition and the value of labour power. As the capitalist system expands, it absorbs more and more people – including children and women – into the wage-labour system, and moves to more remote geographic locations in order to procure raw materials, cheap labour and places to sell commodities. Another dynamic Marx described was the growth of mega-corporations. Capitalist accumulation creates larger and larger corporations who control more and more productive resources, making the international expansion of capitalism inevitable.

Marx and later-day Marxist political economists argue that capitalist accumulation is a highly dynamic but contentious, unstable and ultimately unhealthy economic system. The main contradiction of capitalist production – that goods and services are produced socially by the working class, but are appropriated privately by the capitalist class — results in class conflict, struggle and ultimately change.

In the simplest (if not simplistic) form, the relationship of the production process to all other social phenomena is traditionally designated as the 'base-superstructure' relationship. Political structure, culture and social relations outside the workplace as well as family structure are considered part of the 'superstructure' (that is, not directly involved in the production and reproduction of goods and services). The superstructure is shaped by and serves the dynamics of the 'base' – the material conditions of the production of commodities.

Part of Marx's legacy in economics, and many other disciplines, is Marxist methodology. Borrowing from, but at the same time transforming, the ideas of German philosopher Georg Hegel, Marx employed dialectical (or historical) materialism. This methodology stresses an historical and contradictory nature of unequal power relations based on the material conditions of classes. The method provides a complex examination of the dynamic role and influence of structures and institutions in the production and reproduction of power relations. Relationships among people cannot be understood outside of the structures and institutions which exist to help reproduce those relationships. Dialectical materialism maintains that the way one interprets and intervenes in the world is itself influenced by history and conflict. Marx rejected the notion that knowledge and ideas were fixed.

For Marx and his adherents, Marxist political economy is not just a theory that explains the world, it is a call to change it. Marxism is an explicit political project and much of its historical appeal has been that it is both a theory and a practice. Marx's (and Engels's) work have had profound intellectual and political effects over the last 140 years.

Given that Marxist political economics focuses almost exclusively on class relations, the specific role that gender plays – in both ideological and structural ways – is an area of considerable and highly contested debate. The history of this debate is as old as Marxism itself. In traditional Marxist political economy, the treatment of women's oppression is much like its treatment of other important non-class power relations (such as between nation-states, races, and so on) – it is derivative of class relations. An example of this is most clearly seen in Frederick Engels's 1884 book, *The Origin of the Family, Private Property and the State*, one of the first works to deal specifically with women's relationship to the production process. Here, Engels claimed,

> According to the materialist conception, the determining factor in history is, in the final instance, the production and reproduction of immediate life. This, again, is of a twofold character: on the one side, the production of the means of existence, of food, clothing, shelter and the tools necessary for that production; on the other hand, the production of human beings themselves, the propagation of the species. The social organization under which the people of a particular historical epoch and a particular country live is determined by both kinds of production: by the stage of development of labor on the one hand and of the family on the other. (Engels 1972, p. 71)

In his book, however, Engels only discussed one side of the duality – the ways in which women's role in reproduction was shaped by the production and reproduction of commodities.

Engels's basic argument was that in order to maintain private property through inheritance, men need to know who their heirs are. They therefore enforce a system of patrilineal and patriarchal control through a system of monogamous marriages. For Engels, women's economic dependence on men – which is a direct result of private ownership of the means of production – oppresses women. The elimination of women's oppression will only occur with the abolition of private property and the monogamous family. Eradicating capitalism frees both men and women to love whom they want and fulfil their personal and sexual desires; it liberates workers from alienating work and liberates men and women from alienating marriages.

Feminists – contemporary ones and those writing 100 years ago — have always challenged Marxist understandings of women's oppression. Marxist and socialist thinkers in the late nineteenth and early twentieth century, for example, grappled seriously with women's status under capitalism and even gave it its own name – the 'Woman Question'. A persistent critique of traditional Marxist political economy's treatment of women's unequal status is that women have to face gender oppression that is independent of their class status and in different types of class societies, including socialism (Eisenstein 1979). While wealthy women may have more options and privileges than other women, all women face a set of physical, social and ideological constraints that are different from those faced by men and place women in a vulnerable and unequal position with men. The sexual division of labour typifies all societies across space and time – though the specific work done by women and men varies (Hartmann 1976). Gender oppression is not merely a function of propertied societies.

A second set of criticisms has to do with Marxism's project and focus. In Marxist economic analysis, economic processes are given prominence over any other type of human interaction. Production for exchange, typically men's work, takes precedence over production for use or reproduction, typically women's work. The emphasis on exploitation, which occurs in wage labour production processes, makes secondary (and in some treatments completely ignores) the importance of non-waged work in economic, political and social processes (Folbre 1982). However, non-waged work, like waged work, entails economic, ideological, cultural and social interactions, perceptions and control (Rubin 1976). By not subjecting reproductive work to the same historical and dialectical analysis applied to for-profit production work, much of Marxist analysis is biased and incomplete (Mitchell 1966).

Despite the inadequate, if not anti-feminist, explanation of women's status offered by traditional Marxists, Marxist political economy has remained a seductive model for feminists. Many feminists were active socialists (and later communists) in the late nineteenth and early twentieth century and gravitated toward Marxist and other socialist theories of liberation. For over a century, feminists have looked to Marxist political economy for a framework that argues for transformed political, economic and social relations that will distribute wealth and power more equally – including along gender lines. With the rise of the New Left and feminist movements in the late 1960s and early 1970s, Marxist theory became popular to those interested in understanding and transforming unequal relations (such as between countries or between genders), yet still retained an understanding of class-based oppression.

The model offers at least three important contributions to and insights for feminist economics. The first has to do with Marxist methodology and stresses understanding historical and institutional dynamics, which in the modern period has been a hallmark of many types of feminist analysis. Marxist methodology, in its focus on unequal class power relations, poses a model that poses conflicting interests which always result in struggle and change. The model argues that unequal power relations are unfair and inefficient and that when people mobilize along their similar economic interests, they can together affect the direction of change. For many feminists, including feminist economists, who see gender relations as oppressive to women and systematically embedded in economic institutions, Marxist methodology provides a powerful springboard for thinking and theorizing about gender relations. In addition, Marx's notion that knowledge is itself historically determined has also been an important insight for feminist philosophers and economists using 'standpoint theory' (Harding 1995).

A second important insight provided by Marxist political economy is the important role of reproduction in economic activity and model building. One main form this takes in Marxist political economy is in the labour theory of value itself. A worker's value (that is, wage) will be determined by the amount of time it takes to reproduce that worker. Since reproduction takes place in the home and that work is mainly performed by women, teasing out the labour theory of value allows feminists to raise the questions of the sexual division of labour and the relationship of production to reproduction. The focus on reproduction (even though neglected in many traditional treatments) has the potential to make family structure, the cultural notions of who are 'workers' and who are not and families as an income distribution system, a crucial component of understanding classes, wage structure and protest.

A third important contribution of Marxist political economy to feminist economics is the way in which the dynamic of the process of accumulation affects family labour systems. Marx predicted that women would be drawn into the labour force because they receive lower wages than men. He also saw this as an erosion of family life. Feminists, both at the turn of the century and in modern times, have emphasized the liberatory effects of wage labour. Regardless of where one falls in this debate, the linking of the process of accumulation to the development of the wage labour force is an important contribution to understanding the role of gender in a capitalist society.

By the early 1970s, the group of New Left feminists, who were upset with the New Left's lack of attention to gender but still adhered to Marxist political economy, began calling themselves socialist feminists (Hansen and Philipson 1990). They wanted to use some of the insights of Marxist political economy, including its analysis of classes, both to critique Marxist political economics and to better understand and integrate gender and (sometimes) race into Marxist analysis. And while these feminists, many of them economists, were attracted to and worked fruitfully within a Marxist political economic framework, feminism – and with it socialist feminists – were not readily accepted by many Marxist economists or easily incorporated into Marxist political economy organizations, academic enclaves, culture or journals, often echoing the oppression of women in society. An example of this tension was evident in battles over male dominance that erupted in the Union for Radical Political Economics (URPE – the organization formed in 1968 by radical political economists) in the early 1970s, resulting in the formation of a women's caucus within the organization in 1971, making it the first modern day women's organization in economics. In 1972, the women's caucus published a special issue of URPE's journal, the *Review of Radical Political Economics* (RRPE) on women, the first of four special issues on the political economy of women, all published by 1980 (Vol 4(3), Vol 8(1), Vol 9(3), and Vol 12(2)). Articles in the special issues served as a first important outlet for a socialist feminist economics scholarship and spanned a wide range of feminist economic thinking: the question of how to theorize about women and families, the role of reproductive labour and control, feminist pedagogy, critiques of Marxist and neoclassical treatment of women and families, women's economic history, women in socialist economies and women in labour markets.

One of the most enduring conflicts, intellectual and political, between Marxists and feminists has to do with the nature and source of women's oppression in capitalism (see Humphries 1977 and Hartmann and Markusen 1980 for more on how feminists debated this). Socialist feminists have worked to use the insights of Marxist political economy to theorize about the dynamics between class and gender oppression. Their critique and re-working of Marxist political economy has helped transform Marxist political economy and has also provided an important basis for contemporary feminist economics (Matthaei 1992). Often using Engels's work as a starting point, these contributions are in the tradition of Marxist political economics because they focus on the relationships between reproduction and production in the process of accumulation. However, they are also examples of feminist economics scholarship in that they highlight the distinct, yet related, dynamics of gender oppression within capitalism.

The first serious and sustained theoretical discussion by socialist feminists of women's oppression in capitalism was referred to as the 'domestic labour debates'. The debate focused on the role domestic labour plays in capitalism and created an important, yet unresolved and contentious, theoretical debate on how to use Marxist political economy to understand the role of women's unpaid work in the home by linking it directly to production (for a review of debate, see Himmelweit 1989). The domestic labour debate discussions opened the door for a serious discussion of gender in Marxist economics that did not reduce women's oppression to their class position. The domestic labour debates also sparked a discussion of the direction of political action and political platforms socialist feminists might pursue. 'Wages for housework' campaigns coincided with the domestic labour debate in Britain and in the United States. A focus on reproductive labour also provided a link to the reproductive rights networks that engaged many feminists at the time. The domestic labour debate continued for over a decade with over 50 articles published mostly in the United States and Britain (Molyneux 1979). The role of domestic labour in economic accounting has taken centre stage in current feminist economic research and action.

Following the 'domestic labour debates', socialist feminists contributed a rich theoretical literature concerning women's economic oppression under capitalism. The remainder of this section will focus on three important 'paths' blazed in the 1970s and early 1980s. Each represents original, fruitful and distinct analysis of one of the most enduring conflicts between feminism and Marxism – the question of the source and the dynamics of women's oppression. What unifies them, however, is their emphasis on the relationships of reproduction to production and on the family as a primary location of women's oppression.

One path, referred to as 'dual systems theory', was introduced by Hartmann (1981) in her essay 'The Unhappy Marriage between Marxism and Feminism'. In that essay Hartmann argued that the system of women's oppression – patriarchy – cannot be reduced to capitalist class relations, because it has its own dynamics. Hartmann claimed there exist dual systems of oppression: sometimes these systems operate in tandem and sometimes in opposition.

> We suggest that our society can best be understood once it is recognized that it is organized both in capitalistic and in patriarchal ways. While pointing out tensions between patriarchal and capitalist interests, we argue that the accumulation of capital both accommodates itself to patriarchal social structure and helps to perpetuate it. (Hartmann 1981, p. 3)

Hartmann argued that Marxism is sex-blind. It can easily define certain places in capitalism but does not have the tools to explain why certain faces (for example, women and people of colour) fill those slots. One needs a theory of gender and race to do that. A good example of the use of dual labour systems in a recent work is Amott and Matthaei's (1996) economic history of women in the United States.

Sociologist Michèle Barrett (1980) argued for a different approach. She claimed that the ideological expressions of women's oppression in capitalism are real and too important to see as a reflection of the material base (as Marxists have). Further, Barrett argued that ideology was too connected to the specific class relations of capitalism to relegate it to a separate sphere. Barrett, then, attempted to meld Marxism's materialism with feminist psychoanalytical literature by using French Marxist Louis Althussar's notion of ideology. In *Women's Oppression Today*, Barrett laid out the basis for Althussarian, post-Marxist, postmodernist treatments of gender. Barrett defined ideology as 'a generic term for the processes by which meaning is produced, challenged, reproduced, transformed' (Barrett 1980, p. 97). But ideology is not separate from the relations of production,

> ideology has played an important part in the historical construction of the capitalist division of labour and in the reproduction of labour power. A sexual division of labour and accompanying ideologies of the appropriate meaning of labour for men and women, have been embedded in the capitalist division of labour from its beginnings. (Barrett 1980, p. 98)

Fraad et al. (1994) in a recent mongraph use this type of Athussarian approach to gender.

Lourdes Benería, in an article that appeared in 1979, argued for exploring a different kind of dualism than those explored by either Hartmann or Barrett – that of production and reproduction. Benería returns directly to Engels's original dualism to discuss the relationship of the sexual division of labour in production to women's role in reproduction. But rather than resort to a rather stagnant view of the family and rely on the existence of private property, Benería argues for a closer examination of the social and material conditions of reproduction and the ways in which reproduction and production are related. She suggests three important focal points for this examination: the degree to which men control women's reproductive capacities; the extent to which women perform child care and domestic tasks associated with reproductive labour; and 'the extent to which the allocation of women as agents of production is conditioned by their role in reproduction' (Benería 1979, p. 207). Benería emphasizes the basic contradiction of reproduction for women: the need (and shared objective with men) to produce children versus their lack of control over their reproductive capacities because of the extent of control men have over their own lives as mothers. She argues women's roles in the home shape their role in the non-domestic spheres.

The theoretical issues posed by these feminists using Marxist political economics have not been resolved. Some previously engaged in these debates have moved away from Marxism all together, grabbing their 'tools' and moving to postmodern feminism. Others have lost interest in the immediacy of developing the single theory which can explain gender and class relations across all time and histories and have turned instead to concrete analysis of women's economic situation. Some have used these insights and dead-ends to inform current debates in feminist economic thinking and develop new theories about gender (see, for example, Folbre 1994). Still, the importance of collective action and the role of social structures and institutions in reproducing women's oppression that were initially raised in the theoretical debates over women's relationship to capitalism are the same ones feminist economists grapple with today.

RANDY ALBELDA

See also
Capitalism; Class; Feminism(s); Domestic Labour; Gender; Patriarchy; Socialism.

Bibliography
Albelda, Randy (1997), *Economics and Feminism: Disturbances in the Field*, New York: Twayne Publishers.
Amott, Teresa and Julie Matthaei (1996), *Race, Gender and Work: A Multicultural History of Women in the United States*, 2nd edn, Boston: South End Press.

Barrett, Michèle (1980), *Women's Oppression Today: Problems in Marxist Feminist Analysis*, London: Verso Books.

Benería, Lourdes (1979), 'Reproduction, production and the sexual division of labor', *Cambridge Journal of Economics*, (3), 203–25.

Eisenstein, Zillah (1979), 'Some Notes on the Relationship of Capitalist Patriarchy', in Zillah Eisenstein (ed.), *Capitalist Patriarchy and the Case for Socialist Feminism*, New York: Monthly Review Press, pp. 41–55.

Engels, Frederick (1972), *The Origin of the Family, Private Property and the State*, New York: International Publishers.

Folbre, Nancy (1982), 'Exploitation comes home: a critique of the Marxian theory of family labor', *Cambridge Journal of Economics*, (6), 317–29.

Folbre, Nancy (1994), *Who Pays for the Kids: Gender and the Structure of Constraints*, London: Routledge.

Fraad, Harriet, Stephen Resnick, and Richard Wolff (1994), *Bringing It All Home: Class, Gender and Power in the Modern Household*, Boulder, Colorado: Pluto Press.

Hansen, Karen V. and Irene J. Philipson, (eds) (1990), *Women, Class, and the Feminist Imagination: A Socialist-Feminist Reader*, Philadelphia: Temple University Press.

Harding, Sandra (1995), 'Can feminist thought make economics more objective?', *Feminist Economics*, **1** (1) Spring, 7–32.

Hartmann, Heidi (1976), 'Capitalism, patriarchy and job segregation by sex', *Signs*, **3** (2), 137–69.

Hartmann, Heidi (1981), 'The Unhappy Marriage of Marxism and Feminism', in Lydia Sargent (ed.), *Women and Revolution: A Discussion of the Unhappy Marriage of Marxism and Feminism*, Boston: South End Press, pp. 1–41.

Hartmann, Heidi and Ann Markusen (1980), 'Contemporary Marxist theory and practice: a feminist critique', *Review of Radical Political Economics*, **12** (2), 87–94.

Himmelweit, Susan (1989), 'Domestic Labor', in John Eatwell, Murray Milgate and Peter Newman (eds), *The New Palgrave: Social Economics*, New York: W.W. Norton, pp. 35–9.

Humphries, Jane (1977), 'The working class family, women's liberation, and class struggle: the case of nineteenth century British history', *Review of Radical Political Economics*, **9** (3), 25–41.

Marx, Karl (1967), *Capital: A Critical Analysis of Capitalist Production*, Volume 1, New York: International Publishers.

Matthaei, Julie (1992), 'Marxist–Feminist Contributions to Radical Economics', in Bruce Roberts and Susan Feiner (eds), *Radical Economics*, Norwell, Massachusetts: Kluwer Academic Press, pp. 117–44.

Mitchell, Juliet (1966), 'Women: the longest revolution', *New Left Review*, 40, (November–December).

Molyneux, Maxine (1979), 'Beyond the domestic labour debate', *New Left Review*, 116 (July–August), 3–27.

Rubin, Gayle (1976), 'The Traffic of Women: Notes on the Political Economy of Sex', in Rayna Rapp Reiter (ed.), *Towards an Anthology of Women*, New York: Monthly Review Press, pp. 157–210.

Methodology

The expression 'economic methodology' carries several meanings. Sometimes it refers to the collection of tools and techniques economists use to explore economic relations such as their theoretical and empirical models, surveys, and multivariate regression analysis. At other times methodology is concerned with epistemological processes; here the term refers to the ways in which economists decide what will be considered economic knowledge. As such, it deals with issues of disciplinary authority and legitimation: it addresses questions about who gets to define the domain of economic inquiry, how it is decided which activities will be the subject of economic inquiry, which variables will be considered important economic variables, and which assumptions about the world and the nature of scientific analysis economists will adhere to. Both meanings of the word methodology will be dealt with here, and the more fundamental aspects of epistemology will be addressed first since this is where feminist economics has presented the greatest challenges so far. At the same time it is important to bear in mind that the two meanings of the word are not mutually exclusive but like the two sides of a coin. Sometimes tools and methods are dictated by the theoretical and epistemological positions of the researcher and sometimes the process of inquiry is determined by tools and methods.

It should be remembered that all economic research dealing with women or gender is not necessarily feminist economics. While there is scope for different political persuasions, a feminist point of view implies a critique of male supremacy, a desire to change it and a conviction that it is changeable. Debates about the specific interventions called for and the best means towards emancipatory change are very much part of what characterizes feminist economic discourse. Feminist economists come from a wide spectrum within the discipline of economics, and it would be misleading to try to set up a complete list of characteristics of the ideas and practices that define this new school of thought in economics. However, all feminist economists agree that women's economic contributions and women's lives have been neglected in the writings and analyses of all but a handful of economists until very recently. The exclusion is rooted partly in the pervasive sexism and androcentrism of the field (Pujol 1992), and partly in the difficulty of creating useful new categories of analysis. In addition, new scholarship shows that the writings of women economists, whether they explicitly examine issues in women's lives or not, have been systematically ignored and left out of historical surveys even though women have an early and solid presence in several major publications in economics (Dimand et al. 1995). Feminist economists are also united in their theoretical and practical emphasis on the role of gender in all economic contexts, and the kind of work that explicitly uses gender as a category of analysis – performed by people inside and outside the academy – form the loose and permeable boundaries of this new field (Grapard 1996).

Feminist economists argue that the historically pervasive neglect of gender makes it imperative for all schools of thought in economics to reevaluate their theoretical foundations and practices. The coexistence of the orthodox, or neoclassical, school of thought, alongside several heterodox schools of thought, such as the Austrian, the institutionalist, the Marxist and the Post Keynesian, means that there is not a single, unified set of assumptions about the nature of knowledge, the nature of the real world, and human nature among economists. Feminist economics thus presents a broad methodological critique across the entire discipline of economics as well as specific challenges within each school of thought. Standard works on methodology and economics provide a discussion of the history and problems of economic methodology, whether it emphasizes methodological unity (Blaug [1980] 1992) or diversity (Caldwell 1982). Few of the standard references, however, will discuss and explore the critiques and contributions of the field of feminist economics, because the feminist impact on economic knowledge is so recent.

The great advances in feminist theory over the last 30 years have had an important impact on feminist economics. These developments have been coming from many academic disciplines, but for questions of methodology, work in the philosophy of science has been particularly significant. Philosopher Harding (1986, 1991) points out that feminist criticism raises questions about the social structure and uses of science as well as about the origins, problematics, social meanings, agendas and theories of scientific knowledge-seeking. She examines three feminist theoretical perspectives that all have been important in feminist economics: feminist empiricism, which tries to correct 'bad science'; feminist standpoint theory, which tries to construct knowledge from the perspective of women's lives; and feminist postmodernism, which is suspicious of the Enlightenment loyalties inherent in modernist scientific and epistemological projects.

Because these perspectives are not mutually exclusive, the critiques and contributions presented by feminist economists will often reflect more than one of them. The feminist empiricist tendency will be particularly important for economists who feel that the main problems with economics are the biases resulting from the historical lack of collection and incorporation of data covering the lives of half the human population. Bad science can become a better, more objective science, it is argued, if economists would pay more attention to researching and documenting women's lives.

In contrast to the empiricist position, where social characteristics such as the gender of the inquiring researcher is unimportant, standpoint theory argues that the different life experiences of men and women are strongly associated with the development of particular viewpoints. From the perspective of standpoint theory it is deeply problematic that the world of those who practise economics is overwhelmingly western and male. In hierarchical and gender-stratified societies, the definition of economic issues deemed legitimate and worthwhile to investigate thus reflects the privileged social, economic and political position of men. This has resulted in the development of economic concepts and categories that portray the male experience in the industrialized countries of the West as the norm, and that either ignore or depict as deviant or parasitic the lives of those not fitting the male norm. Standpoint theorists suggest that economic knowledge developed from an outsider's point of view is bound to be more questioning of the conventional assumptions and practices in economics, and such knowledge will therefore greatly enrich the discipline. Economics from women's perspective is thus more likely to consider issues of care as important, and to see the purpose of economic activity as provisioning rather than as maximizing national output and growth. This is not because women are assumed to be naturally more nurturing and caring but because women historically have been in charge of the daily tasks of feeding and taking care of families in ways not shared by most men.

Feminist postmodernism emphasizes specifically feminist concerns as it joins others who present a postmodern or poststructuralist critique of the Cartesian scientific practices associated with the Enlightenment. Like the standpoint theory, the postmodernist critique rejects the possibility of an abstract, individual knower who has access to a disembodied scientific truth. This leads to inquiries and debates about what objectivity might mean in economics research, and whether it is something to strive for. Questioning what is meant by objectivity involves considering how truth claims are validated. Although scholars with an interest in methodological issues will recognize that the facts never speak for themselves, it is still standard practice in neoclassical economics to insist on a strict division between normative and positive questions, and to believe in the possibility of an aperspectival, God's Eyes point of view. In contrast, the idea that all knowledge is situated knowledge is emphasized by Longino (1990) when she points out that objective scientific findings always depend on historically constituted interpretive communities for validation. Feminists question the notion of a disembodied, objective, neutral science, and they suggest that questions of gender are profoundly implicated in the origin of this ideal of impersonal detachment. The Philosopher Bordo (1987, p. 106) thus argues that 'the Cartesian reconstruction of the world is ... a defiant gesture of independence from the female cosmos'.

Postmodernists push the questioning of conventional categories even further. While most standpoint theorists assume there is a concrete meaning to the term 'women' and that it makes sense to say about a theoretical position or a policy option that it is to 'women's advantage', a postmodern view would point to the danger of assuming that 'women' can exist as a universal, ahistorical category. Accordingly, when discourse imposes such a unity, it will necessarily reflect the positions of those who are in a position to define the boundaries of the category women. These issues have been explored most fully in the economic development literature where the impact of western assumptions and policy prescriptions for non-western countries are discussed (Elson 1991; Marchand and Parpart 1995).

In the following discussion, the specific examples from work by feminist economists are not necessarily intended to illustrate one or the other of the feminist paradigms introduced above. As mentioned earlier, they are not mutually exclusive, and they are best seen as signposts that can help in understanding how certain arguments within feminist economics fit into a larger framework of feminist concerns and theoretical developments. Furthermore, it would be a mistake to expect a presentation of a fully formed, alternative, unified feminist methodology. Instead, feminist economic scholars have identified various instances where a feminist critique seems particularly relevant; there is no overarching theory that will put everything in its right place. For most feminist economists, the days for such projects in the social sciences are long gone.

Feminist economists argue that the androcentrism of economics influences and colours the discipline in fundamental ways. The constrained optimization model of neoclassical economics presents a rational economic agent who is detached and independent of social relations outside of those involving contractual trade; this utility maximizing individual represents a purely masculine position (Nelson 1995), and the theoretical position of this 'separative self' (England 1993) makes it ill-suited for modelling the behaviour of those who do not fit his image. In standard economic theory, rational economic man, aka 'Homo Economicus', derives utility, or satisfaction, from consuming goods and services. The origins of the preferences underlying his utility function are not subject to economic analysis, and his utility is not assumed to be influenced by others. In other words, tastes and preferences are considered exogenous to the model, and interpersonal utility comparisons are ruled out. The human bonds and social connections, without which human society could not exist, are thus placed outside the sphere of economic theorizing, and that means that large parts of caring labour, and especially women's labour, remain invisible and unaccounted for in mainstream economic work.

The exclusion of women and female agency is not just a question of leaving half of the human race out of economic discourse; it also influences the theoretical structures and actual practices of economic inquiry, as well as the nature and character of the standard economic agent. By ignoring issues of gender, the foundations of the discourse and practice of economics cannot be understood, and we are missing an opportunity to fully recognize the situatedness of those involved in conventional (read: masculinist) scientific practices.

Nelson (1996, pp. 20–38) argues that a systematic devaluation of women and the feminine in our culture is behind the privileging of the masculine. Her 'gender-value compass' shows how our culture associates positive attributes with masculinity and negative values with femininity, and it reveals the dualism and the masculine biases of the values embodied in neoclassical theory and practices. In accordance with a simple dualistic view, economic reasoning is associated with formal logic and masculinity, and any argument or exposition that is not presented in the prescribed manner will be seen as illogical and inferior. Theoretical mathematical models are seen as the only valid and rigorous means to advance economic knowledge, and without results derived from a theoretical model and its statistical validation, economic inquiry is seen as soft, imprecise and invalid. Other forms of reasoning and different kinds of knowledge are thus considered unscientific and are associated with femininity and inferiority. Nelson argues that replacing the masculine values with more gender-neutral, complementary values will make for a better economics. She emphasizes that the development of a richer theoretical fabric will not come about because women somehow do economics differently but because including values and experiences previously excluded provide better and more complete data to work with, and hence produce a more objective economic science.

A further exploration of the values embodied in economic discourse and practices has been influenced by the postmodern turn in literary criticism, starting with McCloskey's analysis of the rhetoric of economics. McCloskey (1985) argues that economists do not practise what they preach. They do not, in fact, adhere to the strict, rational, scientific methodological principles they usually advocate. Instead, they use rhetorical devices and storytelling in an effort to persuade their colleagues. While McCloskey's work ignores the gendered aspects of economic practices, feminist economists have examined the narrative strategies used in economic discourse in order to document the gendered nature of the stories and metaphors, such as Robinson Crusoe, used by economists (Grapard 1995, Strassmann 1993a). This analysis points to the political dimensions of a discourse that constructs the economic agent and the domain of economics in western, masculinist ways.

Other postmodern influences can be found in the examination of issues of power and representation in economics. Conventional wisdom has it that economic knowledge is created in a free marketplace of ideas, and that good ideas and scientifically valid research will be impartially evaluated and will be published if they meet the quality standards of the profession. Feminist economists have examined the extent to which there is indeed such a free market, and it appears that, in fact, women and other marginalized groups do not have an equal chance at being heard in the profession (Strassmann 1993b; Williams 1993). Consequently, the scholarship thus excluded will introduce a bias in what will be considered knowledge in economics. Until quite recently, exchange in the public marketplace constituted the only proper domain of economics, and there was no economic analysis of the family and private households. However, in the 1960s, the influx of married white women into the labour market in the USA caused the establishment of a new research programme to explain the labour market participation of a non-male worker, that is, of an economic agent whose life and labour outside the labour market needed to be included in the analysis. The historical split between the public and the private spheres, which still produces tension in economics at both the theoretical and practical level, has been explored by political scientists (Elshtain 1981; Pateman 1988) and by feminist economists (Folbre and Hartmann 1988; Folbre 1995; Jennings 1993).

The 'New Home Economics', associated particularly with the work of Gary Becker (1981), has been important in establishing the terms on which women and issues of gender first entered orthodox economic discourse. (In another instance of sexist bias in the profession it is rarely acknowledged that Becker's work was preceded by and based on the contributions of others, especially that of Reid (1934).) This approach uses standard microeconomic theory to model the behaviour of the family. The model embodies the assumptions about rational economic agents questioned by feminist economists, and it operates with a single utility function, that of the 'benevolent patriarch' who ensures consensus through the power of the purse. The model has been widely criticized by feminist economists for its simplistic assumptions and its complacency toward the status quo (Ferber and Birnbaum 1977; Folbre and Hartmann 1988; Bergmann 1995). It also imposes assumptions about altruistic behaviour in the family which are inconsistent with its assumptions about motivations in the market place (England 1993). In addition, in the neoclassical model systematic power inequalities between men and women are presented as 'natural' and unproblematic (Seiz 1992; Woolley 1993). With its emphasis on free choice, the model pays no attention to the structural constraints that disproportionately limits women's choices in the home and the marketplace. It analyses the family in a basic trade model with some prices calculated in terms of time–money combinations, and it supports the status quo through its assumptions about women's and men's stereotypical comparative advantages in the production of market versus nonmarket goods; in a tautological manner, it explains women's lower pay and status in the marketplace by their obligations in the home, while simultaneously explaining women's disproportionate share of household labour by their lower pay, and hence lower opportunity cost, in the market.

Neoclassical economists have recently looked to game theory and bargaining models in order to address issues of the family (Manser and Brown 1980). This has led to a more 'realistic' modelling of decision making and negotiations inside the nuclear family and is seen by many feminist economists as an advance over Becker's model. Bargaining theory acknowledges the presence in the family of individuals with different preferences and it explicitly allows for strategic behaviour in an environment of uncertainty. It can also be useful for analysing how bargaining power is affected by public policy (Lundberg and Pollack 1993). At the same time, feminists wonder how much new knowledge is actually produced by formalizing and modelling individual optimizing behaviour in this way (Seiz 1991). So much of what is unknown, interesting and important about gender and relations of power has to be left out in order for such a model to give predictable, unambiguous results. Feminist economists are interested in qualitative questions such as what factors affect bargaining power, how social norms influence the bargaining process, and how extra-household patterns of power affect bargaining inside the household. In recent feminist economic analysis, such questions are beginning to be explored and the bargaining approach is extended to the interaction between the family, the community and the state (Agarwal 1997).

The pervasive exclusion of much of women's economic activity has led many feminist economists to display a certain scepticism toward the formal model building and the techniques that currently dominate research in the profession. Much of the theoretical and applied research done by feminist economists therefore consists of critically examining the methodological shortcoming of existing frameworks and in proposing methodological changes that will better serve feminist ends.

One of the instances where methodological rethinking has manifested itself is in the area of measuring and valuing unpaid labour (Himmelweit 1995). Traditionally, women's unpaid, domestic labour was considered 'unproductive' by both the neoclassical and Marxist schools of thought, and statisticians decided to leave it out of national accounts (Folbre 1991). In fact, some labour economists still depict the labour force participation decision as involving a tradeoff between market work and leisure. However, as women in industrialized countries entered the labour force in greater numbers, it became obvious that there was a three-way tradeoff between paid market work, unpaid domestic work and leisure. This new categorization is necessary to illuminate factors that are important for explaining people's choices, especially women's. Women's increased labour force participation also raises new issues of public policy, for example the availability of child care. Without a proper theoretical understanding and a good estimate of the value of time spent in unpaid labour, policymakers are likely to underestimate the value of women's time, and to provide suboptimal amounts of public support for dependent care.

The questions of how to put a value on work performed outside the market and of how best to incorporate it into a macroeconomic framework are complex. Feminist economists currently disagree on whether it is politically wise to include women's unpaid labour in the GDP accounts as productive labour. Some argue it will reinforce the status quo by validating the perception that household labour and child care are women's work. Others argue that to have some measure of the magnitude and the value of productive labour that goes uncounted is bound to have far-reaching consequences for social and economic policy and for social norms and institutions (Benería 1992; also see *Feminist Economics*, 2 (3), Fall 1996). They find very useful the satellite accounts based on extensive time-use studies which document the gendered character of the division of labour throughout the world (United Nations Development Program 1995).

Feminist scholars working in the area of economic development have contributed substantially to the literature concerning unpaid labour. In countries where a very large part of production and consumption take place outside the market, the impact of male and market biases have led policymakers to undervalue women's economic contribution to subsistence agriculture, for example, and consequently the result of much development planning has been a decrease in women's relative economic welfare (Benería and Feldman 1992; Elson 1991). Proposals to reconceptualize macroeconomic modelling and structural adjustment policies in order to address questions of gender have recently been developed (Çagatay et al. 1995).

In its earliest days, the research programme of feminist economics has necessarily been focused on identifying and analysing the gender biases in traditional economic models and empirical work. The standard statistical methods used by neoclassical economists rely on large data sets often collected by government agencies. The information contained is necessarily rough and consists of impersonal answers to unambiguous questions since statistical and econometric analyses require measurable and quantifiable variables. In addition to the criticism voiced by others concerning the misuse of statistics and econometrics (McCloskey 1985; Nelson 1996), feminist economists object to the exclusive reliance on quantitative methods. One reason is that the data collected by national statistical agencies usually reflect the gender biases of neoclassical theory. In the case of empirical work on the family and labour force participation, it makes feminist inquiry more difficult that GDP accounts only measure market production; that household income and expenditure surveys do not collect information on intra-household access to resources; and that labour-force surveys reflect notions of the typical male worker. Feminists are therefore working to change the data collection through the revised GDP accounts and household panel data with more information on intra-household differences in resource access and workload (MacDonald 1995).

Because feminist economists are interested in questions that require more nuanced, interpretive accounts, they are often faced with the task of generating their own primary data. While such specialized surveys may lend themselves to standard econometric techniques, the researcher is sometimes in a position where new, qualitative methods of analysis need to be developed. Contrary to popular belief in the profession, this kind of empirical economics is thus not easier than standard econometric work (MacDonald 1995).

As the field of feminist economics matures, these methodological insights thus lead to new ways of conceptualizing economic inquiry and the gathering of data. In contrast to the conventional practice of relying on large data-sets, feminist applications of both quantitative and qualitative research methods tend to put greater faith in people's own voices: interviews, detailed surveys conducted by researchers with specific, complex research questions in mind, participant–observer research and the use of focus groups are part of the current innovative strategies. One researcher found that allowing poor women to participate as researchers – by interviewing other poor women taking part in a job training programme – resulted in a decrease in interviewer bias and improved the response rate (Kim 1997). Extensive conversations allow the participant–observer to understand the institutional constraints and the complex processes that yield certain outcome variables in ways not possible based on survey responses. The use of focus groups involves group interviews with less than a dozen persons where a facilitator and note taker can generate a research hypothesis based on the main concerns expressed by the group, or the group can be asked to address several specific questions that a research team is interested in pursuing. This method has allowed women's concerns to be identified and formalized in a collective forum, and it is particularly well suited for action-oriented research initiatives. Adopting research methods that have been developed in other disciplines such as history, sociology, anthropology and ethnography, as well as interacting with researchers from these fields, thus has clear advantages for areas of inquiry ignored by economists until now (Kim 1997).

Although feminist economists do not necessarily share a common ideological and political perspective, they do have a commitment to methodologies that help formulate theoretical models and practical proposals that will lead to emancipatory change for women. What this means in practice, however, and how specific policy initiatives should be evaluated, is a matter of debate. Some of the work that has been developed from the particular perspective of academic women in industrialized countries has undoubtedly been insufficiently informed by the views and experiences of those who are differently situated. This clearly presents a challenge to feminist methodology: 'To view masculinity and gender interests as the principal forces shaping the discipline, neglecting class, race and nationality, will leave us making claims about the history and shortcomings of orthodox economics that are both too strong and seriously incomplete' (Seiz 1997). The active participation of feminist economists from both the South and the North in a sustained debate and conversation that help define the methodological agenda is undoubtedly necessary to produce invigorating, new feminist scholarship in economics.

ULLA GRAPARD

See also

Dualisms; Development, Theories of; Econometrics; Economic Man; Feminism(s); Game Theory and Bargaining Models; Gross Domestic Product; Gender; History of Economic Thought; Labour Force Participation; Neoclassical Economics; Postmodernism; Rhetoric.

Bibliography

Agarwal, Bina (1997), 'Bargaining and gender relations: within and beyond the household', *Feminist Economics*, **3** (1), 1–51.

Becker, Gary S. (1981), *A Treatise on the Family*, Cambridge: Harvard University Press.

Benería, Lourdes (1992), 'Accounting for women's work: the progress of two decades', *World Development*, **20** (1), 1547–60.

Benería, Lourdes and Shelly Feldman (eds) (1992), *Unequal Burden. Economic Crises, Persistent Poverty and Women's Work*, Boulder: Westview Press.

Bergmann, Barbara (1995), 'Becker's theory of the family: preposterous conclusions', *Feminist Economics*, **1** (1), 141–50.

Blaug, Mark ([1980] 1992), *The Methodology of Economics*, Cambridge: Cambridge University Press.

Bordo, Susan (1987), *The Flight to Objectivity: Essays on Cartesianism and Culture*, Albany: State University of New York Press.

Çagatay, Nilüfer, Diane Elson and Caren Crow (eds) (1995), *Special Issue on Gender, Adjustment, and Macroeconomics, World Development*, **23** (11).

Caldwell, Bruce J. (1982), *Beyond Positivism. Economic Methodology in the Twentieth Century*, London: Allen and Unwin.

Dimand, Mary Ann, Robert W. Dimand, and Evelyn L. Forget (eds) (1995), *Women of Value*, Aldershot and Brookfield: Edward Elgar.

Elshtain, Jean Bethke (1981), *Public Man, Private Woman*, Princeton: Princeton University Press.

Elson, Diane (ed.) (1991), *Male Bias in the Development Process*, Manchester: Manchester University Press.

England, Paula (1993), 'The Separative Self: Androcentric Bias in Neoclassical Assumptions', in Marianne A. Ferber and Julie A. Nelson (eds), *Beyond Economic Man: Feminist Theory and Economics*, Chicago: University of Chicago Press.

Ferber, Marianne and Bonnie Birnbaum (1977), '"The New Home Economics": retrospects and prospects', *Journal of Consumer Research*, **4** (1), 19–28.

Folbre, Nancy (1991), 'The unproductive housewife: Her evolution in nineteenth century thought', *Signs*, **16** (3), 463–84.

Folbre, Nancy (1995), '"Holding hands at midnight": the paradox of caring labor', *Feminist Economics*, **1** (1), 73–92.

Folbre, Nancy and Heidi Hartmann (1988), 'The Rhetoric of Self-Interest: Ideology of Gender in Economic Theory', in Arjo Klamer, Donald McCloskey and Robert M. Solow (eds), *The Consequences of Economic Rhetoric*, Cambridge: Cambridge University Press.

Grapard, Ulla A. (1995), 'Robinson Crusoe: the quintessential man?', *Feminist Economics*, **1** (1), 33–52.

Grapard, Ulla A. (1996), 'Feminist Economics: Let Me Count the Ways', in Fred Foldvary (ed.), *Beyond Neoclassical Economics. Heterodox Approaches to Economic Theory*, Cheltenham: Edward Elgar.

Harding, Sandra (1986), *The Science Question in Feminism*, Ithaca: Cornell University Press.

Harding, Sandra (1991), *Whose Science? Whose Knowledge?*, Ithaca: Cornell University Press.

Himmelweit, Susan (1995), 'The discovery of "unpaid work"', *Feminist Economics*, **1** (2), 1–19.

Jennings, Ann L. (1993), 'Public or Private? Institutional Economics and Feminism', in Marianne A. Ferber and Julie A. Nelson (eds), *Beyond Economic Man: Feminist Theory and Economics*, Chicago: University of Chicago Press.

Kim, Marlene (1997), 'Poor women survey poor women: feminist perspectives in survey research', *Feminist Economics*, 3 (2), 99–117.

Longino, Helen (1990), *Science as Social Knowledge: Values and Objectivity in Scientific Inquiry*, Princeton: Princeton University Press.

Lundberg, Shelley and Robert A. Pollack (1993), 'Separate spheres: bargaining and the marriage market', *Journal of Political Economy*, 101 (6), 988–1010.

MacDonald, Martha (1995), 'Feminist Economics: From Theory to Research', *Canadian Journal of Economics*, 28 (1), 159–76.

Manser, Marilyn and Murray Brown (1980), 'Marriage and household decisionmaking: a bargaining analysis', *International Economic Review*, 21 (1), 31–44.

Marchand, Marianne H. and Janet L. Parpart (eds) (1995), *Feminism/Postmodernism/Development*, London and New York: Routledge.

McCloskey, Donald N. (1985), *The Rhetoric of Economics*, Madison: Wisconsin University Press.

Nelson, Julie A. (1995), 'Feminism and Economics', *Journal of Economic Perspectives*, 9 (2), 131–48.

Nelson, Julie A. (1996), *Feminism, Objectivity and Economics*, London and New York: Routledge.

Pateman, Carole (1988), *The Sexual Contract*, Stanford: Stanford University Press.

Pujol, Michèle A. (1992), *Feminism and Anti-Feminism in Early Economic Thought*, Aldershot: Edward Elgar.

Reid, Margaret (1934), *The Economics of Household Production*, New York: John Wiley.

Seiz, Janet (1991), 'The bargaining approach and feminist methodology', *Review of Radical Political Economics*, 23 (1&2), 22–9.

Seiz, Janet (1992), 'Gender and Economic Research', in Neil de Marchi (ed.), *Post-Popperian Methodology of Economics: Recovering Practice*, Boston and Dordrecht: Kluwer Academic Publishers.

Seiz, Janet (1997), 'Book Reviews', *Feminist Economics*, 3 (1), 179–88.

Strassmann, Diana L. (1993a), 'The stories of economics and the power of the storyteller', *History of Political Economy*, 25 (1), 147–65.

Strassmann, Diana L. (1993b), 'Not a Free Market: The Rhetoric of Disciplinary Authority in Economics', in Marianne A. Ferber and Julie A. Nelson (eds), *Beyond Economic Man: Feminist Theory and Economics*, Chicago: University of Chicago Press.

United Nations Development Programme (1995), *Human Development Report*, New York and Oxford: Oxford University Press.

Williams, Rhonda M. (1993), 'Race, Deconstruction, and the Emergent Agenda of Feminist Economic Theory', in Marianne A. Ferber and Julie A. Nelson (eds), *Beyond Economic Man: Feminist Theory and Economics*, Chicago: University of Chicago Press.

Woolley, Frances R. (1993), 'The feminist challenge to neoclassical economics', *Cambridge Journal of Economics*, 17, 485–500.

Migration

While migration has long been recognized as playing a central role in attaining labour market equilibrium and economic development, only recently have economists paid attention to understanding the gender-specific determinants and consequences of geographic relocation within and across national boundaries. In the last 20 years, both migration theory and an increasing number of empirical studies have begun to treat seriously the potentially different motives for and impact of migration on male and female migrants, with important consequences for the economics of the family, labour markets and rural and urban development policy. Here, three distinct theoretical frameworks for analysing the economic determinants and consequences of migration, each of which place differing emphases on the role of the individual and the household in the migration decision and migration outcomes, are compared and contrasted, and both their gender analytic content and the relevant empirical evidence are evaluated.

Internal migration accounts for nearly half of urban population growth and women constitute approximately 50 per cent of all internal migrants in developing countries. There are, however, marked differences in both the importance of rural–urban population movements and the gender composition of migration across regions. Broadly speaking, men dominate the rural to urban population flows in most of Africa and South Asia, where, with some exceptions, migration is the principal contributor to urban population growth; in Latin America, where natural urban population growth now generally exceeds net migration, women migrate in larger numbers than men (and have done so since at least the 1940s); and rapidly urbanizing and industrializing East and South-East Asian countries also now draw significant numbers of rural women into the cities. Further decomposition of the data by age group shows that, in most countries, women are younger than men when they migrate: while male net rural–urban migration rates peak somewhere over ages 10–24, those for women tend to reach a maximum over age range 10–19 (Singelmann 1993).

The individual migration model, with its roots in the nineteenth century work of Ravenstein (1885, 1889), obtained prominence in the development economics literature with the classic articles by Todaro (1969) and Harris and Todaro (1970). In a development context, the model is strongly associated with the dual sector paradigm, in which surplus labour (labour which does not make a positive contribution to production, including domestic labour) is transferred from the 'subsistence' or 'traditional' agricultural sector of the economy to the 'capitalist' or 'modern' industrial sector, fuelling growth and structural transformation (Lewis 1954). The model characterizes migration as an individual decision in which a person compares her/his expected income in two sectors or geographic areas over a given time horizon. Expectations are based primarily on the probability of finding employment in each sector, although other factors such as crop risk (in the case of agriculture) and the existence of social networks (in the case of urban employment) may also be influential to the migrant's decision. The key result of the model is that, if urban–rural income differentials are high enough, people will migrate even if their chances of actually gaining urban, formal sector employment in the short run are quite low. The principal policy implication is thus that, without raising rural incomes, urban job creation will only attract more migrants, further contributing to unemployment. Thus, individually rational decisions may lead to socially suboptimal outcomes.

Empirical tests of the Todaro model have generally supported the hypotheses of income disparity-induced migration and the importance of human capital (especially formal education) in determining migrant selectivity (Fields 1982; Schultz 1982; Yap 1977). More highly educated young people are more likely to migrate because education increases their probability of obtaining relatively well-paid, formal sector urban employment. The results regarding the deterrent effect of formal sector unemployment have been considerably more mixed, leading some economists to posit an alternative model which incorporates the urban informal sector as an easy-entry employment haven, especially for less-educated migrants and those facing formal sector labour market discrimination, such as women (Cole and Sanders 1985; Eaton 1992). An important result of this latter development is that migration is no longer viewed as a social 'bad' for contributing to urban unemployment and poverty, especially insofar as linkages between the formal and informal sectors allow for complementary employment and income growth.

Both the Todaro model and its more recent adaptations are intended to be 'gender neutral' in the sense that the laws governing migration are assumed to be the same for men and women. The possibility that the determinants of migration differ systematically for men and women remains unexplored; the individual model thus fails to explain the gender selectivity of migration except with reference to individual income and employment differences. Todaro himself has characterized mainstream migration theory as 'sex-specific ... to male migration' and therefore 'special ... rather than general' (Thadani and Todaro 1984, p. 38).

In response to this 'sex specificity', Thadani and Todaro (1984) suggest that a distinguishing feature of female compared to male migration is the importance of marriage as a reason for migration. Their model represents female migration as a function of three sources of income differential: the usual expected rural/urban gap, the 'mobility marriage' differential (defined as an unattached female migrant's chances of achieving a certain expected income through marriage to a male in the modern sector), and the 'customary marriage' differential reflecting the relative probability that an unattached female can find *any* spouse in urban as distinct from rural areas. Behrman and Wolfe (1984) tested this model for a large sample of Nicaraguan households, and found that while the probability of finding a companion motivated a significant amount of female *urban–rural* (and large to small city) migration, women moving from the countryside to the city did so largely for own-labour market reasons. And Findley and Diallo (1993) likewise found that rural Malian women's migration responded to source region economic variables such as average village income and the existence of female income-generating opportunities such as sheep and goat raising, although this migration was most often 'disguised' as being family-related.

From a gender analytic perspective, a fundamental critique of the individual approach is that it treats the migration decision as abstracted from the resource-pooling unit of which the migrant is a member; in other words, it ignores the household-level factors that may influence who migrates and on what terms. Feminist geographers Sylvia Chant and Sarah Radcliffe note that even the development of a specific individual model for female migration runs the risk of treating women as a 'special' group whose participation in migration flows needs to be explained, whereas male migration is seen as relatively unproblematic and reducible to wage rate differentials. They argue that a more comprehensive approach would explore how gender relations affect *both* female and male migration, and the characteristics of the participation of both genders in population moves (Chant and Radcliffe 1992).

Two alternative strands of migration theory address some of the limitations of the individual model by considering two variants of family migration. The first focuses on an entire household's relocation from one area to another, and the second examines the effects of select household members changing their place of residence while remaining effective economic members of the family by virtue of continued resource pooling. The first of these household-level migration models was originally proposed by Mincer (1978), who argued that 'net family gain rather than net personal gain ... motivates migration of households' (Mincer 1978, p. 750). This family migration model is an application of the New Home Economics, which assumes that the preferences of household members can be aggregated together into a common utility function and that income is fully pooled. As a result, some household members may be 'tied movers' or 'tied stayers' in the sense that their own private calculus would dictate an opposite migration decision.

The Mincer model suggests that women are more likely than men to be tied movers, since they exhibit more discontinuous labour market participation and the returns to migration are smaller for individuals with weak labour market attachment. Migration is thus both facilitated by and reinforces gender-based comparative advantage in market and household activities: wives' initial relative specialization in domestic production frees up their husbands to move the family in response to his own labour market opportunities and, since tied movers are more likely to suffer earned income losses when they migrate, women's comparative advantage in domestic labour is further enhanced after relocation. In this regard, Mincer (1978, p. 771) claims that 'tied migration ranks next to child rearing as an important dampening influence in the life-cycle wage evolution of women'.

Empirical evidence from the USA for the 1960s and 1970s suggests that migration is indeed associated with a decrease in women's earnings, and that the gains from migration are larger for married than for single men (Mincer 1978). Econometric tests using developing country data have also been broadly supportive of the 'family migration' hypothesis: in Brazil, Cackley (1993) found that, correcting for migrant selectivity, male but not female wage differentials were significant in explaining married women's migration; and in Costa Rica, Shields and Shields (1989) argue that the negative effect of mothers' education on family migration probabilities reflects the transfer costs of nonmarket household production. A recent study of international immigrants to Canada finds evidence that wives in immigrant families take on 'dead-end' jobs to finance their husbands' investments in human capital until the migrant men can obtain higher-paying, more stable employment (Baker and Benjamin 1997).

Mincer, however, warns against misinterpreting the adverse effects of migration on the labour market experience of some married women as a form of social oppression: 'Such a view ... fails to note that [migration] behavior ... is a product of family welfare maximization. This is Pareto-optimal, since private market losses can be internalized by the family, that is, compensated by a redistribution of gains' (1978, p. 757). In other words, migration which offers differential net individual benefits can be considered incentive compatible for all household members if one accepts the basic premises of the New Home Economics. In particular, the model hinges on the assumption that certain family members' sacrificing of their own income earning potential is compensated for by sharing rules (altruism) which allow them to benefit from overall higher household earnings.

A feminist critique of this version of family migration theory focuses on the presumed consensual nature of the migration decision process and the inevitability of a redistribution of the gains from marriage in the event of a tied move. A model developed by Katz et al. (1998) draws on household bargaining theory to treat the migration decision as a negotiated outcome, with spouses' relative bargaining power and resulting share of the net benefits from migration a function of their fallback positions or threat points. An empirical test of this alternative model using data on migrant married couples in Quito, Ecuador suggests that women with higher levels of education play more active roles in the migration decision, while households in which men participate more fully in household production demonstrate less male bias in the migration decision-making process (Katz et al. 1998).

A second strand of the household approach to migration does make use of a bargaining model, although here the focus is on intergenerational bargaining between non-migrant parents and migrant children in the context of *partial* family migration, that is, where only select household members move but continue to participate in their origin family's economy via mutual remittances. The most influential author in this school has been Oded Stark, who suggests that migration can be interpreted as a household strategy to diversify labour market risk and substitute for incomplete capital markets in rural areas (Stark 1991). His argument is that young migrants serve as financial intermediaries for their families who participate in credit-constrained, risky agricultural undertakings: 'children's primary role as migrants is not to generate an income stream per se, but to act as catalysts for the generation of such a stream by precipitating an income-increasing technological change on the family farm' (Stark 1991, p. 12).

In contrast to the Mincer model, this household approach recognizes that the decision to migrate is often a joint one, part of an 'intertemporal contractual arrangement' between the migrant and her/his family. In this cooperative game framework, both the migrant and nonmigrant parties must 'do better' (in utility or expected income terms) by placing someone in the urban labour market and making remittance transfers, in comparison to the relevant alternatives. Only if the gains to cooperation are positive for each party will the arrangement be incentive compatible – essential if the 'contract' is to be self-enforcing. The terms of the migration contract reflect the relative bargaining powers of the parties. Factors which enhance the nonmigrants' relative position in the absence of remittances, such as large landholdings, policy-induced easing of capital market restrictions, or a high underemployment urban labour market, are predicted to have the counterintuitive effect of increasing migrant remittances, while variables which either weaken the source economy or strengthen the migrant's position may have the opposite impact.

Empirical tests of the household framework have generated interesting results. Data from Botswana, for example, indicate that remittances are larger to families with higher per capita incomes and assets, countering the idea that such contributions are motivated solely by altruism (Lucas and Stark 1985). Another African study found that both the probability of male migration and the level of remittances from sons in Western Kenya were positively influenced by the prospect of land inheritance, especially where there was competition for such inheritance from other adult sons (Hoddinott 1994). Lauby and Stark (1988) make the case that daughters' migration in the Philippines is largely determined by family characteristics and the need for a quick and steady source of remittances, where the latter leads migrant Filipinas into wage labour in large cities, despite better (but slower to develop and less secure) self-employment opportunities in small towns.

From a gender-analytic perspective, this intergenerational household bargaining approach represents a significant advance over prior economic models of migration insofar as it recognizes the strategic interplay between individual interests and collective wellbeing. However, the representation of household decision making and resource allocation is problematic on at least two counts. First, the cooperative game framework implies a symmetry among the parties which ignores the gender and age hierarchies that structure the household economy. In other words, although their fallback positions may differ, players are equal with respect to the rules of the game, meaning that both the weights given to their gains to cooperation and the weights given to their exit options are equal. For example, in the case of youth migration, the roles of filial obligation and obedience (which may themselves be gender-specific) in the determination of remittance levels are likely to be important, but it is difficult to represent such social psychological parameters in a formal model and to measure them empirically. In the Botswana study cited above, Lucas and Stark do not explore the theoretical foundations of the significant systematic gender differences in the factors influencing remittances, in which daughters appear to be motivated by repayment for schooling while sons apparently pursue a strategy to maintain favour in (patrilineal) inheritance.

A second shortcoming of the Stark model is that it assumes that non-migrant household members form a coalition with respect to the migrant based on shared strategic interests. However, it may be the case that individual non-migrants are affected quite differently by a given household member's move, depending on the nature of their interdependence in the rural division of labour and the intra-household remittance flow (who within the household actually sends and receives monetary exchanges with the migrant), both of which typically have strong gender components. While this does not necessarily prevent the formation of a coalition by non-migrants, it does introduce a degree of complexity which might at the minimum influence the terms of the migration 'contract' (Katz 1998). For example, in societies where daughters contribute substantial amounts of labour to domestic production (including child care for younger siblings, freeing up their mothers to pursue income-generating work), their migration may impose substantial costs on their mothers, who are only compensated insofar as remittances directly or indirectly benefit them. A parallel argument could be made for sons who contribute to their father's agricultural work.

A feminist economic model of partial household migration would thus need to address the following questions: what are the gender-specific determinants of bargaining power between parents and children? How are the possibly competing preferences of non-migrants (for example, mothers and fathers in the case of youth migration) over the migration decision reconciled?; and how are inter-personal remittance flows (as distinct from levels) determined? Recent empirical work in Malaysia and the Dominican Republic represent initial attempts to consider these issues. Kusago (1996) uses innovative field methodologies to assess the degree of preference heterogeneity among mothers and fathers of young female migrants, and traces the impact of daughter-to-mother remittances on intra-household resource allocation. De la Brière et al. (1997) investigate gender differences in remittance motives, and find that while young men who plan to return to their places of origin follow a pattern consistent with investment in potential bequests, female migrants with no intention of returning play the role of insurers to their families during economic downturns.

Migration is an important area of research for feminist economics. It is a topic with an active debate over the distinct roles of the individual and the household, and empirical evidence from both developed and developing economies suggests that significant gender differences exist in the determinants and consequences of geographic mobility. Future research should build on advances made in this field by continuing to explore the intra-household dynamics of migration decision making, the differential effects of migration on women and men, and the policy implications of a gendered approach to migration.

ELIZABETH KATZ

See also

Development, Theories of; Family, Economics of; Game Theory and Bargaining Models; Urban and Regional Economics.

Bibliography

Baker, Michael and Dwayne Benjamin (1997), 'The role of the family in immigrants' labour-market activity: an evaluation of alternative explanations', *American Economic Review*, **87** (4), 705–27.

Behrman, Jere R. and Barbara L. Wolfe (1984), 'Micro determinants of female migration in a developing country: labour market, demographic marriage market and economic marriage market incentives', *Research in Population Economics*, **5**, 137–66.

Cackley, Alicia Puente (1993), 'The Role of Wage Differentials in Determining Migration Selectivity By Sex: The Case of Brazil', in United Nations, Department for Economic and Social Information and Policy Analysis, *Internal Migration of Women in Developing Countries*, New York: United Nations, pp. 259–69.

Chant, Sylvia and Sarah A. Radcliffe (1992), 'Migration and Development: The Importance of Gender', in Sylvia Chant (ed.), *Gender and Migration in Developing Countries*, London and New York: Belhaven Press, pp. 1–29.

Cole, William and Richard Sanders (1985), 'Internal migration and urban employment in the third world', *American Economic Review*, **75** (3), 481–94.

De la Brière, Bénedicte, Alain de Janvry, Sylvie Lambert and Elisabeth Sadoulet (1997), *Why Do Migrants Remit? An Analysis for the Dominican Sierra*, FCND Discussion Paper No. 37, Washington, DC: International Food Policy Research Institute.

Eaton, Peter J. (1992), 'Rural–urban migration and underemployment among females in the Brazilian northeast', *Journal of Economic Issues*, **26** (2), 385–95.

Fields, Gary S. (1982), 'Place-to-place migration in Colombia', *Economic Development and Cultural Change*, **30** (3), 539–58.

Findley, Sally E. and Assitan Diallo (1993), 'Social Appearances and Economic Realities of Female Migration in Rural Mali', in United Nations, Department for Economic and Social Information and Policy Analysis, *Internal Migration of Women in Developing Countries*, New York: United Nations, pp. 243–57.

Harris, John R. and Michael P. Todaro (1970), 'Migration, unemployment and development: a two-sector analysis', *American Economic Review*, **60** (1), 126–42.

Hoddinott, John (1994), 'A model of migration and remittances applied to Western Kenya', *Oxford Economic Papers*, **46**, 459–76.

Katz, Elizabeth (1998), 'An Intra-Household Model of Migration and Remittances with Evidence from Ecuador', Paper presented at the Allied Social Science Association meetings, Chicago, Illinois, January 3–5.

Katz, Elizabeth, Andrew R. Morrison and Richard E. Bilsborrow (1998), 'Tied Movers or Bargained Moves? The Determinants of Married Couples' Migration Decision-Making in Ecuador', Paper prepared for the meetings of the Population Association of America, Chicago, Illinois, April 2–4.

Kusago, Takayoshi (1996), 'Female Migration to Export Processing Zones in Malaysia: The Role of Preference Heterogeneity and Intra-Household Power Relations in Family Decision-Making', Ph.D. dissertation, University of Wisconsin–Madison.

Lauby, Jennifer and Oded Stark (1988), 'Individual migration as a family strategy: young women in the Philippines', *Population Studies*, **42**, 473–86.

Lewis, W.A. (1954), 'Economic development with unlimited supplies of labour', *Manchester School*, **22** (2), 139–91.

Lucas, Robert E.B. and Oded Stark (1985), 'Motivations to remit: evidence from Botswana', *Journal of Political Economy*, **93** (5), 901–18.

Mincer, J. (1978), 'Family migration decisions', *Journal of Political Economy*, **86** (5), 749–73.

Ravenstein, E.G. (1885), 'The laws of migration', *Journal of the Royal Statistical Society*, **48**, 167–227.

Ravenstein, E.G. (1889), 'The laws of migration', *Journal of the Royal Statistical Society*, **52**, 241–301.

Schultz, T. Paul (1982), 'Lifetime migration within educational strata in Venezuela: estimates of a logistic model', *Economic Development and Cultural Change*, **30** (3), 559–93.

Shields, Gail M. and Michael P. Shields (1989), 'Family Migration and Nonmarket Activities in Costa Rica', *Economic Development and Cultural Change*, **38** (1), 73–88.

Singelmann, Joachim (1993), 'Levels and Trends of Female Internal Migration in Developing Countries, 1960–1980', in United Nations, Department for Economic and Social Information and Policy Analysis, *Internal Migration of Women in Developing Countries*, New York: United Nations, pp. 77–93.

Stark, Oded (1991), *The Migration of Labor*, New York: Basil Blackwell.

Thadani, Veena N. and Michael P. Todaro (1984), 'Female Migration: A Conceptual Framework', in James T. Fawcett, Siew-Ean Khoo and Peter C. Smith (eds), *Women in the Cities of Asia: Migration and Urban Adaptation*, Boulder, Colorado: Westview Press.

Todaro, Michael P. (1969), 'A model of labor migration and urban unemployment in less developed countries', *American Economic Review*, **59** (1), 138–58.

Yap, Lorene Y.L. (1977), 'The attraction of cities: a review of the migration literature', *Journal of Development Economics*, **4**, 239–64.

Minimum Wage

Low wages have historically been and continue to be a serious problem for women workers in both developed and less-developed countries. Given the large proportion of women who currently work for wages, in countries with minimum wage laws it is frequently the case that a majority of minimum wage workers are women. For example, in the United States, nearly two-thirds are women (IWPR 1995); and in Great Britain at the time that the extremely limited minimum wage laws were abolished in 1993, 80 per cent of covered workers were women (Hart 1994, p. 178). As a result, the minimum wage is of considerable interest to feminist economists who are investigating policies to move women out of poverty. However, as will be discussed below, current-day feminist economists see improving the minimum wage as only one part of a *package* of policies aimed at providing an adequate level of support for women workers and their families.

In addition, a growing movement in the United States and Canada, with a base in organized labour, has been reintroducing the historic demand for a *living* wage, rather than merely a *minimum* wage. Although there is not a large body of feminist writing on this movement, historical feminist analyses suggest that the success of such a movement in raising women's standard of living depends on who gets to determine the meaning of a 'living' wage. Early twentieth century struggles for living wages for women became lengthy debates about what was a suitable standard of living for women (Kessler-Harris 1990). Raising the value of women's work, and demanding 'the rate for the job' appear to be less value-prone strategies. Feminists studying women in less-developed countries add that the level of pay is only one part of the struggle for economic independence for women: their ability to retain *control* over their own pay is equally important.

Feminists were more actively engaged in debate over minimum wages in the early twentieth century, a period in which Great Britain, Australia and New Zealand established industry-specific minimum wages for both male and female workers, and a number of states in the United States established industry-specific minimum wages solely for women. The minimum wage discussions of this period resonate with the classical and Marxian views of distribution, which argue that wages have an exogenous base in societally-determined levels of subsistence, and suggest that this notion of accepted living standards varies by gender, as well as class and race. As such, they provide insight into the origins and persistence of gender-based wage differences. In addition, the minimum wage legislation in the United States raises interesting questions for the equality-versus-difference public policy debate, since a number of its supporters clearly perceived gender-based protective legislation as an opening wedge for class-based protection. Opponents of minimum wages for women, on the other hand, included Alice Paul of the National Women's Party, who believed that any gender-specific protective legislation was detrimental to women's progress. In what follows, this entry will review the very active discussion among feminists in the United States about minimum wages in the early twentieth century, then return to the present literature, which is less specifically focused on this issue.

In the Progressive Era in the early twentieth century, reform-minded feminists in the United States saw minimum wages specifically for women in the sweatshop industries as an important component of protective legislation designed to protect working class women from excessive exploitation. Activists with organizations like the Consumers League (for example, Maude Nathan and Florence Kelly) and the Women's Trade Union League (for example, Maude Swartz) joined league with social investigators (for example, Mary Van

Kleeck of the Russell Sage Foundation) and academics (for example, Emilie Hutchison of Barnard, Dorothy Douglas of the University of Washington) to call for state-by-state legislation to set minimum wages at a level consistent with decency and health for women in specific industries. The ideologies of the reformers differed, as did their motives: from preservation of traditional values to promotion of equality for women and from Christian benevolence to socialist revolution. Accordingly, their reasons for focusing on gender-specific legislation ranged from a strong belief in essential differences between men and women to a pragmatic recognition that protective legislation was more likely to pass scrutiny in the courts than was gender-neutral legislation.

Feminist reformers' arguments could be divided into four basic, not mutually exclusive, categories, which may be labelled pragmatic, strategic, essentialist and social value arguments. Pragmatic arguments pointed out that women were the lowest paid workers, with wages that often left them in desperate circumstances (Hutchison 1919, pp. 15–27). Strategic arguments focused on the inability to pass gender-neutral protective legislation. Supreme Court rulings from the late nineteenth century on tended to reject protective legislation for men as an interference with their freedom of contract; but, after the 1908 Muller vs Oregon decision, protection was allowed for women workers (Kessler-Harris 1990, p. 38).

Third, arguments supporting a minimum wage for women often made reference to their essentially different natures from men. Wage work was to occupy a relatively brief interlude between an early-ending childhood and a life of marriage and motherhood. As such, women's wages were believed to be 'naturally' lower than men's; but because effective mothering was seen as a social good, there was need for public vigilance to assure that women's wages did not fall below the level necessary for health and morality. Women who were weakened by long hours and poor diets jeopardized their all-important future role (Hutchison 1919, p. 82). In California, for example, the slogan of the middle-class club women who were the force behind the minimum wage was: 'Employed womanhood must be protected in order to foster the motherhood of the race' (Women's Bureau 1928, p. 130).

Finally, building on the work of Beatrice and Sidney Webb, many participants in the minimum wage discussions of this period argued that employers who did not pay the full cost of supporting their female employees were 'parasitic' on the community, because they were being, in effect, subsidized by the wages of other family members or by public or private charity (the same, of course, would be true for low-wage male workers) (Hutchison 1919, pp. 82–3). Maud Swartz of the Women's Trade Union League echoed this argument. Employers paying less than a living wage were 'nothing but people who are living on the bounty of the Nation' (Swartz in Women's Bureau 1923, pp. 80–81).

Beginning with Massachusetts in 1912, sixteen states and the District of Columbia passed minimum wages for women (in 1923 the Supreme Court invalidated the Washington DC law; for the next decade only sporadic and largely unsuccessful efforts were made to design gender-specific minimum wage laws). As states began to design their minimum wage guidelines, feminist activists and academics participated in the discussion about what constituted the minimum wage necessary for health and decency, which was the criterion universally adopted as a goal. According to economist Dorothy Douglas, employers generally advocated either a 'pin-money theory', arguing that women's wages need cover only part of their expense (a view Douglas termed 'ultra-reactionary'), or a 'joint-cost theory', which presumed that the worker lived with her family and enjoyed the 'economies of family life', allowing her to survive on a very low wage (Douglas 1920, p. 225). Douglas and Emilie Hutchison went to great lengths to refute the joint-cost argument, arguing that the true costs of a woman living with her family were little less than those of a woman living alone (a woman 'adrift' in the parlance of the day), because her living costs must include her share of the support of her housewife/mother, whose services she employed (Douglas 1920, pp. 245–6; Hutchison 1919, pp. 45–7).

In concert with most feminists of their day, Douglas and Hutchison advocated a minimum wage sufficient to support a woman living away from her family. Not only were the 'economies of family life' overstated, in their view, but also requiring employers to pay a wage sufficient for independence for women was the only way to assure that industry did not become parasitic on the community. These arguments were sufficiently persuasive that every state adopted the woman adrift as the standard for setting minimum wages, despite active lobbying by employers, and their awareness that the majority of women in manufacturing in fact lived with their families (Women's Bureau 1928, p. 75). In practice, however, according to Elizabeth Brandeis, the minimum wage arrived at was almost always a compromise, one in which rates were frequently set below the estimated cost of living (Brandeis 1935, p. 527).

In this discussion of the minimum standard necessary for women, only a few voices spoke up for the notion that women, like men, supported dependants and required not an individual wage, but a family wage (a view Douglas disapprovingly termed 'ultra-radical' (1920, p. 225)). The most prominent exponent of the family-based minimum was Mary Van Kleeck of the Russell Sage Foundation, particularly while she was temporarily head of the Women in Industry Service of the Department of Labor during World War I (*Monthly Labor Review* 1918, pp. 1340–41). These wage principles were not adopted by the government, however, and after the war Van Kleeck drafted a statement of principles again endorsing a family wage for women (Van Kleeck 1919, p. 91). Alice Kessler-Harris argues that the Women in Industry Division was primarily concerned with insuring the women did not undercut the wages of male workers (Kessler-Harris 1990, p. 88). While this was no doubt a concern, Van Kleeck justified the demand for a family wage with the evidence from her own studies, which showed that many women workers helped support dependants (cited in Douglas 1920, p. 238). Van Kleeck's arguments were precursors of current feminist arguments about what constitutes a living wage for women workers; however, in her day she was virtually alone in her views. Most analysts, including most feminists, in the Progressive Era viewed wage labour as appropriate only for unmarried, or at least childless, women; a family wage for women was not only unnecessary, in this view, but sent an undesirable social message that women with children should work for wages.

The gender-specific minimum wage laws of the Progressive Era had a positive effect on wages for women in some of the worst sweatshop industries. However, given their cumbersome industry-by-industry structure, the short period for which most were active, and the small number of states in which they were in effect (not including highly-industrialized New York or Illinois), their effects were fairly minimal. Additionally, all of the state laws exempted domestic and agricultural work from minimum wages, effectively excluding most African-American women from coverage (laundry workers, who were covered, were, however, frequently African-American).

It was not until the Supreme Court reversed itself in 1936 and accepted Washington State's minimum wage for women that the stage was set for an attempt at a national, gender-neutral minimum wage. The Fair Labor Standards Act of 1938 set a flat rate minimum wage applicable to both male and female workers, avoiding questions about living wages, or appropriate styles of living for men and women. However, the law was passed with the justification that the federal government had the right to regulate industries engaged in interstate commerce, and 'commerce' was interpreted as excluding such occupations as agriculture, domestic work, most retailing, and food packing and processing, disproportionately excluding women from coverage (as well as African-American men, who were heavily employed in agriculture) (Hart 1994, p. 152). The law was gradually extended through case-by-case decisions, with, for example, agricultural workers first included in 1966 and domestic workers in 1974 (Hart 1994, p. 169). By the 1990s more than 90 per cent of American workers were covered by the federal minimum wage, and nearly two-thirds of these workers were women.

Feminist economists in the United States at present are working toward reviving the notion of a family wage for women workers, noting that most women support dependants, and that poverty rates are highest for women who are raising children alone. Since the majority of minimum wage workers are women, and single women with children have the lowest earnings, it might be supposed that strategies to create a family wage for women workers might focus on establishing a higher minimum. In fact, however, feminist strategies include increasing the minimum wage as only one component of a plan to improve the condition of women workers and their families. This is in part because the increases in the minimum wage required to bring women single parents and their children out of poverty are so great as to appear politically unfeasible. Figart and Lapidus (1995, p. 64) report that an hourly wage of $5.65 per hour would be required to bring a parent and two children up to the poverty line; $7.14 would be required for a parent and three children. Renwick and Bergmann's Basic Needs Budget, which uses budget-based methodology to measure minimum necessary living costs for a single parent and two children, finds that a wage of $8.70 would be needed to bring the family to this level (Renwick and Bergmann 1993, p. 15). Spalter-Roth and Hartmann (1991) estimate a sufficiency wage necessary to bring a working mother with two children up to the poverty line plus child care costs for one child at $5.80 an hour for full-time, full-year work.

Additionally, feminist economists argue that other strategies provide more substantial benefits to women workers. Figart and Lapidus estimate that comparable worth for women in female-dominated occupations would raise more low income women workers out of poverty than the now-implemented $5.15 minimum wage (1995, p. 70). Renwick and Bergmann advocate subsidized health insurance for single parents whose jobs do not offer it, and free child care for all single parent families (1993, p. 20). Spalter-Roth and Hartmann (1991, p. 85) find that overcoming race and gender discrimination in the work force, creating an abundance of full-time, year-round jobs, and enabling women without high school degrees to earn a GED, are the most effective policies to move low-income women and their families out of poverty. In an era in which women must support themselves and their families over their lifetimes, a wage set at the minimum 'necessary for health and decency' no longer suffices. Feminist economists, while not disparaging the minimum wage as a floor on wages, seek to move women beyond bare subsistence to equity and a wage sufficient to support a family.

MARILYN POWER

See also
Comparable Worth/Pay Equity; Family Wage; Feminization of Poverty; Protective Legislation.

Bibliography
Brandeis, Elizabeth (1935), 'Labor Legislation', in John R. Commons (ed.), *History of Labor in the United States, 1896–1932*, Vol. III, New York: The Macmillan Co.
Douglas, Dorothy W. (1920), 'The cost of living for working women: a criticism of current theories', *Quarterly Journal of Economics*, **34**, February, 225–59.

Figart, Deborah M. and June Lapidus (1995), 'A gender analysis of U.S. labor market policies for the working poor', *Feminist Economics*, **1** (3), 60–81.

Hart, Vivien (1994), *Bound by Our Constitution: Women, Workers, and Minimum Wage Laws in the United States and Britain*, Princeton: Princeton University Press.

Hutchison, Emilie Josephine (1919), *Women's Wages: a Study of the Wages of Industrial Women and Measures Suggested to Increase Them*, New York: Longmans, Green and Co.

Institute for Women's Policy Research (IWPR) (March, 1995), 'Women and the Minimum Wage', Briefing Paper, Washington, DC.

Kessler-Harris, Alice (1990), *A Woman's Wage: Historical Meanings and Social Consequences*, Lexington: University Press of Kentucky.

Monthly Labor Review (1918), 'Conference of Trade-Union Women Under Auspices of U.S. Department of Labor', pp. 190–92.

Renwick, Trudi and Barbara Bergmann (1993), 'A Budget-Based Definition of Poverty', *Journal of Human Resources*, **28**, (Winter), 1–24.

Spalter-Roth, Roberta and Heidi I. Hartmann (1991), *Increasing Working Mothers' Earnings*, Washington, DC: Institute for Women's Policy Research.

Van Kleeck, Mary (1919), 'Federal Policies for Women in Industry', *Annals of the American Academy of Political Science*, (January), 87–94.

Webb, Sidney and Beatrice Webb (1920), *Industrial Democracy*, London: Longmans, Green and Co.

Women's Bureau, U.S. Department of Labor (1923), *Proceedings of the Women's Industrial Conference*, Bulletin 33.

Women's Bureau, U.S. Department of Labor (1928), *The Development of Minimum Wage Laws in the U.S., 1912–1927*, Bulletin 61.

Neoclassical Economics

Neoclassical economics is the predominant school of contemporary economic theory. For most economists, neoclassical economics *is* economics, the standard to which all other schools are compared. Neoclassical economists start from the premise that resources are scarce and human wants are unlimited, and they define economics as the science of choice: the study of how societies allocate scarce resources among alternative uses. In this view economics is an objective, gender-neutral and value-free science that seeks to articulate the laws of economics in the same way that physicists seek to articulate the laws of physical phenomena. It assumes an economic reality that is independent of theoretical observations, the laws of which may be apprehended through the use of the scientific method. Feminist scholars in other social sciences have shown that scientific knowledge claims are inevitably saturated with a variety of contextual values that reflect the gender, class, culture and social location of their practitioners (Kramarae and Spender 1992). Feminist economics brings similar insights to an examination of neoclassical economics, providing a critique of the gender, race and class bias in its theory and methodology. Feminist economists working within the neoclassical tradition are incorporating such insights and expanding the boundaries of neoclassical theory and methodology.

The cornerstone of neoclassical economics is its reliance on supply and demand analysis to explain prices and output simultaneously. It is a theory of value, distribution and output and has its genesis in what has come to be called the marginal revolution in economics in the late nineteenth century. The marginal revolution refers to a shift from thinking about the value of goods and services as a function of their production costs to an understanding of their value as the result of individuals' subjective evaluations. Before the marginal revolution, classical economists assumed that the value of any commodity was objectively determined by how much it cost to produce it. However, actual prices often did not reflect value when defined in this way, partly because an objective conception of value could not account for the usefulness or desirability of goods to consumers. The marginalists were a group of economists who argued that the value of commodities is determined by the utility they provide to consumers, where utility refers to the ability of commodities to satisfy human pleasures, wants and needs. They are referred to as marginalists because they argued that it is not the total utility of a good that determines its value but rather its marginal utility. Marginal means additional or incremental, and so marginal utility refers to the subjective value of an additional unit of a particular commodity. Marginal utility is assumed to decrease as more of a good is consumed: as the consumption of a good increases, the additional satisfaction gained from that consumption decreases.

Marginal analysis remains at the centre of contemporary neoclassical economics. Contemporary models assume that individuals – be they consumers, workers or firms – undertake any economic activity up to the point where the marginal (or additional) benefits of that activity are equal to its marginal costs. This calculus will, in turn, enable consumers to maximize their utility (or satisfaction), and aggregating the results across all consumers then provides the demand schedules for good and services. The supply schedules for goods and services are likewise determined by aggregating the profit-maximizing positions for individual producers. Together demand and supply determine a commodity's price and level of output through their simultaneous interaction. Any imbalance between supply and demand automatically exerts pressure on prices to adjust to a new market clearing level. If no market imperfections are present, then the price system will result in an economically efficient allocation of scarce resources, an allocation that maximizes economic welfare.

It has been noted by feminist economists and others that neoclassical economics is defined by its method of explanation rather than by its domain of study. Two important characteristics of this method are a commitment to methodological individualism and the centrality of rational choice theory. Methodological individualism assumes that analyses of social phenomena start from an analysis of individual behaviour. Thus, an economic system is conceived of as a collectivity of rational economic agents who maximize their utility (or profits, in the case of firms) subject to the constraints placed on them by prices and incomes. Individual economic decisions are coordinated through markets, and economic outcomes are simply the collective results of their choices.

Rational choice simply refers to the ability of individuals to order their preferences (their likes and dislikes) in a manner that is logically consistent and then, given that preference structure, to make choices that maximize their self-interest. The preferences that underlie economic choices are assumed to be fundamentally independent from the constraints on choice, prices and other costs. Rational choice is then understood in terms of constrained optimization techniques: economic agents maximize their wellbeing by engaging in any activity up to the point where the marginal benefits are equal to the marginal costs. Within this framework individuals are assumed to have no contingent obligations or responsibilities, and they interact contractually with one another when it is in their self-interest to do so. The rational economic agent is commonly referred to as 'homo economicus' or 'economic man'.

Feminist economists contest the notion that explanations based on methodological individualism and rational choice theory are the best way to achieve scientific rigour and objectivity. Nelson (1996) argues that the emphasis on choice in economics is related to the Cartesian dichotomy between embodiment and rationality. In this view, the abstract, detached, masculine view represents scientific thinking and is radically removed from the concrete, connected, feminine reality of material life. Nelson argues that making the detached *cogito* the object of study in economics means that nature, the body, children and the need for human connectedness remain cut off from masculine concern. Moreover, the emphasis on scarcity suggests that nature is hostile and stingy. This suggests a conception of man dominating a passive, but nevertheless threatening, nature. Nelson suggests that instead of conceptualizing economics as a theory of choice, it could be conceived of as a theory of provisioning. This would enable feminist economists to direct their attention away from the theoretical modelling of utility-maximizing behaviour and toward examinations of ways to improve people's material wellbeing.

Conceiving of economics in this way entails an examination of the prevailing distinction between positive and normative economic theory. (Positive theory is said to examine the facts of economic life, independent of the values of the investigator; normative theory evaluates those facts in terms of values and goals.) Feminist scholars provide a serious challenge to the positive/ normative distinction through their insistence that the notion of science as an objective enterprise – value free, politically neutral and gender blind – is distinctly androcentric and biased (Harding 1995, Longino 1990).

Harding (1995) shows that although the goal of impartial, value-free research is to eliminate social values and prejudices from science, in practice it eliminates only those values that differ among researchers. Shared, or 'constitutive', values within the scientific community will not be questioned. To the extent that the community excludes women and people of colour, implicit assumptions about race, class and gender will not be apparent. However, a different conception of objectivity, which she terms strong objectivity, rejects the ideal of value neutrality and extends the notion of the scientific method to include an examination of constitutive values and hidden cultural assumptions that remain invisible from the standpoint of the dominant groups. The preoccupation with objectivity and scientific rigour within neoclassical economics, combined with the homogeneity of the economics profession, results in a biased and incomplete economics because there are few opportunities or incentives for examining shared cultural assumptions and values.

Examining the implicit assumptions and values embedded in the neoclassical paradigm is an important part of the feminist economics project. Strassmann (1993) calls attention to the role of values and power in the production of economic knowledge by examining economics as an interpretive community whose members are socialized not to question the primacy of the methodological and theoretical assumptions embedded within the discipline. She reconceptualizes economic theory as storytelling and examines the constitutive values embedded in several common economic stories. The notion of free choice is one such story. Embedded in this story is the assumption that people are able to be responsible for taking care of their own needs and, moreover, that they take only their own needs and wishes into account. Actions that benefit others are accounted for by altruism. Strassmann argues that while these assumptions may indeed be typical of the perceived experiences of adult white male middle-class economists, they fail to capture economic reality for many others such as children, the elderly, the infirm or others who do not have independent access to economic resources. This exclusion is one example of the partial and incomplete nature of typical neoclassical accounts.

Barker (1995) examines the constitutive values embedded in economists' use of the efficiency, or Pareto optimality, criterion. Economic efficiency is simply a way of judging economic outcomes: if there is no way to make anyone better off without making another one worse off, then an outcome is economically efficient. It follows from this criterion that there will be an optimal level of pollution, an optimal level of product safety, an optimal level of resources devoted to child care and even an optimal level of crime. Barker argues that economic efficiency implicitly assumes that measures of economic wellbeing can be collapsed into a single metric, that all values are commensurable and that all human needs can be met through market exchange. These are shared assumptions and values that, in practice, privilege market activities and diminish the significance of nonmarket activities, many of which have traditionally been considered women's work.

The gendered and androcentric nature of *homo economicus* provides other examples of unexamined values in neoclassical theory. The rational economic agent is a self-sufficient individual, existing outside social and cultural influences, with no contingent obligations to anyone. Robinson Crusoe is a paradigm example of such an agent, and he is often used in textbooks to illustrate how individuals allocate their time between work and leisure to maximize their wellbeing. Grapard (1995) asks what the story of a single, white, colonial male living alone (until he is joined by Friday, his native servant) on a desert island can tell us about economics. According to Grapard, the absence of women and Crusoe's relationship with Friday reflect both race and gender exploitation. Economists' appropriation of the story reveals how neoclassical discourse deals with gender and race: it reifies economic man, naturalizes racism and marginalizes women's contributions to economic welfare.

The public/private distinction, which has its origins in liberal political theory, plays an important part in explaining why neoclassical economics has marginalized women's economic contributions. This distinction refers to the theoretical separation between human interactions in the public or political world and those in the private realm of the family. Private or familial relationships are necessary and obligatory; public or political relationships are voluntary and contractual. Pujol's (1992) work shows that neoclassical analysis requires this distinction for its own theoretical consistency. For example, investment in human capital, necessary for reproduction and growth in a capitalist economy, requires that parents must act unselfishly toward their children, and this type of behaviour is at odds with the assumption of self-interest in the neoclassical model. Thus it is implicitly assumed that selfish economic behaviour does not hold within the family unit. Similarly, England (1993) and Folbre and Hartmann (1988) argue that the public/private distinction falsely exaggerates both the atomistic, competitive behaviour of market relationships and the extent of connection, care and altruism within families.

Given its adherence to methodological individualism, the economic analysis of the family presents a potentially serious difficulty for neoclassical theory, a difficulty neatly solved by the New Home Economics. This approach assumes that the head of the household redistributes family income and makes consumption decisions for the rest of the family members. The head is an altruist, cares about the wellbeing of the family and is able to transfer purchasing power to them (Becker 1981). Although the head is not explicitly defined as a man, this conceptualization of the family reflects a patriarchal, Victorian ideal. It treats the family as a unit of cohesive interests and uses the principles of rational choice theory to explain gendered choices and outcomes. Since women are assumed to have a natural inclination for household activities, the sexual division of labour is seen as mutually beneficial to both men and women. Inequalities in the distribution of domestic work and asymmetries in the division of labour are explained as the consequences of individuals' utility maximizing choices (Benería 1995). Benería argues that this analysis leaves out important questions about initial allocations of resources among individuals, including gendered skills, and it does not problematize differences in autonomy and power. Thus the New Home Economics cannot offer transformative analyses of gender inequalities and gender relations (Benería 1995).

Feminist economists working within the neoclassical paradigm stress the importance of documenting differences in the wellbeing of men and women, strive to conduct research that is free from androcentric bias and advocate economic policies that promote gender equity (Woolley 1993). Consequently, the economics of the family and labour markets has received considerable attention from feminist economists working in the neoclassical tradition. For example, Grossbard-Shechtman (1993) provides a theoretical framework that models marriage as an exchange of spousal labour, which is work done by one spouse (usually the wife) that benefits the other. The rewards to spousal labour vary according to the supply and demand for marriage partners. Grossbard-Shechtman argues that characterizing women who are married or cohabiting and not participating in the labour force as spousal workers acknowledges the value of household labour, and opens the door for spousal workers to bargain for the right to be fairly compensated.

Using game-theoretic or strategic bargaining models to analyse the family is another important extension of this research for feminist economists working in the neoclassical tradition. Acknowledging that family relationships will have elements of both conflict and cooperation, these models describe intra-family interactions as a type of strategic bargaining that determines the allocations of resources and responsibilities within the household. Ott's (1995) work provides a clear example. She begins with the observations that bargaining power within marriage depends on the spouses' alternatives in paid employment, and that specialization in market work increases an individual's potential earnings while specialization in household labour entails a loss in earning potential. Therefore a family's division of labour between market and household labour affects not only family income, but also the future labour market opportunities of marriage partners and their bargaining power within the household. Unlike the traditional model, which implies that one person (generally the wife) will specialize in household labour, the bargaining model shows that such specialization can negatively affect both a spouse's earnings potential and his or her wellbeing within the household.

Agarwal (1997) takes a similar approach, but considerably broadens the scope of factors in the analysis, and thus takes the game-theoretic approach beyond its neoclassical roots. She explicitly addresses the complexity of gender relations between men and women and examines the ways these relations impinge on economic outcomes. Characterizing the family as a complex web of relationships, Agarwal argues that the economic wellbeing of particular family members depends upon a variety of factors such as the role of social norms in bargaining, the coexistence of self-interest and altruism, and the role of the household in wider social institutions, all factors typically not considered in neoclassical analysis.

Feminist economists have also noted that women's roles in the household as wives and mothers reinforces a gendered division of labour and rationalizes the wage gap between men and women. On average, women's wages are lower than men's, and labour markets are highly segregated by sex. Occupational segregation means that women are often segregated into lower paying and less prestigious occupations, and gender segregation exists even within occupations. Feminist analysis of occupational segregation challenges the views of traditional neoclassical economists, who do not take gender into account, and hold that these labour market outcomes are determined by supply and demand and are the result of the free market process. Feminist economists have also modified neoclassical explanations of labour market discrimination and the wage gap by explicitly taking into account the social and institutional norms that constrain and shape women's preferences and choices (Bergmann 1986; Humphries 1995; Woolley 1993). Bergmann shows that discrimination in hiring practices causes both occupational segregation and lower earnings for women. Discrimination causes women to be crowded into female-dominated occupations and this crowding increases the supply of labour and lowers women's wages. Thus unfair and discriminatory labour market outcomes are the result of a traditional sexual division of labour institutionalized in the norms and practices of contemporary society.

The efforts of feminist economists to reconstruct economic theory have been informed by both the critiques and the modifications of neoclassical economics. Economics is increasingly being conceptualized as the study of provisioning rather than the science of choice, and methodological individualism, rational choice and contractual exchange are no longer required to be in the centre of the analysis. The role of gender in determining economic outcomes is being explored, and in addition to gender, race, class and sexual orientation are now considered appropriate categories of analysis for economic theorists. This raises an important question: with these changes and modifications is what remains still neoclassical economics or does it become something else, such as feminist political economy? It is not possible to answer this question at this point, and so the ways in which the neoclassical framework will be transformed by feminist economics remains an open question.

DRUCILLA K. BARKER

See also
Economic Man; Family, Economics of; Feminist Economics; Game Theory and Bargaining Models; Labour Markets, Theories of; Marriage, Theories of; Methodology; Wage Gap.

Bibliography
Agarwal, Bina (1997), '"Bargaining" and gender relations: within and beyond the household', *Feminist Economics*, **3** (1), (Spring), 1–50.
Barker, Drucilla K. (1995), 'Economists, social reformers and prophets: a feminist critique of economic efficiency', *Feminist Economics*, **1** (3), 26–39.
Becker, Gary (1981), *A Treatise on The Family*, Cambridge: Cambridge University Press.
Bergmann, Barbara (1986), *The Economic Emergence of Women*, Basic Books.
Benería, Lourdes (1995), 'Toward a greater integration of gender in economics', *World Development*, **23** (11), 1839–50.
England, Paula (1993), 'The Separative Self: Androcentric Bias in Neoclassical Assumptions', in M.A. Ferber and J.A. Nelson (eds), *Beyond Economic Man: Feminist Theory and Economics*, Chicago: University of Chicago Press, pp. 37–53.
Ferber, Marianne, A. and Julie A. Nelson (1993), *Beyond Economic Man*, Chicago: University of Chicago Press.
Folbre, Nancy and Heidi Hartmann (1988), 'The Rhetoric of Self-Interest: Ideology and Gender in Economic Theory', in Arjo Klamer, Donald McCloskey and Robert Solow (eds), *The Consequences of Economic Rhetoric*, Cambridge: Cambridge University Press, pp. 184–206.
Grapard, Ulla (1995) 'Robinson Crusoe: the quintessential economic man?', *Feminist Economics*, **1** (1), (Spring), 33–52.

Grossbard-Shechtman, Shoshana A. (1993), *On the Economics of Marriage*, Boulder: Westview Press.

Harding, Sandra (1995), 'Can feminist thought make economics more objective?', *Feminist Economics*, **1** (1), (Spring), 7–32.

Humphries, Jane (1995), 'Economics, Gender and Equal Opportunities', in J. Humphries and J. Rubery (eds), *The Economics of Equal Opportunities*, Manchester: Equal Opportunities Commission, pp. 55–86.

Kramarae, Cheris and Dale Spender (eds) (1992), *The Knowledge Explosion: Generations of Feminist Scholarship*, New York: Teacher's College Press.

Longino, Helen E. (1990), *Science as Social Knowledge: Values and Objectivity in Scientific Inquiry*, Princeton: Princeton University Press.

Madrick, Jeff (1997), 'Why mainstream economists should take heed', *Feminist Economics*, **3** (1), (Spring), 141–8.

Nelson, Julie, A. (1996), *Feminism, Objectivity, and Economics*, London: Routledge.

Ott, Notburga (1995), 'Fertility and Division of Work in the Family: A Game Theoretic Model of Household Decisions', in Edith Kuiper and Jolande Sap (eds), *Out of the Margin: Feminist Perspectives on Economics*, London: Routledge, pp. 80–99.

Pujol, Michèle (1992), *Feminism and Anti-Feminism In Early Economic Thought*, Aldershot: Edward Elgar.

Strassmann, Diana (1993), 'Not a Free Market: The Rhetoric of Disciplinary Authority in Economics', in M.A. Ferber and J.A. Nelson (eds), *Beyond Economic Man: Feminist Theory and Economics*, Chicago: University of Chicago Press, pp. 54–68.

Woolley, Francis (1993), 'Gender and economics: feminist challenges to neoclassical economics', *Cambridge Journal of Economics*, **17**, 485–500.

Occupational Segregation

Occupational segregation by gender refers to the inequality in the distribution of men and women across different occupational categories. It is a concept that is used to demonstrate that men and women have different jobs. Although various measures of occupational segregation have been proposed, it is most frequently measured using the index of dissimilarity defined by Duncan and Duncan (1955):

$$\text{OSI} = 1/2 \sum |F_i - M_i|,$$

where F_i = the proportion of women in the labour force that is employed in occupation i and M_i = the proportion of men in the labour force that is employed in occupation i. The value of the index can range between zero and 100, with zero representing perfect integration and 100 representing complete segregation. In the USA in 1996, the index of occupational segregation based on nine occupational categories was 33.04 per cent. This value is interpreted as the percentage of women (or men) that would have to change occupations in order for the occupational distributions of men and women to be identical. There is also occupational segregation on the basis of race in the USA (see, for example, King 1992 and Albelda 1986 for historical trends in occupational segregation by gender and race), but segregation on the basis of gender is both more pronounced and more persistent. It is thus an important area of inquiry for feminist economists.

There are both practical and philosophical justifications for feminist analysis of occupational segregation. On a practical level, occupational segregation is an important dimension of gender inequality in the labour market. Its existence is one symptom that women are not given unrestricted access to labour market opportunities. Segregation also has important implications for the wage gap between women and men, as well as for opportunities for advancement in the labour market. Understanding the causes and consequences of occupational segregation is crucial to the formulation of labour market policies. Affirmative action policies, for example, can be interpreted as an attempt to reduce occupational segregation, and comparable worth policies can be viewed in part as an effort to reduce the wage differentials that segregation may cause.

On philosophical and methodological levels, feminist analysis of occupational segregation is important for two reasons. First, it is a topic that facilitates interdisciplinary analysis. As will be discussed below, an adequate understanding of occupational segregation requires feminist economists to move beyond the traditional boundaries of economics. Second, analysis of occupational segregation provides opportunities for critiquing neoclassical economic theories, exposing the gender biases inherent in them and proposing new alternatives.

There are two major neoclassical economic explanations of occupational segregation: human capital theory and theories of discrimination. The human capital explanation of occupational segregation focuses on the supply side of the labour market. It explains segregation as the result of rational decisions made by women to invest in different amounts and types of education and training (see, for example, Polachek 1981). Women are assumed to make different human capital investment decisions primarily because of their expected intermittent labour force participation. Under the assumption that women's labour force participation is not continuous and that skills acquired through human capital investment will depreciate during periods out of the labour force, women will choose to invest in skills and enter occupations for which the depreciation of human capital is relatively low. According to this theory, women would therefore be expected to be concentrated in these occupations, and to be found in small numbers in occupations for which continuous work experience is highly rewarded and the rate of skill depreciation is high.

In contrast to human capital theory, theories of labour market discrimination focus on the demand side of the market in explaining occupational segregation. Becker's (1971) theory relies on the assumption of a 'taste' for discrimination, or prejudice, on the part of employers, workers and/or consumers. In the face of this prejudice, women may simply not be hired for certain kinds of jobs. If employers in certain occupations exhibit a strong taste for discrimination, or workers or consumers associated with these occupations do not want to interact with women workers, then relatively few women will be employed in such occupations. They will be concentrated in occupations for which the taste for discrimination is relatively small or nonexistent.

The theory of statistical discrimination is also used as a means of explaining occupational segregation. According to the theory (see Phelps 1972), employers make hiring decisions on the basis of imperfect information about the future productivity of workers. Since there are costs associated with hiring and training workers, employers will attempt to reduce these costs by ascribing characteristics to potential workers on the basis of the group to which they belong. If women as a group are assumed to be less committed to the labour force, or are assumed to possess certain stereotypical characteristics, then they will not be hired in some jobs. The result will be occupational segregation.

All three of these theories have been critiqued by feminist scholars, as well as by institutional economists and other social scientists. Some of the critiques are based on general challenges to their assumptions of free, rational choice and competitive labour markets. Other critiques focus more explicitly on the specific features of the individual theories, and on the extent to which the predictions of the theories are consistent with real-world evidence.

In the case of human capital theory, feminist scholars have found the assumption of investment decisions made on the basis of free rational choice to be problematic. The theory does not consider the extent to which choices may be mediated by the perception of discrimination against potential entrants into certain fields, or by broader societal influences that may determine what occupational choices are 'appropriate' for women. Moreover, the theory takes the assumption of women's intermittent labour force participation as given – it does not consider economic or social forces that may affect women's labour force continuity.

The patterns of occupational segregation predicted by the theory have also been called into question. England (1982) and England et al. (1988) have conducted empirical studies of occupational segregation that generate results inconsistent with the human capital theory. Specifically, they have found that women are not segregated into occupations with low penalties for intermittent labour force participation, and that women who participate in the labour force continuously are not more likely to be found in occupations that reward such participation.

These findings, along with evidence of occupational crowding developed by Bergmann (1974), suggest that some sort of discrimination is responsible for occupational segregation. But feminists have criticized many theories of discrimination because they take the taste for discrimination as given. Such theories do not provide an explanation of the origins of prejudice in the labour market – it is simply assumed to exist. The conventional neoclassical assumption of fixed and exogenous preferences does not allow for analysis of the motivations or sources of discriminatory behaviour.

Similarly, the theory of statistical discrimination has been criticized by feminist scholars. It tends to legitimize the existence of occupational segregation by explaining it as the outcome of the rational, cost-minimizing behaviour of employers. As Olson (1990) has suggested, this approach tends to deny the existence of sexism in the labour market, and it does not provide a meaningful or useful explanation of why occupational segregation persists.

Dissatisfaction with the assumptions and ideological bases of neoclassical economic models used to explain occupational segregation has led feminist scholars to embrace other intellectual traditions within economics, and to move outside of the discipline for a fuller understanding of the process. Institutional economic models of segmented labour markets (see, for example, Woodbury 1987) are more consistent with the ideals of feminist economics, and offer greater promise for analysing the causes and consequences of occupational segregation.

Institutional segmented labour market models are more amenable to feminist insights into the process of occupational segregation for two important reasons. First, they emphasize that segregation is not simply the result of free, rational choices as manifested in labour supply and demand. The role of constraints on behaviour in determining labour market processes is explicitly recognized. Second, such models do not view labour markets in isolation from the rest of society, but rather emphasize the connections between the two. Occupational segregation is explained by segmented labour market theories in part as a result of the assignment of workers to primary or secondary labour markets. That is, the segregation of women into a small number of occupations does not occur as a result of voluntary, rational choices made by workers, but rather as a result of employers' assignment of workers to jobs on the basis of stereotypes or statistical discrimination. Once assigned to a particular labour market segment, workers tend to acquire the characteristics of their jobs, and this tends to reinforce patterns of occupational segregation.

Segmented labour market theories also explain occupational segregation as a result of the larger social context within which labour markets operate. Labour markets are seen as cultural, as well as economic, institutions and, as such, the rules that govern their operation – and the jobs that men and women hold – parallel the rules and the roles of the larger society.

Feminist scholars have used this social/cultural conception of labour markets to develop more complete explanations of the process of occupational segregation. Some explanations require going outside the discipline of economics and using sociological and psychological theories to explain segregation. According to these approaches, the fact that men and women hold different jobs can be attributed to differences in their psychological makeup – different goals and aspirations, for example – or to the fact that women's and men's socialization processes lead them to choose different jobs. Women's jobs as teachers and nurses, for example, would be seen as natural extensions of their nurturing characteristics. (See Fischer 1987 for a discussion of some of these theories.)

Improvements in neoclassical economic explanations of occupational segregation have been made by feminist economists who have argued that the process cannot be adequately understood by relying solely on supply-side or demand-side theories. They have recognized that a complete understanding of occupational segregation requires a theory that explains how the behaviour of participants in labour markets interacts to determine how certain jobs acquire gender labels, why such labels tend to persist over time, and the conditions under which gender labels may change. Such a theory requires, at least, consideration of both supply and demand factors and, at best, an appreciation of how these factors are shaped by society as a whole.

One such theory has been advanced by Strober (1984), who develops a 'relative attractiveness' model of segregation. This approach argues that occupational segregation occurs because men have the first choice of occupations that are relatively attractive, in terms of compensation, working conditions, and status and prestige. Occupations that are deemed relatively unattractive by men are then left for women to occupy. According to the theory, men have the right of first choice of occupations because of the power conferred on them by society as a whole. Thus, the occupational distribution is not determined simply by forces of labour supply and demand, but also on how these forces are influenced by men's choices and the way in which these choices constrain the opportunities open to women. Changes in the gender label of jobs will occur if an occupation held by men becomes relatively unattractive to them. Strober and others (see Strober 1984; Strober and Arnold 1987 and Strober 1992, for example) have used the theory to explain changing patterns of segregation in schoolteaching, bank telling and several other professions.

A similar theory that incorporates both labour market factors and the way they are situated within society as a whole has been developed by Reskin and Roos (1990). They describe occupational segregation, and changes in the occupational distribution of men and women over time, as the result of a dual queuing process. Labour market processes can be described in terms of a job queue (the ranking of different jobs by workers) and a labour queue (the ranking of workers by employers). The distribution of women and men across occupations will be determined by the way in which the labour queue is mapped onto the job queue or, in other words, how far down in its ranking of workers an employer has to go to fill a certain job. The theory suggests that women are placed at the end of labour queues for a variety of reasons – stereotypes, tradition, or discrimination – and that occupational segregation will be the result.

The nature and extent of occupational segregation will change over time, according to this theory, if there is a change in the structure of either type of queue. If, for example, particular occupations or industries experience growth or decline, if there is a change in the gender composition of the labour force, or there is a change in the nature of work itself in different occupations, then changes in the occupational distribution of women and men would be predicted by the theory. One advantage of this approach to understanding segregation is that it allows explicit consideration of how gender roles themselves, both within the labour market and in society as a whole, help to shape occupational distributions.

These broader theories have been used in the feminist literature to gain a better understanding of what types of societal factors contribute to the persistence of occupational segregation. Feminist research on the impact of technology on occupational segregation (see Burnell 1993 and Hartmann et al. 1986, 1987, for example) and on the impact of urban spatial structure on segregation (see Hanson and Pratt 1995) represent applications of these theories.

Feminist critiques of neoclassical economic explanations for occupational segregation have resulted in the development of new paradigms. By exposing the partiality and shortcomings of neoclassical models, and by drawing on the work of institutional economists and other social scientists, feminist scholarship on occupational segregation has led to a better understanding of its causes and consequences. There are still several areas of inquiry that are fruitful and important for feminist scholars, however. More work needs to be done in order to understand the gender-typing of jobs – that is, how certain occupations come to be associated with women or men. Similarly, racial and ethnic differences in occupational segregation need further investigation, in order to more fully understand both the causes and consequences. Relatively little feminist analysis of cross-cultural patterns of occupational segregation has been done, but this will hopefully improve as more data from developing countries becomes available. Findings in all of these areas should be used as the basis for better labour market policies designed to address the secondary status of women.

BARBARA S. BURNELL

See also
Affirmative Action; Comparable Worth/Pay Equity; Discrimination, Theories of; Human Capital Theory, Labour Force Participation, Labour Markets, Theories of; Labour Market Segmentation; Wage Gap.

Bibliography
Albelda, Randy P. (1986), 'Occupational segregation by race and gender, 1958–1981', *Industrial and Labour Relations Review*, **39** (3), 404–11.

Becker, Gary (1971), *The Economics of Discrimination*, 2nd edn, Chicago: University of Chicago Press.

Beller, Andrea (1984), 'Trends in Occupational Segregation by Sex and Race, 1960–1981', in Barbara Reskin (ed.), *Sex Segregation in the Workplace: Trends, Explanations and Remedies*, Washington, DC: National Academy Press, pp. 11–26.

Bergmann, Barbara (1974), 'Occupational segregation, wages and profits when employers discriminate by race or sex', *Eastern Economic Journal*, **1** (1–2), 103–10.

Blau, Francine and Wallace Hendricks (1979), 'Occupational segregation by sex: trends and prospects', *Journal of Human Resources*, **14** (2), 197–210.

Burnell, Barbara (1993), *Technological Change and Women's Work Experience: Alternative Methodological Perspectives*, Westport, Connecticut: Bergin and Garvey.

Duncan, Otis and Beverly Duncan (1955), 'A methodological analysis of segregation indices', *American Sociological Review*, **20** (2), 210–17.

England, Paula (1982), 'The failure of human capital theory to explain occupational sex segregation', *Journal of Human Resources*, **17** (3), 358–70.

England, Paula, George Farkas, Barbara Kilbourne and Thomas Dou (1988), 'Explaining occupational sex segregation and wages: findings from a model with fixed effects', *American Sociological Review*, **53** (4), 544–58.

Fischer, Charles (1987), 'Toward a more complete understanding of occupational sex discrimination', *Journal of Economic Issues*, **21** (1), 113–38.

Hanson, Susan and Geraldine Pratt (1995), *Gender, Work and Space*, London: Routledge.

Hartmann, Heidi, Robert Kraut and Louise Tilly (1986), *Computer Chips and Paper Clips: Technology and Women's Employment, Vol. 1*, Washington, DC: National Academy Press.

Hartmann, Heidi, Robert Kraut and Louise Tilly (1987), *Computer Chips and Paper Clips: Technology and Women's Employment, Vol. 2*, Washington, DC: National Academy Press.

Jacobsen, Joyce (1994), 'Trends in workforce segregation, 1960–1990', *Social Science Quarterly*, **75** (1), 204–11.

Karmel, T. and M. Maclachlan (1988), 'Occupational sex segregation: increasing or decreasing?', *The Economic Record*, **64** (186), 187–95.

King, Mary (1992), 'Occupational segregation by race and sex, 1940–1988', *Monthly Labour Review*, **115** (4), 30–36.

Olson, Paulette (1990), 'The persistence of occupational segregation: a critique of its theoretical underpinnings', *Journal of Economic Issues*, **24** (1), 161–71.

Phelps, Edmund (1972), 'The statistical theory of racism and sexism', *American Economic Review*, **62** (4), 659–61.

Polachek, Solomon (1981), 'Occupational self-selection: a human capital approach to sex differences in occupational structure', *Review of Economics and Statistics*, **63** (1), 60–69.

Reskin, Barbara and Patricia Roos (1990), *Job Queues, Gender Queues: Explaining Women's Inroads into Male Occupations*, Philadelphia: Temple University Press.

Strober, Myra (1984), 'Toward a Theory of Occupational Sex Segregation', in Barbara Reskin (ed.), *Sex Segregation in the Workplace: Trends, Explanations and Remedies*, Washington, DC: National Academy Press, pp. 144–56.

Strober, Myra (1992), 'The Relative Attractiveness Theory of Gender Segregation: The Case of Physicians', Proceedings of the Annual Meetings of the Industrial and Labour Relations Research Association.

Strober, Myra and Carolyn Arnold (1987), 'The Dynamics of Occupational Segregation Among Bank Tellers', in Clair Brown and Joseph Pechman (eds), *Gender in the Workplace*, Washington, DC: Brookings Institution, pp. 107–48.

Woodbury, Steven (1987), 'Power in the labour market: institutionalist approaches to labour problems', *Journal of Economic Issues*, **21** (4), 1781–1807.

Parental Leave

Parental leave generally refers to an authorized absence from work, with or without pay, by a mother or a father for the purposes of taking care of children, especially newborn or newly adopted children. After the absence, the parent is entitled to return to her or his former employment, either in the same or an equivalent job. Parental leave may be provided voluntarily by employers, as a result of collective bargaining or in compliance with law. Parental leave is a relatively new form of family-related leave focused on caregiving, which can be done by either parent. It is conceptually separate from *maternity leave*, which most often refers to a mother's leave from work in connection with childbirth and the physical recovery period (generally about six to fourteen weeks though it can also extend longer). Parental leave is also separable from the concept of *family care leave*, which refers to leave provided to any worker in order to care for another family member, such as a spouse, parent, child or other close individual, in time of illness or other great need (Ferber and O'Farrell 1991, p. 117).

As a matter of national law, parental leave is predated by maternity leave, which was first introduced in 1878 in Germany, followed by France (in 1928) and Denmark, Finland and Sweden (all in 1937). In Europe declining fertility rates were often cited as the cause for enacting such family friendly policies. Sweden, for example, in addition to maternity leave, enacted policies to reduce income differences between families with more and fewer children in order to encourage adults to want to have more children (Liljestrom 1978). Most other countries enacted maternity leave after World War II (Ferber and O'Farrell 1991), and it was not until 1974 that Sweden became the first country to enact parental leave, extending leave rights to fathers as well as mothers. It is interesting to note that an explicit goal of the Swedish law was to allow families to make their own decisions as to which parent would provide more of the infant care and thus to make it possible for them to equalize family and work roles, if they so desired (Liljestrom 1978). In 1977, Norway extended paid maternity leaves to fathers for the first time: if the mother was employed, the father could take a share of the mother's post-birth 12-week paid leave (although the mother retained a sole right to the first 6 weeks of a total 18 weeks paid leave) and was given rights to additional unpaid leave as well (Henriksen and Holter 1978). In the 1980s, Denmark, Finland and West Germany also increased the part that fathers could take in parental leave (Kamerman 1991). Other countries, including the United States, followed suit, and in 1997 the International Labour Organization (1997) reported that approximately 25 countries provide some type of leave to fathers. More broadly, some type of family care leave, even if limited only to maternity leave, is currently available in nearly all countries.

Parental leave is an important public policy for women workers and their families. Since women still carry out the bulk of family care work in virtually all countries, and since the employment of mothers, particularly mothers of young children, has grown rapidly in many countries, parental leave provides an important way for women to maintain attachment to their jobs while also taking time off to meet children's needs. With the growing employment of mothers, the proportion of families in which both parents work is also therefore increasing rapidly, making the need to balance work and family considerations important for both men and women. Additionally, as families increasingly rely on mothers for at least a portion of their incomes, the right to return to one's job after an absence for the care of children is increasingly important for maintaining families' living standards. Research further suggests that even unpaid leave improves mothers' earnings by facilitating the accumulation of seniority on the job (Spalter-Roth et al. 1990). And for families who rely on mothers' earnings for part or all of their income, paid parental leave can be an important means of stabilizing family income. Paid family care leave is especially important to single mother families, many of whom would have no other family member's earnings to which to turn when the mother must be absent from work for family care reasons.

Paid leave, either parental or maternity, is generally not the only form of income support available to families with children, and so its absence may be more or less devastating financially according to the availability of other income sources. In many countries, poor single mothers and their children are supported by welfare programmes that provide them with income whether or not they work, thereby offering an alternative to paid maternity leave; in addition, some countries also provide income assistance to poor two-parent families. Many countries further provide child or family allowances in the form of monthly cash payments to the mothers of all or most minor children; these too supplement family income whether or not the mother works (Kamerman and Kahn 1978). In many countries, virtually all workers have access to paid sick leave, often provided through a social insurance system, that protects parents' income when they are too ill to work, thus offering another source of income. Finally, tax policy (specifically that related to how the incomes of families with children are taxed and whether the incomes of mothers and fathers are taxed separately or jointly) can also affect how families make use of available leaves and/or absorb the financial impact of having and raising children (McCaffery 1997). Thus the impact of the presence or absence of family-related leave policies on women and their families can only be evaluated in the full policy context, including the extent of anti-discrimination machinery available, in each country.

Both in law and in practice, parental leave continues to be generally less available than maternity leave, and these conceptually separable types of leave are often combined in extended maternity leaves available to mothers only. It is not uncommon, for example, for a country to require that employers provide maternity leaves extending to 12 months or more, a length of time that clearly includes leave for infant care, but only for the mother. In addition, while most countries require paid maternity leave (usually paid in full or in part via a social insurance programme) for several months, extended periods of maternity leave are often unpaid. And in those few countries with laws providing for a combination of paid and unpaid parental leaves, these leaves may extend for periods of up to several years, but the paid portion of the leave is generally considerably shorter (Ferber and O'Farrell 1991; International Labour Organization 1997; Lewis 1997).

These differences among parental leave policies around the world reflect a considerable range of generosity in who is covered, for what reasons, for how long and at how much salary replacement. At one end of the spectrum, Sweden has the most generous parental leave programme in addition to having the oldest law (1974) extending paid leave to fathers. After 180 days of employment (by both the mother and father), the couple currently may share 270 days of leave at 90 per cent of pay (funded by social insurance), followed by 90 additional days of leave paid at a flat rate by the employer, followed by up to 18 months of unpaid leave. This 2.5 years of leave can be spread over the first 4 years of a child's life. In addition, parents in Sweden have up to 90 days of paid leave annually to care for a sick child and 2 days of paid leave for school or child care centre visits (Ferber and O'Farrell 1991). In practice, however, fathers in Sweden use most of these forms of leave much less than do mothers; in 1987, for example, only about 25 per cent of eligible Swedish fathers took parental leave, averaging 26 days of leave, which was still considerably higher than leave taken by only about 5 per cent of eligible fathers in Denmark, Finland, Germany and Norway. To encourage greater leave taking by fathers, in 1996 the European Union directed that a portion of available parental leave be reserved for fathers only rather than allowing the total to be shared for use by either parent (International Labour Organization 1997).

The United States provides an example at the other end of the generosity spectrum, since it still has no federal requirement for the provision of paid maternity leave. Indeed, the first national law requiring any parenting-related leave dates only from 1993, with the passage of federal legislation requiring employers (with 50 or more employees) to provide up to 12 weeks of unpaid leave to either parent to take care of a newborn child or newly adopted child, provided the parent has worked at least one year for 1250 hours or more. (In addition to exempting employers of fewer than 50 workers, it is important to note that in the USA there is no national law requiring employers to provide paid sick or vacation leave.) This 'new child' leave is required to be offered by a covered employer only once every two years, and if both the mother and father work for the same employer, the employer is required to offer it to only one of them (Lenhoff and Subramanian 1998). (It is important to mention that many individual states in the United States do require more generous leaves, especially for the mother surrounding childbirth, and in practice many US employers, especially large ones, do offer short paid maternity leaves in addition to regular paid sick or vacation leaves.) In addition, under the 1993 law, fathers in the USA are eligible to take leave for new child care, and recent research shows that fathers are taking advantage of the new law to take modest amounts of leave surrounding childbirth (US Family and Medical Leave Act Commission 1996). These father-friendly aspects of the US law are among its more positive features. Thus while the United States is one of the few countries in the world without a national law requiring paid maternity leave, it is also one of the few that requires that parental leave extends to fathers. In addition, the US law providing job-guaranteed parental leave is a very broad one, providing for both family care leave (for care of spouses and parents as well as children) and leave for the worker's own illness (the medical leave portion covers the mother's childbirth-related absence). Although all that US employers are required to provide is unpaid leave, few other countries specify that leave can be taken for spousal and parental care as well as child care (Lewis 1997).

The lack of coverage in many countries for fathers and for family situations other than new child care is an important feminist issue because it has the potential to change (or at least to reflect and further advance already changed) cultural attitudes about appropriate work for women and men. Since many feminists argue that women will remain unequal (economically, politically and socially) as long as they remain primarily responsible for family care, shifting a greater proportion of the care of children and family members to men is an important aspect of achieving equality between women and men (Vogel 1993). In many of the countries that lack fathers' rights to caregiving leaves, feminists and others continue to agitate to extend existing leave rights of mothers to fathers. In the United States, for example, the 'fathers' rights' debate in the 1980s was explicit, and several well-placed feminist advocates worked to derail maternity leave legislation that members of Congress were planning to introduce (Radigan 1988). Their concern was that 'special treatment' for women should not be enacted into law because of the fear that these special treatments would be used by employers to discriminate against women (since their special treatment would make women more costly to hire than men). Consequently, these feminists espoused an 'equal treatment' approach and wanted any new legislation to apply to women and men equally. Other feminists, however, felt that women, who are after all the only sex that can actually bear children, needed special treatment in order to enable them to be equal to men in the labour market (Radigan 1988). In the end, with the passage of the federal 1993 Family and Medical Leave Act, the equal treatment philosophy generally won out in the United States since the law extends both medical leave and family care leave equally to men and women. (However, because all the leave seriously considered during this debate was unpaid, it can be argued that feminists did not give up anything, such as wage replacement for working mothers on maternity leave, by insist-ing on a gender-neutral approach.) This gender-neutral approach has led to a continuing issue in the United States as to whether any accommodations can be made for mothers but not for fathers (for example, providing work breaks to facilitate a mother nursing a child or pumping out her breast milk for later use). As the sociologist Vogel (1993) argues, it may be necessary in the United States to add specific considerations that apply to women differen-tially to the basic equal treatment model in order to achieve equal treatment in practice for women. Similar discussions will be necessary in those coun-tries that lag behind in providing leaves to fathers, especially since it is important that their family-related leave policies be made more gender neu-tral if they are to contribute to achieving greater equality between the sexes (Lewis 1997).

Just as feminist activists in the United States have been divided on the best way to approach family friendly policies, so have feminist economists. While many feminist economists generally argue that the United States needs more policies that emphasize family friendly benefits (Folbre 1994), Bergmann (1998) argues family policies that are too generous offer too much paid leave at home and may, for example, work to retard women's achievement of equality. Bergmann's approach is informed by her training in economics in that she fears that given the choices available to women in the labour market (which are often low-wage jobs where women face discrimination), many women might choose to stay home and receive leave benefits. Meantime, these women would be losing human capital and work experience and doom-ing themselves to lower earnings in the future, further reinforcing their tendencies to choose to stay home. Indeed, Bergmann would like to see more government effort focused on enforcing the laws against employment dis-crimination (and more public dollars spent on child care for working parents) and less on helping women to stay home to take care of children.

In general, Bergmann's concerns are shared by many labour economists who consider that policies such as parental leave may have unintended ad-verse effects (Blau and Ferber 1992; Killingsworth 1985). Because these policies can raise the cost of hiring women workers, they may result in women being hired less frequently or in their being less likely to be trained for higher level jobs or promoted to higher-level jobs. Women might even experience general job loss. When the proposed Family and Medical Leave

Act was being debated in the US Congress, for example, the Chamber of Commerce argued that it would be prohibitively expensive for employers to provide even unpaid leaves and that some small businesses might even be forced to close.

Feminist economists and other social scientists have generally tried to challenge these conclusions by conducting empirical research. Trzcinski (1989) surveyed employers to determine how much job turnover typically costs employers and how they currently handle temporary absences, concluding that the costs of providing leave would be less than the current costs of turnover. The Families and Work Institute surveyed four states that had previously implemented parental leave laws and found that businesses were able to comply with little difficulty (Bond 1991). Other studies showed that having leave, especially paid leave, increases women's earnings by increasing their seniority on the job and reducing their turnover (Spalter-Roth et al. 1990) and that maternity protection laws seem to encourage rather than discourage the growth of both female employment and small businesses (Spalter-Roth and Willoughby 1988). The Institute for Women's Policy Research, placing women at the centre of their analysis to interpret the controversy from their point of view, showed that the current costs to women (from not having a guaranteed job to go back to after childbirth) in terms of lost earnings were greater than the costs to employers of providing the leaves (Spalter-Roth and Hartmann 1990).

Feminists have also generally argued that policies that intervene in the market to set minimum labour standards are legitimate and necessary; the 'free' market, they argue, is, in reality, the accumulation of customs, traditions and institutions in which some interests have been better represented than others. To redress the balance, positive action is needed (Bravo 1991). Similarly, some family policy advocates argue that family policies actually help the economic system perform better because they tend to increase productivity in the workplace by enabling workers to both work and meet the family care needs (Bravo 1991).

Much work remains to be done on the implementation and assessment of family care policies and legislation. In order to enhance women's status, further research is warranted on how men can be encouraged to make more use of parental leave and family care policies, so that the term 'working father' becomes as common as 'working mother' or that the term 'nurturer/ worker' is understood to apply to all adults. A related question is whether some family policies work to reinforce women's traditional roles and thus need to be altered to allow women and men more choice in how to allocate their time between work and family pursuits. In addition, further research is needed on how family-friendly reforms in the workplace affect the bottom line of firms' performance and profitability.

More generally, it would be ideal to know which family policies contribute most to women's equality and how they can be encouraged. A related theoretical issue of special importance to feminist economists is how much of the costs of reproducing humans should be placed on families or employers as compared to society more broadly through social insurance schemes. If, as Folbre and Hartmann argue (1988), reproducing ourselves and caring for each other are important human values, how can these values be included in traditional economic models based on profit and utility maximization by 'rational economic men'? Resolution of these issues would contribute to improved understanding of a range of public policies related to women and families, including policies addressing poverty, child care, education, marriage and divorce, taxation and retirement.

HEIDI HARTMANN

See also

Family, Economics of; Family Policy; Income Support and Transfer Policy; Protective Legislation.

Bibliography
Bergmann, Barbara (1998), 'Watch Out for Family Friendly Benefits', *Dollars and Sense*, (January), 10–11.

Blau, Francine D. and Marianne A. Ferber (1992), *The Economics of Women, Men, and Work*, Second Edition, Englewood Cliffs, New Jersey: Prentice-Hall, Inc.

Bravo, Ellen (1991), 'Family Leave: The Need for a New Minimum Standard', in Janet Shibley Hyde and Marilyn J. Essex (eds), *Parental Leave and Child Care: Setting a Research and Policy Agenda*, Philadelphia: Temple University Press, pp. 165–75.

Bond, James T. (1991), *Beyond the Parental Leave Debate: The Impact of Laws in Four States*, New York: Families and Work Institute.

Ferber, Marianne A. and Brigid O'Farrell with La Rue Allen (eds) (1991), *Work and Family: Policies for a Changing Work Force*, Washington, DC: National Academy Press.

Folbre, Nancy (1994), *Who Pays for the Kids? Gender and the Structures of Constraint*, London and New York: Routledge.

Folbre, Nancy and Heidi Hartmann (1988), 'The Rhetoric of Self-Interest: Ideology of Gender in Economic Theory', in Arjo Klamer, Donald N. McCloskey and Robert M. Solow (eds), *The Consequences of Economic Rhetoric*, Cambridge: Cambridge University Press, pp. 184–203.

Henriksen, Hildur Ve and Harriet Holter (1978), 'Norway', in Sheila B. Kamerman and Alfred J. Kahn (eds), *Family Policy: Government and Families in Fourteen Countries*, New York: Columbia University Press, pp. 49–67.

International Labour Organization (1997), *Maternity Protection at Work*, Geneva: International Labour Office.

Kamerman, Sheila B. (1991), 'Parental and Infant Care: U.S. and International Trends and Issues, 1978–1988', in Janet Shibley Hyde and Marilyn J. Essex (eds), *Parental Leave and Child Care: Setting a Research and Policy Agenda*, Philadelphia: Temple University Press, pp. 11–23.

Kamerman, Sheila B. and Alfred J. Kahn (eds) (1978), *Family Policy: Government and Families in Fourteen Countries*, New York: Columbia University Press.

Killingsworth, Mark R. (1985), 'The Economics of Comparable Worth: Analytical, Empirical, and Policy Questions', in Heidi I. Hartmann (ed.), *Comparable Worth: New Directions for Research*, Washington, DC: National Academy Press, pp. 86–115.

Lenhoff, Donna R. and Sandhya Subramanian (1998), 'The Family and Medical Leave Act: 5 years of success', *Perspectives on Work*, **2** (2), 4–7.

Lewis, Suzan (1997), *European Perspectives on Work and Family Issues*, Boston, Massachusetts: The Center for Work and Family, Boston College.

Liljestrom, Rita (1978), 'Sweden', in Sheila B. Kamerman and Alfred J. Kahn (eds), *Family Policy: Government and Families in Fourteen Countries*, New York: Columbia University Press, pp. 19–48.

McCaffery, Edward J. (1997), *Taxing Women*, Chicago, Illinois: University of Chicago Press.

Radigan, Anne L. (1988), *Concept and Compromise: The Evolution of Family Leave Legislation in the U.S. Congress*, Washington, DC: Women's Research and Education Institute.

Spalter-Roth, Roberta and Heidi I. Hartmann (1990), *Unnecessary Losses: Costs to Americans of the Lack of Family and Medical Leave*, Washington, DC: Institute for Women's Policy Research.

Spalter-Roth, Roberta and John Willoughby (1988), *New Workforce Policies and the Small Business Sector: Is Family Leave Good for Business?*, Cleveland, Ohio: 9 to 5, the National Association of Working Women.

Spalter-Roth, Roberta, Claudia Withers and Sheila R. Gibbs (1990), *Improving Employment Opportunities for Women Workers: An Assessment of the Ten Year Economic and Legal Impact of the Pregnancy Discrimination Act of 1978*, Washington, DC: Institute for Women's Policy Research.

Trzcinski, Eileen (1989), 'Issues and Findings from a Connecticut Survey of Employers', paper prepared for the Panel on Employer Policies and Working Families, Committee on Women's Employment and Related Social Issues, National Research Council, Washington, DC.

US Family and Medical Leave Act Commission (1996), *A Workable Balance: Report to Congress on Family and Medical Leave Policies*, Washington, DC: US Department of Labor.

Vogel, Lise (1993), *Mothers on the Job: Maternity Policy in the US Workplace*, New Brunswick, New Jersey: Rutgers University Press.

Patriarchy

Patriarchy is a term which feminists have used to denote a society whose social relationships systematically privilege and empower men. Feminist economists have used the terms patriarchy and patriarchal to refer to economies in which men have power over women, or are empowered *vis-à-vis* women. Some also use the term to denote systems in which fathers (patriarchs) have power over their children as well as their wives (Folbre 1980).

Capitalist economies are patriarchal in that they concentrate women in the lower paid jobs and in unpaid, reproductive work. This practice not only sustains capitalist economies, but also a patriarchal family in which the husband is empowered over his wife and children, not only legally and ideologically, but also economically by his greater access to earnings.

Among economists, the concepts of patriarchy and patriarchal are most used among Marxist-feminist economists, and this entry will focus on their analyses. Such economists, building on Marxist economic theory, have focused on the ways in which economic relationships construct and differentiate the members of society. To Marx's analysis of the ways in which economies create class difference, exploitation and inequality, Marxist-feminists have added an analysis of the ways in which economies create gender difference, oppression and inequality – of the ways that economies are patriarchal. Feminist institutionalists conceptualize the economics of gender similarly to Marxist-feminists, focusing on the ways in which culture and institutions construct and reinforce gender difference and inequality (Jennings 1993). In contrast, mainstream feminist economists, like other mainstream economists, tend to locate the source of gender inequality outside of the purview of economics, in the discriminatory preferences of individuals, which are taken as a given, and then study the ways in which these discriminatory preferences create economic inequality between the sexes (see Blau et al. 1998, for a good synthesis of mainstream analysis of gender and economics).

Patriarchy is maintained by three different levels of social practices: self-conscious choice and struggle by individuals and groups, patriarchal institutions and social practices, and subconscious forces (Matthaei 1992). One of the early feminist economic analyses of patriarchy was provided by Heidi Hartmann in her article, 'Capitalism, Patriarchy, and Job Segregation by Sex'. In this article Hartmann analysed patriarchy as the result of self-conscious choices and organizing by men, arguing that 'male workers have played and continue to play a crucial role in maintaining sexual divisions in the labor process' (1979, p. 208). She traced the development of the family wage system in the nineteenth century USA, showing how men organized through unions to exclude women from the high, family-wage-paying jobs, ensuring women's economic dependence upon their husbands or fathers and thus perpetuating gender inequality in both economic and familial spheres. Feminist historians have shown, however, that women also played a significant role in developing this new form of the sexual division of labour. In particular, middle-class women played an active role in the development of a 'cult of domesticity' that defined women's traditional work in the family as a homemaking career, seen as incompatible with labour force participation, and argued for its social importance as a balance to men's work of 'breadwinning'. The Women's Trade Union League, for example, joined with white male unions in the successful fight for protective legislation, which restricted women's labour force presence (Matthaei 1982, Chapters 5, 6 and 8).

Feminist economists emphasize that patriarchy is also maintained and reproduced through a set of social institutions and practices which are passed down between the generations and taken as given, rather than self-consciously invented. Central among these is the sexual division of labour, which historically has assigned individuals on the basis of their biological sex to either men's or women's work, with men's work centred in interfamilial activities, and women's in child-rearing and intrafamilial work. This division of labour between the sexes turns them into different and complementary genders and provides 'glue' for heterosexual marriage. However the sexual division of labour does not necessarily create inequality and patriarchy. For example, in some Native American nations before the European invasion, women appear to have been economically on a par with men (Amott and Matthaei 1996, Chapter 3; Leacock 1981, Chapter 7).

In patriarchal societies, however, the sexual division of labour excludes women from positions of economic and political power and hence subordinates them to men. Men's struggles to monopolize family wage jobs in the nineteenth century USA, mentioned above, were a successful attempt to reconstruct and perpetuate the sexual division of labour as the economy underwent the tremendous transformation of industrialization. These struggles succeeded largely because the populace already accepted the institution of the sexual division of labour – the existence of distinct categories of men's work and women's work. The resulting assignment and confinement of women to unpaid reproductive work in the home as well as to lower-paid jobs thus became an essential feature of capitalist patriarchy.

Finally, patriarchy exists on a subconscious level: as an early feminist saying put it, 'It is hard to fight an enemy that has outposts in my brain'. As children, we are taught to accept, embrace and work to establish our gender identities. In other words, females and males tend to accept as given the socially constructed definitions of feminine and masculine, womanhood and manhood, believing them to be God- and/or nature-given. They then strive to be women and men, respectively, by acting in the ways society dictates as feminine and masculine. In this way, gendered behaviour is not a self-conscious choice, but an ascribed identity. For a female, growing up with a gender identity has involved believing that one is incapable of doing men's work, and a failure if one does not marry and raise children – beliefs that are reinforced by the social institutions of the sexual division of labour. For this reason 'consciousness-raising', that is, making oneself aware of the expectations of one's gender role and realizing that one does not have to accept it as God- or nature-given, was a key aspect of feminist movement in the 1970s USA, accompanying women's political organizing against labour market discrimination (that is, the sexual division of labour in paid work) (Amott and Matthaei 1996, p. 134).

A central question for feminist economists has been the relationship between patriarchy and capitalism. Early Marxist-feminists, dissatisfied with Marxism's ignoring of gender inequality and with the difficulty of fitting an analysis of patriarchy into existing Marxist categories, put forward and explored the concept of capitalist patriarchy in a series of essays in *Capitalist Patriarchy and the Case for Socialist Feminism* (1979). (Others worked to establish the economic significance of women's domestic labour within the Marxist theoretical framework (Gardiner 1979).) As editor Zillah Eisenstein wrote, 'I choose this phrase [capitalist patriarchy] to emphasize the mutually reinforcing dialectical relationship between capitalist class structure and hierarchical sexual structuring' (p. 5). This dual systems theory was further explored in essays by Heidi Hartmann and by Nancy Folbre and Ann Ferguson in an edited collection entitled *Women and Revolution: A Discussion of the Unhappy Marriage of Marxism and Feminism* (Sargent 1981). These authors argued that whereas capitalism is characterized by class differentiation and the capitalists' exploitation of workers, patriarchy is characterized by gender differentiation and the oppression of women by men. Whereas capitalists extract surplus labour from workers, men extract unpaid household labour from women. Historically, these Marxist-feminists argued, patriarchy and capitalism sometimes work together and sometimes conflict. For example, Ferguson and Folbre (1981) theorized that men's receipt of a 'family wage' and married women's absence from the labour force represented a compromise between capitalists' needs for a wage labour force and men's desire to maintain power over women, including being served by them in the home. A somewhat different version of dual systems analysis which focuses on distinct spheres was put forward by Benería (1979), Chodorow (1979) and Humphries and Rubery (1984), building on Engels's analysis of production and reproduction as both part of a mode of production's material base. These theorists analysed the home and reproduction as the centre of the patriarchal process of men's exploitation of women's unpaid labour, and the labour market as the centre of the capitalist process of the extraction of surplus value.

However, other early Marxist-feminists disagreed with dual systems theory. Josephs (1981) noted that such theories ignored the racial–ethnic oppression which also characterizes capitalism; men of colour, she argued, do not have power over white women. Al-Hibri (1981) criticized the assumption that gender and class are independent forms of oppression, in an essay entitled 'Capitalism is an Advanced Stage of Patriarchy: But Marxism is not Feminism'. Building on these analyses, and on the growing awareness in women's studies that gender oppression was intertwined with race (Hull et al. 1982; hooks 1984; Glen 1985), Marxist-feminist economists Amott and Matthaei (1996) wrote a multicultural history of women's work in the USA. They stressed the fact that patriarchal, class and racial–ethnic processes are interdetermining, and that none of them can be fully understood independently of the others (1996, Chapter 2). For example, they criticized the view that women's performance of unpaid labour for their husbands and fathers in the home is the key to patriarchal oppression, noting that some women, due to class and/or race privilege, do not perform this labour themselves, but rather employ servants, disproportionately women of colour, to do so. In this way class, gender and race are intertwined and interdetermining, so that womanhood does not have definition which is universal across class and race-ethnicity. If this is true, capitalism must be understood not as a system independent of patriarchy, but rather as inherently patriarchal and racist. (For a more fleshed out version of this argument, as well as a summary of different Marxist-feminist approaches to patriarchy, see Matthaei 1992.)

Further, as Al-Hibri (1981) points out, patriarchy and capitalism are not two systems that arose together and are on equal footing in today's economy; rather, patriarchy preceded capitalism by millennia, and capitalism is a form of patriarchy. Capitalist economic systems are inherently patriarchal, and share many similarities with previous forms of patriarchy, which include but are not limited to the empowerment of men over women. Patriarchal societies are also characterized by an engagement in and glorification of war-making – that is, in struggles to dominate and exploit others through the use of force – and they assign these activities, which are highly valued, to men. Conversely patriarchal societies devalue the activities of life-giving and child-rearing, which they assign to women. For this reason, feminist sociologist Mies (1986) calls patriarchal modes of production (including but not limited to capitalist economies) 'predatory modes of production', emphasizing the fact that they are based on enrichment through the violent domination of others, be they other nations or groups, women or wage workers.

These patriarchal characteristics are built into the very nature of capitalism (Matthaei and Amott 1997). The struggle to dominate others through war and colonization – at the root of the modern construction of race – was an essential part of the birth of the first capitalist economies (Cox 1948, Chapter 16). Furthermore the struggle to dominate pervades capitalist economies in the form of the competition between firms for profits and growth, as well as that between workers for jobs and advancement. Money, which gives one power over things and others, becomes the measure of success in these struggles; its valuation is part and parcel of the devaluation of activities that are centred in nurturing and empowering others, in particular child-rearing and unpaid homemaking (Matthaei and Amott 1997).

Competition, war and male domination have characterized social life for so long that many have come to view them as natural, or at least, requisite parts of any desirable or 'civilized' society. However, they are not universal to all societies. Feminist scholars, including Leacock (1981), Buffalohead (1983) and Gimbutas (1991), have identified prepatriarchal societies in precolonial North America and in old Europe. In these societies, they argue, the sexual division of labour did not create inequality between the sexes, because women's work of childrearing was viewed as highly important, creative work, on a par with men's. Social and economic relations were cooperative and egalitarian, rather than competitive and hierarchical, and peaceful coexistence, rather than war and military fortifications, was the norm.

Such a comparison of pre-patriarchal and patriarchal institutions can help feminist economists see the limitations of women's liberation within capitalist patriarchal economies. At present, many advanced capitalist patriarchal societies are experiencing a partial breakdown of the sexual division of labour as a growing share of women are participating in the paid labour force and entering into 'men's jobs'. In most developed countries, a majority of married women are in the labour force (Blau et al. 1998, p. 336), and it is considered 'discrimination', an illegal act, for employers to follow the dictates of the sexual division of labour and assume that women are inherently less qualified for men's jobs (or vice versa), without checking their actual qualifications. Although discrimination is far from eliminated (for example, in the USA in 1988, over two-thirds of the 'wage gap' in the US could not be explained by productivity-related differences (Blau et al. 1998, pp. 189–90)), a privileged and visible subset of females has been able to achieve economic power and status in highly-paid, high-status men's jobs. In 1995, for example, US women constituted 26 per cent of all lawyers, 24 per cent of doctors and 50 per cent of financial managers (US Bureau of the Census 1996, p. 405), and at least 17 per cent of employed women in each major racial–ethnic group had jobs in the upper tier of the primary labour market in 1990 (Amott and Matthaei 1996, pp. 345–7). The median weekly earnings of full-time women workers rose from 62 per cent of men's in 1970 to 75 per cent in 1995 (Blau et al. 1998, p. 135).

These achievements, however, have raised another set of questions for feminist economists and activists. First, women are not benefiting equally from these changes. Even if gender and race discrimination were absent, which they are not, class privilege affects a woman's ability to succeed in the labour market. And labour market hierarchies are alive and well and increasing among women, with 'successful' women relying on the labour of other, less privileged and lower-paid women to perform their reproductive work in their homes, day care centres, or other service work. Second, most women are still burdened with the majority of the unpaid work in the home, the 'double day', and this makes it difficult for them to compete in the labour market on an equal footing with men. For example, in the USA in 1988, employed married women averaged 21 hours a week of housework, compared with 8 hours for men with employed wives (Blau et al. 1998, p. 52). The continuing burden of unpaid work, combined with continuing occupational segregation, meant that almost one-half of all female-headed households with children lived in poverty (Amott and Matthaei 1996, p. 312). Third, and related, capitalist patriarchal values have not changed. Money is the prime value and measure of worth, as well as ticket to survival, and reproductive work for one's family remains unpaid. The economy rewards those who dedicate their lives to their own advancement in the economic competition, and minimize, delegate to others, or otherwise subordinate their family-oriented work; for this reason, prominent feminist economist Bergmann (1986,

Chapters 11 and 12) advocates that housework and childcare be commoditized as completely as possible, so that women can compete equally with men in the labour market. Women, if they are to 'succeed', or often just survive in an era when divorce is commonplace and welfare programmes are being rolled back, are thus being pushed to take on traditionally masculine, competitive values. Conversely, those who actively participate in caring for their families and communities are economically punished.

Thus a new form of patriarchal capitalism is emerging. Whereas in its previous form, capitalist patriarchy was characterized by a rigid sexual division of labour, this new form allows some freedom for the sexes to choose between or combine gender roles. Some women – particularly those with class and race privilege – can enter into 'men's jobs', even positions of economic wealth and power, and men can enter into 'women's jobs', including becoming househusbands. However, the essential structure of the economy has stayed the same, and traditionally masculine activities – now done by both females and males – are valued above traditionally feminine ones, still mostly done by females, but also by some males. The core economic process remains the struggles by firms and workers to dominate others in an economic hierarchy. Thus if discrimination is in the process of being reduced, patriarchy is alive and well, if in an altered form (Matthaei and Amott 1997).

The challenge to feminist economists is to elaborate economic and social theories that can make visible and thus help eliminate the deep structures of patriarchy, rather than taking them as given and natural – just as feminists have made visible and criticized the social construction of gender. This means formulating a critique not only of the sexual division of labour in the home and labour market, but also of the gendered and patriarchal values and processes that are built into capitalist patriarchy. Feminist economists have criticized *neoclassical economics'* core concept of 'rational *economic man*', a self-interested, utility-maximizing, atomistic being, for being both unrealistic and masculinist (England 1993; Strassman 1993). Nelson (1993) suggests a shift in the values underlying economic theory in her call for economics to reconstitute itself as the study of provisioning, rather than the study of choice. Jennings (1993) has pointed out the ways in which mainstream theory shares the 'economism' of capitalist patriarchal culture, 'the social prioritizing of market processes as the desiderata of social well-being' (p. 124). She critiques this economistic view as inherently dualistic and patriarchal, pointing out that '"Economistic" beliefs must be challenged as hierarchical and invidious, and economic principles must be reconnected to the full range of human activities, most of which have provisioning significance' (pp. 125–6).

In this way, feminist economists are pointing towards a vision of an economy whose goal is the provisioning of the essential needs of all people, both material and spiritual. Ecofeminists Mies and Shiva (1993, Chapter 20) argue that true women's liberation is impossible within capitalism, given its inherently patriarchal, violent, inequality-generating and ecologically destructive nature; they present a vision of a 'subsistence economy' characterized by community-based, cooperative, nonhierarchical and ecological institutions. In a similar vein, Matthaei and Amott (1997) argue that feminists, anti-racists and other progressives need to advocate for and work towards new, post-patriarchal post-capitalist economic institutions based on mutuality and equality amidst difference, cooperation, power as the empowerment of oneself and others, and the sacredness of life, both human and non-human. They argue that the seeds of such an economy are already present in the socially-responsible investment and consumer movements which financially support firms that embody progressive, post-patriarchal principles such as gender and race equality, environmentalism and pacifism, and/or which are cooperatively owned and run. In this way, feminist economists are challenging not only the discipline of economics, but also the very economic structure of the present-day capitalist economies.

JULIE MATTHAEI

See also
Capitalism; Class; Domestic Labour; Feminism(s); Gender; Marxist Political Economics; Race.

Bibliography

Al-Hibri, Azizah (1981), 'Capitalism is an Advanced Stage of Patriarchy: But Marxism is not Feminism', in Lydia Sargent (ed.), *Women and Revolution*, Boston, South End Press, pp. 165–93.

Amott, Teresa and Julie Matthaei (1996), *Race, Gender and Work: A Multicultural Economic History of Women in the United States*, Boston: South End.

Benería, Lourdes (1979), 'Reproduction, production, and the sexual division of labour', *Cambridge Journal of Economics*, **3** (3), 203–25.

Bergmann, Barbara (1986), *The Economic Emergence of Women*, New York: Basic Books.

Blau, Francine, Marianne Ferber and Anne Winkler (1998), *The Economics of Women, Men and Work*, 3rd edn, Upper Saddle River, New Jersey: Prentice Hall.

Buffalohead, Priscilla (1983), 'Farmers, warriors, traders: a fresh look at Ojibway women', *Minnesota History*, **48**, (Summer), 226–40.

Chodorow, Nancy (1979), 'Mothering, Male Dominance, and Capitalism', in Zillah Eisenstein (ed.), *Capitalist Patriarchy and the Case for Socialist Feminism*, New York: Monthly Review Press, pp. 83–106.

Cox, Oliver (1948), *Caste, Class, and Race: A Study in Social Dynamics*, New York: Monthly Review Press.

Eisenstein, Zillah (ed.) (1979), *Capitalist Patriarchy and the Case for Socialist Feminism*, New York: Monthly Review Press.

England, Paula (1993), 'The Separative Self: Androcentric Bias in Neoclassical Assumptions', in Marianne Ferber and Julie Nelson (eds), *Beyond Economic Man: Feminist Theory and Economics*, Chicago: University of Chicago Press, pp. 37–53.

Ferguson, Ann and Nancy Folbre (1981), 'The Unhappy Marriage of Patriarchy and Capitalism', in Lydia Sargent (ed.), *Women and Revolution*, Boston: South End Press, pp. 313–38.

Folbre, Nancy (1980), 'Patriarchy in colonial New England', *Review of Radical Political Economics*, **12** (2), (Summer), 2–23.

Gardiner, Jean (1979), 'Women's Domestic Labour', in Zillah Eisenstein (ed.), *Capitalist*

Patriarchy and the Case for Socialist Feminism, New York: Monthly Review Press, pp. 173–89.

Gimbutas, Marija (1991), *Civilization of the Goddess: The World of Old Europe*, San Francisco, California: Harper San Francisco.

Glen, Evelyn Nakano (1985), 'Racial ethnic women's labour', *Review of Radical Political Economics*, **17** (3), (Fall), 86–108.

Hartmann, Heidi (1979), 'Capitalism, Patriarchy, and Job Segregation by Sex', in Zillah Eisenstein (ed.), *Capitalist Patriarchy and the Case for Socialist Feminism*, New York: Monthly Review Press, pp. 206–47.

Hartmann, Heidi (1981), 'The Unhappy Marriage of Marxism and Feminism: Towards a More Progressive Union', in Lydia Sargent (ed.), *Women and Revolution*, Boston: South End Press, pp. 1–41.

hooks, bell (1984), *Feminist Theory: From Margin to Centre*, Boston: South End Press.

Hull, Gloria, Patricia Bell Scott and Barbara Smith (1982), *All the Women are White, All the Blacks are Men, but Some of Us are Brave*, Old Westbury, New York: Feminist Press.

Humphries, Jane and Jill Rubery (1984), 'The reconstitution of the supply side of the labour market: the relative autonomy of social reproduction', *Cambridge Journal of Economics*, **8** (4), 331–46.

Jennings, Ann (1993), 'Public or Private? Institutional Economics and Feminism', in Marianne Ferber and Julie Nelson (eds), *Beyond Economic Man: Feminist Theory and Economics*, Chicago: University of Chicago Press, pp. 111–29.

Josephs, Gloria (1981), 'The Incompatible Menage a Trois: Marxism, Feminism and Racism', in Lydia Sargent (ed.), *Women and Revolution*, Boston: South End Press, pp. 91–108.

Leacock, Eleanor (1981), *Myths of Male Dominance: Collected Articles on Women Cross-Culturally*, New York: Monthly Review Press.

Matthaei, Julie (1982), *An Economic History of Women in America: Women's Work, the Sexual Division of Labour, and the Development of Capitalism*, New York: Schocken Books.

Matthaei, Julie (1992), 'Marxist-Feminist Contributions to Radical Economics', in Bruce Roberts and Susan Feiner (eds), *Radical Economics*, Norwell, Massachusetts: Kluwer Academic Publishers, pp. 117–44.

Matthaei, Julie (1996), 'Why Feminist, Marxist, and Anti-Racist Economics Should be Feminist–Marxist–Anti-Racist Economists', *Feminist Economics*, **2** (1), 22–42.

Matthaei, Julie and Teresa Amott (1997), 'Global Capitalism, Difference, and Women's Liberation: Towards a Liberated Economy', Wellesley College Working Paper 97–03.

Mies, Maria (1986), *Patriarchy and Accumulation on a World Scale: Women in the International Division of Labour*, London: Zed Books.

Mies, Maria and Vandana Shiva (1993), *Ecofeminism*, London: Zed Books.

Nelson, Julie (1993), 'The Study of Choice or the Study of Provisioning? Gender and the Definition of Economics', in Marianne Ferber and Julie Nelson (eds), *Beyond Economic Man: Feminist Theory and Economics*, Chicago: University of Chicago Press, pp. 23–36.

Sargent, Lydia (ed.)(1981), *Women and Revolution: A Discussion of the Unhappy Marriage of Marxism and Feminism*, Boston: South End Press.

Strassman, Diana (1993), 'Not a Free Market: The Rhetoric of Disciplinary Authority in Economics', in Marianne Ferber and Julie Nelson (eds), *Beyond Economic Man*, Chicago: University of Chicago Press, pp. 54–68.

US Bureau of the Census (1996), *Statistical Abstract of the United States: 1996*, Washington, DC: US Government Printing Office.

Pedagogy

Pedagogy is what happens in the classroom. Pedagogy is a description of a set of complex interactions that occur in a classroom between the instructor and his/her students, between and among students, between the instructor and the subject matter, and between the students and the subject matter. The objectives of these interactions can range from the direct transmission of knowledge from one generation to another to the creation of knowledge to transform society. At one end of a pedagogy continuum, the set of interactions that occur in the classroom seems highly structured and the information flow is unidirectional. For example, the relationship between the instructor and his/her students is hierarchical where the instructor is an expert and the student is a novice with regard to the subject matter. Typically, the material is transmitted directly via lectures in a classroom where the instructor stands at the front of the room and students sit in rows of fixed chairs taking notes. Students passively listen and take in the material. There are little, if any, interactions between the instructor and the students or between and among the students. Student understanding of the ideas presented is usually evaluated with a series of tests that elicit an uncritical regurgitation of the material. At the other extreme of the pedagogy continuum, the relationship between the instructor and his/her students is non-hierarchical and multidirectional. The instructor and his/her students are co-investigators with regard to the subject matter. The instructor brings his/her expertise and his/her story of the subject and students bring their own experiences and knowledge and their stories of the subject to the classroom. The information flow is multidirectional. Together they exchange their knowledge through active, although often highly structured, sets of interactions and create new knowledge. Student understanding of the ideas discussed is evaluated by their ability to construct theories and think critically about them in verbal and/or written ways. At both ends of the pedagogy continuum, the knowledge gained can be for its own sake or to use for political interventions to bring about social and economic change.

Feminist instructors are concerned about pedagogy for a variety of reasons. Some feminists may not have had positive experiences in the educational system, they may have witnessed negative effects of the educational system on their own students, or they may have intellectual interests and concerns about teaching. Feminist pedagogy is more than an instructor who defines him/ herself as a feminist and teaches in a classroom. Feminist instructors may be found all along the pedagogy continuum. For example, a feminist instructor may conduct a course in a very hierarchical and unidirectional manner. While there is no one feminist pedagogy, Sandler et al. (1996) note several common themes. Feminist pedagogy questions the neutrality of positivism and objectivity; realizes the importance and legitimacy of personal experience for learning; explores the intersections of race, gender and class and their impact on the subject matter; establishes non-hierarchical interactions between the instructor and the students and between and among students; and empowers students to be active and contributing members of the political process.

Feminist instructors who are conscious of the potential impact of a gender perspective on pedagogical practices are more likely to find themselves on the less hierarchical and multidirectional end of the pedagogy continuum. The importance of feminist pedagogy for economists is twofold. First, feminist pedagogy will transform the economics classroom into a more hospitable place and increase learning for a more diverse student body. Second, the increasing use of feminist pedagogy in economics classrooms will transform the research methodology of economics and thus the discipline.

Feminist pedagogy did not grow out of a vacuum. It is the product of a long history of educational change and ferment. Giroux (1997) describes three streams of educational thought that have evolved over time. Conservative educational thought as typified by Adler (1982) argues that there is a store of artifacts and theory that needs to be passed on to the younger generation. Students are to master specific skills and predetermined forms of knowledge. Which facts and which theories to be passed on and how they are to be passed on are not questioned. Liberal educational thought is exemplified by the works of Dewey (1916) to more recent educators who emphasize multiculturalism (Adams 1992; Schoem 1994). The needs and concerns of students are the starting points for developing pedagogical techniques. The intent is to focus on student-directed learning, to connect knowledge and personal experience, and to facilitate positive interactions among students (Anderson and Adams 1992; Belenky et al. 1986; Bruffe 1993; Johnson et al. 1991; Light 1990; Maher and Tetreault 1994; Meyers and Jones 1993; Smith and Kolb 1985; Tobias 1990). The radical critique of both of these streams of thought is that neither is very forward looking, empowering, or creative. Radical pedagogy, as often typified by Friere (1970) and Giroux (1997), involves first analysing how cultural production is organized and how the power structures within schools reproduce that structure. Second, radical pedagogy tries to construct political strategies for participating in social struggles designed to make schools democratic spheres of influence. Radical educational theorists not only see the classroom as a place where knowledge is transmitted, but also as a place where political activity begins (hooks 1994).

Economics has three comparable streams of educational thought. Conservative economic educators, the majority of economic educators, teach in hierarchically structured, unidirectional classrooms, lecture daily, and transmit the received neoclassical model (Becker 1998; Becker and Watts 1996). The purpose of this enterprise is to teach students to 'think like economists' (Siegfried et al. 1990). The professor and text are the store of all economic knowledge and students are vessels into which it is put. Liberal economic educators are cognizant of the fact that the content of economics courses is narrow, that not all students learn in the same way, and that some voices are not heard (Bartlett 1996, 1997, 1998; Bartlett and Feiner 1992; Bartlett and

Ferber 1998; Bergmann 1987; Ferber 1997). They argue for a more inclusive curriculum, for a variety of teaching techniques or interactions to be incorporated into economics courses, and for a more hospitable dynamic in the classroom. Bartlett and Ferber (1998) talk about humanizing the content and pedagogy of economics classes. Radical economic educators are concerned about how the educational system produces workers for the corporate state. Rather than the educational system generating informed and active citizens, the system produces workers who accept the status quo (Feiner and Roberts 1990). Since most educational systems are patterned after the British educational system, similar patterns are found around the world.

Culley and Portuges (1985, p. 1) note that, 'The phrase "feminist pedagogy" couples the contemporary and the traditional, joining current political movements with a concern for the transmission of knowledge more ancient than the Greek word for teaching'. Feminist pedagogy evolved out of the intersection of female experiences with the educational tradition. Shackelford (1992) identifies three recurring pedagogical themes for economists: ending the oppression of women and other marginalized groups, validating other forms of knowing, and using knowledge for change. To begin the process of incorporating these themes into the economics classroom, feminist instructors must begin to expand the content of their courses and to redefine the types of interactions that take place in the classroom.

Aerni et al. (1999) construct a model that systematically develops several paths that an instructor may take toward a more feminist pedagogy in economics by incorporating more inclusive course content and classroom environments into economics or any combination of the two. They begin with a variant on the McIntosh (1983) multi-stage interactive model for incorporating women into the curriculum. In the first stage, the received neoclassical canon, women are absent. Economics is gender-blind. Economics is taught as if the economic behaviour of the rational economic man was indeed generic and captured the economic behaviour of all people for all time. In the second stage, finding and adding women, the experiences of women are added to the content of the course and then stirred. Economic theory is applied to the special issues of women or used to explain the observed differences in economic behaviour between men and women. The anomalies that often result help to define the third stage – challenging and proposing. Since women's economic behaviour does not always fit the male norm, in this stage existing economic theories are modified or extended. The adjustments take the form of expanded neoclassical economic theories or alternative economic theories. Having exhausted the possibilities of traditional and heterodox economic theory, the fourth stage begins to evolve. This stage would necessitate a redefining of economics as more interdisciplinary and methodologically diverse approaches are sought for understanding economic behaviour.

Aerni et al. then discuss the use of more inclusive pedagogical techniques in individual, group and community learning environments. The individual learning process or environment is typical of most economics courses. The student sits in a lecture hall and learns by him/herself. There is very little interaction between him/her and the instructor and between him/her and other students in the class. The group learning process encourages structured interactions between students. Here, the instructor uses various group exercises, cooperative learning techniques, or team learning (Bartlett 1995, 1998). The instructor plays less of a role in the transmission or creation of knowledge and students play an increasingly significant role in the learning process. Finally, the walls of the classroom are expanded and students learn not only from each other and the instructor, but also from the 'outside world'. Students can learn through service learning assignments (McGoldrick 1998) or from political activism (Lewis 1995).

Aerni et al. argue that to engage in feminist pedagogy, an instructor must develop both a more inclusive course content and a more inclusive learning environment. Inclusive course content taught in a traditional way (in an individualistic and competitive learning environment) is not feminist pedagogy, and the received canon of neoclassical economic theory taught in a more cooperative and community learning environment is not feminist pedagogy either. Instead, Aerni et al. argue that the more inclusive and cooperative the content and interactions in the classroom, the more an instructor's pedagogy approaches feminist pedagogy as outlined by Shackelford (1992). The ultimate feminist pedagogy will never be achieved, however, because it is an evolutionary process that occurs as an economics instructor moves from the gender-free economics found in most classrooms to an inclusive curriculum taught increasingly with cooperative learning techniques in an open classroom. Students, realizing that they are an integral part of the educational community, will learn that they are a part of a political process as well and will be prepared to take an active role in it.

Another dimension to feminist pedagogy that is often ignored is the content of the interactions between the instructor and the students and the students and other students and how personal prejudice, histories and backgrounds can affect these interactions. Hall and Sandler's (1982) initial report on the 'chilly climate' describes how male and female students are treated differently in the classroom and how these minor differences can add up to a hostile learning environment. For example, instructors often communicate a lower status to female students by asking them easier questions. Or, an instructor may yield to the influence of an internalized stereotype, such as focusing on a female student's traditional accomplishments, rather than her intellectual achievements. Female students can be excluded from class participation in subtle ways. Interrupting female students more may silence them. Female students can be treated differently even when they exhibit the same behaviour as male students. For example, a female student asking for help on an assignment may be thought of as not capable of knowing the material while a male student may be thought of as inquisitive. Female students can be given less encouragement by giving them less follow up on their answers as compared with that of male students. Female students can be discouraged through politeness and made to feel singled out. Finally, overt comments about sexuality may have a detrimental effect on female students' learning. While the 'chilly climate' report received a great deal of attention when it was first released, their most recent report (Sandler et al. 1996) suggests that less has been changed than anticipated 15 years ago.

While much is written on how to create a learning environment, very little is written on how to determine the effectiveness of that environment on student understanding of economics. Multiple-choice tests and short answer questions are the norm in economics courses. Students are given few written assignments and even fewer opportunities to debate and make oral presentations. If the delivery methods for the material change, then the evaluation schemes should also change and align with them. For example, it makes very little sense to use multiple-choice questions in a course that has used group learning techniques and has had students engage in service learning assignments. An oral presentation or a written report might give a student an opportunity to better demonstrate the different dimensions of the learning experience. Similarly, a more inclusive content would be remiss, even using an individualistic approach to learning, if the instructors did not ask the student on a more traditional short answer test to explain how the particular economic principle being tested might relate to their own lives. A wider range and more creative alternative assignments are found with feminist pedagogy.

Feminist pedagogy is particularly important for economic thought because it is one vehicle for transforming the discipline from one increasingly out of touch with the economic reality of the majority into one that is contributing to solutions for many of the urgent problems facing individuals and society. Feminist instructors using feminist pedagogy approach the classroom in very different ways than more traditional economic instructors. Non-hierarchical, cooperative interactions are the hallmark of the interactions between the instructor and his/her students. Thus, the connection between teaching and learning is blurred. As a result, a feminist economic instructor who uses feminist pedagogy would begin to see the artificial distinctions between him/herself and his/her research blur also. A feminist researcher's ways of knowing would be more interactive, non-hierarchical and co-investigative. A whole new array of interactions between the researcher, the subject and the context within which they exist would become significant to the study. The feminist economics researcher is more respectful of his/her own relationship with the subject/subjects being studied rather than operating under the illusion of separateness and objectivity. Economic knowledge would then be an evolving process of idea generation rather than a stock of economic theories to be passed on to the next generation. The feminist researcher is more aware of the impact of new knowledge on the socioeconomic–political structures that surround the classroom and vice versa.

Feminist pedagogy has been criticized as representing nothing new. In some respects that criticism is accurate. Feminist pedagogy grew out of a gender analysis of the conservative, liberal and radical traditions found in educational literature. The gendered aspects of these streams of thought went unchallenged until feminists began to approach the subject (Culley and Portuges 1985). Feminist pedagogy improves upon traditional pedagogy. Its more inclusive course content and a more inclusive learning environment help more students learn more effectively (Lage and Tregilia 1996; Light 1990; Johnson et al. 1991). Some conservative economic educators might argue that adding women and people of colour to the course content 'waters down' or 'softens' the curriculum and takes away from the theories and skills that students should be learning or that the new content is sociology, psychology or something other than economics. Of course the question here is what do students learn in traditional economics courses and how do they learn it. Feminist pedagogy is concerned with both of these issues. Liberal educators might argue that progress is being made and that the curriculum is more inclusive, but as Aerni et al. argue, an inclusive curriculum is not necessarily a feminist pedagogy. An inclusive curriculum is but one component of a feminist pedagogy. Radical economics educators might argue that not all feminists who practise feminist pedagogy do it with the intent of constructing knowledge for political change. The question here is what constitutes political change within the system. However, changing the classroom to include more feminist pedagogy would change the social structures around it. All of these criticisms are part of the process and provide direction for research efforts in the field.

The issues for further study by feminist economists are several. First, how does an instructor go about changing the content and set of classroom interactions within institutions of higher education given the set of rewards that exist and the different priority put on teaching and research. Students who expect to come into a classroom and sit back and soak up the information will be disappointed to find him/herself in a classroom where he/she is expected to interact on a daily basis and to take responsibility for their own learning. Second, the role that course evaluations play in the reward system could discourage the development and implementation of feminist techniques and needs to be studied. If the link between theoretical progress is closely correlated with changing classroom interactions between the instructor and his/her students, between and among students, between the subject matter and the instructor and students, then encouraging feminist pedagogical techniques in the classroom would be as important as encouraging basic research itself. Economic instructors who practise feminist pedagogy would find it difficult not to use a more inclusive research methodologies and to establish different relationships with the subject matter. The end result would be better economic research, one that would expand the complexity of economic reasoning and change what it means to 'think like an economist'. As Rich (1979, p. 240) notes, feminist educators have two choices. They can either lend their weight to the forces that keep women oppressed in the educational system or they can consider what 'we have to work against, as well as with, in ourselves, in our students, in the content of the curriculum, in the structure of the institution, in the society at large'. Feminist pedagogy is indeed taking the experiences of women seriously and offers feminist economists another avenue for transforming the economics discipline.

ROBIN L. BARTLETT

See also
Economics Education; Feminist Economics.

Bibliography
Adams, Maurianne (1992), 'Cultural Inclusion in the American College Curriculum', in Laura L.B. Border and Nancy Van Note Chism (eds), *Teaching for Diversity*, No. 49, San Francisco: Jossey-Bass, pp. 5–17.

Adler, Mortimer (1982), *The Paideia Proposal*, New York: Macmillan.

Aerni, April Laskey, Robin L. Bartlett, Margaret Lewis, KimMarie McGoldrick and Jean Shackelford (1999), 'Toward a feminist pedagy in economics', *Feminist Economics*, **5** (1), 29–44.

Anderson, James A. and Maurianne Adams (1992), 'Acknowledging the Learning Styles of Diverse Student Populations: Implications for Instructional Design', in Laura L.B. Border and Nancy Van Note Chism (eds), *Teaching for Diversity*, No. 49, San Francisco: Jossey-Bass, pp. 19–33.

Bartlett, Robin L. (1995), 'A flip of the coin – a roll of the die: an answer to the free-rider problem in economic instruction', *The Journal of Economic Education*, **26** (2), 131–9.

Bartlett, Robin L. (1996), 'Discovering diversity in introductory economics', *Journal of Economic Perspectives*, **19** (2), 141–53.

Bartlett, Robin L. (1997), 'Restructuring Economics 190 R & G: Introductory Economics from a Race and Gender Perspective', in Robin L. Bartlett (ed.), *Introducing Race and Gender into Economics*, New York: Routledge, pp. 3–27.

Bartlett, Robin L. (1998), 'Making Cooperative Learning Work in the Economics Classroom', in William E. Becker and Michael Watts (eds), *Teaching Economics to Undergraduates: Alternatives to Chalk and Talk*, Cheltenham: Edward Elgar, pp. 11–34.

Bartlett, Robin L. and Susan Feiner (1992), 'Balancing the Curriculum: Content, Method, and Pedagogy', *American Economic Review*, **82** (2), 559–64.

Bartlett, Robin L. and Marianne A. Ferber (1998), 'Humanizing Content and Pedagogy in Economics Classrooms', in William B. Wallstad and Phillip Saunders (eds), *Teaching Undergraduate Economics: A Handbook for Instructors*, New York: McGraw Hill.

Becker, William E. (1998), 'Teaching economics to undergraduates', *Journal of Economic Literature*, **35** (3), 1347–73.

Becker, William E. and Michael Watts (1996), 'Chalk and talk: a national survey on teaching undergraduate economics', *American Economics Review*, **86** (2), 448–53.

Belenky, Mary Field, Blythe McVicker Clinchy, Nancy Rule Goldberger and Jill Mattuck Tarule (1986), *Women's Ways of Knowing: The Development of Self, Voice, and Mind*, New York: Basic Books.

Bergmann, Barbara R. (1987), 'Women's roles in the economy: teaching the issues', *Journal of Economic Education*, **18** (20), 393–407.

Bruffe, Kenneth A. (1993), *Collaborative Learning*, Baltimore: The Johns Hopkins Press.

Culley, Margo and Catherine Portuges (eds) (1985), *Gendered Subjects: The Dynamics of Feminist Teaching*, Boston: Routledge and Kegan Paul.

Dewey, John (1916), *Democracy and Education*, New York: Free Press.

Feiner, Susan F. and Bruce B. Roberts (1990), 'Hidden by the invisible hand: Neoclassical economic theory and the textbook treatment of race and gender', *Gender and Society*, **4**, 159–81.

Ferber, Marianne A. (1997) 'Gender and the Study of Economics: A Feminist Critique', in Robin L. Bartlett (ed.), *Introducing Race and Gender into Economics*, New York: Routledge, pp. 147–55.

Friere, Paulo (1970), *Pedagogy of the Oppressed*, New York: The Continuum Publishing Company.

Giroux, Henry A. (1997), *Pedagogy and Politics of Hope: Theory, Culture, and Schooling*, Boulder, Colorado: Westview Press.

Hall, Roberta M. and Bernice R. Sandler (1982), *The Classroom Climate: A Chilly One For Women?*, Washington, DC: Project for the Status and Education of Women, Association of American Colleges.

hooks, bell (1994), *Teaching to Transgress: Education as the Practice of Freedom*, New York: Routledge.

Johnson, David W., Roger T. Johnson and Karl A. Smith (1991), *Cooperative Learning: Increasing College Faculty Instructional Productivity*, ASHE-ERIC Higher Education Report No. 4, Washington, DC: The George Washington University, School of Education and Human Development.

Lage, Maureen and Michael Tregilia (1996), 'The impact of integrating scholarship on women into introductory economies: evidence from one institution', *Journal of Economic Education*, **27** (1), 26–36.

Lewis, Margaret (1995), 'Breaking down the walls, opening up the field: situating the economics classroom in the site of social action', *Journal of Economic Issues*, **29** (2), 555–65.

Light, R.J. (1990), *Explorations with Students and Faculty about Teaching, Learning, and Student Life, First Report 1990*, Cambridge, Massachusetts: Harvard University.

Maher, Francis A. and Mary Kay Thompson Tetreault (1994), *The Feminist Classroom: An Inside Look at How Professors are Transforming Higher Education for a Diverse Society*, New York: Basic Books.

McGoldrick, KimMarie (1998), 'Service learning in economics: A detailed application', *Journal of Economic Education*, **29** (2), 365–76

McIntosh, Peggy (1983), 'Interactive Phases of the Curricular Re-Vision: A Feminist Perspective', Wellesley, Massachusetts: Wellesley College, Center for Research on Women, Working Paper No. 124.

Meyers, C. and T.B. Jones (1993), *Promoting Active Learning Strategies for the Classroom*, San Francisco: Jossey-Bass.

Rich, Adrienne (1979), 'On Taking Women Students Seriously', in *On Lies, Secrets and Silences: Selected Prose 1966–78*, New York: Norton.

Sandler, Bernice Resnick, Lisa A. Silverberg and Roberta M. Hall (1996), *The Chilly Classroom Climate: A Guide to Improve the Education of Women*, Washington, DC: National Association For Women in Education.

Schoem, D. et al. (eds) (1994), *Multicultural Teaching in the University*, Westport, Connecticut: Praeger.

Shackelford, Jean (1992), 'Feminist pedagogy: a means for bringing critical thinking and creativity to the economics classroom', *American Economic Review*, **82** (2), 570–76.

Siegfried, John J., Robin L. Bartlett, W. Lee Hansen, Allen C. Kelley, Donald N. McCloskey and Thomas H. Tietenberg (1990), 'Economics', *Liberal Learning and the Arts and Sciences Major*, Volume 2: Reports from the Field, Washington, DC: Association of American Colleges, pp. 25–42.

Smith, D. and David A. Kolb (1985), *User Guide for the Learning-style Inventory*, Boston: McBer and Company.

Tobias, Sheila (1990), *They're Not Dumb, They're Different: Stalking the Second Tier*, Tucson, Arizona: Research Corporation.

Pensions and Old Age Retirement

The most poignant shared international experience is that income to older women is often not enough, and poverty universally threatens older women more than older men (Smeeding 1997). In the USA, for example, over one-fifth of all women aged 65 years of age or older receive incomes that place them below the poverty line, leading to one of the highest poverty rates for older women in industrialized nations. In fact, nearly three-quarters of the elderly poor in the USA are women (Briceland-Betts 1995).

Where do older women get income? In most industrialized nations, women's access to old age income comes mainly from earnings-related pension programmes (their own or from their husband's work), government income support programmes, personal wealth and, in developing nations, from children (Rix et al. 1998). In the USA, which stands apart from other nations in not having a mandatory retirement age, earnings can also provide a source of income for women in old age. Government programmes are a particularly important source of old age income for women in industrialized nations. Many of these programmes, such as the old age insurance programme typically referred to as 'Social Security' in the USA, reflect the earnings-related 'Bismarckian model' associated with German Chancellor Bismarck's 1889 pension system in which pensions were viewed as a deferred wage, that is, an earned right. In contrast, universal assistance programmes (so-called 'Beveridge-type' systems found in Anglo-Saxon nations outside the USA and in Nordic countries) provide income to those meeting citizenship and residency criteria. These evolved later, in the immediate post-World War II period, and became straightforward means-tested programmes that transferred income to citizens in need (Myles and Quandagno 1996). The structure of these different government income support programmes has important implications for the status of older women. In deferred-wage pension systems, for example, the choices women make (or are limited to) early in their lives to forgo earnings cause them to suffer the long-term consequences of low old-age income (Rix et al. 1998). In universal assistance programmes, however, the guarantee of old age support lessens the likelihood of old age poverty.

Although poverty among older women is higher in the USA than in many other industrialized nations, the World Bank and other international financial organizations promote a version of the mixed public/private pension system found in the USA. Consequently, the characteristics of the current system in the USA, as well as efforts to further privatize this system, have important implications for the economic wellbeing of older women in many nations and will be the focus of this entry.

The US pension system combines four sources of income to the elderly: participation in the mandatory and nearly universal old age insurance programme known as Social Security, voluntary employer-based pensions, private wealth (for example, income from personal assets), and paid employment. Means-tested public assistance is a very small part of retirement income in the USA, accounting for less than 2 per cent for unmarried women and less than 0.5 per cent for married couples (Grad 1996).

The Social Security system in the USA, like most others, is 'progressive' in that it provides higher replacement rates for low-income workers than for higher income workers. However, the programme is not means-tested, so contributors with similar work histories get similar benefits even if one has a large amount of wealth. Non-married older women receive the majority of their retirement income from Social Security, almost 53 per cent, because of the progressive formula, the subsidy to dependants, and the cost-of-living annual adjustments that help those who live longer. Couples, in contrast, receive less than 38 per cent of their income from Social Security (Grad 1996).

With the second source of retirement income, voluntary employer-provided pensions, coverage and generosity varies greatly between occupations, employers and industries. Unfortunately, female-dominated industries in service and wholesale and retail trade have the lowest level of pension coverage. (This is also true in other nations with employer-based voluntary systems.) One-half of American workers have employer-based pensions but only 39 per cent of women workers do, and women's pensions are half the value of men's (Costello and Stone 1995). In 1994, unmarried older women obtained less than 16 per cent of their income from employer pensions (private and government pensions and railroad retirement), while one-fifth of older married couple's incomes come from employer-based voluntary systems (Grad 1996). Legislation has attempted to reduce these discrepancies. The Retirement Equity Act of 1984, for example, reflecting feminist reconceptions of the housewife as a contributor to household income, has provided a significant legislative improvement for married women by making it more difficult for married men to dilute the access of wives to employer-based pensions.

Recent shifts away from 'defined benefit' employer-provided pension plans to 'defined contribution' plans (such as '401(k) plans') pose four major threats to women. First, employers offer higher rates of contributions to higher income workers who are, on average, men. In addition, women live almost 30 per cent longer than men and therefore pay higher rates for annuities or deplete their accounts before they die. Third, defined contribution pensions are not adjusted to make up for losses due to inflation. Since women live longer, inflation has a greater impact on them. Last, because workers choose their own investments, and women tend to invest more conservatively than men (not because of an innate gender difference but because they have lower incomes), such programmes yield significantly less benefits for the same amount of contributions, up to 16 per cent less in one study (Ross 1997).

The third and fourth sources of income for older Americans, wealth and current earnings, have to date received less attention from policymakers. Elderly married couples obtain 16.6 per cent of their income from assets, while they account for 18.9 per cent of the income of unmarried elderly women. Although 22.9 per cent of income to elderly couples comes from earnings, only 8.8 per cent of income to unmarried older women comes from earnings, reflecting the lower labour force participation rates and earnings of older women compared to men (Grad 1996).

Analysts agree that the growth of Social Security benefits, with their indexation for inflation, has enormously decreased the overall rate of old age poverty for women (from 22 per cent in 1971 to 15 per cent in 1991) (Rix et al. 1998). Remarkably, this dramatic decrease in women's old age poverty occurred when most of the population experienced stagnating incomes and increased poverty, but not all elderly women have benefited equally. Older women living alone, for example, still have higher poverty rates than couples, and since more elderly men are in couples, the poverty rate for older women is almost double the male rate of just under 8 per cent (Sandell 1994). In fact, elderly women without husbands have the second highest poverty rates in the USA (non-white children have the highest) at 21 per cent, a rate much higher than any other group of single elderly women in the industrialized nations of the OECD, where the average poverty rate for single elderly women is about 6 per cent.

Additional problems persist. African-American elderly women living alone, for example, have a staggering 75 per cent rate of poverty. Widows are also particularly vulnerable to poverty; when a husband dies the chance the surviving wife will fall into poverty increases 350 per cent. (This 'widow effect' larger in the USA than in other OECD nations (Smeeding 1997).) Further, old age poverty may be made worse because of the elderly's dependence on publicly funded health care and housing. Although these programs have raised the standard of living for elderly women in OECD countries (Smeeding 1997), recent moves to cut government budgets have the potential to counter the gains mentioned above.

These differential effects in old age income and poverty rates have led feminists to argue that the stark gender differences in the quality of life for older people can and must be explained by explicit analyses of the gender biases in public policy and the work force. As part of the overall feminist economic agenda to expose gender differentials in economic experiences, choices and opportunities, feminist economists have, for example, identified patriarchal biases in public policy, the subordinate status of women workers, and the increasing instability of marriages as sources of the greater poverty risk facing elderly women. Such analyses have, in turn, informed feminist economic policy reforms and provide clues for future feminist economic research.

For example, feminists have paid particular attention to pension programmes based on the deferred wage model for the obvious problems that this structure causes for women who are not dependent on males, who live longer than men, and who experience unequal wages and labour market discrimination that result in less coverage and lower payments in employer-provided pensions plans and in lower Social Security benefits. Feminist economists are, of course, not the first to recognize the significance of the political economy of old age income. Marxist political economists, for example, have acknowledged that retirement income was a working class victory, but only a partial one since workers pay for it through deferred wages and a redistribution between wage earners (see, for example, Olson 1982).

Feminist economists have subsequently highlighted the gendered aspects of these redistributional issues. Folbre (1994), for example, examines the patriarchal biases in the historical development of retirement income in the USA (including the fact that the original Social Security Act excluded the female-concentrated industries) and illustrates the inequities that the resulting system has created for women and children. She points out how under the current structure of Social Security, men can abandon their children and still receive decent benefits. In addition, Folbre argues that the Social Security system exploits women's labour, since the benefits of older males are based on the future productivity of children, which is linked to the amount and quality of undervalued female labour.

One specific aspect of the Social Security system that has received a great deal of attention from feminist scholars is the system for defining benefits, which often leads to the non-recognition of women's own labour force participation and to a situation where one-earner couples receive higher benefits then two-earner couples with the same income, a situation known as the 'housewife bonus' (Bergmann 1986; Holden 1996). Under the current system, all workers earn a Social Security pension based on their own earnings record. If the Social Security pension based on her/his own work history is higher than the dependent benefit (which is 50 per cent of the spouse's pension), then the recipient receives her/his own pension; if, however, this pension is lower, then the recipient receives the dependent benefit. In 1994, for example, although most married women were eligible for retired workers benefits, their spouse's benefit was higher. Specifically, less than one-third of women had a worker benefit higher than her spouse's benefit, thus not receiving any credit for her labour force contributions (Holden 1996). This result has led many feminists to argue that when women receive benefits based on the spouse's labour force record, she is unfairly receiving a zero rate of return on her own contributions (Bergmann 1986; Holden 1996).

A suggested reform of Social Security that has received the support of a variety of feminists (see, for example, Bergmann 1986; Blau and Ferber 1992; Holden 1996), is 'earnings sharing'. Under this approach, two equally sized accounts, based on the combined Social Security record for the married couple regardless of how paid and unpaid work is distributed between them, would be established. Thus 'earnings sharing' has been suggested as a way to address both the problems of the wife's work going unrecognized and existing inequities between one-earner and two-earner couples. But despite this proposal's immediate appeal of fairness, research shows that such a change would not affect 90 per cent of couples and could reduce the benefits of low-income one-earner families and women who survive their husbands for a significant length of time (US Department of Health, Education, and Welfare 1978).

Currently, most discussions of Social Security reform in the USA and internationally focus on 'privatization' and include proposals that encourage the transformation of social insurance systems into individual accounts where workers invest in a wide range of assets (World Bank 1994). Privatizing social insurance systems would divert some or all of the mandatory contributions to individual accounts, so instead of people receiving benefits if they meet certain conditions (such as being at retirement age, having dependants and having a record of contributions), workers' retirement benefits would now depend on the size of their individual accounts. Although such a system might meet the feminist goal of equal rates of return between men and women, women's individual accounts are likely to be smaller, and thus their retirement income less adequate, since women typically live longer, earn less and work fewer years than men. In simulations of such reforms in the US economy, and in cases where such reforms have been implemented (such as Chile in 1981), women have, in fact, been found to be worse off than under the current system (Rix et al. 1998).

Another proposal for improving older women's access to income is to increase the means-tested benefits for older women through general revenues.

Briceland-Betts (1995), for example, proposes a system that pays a minimum pension out of general federal revenues up to the poverty line. By increasing the share of old age income from means-tested aid, such a programme could have a significant impact on the problem of high old age poverty among women. However, the proposal calls for more compassion for women rather than any structural change in entitlement and, to date, has been less supported than other reform proposals.

Other proposals aim at changing social values toward children. Burggraf (1997), for example, argues that to promote the value of children, Social Security needs to reward parents for having children. She proposes diverting some of the Social Security taxes currently now paid into the system by employers and workers to a payment to the workers' parents. This proposal rewards adults for having children, since the children would be required to pay their own parents directly rather than contributing to a pool for the nation's parents. This idea raises concerns similar to those associated with privatizing Social Security since the investment in one's children would pay off if the children married well and earned well.

Other reform proposals have focused more explicitly on private pensions and labour market conditions. Ghilarducci (1992), for example, argues that the voluntary employer-based pension system disadvantages women because they have less bargaining power and are concentrated in industries and occupations that have weaker coverage and lower benefits. This leads her to call for a mandatory employer-based pension system that would supplement the existing Social Security system.

One of the most important feminist contributions to the study of old age income security is the reconception of marriage as an independent economic activity where home work and taking care of children and the elderly deserves to be pensioned. This is a contribution that is reflected in existing legislation, such as the Retirement Equity Act of 1984, and needs to guide future feminist work on pensions and retirement. Feminists must ensure that the entitlement to pension income includes recognition of so-called unpaid work; if it does not, success in raising older women's income will depend on political proclivity toward charity. Specific proposals toward pensioning unpaid work include requiring employers to give pension credit for dependent care leaves of absences and for Social Security to give credit for a certain number of years for every child a woman raises (US Department of Health, Education, and Welfare 1978). Research is also needed to evaluate the effects on women's poverty if a couple's Social Security benefit is reduced in order to raise the survivors' benefit.

In addition, national guidelines for pension disbursements in divorce would help improve the retirement income of divorced women, who are particularly vulnerable to poverty (Sandell 1994). Attorneys need more training in this area, and more research needs to be done to assess pension losses in divorce. Also, the labour market status of women during their working years must also be addressed. Since equal access to work and wages will most effectively reduce retirement income inequality, research on the effectiveness of increasing women's labour market power, through unions and collective bargaining for example, needs to be explored.

Ultimately the focus of feminist research and activism in this area must focus directly on the problem of providing adequate income for older women. Feminist research in the area needs to embody four principles: first, all work, including non-paid work, is entitled to be pensioned; second, wives need property rights to husband's pensions; third, retirement income security cannot be evaluated by examining only one piece of the public/private mix of old age income; and fourth, women's economic disadvantages and longer life should not make being old and non-married a formula for poverty. Feminist research guided by these principles offers great promise for developing policies to ensure a more economically secure future for women in old age.

TERESA GHILARDUCCI

See also
Poverty, Measurement and Analysis of; Public Sector Economics/Public Finance; Tax Policy.

Bibliography
Bergmann, Barbara (1986), *The Economic Emergence of Women*, New York: Basic Books.
Blau, Francine D. and Marianne A. Ferber (1992), *The Economics of Women, Men and Work*, 2nd edn, Englewood Cliffs, New Jersey: Prentice Hall.
Briceland-Betts, Deborah (1995), 'Testimony before the Advisory Council on Social Security', for the Older Women's League, March 8.
Burggraf, Shirley P. (1997), *The Feminine Economy and Economic Man*, Reading, Massachusetts: Addison-Wesley.
Costello, Cynthia and Anne J. Stone (eds) (1995), *The American Woman, 1994–1995*, New York: W.W. Norton.
Folbre, Nancy (1994), *Who Pays For the Kids: Gender and the Structures of Constraints*, London: Routledge.
Ghilarducci, Teresa (1992), *Labor's Capital: The Economics and Politics of Private Pensions*, Cambridge, Massachusetts: MIT Press.
Grad, Susan (1996), *Income of the Population 55 or Older*, 1994 U.S. Social Security Administration, Office of Research and Statistics, SSA Publications No. 13–11871, Washington DC: U.S. Government Printing Office.
Holden, Karen (1996), 'Social Security and the Economic Security of Women: Is it Fair?', in Eric Kingson and James H. Schultz (eds), *Social Security in the 21st Century*, New York: Oxford University Press, pp. 91–104.
Myles, John and Jill Quandagno (1996), 'Recent Trends in Public Pension Reform: A Comparative View', in Keith G. Banting and Robin Boadway (eds), *Reform of the Retirement Income Policy: In International and Canadian Perspectives*, Kingston, Ontario: School of Policy Studies, Queen's College, pp. 247–74.
Olson, Laura Katz (1982), *The Political Economy of Aging: The State, Private Power, and Social Welfare*, New York: Columbia University Press.
Rix, Sara, Linda Rosenmann and James H. Schulz (1998), 'Privatization and Older Women's Financial Needs: Gender Differences in Public and Private Targeting', Paper prepared for the

Second International Social Security Association Conference on Social Security, Jerusalem, 25–28 January.

Ross, Jane (1997), 'Testimony Before the Social Security Subcommittee of the House Ways and Means Committee on Social Security Reform: Implications for the Financial Well-Being of Women', General Accounting Office, GAO/T-HEH-97 112, April 10.

Sandell, Steven (1994), 'Women and Social Security', presentation to the Advisory Council on Social Security, October 24.

Smeeding, Timothy M. (1997), 'Reshuffling Responsibilities in Old Age: The United States in a Comparative Perspective', Duplicated paper, Syracuse, New York: Center for Policy Research.

US Department of Health, Education, and Welfare (1978), 'Report of the US Health, Education, and Welfare Department Task Force on the Treatment of Women under Social Security', February.

World Bank (1994), *Averting the Old Age Crisis: Policies to Protect the Old and Promote Growth*, New York: Oxford University Press.

Population

Many thinkers in the late eighteenth and early nineteenth centuries debated the consequences of population growth to economic wellbeing. Early in this debate, most theorists, including Adam Smith, William Goodwin and the Marquis de Condorcet, exhibited the optimism of Enlightenment thinkers that man, as master of his environment, could surmount any obstacles created by population pressures. But not all thinkers shared this optimism, as the 1798 publication of Thomas Robert Malthus's *An Essay on the Principle of Population* clearly demonstrated. In fact, Malthus's work not only captured the public's attention during his lifetime, it also has informed much of the theoretical and policy debates about population growth throughout the world ever since. In what has come to be known as the Malthusian theory of population, Malthus examined the relationship between population growth and economic wellbeing as measured by the food supply. Arguing that food production would grow at an arithmetic rate while population grew geometrically, Malthus concluded that population growth would surpass a country's ability to feed its residents. While he initially believed that only an increasing death rate caused by starvation, famine and disease (Malthus 1798) would balance the two growth rates, in the second edition of this work, published in 1803, Malthus refined his position further when

He gave increasing importance to changes in the birth rate as an alternative way of maintaining the balance between 'population' and 'food'. Essentially he argued that when food was scarce and times were hard, prices rose and men and women were forced to delay their marriages. In turn, this reduced the birth rate and helped to restore the equilibrium between population and resources (including food supplies). (Dyson 1996, p. 4)

Malthus's legacy not only created the foundations for orthodox economic theory through its emphasis on scarce resources, it also established the basis for subsequent developments in population theory and policy. Since Malthus, theoretical economists interested in both economic growth and development have considered population growth to be a key element for understanding these processes. This focus, in turn, has had the following policy consequences. First, Malthus's conjecture that population must be controlled to ensure wellbeing created a climate whereby aid to the poor was considered counterproductive because such a policy would only help the poor increase their numbers. Secondly, Malthusian theory set the tone for post-colonial development theories which assumed that economic 'development' was only possible through population control. This emphasis has consequently raised questions about fertility, reproductive control and sexuality and placed them at the core of contemporary population and development debates, thus making population an issue of great interest to feminist researchers.

While the post-colonial emphasis on population and development began after World War II, it was the 1965 publication of Ester Boserup's *The Condition of Agricultural Growth* that provided feminists with an argument against Malthusian principles. Here Boserup, one of the foremothers of feminist economics, demonstrated a positive relationship between population growth and land use, as evidenced in societies with high population densities that had developed more sophisticated agricultural systems and farm tools. Boserup's empirical study contributed cross-regional examples to the 1970's debate on population by showing that greater density in population in both Asia and Africa tended to increase agricultural innovation and therefore productivity. The increased population would lead to more efficient use of land and an increase in output (Furedi 1997, p. 46). This decidedly questioned the Malthusian idea that population growth had a negative impact on economic wellbeing.

Following Boserup's lead, feminist economists in the late 1970s, such as Benería and Sen (1980), contributed to the analysis by questioning the assumption that modernization had a positive impact on society. They pointed out the differential impact of economic development on men and women as a result of the sexual division of labour, the links between production and reproduction, and the inherent hierarchal structures generated by capitalist institutions (Benería 1995). Their work helped question the success of development through modernization for women.

In addition to questioning population's role in economic development, feminists concerned with women's rights have also entered contemporary debates on population. By identifying connections between economic growth, population growth and women's reproductive rights, many of these scholars have advocated family planning as a human right necessary for women's productive and reproductive health.

Ruth Dixon-Mueller, a sociologist who has written widely on population policy and women's rights, argues that there have been two convergent streams of thought. The first stream originates in concepts of human rights which laid the groundwork for the movement for women's liberation, family planning as a human right and ultimately to the idea of reproductive rights. The second stream makes the connection between economic growth and population growth and from here moves to population control by means of family planning. The second stream

> flows through a series of post-Malthusian theories of classical and neo-classical economists, socialists and Marxists, demographic transitionalists, modern-day Malthusians and free marketeers, each with their own notions of how population growth affects economic growth and their policy implications. Out of Malthus was born the nineteenth century movement for birth control in Europe and North America. (Dixon-Mueller 1993, p. 4)

In the twentieth century this stream then led to a policy emphasis on population control in developing countries.

By the mid 1960s, population control through family planning in developing countries was guided by the policy prescriptive emanating from the evolving field of demography. In particular this reflected the notion that economic outcomes were due to demographic changes and that one could predict ideal population numbers that would then lead to better economic circumstances for all. Demography helped those interested in population control come up with target levels of population growth. The Malthusian legacy continued to flourish at the international policy level, with an uncritical acceptance of the idea that economic wellbeing was inherently connected to the control of population growth.

Some feminists in the South (also referred to as the Third World or developing countries) resisted target driven population control policies by exploring the relationship between science, reproductive technology and capitalism. For example, feminist scholars and activists brought to light the way that pharmaceutical companies and international population service organizations were using Third World women for experimental contraceptive technology or as guinea pigs or dumping grounds for contraceptive technology (Hartman 1987), and formed networks such as FINRRAGE (Feminist International Network for Resistance Against Reproductive and Genetic Engineering). FINRRAGE saw these abuses as the inevitable consequences of the relationship between reproductive technologies and the profit-making incentive of multinational corporations. A schism was created between the reproductive rights position which advocated for the right to have access to contraceptive technology and others who felt that family planning and the use of reproductive technologies helped capitalism sell products to consumers while controlling the social and political culture (Akhter 1993). This schism caused tension between, on the one hand, feminists who argued for family planning and the right to technology; and on the other hand, feminists who found family planning, and the use of reproductive technologies, as a way for capitalism to use women's bodies for profit making and to control the population of poor women in the North (also referred to as developed or industrialized countries) and the South.

A space was opened up in the 1980s that widened the discourse on population by emphasizing the social, cultural and economic factors that influence reproductive health (Ford Foundation 1991). Called 'reproductive health', this new approach expanded a narrow vision of target driven population policy to look more comprehensively at population issues to include such aspects as the quality of care, sexuality and violence, to name a few. It also moved away from the predominantly demographically driven understanding of population and development to a multidisciplinary approach. Even institutions that were traditionally part of the population establishment such as the Population Council, an institution that was active in advocating population control in developing countries, started moving toward a reproductive health approach (Population Council 1994).

It was during this opening of the population discourse that a serious consolidation of feminist perspectives both from the North and the South took place. The reproductive health approach allowed for a discussion of the abuses of population control policy but was able to allow for a right to family planning. The two streams that Dixon-Mueller pointed out were finally able to come to a common understanding.

The International Conference on Population and Development (ICPD) held in Cairo by the United Nations (UN) in 1994 was the most significant global effort by the feminist movement to radically change the discourse on population and the theoretical assumptions behind a target-driven population policy that ignored that women's bodies were at the centre of the debate. In the past the UN Conferences on Population had been a place for governments to reaffirm their commitment to population control policies. In contrast, the Cairo meeting had an unprecedented representation of non-governmental organizations, particularly from the women's movement. In Cairo, women from the North and the South had one of the most distinct and important roles in changing the focus of the conference and the resulting document, the Programme of Action, away from population control to that of reproductive health.

These shifts and, in particular, the focus on women was a crucial and long-awaited change in the analysis of population and development. Gender equity and gender equality, empowerment, reproductive rights and reproductive health were the main focus of the Programme of Action. The importance of male responsibility and the need to pay particular attention to the girl child were crucial to a long-term change in the way population and family planning policies were formulated and implemented (ICPD 1994).

The reproductive health approach also brought about a clearly demedicalized notion of health that examines the social, economic and psychological components of health. The Programme of Action based on this approach expanded the focus to recognize the linkage between population, poverty, patterns of consumption and production. Recognizing the need to understand population growth in a larger context was an important milestone in population policy and discourse. The economic development agenda, though, did not reflect the progressive rhetoric of the rest of the document and maintained economic growth as the overriding principle. The ICPD was the first time that a UN population conference had a particularly feminist agenda. It has reversed, at least, the rhetoric in the population field, giving women a central role.

This shift in the focus of population policy that emerged from ICPD has not, however, been without controversy. Some scholars and activists from the South maintained that the focus on reproductive health was responsible for the neglect of the more important issue of development, inequity between North and South, and the unequal and exploitative transfer of resources. The placement of reproductive health and rights in the centre has been seen as a way to limit women to a primarily reproductive role which does not include the more important need to understand women's economic and social dimensions (Shiva and Shiva 1994, pp. 13–16).

Others feel that ICPD is a step forward insofar as it has shifted the discourse on population to emphasize women and gender issues. Rosalind Petchesky, an influential theorist in the field of reproductive rights, argues that

> the Cairo document begins to approach a conceptual framework of interdependence and non-linear causation that departs significantly from Malthusian thinking. ... Population growth, according to the document, is only one variable in a complex array of interconnected problems, including women's low status, widespread poverty, resource depletion, 'social and economic inequality' and unsustainable patterns of production and consumption. (Petchesky 1995, p. 160)

Because of the ICPD conference and the resulting Programme of Action the population debate has moved beyond the Malthusian principle and now encompasses a much larger set of factors. There is an increasing understanding that family planning programmes in the past have been primarily carried out for the reduction of population growth and not to enhance women's health (Smyth 1996), and there is evidence that the predominantly demographically driven policies of state, national and international bodies are being questioned at all levels. There has been a slow but increasing inclusion of women's health advocates in setting policies and an increasing demand among policymakers to have the input from feminist economists to look at the linkages between economic globalization and reproductive health. There is an awareness that more research needs to be done that employs a wider social science approach to health. International networks are being formed of scholars interested in social science and health. The feminist contribution to this movement is growing with an ever-expanding space being given to feminist research.

The next step for feminists is to challenge assumptions that directly connect population to economic wellbeing, and to clarify the appropriate significance of the variable of population growth in addressing women's health, inequality and environmental degradation. Attention must be paid to the global impact of the profit-making needs of an economic system, removed from the interests of its stakeholders, and that can only survive with a never-ending growth of consumption, regardless of justifiable social needs. Feminists need to be able to demand women's reproductive freedom, gender equality, equity and empowerment for its own sake even if it means that women will then have more children.

RADHIKA BALAKRISHNAN

See also
Development Policies; Development, Theories of; Health Care.

Bibliography
Akhter, Faridha (1993), 'Reproductive Rights: A Critique from the Realities of Bangladeshi Women', unpublished paper.

Benería, Lourdes (1979), 'Reproduction, production and the sexual division of labour', *Cambridge Journal of Economics*, **3**, (September), 203–25.

Benería, Lourdes (1995), 'Toward a greater integration of gender in economics', *World Development*, **23** (11), 1839–51.

Benería, L. and G. Sen (1980), 'Accumulation, reproduction and women's role in economic development: Boserup revisited', *Signs*, **7** (2), 279–98.

Boserup, Ester (1965), *The Condition of Agricultural Growth*, London: Allen and Unwin.

Dixon-Mueller, Ruth (1993), *Population Policy and Women's Rights; Transforming Reproductive Choice*, Westport, Connecticut: Praeger.

Dyson, T. (1996), *Population and Food: global trends and future prospects*, New York: Routledge.

Ford Foundation (1991), *Reproductive Health: A Strategy for the 1990s*, New York: The Ford Foundation.

Furedi, Frank (1997), *Population and Development: A Critical Introduction*, New York: St Martin's Press.

Hartman, Betsy (1987), *Reproductive Right and Wrongs: The Global Politics of Population Control and Contraceptive Choice*, Boston: South End Press.

International Conference on Population and Development (1994), *Summary of Programme for Action*, New York: ICDP.

Malthus, T.R. (1798), *An Essay on the Principle of Population*, in Anthony Flew (ed). Reprinted 1976, Pelican Books.

Petchesky, Rosalind Pollack (1995), 'From population control to reproductive rights: feminist fault lines', *Reproductive Health Matters*, (6), (November), 152–61.

Population Council (1994), 'Reproductive Health Approach to Family Planning', in *Critical Issues in Reproductive Health and Population*, New York: The Population Council.
Shiva, Vandana and Mira Shiva (1994), 'Was Cairo a step forward for third world women', *Third World Resurgence*, (October), 13–16.
Smyth, Ines (1996), 'Gender analysis of family planning: beyond the feminist vs. population control debate', *Feminist Economics*, 2 (2), (Summer), 63–87.

Post Keynesian Economics

Post Keynesian economics refers to the scholarship inspired by the work of John Maynard Keynes and Michal Kalecki. In particular it includes the contributions of Joan Robinson, Richard Kahn, Nicholas Kaldor and contemporary theorists who build upon and extend the main themes and foci of their work. The boundaries of Post Keynesian economics are undetermined in some scholars' work, including all of the above-mentioned, Neo-Ricardian (derived from the work of Pierro Sraffa) economics, institutional economics and a broad body of eclectic heterodox literature (Lavoie 1994, pp. 1–4).

The major components of Post Keynesian analysis which differentiate it from the standard version of the neoclassical synthesis result from four major conceptual differences that infuse all elements of Post Keynesian analysis. Post Keynesians systematically incorporate uncertainty into their analysis, especially in their theory of the firm where it is a key component in the formation of expectations which drive firms' production plans. Post Keynesians use historic time rather than logical time. This impacts on the Post Keynesian understanding of economic processes as dynamic, thus they reject the notion of equilibrium as characterizing the economic system of market economies. In addition to these conceptual differences, Post Keynesian analysis consistently treats the construction of prices as administered, including theories of full-cost pricing, mark-up pricing and target-return pricing which are not viewed as mutually exclusive alternatives (Lavoie 1994, p. 129). Money is treated as endogenous; meaning it is created by its own demand.

The rest of this entry assesses the foundations of Post Keynesian economics to determine whether an explicitly Post Keynesian feminist economics is possible. Then attempts to construct explicitly Post Keynesian economic analyses are reviewed. As noted throughout, a feminist–Post Keynesian analysis must draw on the microfoundations of other heterodox schools of thought to achieve a systematic inclusion of the concept of gender.

The relative paucity of attempts to construct explicitly feminist Post Keynesian economic theories is explained by the emphasis of Post Keynesians on aggregate economic phenomenon. There are two central questions that need to be addressed with regard to the possibility of a feminist Post Keynesian economics: Are the microfoundations of Post Keynesian analyses such as to make, encourage or prohibit the inclusion of gender as a theoretical construct? Will the inclusion of gender in those microfoundations alter the aggregate analyses of Post Keynesian? The answer to the first question is largely dependent on how agency is defined within Post Keynesian theoretical models. In this regard, Lavoie's (1992) exploration of Post Keynesian foundations is helpful.

In his characterization of Post Keynesian theories of choice Lavoie argues that choice is a result of procedural, rather that substantive, rationality. Following Keynes and Simon, Lavoie states, 'When they take decisions, or even when they set their preferences, entrepreneurs and households rely on habits, customs, conventions and norms' (Lavoie 1992, p. 56). Lavoie notes that how habits, customs, conventions and norms are constructed and how they change are areas where Post Keynesians 'still have little to offer by way of an explanation. ... This of course, should be the contribution of the institutionalists and their Veblenian evolutionary economics' (Lavoie 1992, p. 58). Using institutionalist theorizing of human behaviour, which employs culturally constructed categories (including gender), for Post Keynesian microfoundations is likely to enhance the prospects for the development of feminist Post Keynesian analysis.

Lavoie, in a later work, notes innate preferences, preferences based on existing habits and conventions, and preferences that evolve (because the 'behaviour of the consumer, as well as the satisfaction derived from consumption is not independent of the consumption of other consumers') all contribute to the choices consumers make (Lavoie 1994, p. 552). He argues: 'The norms of consumption, while dependent on past standards, will evolve and be set to a large extent either by imitation or by envy' (p. 553). Lavoie's focus on non-independence, social norms and the evolution of past standards in constructing preferences, opens the door to considering the role of gender in the construction of preferences and consumer choice.

Lavoie (1992), in his description of Post Keynesian analyses of theories of firm behaviour, rejects maximization of returns as a motive. Instead he notes that Post Keynesians typically adopt the dual goals of growth and the acquisition of power (economic and social) as the motives for firm behaviour. Again, conceptions of the firm from heterodox economics are prominent including institutionalists (Galbraith, Berle and Means, who reject profit maximization, and focus on increased managerial discretion, risk avoidance and avoidance of market discipline), and Marxists (Baran and Sweezy, who also reject profit maximization in favour of capital accumulation, risk avoidance and 'live and let live' behaviour among corporate capitalists), along with those of Joan Robinson, Alfred Eichner and Jean Marchal.

And finally the Post Keynesian labour market is characterized as follows: 'the labour market does not truly exist; the wage rate is not just another ordinary price: it has much influence on the overall economy; workers are not commodities: norms rule over supply and demand; the demand for and the supply of labour are not well behaved' (Appelbaum 1979; Seccareccia 1991, cited in Lavoie 1992, p. 217). Lavoie's characterization of Post Keynesian views of the labour market is heavily institutional in character. He writes: 'In the market for labour, normative pressures, that is pressures linked to customs and equity, have much more importance than anomic pressures, that is pressures that lack organizational content such as market forces and conjunctural force' (Lavoie 1992, p. 218). Again, since culturally constructed motivations structure behaviour in the labour market there is no barrier to the inclusion of a cultural construct such as gender.

Thus, in Lavoie's presentation of Post Keynesian fundamentals agency is consistently defined in terms of culturally constructed behaviour, thereby allowing for the inclusion of gender constructs and consideration of gendered behaviour as economically significant to the overall operation of the economy. Hence Post Keynesian economics is certainly not hostile to feminist theorizing, and at this time has incorporated theories of human behaviour congenial to and encouraging of incorporating gendered behaviour into its theorizing.

The second question posed above, regarding the impact of incorporating gender on the aggregate theorizing of Post Keynesians, will be deferred until attempts to develop feminist themes or incorporate feminist theory and method into Post Keynesian analyses have been reviewed. The dependence of Post Keynesian economic thought on other heterodox schools to ground the motivation for the economic behaviour of participants in the economy has not precluded a few scholars from attempting to address what have historically been central concerns of feminists from Post Keynesian perspectives, and attempts to expressly combine feminist and Post Keynesian theorizing.

For example, Fuller (1996) articulates an explicitly Post Keynesian view, in sharp contrast with Gary Becker's neoclassical household production approach, of consumption activity. He writes: 'post-Keynesians should adopt essentially a view of consumption activity as a process of cooperation-seeking behaviour through interpersonal communication in which goods have a facilitating role' (Fuller 1996, pp. 603–4). He notes that further work by Post Keynesians is necessary to understand how individuals develop their aims and what conduct is involved in achieving those aims when people are understood as embedded in social relations.

Fuller's conception is a complete rejection of the assumption of global rationality, competition-driven social relations and household-entered production, which characterize Becker's model (Fuller 1996, p. 596). It opens the door to explicit consideration of gender relations as part of the social relations in which individual procedural rationality operates. Thus, gender, manifest in non-household institutions, social rules and norms and physical and environmental constraints, is invited if not recommended explicitly by Fuller's approach. Clearly this process is significantly underway in the feminist literature as recent articles by Agarwal (1997) and Phipps and Burton (1995) demonstrate.

In another example, Levin (1995) explicitly ties Post Keynesian investment theory to feminist epistemological thought through the Post Keynesian 'espousal of radical subjectivism, and ... its notion of the primacy of convention in impacting agent expectations' (Levin 1995, p. 108). The radical subjectivism is important because the understanding of agent knowledge, as radically (or fundamentally) uncertain and inherently subjective, 'breaks the determinate link (associated with Cartesian thought) between the objective world and the knowledge which we possess of the world' (Levin 1995, p. 108). The knowledge upon which investment decisions rest in much Post Keynesian thought, according to Levin, 'is the indeterminate and unstable product of convention' (Levin 1995, p. 109). Levin notes that uncertainty leads to instability, and conventional behaviour contributes to stability in investment expenditure. He also discusses the impact of rumours, social comparison of opinions and fads on investment expenditure. Levin adds to these Post Keynesian themes by exploring the role of emotion on investment. He notes that uncertainty may give rise to cognitive dissonance, when knowledge or beliefs are mutually inconsistent, and that the reduction of this dissonance is an important motivation for behaviour. He notes that to alleviate the dissonance people often change their cognition or pretend not to be ignorant. Falling back on convention is seen as consistent with this latter technique for dealing with dissonance.

Levin argues that Keynes's notion of sentiments can be supplemented with contagion theory which can explain how emotional responses can lead to mass behaviour. Moreover he notes that awareness of the baselessness of our knowledge is used by Keynes to explain the apparent irrational (from a neoclassical perspective) preference for holding money and to understanding the interest rate as a gauge of our emotional insecurity (Levin 1995, p. 114). Levin sees the mutual rejection of Cartesian foundationalist notions of knowledge, the adoption of subjectivism, and the reliance upon convention pushing Post Keynesians in the direction of feminist epistemology. He argues that a combined effort by feminists and Post Keynesians would represent a more compelling and powerful challenge to standard economic theory (Levin 1995, p. 114).

Corcoran and Courant (1987) present an empirical analysis of sex-based occupational segregation consistent with the Post Keynesian approach described by Lavoie above. Their hypothesis is that the sex-based wage gap and sex-based occupational discrimination is not fully eroded over time by competitive forces because it is partially caused by factors such as early sex-role socialization and pre-labour market discrimination (Corcoran and Courant 1987, p. 330). They empirically explore, using the Panel Study of Income Dynamics of the University of Michigan, the significance of unmeasured human capital differences that arise from sex-role socialization in the home and school (Corcoran and Courant 1987, p. 333). The sex-role socialization issues that they find significant are the difference between the course of study of boys and girls; the sex typicality of the mother's occupation; and consistency with traditional sex roles in the household (Corcoran and Courant 1987, pp. 344–5). Corcoran and Courant's exploration of sex-role socialization is limited by the data set employed; more systematic and complete analyses of these phenomena are common in feminist economics, for example Blau et al. (1998).

In her unique contribution Jennings (1994) explicitly addresses the possibility of feminist Post Keynesian analysis in terms of Hyman Minsky's monetary theory of production. She accepts Minsky's endogenous money approach; 'money is the form of wealth that matters in capitalism … money wags the tail of goods; capitalism is not a monetized form of barter, nor have economies organized primarily by barter ever existed', yet she has some fundamental concerns with Minsky's approach (Jennings 1994, p. 557). Jennings notes that this myopic concern with money blinds both Minsky and Post Keynesians to exchange outside fully monetized markets (for example, within the household), as if they had no impact on monetized markets. Thus Minsky's monetary production theory is no better than Becker's microeconomic barter models of the household in the valuation of household labour. Indeed, the Post Keynesian approach may be a bit worse since Becker at least notices the significance of domestic labour. Certainly, in her view, Becker's framework is no worse than Minsky's in terms of ignoring the difference between market and nonmarket activity (Jennings 1994, pp. 559–60).

However, in spite of this concern Jennings also argues that there are two feminist implications that follow from Minsky's approach. First, she notes that the Post Keynesian approach rejects the orthodox claim that money is a veil. This means that Post Keynesians reject the notion that money only shows the effects of real economic activity and is not a cause of real economic activity. If money is a veil over productive activity then activities that yield monetary gain are socially valuable and those that do not yield a monetary gain are not. Thus the non-monetized production of women in traditional household domestic activities is not socially valuable, indeed, this is leisure. Second, she notes that 'it is harder to sell for money than it is to buy' (Jennings 1994, p. 558). Women's labour has been socially constructed as less saleable than men's labour and codified as such in patriarchal social institutions. These cultural constraints on saleability of women's labour combines with the asymmetry with regard to buying and selling for money to systematically disadvantage women. From these observations Jennings argues that 'money is not a veil, but a social prerogative' (Jennings 1994, p. 558).

Jennings notes that monetary theories of production recognize the social power of money, but fail to explore the implications of this social power on women, the family and other gender issues. She issues a three-part challenge that constitute a feminist agenda for macroeconomics. The items on the agenda are an explicit exploration of the behavioural assumptions appropriate to monetary production models; exploration of the nature and impact of current consumption patterns in Post Keynesian models; and exploration of the differential impacts of macroeconomic stabilization policies on groups other than monied interests, especially those in society on the disadvantaged side of our gender, race and class cleavages, in order to understand the social meaning of 'economic scarcity' (Jennings 1994, p. 562). Jennings sees meeting the challenge of constructing a feminist macroeconomics as a joint effort between feminist Post Keynesians and feminist Institutionalists.

Jennings points out that Waring's (1988) critique of the United Nations System of National Accounts provides a beginning to the disaggregation and careful exploration necessary for a feminist macroeconomics. However, she notes that little has been done to build on Waring's work. Thus Jennings explicitly raises the second question posed above for a Post Keynesian feminist economics: since the issue of gender is relegated to the microeconomic foundations of an economic framework that focuses on macroeconomic aggregates, and those working within the framework acknowledge that the microeconomic foundation of their work (increasingly emerging from the institutionalist tradition, for example, Arestis 1996) is significantly underdeveloped theoretically, will the inclusion of gender within those microfoundations have a significant impact on the macroeconomic theorizing of Post Keynesians? Jennings argues it must.

There seems to be little in the way of epistemological or methodological barriers to feminist Post Keynesian theorizing. Instead, the aggregate character of most Post Keynesian theorizing has made it very easy for the Post Keynesians to overlook and neglect feminist concerns. The overall impression that these feminist or near feminist contributions to Post Keynesian thought make is that the theory of human behaviour underlying Post Keynesian thought is significantly underdeveloped. These are most often characterized as underdeveloped microfoundations for the aggregate models and theories developed by Post Keynesians. All of the authors point to non-neoclassical theories of human behaviour as likely sources for inspiration or starting points for the development of this area of Post Keynesian theorizing. Institutional, Marxian, social, humanistic and Austrian economics as well as sociology are drawn upon as sources for alternative foundations.

WILLIAM WALLER

See also

Institutional Economics; Labour Markets, Theories of; Macroeconomics.

Bibliography

Agarwal, Bina (1997), 'Bargaining and gender relations: within and beyond the household', *Feminist Economics*, **3** (1), 1–51.

Appelbaum, E. (1979), 'The Labor Market', in A.S. Eichner (ed.), *A Guide to Post-Keynesian Economics*, White Plains, New York: M.E. Sharpe, pp. 100–119.

Arestis, Philip (1996), 'Post-Keynesian economics: towards coherence', *Cambridge Journal of Economics*, **20**, 111–35.

Blau, Francine D., Marianne A. Ferber and Anne E. Winkler (1998), *The Economics of Women, Men, and Work*, Upper Saddle River, New Jersey: Prentice Hall.

Corcoran, Mary E. and Paul N. Courant (1987), 'Sex-role socialization and occupational segregation: an exploratory investigation', *Journal of Post-Keynesian Economics*, **9** (3), 330–46.

Fuller, Christopher G. (1996), 'Elements of a Post Keynesian alternative to household production', *Journal of Post Keynesian Economics*, **18** (4), 595–607.

Jennings, Ann (1994), 'Towards a feminist expansion of macroeconomics: money matters', *Journal of Economic Issues*, **28** (2), 555–65.

Lavoie, Marc (1992), *Foundations of Post-Keynesian Economic Analysis*, Aldershot: Edward Elgar.

Lavoie, Marc (1994), 'A post-Keynesian approach to consumer choice', *Journal of Post Keynesian Economics*, **16** (4), 539–62.

Levin, Lee B. (1995), 'Toward a Feminist, Post-Keynesian Theory of Investment', in E. Kuiper and J. Sap (eds), *Out of the Margin: Feminist Perspective on Economics*, New York: Routledge, pp. 100–119.

Phipps, Shelley A. and Peter S. Burton (1995), 'Social/institutional variables and behaviour within households: an empirical test using the Luxembourg Income Study', *Feminist Economics*, **1** (1), 151–74.

Seccareccia, M. (1991), 'An alternative to labour-market orthodoxy: the post-Keynesian/institutionalist policy view', *Review of Political Economy*, **3** (1), 43–61.

Waring, Marilyn (1988), *If Women Counted: A New Feminist Economics*, San Francisco: Harper.

Postmodernism

Postmodernism is a concept that entered academic vocabularies during the latter half of the twentieth century. Because postmodernism has seen both academic and popular usage, it defies easy definition. It basically means 'beyond modernism' and suggests that, given the economic and cultural changes in the world at the close of the twentieth century, it is time to go beyond the modernist notions of universal truths, objective knowledge, and unlimited and eternal laws and tendencies. So as the world around us has changed it is also time to change how we come to know and understand it.

The French postmodern philosopher, Michel Foucault, wrote of the postmodern world that

> we are in the epoch of simultaneity: we are in the epoch of juxtaposition, the epoch of the near and far, of the side-by-side, of the dispersed. We are at a moment, I believe, when our experience of the world is less that of a long life

developing through time than that of a network that connects points and intersects with its own skein. (Foucault 1986, p. 22)

Postmodernism is a term that attempts to capture the cultural transformation that the world is now undergoing, in large part due to the globalization of capitalism. Michael Rosenthal says that what it 'often boils down to is an affirmation of plurality and complexity' (Rosenthal 1992, p. 101). In this sense it tries to come to grips with our feelings of 'decentredness', 'discontinuity', 'fragmentation' and 'heterogeneity' that speak to the insecurity and anxiety in today's globalized world (Harvey 1989, 1991).

The effect that postmodernism has had on feminist theory is significant. As Marianne Ferber and Julie Nelson suggest, postmodernism 'probably provides the best basis for a dialogue between feminist theory and economics' (Ferber and Nelson 1993, p. 9). This dialogue begins with deconstructionism and postmodernism's impact in philosophy. Modernist philosophy includes both the empiricist and rationalist traditions, both of which emerge from Cartesian dualism and the confidence that the world can be known by way of eternal truths and universal tendencies. There is in modernist thought a sense that a 'God's eye view' of the world can be taken and that this is grounded from the perspective of a stable subject whose inquiry can discover objective knowledge of a universal and eternal character (Bordo 1990, p. 142; Rorty 1979).

Postmodernism challenges the modernist notion of universal truth, recognizing instead that 'truth' is situated in the particulars of the theorist and is thus not value-free. For feminist theorists, the primary way truth is situated is through gender. For postmodern feminists, this has meant identifying the gendered nature of the underlying principles and assumptions of their discipline's texts. Recognizing the gendered nature of a discipline's principles has, in turn, led feminist economists to question the notions of universal human behaviour underlying neoclassical and Marxist economic analysis and to the recognition that economic theory does, in fact, reflect masculine biases; in other words, the principles underlying economic analysis are, in fact, gendered principles.

Also, postmodern feminist theorists have focused on gender's role in scientific inquiry, leading them to argue that a postmodern conception of objectivity is needed. This has meant that there may be more than one way of looking at an issue and therefore there can be multiple truths, all of which have an element of objectivity. Modernist science has assumed that objectivity implies that its knowledge is value-free. Postmodern feminists have disputed this, and feminist economists have then understood this to mean that much of what passes for economic science is not value-free. It is not truly 'objective' science because there are 'contextual values' within it that make its truths 'situated truths'. Science and its truths are never totally value-free, because scientific discoveries always enter our lives within an already existing world of power relations and institutions. Today's institutional structures, into which 'facts' make their appearance, include patriarchal, race and class hierarchies.

For postmodernists how an issue is analysed is a matter of perspective or 'where one is situated'. What feminist theorists suggest is that modernist science is gendered in its method as well as in much of its truths. As Nelson (1996, p. 133) maintains, 'feminist scholarship suggests that fundamental concepts of Western thought – especially hierarchical dualisms of reason over nature and separation over connection – are fundamentally tied into a gender ideology that also ranks men over women'. More specifically, this means that 'in the Cartesian view, the abstract, general, separated, detached, emotionless, "masculine" approach taken to represent scientific thinking, is radically removed from, and clearly seen as superior to, the concrete, particular, connected, embodied, passionate, "feminine" reality of material life' (Nelson 1996, p. 40). So postmodern feminist theory has deconstructed the scientific method of Cartesianism and found it to have a masculine bias (Badgett 1995).

As feminist philosopher, Sandra Harding, says

> when sciences are already in the service of the mighty, scientific neutrality ensures that 'might makes right'. Feminists in every discipline have argued that androcentric 'might' has all too often appealed to neutrality-maximizing standards in order to justify as 'right' distorted descriptions and explanations of natural and social regularities and their underlying causal tendencies. (Harding 1995, p. 17)

Harding's argument is that rather than abandon objectivity altogether, we should try to increase objectivity by requiring that scientific analysis also reveals the 'contextual values' that underlie all such inquiry. The point is to avoid relativism by maximizing objectivity through values clarification.

What has postmodern feminist theory therefore meant for feminist economics? It has meant that since modernist science, which provides the basis for both neoclassical and Marxist economics, has been masculine and not value-free, feminist economists can start off 'thinking about economic relations from the perspective of women's activities rather than of the conceptual schemes in the dominant institutions, including the discipline of economics, from which women have systematically been excluded' (Harding 1995, p. 24; see Nelson 1993, pp. 23–36). In other words, economics has historically been a discipline of men, focused on the male-dominated economic activities of buying and selling within the public sphere of the market. In addition, 'gender also affects the construction of the discipline in terms of the standpoint from which the world is perceived, and the way the importance and relevance of questions are evaluated' (Ferber and Nelson 1993, p. 2). So even the fundamental concept of 'economic man', or 'homo economicus', is androcentric. Thus the competitive, rational calculating and individualistic human atom that comprises the foundation for all neoclassical economic theory is a very masculine notion and has become universalized as the human nature for all people. But as feminist economists have argued this model of human behaviour is not universal but rather a masculine prototype (Ferber and Nelson 1993).

Feminist economists have also examined the implications from the postmodern critique of the economics discipline's reliance on universal principles. For example, by deconstructing the economic dimensions of a self that is connected, emotional, nurturing and cooperative, feminist economists have developed an economic person who is engaged in valuable economic activities both in and outside of the home (England 1993, p. 40). Thus what is discovered in such a postmodern economic analysis is that women's roles in the economy have been ignored and undervalued, leading Nelson to note that 'the most notable example of masculine bias concerning families in contemporary economics is, of course, simply the general absence of any attention to families at all' (Nelson 1996, p. 61).

Thus the postmodern critique of the 'universal' category of 'homo economicus', or 'economic man', challenges traditional economic thinking. From the more 'situated perspective' of women this is a male-biased concept that narrows the focus to the market and competitive individuals. Nelson then argues for a broadened definition of economics that transcends the emphasis on market-based activities and focuses on 'economic provisioning and the sustenance of life, whether it be through market, household, or government action or whether it be by symmetric exchange, coercion, or gift' (Nelson 1996, p. 36).

Another example of how postmodernism has influenced feminist theory and thus feminist economics concerns the role of women in development projects and issues of Third World nations. Third World women have an image, created in part by the androcentric notion of 'homo economicus', that they are 'helpless, ignorant, vulnerable and impoverished' (Berik 1997, p. 156). Yet the postmodern feminist approach says that such a view ignores the vital role played by Third World women in essential nonmarket provisioning and leads to the modernist approach that 'legitimates the need for technical aid, promotes control by (and dependence on) Northern experts, and stifles Third World women's own participation and knowledge' (Berik 1996, p. 156; see Marchand and Parpart 1995). As the roles played by women in provisioning have begun to be recognized, development policies have begun to change and focus more on grassroots efforts that are more women-centred.

Thus postmodernism has validated the notion that much of what has passed for scientific economic theory has been masculine in character and has therefore helped to reinforce and perpetuate patriarchal domination. Feminist economics as influenced by postmodernism does not simply study women in the economy but attempts to create a wholly new way to theorize economics itself. By doing so, this approach is far more radical and has the potential to influence and shape more fully democratic and humanized economic institutions for the twenty-first century.

Yet there is a downside to postmodernism's message as well. What has occurred with the globalization of capitalism and its cultural transformation is that the means by which people, and in particular women, can define themselves differently from one another have dramatically increased. Postmodernism suggests that women can have multiple identities drawn from different life activities. This makes it harder for them to identify with each other's problems. It then obstructs the process of building broader movements based upon common problems. The logic of the new system seems to divide and fragment. As Haraway states, 'identities seem contradictory, partial, and strategic. With the hard-won recognition of their social and historical constitution, gender, race, and class cannot provide the basis for belief in "essential" unity. There is nothing about being "female" that naturally binds women' (Haraway 1985, pp. 72–3). But Haraway also acknowledges that women are simultaneously beginning to see the value in forging coalitions, thereby potentially avoiding the often debilitating cynicism and passivity that can easily mount and swamp progressive movements.

Postmodern feminist theory attempts to reconcile the legitimate manner in which women may differently determine their identities with the need to unify for gender equality and an end to patriarchy. Feminist economics in particular has to find ways to theorize that reflect the experiences of all women, whether they are Third World, urban and poor, or white and middle-class. This is a major challenge that will require continued theorizing and hard mobilizational work (Fraser 1985; Laclau 1988; Waugh 1989; Seiz 1997).

Many feminist theorists are now arguing for the creation of a 'politics of difference' (Fraser and Nicholson 1990; Young 1990). This will help to clarify remaining differences between women, but then also demonstrate more ways that these differences can be overcome. Building common bonds is the key. This approach recognizes the notion of unity-through-diversity that increasingly has common currency within progressive movements worldwide. Theories that accept the reality of growing diversity are needed so that the process of bringing humankind together for a socially and gender-just world can be constructed more effectively.

DOUG BROWN

See also
Capitalism; Class; Dualisms; Feminism(s); Feminist Economics; Gender; Patriarchy; Race.

Bibliography
Badgett, M.V. Lee (1995), 'The last of the modernists?', *Feminist Economics*, 1, (Spring), 63–65.

Berik, Gunseli (1997), 'Review of *Feminism/Postmodernism/Development*', *Feminist Economics*, 3, (Spring), 153–61.

Bordo, Susan (1990), 'Feminism, Postmodernism, and Gender-Skepticism', in Linda Nicholson (ed.), *Feminism/Postmodernism*, New York: Routledge, pp. 133–56.

England, Paula (1993), 'The Separative Self: Androcentric Bias in Neoclassical Assumptions', in Marianne Ferber and Julie Nelson (eds), *Beyond Economic Man*, Chicago: University of Chicago Press, pp. 37–53.

Ferber, Marianne and Julie Nelson (1993), 'Introduction: The Social Construction of Economics and the Social Construction of Gender', in Marianne Ferber and Julie Nelson (eds), *Beyond Economic Man*, Chicago: University of Chicago Press, pp. 1–22.

Flax, Jane (1990), *Thinking Fragments: Psychoanalysis, Feminism and Postmodernism in the Contemporary West*, Berkeley: University of California Press.

Foucault, Michel (1986), 'Of other spaces', *Diacritics*, 16 (1), (Spring), 22–6.

Fraser, Nancy (1985), 'Michel Foucault: a "young conservative"?', *Ethics*, 96,(October), 165–84.

Fraser, Nancy and Linda Nicholson (1990), 'Social Criticism Without Philosophy: An Encounter Between Feminism and Postmodernism', in Linda Nicholson (ed.), *Feminism/Postmodernism*, New York: Routledge, pp. 19–38.

Haraway, Donna (1985), 'A manifesto for cyborgs: science, technology, and socialist feminism in the 1980s', *Socialist Review*, 15 (2), (March/April), 65–108.

Harding, Sandra (1986), *The Science Question in Feminism*, Ithaca, New York: Cornell University Press.

Harding, Sandra (1995), 'Can feminist thought make economics more objective?' *Feminist Economics*, 1, Winter, 7–32.

Harvey, David (1989), *The Postmodern Condition: An Enquiry into the Origins of Cultural Change*, Cambridge, Massachusetts: Basil Blackwell.

Harvey, David (1991), 'Flexibility: threat or opportunity', *Socialist Review*, 21 (1), (January/March), 65–78.

Jameson, Fredric (1988), 'Regarding Postmodernism – A Conversation with Fredric Jameson', in Andrew Ross (ed.), *Universal Abandon*, Minneapolis: Minnesota, University of Minnesota Press, pp. 3–30.

Jameson, Fredric (1991), *Postmodernism: Or the Cultural Logic of Late Capitalism*, Durham, North Carolina: Duke University Press.

Laclau, Ernesto (1988), 'Politics and the Limits of Modernity', in Andrew Ross (ed.), *Universal Abandon*, Minneapolis, Minnesota: University of Minnesota Press.

Lyotard, Jean-Francois (1984), *The Postmodern Condition: A Report on Knowledge*, Minneapolis, Minnesota: University of Minnesota Press.

Marchand, Marianne and Jane Parpart (eds) (1995), *Feminism/Postmodernism/Development*, New York: Routledge.

Nelson, Julie (1993), 'The Study of Choice or the Study of Provisioning? Gender and the Definition of Economics', in Marianne Ferber and Julie Nelson (eds), *Beyond Economic Man*, Chicago: University of Chicago Press, pp. 23–36.

Nelson, Julie (1996), *Feminism, Objectivity, and Economics*, New York: Routledge.

Nicholson, Linda (1990), 'Introduction', in Linda Nicholson (ed.), *Feminism/Postmodernism*, New York: Routledge, pp. 1–16.

Rorty, Richard (1979), *Philosophy and the Mirror of Nature*, Princeton, New Jersey: Princeton University Press.

Rosenthal, Michael (1992), 'What was postmodernism?', *Socialist Review*, 22 (3), (July/Sept), 83–106.

Seiz, Janet (1997), 'Review of *Beyond Economic Man*', *Feminist Economics*, **3**, (Spring), 179–88.
Waugh, Patricia (1989), *Feminist Fictions: Revisiting the Postmodern*, New York: Routledge.
Young, Iris (1990), 'The Ideal of Community and the Politics of Difference', in Linda Nicholson (ed.), *Feminism/Postmodernism*, New York: Routledge, pp. 300–323.

Poverty, Measurement and Analysis of

How poverty is defined and measured is important for both research and policymaking. It is possible to define poverty as the lack of the bare minimum requirements for supporting life, but most analysts add a social dimension. Adam Smith defined economic poverty as the want of 'necessaries' in which he included 'not only the commodities that are indispensably necessary for the support of life, but whatever the custom of the country renders it indecent for creditable people, even of the lowest order, to be without' (Smith 1776). In more modern language Townsend (1992, pp. 5, 10) has said much the same – that economic poverty can be defined as the lack of sufficient income to fulfil the roles expected of members of society. With this kind of definition, what is considered poverty will vary over time and across countries as the overall standard of living rises. Under all definitions, value judgements concerning what is necessary are inescapable.

In industrialized countries, poverty measures have usually relied on establishing a dividing line, referred to as the 'poverty threshold' or 'poverty line', between the poor and non-poor. Individual or family resources, generally measured in terms of income or expenditures, are then compared with this threshold to determine how many families or individuals are poor.

Poverty thresholds have been established in a variety of ways. Needs-based definitions rely on costing out a minimum basic needs budget. Minimum needs are defined by researchers to reflect standards that they perceive would achieve widespread public approval or by examining actual expenditures of families with incomes below some fraction of the median. If the fraction is set too low this latter method runs the risk of being circular; anyone spending the average of what other low-income people spend is not considered poor. Another way of establishing minimum needs is to ask respondents in surveys what they consider to be the least they or others in their communities could get along on. The process of establishing minimum needs standards is also sometimes bypassed by setting poverty thresholds (adjusted by family size) at some fraction (typically 40–60 per cent) of a country's median family income. The rationale is that families with incomes below these levels would ordinarily have living standards below accepted social norms and would be unable to participate in expected social roles.

The official poverty thresholds in the USA illustrate a needs-based approach that depends directly on only one of the 'necessaries', a minimally adequate budget for food. The thresholds were originally developed in the 1960s by Mollie Orshansky of the Social Security Administration using Department of Agriculture studies of food budgets of families of different sizes. At that time expenditure on food made up about one-third of total family expenditures, and the food budgets were therefore multiplied by three to obtain a poverty threshold. Since then the thresholds have been updated annually to reflect increases in the cost of living (Ruggles 1990, pp. 3–5).

The resource measure used in determining who falls below the poverty line is usually either consumption expenditures or income. Using consumption has the advantage of allowing for smoothing of expenditures through spending of assets. On the other hand, people would ordinarily be considered poor if their consumption depended on begging, stealing or precarious borrowing from family or friends. In practice income is usually chosen because income data are easier to collect through household surveys and probably more accurate than consumption data (Ruggles 1990, pp. 25–7). A related issue is how assets might best be taken into account in measuring poverty – a question that has received much attention, especially in research on poverty among the elderly.

Once a poverty threshold and corresponding resource measure are defined, the poverty of a population may still be measured in a variety of ways. The most widely used measures are based on the resources of individuals or family units, which are assumed to share resources equitably. This implies that each family member has the same poverty status. A poverty rate may then be calculated, measuring the incidence of poverty in the total population or in various subgroups, such as children, single-mother families, or elderly widows. Measures of the intensity of poverty may also be needed. The simplest kind of intensity measure is the poverty gap, which shows the difference between a poverty threshold and the mean income of the population below the threshold. (For a variety of more complex poverty intensity measures see Rodgers and Rodgers 1991.)

Over the years both feminist and mainstream economists have expressed increasing dissatisfaction with some of the poverty measures in common use. Until recently much of the mainstream criticism of US poverty measures has focused on the resource side, contending, for example, that in-kind benefits such as the value of food stamps and housing or health-care subsidies should be counted as income. Feminist economists, on the other hand, have stressed the inadequacy of the poverty thresholds themselves (Ruggles 1990; Renwick and Bergmann 1993). In addition, many feminist economists contend that the poverty of women may be understated when it is assumed that income is shared equally within families (Folbre 1986; Kabeer 1994; Woolley and Marshall 1994; Nelson 1996).

Both of these feminist criticisms are congruent with a broader critique that questions the whole approach of considering economic welfare to be solely a function of resources, however measured. Amartya Sen has argued that 'by focusing poverty study specifically on incomes as such, crucial aspects of deprivation may be entirely lost' (Sen 1992, p. 113). Sen favours focusing instead on 'capabilities to achieve functionings', such as the ability to be well-nourished, to obtain clothing and shelter, and to fulfil culturally-defined roles necessary for social respect. This approach differs from other poverty measurements in requiring close attention to different resources needed by different individuals to achieve comparable functionings. For example, people with physical disabilities may have to incur greater expenses than others in order to hold a job. The relevant concept of resources under the capabilities approach is not the level of income *per se*, but the adequacy of income after taking into account individual variations in needs.

Recognition of the importance of considering differing needs of individuals in different circumstances has informed much of the feminist critique of US poverty measures. Differences based on family size and the effects of using different equivalence scales to estimate the needs of different sized families have been widely discussed in mainstream poverty literature (see Citro and Michael 1995, pp. 159–82), but Ruggles (1990) in her book *Drawing the Line* drew attention to other important differences in needs. From a feminist perspective, one of the most important and innovative of her suggestions was taking into account the necessity of incurring child care expenses in order to earn income. The original poverty thresholds based on 1950s consumption patterns are unlikely to have contained a significant allowance for child care because few mothers of young children were then employed outside of the home.

Moving in the direction of defining an individualized capability-oriented poverty standard, Renwick and Bergmann (1993) calculated a basic needs budget for single-parent families. Included in the budget were allowances for food, housing (adjusted for differences in cost by region), health care, clothing, personal care and income taxes, all adjusted for number and ages of the children. For employed parents additional allowances were included for transportation, payroll taxes and child care, if necessary in order to hold a job. Thresholds were then adjusted to take into account in-kind provision or subsidies for any of these necessities.

Comparing their new poverty measure with poverty data from the US Bureau of the Census, Renwick and Bergmann found many more working poor single parents and a slight reduction in poverty among those dependent on public assistance. In another paper Renwick (1993) extended the analysis to two-parent families with children. Both analyses found official poverty thresholds to be much too low, especially for two-earner couples and employed single parents.

The principle of taking into account differences in basic needs for families in different circumstances recently received further endorsement from a report by the National Research Council (NRC). Commissioned by several federal agencies at the request of the Joint Economic Committee of the US Congress, the report recommended a new poverty measure that allows for most of the same kinds of expenditures and subsidies as the measure advocated by Renwick and Bergmann. The major difference is that instead of having what is essentially an individualized poverty line, the NRC proposed that most adjustments be made to the resource side (Citro and Michael 1995). The income counted in determining poverty would be net of expenses not covered in the basic budget. Researchers at the US Bureau of the Census and the Bureau of Labor Statistics have recently created experimental poverty measures based on the NRC proposal and examined the effects of using these new measures (Garner et al. 1998).

The crucial importance of the poverty measure being used can be illustrated by considering the issue of welfare reform in the USA. In 1996 the Congress passed sweeping changes in welfare law with the intention of forcing most single mothers to work. In the debate on this law that is sure to continue in to the future, it will be much easier to claim that the new law is not causing hardship if the current definitions of income and poverty thresholds are maintained. The NRC's research, as well as that of Renwick and Bergmann, shows that a poverty measure that takes into account expenses incurred in producing earnings will lead to many more employed parents being considered poor (Renwick and Bergmann 1993; Citro and Michael 1995, pp. 262–9).

In an in-depth study of low-income women, Edin and Lein (1997) also found that many working single mothers had higher incomes than those on welfare but that these higher incomes were offset, or more than offset, by higher expenses. Furthermore, low-income working mothers encountered more hardships such as not having sufficient money to pay for rent, food, medical care, or winter clothing for children when compared with non-working mothers who depended on public assistance. These findings imply that other countries that, like the USA, do not provide state-funded child care for all low-income working mothers, are likely to understate poverty when they rely on conventional income-based measures not adjusted for individual needs. This is an area in which feminist research on poverty can continue to play an important role by insisting on the importance of taking into account expenses such as child care and transportation that must be incurred to produce earnings.

Another area in which feminist economics has made an important contribution to poverty measurement and analysis is in questioning whether the family, rather than the individual, is the proper unit to use in measuring poverty. Measures based on family resources assume that resources are divided equitably within families. Many feminist economists have questioned this assumption (see for example, Folbre 1986; Woolley and Marshall 1994; Nelson 1996). Much of the research in this area has focused on developing countries, especially those with cultural practices that strongly discriminate against women. In countries such as India and Bangladesh large differences between males and females can be observed in social indicators such as literacy, access to health care, and rates of malnutrition, morbidity and mortality (Kabeer 1994, pp. 136–61; Sen 1992, pp. 122–4). Ethnographic studies add to the evidence that resources are unequally shared within families in many parts of the developing world. (See examples in Dwyer and Bruce 1988.)

Resource distribution within families has also been a focus of some feminist critiques of the neoclassical literature on the economics of the family (Doss 1996; Woolley and Marshall 1994). In an important contribution Phipps and Burton (1995) showed that making different assumptions about the extent of income pooling and the existence of 'public goods' within families leads to large differences in the measured amount of individual poverty in Canada. Expenditures within families have been shown to depend on who contributes the income; this finding leads to the conclusion that income is not completely pooled (Lundberg et al. 1997). Findlay and Wright (1996) also showed with data from the USA and Italy that if intrahousehold inequality exists, poverty among women is likely to be seriously underestimated. Clearly the poverty status of individuals within families should be an important topic for further feminist research on poverty in industrialized countries as well as in the developing world.

Lois B. Shaw

See also

Child Care; Family, Economics of the; Feminization of Poverty; Income Support and Transfer Policy; Welfare Reform.

Bibliography

Citro, Constance F. and Robert T. Michael (eds) (1995), *Measuring Poverty: A New Approach*, Washington, DC: National Academy Press.

Doss, Cheryl R. (1996), 'Testing among models of intrahousehold resource allocation', *World Development*, **24** (10), 1597–609.

Dwyer, Daisy and Judith Bruce (eds) (1988), *Women and Income in the Third World*, Stanford, California: Stanford University Press.

Edin, Kathryn and Laura Lein (1997), *Making Ends Meet*, New York: Russell Sage Foundation.

Findlay, J. and R.E. Wright (1996), 'Gender, poverty and the intra-household allocation of resources', *Review of Income and Wealth*, **42** (3), (September), 335–51.

Folbre, Nancy (1986), 'Hearts and spades: paradigms of household economics', *World Development*, **14** (2), 245–55.

Garner, Thesia I., Kathleen Short, Stephanie Shipp, Charles Nelson and Geoffrey Paulin (1998),

'Experimental poverty measurement for the 1990s', *Monthly Labor Review*, **121** (3), (March), 39–61.

Kabeer, Naila (1994), *Reversed Realities: Gender Hierarchies in Development Thought*, London: Verso.

Lundberg, Shelley J., Robert A. Pollak and Terence J. Wales (1997), 'Do husbands and wives pool their resources?', *Journal of Human Resources*, **32**, (Summer), 463–80.

Nelson, Julie A. (1996), *Feminism, Objectivity, and Economics*, London and New York: Routledge.

Phipps, Shelley A. and Peter S. Burton (1995), 'Sharing within families: implications for the measurement of poverty among individuals', *Canadian Journal of Economics*, **28** (1), (February), 177–204.

Renwick, Trudi J. (1993), 'Budget-based poverty measurement: 1992 basic needs budgets', *Proceedings of the Social Statistics Section*, Alexandria, Virginia: American Statistical Association, 573–82.

Renwick, Trudi J. and Barbara R. Bergmann (1993), 'A budget-based definition of poverty', *Journal of Human Resources*, **28**, (Winter), 1–24.

Rodgers, John L. and Joan R. Rodgers (1991), 'Measuring the intensity of poverty among subpopulations', *Journal of Human Resources*, **26**, (Spring), 338–61.

Ruggles, Patricia (1990), *Drawing the Line: Alternative Poverty Measures and Their Implications for Public Policy*, Washington, DC: The Urban Institute Press.

Sen, Amartya (1992), *Inequality Reexamined*, Cambridge, Massachusetts: Harvard University Press.

Smith, Adam (1776), 'Taxes upon consumable commodities', *The Wealth of Nations*, Book V, Chapter 2, Article 4.

Townsend, Peter (1992), *The International Analysis of Poverty*, Hemel Hampstead: Harvester-Wheatsheaf.

Woolley, Frances and Judith Marshall (1994), 'Measuring inequality within the household', *Review of Income and Wealth*, **40** (4), (December), 415–31.

Protective Legislation

Protective legislation is the term applied to forms of labour legislation that explicitly target women and children. Historically, the goal of labour legislation has been to mitigate the negative impact of market forces on wage workers. During the late nineteenth and early twentieth centuries, a series of laws were passed in most industrialized countries that extended the state's protection specifically to women workers. These protective legislation laws commonly established maximum hours, restrictions on night work and limits on heavy lifting; they also barred women from specific occupations ostensibly for reasons of health and safety. Some regulations also set minimum wages for female workers, however, these have received far less attention from scholars. In Europe and Australia, but not the USA, maternity leaves were part of protective legislation policies (Wikander et al. 1995).

England, the earliest industrial power, passed the first examples of protective legislation for women in the 1840s. Prior legislation limiting children's hours of work and banning children under nine from textile factories was passed in 1833. Commonly referred to as the Factory Acts, the English laws emerged out of the Ten Hours Movement whose original objective was a gender-neutral reduction in the length of the working day. In order to reconcile state intervention with dominant *laissez-faire* principles, protective legislation was limited to parties defined as 'unfree agents', that is, to women and children. Trade unionists, middle-class reformers and some cotton textile manufacturers supported passage of the Factory Acts. In 1842, women were restricted from working in mines (Humphries 1981). In 1844, they were banned from night work. In 1847, a 10-hour limit was placed on women's work in the textile industry. In 1874, a weekly limit of 56½ hours of work in textile factories was established; these restrictions were extended to other industries in 1878 (Rose 1992). By the 1870s, such restrictions were common throughout Europe (Wikander et al. 1995). Advocates frequently cited the example of such policies in other countries in order to support their cause (see Karlsson in Wikander et al. 1995; Brandeis and Goldmark 1969).

Protective legislation emerged in the United States at the beginning of the twentieth century and was passed at the state, not federal, level. Maximum hours laws were the most prevalent, although other forms of protective legislation were also enacted (see Table 7.1 in Goldin 1990 for a list of maximum hours legislation by state). The labour union movement, Progressive-era reformers and 'social feminists' worked together in support of these initiatives when more general forms of labour legislation were blocked by the Supreme Court. In a 1905 ruling, the Court determined that a gender-neutral New York law setting maximum hours infringed upon the right of free contract (Nickless and Whitney 1997). Thus, once again *laissez-faire* doctrines severely curtailed the development of gender-neutral employment regulations.

In 1908, future Supreme Court justice Louis Brandeis and coauthor Josephine Goldmark submitted a landmark brief in support of an Oregon law restricting hours for women workers only. These legal advocates presented the Court with rationales in favour of gender-specific legislation (Brandeis and Goldmark 1969). Vogel (1993) suggests that the Court especially seized on the justification that there was a larger public interest in women's health and safety, not analogous to men's. The basis for the latter assertion was women's roles as mothers, that is, their responsibility for social reproduction. The Court upheld the legitimacy of protective legislation. This ruling inspired passage of some form of protective legislation in every state. These laws remained in place until 1969 when the Equal Employment Opportunity Commission ruled they conflicted with Title VII of the Civil Rights Act of 1964 (Baer 1978).

However, the development of protective legislation is indicative of more than mere legal opportunism in light of the failure of other labour market regulations. The institutionalization of similar policies in most industrializing countries reflects economic and ideological developments that were widespread during this historical period. In the latter part of the nineteenth century, industrialization was expanding and capital was concentrating. Wage labour was becoming increasingly masculinized. A subtle shift occurred in legal doctrine regarding women, from 'coverture', whereby women were defined as wives and helpmates, to a new legal theory of women's role as mothers and bearers of the future labour force (Vogel 1993). For example, historian Rose (1992) argues that by the 1870s British legislators and reformers increasingly focused their discourse on the problem of working mothers rather than working women in general. Protective legislation was integral to the institutionalization of the doctrine of separate spheres, that is, a male sphere of the polis and the market and a female sphere of domesticity.

Among feminist economists, protective legislation has usually been cited as evidence of the structural basis of barriers to women's full integration into the labour force. Bergmann cites the legal reversal of protective legislation laws as a factor in the 'economic emergence of women' (1986, p. 153). Hartmann (1983, originally published in 1976) has relied upon the history of the protective legislation role to document how the interests of male workers have been accommodated by capitalism. Male trade unionists supported protective legislation in order to maintain their monopoly on skilled labour and their control of women's unpaid reproductive labour. Hartmann contrasts union support of protective legislation for women with their reliance upon organizing and contract negotiations for male workers. By segregating women into low-paid occupations, protective legislation undermined women's economic autonomy and reinforced the gender division of labour between paid and unpaid work in the household. She labelled this social system of male domination 'patriarchy'. Hartmann (pp. 195–6) used her analysis of patriarchy to critique both neoclassical discrimination theories that attributed occupational segregation to irrational tastes and preferences, and radical theories that ascribed labour market segmentation to the actions of capitalists alone.

In contrast, some have argued that the main objective of protective legislation was to reduce the length of the working day 'from behind women's petticoats', a phrase attributed to Thomas Ashton, a factory reform advocate (cited in Rose 1992, p. 60). Labour reformers hoped that limits on the labour of women and children would reduce the hours factories were in operation, effectively regulating men's employment as well as women's. Thus, Baer (1978) distinguishes between the largely altruistic motives that led to the passage of protective legislation and its restrictive effects. However, economic historian Claudia Goldin questions whether protective legislation as actually implemented had such a restrictive impact on women's labour force position. Focusing on maximum hours provisions, Goldin (1990) finds that protective legislation was passed in those states where labour unions had initially fought for general hours reductions. Female employment was not reduced by passage. Her empirical study also indicates that male workers ultimately lowered their hours following passage of limits on female workers.

This confirms Steinberg's (1982, p. 128) contention that protective legislation's initial impact depended more upon where an employee worked than their gender.

Feminist historians and others have noted that protective legislation was supported by many advocates for working women (Kessler-Harris 1985; Vogel 1993). In fact, by the 1920s a rift emerged in the USA between 'social feminists', those with strong ties to the labour movement who favoured protective legislation to ameliorate the conditions for factory workers, and supporters of the newly-proposed Equal Rights Amendment, including the National Women's Party. This ongoing strategic conflict has been labelled the 'Equality versus Difference Debate'. According to historian Kessler-Harris (1985), advocates of protective legislation acknowledged biological differences in reproductive roles as well as socially constructed differences. Their defence of protective legislation was based upon historically contingent circumstances, including the failure of gender-neutral legislative initiatives. However, in the long run such measures reinforced gender inequality. Male workers were defined as the norm, and women came to be viewed as workers with special needs.

In the 1960s, Kessler-Harris (1985) argues, a humanistic and rights-based vision of feminism surpassed social feminism. While the equality legislation that emerged from this movement has contributed to real advances for individual women, the rules of the game require adherence to male norms. Family responsibilities keep many women out of the game, segregated in traditionally female occupations with low pay and limited advancement potential. Few women, therefore, are able to reap the benefits of equality. Thus, Kessler-Harris notes that neither extreme, difference nor equality, has been a completely successful strategy.

The work of Kessler-Harris has sparked intensive discussion among feminist historians over how to overcome the dichotomy between equality and difference (see, for example, Milkman 1986; Baron 1987; Scott 1988; Vogel 1993). Scott (1988), for example, argues that equality should not be construed as predicated upon sameness. Vogel (1993) introduces the concept of 'differential consideration', to refer to 'policies that encase female specificity within a larger gender-neutral context' (pp. 157–8). Within this literature, both the US Family and Medical Leave Act and comparable worth/pay equity have been suggested as gender-neutral policies that can also recognize women's distinct contributions.

The interdisciplinary literature on protective legislation can provide important insights for several streams of research by feminist economists. For example, feminist economists analysing caring labour emphasize the social importance of familial roles (Folbre 1995; Himmelweit 1995). In a similar vein, Kessler-Harris has asserted that 'gender equality will be achieved only when the values of the home ... are brought to the workplace where they can transform work itself' (1985, p. 535). Both literatures critique the individualistic values around which economic institutions are currently structured. As feminist economists evaluate options for structuring public policy, the literature on protective legislation provides a useful conceptual framework (see Figart and Mutari 1998).

The historical literature on protective legislation can also contribute to feminist challenges of traditional economic methodologies. Rose (1992) maintains that the economic calculus of profit-maximization cannot provide a sufficient explanation for the development of policies such as protective legislation. Citing the importance of cultural analyses of labour market institutions, she asserts that 'economic relations were (and are) in part constituted by gender' (p. 7). This assertion challenges the conventional depiction of gender-neutral market forces in both neoclassical economics and Marxist political economy and provides the basis for a feminist economic paradigm.

ELLEN MUTARI

See also
Comparable Worth/Pay Equity; Discrimination, Theories of; Domestic Labour; Family Policy; Family Wage; Minimum Wage; Parental Leave; Patriarchy.

Bibliography
Baer, Judith A. (1978), *The Chains of Protection: The Judicial Response to Women's Labor Legislation*, Westport, Connecticut: Greenwood Press.

Baron, Ava (1987), 'Feminist Legal Strategies: The Powers of Difference', in Beth B. Hess and Myra Marx Ferree (eds), *Analyzing Gender: A Handbook of Social Science Research*, Newbury Park, California: Sage Publications, pp. 474–503.

Bergmann, Barbara R. (1986), *The Economic Emergence of Women*, New York: Basic Books.

Brandeis, Louis D. and Josephine Goldmark (1969), *Women in Industry*, New York: Arno Press.

Figart, Deborah M. and Ellen Mutari (1998), 'Degendering work time in comparative perspective: alternative policy frameworks', *Review of Social Economy*, LVI (4).

Folbre, Nancy (1995), '"Holding hands at midnight": the paradox of caring labor', *Feminist Economics*, 1 (1), 73–92.

Goldin, Claudia (1990), *Understanding the Gender Gap: An Economic History of American Women*, New York: Oxford University Press.

Hartmann, Heidi (1983), 'Capitalism, Patriarchy, and Job Segregation by Sex', in Elizabeth Abel and Emily K. Abel (eds), *The Signs Reader: Women, Gender and Scholarship*, Chicago: University of Chicago Press, pp. 193–225.

Himmelweit, Susan (1995), 'The discovery of "unpaid work": the social consequences of the expansion of "work"', *Feminist Economics*, 1 (2), 1–19.

Humphries, Jane (1981), 'Protective legislation, the capitalist state, and working class men: the case of the 1842 Mines Regulation Act', *Feminist Review*, 7, 1–34.

Kessler-Harris, Alice (1985), 'The Debate Over Equality for Women in the Workplace: Recognizing Differences', in Naomi Gerstel and Harriet Engel Gross (eds), *Families and Work*, Philadelphia: Temple University Press, pp. 520–39.

Kessler-Harris, Alice (1990), *A Woman's Wage: Historical Meanings and Social Consequences*, Lexington: The University Press of Kentucky.

Milkman, Ruth (1986), 'Women's History and the Sears Case', *Feminist Studies*, 12 (2), 375–400.

Nickless, Pamela J. and James D. Whitney (1997), 'Protective Labor Legislation and Women's Employment', in Robin L. Bartlett (ed.), *Introducing Race and Gender into Economics*, London: Routledge, pp. 31–41.

Rose, Sonya, (1992), *Limited Livelihoods: Gender and Class in Nineteenth-Century England*, Berkeley: University of California Press.

Scott, Joan Wallach (1988), *Gender and the Politics of History*, New York: Columbia University Press.

Steinberg, Ronnie (1982), *Wages and Hours: Labor and Reform in Twentieth-Century America*, New Brunswick: Rutgers University Press.

Vogel, Lise (1993), *Mothers on the Job: Maternity Policy in the U.S. Workplace*, New Brunswick: Rutgers University Press.

Wikander, Ulla, Alice Kessler-Harris and Jane Lewis (eds) (1995), *Protecting Women: Labor Legislation in Europe, the United States, and Australia, 1880–1920*, Urbana: University of Illinois Press.

Public Sector Economics/Public Finance

Public sector economics examines the role and functioning of the public or government sector within the economy. Before the 1960s, this branch of economics was known as public finance, a term now associated with the subfield studying the revenues and expenditures of the state. Questions addressed by public sector economics include: What is the appropriate role for the market versus the public sector in the economy? What quantity, and quality, of goods and services should be provided directly by the public sector? Which subsidies, taxes or regulations should be used by governmental bodies to raise revenue and modify market outcomes? How should public preferences be gauged? How should the effectiveness of government expenditures be evaluated? The varying size and functions of the government sector in different countries are indicative of the extent of differing views on the public sector and in the field of public sector economics.

Since its origin, feminist economics has addressed the issues associated with public sector economics from a gendered perspective. Early feminist writers in this field linked the restrictions on women's property rights and on their access to employment and income to the relegation of women to roles in the 'private' sphere and the associated limitations on their economic rights and political power. Much of what feminists have had to say about economic and political theory constitutes both a critique of public sector economics and the beginnings of an alternative approach.

Ancient writings offering guidance on financial matters to monarchs and other representatives of state power are the predecessors of today's literature in public sector economics. The origins of modern theories of public finance, as well as the entire discipline of economics, are usually traced to Adam Smith's *Wealth of Nations* (1776), however. In public finance, David Hume's *A Treatise of Human Nature* (1739) was also of special significance, since in it Hume addressed the free rider problem, that is, the question of why the market does not provide public goods, such as national defence. But Smith and other political economists of that period ensconced women in the private household sphere, a sphere into which the government ought not intervene. In the nineteenth century, John Stuart Mill and Harriet Taylor (1848) and Friedrich Engels (1884), pioneers of modern feminist economics, responded at length to the thought of Smith, Hume and others on women's economic status *vis-à-vis* the state, addressing such issues as restrictions on women's property rights, the origins of the family and the state, and the role played by the state in the wages and conditions of women's employment. Their writings, particularly the socialist and Marxist schools of thought on women, influenced the development of demands made by feminists working to improve women's status in society.

At the turn of the century, feminist efforts to understand and end women's subordinate position continued to be heavily influenced by theories which linked this subordinate position to women's role in the economy and their exclusion from equal participation in the state. For example, in the United States Susan B. Anthony stressed the connection between women's lack of suffrage, the male-dominated character of the state and exploitation of women workers (Hymowitz and Weissman 1978, pp. 115–21). Charlotte Perkins Gilman, and later Margaret Reid, contested the isolation of the domestic or 'private' sphere from the 'public' sphere of market production and government, and the undervaluation of women's role in the household. Gilman (1898) stressed the need for women's increased participation in the public sphere, both in the workplace and in representative political bodies. Reid (1934) focused on the household, and she appealed to the state to recognize the economic value of women's role in the household and to formulate policies in support of women's family responsibilities.

The growth of the welfare state internationally in the first part of the twentieth century, and the accompanying ideology accepting the responsibility of the state to address the unmet basic needs of citizens, has been convincingly linked to the political demands of women trying to improve the economic situation of themselves, their families and communities (see Piven 1990, pp. 250–64; Sapiro 1990, pp. 36–54). The exploration by the women's movement of the idea that the personal is political also moved the discussion of the economics of marriage and the family to the political sphere, and so has impacted the understanding of the economics of public policy. As a result of challenging traditional divisions, feminists have influenced and redefined the appropriate role for the state, and in so doing have pushed out the frontier of public sector economics. These changes are reflected in welfare legislation, in equal opportunity and equal rights legislation, in affirmative action, in family leave and pay equity legislation, as well as in divorce law and other family-related legislation. Feminists, in turn, continue to grapple with the question of why the market, and society, so often fail women, and in these efforts, ideas from public sector economics have impacted feminists' conception of the current functioning of the public sector and its limitations.

Feminists are questioning some of the foundational concepts of public economics, re-examining not only economists' understanding of the nature of the state, but also their depiction of human behaviour. In particular, feminist economists are re-examining traditional views on the role of the public sector, the institutions of the state, taxation, and the evaluation of government expenditures and programmes. The findings and conclusions of these analyses, surveyed briefly below, imply the need to rethink the field.

Public sector economics, as it exists in market-dominated economies, builds on the assumption that only where market failure occurs should government intervention be considered. Under this theory, market failure is acknowledged to be a frequent occurrence, however, happening in cases where externalities or public goods exist, as well as in a myriad of other cases including those of incomplete markets, imperfect information, or barriers to entry. Government intervention to remedy problems occasioned by market failure may take several forms, including the use of subsidies, taxation, regulation or legislation. Public sector economics assesses the desirability of alternative government interventions, with the aim of improving social welfare, as that concept is explicated by economic theory.

Feminists are contesting many tenets of this approach, starting with the issue of the appropriate role for government *vis-à-vis* the market. They subsume this question under the prior problem of how to structure society. Questions raised by feminists pointing to the need for this change in focus include: What is the cause of society's undervaluation of women's work, especially work in the home? What adverse effects does a market economy have on the ethical base of society? How should society respond? (See Weisskopf and Folbre 1996.) In addition, feminists ask 'If the family as currently structured breeds injustice and unfair treatment of women and dependents, what is the remedy?' (Okin 1989).

This exploration of how to structure society has been far-ranging. There has been concern with voice and empowerment, and with conditions fostering the creative expression of authentic voice. There has been examination of industry and government, but especially of the family, a basic construction site in the building of a better society. Accordingly, feminist economists attack the oppositional distinction between public and private spheres, which would place family matters outside the public forum and so deny women a collective voice in how their lives are structured. They argue that economic theory renders invisible the many unpaid tasks performed within the family, as well as the inequities perpetuated by women's subordinate economic position. The value of unpaid, caring labour performed by women and men in meeting the needs of family, relatives and community in fact is equal to 21–90 per cent of GNP, depending on the country, according to estimates by Cloud and Garrett (1996). The exclusion of these activities from national income accounting and their general neglect in economic analyses tends to remove much of what women do from consideration in policy debates and so results in sometimes fatally flawed decisions (Waring 1988). From a slightly different perspective, the widespread benefits of women's unpaid labour to the population and the economy give it many of the characteristics of a public good – a controversial designation which, if accepted, would require inclusion of this labour and its benefits in policy discussions (Folbre 1994).

In addition, feminists argue that economists are mistaken in treating self-interest as the sole motivation driving human behaviour that need be considered in the economic model. Pursuit of the 'greatest good' or the public interest, purportedly the goal of much public policy, inherently involves motivations other than self-interest. Effective voices speaking for future generations and for dependent populations cannot emerge within the context of narrow self-interest. Held (1984) points out that the individual pursuit of gain may in fact be incompatible with the development of trust required within society for the pursuit of collective goals, and does not in fact adequately account for a broad spectrum of human behaviour.

The basic tool for assessing the desirability of various government interventions, welfare theory, not surprisingly is also challenged by feminist economists. Group interests and preferences are not simply aggregations of individual voices seeking their isolated individual welfares. Yet welfare theory assumes that social preferences can be understood as such aggregations, and so ignores the realities of interdependency and cooperation. Interdependencies in fact determine individuals' access to the 'goods' of human life. If the welfare of an individual is interdependent with that of others, whether statically or dynamically, the nature of these interrelationships must be explicitly recognized, particularly when the tradeoffs common to power relationships are operating (Hill 1998). The use of income, wealth and consumption levels as the empirical measures of wellbeing is also problematic, resulting in the neglect of the very functionings that constitute human wellbeing.

Feminist critiques imply, in the end, that all social activity is appropriate domain for inquiry by economists studying public policy, and that all tools that contribute to the understanding of human behaviour are valid for this purpose. But if all social activity is now subject to analysis, the question of public sector economics continuing as a specific or separate field is raised. Further, if that analysis is conducted by using a wide range of social science tools, is that still economics? This latter question, increasingly asked by feminist economists across fields, has led some to tackle the issue as a question of how the discipline and profession are self-defined (Strassman 1990).

Another aspect of public sector economics that has garnered attention from feminist economists relates to the institutions of the state. In mainstream economics, the class and gender composition of the state is not considered relevant and so is not discussed. Whether economists are attempting to ascertain consumer demand or design an appropriate voting mechanism, the state is treated in the analysis as an impersonal arbiter or the executive agent for the voting public. The policy decisions made by the state are not considered in terms of any groups of individuals involved in the process; rather citizens are viewed simply as consumers differentiated solely by their preferences with respect to public goods. Any dynamics arising from interactions between various groups do not fit into the analytical framework and so cannot be considered. At the next stage, the problems associated with implementation of these decisions which arise from dissension between groups are similarly outside the purview of public sector economics, with the result that biases in implementation are not discovered until programme outcomes are analysed.

Feminists looking at the public sector and the process of public sector decision making note that mechanisms of choice are embedded in social institutions in which unequal power relationships are protected. The role of the state in perpetuating the economic dependency of women, as well as the potential and actual advances for women that have come as a result of political and legislative processes, are noted and debated by feminists. MacKinnon (1989), a legal theorist, draws out the implications of understanding the state as a male construction. Under the male-dominated state, the norm, which in fact is inequality, is treated as equitable, with state intervention only justified where extraordinary circumstances exist. At the same time, the state is an important arena for feminist struggle, and women through their participation in public debate have changed its nature and ideology (Charlton et al. 1989; Gordon 1990).

Feminists are also involved in emerging efforts to introduce ethics into economic analysis, which raises important questions for public sector economics. It is argued that majority rule, treated as a cornerstone of Western democracy in political theory, does not result in the protection of the just interests of the minority; and the market mechanism, resting in effect on votes measured in monetary units, does not address economic justice or the economic needs of all in the marketplace. Women are often acutely aware of the ethical shortcomings of the conduct of the public sector as reflected in its budgetary priorities, legislative processes and legal system. Held (1984) and Okin (1989) address some of these issues, and also ask why current theories of justice have not had more impact. They note that these theories, including that of Rawls, are often excessively abstract and contribute to the deferral of meaningful change through their pursuit of unattainable and even undesirable optimal solutions.

Much of traditional public finance addresses the issue of taxation, from the viewpoint of the state's concerns for revenue stability and economic efficiency, but also from the perspective of equity. Microeconomic theory is used to analyse taxes as an external intervention in the market, imposing deadweight (or efficiency) losses on consumers and suppliers of the products or factors taxed. The distribution of the tax burden among businesses and households, and the impact on the leisure/work choice are also analysed. The criteria most commonly used in determining the equity of a given tax are that of the benefit principle (examining the relationship between taxes paid and benefits received) and that of the progressivity or regressivity of a tax with respect to income (examining the relationship between taxes paid and income levels).

Several groups, including feminists, however, are going beyond equity and efficiency criteria to examine class and gender bias in the tax structure. Internationally, income taxes are often, and perhaps usually, structured in ways that result in a higher effective tax rate on women's earned income, thereby discouraging their labour force participation (Stotsky 1996). Regressive taxes, such as the sales tax, also tend to affect women more negatively then men, given their lower income levels. One related area of debate among feminists is the current non-taxation of housework. Housework provides income in kind to a household. Some believe that the recognition of the income provided by the work of women at home requires that this income be subject to tax, just as the income from jobs done for neighbours is counted as part of the tax base, in order to maintain equity between families with and those without a stay-at-home spouse (Bergmann 1986, p. 212). Others argue that much of this work in effect is a public good that is undersupplied, with the implication being that it should be subsidized (Folbre 1994). Folbre also contends that the use of bonds, which are financed by a tax on future generations, places a special burden on women, who ensure the supply of this public good. The reduction of a child's future income may mean a reduction in the child's support of aging parents, or may divert parents' future income toward financing that child's education and other future needs. Biases in the calculation of the consumer price index (the cost of nappies, for example, may not be included in the package of goods bought by a household) can also adversely affect women's tax obligations, and an argument can be made for redress through adjustment of current tax provisions (Renwick 1997).

Cost–benefit analysis, in which the discounted value of future net benefits is compared with the similarly discounted costs of investment, is the primary tool used to evaluate public expenditures. In theory, the present values generated by alternative uses of public funds should be compared, after adjustment for market failures, including undervaluation of the future by those living in the present. The alternatives with the greatest present value or the highest internal rate of return then should be ranked highest for funding. Feminist critiques of the shortcomings of economic theory apply here, especially the dismal failure of the market to place appropriate value on several of the expected outcomes of any project. Reasons for this failure include the neglect of the value of nonmarket work, the failure to evaluate the ethical outcomes or the effects on the quality of life of a project; in other words, if caring labour or the fostering of altruism are not valued by the market, they cannot enhance a project's value. One recurring problem in this area is the need to evaluate the worth of a life or of the time of different persons. In this, there is a heavy reliance on the current and future earnings stream of a person. One feminist critique of this approach is that of McCloskey (1993), who notes that a better way to estimate the worth of a person would be to use the value placed on her or him by all others, not just employers.

The goal of feminist economics, to improve the condition of women in society, appears to be part of that of public sector economics, whose aim can be stated as the improvement of social wellbeing. In practice, however, public sector economics has neglected the effects of public policy on women, and in many cases has not only assumed but helped to maintain women's economic dependency (Sapiro 1990). While welfare economics is changing, moving beyond measurement of an individual's consumption of goods and services as a proxy for his or her wellbeing, it remains based on an individualistic approach, in which social relationships are considered only through their effects on an individual's access to goods, services and functionings, for example more rights and freedoms are represented by increased access (Sen 1992). The quality of relationships, however, needs to be incorporated into welfare economics in an intrinsic manner that preserves in theory the importance in fact of love, justice, caring and social power.

In a related arena, the problem of social decision making remains at the heart of public economics, and feminist interest in social choice in concrete settings has emphasized the necessity of attention to the rich complexity of institutional realities (Bergmann 1986, pp. 299–315). The divergence of the state from principles of equity and justice points to the need for rethinking the ethical basis of current governmental forms and decision-making procedures. Feminist concern with equity within the family and with adequate voice and representation of the needs of dependants as well as of women can move forward current efforts to incorporate ethics into public economics. The work of feminist philosophers and political scientists such as Held (1984) and Okin (1989) as well as that of legal scholars (Weisberg 1993; MacKinnon 1989) will influence future work by feminist economists addressing the nature of the state, as will studies of the gender, class and racial dimensions of governmental programmes and policies.

Feminist recognition of human motivations beyond self-gain, and belief in the value of cooperation and caring, have brought more attention to the question of how positive motivations beyond self-gain operate. Recent findings by brain neurologists (Damasio 1994) have also shed light on the essential role of emotions in the ability to make decisions, which is revolutionizing the very concept of rationality. In the future, feminists and others will be incorporating a richer understanding of how humans function into their analyses. The potential for drawing upon positive motivations more systematically and surely in the design of public institutions and publicly-funded projects can be developed by feminist researchers, especially where the target population is dependent, disadvantaged or otherwise voiceless, such as wildlife or the environment.

MARIANNE T. HILL

See also
Economic Man; Economic Welfare; Gross Domestic Product; Income Support and Transfer Policy; Neoclassical Economics; Tax Policy.

Bibliography
Bergmann, B. (1986), *Economic Emergence of Women*, New York: Basic Books.

Charlton, S.E., J. Everett and K. Staudt (eds) (1989), *Women, the State and Development*, Albany: State University of New York Press.

Cloud, K. and N. Garrett (1996), 'A modest proposal for inclusion of women's household human capital production', *Feminist Economics*, 2 (3), 93–119.

Damasio, A. (1994), *Descartes' Error*, New York: Grosset/Putnam.

Ferber, M. and J. Nelson (eds) (1993), *Beyond Economic Man: Feminist Theory and Economics*, Chicago: University of Chicago Press.

Folbre, N. (1994), 'Children as public goods', *American Economic Review*, **84** (2), (May), 86–90.

Folbre, N. and H. Hartmann (1988), 'The Rhetoric of Self-Interest', in A. Klamer, D. McCloskey and R. Solow (eds), *The Consequences of Economic Rhetoric*, Cambridge: Cambridge University Press.

Fraser, N. (1990), 'Struggle Over Needs', in L. Gordon (ed.), *Women, the State, and Welfare*, Madison: University of Wisconsin Press, pp. 199–225.

Gordon, L. (ed.) (1990), *Women, the State, and Welfare*, Madison: University of Wisconsin Press.

Held, V. (1984), *Rights and Goods*, New York: Free Press.

Hill, M. (1998), 'On Power and Well-Being', Working Paper 9806, Center for Policy Research and Planning, Mississippi Institutions of Higher Learning, Jackson, Mississippi.

Hymowitz, C. and M. Weissman (1978), *A History of Women in America*, New York: Bantam Books.

MacKinnon, C. (1989), *Toward a Feminist Theory of the State*, Cambridge: Harvard University Press.

McCloskey, D. (1993), 'Some Consequences of a Conjective Economics', in M. Ferber and J. Nelson (eds), *Beyond Economic Man: Feminist Theory and Economics*, Chicago: University of Chicago Press.

Okin, S.M. (1989), *Justice, Gender and the Family*, New York: Basic Books.

Piven, F.S. (1990), 'Ideology and the State', in L. Gordon (ed.), *Women, the State, and Welfare*, Madison: University of Wisconsin Press, pp. 250–64.

Reid, M.G. (1934), *Economics of Household Production*, New York: John Wiley.

Renwick, T. (1997), 'Basic Needs Budgets', Unpublished paper presented at Allied Social Sciences Associations meeting, New Orleans.

Sapiro, V. (1990), 'The Gender Basis of American Social Policy' in L. Gordon (ed.), *Women, the State, and Welfare*, Madison: University of Wisconsin Press, pp. 36–54.

Sen, A. (1992), *Inequality Reexamined*, New York: Russell Sage Foundation.

Stotsky, J.G. (1996), *Gender Bias in Tax Systems*, International Monetary Fund Working Paper 96/99.

Strassmann, D. (1990), 'Not a Free Market: The Rhetoric of Disciplinary Authority in Economics', in M. Ferber and J. Nelson (eds), *Beyond Economic Man: Feminist Theory and Economics*, Chicago: University of Chicago Press, pp. 54–68.

Waring, M. (1988), *If Women Counted*, San Francisco: Harper Press.

Weisberg, D.K. (ed.) (1993), *Feminist Legal Theory. Foundations*, Philadelphia: Temple University Press.

Weisskopf, T. and N. Folbre (1996), 'Debating markets', *Feminist Economics*, 2 (1), (Spring), 69–85.

Race

Like gender, race is an idea and a social construct, as well as a category of analysis for social scientists. Race is based on perceived physical differences and rationalized as 'natural' and/or 'God-given'. Whereas gender creates differences and inequality according to biological sex, race differentiates individuals according to skin colour, physical features or ancestry (Amott and Matthaei 1996, Chapter 2).

Throughout history human beings have lived in societies with distinct languages, cultures and economic institutions. These social differences, known as ethnic differences, have been perpetuated by marriage within, but rarely between, social groups. While ethnic differences are interconnected, in the contemporary world, with race, they are not synonymous with it, and they can and have existed independently of it; in particular, ethnic differences have always existed, whereas race is a relatively recent social category (Cox 1948).

Race as it is currently conceptualized developed out of seventeenth- and eighteenth-century European thought, accompanying the process of European colonization of the world. As such, it is of European origin. The concept of race was first embedded in the Christian world view; racial theorists argued that non-Europeans were not descended from Adam and Eve as Europeans were. With the growth of Western science and its secular world view in the nineteenth century, racial–ethnic differences and inequality were attributed directly to biology. Human beings were seen as being divided into biologically distinct and unequal races. Europeans, as 'whites', were viewed as occupying the top of the racial hierarchy, with the right and duty to dominate those who were non-European and non-white ('white man's burden'). The different social and economic practices of non-European societies were viewed by nineteenth-century Europeans as 'savage', and in need of the 'civilizing' influence of whites (Omi and Winant 1986; Hodges et al. 1975; Banton and Harwood 1975).

European racial theories were used to justify a set of economic and social practices – in particular colonization and slavery – which in fact made the 'races' socially and economically unequal (Cox 1948; Hodges et al. 1975). In this way racism and the practices which embody it became self-fulfilling prophecies. Claiming that non-whites were inherently inferior, whites segregated and subordinated them socially, economically and politically. Furthermore, by preventing intermarriage between people of colour and whites, whites perpetuated physical and ethnic differences as well as social and economic inequality between themselves and people of colour across the generations (Amott and Matthaei 1996, Chapter 2 and Part II). As feminist economist Rhonda Williams has pointed out, European racial theories were also masculinist and gendered. For example, arguments about intellectual inferiority focused on men of colour and compared their brains to those of white women. 'For the nineteenth century race and gender scientists, the lower races represented the "female" type of the human species, and females the "lower race" of gender' (1993, p. 149). She also noted the ways in which race and gender constructs share common roots in the Cartesian world view, whose conceptual dualisms – including reason vs. emotion, culture vs. nature, mind vs. body, normal vs. pathological, active vs. passive – constructed European men as superior, and women and non-Europeans as inferior beings, needing to be dominated by them (pp. 144–5).

Few scientists today claim that there are biological factors which create unequal races of human beings (a prominent exception is Hernstein and Murray 1994). In a growing number of countries, explicitly racist laws and practices have been overturned by civil rights struggles, and rigid 'colour bars' have been eliminated, allowing some people of colour to move up above some whites in the economic hierarchy. Nevertheless, even in such liberal countries, deep-seated attitudes and institutions continue to differentiate people according to 'race'. For example, in the United States the continued race-typing of jobs by establishment or region, residential and school segregation, and inheritance patterns (which connect race to class and hence help perpetuate racial hierarchies) play major roles, as do persistent and strong social taboos against 'miscegenation' (intermarriage) combined with the persistence of race as a concept through which people identify themselves and others (Amott and Matthaei 1996, Part II; Omi and Winant 1986).

Feminist economists, as well as feminists in general, have tended to ignore race (and class) in their theorizing about gender, particularly in the 1970s and early 1980s; some early examples of this are Kreps (1976) and Eisenstein (1979). This tendency has been most pronounced among white feminists, and has been most loudly criticized by feminists of colour, including Barbara Smith (Hull et al. 1982), hooks (1985), Glenn (1985), Malveaux (1985, 1986), and Williams (1993). As feminists of colour have pointed out, race-blind feminist analysis erases the substantial differences that exist between the experiences of women of different racial–ethnic and class groups, as well as the oppressive relationships that exist among women. Race-blind feminist analysis also tends inadvertently to posit the experiences of white women as the universal, as suggested by the title of an early anthology of black women's studies, *All the Women are White, All the Blacks are Men, But Some of Us are Brave* (Hull et al. 1982).

Many white feminist economists, for example, have viewed married women's assignment to the unpaid work of child care and housekeeping for their families as core to the sexual division of labour and to 'women's oppression' (Hartmann 1979; Matthaei 1982; Bergmann 1986). However, as feminist analysts of colour have pointed out, such a theoretical framework denies the reality of women's lives, as they are differentiated by race and class (Josephs 1981; Glenn 1985; hooks 1985). For example, many middle- and upper-class women, disproportionately white, have been able to delegate much of their own housework and child care to other, less affluent women, disproportionately women of colour, who often are then prevented from taking adequate care of their own families. This disruption of family relationships was a key aspect of the oppression of many women of colour in the USA during the nineteenth century as well, especially among African slaves, Native Americans on reservations, and Asian immigrants' families (Glenn 1985; Dill 1988; Amott and Matthaei 1996, Part II).

Feminist economists also have tended to focus exclusively on gender in their studies of occupational segregation, ignoring race differences and hierarchies among women. This was especially true in early studies (Blaxall and Reagan 1976; Lloyd and Niemi 1979). However, there is a substantial and growing body of research by feminist economists (as well as by feminist social scientists) which studies racial differences among women, and/or the interconnections between race, gender and class hierarchies.

Most early feminist work done in the USA that dealt with race and gender simultaneously concentrated on black women, and comparisons between black and white women. Phyllis Wallace, an African-American woman who served as chief economist for the Civil Rights Commission, was a trail blazer in this regard; she played an active role in anti-discrimination policymaking and enforcement and published extensively in the area of gender, race and employment discrimination (Wallace 1974, 1982; Wallace and Lamond 1977; Wallace et al. 1980). Feminist economists noted that black women had experienced a dramatic shift out of household service and into clerical and professional jobs in the post-World War II period, which made their occupational distribution more similar to that of white women. Accompanying this occupational shift, black women's earnings rose from 53 per cent of white women's in 1950 to 96 per cent in 1978 (Albelda 1985). Even so, as Malveaux (1982, 1985, 1986), Williams (1988) and Burbridge (1994) pointed out, many significant economic differences remained between black and white women: black women experienced much higher unemployment rates, rates of female-headship of families and poverty rates than did white women, as well as significantly different occupational distributions. Further, between 1980 and 1997, black women's earnings fell from 93 per cent of white women's to only 84 per cent (US Department of Labor 1981, 1998). In the late 1980s and 1990s, feminist economists' research on race has broadened from studies of black and white women to the study of the broad spectrum of racial–ethnic groups, and the distinctiveness of each minority group's experience of racism has been recognized. For example, Amott and Matthaei (1996) wrote an economic historical study of women in the United States which presented, compared and contrasted the experiences of Indian, Chicana, white, black, Japanese-American, Chinese-American, Filipina-American and Puerto Rican women. They found both significant similarities and persistent differences among women of different racial–ethnic and class backgrounds as they moved from qualitatively distinct labour systems in the eighteenth and nineteenth centuries (tribal, plantation, hacienda and family) into wage labour markets in the twentieth century in which jobs were simultaneously sex- and race-typed (1996, Chapter 9). While whiteness still brings a premium for women in the economy, Chinese-, Japanese- and Filipina-American women employed full time all have higher median incomes than European American women workers, while island Puerto Rican women earn about a third of their European-American counterparts (Amott and Matthaei 1996, p. 348).

Conceptually, feminists have become increasingly aware that an analysis of racial oppression (or privilege) cannot simply be added onto an analysis of gender as a separate and independent phenomenon. As hooks (1985) insisted, women do not share a common experience of gender oppression (or privilege). Rather, gender oppression itself is experienced differently by a woman according to her racial–ethnic and class position (Spelman 1988), as noted in the above discussion of 'women's traditional work' of child-rearing. Similarly, race is experienced differently according to gender. For example, the oppression experienced by enslaved African-American women was distinct from that of men because of their vulnerability to sexual abuse and rape, and because of their role as reproducers of slaves for the owner. Furthermore, gender inequality and oppression exist within communities of colour in the form of unequal access to the labour market and unequal allocation of unpaid work in the home, for example. Thus, feminist economic theory cannot adequately understand gender if it ignores race, just as anti-racist theories are inadequate if they ignore gender. These complicated interconnections between gender, race and class are explored in a number of recent studies and anthologies (for example King 1992; Badgett and Williams 1994; Power and Rosenberg 1995; Chow et al. 1996).

The interconnectedness of gender, race and class also means that the world view of mainstream, neoclassical economics is not masculinist in some universal sense, as suggested by many feminist economists (for example Nelson 1993; England 1993) – but also simultaneously white/European (Williams 1993), class-privileged, and species-ist (Plumwood 1993, pp. 67–8). Conversely, as Matthaei (1996) argues, feminist economists must be anti-racist and Marxist if they are truly to be feminist economists, since they cannot understand the meaning of gender for all women (and men) if they ignore race and class.

Similarly, feminist economists' policy prescriptions and future visions will be of limited appeal if they do not directly deal with race and class differences among women (Matthaei 1996). The difficult challenge to feminist economists, policymakers and activists is to highlight the importance of gender differentiation and inequality without falsely assuming a common experience of womanhood across race and class, and without implying that gender oppression is either clearly distinct from race and class processes or more important than they are. This leads to the support of anti-discrimination, affirmative action, and comparable worth policies – which will place those who are women and/or people of colour on a more equal footing with men and whites in the labour market competition. However, such support must be accompanied by the knowledge that, even if discrimination were to be eradicated, these policies would not eliminate inherited class privileges, disproportionately held by whites, or the disadvantaging of those who do unpaid reproductive work, disproportionately women (Malveaux 1986; Matthaei and Amott 1988). Nor will they end the existence of an economic hierarchy, intrinsic to capitalist economies, in which a few are privileged and the vast majority exploited, even if women and people of colour are equally represented among the privileged (Matthaei 1996). Thus Matthaei and Amott (1997) have urged feminists to envision and work towards radical restructuring of the economy so as to eradicate hierarchy and competition *per se*, replacing them with institutions that are cooperative, egalitarian and ecological, and which value reproductive work.

JULIE MATTHAEI

See also
Class; Dualisms; Feminism(s); Gender.

Bibliography
Albelda, Randy (1985), '"Nice work if you can get it": segmentation of white and black women workers in the post-war period', *Review of Radical Political Economics*, **17** (3), 72–85.

Almquist, Elizabeth (1972), *Minorities, Gender and Work*, Lexington, Massachusetts: D.C. Heath.

Amott, Teresa and Julie Matthaei (1996), *Race, Gender and Work: A Multicultural Economic History of Women in the United States*, Boston: South End Press.

Badgett, Lee and Rhonda Williams (1994), 'The Changing Contours of Discrimination: Race, Gender, and Structural Economic Change', in Michael Bernstein and David Adler (eds), *Understanding American Economic Decline*, New York: Cambridge University Press, pp. 313–29.

Banton, Michael and Jonathan Harwood (1975), *The Race Concept*, New York: Praeger.

Blaxall, Martha and Barbara Reagan (eds) (1976), *Women and the Workplace: The Implications of Occupational Segregation*, Chicago: University of Chicago Press.

Bergmann, Barbara (1986), *The Economic Emergence of Women*, New York: Basic Books.

Burbridge, Lynn (1994), 'The reliance of African-American women on government and third-sector employment', *American Economic Review*, **84** (2), 103–7.

Chow, Esther Ngan-Ling, Doris Wilkinson and Maxine Baca Zinn (eds)(1996), *Race, Class, and Gender: Common Bonds, Different Voices*, London: Sage Publications.

Cox, Oliver (1948), *Caste, Class, and Race: A Study in Social Dynamics*, New York: Monthly Review Press.

Dill, Bonnie Thornton (1988), 'Our mothers' grief: racial ethnic women and the maintenance of families', *Journal of Family History*, **13** (4), 415–31.

Eisenstein, Zillah (ed.) (1979), *Capitalist Patriarchy and the Case for Socialist Feminism*, New York: Monthly Review Press.

England, Paula (1993), 'The Separative Self: Androcentric Bias in Neoclassical Assumptions', in Marianne Ferber and Julie Nelson (eds), *Beyond Economic Man: Feminist Theory and Economics*, Chicago: University of Chicago Press, pp. 37–53.

Glenn, Evelyn Nakano (1985), 'Racial Ethnic Women's Labor', *Review of Radical Political Economics*, **17** (3), (Fall), 86–108.

Hartmann, Heidi (1979), 'Capitalism, Patriarchy, and Job Segregation by Sex', in Zillah Eisenstein (ed.), *Capitalist Patriarchy and the Case for Socialist Feminism*, New York: Monthly Review Press, pp. 206–47.

Hernstein, Richard and Charles Murray (1994), *The Bell Curve: Intelligence and Class Structure in American Life*, New York: The Free Press.

Hodges, John et al. (1975), *The Cultural Bases of Racism and Group Oppression*, Berkeley: Two Riders Press.

hooks, bell (1985), *Feminist Theory: From Margin to Center*, Boston: South End Press.

Hull, Gloria, Patricia Bell Scott and Barbara Smith (1982), *All the Women are White, All the Blacks are Men, but Some of Us are Brave*, Old Westbury, New York: Feminist Press.

Josephs, Gloria (1981), 'The Incompatible Menage a Trois: Marxism, Feminism and Racism', in Lydia Sargent (ed.), *Women and Revolution*, Boston: South End Press, pp. 91–108.

King, Mary (1992), 'Occupational segregation by race and sex, 1940–1988', *Monthly Labor Review*, **115** (4), 30–37.

Kreps, Juanita (ed.)(1976), *Women and the American Economy: A Look to the 1980s*, Englewood Cliffs, New Jersey: Prentice-Hall.

Lloyd, Cynthia and Beth Niemi (1979), *The Economics of Sex Differentials*, New York: Columbia University Press.

Malveaux, Julianne (1982), 'Moving Forward, Standing Still: Women in White Collar Jobs', in Phyllis Wallace (ed.), *Women in the Workplace*, Boston: Auburn House, pp. 101–65.

Malveaux, Julianne (1985), 'The economic interests of black and white women: are they similar?', *Review of Black Political Economy*, **14** (1), (Summer), 5– 27.

Malveaux, Julianne (1986), 'Comparable Worth and Its Impact on Black Women', in Margaret Simms and Julianne Malveaux (eds), *Slipping Through the Cracks: The Status of Black Women*, New Brunswick, New Jersey: Transaction Publishers, pp. 54–82.

Matthaei, Julie (1982), *An Economic History of Women in America: Women's Work, the Sexual Division of Labor, and the Development of Capitalism*, New York: Schocken Books.

Matthaei, Julie (1996), 'Why Marxist, feminist, and anti-racist economists should be Marxist–feminist–anti-racist economists', *Feminist Economics*, **2** (1), 22–42.

Matthaei, Julie and Teresa Amott (1988), 'The promise of comparable worth: a socialist–feminist perspective', *Socialist Review*, **88** (May–June), 101–17.

Matthaei, Julie and Teresa Amott (1997), 'Global Capitalism, Difference, and Women's Liberation: Towards a Liberated Economy', Wellesley College Working Paper 97–03.

Nelson, Julie (1993), 'The Study of Choice or the Study of Provisioning? Gender and the Definition of Economics', in Marianne Ferber and Julie Nelson (eds), *Beyond Economic Man*, Chicago: University of Chicago Press, pp. 23–36.

Omi, Michael and Howard Winant (1986), *Racial Formation in the United States: From the 1960s to the 1980s*, New York: Routledge & Kegan Paul.

Plumwood, Val (1993), *Feminism and the Mastery of Nature*, New York: Routledge.

Power, Marilyn and Sam Rosenberg (1995), 'Race, class, and occupational mobility: black and white women in service work in the United States', *Feminist Economics*, **1** (3), 40–59.

Spelman, Elizabeth V. (1988), *Inessential Woman: Problems of Exclusion in Feminist Thought*, Boston: Beacon Press.

US Department of Labor (1981), *Employment and Earnings*, **28** (1), (January).

US Department of Labor (1998), *Employment and Earnings*, **45** (1), (January).

Wallace, Phyllis (1974), *Pathways to Work: Unemployment Among Black Teenage Females*, Lexington, Massachusetts: Lexington Books.

Wallace, Phyllis (ed.) (1982), *Women in the Workplace*, Boston, Massachusetts: Auburn House Publishing Co.
Wallace, Phyllis and Annette LaMond (1977), *Women, Minorities, and Employment Discrimination*, Lexington, Massachusetts: Lexington Books.
Wallace, Phyllis, with Linda Datcher and Julianne Malveaux (1980), *Black Women in the Labor Force*, Cambridge, Massachusetts: MIT Press.
Williams, Rhonda (1988), 'Beyond Human Capital: Black Women, Work, and Wages', Wellesley College Center for Research on Women, Working Paper No. 183.
Williams, Rhonda (1993), 'Race, Deconstruction, and the Emergent Agenda of Feminist Economic Theory', in Marianne Ferber and Julie Nelson (eds), *Beyond Economic Man: Feminist Theory and Economics*, Chicago: University of Chicago Press, pp. 144–53.

Rhetoric

The term 'rhetoric' refers to the effective and persuasive use of language and is a much richer concept than its popular and dismissive connotation of 'talk as mere rhetoric'. With its explicit emphasis on human deliberation and action and how adherence is gained from particular audiences for particular positions, rhetorical analysis has proven to be very useful to feminist economists. It has inspired several important lines of feminist economic inquiry, providing new critiques of economic theory and the economics profession, and suggesting a theoretical foundation for new approaches to feminist economic theory.

Feminist economic rhetorical inquiry can be divided into three general categories or approaches, reflecting these different contributions. The first category of analysis criticizes the gendered nature of economics, exposing the economic subjects, theories and methods which essentialize maleness and femaleness rather than recognizing that gender roles are socially constructed. This approach, which has received the greatest attention by scholars of economics, borrows from the methods of postmodernist literary and cultural criticism to question the limitations imposed upon economic theory and methodology by gendered assumptions embedded in economic discourse. The second approach challenges the 'gatekeeping function' of economic discourse, exposing the rhetorical and linguistic conventions in academic economics which unfairly inhibit the participation of women economists in academic economic debate. While these first two approaches are forms of critical analysis, challenging the legitimacy of gendered economics from a feminist perspective, the third approach is theoretical, calling for the development of feminist economic theory grounded in rhetorical theory. Although the third approach is currently the least developed, it holds great promise.

The emergence of feminist economics introduces a new complexity to the traditional disagreements among contemporary schools of economic thought, such as neoclassical (or 'mainstream'), Marxist and institutionalist economics. Feminist economists can define themselves within any of these schools of thought, but feminist economics brings new perspectives and challenges to each. To date, the critical rhetorical approaches used by feminist economists have been aimed primarily (though not exclusively) at challenging the assumptions of neoclassical economics, because it is the theory that dominates academic economics in the United States and because it does not include either culture or gender as a category of analysis. This entry will provide an overview of the three categories of feminist economic rhetorical analyses as they have developed in the United States and offer suggestions for further feminist economic inquiry in this area.

The gendered economy: contested metaphors

An example of feminist criticism of gendered economic discourse is found in Gibson-Graham (1996), *The End of Capitalism (as we knew it)*. Gibson-Graham examined the criticism of globalization by American left-leaning economists or social critics and found it reproduced the gendered construction of rape; that is, globalization was represented as the 'capitalist penetration' of hapless cultures, so that 'rape became *globalization*, men became *capitalism* or its agent the *multinational corporation (MNC)*' (Gibson-Graham 1996, p. 121). This locution was deemed objectionable on two grounds: it reproduces an understanding of women as either having been raped or as 'rapable', their sexuality defined by the violence that either has been or might be visited upon them; and it obscures attention to the dynamics of global capitalism because it represents the receiving nations as passive victims.

The critical approach taken by Gibson-Graham reflects the critical method used in the field of cultural studies (Hall 1997); that is, to *intervene* in a particular discourse by *interrogating* the underlying assumptions, thereby creating the grounds for *contesting* the cultural norms, values, beliefs or myths ('meta-messages') implicit in the discourse, and which are therefore reproduced by their use. The aim is to notice where the use of language affects, shapes, or determines social practice and hence has a material effect on social relations.

Contesting the gendered metaphors of mainstream economics has opened economic theory to feminist perspectives. Nelson (1992) has argued that high value is attributed to subjects of economic inquiry perceived as 'masculine' in a culture where values are gendered. As a foundational concept for mainstream economic thought, 'economic man' – the agent for exchanges based on rational choice in the marketplace – has been the subject of feminist interrogation. 'Economic man' is typically represented in economics textbooks and theory as autonomous, lacking in empathy, and uninfluenced by social relations. Grapard (1995) interrogated these assumptions through an analysis of the frequent use of Robinson Crusoe as the exemplary 'economic man'; and Samson (1995) argued that feminist interrogation of the 'Robinson Crusoe trade allegory' revealed the race and gender biases entailed in neoclassical economics. Joseph Persky called for a reconsideration of John Stuart Mill's construction of 'economic man' as a 'useful reference point for comparative economics and feminist economics' (Persky 1995, p. 221). England (1993) examined the androcentric bias in mainstream assumptions about the economics of the marketplace. Together, these analyses demonstrate that the reliance on the term 'economic man' has a number of significant consequences: it privileges an idiosyncratic understanding of 'rational choice' as confined to the desire to maximize pleasure and avoid pain within resource constraints, and it legitimates excluding from both mainstream economic theory and the teaching of economics the consideration of social relations within families, unpaid labour, and issues of exploit and domination relevant to race, class and gender.

Professional gatekeeping: economic discourse as social practice

In the United States, university economics faculty are predominately male. Feminist economists argue that institutional practices and gendered interpersonal communication styles serve a 'gatekeeping' function, restricting access to women and especially to non-mainstream economists. Nancy Folbre argued that feminists should concern themselves not only with the intellectual practices that give rise to economic theories, but also with the social and economic practices outside the university that restrict participation in academic economic discourse, particularly how the 'unequal distribution of financial and human capital' has the effect of excluding potential contributors to social scientific discourse (Folbre 1993, p. 167). In a similar vein, Feiner and Morgan (1987) and Feiner and Roberts (1990) considered the implications of how future economists are taught. They found that the reductionist and exclusionary approaches of mainstream economic theory result in the omission of the economic issues relevant to class, race and gender from economics textbooks. Diana Strassman contested the 'notion of science as a social practice where free scrutiny and open participation lead to a sorting and ranking of ideas according to their worthiness' because it obscured crucial questions such as 'who gets to participate and who gets excluded?'; in short, the relationship between 'rhetoric and power in economics' has remained 'largely unexamined' (Strassman 1993b, p. 149).

In the wake of a heated exchange which took place in May and June, 1994 on a feminist economic electronic list, *femecon-l*, protracted attention was given to how gendered interpersonal communication styles contribute to the marginalization of women in academic economics. The exchange, which was about the role of conceptions of the market in feminist economics, was often vitriolic. The tone of the discussion became the topic of another extended debate about how to foster the free exchange of ideas, and the degree to which aggressive language discouraged potential participants.

The question was sufficiently significant that the 'Dialogue' section of an issue of the new journal *Feminist Economics* was devoted to its consideration (*Feminist Economics*, 2 (1), 1996). An edited portion of the transcript was followed by comments from a number of contributors addressing how the modes of argumentation and interpersonal communication were unfairly exclusionary of feminist and/or heterodox economic thought. Lynn Duggan and Jennifer Olmsted, for example, criticized the edited transcript for apparent gender bias because it included three men and one woman, which misrepresented the gender mix of the interlocutors who contributed to the discussion on *femecon-l*. Had the transcript represented the proportion of men and women participating in the debate, they argued, 'the role of culture in defining markets' and, hence, the economic implications of women's social roles, would have been included rather than excluded (Duggan and Olmsted 1996, p. 87). Richard Wilk questioned how there could be a 'free market' of ideas when those participating in economic debate can 'never be free of gender bias' (Wilk 1996, p. 90). Feiner (1996) argued that the conventions common to economic discourse have a silencing effect on women's voices. She both advocated and demonstrated a feminist economic discourse that is enriched by the 'poetic imagination'. Robertson (1996) offered a rhetorical analysis of the debate's transcript in order to reveal the 'barriers to the effective production of economic knowledge from a feminist perspective'. She called for a redefinition of economic discourse as a 'species of persuasive discourse that shapes the civic order' (Robertson 1996, pp. 98, 111).

In the next issue of *Feminist Economics*, Roxane and Stephen Gudeman provided an empirical linguistic analysis of the entire archive of the debate. They found that male contributors were overrepresented in contributions relevant to the debate about economic ideas; female contributors tended to make an effort to contribute to or comment on how the debate was affecting social relations. They focused especially on the overrepresentation of Donald McCloskey, whom they designated a 'special case' because he 'diverged' from the other statistical categories 'by using linguistic markers that signify greater power, prestige, and adversariality' (Gudeman and Gudeman 1996, p. 22). This conclusion made even more problematic the consideration of the 'gatekeeping' function exercised by male academic economists because McCloskey's methodology of rhetorical inquiry in his *Rhetoric of Economics* (McCloskey 1985) was widely appreciated for opening the door of mainstream economic discourse to feminist perspectives.

A consideration of the gendered aspects of interpersonal communication in economics provides an opportunity both to note and clarify authorial identity decisions made by some contributors mentioned in this entry. Donald McCloskey announced publicly his transition to Dierdre McCloskey approximately eighteen months after the exchange on *femecon-1* and currently publishes under that name. The author of *The End of Capitalism (as we knew it)* (Gibson-Graham 1996), is a merging of the names of the two female economists who co-authored the book, Julie Graham and Katherine Gibson. This team borrows from the practice of nineteenth century British women novelists, most notably George Eliot, who adopted male-sounding names when women were discouraged from publishing novels.

Rhetorical theory and economic inquiry: economic inquiry redefined as argument

The potential for using rhetorical theory as a grounds for feminist economic theory has its origins in the philosophical challenges to the claims of objectivity made by scientific positivists in the natural and physical sciences. Rorty (1979), among others, argued that language and meaning could not be so decontextualized from their historical and cultural origins as to warrant the claims to value-free objectivity which formed the basis for modern scientific inquiry. The criticism of the scientific method posed a considerable challenge to mainstream economists because they claimed their methodology was a positive science. McCloskey responded to this challenge with *The Rhetoric of Economics* (McCloskey 1985), which appeared shortly after the publication of his path-breaking essay 'The Rhetoric of Economics' in the *Journal of Economic Literature* (McCloskey 1983). McCloskey's approach was not feminist but, as mentioned above, his work played an important role in encouraging feminist economic postmodernist criticism, and came at the same time as important feminist critiques of the scientific method and of objectivity (Bordo 1986, 1987; Harding 1986).

McCloskey was seen as important to feminist economics for two reasons. First, the argument that economic discourse should be understood as a form of persuasive argument rather than as an objective science was made by a conservative, mainstream economist, who had only recently left the prestigious, generally conservative economics faculty at the University of Chicago to accept an endowed chair at the University of Iowa, rather than by a heterodox and/or feminist economist. This lent particular authority and weight to the critique. Second, McCloskey included literary criticism in his definition of rhetoric, which encouraged feminist economists to draw upon feminist literary and cultural criticism to criticize gendered economics. While many feminist economists disagreed with McCloskey's defence of the tenets of conservative mainstream economics, they also acknowledged the role McCloskey played in opening an arena for feminist economic discourse. Feminist economics have introduced fundamental explorations of the discipline's biases and exclusions, going beyond the limiting constraints of McCloskey's approach.

Economic stories: epistemology, methods and narratives

The challenge to the authority of mainstream economic methodology has led feminist economists to argue for reconceptualizing economic theory. One approach has been to understand economic discourse as partial narratives which reproduce particular valuational and epistemological assumptions. These define not only what is studied, but how it is characterized or understood. Diana Strassman made this point when she substituted the word 'story' for 'theory' in her criticism of 'The Story of the Marketplace of Ideas', 'The Story of the Woman of Leisure', and 'The Story of Free Choice'. Strassman argued that because mainstream economic discourse 'requires that explanatory accounts be built on the foundational assumptions of self-interested individualism and contractual exchange', it insulates itself 'against accounts built on alternative assumptions' (Strassman 1993a, p. 55). The attention to economic theory as analogous to fiction has a tactical utility for the larger strategy of legitimating feminist discourse within mainstream economics. Strassman argued that the fundamental constructions of mainstream economic thought are flawed in the same way as all narratives because they can be only partial explanations; hence, room needs to be made at the table – especially for feminist thought, but also for other standpoints as well – for multivocality, for a greater diversity of narratives in order to broaden the perspective. Seiz (1995, p. 110) also argued that the critique of scientific methodology means acknowledging that '(1) inquirers can never be certain whether claims about the world are true; (2) scientific inquiry is permeated with "internal" and "external" values; and (3) all beliefs are affected by inquirers' social locations'.

The interest in how the 'social locations' of economists have determined their economic discourse has resulted in critical attention being paid to the relationship between cultural conceptions of masculinity and dominant economic theories and methods. Feiner (1994), for example, applied feminist psychological theories of masculine consciousness formation to explain how the selection process for academic economists has resulted in a profession dominated by males who reproduce their socially constructed concepts of self when they describe the market as an all-giving 'mother'. Nelson (1993, p. 121) saw a gender ideology favouring an 'unbalanced masculinity' as determining the fixation on scholarly 'detachment' in economic discourse, and traced the changing conception of 'scientific impartiality' in economics professional statements of aim and mission from 1885 forward.

Rhetorical criticism and rhetorical theory

There is an important difference between using rhetorical criticism to contest gendered economics and using rhetorical theory as a foundation for feminist economic theory. Strassman and Polanyi (1995) have pointed out that the critique of the neoclassical paradigm 'is a vital intellectual contribution in its own right'. Certainly, the critique of the metaphor 'economic man' on the grounds that it reproduces a cultural bias in favour of patriarchal hegemony is valuable because it opens the eyes to the bias in an explanation which otherwise seems natural and complete, a bias that has the effect of placing unwarranted limits on economic inquiry and which marginalizes women's economic roles.

The critical inquiry does not, however, answer the question of how economic inquiry *ought* to be conducted; nor does it offer an epistemological or methodological approach that would indicate how to choose among competing economic theories, although feminist economists have confronted this problem. Seiz called for an 'epistemological "middle ground"' located between the extremes of the claims of positivist science to establishing certainty and the relativism that follows as a consequence of the postmodern critique (Seiz 1995, p. 110). Nelson (1996) analysed sexist bias in scientific method, theory and the subjects chosen for economic analysis, and argued that a view of economics that is less driven by masculine assumptions would change macroeconomic and empirical methods. Milberg and Pietrykowski (1994) argued that poststructuralist and feminist approaches which ground theory in the relation between the individual and society are incompatible with neoclassical thought, but 'significantly enhance' Marxian economic analysis of production and consumption.

The recognition that economic theory and method are necessarily valuational and socially constructed means that economic discourse can be 'read' as a form of 'storytelling', as advocated by Strassman; or that it can be understood as a form of persuasive argument, as advocated by McCloskey. Both advocate attention to how adherence is gained for economic propositions; but a clearer set of theoretical grounds are needed to determine how adherence 'ought' to be gained, or what ought to constitute legitimate economic arguments. Waller and Robertson (1990) faulted McCloskey's approach in *Rhetoric of Economics* (McCloskey 1985) because it confined rhetorical analysis to exploring how adherence is gained for the tenets of mainstream economics – tenets which were regarded as beyond questioning. McCloskey's method offered an expedient way to preserve the basic tenets of mainstream economic thought in the face of the onslaught mounted against positivist methodology. Waller and Robertson argued that the critique of the positivist methodology of mainstream economics leads to a much broader set of implications. The conclusion to be drawn is that 'the study of economics is the study of the social manifestations and consequences of valuational decisions' (Waller and Robertson 1993, p. 160). This means that economic thought is a form of persuasive discourse about society and how social relations ought to be shaped, rather than a science that describes self-perpetuating natural laws.

Lewis and Sebberson (1992) also objected to the limited vision McCloskey offers of the potential usefulness of rhetorical theory. They focused specifically on how a broader understanding of rhetorical theory provides a potential foundation for feminist economics. As a school of thought, feminist economics is grounded in the insight that economic discourse is about choosing what factors will make for a better society. As a form of 'social knowledge', economic discourse ought to be understood as persuasive practice determining social relations and as engaged in establishing dialectical relationships.

The future of rhetoric in feminist economics

The criticism of gendered economics has challenged embedded patriarchal assumptions about family, unpaid labour and the economic and social roles of women. A feminist criticism is inevitably grounded in the question of who counts as an economic agent, and in contesting economic discourse that obscures the role of women in the economy or in producing economic knowledge. A second important assumption is that gender roles are assigned and redefined as a result of social constructions and practices, rather than being fixed and natural. A consideration of both elements leads to the question of how feminist economics can avoid challenging the fundamental assumptions of mainstream economic thought, given that it depends upon a conception of economic agency that is theoretical and hence atemporal rather than historical; fixed rather than subject to the dynamics of social processes of definition; and gendered as masculine.

Attention to the social practices in economics which either inhibit the participation of female economists or erect barriers to feminist economics grounds feminist economic thought in a consideration of the social, historical and cultural forces that motivate the production of economic knowledge. The perspective offered by linguistic anthropology has contributed to this understanding in valuable ways. The limitation is that it describes typical communication practices and notices how they are used to signify dominance, exclusion or authority; however, such analysis alone does not indicate how barriers to communication ought to be rectified. This is particularly a problem if communication styles are coded as fixedly 'female' and 'male'. In addition, attention only to the category of 'gender' can prevent attention to those barriers arising from race, class or other socially constructed categories of identity.

Another avenue for rhetorical criticism by feminist economists is to analyse how the barriers to women's participation in academic economics have been circumvented. More attention is needed to both the social history of women economists and their contributions, and to women novelists, journalists and essayists who have filled the void created by academic economics by writing about women's economic roles in relation to their social, biological and political roles.

Collectively, the various feminist critical approaches to gendered economics offer a way to redefine the role of women as historical agents in the economy and in the production of economic knowledge. The critical approaches offer a way to examine how adherence is gained for economic thought. They challenge those methods that rely upon reproducing assumptions based upon unfair, biased or blinkered conceptions of gender.

The critical approach does not, however, indicate what warrants should be used to choose among competing economic theories, and it is sometimes perceived as irrelevant to considering the real effects of the economy on women. Parpart (1993, p. 439) noted that many feminists concerned with issues of poverty and development in the Third World 'have rejected both feminism and postmodernism, dismissing them as First World preoccupations, if not indulgences'. Her exploration of the relevance of postmodern feminism for addressing real economic issues points toward the problem of linking the feminist postmodernist critical framework with both feminist economic theory and policy or applied economics. This challenge is further explored by Connelly et al. (1995) who wanted a 'more open, inclusive and multifaceted approach to the teaching, research and practice of development, especially for women' (Connelly et al. 1995, p. 17).

The future of rhetorical economic criticism from a feminist perspective will depend to a great extent upon a consideration of what legitimate warrants there are for either seeking or granting adherence to economic theory, methodology and subjects. There are three assumptions about economic discourse defined as persuasive discourse which offer a potential grounding for a feminist economic theory: that academic economic discourse is entailed in the production of the economic order; that economic discourse entails both culturally-derived ontological assumptions about human nature and teleological assumptions – culturally-conditioned beliefs about ultimate social ends or purposes – which should be made apparent as arguable propositions; and the production of economic knowledge ought to be concerned with social provisioning if it is to have any social utility beyond sustaining an academic industry in publications and conferences. The value of analysing gendered economics thus holds promise for opening the economics profession to a more varied array of voices, but also for allowing a more socially-grounded approach to economic theory and policy.

LINDA ROBERTSON

See also

Economic Man; Economics Education; Feminist Economics; Gender; History of Economic Thought; Methodology; Neoclassical Economics; Postmodernism.

Bibliography

Bordo, Susan (1986), 'The Cartesian masculinization of thought', *Signs*, **11**, 439–56.

Bordo, Susan (1987), *The Flight to Objectivity*, Albany: State University of New York Press.

Connelly, Patricia M., Tania Murray Li, Martha Macdonald and Jane L. Parpart (1995), 'Restructured worlds/restructured debates: globalization, development and gender', *Canadian Journal of Development Studies*, Special Issue, 17–38.

Duggan, Lynn and Jennifer Olmsted (1996), 'Where has all the gender gone?', *Feminist Economics*, **2** (1), 86–9.

England, Paula (1993), 'The Separative Self: Androcentric Bias in Neoclassical Assumptions', in Marianne A. Ferber and Julie A. Nelson (eds), *Beyond Economic Man: Feminist Theory and Economics*, Chicago: University of Chicago Press.

Feiner, Susan F. (1994) 'Reading neoclassical economics: toward an erotic economy of sharing', *Studies in Psychoanalytic Theory*, **3** (2), (Fall), 50–67.

Feiner, Susan F. (1996), 'A paradigm of our own', *Feminist Economics*, **2** (2), (Summer), 94–7.

Feiner, Susan F. and Barbara A. Morgan (1987), 'Women and minorities in introductory economics textbooks: 1987–1984', *Journal of Economic Education*, **18** (4), 376–92.

Feiner, Susan F. and Bruce Roberts (1990), 'Hidden by the invisible hand: neoclassical economic theory and the textbook treatment of race and gender', *Gender and Society*, **4** (2), (June), 159–81.

Folbre, Nancy (1993), 'How does she know? Feminist theories of gender bias in economics', *History of Political Economy*, **25** (1), 167–84.

Gibson-Graham, J.K. (1996), *The End of Capitalism (as we knew it): A Feminist Critique of Political Economy*, Oxford: Blackwell Publishers.

Grapard, Ulla (1995), 'Robinson Crusoe: the quintessential economic man?', *Feminist Economics*, **1** (1), 33–52.

Gudeman, Roxanne Harvey and Stephen Gudeman (1996), 'Gender, market and community on Femecon in May and June 1994', *Feminist Economics*, **2** (2), (Summer), 1–39.

Hall, Stuart (ed.) (1997), *Representation: Cultural Representations and Signifying Practices*, London: Sage.

Harding, Sandra (1986), *The Science Question in Feminism*, Ithaca: Cornell University Press.

Lewis, Margaret and David Sebberson (1992), 'Why McCloskey's Rhetoric is not Feminist', Unpublished, Presented at the International Association for Feminist Economics, Washington, DC.

McCloskey, Donald (1983), 'The rhetoric of economics', *Journal of Economic Literature*, **31** (June), 434–61.

McCloskey, Donald (1985), *The Rhetoric of Economics*, Madison: University of Wisconsin Press.

Milberg, William S. and Bruce A. Pietrykowski (1994), 'Objectivism, relativism and the importance of rhetoric for Marxist economics', *Review of Radical Political Economy*, **26** (1), 85–109.

Nelson, Julie A. (1992), 'Gender, metaphor, and the definition of economics', *Economics and Philosophy*, **8** (1), (Spring), 103–25.

Nelson, Julie A. (1993), 'Value-free or valueless? Notes on the pursuit of detachment in economics', *History of Political Economy*, **25** (1), 121–45.

Nelson, Julie A. (1996), *Feminism, Objectivity, and Economics*, London and New York: Routledge.

Parpart, Jane L. (1993), 'Who is the "other"?: A postmodern feminist critique of women and development theory and practice', *Development and Change*, **24** (3), 439–64.

Persky, Joseph (1995), 'The ethology of homo economicus', *Journal of Economic Perspectives*, **9** (2), 221–31.

Robertson, Linda (1996), '"Debating markets", a rhetorical analysis of economic discourse', *Feminist Economics*, **2** (1), 93–113.

Rorty, Richard (1979), *Philosophy and the Mirror of Nature*, Princeton: Princeton University Press.

Samson, Melanie (1995), 'Towards a "Friday" model of international trade: a feminist deconstruction of race and gender bias in the Robinson Crusoe trade allegory', *Canadian Journal of Economics*, **28** (1), 143–58.

Seiz, Janet A. (1995), 'Epistemology and the tasks of feminist economics', *Feminist Economics*, **1** (3), 110–18.

Strassman, Diana (1993a), 'Not a Free Market: The Rhetoric of Disciplinary Authority in Economics', in Marianne A. Ferber and Julie A. Nelson (eds), *Beyond Economic Man: Feminist Theory and Economics*, Chicago: University of Chicago Press.

Strassman, Diana (1993b), 'The stories of economics and the power of the storyteller', *History of Political Economy*, **25** (1), 147–65.

Strassman, Diana and Livia Polanyi (1995), 'Shifting the paradigm: value in feminist critiques of economics', *Forum for Social Economics*, **25** (1), 3–19.

Waller, William T., Jr and Linda R. Robertson (1990), 'Why Johnny (Ph.D., economics) can't read: a rhetorical analysis of Thorstein Veblen and a response to Donald McCloskey's *Rhetoric of Economics*', *Journal of Economic Issues*, (December), 1027–44.

Waller, William T., Jr and Linda R. Robertson (1993), 'Commentary by William T. Waller and Linda Robertson', in Marc R. Tool (ed.), *Institutional Economics: Theory, Method, Policy*, Boston: Kluwer Academic Publishers, pp. 160–72.

Wilk, Richard (1996), 'Taking gender to market', *Feminist Economics*, **2** (1), 90–93.

Sexual Orientation

The direction of a person's primary erotic attraction towards people of the same sex, towards those of the other sex or towards people of either sex defines conceptually, though unobservably, that individual's sexual 'orientation'. This notion has been operationalized by using self-reported identities or by using measures of observed or reported behaviour (for example, the Kinsey scale). Sexual orientation has been treated as a significant character trait for over a century, but these formulations are still fluid with some articulations being more biologically slanted ('essentialist' approaches) and with some based more on socially evolved behaviours and beliefs ('constructionist' approaches). Analysis of sexual orientations is vital for feminist economics because, first, perceptions of gender and of sexual orientation (mediated by cognitive codes) interact in their impacts on markets and, second, markets, in turn, affect these cognitive codes which influence human perceptions of both gender and sexual orientation.

Transgender (adopting outward modes hegemonically associated with the sex other than one's own), transsexual (surgically and hormonally adopting physical characteristics typically associated with the sex other than that determined by one's genetic code) and intersexual (breaking the genetic dichotomy of male/female) people also transgress dominant gender roles boldly. Though transgenders do not fit within the definition of sexual orientation given above, they are intimately tied to how an array of orientations arose as part of the social reconstruction of gender roles, described below, at the end of the nineteenth century in Anglo-based cultures. Transgendered behaviour has also been linked historically to gendered differences in the operation of labour markets. For these reasons, ignoring transgenders in an overview of ties between feminist economics and sexual orientation would be an erasure which, for some, would signal obeisance to norms which serve to maintain the gender hierarchy.

The relevance of sexual orientations to feminist thinking can be hinted at by recalling Rich's (1986, p. 229) account of how 'profoundly weakened' feminist theory is when it silences consideration of lesbian sexuality. As an example of this theoretical weakness, consider economic models of the family. Lee Badgett has shown the significance for feminist economists of what she calls 'two separate analytical axes'; namely gender ('social meaning given to biological differences') and sexual orientation ('sexuality based on the gender of one's sex partners') (Badgett 1995b, pp. 122–4). Using only one analytical axis, gender, tends to limit economists' field of vision and points of reference to one kind of family structure, the male–female couple and nuclear family. One deleterious effect of this focus is that it eliminates theoretical and empirical strategies that could illuminate the importance of gender norms and legal institutions (in addition to rational choice and bargaining power) in determining women's economic well-being.

Within feminist thought more broadly, challenges to an exclusively gendered analytical focus have arisen in many contexts. From its beginnings, at least some feminist theorists have insisted on the need to resist universalizing gender categories: 'Black feminists, for example, have reminded their white sisters that race, nationality, sexuality, etc., construct the meaning/experience of gender – there is no unifying "woman"' (Williams 1993). King's (1994) insightful historical account of feminist theory highlights important (and the later neglect of) black women's theoretical contributions to, as well as the central role of lesbians in, early feminist theory and politics. Recognizing women's multiple identities related to sexual orientation, race, class and nationality dramatically expands the ambitions of feminist theory but, as Audre Lorde and others argued, might also improve the ability of feminists to 'dismantle the master's house': 'For difference must be not merely tolerated, but seen as a fund of necessary polarities between which our creativity can spark like a dialectic' (Lorde, p. 1983). Thus concerns about sexual orientation (and other identities) have been at the heart of many feminist theorists' analyses.

A variety of frameworks in political economy and feminist theory are used to think about the positions of lesbian, bisexual, gay and transgender people in societies. Some rest on libertarian thinking about markets and individual rights *vis-à-vis* governments; some focus on sociological and institutional descriptions of social institutions; and others use Marx's labour theory of value as a source of intuition to understand the dominance of patriarchal heteronormativity and the erasure of female erotic pleasure and of lesbian relations (for example, Gottlieb 1984), while much work focuses on policy issues which are currently of pressing importance using a rather neoclassical notion of 'discrimination'. A new approach focusing on the origin of social conceptualizations of sexual orientations and on their overlap and instability *vis-à-vis* other identities is the focus of what has recently come to be called queer theory. This thinking has been developed most intensively in more literary types of cultural analysis, and it is an approach fraught with emotionally intense and ideologically divisive scholarly argument. While queer theory is certainly not the only approach used to understand the social roles of sexual orientations, it is distinctive in that it appears to have been created first to understand the sharply different roles that sexual orientations have played in Western cultures over the last 2500 years (Cornwall 1998), and only then has it been adapted for use in other fields. For this reason it is sketched briefly here.

The term queer theory was first used by de Lauretis (1991, p. iv) to describe 'the conceptual and speculative work involved in discourse production, and ... the necessary critical work of deconstructing our own discourses and their constructed silences'. This analysis of discourse is based on the notion of 'discursive structure', which is the complex web of unconscious lingual associations made via the neural networks in human brains which guide, often in a probabilistic and certainly in a non-conscious way, how we make inferences about what is 'true'; hence, Foucault's (1966, pp. 13, 68, 89; 1972, p. 191) term, 'épistème'. In short, discursive structures are (largely) linguistic cognitive structures which develop as individuals learn their mother tongues and as they learn to understand, to map, their social embeddedness. This offers a deep lingual basis for thinking and acting within social norms.

Understanding how discursive structures channel thinking about queer identities rests on two notions, Otherness and Abjection, which have come to be tied to erotic feelings and actions. 'Other' must be understood as a foundational category, a background against which visible social categories are (usually implicitly) defined, and as being linked to the operation of a social hierarchy. The way Queer implicitly defines heterosexuality parallels the role of Feminine in defining maleness (Butler 1993, Chapter 1) and the role of Blackness as the mostly implicit background against which whiteness in America has been constructed (Morrison 1992). This conceptual role is illustrated by the evolution at the end of the nineteenth century in Anglo-based cultures of definitions of sexualities. What is now called 'heterosexuality' slowly gained its present meaning by not being any of the numerous, finely specified 'deviancies', the 'homosexualities', which were created to name certain 'types of person' then seen as seriously flawed. Homosexuality marked the limit of what was socially thinkable, or at least utterable ('love that dare not speak its name'), that is, it defined the boundary of linguistically normative behaviour.

The linguistic basis for norms or identities can be illustrated, following Butler (1993, p. 13), by looking at gender norms. They are effective to the extent that they are cited as such and that they compel such citations ('prove you are a man/lady'); that is, to the extent they are 'reiterated'. Our thinking does this by naming us and so sexing us with culturally assigned connotations which place us in social space. Such naming is a 'performative', a speech act performing the sexing through its utterance which gains credibility through the anticipation of these reiterated citations. These notions of performatives and of other speech acts have come to play a central role in queer as well as in feminist theory.

This intimate tie between feminist and queer thinking also stems from the fact that, in American culture, for example, the specification of 'gender-appropriate' erotic playmates and love objects, as well as other behaviours, is an especially salient part of gender norms, violations of which are punished by labelling the violator as 'queer' and thereby sanctioning action against this person. The frequently extreme violence with which this marking of sexual violators as social outcasts is executed manifests the second key notion in queer theory: abjection based on erotic thoughts and behaviour. Abjection designates who is outside sociality, who is a 'monster' (Butler 1997, p. 136), not a person: 'I would rather die than do or be that!' (Butler 1993, p. 243 and, for analogous abjection of transgenders, see Stryker 1994). Abjection has roots in feminist theory going back, for example (and possibly over her protests), to articulations by Kristeva (1982) who described how, in the preverbal, deepest learning and mental formatting beginning with babies, people develop perceptions of most-feared horrors which they may conflate with excrement which is threateningly close to, even part of, their 'selves', perceptions which are then reiterated in social interactions, consciously and/or unconsciously, throughout their lives.

This unification of Other and Abject in the concept Queer has proven useful to understand the power and inertia characteristic of social hierarchies tied to what are so easily, often glibly referred to as 'identities'. Reading Queer as mere difference, as simply being a mathematical reflection across an arbitrary and rather inconsequential boundary is easy when 'lesbian chic' and hints of homoerotic maleness are commodified and attached to widely advertised consumption goods as sorting devices to create market niches and so to facilitate price discrimination. These media-intensive images convey a dangerously false sense of equality in a carnival of identities.

Thus queer theory would seem to have a special role in developing new ways of analysing social identities and their interaction since, like feminist and race studies, queer theory is inherently sited in the interstices of epistemological space – between and across established disciplinary boundaries (Foucault 1966, pp. 358–59) – and so it must develop analytical methods and discourses not presently available in the disciplines already within the academic canon. Furthermore, because sexual orientation is a newcomer to social analysis and so has been less reified in its distinctness than have some other cultural markers, it is less easily mistaken as constituting a person's 'whole identity' so that sexual orientation offers useful intuition into seeing identity as multidimensional, as fractured into many shards, as 'over-determined'.

Queer theory is also distinctive because its particular focus, sexual orientation, cannot easily be foisted off essentialistically as being an obviously distinguishing trait and then either dismissed from further thought or used as an obvious (and so not meriting further inquiry) explanatory device as are, all too often, sex, skin colour, shape of eyes and so on. To the contrary, erotic preferences make very clear how hidden, how 'unconscious', some factors shaping human 'thinking', human behaviour and, thus, human identities can be. The evolution of the concept of the unconscious ('l'impensé') at the end of the last century is one of Foucault's key points in his discussion of what he termed 'human sciences' (1966, Chapter 10); subsequently, it has served as the central focus of much queer theory and, since it is, by definition, not directly consciously observable, this focus enforces some tentativeness about what queer theory 'is' and about what it 'proves'. For economists, this focus can contribute to the profession's debates about the opposition between 'rational choice' theory and institutional and behavioural approaches.

This description of queer theory can easily be misinterpreted as focusing primarily on (the identities of) individuals. However, queerness can be seen as not so much a trait of an individual person as it is the opposite reflection of a historically, geographically and culturally contingent social structure labelled 'heteronormativity'.

Heteronormativity is an ambitious descriptor of concepts of and of constraints on humans; it is a composite of signalling devices, serving now in Euro-influenced cultures to mark 'respectable' behaviour. It is not imposed externally on individuals like a dictum from some tyrant; rather it operates hidden under the cover of unconsciousness within each individual. Its power comes not from its physical intensity, but rather from its inexorable signalling of shame, of guilt over what is desired, a longing that remains unspeakable, unrepresentable, corrupted by a heightened 'conscience' (Butler 1997, p. 183).

Heteronormativity takes 'individuals' as the social atom for political concepts giving rise to 'methodological individualism' (Elshtain 1981, pp. 108–9). This is closely linked in liberal thinking with the social evolution of the ethically and politically charged distinction between public and private domains of human space, with queer perspectives questioning the enforced relegation of erotic articulations to private space. Heteronormativity also assumes that couples (and marriage) are the 'natural' social atom for erotic articulations of human behaviour and so gives ethical priority to the dichotomy of monogamous versus promiscuous behaviour. (For more detail on the evolution of the doctrine of sexual monopoly known as 'monogamy' and on the erasure of the legitimacy of all erotic pleasure separate from procreation, see Foucault 1984a, 1984b; Brooten 1996; Jordan 1997.)

Heteronormativity still carries residue from the misogynistic assignment to women of the social role of embodying erotic stimulation, an assignment constructed in the last half of the last century as the saint/slut dichotomy evolved to disempower women in many activities (D'Emilio and Freedman 1988; Amott and Matthaei 1991; Matthaei 1995). Foucault also points out the 'medicalization of [women's] bodies and their sex ... carried out in the name of the responsibility they owed to the health of their children, the solidity of the family institution, and the safeguarding of society' (1978, pp. 146–7). Thus the bourgeois 'family was the crystal in the deployment of [the new concept] sexuality' (1978, p. 111) and the social role of mothers evolved into their being enforcers of the new norms of sexuality within the home.

As feminist theory more generally has benefited from recognizing the importance of sexual orientation, so too is feminist economic theory slowly recognizing its role. Considering the analytical category of sexual orientation pushes feminist economists to realize which women are excluded from many feminist analyses – lesbians and bisexual women – and to rethink some of the basic concerns at the heart of feminist economics, such as family, gender and sexuality. Feminist economics can gain from an awareness of new work tying sexual orientations to markets in two ways: first, empirical studies mark and measure the impact that differences in sexual orientations, interacting with gender, have on observed market results and, second, more queerly theoretical perspectives reveal the impact of markets and economic institutions on social conceptualizations of sexual orientations and how they interact with conceptualizations of gender. The first perspective has only recently attracted the attention of economists, while many academics providing insight into the second angle are not economists.

A breakthrough piece by Badgett on the empirical impact of sexual orientations on markets offers strong evidence of inequality in earnings by sexual orientation when age, education, experience, occupation and region are held constant (Badgett 1995a). Badgett's work is path-breaking for being the first to use well-established econometric techniques to ascertain that there is, indeed, earnings inequality tied to erotic preferences. In particular, her use of mainstream econometric techniques offers strong evidence against the populist belief that lesbian, gay and bisexual people, especially male couple households, have incomes above those of comparable straight households (Badgett 1997a).

This work is also path-breaking for its ingenuity in overcoming the lack of data on earnings differentiated by sexual orientation, using information on sexual behaviour to infer sexual orientation categories. The analysis of 1990 US Census data by Klawitter and Flatt (1998) required similar creativity in matching up households with same-sex 'unmarried partners', a new term in the 1990 Census. Because orientations other than straight (for example, lesbian, bisexual, gay and transgender) have been at an extreme social boundary, a boundary connoting disgust and shame, it has been politically impossible to get federal funding for efforts to collect such data directly as well as being very difficult to get individuals to reliably describe their sexual orientations (see also Klawitter 1998, p. 58). This is just one contemporary example of the significant role played by heteronormative notions of respectability in erasing, from academic work as well as from overtly political discussion, lesbigayer positive analysis.

Finally, and most importantly for feminist economists, this econometric work (Badgett 1995a; Klawitter and Flatt 1998; Badgett and King 1997) demonstrates the value of accounting for both gender and sexual orientation when looking at data on earnings and occupational choices. The statistical significance and magnitude of differences by sexual orientation depend on gender: gay/bisexual men earn significantly less than heterosexual men, but lesbian/bisexual women's earnings are statistically insignificantly different from heterosexual women's earnings. Thus any analysis which ignores the interaction between sexual orientation and gender can be misleading.

Some theorizing and some noneconometric empirical work on particular markets other than labour markets have suggested that sexuality might also influence the allocation of people in urban areas (Knopp 1997) or affect the allocation of capital to firms and investments (Badgett 1997b). Even distinctions among commodities are often contingent on overt or imputed sexual orientations of the intended buyers of a particular consumer product (on marketing, see Gluckman and Reed 1997, Chapter 1; Baker 1997).

Feminist economists have begun to look at how analysis of family structures changes when account is taken of differences in sexual orientations. Larson (1992), Badgett (1995b), Brown (1998), Giddings (1998), and Rose and Bravewomon (1998) all argue that traditional economic models of the family, whether feminist or nonfeminist, fail to capture important determinants of the well-being of gay and lesbian people's families, given differences in gender configurations and in the institutional structures available to support different kinds of families.

An expanded view of the family embracing a more complex meaning of 'gender' opens theorizing and policy discussions, in economics generally as well as in feminist economics, to new sources of intuition in marrying analysis of gender norms and institutional contexts with approaches based on rational choice and bargaining power. Thus Badgett (1995b) shows that Becker's (1991) analysis of the complementarity of men's and women's familial roles leads to results contradicting his predictions when applied to same-sex couples. Further, legal institutions defining, taxing and adjudicating marriage/divorce, child custody/adoption, medical benefits for 'dependants' and hospital-visitation and funeral rights impose distinctly different transaction costs on different-sex and same-sex couples. Finally, the a priori restriction of analysis to erotic and household dyads omits the possibility of even considering the impacts on fertility and labour-force participation decisions arising from alternative patterns of relationships among individuals.

Sexual orientation's impact on feminist economics can also be seen through queerly theoretical, historical study of the interaction between markets and socially constructed notions of gender and sexual orientation. This analysis goes back to Foucault (1978), who traced the birth of the very concept of sexuality to the rise of markets. The growth of markets and the concomitant rise of a bourgeois merchant class brought about new meanings and constraints for particular groups of women (merchants' wives) and children, whose sexual behaviour was redefined, and it also led to 'a psychiatrization of perverse pleasure' (Foucault 1978, p. 105), that is, the creation of the 'character trait' of homosexuality.

The themes developed by Foucault have been extended by studies of the evolution of notions of gender at the end of the nineteenth century in the United States simultaneously with the articulation of notions of homo- and heterosexuality. Chauncey (1994, pp. 114–18) mapped the link between, on the one hand, the growth of men working in less clearly 'masculine' jobs in offices rather than in physically demanding work and, on the other hand, the construction of 'men' as 'not women', replacing the former concept of 'not boys'. Chauncey tied this to the evolving discursive structures as indicated, for example, in the growth of misogynistic taunts such as 'sissy', 'pussy-foot', 'Nancy' and 'she-men' as penalties for 'inappropriate' male behaviour. Chauncey and also Faderman (1991) trace some of the details of the construction, via lingual cognitive codes, of class boundaries as well as concepts of gender and sexuality and their links to changes in the economics of families and the evolution of labour and product markets, churches and new occupations.

The rise of gay identities has been linked to market-induced shifts in families and in wage labour markets. D'Emilio (1983) traces both the declining economic significance of traditional families and the development of a gay identity to the growing availability of wage labour in urban areas. Both D'Emilio and Weeks (1979, 1981) explain how gender segregation in workplaces and in social institutions, such as clubs, baths, bars and other 'public' spaces, facilitated the development of a gay male sexual identity. Chauncey also shows how this birth of gay male culture interacted with changing social roles for women, since urban areas offered 'relatively cheap accommodations and the availability of commercial domestic services for which men traditionally would have depended on the unpaid household labour of women' (1994, pp. 133–5).

Matthaei (1995, pp. 31–2) notes that D'Emilio's 'argument is much stronger for men than for women' (see also Chauncey 1994, p. 27). The very different values which evolved for women compared to men in the last half of the nineteenth century in American culture (D'Emilio and Freedman 1988) and the very different earnings levels resulting from the sex-segregation of labour markets (Matthaei 1995, p. 13) led to rather different manifestations of same-sex eroticism for women than for men. These manifestations of homosociality for both men and women in the nineteenth century appear to have been amplified by the 'rigid sexual division of labour' then (Matthaei 1995, pp. 15–16). But increased access by both black and white women to college education opened up new occupations 'viewed as naturally feminine – teaching, social work, librarianship, and nursing, as well as social activism/social homemaking' which enabled 'educated, middle-class females ... to live with other females as life partners, without one member of the couple having to pass as a man (an opportunity which working-class women did not have)' (Matthaei

1995, p. 17). The movement for women's college education together with the bans on employing married women, especially in teaching and clerical jobs through the 1940s, served to discourage women from heterosexual marriage. Evidence for this is the fact that 'rates of non-marriage were much higher among college graduates than among non-graduates' (Matthaei 1995, p. 17). In what might be seen as some sort of social dialectic, a 'heterosexual counterrevolution' followed in the 1910s and 1920s constructing unmarried women as 'sexless spinsters and prudes' (Chauncey 1994, p. 118; Faderman 1991, pp. 88–92). More recently, the enormous growth in so-called (public) 'labour force participation' of women has led to an 'increase in the numbers of women who are economically independent of men [which] has had an important effect on sexuality' and on marriage (Matthaei 1995, p. 26).

This historical and institutional work suggests that what is 'lesbian' and what is 'gay' are fluid, are historically contingent on other social constructions and, perhaps, can be viewed as dependent on discursive structures. This dependence may be best modelled as a general-equilibrium type of simultaneity or interdependence in the social articulation of gender and sexuality as well as of race and class, on the one hand, and of labour and product markets on the other. This interdependence between the cognitive codes influencing people's thinking at any point in time and the operation of markets has recently been reflected in theoretical economics as 'queer political economy' by Cornwall (1997). This interaction between inherited discursive structures and the functioning of markets exposes a danger for economists who are mentally conditioned to seek discrete, firm economic identities which can be captured by yes/no decisions (zero/one dummy variables) across history.

Lesbian, gay and bisexual studies share with feminist and race theory interest in the social articulation of cognitive codes which stigmatize bodies and so amplify inequality and inefficiency. This interest in the perception of bodies differs from both neoclassical analysis and Classical Marxian analysis which have constructed analytical methods that ignore 'desiring bodies' and instead model the interaction in markets of bodiless actors (actors as ciphers) whose 'desires' have been largely erased (Cornwall 1996, 1997). Thus the distinctness of sexual orientation from gender, even though the two are intimately tied, suggests an agenda of research within feminist economics that seeks ways to grapple with, first, the impact on markets of the interactions of perceptions of gender and of sexual orientation and, second, how markets, in turn, affect this maelstrom of interacting perceptions. Echoing Adrienne Rich's comment cited earlier, it might be argued that a feminist economics which ignores sexual orientation is 'profoundly weakened' since a notion of sexual division of labour 'rooted in a division between the sexes … [implicitly] assumes a male–female distinction within the family … [and] the invisibility of same-sex couples (and of individuals not in a couple) within feminist economists' ideas of "a family" leads to an incomplete political agenda' (Badgett 1995b, p. 127; see also Rubin 1975, p. 80). Badgett (1995b, p. 130) further notes that 'rather than dealing with sexual orientation by either squeezing one form of gay family (the same-sex couple) into the heterosexual model or by developing an entirely separate model of [lesbian, gay, and bisexual people's] families, feminist economists could contribute to the development of a theory explaining the existence and dynamics of many kinds of family structures'. Matthaei (1998) invites study of the interaction between feminism and lesbianism operating through the 'marriage market'. To advance this agenda of research within feminist economics, work is needed to increase the availability of data on the sexual orientations of market participants, and, to achieve this, it is also necessary to transform existing theoretical constructs which abject same-sex erotics just as unpaid work within a household was once considered beyond the bounds of respectability for economists.

RICHARD CORNWALL AND LEE BADGETT

See also
Feminism(s); Gender; Postmodernism; Race.

Bibliography
Amott, Teresa L. and Julie A. Matthaei (1991), *Race, Gender, and Work: A Multicultural Economic History of Women in the United States*, Boston: South End Press.

Badgett, M.V. Lee (1995a), 'Wage effects of sexual orientation discrimination', *Industrial and Labour Relations Review*, **48**, (July), 726–39.

Badgett, M.V. Lee (1995b), 'Gender, sexuality, and sexual orientation: all in the feminist family?', *Feminist Economics*, **1** (1), 121–39.

Badgett, M.V. Lee (1997a), 'Beyond Biased Samples: Challenging the Myths on the Economic Status of Lesbians and Gay Men', in Amy Gluckman and Betsy Reed (eds), *Homo Economics: Capitalism, Community and Lesbian and Gay Life*, New York: Routledge, pp. 65–71.

Badgett, M.V. Lee (1997b), 'Thinking Homo/Economically', in Martin Duberman (ed.), *A Queer World: The Center for Lesbian and Gay Studies Reader*, New York: New York University Press, pp. 467–76.

Badgett, M.V. Lee and Mary C. King (1997), 'Lesbian and Gay Occupational Strategies', in Amy Gluckman and Betsy Reed (eds), *Homo Economics: Capitalism, Community and Lesbian and Gay Life*, New York: Routledge, pp. 73–86.

Baker, Dan (1997), 'A History in Ads: The Growth of the Gay and Lesbian Market', in Amy Gluckman and Betsy Reed (eds), *Homo Economics: Capitalism, Community and Lesbian and Gay Life*, New York: Routledge, pp. 11–20.

Becker, Gary (1991), *Treatise on the Family*, enlarged edn, Cambridge: Harvard University Press.

Brooten, Bernadette J. (1996), *Love Between Women: Early Christian Responses to Female Homoeroticism*, Chicago: The University of Chicago Press.

Brown, Cara L. (1998), 'Sexual orientation and labour economics', *Feminist Economics*, **4** (2), 89–95.

Butler, Judith (1993), *Bodies That Matter: On The Discursive Limits of 'Sex'*, New York: Routledge.

Butler, Judith (1997), *The Psychic Life of Power: Theories in Subjection*, Stanford, California: Stanford University Press.

Chauncey, George (1994), *Gay New York: Gender, Urban Culture, and the Making of the Gay Male World, 1890–1940*, New York: BasicBooks HarperCollins.

Cornwall, Richard R. (1996), 'Rethinking Marxism Queerly', presented at Politics and Languages of Contemporary Marxism Conference, 5–8 December, University of Massachusetts, Amherst.

Cornwall, Richard R. (1997), 'Deconstructing silence: the queer political economy of the social articulation of desire', *Review of Radical Political Economics*, **29** (1), (March), 1–130.

Cornwall, Richard R. (1998), 'A primer on queer theory for economists interested in social identities', *Feminist Economics*, **4** (2), Summer, 73–82.

D'Emilio, John (1983), 'Capitalism and gay identity', in Ann Snitow et al. (eds), *Powers of Desire: The Politics of Sexuality*, New York: Monthly Review Press. Reprinted in Henry Abelove, Michele Ann Barale and David Halperin (eds), (1993), *The Lesbian and Gay Studies Reader*, New York: Routledge.

D'Emilio, John and Estelle B. Freedman (1988), *Intimate Matters: A History of Sexuality in America*, New York: Harper & Row.

Elshtain, Jean Bethke (1981), *Public Man, Private Woman: Women in Social and Political Thought*, Princeton, New Jersey: Princeton University Press.

Faderman, Lillian (1991), *Odd Girls and Twilight Lovers: A History of Lesbian Life in Twentieth-Century America*, New York: Columbia University Press.

Foucault, Michel (1966), *Les mots et les choses: Une archeologie des sciences humaines*, Paris: Gallimard.

Foucault, Michel (1972), *The Archaeology of Knowledge and The Discourse on Language*, Trans. A.M. Sheridan Smith, New York: Pantheon.

Foucault, Michel (1978), *The History of Sexuality, vol. 1: An Introduction*, Trans. Robert Hurley, 1990 edn, New York: Vintage Books, Random House.

Foucault, Michel (1984a), *The History of Sexuality, vol. 2, The Use of Pleasure*, Trans. Robert Hurley, 1990 edn, New York: Vintage Books, Random House.

Foucault, Michel (1984b), *The History of Sexuality, vol. 3, The Care of the Self*, Trans. Robert Hurley, 1988 edn, New York: Vintage Books, Random House.

Giddings, Lisa A. (1998), 'Political economy and the construction of gender: the example of housework within same-sex households', *Feminist Economics*, **4** (2), 97–106.

Gluckman, Amy and Betsy Reed (1997), *Homo Economics: Capitalism, Community and Lesbian and Gay Life*, New York: Routledge.

Gottlieb, Rhonda (1984), 'The political economy of sexuality', *Review of Radical Political Economics*, **16** (1), 143–65.

Jordan, Mark (1997), *The Invention of Sodomy in Christian Theology*, Chicago: University of Chicago Press.

King, Katie (1994), *Theory in its Feminist Travels*, Bloomington, Indiana: University Press.

Klawitter, Marieka M. (1998), 'Why aren't more economists doing research on sexual orientation?', *Feminist Economics*, **4** (2), 55–9.

Klawitter, Marieka M. and Victor Flatt (1998), 'The effects of state and local antidiscrimination policies for sexual orientation', *Journal of Policy Analysis and Management*, **17** (4), 658–86.

Knopp, Lawrence (1997), 'Gentrification and Gay Neighborhood Formation in New Orleans: A Case Study', in Amy Gluckman and Betsy Reed (eds), *Homo Economics: Capitalism, Community and Lesbian and Gay Life*, New York: Routledge, pp. 45–63.

Kristeva, Julia (1982), *Powers of Horror: An Essay on Abjection*, Trans. Leon S. Roudiez, New York: Columbia University Press.

Larson, Kathryn (1992) 'The Economics of Lesbian Households', in R. Spalter-Roth, D. Clearwaters, M. Gish and S.A. Markham (eds), *Exploring the Quincentennial: The Policy Challenges of Gender, Diversity, and International Exchange*, Institute for Women's Policy Research, pp. 251–7.

de Lauretis, Teresa (1991), 'Queer theory: lesbian and gay sexualities. An introduction', *Differences: A Journal of Feminist Cultural Studies*, **3** (2), iii–xviii.

Lorde, Audre (1983), 'The Master's Tools Will Never Dismantle the Master's House', in Cherrie Moraga and Gloria Anzaldua (eds), *This Bridge Called My Back*, New York: Kitchen Table Press.

Matthaei, Julie (1995), 'The sexual division of labour, sexuality, and lesbian/gay liberation:

towards a Marxist-feminist analysis of sexuality in US capitalism', *Review of Radical Political Economics*, **27** (2), 1–37.

Matthaei, Julie (1998), 'Some comments on the role of lesbianism in feminist economic transformation', *Feminist Economics*, **4** (2), 83–8.

Morrison, Toni (1992), *Playing in the Dark: Whiteness and the Literary Imagination*, Cambridge, Massachusetts: Harvard University Press.

Rich, Adrienne (1986), 'Compulsory heterosexuality and lesbian existence', in *Blood, Bread, and Poetry, Selected Prose 1978–1985*, New York: W.W. Norton & Company. Reprinted in Henry Abelove, Michele Ann Barale and David M. Halperin (eds) (1993), *The Lesbian and Gay Studies Reader*, New York: Routledge. Page citations taken from latter source.

Rose, Nancy E. and Lynn Bravewoman (1998), 'Family webs: a study of extended families in the lesbian/gay/bisexual community', *Feminist Economics*, **4** (2), 107–9.

Rubin, Gayle (1975), 'The traffic in women: notes on the "political economy" of sex', in Rayna R. Reiter (ed.), *Towards an Anthropology of Women*, New York: Monthly Review Press, pp. 157–210.

Stryker, Susan (1994), 'My words to Victor Frankenstein above the village of Chamounix: performing transgender rage', *GLQ*, **1** (3), 237–54.

Weeks, Jeffrey (1979), *Coming Out: Homosexual Politics in Britain, from the Nineteenth Century to the Present*, New York: Quartet Books.

Weeks, Jeffrey (1981), *Sex, Politics and Society: The Regulation of Sexuality Since 1800*, London: Longman.

Williams, Rhonda M. (1993), 'Race, Deconstruction, and the Emergent Agenda of Feminist Economic Theory', in Marianne A. Ferber and Julie A. Nelson (eds), *Beyond Economic Man*, Chicago: University of Chicago Press.

Socialism

The term socialism has been used to describe economic systems including the Soviet Union and China; economic, political and social theories; and visions for economic justice. In each of these uses socialism provides a foil for capitalism. As an economic system, socialism is the alternative to capitalism. As theory, socialism provides an analysis of oppression under capitalism. As a vision for economic justice, socialism also provides hope of nonoppressive economic structures that could replace capitalism. For feminist economists, socialism provides opportunities to investigate the relationship between economic systems and women's oppression, with women's status in different economic systems providing useful empirical information. Socialist theories further contribute to the analysis of women's oppression, while socialist feminist visions for future economic structures provide hope for improving women's lives. First, this entry will explore the definition of socialism as an economic system. Second, the features of socialist theories that are most relevant for feminist economic analyses are discussed. Third, socialist visions of alternative economic structures are described.

Most economics textbooks define socialism as a failed economic system. The textbook definition of socialism is a system in which the means of production are socially owned in contrast to private ownership in capitalism. Socially owned has generally been interpreted as state ownership. Alternative forms of collective ownership, such as the Kibbutzim in Israel or the Mondragon worker cooperatives in the Basque region of Spain, are usually ignored. Economics textbooks typically associate socialism with central planning, in which a state bureaucracy controls the allocation of goods and resources. Market socialism, in which the state alters behaviour by controlling the prices, is sometimes presented as an alternative. Consequently, discussions of socialism's theoretical defects emphasize the lack of incentives in the absence of private ownership and the lack of information that central planners and state pricing agencies would encounter. Empirical defects include the stagnating growth rates of the Soviet Union, the poor quality of goods produced in centrally planned economies, various measures of wasted resources and, finally, the collapse of the Soviet Union and the decision to reform the system in China.

Many believe these criticisms of the Russian and Chinese experiments provide a refutation of socialism as a viable economic system. However, measuring the viability of an economic system implies a specific set of goals. In this case, the stagnating growth in the Soviet Union defines nonviability. Feminists have questioned growth as the primary goal of economic systems, emphasizing quality of life and human development goals instead. Thus, a feminist evaluation of socialism as an economic system requires a different set of criteria, which might include low poverty levels, high educational attainment, long life expectancy, and a high share of control over income for women. Using these measures socialist countries tend to perform better than countries with comparable income levels.

Feminists are critical of the experiments in Russia and China. The ideologies that motivated these revolutions emphasized hierarchies based on class allowing gender only secondary status, and ignoring ethnicity and other characteristics that differentiate economic actors. Women's labour force participation rates were higher, but the gender division of labour persisted, relegating women to poorly paid low status jobs. Experiments with the socialization of housework were short lived. Housework was not considered productive and was thus not given priority. Planners failed to take advantage of technological innovations that could have reduced the burden of housework.

As a result, many feminists have rejected socialism as a mechanism for the liberation of women. However, the failure to fully liberate women in socialist economies does not imply that these women were worse off than women in capitalist economies. The liberation of women may be independent of the economic system. Alternatively, socialism may be a necessary, but insufficient condition for the liberation of women. Although women continued to face a double day, policies such as maternity leave, enterprise-based child care and job security, provided greater support for family responsibilities than capitalist states did (Hopkins 1995). Furthermore, any differences in status may be attributed to other factors, such as cultural norms, rather than the economic system. The value of the increased acceptance of women's economic independence that socialist ideologies promoted should also not be ignored. Finally, Russia and China do not comprise the entire range of socialist experiments. In Nicaragua, for example, extensive involvement by women in the revolution resulted in explicit government policy that indicated that the struggle against sex discrimination would not be put off and that it would require more than the liberation of the working class.

The possibility of a liberatory socialism challenges the narrow definition of socialism presented in economics textbooks. Studying socialism as economic, political and social theories and as visions for economic justice can allow feminist economists to investigate the possibilities for alternative economic structures that are liberatory. Socialist theories, from pre-Marxian 'utopian' variants, through Marxism to forms of democratic socialism, are primarily critiques of capitalism exposing unequal power relations. Socialist feminist theories are both derivations of these traditions and criticisms of the neglect of gender. Socialism, for socialist feminists, is an analysis of unequal power relations in economic, political and social processes that recognizes the importance of gender, class and race as social categories.

Karl Marx, the writer most closely associated with socialism, did not include an analysis of women's oppression in his critique of capitalism. However, his collaborator, Friedrich Engels, did make an influential, but ambiguous, contribution in his *The Origin of the Family, Private Property, and the State* (1884). Drawing on the Marxian analysis of capitalism, Engels argued that the process of social evolution, specifically the ownership of private property and the exclusion of women from social production, was the source of women's oppression. However, because Engels (like Marx) focused on class hierarchies, this analysis absolved working class men of any responsibility for patriarchy and the oppression of women.

Engels was responding to German social democrat August Bebel. In *Women and Socialism* (1879), Bebel linked women's oppression, and all oppression, to economic dependence and a lack of independent property rights. Bebel did not question women's primary responsibility for child care and shared the Marxist view that technological innovation would soon make housework unnecessary. However, according to feminist economic historian Nancy Folbre, Bebel did contest the orthodox Marxist view in his 'refusal to blame women's oppression simply on the interests of the ruling class' (Folbre 1993, p. 105).

Folbre (1993) argues that by focusing on Marxian analyses, many scholars have overlooked the important connections between feminist and socialist theory. She argues that pre-Marxian and other 'utopian' socialists anticipated many of the criticisms of economic theory made by contemporary feminists.

For example, the social reformer William Thompson, writing in the 1820s, explicitly linked his criticism of individual competition to women's situation. He argued that men's greater physical strength and the interruptions in women's employment required by reproduction disadvantaged women, and he criticized the inefficiencies of the system of domestic labour. With Anna Wheeler, Thompson also developed a critique of patriarchy that criticized the economic assumption that men are self-interested with each other, but altruistic with women and children. This critique of a dualistic and contradictory theory of political economy was central to Thompson's advocacy of a socialist community (Folbre 1993).

By the turn of the century, socialist feminist Charlotte Perkins Gilman was providing an independent voice based on her own experience. Gilman attributed women's oppression to the domestic division of labour between men and women. Thus, unlike her male predecessors, Gilman argued that both parents should be responsible for raising children. She consequently advocated for the socialization of housework, which would free men and women from the burdens of cooking and cleaning (Gilman 1966).

Later in the century, in the women's liberation movement of the 1970s, socialist analyses of women's oppression focused on women's position in the labour market and as unpaid domestic workers. Because women were observed to be disproportionately represented at the bottom of the labour hierarchy, it was argued that women were oppressed both as workers and as women. Further, because women also bore primary responsibility for child care and other household labour, they were disadvantaged in the competition for good jobs. Thus gender ideology was identified in socialist feminist analyses as playing an important role in women's labour market position. These analyses demonstrated how socially constructed beliefs about what work was appropriate for women and about the value of 'male' versus 'female' jobs had created oppressive economic structures. Subsequent analyses not only examined women's oppression resulting from connections between gender and class, but were also expanded to include other forms of oppression, such as racism. However, much more work on the relationships between different forms of oppression is needed, making these connections an important topic for feminist economic theorists to explore.

Socialist feminists differ on the source of women's exploitation in the household. Following the Marx/Engels school of thought, Marxist feminists attribute this exploitation to the capitalist employers of working class male breadwinners. Integrating the insights of radical feminism, socialist feminists recognized patriarchal power exercised by working class male heads of households (Hartmann 1981). Despite disagreements about the relationship between capitalism and patriarchy and about whether or not domestic labour constituted a mode of production, socialist feminists were united by the recognition that women's liberation would not result solely from the removal of capitalist exploitation. Recognizing family as a locus of patriarchal oppression meant that a truly liberatory socialism also needed to eliminate patriarchy. How to organize caring labour in a non-exploitive manner remains an important topic of research for many socialist feminist economists.

Another variant of socialist feminism, materialist ecological feminism, extends the critique beyond class, gender and race to include the economic exploitation of the environment. The domination of women is connected to the domination of nature. In the capitalist global economy, women's bodies and nature are both commodified and valued only in their ability to generate profits (Mies and Shiva 1993). These exploitive relationships develop from the logic of capitalism, and can also apply to people of colour, domestically as racism, and internationally as neo-colonialism. Thus, for materialist ecological feminists, oppression of women, people of colour and the environment are interrelated and are derived from capitalism (Kirk 1997).

Socialist theories provide the basis for socialism as a vision for economic justice. Benería (1989) describes the necessary concerns of a feminist socialist developing a vision for an alternative economic system. First, understanding the interaction between gender and class in women's lives must be at the foundation of any policies to change the system. It is not enough to be allowed to compete for a few good jobs, when so many jobs are part-time and low-paid. Thus, for socialism to be feminist it must address issues of 'control, exploitation, and organization of economic life' (Benería 1989, p. 328). Second, a feminist socialism must address not only the material aspects of women's lives, but also their interaction with the ideological aspects of women's lives. For example, if a feminist socialism is to eliminate women's oppression, gender roles need to change. Understanding how gender roles are constructed and maintained is necessary to build institutions and policies that support women's liberation. Third, the sexual division of labour in the household needs to be addressed. Although the socialist experiments in Eastern Europe and Russia did a better job of providing services like child care than did capitalist economies, policies tended to reinforce the traditional division of labour between men and women (Hopkins 1995). Fourth, a feminist socialism should be democratic. Feminist traditions of collective decision making are not consistent with the hierarchical party control of the socialist experiments in Russia, China and Eastern Europe. Finally, production under a feminist socialism needs to respond to social needs, not just individual consumer needs. While capitalist firms respond only to the profit motive, socialist feminist firms would also respond to the needs of their workers to combine work and family responsibilities, to concern for the environment and to fair labour practices.

Mitter (1991) argues that any future for socialism is going to have to emerge from the grass roots alternative labour movements. Mitter cites examples from India, in which 'networks of vulnerable and casualised women workers' have developed visions of alternative economic structures (Mitter 1991, p. 115). These visions address feminist concerns because they are based on the experiences of actual women, as articulated by the most vulnerable women. Transformation of women's power within the family through collective action is at the core of these developments. These grass roots women's groups focus on issues such as child care, sexual harassment and independent income-generating activities for women, rather than on the wage-bargaining of traditional union structures. Mitter argues that making links between these groups – most of which develop to address specific issues – and national and international goals for a just society is necessary for any future socialism.

Many feminists in search of alternative economic structures have abandoned the dualism of capitalism and socialism. Advocates for both economic systems tend to obscure women's lives by ignoring relationships within the family, because both systems tend to be defined by formal production processes. The binary categories of capitalism and socialism generate an entire list of dualisms that distort the opportunities for change in economic structures. Most economies are actually mixed economies with some private and some state ownership, some government planning, some planning at the enterprise level and some market influence over individual decisions. Benería (1989) points out that privately-owned small businesses and limited market influences are not inconsistent with a feminist socialism. Feminists, including socialist feminists, have not developed a consensus on the role of the market and commodification of goods, such as caring services, in a more just society.

Matthaei and Amott do not use the term socialism, but step out of the dualism by writing in more general terms about alternatives to the specific global capitalism in which we find ourselves (Matthaei and Amott 1997). Like Mitter, Matthaei and Amott make an appeal for grass roots reformism, that would allow individual women to have autonomy and would promote change without requiring the overthrow of the government. Their feminist alternative focuses on rejecting patriarchal values of violence and domination, embodied in the notion of 'freedom and self-expression as the struggle to subordinate others' (Matthaei and Amott 1997, p. 23). These patriarchal values should then be replaced with feminist values, such as the 'power to give and nurture life'. The way to achieve these values is through creating structures that reflect these values. Given the present political context, the structures must be constructed within otherwise capitalist systems. These structures might include consumer unions that demand that producers of the products they purchase reflect such values as environmentalism and fair labour practices; alternative investment strategies that consider not just profits, but social values; and cooperative firms based on worker control.

New visions of socialism have proliferated since 1989. Rigid definitions based on the absence of private property and complete rejection of markets have given way to broad collections of structures and strategies for meeting socialist goals. There is a great deal of work for feminist economists to discover the opportunities for women's liberation from potential economic structures and to continue to identify and criticize economic structures that oppress women. If new visions of economic alternatives to capitalism are going to be successful, feminist economists will need to continue developing more complete (that is, more inclusive) studies of women's oppression in existing systems and theoretical frameworks, and they will need to participate as scholars and activists in bringing about this new vision for a non-oppressive society.

BARBARA HOPKINS

See also

Capitalism; Class; Domestic Labour; Economic History, China; Economic History, Russia; Marxist Political Economics; Race.

Bibliography

Benería, Lourdes (1989), 'Capitalism and Socialism: Some Feminist Questions', in Sonia Kruks, Rayna Rapp and Marilyn B. Young (eds), *Promissory Notes: Women in the Transition to Socialism*, New York: Monthly Review Press.
Folbre, Nancy (1993), 'Socialism, Feminist and Scientific', in Marianne A. Ferber and Julie A. Nelson (eds), *Beyond Economic Man: Feminist Theory and Economics*, Chicago: The University of Chicago Press.
Gilman, Charlotte Perkins (1966), *Women and Economics*, New York: Harper and Row.
Hartmann, Heidi (1981), 'The Unhappy Marriage of Marxism and Feminism: Towards a More Progressive Union', in Lydia Sargent (ed.), *Women and Revolution*, Boston: South End Press.
Hopkins, Barbara (1995), 'Women and Children Last', in Edith Kuiper, Jolande Sap et al. (eds), *Out of the Margin: Feminist Perspectives on Economics*, London: Routledge.
Kirk, Gwyn (1997), 'Standing on Solid Ground: A Materialist Ecological Feminism', in R. Hennessy and C. Ingraham (eds), *Materialist Feminism: A Reader in Class, Difference, and Women's Lives*, London: Routledge.
Matthaei, Julie and Teresa Amott (1997), 'Global Capitalism, Difference, and Women's Liberation: Towards a Liberated Economy', *Wellesley College Working Paper*, 97–103.
Mies, Maria and Vandana Shiva (1993), *Ecofeminism*, London; Zed.
Mitter, Swasti (1991), 'Socialism out of the common pots', *Feminist Review*, **39**, 113–18.

Structural Adjustment Policies

Structural adjustment policies (SAPs) refer to high-powered austerity programmes implemented in many countries across the globe since the early 1980s and propelled by international financial loans tied to International Monetary Fund (IMF) and World Bank conditionalities. From Africa to Asia, Latin America and Eastern Europe, over 100 countries have applied similar packages, despite significant differences in their economies. Earlier versions of these types of policies had been part of stabilization plans imposed by the IMF during the post-World War II period on countries with chronic balance of payments problems. What was new with SAPs was their wider scope and their connection with the foreign debt problem that developed in the late 1970s and early 1980s. The accumulated debt was the result of a variety of factors – from the oil crisis of the 1970s to the very lax lending policies that resulted from the accumulation of petrodollars in international banks, and from the rise in interest rates in the United States in the late 1970s to the withdrawal of large amounts of funds from indebted countries resulting from fears of devaluation and the growing trade and balance of payments deficits. In addition, falling prices of commodities exported from Third World countries further intensified these external economic shocks.

Two of the first SAPs packages were adopted by the Philippines in September 1980 and Mexico in August 1982, both under the close guidance of the IMF and the World Bank. The public announcement by the Mexican government that it could no longer meet its debt payments and the importance of Mexico as one of the largest Latin American countries made this case particularly significant. Hence, the Mexican package was viewed as the response of the international financial community to the prevailing fear of the global crisis that could have developed if many governments defaulted. The package consisted of a set of tough policy measures adopted as a condition for the new loans, amounting to $5.3 billion and put together with help from the IMF, the World Bank, the US government and international commercial banks. The goal was to return Mexico to economic health and generate resources that would help pay its debt. Additionally, the standard set of policies which would have tremendous consequences for the lives of millions of people was adopted without public discussion, setting the model followed by other countries across the globe during the 1980s and 1990s.

Since their inception, SAPs were inspired by the neoliberal model associated with the 'Washington Consensus', that is, an emphasis on the market as the main allocator of economic resources and a corresponding decrease in the role of government. Although some details might have varied from country to country, the basic characteristics can be summarized as falling in four major policy areas. First, a common starting point is the adjustment in the area of foreign exchange, beginning with currency devaluation in order to deal with normally overvalued currencies. This leads to an automatic increase in the price of imports, followed by that of domestic prices and inflationary trends.

Second, drastic cuts in government spending are used not only to reduce deficits in the public sector but also to shift resources and economic activity from the public to the private sector. They are also used to decrease aggregate demand in order to stem inflation. These cuts reduce or eliminate government services and subsidies, such as in education, health and other sectors, that contribute to the social wage, particularly of low income groups. Another aspect of the reduction of the government's role in the economy is the process of privatization of public firms. Although privatization might serve the important function of reducing the domestic deficit and eliminating inefficient and even corrupt activities in the public sector, it has also played a significant role in the imposition of the market over welfare and human development criteria in the functioning of the economy.

Third, SAPs have been used to stimulate deep economic restructuring through market deregulation, including labour and capital markets. This in turn creates strong pressures to restructure production, which leads to the introduction of new technologies, reorganization of labour processes and an emphasis on efficiency and 'modernization'. Fourth, this process is reinforced by trade liberalization and the easing of rules regulating foreign investment, increasing the degree of globalization of the economy and emphasizing the production of tradables over non-tradables. This reinforces the need to strive for more efficient production so as to be able to compete in international markets and reverse the external debt problem.

To sum up, orthodox SAPs represent deep economic and social changes aimed at a variety of objectives: increasing productivity levels even though, at least during the initial stages, at lower real wages; eliminating waste and inefficiency while 'rationalizing' the economy according to the signals dictated by an expanding market; achieving a higher degree of openness to foreign competition and integration in the global economy through trade and financial liberalization; altering economic and social relations and shifting the distribution of resources, rights and privileges towards social groups benefiting from the market; responding to the needs and interests of international capital and powerful global and domestic interests, including the large financial institutions, transnational corporations and international organizations such as the World Bank and the IMF; and reaching the final objective of returning to acceptable levels of economic growth and stability.

Almost two decades after the initial SAPs were adopted, have these goals been achieved? In the short run, the impact of SAPs is felt strongly throughout the economy and among all social groups. Higher import prices affect producers and consumers although trade liberalization may result in cheaper prices for some imports. At the same time, those linked to exports and the financial sector see their fortunes grow. Government budget cuts and foreign competition generate unemployment in some sectors and often force many domestic producers out of the market, with subsequent multiplier effects. All of these can result in negative rates of growth, as in the case of the 'lost decade' in Latin America during the 1980s. The average per capita GNP for the region as a whole was 8 per cent less in 1989 than in 1980 – equivalent, in real terms, to its 1977 level (ECLAC 1990). The fall in per capita income under SAPs is accompanied by shrinking household budgets for a large proportion of the population, downward social mobility, increasing poverty rates and other social ills (Taylor 1988; ECA 1989; ECLAC 1995). At the same time, higher unemployment rates place downward pressure on wages which, together with inflationary pressures, contribute to the deteriorating position of labour. This is justified with the expectation that it will reverse the initial economic conditions and therefore return the economy to rising employment and living standards.

In the long run, however, the rationale behind SAPs is that they will result in a more efficient economy with positive growth. The record shows that in many ways this has been the case – at least in the short run – although at high social costs. In such cases, macroeconomic indicators have led to optimistic evaluations, with renewed economic activity and positive growth rates, inflationary tendencies under control, high levels of net foreign investment, significant increases in trade and buoyant stock markets (World Bank 1992–94; ECLAC 1995). At the same time, case studies at the micro level and reports on people's daily lives portray a more negative view, documenting hardships of survival, social tensions and increasing economic and social inequalities – implying that even optimistic macroeconomic results do not trickle down easily to the population at large (Cornia et al. 1987; Elson 1991; Benería and Feldman 1992; Floro 1995).

Thus, two major critiques of SAPs have emerged. The first emphasizes the social costs of adjustment and their gender dimensions. The second calls attention to the ineffectiveness of SAPs in the long run. One of the initial critiques of SAPs was published by UNICEF (Cornia et al. 1987). It included empirical studies documenting different aspects of the harder and longer-than-expected social costs of adjustment and argued in favour of an 'adjustment with a human face'. Although it did not underline any specific gender bias, subsequent research showed the extent to which SAPs have not been gender-neutral. Feminist critiques emerged, pointing out ways in which the hardships of adjustment were unequally distributed, displaying not only a bias against specific groups of people – mostly a class bias – but also a gender bias. Empirical research has shown that gender biases are due to several different reasons. First, given the division of labour and women's role in the household economy, austerity programmes and shrinking household budgets intensify women's domestic and reproductive work (Moser 1989; Floro 1995). In this sense, greater efficiency and lower costs of production might in fact represent a transfer of costs from the market to the sphere of the household (Elson 1991). Second, budget cuts in essential services such as health, education and housing tend to affect especially the poor and to increase women's responsibilities in family care (Benería and Feldman 1992; Lind 1992; Barrig 1996). Third, lower real incomes force new household members to participate in the paid labour force – particularly women and the young, given their historically lower participation rates – often under the precarious conditions of the informal sector (Tripp 1992; Moser 1989; Manuh 1994). Fourth, low wages in the export sector, particularly women's wages in labour-intensive industries, is a significant factor in keeping exports competitive (Standing 1989; Çagatay et al. 1995b).

All of this implies that macroeconomic policies are not socially and gender-neutral as normally assumed. As Elson (1991) has argued, apparently neutral concepts such as productivity increases and resource-switching assume that human resources are free and can be 'costlessly transferable between different activities' and that 'households and people will not fall apart under the stress of the decisions that adjustment requires' (p. 168). To be sure, these critiques of SAPs have been subject to debate on the basis that they have been made from case studies that could not be generalized. In addition, the critiques are more conclusive for some countries and regions, such as Latin America, than for others (Sahn et al. 1994; ECLAC 1995). However, the accumulated evidence of many studies makes a strong case for the feminist critiques, which even sceptics have admitted.

In addition to analysing the gender dimensions of the impact, feminists have also emphasized that existing gender inequalities might be an obstacle to efficient allocation of resources and the success of SAPs. For example, empirical work on sub-Saharan Africa has shown that farmers might not respond to policy incentives as a result of constraints set up by the traditional gender division of labour (Palmer 1991; Çagatay et al. 1995b; Elson 1995). Likewise, some of the social investment funds set up in many countries to deal with the most urgent problems of adjustment have missed the opportunity of tapping women's skills and providing sources of livelihood for them due to the dubious assumption that funds going to men will benefit women and their families (Benería and Mendoza 1995).

SAPs have also been critiqued on the basis of their mixed results and impact on sustainability. Structural adjustment has succeeded in solving the debt problem for the international financial community, keeping debt payments flowing. At the country and regional level, however, the debt continues to represent a burden for its citizens (Benería 1996). It has been argued that many countries and regions have moved from a debt crisis to a crisis of development, with low or unstable growth rates and vulnerable economic and social conditions (ECLAC 1995). The Mexican crisis of 1994 typified this problem. Despite several years of optimistic trends in the early 1990s, Mexico had to be rescued again by the international community, with a financial package that surpassed the $50 billion mark, ten times larger than the 1992 package (Benería 1996). Likewise, the 1997 South-East Asian economic crisis raised similar issues, particularly the dependency on unregulated external capital, this time in economies viewed as having provided a successful development model (Bello 1997; Kohr 1998).

Likewise, these critiques point to the precariousness of the economic and social model promoted by SAPs, underlining the growing evidence of economic and social inequalities which feed social tensions and contribute to growing crime rates, urban squalor and environmental degradation. This has led some authors to view these trends as leading to a 'socially unsustainable' development model, not only in countries in which SAPs were originally implemented but also in cases of more recent implementation, such as in Eastern Europe (ECA 1989; ECLAC 1995; Slomczynski and Shabad 1997).

One of the common responses to critiques of SAPs is that there was no alternative given the economic conditions of many countries. Thus, the 1980s and 1990s witnessed a standardization of adjustment policies despite the different conditions prevailing in their economies. The implementation of similar packages in the Eastern European countries since 1989 and in South-East Asia since the outburst of the 1997 crisis illustrates this trend. Hence, for the most part, alternative paths to adjustment were not given an opportunity. In Mexico, for example, the IMF-inspired package adopted in 1982 prevailed over the more structuralist 'managed adjustment' policies promoted by a different team of economists working with the Ministry of Industry (Singh 1991). The alternative package included a series of trade and exchange rate controls, bank nationalization and direct negotiations with international commercial banks; its aim was to deal with the crisis without creating shocks and painful adjustments. It also included the formation of a common front of Latin American countries to negotiate the debt collectively so as to increase their bargaining power (Bener\u00eda 1996). Thus, the historical opportunity to try an alternative path was missed.

An alternative strategy would include policies to induce growth and efficiency as well as equity, including a more equal distribution of the debt burden. In this sense, feminist economics has made an important contribution to a discussion of alternatives, suggesting, for example, how the more prevalent gender analysis at the micro level has macroeconomic implications along the following lines (Bener\u00eda 1995; \u00c7agatay et al. 1995a; Elson 1995).

First, alternative policies should not assume that people have an infinite capacity to bear the costs of adjustment. The literature has illustrated the tremendous endurance of people, but at the high costs of suffering and depletion of human resources. Second, the hidden costs of adjustment should be taken into consideration, including health-related problems, discontinuities in children's schooling due to women's work intensification, infrastructure and ecological deterioration, and increased crime and violence. Third, alternative packages should include two types of policy: short-run compensatory measures to deal with the most urgent needs resulting from SAPs, and longer-term transformative measures – such as distributive policies focusing on property rights and income – generating changes in the division of labour between paid and unpaid work, educational and retraining programmes and productivity increases in agriculture and other sectors. Fourth, there should be a clear recognition of the links between the paid and unpaid sectors of the economy and between productive and reproductive work. This is crucial if we are to view macroeconomic models as a tool to design policies for the provisioning of needs and maximization of social welfare and not just as a way of maximizing efficiency and economic growth. Fifth, gender equality can contribute to achieving macroeconomic objectives. Thus, anti-discriminatory policies might result in a more efficient allocation of resources. For example, given the empirical evidence showing that women's control of income contributes more than men's to household welfare and family nutrition (Dwyer and Bruce 1988; Elson 1991), income schemes addressed to women can meet both efficiency and anti-discriminatory goals.

These contributions of feminist economics have also resulted from an effort at engendering macroeconomics at the conceptual and practical levels (Çagatay et al. 1995a). With an emphasis on understanding gender relations and addressing gender inequalities, different authors have demonstrated the usefulness of such an approach for growth theory, resource allocation and distribution, labour market analysis, public finance, time allocation and policy initiatives, among others. Still at an incipient stage, a similar effort at engendering international trade is also a recent contribution of feminist economics to our understanding of the effects of SAPs (Joekes and Weston 1994). Although originated among gender and development circles, this body of work has wide relevance for feminist economics in general.

LOURDES BENERIA

See also
Development Policies; Development, Theories of; Economic Restructuring; Globalization; Growth Theory (Macro Models); International Economics.

Bibliography
Barrig, Maruja (1996), 'Women's Collective Kitchens and the Crisis of the State in Peru', in J. Friedmann, R. Albers and L. Autler (eds), *Emergences: Women's Struggles for Livelihood in Latin America*, Los Angeles: UCLA Latin American Studies Center, pp. 59–77.

Bello, Walden (1997), 'Addicted to capital. The ten-year high and present day withdrawal frame of South East Asia's economies', University of the Philippines, Center for Political Studies Issues and Letters, 6 (9–10).

Benería, Lourdes (1995), 'Towards a Greater Integration of Gender in Economics', in Çagatay et al. (eds), Special issue on 'Gender, Adjustment and Macroeconomics', *World Development*, 23 (11), pp. 1839–950.

Benería, Lourdes (1996), 'The Legacy of Structural Adjustment in Latin America', in L. Benería and M.J. Dudley (eds), *Economic Restructuring in the Americas*, Ithaca, New York: Latin American Studies Program, Cornell University, pp. 3–30.

Benería, Lourdes and Shelley Feldman (1992), *Unequal Burden; Economic Crises, Persistent Poverty and Women's Work*, Boulder: Westview Press.

Benería, Lourdes and Breny Mendoza (1995), 'Structural adjustment and social investment funds: the case of Honduras, Mexico and Nicaragua', *The European Journal of Development Research*, **7** (1), (June), 53–76.

Çagatay, Nilufer, Caren Grown and Diane Elson (eds) (1995a), Special issue on 'Gender, Adjustment and Macroeconomics', *World Development*, **23** (11).

Çagatay, Nilufer, Caren Grown and Diane Elson (1995b), 'Introduction', Special issue on 'Gender, Adjustment and Macroeconomics', *World Development*, **23** (11), 1827–38.

Cornia, Giovanni, Richard Jolly and Frances Stewart (eds) (1987), *Adjustment with a Human Face*, Vol. 1, New York: UNICEF/Clarendon Press.

Dwyer, Daisy and Judith Bruce (eds) (1988), *A Home Divided: Women and Income in Third World Countries*, Stanford: Stanford University Press.

ECA (Economic Commission for Africa) (1989), *Adjustment with Transformation, ECA/CM 15/6/Rev. 3*, Addis Ababa: United Nations.

ECLAC (Economic Commission for Latin America and the Caribbean) (1990), *Transformación Productiva con Equidad*, Santiago de Chile.

ECLAC (1995), *Social Panorama of Latin America*, Santiago de Chile.

Elson, Diane (1991), *Male Bias in the Development Process*, Manchester: Manchester University Press.

Elson, Diane (1995), 'Gender Awareness in Modeling Structural Adjustment', in Çagatay et al. (eds), Special issue on 'Gender, Adjustment and Macroeconomics', *World Development*, **23** (11), pp. 1851–68.

Floro, M. Sagrario (1995), 'Economic Restructuring, Gender and the Allocation of Time', in Çagatay et al. (eds), Special issue on 'Gender, Adjustment and Macroeconomics', *World Development*, **23** (11), pp. 1913–30.

Joekes, Susan and Ann Weston (1994), *Women and the New Trade Agenda*, New York: UNIFEM.

Kohr, Martin (1998), 'IMF policies in Asia come under fire', *Third World Economics*, No. 176, 1–15 January.

Lind, Amy (1992), 'Power, Gender and Development: Popular Women's Organizations and the Politics of Needs in Ecuador', in Arturo Escobar and Sonia Alvarez (eds), *The Making of Social Movements in Latin America*, Boulder: Westview Press, pp. 134–49.

Manuh, Takyiwaa (1994), 'Ghana: Women in the Public and the Informal Sectors Under the Economic Recovery Programme', in Pamela Sparr (ed.), *Mortgaging Women's Lives. Feminist Critiques of Structural Adjustment*, London: Zed Books, pp. 61–77.

Moser, Caroline (1989), 'The impact of recession and adjustment at the micro level: low income women and their households in Guayaquil, Ecuador', *The Invisible Adjustment: Poor Women and the Economic Crisis*, New York: UNICEF.

Palmer, Ingrid (1991), *Gender and Population in the Adjustment of African Economies: Planning for Change*, Geneva: ILO.

Sahn, David, Paul Rorosh and Stephen Younger (1994), 'Economic Reform in Africa: A Foundation for Poverty Alleviation', Cornell University Food and International Nutrition Program, Working Paper No. 72.

Singh, Ajit (1991), 'Employment and output in a semi-industrial economy: modeling alternative policy options in Mexico', in A. Dutt and K. Jameson (eds), *New Directions in Development Economics*, Aldershot: Edward Elgar.

Slomczynski, Kazimierz and Goldy Shabad (1997), 'Systemic transformation and the salience of class structure in Central Europe', *European Politics and Societies*, **II** (1), (Winter).

Sparr, Pamela (ed.) (1994), *Mortgaging Women's Lives. Feminist Critiques of Structural Adjustment*, London: Zed Books.

Standing, Guy (1989), 'Global feminization through flexible labour', *World Development*, **17** (7), 1077–96.

Taylor, Lance (1988), *Varieties of Stabilization Experience. Towards Sensible Macroeconomics in the Third World*, New York: Clarendon Press. Oxford.

Tripp, Aili Mari (1992), 'The Impact of Crisis and Economic Reform on Women in Urban

Tanzania', in L. Benería and S. Feldman (eds), *Unequal Burden; Economic Crises, Persistent Poverty and Women's Work*, Boulder: Westview Press, pp. 159–80.
UNDP (United Nations Development Programme) (1995), *The Human Development Report*, Oxford University Press.
World Bank, *World Development Report (1992–94)*, Oxford University Press.

Tax Policy

A tax system is defined as 'a set of taxes imposed on several goods' (Bruce 1998, p. 446). Since a government can generate the same amount of tax revenue from a variety of tax systems, economic theory dictates that the system should be both efficient and fair. An efficient tax system is traditionally defined as one that minimizes interference with economic decisions, and thus the allocation of resources, in otherwise efficient markets (for example, markets where the marginal social benefits are just equal to the marginal social costs of production). When economic decision makers (such as consumers, producers or workers) change their behaviour in response to a tax, by, for example, buying less of a taxed product using less of a taxed input, or working fewer hours, the tax is seen to have 'distorted' economic behaviour and consequently the allocation of resources.

A tax system is considered fair if it is horizontally and vertically equitable. Horizontal equity is achieved when individuals of the same economic capacity (for example, the same income) pay the same amount of taxes per year or over a lifetime. Therefore, when two individuals who earn the same income but pay differing amounts of taxes because the sources of the incomes are different, horizontal equity is violated. Vertical equity is achieved when individuals of differing economic ability pay different amounts of taxes, meaning that those with higher incomes should pay more than those with lower incomes. However, the lack of agreement on which taxpaying units are equal and thus deserve equal treatment under the tax code and which are unequal has resulted in much debate on the fairness of tax systems. Another source of contention is how much more in taxes should a unit with higher income pay in comparison to a unit with lower income. That is, should the tax schedule be progressive, meaning that higher-income units face a higher average tax rate than lower-income units and, if so, how progressive should the schedule be.

Feminist economists assert that many aspects of current tax systems are neither equitable or efficient. They challenge the traditional view of horizontal equity, suggesting that tax policy has been strongly influenced by patriarchal interpretations of what constitutes 'equal' and thus what constitutes the proper taxpaying unit (Nelson 1996, p. 97). Because the definition of the proper tax unit was developed during a time when the single-income family with the husband working full time outside the home and the wife working as homemaker dominated, contemporary tax systems severely penalize two-income families and favour the traditional, single-income family. In addition, many economists (feminist and traditional) have been concerned that several aspects of government tax policy distort the labour force participation decision of many women, in effect penalizing women who seek to work outside the home. Since most feminist discussions have focused on income and social security taxes, this entry will examine policies concerning these taxes in the context of the United States.

Income tax policies in the United States were developed when the one-earner family was the norm, resulting in a system biased in favour of this traditional family structure. Between 1913 and 1948, for example, all individuals' taxes were based on the same progressive rate schedule. Because of the income tax's progressivity, a taxpayer had an incentive to transfer some of his income to a spouse with little or no income in order to lower his tax liability. This was allowed only in 'community property' states, however, in which each spouse had a legally defined interest in most income received during a marriage. In 1948, the tax system was changed to allow all married couples the benefits of 'income splitting': married couples could file a joint return in which their combined income would be split in half, with taxes paid on each half regardless of the actual distribution of earnings between the spouses. Though this had very little impact on spouses with similar earnings, it resulted in a substantial 'marriage tax benefit' for those taxpaying units comprised of spouses of unequal earnings, that is the traditional breadwinner–homemaker family which, at the time, comprised the majority of the taxpaying population (O'Neill 1983, p. 3).

As a result, single persons without dependants were paying taxes that were as much as 40 per cent higher than a married couple with the same amount of taxable income filing a joint return (O'Neill 1983, p. 4). In response, Congress enacted a more generous rate schedule for singles designed to ensure payment of no more than 20 per cent of the tax of an equal-income married couple filing jointly. Married couples choosing to file separately could not use the new rates for single taxpayers, however, and were (and still are) subject to a less generous 'married-filing-separately' schedule. As a result, many two-earner couples pay a combined tax that is considerably higher than the taxes paid by two single persons with the same income. It is this feature that is often referred to as the 'marriage tax penalty'.

Feminist economists have argued that the US income tax system favours traditional, patriarchal marriages in which the male is the sole earner and the wife is economically dependent on her husband. One reason for their position stems from the previously mentioned 'marriage tax benefit' vs. 'marriage tax penalty'. When two workers with similar incomes marry, their tax burden increases above what they would pay if they remained single. In contrast, when a single worker marries someone not in the paid labour force, the income tax paid by the worker is lowered because the same income is then taxed at the lower rate for married couples, resulting in a favourable bias towards traditional marriage arrangements. This violates the concept of horizontal equity since a household comprised of two married wage earners with similar earnings pays more in taxes than a one-earner married couple with the same level of total earnings (Rosen 1987; Feenberg and Rosen 1995; Alm and Whittington 1996; McCaffery 1997).

The Economic Recovery Tax Act of 1981 initiated a reform that partially reduced the marriage tax, by allowing married couples to deduct 10 per cent of the earnings of the lower income spouse. The Tax Reform Act of 1986 eliminated this deduction, however, on the theory that the lower marginal tax rates instituted by this law would provide the necessary relief from the marriage penalty. Although this Act lowered the marriage penalty on average, evidence shows that it still exists and is in fact larger for low-income couples (Feenberg and Rosen 1995).

One of the reasons that the marriage penalty is larger for low-income couples is that the government terminates various benefit programmes for lower-income couples, most notably the earned income tax credit, when a couple marries. This particular benefit provides a refundable tax credit equal to a certain percentage of earned income to low-income working families. The amount of the credit is phased out, however, for taxpayers whose adjusted gross income exceeds a certain amount. So, for example, a tax penalty of $727 for a family in which each spouse earns $25 000 becomes a penalty of $3717 for a family in which each spouse earns $10 000, due to the loss of the earned income tax credit (Feenberg and Rosen 1995).

Horizontal equity is further violated by not counting and taxing the value of goods and services produced in the home. A couple comprised of two individuals earning $20 000 each in the market, which is taxed, and producing $10 000 worth of goods and services each in the home, face higher taxes on their $60 000 total income than the couple comprised of one individual earning $30 000 of taxable income in the market and one spouse producing $30 000 worth of goods and services in the home. Though the two couples possess the same level of economic wellbeing – in this example valued at $60 000 – they are not treated equally. It has been argued that the first couple has a higher ability to pay taxes, and thus should face higher taxes. Alternatively, however, if household services are counted as income, the ability to pay of an earner-and-homemaker couple with a given money income will be higher than that of a household in which earning the same money income requires that both adults work outside of the home. The two-earner couple has less time for leisure, and more need for money to pay for market goods to replace home production (Nelson 1996, p. 104).

Research shows that the marriage tax does distort individuals' behaviour and thus violate economic efficiency. One study found that the marriage tax penalty reduced the probability of marriage by unmarried taxpaying women and increased the probability of divorces by married taxpaying women (Alm and Whittington 1995). Another study found no effect on the marriage rate, but found that the tax did affect the timing of marriage. Specifically, taxpayers contemplating marriage were likely to postpone marriage from the last few months of a year to the beginning months of the following year (Sjoquist and Walker 1995).

Income tax policy can distort a married woman's labour force participation decision, another breach of economic efficiency. Since market work is taxed and home production is not, it creates a disincentive for married women to participate in the labour force. This disincentive is further promoted by the progressivity of the tax system. Joint tax filing by married couples in the progressive tax system results in the lower-earning spouse, who usually is the wife, facing a higher marginal tax rate on her first dollar earned than she would have as an individual and than her husband. In fact, the tax rate would depend on the level of her spouse's earnings (McCaffery 1997, p. 20; O'Neill 1983, p. 3). Married women have more elastic labour supply schedules than their husbands, meaning that they are more responsive to wage changes (Atkinson 1995). In light of this evidence, efficiency requires taxing wives at a *lower* rate compared to their husbands.

An additional disincentive is created by the inadequacy of deductions for child care and other work-related expenses, estimated to be up to 68 per cent of the second income of middle- and upper-income two-earner couples (Hanson and Ooms 1991). When the secondary wage earning wife enters the workforce, she not only pays a higher percentage of her income to taxes, she must also pay for those costs resulting from her decision to work outside the home, the most significant being child care. Theoretically, the costs of earning income should be deducted from total income in order to arrive at taxable income. However, because of the difficulty of determining which expenses are legitimate costs of earning income as opposed to consumption items, the lump-sum deduction is available for all taxpayers. The problem is that this deduction exhibits a marriage penalty: in 1996 in the USA, for example, the standard deduction for single taxpayers was $4000, but only $6700 for married couples filing jointly. The child care tax credit in particular is woefully lacking for most families, and even non-existent for most low-income families since it is nonrefundable, meaning that they benefit only if they pay a positive income tax, which is not the case for many due to the earned income tax credit.

Lower-earning spouses face further inequities and distortions in the US Social Security system. 'Social security' is generally defined as a system for partially replacing earnings when a worker retires or dies. In the USA, social security is provided through the Old Age, Survivor's and Disability Insurance (OASDI) programme, which is financed by a payroll tax with a regressive structure, meaning lower-income workers pay a higher average rate than higher-income workers do (Committee on Ways and Means 1993,

p. 79). The system's regressivity, combined with the lack of deductions for spouses or dependants, penalizes the second earner in a married couple. In addition, equal contributions into the system do not result in equal benefits for all individuals or families. A one-earner couple pays taxes on the earner's wages, and receives his or her benefits plus an additional 50 per cent for a dependent spouse. For a two-earner couple, the second earner can receive the greater of her own contributions' worth of benefits or half of her spouse's benefits. If this second earner receives more benefits from half of her spouse's benefits, she is paying the full amount of taxes on her earnings and yet not receiving the benefit. The rate of return on taxes paid by the one-earner family is therefore higher, resulting in a subsidy to the 'traditional' family in which the wife is a dependant (O'Neill 1983, p. 15). Thus current social security policy is likely to be a deterrent to labour force participation among wives, for they get little or no return on their required payroll taxes.

Feminist proposals for reform of tax policy in the United States have addressed both equity and efficiency issues. Feminist proposals for income tax reform, for example, suggest that the tax system should be marriage neutral, meaning that two individuals' tax burdens should not change when they marry. This would be achieved if each person were taxed as individuals so as to eliminate both the work incentive and the marriage penalty. Under separate filing, married women who work outside the home would face an initial zero bracket, just as their husbands do (McCaffery 1997, p. 278).

Taxing household production is another alternative to the current tax system. Besides promoting horizontal equity between households of equal economic wellbeing, it would recognize the economic value of housework. This has received little serious attention, however, primarily due to the difficulties of obtaining reliable, acceptable estimates of the value of housework. In addition, feminists are split on whether formally valuing housework and thus encouraging domesticity of women is desired (Blau et al. 1998, p. 61).

Feminist economists have also argued that larger child-care deductions would allow more wives to consider working and would increase the funds available for child care. In addition, a secondary-earner deduction would help meet the added costs of commuting, clothing, meals and other work-related costs that result from having two earners in a family (McCaffery 1997).

'Earnings sharing' has been proposed as a method of promoting equity and efficiency in the US Social Security system (Steurle and Bakija 1994). Under this proposal, an equal share of total household earnings is assigned to each spouse, and each partner would receive a benefit based on half the couple's combined earnings. The spousal benefits of the current system would disappear, eliminating the advantage of one-earner families, and would thus be more supportive of labour force participation than the current system. The proposed system would move in the direction of greater horizontal equity, in that equal contributions yield equal benefits. A further advantage is that this proposal recognizes the contribution of market and nonmarket production to family welfare.

Feminist economists conclude that the current tax system which promotes male individualism and female subservience needs to be reformed. Nelson (1996, p. 108) advocates taxing all able-bodied earners individually and allowing larger exemptions for true dependants, those unable to support themselves because they are too young, too old, or chronically disabled and who rely on the earner for their economic support. The nonearning adult is not treated as a dependant, but would not file taxes either. This system is marriage neutral, eliminates the work disincentives for second earners, and implicitly takes into account household production by disallowing an exemption for the full-time homemaker. As Nelson argues, 'able-bodied adults are never engulfed, in this definition: even if they are nonearners, their productive capacity is recognized and they are never considered as dependents' (Nelson 1996, p. 110).

In further research, feminist economists need to study the relationships between tax policies and outcomes important to women, including but not limited to women's labour force participation decision, whether it is part time or full time, second-shift work or contingent employment. Other outcomes include the effect on bargaining power within a marriage, fertility, divorce and the overall economic status of women. In addition, feminist economists in the USA might study the experience of other countries that already have some form of individual-plus-dependants taxation and separate filing, particularly as more thought and analysis is given to the issue of which relationships should be considered important for tax purposes (Nelson 1996, p. 108). Tax and social security policies on property income, parental leave, child allowances, a family wage, support for dependant care and fringe benefits should also be evaluated in light of their expected outcomes and the underlying assumptions about relationships. Finally, feminist analysis of other tax policies such as the value added tax, wealth taxes, excise taxes and the earned income tax credit is encouraged.

DONNA M. ANDERSON

See also

Family Wage; Income Support and Transfer Policy; Labour Force Participation; Pensions and Old Age Retirement; Public Sector Economics/Public Finance.

Bibliography

Alm, James and Leslie A. Whittington (1995), 'Does the income tax affect marriage decisions?', *National Tax Journal*, **48**, 565–92.

Alm, James and Leslie A. Whittington (1996), 'The rise and fall and rise ... of the marriage tax', *National Tax Journal*, **44**, 571–89.

Atkinson, Anthony B. (1995), *Public Economics in Action: The Basic Income/Flat Tax Proposal*, Oxford: Clarendon Press.

Blau, Francine D., Marianne A. Ferber and Anne E. Winkler (1998), *The Economics of Women, Men, and Work*, Upper Saddle River, New Jersey: Prentice-Hall, Inc.

Bruce, Neil (1998), *Public Finance and the American Economy*, New York: Addison-Wesley Educational Publishers, Inc.

Committee on Ways and Means (1993), *Overview of Entitlement Programs: 1993 Green Book*, Washington, DC: US Government Printing Office, p. 79.

Feenberg, Daniel R. and Harvey S. Rosen (1995), 'Recent developments in the marriage tax', *National Tax Journal*, **48** (1), 91–101.

Hanson, Sandra L. and Theodore Ooms (1991), 'The economics costs and rewards of two-earner, two-parent families', *Journal of Marriage and the Family*, **53**, 622–34.

Leader, Shelah Gilbert (1983), 'Fiscal Policy and Family Structure', in Irene Diamond (ed.), *Families, Politics and Public Policy: A Feminist Dialogue on Women and the State*, New York: Longman, pp. 139–47.

McCaffery, Edward J. (1997), *Taxing Women*, Chicago: Chicago Press.

Nelson, Julie A. (1991), 'Tax reform and feminist theory in the USA: incorporating human connection', *Journal of Economic Studies*, **18** (5/6), 11–29.

Nelson, Julie A. (1996), *Feminism, Objectivity and Economics*, New York: Routledge.

O'Neill, June (1983), 'Family Issues in Taxation', in Rudolph G. Penner (ed.), *Taxing the Family*, Washington, DC: American Enterprise Institute for Public Policy Research, pp. 1–22.

Pechman, Joseph A. and Gary V. Engelhardt (1990), 'The income tax treatment of the family: an international perspective', *National Tax Journal*, **43** (1), 1–22.

Rosen, Harvey S. (1987), 'The marriage penalty is down but not out', *National Tax Journal*, **40** (1), 567–75.

Sjoquist, David L. and Mary Beth Walker (1995), 'The marriage tax and the rate and timing of marriage', *National Tax Journal*, **48**, 547–58.

Steurle, Eugene C. and Jon M. Bakija (1994), *Retooling Social Security for the 21st Century*, Washington, DC: Urban Institute Press.

Technological Change

Technological change emerged as a field of study in economics in the context of post-World War II research on economic growth and development. According to the neoclassical tradition, the sources of economic growth were considered to be population growth and thrift, the former providing labour, the latter being the source of capital investment. Increasing labour and capital inputs were considered necessary to increase production. However, several studies beginning in the 1950s rejected the traditional explanations of economic growth by showing that growth of the US economy was due mostly to increased efficiency rather than increased quantity of inputs (Abramovitz 1956; Solow 1957; Kendrick 1973). This became known as the residual hypothesis, the residual being the increase in output not attributable to an increase in inputs and interpreted as a measure of technological change (Metcalfe 1987).

While economic growth at the national level is generally measured by changes in gross domestic product (GDP), the total factor productivity (TFP) measurement may be used in order to compensate for the growth in inputs and to provide an estimate of the output gains from changes in efficiency and technological change. TFP is the ratio of an index of aggregate output to an index of aggregate inputs. There are three approaches to measuring TFP: index numbers or growth accounting (Diewert 1981), econometric (Capalbo and Antle 1988) and non-parametric (Chavas and Cox 1992).

Postwar research on TFP focused attention on the economic impacts of technological change, and since then researchers have investigated three general areas: innovation and invention, diffusion and measurement of technological change (Metcalfe 1987). Research on invention and innovation examines the forces that cause products and processes to be developed and applied (Binswanger and Ruttan 1978). Research on diffusion of technology examines the cumulative adoption rate, the pace of adoption, and what characteristics of the firm and the decision maker influence technology adoption (Griliches 1957; Rogers and Stanfield 1968; Feder et al. 1985). The subfield of measurement and explanation of technological change has focused on separating growth in inputs versus growth in efficiency as sources of output growth (Capalbo and Antle 1988).

Within the subfield of measurement, researchers determine the best methods to measure aggregate outputs and inputs, and what factors are driving the 'residual', that is, what is driving the growth in efficiency and technical change. Factors conventional economists have looked at include: human capital formation, policy changes, R&D, and so on (Nelson and Phelps 1966; Feder et al. 1985). Thus, the debate in determining what is the rate of technological change (and what is driving it) hinges on measurement issues. What is counted and how it is valued determines what the measure of economic growth is, and hence what TFP is, and what is 'left over' is attributed to technological change and efficiency gains. So whether women's contribution to technological change is recognized depends on whether their work is counted and how it is valued.

The focus of traditional research on technological change has been on developed countries. However, feminist economic critiques of technological change and the way it is studied came from studies of developing countries, especially when it became apparent that development policies were failing as a result of policymakers not recognizing the role women played in these economies. The feminist critique of the field of technological change originates in a critique of both national accounts and TFP, which fail to take into account many unpaid, primarily female activities. It is only recently and only among a very limited number of developed countries where household production and unpaid labour have been recognized in adjusting government accounts. Researchers estimate that if this were applied to all government accounts, such activities would augment most countries GDP by about 25–30 per cent (UN 1991). However, in most cases, the contribution of women's unpaid work continues to go unrecognized in measuring technological change.

Problems arise when women's work, their knowledge and their output is not seen, counted or recognized, or when it is attributed to men. For example, when comparing productivity measures in agriculture, many studies use output per male worker. Since women provide much of the labour in agriculture (75 per cent in Africa), and the variation between countries is quite high (UN 1991), this is not a meaningful measure of productivity. Hence, comparisons over time which attempt to capture technological change are also not meaningful.

Recognized problems exist in counting women's outputs and inputs. For example, in agriculture, women tend to grow traditional crops or crops for household consumption. Women also tend to be involved in the informal sector, through such activities as barter, petty sales, domestic work and piecework. National statistics on both home production and the informal sector are notoriously poor and most countries do not include them in their statistics (Hedman et al. 1996). In addition, women's contribution to household welfare (child and elderly care, housework, cooking) is simply not counted, except for attempts in a few developed countries. In industrialized countries, between 30 to 60 per cent of GNP has gone unaccounted by failing to take into account women's unpaid work (Castles 1990), and the percentages are probably higher in less industrialized countries. On the input side, women's labour in agriculture and self-employment is rarely counted because most of this work is unpaid (Hedman et al. 1996). Thus, TFP measures and technical change measures derived from them typically omit much of the contribution of women. Thus a resulting debate is whether apparent growth in GDP (and hence TFP and technical change) is merely the monetarization of women's unpaid activities, as more women work for wages and must now purchase goods and services which previously were produced at home, and hence not counted (Harvey 1996; Ironmonger 1985).

A conventional policy application of the measurement of technological change which is linked to the subfields of innovation and adoption is to explore biases in technological change, for example, whether technologies have been saving or using in land, capital or labour (Binswanger and Ruttan 1978). The neoclassical assumption is that technological innovation and adoption, and hence the rate of technological change, has been driven by relative prices. Thus, policymakers devise policies to bring about technological change by subsidizing particular factors of production, such as subsidized credit or tax policies in agriculture to encourage investment in capital and to free up labour for off-farm employment. However, since labour inputs in agriculture, particularly those of women, are often poorly counted, there is some question as to how reliable estimates of such factor biases have been.

Given the conventional view within the subfield of innovation that relative prices are the underlying force for technological development, much of the mainstream literature has examined how labour saving technology has been developed in response to high labour costs (Binswanger and Ruttan 1978). However, since unpaid, largely female, labour is not counted, feminists have questioned whether technologies that have been developed are truly labour saving of both paid and unpaid labour, are useful for women, and are developed and extended in such a way that women can use them (IFAD/FAO/FARMESA 1998; Rowbotham 1995). This omission of women in technology policy assessment creates further problems for women. Examples include the introduction of motorized rice hullers in Java, where 1.2 million landless women employed in hand pounding of rice were thrown out of work (FAO 1996), while oil extraction and fish processing technologies in Africa (Martinson 1992) and milking technology in Chile (FAO 1991) displaced female labour with higher paid male labour. Had the gender division of labour and wage differentials been taken into account, it is unlikely that these technologies would have appeared economically attractive enough to be developed or implemented.

Feminists have also questioned the degree to which cultural values are embedded in technological innovation, challenging the assumption that science and innovation are neutral, inevitable forces, with automatic benefits (Saito et al. 1994). These feminists have sought to challenge both technological determinism as well as cultural stereotypes of male and female identity (Rowbotham 1995). As an example, a study of tools and implements in Africa found that very little research had been done to develop tools appropriate for women, who did most of the agricultural labour. The researchers attributed this lack of interest in the needs of women to a variety of cultural perceptions. For example, commercial manufacturers did not perceive that women did agricultural work; local blacksmiths did not perceive that women bought tools; and it was generally held that anything that made women's jobs easier contributed to their 'laziness' (IFAD/FAO/FARMESA 1998).

An alternative feminist perspective of innovation is whether women do science differently than men and whether they would or do develop technology that is different from men's. Historical studies of innovation reveal that women have had a greater role in technology development and thought than is generally acknowledged (Rowbotham 1995). The invisibility of women's contributions to technology innovation can be attributed to a failure to measure and count women's unpaid work, as well as the perception that such work is not 'technical' because technology is regarded as being high-cost and hardware based, rather than knowledge or skill based (Appleton 1995). In 22 case studies of technical innovations by women from 16 developing countries, it is demonstrated that women's work is highly technical, that the technological needs and priorities of women are indeed different from men's, and that women utilize different channels to communicate technical information and skills (Appleton 1995).

Research within the subfield of the diffusion of technology examines how individuals or firms adopt technology and how their characteristics influence technology adoption (Griliches 1957; Rogers and Stanfield 1968; Feder et al. 1985). In the conventional technology adoption model, the unit of analysis is generally the firm, not the household, with the male head of household assumed to be the sole decision maker in the case of family businesses. Technology itself is viewed as predetermined, always beneficial and with eventual adoption (Griliches 1957). Conventional research has focused on determining which characteristics of the decision maker make him more likely to adopt a technology and what is the trajectory of cumulative adoption (Rogers and Stanfield 1968; Feder et al. 1985). A common factor examined in these technology adoption models is human capital (Nelson and Phelps 1996).

The assumptions of these conventional adoption models are not borne out when individuals themselves are asked how decisions are made; women are indeed decision makers. For example, farm men and women indicate that technology and other long-term decisions are largely joint decisions, with individuals making decisions over day to day aspects of processes to which they respectively contribute labour (Zepeda et al. 1997; Saito et al. 1994). Empirical testing rejects the conventional technology adoption model utilized since Griliches (1957), as well as a unitary household model of adoption, and indicates that a bargaining framework better fits the technology choice decision (Zepeda and Castillo 1997). The implication is that conclusions drawn from the conventional technology adoption model about the trajectory of adoption and the factors influencing adoption are misleading because the underlying theory and assumptions cannot be supported. In other words, technology decisions need to be modelled as joint or household decisions.

Feminists have also questioned women's access to technology (Martinson 1992; Saito et al. 1994). Some feminists see women as excluded from technology development and transfer, and seek to improve women's access (Martinson 1992; Saito et al. 1994). They argue that technology may be directed towards men, bypass women or displace women (Boserup 1970; Standing 1992). As an example of how the introduction of technology can worsen the economic situation of women, mechanization of irrigation replaced female with male labour, displacing, in Bangladesh alone, between 3.5 and 5 million days of labour per year (FAO 1996).

Feminists have identified six factors that differentiate men's and women's technology adoption preferences and patterns (Martinson 1992). The first three represent gendered cultural norms. First, there is the gender division of labour; women often have specific, culturally defined roles. Additionally, women often experience severe time constraints due to culturally defined household duties and often there are cultural restrictions on using machinery (or animal traction, IFAD/FAO/FARMESA 1998), which could enhance women's productivity. The fourth and fifth factor represent differential access to institutions. Women also often have limited access to cash or credit to purchase technology and may have no collateral because land is legally or traditionally held by men. Women have limited education and training opportunities, particularly in Africa. This is particularly important because human capital has repeatedly been found to be a limiting factor to adoption and implementation of technology (Nelson and Phelps 1966; Rogers and Stanfield 1968). Finally, technology affects income and, hence, power and gender relations. New technology is often linked to increased profits or cash crops and undermines women's traditional roles in production and processing. As a study in Africa concluded, 'For a man, a crop means income. For a woman, a crop means food. Whenever cash is involved, men also become involved' (IFAD/FAO/FARMESA 1998, p. 64).

To summarize, feminist economic thought offers much to improve the accuracy of measurement of technological change, and to expand the understanding of the processes of innovation and adoption. Researchers who focus on monetary transactions cannot accurately measure economic growth or, consequently, TFP or technological change because they ignore many of the roles played by women. In addition, while measurement recommendations exist, they need to be more widely implemented (Castles 1990; Hedman et al. 1996, Harvey 1996; Ironmonger 1985; UN 1991). As feminist scholars and policymakers examining the development and transfer of technology have argued, researchers need to recognize women's work as technical (Rowbotham 1995), recognize technological innovations by women (Appleton 1995), as well as develop and transfer technology in ways that meets women's needs (IFAD/FAO/FARMESA 1998; Martinson 1992, Saito et al. 1994; Standing 1992). Finally, in developing theory and modelling technology decisions, researchers need to incorporate women's role in the choice process (Zepeda and Castillo 1997; Zepeda et al. 1997).

The issues of theory and data offer further challenges to feminist economists working in the field of technological change. Researchers are beginning to modify existing or develop new recommendations and theory regarding the innovation, diffusion and measurement of technological change. Continued research is needed to develop economic theory that permits multiple decision makers with different preferences. Additionally, economic theory must account for the effects of cultural norms and existing political and economic institutions if technological change is to be fully understood and policies promoting this change are to be effective. Work is also needed to examine whether development of technology for activities largely performed by women can best be explained in the context of existing economic models of innovation, or whether new theory is needed to explain how women innovate.

Although much theoretical work remains to be done, without data empirical testing is impossible. Data is perhaps the keystone to advances in a feminist approach to technological change. Topics which require such data include the development of 'real' measures of economic growth and technological change which include women's inputs and outputs in determining measures of productivity. Would estimated technological change biases be different if women's contribution were counted? How different would international comparisons and comparisons over time appear with such data? What implications would this have for policy, particularly R&D expenditures, education and extension? Finally, these data questions may lead feminist economists to question not only what drives technological change but also the very definition of economic growth itself.

LYDIA ZEPEDA

See also

Agriculture (Third World); Economic Growth (Macro Models); Gross Domestic Product.

Bibliography

Abramovitz, M. (1956), 'Resource and output trends in the United States since 1870', *American Economic Review, Papers and Proceedings*, **46**, (May), 5–23.
Appleton, H. (ed.) (1995), *Do It Herself: Women and Technical Innovation*, London: Intermediate Technology Publications.
Binswanger, H.P. and V.W. Ruttan (1978), *Induced Innovation: Technology, Institutions and Development*, Baltimore: Johns Hopkins University Press.
Boserup, E. (1970), *Women's Role in Economic Development*, London: George, Allen and Unwin.
Capalbo, S.M. and J.M. Antle (eds) (1988), *Agricultural Productivity: Measurement and Explanation*, Washington, DC: Resources for the Future.
Castles, I. (1990), *Measuring Unpaid Household Work: Issues and Experimental Estimates*, Information Paper no. 5236.0, Sydney: Australian Bureau of Statistics.
Chavas, J.-P. and T. Cox (1992), 'A nonparametric analysis of the influence of research on agricultural productivity', *American Journal of Agricultural Economics*, **74**, 583–91.
Diewert, W.E. (1981), 'The Economic Theory of Index Numbers: A Survey', in A. Deaton, (ed.), *Essays in the Theory and Measurement of Consumer Behaviour in Honour of Sir Richard Stone*, London: Cambridge University Press.
FAO (1991), *The Impact of Technology on the Productive Activities of Women in Latin America and the Caribbean*, Rome: Food and Agricultural Organization, Women in Agricultural Production and Rural Development Service.
FAO (1996), *Women: the Key to Food Security*, Rome: Food and Agricultural Organization, Women and Population Division.
Feder, G., R.E. Just and D. Zilberman (1985), 'Adoption of agricultural innovations in developing countries: a survey', *Economic Development and Cultural Change*, **55**, 255–98.
Griliches, Z. (1957), 'Hybrid corn: an exploration in the economics of technological change', *Econometrica*, **25**, 501–22.
Harvey, A.S. (1996), 'The measurement of household time allocation: data needs, analytical

approaches, and standardization', *Journal of Family and Economic Issues*, **17**, (Winter), 261–80.

Hedman, B., F. Perucci and P. Sundstrom (1996), *Engendering Statistics: A Tool for Change*, Stockholm: Statistics Sweden.

IFAD/FAO/FARMESA (1998), *The Potential for Improving Production Tools and Implements Used by Women Farmers in Africa*, Rome: International Fund for Agricultural Development, Food and Agriculture Organization, and Farm Level Research Methods in Eastern and Southern Africa.

Ironmonger, D. (1985), *Household Work: Productive Activities, Women and Income in Household Economy*, Sydney: Allen and Unwin.

Kendrick, J. (1973), *Postwar Productivity Trends in the United States, 1948–1969*, New York: National Bureau of Economic Research.

Martinson, V.A. (1992), 'Constraints to Adoption of New Technologies by Women in Developing Countries', FAO Research Development Centre, Working paper series (no. 12), Rome: FAO.

Metcalfe, S. (1987), 'Technical Change', in J. Eatwell, M. Milgate and P. Newman, (eds), *The New Palgrave Dictionary of Economics*, **4**, New York: Stockson Press.

Nelson, R.R. and E.S. Phelps (1966), 'Investment in humans, technological diffusion, and economic growth', *American Economic Review*, **56**, 69–82.

Rogers, E. and J.D. Stanfield (1968), 'Adoption and Diffusion of New Products: Emerging Generalizations and Hypotheses', in F.M. Bass et al. (eds), *Application of the Sciences in Marketing Management*, New York: Wiley and Sons.

Rowbotham, S. (1995), 'Feminist Approaches to Technology: Women's Values or a Gender Lens?', in S. Mitter and S. Rowbotham, (eds), *Women Encounter Technology: Changing Patterns of Employment in the Third World*, London: Routledge.

Saito, K., H. Mekonnen and D. Spurling (1994), *Raising the Productivity of Women Farmers in Sub-Saharan Africa*, World Bank Discussion Paper 230, Washington DC: The World Bank.

Solow, R. (1957), 'Technical change and the aggregate production function', *Review of Economics and Statistics*, **39** (August), 312–20.

Standing, H. (1992), 'Employment', in L. Ostergaard, (ed.), *Gender and Development: A Practical Guide*, London: Routledge.

UN (1991), *The World's Women: Trends and Statistics, 1970–1990*, New York: United Nations.

Zepeda, L. and M. Castillo (1997), 'The role of husbands and wives in farm technology choice', *American Journal of Agricultural Economics*, **79**, 583–8.

Zepeda, L., M. Goodale, C. Lay, K. McSweeney and D. Undersander (1997), 'The results of four Wisconsin focus groups: the role of husbands and wives in farm decisions', *Review of Agricultural Economics*, **19**, 291–307.

Unemployment and Underemployment

Unemployment and underemployment rates are important barometers of the state of the macroeconomy and the human condition. The unemployment rate indicates economic hardship because it shows the extent to which individuals are not working and, thus, not earning income. But the consequences of unemployment are far more extensive. As Sen (1997, p. 169) points out, 'The penalties of unemployment include not only income loss, but also far-reaching effects on self-confidence, work motivation, basic competence, social integration, racial harmony, gender justice, and the appreciation and use of individual freedom and responsibility'. He goes on to list ten 'diverse penalties of massive unemployment' that economists, including feminist economists, have discussed. These penalties are loss of current output and fiscal burdens, loss of freedom and social exclusion (job-related insurance, pension entitlements, social activities), skill loss, psychological harm (shown to be particularly severe for young women), ill health and mortality, motivation loss and resignation (also severe for young women), loss of human relations and family life, racial and gender inequality, loss of social values and responsibility, and organization inflexibility and technical conservatism (caused by fear of unemployment) (Sen 1997, pp. 161–4).

International comparisons of unemployment rates reflect differences in countries' use of human resources in production, their economic performance, and the economic wellbeing of their populations. Changes in countries' unemployment rates reflect the business cycle, that is, the overall fluctuations in the rate at which the economy produces goods and services. The unemployment rate is countercyclical, so that when the economy is operating at full capacity at 'peaks' in the business cycle, the unemployment rate is low. At the cycle's 'trough' the unemployment rate is high.

The measurement of unemployment is well-defined. The Bureau of Labor Statistics (BLS) in the USA, for example, states that one is unemployed if jobless during the survey week, available for work and actively looking for work during the previous four weeks. Different countries use alternative measures of unemployment. To account for such measurement differences, international publications, such as *Main Economic Indicators* (1997), published by the Organisation for Economic Cooperation and Development (OECD), and Yearbook of Labour Statistics (1997) from the International Labour Office (ILO), use a definition of unemployment that conforms to the ILO guidelines. The resulting unemployment rates show the number of unemployed as a percentage of the labour force and are consistent with the BLS definition for the USA.

Though it provides one measure of the state of the economy, the unemployment rate is not adequate as a broad measure of the underutilization of labour. It obscures the problems of discouraged workers, involuntary part-time workers and others whose skills are not being used efficiently. Measures of underemployment capture these other groups. Underemployment has no single definition or measurement method and has been used in different ways by economists as compared to sociologists, anthropologists, management researchers and psychologists. Economists are usually interested in measuring economic hardship, sociologists in social or socioeconomic distress, and management researchers in the connection between job satisfaction and performance. Feminist writings have incorporated all of these approaches, although the definitions of underemployment have not been constructed by feminist researchers. The economics definition, as explained by Feldman (1996) for US underemployment measures, relates the actual job requirements to the efficient use of labour. He identifies five job characteristics that imply underemployment: formal education beyond the job requirements, involuntary employment outside one's own area of formal education for employment, higher level work skills and more work experience than the job requires, involuntary part-time, temporary, or intermittent employment, and a wage 20 per cent or more below the previous job (or for a new entrant, below the average of similarly educated new entrants). The last is often omitted in economic studies, since economists tend to use BLS data which does not include detailed wages.

The sociology tradition uses the Labour Utilization Framework (LUF) developed by Hauser (1974) and refined by Clogg and Sullivan (1983), a framework which has been particularly useful in studies of feminist concern. The objective is to measure those 'not adequately employed' based on information from the US Current Population Survey (CPS). The underemployed include the sub-unemployed (discouraged workers, those who have given up searching for a job), the unemployed (as defined by the BLS), the underemployed by virtue of working low hours, the underemployed by low income (based on government definitions of poverty), and the underemployed by mismatch of education or skills. A residual category, the difference between total labour force and the five above categories, is defined as 'adequately employed'. A major point of difference between the two concepts is whether unemployment is a component of underemployment, as in the work of Hauser (1974) and Clogg and Sullivan (1983), or is a separate category as in the economics tradition.

The relationship between unemployment and underemployment is a complex one; looking solely at unemployment may obscure the extent of economic hardship which stems from underemployment. It is very important to recognize that a person can be fully employed working long hours and yet be underemployed. This distinction is particularly critical in studies of gender and employment in developing countries (roughly, those defined by the World

Bank (1997) as 'low income countries' with per capita GNP of $730 or below in 1995), newly-industrialized countries or NICs (such as Taiwan, Korea, Singapore and Hong Kong) and transitional economies of the former Soviet Union. In such economies the sexual division of labour has been found to be particularly significant in placing limits on the types of work women can do, thus contributing to underemployment (Mohiuddin 1997). Also, in her work on women and development, Boserup (1990) explains that both ownership and training in technology are often focused on men so that economic development creates a widening gap between the training levels or 'credentials' of men and women. Women's unemployment rates might be low while the underemployment of women is high because of lack of adequate access to capital in the forms of education, machines, and land.

Economic works on gender/racial differences and unemployment/underemployment

Feminist scholars, both economists and other social scientists, have been concerned with the unemployment/underemployment issues described by Sen (1997). These concerns are evident in studies of developing countries, transitional economies, comparisons of women's conditions in urban and rural settings and in formal and informal sectors. The informal sector, as defined by Ward and Pyle (1995), consists of unregulated waged labour (for example, transnational companies subcontracting piecework into the home) and/or self-employed labour. Feminist scholars' efforts to identify and understand underemployment are warranted, since the incidence of underemployment is higher for women than men (De Anda 1994; Tipps and Gordon (1985). For example, Tipps and Gordon find that women in the USA are more likely to experience reduced hours through involuntary part-time work, the percentage of workers with marginal jobs (skills mismatch) is highest for women, and the highest rates of underemployment through low pay are for women. Others have reported that the rate of discouraged workers is higher among women than men (Lichter 1989), though more recently the rate is reported to be about the same between men and women (Blau et al. 1998, p. 251).

A typical approach to unemployment research by feminist and other economists is to make demographic comparisons of unemployment rates, since these are readily available. Much of this research covers the USA in the 1970s and early 1980s. Blau et al. (1998, pp. 243–54) include a review of research on gender and unemployment. Among the findings they report are, first, that the gender unemployment rate differential has essentially disappeared in the USA since the 1970s and early 1980s when women's unemployment rate was higher than men's, especially in business cycle peaks. Second, the rate of discouraged workers has decreased, due in part to a change in the measurement method in 1994, and has fallen more for women than for men. Third, they cite data showing that a larger proportion of women than men are employed part time for economic reasons, one component of underemployment.

Other unemployment rate research has focused on race and location differentials. Badgett (1994) finds that black workers' addition to unemployment increased from 1970 to 1990 and employment opportunities declined while the unemployment situation of white women improved. De Anda (1994), applying the LUF methodology and studying men and women of Mexican origin in the USA (those identified by sample respondents as Mexican-Americans, Mexicano or Chicano), finds that Mexican women are more disadvantaged in the US workforce than their male counterparts. Rural–urban comparisons have also been drawn. Lichter (1989) points out that the available supply of low-wage and low-skill female labour has attracted certain industries in the rural USA, which perpetuates the under-utilization of rural women's labour resources.

The unemployment patterns of women over recessions in four countries – the USA, UK, France and Italy – are analysed and methodological issues are explored in Rubery (1988). The neoclassical theory of a competitive homogeneous labour market is rejected by the authors in Rubery in favour of a labour market segmentation approach. The perspective of the authors is that fundamental social and industrial organization and historical forces create the conditions for country differences in women's employment and unemployment; labour force gender differences are more than deviations from an otherwise neoclassical world. At the same time, some common trends in the countries towards industry deregulation, higher job qualifications of women and larger labour market participation of women are found.

Studies of US unemployment rate behaviour in the 1970s and early 1980s find that the women's unemployment rate tended to be higher than the men's, with this unemployment gap larger in expansions. A major explanation of the higher women's rate is the lower labour force attachment of women than men (Blau et al. 1998). Lower labour force attachment resulted in more frequent exits and entries to the labour force; this had a number of consequences. Frequent reentry was associated with higher unemployment levels as women spent more time seeking jobs. Also lower job tenure resulted in lower acquisition of skills, while absences from the labour force implied depreciation of skills. Intermittent employment reduced women's experience and wages and thus contributed to both unemployment and underemployment. Feldman (1996) adds that women may have been more willing than men to settle for lower wages and low-skill jobs that would enable them to meet the expectations of both career and family responsibilities. Thus women's lower attachment to the labour force and their more frequent reentry (or higher turnover) required that they spend more time searching for jobs, increasing women's unemployment rates. Discrimination is also mentioned as a potential problem for women (DeBoer and Seeborg 1989).

The fact that the women's unemployment rate rises in recessions has also been explained by the 'buffer hypothesis'. Humphries (1988) describes this hypothesis, which is that women are the last hired in expansions and the first to be fired in recessions. One explanation is job search theory which states that women's labour force attachment, thus job tenure and skill levels, are lower than men's, therefore women are most likely to be let go in recessions. Also, if women leave the labour market more frequently than men, women might be more likely to reenter the job market in recessions when job searches are protracted. A further explanation of the buffer hypothesis is the Marxist theory of a reserve army of unemployed, in this case consisting of women (Miller 1990). The buffer hypothesis predicts more pronounced business cycle behaviour of women's unemployment rates than men's, which is not the US historical experience. Offsetting the volatility of women's rates is the fact that many women become discouraged and drop out of the labour force in recessions, thus increasing their underemployment rather than the measured unemployment rate.

The employment gap in the USA narrowed and became more complex during the 1980s, with the 1982 recession the first time in the postwar period that the women's overall unemployment rate dropped below the men's. This pattern, roughly equal unemployment rates with men's rates rising above women's in recessions, has persisted through the 1990s. Economists have proposed various explanations for the post-1982 narrowing of the unemployment gap between male and female rates. Two explanations are offered by DeBoer and Seeborg (1989). The first cites a convergence of participation patterns, that is, the increasing labour force attachment of women and the decreasing attachment of men. Their second explanation, accounting for about half of the effect, is that the secular decline of male-dominated industries and the increase in service-oriented industries, which employ relatively more women, have been relevant to the secular tendency for the gap to narrow. Blau et al. (1998) add that with the advent of the 'baby bust', there are fewer new entrants to the labour market competing with women for entry level jobs, thus lowering their unemployment.

Why does the men's rate rise above the women's in recessions? Two explanations offered are the 'substitution hypothesis' whereby employers substitute cheaper women workers for men in recessions and the 'segmentation hypothesis' which states that women's jobs are segmented into industries and occupations that are less prone to cyclical variation (Humphries 1988). While DeBoer and Seeborg (1989) focus on industrial segmentation by gender, Rives and Turner (1987) and Miller (1990) studied the occupational segmentation of labour by gender. They explain changes in the gender unemployment gap by a combination of the concentration of women in occupations least affected by business cycles and the restructuring of the economy in ways that increase the relative importance of those occupations compared to the most cyclical occupations, namely, production work in basic industry. Miller also divides occupations into 'middle class' and 'working class', finding that gender differences in patterns of unemployment rates are negligible in the former and substantial in the latter. Humphries's evidence, including earnings patterns that show a smaller gender wage gap in recessions, supports segmentation hypotheses over substitution or buffer hypotheses. She concludes, however, that these hypotheses can all be valid if applied to particular subsectors of economies.

Economic restructuring effects on unemployment/underemployment

Feminist scholars have been particularly concerned with women's unemployment/underemployment in the contexts of economic development and economic restructuring. Global economic restructuring refers to the system whereby research and management activities in transnational companies take place in developed countries, whereas the assembly line work, or processing for export, occurs in lesser developed countries (LDCs) and newly-industrializing countries (NICs). The concern of scholars has focused on the employment impacts in LDCs and NICs. These countries, encouraged by the World Bank or the International Monetary Fund (IMF) often establish structural adjustment policies, roughly defined as the development policies to reshape the economy to be more free-market oriented (Sparr 1994; Ward and Pyle 1995). The jobs created (for example, making computer chips or assembling electronic equipment) tend to be sited in export processing zones, areas that have restrictions on worker rights to organize and only limited health and safety requirements. Women dominate these processing jobs, which are low level subordinate jobs, dead end, low wage relative to men's wages, and vulnerable to industrial downturns and economic crises (Ward and Pyle 1995). Downturns create higher unemployment rates and also push women into the service sector and informal sector. Sparr (1994), in her strong critique of the impact of structural adjustment policies, concludes that more women than men become unemployed, working conditions for women deteriorate, women become poorer, wage differentials grow and women's unpaid work escalates. Sparr cites research (including case studies in her book) which show one or more of these effects in such countries as Egypt, Ghana, Turkey, Nigeria, Sri Lanka, Mexico, Brazil, Argentina and Venezuela. To the extent that global restructuring has 'marginalized' women workers into low-skilled, low-paid, intermittent or part-time labour, it is important to focus on underemployment as well as unemployment to understand women's economic status. Many jobs in both formal and informal sectors have underemployment characteristics such as low wages, low skill requirements, and susceptibility to downturns in the economy.

In economies in transition from communism, economic restructuring associated with changing from a planned to a market economy has also had differential impacts on women (Aslanbeigui et al. 1994; Leven 1997). Economies in transition and also developing economies have experienced increased instability in women's employment and underemployment rates over the last two decades. Under communism, equal rights, including employment rights, for women were a stated policy, though little was done to change the basic values of citizens to reflect that policy. Restructuring and market reform, rather than creating a gender-neutral market mechanism, have opened the way for economic agents to react negatively to the equality doctrine and increase gender discrimination in employment practice. For example, women more often than men have been the target of layoffs when economic crises occur, pushing them into unemployment or into underemployment in the informal sector. Women also face a larger long-term employment threat than men in these countries (International Labour Office 1996). Hopkins (1995, p. 257) notes that women 'bear a heavier burden of unemployment in the transition from socialism to capitalism'. She cites studies that show women as 50–75 per cent of the unemployed in Russia and over 50 per cent in Poland.

In industrialized countries, the decline in the industrial sector combined with growth in the service sector exacerbate underemployment (Tilly 1991). For example, Tilly finds that post-1979 growth in US industries has relied on a part-time, low-wage, low-skill, flexible work force. This work force is dominated by women. Peterson (1994, p. 117) reports that some economists contend that contingent work is the private sector's response to women's preference for flexible work schedules, a response which ignores the costs to women. In general, US employers have come to rely more heavily on contingent employment. Similarly, in the European Economic Community between 1983 and 1987, over three-quarters of the new jobs were held by women and fully 60 per cent of the jobs involved part-time employment (Rantalaiho and Julkunen 1994).

As the previous discussions have suggested, two directions for future research by feminist economists on unemployment and underemployment are evident. First, updated analyses of unemployment could be conducted in light of recent changes in the structure of industries and labour markets. With notable exceptions, much of the research on gender and ethnic differences in unemployment appeared in the 1970s and 1980s. New assessments of the gender and racial patterns of unemployment would be valuable, since these appear to be evolving.

A second direction for future research stems from the need for greater emphasis on the economics of underemployment. Current economic statistics do not adequately capture the extent of underemployment. Approaches such as those of Hauser (1974), Clogg and Sullivan (1983) and Ruiz-Quintanilla and Claes (1996) might be useful to feminist economists seeking data on the underemployed To date, non-economist feminist scholars have been responsible for many of the contributions to understanding underemployment (though they do not often use the term), particularly in the context of developing economies. Given current global trends in economic restructuring and increased use of contingent labour, official unemployment rates are likely to become less accurate indicators of economic hardship and underemployment measures to become more relevant.

Michie (1997, p. 7) states that 'unemployment is both an immense social evil and a colossal economic waste'. He goes on to call unemployment 'unjust and inefficient'. Feminist economics could make substantial contributions to understanding and, perhaps, ameliorating, the extent and hardships of unemployment and underemployment.

KIM SOSIN AND JANET M. RIVES

See also
Contingent Labour Force; Development Policies; Economic Restructuring; Informal Sector; Labour Market Segmentation; Labour Markets, Theories of; Macroeconomics; Occupational Segregation; Structural Adjustment Policies.

Bibliography

Aslanbeigui, Nahid, Steven Pressman and Gale Summerfield (1994), *Women in the Age of Economic Transformation*, London: Routledge.

Badgett, M.V. Lee (1994), 'Rising black unemployment: changes in job stability or in employability?', *The Review of Black Political Economy*, **22**, (Winter), 55–75.

Blau, Francine, Marianne Ferber and Anne E. Winkler (1998), *The Economics of Women, Men, and Work*, Upper Saddle River, New Jersey: Prentice Hall.

Boserup, Ester (1990), 'Economic Change and the Roles of Women', in Irene Tinker (ed.), *Persistent Inequalities: Women and World Development, 1962–81*, New York: Oxford University Press, pp. 14–24.

Clogg, Clifford C. and Teresa Sullivan (1983), 'Labour force composition and underemployment trends, 1969–1980', *Social Indicators Research*, **12**, 117–52.

De Anda, Roberto M. (1994), 'Unemployment and underemployment among Mexican-origin workers', *Hispanic Journal of Behavioral Sciences*, **16** (2), 163–75.

DeBoer, Larry and Michael C. Seeborg (1989), 'The unemployment rates of men and women: a transition probability analysis', *Industrial and Labour Relations Review*, **42** (3), 404–14.

Feldman, Daniel C. (1996), 'The nature, antecedents and consequences of underemployment', *Journal of Management*, **22** (3), 385–407.

Hauser, P.M. (1974), 'The measurement of labour utilization', *Malayan Economic Review*, **19** (1), 1–17.

Hopkins, Barbara E. (1995), 'Women and Children Last: A Feminist Redefinition of Privatization and Economic Reform', in Edith Kuiper and Jolande Sap (eds), *Out of the Margin: Feminist Perspectives on Economics*, London: Routledge, pp. 249–63.

Humphries, Jane (1988), 'The experience of American women in three post-war recessions', in Jill Rubery (ed.), *Women and Recession*, London: Routledge and Kegan Paul.

International Labour Office (1996), *World Employment*, Geneva: ILO.

International Labour Office (1997), *Yearbook of Labour Statistics*, Geneva: ILO.

Leven, Bozena (1997), 'The Welfare of Polish Women Before and During the Transition' in Janet M. Rives and Mahmood Yousefi (eds), *Economic Dimensions of Gender Inequality: A Global Perspective*, Westport, Connecticut: Greenwood Press, pp. 185–202.

Lichter, Daniel T. (1989), 'The underemployment of American rural women: prevalence, trends and spatial inequality', *Journal of Rural Studies*, 5 (2), 199–208.

Michie, Jonathan (1997), 'Introduction', in Jonathan Michie and John Grieve Smith (eds), *Employment and Economic Performance: Jobs, Inflation, and Growth*, New York: Oxford University Press, pp. 1–8.

Miller, John A. (1990), 'Women's unemployment patterns in postwar business cycles: class difference, gender segregation of work and deindustrialization', *The Review of Radical Political Economics*, 22 (4), 87–110.

Mohiuddin, Hasmeen Niaz (1997), 'Gender Inequality in the Pakistan Labour Market: Myth and Reality', in Janet M. Rives and Mahmood Yousefi (eds), *Economic Dimensions of Gender Inequality: A Global Perspective*, Westport, Connecticut: Greenwood Press, pp. 167–84.

Organisation for Economic Cooperation and Development (1997), *Main Economic Indicators*, Paris: OECD.

Peterson, Janice (1994), 'Traditional Economic Theories and Issues of Gender: The Status of Women in the United States and the Former Soviet Union', in Janice Peterson and Doug Brown (eds), *The Economic Status of Women under Capitalism*, Aldershot: Edward Elgar, pp. 113–27.

Rantalaiho, Liisa and Raija Julkunen (1994), 'Women in Western Europe: socioeconomic restructuring and crisis in gender contracts', *Journal of Women's History*, 5 (3), 11–29.

Rives, Janet and Keith Turner (1987), 'Women's occupations as a factor in their unemployment rate volatility', *Quarterly Review of Economics and Business*, 27 (4), 55–64.

Rubery, Jill (1988), *Women and Recession*, London: Routledge and Kegan Paul.

Ruiz-Quintanilla, S. Antonio and Rita Claes (1996), 'Determinants of underemployment of young adults: a multi-country study', *Industrial and Labour Relations Review*, 49 (3), 424–38.

Sen, Amartya (1997), 'Inequality, unemployment, and contemporary Europe', *International Labour Review*, 136 (2), 155–72.

Sparr, Pamela, (1994), 'Feminist Critiques of Structural Adjustment', in Pamela Sparr (ed.), *Mortgaging Women's Lives: Feminist Critiques of Structural Adjustment*, London: Zed, pp. 13–39.

Tilly, Chris (1991), 'Reasons for the continuing growth of part-time employment', *Monthly Labor Review*, 114 (3), 10–18.

Tipps, Havens C. and Henry A. Gordon (1985), 'Inequality at work: race, sex, and underemployment', *Social Indicators Research*, 16 (3), 35–49.

Ward, Kathryn B. and Jean Larson Pyle (1995), 'Gender, industrialization, and development', *Development*, (1), 67–71.

World Bank (1997), *World Development Report*, New York: Oxford University Press.

Unions and Union Organizing

Feminism has a tradition of both research on the subject of unions and activism within unions. Researchers have examined the interaction of unions with women workers while activists have applied feminist theory either to improve union responsiveness to women members or to build unions composed primarily of women. One of the most difficult aspects of unionism is the contradictory nature of the role of unions in women's lives. The same union will frequently provide better pay and benefits (for example, pensions, medical care) for union women at exactly the same time as they discriminate against those same women members. Thus while unions are frequently the only defence for workers in menial jobs, the same unions may passively or actively discourage women from entering leadership positions. In addition, unions do not frequently or effectively bargain issues which relate to women's double role as housewife and wage worker, such as benefits for part-time work (Blau et al. 1998; Cook et al. 1984; Cunnism and Stageman 1995; Long 1996; Milkman 1990). Finally, there is also an implicit racial and ethnic dimension to this discussion. In the United States, for example, women who are not of European ancestry are disproportionally employed in menial jobs and need union protection even more than other segments of working women. At the same time, these women are the least represented in union leadership ranks (Jones 1995). And while ethnic minorities vary from country to country, similar results obtain: women not from the local dominant culture tend to be employed in the most menial jobs and to receive the worst wages (see, for example, Tsurumi 1990) and they also tend to be poorly represented by and in unions.

In all industrial countries, women were a significant part of the workforce and the union movement during the nineteenth and early twentieth century. However, virtually all long-standing unions worldwide have a history of either admitting women as marginal members who are not allowed to participate fully or of excluding women altogether (Cook et al. 1984). An early example of this gender bias can be found in the National Agricultural Laborer's Union (NALU), which was formed in England in 1872 as the first national farm workers' union. While NALU organized 12 per cent of male farm workers at the height of their influence, they never admitted women. Instead, NALU actively campaigned to have women removed from the fields as wage labourers, pushing for public policies which confined women to the household (Sayer 1995), a pattern that was repeated in early unions in every industrial country. Yet women persisted in taking part in the union movement in all these countries, either by forming gender separate organizations (for example, Sons and Daughters of St Crispin) or by demanding representation from all male organizations. In the United States, for example, the organizers and participants of the first recorded mill strikes were all women and children (Hymowitz and Weissman 1978), and Blewett (1988) documents that the first two unions in the Massachusetts shoe industry were formed by women shoebinders.

Why? Simply, there were tremendous economic incentives for women to unionize – their gender was used as a universal excuse to pay the worst wages, their labour was doubly exploited in the market place and in the household and there was a lack of social protection for all wage workers during the nineteenth century. Ware (1924) described the phenomena of women mill hands organizing in Lowell, Massachusetts decades before the first male unions. To explain why this early union activity was all female, he noted that legal restrictions on alternatives to wage work for women (particularly married women in the USA who were unable to own property or receive their own wages) and the narrow definitions of gender appropriate labour took away any illusions mill hands had of either moving up to management or into business ownership.

Worldwide the pattern of early unions was to organize, win key demands and then collapse. However, by the late 1850s and early 1860s in the USA, there were permanent unions in all large cities and rural industrial areas throughout the northeast (Gutman 1989), and in 1869 the first national union, the Noble Order of the Knights of Labor, was formed. The Knights are important in discussions of women and unions because they were unique in allowing equal membership regardless of gender. (Interestingly, the Knights extended full membership to freed Africans, but refused to extend membership to Chinese labourers.) In the heyday of their public years, 1878–83, they had an estimated female membership of over 50 000 (Kessler-Harris 1981) and an estimated total membership of 500 000. In 1886, factional strife, part of which centered around objections to the equal status of women and African-Americans, led to a split in the organization with 316 000 skilled male labourers leaving to form the American Federation of Labor (AFL) (Fink 1977).

This split between the Knights and the AFL reflected the contradictions faced by labouring women in the international union movement. On the one hand, women were an integral part of the working class, but on the other, their involvement in wage labour was depicted negatively from many sides. Skilled men saw women as threats to their preferential position as highly paid labour, and industrialists saw unionized women as a threat to large pools of cheap labour in countries where manufacturing was rapidly expanding.

Moving to the twentieth century, this pattern of women being both unionized and marginalized has become the norm. Nowhere are women in leadership positions in numbers which reflect their membership numbers in unions. With a handful of exceptions, unions do not address the universal needs of women to combine traditional household labour and wage work. While it would be impossible to spell out the specifics of individual unions from many countries in such a small space, the following example from Poland is typical of the gendered contradictions between women and the labour movement.

Long (1996) takes an anthropologist's look at the gender contradictions within Poland's Solidarity, the first independent trade union in the Soviet bloc prior to the fall of the communist government in the USSR. She specifically examines working class women in industry (as opposed to intellectual or farm women). Roughly equal numbers of men and women stood side by side fighting for democratic rights to organize into unions independent of the communist state during the period when Solidarity was illegal. Once the organization won local and worldwide recognition, women's special work conditions were either ignored or women were actively discriminated against by Solidarity leadership. While women have always provided the vast majority of staffing for Solidarity, only two women have held national leadership positions – Anna Walentynowicz and Alina Pienkowska – and those positions were in textiles and teaching where most women work.

Generally, Solidarity has not addressed either the double burden of home and work faced by Polish women or government attempts to outlaw both birth control and the right to abortion. To address some of these issues, a women's section of Solidarity was formed in 1989, but it was banned by the organization's leadership in July 1991 *for pro-choice activities*. By disallowing this women's section, Solidarity has effectively stopped women organizing in the low-paid industries in which they are concentrated (for example, textiles) areas already suffering from lack of union organization.

Solidarity certainly is not the only twentieth-century union with more rhetoric than reality when it comes to defending the rights of working women. As Cook et al. (1984) noted when discussing the generalized nature of sexism in labour organizations, unions are latecomers to the acceptance of the goal of equity for women in the workplace. Regardless of orientation – socialist, Christian, or nonpartisan – the stated goals of unions have tended to be much more progressive on issues of sexual equality, both within the union and in the market place than have their practical programmes.

Today, with a few exceptions, most unions still ignore issues particularly related to women. As one example, only unions in Sweden effectively represent part-time employees, overwhelmingly women, by negotiating benefits such as retirement pensions and medical care that are usually associated with full-time work. Throughout the rest of the world, unions completely ignore the part-time labour of women who combine their traditional household labour with the necessity of earning wages. And in the most obvious sign of union discrimination against women in the twentieth century, women continue their absence at leadership levels worldwide – despite longstanding and, in many cases, majority membership in unions. As long as the rhetoric of unions continues to be separated from practice by such an abyss, this situation is likely to continue into the twenty-first century.

These contradictions between the needs of labouring women for protection in the workplace and the discrimination against women in labour organizations have created ongoing difficulties for feminists seeking to place unions within feminist theory or on the agenda for feminist activities. For example, one recurring criticism of the US women's movement addresses the needs of middle and upper-class women of European origins (Guy-Sheftall 1995).

Women who work in menial occupations or who come from diverse racial and ethnic origins tend to be marginalized within the feminist movement. There has been enough truth in this accusation for many feminists to work at trying to incorporate race and class dimensions into their work.

In the 1960s and 1970s, feminists began researching the basic need/discrimination contradiction and some descriptive work has now been published, primarily incorporating statistics about union women, as in the economic principles text by Blau et al. (1998). There have also been an impressive number of descriptive studies produced by historians, sociologists and anthropologists examining the involvement of women with unions (Cook et al. 1984; Lamphere 1987; Milkman 1987; Gutman 1989; Gabin 1990; Zappi 1991; Cunnism and Stageman 1995; Long 1996). Closely related is the work by African-American feminists who also provide observational information on black women in unions. These authors have frequently incorporated the contradictions faced by black women in unions into their theoretical work (Guy-Sheftall 1995).

Building on some of the descriptive work, early Marxist-feminists (for example, Hartmann 1976, 1981) held that discrimination in unions and the concept of the family wage were one way in which men continued to enforce and benefit from domestic labour. By preventing women from seeking out well-paid union jobs, men were instrumental in maintaining the gender hierarchy. As long as women were unable to gain access to economic power in the market place, men were able to continue to exchange economic power for domestic labour performed in the home.

Feminists from all schools of thought have also examined the maleness of union culture. Some have been activists who put their theory into practice, establishing a number of women's unions and groups aimed specifically at women workers such as the Coalition of Labor Union Women (CLUW), Nine to Five, and Seiu District 925 (Milkman 1990; Long 1996; Cunnism and Stageman 1995).

There are strengths and weaknesses associated with all this work by scholars and activists. Descriptive and theoretical work by social scientists and African-American scholars, for example, has successfully carved a place for working women on the feminist agenda. This recognition of multi-faceted definitions of gender when applied across class, race and ethnic lines has been extremely valuable in extending the boundaries of feminist debate. However, this body of work tends to provide testimony with no answer. Descriptive pictures of women in unions have provided no resolution to the need/discrimination contradiction. This lack of resolution is partly due to the lack of a theoretical framework and partly due to the complexity of finding universal solutions which apply to the different class, race and ethnic contradictions faced by women.

The Marxist-feminist theoretical view was successful in explaining some union discrimination. The motivation of maintaining male privilege in domestic labour did indeed lead to either exclusion of women from unions or discrimination against women within unions. The weakness of this answer was that it did not explain those times when male-dominated unions acted on behalf of women. For example, the Teamsters have organized more women workers than any other union in the twentieth century and the United Auto Workers was the first union to publicly sponsor the Equal Rights Amendment. Both unions, however, maintain an almost complete absence of women in leadership positions.

Activist feminists have worked to carve more space for women in unions, and their primary strength is that they have recognized the need/discrimination contradiction. In the United States, for example, CLUW has had some success in forcing unions to include women in leadership and in recognizing the legitimacy of women's issues. The problem has been that CLUW's membership has been drawn from women already in union leadership positions, and it has not focused resources on incorporating rank and file women or organizing the unorganized. Another activist group, Nine to Five, organized on the theory that the *process* of union organizing was different for women, but they have had limited success because of a legal structure in the workplace which grants only unions the right to negotiate between employers and employees. As a result, Nine to Five formed SEIU District 925 which has brought in new women union members in civil service (Milkman 1987).

Most of the criticisms developed in the 1970s and 1980s – that unions tend to protect male privilege to the detriment of their women members and that they ignore issues related to women's unique position between wage work and housework – stand unchanged in the 1990s (Milkman 1990; Guy-Sheftall 1995). There has been little recent work on women in unions, and what there is tends to simply add newer statistics to descriptive work (Blau et al. 1998) or to focus narrowly on ethnographic work (Long 1996; Tsunami 1990). There remains a vacuum of research and theoretical thinking in this area which sorely needs to be filled. More specifically, feminist economists, along with other scholars and activists, need to explain why the focus of practical policies in unions continues to discriminate against women workers, and then bring that understanding to finding solutions to the need/discrimination contradiction.

MARGARET S. COLEMAN

See also

Double Day/Second Shift; Labour Market Segmentation.

Bibliography

Bergmann, Barbara R. (1996), *In Defense of Affirmative Action*, New York: Basic Books.

Blau, Francine D., Marianne A. Ferber and Anne E. Winkler (1998), *The Economics of Women, Men, and Work*, 3rd edn, Upper Saddle River, New Jersey: Prentice-Hall.

Blewett, Mary H. (1988), *Men, Women, and Work. Class, Gender, and Protest in the New England Shoe Industry, 1780–1890*, Urbana and Chicago: University of Illinois Press.

Cook, Alice H., Val R. Lorwin and Arlene Kaplan Daniels (eds) (1984), *Women and Trade Unions in Eleven Industrial Countries*, Philadelphia: Temple University Press.

Cunnism, Sheila and Jane Stageman (1995), *Feminizing Unions: Challenging the Culture of Masculinity*, Aldershot, Brookfield Massachusetts, Hong Kong, Singapore, Sydney: Avebury.

Fink, Gary M. (ed.) (1977), *Labor Unions*, Westport, Connecticut: Greenwood Press.

Gabin, Nancy F. (1990), *Feminism in the Labor Movement. Women and the United Auto Workers, 1935–1975*, Ithaca and London: Cornell University Press.

Gutman, Herbert G. (1989), *Who Built America? Volume One from Conquest and Colonization Through Reconstruction and the Great Uprising of 1877*, New York: Pantheon Books.

Guy-Sheftall, Beverly (ed.) (1995), *Words of Fire: An Anthology of African-American Feminist Thought*, New York: The New Press.

Hartmann, Heidi (1976), 'Capitalism, Patriarchy, and Job Segregation by Sex', in Martha Blaxall and Barbara Reagan (eds), *Women and the Work Place: The Implications of Occupational Segregation*, Chicago: University of Chicago Press.

Hartmann, Heidi (1981), 'The family as the locus of gender, class and political struggle: the example of housework', *Signs: Journal of Women in Culture and Society*, **6**, 366–94.

Hymowitz, Carol and Michaele Weissman (1978), *A History of Women in America*, New York: Bantam Books.

Jones, Claudia (1995), 'An End to the Neglect of the Problems of the Negro Woman', [*Political Affairs*, 1947, reprinted in Buzz Johnson's, 1985, *I Think of My Mother: Notes on the Life and Times of Claudia Jones*, London: Karia Press.] in Beverly Guy-Sheftall, (ed.), *Words of Fire: An Anthology of African-American Feminist Thought*, New York: The New Press.

Kessler-Harris, Alice (1981), *Women Have Always Worked*, New York: The Feminist Press.

Lamphere, Louise (1987), *From Working Daughters to Working Mothers, Immigrant Women in a New England Industrial Community*, Ithaca: Cornell University Press.

Long, Kristi S. (1996), *We All Fought for Freedom: Women in Poland's Solidarity Movement*, Boulder, Colorado: Westview Press.

Milkman, Ruth (1987), *Gender at Work: The Dynamics of Job Segregation by Sex during World War II*, Urbana: University of Illinois Press.

Milkman, Ruth (1990), 'Gender and Trade Unionism in Historical Perspective', in Louise A. Tilly and Patricia Gurin (eds), *Women, Politics, and Change*, New York: Russell Sage Foundation.

Sayer, Karen (1995), *Women of the Fields: Representations of Rural Women in the Nineteenth Century*, Manchester and New York: Manchester University Press.

Tsurumi, E. Patricia (1990), *Factory Girls: Women in the thread mills of Meijji, Japan*, Princeton, New Jersey: Princeton University Press.

Ware, Norman (1924), *The Industrial Worker, 1840–1860. The Reaction of American Industrial Society to the Advance of the Industrial Revolution*, Boston and New York: Houghton Mifflin Company, Cambridge: The Riverside Press.

Interview

Moore, Bernard (1997), Labor Organizer for SEIU 32B–32J.

Urban and Regional Economics

Urban and regional economics breaks with the 'science fiction of life lived on the head of a pin' (Hanson 1992, p. 585), to concentrate on analysing location decisions, spatial interrelationships between economic actors and the role of state policies in fostering or containing spatial differentiation; these include housing, transport, environmental, industrial location, local economic development policies and local public finance. Mainstream urban economics and regional science, based in the neoclassical paradigm, remain almost entirely gender-blind (Burnell 1997), but the political economy approach to the urban and the regional has fostered a feminist economic geography. This approach shares the critiques of conventional economic reasoning of feminist economics, and mirrors many of the debates within feminist economics, drawing on postmodern developments within geography.

Early feminists identified 'man-made spaces' as constricting the options open to women (Hayden 1981), long before Betty Friedan located 'the problem which has no name' in the comfortable suburbs of western society. With the development of feminist history from the 1970s, the separation of male and female spheres was detailed from the micro (household) level to the more macro (urban) level. Feminist geography built on this spatial analysis of domestic labour and hence contained an implicit, and later more explicit, challenge to conventional geography. Tensions about the place of domestic labour in human geography are still rife, while conventional urban and regional economics continues to write the domestic world out of account.

The central organizing principle of feminist urban analysis through the 1970s and 1980s focused on the 'fossilization' of the sexual division of labour 'into concrete space' (England 1991, p. 13), characterized as a divide between 'Masculine Cities and Feminine Suburbs' (Saegert 1980). This fuelled a wide range of empirical studies of the constrained physical mobility of women. Madden (1973, 1977), for example, argued that married women's limited mobility enabled employers to gain advantageous spatial monopsony, a point taken up by feminists working in the political economy tradition as an aspect of capitalist restructuring strategies. Both Massey (1984) and Nelson (1986) point to capitalist exploitation of women's 'spatial entrapment'. Massey, for example, builds her analysis of spatial divisions of labour on a wider conceptualization of the gendered workforce, in which male trade union organization in core areas is counterposed to 'green', compliant female labour in the periphery. In doing this she begins to identify a geography of gender relations, which, in its early formulations, is structured by capital. From the mid 1980s the centrality given to economic relations in such accounts diminished, as did the implicit assumption of an undifferentiated patriarchal order. Thus feminist economic geography of the 1990s took up and developed the spatial dimension to identity construction and, with this, the analysis of difference between women. From this discussion the original motif of spatially separate gender spheres was identified as ethnocentric and class bound. Far from having short commutes, inner-city black women were forced into long and difficult journeys to work because they were directly excluded from better city centre jobs.

Importance to feminist economic theory
Feminist geography emphasizes how women are differentiated from men as economic actors by their more constrained mobility, but it also shows how differences between women stem from, and interrelate with, differences in location. In this perspective, 'place' is not just a metaphor of difference but a concrete lived experience that fosters social division.

Critiques of conventional urban and regional analysis operate at a number of different levels, reflecting broader feminist engagements with conventional social science. Thus, from the 1970s a number of women, reacting to the absence of empirical research on women's paid and unpaid work in urban and rural settings, sought to add women into the analysis, as did some men. Behind this lay a critique of urban planning and policy as organized to reinforce women's domesticity. This analysis began to incorporate gender relations, as questions of safety from male violence became important. Regional planning and policy have, however, remained largely free of criticism, except for some studies of the particular costs to women of restructuring strategies. The multi-faceted, multi-disciplinary 'localities' approach to urban and regional change offered some reconciliation of feminist concerns with those of mainstream urban analysis as does the newer analysis of flexibilization, regulation theory and 'queer geography', but quantitative regional science remains untouched by feminist analysis, and is in a state of some decline (Warf 1995).

The classic economic model of the urban land market is built on the assumption of a monocentric city in which all employment is at the centre. In this model, households locate at different distances from the city centre according to the value they place on housing space relative to the cost and inconvenience of commuting (Alonso 1964). Thus the suburbanization of households with full-time housewives and mothers is seen to arise from utility maximization among unitary households. Workers, who are assumed to be male, are seen to locate after acquiring a job, thus writing married women employees out of the model entirely. Kain (1962, p. 154), though, has suggested a more realistic account arguing that, 'households adjust their place of residence to the man's job location and their residential preferences, after which the woman adjusts her job location to the given family residence'. This approach has been criticized for being based on 'an economically irrational assumption that women are casual or secondary workers' (White 1977, p. 42). To date, however, female urban economists have sought only to add suburban employment locations into an otherwise undisturbed model.

The main critical analysis by economists focuses on the limitation of the model for forecasting and policy, specifically in relation to housing demand. Madden (1980), for example, asks whether the rising employment by married women will change residential preferences, and concludes that it will not, largely because employment opportunities are not clustered in the central city, as the simple model assumes. Her findings show that residential location is almost exclusively male-centred, but she does not explore the implications.

The household is treated in urban economics very much as a black box. Kristensen (1997), however, raises the idea that there are 'gender specific utility functions' and suggests that women's preferences for housing are structured by their employment status. He also points to a barely articulated criticism that urban residential location models ignore the work involved in the upkeep of the home, and argues that, other things being equal, employed women seek to reduce domestic labour and will hence opt for smaller houses. Thus one fundamental proposition, that increasing income is associated with increasing demand for household space, is brought into question. For his Danish sample Kristensen found that residential location is affected by who, within the household, earns the money.

This recognition of the importance of gender in residential location mirrors debate among geographers and sociologists about the gendered nature of gentrification (Bondi 1991). Does gentrification reflect the marginal status of lone women in the market for owner-occupied housing, or more of a desire of lone women and lesbian households to seek out congenial neighbours, or the rise of the dual career households? Mainstream urban economists have barely acknowledged the question.

Another concern is the blindness in the debate on suburban residential location and women's shorter work journeys: this has been the failure to distinguish between women according to the control they have over household residential location, that is, between lone women and women with partners. This arises from a tendency to assume a single household utility function in all households (Hanson and Pratt 1995). Thus suburbanization is not a male conspiracy; rather, as domestic producers, and especially as mothers, women have sought suburban homes.

The focus of feminist criticism has been the failure of conventional urban analysis to recognize the impact of child care responsibilities on the mobility of women in the city. This criticism involves three debates that dovetail into one another: firstly, the reasons for women's shorter journey to work; secondly, the implications for women's employment and their pay; and thirdly, the generality of the finding of shorter journey times across all employed women.

While most feminist geographers emphasize the domestic division of labour to explain women's shorter commutes, the empirical findings suggest that single women without children commute the shortest distance and hence that other factors are important. In British studies gender differences in incomes and in access to cars – 'men's love affair with the car' – are seen to give men larger job search areas and greater employment choices (Campbell 1993).

From the 1970s on, some writers argued that women's lesser spatial mobility contributed to the gender wage gap (Fuchs 1988) and that low female incomes were a consequence of lower mobility, rather than a cause (Hanson and Pratt 1995). However, short journeys to work are not in themselves a problem. For single women and women with a strong say in where the household locates, they reflect a relatively unconstrained choice, particularly when contrasted with black and ethnic minority women, whose journeys to work are as long as those of their male counterparts. Even though residential location for married women tends to be male-centred and even though 'women's work' is more subject to spatial monopsony, Madden and Chiu (1990) found that the wage gap between women and their partners in the USA was much the same wherever they lived.

At the individual level, it is possible for women to circumvent spatial constraints, but spatiality remains a key feature differentiating male and female jobs. It takes two forms: first, archetypical female jobs are relatively ubiquitous with low levels of specialization (Singell and Lillydahl 1986). Women can therefore move relatively freely between jobs as a 'trailing wife' (Bruegel 1996). Secondly, they are relatively static, rarely involving long distance travel and overnight stays; women are kept 'in place' geographically and hierarchically at one and the same time.

The constrained mobility of women produces a geography of labour force participation which yields reserve armies of labour at both a regional and local level (Green 1994). It also makes for variation in the occupational profile of women in different areas and some differences in the scale of sex segregation and in the gender typing of jobs (Lorence 1992). Women's jobs and men's jobs may be universally differentiated along similar axes, but at the detailed level jobs done by women in areas of long-term labour shortage have been found to be done by men where jobs for men are relatively scarce. Two important issues arise from this: first that location decisions of firms are not gender blind – restructuring and relocation decisions are highly sensitive to the specific attributes of local gendered labour forces. Nelson (1986) argues, for example, that the relocation of back office functions to suburban locations in California reflected a desire to switch from a labour force of young black women to a more loyal, spatially constrained workforce of suburban white women.

Secondly, at the regional level, differences in the degree to which households are dependent on a sole male wage create a geography of gender relations (Massey 1984, Murgatroyd et al. 1985), but as with the categorization of different nation-states by patriarchal form, this is not a static geography. Local gender relations are subject to (sometimes countervailing) flows of capital, national policy initiatives and the spread of ideas and values (Perrons 1995). Nevertheless, the geographical basis of difference amongst women, rooted in limited geographical mobility, is an important part of a feminist economic geography. It has been shown to inform patterns of political activity amongst women (Mackenzie 1989). Collectively, women are not simply to be seen as victims caught in a spatial trap, but as active shapers of the local geography of public facilities and amenities, including transport provision.

Within this framework, feminist geographers and planners as well as a number of younger male writers have sought to uncover the way men wield power, as men, in the construction and development of the city. McDowell's (1997) analysis of the City of London as an embodiment of upper-class male values and norms and Massey's (1996) account of masculinity and high tech in South East England are valuable contributions to a feminist urban economics. Tickell and Peck (1996) have incorporated such insights in an analysis of business power in new urban governance in Britain, showing how the political economy of urbanism is increasingly open to feminist thinking.

Individually women are not equally spatially constrained. A gender analysis of migration patterns shows that cities at the top of the urban hierarchy attract highly qualified women and export women involved full time in child care. This makes for a particularly polarized picture of difference amongst women in global cities, expanded, particularly in New York, as Sassen (1991) shows, by patterns of international migration and ethnic discrimination. There is then an urban dimension to patterns of difference between women. Analysis of ethnic minority women's position in a number of large cities points to the way one group of women have been able to overcome domestic and spatial constraints by employing other women, often from very distant locations, to service needs within and outside the household.

There is then a sense that the analysis of spatiality in the construction of women's labour reflects past practice; that higher car ownership and increasing levels of household headship amongst women and large-scale relocation of city centre employment into residential neighbourhoods, as well as increasing levels of international migration on the part of women, is superseding any simple picture of spatial constraint. But the increasing distances women now drive have costs and may reflect highly constrained, gendered, choices. Women are spending more time ferrying children across the city, except where they are able to employ others to do so, or, at the other end of the income scale, where they are not in a position to take their children anywhere very much. Technological changes which increase the ability of men and women to work from home and to move to remoter places also raise research questions. However constricting the separation of home and work, the merging of the two in space and time is unlikely to be liberating. Lastly, there are a series of policy questions raised by the 'joint' purchase and ownership of housing and the concept of a family home. These serve to gender both homelessness and poverty in old age, the one towards men and the other towards women. Here the future of feminist urban economics links closely with developments in feminist social policy.

IRENE BRUEGEL

See also

Labour Market Segmentation; Labour Markets, Theories of; Migration.

Bibliography

Alonso, W. (1964), *Location and Land Use*, Cambridge, Massachusetts: Harvard University Press.

Bondi, L. (1991), 'Gender divisions and gentrification', *Transactions of British Institute of Geographers*, **16** (4), 190–98.

Bruegel, I. (1996), 'The Trailing Wife: A Declining Breed?', in Kate Purcell, R. Crompton and D. Gallie (eds), *Changing Forms of Employment: Organisation, Skills, Gender*, London: Routledge, pp. 235–58.

Burnell, B. (1997), 'Spatial dimensions of occupational segregation', *Feminist Economics*, **3** (3), 69–86.

Campbell, B. (1993), *Goliath*, London: Methuen.

Duncan, S. (1996), 'The Diverse Worlds of European Patriarchy', in M.D. Garcia-Ramon and J. Monk (eds), *Women of the European Union*, London: Routledge.

England, K. (1991), 'Gender relations and the spatial structure of the city', *Geoforum*, **22** (2), 135–47.

Fuchs, V. (1988), *Women's Quest for Economic Equality*, Cambridge, Massachusetts: Harvard University Press.

Green, A. (1994), 'The geography of changing female activity rates: issues and implications for policy and methodology', *Regional Studies*, **28** (6), 633–9.

Hanson, S. (1992), 'Geography and feminism: worlds in collision', *Annals Association of American Geographers*, **82** (4), 569–86.

Hanson, S. and G. Pratt (1995), *Gender, Work and Space*, London: Routledge.

Hayden, D. (1981), *The Grand Domestic Revolution: A History of Feminist Designs for American Homes, Neighborhoods, and Cities*, Cambridge, Massachusetts: MIT Press.

Kain, J. (1962), 'The journey to work as a determinant of residential location, *Papers of the Regional Science Association*, **9**, 137–60.

Kristensen, G. (1997), 'Women's economic progress and the demand for housing', *Urban Studies*, **34** (3), 403–18.

Lorence, J. (1992), 'Service sector growth and metropolitan occupational sex segregation', *Work and Occupations*, **19** (2), 128–56.

Mackenzie, S. (1989), 'Restructuring the Relations of Work and Life: Women as Environmental Actors; Feminism as Geographical Analysis', in S. Mackenzie and A. Kobayashi (eds), *Remaking Human Geography*, London: Unwin.

Madden, J.F. (1973), *The Economics of Sex Discrimination*, Lexington, Massachusetts: D.C. Heath.

Madden, J.F. (1977), 'A spatial theory of sex discrimination', *Journal of Regional Science*, **17** (3), 369–80.

Madden, J.F. (1980), 'Urban land use and the growth in two earner households', *American Economic Review*, **70**, 191–7.

Madden, J. and Chen Chiu L. (1990), 'Wage effects of residential location: commuting constraints on married women', *Urban Studies*, **27** (3), 353–70.

Massey, D. (1984), *Spatial Divisions of Labour: Social Structures and the Geography of Production*, Basingstoke: Macmillan.

Massey, D. (1994), *Space, Place and Gender*, Oxford: Polity.

Massey, D. (1996), 'Masculinity, dualisms and high technology', *Transactions of Institute of British Geographers*, **20**, 487–99.

McDowell, L. (1997), *Capital Culture: Gender at Work in the City*, Oxford: Blackwell.

Murgatroyd, L., M. Savage, D. Shapiro et al. (1985), *Localities, Class and Gender*, London: Pion.

Nelson, K. (1986), 'Labour Demand, Labour Supply and the Suburbanisation of Low Wage Office Work', in A. Scott and M. Storper (eds), *Production, Work Territory*, London: Allen Unwin.

Perrons, D. (1995), 'Gender inequalities in regional development', *Regional Studies*, **29** (5), 465–76.

Rose, D. (1989), 'A Feminist Perspective of Employment Restructuring', in J. Wolch and M. Dear (eds), *The Power of Geography*, Boston: Unwin Hyman.

Saegert, S. (1980), 'Masculine Cities and Feminine Suburbs: Polarised Ideas, Contradictory Realities', in C. Stimpson (ed.), *Women and the American City*, Chicago: University of Chicago Press.

Sassen, S. (1991), *The Global City: New York, London, Tokyo*, Princeton: Princeton University Press.

Singell, L. and J. Lillydahl (1986), 'An empirical analysis of commute to work patterns of males and females', *Urban Studies*, **23** (2), 119–29.

Tickell, A. and J. Peck (1996), 'The return of Manchester men: men's words and men's deeds in the remaking of the local state', *Transactions of British Institute of Geographers*, **21**, 595–616.

Vaiou, D. (1992), 'Gender divisions in urban space: beyond the rigidity of dualistic classifications', *Antipode*, **24** (4), 247–62.

Warf, B. (1995), 'Separated at birth: regional science and social theory', *International Regional Science Review*, **18** (2), 185–93.

White, Michelle (1977), 'A model of residential location choice and commuting by men and women', *Journal of Regional Science*, **17** (1), 41–52.

Value

Contested concepts of value and valuation have been central to the discipline of economics, at least from the time of Adam Smith. Two areas of disagreement have been of particular importance: the relationship of market price to value, and the nature of the process of valuation, different understandings of which are basic to differences among the schools of thought described elsewhere in this volume. Recognition that value is socially determined, and not perfectly and naturally measured in market prices, is a distinguishing characteristic of feminist economics.

That economics, alone of the social sciences and related applied disciplines, has been so concerned with the meaning and source of value is explained by the dual roots of the discipline in moral philosophy and in modern social science. As moral philosophy, economics has been concerned with whether prices were 'just' and conformed with social and religious expectations, while as a modern social science, economics has sought to explain the processes whereby prices are determined and change in complex market economies. This has led economists, such as Smith in *The Wealth of Nations* (1776), to describe not only how prices were set in market places, but also to justify that price is, in fact, a fair indicator of a commodity's value. In Smith's case, this dual concern, along with his aim of ending British state control of trade, led to his advocacy of laissez-faire and market determination of prices and of trade. Market determination, Smith argued, would tend to produce a socially desirable valuation of commodities (which for Smith meant a natural valuation) through the harmonious workings of the invisible hand.

Smith's efforts to explain what gives rise to the value of goods in exchange began a long debate over 'value' in the discipline of economics. For the classical economists the search for the determinants of value was a search for the common element in all commodities that allowed comparison of value. The ratios of that common element would be the determinant of natural or normal prices, toward which, in Smith's argument, market prices would tend.

Smith himself was inconsistent, speaking at times of value as that contributed by the quantity/quality of labour involved in the production of a good, and at other times as a summation of costs. However, as he wrote before the industrial revolution, direct labour costs were the major costs in the production of goods so that the inconsistency was not terribly important. David Ricardo in *Principles of Political Economy* (1817) made Smith's logic neater, and by building his theory squarely on the labour theory of value he led the way to Karl Marx's (*Das Kapital* 1867) deduction that, in a world where machinery was more and more used, workers would be deprived of increasing shares of the value that they contributed. To Smith's harmonious world the idea of 'surplus value' and exploitation was added.

For the classical economists it was the clash of interests among the major groups of English society, the landowners, the capitalists and the workers, that determined price, and it was the equity (or inequity) and consequences of the shares received by these classes that was of great interest. In response to Marx's dramatic conclusions about the future of capitalism, and because of changing economic conditions and questions, most economists soon shifted their focus away from the labour theory of value.

For the neoclassical economists who wrote after the 1870s, appreciation of markets as a desirable way to organize the provisioning of society remained at the heart of the discipline, as did the Smithian need to justify market-determined prices as equivalent to natural values. However, focus shifted from class to individual interests; the question was no longer whether the landlords or capitalists would get an unfair share of the dividends produced by economic growth. In the rapidly industrializing, and richer, world of the late nineteenth century, the question was whether individuals would obtain their rightful shares. For most economists after the 1870s the measure of value became 'utility', the satisfaction received by an individual from the consumption of goods and services, rather than the amount of labour required for production. Although not measurable, the concept of utility served to legitimate the idea that only individuals could determine the value that goods and services had for them. As Alfred Marshall codified the new way of thinking in his *Principles of Economics* (1890), price was the product of individual rather than class interaction. Individual firms supplied; individual consumers purchased. In the absence of evidence of monopolistic power, tariff protection or other 'interferences' with the normal market determination of prices, Marshall argued, the equilibrium prices that resulted from the interaction of firms and individuals could be assumed to be accurate reflections of fair costs to the firms and of individual tastes and preferences.

In neoclassical economics equilibrium prices are the equivalent of Smith's normal, or real, prices and much of modern welfare economics involves showing how departures from those equilibrium prices entail welfare losses for society. These conclusions turn on the proposition that prices are a true reflection of value and that value is assumed to derive from individual tastes and preferences, the investigation of which is usually assumed to lie beyond the boundaries of economic analysis. The conviction that price and value are guaranteed to be the same (save where monopoly, monopsony, or government 'interference' intrude) is so complete for most modern neoclassical economists that there is little awareness that the concept of value was and is an issue in economics.

Three alternative and overlapping approaches to the analysis of value coexist in modern economics with the neoclassical concept of value. The first of these involves a continuation of Ricardian and Marxian economics. In modern Marxian economics emphasis is placed on the exploitation of workers that results from the fact that workers produce more goods and services than required by their standard of living. The 'surplus value' that results accrues to the non-working classes in capitalist societies. For those working in the Ricardian and Marxist traditions, market prices do not result in an equitable division of the output of society. However, within this tradition value continues to be understood as a characteristic of the valued object. In particular, the value is determined by the amount of embodied labour.

An alternative approach – that of institutional economics – treats value as the consequence of a process, where the process is the focus of analysis. For institutional economists there is no search for a common element, the ratio of the embodiment of which determines the ratio of values among goods and services. Instead values and prices are understood as determined by a variety of kinds of interactions among firms, consumers, courts, legislative and other government bodies, interest groups, non-consuming individuals and the powerful force of customary practice. Valuing is a process of social learning and of the use of social power by all groups involved. To illustrate: recent learning indicates that eating more fresh fruits and vegetables is important for health. This information is spread in a variety of ways, all self-serving in varying degrees and ways, by the groups involved in spreading the word; advertising of diet supplements and articles in medical journals coexist. The message is received in a wide variety of contexts that are determined by class, income, education, group-perception and pressure. As new learning occurs, and as new opportunities are taken by producers, consumers, governments and other groups, the process of valuing goes on and the valuations of the moment change. Prices of goods and goods are in part determined in this process, though price and value are not the same thing.

Unlike institutional economics, neither neoclassical economics nor Marxian economics make the process of valuation central to analysis. In contrast to the institutionalists, neoclassicists would say that, for reasons usually held to be beyond the realm of economic analysis, the demand for fresh fruits and vegetables has shifted, leading to higher prices in the short run and new equilibrium long-run prices determined by the elasticity of supply in response to the change of demand. The focus of attention is on the change of prices and the 'efficiency' of those prices in reflecting consumer preferences, resource availability and the state of technology. The Marxian approach is similar in that focus is on prices (and especially on wages as the price of labour). However, in Marxian analysis emphasis is on the inequity of the consequences, as owners of capital are in a position to reap unjustified rewards from the changing demand of consumers.

Modern feminist economists have developed the third approach to value, one that has elements in common with Marxist and with institutional economics. The distinctive focus of feminist economics is upon the role that gender plays in the process of valuation. The approaches of feminist economists to distributional issues, to discrimination, to the indivisibility of women's work in nonmarket sectors of the economy, to comparable worth and pay equity and to family policy involve three major departures from the neoclassical treatment of value.

The first departure is the recognition that market prices are not the normal or inevitable consequences of impersonal forces that play out in the economy. From Smith through the modern neoclassicals the power of groups in society to affect economic outcomes has, with some notable exceptions, been largely ignored by economists. Even within Marxist economics, the interactions among capitalists and labourers are largely impersonal; the actors are puppets moved by larger and impersonal forces. Neoclassical economists have incorporated 'rent-seeking', monopoly and monopsony and other interferences with the normal, but the range of activity over which power is recognized has been limited by the narrow focus of the approach. Only labour economists in the mainstream of economists have had much to say about other kinds of power as almost of necessity they have had to incorporate gender, race, ethnicity and class into their analyses.

Feminist economists, on the other hand, have been aware of the importance of power in determining the value placed on different kinds of activities. At its rawest, the power exercised by firms in declaring 'women's work' to be worth less than that of men illustrates the importance of power in determining value and price. At more subtle, but equally important, levels, the power of shared notions about the relative worth of parking lot attendants and day care workers, provides additional illustration of how values can seem badly skewed to those who view from the perspective of the powerless (Attewell 1990, p. 428; Bergmann 1986; Ferber 1982). In focusing on power, feminist economists share the Marxist economist's view that distribution is exploitive of those who contribute larger value than they receive. At the same time, they share the institutional economist's view that distribution is understood as a consequence of interaction of a variety of groups, and not simply as consequence of the conflicting interests of labour and capital.

The second departure for feminist economics from neoclassical value theory is a logical consequence of the first departure. If distribution is exploitive because some contribute more than they receive, it seems reasonable to ask what the measure of value is. One approach taken by feminist economists has been to offer alternative concepts of value to those already available in classical and neoclassical economics. In the work of a number of feminist economists (Bergmann 1986; Ferber 1982; Folbre 1994; Waring 1988) emphasis is put on the role of women in provisioning of society and in social reproduction, and on the value to society of these contributions.

With the growing importance of buying and selling in Western and industrializing economies in the nineteenth and twentieth centuries, those services not provided as commodities ceased to be thought of as economic. Women's work in raising children and in caring for families became distinctly non-economic and in the process lost 'value'. After the 1870s, when, for most economists, price and value became increasingly the same, 'women's work', because it had no price, had no value, at least of the ordinary economic sort. Feminist economists have reacted strongly to this conclusion. Even though there are strong differences over whether imputation and inclusion of monetary values in national income accounts of women's contributions in the home are an appropriate remedy, there is little disagreement that women contribute more economic value than has been generally recognized.

It is important to note that the agreement that women make undervalued contributions to social reproduction involves a different set of issues than does the equally agreed to proposition that women are often treated prejudicially in labour markets. The question of how the contribution of women (or men, for that matter) to the care and raising of children, to the mental and physical health of families and to social reproduction in general should be valued is a question of how to value, in ways that affect the distribution of income, non-marketed services. Neoclassical economists would suggest using shadow prices (that is, an estimate of what price would be if the services were marketed), but this requires the assumption that market prices are indeed appropriate ways to value the services in question. Another way is to adopt, and to recognize the legitimacy of, entirely nonmarket processes of income distribution.

Such non-market distributive processes have been at the heart of income maintenance programmes widely adopted in the industrialized nations in the twentieth century. The programmes are rooted in recognition that not all that society values has a market price, and not all market processes, even though unfettered by government or monopoly, yield prices that are 'right' in the eyes of society. Welfare programmes are rooted in recognition that valuation is a complex social and political process, of which markets are but one aspect.

This recognition leads to the third departure for feminist economics from the standard neoclassical approach. Feminist economists who argue that the current distribution is unfair and/or incomplete, recognize, as do the institutionalists, that there is no natural measure of value. Value is socially constructed through an ongoing process, and prices and distributional consequences are always a consequence of the current play of interests, policies and customs. From this follows the third departure. Feminist economists are activists with respect to values, and in this too they share with the Marxists and the institutionalists. Marxist economists are necessarily committed to a belief that the currently existing capitalist economies either will, or should, be replaced by economic systems in which surplus value accrues to workers, either as individuals, or collectively through public goods. The world is to be changed. Institutional economists, because they see both values and prices as part of ongoing processes, also see current values and prices as changeable. Efforts to change the current values of groups in society are an ever-present part of society – in modern societies these efforts take the form of advertising, but also of education, of science, and of political processes. And for feminist economists, growing recognition of the value of women's economic contributions can and must improve women's economic status.

The idea that economists can be simple truth-seekers who discover a natural economy not affected by power and persuasion is rejected by feminists (Harding 1995). That rejection entails rejection of the idea that value is to be discovered; instead values are about valuation and that is what economists should study. The goal for feminist economics is to understand and describe the *social* (including economic) processes of valuation, and particularly to understand the role that gender plays in those processes. Feminist economics has already enriched both the Marxian and institutional approaches to the study of value by calling attention to the importance of gender. This enrichment should continue in future research. Further, feminist economists may be able to cause neoclassical economists to reexamine the importance of the dual roots of economics for treatment of the relationship between price and value. Thus research in feminist economics has the potential to encourage a general reexamination of assumptions about value.

ANNE MAYHEW

See also
Comparable Worth/Pay Equity; Family Policy; Feminist Economics; Institutional Economics; Marxist Political Economics.

Bibliography
Attewell, Paul (1990), 'What is skill?', *Work and Occupations*, **17**, (November), 422–48.
Bergmann, Barbara (1986), *The Economic Emergence of Women*, New York: Basic Books.
Ferber, Marianne (1982), 'Women and work: issues of the 1980s: a review article', *Signs*, **8** (2), (Winter), 273–95.
Folbre, Nancy (1994), *Who Pays for the Kids? Gender and the Structures of Constraint*, New York: Routledge.
Harding, Sandra (1995), 'Can feminist thought make economics more objective?', *Feminist Economics*, (Spring), 7–32.
Waring, Marilyn (1988), *If Women Counted: A New Feminist Economics*, San Francisco: Harper Collins.

Volunteer Labour

The broadest definition of volunteer labour includes work hours provided in exchange for a stipend or no remuneration, either within or outside an organizational structure. Within the organizational or 'formal' sector, volunteers contribute to arts and cultural associations, including museums, zoos and broadcasting. They belong to religious, civic and social organizations, which may or may not purport to benefit the public good. Formal-sector volunteers contribute to education, health services, environmental activities, human services, international/foreign affairs, foundations, recreation services, work-related organizations, youth development, crime prevention, resident associations and fire fighting. Some research includes definitions of voluntarism as membership in associations defined loosely as people contributing membership dues by mail. Outside organizational structures, 'informal' volunteers may aid neighbours or friends with child care or transportation, grocery shopping or nursing care.

Volunteer labour is a significant source of labour input for many US organizations. In 1994, volunteer time provided 36 per cent of total employment to the independent (nonmarket, nongovernment) sector in the USA (down from 41 per cent in 1987), but only 9 per cent of government employment and a negligible percentage of business employment. These percentages correspond to an estimated 89 million adults contributing over 19 billion hours, providing the equivalent of 8.8 million full-time employees, whose assigned value, by one measure, was $182 billion (Hodgkinson 1996).

The demographic profile of the average US volunteer has changed over time. A 1965 survey showed that the typical volunteer was a married, unemployed woman, and this was still true in 1974 (Schram and Dunsing 1981). However, evidence suggests that by the early 1990s women were only slightly more likely than men to volunteer. People most likely to volunteer in the formal sector are between 35 and 44 years old, have average household incomes of $50 000 or more, are college graduates, employed part time, married and are members of religious organizations (Hodgkinson 1996). Participation in voluntary activity varies broadly within racial and ethnic groups (Fischer and Schaffer 1993). To the extent that women and minorities are disproportionately involved in informal volunteer networks, surveys that count only formal voluntary activity may be systematically biased.

The key point of consensus on gender and voluntarism is that sex segregation and conformity to traditional gender roles in volunteering mirrors occupational segregation in the paid labour force (Daniels 1988; Fischer and Schaffer 1993; McPherson and Smith-Lovin 1986). Women are more likely than men to volunteer in largely female associations, although a majority of those associations have male leadership and/or serve as 'auxiliaries' to men's associations and male-run institutions. Women's volunteer roles are more likely than are men's to lack an internal promotion ladder to more prestigious or powerful volunteer positions or to paid staff positions.

A popular perception holds that women's entry into the paid labour force drained the volunteer labour pool. However, during the past 30 years of women's entry in the paid labour force, volunteer activity has been quite stable. The Bureau of Labor Statistics estimates that the percentage of US Americans who volunteered rose from 18 per cent in 1965 to 24 per cent in 1974 then declined to 20 per cent in 1989 (although the three surveys were not directly comparable over time) (Hayghe 1991). A Gallup survey (Hodgkinson 1996) shows voluntarism in the USA peaked in 1989 at 54 per cent, rising from 45 per cent in 1987, fell during the 1990–91 recession, then recovered somewhat. By 1993, 48 per cent of US American adults volunteered an average of four hours per week. The range of estimates reflects the range of definitions of voluntary activity.

International scholars note that voluntarism is perceived differently across cultures. Voluntary activity is framed by the degree of economic development that determines the supply of private resources (time and after-tax income) and by the legal and social structures that bolster or restrict development of associations. Various religious teachings shape the tendency to volunteer. For example the minor emphasis on altruism and philanthropy in Japanese religious traditions may help explain a less extensive voluntary sector in Japan (Hardacre 1991) than in the USA, while the Catholic culture and its emphasis on charity is the root of voluntarism in Italy (Perlmutter 1991). Key differences by country also include the role of the state in providing social services. Some governments virtually crowd out the voluntary sector. For example 'Swedish central authority has expanded so much that whether any organized activity remains outside the state is singularly problematic' (Boli 1991, p. 95). Fiscal policy provides incentives or disincentives to participate in voluntary associations, for example, in the USA with tax incentives (Hochman and Rodgers 1986; Weisbrod 1992), or in Israel with direct government funding of non-profit organizations (Jaffe 1991) where much of the country's voluntary activity occurs. More homogeneous countries such as Sweden and Japan are less likely to develop voluntary associations (Cheung 1992), perhaps because people do not need to seek out groups with similar interests or background. Similarly in France such cultural factors as low geographic mobility, strong neighbourhood cohesion and family stability provide social outlets outside of organizations (Veugelers and Lamont 1991). It is important to note that no comparable figures are available for direct comparison of the extent of voluntarism across countries. Consequently, this fact, along with the focus in the literature on the US volunteer labour experience, leads the following discussion to a similar focus.

Volunteer labour parallels the public/private duality of women's lives. Volunteer labour is 'public' or outside the home, similar to labour market experiences, yet largely unpaid, like the home and family responsibilities of the 'private' sphere. Volunteer labour is of interest to feminist scholars across disciplines because of its practical role in women's lives, its contribution to social and economic life and its relationship to women's paid labour market experience.

Clearly women value volunteer work enough to make significant contributions of unpaid time. Despite professional and personal responsibilities, roughly 50 per cent of US women volunteer an average of four hours per week (Hodgkinson 1996). Volunteers contribute to families, communities and economies, yet because such labour is not assigned a wage value, it is one of the many ways in which women's contributions to GDP remains uncounted. In the US policy arena a clear understanding of the voluntary sector's role in maintaining communities is also of import in such political environments as the government ceding of responsibility for social service programmes during the 1990s. Moreover non-profit tax status is being redefined to restrict the advocacy role of non-profit organizations, making volunteers more critical to stretch the shrinking resources of organizations that work for social change.

Volunteer labour contributed to the evolution of women's labour market experience. Until relatively recently the voluntary sector provided women's primary public venue. Until the mid-nineteenth century, women in the USA could not own property or control their earnings even if they could find paid employment. But as volunteers in charitable organizations women could raise funds, pay wages and manage investments (Ginzberg 1990). By the mid twentieth century, many women worked as volunteers because of the 'unsuitability or impracticality of paid employment' for middle- and upper-income women. Although today some women volunteer for the same reason, 'many women who once gave all their working time to the cause of voluntarism now enter salaried employment' (Daniels 1988, p. 11).

Despite the variety of sources of interest in volunteer labour, it is not well researched. Allowed to broaden their analytical framework beyond market economics, feminist economists would be likely candidates to examine volunteer labour. However they have been utterly silent on the subject, leaving any feminist perspective on volunteer labour to such other disciplines as sociology, psychology and history. In general research on volunteer labour attempts to explain why people volunteer. Employment-related reasons to volunteer include building human capital that may be useful in the paid labour market and building networks that generate job opportunities and support job efforts (for example, informal child care arrangements). People may volunteer in order to provide social, nonmarket goods for consumption by themselves and their families. In addition, people may volunteer in order to contribute to the welfare of their communities.

As noted, employment-related reasons for providing volunteer labour include building human capital and participating in employment-enhancing networks. Mueller (1975) finds that US women volunteer primarily in order to build and maintain human capital and to aid in job search. Canadian women and men are roughly equally interested in the labour market benefits of volunteering (Day and Devlin 1997). However those benefits accrue differently to women and men. For example women who volunteer for religious organizations earn less than women who do not volunteer. Men do not incur those wage penalties. Participation in such business-related organizations as the Chamber of Commerce is associated with higher wages for both women and men, but women are less likely to participate in such groups. Women are less likely to hold leadership positions in all types of voluntary organizations. Day and Devlin (1997, p. 715) conclude, 'the negligible returns to women suggest either that women are not gaining [relevant labour market] experience, or that discrimination against women in the labour market extends to the valuation of their volunteer experience as well'. They estimate that the difference in their relative labour-market return to volunteering may account for as much as one-third of the wage gap, the difference between average wages earned by women and men. Daniels (1988) also finds that despite successful, long-term careers as volunteers, US women in her study could not move to paid positions of equivalent authority or status.

Sociologists McPherson and Smith-Lovin (1982, 1986) examine the importance of voluntary associations as networks useful in the job market, exposing members to useful information and potentially important acquaintances. They assert that larger organizations provide more contacts, while cross-gender organizations imply access to resources outside women's traditional domains. To the extent these organizational characteristics are beneficial in the labour market, the benefits accrue disproportionately to men. Men are more likely than are women to belong to larger organizations, which tend to be less homogeneous. Although women and men participate in voluntary associations at similar rates, women, especially those not employed, typically volunteer in groups that are all female or only slightly mixed. Such patterns produce substantial differences in the labour market resources available to women and men in the voluntary sector.

In addition to volunteering out of employment-related motivations, people also volunteer to influence levels of such social, nonmarket goods as recreational, cultural and educational activities. In the USA women and men are more likely to volunteer if they have school-age children. In a 1989 Bureau of Labor Statistics survey, 19.1 per cent of women and 16.8 per cent of men with no children under 18 years old reported volunteering in the preceding year. Of their counterparts with children 6–17 years old, 27.8 per cent of women and 23.2 per cent of men volunteered (Hayghe 1991). Through their children's schools, sports or religious activities, parents have many opportunities to volunteer.

Mueller examines 'volunteer output' as 'one of the inputs that go into the production of child services' (1975 p. 331), hypothesizing that the presence of preschoolers would decrease voluntarism because of time constraints. Instead, she finds that voluntarism increases with preschoolers and has no relationship with the presence of school-age children in the home. She concludes that her results reinforce the employment-related rather than child services provision motivation for volunteering.

Most volunteers report altruism as their primary motivator (Fischer and Schaffer 1993). It is here that feminist economists have spoken most loudly, not in building a body of research, but in volunteering themselves. Working for social change and economic wellbeing, they have educated people who work with low-income families as well as members of those families, written for popular media on issues of economic policy and justice, and provided research to activists and advocates in low-income communities and feminist organizations. There is, however, no feminist economic critique of the literature on volunteer labour, nor of the virtual dearth of research in the area. What critique exists is of the practice of voluntarism itself, asserting it undermines women's wages and allows government to underfund social programmes.

Sociologists Steinberg and Jacobs (1994) contend that to perform a job as a volunteer affirms the underlying assumption that the job is socially productive but not necessarily economically productive. When such tasks become paid work, then it is low-waged work, affecting women's position in the market wage distribution and contributing to biases incorporated into comparable worth efforts. There has been no empirical examination of this assertion.

Preston (1989) tests whether volunteers effectively compete with paid workers. Focusing on the nonprofit sector where volunteers comprise roughly 40 per cent of staff, she finds a small but growing penalty for women working in the nonprofit sector relative to women's average wages economy-wide but no evidence that the presence of volunteers suppress wages. Preston concludes that the psychological benefits of performing socially beneficial work in the nonprofit sector compensate for the wage differential. However she finds no wage difference between sectors for the same type of work, for example, clerical work in nonprofit and for profit organizations, suggesting it is the undervaluing of occupations and industries dominated by women rather than some inherent compensation of working for a nonprofit organization that drives the wage penalty.

The early position of the National Organization of Women as reported by Daniels (1988) was that government would fund social services if women were not offering free, regular labour to provide the services below market cost. However Menchik and Weisbrod (1981) find no substitutability between volunteer provision and local government provision of public goods, but admit inconclusive results. Smith and Freedman (1972) contend that volunteers divert concern and energy from promoting structural, social change. However, volunteers in more traditional roles assert they are in superior positions to challenge institutions because they cannot be threatened with loss of salary (Daniels 1988).

Conventional as well as feminist analysis of volunteer labour suffers from its lack of class analysis. Income has been repeatedly shown to be the single most important determinant of formal volunteer activity, with high-income people most likely to volunteer. Thus much of the focus has been on upper-class, institutional philanthropy that some contend is born of a *noblesse oblige* that says community service somehow justifies class privilege (Daniels 1988). Similarly the literature has not presented a clear race analysis or examination of the varied voluntary activity within ethnic and racial groups.

Despite the fact that volunteers list altruism and provision of services for children as key motivators (Fischer and Schaffer 1993), the existing literature finds little empirical evidence beyond employment-related reasons for volunteering. Given that the tools employed to date are primarily market-driven, these results do not surprise. Feminist economists have ample room to look to more comprehensive explanations for volunteer labour activity.

Of key importance, work in the field warrants serious class and race analysis. The field needs a sound theory of volunteer labour supply that more fully addresses nonmarket as well as market motivations for volunteering. Feminist economists have examined women's 'double shifts' of paid work and dependant care. Closer scrutiny of volunteer labour as providing activities and opportunities for one's family would be a useful addition to this literature. The field needs to explore how volunteer labour affects the paid labour market experience of women who volunteer and of women in general. To what extent does volunteer work help move women into the paid labour market in desirable jobs at desirable wages? Do volunteers serve to suppress women's wages or to displace women workers? Economists need to examine the sex segregation in volunteer activities that mirrors the labour force. If not constrained by economic rationalizations of occupational segregation, why do women and men perform gendered activities in volunteer work? Such a study might inform our understanding and bolster social/institutional arguments concerning the role of occupational segregation in the gender wage gap. With insight into the role of families and communities, feminist economists could also affect policy discourse by examining the extent to which the voluntary sector is likely and able to compensate for budget reallocations away from income maintenance and social service programmes.

SUSAN K. TAYLOR

See also
Gross Domestic Product; Occupational Segregation; Wage Gap.

Bibliography
Boli, John (1991), 'Sweden: Is There a Viable Third Sector?', in Robert Wuthnow (ed.), *Between States and Markets: The Voluntary Sector in Comparative Perspective*, Princeton, New Jersey: Princeton University Press, pp. 94–124.
Cheung, Paul P.L. (1992), 'The Development of Private Philanthropy in Singapore', in Kathleen D. McCarthy, Virginia Ann Hodgkinson and Russy D. Sumariwalla (eds), *The Nonprofit Sector in the Global Community: Voices from Many Nations*, San Francisco: Jossey-Bass Publishers, pp. 454–65.
Daniels, Arlene Kaplan (1988), *Invisible Careers: Women Civic Leaders from the Volunteer World*, Chicago: The University of Chicago Press.
Day, Kathleen M. and Rose Anne Devlin (1997), 'Can volunteer work help explain the male–female earnings gap?', *Applied Economics*, **29** (6), (June), 707–21.
Fischer, Lucy Rose and Kay Banister Schaffer (1993), *Older Volunteers: A Guide to Research and Practice*, Newbury Park, California: Sage Publications.
Ginzberg, Lori D. (1990), *Women and the Work of Benevolence: Morality, Politics, and Class in the Nineteenth-Century United States*, New Haven: Yale University Press.
Hardacre, Helen (1991), 'Japan: The Public Sphere in a Non-Western Setting', in Robert Wuthnow (ed.), *Between States and Markets: The Voluntary Sector in Comparative Perspective*, Princeton, New Jersey: Princeton University Press, pp. 217–42.
Hayghe, Howard V. (1991), 'Volunteers in the U.S.: who donates the time?', *Monthly Labor Review*, **114** (2), (February), 17–23.
Hochman, Harold M. and James D. Rodgers (1986), 'The Optimal Tax Treatment of Charitable Contributions', in Susan Rose-Ackerman (ed.), *The Economics of Nonprofit Institutions: Studies in Structure and Policy*, New York: Oxford University Press, pp. 224–45.
Hodgkinson, Virginia Ann (1996), *Nonprofit Almanac 1996–1997: Dimensions of the Independent Sector*, fifth edn, San Francisco: Jossey-Bass Publishers.
Jaffe, Eliezer D. (1991), 'Israel: State, Religion, and the Third Sector', in Robert Wuthnow (ed.), *Between States and Markets: The Voluntary Sector in Comparative Perspective*, Princeton, New Jersey: Princeton University Press, pp. 189–216.
McPherson, J. Miller and Lynn Smith-Lovin (1982), 'Women and weak ties: differences by sex in the size of voluntary organizations', *American Journal of Sociology*, **87** (4), (January), 883–904.
McPherson, J. Miller, and Lynn Smith-Lovin (1986), 'Set segregation in voluntary associations', *American Sociological Review*, **51** (1), (February), 61–79.
Menchik, Paul and Burton A. Weisbrod (1981), 'Volunteer Labor Supply in the Provision of Collective Goods', in Michelle J. White (ed.), *Nonprofit Firms in a Three Sector Economy*, Washington, DC: The Urban Institute, pp. 163–81.
Mueller, Marnie W. (1975), 'Economic determinants of volunteer work by women', *Signs: Journal of Women in Culture and Society*, **1** (2), (Winter), 325–38.
Preston, Anne (1989), 'The nonprofit worker in a for-profit world', *Journal of Labor Economics*, **7** (4), (October), 438–63.
Perlmutter, Ted (1991), 'Italy: Why No Voluntary Sector?', in Robert Wuthnow (ed.), *Between States and Markets: The Voluntary Sector in Comparative Perspective*, Princeton, New Jersey: Princeton University Press, pp. 157–88.
Schram, Vicki R. and Marilyn M. Dunsing (1981), 'Influences on married women's volunteer work participation', *Journal of Consumer Research*, **7** (4), (March), pp. 372–9.
Smith, Constance E. and Anne Freedman (1972), *Voluntary Associations: Perspectives on the Literature*, Cambridge, Massachusetts: Harvard University Press.
Steinberg, Ronnie J. and Jerry A. Jacobs (1994), 'Pay Equity in Nonprofit Organizations: Making Women's Work Visible', in Teresa Odendahl and Michael O'Neill (eds), *Women and Power in the Nonprofit Sector*, San Francisco: Jossey-Bass Publishers, pp. 79–120.
Veugelers, Jack and Michele Lamont (1991), 'France: Alternative Locations for Public Debate',

in Robert Wuthnow (ed.), *Between States and Markets: The Voluntary Sector in Comparative Perspective*, Princeton, New Jersey: Princeton University Press, pp. 125–56.

Weisbrod, Burton A. (1992), 'Tax Policy Toward Nonprofit Organizations: A Ten-Country Survey', in Kathleen D. McCarthy, Virginia A. Hodgkinson and Russy D. Sumariwalla (eds), *The Nonprofit Sector in the Global Community: Voices from Many Nations*, San Francisco: Jossey-Bass Publishers, pp. 29–50.

Wuthnow, Robert (1991), *Between States and Markets: The Voluntary Sector in Comparative Perspective*, Princeton, New Jersey: Princeton University Press.

Wage Gap

The gender-based wage gap or wage differential is one of the most important statistical indicators of women's economic status. It provides the inspiration for much of the research within economics on discrimination in the labour market. This singular measure, in fact, provides the proxy for many studies of wage discrimination. However, feminist economists consider a multiplicity of measures and methodologies for evaluating women's economic status.

Measurement of the wage gap seems straightforward. In the popular press, the gap is often referred to incorrectly. The less-than-parity wage ratio is commonly called 'the wage gap', but this is statistically inaccurate. To figure the wage gap, first calculate the female-to-male wage ratio, or the average or median wage (or earnings) of women divided by the same gauge for men – measured annually, monthly, weekly or hourly. Earnings are usually for full-time year-round workers. The wage gap, then, equals 1.00 or 100 percent minus the wage ratio. For example, in dollars, if the wage ratio were 65 cents or 65 per cent, the wage gap is 100 per cent less 65 per cent or 35 per cent. In the USA, for example, women who worked year-round and full time in 1996 earned only 75 per cent of men's median weekly earnings, a 25 per cent (or 25 cent) gap. (US statistics are published annually by the Department of Labor.)

Considerable attention is paid to the trend in the wage gap over time as a measure of women's economic progress. Progress has been slow. In the USA, the wage gap measured 40 cents in 1963, when the US Congress passed the Equal Pay Act mandating that men and women receive equal pay for equal work, and it was still 40 cents in 1980. The gap narrowed by 11 cents from 1980 to 1990, but according to the National Committee on Pay Equity and the Institute for Women's Policy Research, over half of the narrowing in the 1980s was due to a decline in men's real wages. In real terms, the gap has hardly budged in the 1990s.

Using data from the International Labour Office *Yearbook of Labour Statistics*, Jacobsen (1994, pp. 378–9) reports that many advanced industrialized countries, notably Australia and Scandinavian countries, have female-to-male wage ratios higher than the USA. However, countries such as Japan and the United Kingdom have lower wage ratios than the USA, thus making it difficult to generalize about cross-country trends. Nevertheless, the earnings gap tends to be smaller in countries that emphasize egalitarian wage policies in general and in countries with centralized collective bargaining. It tends to be largest in countries such as Japan that emphasize a traditional role for women and in countries with individually- and market-driven wage determination (Gunderson 1994, p. 13).

In their comparative work on eight industrialized nations, Blau and Kahn (1992, 1994) found that women benefit from a lower wage gap in countries such as Sweden, Norway and Australia with less overall earnings inequality. These countries blend centralized wage setting with generally strong collective bargaining that reduces both interfirm and interindustry wage variation. In fact, Blau and Kahn project that the gender pay gap would have narrowed further between 1975 and 1987 were it not for an increase in overall inequality. The contribution of centralized bargaining, culture and social policy, and country-specific structures and institutions in narrowing the wage gap is further supported by studies of Germany, Italy, the United Kingdom and Australia by Rubery (1992) and Hunter and Rimmer (1995). The role of government labour market regulation and centralized pay determination through industry-wide agreements may play more of a role in gender pay equality than gender-specific equal pay directives or equality legislation, according to these authors.

Reliable, consistent data on the gender-based earnings differential is more difficult to find for developing and formerly socialist counties. In general, women in developing countries have larger wage gaps and are concentrated in low-waged work in both the formal and informal sectors of the economy (Jacobsen 1994, Chapter 12). Some evidence suggests that women in postsocialist countries such as Poland and Romania had wage gaps on a par with other countries in western and eastern Europe in the 1980s (see Aslanbeigui et al. 1994).

The wage gap is the single measure of discrimination in traditional economic analysis. In Jane Humphries's view,

> Differences between men's and women's pay and associated employment segregation have probably attracted more attention from neo-classical economists than any other gender-related issue. Observed differences in pay constitute *prima-facie* evidence of inequality and suggest that the labour market may not be a level playing field. (1995, p. 59)

Therefore, economists and sociologists, both feminist and non-feminist, have studied the causes of the wage gap in order to debate the extent of labour market discrimination. Among the perspectives are theories of human capital, compensating differentials, dual and internal labour markets, labour market segmentation, capitalist competition, structural and poststructual analyses.

Neoclassical economists typically define labour market discrimination as remunerating employees differently when they have equivalent productivity, and argue that employment discrimination is not easily measurable. Instead discrimination is attributed to a residual, the unexplained portion of the differential in wages. This residual technique, developed by Oaxaca (1973), estimates separate wage regressions by gender. It decomposes the gender wage gap into two parts: differential means or characteristics (such as education and experience), and differential coefficients, or returns to characteristics.

To neoclassical economists, a significant part of the wage gap can be explained by the market, or by differences in education and human capital endowments, as well as by additional measures of productivity. The second portion, the unexplained residual after accounting for gendered differences in measurable independent variables, is termed discrimination.

Some mainstream economists continue to assert that the residual would be small or zero if the model could be correctly specified. Others argue that younger cohorts of women with greater labour force attachment are fuelling a decline in the wage gap. However, earnings differences between women and men tend to widen over the life cycle as women become trapped in dead-end jobs. In each of the last four decades, younger women in the USA have faced lower wage gaps than older women. Feminist economists maintain that the wage gap will not wither away if we merely wait for young women to make different choices than their mothers.

Dissatisfied with the limits of neoclassical approaches to explaining the wage gap, many feminist economists are convinced that labour market segmentation, as well as other institutional variables and nonmarket factors, exert significant influences on wage differentials. The wage gap and its relative decline are due to more than measurable productivity differences (see Gunderson 1989; Sorensen 1991). Neoclassical frameworks are characterized by circular causality; low wages both explain and are explained by women's lower human capital investments. Feminist economists assert that differences in productivity reflect and are conditioned by larger social institutions rather than merely individual rational decision making (see Humphries 1995). The long history of the gendered division of labour, the practice that women are not considered deserving of a family wage, and discrimination in hiring and advancement all lead to pay inequity.

Specifically, a major reason for the wage gap is that men and women do not work together. In a national labour force in the USA that is 47 per cent female, six out of ten women still work in female-dominated occupations, particularly in a growing service sector. Most women are clerical and professional specialty workers, especially African-American women who left domestic service to replace white women in offices. About eight of ten men are employed in male-dominated occupations, especially craft and managerial or administrative work. Relatively few occupations are truly integrated, as evidenced by visits to individual workplaces. The wage gap is narrower in female-dominated occupations where overall average pay is lower, although men still earn more than women in jobs such as secretary, cashier, social worker and nurse. This not only suggests that men's earnings exceed women's, but that traditionally women's work is devalued in the economy. (For general data on occupational segregation in the USA and other countries, see Bergmann 1986, Chapters 4 and 5; Blau et al. 1998, Chapters 5 and 11.)

Treiman and Hartmann (1981) were among the first to demonstrate that the percentage female in an occupation was negatively associated with wages and to explore techniques for overcoming such wage discrimination. Their methodology has been replicated and extended by numerous empirical studies (see England 1992, Chapter 1 for a summary). By shifting the direction of studies to occupational segregation, feminist economists isolated a new directly measurable variable: the impact of percentage female in an occupation on the wage. The effect of occupational segregation on the wage gap has been used to document the need for policies mandating comparable worth/pay equity.

Over 100 countries have ratified the International Labour Office's Equal Pay Convention (No. 100) and Recommendation (No. 90) on equal pay for work of equal value. Broader than limited equal pay for equal work standards, the ILO standard calls upon member countries to apply equal pay through laws, regulations, and/or collective agreements (ILO 1986; Gunderson 1994). In not ratifying the convention, the USA is a notable exception among industrialized counties. Equal value is also a principle within the Equal Pay Directive (1975) of the European Union.

Avenues for future research on the wage gap include the development of alternative indicators of women's economic status. Feminists have pointed out that the singular indicator of the gender wage gap reveals less than it conceals. Men's declining real wages in several industrialized countries and the increased polarization of wages and income among women point to the weakness of focusing exclusively on the average wage gap (Humphries and Rubery 1992; Armstrong 1996). Global economic restructuring has accelerated a 'harmonizing down' of men's and women's relative wages. Further, the wage gap for African-American women and women of Latina descent has always been greater than for white women. Most traditional empirical studies isolate the gender wage gap from the race-based wage gap, neglecting the interaction of various forms of wage discrimination. In addition, the emphasis on relative wages obscures other kinds of and sources of discrimination in hiring, job assignment, promotion and sexual harassment that deserve investigation. Finally, feminist economists should continue their research on public policies that improve all women's absolute standard of living in addition to their relative economic position.

DEBORAH M. FIGART

See also

Comparable Worth/Pay Equity; Discrimination, Theories of; Economic Restructuring; Family Wage; Human Capital Theory; Income Support and Transfer Policy; Labour Market Segmentation; Occupational Segregation.

Bibliography

Armstrong, Pat (1996), 'The Feminization of the Labour Force: Harmonizing Down in-a Global Economy', in Isabella Bakker (ed.), *Rethinking Restructuring: Gender and Change in Canada*, Toronto: University of Toronto Press, pp. 29–54.

Aslanbeigui, Nahid, Steven Pressman and Gale Summerfield (eds) (1994), *Women in the Age of Economic Transformation: Gender Impact of Reforms in Post-Socialist and Developing Countries*, London: Routledge.

Bergmann, Barbara R. (1986), *The Economic Emergence of Women*, New York: Basic Books.

Blau, Francine D. and Lawrence Kahn (1992), 'The gender earnings gap: learning from international comparisons', *American Economic Review*, **82** (2), 533–38.

Blau, Francine D. and Lawrence Kahn (1994), 'Rising inequality and the U.S. gender gap', *American Economic Review*, **84** (2), 23–33.

Blau, Francine D., Marianne A. Ferber and Anne E. Winkler (1998), *The Economics of Women, Men, and Work*, 3rd edn, Upper Saddle River, New Jersey: Prentice-Hall.

England, Paula (1992), *Comparable Worth: Theories and Evidence*, New York: Aldine de Gruyter.

Gunderson, Morley (1989), 'Male–female wage differentials and policy responses', *Journal of Economic Literature*, **27** (1), 46–72.

Gunderson, Morley (1994), *Comparable Worth and Gender Discrimination: An International Perspective*, Geneva: International Labour Office.

Humphries, Jane (1995), 'Economics, Gender, and Equal Opportunities', in Jane Humphries and Jill Rubery (eds), *The Economics of Equal Opportunities*, Manchester: Equal Opportunities Commission, pp. 55–86.

Humphries, Jane and Jill Rubery (1992), 'The Legacy for Women's Employment: Integration, Differentiation and Polarisation', in Jonathan Michie (ed.), *The Economic Legacy: 1979–1992*, London: Academic Press, pp. 236–55.

Hunter, Laurie and Sheila Rimmer (1995), 'An Economic Exploration of the UK and Australian Experiences', in Jane Humphries and Jill Rubery (eds), *The Economics of Equal Opportunities*, Manchester: Equal Opportunities Commission, pp. 245–73.

International Labour Office (ILO) (1986), *Equal Remuneration: General Survey by the Committee of Experts on the Application of Conventions and Recommendations*, Geneva: ILO.

Jacobsen, Joyce P. (1994), *The Economics of Gender*, Cambridge, Massachusetts: Blackwell Publishers.

Oaxaca, Ronald (1973), 'Male female wage differentials in urban labor markets', *International Economic Review*, **14** (3), 693–709.

Rubery, Jill (1992), 'Pay, gender and the social dimension to Europe', *British Journal of Industrial Relations*, **30** (4), 605–21.

Sorensen, Elaine (1991), *Exploring the Reasons Behind the Narrowing Gender Gap in Earnings*, Washington, DC: The Urban Institute Press.

Treiman, Donald J. and Heidi I. Hartmann (eds) (1981), *Women, Work, and Wages: Equal Pay for Jobs of Equal Value*, Washington, DC: National Academy Press.

Welfare Reform

In most industrialized countries, the term welfare typically includes a wide set of income support and transfer programmes such as unemployment insurance, family allowances and old-age support. In the United States, however, people associate welfare with a handful of programmes that serve low-income families and individuals. These include Food Stamps (vouchers that can be used to purchase food), Medicaid (health care coverage for low-income persons and families), and cash assistance to families with children.

Welfare programmes are defined more narrowly in the United States than in its industrial counterparts, both in terms of coverage and size of benefits. In addition, the United States has taken a particularly severe approach to welfare reform in the last decade. Consequently, this entry will focus on recent changes in welfare policy in the United States and the relevance of such an approach to welfare reform for feminist economics.

The programme most closely identified as 'welfare' in the United States has been Aid to Families with Dependent Children (AFDC), providing cash assistance to single mother families and reaching 12.7 million people (4.7 per cent of the USA population) in 1996 (Committee on Ways and Means, US House of Representatives 1998). While many countries have recently instituted reforms to both lower the level and narrow the scope of income assistance to single mother families, only the United States has dismantled its programme. In 1996, the federal government abolished the AFDC programme and established a block grant called Temporary Assistance for Needy Families (TANF). The federal government will give states a fixed sum of money to be spent on needy families and states must match 75 per cent of that money. States alone determine who is needy and are free to terminate benefits if recipients do not comply with specific work or reporting rules or if families have used benefits for a specified period of time (as short as 21 months in Connecticut), regardless of need.

The AFDC programme, originally called Aid to Dependent Children (ADC), was established in 1935 as part of the Social Security Act which included the old-age insurance programme (referred to as Social Security in the United States) and unemployment insurance. Welfare legislation then was part and parcel of federal legislation that recognized not all families could support themselves by male breadwinning wages, based on an assumed standard family wage. AFDC was fashioned after state programmes enacted during the Progressive Era a few decades earlier, as states struggled to stem poverty among households with children in which the male bread earner was absent (Gordon 1994). In addition, the 1935 legislation – passed at the height of the US depression – was intended to keep single mothers out of the labour force. The programme was funded via a matching grant – the federal government matched every dollar (and for some states even more) that a state spent. The federal government set eligibility requirements while states set benefit levels. AFDC was an entitlement programme in that anyone who met eligibility requirements was entitled to receive benefits.

The programme's emphasis has changed over time. Most notably, since the 1970s, there has been much more emphasis on moving recipients into paid work and collecting payments from fathers. Provisions in the 1935 law allowed states to 'experiment' with different rules, and throughout the 1970s and 1980s states reformed their programmes, often by encouraging training and paid work, discouraging behaviours that are seen as not promoting paid work, and reducing or eliminating benefits for women who do not disclose paternity of children (Mink 1998). In 1988, the Federal government passed the Family Support Act which set into place work requirements for AFDC recipients but also extended child care and health care benefits for a full year to recipients who leave AFDC because of increased earnings.

Although conservatives have always been opposed to AFDC, attacks intensified in the 1980s. President Ronald Reagan made his assault on welfare mothers a key theme during his presidency, relying heavily on the work of George Gilder and Charles Murray, coining the term 'welfare queen'. And while AFDC has historically accounted for about 1 per cent of the federal budget and about 3 per cent of state budgets, by the early 1990s national and state politicians from both political parties were successfully calling for crackdowns on welfare mothers. Welfare recipients were often painted as immoral (having too many babies out of wedlock) and lazy (not willing to get and hold a job), despite research to the contrary (for example, Moffitt 1992). In 1992, presidential candidate Bill Clinton received positive responses to his promise to 'end welfare as we know it'. By 1996, 40 states had reformed their welfare policies – typically including a few 'carrots' and lots of 'sticks' (Committee on Ways and Means, US House of Representatives 1998). The main emphasis was on replacing public assistance with earnings as quickly as possible, punishing certain behaviours, and cracking down on 'deadbeat dads'.

Welfare reform in the United States culminated with the Personal Responsibility and Work Opportunity Reconciliation Act of 1996 in which AFDC was abolished. No longer does meeting eligibility requirements entitle poor families to assistance, since states define needy any way they see fit. And while the act passes responsibilities on to the states, there are still some federal strings attached. In 1998, 30 per cent of TANF recipients in a state must have worked 20 hours a week which must grow to 50 per cent working 30 hours per week by 2002 (education and training programmes do not meet the work participation requirements). Importantly, for the first time federal cash assistance is now time limited to five years (60 months) for a lifetime.

There are four important reasons why welfare and its reform are feminist economic issues. First, and most immediately, the level of welfare payments and the regulations on welfare receipt make up the 'safety net' for any woman with a child. Currently, one woman in six is a single mother and every child born today has a one out of two likelihood of growing up in a single parent family in his or her lifetime. About one-third of all single mothers in the United States received AFDC (Albelda and Tilly 1997).

Second, when welfare benefits are reduced, eligibility rules tightened, or workfare (unpaid labour) requirements added, more women enter the work force. Most welfare recipients have limited education and consequently compete at the low end of the labour market. At each level of the labour market, workers feel competitive pressure from those just a little below. Since many women fill the ranks of the low-wage labour force, recent welfare reform will place downward pressure on women's wages.

Third, welfare policies indicate what the political and economic systems think of women's work. AFDC/TANF is designed to provide the income supplements mothers need when they lack male income. In January 1997, the median welfare payment for a family of three was 34 per cent of the poverty line, which was $12 802 per year or $1068 a month. The maximum AFDC benefit for a family of three in the most generous state – New York (Suffolk County) – was $703 a month, while the least generous state – Mississippi – was $120 (Committee on Ways and Means, US House of Representatives 1998, pp. 418–19). Even adding in the cash value of Food Stamps, welfare leaves families below the poverty level. In 1997, the monthly value of AFDC and Food Stamps combined for a family of three in New York was $922 and in Mississippi was $435. In the median state, the combined package was worth 62 per cent of the poverty line (Committee on Ways and Means, US House of Representatives 1998, pp. 416–18). By keeping payments so low, the political system ratifies an economic system that pays women far less than men, and does not value (in terms of income) the work of caring for families.

Finally, welfare reform debates in the United States debase low-income women and call into question some of their fundamental rights. Over the last two decades the political debate on welfare has been characterized by a narrow understanding of the issues, driven by a set of myths and stereotypes that typically involve images of 'wombs gone wild' (especially teenagers' wombs) or women sitting at home for years on end collecting reams of money. These myths mask the reality of women's lives and call into question mothers' ability to make individual choices about their family situations – including the right to have children and whether or not to live with or marry the father of their children. The discussions on welfare mothers too often take place absent the larger economic, political, and social context of abject poverty and domestic abuse.

Economists have long been active in welfare reform debates via their analyses of poverty. But like many, if not most, economic treatments, the issue of gender has been ignored or downplayed. Traditionally, economists have offered two types of approaches to poverty. One approach examines the macroeconomic and structural causes of poverty (see Tobin 1994). These types of analyses tend to focus on inner-city employment opportunities for men and avenues for economic growth. The second focus uses microeconomic modelling to ferret out individual behaviour responses to economic incentives built into poverty programmes (see Moffitt 1992). These include analysis of work and marriage responses to the amount of income disregard (the benefits recipients lose for every dollar they receive as earnings), changes in eligibility rules which exclude families with two parents, and benefit levels or reductions.

Feminist economists have added an important, new dimension to discussions of poverty and welfare reform by integrating the ways in which gender matters in welfare reform. Responding to macroeconomic level analysis, feminist economists have noted that promoting men's employment and community economic development that does not pay attention to the issues facing women's employment, notably dependant care responsibilities, will likely not work in alleviating poverty among single mothers and will not serve the needs of many low-income families. Specifically, feminists (including feminist economists) have noted that employment – specifically job creation – may not be the right solution to mothers' poverty. On the microeconomic level, feminist economists have consistently argued that mothers' employment opportunities and hence their individual responses to policy changes are circumscribed by child rearing and gender discrimination in labour markets. Welfare reform discussions by feminist economists bring to the fore analysis of the short- and long-term benefits and costs of marriage for women, the dynamics of child-bearing decisions, and the relationship of the women's economic independence to larger economic phenomena and public policies.

What distinguishes many feminist economists' understanding of welfare receipt from other treatments – ranging from conservative to progressive treatment of the urban poor – is that they see women who turn to welfare not as having behaviour disorders (caused either by underlying structural events such as lack of employment opportunities for men or 'bad' habits caused by welfare receipt itself) but as pursuing a survival strategy (often of last resort) because both the labour market and family support systems have failed them as they attempt to raise their children.

Contributions to a feminist analysis of welfare receipt and welfare reform span a variety of disciplines (history, sociology, political science and economics) and topics. One important contribution feminist economists have made is in improving understandings of why single mothers are poor and hence need and deserve public assistance (for example, Folbre 1984; Sawhill 1988; Albelda and Tilly 1997). Usually feminist economic analysts argue that women's economic activity in households, namely child rearing, is important work. If (or when) traditional family structures break down, that work is no longer financially supported by individual men but still needs to be valued and provided regardless of whether or not fathers are present.

Another crucial area in which feminist economists have contributed is in providing valuable empirical research detailing the relationship between welfare receipt and child bearing, employment and marriage. The literature is extensive and only a few are mentioned here. McCrate's (1992) discussion of why teen mothers might rationally choose parenthood calls into question the current policy emphasis of blaming teen pregnancy on welfare receipt. Blank's extensive work on employment dynamics and welfare receipt has consistently enriched our understanding of the unlikely potential of replacing cash assistance with jobs without either better jobs or more wage supports (Blank and Ruggles 1994; Blank 1995a). The Institute for Women's Policy Research has produced several important studies on how women utilize cash assistance, providing a much richer and complex understanding of the ways in which welfare recipients cycle in and out of jobs – often using welfare as a form of unemployment insurance – and how recipients carefully package income from work, family and the government (see, for example, Spalter-Roth et al. 1995). Feminist economic work on the decline in marriage and increase in out-of-wedlock births has placed popular assumptions and attacks on welfare mothers in perspective (Blank 1995b), has shown what is effective for replacing earnings with welfare (Petersen 1995) and offered realistic analysis on the potential of child support (Beller and Graham 1993).

A third important contribution has been the historical analysis of welfare and welfare reform and tracing the deeply gendered nature of public policy. For example, Abramovitz (1996) follows the imposition of 'work ethic' and the 'family ethic' (that a woman should marry a man capable of supporting her) in her analysis of the history of welfare reform. She, along with Gordon (1994), has provided a distinctly feminist basis for interpreting relief policies for men as very distinct from those for women. Rose (1993, 1995) has traced the benefits and problems of government generated jobs for men and women.

Feminist economists have been in the forefront of providing accessible, accurate information on the economic situation of poor women and their children from a feminist perspective and in presenting alternative welfare reform proposals (Albelda and Tilly 1997; Albelda et al. 1996; Bergmann and Hartmann 1995; Blank 1997; Figart and Lapidus 1995; Seavey 1996). The parameters of those proposals are similar and typically reach beyond the policies directed toward current welfare recipients. With women's economic independence and the reduction of poverty as the goals, feminist economic prescriptions emphasize policies which recognize the link between child rearing and employment and seek to make both options more viable for all families. At a fundamental level, feminist economists include in their proposals the provisions of universal health care coverage and some guaranteed form of cash assistance for single mothers who cannot do paid labour. Second, they argue that the United States needs to make a stronger commitment to sharing the costs of child rearing. The proposals range from establishing children's allowances to expanding the availability and funding for child care to establishing paid family leave. Third, they generate policies directed toward the labour market that would make employment a viable economic alternative to welfare for low-income single mothers. The set of policies vary but typically include income or in-kind supplements to low-income workers, legislative policies that improve women's wages such as increases in the minimum wage or comparable worth legislation, increased education and training opportunities, and improved transportation. And while feminist policies have not taken centre stage in current policy debates, they do provide hope and the needed ammunition for a time when the United States is ready for a more equitable and economically productive set of reforms that do not seek to punish the poor, but rather serve to enrich all families' lives.

RANDY ALBELDA

See also

Child Support; Family Policy; Feminization of Poverty; Income Support and Transfer Policy; Poverty, Measurement and Analysis of.

Bibliography

Abramovitz, Mimi (1996), *Regulating the Lives of Women: Social Welfare Policy from Colonial Times to the Present*, Revised Edition, Boston: South End Press.

Albelda, Randy and Chris Tilly (1997), *Glass Ceilings and Bottomless Pits: Women's Work, Women's Poverty*, Boston, Massachusetts: South End Press.

Albelda, Randy, Nancy Folbre and the Center for Popular Economics (1996), *The War on the Poor: A Defense Manual*, New York: The New Press.

Beller, Andrea and John Graham (1993), *Small Change: The Economics of Child Support*, New Haven: Yale University Press.

Bergmann, Barbara and Heidi Hartmann (1995), 'A welfare reform based on help for working parents', *Feminist Economics*, 1 (2), (Summer), 85–9.

Blank, Rebecca M. (1995a), 'Teen pregnancy: government programs are not the cause', *Feminist Economics*, 1 (2), (Summer), 47–58.

Blank, Rebecca M. (1995b), 'Outlook for the U.S. Labor Market and Prospects for Low-Wage Entry Jobs', in Demetra Smith Nightingale and Robert H. Haveman (eds), *The Work Alternative: Welfare Reform and the Realities of the Job Market*, Washington, DC: The Urban Institute, pp. 33–70.

Blank, Rebecca M. (1997), *It Takes a Nation: A New Agenda for Fighting Poverty*, New York: Russell Sage.

Blank, Rebecca M. and Patricia Ruggles (1994), 'Short-term recidivism among public-assistance recipients', *American Economic Review*, 84 (2), 49–53.

Committee on Ways and Means, US House of Representatives (1998), *1998 Green Book: Overview of Entitlement Programs*, Washington, DC: US Government Printing Office.

Figart, Deborah M. and June Lapidus (1995), 'A gender analysis of U.S. labor market policies for the working poor', *Feminist Economics*, 1 (3), 60–81.

Folbre, Nancy (1984), 'The pauperization of motherhood: patriarchy and social policy in the U.S.', *Review of Radical Political Economics*, 16 (4), 72–88.

Gordon, Linda (1994), *Pitied But Not Entitled: Single Mothers and the History of Welfare, 1890–1935*, New York: Free Press.

McCrate, Elaine (1992), 'Expectations of adult wages and teenage childbearing', *International Review of Applied Economics*, 6 (3), 309–28.

Mink, Gwendolyn (1998), *Welfare's End*, Ithaca, New York: Cornell University Press.

Moffitt, Robert (1992), 'Incentive effects of the U.S. welfare system: a review', *Journal of Economic Literature*, **30**, (March), 1–61.

Petersen, Carol (1995), 'Female-headed families on AFDC: who leaves welfare quickly and who doesn't', *Journal of Economic Issues*, **29** (2), (June), 619–29.

Rose, Nancy (1993), 'Gender, race, and the welfare state: government work programs from the 1930s to the present', *Feminist Studies*, **19** (7), 319–42.

Rose, Nancy (1995), *Workfare or Fair Work? Women, Welfare, and Government Work Programs*, New Brunswick, New Jersey: Rutgers University Press.

Sawhill, Isabel (1988), 'Poverty in the U.S.: why is it so persistent?', *Journal of Economic Literature*, **27** (3), 1073–119.

Seavey, Dorothy K. (1996), *Back to Basics: Women's Poverty and Welfare Reform*, Special Report CRW 13, Wellesley, Massachusetts: Wellesley College Center for Research on Women.

Spalter-Roth, Roberta, Beverly Burr, Heidi Hartmann and Lois Shaw (1995), *Welfare That Works: The Working Lives of AFDC Recipients*, Washington, DC: Institute for Women's Policy Research.

Tobin, James (1994), 'Poverty in Relation to Macroeconomic Trends, Cycles, and Policies', in Sheldon Danziger, Gary Sandefur and Daniel Weinberg (eds), *Confronting Poverty: Prescriptions for Change*, Cambridge, Massachusetts: Harvard University Press, pp. 147–67.

Recommended internet sources: www.welfareinfo.org; epn.org

Women in the Economics Profession

The discipline of economics was transformed into a profession during the last two decades of the 19th century. In the years since then, women have been and remain significantly underrepresented in the economics profession, accounting for about 23 per cent of new PhDs by the mid 1990s, holding 11 per cent of academic jobs and less than 6 per cent of full professorships (Kahn 1995, pp. 194–5). The gender structure of the profession has elicited two main responses from the profession over the past 30 years. First, it has engendered scholarship mainly by women economists into the historical roots of the imbalance and on overlooked women economists of the past. Second, the idea, born in the 1960s, that the patterns of the past could be changed if women were actively encouraged by the profession resulted in the establishment in 1971 of the Committee on the Status of Women in the Economics Profession (CSWEP) of the American Economic Association (AEA). The purpose of CSWEP is to support women as professional economists and to encourage ongoing research into their status.

The historical record of the economics profession contains very few women. The standard biographical dictionary *Who's Who in Economics: A Biographical Dictionary of Major Economists 1700–1986* (Blaug 1986) includes eight women out of almost 400 economists no longer living. These numbers illustrate the historic male dominance of the discipline. However recent scholarship is recovering women economists of the past who have been ignored and a *Biographical Dictionary of Women Economists* is currently being compiled (Dimand et al. forthcoming). Recovering these women economists is significant because it challenges the notion of a virtually womenless history of the economics profession. It also raises the question of how and why they came to be overlooked. Feminist scholars have found answers in the process of professionalization that occurred in economics at the turn of the century.

Much of the history of economics as a profession that has been written is for the United States (Church 1974; Coats 1960, 1985, 1988; Furner 1975; Parrish 1967; Ross 1991). The professionalization of economics in America coincided with the growth of graduate education for men in the United States and with the emergence of academic professionalism in universities. Before the Civil War, a college education was the primary form of higher education in the USA. Students interested in advanced study went to European universities; by 1900 that had changed. The university had replaced the college as the leading US educational institution, with the PhD as the highest degree. College and university teaching was becoming a career for professionals – experts certified with PhDs, membership in one of the growing scholarly associations, and with publishing outlets in the newly established specialty, research journals.

The professionalization of economics was part and parcel of this rise of the American university and of academic professionalism. In 1880 only three men in leading US universities devoted most of their time to teaching political economy. By 1900 there were 51 chairs in economics and American universities had granted 87 PhDs in economics (Coats 1988, p. 345; Parrish 1967, p. 11). These USA-trained economists were bent on ensuring that a career as an economist would be respected, influential, and well paid. To accomplish this meant controlling who could be considered a professional economist. Struggles over the appropriate role and mission of economists permeated the early years of the AEA, which was created in 1885. However by the turn of the century what it meant to be a professional economist had been more or less established (see, for example, Furner 1975, pp. 145–60, 258–60). Professional economists were specialists skilled in the use of the scientific method; thus they should have a PhD and membership in the AEA. Economists as experts should publish in the scholarly journals; publishing in the popular press was for amateurs. Professional economists should influence policy indirectly as academicians, one step removed from active participation in economic reform movements, which were seen as unscientific and lacking in objectivity. The rise of the university and academic professionalism, and the emergence of a consensus on the self-definition of the professional economist, affected men and women in profoundly different ways, explaining in part the historic gender structure in economics (and other professions) (Glazer and Slater 1987, pp. 223–4).

The growth of graduate education for men coincided with the growth in college education for women. As more women earned their undergraduate

degrees they lobbied for entrance into the newly established graduate programmes. However, these graduate programmes with few exceptions were
not coeducational. They were patterned on programmes at German universities that had never admitted women. Women intellectuals fought persistently
for admission to leading graduate schools, especially during the 1890s, and
by 1910 many of the American, British and German universities had opened
their PhD programmes to women (Rossiter 1982, pp. 34–51).

This meant that women interested in economics could satisfy an important
requirement for becoming an economist: having a PhD. By 1910 about 10 per
cent of all US PhD students in economics were women. By 1918, 18 per cent
of American PhDs in economics were received by women, a pre-1980s peak
(Libby 1984, p. 273). In addition, women could (and did) join the AEA.
Unlike some other scholarly associations that barred women members, the
AEA was always open to women and there was a woman (Katherine Coman)
on its inaugural Council. Women could also publish in economics journals
although it is not clear that they had equal access to them. For example, of the
six main economics journals of the early twentieth century, three of them
(*Journal of Political Economy, Publications of the American Economic Association* and *Annals of the American Academy of Political and Social Science*)
contain a significant number of articles by women. The other three (*Quarterly Journal of Economics, Yale Review* and *Political Science Quarterly*)
contain almost none (Hammond 1993, p. 367).

It was extremely difficult for women PhDs to find academic employment
teaching economics. If they were not married women's colleges and a few of
the Midwestern teaching colleges and land-grant universities would hire women
to teach economics (notably, the Universities of Nebraska and Chicago and
Stanford University (Libby 1984, p. 284)), but these positions were few in
numbers. This dearth of opportunities to teach was a crucial barrier to women
in the economics profession as the teaching position was one of the most
important criteria for recognition as a professional economist (Coats 1985,
p. 1699; Furner 1975, p. 144). Why were economics departments reticent to
hire women as professors? This was due, in part, to the 'separate spheres'
gender ideology of the time which characterized the feminine as soft, passive
and domestic at a time when social science academics, economists included,
were trying to gain a reputation for being rational, hard and objective, characteristics associated with the masculine (Gordon 1990, pp. 4–5; Ross 1991,
pp. 59–60; Rossiter 1982, p. xv). Moreover, in the early years of the twentieth century there was a backlash against women in the universities. The
considerable success of women students, particularly at the undergraduate
level, was seen to come at the expense of male students, threatening
effeminization of the university. The universities responded by adopting quotas, segregating classes or establishing separate women's colleges (Gordon

1990, pp. 42–3; Rosenberg 1982, pp. 43–8, 112–17). This further weakened support for women's access to college and university teaching positions.

Given the scarcity of academic jobs in economics departments several early women economists, along with women colleagues from chemistry, biology, sociology and the law, migrated to academic careers in one of the new interdisciplinary 'feminine' programmes like domestic management, home economics, sanitary science and social work, or they took subfaculty positions as deans of women (Ross 1991, p. 70; Rossiter 1982, pp. 51–64). Others pursued their careers entirely outside the academy. As Libby reports the largest employers of women economists before 1925 were the US Department of Labor's Women and Children's Bureau and the Women's Educational and Industrial Union of Boston, a leading publisher of studies on working women (Libby 1984, p. 284). Still others turned to employment in the settlements, charitable institutions usually associated with universities that were designed to investigate and alleviate conditions of urban poverty.

Each of these choices served to separate women economists from their male counterparts who were gaining professional reputations teaching and researching economics in university economics and social sciences departments. In addition, these employment choices naturally led women economists to research topics of family decision making, household consumption and standards of living, and women and children in the workforce, topics that were outside the contemporary, male-defined economics mainstream which centred on tariffs, trust, railroads, banks and money, agricultural prices and land policy (Parrish 1967). Women settlement workers also wrote articles, based on data they gathered from settlement neighbourhoods, proposing policies addressing poverty and other social problems and then lobbied vigorously for the corresponding social welfare legislation (Rosenberg 1982, pp. 33–5). They were often quite successful in their lobbying efforts, and many current social welfare policies have their roots in the Progressive era research and activism of these well-educated women settlement workers. However this did not earn them inclusion in the ranks of professional economists because settlement jobs were not full-fledged academic jobs and because the social reform activism associated with settlement work was increasingly considered by economists to lack objectivity, to be unscholarly, and thereby fall outside the realm of professional economics (Furner 1975, p. 160; Ross 1991, pp. 158–61).

To summarize, as the discipline of economics became academicized, as it marginalized topics of interest to women economists, and as it turned away from social reform, it simultaneously turned away from women as economists. The universities were increasingly, albeit grudgingly, willing to provide women with a graduate economics education, but they were not willing to employ or promote them on an equal basis with men (Glazer and Slater 1987, pp. 11–12; Gordon 1990, p. 118). Women PhDs responded by turning to employment in the less-prestigious 'feminine' disciplines, in government and quasi-government research jobs studying women and children, and in settlements (or they married and left the workforce). Each of these choices put women outside the accepted definition of professional economist and contributed to their lack of visibility in the historical record of economics. Women also responded by earning fewer PhDs in economics. From its 1918 peak of 18 per cent, the proportion of PhDs earned by women dropped to around 10 per cent by the 1920s and stayed there until it began its slow climb through the 1980s and 1990s (Libby 1984, p. 273).

In the 1970s the feminist revolution opened the collective eyes of the profession to the gender imbalance, and research into the contemporary status of women as economists began. The 1974 meeting of the American Economic Association contained a session devoted to 'The Supply and Mobility of Women Economists'. Three papers from that session were published in the *American Economic Review* and were among the first to use CSWEP-generated data to investigate the low representation of women in the profession 75 years after its formation. It is striking that each of the three papers takes as a given that women economists faced significant sex discrimination and barriers to academic employment and advancement. Amsden and Moser (1975, p. 91) concluded in their study of the 1973–74 job market that 'even with affirmative action programs, improvements for women economists seem marginal'. Strober (1975) used 1974–75 data to study why women chose to become economists (primarily because they liked the subject matter, wanted to solve social problems, or were interested in applying mathematics) and why women dropped out of PhD programmes (because their interests changed or because future financial rewards and job opportunities were limited). She also found that women in the mid 1970s, like their turn-of-the-century forebears, were more likely than men to enter the fields of labour economics and welfare programmes, consumer economics, and urban and regional economics (p. 96). Reagan (1975), acknowledging economics as a 'stereotypically male profession' (p. 100), found that barriers to full career development faced by women, especially men's attitudes toward women colleagues, were important sources of the wage differential between male and female economists.

With CSWEP support, research on women in the economics profession has slowly increased, especially in the 1990s. Important publications include Barbezat (1992); Blank (1991); Broder (1993a, 1993b), Ferber and Teiman (1980); Formby et al. (1993); Hirschfield et al. (1995); Kahn (1993); McDowell and Smith (1992); McMillen and Singell (1994); and Singell and Stone (1993). Kahn (1995) reviews this literature and assesses the record of women's place in the economics profession as it faces the next turn of the century.

Kahn reports that there are several dimensions of the career paths of economists where a hypothesis of gender discrimination is not strongly supported by the evidence. These include the areas of undergraduate grades in economics; the graduate admissions process; quality of first jobs for tenure-track academics and for nonacademics; access to journals; and nonacademic salaries. However gender discrimination cannot be ruled out at several other important junctures in an economist's career. Women are far less likely than men to major in economics and consistently achieve lower scores on the Graduate Record Exam. Fewer women than men economics majors decide to enter PhD programmes and women drop out of PhD programmes at a decidedly higher rate than men do. More women than men have non-tenure-track first jobs and first jobs in liberal arts colleges. In addition, there is widespread evidence of a statistically significant gender gap in academic salaries and in promotion rates for women academic economists.

Kahn's study suggests that the record of the profession with respect to gender discrimination is mixed. There appear to be discriminatory barriers at some points along the career path but not at others. But whether due to discrimination or not, the economics profession remains, as it has throughout its history, largely male. The profession starts off attracting fewer women at the undergraduate level (30 per cent of economics majors are women) and loses its women members at every point along the career path: 28 per cent of those entering graduate economics programmes are women; 23 per cent of economics PhDs are earned by women; 11 per cent of academic economics positions are held by women; 20 per cent of non-tenure-track and 8 per cent of tenured academic positions are held by women; 6 per cent of full professors are women, dropping to 4 per cent if one looks only at PhD-granting departments (Kahn 1995, p. 195). These statistics indicate improvements relative to the year 1900 but not a propitious start to the year 2000.

Despite the continuing small proportion of women in the economics profession, in the early 1990s feminist perspectives on economics and the economics profession began to gain academic credibility (see, for example, Ferber and Nelson 1993). Feminist theorists attempt to identify distortions that have entered into economics because of its historical masculine dominance and to broaden and improve economics by questioning its core assumptions, values, methodologies and policy prescriptions in light of potential gender influences. In 1992 the International Association for Feminist Economics (IAFFE) was founded to promote research and policy recommendations on gender-related economic issues. A burst of new research followed and is slowly beginning to influence the profession (see Nelson 1995 and Albelda 1997). In 1995 IAFFE launched its official journal, *Feminist Economics,* to create a forum for feminist scholarship and inquiry. The Council of Editors of Learned Journals named the journal the 'best new journal' of 1997 in recognition of the quality and importance of this new research.

CLAIRE HOLTON HAMMOND

See also
Committee on the Status of Women in the Economics Profession; Feminist Economics; International Association for Feminist Economists.

Bibliography
Albelda, Randy (1997), *Economics and Feminism: Disturbances in the Field*, New York: Twayne Publishers.
Amsden, Alice and Collette Moser (1975), 'Job search and affirmative action', *American Economic Review*, **65**, (May), 83–91.
Barbezat, Debra (1992), 'The market for new Ph.D. economists', *Journal of Economic Education*, **23**, (Summer), 262–76.
Blank, Rebecca (1991), 'The effects of double-blind versus single-blind reviewing: experimental evidence from the *American Economic Review*', *American Economic Review*, **81**, 1041–67.
Blaug, Mark (ed.) (1986), *Who's Who in Economics: A Biographical Dictionary of Major Economists 1700–1986*, 2nd edn, Cambridge: The MIT Press.
Broder, Ivy (1993a), 'Professional achievements and gender differences among academic economists', *Economic Inquiry*, **31**, 116–27.
Broder, Ivy (1993b), 'Review of NSF economics proposals: gender and institutional patterns', *American Economic Review*, **83**, (September), 964–70.
Church, Robert L. (1974), 'Economists as experts: the rise of an academic profession in the US, 1870–1920', in Lawrence Stone (ed.), *The University in Society. Vol. II. Europe, Scotland and the USA from the 16th to the 20th Century*, Princeton: Princeton University Press, pp. 571–609.
Coats, A.W. (1960), 'The first two decades of the American Economic Association', *American Economic Review*, **50**, (September), 555–74.
Coats, A.W. (1985), 'The American Economic Association and the economics profession', *Journal of Economic Literature*, **23**, (December), 1697–1727.
Coats, A.W. (1988), 'The Education Revolution and the Professionalization of American Economics', in William Barber (ed.), *Breaking the Academic Mould: Economists and American Higher Learning in the Nineteenth Century*, Middletown: Wesleyan University Press, pp. 340–75.
Dimand, Robert, Mary Ann Dimand and Evelyn Forget (forthcoming), *Biographical Dictionary of Women Economists*, Lyme, New Hampshire: Edward Elgar Publishing.
Ferber, Marianne and Julie A. Nelson (1993), *Beyond Economic Man: Feminist Theory and Economics*, Chicago: University of Chicago Press.
Ferber, Marianne and Michelle Teiman (1980), 'Are women at a disadvantage in publishing journal articles?', *Eastern Economic Journal*, **6**, 89–93.
Formby, John, William Gunther and Ryoichi Sakano (1993), 'Entry level salaries of academic economists: does gender or age matter?', *Economic Inquiry*, **31**, 128–38.
Furner, Mary (1975), *Advocacy and Objectivity: A Crisis in the Professionalization of American Social Sciences, 1865–1905*, Lexington: The University Press of Kentucky.
Glazer, P.M. and M. Slater (1987), *Unequal Colleagues: The Entrance of Women into the Professions, 1890–1940*, New Brunswick: Rutgers University Press.
Gordon, Lynn (1990), *Gender and Higher Education in the Progressive Era*, New Haven: Yale University Press.
Hammond, Claire (1990), 'Women and the Professionalization of Economics', Paper for the Southern Economic Association Meetings, New Orleans.
Hammond, Claire (1993), 'American women and the professionalization of economics', *Review of Social Economy*, **51**, (Fall), 347–70.
Hirschfeld, Mary, Robert L. Moore and Eleanor Brown (1995), 'Exploring the gender gap on the GRE subject test in economics', *Journal of Economic Education*, **26**, (Winter), 3–15.
Kahn, Shulamit (1993), 'Gender differences in academic career paths of economists', *American Economic Review*, **93**, (May), 52–56.
Kahn, Shulamit (1995), 'Women in the economics profession', *The Journal of Economic Perspectives*, **9**, (Fall), 193–205.

Libby, Barbara (1984), 'Women in Economics before 1940', in Edwin Perkins (ed.), *Essays in Economic and Business History*, Vol. III, Los Angeles: Economic and Business Historical Society, pp. 273–90.

Libby, Barbara (1987), 'A statistical analysis of women in the economics profession, 1900–1940', *Essays in Economics and Business History*, 5, 179–89.

McDowell, John and Janet Smith (1992), 'The effect of gender sorting on propensity to coauthor: implications for academic promotion', *Economic Inquiry*, 30, (January), 68–82.

McMillen, Daniel P. and Larry D. Singell (1994), 'Gender differences in first jobs for economists', *Southern Economic Journal*, 60, (January), 701–14.

Nelson, Julie A. (1995), 'Feminism and economics', *Journal of Economic Perspectives*, 9, (Spring), 131–48.

Parrish, John B. (1967), 'The rise of economics as an academic discipline: the formative years to 1900', *Southern Economic Journal*, 34, (July), 1–16.

Reagan, Barbara (1975), 'Two supply curves for economists? Implications of mobility and career attachment of women', *American Economic Review*, 65, (May), 100–107.

Rosenberg, Rosalind (1982), *Beyond Separate Spheres: Intellectual Roots of Modern Feminism*, New Haven: Yale University Press.

Ross, Dorothy (1991), *The Origins of American Social Science*, Cambridge: Cambridge University Press.

Rossiter, Margaret (1982), *Women Scientists in America: Struggles and Strategies to 1940*, Baltimore: Johns Hopkins University Press.

Singell, Larry D. and Joe Stone (1993), 'Gender differences in Ph.D. economists' careers', *Contemporary Policy Issues*, 11, 95–106.

Strober, Myra (1975), 'Women economists: career aspirations, education, and training', *American Economic Review*, 65, (May), 92–9.

Women's Budgets

The terms 'gender sensitive budgets', 'gender budgets', 'women's budgets' and 'women's budget statements' refer to a variety of processes and tools aimed at facilitating an assessment of the gendered impacts of government budgets. In the evolution of these exercises, the focus has been on auditing government budgets for their impact on women and girls. This has meant that, to date, the term 'women's budget' has gained widest use. Recently, however, these budget exercises have begun using gender as a category of analysis so the terminology 'gender sensitive budgets' is increasingly being adopted. It is important to recognize that 'women's budgets' or 'gender sensitive budgets' are not separate budgets for women, or for men. They are attempts to break down, or disaggregate, the government's mainstream budget according to its impact on women and men, and different groups of women and men, with cognizance being given to the society's underpinning gender relations.

Women's budgets have been implemented in both industrialized and developing countries. While there are variations between countries in the form these exercises have taken, they share similar assumptions about the importance of the government budget for gender. Women's budget exercises recognize that government budgets command substantial resources and that the state is an influential force in shaping gender outcomes. Also, government budgets impact on individuals and groups directly by design and indirectly as part of general policy. Budgets can impact differently on women and men, and different groups of women and men, through the provision of government goods and services, public sector employment opportunities, income transfers and the raising of taxation revenues as well as through their influence on the macroeconomic aggregates of output, employment, prices, investment and demand. By asking questions about the direct and indirect impacts and the equity and efficiency outcomes of government budgets on women and men, women's budgets force re-evaluation of a long held assumption that government budgets and economic policies generally are 'gender neutral' in their impact (Sharp and Broomhill 1990). This perception has been maintained with the traditional presentation of budgets in terms of financial aggregates without specific mention of either women or men (Elson 1997). Even policies and resource allocations which aim initially to give advantages to a specific group, such as taxation concessions to export businesses, tend to be portrayed as ultimately benefiting all the community. Such presentations belie the fact that women and men tend to occupy different and unequal economic and social positions and roles; they undertake different activities, face different constraints and accordingly make different choices. Consequently, there is considerable scope for women and men to be affected by, and respond differently to, budgetary policy (Elson 1997; Himmelweit 1998). Women's budgets provide a mechanism for systematically uncovering these issues and, in doing so, challenge the 'gender blindness' of traditional economic policy.

Women's budget exercises differ markedly between countries in their scope, whether they are conducted inside or outside of government and its budgetary processes (that is, location), and in their politics (Budlender and Sharp 1998). These factors have been shown to be important in shaping the successes and limitations of these exercises (Sawer 1990, 1996; Sharp and Broomhill 1990, 1999). The first and longest running audits of the budget's impact on women and girls was undertaken by the Australian Federal and State governments during the 1980s and 1990s. These women's budgets were constructed and undertaken entirely within the structures of the state and were characterized by a unique politics arising from feminists working within the state. South Africa was the next country to implement a comprehensive and continuous women's budget exercise. It began in 1996 as a community-based exercise in post-apartheid South Africa, but was unique in having the support of the women's sub-committee of the South African Parliament's Joint Standing Committee on Finance. In the following year a more limited exercise within the state began. In 1994 the National Commission on the Role of Filipino Women began a unique women's budget exercise to audit the Philippines national government's Gender and Development budgetary allocations. Several Commonwealth countries are scheduled to take part in a gender-sensitive budget exercise conducted within government as part of a pilot project endorsed at the 1996 regular meeting of Commonwealth Ministers for Women's Affairs. South Africa was the first government to participate in the Commonwealth countries' pilot project in 1997 and it has since been joined by Sri Lanka and Barbados. St Kitts and Fiji are investigating joining the pilot project. In addition, the governments of Namibia and Mozambique initiated gender-sensitive budget exercises in 1998 and non-government groups in Uganda, Tanzania, Zimbabwe, Switzerland, Canada and Britain have also been developing exercises.

Women's budget analyses have emerged out of feminist practical politics seeking to change government policies. To date they have been the subject of limited research for their theoretical underpinnings and capacities to achieve change. As such, women's budgets provide a new terrain for feminist economic thought, and some feminist activists and academics have begun the process of making theoretical connections. The main areas to which connections have been made are feminist theories of the state and feminist critiques and reconstructions of macroeconomics.

The question of the role of the state in relation to women's economic position has been raised and debated extensively by feminists. Women's budgets offer opportunities to inform and be informed by this theoretical debate. In Australia, where women's budgets originated, this has been enabled by the fact that feminist politics has for three decades had a significant space within the state itself. An early analysis of women's budgets argued that the longer-term significance of women's budgets needs to be assessed in the context of the overall role of the state in relation to women's economic position (Sharp and Broomhill 1990). Several feminist analyses of women's budgets acknowledged that these exercises offer a potentially positive role for the state to play in raising women's economic position. In particular, these analyses argue that national machinery introduced for integrating gender into government policy is ultimately limited unless attention is paid to the budgetary dimension (Sawer 1990; Budlender 1996). National machinery for women which provides policy oversight, monitoring and advocacy needs to be followed through in terms of its implications for the budget (Goetz 1995).

Other analyses, however, caution against assuming that the state will respond positively even when the processes or 'machinery of government' for promoting gender equality have been established. Historically, the role of the state in influencing women's economic position in society has been complex and, in some respects, contradictory (Sharp and Broomhill 1988, 1990). While it is clear that the various agencies of the capitalist state, and the government in particular, have played an important role in sustaining the structures within which women are subordinated in society, the state has also acted as an agent for progressive changes to improve women's economic position. Women's budgets themselves reflect this contradiction. On the one hand, their existence illustrates that pressure from feminists in the political process has been successful in forcing governments at least to acknowledge women's specific economic interests. On the other hand, the potentially progressive role of women's budgets envisaged by their architects remains only partially fulfilled as a result of other conservative pressures placed on the state. Paramount among these are the gender-blind set of economic policymaking assumptions and a strong ideological bias against state intervention to achieve equity goals for specific groups. Feminists too have played some role in reinforcing a narrow agenda of women's budgets by focusing on the distribution of government welfare expenditures and largely ignoring the impacts of taxation and revenue raising generally. An important step in making women's budgets more effective requires considerable political pressure to be exerted upon the state by women's groups and their supporters. Ideally this approach would incorporate a feminist politics which pressures the state from within as well as from outside (Sharp and Broomhill 1990).

The second area where feminists have forged theoretical connections has been between gender-sensitive budget exercises and the emerging feminist economic critique of macroeconomics. Central to this view is the idea that a gender-neutral approach to national budgets can undermine macroeconomic policies by ignoring women's economic contributions in the form of unpaid work in the household, voluntary community work, subsistence and informal sector employment. These economic contributions are deemed significant in how the economy operates. They are based on a gender division of labour which gives rise to gender differences which are structural to the economy. In this way feminist economists have created a space to argue that gender matters for policy efficiency as well as for equity. Studies of developing countries have shown, for example, that reducing gender inequality in education enrolments, the labour market or women's unpaid time burdens leads to rises in productivity, national income and economic growth (Elson 1997).

The feminist critique of conventional macroeconomics further argues that effective budgets (as well as other macroeconomic policy instruments) require a conceptual framework which incorporates the gendered care economy into the total flow of national income and output. In so doing, interactions between paid and the unpaid activities critical to macroeconomic policy will be brought into view (Bakker 1997; Benería 1995; Çagatay et al. 1995; Elson 1998). A starting point for this analysis has been to introduce the unpaid household and community care sector into the circular flow model of the economy. The unpaid care sector, aided by inputs provided by the public sector, is argued to underpin macroeconomic growth because it plays a crucial role in producing the labour force and developing and maintaining the social context in which economic activities take place (including the creation of social assets such as sense of community, responsibility and trust). Thus, in contrast to conventional macroeconomics, which ignores how the labour force comes into existence, labour is theorized as an input into production which is itself produced. Furthermore, long-run decisions about social reproduction are expected to have an influence on the quality and quantity of labour available to the productive or paid economy (Walters 1995). Thus, budgetary policies, through their impact on household decisions, the labour market and the availability of government services, potentially have significant feedback effects on quantity and quality of care activities.

One way in which the interdependency of the paid and the unpaid sectors of the economy has been drawn out has been to stress the complementarity of private production and public investment in health, education, infrastructure and market access, a matter emphasized by 'new growth theory' (Bakker 1997; Palmer 1995). Utilizing this framework feminists have pointed to the positive link between equity and growth while noting that women's economic contribution is characterized by biased or absent markets arising out of inequitable gender relations which need to be taken into account for efficient policy. Segmented labour markets which result in women systematically receiving lower wages than men because of a lower sociocultural value being assigned to women's work are an example of biased markets, while significant absent markets characterize much of the reproduction of the labour force which is work primarily done by women without any cost being accounted for by the market-based economy. The latter amounts to a socially determined tax being placed on women's labour (Palmer 1995). Conventional macroeconomic theory which advocates policies of cutbacks in public sector investments in areas such as health and education ignores the capacity of these expenditures to reduce gender inequities and promote economic growth by creating or stimulating missing or segmented markets. That is, conventional macroeconomic theory and policy, by ignoring the ways in which gender relations contribute to distortions in resource allocations caused by absent and biased markets, can advocate budgetary reductions which are likely to aggravate these distortions by 'crowding out' women's contribution to economic growth (Palmer 1995). A key conclusion of the feminist critique of macroeconomics is therefore that gender inequalities are not only unfair but costly.

A number of other theoretical implications will undoubtedly continue to emerge from the experience of women's budgets. There remains a need for ongoing feminist research which critiques traditional budgets and their resource allocations for their equity, efficiency and effectiveness. Tools of public finance analysis such as public expenditure and taxation incidence need to be evaluated for their capacities to incorporate gender, and the potential contribution of qualitative assessments of the impacts of government expenditure and revenue raising needs attention. The research agenda could be fruitfully extended to examine how the value of caring labour might be budgeted for in policy as well as continuing to theorize the role of the caregiver in the macroeconomy. A feminist research agenda would also include an analysis of which institutional processes and structures foster government budgetary accountability and which ones do not. This would include examining the capacities of institutions of treasury, finance and public enterprises to engender their approach to programmes and policies. At a broader level there is a need for further research on the gendered impact of globalization and restructuring and the consequences of the state adopting neoliberal policies for women's economic position and gender relations. The implementation of women's budgets in a diverse range of countries have also brought to the forefront additional questions for a feminist research agenda. Of particular interest to feminist economists and feminists more generally is how feminist analyses of budgets might take into account women's and men's experiences in terms of gender, race and class. Finally, the experience of countries undertaking gender-sensitive budget exercises is yet to be comprehensively researched, along with a comparison of the findings.

RHONDA SHARP

See also
Domestic Labour; Economic Restructuring; Macroeconomics; Public Sector Economics/Public Finance; Tax Policy.

Bibliography
Bakker, Isabella (1997), 'Integrating Paid and Unpaid Work into Economic Growth and Human Development Strategies', Paper presented at the United Nations Development Program sponsored workshop on Integrating Paid and Unpaid Work into National Policies, Seoul, Republic of Korea, May 28–30.
Benería, Lourdes (1995), 'Towards a greater integration of gender in economics', *World Development*, **23** (11), 1839–50.
Budlender, Debbie (ed.) (1996), *The Women's Budget*, Cape Town: Institute for Democracy in South Africa.
Budlender, Debbie (ed.) (1997), *The Second Women's Budget*, Cape Town: Institute for Democracy in South Africa.
Budlender, Debbie and Rhonda Sharp with Kerri Allen (1998), *How to do a Gender-Sensitive Budget: Contemporary Research and Practice*, Canberra and London: Australian Agency for International Development and Commonwealth Secretariat.
Çagatay, Nilufer, Diane Elson and Caren Grown (1995), 'Introduction to gender, adjustment and macroeconomics', *World Development*, **23** (11), 1827–36.
Elson, Diane (1997), 'Gender-neutral, Gender-blind, or Gender-sensitive Budgets? Changing the Conceptual Framework to Include Women's Empowerment and the Economy of Care', Background paper for the Preparatory Mission to South Africa to Integrate Gender into National Budgetary Policies and Procedures in the Context of Economic Reform, London: Commonwealth Secretariat.

Elson, Diane (1998), 'The economic, the political and the domestic: businesses, states and households in the organisation of production', *New Political Economy*, 3 (2), 189–208.

Goetz, A.M. (1995), 'The Politics of Integrating Gender into State Development Processes: Politics, Opportunities and Constraints in Bangladesh, Chile, Jamaica, Mali, Morocco and Uganda', Geneva: United Nations Institute for Social Development.

Himmelweit, Susan (1998), 'Care and the Budgetary Process', Paper presented at the Conference Out of the Margin 2: Feminist Approaches to Economics, held at the University of Amsterdam, Amsterdam, The Netherlands, 2–5 June.

Palmer, Ingrid (1995), 'Public finance from a gender perspective', *World Development*, 32 (11), 1981–6.

Sawer, Marian (1990), *Sisters in Suits: Women and Public Policy in Australia*, Sydney: Allen and Unwin.

Sawer, Marian (1996), 'Femocrats and Ecorats: Women's Policy Machinery in Australia, Canada and New Zealand', Occasional Paper No 6, Geneva: United Nations Research Institute for Social Development.

Sharp, Rhonda and Ray Broomhill (1988), *Shortchanged: Women and Economic Policies*, Sydney: Allen and Unwin.

Sharp, Rhonda and Ray Broomhill (1990), 'Women and government budgets', *Australian Journal of Social Issues*, 25 (1), 1–14.

Sharp, Rhonda and Ray Broomhill (1999), 'Australia's role in the development of gender-sensitive budgets', Paper presented at the United Nations Development Programme in Partnership with UNIFEM, Workshop on Pro-Poor, Gender and Environment-Sensitive Budgets, New York, USA, 28–30 June.

Summers, Anne (1986), 'Mandarins or Missionaries: Women in the Federal Bureaucracy', in Norma Grieve and Ailsa Burns (eds), *Australian Women: New Feminist Perspectives*, Melbourne: Oxford University Press.

Walters, Bernard (1995), 'Engendering macroeconomics: a reconsideration of growth theory', *World Development*, 23 (11), 1869–80.

Index

Aaron, H. 427
Aaronson, S. 72, 74
Abel, E.K. 42
Abell, J.D. 27
Abjection 672, 673
Abramovitz, M. 461, 467, 469, 702, 755
Abuse Prevention Act (1978) 124
accumulation 536, 537
Acker, J. 74, 111, 517
activism 162–7, 347
   China 181–3
   India 205–8
   Singapore 242
   South America 248, 254
   United States 270
   Western Europe 274, 277, 280
Acton, J. 169
Adams, A.E. 429
Adams, M. 602
Addison, T. 102
Adelman, I. 275
Adler, M. 602
Aerni, A.L. 315, 369, 487, 603, 604, 606
affirmative action 1–7, 24, 399, 645
Africa
   agriculture 10, 14
   banking and credit 28, 29
   child support 49, 53
   development theories 96
   economic restructuring 293
   environmental and natural resource
      economics 325
   imperialism 453
   income distribution 460, 461
   International Association for Feminist
      Economics 489
   international economics 495
   migration 556
   population 617
   technological change 704, 705, 707
   unions 720
African-Americans 268, 270
   feminism 353
   glass ceiling 397

   health 430
   labour force participation 502
   minimum wage 567
   pensions and old age retirement 611
   unions 720, 722
   wage gap 748, 749
Afshar, H. 419
Aganwadis (courtyards) 41
Agarwal, B. 14, 203, 205, 488, 532, 551,
   575, 625
   environmental and natural resource
      economics 324, 325, 326
   family 332, 333
   feminist economics 363, 364, 366,
      368, 369
   game theory 382, 384, 385, 386, 388
age 115
   at marriage 115
   capitalism 36
   discrimination 107, 111
   domestic abuse 125
   feminism 354
   health 427
   sexual orientation 675
   Sub-Saharan Africa 259, 261
agency theory 469, 623
Agnihotri, I. 206–7
agriculture 9–16, 704, 705
Ahmed, L. 220
Aid to Families with Dependent
   Children 465, 466, 470, 751, 752,
   753
Akerlof, G. 515
Akhter, F. 619
Akyeampong, E. 172
Al-Qudsi, S. 223
Albania 185
Albelda, R. 61, 108, 401, 470, 517, 578,
   655, 762
   feminization of poverty 373–4, 377
   income distribution 457, 460, 462
   labour market segmentation 507–8
   welfare reform 752, 754, 755
Albrecht, L.J. 214